ESSENTIAL READINGS IN
COMPARATIVE
POLITICS

FIFTH EDITION

ESSENTIAL READINGS IN
COMPARATIVE
POLITICS

FIFTH EDITION

PATRICK H. O'NEIL | RONALD ROGOWSKI

W. W. NORTON & COMPANY
NEW YORK · LONDON

W. W. Norton & Company has been independent since its founding in 1923, when William Warder Norton and Mary D. Herter Norton first published lectures delivered at the People's Institute, the adult education division of New York City's Cooper Union. The firm soon expanded its program beyond the Institute, publishing books by celebrated academics from America and abroad. By mid-century, the two major pillars of Norton's publishing program—trade books and college texts—were firmly established. In the 1950s, the Norton family transferred control of the company to its employees, and today—with a staff of four hundred and a comparable number of trade, college, and professional titles published each year—W. W. Norton & Company stands as the largest and oldest publishing house owned wholly by its employees.

Editor: Peter Lesser
Associate Editor: Samantha Held
Project Editor: Linda Feldman
Managing Editor, College: Marian Johnson
Managing Editor, College Digital Media: Kim Yi
Production Manager: Elizabeth Marotta
Media Editor: Spencer Richardson-Jones
Associate Media Editor: Michael Jaoui
Media Editorial Assistant: Ariel Eaton
Marketing Manager, Political Science: Erin Brown
Text Design: Faceout Studio
Art Director: Hope Miller Goodell
Permissions Manager: Megan Schindel
Permissions Clearer: Bethany Salminen
Composition: Six Red Marbles
Manufacturing: Quad Graphics—Fairfield

ISBN: 978-0-393-93898-2 (pbk.)

W. W. Norton & Company, Inc., 500 Fifth Avenue, New York, N.Y. 10110
www.wwnorton.com

W. W. Norton & Company Ltd., Castle House, 15 Carlisle Street, London W1D 3BS

3 4 5 6 7 8 9 0

CONTENTS

PREFACE

Comparative politics, as a field, lacks an agreed upon core. While to some degree this is true of political science as a whole, the study of comparative politics has been especially plagued by disagreements over what merits study and how to go about this study. Whereas the study of international relations (political relations between countries) draws upon a set of key ideas and scholarship, only recently has a similar consensus arisen within comparative politics. Even now, scholars vary widely in the questions, approaches, and evidence that they bring to bear. It was this very problem that led to the creation of the *Essentials* set of texts in comparative politics.

Bringing together the "essentials" of comparative politics in a volume of manageable dimensions presented us with a serious challenge, but also, in our view, an irresistible opportunity. Where textbooks inevitably only summarize the original literature, if they discuss it at all, we have long thought it crucial—not least in our own teaching—to expose our students to the key works and original ideas and to show how they fit together in a larger and more generous understanding of comparative politics. Thus when Ann Shin and Roby Harrington suggested, on behalf of Norton, that we collaborate on a set of original readings to complement *Essentials of Comparative Politics*, we quickly overcame our initial trepidation and took up the challenge.

The readings have been chosen and organized to serve a number of purposes. On most topics, we have combined one or more "classic" pieces—widely recognized as having shaped the present field—with more recent influential contributions. Other works provide valuable surveys of changes in the field over time. Where possible, we have juxtaposed contending views on a topic, giving readers the opportunity to weigh the merits of competing arguments. Finally, we have sought to include a number of shorter and contemporary pieces that help link theory to current political events and developments. The headnotes to each chapter explain more fully our rationale for including the readings we did. The chapters of this volume parallel those of *Essentials of Comparative Politics*, often tying directly to concepts addressed in that textbook. They are also meant to flesh out ideas and developments addressed in *Cases in Comparative Politics*.

The reader begins with an overview of some of the ideas and debates concerning the study of comparative politics itself. From there, we investigate the key concepts of the state and sovereignty, and how scholars have thought about its rise, fall, and failure. We then consider national and ethnic identities and their relationship to political stability and violent conflict. Our discussion of political economy helps trace the relationship between states, markets, and property, while the chapters on democratic and nondemocratic regimes consider how democracies emerge, the foundations of nondemocratic rule, and the prospects for democracy and democratization around the world. This discussion then leads to the chapter on political violence, with its particular focus on terrorism and revolution. From here, we lay out readings on developed, developing, and communist and post-communist countries, attempting to apply some of the ideas addressed in earlier chapters to understanding these parts of the world. Finally, our chapter on globalization considers the ways in which this process may—or may not—shape the role and place of domestic and international politics in the future, why and how globalization is being resisted, and what this means for the future study of comparative politics. Hopefully, this material will provide the reader a sense of the core issues and ideas within comparative political scholarship and the field's relationship to real world issues. The readings also build upon and often reference each other, giving the reader a sense of how they are interconnected as a single body of scholarship. While comparative politics may be diverse and even fractious, the readings underscore the perennial questions and concepts that drive our teaching and research.

While this collection is addressed primarily to undergraduates who are deepening their knowledge of comparative politics, we intend it also as a contribution—and in our view a highly necessary one—to *intra*disciplinary professional dialogue. Far too many graduate students and practicing scholars, in our view, are forgetting or ignoring the impressive depth and breadth of comparative politics. We thus intend this volume as both an introduction and a remedy. Now, in its fifth edition, we have refined and improved our selections, seeking to strike a balance between complexity and accessibility.

We owe deep and extensive thanks to the various individuals who contributed to this work. Ann Shin played a critical role in initiating this project, reviewing our choices and helping us maintain order in the face of constant changes, updates, and second thoughts. Aaron Javsicas and Jake Schindel improved our offerings in the third and fourth editions, and Samantha Held has guided our revisions in this edition. Our thanks, too, to those external reviewers who considered our selections and provided important suggestions on how the reader might be improved. Finally, thanks to all those students with whom we have shared these readings in the past. Their responses, tacit and explicit, greatly influenced our selections and rationale. We hope that this range of materials can serve comparative politics courses across a range of levels, and that students and faculty alike will find them both wide-ranging and compelling.

Patrick O'Neil
Ron Rogowski
May 2017

1 WHAT IS COMPARATIVE POLITICS?

The ancestry of comparative politics can be traced back to ancient Greece and Aristotle and to the classic social theorists of the Renaissance and Enlightenment. From the field's modern revival in the late nineteenth century until the mid-1950s, it was a predominantly legalistic, normative, and descriptive enterprise. It focused on legal texts; it argued about how institutions should be, rather than analyzing their actual characteristics; and it described—often in numbing detail—how countries' institutions worked. However, comparison of countries' institutions was usually limited to a few cases (most often, the major European countries and the United States), and political scientists demonstrated scant interest in what we would now call the comparative method. As comparative politics scholar Roy Macridis once wrote, in that era the field was "configurative" rather than comparative.

All of this changed with stunning rapidity in the late 1950s and the 1960s, when leading comparativists rediscovered the "grand tradition" in social theory, particularly the works of Karl Marx and Max Weber. Also, through such works as Anthony Downs's *An Economic Theory of Democracy* (1957) and Seymour Martin Lipset's *Political Man* (1960), political scientists explored the possibilities of quantitative, game-theoretic, and economic approaches. From the early 1970s on, an increasing share of scholarly articles used quantitative methods, and during the 1980s and 1990s, the rational-choice perspective came to underlie some of the most significant work in comparative politics. The most recent contributions to the field, while usually taking rational choice as their starting point, have begun to explore the deviations from strict rationality studied by Daniel Kahneman and Amos Tversky. Increasingly, empirical work has employed various methods of experimentation.

In a work that has already become a modern classic, "Research Traditions and Theory in Comparative Politics: An Introduction" (1997), Mark I. Lichbach and Alan S. Zuckerman give a brilliant capsule history of these developments and focus our attention on what they and many others regard as the three major theories that eventually emerged in the field of comparative politics: the cultural, the structural, and the rational-choice approaches. Lichbach and Zuckerman trace the intellectual antecedents of these approaches, examine the reasons for their ascendance, and address the research questions that each theory pushes to the fore.

Lichbach and Zuckerman also note that, despite their disagreements, today's comparativists agree on the need for comparison and explanation. Most would also agree with the great sociologist Max Weber that social-scientific explanation is best achieved by what we now call a model—or, as Weber put it, a conjecture or hypothesis about people's behavior that (1) "makes sense" in terms of what we already know about how people think; (2) is "fertile," meaning that it logically implies predictions about behavior that we are not immediately studying; and (3) is "testable," particularly in a comparative setting.

We can also divide comparativists into those who emphasize area studies—close knowledge of a country or region (the Middle East, Latin America, Africa, China, Nigeria)—and those who stress the "science" in "social science," seeking general laws of political behavior and institutions that would apply in all areas of the world. In Lichbach and Zuckerman's terms, almost all culturalists fall into the first category, and almost all rationalists into the second. Structuralists divide between the two, often focusing on a close comparison of similar cases (for example, major revolutions or civil wars). Increasingly, these distinctions came to be overshadowed by the one between "quantitative" and "qualitative" scholars. Although almost all rationalists and most structuralists use quantitative (or, more rarely, experimental) methods in their empirical work, culturalists are more likely to conduct qualitative or multi-method research.

Gary King, Robert O. Keohane, and Sidney Verba's pathbreaking textbook, *Designing Social Inquiry* (1994), set itself the ambitious goal of bridging the divides between qualitative and quantitative, and between cultural/structural and rational-choice, work in comparative politics. The difference, KKV (King-Keohane-Verba) contended, was stylistic, not fundamental. Whether one studied a few cases (or even just one) in depth, or many more on only a few dimensions, the same standards of scientific inference must (and, indeed, among practitioners usually did) apply. Exactly as Lichbach and Zuckerman (and, long before them, Weber) had argued, KKV insisted that good comparative theory must be fertile, testable, and tentative, and must seek to simplify complexity.

John Stuart Mill, among the most brilliant and fertile thinkers of the nineteenth century, addressed many of these same issues in an astonishingly perceptive and foresighted way in *A System of Logic*—one that, indeed, takes up some of the questions raised both in the quantitative-qualitative debate and within quantitative work. While his language may strike us as somewhat archaic (Mill, after all, was writing in 1843), his points remain entirely fresh. While qualitative scholars have often cited Mill's "method of agreement" and "method of difference," they have curiously overlooked his even more important "method of concomitant variation," without which (as he emphasized) "we should be forever unable to determine a cause." Similarly, quantitative scholars have usually failed to note that Mill's "method of concomitant variation" stressed the possible invalidity of what we would now call "out of sample" inference; and neither quantitative nor qualitative researchers have noted that Mill's "method of difference" allowed reliable causal inference only through controlled experimentation. All three methods are summarized here and will be discussed in this chapter's selection from Mill.

Condensing Mill's argument drastically, and inevitably with some distortion: (a) If we find that in every case of some phenomenon we seek to explain (e.g., the rise of dictatorship) one antecedent factor (e.g., a major economic downturn) was present, while no other conjectured cause (e.g., defeat in war, ethnic conflict, a powerful landowning elite) linked all of the observed cases, we would be justified in at least hypothesizing that the common factor (here, economic downturn) was the cause. This would be the "method of agreement," which Mill stresses is by no means conclusive. (b) If, on the other hand, all factors except one were identical among a large set of observed cases (e.g., all have a powerful landowning elite, all have been defeated in war, etc.), but dictatorship arose only where one additional factor (again, take as our example a sharp economic downturn) was present, we would be far more justified in inferring that unique factor to be the cause of this phenomenon. This Mill calls, reasonably enough, the "method of difference"; and, as he observes, the acid test is one of experimentation, where we would insert or remove that presumed cause by intervention, or what today is called "treatment." Because with many social phenomena we cannot (or, at least in Mill's day, could not) perform such an experiment, Mill really argues here for what we would call "control variables." Absent experimentation, however, even the method of difference allows no secure causal inference.

Stronger support for causal inference in such non-experimental cases, Mill argues, comes from (c) the "method of concomitant variation"—that is, our observation that, controlling for all other factors, the phenomenon we seek to explain and the imputed cause covary monotonically. In other words, as the supposed cause increases, so does its alleged effect. In a yet more sophisticated way, Mill notes that (1) the functional form of the covariation need not be rigidly specified (it can be quadratic, linear, logarithmic, or something else altogether); and (2) even when we have established such a relationship within our set of observations, we can infer nothing about observations outside our sample. If, for example, the lowest per capita income we observe is $2 per day, we cannot simply extrapolate any observed relationship between per capita income and, let us say, political stability, for cases where per capita income is 50 cents per day.

Note how Mill bridges here the quantitative, qualitative, and experimental aspects of comparison. We can use observational methods of agreement and difference to inform qualitative work; we can yet more powerfully infer causation by the method of concomitant variation; and, in the ideal case, we use the method of difference in an experimental setting to gain the greatest confidence that we have established a causal relationship.

Given the technology of his age, Mill doubted that experimentation would be possible in the social sciences. But beginning in the 1940s, psychologists began to perform laboratory experiments; in the 1960s, political scientists followed suit, especially to determine whether humans actually performed as game theory said they would. Ronald Rogowski notes that only in the last two decades, and because of such newly available technologies as the Internet, has experimentation moved outside the laboratory and begun, in fact, to dominate empirical work in political science. It has done so for precisely the reason that Mill advanced: it allows the most reliable way of applying the "method of difference," of establishing what one factor among many, when varied by the experimenter, actually produces the effect that theory predicts.

In practice, comparativists today choose freely among methods. Although quantitative ones predominate, they are often supplemented by qualitative work, including the examination of documents, interviews, and news reports. Crucial experiments, such as those on the effectiveness of a theoretically important intervention, are performed with ever-greater frequency. And although the rational-choice perspective is by far the dominant one, all practicing comparativists are aware of that approach's limits: cultural taboos or resentments, for example, or such structural factors as the geographic distribution of employment, may trump economic self-interest (a point to which we will return later in this volume as we examine nationalism, ethnicity, and opposition to globalization).

Mark I. Lichbach and Alan S. Zuckerman
RESEARCH TRADITIONS AND THEORY IN COMPARATIVE POLITICS: AN INTRODUCTION

The Common Heritage of Comparative Politics

Comparativists inherit their dream of theorizing about politics from the founders of social theory. Their intellectual forebears represent the pantheon of Western thought. In the classic survey of the field's intellectual origins, Harry Eckstein (1963) highlights the past masters.

> Comparative politics . . . has a particular right to claim Aristotle as an ancestor because of the primacy that he assigned to politics among the sciences and because the problems he raised and the methods he used are similar to those still current in political studies (Eckstein 1963: 3).

From *Comparative Politics: Rationality, Culture, and Structure* (New York: Cambridge University Press, 1997), pp. 3–10.

Machiavelli and Montesquieu, Hobbes and Smith are the progenitors who lived during the Renaissance and the Enlightenment. The classic theorists of social science—Karl Marx, Max Weber, Emile Durkheim, Vilfredo Pareto, Gaetano Mosca, and Roberto Michels—established the field's research agenda, mode of analysis, and contrasting theoretical visions. Several seminal theorists of contemporary political science—Harry Eckstein, David Apter, Robert Dahl, Seymour Lipset, Karl Deutsch, Gabriel Almond, and Sidney Verba—drew on this heritage to rebuild and reinvigorate the field of comparative politics. A shared, grand intellectual vision motivates comparativists.

Comparativists want to understand the critical events of the day, a position that ensures that dreams of theory address the political world as it exists, not formal abstractions or utopias. Just as Marx and Weber responded to the fundamental transformations associated with the rise of capitalism, just as Marx developed a general strategy for a socialist revolution and Weber grappled with the theoretical and normative demands of the bureaucratic state, and just as Mosca, Pareto, and Michels strove to understand the possibilities and limits of democratic rule, students of comparative politics examine pressing questions in the context of their immediate political agenda. The contemporary study of comparative politics therefore blossomed in response to the political problems that followed World War II. New forms of conflict emerged: Communist threats; peasant rebellions and revolutions; social movements, urban riots, student upheavals, military coups, and national liberation struggles swept the world. Government decisions replaced markets as foci for economic development. New states followed the disintegration of colonial empires, and the worldwide movement toward democratic rule seemed to resume after the fascist tragedies. The challenges of the current era—domestic conflict, state-building, the political bases of economic growth, and democratization, to note but a few—stand at the center of today's research, indicating that the need to respond to contemporary issues guides the field.

Comparative politics therefore asserts an ambitious scope of inquiry. No political phenomenon is foreign to it; no level of analysis is irrelevant, and no time period beyond its reach. Civil war in Afghanistan; voting decisions in Britain; ethnic conflict in Quebec, Bosnia, and Burundi; policy interactions among the bureaucracies of the European Union in Brussels, government agencies in Rome, regional offices in Basilicata, and local powers in Potenza; the religious bases of political action in Iran, Israel, and the United States; the formation of democracies in Eastern Europe and the collapse of regimes in Africa; and global economic patterns are part of the array of contemporary issues that stand before the field. Questions about the origins of capitalism; the formation of European states; the rise of fascism and the collapse of interwar democracies; and the transition to independence after colonial rule are

some of the themes of past eras that still command our attention.

Second, comparativists assert an ambitious intellectual vision in that they approach these substantive concerns with general questions in mind. Anyone who studies the politics of a particular country—whether Germany or Ghana, the United Arab Emirates or the United States of America—so as to address abstract issues does comparative politics. Anyone who is interested in who comes to power, how, and why—the names, places, and dates of politics in any one place or other—in order to say something about the politics of succession or the determinants of vote choice is a comparativist. In other words, students of comparative politics examine a case to reveal what it tells us about a larger set of political phenomena, or they relate the particulars of politics to more general theoretical ideas about politics.

Comparativists therefore insist that analysis requires explicit comparisons. Because events of global historical significance affect so many countries in so short a period of time, studies of single countries and abstract theorizing are woefully inadequate to capture epoch-shaping developments. More than three decades ago, when the founders of the contemporary field of comparative politics initiated the most recent effort to merge theory and data in the study of politics, they therefore established another of the field's guiding principles: The proper study of politics requires systematic comparisons.[1]

Finally, comparativists assert a grand intellectual vision in that their generalizations are situated in the context of the Big Questions of social thought: Who rules? How are interests represented? Who wins and who loses? How is authority challenged? Why are some nations "developed"? These questions have produced much contemporary theorizing about the connections among social order, the state, civil society, and social change, especially in democracies. Comparativists engage the basic issues that inform social and political thought.

In sum, comparative politics follows the lead of the grand masters in their approach to substantive issues, to the scope of inquiry, to the nature of theory-building, and to the enduring problems of social thought. As comparativists address politically significant matters, explore a range of political phenomena, propose general explanatory propositions based on systematic evidence from multiple cases, and address Big Questions, they move along a path first marked by the founders of social science.

The Competing Traditions in Comparative Politics

In spite of this shared dream, long-standing disagreements separated the field's forebears and contrasting research schools characterize current efforts to build theories in comparative politics. When many of today's senior scholars were graduate students, their training included courses that compared psychological and culturalist approaches, institutional studies of political organizations, structural-functional and systems analyses, cybernetics and modes of information theory, pluralist, elitist, and Marxist analyses, modernization theory and its alternatives of dependency and world-systems theories, and rational choice theory, to name the most obvious. Most of these perspectives have disappeared and some have formed new combinations. Today, rational choice theories, culturalist approaches, and structural analyses stand as the principal competing theoretical schools in comparative politics. Rational choice theorists follow a path laid out by Hobbes, Smith, and Pareto; culturalists continue work begun by Montesquieu and developed by Weber and Mosca; and structuralists build on Marx's foundations and add to Weber's edifice. The themes and debates of contemporary comparative politics are therefore rooted in the enduring questions of social thought. They continue to lie at the center of work in all the social sciences.

Rationalists begin with assumptions about actors who act deliberately to maximize their advantage. This research school uses the power of mathematical reasoning to elaborate explanations with impressive scope. Analysis begins at the level of the individual and culminates in questions about collective actions, choices, and institutions. Following the path first charted by Downs (1957), Olson (1968), and Riker (1962), rational choice theory has spread to address diverse problems: from electoral choice to revolutionary movements, from coalitions to political economy, and from institution formation to state-building. Here, the clarity of mathematical reasoning takes pride of place; powerful abstract logics facilitate a shared understanding among the members of the research school.

As comparativists engage in fieldwork in diverse societies, they grapple with the need to understand varied ways of life, systems of meaning, and values. As students who cut their teeth on the abstractions of modernization and dependency theory encounter the realities of particular villages, political parties, and legislatures, they seek to ground their observations in the politics that is being analyzed. Following the lead of social and cultural anthropologists, many comparativists adhere to Geertz's (1973) admonition to provide "thick descriptions." Culturalists therefore provide nuanced and detailed readings of particular cases, frequently drawn from fieldwork, as they seek to understand the phenomena being studied. This stance usually joins strong doubts about both the ability to generalize to abstract categories and the ability to provide explanations that apply to more than the case at hand.

Structuralists draw together long-standing interests in political and social institutions. Many emphasize the formal organizations of governments; some retain Marx's concern with class relations; some study political parties and interest groups; some combine these into analyses of how states and societies interact; and some emphasize the themes of political economy. Although these scholars display diverse patterns of reasoning, from mathematical models to verbal arguments, and many modes of organizing empirical evidence, they continue to follow Marx's and Weber's contention that theory and data guide social analysis.

* * * These research traditions take strong positions on the methodological issues that divide

comparativists.[2] Rational choice theorists seek to maximize the ability to provide universal laws that may be used in nomothetic explanations. They consider problems of reliability—the concern with the evidence required to support generalizations from the particular to sets of cases—as a challenge to research design. Cultural interpreters maximize the importance of reliability as they describe the constellations of particular cases and minimize the value of generalist research expectations. They interpret particular events, decisions, and patterns, eschewing any need to tie explanations to general principles. Structural analysts who follow Marx offer universal theories that include causal accounts. At the same time, they struggle to tie reliable descriptions into powerful generalizations; they grapple self-consciously with the requirements of case selection and how best to move from the particular analysis to the set of cases about which they seek to theorize. Comparativists' long-standing debates over method thus reappear in the three research traditions.

However, * * * the dispute among the schools goes beyond the ideographic-nomothetic divide. The traditions differ with respect to ontology: Rationalists study how actors employ reason to satisfy their interests, culturalists study rules that constitute individual and group identities, and structuralists explore relations among actors in an institutional context. Reasons, rules, and relations are the various starting points of inquiry. The traditions also differ with respect to explanatory strategy: Rationalists perform comparative static experiments, culturalists produce interpretive understandings, and structuralists study the historical dynamics of real social types. Positivism, interpretivism, and realism are the possible philosophies of social science.

Moreover, * * * no school displays a rigid and uniform orthodoxy. Rationalists debate the utility of relaxing the core assumption that defines individuals as maximizers of their self-interest. They differ as well over the proper form of explanation, some seeking covering laws and others proposing causal accounts, as they debate the necessity of transform-

ing formal models into accounts of events. Continuing the debate initiated by Marx and Weber, structuralists differ over the ontological status of their concepts: Are social class, ethnicity, state, and other concepts that characterize this research school natural types? Are political processes best seen as determined and closed ended or probabilistic and open-ended processes? Structuralists differ as well over the utility of nomothetic and causal explanations. Culturalists disagree over the theoretical importance of generalizations drawn from their fieldwork. May one derive or test general propositions from the analysis of a particular village? Do public opinion surveys provide an adequate picture of people's goals, values, and identities? They differ over the nature of explanation in comparative politics as well. Some culturalists reject any form of covering law or causal accounts, offering only interpretations of political life in particular places; others move toward the mainstream of comparative politics, incorporating values and systems of meaning into theories that adhere to the standard forms of explanation. In short, * * * ideal-type rationalists, culturalists, and structuralists need to be identified so that we may recognize how practicing comparativists employ a battery of ideal-type strategies in their concrete empirical work.

Comparative politics is dominated today by rationalist, culturalist, and structuralist approaches. What explains the imperialist expansion of these schools and the disappearance of earlier approaches? [For one thing, t]hese schools share an ontological and epistemological symmetry. They offer—indeed force—choices along the same dimensions. Furthermore, at a more fundamental level, the themes of the research schools rest at the heart of the human sciences. Reason, rules, and relations are unique to social theory. Focusing on these themes sets research in the social sciences apart from the physical sciences, providing a fundamental basis on which to theorize about political phenomena. Rationalist, culturalist, and structuralist theories are thus embedded in strong research communities, scholarly traditions, and analytical languages.

NOTES

1. Classic works that appeared to herald the emergence of comparative politics as a subdiscipline of political science include Almond and Coleman (1960), Almond and Verba (1963), Beer and Ulam (1958), Dahl (1966; 1971), Eckstein and Apter (1963), Holt and Turner (1970), Huntington (1968), La Palombara and Weiner (1966), Lipset and Rokkan (1967), Moore (1966), Przeworski and Teune (1970), Pye and Verba (1965), Riker (1962), and Sartori (1970). At the same time, two journals, *Comparative Politics* and *Comparative Political Studies*, appeared, helping to institutionalize the subfield.

2. There is also a long-standing debate in comparative politics about methodology. As comparativists propose explanations that cover sets of cases, perhaps based on causal accounts, they grapple with questions that relate to theory-building, concept formation, and case selection: How do concepts carry across cases? What is the value of treating concepts as variables that are measured by indicators? What is the proper use of case-specific information in theories that cover many cases? How does the choice of cases affect the general propositions offered? Are there requirements that define the number of cases that need to be included in an analysis? What is the relevance of single case studies to the development of theory? How can single case studies be used to speak to general sets of phenomena? Is it possible or desirable to include all relevant instances in the analysis? Is it possible to devise an adequate methodology that permits powerful generalizations based on the observation of a small number of cases? These questions raise problems of external validity, the ability to generalize beyond the case being observed.

   Nearly thirty years ago, Sartori (1970) drew attention to fundamental questions of concept formation. At that same time, Lijphart (1971) and Przeworski and Teune (1970) initiated a controversy about the proper methodology of comparative research, in which Eckstein (1975), Ragin (1987), Ragin and Becker (1992), and Skocpol and Somers (1980) have offered significant alternative positions (see Collier 1993 for a review of this literature). Most recently, Collier and Mahon (1993), Collier (1993), and Sartori (1994) illustrate further developments concerning the proper formation of concepts, and King, Keohane, and Verba (1994; 1995) initiated a productive debate over issues of research design in comparative politics. On the latter, see especially Bartels (1995), Brady (1995), Caporaso (1995), Collier (1995), Laitin (1995), Mohr (1996), Rogowski (1995), and Tarrow (1995). There is a natural affinity between studies of research design and comparative method that is frequently overlooked. King, Keohane, and Verba (1994; 1995) argue that there is only one scientific method. Hence, their strictures resemble those proposed by Cook and Campbell (1979).

REFERENCES

Almond, Gabriel A., and James S. Coleman, eds. 1960. *The Politics of Developing Areas.* Princeton: Princeton University Press.

Almond, Gabriel A., and Sidney Verba. 1963. *The Civic Culture: Political Attitudes and Democracy in Five Nations.* Princeton, NJ: Princeton University Press.

Bartels, Larry. 1995. "Symposium on Designing Social Inquiry." *The Political Methodologist,* 6:8–11.

Beer, Samuel H., and Adam B. Ulam, eds. 1958. *Patterns of Government: The Major Political Systems of Europe.* New York: Random House.

Brady, Henry E. 1995. "Symposium on *Designing Social Inquiry.*" *The Political Methodologist,* 6:11–14.

Caporaso, James. 1995. "Research Design Falsification, and the Qualitative-Quantitative Divide," *American Political Science Review* 89:457–60.

Collier, David. 1993. "The Comparative Method." In Ada W. Finifter, ed., *Political Science: The State of the Discipline II.* Washington, D.C.: American Political Science Association.

———. 1995. "Translating Quantitative Methods for Qualitative Researchers: The Case of Selection Bias." *American Political Science Review* 89:461–6.

Collier, David, and James Mahon. 1993. "Conceptual 'Stretching' Revisited: Adapting Categories in

Comparative Analysis." *American Political Science Review* 87: 845–55.

Cook, Thomas D., and Donald T. Campbell. 1979. *Quasi-Experimentation: Design and Analysis Issues for Field Settings.* Boston: Houghton Mifflin.

Dahl, Robert A., ed. 1966. *Political Oppositions in Western Democracies.* New Haven: Yale University Press.

———. 1971. *Polyarchy: Participation and Opposition.* New Haven: Yale University Press.

Downs, Anthony. 1957. *An Economic Theory of Democracy.* New York: Harper & Row.

Eckstein, Harry. 1963. "A Perspective on Comparative Politics, Past and Present." In Harry Eckstein and David E. Apter, eds., *Comparative Politics: A Reader.* New York: The Free Press of Glencoe.

———. 1975. "Case Study and Theory in Political Science." In Fred Greenstein and Nelson Polsby, eds., *Handbook of Political Science VII.* Reading, MA: Addison-Wesley.

Eckstein, Harry, and David E. Apter, eds. 1963. *Comparative Politics: A Reader.* New York: The Free Press of Glencoe.

Geertz, Clifford. 1973. *The Interpretation of Cultures.* New York: Basic Books.

Holt, Robert T., and John E. Turner, eds. 1970. *The Methodology of Comparative Research.* New York: The Free Press.

Huntington, Samuel P. 1968. *Political Order in Changing Societies.* New Haven: Yale University Press.

King, Gary, Robert O. Keohane, and Sidney Verba. 1994. *Designing Social Inquiry: Scientific Inquiry in Qualitative Research.* Princeton, NJ: Princeton University Press.

———. 1995. "The Importance of Research Design in Political Science." *American Political Science Review* 89:475–81.

Laitin, David. 1995. "Disciplining Political Science." *American Political Science Review* 89:454–6.

La Palombara, Joseph, and Myron Weiner, eds. 1966. *Political Parties and Political Development.* Princeton, NJ: Princeton University Press.

Lijphart, Arend. 1971. "Comparative Politics and Comparative Method." *American Political Science Review* 65:682–93.

Lipset, Seymour M., and Stein Rokkan, eds. 1967. *Party Systems and Voter Alignments: Cross-National Perspectives.* New York: The Free Press.

Mohr, Lawrence. 1996. *The Causes of Human Behavior: Implications for Theory and Method in the Social Sciences.* Ann Arbor: University of Michigan Press.

Moore, Barrington, Jr. 1966. *Social Origins of Dictatorship and Democracy: Lord and Peasant in the Making of the Modern World.* Boston: Beacon Press.

Olson, Mancur, Jr. 1968. *The Logic of Collective Action: Public Goods and the Theory of Groups.* New York: Schocken.

Przeworksi, Adam, and Henry Teune. 1970. *The Logic of Comparative Social Inquiry.* New York: Wiley-Interscience.

Pye, Lucien W., and Sidney Verba, eds. 1965. *Political Culture and Political Development.* Princeton, NJ: Princeton University Press.

Ragin, Charles. 1987. *The Comparative Method.* Berkeley: University of California Press.

Ragin, Charles C., and Howard S. Becker, eds. 1992. *What Is a Case? Exploring the Foundations of Social Inquiry.* Cambridge, UK: Cambridge University Press.

Riker, William H. 1962. *The Theory of Political Coalitions.* New Haven, CT: Yale University Press.

Rogowski, Ronald. 1995. "The Role of Theory and Anomaly in Social-Scientific Inference." *American Political Science Review* 89:467–70.

Sartori, Giovanni. 1970. "Concept Misformation in Comparative Politics." *American Political Science Review* 64:1033–53.

———. 1994. "Compare Why and How: Comparing, Miscomparing, and the Comparative Method." In Mattei Dogan and Ali Kazancigil, eds., *Comparing Nations: Concepts, Strategies, Substance.* Oxford: Blackwell.

Skocpol, Theda, and Margaret Somers. 1980. "The Uses of Comparative History in Macrosocial Inquiry." *Comparative Studies in Society and History* 22:174–97.

Tarrow, Sidney. 1995. "Bridging the Qualitative-Quantitative Divide in Political Science." *American Political Science Review* 89:471–4.

Gary King, Robert O. Keohane, and Sidney Verba
THE *SCIENCE* IN SOCIAL SCIENCE

■ ■ ■

For several decades, political scientists have debated the merits of case studies versus statistical studies, area studies versus comparative studies, and "scientific" studies of politics using quantitative methods versus "historical" investigations relying on rich textual and contextual understanding. Some quantitative researchers believe that systematic statistical analysis is the only road to truth in the social sciences. Advocates of qualitative research vehemently disagree. This difference of opinion leads to lively debate; but unfortunately, it also bifurcates the social sciences into a quantitative-systematic-generalizing branch and a qualitative-humanistic-discursive branch. As the former becomes more and more sophisticated in the analysis of statistical data (and their work becomes less comprehensible to those who have not studied the techniques), the latter becomes more and more convinced of the irrelevance of such analyses to the seemingly non-replicable and nongeneralizable events in which its practitioners are interested.

A major purpose of this book is to show that the differences between the quantitative and qualitative traditions are only stylistic and are methodologically and substantively unimportant. All good research can be understood—indeed, is best understood—to derive from the same underlying logic of inference. Both quantitative and qualitative research can be systematic and scientific. Historical research can be analytical, seeking to evaluate alternative explanations through a process of valid causal inference. History, or historical sociology, is not incompatible with social science (Skocpol 1984: 374–86).

Breaking down these barriers requires that we begin by questioning the very concept of "qualitative" research. We have used the term in our title to signal our subject matter, not to imply that "qualitative" research is fundamentally different from "quantitative" research, except in style.

Most research does not fit clearly into one category or the other. The best often combines features of each. In the same research project, some data may be collected that is amenable to statistical analysis, while other equally significant information is not. Patterns and trends in social, political, or economic behavior are more readily subjected to quantitative analysis than is the flow of ideas among people or the difference made by exceptional individual leadership. If we are to understand the rapidly changing social world, we will need to include information that cannot be easily quantified as well as that which can. Furthermore, all social science requires comparison, which entails judgments of which phenomena are "more" or "less" alike in degree (i.e., quantitative differences) or in kind (i.e., qualitative differences).

* * * Neither quantitative nor qualitative research is superior to the other, regardless of the research problem being addressed. Since many subjects of interest to social scientists cannot be meaningfully formulated in ways that permit statistical testing of hypotheses with quantitative data, we do not wish to encourage the exclusive use of quantitative techniques. We are not trying to get all social scientists out of the library and into the computer center, or to replace idiosyncratic conversations with structured interviews. Rather, we argue that nonstatistical research will produce more reliable results if researchers pay attention to the rules of scientific inference—rules that are sometimes more clearly stated in the style of quantitative research. Precisely defined statistical methods that undergird quantitative research represent abstract formal models

From *Designing Social Inquiry: Scientific Interest in Qualitative Research* (Princeton, NJ: Princeton University Press, 1994), pp. 4–12.

applicable to all kinds of research, even that for which variables cannot be measured quantitatively. The very abstract, and even unrealistic, nature of statistical models is what makes the rules of inference shine through so clearly.

The rules of inference that we discuss are not relevant to all issues that are of significance to social scientists. Many of the most important questions concerning political life—about such concepts as agency, obligation, legitimacy, citizenship, sovereignty, and the proper relationship between national societies and international politics—are philosophical rather than empirical. But the rules are relevant to all research where the goal is to learn facts about the real world. Indeed, the distinctive characteristic that sets social science apart from casual observation is that social science seeks to arrive at valid inferences by the systematic use of well-established procedures of inquiry. Our focus here on empirical research means that we sidestep many issues in the philosophy of social science as well as controversies about the role of postmodernism, the nature and existence of truth, relativism, and related subjects. We assume that it is possible to have some knowledge of the external world but that such knowledge is always uncertain.

Furthermore, nothing in our set of rules implies that we must run the perfect experiment (if such a thing existed) or collect all relevant data before we can make valid social scientific inferences. An important topic is worth studying even if very little information is available. The result of applying any research design in this situation will be relatively uncertain conclusions, but so long as we honestly report our uncertainty, this kind of study can be very useful. Limited information is often a necessary feature of social inquiry. Because the social world changes rapidly, analyses that help us understand those changes require that we describe them and seek to understand them contemporaneously, even when uncertainty about our conclusions is high. The urgency of a problem may be so great that data gathered by the most useful scientific methods might be obsolete before it can be accu-

mulated. If a distraught person is running at us swinging an ax, administering a five-page questionnaire on psychopathy may not be the best strategy. Joseph Schumpeter once cited Albert Einstein, who said "as far as our propositions are certain, they do not say anything about reality, and as far as they do say anything about reality, they are not certain" (Schumpeter [1936] 1991:298–99). Yet even though certainty is unattainable, we can improve the reliability, validity, certainty, and honesty of our conclusions by paying attention to the rules of scientific inference. The social science we espouse seeks to make descriptive and causal inferences about the world. Those who do not share the assumptions of partial and imperfect knowability and the aspiration for descriptive and causal understanding will have to look elsewhere for inspiration or for paradigmatic battles in which to engage.* * *

Defining Scientific Research in the Social Sciences

Our definition of "scientific research" is an ideal to which any actual quantitative or qualitative research, even the most careful, is only an approximation. Yet, we need a definition of good research, for which we use the word "scientific" as our descriptor.[1] This word comes with many connotations that are unwarranted or inappropriate or downright incendiary for some qualitative researchers. Hence, we provide an explicit definition here. As should be clear, we do not regard quantitative research to be any more scientific than qualitative research. Good research, that is, scientific research, can be quantitative or qualitative in style. In design, however, scientific research has the following four characteristics:

1. **The goal is inference.** Scientific research is designed to make descriptive or explanatory *inferences* on the basis of empirical information about the world. Careful descriptions of specific phenomena are often indispensable

to scientific research, but the accumulation of facts alone is not sufficient. Facts can be collected (by qualitative or quantitative researchers) more or less systematically, and the former is obviously better than the latter, but our particular definition of science requires the additional step of attempting to infer beyond the immediate data to something broader that is not directly observed. That something may involve *descriptive inference*—using observations from the world to learn about other unobserved facts. Or that something may involve *causal inference*—learning about causal effects from the data observed. The domain of inference can be restricted in space and time—voting behavior in American elections since 1960, social movements in Eastern Europe since 1989—or it can be extensive—human behavior since the invention of agriculture. In either case, the key distinguishing mark of scientific research is the goal of making inferences that go beyond the particular observations collected.

2. **The procedures are public.** Scientific research uses explicit, codified, and *public* methods to generate and analyze data whose reliability can therefore be assessed. Much social research in the qualitative style follows fewer precise rules of research procedure or of inference. As Robert K. Merton ([1949] 1968:71–72) put it, "The sociological analysis of qualitative data often resides in a private world of penetrating but unfathomable insights and ineffable understandings. . . . [However,] science . . . is public, not private." Merton's statement is not true of all qualitative researchers (and it is unfortunately still true of some quantitative analysts), but many proceed as if they had no method—sometimes as if the use of explicit methods would diminish their creativity. Nevertheless, they cannot help but use some method. Somehow they observe phenomena, ask questions, infer information about the world from these observations, and

make inferences about cause and effect. If the method and logic of a researcher's observations and inferences are left implicit, the scholarly community has no way of judging the validity of what was done. We cannot evaluate the principles of selection that were used to record observations, the ways in which observations were processed, and the logic by which conclusions were drawn. We cannot learn from their methods or replicate their results. Such research is not a *public* act. Whether or not it makes good reading, it is not a contribution to social science.

All methods—whether explicit or not—have limitations. The advantage of explicitness is that those limitations can be understood and, if possible, addressed. In addition, the methods can be taught and shared. This process allows research results to be compared across separate researchers and research projects studies to be replicated, and scholars to learn.

3. **The conclusions are uncertain.** By definition, inference is an imperfect process. Its goal is to use quantitative or qualitative data to learn about the world that produced them. Reaching perfectly certain conclusions from uncertain data is obviously impossible. Indeed, uncertainty is a central aspect of all research and all knowledge about the world. Without a reasonable estimate of uncertainty, a description of the real world or an inference about a causal effect in the real world is uninterpretable. A researcher who fails to face the issue of uncertainty directly is asserting either that he or she knows everything perfectly or that he or she has no idea how certain or uncertain the results are. Either way, inferences without uncertainty estimates are not science as we define it.

4. **The content is the method.** Finally, scientific research adheres to a set of rules of inference on which its validity depends. Explicating the most important rules is a major task of this

book.[2] The content of "science" is primarily the methods and rules, not the subject matter, since we can use these methods to study virtually anything. This point was recognized over a century ago when Karl Pearson (1892:16) explained that "the field of science is unlimited; its material is endless; every group of natural phenomena, every phase of social life, every stage of past or present development is material for science. The unity of all science consists alone in its method, not in its material."

These four features of science have a further implication: science at its best is a *social enterprise.* Every researcher or team of researchers labors under limitations of knowledge and insight, and mistakes are unavoidable, yet such errors will likely be pointed out by others. Understanding the social character of science can be liberating since it means that our work need not be beyond criticism to make an important contribution—whether to the description of a problem or its conceptualization, to theory or to the evaluation of theory. As long as our work explicitly addresses (or attempts to redirect) the concerns of the community of scholars and uses public methods to arrive at inferences that are consistent with rules of science and the information at our disposal, it is likely to make a contribution. And the contribution of even a minor article is greater than that of the "great work" that stays forever in a desk drawer or within the confines of a computer.

Science and Complexity

Social science constitutes an attempt to make sense of social situations that we perceive as more or less complex. We need to recognize, however, that what we perceive as complexity is not entirely inherent in phenomena: the world is not naturally divided into simple and complex sets of events. On the contrary, the perceived complexity of a situation depends in part on how well we can simplify reality, and our capacity to simplify depends on whether we can specify outcomes and explanatory variables in a coherent way. Having more observations may assist us in this process but is usually insufficient. Thus *"complexity" is partly conditional on the state of our theory.*

Scientific methods can be as valuable for intrinsically complex events as for simpler ones. Complexity is likely to make our inferences less certain but should *not* make them any less scientific. Uncertainty and limited data should not cause us to abandon scientific research. On the contrary: the biggest payoff for using the rules of scientific inference occurs precisely when data are limited, observation tools are flawed, measurements are unclear, and relationships are uncertain. With clear relationships and unambiguous data, method may be less important, since even partially flawed rules of inference may produce answers that are roughly correct.

Consider some complex, and in some sense unique, events with enormous ramifications. The collapse of the Roman Empire, the French Revolution, the American Civil War, World War I, the Holocaust, and the reunification of Germany in 1990 are all examples of such events. These events seem to be the result of complex interactions of many forces whose conjuncture appears crucial to the event having taken place. That is, independently caused sequences of events and forces converged at a given place and time, their interaction appearing to bring about the events being observed (Hirschman 1970). Furthermore, it is often difficult to believe that these events were inevitable products of large-scale historical forces: some seem to have depended, in part, on idiosyncracies of personalities, institutions, or social movements. Indeed, from the perspective of our theories, chance often seems to have played a role: factors outside the scope of the theory provided crucial links in the sequences of events.

One way to understand such events is by seeking generalizations: conceptualizing each case as a member of a *class of events* about which meaningful generalizations can be made. This method often works well for ordinary wars or revolutions, but some wars and revolutions, being much more extreme than others, are "outliers" in the statistical distribution. Furthermore, notable early wars or revolutions may exert such a strong impact on subsequent events of the same class—we think again of the French Revolution—that caution is necessary in comparing them with their successors, which may be to some extent the product of imitation. Expanding the class of events can be useful, but it is not always appropriate.

Another way of dealing scientifically with rare, large-scale events is to engage in counterfactual analysis: "the mental construction of a course of events which is altered through modifications in one or more 'conditions'" (Weber [1905] 1949:173). The application of this idea in a systematic, scientific way is illustrated in a particularly extreme example of a rare event from geology and evolutionary biology, both historically oriented natural sciences. Stephen J. Gould has suggested that one way to distinguish systematic features of evolution from stochastic, chance events may be to imagine what the world would be like if all conditions up to a specific point were fixed and then the rest of history were rerun. He contends that if it were possible to "replay the tape of life," to let evolution occur again from the beginning, the world's organisms today would be completely different (Gould 1989).

A unique event on which students of evolution have recently focused is the sudden extinction of the dinosaurs 65 million years ago. Gould (1989:318) says, "we must assume that consciousness would not have evolved on our planet if a cosmic catastrophe had not claimed the dinosaurs as victims." If this statement is true, the extinction of the dinosaurs was as important as any historical event for human beings; however, dinosaur extinction does not fall neatly into a class of events that could be studied in a systematic, comparative fashion through the application of general laws in a straightforward way.

Nevertheless, dinosaur extinction can be studied scientifically: alternative hypotheses can be developed and tested with respect to their observ-able implications. One hypothesis to account for dinosaur extinction, developed by Luis Alvarez and collaborators at Berkeley in the late 1970s (Alvarez 1990), posits a cosmic collision: a meteorite crashed into the earth at about 72,000 kilometers an hour, creating a blast greater than that from a full-scale nuclear war. If this hypothesis is correct, it would have the observable implication that iridium (an element common in meteorites but rare on earth) should be found in the particular layer of the earth's crust that corresponds to sediment laid down sixty-five million years ago; indeed, the discovery of iridium at predicted layers in the earth has been taken as partial confirming evidence for the theory. Although this is an unambiguously unique event, there are many other observable implications. For one example, it should be possible to find the meteorite's crater somewhere on Earth (and several candidates have already been found).[3]

The issue of the cause(s) of dinosaur extinction remains unresolved, although the controversy has generated much valuable research. For our purposes, the point of this example is that scientific generalizations are useful in studying even highly unusual events that do not fall into a large class of events. The Alvarez hypothesis cannot be tested with reference to a set of common events, but it does have observable implications for other phenomena that can be evaluated. We should note, however, that a hypothesis is not considered a reasonably certain explanation until it has been evaluated empirically and passed a number of demanding tests. At a minimum, its implications must be consistent with our knowledge of the external world; at best, it should predict what Imre Lakatos (1970) refers to as "new facts," that is, those formerly unobserved.

The point is that even apparently unique events such as dinosaur extinction can be studied scientifically if we pay attention to improving theory, data, and our use of the data. Improving our theory through conceptual clarification and specification of variables can generate more observable implications and even test causal theories of unique events such as dinosaur extinction. Improving our data allows us to observe more of these observable implications, and improving our use of data permits more of these implications to be extracted from existing data. That a set of events to be studied is highly complex does not render careful research design irrelevant. Whether we study many phenomena or few—or even one—the study will be improved if we collect data on as many observable implications of our theory as possible.

NOTES

1. We reject the concept, or at least the word, "quasi-experiment." Either a research design involves investigator control over the observations and values of the key causal variables (in which case it is an experiment) or it does not (in which case it is nonexperimental research). Both experimental and nonexperimental research have their advantages and drawbacks; one is not better in all research situations than the other.

2. Although we do cover the vast majority of the important rules of scientific inference, they are not complete. Indeed, most philosophers agree that a complete, exhaustive inductive logic is impossible, even in principle.

3. However, an alternative hypothesis, that extinction was caused by volcanic eruptions, is also consistent with the presence of iridium, and seems more consistent than the meteorite hypothesis with the finding that all the species extinctions did not occur simultaneously.

REFERENCES

Alvarez, Walter, and Frank Asaro. 1990. "An Extraterrestrial Impact." *Scientific American* (October): 78–84.

Gould, Stephen J. 1989. *Wonderful Life: The Burgess Shale and the Nature of History.* New York: Norton.

Hirschman, Albert O. 1970. "The Search for Paradigms as a Hindrance to Understanding." *World Politics* 22, no. 3 (April): 329–43.

Lakatos, Imre. 1970. "Falsification and the Methodology of Scientific Research Programs." In I. Lakatos and A. Musgrave, eds. *Criticism and the Growth of Knowledge.* Cambridge: Cambridge University Press.

Merton, Robert K. [1949] 1968. *Social Theory and Social Structure.* Reprint. New York: Free Press.

Pearson, Karl. 1892. *The Grammar of Science.* London: J. M. Dent & Sons, Ltd.

Schumpeter, Joseph A. [1936] 1991. "Can Capitalism Survive?" In Richard Swedberg, ed. *The Economics of Sociology and Capitalism,* Princeton: Princeton University Press.

Skocpol, Theda. 1984. "Emerging Agendas and Recurrent Strategies in Historical Sociology." In Theda Skocpol, ed. *Vision and Method in Historical Sociology.* New York: Cambridge University Press.

Weber, Max. [1905] 1949. "Critical Studies in the Logic of the Cultural Sciences." In Max Weber, ed. *The Methodology of the Social Sciences.* Translated and edited by Edward A. Shils and Henry A. Fluch. New York: Free Press.

John Stuart Mill
OF THE FOUR METHODS OF EXPERIMENTAL INQUIRY

The simplest and most obvious modes of singling out from among the circumstances which precede or follow a phenomenon, those with which it is really connected by an invariable law, are two in number. One is, by comparing together different instances in which the phenomenon occurs. The other is, by comparing instances in which the phenomenon does occur, with instances in other respects similar in which it does not. These two methods may be respectively denominated, the Method of Agreement, and the Method of Difference.

■　■　■

The mode of discovering and proving laws of nature * * * proceeds upon the following axiom: Whatever circumstance can be excluded, without prejudice to the phenomenon, or can be absent notwithstanding its presence, is not connected with it in the way of causation. The casual circumstances being thus eliminated, if only one remains, that one is the cause which we are in search of: if more than one, they either are, or contain among them, the cause: and so, *mutatis mutandis*, of the effect. As this method proceeds by comparing different instances to ascertain in what they agree, I have termed it the Method of Agreement: and we may adopt as its regulating principle the following canon:—

First Canon

If two or more instances of the phenomenon under investigation have only one circumstance in common, the circumstance in which alone all the instances agree, is the cause (or effect) of the given phenomenon.

Quitting for the present the Method of Agreement, to which we shall almost immediately return, we proceed to a still more potent instrument of the investigation of nature, the Method of Difference.

■　■　■

It is scarcely necessary to give examples of a logical process to which we owe almost all the inductive conclusions we draw in daily life. When a man is shot through the heart, it is by this method we know that it was the gun-shot which killed him: for he was in the fulness of life immediately before, all circumstances being the same, except the wound.

The axioms which are taken for granted in this method are evidently the following: Whatever antecedent cannot be excluded without preventing the phenomenon, is the cause, or a condition, of that phenomenon; Whatever consequent can be excluded, with no other difference in the antecedents than the absence of a particular one, is the effect of that one. Instead of comparing different instances of a phenomenon, to discover in what they agree, this method compares an instance of its occurrence with an instance of its non-occurrence, to discover in what they differ. The canon which is the regulating principle of the Method of Difference may be expressed as follows:—

Second Canon

If an instance in which the phenomenon under investigation occurs, and an instance in which it does not occur, have every circumstance save one in common, that one occurring only in the former; the circumstance in which alone the two instances differ, is the

From John Stuart Mill, *A System of Logic: Ratiocinative and Inductive* (London: John W. Parker, 1843), Chapter 8.

effect, or cause, or a necessary part of the cause, of the phenomenon.

■ ■ ■

Of these methods, that of Difference is more particularly a method of artificial experiment; while that of Agreement is more especially the resource we employ where experimentation is impossible.

■ ■ ■

In the spontaneous operations of nature there is generally such complication and such obscurity, they are mostly either on so overwhelmingly large or on so inaccessibly minute a scale, we are so ignorant of a great part of the facts which really take place, and even those of which we are not ignorant are so multitudinous, and therefore so seldom exactly alike in any two cases, that a spontaneous experiment, of the kind required by the Method of Difference, is commonly not to be found. When, on the contrary, we obtain a phenomenon by an artificial experiment, a pair of instances such as the method requires is obtained almost as a matter of course, provided the process does not last a long time.* * * It thus appears that in the study of the various kinds of phenomena which we can, by our voluntary agency, modify or control, we can in general satisfy the requisitions of the Method of Difference; but that by the spontaneous operations of nature those requisitions are seldom fulfilled.

The reverse of this is the case with the Method of Agreement. We do not here require instances of so special and determinate a kind. Any instances whatever, in which nature presents us with a phenomenon, may be examined for the purposes of this method; and if *all* such instances agree in anything, a conclusion of considerable value is already attained. We can seldom, indeed, be sure that this one point of agreement is the only one; but our ignorance does not, as in the Method of Difference, vitiate the conclusion; the certainty of the result, as far as it goes, is not affected. We have ascertained

one invariable antecedent or consequent, however many other invariable antecedents or consequents may still remain unascertained.* * *

It thus appears to be by the Method of Difference alone that we can ever, in the way of direct experience, arrive with certainty at causes. The Method of Agreement leads only to * * * uniformities in which the question of causation must for the present remain undecided.* * * And hence it is that the Method of Agreement * * * is more emphatically the method of investigation on those subjects where artificial experimentation is impossible; because on those it is, generally, our only resource of a directly inductive nature; while, in the phenomena which we can produce at pleasure, the Method of Difference generally affords a more efficacious process, which will ascertain causes as well as mere laws.

■ ■ ■

If, therefore, there were no other methods of experimental investigation * * * we should be for ever unable to determine the * * * cause. But we have still a resource. Though we cannot exclude an antecedent altogether, we may be able to produce, or nature may produce for us, some modification in it. By a modification is here meant, a change in it, not amounting to its total removal. If some modification in the antecedent A is always followed by a change in the consequent *a*, the other consequents *b* and *c* remaining the same; or, *vice versá*, if every change in *a* is found to have been preceded by some modification in A, none being observable in any of the other antecedents; we may safely conclude that *a* is, wholly or in part, an effect traceable to A, or at least in some way connected with it through causation.

■ ■ ■

Let us now suppose the question to be, what influence the moon exerts on the surface of the earth. We cannot try an experiment in the absence of the moon, so as to observe what terrestrial phenomena her annihilation would put an end to; but when we find that all the variations in the *position* of the moon are followed by corresponding variations in the time and place of high water, the place being always either on the side of the earth which is nearest to, or on that which is most remote from, the moon, we have ample evidence that the moon is, wholly or partially, the cause which determines the tides.

■ ■ ■

The method by which these results were obtained, may be termed the Method of Concomitant Variations: it is regulated by the following canon:—

Fifth Canon
Whatever phenomenon varies in any manner whenever another phenomenon varies in some particular manner, is either a cause or an effect of that phenomenon, or is connected with it through some fact of causation.

The last clause is subjoined, because it by no means follows when two phenomena accompany each other in their variations, that the one is cause and the other effect. The same thing may, and indeed must happen, supposing them to be two different effects of a common cause: and by this method alone it would never be possible to ascertain which of the two suppositions is the true one. The only way to solve the doubt would be that which we have so often adverted to, viz., by endeavouring to ascertain whether we can produce the one set of variations by means of the other.* * * If we cannot ourselves produce the variations, we must endeavour, though it is an attempt which is seldom successful, to find them produced by nature in some case in which the pre-existing circumstances are perfectly known to us.

■ ■ ■

The case in which this method admits of the most extensive employment, is that in which the variations of the cause are variations of quantity. Of such variations we may in general affirm with safety, that they will be attended not only with variations, but with similar variations, of the effect.* * * Suppose, then, that when A changes in quantity, *a* also changes in quantity, and in such a manner that we can trace the numerical relation which the changes of the one bear to such changes of the other as take place within our limits of observation. We may then, with certain precautions, safely conclude that the same numerical relation will hold beyond those limits. If, for instance, we find that when A is double, *a* is double; that when A is treble or quadruple, *a* is treble or quadruple; we may conclude that if A were a half or a third, *a* would be a half or a third, and finally, that if A were annihilated, *a* would be annihilated, and that *a* is wholly the effect of A, or wholly the effect of the same cause with A. And so with any other numerical relation according to which A and *a* would vanish simultaneously; as for instance if *a* were proportional to the square of A. If, on the other hand, *a* is not wholly the effect of A, but yet varies when A varies, it is probably (to use a mathematical phrase) a function not of A alone but of A and something else: its changes will be such as would occur if part of it remained constant, or varied on some other principle, and the remainder varied in some numerical relation to the variations of A. In that case, when A diminishes, *a* will seem to approach not towards zero, but towards some other limit: and when the series of variations is such as to indicate what that limit is, if constant, or the law of its variation if variable, the limit will exactly measure how much of *a* is the effect of some other and independent cause, and the remainder will be the effect of A (or of the cause of A).

■ ■ ■

There is * * * uncertainty affecting the inference that the law of variation which the quantities observe within our limits of observation, will hold beyond those limits. There is of course, in the first instance, the possibility that beyond the limits, and in circumstances therefore of which we have no direct experience, some counter-acting cause might develop itself; either a new agent, or a new property of the agents concerned, which lies dormant in the circumstances we are able to observe. This is an element of uncertainty which enters largely into all our predictions of effects; but it is not peculiarly applicable to the Method of Concomitant Variations. The uncertainty, however, of which I am about to speak, is characteristic of that method; especially in the cases in which the extreme limits of our observation are very narrow, in comparison with the possible variations in the quantities of the phenomena. Any one who has the slightest acquaintance with mathematics, is aware that very different laws of variation may produce numerical results which differ but slightly from one another within narrow limits; and it is often only when the absolute amounts of variation are considerable, that the difference between the results given by one law and by another, becomes appreciable. When, therefore, such variations in the quantity of the antecedents as we have the means of observing, are but small in comparison with the total quantities, there is much danger lest we should mistake the numerical law, and be led quite to miscalculate the variations which would take place beyond the limits; a miscalculation which would vitiate any conclusion respecting the dependence of the effect upon the cause, which could be founded upon those variations.

Ronald Rogowski

THE RISE OF EXPERIMENTATION IN POLITICAL SCIENCE

Three reasons may be advanced for the surge in experimental studies in political science since the turn of the millennium: (i) technological advance; (ii) demands for greater rigor and replicability from funding agencies, peer reviewers, and informed publics; and (iii) most importantly, the greater ability of experiments—some, assuredly not all—to prove what causes political phenomena.

That there has been a huge rise is hardly in dispute. The share of articles in leading journals that report on results of some kind of experiment has risen sharply (Figure 1.1); articles that themselves report on the rise have multiplied (Druckman, Green, Kuklinski, & Lupia, 2006; McDermott, 2002);

and not only handbooks (notably Druckman, Green, Kuklinski, & Lupia, 2011) and how-to manuals on experimentation (Gerber & Green, 2012) have appeared but, starting in 2014, a new journal devoted entirely to experimental work.[1]

Less evident has been a shift toward new and different kinds of experimentation. The once-dominant laboratory experiments, conducted chiefly among undergraduate subjects at major universities, have yielded to *survey, field, and "natural"* experiments. In each case, the Holy Grail is fully randomized "treatment" of some presumably representative set of subjects. If, for example, a random subset of voters is allowed to register more conveniently, by how much, if at all, does the turnout of that "treated" subset change? The virtue of random assignment, no less in politics than in medicine, is that it presumably controls for all other sources of variance in the outcome. If assignment is truly random, then

From Robert A. Scott, Marlis C. Buchmann, and Stephen M. Kosslyn, eds., *Emerging Trends in the Social and Behavioral Sciences: An Interdisciplinary, Searchable, and Linkable Resource* (Hoboken, NJ: John Wiley & Sons, Inc., 2016), pp. 1–11.

Figure 1.1 Experimental Articles in APSR, 1950–2014

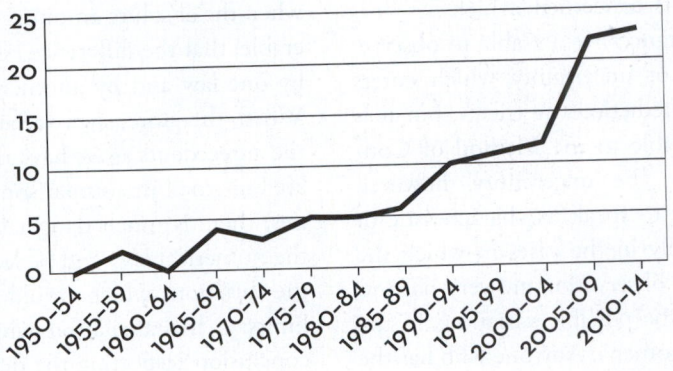

Note: Between 1906 and 1954, no experimental articles appeared.

the members of the "control" and the "treatment" group can differ hardly at all in their composition by gender, age, political inclination, previous voting history, or indeed any other characteristic. They should of course also not differ in their awareness of whether they have been "treated," so most experiments take care to hew to a "single blind" standard, in which such knowledge is withheld from the subjects; few, so far, have also attained the medical "gold standard" of double-blindedness (in which the researchers, too, remain ignorant of who has, and has not, been treated until the study is complete).

Survey experiments best exemplify the effects of newer technology and most readily achieve true randomness. Services such as YouGov, now available in 37 countries (https://yougov.co.uk/about/our-panel/), offer cheap and ready access to nationally representative panels of Internet responders, who can then be randomly divided into various treatment and control groups. In the pioneering study by Michael Tomz and Jessica Weeks (2013), for example, respondents in the United Kingdom and the United States were presented with an identical scenario—a hypothetical country is surreptitiously developing a nuclear weapon—and asked whether a preemptive strike was justified. In half the sample, however, the fictitious country was described as a

democracy, and in the other half as an autocracy. In both countries, respondents were far likelier to endorse a preemptive attack against the autocracy, thus suggesting a potent reason for the prevalence of the "democratic peace," that is, the rarity of armed conflict between democratic states.

What this example also demonstrates, however, along with many others, is the well-known problem of "external validity," is the Internet panel fully representative of the citizenry, would subjects respond in the same way to an actual crisis as to the hypothetical one, how easily could leaders persuade them that a threatening democratic state was actually an autocracy, and so on? We already have some evidence, albeit from a less fraught issue area, that people's responses to hypothetical choices fail to predict how they will behave when faced with the same real choices, with real consequences (Barabas & Jerit, 2010).

Field experiments face far fewer problems of external validity, approximating as they do the "silver standard" of randomized (but by no means double-blind) field tests (RFTs; cf. Manzi, 2012, p. 77). In the typical case, as indeed in what is usually credited as the very first experiment in political science (Gosnell, 1926), voters, legislators, voting districts, or even the coverage areas of television stations (Gerber, Gimpel, Green, & Shaw, 2011) are randomly assigned some treatment—a get-out-the vote mailing, a mailing that invokes peer pressure by listing which of their neighbors recently voted, a specific television advertisement, the same advertisement in a different but widely spoken language (usually Spanish)—while others are assigned a different treatment or no treatment at all. The differences in response constitute powerful evidence both of the effect (or lack thereof) and of its magnitude.

Even here, doubts about external validity may arise: would voters in, say, Kansas respond in the same way as voters have been demonstrated to do in, for example, Connecticut or Texas? However, the greater obstacles to such experiments are ones of expense and nondeception. Mailings are expensive, door-to-door campaigns even more so; ethical researchers cannot run ads or send mailers that falsely imply they come from a given candidate, political party, or official agency; nor can the treatment involve untruths (e.g., attributing to a candidate something she never said or a political affiliation he does not have).

Scholars have proven remarkably adept at avoiding these pitfalls. In "endorsement" surveying, for example, one can state a position that opposing sides have in fact taken (Taliban vs ASIF; Republicans vs Democrats) but in half of the sample attribute it solely to one group (e.g., Taliban), in the other half to their opponents (in this case, ASIF) and in each case ask respondents whether they agree with that position (Lyall, Blair, & Imai, 2013). If support differs markedly according to which side is named as having "endorsed" the position, that may be taken as tacit support of the one side or the other. On even more delicate topics, or ones where respondents may fear that their answers will elicit retribution, "list" or "noise-introducing" techniques may be used (Blair, 2015; Blair, Imai, & Lyall, 2014).[2] Equally inventive, and involving even more delicate issues of funding and of scholarly detachment, was a pioneering study in which researchers persuaded a primary election candidate for statewide office in Texas to permit them to assign his different television ads, in English and in Spanish, randomly to different metropolitan areas (Gerber *et al.*, 2011). Because the campaign was also funding rolling surveys, it proved possible to measure not only the impact of a given advertisement but the duration of the impact. (For attack ads, the effect waned quickly.)

Some of the most daring and original field experiments have been performed in poorer and less stable countries, even in ones that have experienced recent civil war or genocide. In Rwanda, for example, Paluck and Green (2009) ascertained, again by random assignment of subjects in a small set of rural villages that had experienced the genocide, whether regular viewing of a government-sponsored *telenovela* that subtly advocated ethnic reconciliation (vs a "control" set of videos on AIDS prevention) actually changed expressed attitudes and—far more difficult to pin down—behaviors.[3]

Finally, and most controversially, *natural experiments* have proliferated. In these, there is no attempt to assign subjects or regions randomly; rather, evidence is advanced that some exogenous event—the building of an express highway (Shami, 2012), the drawing or redrawing of state, regional, or electoral district boundaries (Ansolabehere, Snyder, & Stewart, 2000), which party held power in London at the time a given Indian province was subjected to British rule (Banerjee & Iyer, 2005), whether military recruits from a given area experienced combat (Jha & Wilkinson, 2012)—has yielded a "quasi-random" assignment of units or persons to "treatment" and "control" groups. An important subset of natural experiments (although not always so regarded) involves so-called regression discontinuity analyses, in which cases on slightly to one side of a "discontinuity" are compared with those on the other side. In one of the most common examples of such studies, the researcher compares parliamentary candidates who narrowly won their seats with rival candidates who narrowly lost. Here the assumption is maintained that such narrow victories and defeats—whether a candidate receives 49.9% or 50.1% of the vote—are essentially decided by chance, so that in all other respects these narrow winners are identical to the narrow losers. [See, for one recent example, Eggers and Hainmueller (2009).]

Interestingly, one of the earliest known practitioners of the natural experiment was Abraham Lincoln. In the debates in the 1850s over whether to permit slavery to expand into the territories, Lincoln's adversary Stephen Douglas argued that the legal status of slavery did not matter: slavery flourished where soil and climate encouraged plantation agriculture, withered where they did not. In rebuttal, Lincoln in his famous "Cincinnati Speech" of September 17, 1859 (Lincoln, 1897), offered a persuasive natural experiment:

> Let us take an illustration between the States of Ohio and Kentucky. Kentucky is separated by this River Ohio, not a mile wide. A portion of Kentucky, by reason of the course of the Ohio, is further north than this portion of Ohio, in which we now stand. Kentucky is entirely covered with slavery; Ohio is entirely free from it. What made that difference? Was it climate? No! A portion of Kentucky was further north than this portion of Ohio. Was it soil? No! There is nothing in the soil of the one more favorable to slave labor than the other. It was not climate or soil that caused one side of the line to be entirely covered with slavery, and the other side free of it. What was it? Study over it. Tell us, if you can, in all the range of conjecture, if there be anything you can conceive of that made that difference, other than that there was no law of any sort keeping it out of Kentucky, while the Ordinance of '87 kept it out of Ohio.

Yet, as Lincoln was wise enough to note, the presumption of "quasirandomness" remains always rebuttable in natural experiments. There may indeed be some difference in "all the range of conjecture" that determines or explains the contrast between the supposed treatment and control groups, or that shows them to differ substantially from each other in some way that random assignment could not yield. If, in a regression discontinuity analysis, three-quarters of the narrow victories in Congressional races go to Republicans, while three-quarters of the narrow losers are Democrats, the quasi-random assumption is violated in an important way. If the systems of land tenure imposed by the British in India resulted more from preexisting post-Mughal institutions than from the colonial masters' prevailing ideology (Foa, 2015), we can no longer assume random assignment. Had it been the case—and the authors take care to show that it was not—that combat experience of Indian soldiers in World War II had been confined largely to groups that the British had regarded as "warlike castes," again the assignment to treatment or control would have been far from random.

Trenchant criticisms of some early natural experiments along these lines have been raised, most pithily in an article aptly entitled, "When 'Natural Experiments' Are Neither Natural nor Experiments" [Sekhon and Titiunik (2012); but see also Imai, Keele, Tingley, and Yamamoto (2011)]. Such exposés by no means rule out natural experiments—Lincoln's remains persuasive to the present day—but they do raise a warning flag: one must demonstrate convincingly that a "quasi" (literally: "as if") random assignment has a high likelihood of being close to random.

In a few extraordinarily lucky instances, a natural experiment offers full and undoubted randomization. Robert F. Erikson and Laura Stoker (2011), for example, exploited the Vietnam-era draft lottery, in which men's birthdays were literally chosen by being drawn from a rotating drum, to establish that having been assigned a low "draft number" and hence exposed to a risk of conscription was strongly and enduringly associated with more pacifist and leftist political attitudes.

Finally, *laboratory experiments* continue to be performed, but they seem to be fading from the mainstream journals. From 2012 to the present (Autumn 2015), for example, only two articles based on laboratory experiments have appeared in the *APSR*, about 10% of the total number of experimental papers published during that time. What seems to have undermined this kind of experimental work is a growing skepticism about its external validity: do ordinary people, or actual decision-makers, behave in the same way as undergraduate subjects sitting before a computer? In some cases, practitioners of this approach have actually tried to buttress their findings by replicating their studies among more representative subjects. Laboratory experiments probably convince best when they tap basic human characteristics—our propensity to miscalculate odds, or to draw false inferences by "thinking fast" (Kahneman, 2011)—rather than specifically political reactions. In other words, it seems that laboratory experiments are migrating to the domain of psychology and away from political science.

The trend therefore is clear; but what has driven it? The first factor, as mentioned earlier, is simply improved technology. By a corollary of "Moore's Law," computerization has made all kinds of experiments cheaper and easier to do, albeit by varying margins. Survey experiments would have been impossible, or at the very least prohibitively expensive, in the precomputer age. Field experiments have been aided by video technology, smart phones (e.g., to register responses instantly or to photograph electoral irregularities), and faster communications from the field to a central data-gathering point. Even laboratory experiments have benefited significantly: subjects who once registered their responses laboriously, often on paper, now do so instantly from a computer screen. In addition, natural experiments are more easily elicited through such innovations as digitized archives and GIS mapping.

A second factor, often underestimated, has involved demands from politicians, opinion makers, and even informed publics for clearer, more convincing, and more reliable findings, ones on which policymakers can actually rely. The critic Jim Manzi (2012), whose work the *New York Times* columnist David Brooks (2012) popularized, contends that in the most important recent crises—the Great Recession, the Iranian nuclear threat, rising income inequality, overtime variations in crime rates—the social sciences, including economics, have relied on models that, while "useful" and "interesting," do "not establish a causal relationship with sufficient certainty to [permit] rational prediction of the effect of a change in policy" (Manzi, 2012, p. 105). In his view, only fully randomized testing can establish causation

with sufficient certainty; and such testing must set itself more modest goals, elucidating pieces of the puzzle—as, in fact, most recent experiments do.

While much of the rising political opposition to governmental funding of the social sciences betrays simply a "shoot the messenger" attitude toward findings the politicians or opinion leaders dislike (cf. Rogowski, 2013), political science in particular renders itself vulnerable to attack on precisely the ground Manzi and Brooks suggest: weak and tentative causal inference, occasioned entirely by lack of fully randomized testing. To draw an unhappy parallel, if medicine still relied on anecdote and induction, the National Institutes of Health might be similarly subject to political attack. Even massively evidence-supported science, of course, can be attacked by the ignorant, the deluded, or the meretricious[4]—think only of the current controversies over global warming, vaccines, and genetically modified organisms—but refuting such nonsense is far easier if the truth is supported by extensive and repeated randomized tests, as for example in the case of the vaccine controversy.

Peer reviewers for major journals in political science, to judge by the experience of the *APSR* and other leading outlets, have begun, if not to reject other modes of inquiry, to credit far more the findings of experimental research. More specifically, the now-frequent criticism of endogeneity, that is, of possible reverse causation or of causation of two correlated variables from a third factor not considered, has felled many an otherwise convincing paper;[5] and the by-now conventional answer of employing a clearly exogenous instrumental variable (IV) can never be as convincing as a randomized experiment—although, of course, such experimentation is hardly possible in the case of historical data.

The National Science Foundation (NSF) is moving only glacially in this direction, likely to its political detriment. Of 237 NSF political science awards with start dates in the 4 years between September 1, 2011, and August 31, 2015, 16, or not quite 7%, included the words "experiment" or "experimental" in their titles, and the trend appeared virtually flat:

6% in the first 2 years, just under 8% in the last two.[6] Yet as it becomes evident that the few experimental projects they have funded have been among those with highest impact, and as it becomes more urgent to fend off political attacks, one suspects that a greater share of funding will go to experimental work. For now, however, some of the most startling and fine-grained studies, including notably the one from the Texas primary election, are being funded by campaigns, other private sources, or smaller foundations.

The parallel shift in economics, albeit more recent, seems also to be more rapid, particularly in development economics, where the work of Abhijit Banerjee and Esther Duflo (2011) has proved revolutionary and is rapidly coming to dominate. The World Bank, the Inter-American Development Bank, and the governments of Indonesia and India, among many others, have tested policy innovations through randomized controlled trials (RCTs) (*Economist*, 2013, 2015).

The final advantage, and certainly the most important one, is sheer scientific beauty and honesty. We understand almost immediately that a fully randomized experiment convinces us as no nonexperimental method can. At their best, the findings of randomized experiments in political science are as exciting and important as those of the earliest ones in medicine—which, surprisingly, date only from the late 1930s (Manzi, 2012, Chapter 7).

It should go without saying that many important questions in political science, especially ones of historical causation, cannot be addressed by randomized trial—although even in cases from the past, there is great value in searching, as Lincoln did and Banerjee and Iyer have done, for some natural experiment. Other large questions will have to be addressed piecemeal: Tomz and Weeks have by no means solved the whole puzzle of the democratic peace, but they have certainly shed important light on how much of it is due, precisely as Immanuel Kant originally argued, to citizens' reluctance, on both moral and practical grounds, to enter combat with another democracy. Furthermore, we do not know whether, in general,

exposing citizens to the risks of combat by conscription makes them in later years more bellicose or more pacific (or neither); but thanks to Erikson and Stoker, we now know for certain that, in the case of the United States during the Vietnam war, it made potential draftees lastingly more pacific.

It requires little courage to make bold predictions about a future in which one will no longer be alive, but I will at least speculate that, 50 years from now, experimentation will play much the same role in political science as it now does in medicine, and with similar results in public confidence and material support. If I am wrong, and if political science remains a largely nonexperimental science, it will continue to be treated with skepticism and stinginess—and, I fear, rightly so.

NOTES

1. *Journal of Experimental Political Science*, eds. Rebecca B. Morton and Joshua A. Tucker. Cambridge Journals.

2. These techniques obscure the responses of individuals—in that sense, they introduce "noise" into the "signals" from individual respondents—but still permit valid inference from the set of respondents as a whole. In the "list" technique, respondents are asked only to indicate *how many* of the items on a larger list they endorse, not which ones. In the survey in Afghanistan, for example, the question asked was, "I'm going to read you a list with the names of different groups and individuals on it. After I read the entire list, I'd like you to tell me how many of these groups and individuals you broadly support, meaning that you generally agree with the goals and policies of the group or individuals. Please don't tell me which ones you generally agree with; only tell me how many groups or individuals you broadly support" (Blair *et al.*, 2014, p. 1045).

3. Pushed too far, such field experiments raise ethical concerns: Are subjects, for example, being deceived or being surreptitiously observed? A different concern is that some less developed countries can become

such frequent loci of field experiments that subjects become too knowledgeable, or even jaded.

4. Thus tobacco companies massively funded research that cast doubt on the link (which they knew perfectly well to be irrefutable) between smoking and lung cancer; and, in more recent years, large oil companies have sought to create controversy over man-made global warming, while in private they not only accepted its reality but were taking measures to protect their own investments against such consequences as rising ocean levels (Krauss, 2015; Lieberman & Rust, 2015).

5. I speak here, albeit only impressionistically, from my 4-year experience (2008–2012) as lead editor of the *APSR*.

6. Search on NSF Awards database (http://www.nsf.gov/awardsearch/), using "advanced search" function and keying for SBE Directorate and Program "political science," within the specified dates. Search conducted on October 16, 2015.

REFERENCES

Ansolabehere, S., Snyder, J. M., Jr., & Stewart, C., III, (2000). Old voters, new voters, and the personal vote. *American Journal of Political Science, 44*, 17–34.

Banerjee, A., & Duflo, E. (2011). *Poor economics: A radical rethinking of the way to fight global poverty.* New York, NY: PublicAffairs.

Banerjee, A., & Iyer, L. (2005). History, institutions, and economic performance: The legacy of colonial land tenure systems in India. *American Economic Review, 95*, 1190–1213.

Barabas, J., & Jerit, J. (2010). Are survey experiments externally valid? *American Political Science Review, 104*, 226–242.

Blair, G. (2015). Survey methods for sensitive topics. *APSA Comparative Politics Newsletter.*

Blair, G., Imai, K., & Lyall, J. (2014). Comparing and combining list and endorsement experiments: Evidence from Afghanistan. *American Journal of Political Science, 58*, 1043–1063.

Brooks, D. (2012). Is our children learning? *The New York Times*, 26 April.

Druckman, J. N., Green, D. P., Kuklinski, J. H., & Lupia, A. (2006). The growth and development of experimental research in political science. *American Political Science Review, 100*, 627–635.

Druckman, J. N., Green, D. P., Kuklinski, J. H., & Lupia, A. (Eds.) (2011). *Cambridge handbook of the experimental political science.* Cambridge, England: Cambridge University Press.

Economist, The. (2013). Random harvest: Once treated with scorn, randomised control trials [sic] are coming of age. 14 December.

Economist, The. (2015). Randomized controlled trials: Measure for measure. 12 December.

Eggers, A. C., & Hainmueller, J. (2009). MPs for sale? Returns to office in postwar British politics. *American Political Science Review, 103*, 1–21.

Erikson, R. F., & Stoker, L. (2011). Caught in the draft: The effects of Vietnam draft lottery status on political attitudes. *American Political Science Review, 105*, 221–237.

Foa, R. (2015). *The pre-colonial origins of state capacity: Evidence from Indian districts.* Delivered at annual meeting of the American political science association, San Francisco.

Gerber, A., Gimpel, J. G., Green, D. P., & Shaw, D. R. (2011). How large and long-lasting are the persuasive effects of televised campaign ads? Results from a randomized field experiment. *American Political Science Review, 105*, 135–150.

Gerber, A., & Green, D. P. (2012). *Field experiments: Design, analysis, and interpretation.* New York, NY: W. W. Norton & Co.

Gosnell, H. F. (1926). An experiment in the stimulation of voting. *American Political Science Review, 20*, 869–874.

Imai, K., Keele, L., Tingley, D., & Yamamoto, T. (2011). Unpacking the black box of causality: Learning about causal mechanisms from experimental and observational studies. *American Political Science Review, 105*, 765–789.

Jha, S., & Wilkinson, S. (2012). Does combat experience foster organizational skill? Evidence from ethnic cleansing during the Partition of South Asia. *American Political Science Review, 106*, 883–907.

Kahneman, D. (2011). *Thinking fast and slow.* New York, NY: Farrar, Straus, and Giroux.

Krauss, C. (2015). More oil companies could join Exxon Mobil as focus of climate investigations. *New York Times*, 6 November.

Lieberman, A., & Rust, S. (2015). Big oil companies united to fight regulations—but spent millions bracing for climate change. *Los Angeles Times*, 31 December.

Lincoln, A. (1897). *Political debates between Lincoln and Douglas.* Cleveland, OH: Burrows Bros. Co., 1897; Bartleby.com, 2001. Retrieved from www.bartleby.com/251/.

Lyall, J., Blair, G., & Imai, K. (2013). Explaining support for combatants during wartime: A survey experiment in Afghanistan. *American Political Science Review, 107*, 679–705.

McDermott, R. (2002). Experimental methods in political science. *Annual Review of Political Science, 5*, 31–61.

Manzi, J. (2012). *Uncontrolled: The surprising payoff of trial-and-error for business, politics, and society.* New York, NY: Basic Books.

Paluck, E. L., & Green, D. P. (2009). Deference, dissent, and dispute resolution: An experimental intervention using mass media to change norms and behavior in Rwanda. *American Political Science Review, 103*, 622–644.

Rogowski, R. (2013). Shooting (or ignoring) the messenger. *Political Studies Review, 11*, 216–221.

Sekhon, J. S., & Titiunik, R. (2012). When natural experiments are neither natural nor experiments. *American Political Science Review, 106*, 35–57.

Shami, M. (2012). Collective action, clientelism, and connectivity. *American Political Science Review, 106*, 588–606.

Tomz, M., & Weeks, J. (2013). Public opinion and the democratic peace. *American Political Science Review, 107*, 849–865.

2 THE STATE

At the center of most discussions of comparative politics lies the state, the organization that wields power over people and territory. In this chapter, we will consider the ways in which we think about and measure the state and how these have changed over time. A theoretical discussion of the state is complemented by more concrete discussions of the challenges that states confront in the current international system.

Many scholars rely heavily on the work of Max Weber, often cited as one of the forefathers of modern social science. In addition to political science, the fields of sociology and economics also owe a debt to Weber. Indeed, at the time of his writing during the late nineteenth and early twentieth centuries, these fields were not clearly distinguished from each other. "Politics as a Vocation" (1918) was a speech originally presented at Munich University, in which Weber sought to lay out some of the most basic ways in which he understood political power. Weber provided the modern definition of the state (a monopoly of force over territory) and from there outlined what he believed to be the central forms of political authority (traditional, charismatic, rational-legal). According to Weber, the development of the modern state occured alongside the growing domination of the bureaucracy and rational-legal authority—politics as a profession, rather than a calling or an inherited role. Thus, charismatic or traditional leaders gave way to the modern professional state. In spite of the profound influence of Weber's work, by the mid-twentieth century state-focused analysis began to lose favor, particularly in the United States. Swept up in the so-called behavioral revolution, political scientists began to concentrate more on societal factors and individual political behavior, downplaying the degree to which the state itself was an important source of politics.

However, over the past three decades, political scientists have returned their attention to the idea of state power and how the state's autonomy and capacity can shape such things as the emergence of democracy or economic progress (topics that we discuss in Chapters 4 and 5). Comparative politics has again become a much more state-focused field of study, and a wide range of contemporary scholars have refocused on the state as an important variable. Jeffrey Herbst's "War and the State in Africa" (1990) draws on historical studies of state formation in Europe to consider whether we can expect similar outcomes in other parts of the world, such as Africa. In Europe, the author notes, interstate war was a critical component in the development of the modern state, helping to improve taxation, administration, and the development of symbols to establish national identity, a process that occurred over many centuries. In Africa, however, states have not formed out of a long process of warfare, but rather are the remnants of empires that once dominated the continent. These states are ill-equipped to carry out most administrative tasks and lack the kind of national unity that can help build state legitimacy. There is a terrible irony, then: the absence of interstate war across Africa has left the continent with an array of weak states that cannot secure either prosperity or security. Indeed, one could go so far as to argue that the lack of war between states has resulted in horrible wars within them, such as the civil conflicts in Liberia or the genocide in Rwanda. Herbst is skeptical that peaceful state-building policies could be an alternative to war, and though he does not suggest that war between countries should be welcomed in Africa in order to build stronger states, it is hard not to draw such an uncomfortable conclusion. In the foreseeable future, the author anticipates an Africa of "permanently weak states."

In the years since Herbst's work was written, Africa and other parts of the world have seen the rise of something worse than the weak states Herbst discusses: what are known as "failed states." From the former Soviet Union to Latin America, Asia, and Africa, various countries have teetered on the edge or plunged into the abyss of state failure, where the most basic functions of the state—including the monopoly of force—have broken down, leading to civil conflict and anarchy. Failed states have become a tremendous concern, not only because of the suffering that such state failures cause but also because of the fear that failed states often provide the perfect breeding ground for terrorism. Robert I. Rotberg considers this in "The New Nature of Nation-State Failure" (2002). When states fail, we see greater civil conflict, weak infrastructure, inequality, corruption, and economic decline. As we learned from Herbst, it is very difficult to build a strong state; for a failed state, this task is even more difficult. Policy makers, Rotberg argues, should take more care to identify and strengthen states in danger of collapse before they are beyond assistance and become an international threat.

Scholars are concerned about not only the power of the state but also the state's future direction. In "Sovereignty" (2001), Stephen D. Krasner takes on many of the recent arguments that, in one way or another, suggest the decline of the state as a major political actor. In spite of such factors as globalization and political integration, the state is still very much alive and will continue to be the driving force in domestic and international politics. The state has a long historical pedigree and an enormous impact on central questions in human development—and it is not going away anytime soon.

Max Weber
POLITICS AS A VOCATION

This lecture, which I give at your request, will necessarily disappoint you in a number of ways. You will naturally expect me to take a position on actual problems of the day. But that will be the case only in a purely formal way and toward the end, when I shall raise certain questions concerning the significance of political action in the whole way of life. In today's lecture, all questions that refer to what policy and what content one should give one's political activity must be eliminated. For such questions have nothing to do with the general question of what politics as a vocation means and what it can mean. Now to our subject matter.

What do we understand by politics? The concept is extremely broad and comprises any kind of *independent* leadership in action. One speaks of the currency policy of the banks, of the discounting policy of the Reichsbank, of the strike policy of a trade union; one may speak of the educational policy of a municipality or a township, of the policy of the president of a voluntary association, and, finally, even of the policy of a prudent wife who seeks to guide her husband. Tonight, our reflections are, of course, not based upon such a broad concept. We wish to understand by politics only the leadership, or the influencing of the leadership, of a *political* association, hence today, of a *state*.

But what is a "political" association from the sociological point of view? What is a "state"? Sociologically, the state cannot be defined in terms of its ends. There is scarcely any task that some political association has not taken in hand, and there is no task that one could say has always been exclusive and peculiar to those associations which are designated as political ones: today the state, or historically, those associations which have been the predecessors of the modern state. Ultimately, one can define the modern state sociologically only in terms of the specific *means* peculiar to it, as to every political association, namely, the use of physical force.

"Every state is founded on force," said Trotsky at Brest-Litovsk. That is indeed right. If no social institutions existed which knew the use of violence, then the concept of "state" would be eliminated, and a condition would emerge that could be designated as "anarchy," in the specific sense of this word. Of course, force is certainly not the normal or the only means of the state—nobody says that—but force

is a means specific to the state. Today the relation between the state and violence is an especially intimate one. In the past, the most varied institutions—beginning with the sib—have known the use of physical force as quite normal. Today, however, we have to say that a state is a human community that (successfully) claims the *monopoly of the legitimate use of physical force* within a given territory. Note that "territory" is one of the characteristics of the state. Specifically, at the present time, the right to use physical force is ascribed to other institutions or to individuals only to the extent to which the state permits it. The state is considered the sole source of the "right" to use violence. Hence, "politics" for us means striving to share power or striving to influence the distribution of power, either among states or among groups within a state.

This corresponds essentially to ordinary usage. When a question is said to be a "political" question, when a cabinet minister or an official is said to be a "political" official, or when a decision is said to be "politically" determined, what is always meant is that interests in the distribution, maintenance, or transfer of power are decisive for answering the questions and determining the decision or the official's sphere of activity. He who is active in politics strives for power either as a means in serving other aims, ideal or egoistic, or as "power for power's sake," that is, in order to enjoy the prestige-feeling that power gives.

Like the political institutions historically preceding it, the state is a relation of men dominating men, a relation supported by means of legitimate (i.e., considered to be legitimate) violence. If the state is to exist, the dominated must obey the authority claimed by the powers that be. When and why do men obey? Upon what inner justifications and upon what external means does this domination rest?

To begin with, in principle, there are three inner justifications, hence basic *legitimations* of domination.

First, the authority of the "eternal yesterday," i.e., of the mores sanctified through the unimaginably ancient recognition and habitual orientation to

From H. H. Gerth and C. Wright Mills, eds., trans, *From Max Weber: Essays in Sociology* (New York: Galaxy, 1958), pp. 77–87.

conform. This is "traditional" domination exercised by the patriarch and the patrimonial prince of yore.

There is the authority of the extraordinary and personal *gift of grace* (charisma), the absolutely personal devotion and personal confidence in revelation, heroism, or other qualities of individual leadership. This is "charismatic" domination, as exercised by the prophet or—in the field of politics—by the elected war lord, the plebiscitarian ruler, the great demagogue, or the political party leader.

Finally, there is a domination by virtue of "legality," by virtue of the belief in the validity of legal statute and functional "competence" based on rationally created *rules*. In this case, obedience is expected in discharging statutory obligations. This is domination as exercised by the modern "servant of the state" and by all those bearers of power who in this respect resemble him.

It is understood that, in reality, obedience is determined by highly robust motives of fear and hope—fear of the vengeance of magical powers or of the power-holder, hope for reward in this world or in the beyond—and besides all this, by interests of the most varied sort. Of this we shall speak presently. However, in asking for the "legitimations" of this obedience, one meets with these three "pure" types: "traditional," "charismatic," and "legal."

These conceptions of legitimacy and their inner justifications are of very great significance for the structure of domination. To be sure, the pure types are rarely found in reality. But today we cannot deal with the highly complex variants, transitions, and combinations of these pure types, which problems belong to "political science." Here we are interested above all in the second of these types: domination by virtue of the devotion of those who obey the purely personal "charisma" of the "leader." For this is the root of the idea of a *calling* in its highest expression.

Devotion to the charisma of the prophet, or the leader in war, or to the great demagogue in the *ecclesia* or in parliament, means that the leader is personally recognized as the innerly "called" leader of men. Men do not obey him by virtue of tradition or statute, but because they believe in him. If he is more than a narrow and vain upstart of the moment, the leader lives for his cause and "strives for his work." The devotion of his disciples, his followers, his personal party friends is oriented to his person and to its qualities.

Charismatic leadership has emerged in all places and in all historical epochs. Most importantly in the past, it has emerged in the two figures of the magician and the prophet on the one hand, and in the elected war lord, the gang leader and *condotierre* on the other hand. *Political* leadership in the form of the free "demagogue" who grew from the soil of the city state is of greater concern to us; like the city state, the demagogue is peculiar to the Occident and especially to Mediterranean culture. Furthermore, political leadership in the form of the parliamentary "party leader" has grown on the soil of the constitutional state, which is also indigenous only to the Occident.

These politicians by virtue of a "calling," in the most genuine sense of the word, are of course nowhere the only decisive figures in the crosscurrents of the political struggle for power. The sort of auxiliary means that are at their disposal is also highly decisive. How do the politically dominant powers manage to maintain their domination? The question pertains to any kind of domination, hence also to political domination in all its forms, traditional as well as legal and charismatic.

Organized domination, which calls for continuous administration, requires that human conduct be conditioned to obedience towards those masters who claim to be the bearers of legitimate power. On the other hand, by virtue of this obedience, organized domination requires the control of those material goods which in a given case are necessary for the use of physical violence. Thus, organized domination requires control of the personal executive staff and the material implements of administration.

The administrative staff, which externally represents the organization of political domination, is, of course, like any other organization, bound by obedience to the power-holder and not alone by the concept of legitimacy, of which we have just spoken. There are two other means, both of which appeal to personal interests: material reward and social honor. The fiefs of vassals, the prebends of patrimonial officials, the salaries of modern civil servants, the honor of knights, the privileges of estates, and the honor of the civil servant comprise their respective wages. The fear of losing them is the final and decisive basis for solidarity between the executive staff and the power-holder. There is honor and booty for the followers in war; for the demagogue's following, there are "spoils"—that is, exploitation of the dominated through the monopolization of office—and there are politically determined profits and premiums of vanity. All of these rewards are also derived from the domination exercised by a charismatic leader.

To maintain a dominion by force, certain material goods are required, just as with an economic organization. All states may be classified according to whether they rest on the principle that the staff of men themselves *own* the administrative means, or whether the staff is "separated" from these means of administration. This distinction holds in the same sense in which today we say that the salaried employee and the proletarian in the capitalistic enterprise are "separated" from the material means of production. The power-holder must be able to count on the obedience of the staff members, officials, or whoever else they may be. The administrative means may consist of money, building, war material, vehicles, horses, or whatnot. The question is whether or not the power-holder himself directs and organizes the administration while delegating executive power to personal servants, hired officials, or personal favorites and confidants, who are non-owners, i.e., who do not use the material means of administration in their own right but are directed by the lord. The distinction runs through all administrative organizations of the past.

These political associations in which the material means of administration are autonomously controlled, wholly or partly, by the dependent administrative staff may be called associations organized in "*estates*." The vassal in the feudal association, for instance, paid out of his own pocket for the administration and judicature of the district enfeoffed to him. He supplied his own equipment and provisions for war, and his subvassals did likewise. Of course, this had consequences for the lord's position of power, which only rested upon a relation of personal faith and upon the fact that the legitimacy of his possession of the fief and the social honor of the vassal were derived from the overlord.

However, everywhere, reaching back to the earliest political formations, we also find the lord himself directing the administration. He seeks to take the administration into his own hands by having men personally dependent upon him: slaves, household officials, attendants, personal "favorites," and prebendaries enfeoffed in kind or in money from his magazines. He seeks to defray the expenses from his own pocket, from the revenues of his patrimonium; and he seeks to create an army which is dependent upon him personally because it is equipped and provisioned out of his granaries, magazines, and armories. In the association of "estates," the lord rules with the aid of an autonomous "aristocracy" and hence shares his domination with it; the lord who personally administers is supported either by members of his household or by plebeians. These are propertyless strata having no social honor of their own; materially, they are completely chained to him and are not backed up by any competing power of their own. All forms of patriarchal and patrimonial domination, Sultanist despotism, and bureaucratic states belong to this latter type. The bureaucratic state order is especially important; in its most rational development, it is precisely characteristic of the modern state.

Everywhere the development of the modern state is initiated through the action of the prince. He paves the way for the expropriation of the autonomous and "private" bearers of executive power who stand beside him, of those who in their own right possess the means of administration, warfare, and financial organization, as well as politically usable goods of all sorts. The whole process is a complete parallel to the development of the capitalist enterprise through gradual expropriation of the independent producers. In the end, the modern state controls the total means of political organization, which actually come together under a single head. No single official personally owns the money he pays out, or the buildings, stores, tools, and war machines he controls. In the contemporary "state"—and this is essential for the concept of state—the "separation" of the administrative staff, of the administrative officials, and of the workers from the material means of administrative organization is completed. Here the most modern development begins, and we see with our own eyes the attempt to inaugurate the expropriation of this expropriator of the political means, and therewith of political power.

The revolution [of Germany, 1918] has accomplished, at least in so far as leaders have taken the place of the statutory authorities, this much: the leaders, through usurpation or election, have attained control over the political staff and the apparatus of material goods; and they deduce their legitimacy—no matter with what right—from the will of the governed. Whether the leaders, on the basis of this at least apparent success, can rightfully entertain the hope of also carrying through the expropriation within the capitalist enterprises is a different question. The direction of capitalist enterprises, despite far-reaching analogies, follows quite different laws than those of political administration.

Today we do not take a stand on this question. I state only the purely *conceptual* aspect for our consideration: the modern state is a compulsory association which organizes domination. It has been successful in seeking to monopolize the legitimate use of physical force as a means of domination within a territory. To this end the state has combined the material means of organization in the hands of its leaders, and it has expropriated all autonomous functionaries of estates who formerly controlled these means in their own right. The state has taken their positions and now stands in the top place.

During this process of political expropriation, which has occurred with varying success in all countries on earth, "professional politicians" in another sense have emerged. They arose first in the service of a prince. They have been men who, unlike the charismatic leader, have not wished to be lords themselves, but who have entered the *service* of political lords. In the struggle of expropriation, they placed themselves at the princes' disposal and by managing the princes' politics they earned, on the one hand, a living and, on the other hand, an ideal content of life. Again, it is *only* in the Occident that we find this kind of professional politician in the service of powers other than the princes. In the past, they have been the most important power instrument of the prince and his instrument of political expropriation.

Before discussing "professional politicians" in detail, let us clarify in all its aspects the state of affairs their existence presents. Politics, just as economic pursuits, may be a man's avocation or his vocation. One may engage in politics, and hence seek to influence the distribution of power within and between political structures, as an "occasional" politician. We are all "occasional" politicians when we cast our ballot or consummate a similar expression of intention, such as applauding or protesting in a "political" meeting, or delivering a "political" speech, etc. The whole relation of many people to politics is restricted to this. Politics as an avocation is today practiced by all those party agents and heads of voluntary political associations who, as a rule, are politically active only in case of need and for whom politics is, neither materially nor ideally, "their life" in the first place. The same holds for those members of state counsels and similar deliberative bodies that function only when summoned. It also holds for rather broad strata of our members of parliament who are politically active only during sessions. In the past, such strata were found especially among the estates. Proprietors of military implements in their own right, or proprietors of goods important for the administration, or proprietors of personal prerogatives may be called "estates." A large portion of them were far from giving their lives wholly, or merely preferentially, or more than occasionally, to the service of politics. Rather, they exploited their prerogatives in the interest of gaining rent or even profits; and they became active in the service of political associations only when the overlord of their status-equals especially demanded it. It was not different in the case of some of the auxiliary forces which the prince drew into the struggle for the creation of a political organization to be exclusively at his disposal. This was the nature of the *Rate von Haus aus* [councilors] and, still further back, of a considerable part of the councilors assembling in the "Curia" and other deliberating bodies of the princes. But these merely occasional auxiliary forces engaging in politics on the side were naturally not sufficient for the prince. Of necessity, the prince sought to create a staff of helpers dedicated wholly and exclusively to serving him, hence making this their major vocation. The structure of the emerging dynastic political organization, and not only this but the whole articulation of the culture, depended to a considerable degree upon the question of where the prince recruited agents.

A staff was also necessary for those political associations whose members constituted themselves politically as (so-called) "free" communes under the complete abolition or the far-going restriction of princely power.

They were "free" not in the sense of freedom from domination by force, but in the sense that princely power legitimized by tradition (mostly religously sanctified) as the exclusive source of all authority was absent. These communities have their historical home in the Occident. Their nucleus was the city as a body politic, the form in which the city first emerged in the Mediterranean culture area. In all these cases, what did the politicians who made politics their major vocation look like?

There are two ways of making politics one's vocation: Either one lives "for" politics or one lives "off" politics. By no means is this contrast an exclusive one. The rule is, rather, that man does both,

at least in thought, and certainly he also does both in practice. He who lives "for" politics makes politics his life, in an internal sense. Either he enjoys the naked possession of the power he exerts, or he nourishes his inner balance and self-feeling by the consciousness that his life has *meaning* in the service of a "cause." In this internal sense, every sincere man who lives for a cause also lives off this cause. The distinction hence refers to a much more substantial aspect of the matter, namely, to the economic. He who strives to make politics a permanent *source of income* lives "off" politics as a vocation, whereas he who does not do this lives "for" politics. Under the dominance of the private property order, some—if you wish—very trivial preconditions must exist in order for a person to be able to live "for" politics in this economic sense. Under normal conditions, the politician must be economically independent of the income politics can bring him. This means, quite simply, that the politician must be wealthy or must have a personal position in life which yields a sufficient income.

This is the case, at least in normal circumstances. The war lord's following is just as little concerned about the conditions of a normal economy as is the street crowd following of the revolutionary hero. Both live off booty, plunder, confiscations, contributions, and the imposition of worthless and compulsory means of tender, which in essence amounts to the same thing. But necessarily, these are extraordinary phenomena. In everyday economic life, only some wealth serves the purpose of making a man economically independent. Yet this alone does not suffice. The professional politician must also be economically "dispensable," that is, his income must not depend upon the fact that he constantly and personally places his ability and thinking entirely, or at least by far predominantly, in the service of economic acquisition. In the most unconditional way, the rentier is dispensable in this sense. Hence, he is a man who receives completely unearned income. He may be the territorial lord of the past or the large landowner and aristocrat of the present who receives ground rent. In Antiquity and the Middle Ages they who received slave or serf rents or in modern times rents from shares or bonds or similar sources—these are rentiers.

Neither the worker nor—and this has to be noted well—the entrepreneur, especially the modern, large-scale entrepreneur, is economically dispensable in this sense. For it is precisely the entrepreneur who is tied to his enterprise and is therefore *not* dispensable. This holds for the entrepreneur in industry far more than for the entrepreneur in agriculture, considering the seasonal character of agriculture. In the main, it is very difficult for the entrepreneur to be represented in his enterprise by someone else, even temporarily. He is as little dispensable as is the medical doctor, and the more eminent and busy he is the less dispensable he is. For purely organizational reasons, it is easier for the lawyer to be dispensable; and therefore the lawyer has played an incomparably greater, and often even a dominant, role as a professional politician. We shall not continue in this classification; rather let us clarify some of its ramifications.

The leadership of a state or of a party by men who (in the economic sense of the word) live exclusively for politics and not off politics means necessarily a "plutocratic" recruitment of the leading political strata. To be sure, this does not mean that such plutocratic leadership signifies at the same time that the politically dominant strata will not also seek to live "off" politics, and hence that the dominant stratum will not usually exploit their political domination in their own economic interest. All that is unquestionable, of course. There has never been such a stratum that has not somehow lived "off" politics. Only this is meant: that the professional politician need not seek remuneration directly for his political work, whereas every politician without means must absolutely claim this. On the other hand, we do not mean to say that the propertyless politician will pursue private economic advantages through politics, exclusively, or even predominantly. Nor do we mean that he will not think, in the first place, of "the subject matter." Nothing would be more incorrect. According to all experience, a care for the economic "security" of his existence is consciously or unconsciously a cardinal point in the whole life orientation of the wealthy man. A quite reckless and unreserved political idealism is found if not exclusively at least predominantly among those strata who by virtue of their propertylessness stand entirely outside of the strata who are interested in maintaining the economic order of a given society. This holds especially for extraordinary and hence revolutionary epochs. A non-plutocratic recruitment of interested politicians, of leadership and following, is geared to the self-understood precondition that regular and reliable income will accrue to those who manage politics.

Either politics can be conducted "honorifically" and then, as one usually says, by "independent," that is, by wealthy, men, and especially by rentiers. Or, political leadership is made accessible to propertyless men who must then be rewarded. The professional politician who lives "off" politics may be a pure "prebendary" or a salaried "official." Then the politician receives either income from fees and perquisites for specific services—tips and bribes are only an irregular and formally illegal variant of this category of income—or a fixed income in kind, a money salary, or both. He may assume the character of an "entrepreneur," like the *condottiere* or the holder of a farmed-out or purchased office, or like the American boss who considers his costs a capital investment which he brings to fruition through exploitation of his influence. Again, he may receive a fixed wage, like a journalist, a party secretary, a modern cabinet minister, or a political official. Feudal fiefs, land grants, and prebends of all sorts have been typical, in the past. With the development of the money economy, perquisites and prebends especially are the typical rewards for the following of princes, victorious conquerors, or successful party chiefs. For loyal services today, party leaders give offices of all sorts—in parties, newspapers, co-operative societies, health insurance, municipalities, as well as in the state. *All* party struggles are struggles for the patronage of office, as well as struggles for objective goals.

Jeffrey Herbst
WAR AND THE STATE IN AFRICA

Most analyses assume that in Africa, as elsewhere, states will eventually become strong. But this may not be true in Africa, where states are developing in a fundamentally new environment. Lessons drawn from the case of Europe show that war is an important cause of state formation that is missing in Africa today. The crucial role that war has played in the formation of European states has long been noted. Samuel P. Huntington argued that "war was the great stimulus to state building," and Charles Tilly went so far as to claim that "war made the state, and the state made war."[1] Similarly, two of the most successful states in the Third World today, South Korea and Taiwan, are largely "warfare" states that have been molded, in part, by the near constant threat of external aggression. However, studies of political development and state consolidation in Africa and many other parts of the Third World have all but ignored the important role that war can play in political development.

The role of war has not been examined because the vast majority of states in Africa and elsewhere in the world gained independence without having to resort to combat and have not faced a security threat since independence.[2] Those scholars who have analyzed the military in the developing world have studied the armed forces' role in economic and political processes but have not examined the changes that war could potentially effect on a state.[3] Studying the military and studying warfare are not the same, especially in the area of state consolidation, because warfare has independent effects on economic policies, administrative structures, and the citizenry's relationship with the state that have very little to do with the military.[4] Finally, beyond the usual problem of trying to study the impact

of a factor that is missing, there is a less excusable normative bias which has sometimes prevented students of politics from examining the effects of war. The question of whether it is only possible to create a nation out of "blood and iron" is apparently one that many analysts find too disturbing to examine.[5]

Comparison of the European case with that of Africa is therefore crucial to understanding whether the analogy holds. War in Europe played an important role in the consolidation of many now-developed states: war caused the state to become more efficient in revenue collection; it forced leaders to dramatically improve administrative capabilities; and it created a climate and important symbols around which a disparate population could unify. While there is little reason to believe that war would have exactly the same domestic effects in Africa today as it did in Europe several centuries ago, it is important to ask if developing countries can accomplish in times of peace what war enabled European countries to do. I conclude that they probably cannot because fundamental changes in economic structures and societal beliefs are difficult, if not impossible, to bring about when countries are not being disrupted or under severe external threat.

The next section of this article outlines how war affected state formation in Europe, with particular attention to two crucial developments: the creation of centralized and efficient structures to collect taxes, and the development of nationalism. I then compare the European experience of state building through warfare to the relative peace that Africa has experienced since the 1960s. While African states have benefited from peace, their development has been stunted by the very problems that war helped European countries to solve. I then evaluate the possibilities that African states might develop strategies

From *International Security* 14, no. 4. (Spring 1990), pp. 117–39.

to solve these fundamental problems in times of peace. I conclude that some states will probably be unsuccessful in finding ways of building the state in times of peace and will therefore remain permanently weak. Accordingly, the international community will have to develop non-traditional policies for helping a new brand of states: those that will continue to exist but that will not develop. Other states, perceiving that peace locks them into a permanently weak position, may be tempted to use war as a means of resolving their otherwise intractable problems of state consolidation.

Effects of War on State Consolidation: The European Case

It is instructive to look at war's impact on European societies because, as will be noted below, war in Europe helped alleviate some of the problems that affect African countries today. At the most basic level, war in Europe acted as a filter whereby weak states were eliminated and political arrangements that were not viable either were reformed or disappeared. Weak states do exist in Europe today—Belgium is one example—but the near-constant threat of war did prompt most states to become stronger to survive. The contrast between this evolutionary development and the current situation in the Third World, where even states that are largely dependent on foreign aid will continue to exist for the foreseeable future, is dramatic. It is, of course, important not to generalize too much because war had many different effects over time, and even in the same period states reacted in a variety of ways to external threats. However, war did affect the ability of European states to increase taxation and contributed to the forging of national identities in many countries. It is therefore important to examine the potential impact of external threat to better understand state consolidation in the Third World.

Taxes

Perhaps the most noticeable effect of war in European history was to cause the state to increase its ability to collect significantly more revenue with greater efficiency and less public resistance. Given the freedom of European states to attack each other, those states that could raise money quickly could successfully threaten their neighbors with a war that might lead to significant damage or even complete destruction. Richard Bean writes, "Once the power to tax had been successfully appropriated by any one sovereign, once he had used that power to bribe or coerce his nobility into acquiescence, that state could face all neighboring states with the choice of being conquered or of centralizing authority and raising taxes."[6] While success in war depends on many factors including technology, tactics, and morale of the troops, raising sufficient revenue was a necessary condition to prevent defeat. States that did not raise sufficient revenue for war perished. As Michael Mann notes, "A state that wished to survive had to increase its extractive capacity to pay for professional armies and/or navies. Those that did not would be crushed on the battlefield and absorbed into others—the fate of Poland, of Saxony, of Bavaria in [the seventeenth and eighteenth centuries].... No European states were continuously at peace. It is impossible to escape the conclusion that a peaceful state would have ceased to exist even more speedily than the militarily inefficient actually did."[7]

War affects state finances for two reasons. First, it puts tremendous strains on leaders to find new and more regular sources of income. While rulers may recognize that their tax system is inadequate, a war may be the only thing that forces them to expend the necessary political capital and undertake the coercion required to gain more revenue. For instance, in Mann's study of taxation in England between 1688 and 1815, he finds that there were six major jumps in state revenue and that each corresponds with the beginning of a war.[8] The association between the need to fight and the need to collect revenue is perhaps clearest in Prussia, where the main tax collection agency was called the General War Commissariat.[9]

Second, citizens are much more likely to acquiesce to increased taxation when the nation is at war, because a threat to their survival will overwhelm other concerns they might have about increased taxation. In fact, taxation for a war can be thought of as a "lumpy" collective good: not only must the population pay to get the good, but it must also pay a considerable amount more than the current level of taxation, because a small increase in revenue is often not enough to meet the new security threat facing the state.[10] In this way, taxation for a war is like taxation for building a bridge: everyone must pay to build the bridge and a small increase in revenue will not be enough, because half a bridge, like fighting half a war, is useless.

Thus, war often causes a "ratchet effect" whereby revenue increases sharply when a nation is fighting but does not decline to the *ante bellum* level when hostilities have ceased.[11] Once governments have invested the sunken costs in expanding tax collection systems and routinized the collection of new sources of revenue, the marginal costs of continuing those structures are quite low and the resources they collect can be used for projects that will enhance the ruling group's support.

While it is not a universal rule, war in other societies at other times often played the same kind of role that war did in Europe. For instance, Joseph Smaldone writes in his study of the Sokoto Caliphate (in what is now Nigeria) between 1500 and 1800:

War was the principal instrument for the establishment and extension of political authority over subject people and foreign territory, and for the organization, maintenance, and reinforcement of that authority. The demands of perennial war evoked institutions to subordinate the sectors of society crucial to the interests of these militarized polities. The permanent requirement to mobilize human and material resources for military purposes [i.e., taxation] intensified tendencies toward the monopolization of power and the elaboration of auxiliary institutions of social control.[12]

Similarly, the South Korean and Taiwanese states have been able to extract so many resources from their societies in part because the demands to be constantly vigilant provoked the state into developing efficient mechanisms for collecting resources and controlling dissident groups.[13] A highly extractive state also could cloak demands for greater resources in appeals for national unity in the face of a determined enemy.

Nationalism

War also had a major impact on the development of nationalism of Europe. Indeed, the presence of a palpable external threat may be the strongest way to generate a common association between the state and the population. External threats have such a powerful effect on nationalism because people realize in a profound manner that they are under threat because of who they are as a nation; they are forced to recognize that it is only as a nation that they can successfully defeat the threat. Anthony Giddens recounts the effects of World War I: "The War canalized the development of states' sovereignty, tying this to citizenship and to nationalism in such a profound way that any other scenario [of how the international system would be ordered] came to appear as little more than idle fantasy."[14] Similarly, Michael Howard notes the visceral impact of wars on the development of nationalism throughout Europe:

Self-identification as a Nation implies almost by definition alienation from other communities, and the most memorable incidents in the group-memory consisted in conflict with and triumph over other communities. France *was* Marengo, Austerlitz and Jena: military triumph set the seal on the new-found national consciousness. Britain *was* Trafalgar—but it had been a nation for four hundred years, since those earlier battles Crecy and Agincourt. Russia *was* the triumph of 1812. Germany *was* Gravelotte and Sedan.[15]

In Europe there was an almost symbiotic relationship between the state's extractive capacity and nationalism: war increased both as the population was convinced by external threat that they should pay more to the state, and as, at the same time, the population united around common symbols and memories that were important components of nationalism. Fighting wars may be the only way whereby it is possible to have people pay more taxes and at the same time feel more closely associated with the state.

The Absence of Interstate War in the Modern Era

While trying to study the chaos caused by administrative disintegration, the forceful crushing of ethnic challenges, and large-scale human rights abuses, many scholars have generally assumed that poor countries today face even more external challenges than European states did in their formative periods.[16] In fact, since the end of the Second World War, very few Third World states have fought interstate wars of the type that affected the evolution of European states. The few Third World interstate wars that have occurred (e.g., India-Pakistan, Iran-Iraq, China-Vietnam) have obscured the fact that the vast majority of Third World states most of the time do not face significant external threats. States like Israel, South Korea, or Taiwan, where national survival has been a real consideration in national politics, are exceptional and even these countries have survived intact.

Even in Africa, the continent seemingly destined for war given the colonially-imposed boundaries and weak political authorities, there has not been one involuntary boundary change since the dawn of the independence era in the late 1950s, and very few countries face even the prospect of a conflict with their neighbors. Most of the conflicts in Africa that have occurred were not, as in Europe, wars of conquest that threatened the existence of other states, but conflicts over lesser issues that were resolved without threatening the existence of another state.

For instance, Tanzania invaded Uganda in 1979 to overthrow Idi Amin, not to conquer Uganda. Similarly, the war in the Western Sahara is a colonial question, not a conflict between independent states. Even South Africa's destabilization efforts against its neighbors are primarily attempts to influence the policies of the majority-ruled countries, not to change the borders of the region. Lesotho or Swaziland would not exist today if South Africa had any real territorial ambitions. In the few conflicts that did have the potential to threaten fundamentally the existence of states—Somalia's attempt to invade Ethiopia in the 1970s and Libya's war against Chad in the 1970s and 1980s—the aggressor did not succeed.[17]

African states have seldom fought interstate wars and the continent has not witnessed significant boundary changes, because independent leaders have continued the system of boundary maintenance that the colonial powers first developed to regulate the scramble for Africa in the late 1800s.[18] African leaders recognized in the early 1960s that a potentially large number of groups would want to secede from the states they are presently in, to join others or create entirely new ones. In order to prevent the continent from being thrown into the chaos of large-scale boundary changes in which the stability and integrity of any state could be threatened, they created a system of explicit norms, propounded by the Organization of African Unity in 1963, which declared any change in the inherited colonial boundaries to be illegitimate. Most of the continent has, accordingly, refused to recognize boundary changes (e.g., Biafra, Eritrea) even where the principle of self-determination might have led them to do so. This system has been successful in preserving African national boundaries and has so far deterred almost all countries from initiating the kind of conquest wars that were so common in European history. The system that maintained the inherited borders as inviolate was strengthened somewhat inadvertently, because two of the largest states on the continent (Nigeria and Zaire), which could conceivably have threatened their much smaller neighbors, faced significant secessionist threats (from the Ibo and Kataganese respectively) and therefore worked resolutely to strengthen the norm that the borders should not be changed.

The stability of new states, especially in Africa, is a remarkable development given that the vast majority of the over one hundred countries in the Third World that have gained their independence since 1945 are poor, have weak administrative structures, and consist of populations that are splintered along regional or ethnic lines. In other words, they are precisely the kinds of states that before 1945 were routinely invaded and taken over by stronger states in their region or by external powers. Yet, very few states in the Third World, despite their evident military and political weaknesses, face any significant external threat.

In contrast, Tilly estimates, the "enormous majority" of states in Europe failed. Peace was the exception and long periods with no major fighting were almost unknown, as for centuries weak states were routinely defeated and populations regularly absorbed by foreign rulers.[19] The psychology of Europe in its formative centuries, where state survival was a very real issue of constant concern to leaders, is so different from the outlook facing Third World leaders today as to suggest that there has been a fundamental change in the survival prospects of weak states and that control of territory is no longer correlated with military power.[20]

Problems of State Consolidation in Africa

African states face numerous problems in their efforts to consolidate power. They are poor, short of trained manpower, and confront societies that are often fragmented and have little orientation to the state as a whole. Many other Third World nations face these same problems although they are often most extreme in Africa, given the poverty of the continent and the fragility of the states. Elites can come to power but, given the precariousness of control in countries where rules governing leadership and succession have not been institutionalized, they may be displaced. Once they lose power, or are prevented from gaining it, ambitious politicians have no other opportunity to accumulate wealth or power because the state controls the badges of status and many of the free-floating resources in the economy, such as they are.[21] Even when they do control the apex of the state, elites may feel that because of their country's vulnerability to exogenous shocks (e.g., sudden sharp drops in the price of their raw material exports) and the presence of sophisticated multinational enterprises and well-connected minority groups (e.g., Lebanese in West Africa, Indians in East Africa), they are not really in control of their own destiny and therefore are vulnerable. As a result of their gross insecurities, these "lame Leviathans"[22] try desperately to control ever-greater parts of society through outright ownership or regulation. However, since they are weak, their efforts are almost inevitably clumsy, heavy-handed, and authoritarian.

Therefore, although the average state in Africa compared to other states is small (as measured by government spending as a percentage of gross domestic product [GDP]),[23] it appears to be too large because its clumsy extractive efforts cause so much damage compared to the benefits that it delivers. Thus arises the image of so many African states as "overdeveloped" or "swollen."[24] The problems confronted by states in Africa can be illustrated by comparing their experience with European states in two areas where war had a significant impact: the state's ability to extract resources through taxes, and the degree of nationalism in the countries south of the Sahara.

A classic example of how weak state power causes the state to institute desperate and self-defeating economic policies is in the area of government revenue. Government revenue poses a major problem for all African states and many others in the Third World. These states are desperately short of revenue to fund even minimal state services (e.g., pay nurses' salaries, buy books for schools, supply transport for agricultural extension services) that their populations have long been promised. In addition to these recurrent costs, Third World countries are in need of more extensive and more efficient tax systems because the process of development requires large expenditures on infrastructure to promote economic activity throughout the country and to handle the ramifications of development, especially the large expenses incurred by urbanizing countries.[25] W. Arthur Lewis estimates that the public sector in Third World countries should be spending on the order of 20 percent of GDP on services, exclusive of defense and debt repayment.[26] However, when defense (2.5 percent of GDP) and debt repayments (3.4 percent of GDP) are subtracted, the average African country spends only 15.7 percent of its GDP on all government functions.[27] While these figures are only rough estimates given the problems associated with African economic statistics, they do illustrate the extent of the fiscal crisis facing African states.

Due to the weakness of administrative and statistical structures in Africa, many governments rely on taxation of foreign trade, because imports and exports must physically pass through a relatively small number of border posts that can be easily manned. Thus, the average African state depends on revenue from tariffs for 20.5 percent of total revenue, compared to all developing countries which, on average, gain 12.9 percent of their revenue from tariffs, and industrialized countries where tariffs account for only 1.3 percent of total revenue.[28]

Unfortunately, funding the state through indirect taxes on foreign trade damages national economies because leaders are compelled to erect ever-greater administrative controls on imports. These tariffs promote corruption, smuggling and, most importantly, overvalued exchange rates, because governments grow to rely on administrative controls rather than the market to regulate imports. Overvalued exchange rates in turn lead to widespread damage within poorer economies as exporters are universally hurt, the population is encouraged to become dependent on imported food, and black markets quickly develop to take advantage of distorted prices.[29] Beyond the immediate damage caused by a tax system dependent on imports and exports, this *type* of tax system is particularly inappropriate for Third World countries. These countries need guarantees of slow and steady increases in government revenue above the rate of economic growth in order to accomplish the tasks crucial to development: build transport and communications systems, establish utilities, and create educational systems.[30]

Another major problem facing leaders in Africa is the absence of a strong popular identity with the state. The lack of a popular consensus over national purpose both aggravates the state's clumsy efforts to extract resources and is itself exacerbated by an insecure, authoritarian elite. Indeed, the picture of African societies widely accepted today is of populations trying desperately to escape the clutches of the state, rather than becoming more involved in it, and certainly not willing to pay more taxes to it.[31] Twenty-five years after "the nationalist period," there are few signs of nationalism in most African countries despite the now *pro forma* exhortations from propaganda organs to engage in state-building. Indeed, the majority of states still have difficulty creating viable symbols to attract the loyalties of their citizens.

Not surprisingly, therefore, there are today very few attempts in African countries to forge a national consensus on major issues, much less a national identity. For instance, most formulas to decrease interethnic tension concentrate only on ameliorating the negative aspects of ethnic conflict by accomodating it through decentralized government structures and preferential policies.[32] However, formulas such as federalism often are inappropriate in countries where national institutions are not strong. Federalist solutions broke down in Sudan and Uganda, among other places, because the incentives for leaders to attempt to gain total control were much greater than the barriers posed by recently adopted institutional arrangements.[33] Moreover, no matter how well accommodationist formulas of intra-societal conflict work, almost everyone in Africa and elsewhere in the Third World would agree that a more basic national loyalty by all societal groups would still be desirable. However, the means by which to induce a disparate society to identify more with the nation-state are unknown in Africa and few in the current era are even attempting to speculate on how to develop a national consensus.

Difficulties of State Consolidation without War

War in Europe played such an important role in the evolution of the state mechanism and society's relationship with the state because it is extraordinarily difficult, outside times of crisis, to reform elemental parts of the governmental system, such as the means of taxation, or to effect a real change in national identity. For instance, since taxes are so consequential to every business decision, the tax system over time reflects a large number of political bargains made by the state with different interest groups. Often governments find it too politically difficult to provide direct subsidies to those they want to favor, so the tax system is a convenient backdoor to aid politically important groups without incurring opprobrium. The political bargains that constitute the tax system develop a momentum of their own because individuals and businesses base their future economic decisions on the incentives and disincentives in the existing tax code. Indeed, Joseph Schumpeter called the fiscal system "a collection of hard, naked facts" and claimed that "the spirit of a people, its cultural level, its social structure, the deeds its policy may prepare—all this and more is written in its fiscal history, stripped of all phrases."[34]

Therefore, even minor changes such as alterations in the level of taxation or shifts in the tax burden, as the United States and most Western European countries have made in the last few years, engender tremendous political battles. Not only the previously favored political groups but all those that simply followed the signals sent out by government will forcefully oppose fiscal reform. Greater changes in the nature of the tax system are even more difficult. Edward Ames' and Richard Rapp's conclusion that

tax systems "last until the end of the government that instituted them" and that tax systems in some European countries survived "almost intact" from the thirteenth and fourteenth centuries until the late eighteenth century may be an exaggeration, but their conclusions suggest just how much inertia a particular system for collecting government revenue can develop over time.[35] Other than war, no type of crisis demands that the state increase taxes with such forcefulness, and few other situations would impel citizens to accept those demands, or at least not resist them as strongly as they otherwise might have. It is therefore hard to counter Tilly's argument that "the formation of standing armies provided the largest single incentive to extraction and the largest single means of state coercion over the long run of European state-making."[36]

Domestic security threats, of the type African countries face so often, may force the state to increase revenue; however, these crises are almost never as grave as the type of external threat the European states had to confront, because they do not threaten the very existence of the state. In addition, domestic conflicts result in fragmentation and considerable hostility among different segments of the population. As a result, the state does not necessarily achieve the greater revenue efficiency gains engendered by an external crisis. Indeed, in a civil war—as in Nigeria in the late 1960s—parts of the state are fighting against each other, which hardly promotes efficiency in tax collection. Public acceptance of tax increases, a crucial factor in allowing European states to extract greater resources in times of war, will be a much more complicated issue in civil disputes. As Mann notes, "the growth of the modern state, as measured by finances, is explained primarily not in domestic terms but in terms of geopolitical relations of violence."[37]

The obstacles posed by large peasant populations, significant nonmonetarized sectors, and widespread poverty are, of course, important contributors to the revenue crisis of the African state. However, these problems do not fully explain why poor states do not extract greater resources from society in a manner that is less economically harmful. Factors such as political will, administrative ability, and the population's willingness to be taxed—issues that can be affected by the decisions of political leaders—are also crucial in understanding why states are unable to achieve their potential level of taxation in a benign manner.[38] For instance, Margaret Levi successfully shows that in such diverse cases as republican Rome, France and England in the Middle Ages, eighteenth-century Britain, and twentieth-century Australia, levels of taxation were affected primarily by political constraints faced by rulers, despite the fact that most of these economies also posed significant barriers to increased tax collection.[39]

Nor has there been any success in developing means to cause the population to identify more with the state, other than fighting a war. Nationalism, which was never nearly as strong or widespread (especially outside the major cities) in Africa as many had thought, was palpable in the late colonial period because there was a "relevant other"— the colonialists—who could be easily identified as oppressors and around which a nominal national identity could be built.[40] However, since independence in most African countries, there has been no "relevant other" to oppose, so it has been extremely difficult to create nationwide symbols of identity. There has therefore been no way of generating a national identity in Africa such as wars forged in Europe. Anthony Smith writes, "the central difficulty of 'nation-building' in much of Africa and Asia is the lack of any shared historical mythology and memory on which state elites can set about 'building' the nation. The 'nation' [is built up] from the central fund of culture and symbolism and mythology provided by shared historical experiences."[41] The result is the anomie in most African countries today.

It could be argued that the lack of nationalism simply reflects the fact that African countries are artificial groupings of disparate peoples and therefore are not really nation-states. However, no "natural" nation-states are mature at birth with populations that have readily agreed to a central identity. Rather, the goal of those who want to create the nation-state is to convince different groups that they do, in fact, share a common identity. This is why even in Europe, which today seems to have nation-states that are more "natural" than Africa's, war had such a crucial role to play in the forging of common identities.

Indeed, the symbiotic relationship that war fostered in Europe between tax collection and nationalism is absent in Africa, precisely because there is no external threat to encourage people to acquiesce in the state's demands, and no challenge that causes them to respond as a nation. Instead, the African state's clumsy efforts at greater extraction are met by popular withdrawal rather than by a populace united around a common identity.

Of course, not all wars led to the strengthening of administrative institutions and greater nationalism. For example, Joseph Strayer notes that the Hundred Years War "was so exhausting for both sides that it discouraged the normal development of the apparatus of the state. There was a tendency to postpone structural reforms, to solve problems on an ad hoc basis rather than [to create] new agencies of government, to sacrifice efficiency for immediate results."[42] However, the Hundred Years War was exceptional because of its length and it therefore did not allow rulers to consolidate the gains usually achieved after facing a short period of external danger. Yet overall, the historical record suggests that war was highly efficient in promoting state consolidation in Europe, and that it would be much more difficult for states to accomplish the same tasks in peacetime.

Are There Peaceful Routes to State Consolidation?

Since African and other Third World countries need to transform important parts of their governmental systems, including their fiscal arrangements, and to promote nationalism, but do not have the traditional avenue of war to aid them, the immediate question is whether they can follow a path other than that adopted by Europe to consolidate state power and to develop new national identities to reduce the divisions between society and the state.

Once again it is interesting to focus on government revenue because the issue is so decisive in its own right and because tax systems are such a good reflection of the basic bargains in society. In an age with reduced levels of interstate war, African countries are faced with the problem of trying to increase the capacity of the state without being able to use wars to "ratchet up" the state's extractive ability. Given the evidence of European fiscal inertia, it is clear that it will be even more difficult to institute major reforms when states are operating in normal circumstances. The one clear chance African countries did have to institute major reforms was at independence, because at that moment political arrangements were in such flux that significant new initiatives could be undertaken. Indeed, some African countries (e.g., Mozambique, Angola) did make massive changes in their political economy (e.g., nationalization, collectivization); unfortunately, these particular reforms were economically ruinous because their socialist policies distorted economies even more than in most African countries. Once independence becomes the normal situation, as it has in African countries, it becomes extraordinarily difficult for leaders to make basic reforms of political arrangements, such as fiscal systems, which might hurt powerful groups. As Peter Bachrach and Morton Baratz noted in the context of American politics, dominant values, myths, rituals, and institutions quickly ossify so that crucial issues, such as fiscal reform, are not even on the agenda.[43] There appears to be no impetus from inside African countries to disrupt the current fiscal arrangements significantly. Indeed, much of the argument that there is currently a significant economic crisis in Africa, and that this crisis was caused by malfunctioning government policies, came from outside the continent.[44]

However, it could be argued that structural adjustment, pressed on African countries by the International Monetary Fund (IMF), the World Bank, and bilateral donors, could serve many state-making functions. As external actors dedicated to fundamental reforms of the economy and of the way the state operates, the IMF and other donors are not subject to the same rigidities that paralyze domestic reformers. The IMF and other actors who insist on fundamental reform could pressure African states for significant changes in their tax system. Demands from an external actor are similar to war, in that a leader can legitimately argue to its population that it has no choice in asking them to make very difficult sacrifices because it is under too much external pressure.

It would be a major mistake, however, to take too far the analogy between pressure from actors such as the IMF and the effects of war. For instance, war produced such spectacular gains in governmental efficiency because the state itself felt threatened. The IMF, or any other actor, cannot produce that feeling; indeed, structural adjustment has been least successful when it has tried to address the issues of how the state itself operates in areas such as public enterprises or fiscal arrangements.[45] The cost to the state itself in failing to adopt a structural adjustment program can be severe, but falls far short of what war would threaten. The IMF will never cause a state to disappear. At worst, a state can simply opt for the high cost of breaking off relations with the IMF.

Nor does external pressure of the type the Fund exerts produce any change in national identity. While leaders can occasionally rally people against the external threat posed by "imperialists," these sentiments usually are not long-lasting because the population may be unable to distinguish between international actors supposedly draining away the nation's funds during a structural adjustment exercise, and those national leaders who led their country into such a spectacular economic debacle. While Europe's leaders in previous centuries hardly treated their populations well by modern standards, it was usually unambiguous that people would be better off if they won the war than if they lost.

The prospects of structural adjustment fostering some kind of nationalism based on resisting foreigners is also limited because the IMF is not really a "relevant other" to a largely peasant population, and cannot induce changes in national consciousness of the type that wars in Europe produced. Unlike a war where the entire population was threatened because of its national identity, structural adjustment will help certain groups unambiguously (e.g., peasants who grow export crops), clearly hurt some (e.g., the urban population dependent on imported food), and have ambiguous effects on many others. Further, the intensity in shared experience that a war generates simply cannot be replicated by, say, protracted negotiations over the IMF's Extended Fund Facility.

The Likelihood of War in Africa

If internal reform seems improbable and there is no other external threat that can perform quite the same role as war, the question becomes whether at some point in the future African leaders will begin to see war as a potential avenue for state-making. Some leaders may look to war simply because they are truly concerned about the fate of the nation and see no other option. Others may not be concerned particularly with nation-building, but may find that their countries have suffered economic decline for so long that the possibilities for their own personal enrichment have become severely limited, and therefore will seek to seize the assets of other countries. So far, the system that has preserved the continent's boundaries has not been significantly tested because most leaders considered it obvious that they were better off with their inherited boundaries than they would be in a chaotic war situation where sovereignty or considerable territory might be lost. However, especially in the context of decades of economic decline, it is possible that some African leaders may recalculate the benefits of a peace that locks them into perpetual weakness. Instead, they may try to increase their state's extractive ability and divert their citizens from inter-ethnic squabbles by seizing upon the multitude of provocations, always present, to provoke a fight with neighboring states.

Paul Colinvaux presents the extreme case for the prospects of interstate war in Africa:

> Africa holds the greatest possibilities for the aspiring general. . . . That there will be battles between African nations as they build their African continent in a new image is as certain as anything in history. For each country there must come times when wealth, hopes, ambitions, and numbers all rise together. It then needs only access to high-quality weapons for an aggression to be an attractive undertaking.[46]

If significant interstate wars break out when provocations are small but elites realize what war could do for the state and the nation, it would not be a strikingly new development. Rather, increased interstate warfare in Africa would simply be a return to the European norm. Whether war in Africa today would actually bring about the same kind of changes that it did in Europe centuries ago is unclear, but the possibility that leaders might become so desperate that they try in some fundamental way to alter the political rules under which their nations function should not be ignored.

Many are the possible provocations that could bring about significant interstate war in Africa. Certainly, there are plenty of border disputes and fragments of ethnic groups that need to be rescued from "foreign domination" to provide enough rationalization for hostile action against other African countries. Conflicts between language blocs (e.g., English versus French),[47] disputes over control of crucial rivers and railroads (especially given the number of land-locked countries), or the simple need to have more land for populations that double every twenty years provide many other potential reasons for war in Africa. More than a few African leaders might someday agree with Bismarck, a brilliant consolidator of a "new nation," on the only real way to unite a fragmented people:

> Prussia . . . , as a glance at the map will show, could no longer wear unaided on its long narrow figure the panoply which Germany required for

its security; it must be equally distributed over all German peoples. We should get no nearer the goal by speeches, associations, decisions of majorities; we should be unable to avoid a serious contest, a contest which could only be settled by blood and iron.[48]

Although African countries had more or less equal defense capabilities at independence, the growing differential in force projection capabilities has led some to suggest that Africa will experience much greater resort to force in the future. Inventories of tanks and other armored vehicles as well as artillery, jet fighters, and naval craft have increased considerably throughout the continent. For instance, just in the period between 1966 and 1981, the number of countries in sub-Saharan Africa with tanks increased from two to eighteen, the number with field artillery went from seven to thirty-six, the number with light armor went from thirteen to thirty-six, and the number possessing jet aircraft went from six to twenty-one.[49] Countries such as Nigeria and Zaire have developed military capabilities that are far greater than their neighbors'. So far, the assurance of stability that is the central advantage of the current African state system has almost always been more attractive than whatever reasons African leaders may have had to begin conflict with their neighbors. However, as President Nyerere of Tanzania showed when he invaded Uganda to depose Idi Amin, even strong proponents of African norms can be driven to interstate conflict if they believe that the costs of not acting are high enough. In the future, African leaders may find that, despite all their efforts, economic reform cannot progress and they cannot get their citizenry to unite around national symbols; it is conceivable that then the deterrent value of the norms of sovereignty may seem much less powerful than they do now. If these norms no longer provided protection to a large number of states, they would lose all meaning throughout the African continent. While the timing of these wars is not predictable, it should be obvious that the incentives that African leaders have to incite wars for the purposes of state-making are significant and may become much

stronger in the future when the futility of domestic reform during times of business as usual, that is, peace, becomes clear.

The Permanently Weak State: A New Development

Much of this discussion has focused on the potential opportunities for African states that, in a European-type state system, might have engaged in battle, won (or at least not lost too badly), and thereby used war in order to further state-building. However, it should be recognized that another class of states in Africa is directly affected by the current absence of war: those states that would have lost badly and would have been absorbed by the winners. These states range from those that are just geographic anachronisms left by colonialism (e.g., The Gambia, Djibouti), and very small states in the shadow of giants (e.g., Benin and Togo, close to Nigeria, or Rwanda and Burundi bordering Zaire), to those that simply lack significant resources for development or defense (e.g., Mali, Mauritania). In Europe during the formative centuries, disintegration of weak states like these was a regular occurrence. Weak states that were defeated then became the poorer regions of richer countries, but at least they had a chance to share in the revenue and resources of a viable state. Yet the absence of a truly competitive state system that penalizes military weakness means that even those states that have no other prospects than long-term dependence on international aid will survive in their crippled form for the foreseeable future. Perhaps the only task of state consolidation that these otherwise weak states can accomplish is to physically capture their populations within the stable boundaries of the African state system.[50]

The presence of permanently weak states that will not be eliminated is a new development in international relations and one that poses novel development challenges. All theoretical work on development so far, no matter what the ideological predisposition of the authors, has implicitly assumed that somehow the nation-states as they currently exist are viable arrangements for development, if only they follow the proper strategies and receive enough help from the international community. This assumption was appropriate for the European context where centuries of war had eliminated states that simply were not viable. However, for Africa, whose states have not been tested by an international system that severely punishes political weakness, there is little reason to believe that many of them will be able to have a favorable enough geographic position, control adequate natural resources, gain the support of a significant portion of their populations, and construct strong administrative structures to ever develop. In the long term, these states may disappear if interstate wars finally do break out in Africa.

In the meantime, what is to be done with states that exist but cannot develop? It is far too early to write off any state's prospects. We have been wrong about the development prospects of many states both in Africa (where scholars were too optimistic) and elsewhere in the world, such as East Asia.[51] It would also be morally unacceptable simply to allow these countries to gradually slide from the world's view into a twilight of perpetual poverty because nature and history have been unkind to them. However, thought must be given to nontraditional alternatives for aid to states that in previous times would simply have been defeated and absorbed by stronger neighbors in a war. For instance, the international community might consider rewarding those countries in the Third World that have taken in economic migrants from non-viable states.[52] The West could consider providing additional aid to those countries willing to engage in some kind of regional integration to mitigate the problems of unchanging boundaries, much as countries that have adopted more rational economic policies have attracted greater aid from donors. The world may simply have to recognize that a certain number of countries are locked into non-viable positions, and develop a long-term approach to their welfare rather than acting surprised every time the inevitable famine or ecological disaster occurs.

Conclusion

It is important not to glorify war. The wars that Europe went through caused immense suffering for generations and wholesale destruction of some societies. Yet it is undeniable that out of this destruction emerged stronger political arrangements and more unified populations. No one would advocate war as a solution to Africa's political and economic problems, where the costs of interstate war could be even higher than in Europe. It is doubtful that, if African countries do start fighting wars, they will undergo exactly the same processes of state consolidation that war engendered in Europe. However, it should be recognized that there is very little evidence that African countries, or many others in the Third World, will be able to find peaceful ways to strengthen the state and develop national identities. In particular, the prospects for states that will not disappear, but simply cannot develop, must be examined. At the same time, we must recognize the possibility that some African leaders in the future may come to believe that the costs of peace—limits on reform possibilities and a fragmented population—are so high that war may not seem like such an undesirable alternative. If African leaders do indeed make this calculation, the suffering that Africa has seen in the last twenty-five years may only be a prelude to much more dangerous developments.

NOTES

1. Samuel P. Huntington, *Political Order in Changing Societies* (New Haven: Yale University Press, 1968), p. 123; and Charles Tilly, "Reflections on the History of European State-Making," in Charles Tilly, ed., *The Formation of National States in Western Europe* (Princeton: Princeton University Press, 1975), p. 42. An important recent addition to this literature is Brian M. Downing, "Constitutionalism, Warfare and Political Change in Early Modern Europe," *Theory and Society*, Vol. 17, No. 1 (January 1988), pp. 7–56. The general literature on warfare's effect on society is voluminous. An

early work which concentrates on some of the themes examined here is Hans Delbrück, *History of the Art of the War within the Framework of Political History*, Vol. III, trans. Walter J. Renfroe, Jr. (Westport, Conn.: Greenwood Press, 1982).

2. For instance, in Morris Janowitz's classic study of the military in the developing world, the political, social, and economic functions of the military are studied extensively but the potential effects of war, or of peace, are not analyzed. Morris Janowitz, *The Military in the Political Development of New Nations: An Essay in Comparative Analysis* (Chicago: University of Chicago Press, 1964), p. 12.

3. The literature is reviewed by Henry Bienen, "Armed Forces and National Modernization: Continuing the Debate," *Comparative Politics*, Vol. 16, No. 1 (October 1983), pp. 1–16.

4. Gabriel Ardent, "Financial Policy and Economic Infrastructure of Modern States and Nations," in Tilly, *The Formation of National States*, p. 89.

5. A useful corrective to the conventional view is provided by John A. Hall, "War and the Rise of the West," in Colin Creighton and Martin Shaw, eds., *The Sociology of War and Peace* (London: Macmillan, 1987).

6. Richard Bean, "War and the Birth of the Nation State," *Journal of Economic History*, Vol. 33, No. 1 (March 1973), p. 220.

7. Michael Mann, "State and Society, 1130–1815: An Analysis of English State Finances," in Mann, *States, War and Capitalism: Studies in Political Sociology* (Oxford: Basil Blackwell, 1988), p. 109.

8. Michael Mann, *The Sources of Social Power* (Cambridge: Cambridge University Press, 1986), p. 486.

9. Michael Duffy, "The Military Revolution and the State, 1500–1800," in Michael Duffy, ed., *The Military Revolution and the State, 1500–1800*, Exeter Studies in History No. 1 (Exeter, U.K.: University of Exeter, 1980), p. 5.

10. "Lumpy" goods are products which are not useful if only part is purchased. Margaret Levi, *Of Rule and Revenue* (Berkeley: University of California Press, 1988), pp. 56–57.

11. Mann, *Sources of Social Power*, pp. 483–490.

12. Joseph P. Smaldone, *Warfare in the Sokoto Caliphate: Historical and Sociological Perspectives* (Cambridge: Cambridge University Press, 1977), p. 139. The same point is made by Richard L. Roberts in his *Warriors, Merchants, and Slaves: The State and the Economy in the Middle Niger Valley, 1700–1914* (Palo Alto: Stanford University Press, 1987), p. 20.

13. Joel S. Migdal, *Strong Societies and Weak States: State-Society Relations and State Capabilities in the Third World* (Princeton: Princeton University Press, 1988), p. 274.

14. Anthony Giddens, *The Nation-State and Violence*, vol. II of *A Contemporary Critique of Historical Materialism* (Berkeley: University of California Press, 1985), p. 235.

15. Michael Howard, *War and the Nation State* (Oxford: Clarendon Press, 1978), p. 9. Emphasis in the original.

16. See, for instance, Joseph LaPalombara, "Penetration: A Crisis of Governmental Capacity," in Leonard Binder, et al., *Crises and Sequences in Political Development* (Princeton: Princeton University Press, 1971), p. 222.

17. In 1977 Somalia, as part of its irredentist project to create "Greater Somalia," invaded Ethiopia in the hope of annexing the Ogaden; the Ethiopians, with significant help from the Soviet Union and Cuba, defeated Somalia in 1978. David D. Laitin and Said S. Samatar, *Somalia: Nation in Search of a State* (Boulder, Colo.: Westview, 1987), pp. 140–143. In 1973 Libyan forces invaded Chad by moving forces into the disputed Aozou strip. The Libyan military presence gradually expanded until a dramatic series of conflicts with the Chadian government (heavily supported by France and the United States) in 1987 forced the Libyans to agree to an end to hostilities. John Wright, *Libya, Chad and the Central Sahara* (London: Hurst, 1989), pp. 126–146.

18. This argument is developed in Jeffrey Herbst, "The Creation and Maintenance of National Boundaries in Africa," *International Organization*, Vol. 43, No. 4 (Fall 1989), pp. 673–692.

19. Tilly, "Reflections on the History of European State-Making," p. 38.

20. Ibid., p. 81.

21. Richard Hodder-Williams, *An Introduction to the Politics of Tropical Africa* (London: Allen and Unwin, 1984), p. 95.

22. Thomas M. Callaghy, "The State and the Development of Capitalism in Africa: Theoretical, Historical, and Comparative Reflections," in Donald Rothchild and Naomi Chazan, eds., *The Precarious Balance: State and Society in Africa* (Boulder, Colo.: Westview, 1988), p. 82.

23. The share of total gross domestic product of sub-Saharan African states is smaller, at 21.6 percent, than the developing country average of 25.5 percent. (Both figures are from 1984.) International Monetary Fund (IMF), *Government Finance Statistics Yearbook 1988* (Washington, D.C.: IMF, 1988), p. 94.

24. See, for instance, Larry Diamond, "Class Formation in the Swollen African State," *The Journal of Modern African Studies*, Vol. 25, No. 4 (December 1987), pp. 592–596; and Nzongola-Ntalaja, "The Crisis of the State in Post-Colonial Africa," in Nzongola-Ntalaja, *Revolution and Counter-Revolution in Africa* (London: Zed Books, 1987), p. 85.

25. W. Arthur Lewis, *The Evolution of the International Economic Order* (Princeton: Princeton University Press, 1978), p. 39.

26. W. Arthur Lewis, *Development Planning: The Essentials of Economic Policy* (New York: Harper and Row, 1966), p. 115.

27. Calculated from IMF, *Government Finance Statistics Yearbook 1988*, pp. 58, 74, and 94.

28. Calculated from ibid., p. 54.

29. See World Bank, *Accelerated Development in Sub-Saharan Africa: An Agenda for Action* (Washington, D.C.: World Bank, 1981), pp. 24–30.

30. Alex Radian, *Resource Mobilization in Poor Countries: Implementing Tax Policies* (New Brunswick, NJ: Transaction Books, 1980), pp. 13–17.

31. See Rothchild and Chazan, *The Precarious Balance*.

32. See, for instance, Donald L. Horowitz, *Ethnic Groups in Conflict* (Berkeley: University of California Press, 1985), pp. 563–680.

33. Buganda had a degree of autonomy when Uganda gained independence and the Kabaka, the traditional ruler of the Buganda people, was the country's first president. However, this arrangement fell apart in 1966 when then Prime Minister Milton Obote overthrew the Kabaka and invaded Buganda. Crawford Young, *The Politics of Cultural Pluralism* (Madison: University of Wisconsin Press, 1976), pp. 149–156. In 1983, President Gaafar Mohamed Nimeiri of the Sudan effectively abrogated the Addis Ababa agreement which had given autonomy to Southern Sudan. The Sudan has been embroiled in a civil war ever since. Mansour Khalid, *Nimeiri and the Revolution of Dismay* (London: KPI, 1985), pp. 234–240.

34. Joseph A. Schumpeter, "The Crisis of the Tax State," in Alan T. Peacock, et al., eds., *International Economic Papers*, No. 4 (London: Macmillan, 1954), pp. 6–7.

35. Edward Ames and Richard T. Rapp, "The Birth and Death of Taxes: A Hypothesis," *Journal of Economic History*, Vol. 37, No. 1 (March 1977), p. 177.

36. Tilly, "Reflections on the History of European State-Making," p. 73.

37. Mann, *Sources of Social Power*, p. 490.

38. Raja J. Chelliah, "Trends in Taxation in Developing Countries," *International Monetary Fund Staff Papers*, Vol. 18, No. 2 (July 1971), p. 312. On the possibility of changing fiscal arrangements in Africa, see Dennis Anderson, *The Public Revenue and Economic Policy in African Countries*, World Bank Discussion Paper No. 19 (Washington, D.C.: World Bank, 1987), pp. 14–15.

39. For instance, see Levi, *Of Rule and Revenue*, p. 105.

40. The importance of the "relevant other" concept in developing group cohesion is explored by Young, *The Politics of Cultural Pluralism*, p. 42.

41. Anthony D. Smith, "State-Making and Nation-Building," in John A. Hall, ed., *States in History* (Oxford: Basil Blackwell, 1986), p. 258.

42. Joseph R. Strayer, *On the Medieval Origins of the Modern State* (Princeton: Princeton University Press, 1970), p. 60.

43. Peter Bachrach and Morton S. Baratz, "Two Faces of Power," *American Political Science Review*, Vol. 56, No. 4 (December 1962), p. 950.

44. For instance, the World Bank's report, *Accelerated Development in Sub-Saharan Africa*, was crucial in

noting the dimensions of Africa's economic crisis; it set the agenda for reform of African economies.

45. Jeffrey Herbst, "Political Impediments to Economic Rationality: Why Zimbabwe Cannot Reform its Public Sector," *The Journal of Modern African Studies*, Vol. 27, No. 1 (March 1989), pp. 67–85.

46. Paul Colinvaux, *The Fates of Nations: A Biological Theory of History* (London: Penguin, 1980), pp. 219–220.

47. Ibid., p. 219.

48. Otto, Prince von Bismarck, *Bismarck, the Man and the Statesman: Being the Reflections and Reminiscences of Otto, Prince von Bismarck, Written and Dictated by Himself after his Retirement from Office*, translated under the supervision of A. J. Butler, Vol. I (New York: Harper and Brothers, 1899), p. 313.

49. William G. Thom, "Sub-Saharan Africa's Changing Military Capabilities," in Bruce E. Arlinghaus and Pauline H. Baker, eds., *African Armies: Evolution and Capabilities* (Boulder, Colo.: Westview, 1986), p. 101. See also Walter L. Barrows, "Changing Military Capabilities in Black Africa," in William Foltz and Henry Bienen, eds., *Arms and the African: Military Influence and Africa's International Relations* (New Haven: Yale University Press, 1985), p. 99 and p. 120; and Henry Bienen, "African Militaries as Foreign Policy Actors," *International Security*, Vol. 5, No. 2 (Fall 1980), p. 176.

50. See Jeffrey Herbst, "Migration, the Politics of Protest, and State Consolidation in Africa," *African Affairs*, Vol. 89, No. 355 (April 1990), pp. 183–203.

51. In the 1950s American administrations debated whether South Korea could achieve any increase in living standards and if American aid should be devoted to simply preventing the country from getting poorer. Clive Crook, "Trial and Error," *The Economist*, September 23, 1989, p. 4.

52. See Jeffrey Herbst, "Migration Helps Poorest of Poor," *Wall Street Journal*, June 15, 1988, p. 12.

Robert I. Rotberg

THE NEW NATURE OF NATION-STATE FAILURE

Nation-states fail because they can no longer deliver positive political goods to their people. Their governments lose legitimacy and, in the eyes and hearts of a growing plurality of its citizens, the nation-state itself becomes illegitimate.

Only a handful of the world's 191 nation-states can now be categorized as failed, or collapsed, which is the end stage of failure. Several dozen more, however, are weak and serious candidates for failure. Because failed states are hospitable to and harbor nonstate actors—warlords and terrorists—understanding the dynamics of nation-state failure is central to the war against terrorism. Strengthening weak nation-states in the developing world has consequently assumed new urgency.

Defining State Failure

Failed states are tense, deeply conflicted, dangerous, and bitterly contested by warring factions. In most failed states, government troops battle armed revolts led by one or more rivals. Official authorities in a failed state sometimes face two or more insurgencies,

From *The Washington Quarterly* 25, no. 3 (Summer 2002), pp. 85–96.

varieties of civil unrest, differing degrees of communal discontent, and a plethora of dissent directed at the state and at groups within the state.

The absolute intensity of violence does not define a failed state. Rather, it is the enduring character of that violence (as in Angola, Burundi, and Sudan), the direction of such violence against the existing government or regime, and the vigorous character of the political or geographical demands for shared power or autonomy that rationalize or justify that violence that identifies the failed state. Failure for a nation-state looms when violence cascades into all-out internal war, when standards of living massively deteriorate, when the infrastructure of ordinary life decays, and when the greed of rulers overwhelms their responsibilities to better their people and their surroundings.

The civil wars that characterize failed states usually stem from or have roots in ethnic, religious, linguistic, or other intercommunal enmity. The fear of "the other" that drives so much ethnic conflict may stimulate and fuel hostilities between ruling entities and subordinate and less-favored groups. Avarice also propels antagonism, especially when discoveries of new, frequently contested sources of resource wealth, such as petroleum deposits or diamond fields, encourage that greed.

There is no failed state without disharmonies between communities. Yet, the simple fact that many weak nation-states include haves and have-nots, and that some of the newer states contain a heterogeneous collection of ethnic, religious, and linguistic interests, is more a contributor to than a root cause of nation-state failure. In other words, state failure cannot be ascribed primarily to the inability to build nations from a congeries of ethnic groups. Nor should it be ascribed baldly to the oppression of minorities by a majority, although such brutalities are often a major ingredient of the impulse toward failure.

In contrast to strong states, failed states cannot control their borders. They lose authority over chunks of territory. Often, the expression of official power is limited to a capital city and one or more ethnically specific zones. Indeed, one measure of the extent of a state's failure is how much of the state's geographical expanse a government genuinely controls. How nominal is the central government's sway over rural towns, roads, and waterways? Who really rules up-country, or in particular distant districts?

In most cases, driven by ethnic or other intercommunal hostility or by regime insecurity, failed states prey on their own citizens. As in Mobutu Sese Seko's Zaire or the Taliban's Afghanistan, ruling cadres increasingly oppress, extort, and harass the majority of their own compatriots while favoring a narrowly based elite. As in Zaire, Angola, Siaka Stevens's Sierra Leone, or Hassan al-Turabi's pre-2001 Sudan, patrimonial rule depends on a patronage-based system of extraction from ordinary citizens. The typical weak state plunges toward failure when this kind of ruler-led oppression provokes a countervailing reaction on the part of resentful groups or newly emerged rebels.

Another indicator of state failure is the growth of criminal violence. As state authority weakens and fails, and as the state becomes criminal in its oppression of its citizens, so general lawlessness becomes more apparent. Gangs and criminal syndicates assume control over the streets of the cities. Arms and drug trafficking become more common. Ordinary police forces become paralyzed. Anarchy becomes more and more the norm. For protection, citizens naturally turn to warlords and other strong figures who express ethnic or clan solidarity, thus projecting strength at a time when all else, including the state itself, is crumbling.

Fewer and Fewer Political Goods

Nation-states exist to deliver political goods—security, education, health services, economic opportunity, environmental surveillance, a legal framework of order and a judicial system to administer it, and fundamental infrastructure requirements such as roads and communications facilities—to their citizens. Failed states honor these obligations in the breach. They increasingly forfeit their function as providers of political goods to warlords and other nonstate actors. In other words, a failed state is no longer able or willing to perform the job of a nation-state in the modern world.

Failed states are unable to provide security—the most central and foremost political good—across the whole of their domains. Citizens depend on states and central governments to secure their persons and free them from fear. Because a failing state is unable to establish an atmosphere of security nationwide and is often barely able to assert any kind of state power beyond a capital city, the failure of the state becomes obvious even before rebel groups and other contenders threaten the residents of central cities and overwhelm demoralized government contingents, as in contemporary Liberia and recent Sierra Leone.

Failed states contain weak or flawed institutions—that is, only the executive institution functions. If legislatures exist at all, they are rubber-stamp machines. Democratic debate is noticeably absent. The judiciary is derivative of the executive rather than being independent, and citizens know that they cannot rely on the court system for significant redress or remedy, especially against the state. The bureaucracy has long ago lost its sense of professional responsibility and exists solely to carry out the orders of the executive and, in petty ways, to oppress citizens. The military is possibly the only institution with any remaining integrity, but the armed forces of failed states are often highly politicized, without the esprit that they once exhibited.

Deteriorating or destroyed infrastructures typify failed states. Metaphorically, the more potholes (or main roads turned to rutted tracks), the more likely a state will exemplify failure. As rulers siphon funds from the state, so fewer capital resources are available for road crews, and maintaining road or rail access to distant provinces becomes less and less of a priority. Even refurbishing basic navigational aids along arterial waterways, as in the Democratic Republic of the Congo (DRC), succumbs to neglect. Where the state still controls the landline telephone system, that form of political and economic good also betrays a lack of renewal, upkeep, investment, and bureaucratic interest. Less a metaphor than a daily reality is the index of failed connections, repeated required dialing, and interminable waits for repair or service. If state monopolies have permitted private entrepreneurs to erect cell telephone towers and offer mobile telephone service, cell telephones may already have rendered the government's landline monopoly obsolete. In a state without a government, such as Somalia, the overlapping system of privately provided cell telephone systems is effective.

In failed states, the effective educational and health systems either have been privatized (with a resulting hodgepodge of shady schools and medical clinics in the cities) or have slowly slumped to increasingly desperate levels of decrepitude. Teachers, physicians, nurses, and orderlies are paid late or not at all, and absenteeism rises. Textbooks and essential medicines become scarce. X-ray machines cannot be repaired. Reports to the relevant ministries go unanswered; and parents, students, and patients—especially rural ones—slowly realize that the state has abandoned them to the forces of nature and to their own devices. Sometimes, where a failed state is effectively split (Sudan), essential services are still provided to the favored half (northern Sudan) but not to the half engulfed by war. Most of the time, however, the weakened nation-state completely fails to perform. Literacy falls, infant mortality rises, the AIDS epidemic overwhelms any health infrastructure that exists, life expectancies plummet, and an already poor and neglected citizenry becomes even poorer and more immiserated.

Failed states provide unparalleled economic opportunity, but only for a privileged few. Those close to the ruler or the ruling oligarchy grow richer while their less-fortunate brethren starve. Immense profits can be made from currency speculation, arbitrage, and knowledge of regulatory advantages. But the privilege of making real money when everything else is deteriorating is confined to clients of the ruling elite or to especially favored external entrepreneurs. The responsibility of a nation-state to maximize the well-being and personal prosperity of all of its citizens is conspicuously absent, if it ever existed.

Corruption flourishes in failed states, often on an unusually destructive scale. Petty or lubricating corruption is widespread. Levels of venal corruption escalate, especially kickbacks on anything that can be put out to bid, including medical supplies, textbooks, bridges; unnecessarily wasteful construction projects solely for the rents they will generate; licenses for existing and nonexisting activities; the appropriating by the ruling class of all kinds of private entrepreneurial endeavors; and generalized extortion. Corrupt ruling elites invest their gains overseas, not at home. A few build numerous palaces or lavish residences with state funds. Military officers always benefit from these corrupt regimes and feed ravenously from the same illicit troughs as their civilian counterparts.

An indicator, but not a cause, of failure is declining real national and per capita levels of gross domestic product (GDP). The statistical foundations of most states in the developing world are shaky, most certainly, but failed states—even, or particularly, failed states with abundant natural resources—show overall worsening GDP figures, slim year-to-year growth rates, and greater disparities of income between the wealthiest and poorest fifths of the population. High official deficits (Zimbabwe's reached 30 percent of GDP in 2001) support lavish security spending and the siphoning of cash by elites. Inflation usually soars because the ruling elite raids the central bank and prints money. From the resulting economic insecurity, often engineered by rulers to maximize their own fortunes and their own political as well as economic power, entrepreneurs favored by the prevailing regime can reap great amounts of money. Smuggling becomes rife. When state failure becomes complete, the local currency falls out of favor, and some or several international currencies take its place. Money changers are everywhere, legal or not, and arbitrage becomes an everyday national pursuit.

Sometimes, especially if climatic disasters intervene, the economic chaos and generalized neglect that is endemic to failed states can lead to regular food scarcities and widespread hunger—even to episodes of starvation and resulting international humanitarian relief efforts. Natural calamities can overwhelm the resources even of nonfailed but weak states in the developing world. But when unscrupulous rulers and ruling elites have consciously sucked state competencies dry, unforeseen natural disasters or man-made wars can drive ignored populations over the edge of endurance into starvation. Once such populations have lost their subsistence plots or sources of income, they lose their homes, forfeit already weak support networks, and are forced into an endless cycle of migration and displacement. Failed states offer no safety nets, and the homeless and destitute become fodder for anyone who can provide food and a cause.

A nation-state also fails when it loses a basic legitimacy—when its nominal borders become irrelevant and when one or more groups seek autonomous control within one or more parts of the national territory or, sometimes, even across its borders. Once the state's capacity deteriorates and what little capacity still remains is devoted largely to the fortunes of a few or to a favored ethnicity or community, then there is every reason to expect less and less loyalty to the state on the part of the excluded and the disenfranchised. When the rulers are seen to be working for themselves and their kin, and not for the state, their legitimacy, and the state's legitimacy, plummets. The state increasingly is perceived as owned by an exclusive class or group, with all others pushed aside.

Citizens naturally become more and more conscious of the kinds of sectional or community loyalties that are their main recourse and their only source of security and economic opportunity. They transfer their allegiances to clan and group leaders, some of whom become warlords. These warlords or other local strongmen derive support from external and local supporters. In the wilder, more marginalized corners of failed states, terror can breed along with the prevailing anarchy that emerges from state breakdown and failure.

A collapsed state is an extreme version of a failed state. It has a total vacuum of authority. A collapsed state is a mere geographical expression, a black hole into which a failed polity has fallen. Dark energy exists, but the forces of entropy have overwhelmed the radiance that hitherto provided some semblance of order and other vital political goods to the inhabitants embraced by language affinities or borders. When a state such as Somalia collapses (or Lebanon and Afghanistan a decade ago and Sierra Leone in the late 1990s), substate actors take over. They control regions and subregions, build their own local security apparatuses, sanction markets or other trading arrangements, and even establish an attenuated form of international relations. By definition, they are illegitimate and unrecognized, but some may assume the trappings of a quasi-state, such as Somaliland in northern Somalia. Yet, within the collapsed state prevail disorder, anomic behavior, and the kinds of anarchic mentality and entrepreneurial pursuits—especially gun and drug running—that are compatible with networks of terror.

Contemporary State Failure

This decade's failed states are Afghanistan, Angola, Burundi, the DRC, Liberia, Sierra Leone, and Sudan. These seven states exemplify the criteria of state failure. Beyond those states is one collapsed state: Somalia. Each of these countries has typified state failure continuously since at least 1990, if not before. Lebanon was once a failed state. So were Bosnia, Tajikistan, and Nigeria. Many other modern states approach the brink of failure, some much more ominously than others. Others drift disastrously downward from weak to failing to failed.

Of particular interest is why and how states slip from endemic weakness (Haiti) toward failure, or not. The list of weak states is long, but only a few of those weak and badly governed states necessarily edge into failure. Why? Even the categorization of

a state as failing—Colombia and Indonesia, among others—need not doom it unquestionably to full failure. Another critical question is, what does it take to drive a failing state into collapse? Why did Somalia not stop at failure rather than collapsing?

Not each of the classical failed and collapsed states fully fills all of the cells on the matrix of failure. To be termed a failure, however, a state certainly needs to demonstrate that it has met most of the explicit criteria. "Failure" is meant to describe a specific set of conditions and to exclude states that only meet a few of the criteria. In other words, how truly minimal are the roads, the schools, the hospitals, and the clinics? How far has GDP fallen and infant mortality risen? How far does the ambit of the central government reach? How little legitimacy remains? Most importantly, because civil conflict is decisive for state failure, can the state still provide security to its citizens and to what extent? Continuously? Only on good days and nights? Has the state lost control of large swaths of territory or only some provinces and regions?

Several test cases are interesting. Sri Lanka has been embroiled in a bitter and destructive civil war for 19 years. The rebel Liberation Tigers of Tamil Eelam (LTTE), a Tamil separatist insurgency, has at times in the last decade controlled as much as 15 percent of Sri Lanka's total land mass. Additionally, with relative impunity, the LTTE has been able to assassinate prime ministers, bomb presidents, kill off rival Tamils, and last year even wreak destruction at the nation's civil aviation terminal and main air force base. But, as unable as the Sinhala-dominated governments of Sri Lanka have been to put down the LTTE rebellion, so the nation-state has remained merely weak, never close to failure. For 80 percent of Sri Lankans, the government performs reasonably well. Since the early 1990s, too, Sri Lanka has exhibited robust levels of economic performance. The authority of successive governments, even before the recent ceasefire, extended securely to the Sinhala-speaking 80 percent of the country, and the regime recaptured some of the contested Tamil areas. Before the truce, road maintenance, educational and medical services, and the other necessary political goods continued to be delivered despite the civil war, to some limited degree even into the war-torn parts of the country. For all of these reasons, despite a consuming internal conflict founded on majority-minority discrimination and deprivation and on ethnic and religious differences, Sri Lanka has successfully escaped failure.

Indonesia is another example of weakness avoiding failure despite widespread insecurity. As the world's largest Muslim nation, its far-flung archipelago harbors the separatist wars of Aceh in the west and Papua (Irian Jaya) in the east, plus Muslim-Christian conflict in Ambon and the Mulukus, Muslim-Christian hostility in Sulawesi, and ethnic xenophobic outbursts in West Kalimantan. Given all of these conflictual situations, none of which have become less bitter since the end of Suharto's dictatorship, suggesting that Indonesia is approaching failure is easy. Yet, as one argument goes, only the insurgents in Aceh and Papua want to secede from the state; and, even in Aceh, official troops have the upper hand. Elsewhere, hostilities are intercommunal and not directed against the government or the state. Unlike the low-level war in Aceh, they do not threaten the integrity and resources of the state. Overall, most of Indonesia is still secure and is "glued" together well by an abiding sense of nationalism. The government still projects power and authority. Despite dangerous economic and other vicissitudes in the post-Suharto era, the state provides most of the other necessary political goods and remains legitimate. Indonesia need not be classified as anything other than a weak state, but the government's performance and provision of security should be monitored closely.

What about Colombia? An otherwise well-endowed, prosperous, and stable state has the second-highest murder rate per capita in the world, its politicians and businessmen wear flak jackets and travel with armed guards, and three private armies control relatively large chunks of its territory with impunity. The official defense and political estab-lishment has effectively ceded authority in those zones to the insurgencies and to drug traffickers. Again, why should Colombia not be ranked as a failed state? Although it could deteriorate into further failure, at present the Colombian government still performs for the 70 percent of the nation that remains under official authority. It provides political goods, even some improving security, for the large part of the state under official authority. When and if the government of Colombia can reassert itself into the disputed zones and further reduce drug trafficking, the power of the state will grow and a weak, endangered state such as Colombia can move away from possible failure toward the stronger side of the equation.

Zimbabwe is an example of a once unquestionably strong African state—indeed, one of the strongest—that has fallen rapidly through weakness to the very edge of failure. All that Zimbabwe lacks in order to join the ranks of failed states is a widespread internal insurgent movement directed at the government, which could still emerge. Meanwhile, per capita GDP has receded by 10 percent annually for two years. During the same period, inflation has galloped from 30 percent to 116 percent. The local currency has fallen against the U.S. dollar from 38:1 to 400:1. Foreign and domestic investment have largely ceased. Health and educational services are almost nonexistent and shrinking further. Road maintenance and telephone service are obviously suffering. Judicial independence survives, but barely, and not in critical political cases. The state has also been preying on its own citizens for at least two years. Corruption is blatant and very much dominated by the avaricious ruling elite. Zimbabwe is an example of a state that, like Sierra Leone and the DRC at earlier moments in history, has been driven into failure by human agency.

Indonesia, Colombia, Sri Lanka, and Zimbabwe are but four among a large number of nation-states (two dozen by a recent count) that contain serious elements of failure but will probably avoid failure, especially if they receive sufficient outside assistance.

They belong to a category of state that is designated weak but that encompasses and spreads into the category of failing—the precursor to true failure. Haiti, Chad, and Kyrgyzstan, from three continents, are representative examples of perpetual weakness. Argentina has recently joined an analogous rank; Russia was once a candidate. Fiji, the Solomon Islands, Tajikistan, Lebanon, Nigeria, Niger, and Burkina Faso remain vulnerable to further deterioration. Even Kenya is a weak state with some potential for definitive failure if ethnic disparities and ambitions provoke civil strife.

The list of states in weakness is longer and hardly static. Some of the potentially stronger states move in and out of weakness and nearer or farther from failure. Others are foreordained weak. Particular decisions by ruling groups would be needed to destabilize members of this second group further and drive them into failure.

The Hand of Man

State failure is man-made, not merely accidental nor—fundamentally—caused geographically, environmentally, or externally. Leadership decisions and leadership failures have destroyed states and continue to weaken the fragile polities that operate on the cusp of failure. Mobutu's kleptocratic rule extracted the marrow of Zaire/DRC and left nothing for his national dependents. Much of the resource wealth of that vast country ended up in Mobutu's or his cronies' pockets. During four decades, hardly any money was devoted to uplifting the Congolese people, improving their welfare, building infrastructures, or even providing more than rudimentary security. Mobutu's government performed only for Mobutu, not for Zaire/DRC.

Likewise, oil-rich Angola continues to fail because of three decades of war, but also because President Eduardo dos Santos and his associates have refused to let the Angolan government deliver more than basic services within the large zone that they control. Stevens (1967–1985) decapitated the Sierra Leonean state in order to strengthen his own

power amid growing chaos. Sierra Leone has not yet recovered from Stevens's depredations. Nor has Liberia been resuscitated in the aftermath of the slashing neglect and unabashed greed of Samuel Doe, Prince Johnson, and Charles Taylor. In Somalia, Mohammed Siad Barre arrogated more and more power and privilege to himself and his clan. Finally, nothing was left for the other pretenders to power. The Somali state was gutted, the abilities of the Somali government to provide political goods endlessly compromised, and the descent into failure and then full collapse followed.

President Robert Gabriel Mugabe has personally led Zimbabwe from strength to the precipice of failure. His high-handed and seriously corrupt rule bled the resources of the state into his own pocket, squandered foreign exchange, discouraged domestic and international investment, subverted the courts, and this year drove his country to the very brink of starvation. In Sri Lanka, Solomon and Sirimavo Bandaranaike, one after the other, drove the LTTE into reactive combat by abrogating minority rights and vitiating the social contract on which the country called Ceylon had been created. In Afghanistan, Gulbuddin Hakmatyar and Burrhan ul-Din Rabani tried to prevent Afghans other than their fellow Pushtun and Tajik nationals from sharing the perquisites of governance; their narrowly focused, self-enriching decisions enabled the Taliban to triumph and Afghanistan to become a safe harbor for terrorists.

Preventing State Failure

Strengthening weak states against failure is far easier than reviving them after they have definitively failed or collapsed. As the problem of contemporary Afghanistan shows, reconstruction is very long, very expensive, and hardly a smooth process. Creating security and a security force from scratch, amid bitter memories, is the immediate need. Then comes the re-creation of an administrative structure—primarily re-creating a bureaucracy and finding the funds with which to pay the erstwhile bureaucrats and policemen. A judicial method is required, which means the establishment or reestablishment of a legitimate legal code and system; the training of judges, prosecutors, and defenders (as attempted recently in East Timor); and the opening of courtrooms and offices. Restarting the schools, employing teachers, refurbishing and re-equipping hospitals, building roads, and even gathering statistics—all of these fundamental chores take time, large sums of money (especially in war-shattered Afghanistan), and meticulous oversight in postconflict nations with overstretched human resources. Elections need not be an early priority, but constitutions must be written eventually and elections held in order to encourage participatory democracy.

Strengthening states prone to failure before they fail is prudent policy and contributes significantly to world order and to minimizing combat, casualties, refugees, and displaced persons. Doing so is far less expensive than reconstructing states after failure. Strengthening weak states also has the potential to eliminate the authority and power vacuums within which terror thrives.

From a policy perspective, however, these are obvious nostrums. The mechanisms for amelioration are also more obvious than obscure. In order to encourage responsible leadership and good governance, financial assistance from international lending agencies and bilateral donors must be designed to reinforce positive leadership only. Outside support should be conditional on monetary and fiscal streamlining, renewed attention to good governance, reforms of land tenure systems, and strict adherence to the rule of law. External assistance to create in-country jobs by reducing external tariff barriers (e.g., on textiles) and by supporting vital foreign direct investment is critical. So is support for innovations that can reduce importation and exportation transport expenditures for the weak nations, improve telephone and power systems through privatization, open predominantly closed economies in general, create new incentives for agricultural productivity, and bolster existing security forces through training and equipment.

All these ingredients of a successful strengthening process are necessary. The developed world can apply tough love and assist the developing and more vulnerable world to help itself in many more similarly targeted ways. In addition to the significant amounts of cash (grants are preferred over loans) that must be transferred to help the poorer nations help themselves, however, the critical ingredient is sustained interest and sustained assistance over the very long run. Nothing enduring can be accomplished instantaneously. If the world order wants to dry up the reservoirs of terror, as well as do good more broadly, it must commit itself and its powers to a campaign of decades, not months. The refurbishment and revitalization of Afghanistan will take much more than the $4.7 billion pledged and the many years that Secretary of State Colin L. Powell has warned the U.S. people will be necessary to make Afghanistan a self-sufficient state. Strengthening Indonesia, for example, would take a concerted effort for decades. So would strengthening any of the dangerous and needy candidates in Africa or in Central Asia.

Preventing state failure is imperative, difficult, and costly. Yet, doing so is profoundly in the interest not only of the inhabitants of the most deprived and ill-governed states of the world, but also of world peace.

Satisfying such lofty goals, however—making the world much safer by strengthening weak states against failure—is dependent on the political will of the wealthy big-power arbiters of world security. Perhaps the newly aroused awareness of the dangers of terror will embolden political will in the United States, Europe, and Japan. Otherwise, the common ingredients of zero-sum leadership; ethnic, linguistic, and religious antagonisms and fears; chauvinistic ambition; economic insufficiency; and inherited fragility will continue to propel nation-states from weakness toward failure. In turn, that failure will be costly in terms of humanitarian relief and postconflict reconstruction. Ethnic cleansing episodes will recur, as will famines, and in the thin and hospitable soils of newly failed and collapsed states, terrorist groups will take root.

Stephen D. Krasner
SOVEREIGNTY

The idea of states as autonomous, independent entities is collapsing under the combined onslaught of monetary unions, CNN, the Internet, and nongovernmental organizations. But those who proclaim the death of sovereignty misread history. The nation-state has a keen instinct for survival and has so far adapted to new challenges—even the challenge of globalization.

"The Sovereign State Is Just about Dead"

Very Wrong

Sovereignty was never quite as vibrant as many contemporary observers suggest. The conventional norms of sovereignty have always been challenged. A few states, most notably the United States, have had autonomy, control, and recognition for most of their existence, but most others have not. The politics of many weaker states have been persistently penetrated, and stronger nations have not been immune to external influence. China was occupied. The constitutional arrangements of Japan and Germany were directed by the United States after World War II. The United Kingdom, despite its rejection of the euro, is part of the European Union.

Even for weaker states—whose domestic structures have been influenced by outside actors, and whose leaders have very little control over transborder movements or even activities within their own country—sovereignty remains attractive. Although sovereignty might provide little more than international recognition, that recognition guarantees access to international organizations and sometimes to international finance. It offers status to individual leaders. While the great powers of Europe have eschewed many elements of sovereignty, the United States, China, and Japan have neither the interest nor the inclination to abandon their usually effective claims to domestic autonomy.

In various parts of the world, national borders still represent the fault lines of conflict, whether it is Israelis and Palestinians fighting over the status of Jerusalem, Indians and Pakistanis threatening to go nuclear over Kashmir, or Ethiopia and Eritrea clashing over disputed territories. Yet commentators nowadays are mostly concerned about the erosion of national borders as a consequence of globalization. Governments and activists alike complain that multilateral institutions such as the United Nations, the World Trade Organization, and the International Monetary Fund overstep their authority by promoting universal standards for everything from human rights and the environment to monetary policy and immigration. However, the most important impact of economic globalization and transnational norms will be to alter the scope of state authority rather than to generate some fundamentally new way to organize political life.

"Sovereignty Means Final Authority"

Not Anymore, If Ever

When philosophers Jean Bodin and Thomas Hobbes first elaborated the notion of sovereignty in the 16th and 17th centuries, they were concerned with establishing the legitimacy of a single hierarchy of domestic authority. Although Bodin and Hobbes accepted the existence of divine and natural law, they both (especially Hobbes) believed the word of the sovereign was law. Subjects had no right to revolt. Bodin and Hobbes realized that imbuing the sovereign with

From *Foreign Policy* (January/February 2001), pp. 20–29.

such overweening power invited tyranny, but they were predominately concerned with maintaining domestic order, without which they believed there could be no justice. Both were writing in a world riven by sectarian strife. Bodin was almost killed in religious riots in France in 1572. Hobbes published his seminal work, *Leviathan*, only a few years after parliament (composed of Britain's emerging wealthy middle class) had executed Charles I in a civil war that had sought to wrest state control from the monarchy.

This idea of supreme power was compelling, but irrelevant in practice. By the end of the 17th century, political authority in Britain was divided between king and parliament. In the United States, the Founding Fathers established a constitutional structure of checks and balances and multiple sovereignties distributed among local and national interests that were inconsistent with hierarchy and supremacy. The principles of justice, and especially order, so valued by Bodin and Hobbes, have best been provided by modern democratic states whose organizing principles are antithetical to the idea that sovereignty means uncontrolled domestic power.

If sovereignty does not mean a domestic order with a single hierarchy of authority, what does it mean? In the contemporary world, sovereignty primarily has been linked with the idea that states are autonomous and independent from each other. Within their own boundaries, the members of a polity are free to choose their own form of government. A necessary corollary of this claim is the principle of nonintervention: One state does not have a right to intervene in the internal affairs of another.

More recently, sovereignty has come to be associated with the idea of control over transborder movements. When contemporary observers assert that the sovereign state is just about dead, they do not mean that constitutional structures are about to disappear. Instead, they mean that technological change has made it very difficult, or perhaps impossible, for states to control movements across their borders of all kinds of material things (from coffee to cocaine) and not-so-material things (from Hollywood movies to capital flows).

Finally, sovereignty has meant that political authorities can enter into international agreements. They are free to endorse any contract they find attractive. Any treaty among states is legitimate provided that it has not been coerced.

"The Peace of Westphalia Produced the Modern Sovereign State"

No, It Came Later

Contemporary pundits often cite the 1648 Peace of Westphalia (actually two separate treaties, Münster and Osnabrück) as the political big bang that created the modern system of autonomous states. Westphalia—which ended the Thirty Years' War against the hegemonic power of the Holy Roman Empire—delegitimized the already waning transnational role of the Catholic Church and validated the idea that international relations should be driven by balance-of-power considerations rather than the ideals of Christendom. But Westphalia was first and foremost a new constitution for the Holy Roman Empire. The preexisting right of the principalities in the empire to make treaties was affirmed, but the Treaty of Münster stated that "such Alliances be not against the Emperor, and the Empire, nor against the Publick Peace, and this Treaty, and without prejudice to the Oath by which every one is bound to the Emperor and the Empire." The domestic political structures of the principalities remained embedded in the Holy Roman Empire. The Duke of Saxony, the Margrave of Brandenburg, the Count of Palatine, and the Duke of Bavaria were affirmed as electors who (along with the archbishops of Mainz, Trier, and Cologne) chose the emperor. They did not become or claim to be kings in their own right.

Perhaps most important, Westphalia established rules for religious tolerance in Germany. The treaties gave lip service to the principle (*cuius regio, eius religio*) that the prince could set the religion of this territory—and then went on to violate this very principle through many specific provisions. The signatories agreed that the religious rules already in effect would stay in place. Catholics and Protestants in German cities with mixed populations would share offices. Religious issues had to be settled by a majority of both Catholics and Protestants in the diet and courts of the empire. None of the major political leaders in Europe endorsed religious toleration in principle, but they recognized that religious conflicts were so volatile that it was essential to contain rather than repress sectarian differences. All in all, Westphalia is a pretty medieval document, and its biggest explicit innovation—provisions that undermined the power of princes to control religious affairs within their territories—was antithetical to the ideas of national sovereignty that later became associated with the so-called Westphalian system.

"Universal Human Rights Are an Unprecedented Challenge to Sovereignty"

Wrong

The struggle to establish international rules that compel leaders to treat their subjects in a certain way has been going on for a long time. Over the centuries the emphasis has shifted from religious toleration, to minority rights (often focusing on specific ethnic groups in specific countries), to human rights (emphasizing rights enjoyed by all or broad classes of individuals). In a few instances states have voluntarily embraced international supervision, but generally the weak have acceded to the preferences of the strong: the Vienna settlement following the Napoleonic wars guaranteed religious toleration for Catholics in the Netherlands. All of the successor states of the Ottoman Empire, beginning with

Greece in 1832 and ending with Albania in 1913, had to accept provisions for civic and political equality for religious minorities as a condition for international recognition. The peace settlements following World War I included extensive provisions for the protection of minorities. Poland, for instance, agreed to refrain from holding elections on Saturday because such balloting would have violated the Jewish Sabbath. Individuals could bring complaints against governments through a minority rights bureau established within the League of Nations.

But as the Holocaust tragically demonstrated, interwar efforts at international constraints on domestic practices failed dismally. After World War II, human, rather than minority, rights became the focus of attention. The United Nations Charter endorsed both human rights and the classic sovereignty principle of nonintervention. The 20-plus human rights accords that have been signed during the last half century cover a wide range of issues including genocide, torture, slavery, refugees, stateless persons, women's rights, racial discrimination, children's rights, and forced labor. These UN agreements, however, have few enforcement mechanisms, and even their provisions for reporting violations are often ineffective.

The tragic and bloody disintegration of Yugoslavia in the 1990s revived earlier concerns with ethnic rights. International recognition of the Yugoslav successor states was conditional upon their acceptance of constitutional provisions guaranteeing minority rights. The Dayton accords established externally controlled authority structures in Bosnia, including a Human Rights Commission (a majority of whose members were appointed by the Western European states). NATO created a de facto protectorate in Kosovo.

The motivations for such interventions—humanitarianism and security—have hardly changed. Indeed, the considerations that brought the great powers into the Balkans following the wars of the 1870s were hardly different from those that engaged NATO and Russia in the 1990s.

"Globalization Undermines State Control"

No

State control could never be taken for granted. Technological changes over the last 200 years have increased the flow of people, goods, capital, and ideas—but the problems posed by such movements are not new. In many ways, states are better able to respond now than they were in the past.

The impact of the global media on political authority (the so-called CNN effect) pales in comparison to the havoc that followed the invention of the printing press. Within a decade after Martin Luther purportedly nailed his 95 theses to the Wittenberg church door, his ideas had circulated throughout Europe. Some political leaders seized upon the principles of the Protestant Reformation as a way to legitimize secular political authority. No sovereign monarch could contain the spread of these concepts, and some lost not only their lands but also their heads. The sectarian controversies of the 16th and 17th centuries were perhaps more politically consequential than any subsequent transnational flow of ideas.

In some ways, international capital movements were more significant in earlier periods than they are now. During the 19th century, Latin American states (and to a lesser extent Canada, the United States, and Europe) were beset by boom-and-bust cycles associated with global financial crises. The Great Depression, which had a powerful effect on the domestic politics of all major states, was precipitated by an international collapse of credit. The Asian financial crisis of the late 1990s was not nearly as devastating. Indeed, the speed with which countries recovered from the Asian flu reflects how a better working knowledge of economic theories and more effective central banks have made it easier for states to secure the advantages (while at the same time minimizing the risks) of being enmeshed in global financial markets.

In addition to attempting to control the flows of capital and ideas, states have long struggled to manage the impact of international trade. The opening of long-distance trade for bulk commodities in the 19th century created fundamental cleavages in all of the major states. Depression and plummeting grain prices made it possible for German Chancellor Otto von Bismarck to prod the landholding aristocracy into a protectionist alliance with urban heavy industry (this coalition of "iron and rye" dominated German politics for decades). The tariff question was a basic divide in U.S. politics for much of the last half of the 19th and first half of the 20th centuries. But, despite growing levels of imports and exports since 1950, the political salience of trade has receded because national governments have developed social welfare strategies that cushion the impact of international competition, and workers with higher skill levels are better able to adjust to changing international conditions. It has become easier, not harder, for states to manage the flow of goods and services.

"Globalization Is Changing the Scope of State Control"

Yes

The reach of the state has increased in some areas but contracted in others. Rulers have recognized that their effective control can be enhanced by walking away from issues they cannot resolve. For instance, beginning with the Peace of Westphalia, leaders chose to surrender their control over religion because it proved too volatile. Keeping religion within the scope of state authority undermined, rather than strengthened, political stability.

Monetary policy is an area where state control expanded and then ultimately contracted. Before the 20th century, states had neither the administrative competence nor the inclination to conduct independent monetary policies. The mid-20th-century effort to control monetary affairs, which was associated with Keynesian economics, has now been reversed due to the magnitude of short-term capital flows and the inability of some states to control inflation. With the exception of Great Britain, the major European states have established a single monetary authority. Confronting recurrent hyperinflation, Ecuador adopted the U.S. dollar as its currency in 2000.

Along with the erosion of national currencies, we now see the erosion of national citizenship—the notion that an individual should be a citizen of one and only one country, and that the state has exclusive claims to that person's loyalty. For many states, there is no longer a sharp distinction between citizens and noncitizens. Permanent residents, guest workers, refugees, and undocumented immigrants are entitled to some bundle of rights even if they cannot vote. The ease of travel and the desire of many countries to attract either capital or skilled workers have increased incentives to make citizenship a more flexible category.

Although government involvement in religion, monetary affairs, and claims to loyalty has declined, overall government activity, as reflected in taxation and government expenditures, has increased as a percentage of national income since the 1950s among the most economically advanced states. The extent of a country's social welfare programs tends to go hand in hand with its level of integration within the global economy. Crises of authority and control have been most pronounced in the states that have been the most isolated, with sub-Saharan Africa offering the largest number of unhappy examples.

"NGOs Are Nibbling at National Sovereignty"

To Some Extent

Transnational nongovernmental organizations (NGOs) have been around for quite a while, especially if you include corporations. In the 18th century, the East India Company possessed political power (and even an expeditionary military force) that rivaled that of many national governments. Throughout the 19th century, there were transnational movements to abolish slavery, promote the rights of women, and improve conditions for workers.

The number of transnational NGOs, however, has grown tremendously, from around 200 in 1909 to over 17,000 today. The availability of inexpensive and very fast communications technology has made it easier for such groups to organize and make an impact on public policy and international law—the international agreement banning land mines being a recent case in point. Such groups prompt questions about sovereignty because they appear to threaten the integrity of domestic decision making. Activists who lose on their home territory can pressure foreign governments, which may in turn influence decision makers in the activists' own nation.

But for all of the talk of growing NGO influence, their power to affect a country's domestic affairs has been limited when compared to governments, international organizations, and multinational corporations. The United Fruit Company had more influence in Central America in the early part of the 20th century than any NGO could hope to have anywhere in the contemporary world. The International Monetary Fund and other multilateral financial institutions now routinely negotiate conditionality agreements that involve not only specific economic targets but also domestic institutional changes, such as pledges to crack down on corruption and break up cartels.

Smaller, weaker states are the most frequent targets of external efforts to alter domestic institutions, but more powerful states are not immune. The openness of the U.S. political system means that not only NGOs but also foreign governments can play some role in political decisions. (The Mexican government, for instance, lobbied heavily for the passage of the North American Free Trade Agreement.) In fact, the permeability of the American polity makes the United States a less threatening partner; nations are more willing to sign on to U.S.-sponsored international arrangements because they have some confidence that they can play a role in U.S. decision making.

"Sovereignty Blocks Conflict Resolution"

Yes, Sometimes

Rulers as well as their constituents have some reasonably clear notion of what sovereignty means—exclusive control within a given territory—even if this norm has been challenged frequently by inconsistent principles (such as universal human rights) and violated in practice (the U.S.- and British-enforced no-fly zones over Iraq). In fact, the political importance of conventional sovereignty rules has made it harder to solve some problems. There is, for instance, no conventional sovereignty solution for Jerusalem, but it doesn't require much imagination to think of alternatives: divide the city into small pieces; divide the Temple Mount vertically with the Palestinians controlling the top and the Israelis the bottom; establish some kind of international authority; divide control over different issues (religious practices versus taxation, for instance) among different authorities. Any one of these solutions would be better for most Israelis and Palestinians than an ongoing stalemate, but political leaders on both sides have had trouble delivering a settlement because they are subject to attacks by counterelites who can wave the sovereignty flag.

Conventional rules have also been problematic for Tibet. Both the Chinese and the Tibetans might be better off if Tibet could regain some of the autonomy it had as a tributary state within the traditional Chinese empire. Tibet had extensive local control but symbolically (and sometimes through tribute payments) recognized the supremacy of the emperor. Today, few on either side would even know what a tributary state is, and even if the leaders of then Tibet worked out some kind of settlement that would give their country more self-government,

there would be no guarantee that they could gain the support of their own constituents.

If, however, leaders can reach mutual agreements, bring along their constituents, or are willing to use coercion, sovereignty rules can be violated in inventive ways. The Chinese, for instance, made Hong Kong a special administrative region after the transfer from British rule, allowed a foreign judge to sit on the Court of Final Appeal, and secured acceptance by other states not only for Hong Kong's participation in a number of international organizations but also for separate visa agreements and recognition of a distinct Hong Kong passport. All of these measures violate conventional sovereignty rules, since Hong Kong does not have juridical independence. Only by inventing a unique status for Hong Kong, which involved the acquiescence of other states, could China claim sovereignty while simultaneously preserving the confidence of the business community.

"The European Union Is a New Model for Supranational Governance"

Yes, but Only for the Europeans

The European Union (EU) really is a new thing, far more interesting in terms of sovereignty than Hong Kong. It is not a conventional international organization because its member states are now so intimately linked with one another that withdrawal is not a viable option. It is not likely to become a "United States of Europe"—a large federal state that might look something like the United States of America—because the interests, cultures, economies, and domestic institutional arrangements of its members are too diverse. Widening the EU to include the former communist states of Central Europe would further complicate any efforts to move toward a political organization that looks like a conventional sovereign state.

The EU is inconsistent with conventional sovereignty rules. Its member states have created supranational institutions (the European Court of Justice, the European Commission, and the Council of Ministers) that can make decisions opposed by some member states. The rulings of the court have direct effect and supremacy within national judicial systems, even though these doctrines were never explicitly endorsed in any treaty. The European Monetary Union created a central bank that now controls monetary affairs for three of the union's four largest states. The Single European Act and the Maastricht Treaty provide for majority or qualified majority, but not unanimous, voting in some issue areas. In one sense, the European Union is a product of state sovereignty because it has been created through voluntary agreements among its member states. But, in another sense, it fundamentally contradicts conventional understandings of sovereignty because these same agreements have undermined the juridical autonomy of its individual members.

The European Union, however, is not a model that other parts of the world can imitate. The initial moves toward integration could not have taken place without the political and economic support of the United States, which was, in the early years of the Cold War, much more interested in creating a strong alliance that could effectively oppose the Soviet Union than it was in any potential European challenge to U.S. leadership. Germany, one of the largest states in the European Union, has been the most consistent supporter of an institutional structure that would limit Berlin's own freedom of action, a reflection of the lessons of two devastating wars and the attractiveness of a European identity for a country still grappling with the sins of the Nazi era. It is hard to imagine that other regional powers such as China, Japan, or Brazil, much less the United States, would have any interest in tying their own hands in similar ways. (Regional trading agreements such as Mercosur and NAFTA have very limited supranational provisions and show few signs of evolving into broader monetary or political unions.) The EU is a new and unique institutional structure, but it will coexist with, not displace, the sovereign-state model.

3 NATIONS AND SOCIETY

The readings presented in this chapter address three basic issues: nationalism, the role of ethnic conflict in civil war, and whether ethnic diversity and segregation lead to worse political and economic results.

Certainly until the sixteenth century, and plausibly even until the eighteenth, nationalism in the modern sense did not exist. People were loyal to a particular lord or locality, but not to a linguistically or ethnically defined nation, and no one was surprised that the typical state or empire embraced a large variety of languages and ethnicities. How, then, did modern nationalism become so powerful a force, and why are most states today *nation-states*, that is, ones that have, or seek, a single national identity (including, in most cases, a single language)?

In his 1962 book, *The Age of Revolution: 1789–1848*, the eminent historian Eric Hobsbawm wrote what many comparativists still regard as the most convincing account of how modern nationalisms arose, with clear implications for present-day ethnic conflicts around the globe. Hobsbawm's crucial insight—that nationalism is always linked to the rapid rise of an indigenous middle class and to the spread of literacy in the native language—remains valid today and has been stressed in analyses of (among many others) Irish, Québecois, Basque, Eritrean, Catalan, and Kurdish nationalism. One should also remember, as Hobsbawm notes, that a sizeable proportion of the "national" languages claimed by such groups—among them Croatian, Romanian, Gaelic, Norwegian, Czech, and modern Hebrew—were more invented (that is, constructed out of a welter of dialects or the imagined evolution of an ossified language) than revived.

Ethnic divisions sometimes lead to violent conflict, inflicting heavy costs on societies both poor (Nigeria, Rwanda, Sri Lanka) and rich (Northern Ireland, Spain, Russia). In the 1990s, some economists held that ethnic fragmentation alone, at least in Africa, led directly to bad policies, weak trust, and continuing poverty. They thus provided a dual rationale for ethnically unified states, or for the secession of "nations" that formed within existing states.

Such violence, particularly civil war, undoubtedly inhibits economic growth. But Paul Collier and other World Bank economists argued that most civil wars have been a result of "greed" rather than "grievance." Conflict was often all about, and fueled by, huge and readily marketable reserves of valuable natural resources (oil, diamonds, copper ore, mahogany). In 2003, the comparativists James D. Fearon and David D. Laitin addressed these questions in a famous article (excerpted in this chapter) titled "Ethnicity, Insurgency, and Civil War." They showed that ethnically diverse societies were no more likely than homogeneous ones to experience civil war; rather, the chief causes were poverty, political instability, and a terrain that favored insurgency. At about the same time, Alberto Alesina and Eliana La Ferrara, in their 2005 article "Ethnic Diversity and Economic Performance," reestablished that ethnic diversity, at least in poor societies, inhibited economic growth, even after other plausible causes had been taken into account. On the other hand, they pointed to the possibility, particularly in wealthy societies, that ethnic diversity could accelerate economic growth by providing complementary skills and insights.

Surprisingly, most of the early research looked only at the degree of ethnic fragmentation in societies: more precisely, the likelihood that two randomly chosen individuals would belong to different ethnic groups.[1] Yet common sense tells us that differences in the wealth of ethnic groups, or in the degree to which they are physically separate from one another, matter also. In the article excerpted here, Kate Baldwin and John D. Huber (2010) show that where ethnic groups differ radically in wealth, government services are poorly provided—one possible reason that fractionalization inhibits economic growth. The final study in this chapter, by Lars-Erik Cederman, Nils B. Weidman, and Kristian Skrede Gleditsch (2011), comes to the surprising conclusion that both the richest and poorest ethnic groups are more likely to initiate violent conflict than those in the middle, and that this effect is strongest where those groups are regionally concentrated.

Nationalism and ethnicity remain among the most active research areas in comparative politics, and data on ethnicity (and on the wealth and location of ethnic groups) are becoming steadily better. Yet one deep mystery endures: How has the "nation" been able, at least for the past century and a half, to elicit the degree of loyalty and self-sacrifice that its citizens have exhibited in both interstate and civil wars?

NOTE

1. If one ethnic group constitutes 20 percent of a society, the probability that two randomly chosen citizens will both be members of this group is $(.2)^2$, or .04. If another group constitutes 30 percent of the society, the likelihood that two randomly chosen citizens will both belong to this ethnic group is $(.3)^2 = .09$. If the remaining half of the population belongs to a third ethnic group, the probability that the two random individuals will belong to this third group is $(.5)^2 = .25$. Thus, the probability that any two randomly chosen people will be coethnics (i.e., belong to the same group, regardless of which of the three it is) must be the sum of these probabilities: $.04 + .09 + .25 = .38$. And the probability that the two random people are *not* coethnics is just $1 - .38 = .62$. Generalizing to any number n of ethnic groups in a society, where p_i represents the share of the population that belongs to a given ethnic group, most work defines an *ethnic fractionalization index* (ELF) as $1 - (\sum p_i^2)$. Economists recognize this as a "Herfindahl index."

Eric Hobsbawm
NATIONALISM

Every people has its special mission, which will cooperate towards the fulfilment of the general mission of humanity. That mission constitutes its nationality. Nationality is sacred.

ACT OF BROTHERHOOD OF
YOUNG EUROPE, 1834

The day will come . . . when sublime Germania shall stand on the bronze pedestal of liberty and justice, bearing in one hand the torch of enlightenment, which shall throw the beam of civilization into the remotest corners of the earth, and in the other the arbiter's balance. The people will beg her to settle their disputes; those very people who now show us that might is right, and kick us with the jackboot of scornful contempt.

FROM SIEBENPFEIFFER'S SPEECH
AT THE HAMBACH FESTIVAL, 1832

After 1830, as we have seen, the general movement in favour of revolution split. One product of this split deserves special attention: the self-consciously nationalist movements.

The movements which best symbolize this development are the 'Youth' movements founded or inspired by Giuseppe Mazzini shortly after the 1830 revolution: Young Italy, Young Poland, Young Switzerland, Young Germany, and Young France (1831–6) and the analogous Young Ireland of the 1840s, the ancestor of the only lasting and successful revolutionary organization on the model of the early nineteenth-century conspiratory brotherhoods, the Fenians or Irish Republican Brotherhood, better known through its executive arm of the Irish Republican Army. In themselves these movements were of

no great importance; the mere presence of Mazzini would have been enough to ensure their total ineffectiveness. Symbolically they are of extreme importance, as is indicated by the adoption in subsequent nationalist movements of such labels as 'Young Czechs' or 'Young Turks.' They mark the distintegration of the European revolutionary movement into national segments. Doubtless each of these segments had much the same political programme strategy, and tactics as the others, and even much the same flag—almost invariably a tricolour of some kind. Its members saw no contradiction between their own demands and those of other nations, and indeed envisaged a brotherhood of all, simultaneously liberating themselves. On the other hand each now tended to justify its primary concern with its own nation by adopting the role of a Messiah for all. Through Italy (according to Mazzini), through Poland (according to Mickiewicz), the suffering peoples of the world were to be led to freedom; an attitude readily adaptable to conservative or indeed imperialist policies, as witness the Russian Slavophils with their championship of Holy Russia, the Third Rome, and the Germans who were subsequently to tell the world at some length that it would be healed by the German spirit. Admittedly this ambiguity of nationalism went back to the French Revolution. But in those days there had been only *one* great and revolutionary nation and it made sense (as indeed it still did) to regard it as the headquarters of all revolutions, and the necessary prime mover in the liberation of the world. To look to Paris was rational; to look to a vague "Italy," "Poland," or "Germany" (represented in practice by a handful of conspirators and emigrés) made sense only for Italians, Poles, and Germans.

If the new nationalism had been confined only to the membership of the national-revolutionary brotherhoods, it would not be worth much more

From *The Age of Revolution: 1789–1848* (London: Weidenfeld & Nicholson, 1962), pp. 163–77. Some of the author's notes have been omitted.

attention. However, it also reflected much more powerful forces, which were emerging into political consciousness in the 1830s as the result of the double revolution. The most immediately powerful of these were the discontent of the lesser landowners or gentry and the emergence of a national middle and even lower-middle class in numerous countries, the spokesmen for both being largely professional intellectuals.

The revolutionary role of the lesser gentry is perhaps best illustrated in Poland and Hungary. There, on the whole, the large landed magnates had long found it possible and desirable to make terms with absolutism and foreign rule. The Hungarian magnates were in general Catholic and had long been accepted as pillars of Viennese court society; very few of them were to join the revolution of 1848. The memory of the old *Rzeczpospolita* made even Polish magnates nationally minded, but the most influential of their quasi-national parties, the Czartoryski connection, now operating from the luxurious emigration of the Hotel Lambert in Paris, had always favoured the alliance with Russia and continued to prefer diplomacy to revolt. Economically they were wealthy enough to afford what they needed, short of really titanic dissipation, and even to invest enough in the improvement of their estates to benefit from the economic expansion of the age, if they chose to. Count Széchenyi, one of the few moderate liberals from this class and a champion of economic improvement, gave a year's income for the new Hungarian Academy of Sciences—some 60,000 florins. There is no evidence that his standard of life suffered from such disinterested generosity. On the other hand the numerous gentlemen who had little but their birth to distinguish them from other impoverished farmers—one in eight of the Hungarian population claimed gentlemanly status—had neither the money to make their holdings profitable nor the inclination to compete with Germans and Jews for middle-class wealth. If they could not live decently on their rents, and a degenerate age deprived them of a soldier's chances, then they might, if not too ignorant, consider the law,

administration, or some intellectual position, but no bourgeois activity. Such gentlemen had long been the stronghold of opposition to absolutism, foreigners, and magnate rule in their respective countries, sheltering (as in Hungary) behind the dual buttress of Calvinism and county organization. It was natural that their opposition, discontent, and aspiration for more jobs for local gentlemen should now fuse with nationalism.

The national business classes which emerged in this period were, paradoxically, a rather less nationalist element. Admittedly in disunited Germany and Italy the advantages of a large unified national market made sense. The author of *Deutschland über Alles* apostrophized

> Ham and scissors, boots and garters,
> Wool and soap and yarn and beer,

because they had achieved, what the spirit of nationality had been unable to, a genuine sense of national unity through customs union. However, there is little evidence that, say, the shippers of Genoa (who were later to provide much of the financial backing for Garibaldi) preferred the possibilities of a national Italian market to the larger prosperity of trading all over the Mediterranean. And in the large multinational empires the industrial or trading nuclei which grew up in particular provinces might grumble about discrimination, but at bottom clearly preferred the great markets open to them now to the little ones of future national independence. The Polish industrialists, with all Russia at their feet, took little part as yet in Polish nationalism. When Palacky claimed on behalf of the Czechs that "if Austria did not exist, it would have to be invented," he was not merely calling on the monarchy's support against the Germans, but also expressing the sound economic reasoning of the economically most advanced sector of a large and otherwise backward empire. Business interests were sometimes at the head of nationalism, as in Belgium, where a strong pioneer industrial community regarded itself, with doubtful reason, as disadvantaged under the rule of the powerful Dutch merchant community, to which it had been hitched in 1815. But this was an exceptional case.

The great proponents of middle-class nationalism at this stage were the lower and middle professional, administrative and intellectual strata, in other words the *educated* classes. (These are not, of course, distinct from the business classes, especially in backward countries where estate administrators, notaries, lawyers, and the like are among the key accumulators of rural wealth.) To be precise, the advance guard of middle-class nationalism fought its battle along the line which marked the educational progress of large numbers of "new men" into areas hitherto occupied by a small elite. The progress of schools and universities measures that of nationalism, just as schools and especially universities became its most conscious champions: the conflict of Germany and Denmark over Schleswig-Holstein in 1848 and again in 1864 was anticipated by the conflict of the universities of Kiel and Copenhagen on this issue in the middle 1840s.

The progress was striking, though the total number of the "educated" remained small. The number of pupils in the French state *lycées* doubled between 1809 and 1842, and increased with particular rapidity under the July monarchy, but even so in 1842 it was only just under 19,000. (The total of all children receiving secondary education then was about 70,000.) Russia, around 1850, had some 20,000 secondary pupils out of a total population of sixty-eight million. The number of university students was naturally even smaller, though it was rising. It is difficult to realize that the Prussian academic youth which was so stirred by the idea of liberation after 1806 consisted in 1805 of not much more than 1,500 young men all told; that the *Polytechnique*, the bane of the post-1815 Bourbons, trained a total of 1,581 young men in the entire period from 1815 to 1830, i.e., an annual intake of about one hundred. The revolutionary prominence of the students in the 1848 period makes us forget that in the whole continent of Europe, including the unrevolutionary British Isles, there were probably not more than 40,000 university students in all. Still their numbers rose. In Russia it rose from 1,700 in 1825 to 4,600 in 1848. And even if they did not, the transformation of society and the universities . . . gave them a new consciousness of themselves as a social group. Nobody remembers that in 1789 there were something like 6,000 students in the University of Paris, because they played no independent part in the Revolution. But by 1830 nobody could possibly overlook such a number of young academics.

Small *elites* can operate in foreign languages; once the cadre of the educated becomes large enough, the national language imposes itself (as witness the struggle for linguistic recognition in the Indian states since the 1940s). Hence the moment when textbooks or newspapers in the national language are first written, or when that language is first used for some official purpose, measures a crucial step in national evolution. The 1830s saw this step taken over large areas of Europe. Thus the first major Czech works on astronomy, chemistry, anthropology, mineralogy, and botany were written or completed in this decade; and so, in Rumania, were the first school textbooks substituting Rumanian for the previously current Greek. Hungarian was adopted instead of Latin as the official language of the Hungarian Diet in 1840, though Budapest University, controlled from Vienna, did not abandon Latin lectures until 1844. (However, the struggle for the use of Hungarian as an official language had gone on intermittently since 1790.) In Zagreb, Gai published his *Croatian Gazette* (later: *Illyrian National Gazette*) from 1835 in the first literary version of what had hitherto been merely a complex of dialects. In countries which had long possessed an official national language, the change cannot be so easily measured, though it is interesting that after 1830 the number of German books published in Germany (as against Latin and French titles) for the first time consistently exceeded 90 percent; the number of French ones after 1820 fell below 4 percent.[1] More generally the expansion of publishing gives us a comparable indication. Thus in Germany the number of books published remained much the same in 1821 as in 1800—about 4,000 titles a year—but by 1841 it had risen to 12,000 titles.

Of course the great mass of Europeans, and of non-Europeans, remained uneducated. Indeed, with the exception of the Germans, the Dutch, Scandinavians, Swiss, and the citizens of the USA, no people can in 1840 be described as literate. Several can be described as totally illiterate, like the Southern Slavs, who had less than one-half percent literacy in 1827 (even much later only one percent of Dalmatian recruits to the Austrian army could read and write), or the Russians, who had two percent (1840), and a great many as almost illiterate, like the Spaniards, the Portuguese (who appear to have had barely 8,000 children in all *at school* after the Peninsular War) and, except for the Lombards and Piedmontese, the Italians. Even Britain, France, and Belgium were 40 to 50 percent illiterate in the 1840s. Illiteracy is no bar to political consciousness, but there is, in fact, no evidence that nationalism of the modern kind was a powerful mass force except in countries already transformed by the dual revolution: in France, in Britain, in the USA and—because it was an economic and political dependency of Britain—in Ireland.

To equate nationalism with the literate class is not to claim that the mass of, say, Russians did not consider themselves "Russian" when confronted with somebody or something that was not. However, for the masses in general the test of nationality was still religion: the Spaniard was defined by being Catholic, the Russian by being Orthodox. However, though such confrontations were becoming rather more frequent, they were still rare, and certain kinds of national feeling, such as the Italian, were as yet wholly alien to the great mass of the people, who did not even speak the national literary language but mutually almost incomprehensible *patois*. Even in Germany patriotic mythology has greatly exaggerated the degree of national feeling against Napoleon. France was extremely popular in Western Germany, especially among soldiers, whom it employed freely. Populations attached to the Pope or the Emperor might express resentment against their enemies, who

happened to be the French, but this hardly implied any feelings of national consciousness, let alone any desire for a national state. Moreover, the very fact that nationalism was represented by middle class and gentry was enough to make the poor man suspicious. The Polish radical-democratic revolutionaries tried earnestly—as did the more advanced of the South Italian Carbonari and other conspirators—to mobilize the peasantry even to the point of offering agrarian reform. Their failure was almost total. The Galician peasants in 1846 opposed the Polish revolutionaries even though these actually proclaimed the abolition of serfdom, preferring to massacre gentlemen and trust to the Emperor's officials.

The uprooting of peoples, which is perhaps the most important single phenomenon of the nineteenth century, was to break down this deep, age-old and localized traditionalism. Yet over most of the world up to the 1820s hardly anybody as yet migrated or emigrated, except under the compulsion of armies and hunger, or in the traditionally migratory groups such as the peasants from Central France who did seasonal building jobs in the north, or the travelling German artisans. Uprooting still meant, not the mild form of homesickness which was to become the characteristic psychological disease of the nineteenth century (reflected in innumerable sentimental popular songs), but the acute, killing *mal de pays* or *mal de cœur* which had first been clinically described by doctors among the old Swiss mercenaries in foreign lands. The conscription of the revolutionary wars revealed it, notably among the Bretons. The pull of the remote northern forests was so strong that it could lead an Estonian servant-girl to leave her excellent employers the Kügelgens in Saxony, where she was free, and return home to serfdom. Migration and emigration, of which the migration to the USA is the most convenient index, increased notably from the 1820s, though it did not reach anything like major proportions until the 1840s, when one and three-quarter millions crossed the North Atlantic (a little less than three times the figure for the 1830s). Even so, the only major migratory nation outside the British Isles was as yet the

German, long used to sending its sons as peasant settlers to Eastern Europe and America, as travelling artisans across the continent and as mercenaries everywhere.

We can in fact speak of only one Western national movement organized in a coherent form before 1848 which was genuinely based on the masses, and even this enjoyed the immense advantage of identification with the strongest carrier of tradition, the Church. This was the Irish Repeal movement under Daniel O'Connell (1785–1847), a golden-voiced lawyer–demagogue of peasant stock, the first—and up to 1848 the only one—of those charismatic popular leaders who mark the awakening of political consciousness in hitherto backward masses. (The only comparable figures before 1848 were Feargus O'Connor [1794–1855], another Irishman, who symbolized Chartism in Britain, and perhaps Louis Kossuth [1802–1894], who may have acquired something of his subsequent mass prestige before the 1848 revolution, though in fact his reputation in the 1840s was made as a champion of the gentry, and his later canonization by nationalist historians makes it difficult to see his early career at all clearly.) O'Connell's Catholic Association, which won its mass support and the not wholly justified confidence of the clergy in the successful struggle for Catholic Emancipation (1829), was in no sense tied to the gentry, who were in any case Protestant and Anglo-Irish. It was a movement of peasants, and such elements of a native Irish lower-middle class as existed in that pauperized island. 'The Liberator' was borne into leadership by successive waves of a mass movement of agrarian revolt, the chief motive force of Irish politics throughout that appalling century. This was organized in secret terrorist societies which themselves helped to break down the parochialism of Irish life. However, his aim was neither revolution nor national independence, but a moderate middle-class Irish autonomy by agreement or negotiation with the British Whigs. He was, in fact, not a nationalist and still less a peasant revolutionary but a moderate middle-class autonomist. Indeed, the chief criticism which has been not unjustifiably raised against him by later Irish nationalists (much as the more radical Indian nationalists have criticized Gandhi, who occupied an analogous position in his country's history) was that he could have raised all Ireland against the British, and deliberately refused to do so. But this does not alter the fact that the movement he led was genuinely supported by the mass of the Irish nation.

■   ■   ■

Outside the zone of the modern bourgeois world there were, however, movements of popular revolt against alien rule (i.e., normally understood as meaning rule by a different religion rather than a different nationality) which sometimes appear to anticipate later national movements. Such were the rebellions against the Turkish Empire, against the Russians in the Caucasus, and the fight against the encroaching British raj in and on the confines of India. It is unwise to read too much modern nationalism into these, though in backward areas populated by armed and combative peasants and herdsmen, organized in clan groups and inspired by tribal chieftains, bandit-heroes, and prophets, resistance to the foreign (or better, the unbelieving) ruler could take the form of veritable people's wars quite unlike the elite nationalist movements in less Homeric countries. In fact, however, the resistance of Mahrattas (a feudal-military Hindu group) and Sikhs (a militant religious sect) to the British in 1803–18 and 1845–49 respectively has little connection with subsequent Indian nationalism and produced none of their own.[2] The Caucasian tribes, savage, heroic, and feud-ridden, found in the puritan Islamic sect of Muridism a temporary bond of unity against the invading Russians and in Shamyl (1797–1871) a leader of major stature; but there is not to this day a Caucasian nation, but merely a congeries of small mountain peoples in small Soviet republics. (The Georgians and Armenians, who have formed nations in the modern sense, were not involved in the Shamyl movement.) The Bedouin, swept by puritan religious sects like the

Wahhabi in Arabia and the Senussi in what is today Libya, fought for the simple faith of Allah and the simple life of the herdsman and raider against the corruption of taxes, pashas, and cities; but what we know as Arab nationalism—a product of the twentieth century—has come out of the cities, not the nomadic encampments.

Even the rebellions against the Turks in the Balkans, especially among the rarely subdued mountain peoples of the south and west, should not be too readily interpreted in modern nationalist terms though the bards and braves of several—the two were often the same, as among the poet-warrior bishops of Montenegro—recalled the glories of quasi-national heroes like the Albanian Skanderbeg and the tragedies like the Serbian defeat at Kossovo in the remote battles against the Turks. Nothing was more natural than to revolt, where necessary or desirable, against a local administration of a weakening Turkish Empire. However, little but a common economic backwardness united what we now know as the Yugoslavs, even those in the Turkish Empire, and the very concept of Yugoslavia was the product of intellectuals in Austro-Hungary rather than of those who actually fought for liberty.[3] The Orthodox Montenegrins, never subdued, fought the Turks, but with equal zest they fought the unbelieving Catholic Albanians and the unbelieving, but solidly Slav, Moslem Bosnians. The Bosnians revolted against the Turks, whose religion many of them shared, with as much readiness as the Orthodox Serbs of the wooded Danube plain, and with more zest than the Orthodox "old Serbs" of the Albanian frontier area. The first of the Balkan peoples to rise in the nineteenth century were the Serbs under a heroic pig-dealer and brigand Black George (1760–1817), but the initial phase of his rising (1804–7) did not even claim to be against Turkish rule, but on the contrary for the Sultan against the abuses of the local rulers. There is little in the early history of mountain rebellion in the Western Balkans to suggest that the local Serbs, Albanians, Greeks, and others would not in the early nineteenth century have been satisfied with the sort of non-national autonomous principal-

ity which a powerful satrap, Ali Pasha "the Lion of Jannina" (1741–1822), for a time set up in Epirus.

In one and only one case did the perennial fight of the shepherding clansmen and bandit-heroes against *any* real government fuse with the ideas of middle-class nationalism and the French Revolution: in the Greek struggle for independence (1821–30). Not unnaturally Greece therefore became the myth and inspiration of nationalists and liberals everywhere. For in Greece alone did an entire people rise against the oppressor in a manner which could be plausibly identified with the cause of the European left; and in turn the support of the European left, headed by the poet Byron who died there, was of very considerable help in the winning of Greek independence.

Most Greeks were much like the other forgotten warrior-peasantries and clans of the Balkan peninsula. A part, however, formed an international merchant and administrative class also settled in colonies or minority communities throughout the Turkish Empire and beyond, and the language and higher ranks of the entire Orthodox Church, to which most Balkan peoples belonged, were Greek, headed by the Greek Patriarch of Constantinople. Greek civil servants, transmuted into vassal princes, governed the Danubian principalities (the present Rumania). In a sense the entire educated and mercantile classes of the Balkans, the Black Sea area, and the Levant, whatever their national origins, were hellenized by the very nature of their activities. During the eighteenth century this hellenization proceeded more powerfully than before, largely because of the marked economic expansion which also extended the range and contacts of the Greek diaspora. The new and thriving Black Sea grain trade took it into Italian, French, and British business centres and strengthened its links with Russia; the expansion of Balkan trade brought Greek or Grecized merchants into Central Europe. The first Greek language newspapers were published in Vienna (1784–1812). Periodic emigration and resettlement of peasant rebels further reinforced the exile communities. It was among this cosmopolitan diaspora that the ideas of the French Revolution—liberalism, nationalism, and the methods of political organization by masonic secret societies—took root. Rhigas (1760–98), the leader of an early obscure and possibly pan-Balkanist revolutionary movement, spoke French and adapted the *Marseillaise* to Hellenic conditions. The *Philiké Hetairía*, the secret patriotic society mainly responsible for the revolt of 1821, was founded in the great new Russian grain port of Odessa in 1814.

Their nationalism was to some extent comparable to the elite movements of the West. Nothing else explains the project of raising a rebellion for Greek independence in the Danube principalities under the leadership of local Greek magnates; for the only people who could be described as Greeks in these miserable serf-lands were lords, bishops, merchants, and intellectuals. Naturally enough that rising failed miserably (1821). Fortunately, however, the Hetairía had also set out to enrol the anarchy of local brigand-heroes, outlaws, and clan chieftains in the Greek mountains (especially in the Peloponnese), and with considerably greater success—at any rate after 1818—than the South Italian gentlemen Carbonari, who attempted a similar proselytization of their local banditti. It is doubtful whether anything like modern nationalism meant much to these "klephts," though many of them had their "clerks"—a respect for and interest in book-learning was a surviving relic of ancient Hellenism—who composed manifestoes in the Jacobin terminology. If they stood for anything it was for the age-old ethos of a peninsula in which the role of man was to become a hero, and the outlaw who took to the mountains to resist any government and to right the peasant's wrongs was the universal political ideal. To the rebellions of men like Kolokotrones, brigand and cattle-dealer, the nationalists of the Western type gave leadership and a pan-hellenic rather than a purely local scale. In turn they got from them that unique and awe-inspiring thing, the mass rising of an armed people.

The new Greek nationalism was enough to win independence, though the combination of middle-class leadership, klephtic disorganization, and great power intervention produced one of those petty caricatures of the Western liberal ideal which were to become so familiar in areas like Latin America. But it also had the paradoxical result of narrowing Hellenism to Hellas, and thus creating or intensifying the latent nationalism of the other Balkan peoples. While being Greek had been little more than the professional requirement of the literate Orthodox Balkan Christian, hellenization had made progress. Once it meant the political support for Hellas, it receded, even among the assimilated Balkan literate classes. In this sense Greek independence was the essential preliminary condition for the evolution of the other Balkan nationalisms.

Outside Europe it is difficult to speak of nationalism at all. The numerous Latin American republics which replaced the token Spanish and Portuguese Empires (to be accurate, Brazil became and remained an independent monarchy from 1816 to 1889), their frontiers often reflecting little more than the distribution of the estates of the grandees who had backed one rather than another of the local rebellions, began to acquire vested political interests and territorial aspirations. The original pan-American ideal of Simón Bolívar (1783–1830) of Venezuela and San Martín (1788–1850) of the Argentine was impossible to realize, though it has persisted as a powerful revolutionary current throughout all the areas united by the Spanish language, just as pan-Balkanism, the heir of Orthodox unity against Islam, persisted and may still persist today. The vast extent and variety of the continent, the existence of independent foci of rebellion in Mexico (which determined Central America), Venezuela, and Buenos Aires, and the special problem of the centre of Spanish colonialism in Peru, which was liberated from without, imposed automatic fragmentation. But the Latin American revolutions were the work of small groups of patricians, soldiers and gallicized *évolués*, leaving the mass of the Catholic poor-white population passive and the Indians indifferent or hostile. Only in Mexico was independence won by the initiative of a popular agrarian, i.e., Indian, movement marching under the banner of the Virgin of Guadalupe, and Mexico has consequently ever since followed a different and politically more advanced road from the remainder of continental Latin America. However, even among the tiny layer of the politically decisive Latin Americans it would be anachronistic in our period to speak of anything more than the embryo of Colombian, Venezuelan, Ecuadorian, etc., "national consciousness."

Something like a proto-nationalism, however, existed in various countries of Eastern Europe, but paradoxically it took the direction of conservatism rather than national rebellion. The Slavs were oppressed everywhere, except in Russia and in a few wild Balkan strongholds, but in their immediate perspective the oppressors were, as we have seen, not the absolute monarchs, but the German or Magyar landlords and urban exploiters. Nor did the nationalism of these allow any place for Slav national existence: even so radical a programme as that of the German United States proposed by the republicans and democrats of Baden (in Southwest Germany) envisaged the inclusion of an Illyrian (i.e., Croat and Slovene) republic with its capital in Italian Trieste, a Moravian one with its capital in Olomouc, and a Bohemian one led by Prague. Hence the immediate hope of the Slav nationalists lay in the emperors of Austria and Russia. Various versions of Slav solidarity expressed the Russian orientation, and attracted Slav rebels— even the anti-Russian Poles—especially in times of defeat and hopelessness as after the failure of the risings in 1846. "Illyrianism" in Croatia and a moderate Czech nationalism expressed the Austrian trend, and both received deliberate support from the Habsburg rulers, two of whose leading ministers—Kolowrat and the chief of the police system, Sedlnitzky—were themselves Czechs. Croatian cultural aspirations were protected in the 1830s, and by 1840 Kolowrat actually proposed what was later to prove so useful in the 1848 revolution, the appointment of a Croat military *ban* as chief of Croatia, and with control over the military frontier with Hungary, as a counterweight to the obstreperous Magyars. To be a revolutionary in 1848 therefore came to be virtually identical with

opposition to Slav national aspirations; and the tacit conflict between the "progressive" and the "reactionary" nations did much to doom the revolutions of 1848 to failure.

Nothing like nationalism is discoverable elsewhere, for the social conditions for it did not exist. In fact, if anything, the forces which were later to produce nationalism were at this stage opposed to the alliance of tradition, religion, and mass poverty which produced the most powerful resistance to the encroachment of Western conquerors and exploiters. The elements of a local bourgeoisie which grew up in Asian countries did so in the shelter of the foreign exploiters whose agents, intermediaries and dependants they largely were. The Parsee community of Bombay is an example. Even if the educated and "enlightened" Asian was not a *compradore* or a lesser official of some foreign ruler or firm (a situation not dissimilar to that of the Greek diaspora in Turkey), his first political task was to Westernize— i.e., to introduce the ideas of the French Revolution and of scientific and technical modernization among his people, against the united resistance of traditional rulers and traditional ruled (a situation not dissimilar to that of the gentlemen-Jacobins of Southern Italy). He was therefore doubly cut off from his people. Nationalist mythology has often obscured this divorce, partly by suppressing the link between colonialism and the early native middle classes, partly lending to earlier anti-foreign resistance the colours of a later nationalist movement. But in Asia, in the Islamic countries, and even more in Africa, the junction between the *évolués* and nationalism, and between both and the masses, was not made until the twentieth century.

Nationalism in the East was thus the eventual product of Western influence and Western conquest. This link is perhaps most evident in the one plainly Oriental country in which the foundations of what was to become the first modern colonial nationalist movement[4] were laid: in Egypt. Napoleon's conquest introduced Western ideas, methods, and techniques, whose value an able and ambitious local soldier, Mohammed Ali

(Mehemet Ali), soon recognized. Having seized power and virtual independence from Turkey in the confused period which followed the withdrawal of the French, and with French support, Mohammed Ali set out to establish an efficient and Westernizing despotism with foreign (mainly French) technical aid. European left-wingers in the 1820s and '30s hailed this enlightened autocrat, and put their services at his disposal, when reaction in their own countries looked too dispiriting. The extraordinary sect of the Saint-Simonians, equally suspended between the advocacy of socialism and of industrial development by investment bankers and engineers, temporarily gave him their collective aid and prepared his plans of economic development. * * * They thus also laid the foundation for the Suez Canal (built by the Saint-Simonian de Lesseps) and the fatal dependence of Egyptian rulers on vast loans negotiated by competing groups of European swindlers, which turned Egypt into a centre of imperialist rivalry and anti-imperialist rebellion later on. But Mohammed Ali was no more a nationalist than any other Oriental despot. His Westernization, not his or his people's aspirations, laid the foundations for later nationalism. If Egypt acquired the first nationalist movement in the Islamic world and Morocco one of the last, it was because Mohammed Ali (for perfectly comprehensible geopolitical reasons) was in the main paths of Westernization and the isolated self-sealed Sherifian Empire of the Moslem far west was not, and made no attempts to be. Nationalism, like so many other characteristics of the modern world, is the child of the dual revolution.

NOTES

1. In the early eighteenth century only about 60 percent of all titles published in Germany were in the German language; since then the proportion had risen fairly steadily.

2. The Sikh movement has remained largely *sui generis* to this day. The tradition of combative Hindu resistance in Maharashtra made that area an early centre of the Indian nationalism, and provided some of its earliest—and highly traditionalist—leaders, notably B. G. Tilak; but this was at best a regional and far from dominant strain in the movement. Something like Mahratta nationalism may exist today, but its social basis is the resistance of large Mahratta working class and underprivileged lower-middle class to the economically and until recently linguistically dominant Gujeratis.

3. It is significant that the present Yugoslav regime has broken up what used to be classed as the Serb nation into the much more realistic sub-national republics and units of Serbia, Bosnia, Montenegro, Macedonia, and Kossovo-Metohidja. By the linguistic standards of nineteenth-century nationalism most of these belonged to a single "Serb" people, except the Macedonians, who are closer to the Bulgarians, and the Albanian minority in Kosmet. But in fact they have never developed a single Serb nationalism.

4. Other than the Irish.

James D. Fearon and David D. Laitin
ETHNICITY, INSURGENCY, AND CIVIL WAR

Between 1945 and 1999, about 3.33 million battle deaths occurred in the 25 interstate wars that killed at least 1,000 and had at least 100 dead on each side. These wars involved just 25 states that suffered casualties of at least 1,000 and had a median duration of not quite 3 months. In contrast, in the same period there were roughly 127 civil wars that killed at least 1,000, 25 of which were ongoing in 1999. A conservative estimate of the total dead as a direct result of these conflicts is 16.2 million, five times the interstate toll. These civil wars occurred in 73 states—more than a third of the United Nations system—and had a median duration of roughly six years.[1] The civil conflicts in this period surely produced refugee flows far greater than their death toll and far greater than the refugee flows associated with interstate wars since 1945. Cases such as Afghanistan, Somalia, and Lebanon testify to the economic devastation that civil wars can produce. By these crude measures, civil war has been a far greater scourge than interstate war in this period, though it has been studied far less.

What explains the recent prevalence of violent civil conflict around the world? Is it due to the end of the Cold War and associated changes in the international system, or is it the result of longer-term trends? Why have some countries had civil wars while others have not? and Why did the wars break out when they did? We address these questions using data for the period 1945 to 1999 on the 161 countries that had a population of at least half a million in 1990.

The data cast doubt on three influential conventional wisdoms concerning political conflict before and after the Cold War. First, contrary to common opinion, the prevalence of civil war in the 1990s was *not* due to the end of the Cold War and associated changes in the international system. The current level of about one in six countries had already been reached prior to the breakup of the Soviet Union and resulted from a steady, gradual accumulation of civil conflicts that began immediately after World War II.

Second, it appears *not* to be true that a greater degree of ethnic or religious diversity—or indeed any particular cultural demography—by itself makes a country more prone to civil war. This finding runs contrary to a common view among journalists, policy makers, and academics, which holds "plural" societies to be especially conflict-prone due to ethnic or religious tensions and antagonisms.

Third, we find little evidence that one can predict where a civil war will break out by looking for where ethnic or other broad political grievances are strongest. Were this so, one would expect political democracies and states that observe civil liberties to be less civil war–prone than dictatorships. One would further anticipate that state discrimination against minority religions or languages would imply higher risks of civil war. We show that when comparing states at similar levels of per capita income, these expectations are not borne out.

The main factors determining both the secular trend and the cross-sectional variation in civil violence in this period are not ethnic or religious differences or broadly held grievances but, rather, conditions that favor *insurgency*. Insurgency is a technology of military conflict characterized by small, lightly armed bands practicing guerrilla warfare from rural base areas. As a form of warfare insurgency can be harnessed to diverse political

From *American Political Science Review* 97, no. 1 (2003), pp. 75–90.

agendas, motivations, and grievances. The concept is most closely associated with communist insurgency, but the methods have equally served Islamic fundamentalists, ethnic nationalists, or "rebels" who focus mainly on traffic in coca or diamonds.

We hypothesize that financially, organizationally, and politically weak central governments render insurgency more feasible and attractive due to weak local policing or inept and corrupt counterinsurgency practices. These often include a propensity for brutal and indiscriminate retaliation that helps drive noncombatant locals into rebel forces. Police and counterinsurgent weakness, we argue, is proxied by a low per capita income. Shocks to counterinsurgent capabilities can arise from political instability at the center or the sudden loss of a foreign patron. On the rebel side, insurgency is favored by rough terrain, rebels with local knowledge of the population superior to the government's, and a large population. All three aid rebels in hiding from superior government forces. Foreign base camps, financial support, and training also favor insurgency.

Our data show that measures of cultural diversity and grievances fail to postdict civil war onset, while measures of conditions that favor insurgency do fairly well. Surely ethnic antagonisms, nationalist sentiments, and grievances often motivate rebels and their supporters. But such broad factors are too common to distinguish the cases where civil war breaks out. Also, because insurgency can be successfully practiced by small numbers of rebels under the right conditions, civil war may require only a small number with intense grievances to get going.

Using data on about 45 civil wars since 1960, Collier and Hoeffler (1999, 2001) find similarly that measures of "objective grievance" fare worse as predictors than economic variables, which they initially interpreted as measures of rebel "greed" (i.e., economic motivation).[2] More recently, they argue that rebellion is better explained by "opportunity" than by grievance (cf. Eisinger 1973 and Tilly 1978) and that the main determinant of opportunity is the availability of finance and recruits for rebels. They proxy these with measures of primary commodity exports and rates of secondary-school enrollment for males. We agree that financing is one determinant of the viability of insurgency. We argue, however, that economic variables such as per capita income matter primarily because they proxy for state administrative, military, and police capabilities. We find no impact for primary commodity exports, and none for secondary schooling rates distinct from income. Our theoretical interpretation is more Hobbesian than economic. Where states are relatively weak and capricious, both fears and opportunities encourage the rise of would-be rulers who supply a rough local justice while arrogating the power to "tax" for themselves and, often, for a larger cause.

Civil War since 1945

■ ■ ■

Trends over Time

Figure 3.1 shows the number of countries with ongoing civil wars by year from 1945 to 1999. Since the number of independent states grew sharply in this period, it also shows the proportion of countries with at least one ongoing war in each year.

The graph indicates that, contrary to popular belief, the prevalence of civil wars in the 1990s is *not* due to effects of the end of the Cold War. The 1999 level of 25 ongoing wars had already been reached by the mid-1980s. Conflicts associated with the Soviet collapse were partly responsible for the sharp increase in the early 1990s, but a marked *decline* has followed.[3]

One might conjecture that more and more civil wars are breaking out over time, thus producing the secular increase. This is incorrect. The rate of outbreak is 2.31 per year since 1945, highly variable but showing no significant trend up or down. The secular increase stems from the fact that civil wars have ended at a rate of only about 1.85 per year. The result has been a steady, almost-linear accumulation of unresolved conflicts since 1945.

Figure 3.1 Number and Percentage of Countries with Ongoing Civil Wars by Year from 1945 to 1999

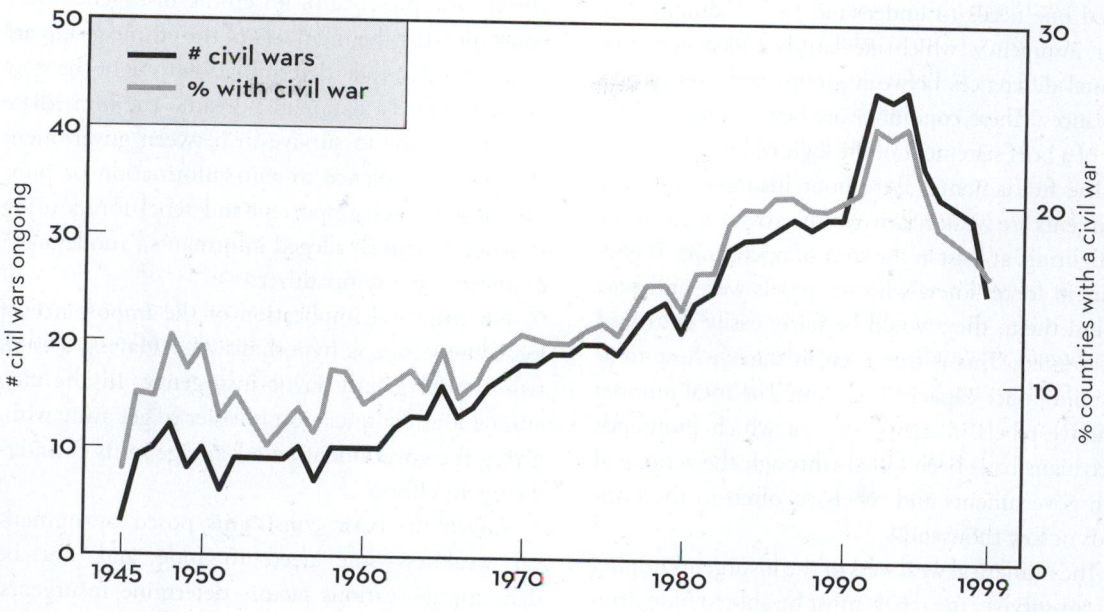

Put differently, states in the international system have been subject to a more or less constant risk of violent civil conflict over the period, but the conflicts they suffer have been difficult to end. The average duration of the civil wars in progress has increased steadily from two years in 1947 to about 15 years in 1999. From a policy perspective this suggests caution about seeing as a temporary "blip" the sorts of military and political problems Western foreign policy makers have faced recently in Kosovo, Macedonia, Bosnia, Somalia, Haiti, East Timor, Colombia, and elsewhere.

Ethnicity, Discrimination, and Grievances

During the Cold War, political scientists and sociologists often sought to trace rebellion to economic inequality (Muller 1985; Paige 1975; Russett 1964), to rapid economic growth said to destabilize traditional rural social systems (Huntington 1968;

Scott 1976), or to frustrations arising from the failure to gain expected benefits of economic modernization (Gurr 1971). A few scholars argued that the real source of rebellion was often ethnic nationalism (Connor 1994), and a rich literature on the sources of nationalist mobilization developed in comparative politics (e.g., Anderson 1983, Deutsch 1953, and Gellner 1983). With the collapse of the Soviet Union and Yugoslavia, such culturalist perspectives became a dominant frame for interpreting inter- and intranational conflict (e.g., Huntington 1996).

■ ■ ■ ■

Insurgency

If many post-1945 civil wars have been "ethnic" or "nationalist" as these terms are usually understood, then even more have been fought as *insurgencies*. Insurgency is a technology of military conflict characterized by small, lightly armed bands practicing guerrilla warfare from rural base areas. To explain why some countries have experienced civil wars in this period one needs to understand the conditions that favor insurgency, which are largely independent of cultural differences between groups and even group grievances. These conditions are best summarized by way of a brief statement of the logic of insurgency.[4]

The fundamental fact about insurgency is that insurgents are weak relative to the governments they are fighting, at least at the start of operations. If government forces knew who the rebels were and how to find them, they would be fairly easily destroyed or captured. This is true even in states whose military and police capacities are low. The total number of active rebels in many wars in which thousands of civilians have been killed (through the actions of both governments and rebels) is often in the hundreds or low thousands.

The numerical weakness of the insurgents implies that, to survive, the rebels must be able to hide from government forces. Several hypotheses follow.

H_8: The presence of (a) rough terrain, poorly served by roads, at a distance from the centers of state power, should favor insurgency and civil war. So should the availability of (b) foreign, cross-border sanctuaries and (c) a local population that can be induced not to denounce the insurgents to government agents.

Much scholarly writing holds that ethnic or class solidarity and grievances are necessary for H_{8c}, the local population's support of active rebels. In line with Kriger (1992) and some analysts of communist insurgencies (e.g., Clutterbuck 1967, Leites and Wolf 1970, and Thompson 1966), we argue that while grievances and ethnic solidarity can be helpful in this regard, they are not necessary. Instead, the key to inducing the local population not to denounce the active rebels is *local knowledge*, or information about who is doing what at the village level. Local knowledge allows the active rebels to threaten retribution for denunciation credibly.[5] Ethnic insurgents use this informational advantage to great effect, often

threatening and inflicting unimaginably harsh sanctions on "their own" people (Kalyvas 1999; Kriger 1992). The presence of an ethnic insurgency does not imply that the members of the ethnic group are of one mind in their determination to fight the state till they realize a nationalist dream. The immediate concern is how to survive in between government forces using violence to gain information or punish alleged rebel supporters and rebel forces using violence to punish alleged informants, "moderates," or government sympathizers.

An empirical implication of the importance of local knowledge is hypothesis H_{8d}: Having a *rural base* should greatly favor insurgency. In the city, anonymous denunciation is easier to get away with, giving the government an advantage in its counterinsurgent efforts.

Given the basic constraints posed by numerical weakness—the need to hide and not be denounced—various factors determine insurgents' ability to wage war. To survive, rebels need arms and matériel, money to buy them, or smugglable goods to trade for them. They need a supply of recruits to the insurgent way of life, and they may also need information and instruction in the practical details of running an insurgency.[6]

Most important for the prospects of a nascent insurgency, however, are *the government's police and military capabilities and the reach of government institutions into rural areas*. Insurgents are better able to survive and prosper if the government and military they oppose are relatively weak—badly financed, organizationally inept, corrupt, politically divided, and poorly informed about goings-on at the local level.

Effective counterinsurgency requires government forces to distinguish active rebels from noncombatants without destroying the lives and living conditions of the latter. This is an extremely difficult political, military, and organizational problem even for well-equipped and well-paid modern militaries; witness the U.S. military's failures in Vietnam (Avant 1994; Krepinevich 1986), early British efforts in Northern Ireland (Kennedy-Pipe 1997), or Soviet efforts in Afghanistan. For less well-financed and bureaucratically competent states, the problem appears to be nearly insoluble. Such states either cannot prevent the abuse of local powers by field commanders or may even permit these abuses as a sort of tax farming to the military. That is, they "pay" the soldiers with the opportunity to loot and pillage, a practice that tends to sustain rather than end insurgencies (see Keen 1998 for examples). Thus, we have the following hypothesis.

H_9: Proxies for the relative weakness or strength of the insurgents—their odds of being killed or captured for a given level of counterinsurgent effort by the government—should be associated with the likelihood that a country develops a civil war. In particular, a *higher per capita income* should be associated with a lower risk of civil war onset because (a) it is a proxy for a state's overall financial, administrative, police, and military capabilities, and (b) it will mark more developed countries with terrain more "disciplined" by roads and rural society more penetrated by central administration.

There is an additional reason why a lower per capita income should favor the technology of insurgency: (c) Recruiting young men to the life of a guerrilla is easier when the economic alternatives are worse. Though we try below, it is difficult to find measures to distinguish among these three mechanisms associating a low per capita income with civil war onset. We believe that the strong results for per capita income reported below are due largely to its acting as a proxy for state military and police strength relative to potential insurgents (a and b in H_9). The fact that measures such as the percentage of young males and male secondary schooling rates predict less well than per capita income is consistent with this conjecture, though not definitive.

Additional factors that would be expected to affect (or proxy) the strength of an insurgent band relative to a state follow.

H_{10}: The political and military technology of insurgency will be favored, and thus civil war

made more likely, when potential rebels face or have available the following.

(a) A newly independent state, which suddenly loses the coercive backing of the former imperial power and whose military capabilities are new and untested (Fearon 1998).

(b) Political instability at the center, which may indicate disorganization and weakness and thus an opportunity for a separatist or center-seeking rebellion.

(c) A regime that mixes democratic with autocratic features, as this is likely to indicate political contestation among competing forces and, in consequence, state incapacity. (In contrast, pure autocracy tends to reflect the successful monopolization of state coercive and administrative power by an individual or group.)

(d) A large country population, which makes it necessary for the center to multiply layers of agents to keep tabs on who is doing what at the local level and, also, increases the number of potential recruits to an insurgency for a given level of income.

(e) A territorial base separated from the state's center by water or distance—for example, East Pakistan (now Bangladesh) from West Pakistan or Angola from Portugal.

(f) Foreign governments or diasporas willing to supply weapons, money, or training.

(g) Land that supports the production of high-value, low-weight goods such as coca, opium, diamonds, and other contraband, which can be used to finance an insurgency.

(h) A state whose revenues derive primarily from oil exports. Oil producers tend to have weaker state apparatuses than one would expect given their level of income because the rulers have less need for a socially intrusive and elaborate bureaucratic system to raise revenues—a political "Dutch disease" (Chaudhry 1989; Karl 1997; Wantchekon 2000). At the same time, oil revenues raise the value of the "prize" of controlling state power.

Partially excepting f, none of these conditions crucially involves cultural differences, ethnic minority status, or group grievances. We do not claim that these factors provide no help to would-be insurgents in specific cases. But, to reiterate, grievances and ethnic differences are too common to help distinguish the countries and years that see civil wars, and in any event the technology of insurgency does not require strong popular grievances or ethnic solidarities to operate effectively. The latter point suggests a contrast to H_4–H_6.

H_{11}: After controlling for per capita income (or other measures of state strength), neither political democracy, the presence of civil liberties, higher income inequality, nor nondiscriminatory linguistic or religious policies should associate strongly with lower odds of civil war. Given the right environmental conditions, insurgencies can thrive on the basis of small numbers of rebels without strong, widespread, popular support rooted in grievances and, hence, even in democracies.

As for measures, for "rough terrain" we use the proportion of the country that is "mountainous" according to the codings of geographer A. J. Gerard.[7] This does not pick up other sorts of rough terrain that can be favorable to guerrillas such as swamps and jungle, and it takes no account of population distributions or food availability in relation to mountains; but it is the best we have been able to do for H_{8a}. For H_9 we use Penn World Tables and World Bank data on per capita income, estimating missing values using data on per capita energy consumption.[8] For H_{10a} (new states) we mark countries in their first and second years of independence; for H_{10b} (political instability) we use a dummy variable indicating whether the country had a three-or-greater change on the Polity IV regime index in any of the three years prior to the country-year in question.[9] For countries that mix democratic and autocratic features (called "anocracies" or "semi-democracies" in the international relations literature and "praetorian regimes" by Huntington 1968)

we mark regimes that score between –5 and 5 on the difference between Polity IV's democracy and autocracy measures (the difference ranges from –10 to 10). Country population (H_{10d}) is based largely on World Bank figures. For oil exporters we marked country-years in which fuel exports exceeded one-third of export revenues, using World Bank data.[10] We coded a dummy variable for states with noncontiguous territory ourselves (H_{10e}).[11]

The remaining hypotheses (H_{8b}–H_{8d}, H_{10f} and H_{10g}) present more difficult measurement challenges. Whether availability of a rural base favors civil war (H_{8d}) is better tested in a research design where ethnic groups are the unit of analysis, so that groups with different geographic concentrations can be compared.[12]

Although it is possible to code rebellions in progress for whether the rebels receive shelter and support from foreign countries (H_{8b}, H_{10f}), the potential availability of these aids to rebel strength is difficult to observe prior to the onset of fighting. In two special cases, the potential availability of support from a foreign power to *governments* is observable—in Soviet policy (the "Brezhnev doctrine") in Eastern Europe and French policy with regard to its former colonies in sub-Saharan Africa.[13] We would expect such support to increase the relative advantage of government forces against potential insurgents and thus associate with lower rates of civil war onset. We also consider a more tenuous measure of potential support to rebels—the number of civil wars ongoing in neighboring countries—which might yield more easily available weapons, training, or the presence of experienced guerrillas.[14]

Empirical Analysis

Our central hypotheses concern the relationship between ethnic and religious diversity or structure, on the one hand, and the susceptibility of a country to civil war, on the other. Several multivariate analyses of the country-year data are presented below, but the main story emerging from them is made clear by the contour plot in Figure 3.2.

Figure 3.2 Probability of Civil War Onset per Five-Year Period

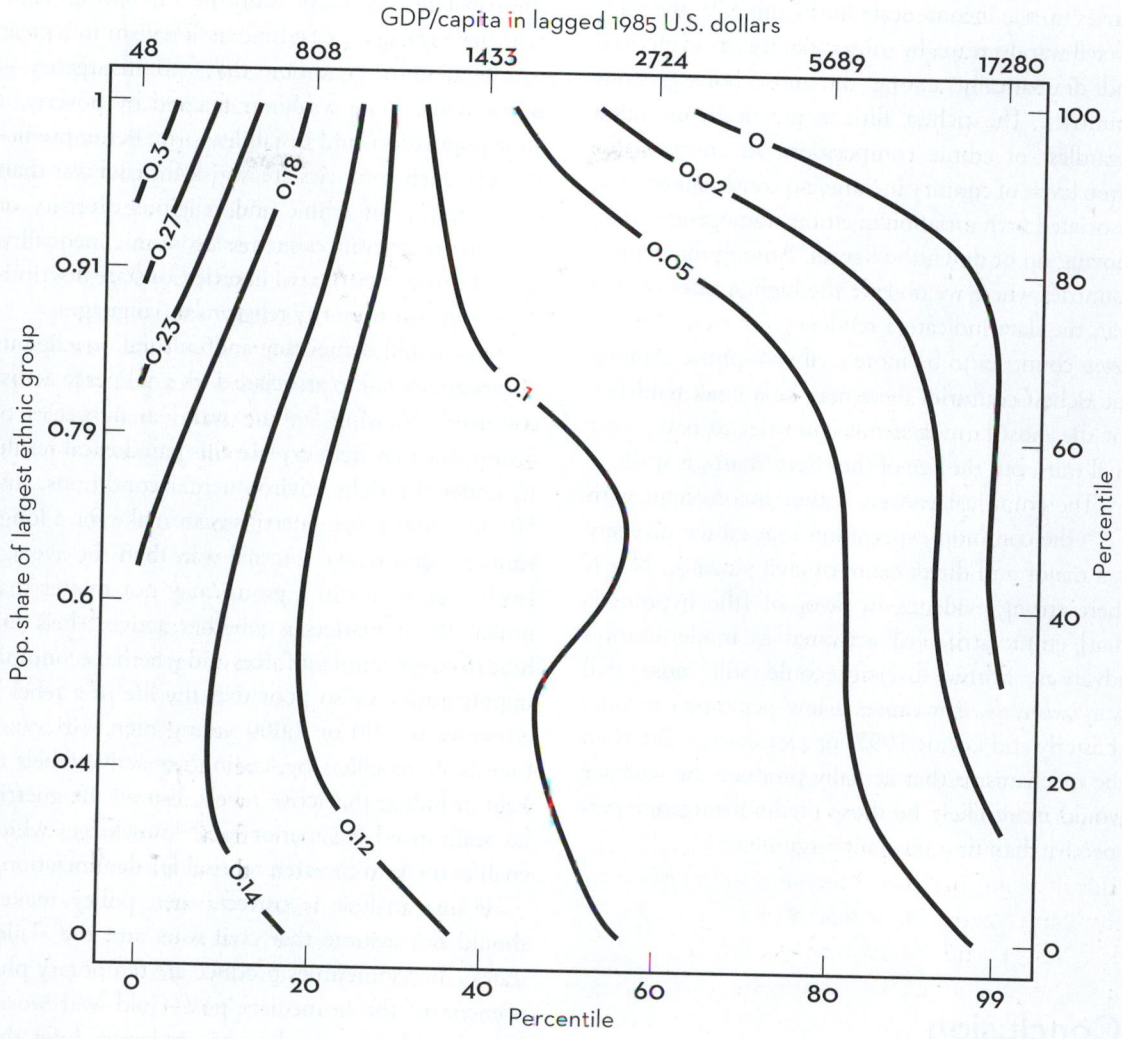

Are More Diverse Countries Prone to Civil War?

Figure 3.2 shows how probabilities of civil war onset vary at different percentiles for country income (on the *x* axis, measured in lagged 1985 dollars) and ethnic homogeneity (on the *y* axis, measured by the population share of the largest ethnic group). The lines in the plot show the probability of war onset in the next five years for a country at the given level of income and ethnic homogeneity. For example, countries at the twentieth percentile in terms of the size of their largest ethnic group—thus quite ethnically *diverse*—but at the eightieth percentile on income have had about a 5% chance of civil war outbreak in the next five years. In contrast, countries at the eightieth percentile on ethnic homogeneity and at the twentieth percentile on income had a 15% chance of war in the next five years.[15]

Note that *for any level of ethnic diversity*, as one moves up the income scale (in Figure 3.2), the odds of civil war decrease, by substantial factors in all cases and dramatically among the most homogeneous countries. The richest fifth is practically immune regardless of ethnic composition. In contrast, for given levels of country income, no consistent effect is associated with variation in ethnic homogeneity (i.e., moving up or down the figure). Among the poorest countries where we observe the highest rates of civil war, the data indicate a tendency for *more homogeneous* countries to be more civil war–prone. Among the richest countries there may be a weak tendency for the most homogeneous countries to have fewer civil wars, but the size of the effect, if any, is small.

The empirical pattern is thus inconsistent with * * * the common expectation that ethnic diversity is a major and direct cause of civil violence. Nor is there strong evidence in favor of [the hypothesis that] ethnic strife [is] activated as modernization advances. Ethnic diversity could still cause civil war *indirectly*, if it causes a low per capita income (Easterly and Levine 1997) or a weak state. But then the mechanisms that actually produce the violence would more likely be those of the insurgency perspective than the culturalist arguments.

■ ■ ■

Conclusion

The prevalence of internal war in the 1990s is mainly the result of an accumulation of protracted conflicts since the 1950s rather than a sudden change associated with a new, post–Cold War international system. Decolonization from the 1940s through the 1970s gave birth to a large number of financially, bureaucratically, and militarily weak states. These states have been at risk for civil violence for the whole period, almost entirely in the form of insurgency, or rural guerrilla warfare. Insurgency is a mode of military practice that can be harnessed to various political agendas, be it communism in Southeast

Asia and Latin America, Islamic fundamentalism in Afghanistan, Algeria, or Kashmir, right-wing "reaction" in Nicaragua, or ethnic nationalism in a great many states. The conditions that favor insurgency—in particular, state weakness marked by poverty, a large population, and instability—are better predictors of which countries are at risk for civil war than are indicators of ethnic and religious diversity or measures of grievances such as economic inequality, lack of democracy or civil liberties, or state discrimination against minority religions or languages.

How could democracy and cultural or religious homogeneity fail to associate with civil peace across countries? Viewing "ethnic wars" as a species of insurgency may help explain this paradoxical result. If, under the right environmental conditions, just 500 to 2,000 active guerrillas can make for a long-running, destructive internal war, then the average level of grievance in a group may not matter that much. What matters is whether active rebels can hide from government forces and whether economic opportunities are so poor that the life of a rebel is attractive to 500 or 2,000 young men. Grievance may favor rebellion by leading nonactive rebels to help in hiding the active rebels. But all the guerrillas really need is superior local knowledge, which enables them to threaten reprisal for denunciation.

If our analysis is correct, then policy makers should not assume that civil wars and the "failed states" they sometimes produce are temporary phenomena of the immediate post–Cold War world. Nor should policy makers or academics infer that ethnic diversity is the root cause of civil conflict when they observe insurgents in a poor country who mobilize fighters along ethnic lines. Instead, the civil wars of the period have structural roots, in the combination of a simple, robust military technology and decolonization, which created an international system numerically dominated by fragile states with limited administrative control of their peripheries.

Regarding policy implications, the spread of democracy and tolerance for ethnic and religious minorities should be major foreign policy goals because they are desirable for their own sake, but not with the expectation that they are "magic bullets" for the prevention or resolution of civil war. Sometimes recommended as a general international policy for resolving ethnic civil wars (e.g., Kaufmann 1996), ethnic partitions should be viewed as having large international implications and high costs. International support for partition would increase the expected benefits for rebels, who, we have argued, may be able to get a nasty civil war going on the basis of small numbers when the conditions for insurgency are right.

Policies to redress grievances, or, in the limit, partition, *could* be important to resolve ongoing conflicts. We cannot say on the basis of this research, which focused on civil war onset rather than termination. We find little evidence that civil war is predicted by large cultural divisions or broadly held grievances. But it seems quite clear that intense grievances *are produced by* civil war—indeed, this is often a central objective of rebel strategy. These could well pose obstacles to settlement.

Regarding prevention, our analysis suggests that while economic growth may correlate with fewer civil wars, the causal mechanism is more likely a well-financed and administratively competent government. In specific terms, international and nongovernmental organizations should develop programs that improve legal accountability within developing world militaries and police, and make aid to governments fighting civil wars conditional on the state observing counterinsurgency practices that do not help rebels recruit militias. Governments that follow horrible, war-perpetuating counterinsurgency practices or are so corrupt as to be helpless should be left on their own or, when there are major implications for regional stability or international terrorism, be viewed as candidates for "neotrusteeship" under the United Nations or regional military and political organizations such as NATO and the European Union. The latter system, which we already see operating, in effect, in Bosnia, Kosovo, and East Timor, should be rationalized so as to improve internal coordination among the many players involved in such operations.

NOTES

1. The interstate war data derive from Singer and Small 1994, updated to include the Kargil and Eritrean wars. The bases for the civil war estimates are discussed below.

2. There are 79 wars in their sample, but they lose about 34 due to missing values on explanatory variables, which are mainly economic. Standard economic data tend to be missing for countries that are poor and civil war–torn. This highly non-random listwise deletion may account for some of the differences between our results.

3. Gurr (2000) notes the late-1990s decline in ethic war and argues that the trend reflects improved management strategies by states and international organizations. The basic pattern in Figure 3.1 is not an artifact of the way we have coded "civil war"; it is observed in a broad range of other data sets on violent domestic conflict for this period (e.g., Gleditsch et al. 2002).

4. Though our formulations differ, we have been influenced here by Stathis Kalyvas's work on the Greek civil war. The literature on guerrilla warfare is extensive; see, for examples, Desai and Eckstein 1990, Griffith 1961, and Laqueur 1976.

5. A "second-order" mechanism by which ethnicity may favor insurgency is that ethnic minorities are sometimes marked by dense social networks that are isolated from dominant group networks, thus giving an informational advantage to local rebels (Fearon and Laitin 1996). But such an advantage does not require ethnic distinctiveness.

6. In the case literature one frequently finds either that rebels' leaders have spent time at guerrilla training camps in, for example, Libya, Afghanistan, Lebanon, or Mozambique (in the 1970s) or that they gained guerrilla experience in one insurgency that applied in pursuing another.

7. Gerard produced this measure for the DECRG project on civil wars at the World Bank. Our sample of countries differs slightly, so we estimated values for 21 missing countries using the difference between the highest and the lowest point of

elevation in each country, which is well correlated with the mountains measure (0.78 in logs).

8. We used income growth rates from the World Development Indicators 2001 to extend the estimates in the Penn World Tables 5.6 and then used the per capita energy consumption estimates provided by the COW project to estimate additional missing values. For details see Fearon and Laitin 2003.

9. For this variable, "transition periods" and "interruptions" (which indicate a "complete collapse of central authority") are coded as instability; foreign occupations are treated as missing.

10. The data are for five-year intervals beginning in 1960; we interpolated for years after 1960, set the value to that in 1960 for years prior to 1960, and used country-specific sources for a few countries without World Bank coverage.

11. Countries with territory holding at least 10,000 people and separated from the land area containing the capital city either by land or by 100 km of water were coded as "noncontiguous." Ignoring the colonial empires, 25 of our 161 countries meet this criterion at some time since 1945.

12. Using the Phase III Minorities at Risk (MAR) data, Fearon and Laitin (1999) found that groups without a rural base area were far less likely to be engaged in violent conflict with the state, even after controlling for various country- and group-specific factors. Toft (1996) was the first to note and examine the strong bivariate relationship in the MAR data.

13. U.S. support to rightist regimes in Latin America during the Cold War might also qualify, although this was perhaps more offset by support for armed insurgency in this area from the Soviet Union and Cuba.

14. The presence of valuable minerals or the suitability of land for the cultivation of narcotics is also codable in principle, but at present we lack such measures (H_{10e}). Nor do we have measures for the comparative disadvantage of governments in access to village-level information (H_{8c}).

15. The figure was produced using R's locfit package, with a smoothing parameter of 0.9, and transforming annual probabilites of outbreak to five-year equivalents. The figure looks highly similar if we use other measures of ethnic diversity, such as fractionalization.

REFERENCES

Anderson, Benedict. 1983. *Imagined Communities.* London: Verso.

Avant, Deborah D. 1994. *Political Institutions and Military Change.* Ithaca, NY: Cornell University Press.

Chaudhry, Kiren Aziz. 1989. "The Price of Wealth: Business and State in Labor Remittance and Oil Economies." *International Organization* 43 (1): 101–45.

Clutterbuck, Richard L. 1967. *The Long, Long War: The Emergency in Malaya.* London: Cassell.

Collier, Paul, and Anke Hoeffler. 1999. "Justice Seeking and Loot-seeking in Civil War," World Bank. Typescript. http://econ.worldbank.org/programs /conflict/library (November 18, 2002).

Collier, Paul, and Anke Hoeffler. 2001. "Greed and Grievance in Civil War." World Bank. Typescript. http://econ.worldbank.org/programs/library (November 18, 2002).

Connor, Walker. 1994. *Ethnonationalism.* Princeton, NJ: Princeton University Press.

Desai, Raj, and Harry Eckstein. 1990. "Insurgency: The Transformation of Peasant Rebellion." *World Politics* 42 (4): 441–66.

Deutsch, Karl W. 1953. *Nationalism and Social Communication.* Cambridge, MA: MIT Press.

Easterly, William, and Ross Levine. 1997. "Africa's Growth Tragedy: Policies and Ethnic Divisions." *Quarterly Journal of Economics* 112 (4): 1203–50.

Eisinger, Peter. 1973. "The Conditions of Protest Behavior in American Cities." *American Political Science Review* 67: 11–28.

Fearon, James D. 1998. "Commitment Problems and the Spread of Ethnic Conflict." In *The International Spread of Ethnic Conflict,* eds. David A. Lake and Donald Rothchild. Princeton, NJ: Princeton University Press.

Fearon, James D., and David D. Laitin. 1996. "Explaining Interethnic Cooperation." *American Political Science Review* 4: 715–35.

———. 1999. "Weak States, Rough Terrain, and Large-Scale Ethnic Violence since 1945." Presented at the

Annual Meetings of the American Political Science Association, Atlanta, GA.

———. 2003. "Additional Tables for "Ethnicity, Insurgency, and Civil War." www.stanford.edu/group/ethnic/.

Gellner, Ernest. 1983. *Nations and Nationalism*. Ithaca, NY: Cornell University Press.

Gleditsch, Nils, Havard Strand, Mikael Eriksson, Margareta Sollenberg, and Peter Wallensteen. 2002. "Armed Conflict 1946–2001: A New Dataset." *Journal of Peace Research* 39 (5): 615–37.

Griffith, Samuel B., ed. 1961. *Mao Tse-Tung on Guerrilla Warfare*. New York: Praeger.

Gurr, Ted R. 1971. *Why Men Rebel*. Princeton, NJ: Princeton University Press.

Gurr, Ted R. 2000. *Peoples versus States*. Washington, DC: United States Institute of Peace Press.

Huntington, Samuel P. 1968. *Political Order in Changing Societies*. New Haven, CT: Yale University Press.

Huntington, Samuel P. 1996. *The Clash of Civilizations and the Remaking of World Order*. New York: Simon & Schuster.

Kalyvas, Stathis. 1999. "Wanton and Senseless? The Logic of Massacres in Algeria." *Rationality and Society* 11 (3): 243–85.

Karl, Terry L. 1997. *The Paradox of Plenty*. Berkeley: University of California Press.

Kaufmann, Chaim. 1996. "Possible and Impossible Solutions to Ethnic Civil Wars." *International Security* 20 (4): 136–75.

Keen, David. 1998. *The Economic Functions of Violence in Civil Wars*. London: Oxford University Press.

Kennedy-Pipe, Caroline. 1997. *The Origins of the Present Troubles in Northern Ireland*. London: Longman.

Krepinevich, Andrew F. 1986. *The Army and Vietnam*. Baltimore, MD: Johns Hopkins University Press.

Kriger, Norma J. 1992. *Zimbabwe's Guerrilla War*. New York: Cambridge University Press.

Laqueur, Walter. 1976. *Guerrilla Warfare*. New Brunswick, NJ: Transaction Books.

Leites, Nathan, and Charles Wolf. 1970. *Rebellion and Authority*. Chicago, IL: Markham.

Muller, Edward N. 1985. "Income Inequality, Regime Repressiveness, and Political Violence." *American Sociological Review* 50: 47–61.

Paige, Jeffery M. 1975. *Agrarian Revolution*. New York: Free Press.

Russett, Bruce M. 1964. "Inequality and Instability." *World Politics* 16: 442–54.

Scott, James C. 1976. *The Moral Economy of the Peasant*. New Haven: Yale University Press.

Singer, J. David, and Melvin H. Small. 1994. "Correlates of War Project: International and Civil War Data, 1816–1992." ICPSR 9905, April.

Thompson, Robert G. 1966. *Defeating Communist Insurgency*. London: Chatto and Windus.

Tilly, Charles. 1978. *From Mobilization to Revolution*. Reading, MA: Addison-Wesley.

Wantchekon, Leonard. 2000. "Why Do Resource Dependent States Have Authoritarian Governments?" Ms., Yale University.

Alberto Alesina and Eliana La Ferrara

ETHNIC DIVERSITY AND ECONOMIC PERFORMANCE

Introduction

New York and Los Angeles are among the two most troubled American cities in terms of racial relations; at the same time they are constant producers of innovation in the arts and business. The United States itself is an economically successful melting pot, but many of its social problems are related to racial and ethnic cleavages. The "tragedy of Africa" is, according to many, largely a result of ethnic conflict, which is indeed pervasive in many parts of the developing world. So, what are the pros and cons of "diversity," being that racial, ethnic, religious, or linguistic?

The potential costs of diversity are fairly evident. Conflict of preferences, racism, and prejudices often lead to policies that are at the same time odious and counterproductive for society as a whole. The oppression of minorities may lead to political unrest or even civil wars. But a diverse ethnic mix also brings about variety in abilities, experiences, and cultures that may be productive and may lead to innovation and creativity. In what follows, we try to highlight the trade-off between the benefits of "diversity" and the costs of heterogeneity of preferences in a diverse multiethnic society.

■ ■ ■

So, is diversity "good" or "bad"? Fragmented societies are often more prone to poor policy management and pose more politico-economic challenges than homogenous ones; it is easy to find rather voluminous evidence on this point. However,

to the extent that not all diverse societies are a failure but in fact some work much better than others, and in fact rather well, it is important to understand why and how. We propose a simple theoretical framework in which the skills of individuals from different ethnic groups are complementary in the production process for a private good, implying that more diversity translates into increased productivity. On the other hand, individual utility also depends on the consumption of a shared public good and, since different ethnic groups may have different preferences on the type of public good to provide, increased diversity lowers the utility from public good consumption. The size of the public sector and the number of ethnic groups are determined by the trade-off between these two forces. We verify the consistency of this theory using repeated cross-sectional data on countries * * * and we find that, while *ceteris paribus* increases in ethnic diversity are associated with lower growth rates, the interaction between diversity and the income level of the community under study is positive. This suggests that ethnic diversity can be beneficial (or at least less detrimental) at higher levels of development. One potential explanation for this effect is that the productivity benefits of skill complementarities are realized only when the production process is sufficiently diversified, as in advanced economies. Another—possibly complementary—explanation is that richer societies have developed institutional features that allow them to better cope with the conflict element intrinsic in diversity and isolate or moderate its negative effects. From the micro to the macro level, in fact, the importance of adequate "rules of the game" to manage diversity is stressed by all disciplines.

From *Journal of Economic Literature* 42 (September 2005), pp. 762–800.

* * * [W]e need to clarify what we, and the literature which we review, mean by various terms like "diversity," "fractionalization," "ethnicity," "race," etc. The empirical literature on cross-country studies has typically used various measures of ethno-linguistic fractionalization. An "ethno-linguistic group" (often referred for brevity as "ethnic group") is identified by a language only in some cases and in other cases by language and skin color or other physical attributes; a variety of indexes have been suggested and we will discuss below similarity and differences. * * * We will use the terms "fractionalization" and "diversity" when we want to be generic and not refer to any particular type of identifying characteristics of the groups; we will use "ethnic," "racial," "religious fragmentation," and "diversity" when we want to be more specific. With the term "diverse society" . . . we mean a nonhomogenous place. The term "fractionalization," on the other hand, will be directly related to a specific measure of number and size of groups: specifically, a more fractionalized place is one in which the probability the two randomly drawn individuals belong to the same group is lower. In surveying the existing literature, we do not touch on the question of what identifies an ethnic group and we take the classifications adopted by the authors as given.

∎ ∎ ∎

Theories on Diversity

The goal of this section is to briefly highlight some basic economic forces underlying the relationship between ethnic diversity and economic performance.

∎ ∎ ∎

Some "Microfoundations"

First diversity can affect economic choices by directly entering individual *preferences*. Early work on social identity theory has established that patterns of inter-group behavior can be understood considering that individuals may attribute positive utility to the well-being of members of their own group and negative utility to that of members of other groups (see e.g., Henri Tajfel, Michael Billig, Robert P. Bundy, and Claude Flament 1971). A recent formalization of this concept is the analysis of group participation by Alesina and La Ferrara (2000), where the population is heterogeneous and individual utility from joining a group depends positively on the share of group members of one's own type and negatively on the share of different types.[1]

Second, diversity can affect economic outcomes by influencing the *strategies* of individuals. Even when individuals have no taste for or against homogeneity, it may be optimal from an efficiency point of view to transact preferentially with members of one's own type if there are market imperfections. For example, Avner Greif (1993) argues that traders in Medieval times formed coalitions along ethnic lines in order to monitor agents by exchanging information on their opportunistic behavior. Ethnic affiliation helped sustain a reputation mechanism in the presence of asymmetric information. But strategies can be conditional on one's ethnic identity also in the presence of perfect information.

∎ ∎ ∎

Finally, diversity may enter the *production* function. People differ in their productive skills and, more fundamentally, in the way they interpret problems and use their cognitive abilities to solve them. This can be considered the origin of the relationship between individual heterogeneity and innovation or productivity. An elegant formalization of this concept is provided by Lu Hong and Scott E. Page (1998), who prove two key results on this point. First, a group of "cognitively diverse" problem solvers can find optimal solutions to difficult problems; second, under certain conditions, a more diverse group of people with limited abilities can outperform a more homogeneous group of high-ability problem solvers. The intuition is that an individual's likelihood of improving decisions depends more on her having a different perspective from other group members than on her own high expected score.

■ ■ ■

SUMMING UP THE IMPLICATIONS OF THE THEORY The potential benefits of heterogeneity come from variety in production. The costs come from the inability to agree on common public goods and public policies. One testable implication is that more heterogeneous societies may exhibit higher productivity in private goods but lower taxation and lower provision of public goods (in relative terms). The benefits in production from variety in skills are more likely to be relevant for more advanced societies. While in poor economies ethnic diversity may not be beneficial from the point of view of productivity, it may be so in rich ones. The more unwilling to share public goods or resources are the different groups, the smaller the size of jurisdictions.[2] The larger the benefits in production from variety, the larger the size. If variety in production can be achieved without sharing public goods, different groups will want to create smaller jurisdictions to take advantage of homogeneity in the enjoyment of the public good.

■ ■ ■

The Consequences of Fragmentation

Countries

EFFECTS ON PRODUCTIVITY AND INCOME LEVEL Economists have started to pay attention to the effects of racial fragmentation across countries at least since a paper by William Easterly and Ross Levine (1997) who argued that, *ceteris paribus*, more racially fragmented countries grow less and

that this factor is a major determinant of Africa's poor economic performance.[3] Several subsequent papers confirmed these results in the context of cross-country growth regressions. In their overview of Africa's problems, Paul Collier and Jan Willem Gunning (1999) also place much emphasis on ethno–linguistic fractionalization (coupled with low political rights) as a major explanation for the lack of social capital, productive public goods, and other growth-enhancing policies.

Easterly and Levine's paper, and much of the literature that followed, used as a measure of fragmentation the probability that two randomly drawn individuals from the unit of observation (say, country) belong to two different groups. Their ethno–linguistic fractionalization (ELF) measure is a Herfindahl-based index defined as follows:

$$ELF = 1 - \sum_i s_{i}^2$$

where s_i is the share of group i over the total of the population. This index represents the probability that two randomly drawn individuals from the population belong to different ethnic groups. The source used by Easterly and Levine to construct the ethno–linguistic groups is the Atlas Narodov Mira, originally compiled by Soviet researchers. Apart from issues of measurement (to which we return below), the robustness of Easterly and Levine's results has been called into question by Jean-Louis Arcand, Patrick Guillaumont, and Sylviane Guillaumont Jeanneney (2000) due to problems of data missingness.[4] Despite the criticisms, subsequent estimates have taken Easterly and Levine's results as a benchmark, and have confirmed them.

Using the updated data set of Alesina, Arnaud Devleeschauwer, Easterly, Sergio Kurlat, and Romain Wacziarg (2003), we now test whether the negative correlation between ethnic fragmentation and growth holds irrespective of the level of economic development or, as our model suggests, is mitigated when the benefits of heterogeneity for productivity are taken into account. Alesina et al. (2003) construct two indices with the same structure as above but using two different (although closely related) characterizations of groups. One is more comprehensive, is labeled *ELF*, and extends the Easterly and Levine index by differentiating groups that may speak the same language but have different ethnicity based upon certain physical characteristics. A striking example would be blacks and whites in the United States, or various ethnic groups in Latin America all speaking the same language, often that of a former colonizer.[5] The second index relies exclusively on language spoken.

Table 3.1 shows some standard growth regressions adopting the baseline specification of Alesina et al. (2003). The dependent variable is the growth rate of GDP per capita from 1960 to 2000 and we use a SUR method in four ten-year periods. The first two columns use the more comprehensive index of fractionalization (which we label *ELF*), while columns 3 and 4 use the one based solely on language. Columns 1 and 3 show a baseline regression with very few controls: regional dummies, initial income, and schooling. Columns 2 and 4 include additional controls, such as measures of political stability and quality of policy. One may argue (and in fact we explore this point below) that the effect of fractionalization on growth may go through exactly these variables; therefore by controlling for these variables one may underestimate the effects of fractionalization on growth. Overall, table 3.1 shows considerable support for the negative effects of fractionalization on growth.[6] In terms of magnitude, the estimates in column 1 suggest that, *ceteris paribus*, going from perfect homogeneity to maximum heterogeneity (i.e., increasing *ELF* from 0 to 1) would reduce a country's growth rate by 2 percentage points per year. Increasing ethnic fractionalization by one standard deviation would reduce growth by 0.6 percentage points per year. These are quite sizeable effects. All the other controls have signs consistent with the vast literature on growth.

An important question is whether or not these negative effects from ethnic fractionalization on growth depend on the level of income or other features of society. * * * Table 3.2 adds to all the regressions of table 3.1 an interaction term between fractionalization and GDP per capita. In all four regressions, the interaction of initial GDP per capita and fractionalization has the expected (positive) sign, suggesting that indeed fractionalization has more negative effects at lower levels of income. In two out of four regressions, this effect is strongly statistically significant.

Collier (2000) argues that fractionalization has negative effects on growth and productivity only in nondemocratic regimes, while democracies manage to cope better with ethnic diversity. This is an important result worth exploring further. It is well known that per capita GDP and democracy are positively correlated: richer countries are more democratic. From a statistical point of view, this high correlation makes it quite difficult to disentangle the effects of democracy from the effects of the level of income on any dependent variable that might be affected by either one or both.[7] Table 3.3 considers the effects of the interaction of ethnic and language fractionalization with the Gastil index of democracy. This index is *decreasing* in the level of democracy so the expected sign on the interaction with fractionalization is negative. The estimates in table 3.3 are consistent with Collier's findings that fractionalization has less negative effects in democracies.

Table 3.4 uses the two basic specifications to try to disentangle the effects of income and democracy. Since we are adding several variables with interactions, we use the simpler specification. Overall, the effect of income seems more robust and more precisely estimated than the effect of democracy. However, these results have to be taken cautiously given the high correlation between democracy and GDP per capita.

The punch line is that rich democracies are more capable of "handling" productively ethnic diversity. Note, however, that as argued above, the variable "democracy" may be endogenous to ethnic diversity. It may be the case that racially fragmented societies that choose democratic institutions are also those in which ethnic cleavages are less deep and/or the

Table 3.1 Fractionalization and Long-Run Growth (dependent variable is growth of per capita GDP)

Variable	ETHNIC		LANGUAGE	
	1	2	3	4
Dummy for the 1960s	0.059 (3.357)	0.153 (5.144)	0.065 (3.563)	0.156 (5.248)
Dummy for the 1970s	0.057 (3.093)	0.158 (5.222)	0.062 (3.280)	0.161 (5.333)
Dummy for the 1980s	0.036 (1.940)	0.141 (4.601)	0.042 (2.213)	0.145 (4.725)
Dummy for Sub-Saharan Africa	–0.008 (–1.630)	–0.016 (2.853)	–0.009 (–2.026)	–0.014 (–2.595)
Dummy for Latin America and the Caribbean	–0.016 (–4.458)	–0.011 (–2.923)	–0.019 (–5.252)	–0.018 (–4.201)
Log of initial income	–0.004 (–1.499)	–0.018 (–3.767)	–0.004 (–1.660)	–0.018 (–3.724)
Log of schooling	0.012 (2.767)	0.005 (1.092)	0.011 (2.627)	0.008 (1.669)
Assassinations		–21.342 (2.212)		–13.988 (–1.010)
Financial Depth		0.012 (1.798)		0.010 (1.652)
Black Market premium		–0.021 (4.738)		–0.022 (–4.953)
Fiscal Surplus/GDP		(0.128) 3.369		0.132 (3.474)
Log of telephones per worker		(0.006) 2.078		0.004 (1.488)
Fractionalization	–0.020 (–3.005)	–0.014 (–1.795)	–0.019 (–2.979)	–0.021 (–2.881)
No. of Observations	82; 88; 94	40; 69; 66	82; 86; 92	39; 68; 65
R-squared	.23; .17; .35	.32; .43; 54	.21; .21; .30	.36; .47; .52

(t-statistics in parentheses)
Estimated Using Seemingly Unrelated Regressions: a separate regression for each ten-year period.

Table 3.2 Fractionalization and Long-Run Growth (dependent variable is growth of per capita GDP)

Variable	ETHNIC		LANGUAGE	
	1	2	3	4
Dummy for the 1960s	0.064 (2.522)	0.220 (5.116)	0.098 (3.910)	0.253 (6.827)
Dummy for the 1970s	0.061 (2.369)	0.226 (5.179)	0.096 (3.735)	0.260 (6.897)
Dummy for the 1980s	0.041 (1.542)	0.209 (4.757)	0.077 (2.951)	0.245 (6.411)
Dummy for Sub-Saharan Africa	−0.007 (−1.574)	−0.014 (−2.479)	−0.007 (−1.478)	−0.011 (−2.138)
Dummy for Latin America and the Caribbean	−0.016 (−4.386)	−0.013 (−3.233)	−0.021 (−5.517)	−0.019 (−4.787)
Log of initial income	−0.005 (−1.297)	−0.027 (−4.253)	−0.008 (−2.420)	−0.031 (−5.523)
Log of schooling	0.012 (2.775)	0.006 (1.112)	0.011 (2.599)	0.009 (1.966)
Assassinations		−21.880 (−2.311)		−16.919 (−1.303)
Financial Depth		0.011 (1.649)		0.008 (1.385)
Black Market premium		−0.021 (−4.736)		−0.020 (−4.729)
Fiscal Surplus/GDP		0.136 (3.618)		0.146 (4.048)
Log of telephones per worker		0.007 (2.532)		0.005 (1.969)
Fractionalization	−0.031 (−0.655)	−0.129 (−2.319)	−0.083 (−1.851)	−0.214 (−4.382)
Fractionalization * log of initial income	0.001 (0.227)	0.015 (2.084)	0.008 (1.279)	0.025 (3.977)
No. of Observations	82; 88; 94	40; 69; 66	80; 86; 92	39; 68; 65
R-squared	.23; .18; .35	.27; .48; .55	.22; .25; .28	.36; .55; .56

(t-statistics in parentheses)
Estimated Using Seemingly Unrelated Regressions: a separate regression for each ten-year period.

Table 3.3 Fractionalization, Democracy, and Long-Run Growth (dependent variable is growth of per capita GDP)

Variable	ETHNIC		LANGUAGE	
	1	2	3	4
Dummy for the 1960s	0.059 (3.290)	0.153 (5.090)	0.073 (3.897)	0.159 (5.331)
Dummy for the 1970s	0.056 (2.869)	0.155 (4.983)	0.069 (3.418)	0.162 (5.220)
Dummy for the 1980s	0.035 (1.790)	0.137 (4.358)	0.050 (2.420)	0.146 (4.632)
Dummy for Sub-Saharan Africa	–0.008 (–1.628)	–0.014 (–2.493)	–0.006 (–1.371)	–0.010 (–1.805)
Dummy for Latin America and the Caribbean	–0.016 (–4.521)	–0.012 (–3.017)	–0.020 (–5.324)	–0.017 (–4.087)
Log of initial income	–0.004 (–1.619)	–0.019 (–3.933)	–0.006 (–2.274)	–0.019 (–4.029)
Log of schooling	0.012 (2.842)	0.007 (1.351)	0.013 (3.108)	0.010 (1.959)
Assassinations		–23.495 (–2.423)		–14.057 (–1.045)
Financial Depth		0.012 (1.951)		0.012 (1.897)
Black Market premium		–0.021 (–4.828)		–0.023 (–5.169)
Fiscal Surplus/GDP		0.117 (3.060)		0.131 (3.520)
Log of telephones per worker		0.006 (2.185)		0.004 (1.610)
Fractionalization	–0.014 (–1.856)	–0.002 (–0.233)	–0.017 (–2.187)	–0.008 (–0.877)
Democracy	0.001 (0.867)	0.003 (1.833)	0.002 (1.390)	0.002 (2.064)
Fractionalization * Democracy	–0.002 (–1.230)	–0.005 (–1.871)	–0.003 (–1.885)	–0.005 (–2.489)
No. of Observations	82; 87; 93	40; 69; 66	80; 85; 90	39; 68; 65
R-squared	.23; .19; .34	.33; .46; .53	.21; .26; .27	.35; .52; .52

(t-statistics in parentheses)
Estimated Using Seemingly Unrelated Regressions: a separate regression for each ten-year period.

Table 3.4 Fractionalization, Democracy, and Long-Run Growth (dependent variable is growth of per capita GDP)

Variable	ETHNIC	LANGUAGE
	1	3
Dummy for the 1960s	0.118 (4.689)	0.138 (5.593)
Dummy for the 1970s	0.115 (4.356)	0.135 (5.197)
Dummy for the 1980s	0.096 (3.562)	0.117 (4.426)
Dummy for Sub-Saharan Africa	−0.005 (−1.053)	−0.003 (−0.668)
Dummy for Latin America and the Caribbean	−0.017 (−4.793)	−0.020 (−5.267)
Log of initial income	−0.012 (−3.398)	−0.014 (−4.247)
Log of schooling	0.012 (2.878)	0.012 (2.979)
Fractionalization	−0.149 (−3.510)	−0.170 (−4.135)
Fractionalization * log of initial income	0.017 (3.233)	0.020 (3.769)
Democracy	0.001 (0.665)	0.001 (1.228)
Fractionalization * Democracy	−0.002 (−1.067)	−0.003 (−1.944)
No. of Observations	82; 87; 93	80; 85; 90
R-squared	.21; .33; .30	.20; .39; .25

(t-statistics in parentheses)
Estimated Using Seemingly Unrelated Regressions: a separate regression for each ten-year period.

power distribution of groups is such that none can impose a nondemocratic rule.

Related to the issue of how democracy interacts with ethnic conflict and with the level of development is the role played by institutions in general. Easterly (2001) constructs an index of institutional quality aggregating Stephen Knack and Philip Keefer's (1995) data on contract repudiation, expropriation, rule of law, and bureaucratic quality. He finds that the negative effect of ethnic diversity is significantly mitigated by the presence of "good" institutions and the marginal effect of ethnic diversity at the maximum level of institutional development is actually zero. Again, the institutional variables used as explanatory factors are likely not exogenous and more work needs to be done to assess the marginal impact of institutional arrangements. Nonetheless, it seems important to take into account that, whatever the mechanisms relating ethnic diversity to economic growth, channeling diversity toward productive uses may require a particular set of "rules of the game."

EFFECTS ON PUBLIC POLICIES An important prediction of our model is that the propensity to supply true public goods should be lower in more ethnically fragmented societies.

■ ■ ■

Rafael La Porta, Florencio Lopez-de-Silanes, Andrei Shleifer, and Robert Vishny (1999) and Alesina et al. (2003) show that ethnic fragmentation is negatively correlated with measures of infrastructure quality, literacy, and school attainment and positively correlated with infant mortality. These correlations are very strong in regressions without income per capita (that may be endogenous to ethnic fragmentation). They lose some of their significance in regressions where on the right hand side one controls for GDP per capita.[8] In any case, neither of these studies argues that ethnic fragmentation is the only cause of "poor quality of government": La Porta et al. (1999), for instance, argue that legal origins are at least as important.

An interesting related question regards the size of public transfers rather than public goods. For a large sample of countries, Alesina, Edward Glaeser, and Bruce Sacerdote (2001) show an inverse relationship between the size of government social spending and transfers relative to GDP on the one hand, and ethnic fractionalization on the other. One explanation is that altruism does not travel well across ethnic lines. Relating this point to the model above, one can view redistributive policies as a "public good" in a society that values equality as a public benefit. On this point, a comparison between the United States and Europe seems especially suggestive. In the United States, welfare spending and redistributive policies are much smaller than in Europe, consistent with the fact that the United States is much more racially and ethnically diverse than most countries in Continental Europe, a point explored in much detail by Alesina and Glaeser (2004). One implication of this analysis is that, to the extent that Western European countries will become more ethnically fragmented, their welfare systems will be under stress.

■ ■ ■

A line of research by Alesina and Enrico Spolaore (1997, 2003), Alesina, Spolaore, and Wacziarg (2000), and Spolaore and Wacziarg (2002) emphasizes the role of racial conflict as a determinant of the number and size of countries. The argument is as follows. The size of a country emerges from a trade-off between the benefits of scale (broadly defined) and the cost of heterogeneity of preferences in the population. Benefits of size include economies of scale in the production of some public goods, internalization of policy externalities, the size of the market, defense and protection from foreign aggression, and regional insurance schemes. The costs of heterogeneity arise because, in large and diverse countries, individuals with different preferences have to share common policies so the average utility of these policies is decreasing with heterogeneity. Empirically, racial fragmentation is often associated with differences in preferences, so racial cleavages are a major determinant of the determination of borders, secessions, and various centrifugal forces.[9]

A potentially testable implication of this approach is that, as the benefits of size diminish, then it becomes more likely that countries can split into more homogenous smaller political entities. One building bloc of this argument is of course that openness to trade is particularly beneficial for small countries. Results by Alberto F. Ades and Glaeser (1999), Alesina, Spolaore, and Wacziarg (2000), and Francisco Alcala and Antonio Ciccone (2004) suggest that, as freedom of trade increases, the benefit of size for economic growth diminishes. In a completely autarkic world, the political size of a country also determines its economic size; in a world of free trade they become more disjoint. That is, from an "economic" point of view (our production of private goods in the simple model above), trade makes economic size "larger." On the other hand, since countries can retain their independence while trading, they do not have to share common public policies on which there are differences of opinions. In ethnically diverse societies, then, increased economic integration should make it more likely that conflicts are resolved with breakdown of countries. Some insights on this issue can be gathered from the political science literature on partition as a solution to ethnic civil war, supported among others by Chaim D. Kaufmann (1996, 1998). A critical assessment of the view that separation is the best solution for civil wars generated by ethnic conflict is provided by Nicholas Sambanis (2000), who uses a cross-sectional data set of all civil wars since 1944 and estimates the probability of partition as a function of the type of civil war (ethnic/religious as opposed to ideological) and of several socioeconomic factors, among which ethnic heterogeneity of the population.

The relationship between ethnic heterogeneity and the likelihood of country breakdowns is also mediated by the role of natural resources, and this is a particularly relevant issue for developing countries. Natural resource discoveries tend to be located in remote areas at the periphery of a country, as resources more centrally located have likely been discovered already. It is often the case that people living in peripheral areas have ethnic identities that do not coincide with the majority of the country as a whole. The availability of new natural resources makes these regions more economically viable on their own and therefore increases pressure for separation or autonomy.[10]

In addition to economies of scale, another benefit of country size is defense and protection from aggressions, so as the world becomes more peaceful one should observe centrifugal forces. Alesina and Spolaore (2003) discuss historical evidence, arguing that this implication is consistent with the data concerning the evolution of country size, international trade, and threats of conflicts. Recently, the collapse of the Soviet Union, by reducing the threat of an East–West conflict, has certainly facilitated political separatism in Eastern Europe. Samuel P. Huntington (1998) notes how the end of the Cold War allowed the realignment of peoples into countries that better reflected homogenous "civilizations." In most cases, this movement meant breakdown of countries and in a few cases movement toward reunification.

Finally, an important issue is the relationship between ethnic heterogeneity, country formation, and democracy. Alesina and Spolaore (2003) discuss the effect of authoritarian systems on measured racial, linguistic, or religious fragmentation and country size. Dictators prefer large countries for several reasons. One is that they can extract rents from larger populations; another one is that they can support with size their bellicose attitudes. Historically, one of the main problems of dictators has been to repress ethnic conflict in an attempt to create artificially homogeneous countries—an issue to which we return below when we discuss the endogeneity of the notion of fragmentation. In fact, dictators often use racial hatred to create support for the dominance of one group over others, a result consistent with models and empirical evidence by Glaeser (2002). One of the implications of this artificial repression of diversity is that centrifugal forces typically explode when dictators fall, as happened for example in the Soviet Union, Spain, Yugoslavia, and Iraq. James D. Fearon (1998) provides an insightful game theoretic model of civil wars that follow the collapse of dictators.

Conclusions and Policy Implications

We proposed a model in which public good provisions were lower in fragmented societies while productivity may be positively related to variety. Is the evidence consistent with it? We certainly found overwhelming evidence supporting the first part of the proposition. As for the productivity effects of diversity, the picture is complex. It is somehow easy to point to economic failures of fractionalized societies, but this is not a general phenomenon. Rich democratic societies work well with diversity, in the case of the United States very well in terms of growth and productivity. Even within the developing world, similar levels of ethnic diversity are associated with very different degrees of conflict and interethnic cooperation. Useful theoretical progress would incorporate in a model like this more realistic institutional features that would distinguish cases in which the economy manages to actually take advantage more or less well of the potential benefits of variety in production.

What are the policy implications of all of the above? The issue is quite difficult and politically charged and it is relevant in at least two areas: immigration policies and local policies that may increase or decrease racial integration. The implication of promoting racial homogeneity is unappealing and probably incorrect both in the short and in the long run. David D. Laitin (1994) provides an interesting example concerning language in Ghana. After independence, this country faced the question of which language to adopt as the official one. Using English had the advantage of its being understood by most and of not favoring one ethnic group over another. On the other hand, it was the language of a colonizer. Laitin argues that a solution with multiple languages

may dominate that of a single homogenous language. The benefit of homogeneity had to be traded off against other considerations (national pride, ethnic balance, etc.).[11] On the other hand, peaceful separation and country breakdown may be perfectly reasonable solutions to racial or cultural diversity.

Globalization also has important implications for ethnic politics. To the extent that small countries can prosper in a world of free trade, then peaceful separatism of certain minorities should not be viewed as threatening, at least from an economic point of view. As far as domestic social policy is concerned, the question is to what extent favoring racial mixing (say with affirmative action) promotes harmony, an issue that would require an entirely separate paper. The starting point would be Arend Lijphart's (1977) seminal contribution that provides a notion of power sharing denoted as "consociational democracy." The key features of this type of democracy should be a coalition government in which "all significant segments of the plural society" are represented, with a proportionality system, a mutual veto, and a federalist structure.[12] He highlights the conditions under which power sharing is likely to succeed, namely, a relative balance of power and economic equality among the different groups. Most importantly, he argues that different groups are most likely to find an agreement when they have to face *external* threats. This makes power sharing schemes difficult to implement and ultimately unstable in some developing countries (e.g., Africa) where most threats to the state come from within. Among recent examples of power sharing agreements that have failed due to internal conflicts are those of Angola and Rwanda. On the other hand, South Africa and Somaliland have managed to successfully implement consociationalist schemes. Ian S. Spears (2002) reports that, in addition to the presence of an "external" threat (Mogadishu), in the case of Somaliland a deeply rooted tradition of power sharing among the elders of local clans may have contributed to the viability of such schemes. However, this calls into question the effectiveness of power sharing as a means of *generating* interethnic cooperation: indeed power sharing may well be the *result* of preexisting attitudes toward interethnic cooperation. Philippe Aghion, Alesina, and Francesco Trebbi (2004a) in fact report that racial and ethnic fractionalization are empirically inversely related to forms of consociativism and widespread proportional representation.[13]

The issue of multiethnicity is especially relevant for current Europe. In fact, while the United States has been a melting pot throughout most of its history, Western European countries have been much more ethnically homogeneous. However, with the opening of borders within the European Union and its expansion to the East, in addition to increasing migration from Africa and other neighboring areas, member countries of the European Union will become less and less homogeneous; in fact the issue of multiethnicity will be one of the major challenges for Europe in the near future.

With this survey, we have tried to assess the costs and benefits of ethnic fragmentation and the policy issues arising in diverse societies. In a more and more integrated world, the question of how different people can peacefully interact is the critical problem for the next many decades.

NOTES

1. A "business counterpart" of the preference element in diversity may be seen in the theories of "customer discrimination." According to these theories, businesses whose employees reflect the ethnic mix of the communities in which they operate perform better than those who do not, as customer satisfaction increases from interacting with service providers similar to themselves.

2. In principle, various ethnic groups could segregate within the same jurisdiction and use different public goods. However, segregation is often imperfect, may entail other costs, and some public goods are by nature jurisdiction wide.

3. An early and never published paper by David Canning and Marianne Fay (1993) used ethnic fractionalization as an instrument for growth.

4. Arcand, Guillaumont, and Guillaumont Jeanneney (2000) note that African countries constitute only 27 of the 172 observations in Easterly and Levine's main regression, and highlight the potential sample selection bias generated by the fact that the data is missing precisely for those countries (in Africa) that have experienced slower growth.

5. In fact, several countries in Latin America appear as more fractionalized compared to Easterly and Levine's classification using this more comprehensive index. See Alesina et al. (2003) for more details.

6. These results are very similar to those reported by Alesina et al. (2003). The only difference is that they use both a linear and a quadratic term for initial per capita income. We use only the linear one because below we explore interactions of the initial level of income with other variables and we want to keep a simpler specification. In any case results with a quadratic term for initial income are very similar for our variables of interest.

7. This is a well known and common stumbling block for anybody who has tried to estimate empirically the costs and benefit of democracy on economic variables, a vast literature that we do not review here; see Jose Tavares and Wacziarg (2001) for one of the most recent and careful contributions.

8. Another variable that is correlated with racial fragmentation is "latitude" and this high correlation makes it sometimes difficult to disentangle the two effects separately, although it is unclear why latitude per se (leaving aside its possible effects on GDP per capita) should affect public policies. Often both variables (latitude and fragmentation) used together are insignificant while they are significant if used separately.

9. Patrick Bolton and Gerard Roland (1997) explore how income differences and redistribution may lead to breakdown of countries.

10. We are grateful to a referee for suggesting this point.

11. For a recent application to language diversity in the European Union and a measure of the "disenfranchisement" that would arise from a reduction in the number of EU working languages, see Victor Ginsburgh, Ignacio Ortuno-Ortin, and Shlomo Weber (forthcoming).

12. Lijphart (1977), p. 25.

13. Note that while proportional representation and consociationalist schemes may diffuse racial tension, their presence is also empirically associated with difficulties in pursuing adequate fiscal policies, larger budget deficits, and macroeconomic policy instability. For extensive empirical evidence, see Torsten Persson and Guido Tabellini (2003).

REFERENCES

Ades, Alberto F., and Edward L. Glaeser. 1995. "Trade and Circuses: Explaining Urban Giants." *Quarterly Journal of Economics*, 110(1): 195–227.

Ades, Alberto F., and Edward L. Glaeser. 1999. "Evidence on Growth, Increasing Returns, and the Extent of the Market." *Quarterly Journal of Economics*, 114(3): 1025–45.

Aghion, Philippe, Alberto Alesina, and Francesco Trebbi. 2004a. "Endogenous Political Institutions." *Quarterly Journal of Economics*, 119(2): 565–611.

Aghion, Philippe, Alberto Alesina, and Francesco Trebbi. 2004b. "Choosing Electoral Rules: Evidence from US Cities." Unpublished.

Alcala, Francisco, and Antonio Ciccone. 2004. "Trade and Productivity." *Quarterly Journal of Economics*, 119(2): 613–46.

Alesina, Alberto, Reza Baqir, and William Easterly. 1999. "Public Goods and Ethnic Divisions." *Quarterly Journal of Economics*, 114(4): 1243–84.

Alesina, Alberto, Reza Baqir, and William Easterly. 2000. "Redistributive Public Employment." *Journal of Urban Economics*, 48(2): 219–41.

Alesina, Alberto, Reza Baqir, and Caroline Hoxby. 2004. "Political Jurisdictions in Heterogeneous Communities." *Journal of Political Economy*, 112(2): 348–96.

Alesina, Alberto, Robert J. Barro, and Silvana Tenreyro. 2002. "Optimal Currency Areas," in *NBER Macroeconomics Annual 2002*. Mark Gertler and Kenneth Rogoff, eds. Cambridge: MIT Press, 301–55.

Alesina, Alberto, Arnaud Devleeschauwer, William Easterly, Sergio Kurlat, and Romain Wacziarg. 2003. "Fractionalization." *Journal of Economic Growth*, 8(2): 155–94.

Alesina, Alberto, and Edward L. Glaeser. 2004. *Fighting Poverty in the US and Europe: A World of Difference*. Oxford and New York: Oxford University Press.

Alesina, Alberto, Edward Glaeser, and Bruce Sacerdote. 2001. "Why Doesn't the United States Have a European-Style Welfare State?" *Brookings Papers on Economic Activity*, 2: 187–254.

Alesina, Alberto, and Eliana La Ferrara. 2000. "Participation in Heterogeneous Communities." *Quarterly Journal of Economics*, 115(3): 847–904.

Alesina, Alberto, and Eliana La Ferrara. 2002. "Who Trusts Others?" *Journal of Public Economics*, 85(2): 207–34.

Alesina, Alberto, and Enrico Spolaore. 1997. "On the Number and Size of Nations." *Quarterly Journal of Economics*, 112(4): 1027–56.

Alesina, Alberto, and Enrico Spolaore. 2003. *The Size of Nations*. Cambridge: MIT Press.

Alesina, Alberto, Enrico Spolaore, and Romain Wacziarg. 2000. "Economic Integration and Political Disintegration." *American Economic Review*, 90(5): 1276–96.

Alesina, Alberto, and Romain Wacziarg. 1998. "Openness, Country Size and Government." *Journal of Public Economics*, 69(3): 305–21.

Anderson, Benedict. 1983. *Imagined Communities*. London: Verso.

Arcand, Jean-Louis, Patrick Guillaumont, and Sylviane Guillaumont Jeanneney. 2000. "How to Make a Tragedy: On the Alleged Effect of Ethnicity on Growth." *Journal of International Development*, 12(7): 925–38.

Bannon, Alicia, Edward Miguel, and Daniel Posner. 2004. "Sources of Ethnic Identification in Africa." University of California at Los Angeles. Mimeo.

Barr, Abigail. 2003. "Trust and Expected Trustworthiness: Experimental Evidence from Zimbabwean Villages." *Economic Journal*, 113(489): 614–30.

Bates, Robert H. 2000. "Ethnicity and Development in Africa: A Reappraisal." *American Economic Review*, 90(2): 131–34.

Berman, Eli. 2000. "Sect, Subsidy, and Sacrifice: An Economist's View of Ultra-Orthodox Jews." *Quarterly Journal of Economics*, 115(3): 905–53.

Bernard, Tanguy, Alain de Janvry, and Elisabeth Sadoulet. 2004. "Social Resistance to Institutional Change: Explaining the Emergence of Differentiating Organizations in Rural Senegal." University of California at Berkeley. Mimeo.

Biggs, Tyler, Mayank Raturi, and Pradeep Srivastava. 2002. "Ethnic Networks and Access to Credit: Evidence from the Manufacturing Sector in Kenya." *Journal of Economic Behavior and Organization*, 49(4): 473–86.

Bigsten, Arne, Peter Kimuyu, and Karl Lundvall. 2000. "Informality, Ethnicity, and Productivity: Evidence from Small Manufacturers in Kenya." Göteborg University Department of Economics Working Paper No. 27.

Blanchard, Olivier Jean, and Lawrence F. Katz. 1992. "Regional Evolutions." *Brookings Papers on Economic Activity* 1: 1–61.

Bloch, Francis, and Vijayendra Rao. 2001. "Statistical Discrimination and Social Assimilation." *Economics Bulletin*, 10(2): 1–5.

Bolton, Patrick, and Gerard Roland. 1997. "The Breakup of Nations: A Political Economy Analysis." *Quarterly Journal of Economics*, 112(4): 1057–90.

Bossert, Walter, Conchita D'Ambrosio, and Eliana La Ferrara. 2005. "A Generalized Index of Fractionalization." Bocconi University and University of Montreal. Mimeo.

Bossert, Walter, Prasanta K. Pattanaik, and Yongsheng Xu. 2003. "Similarity of Options and the Measurement of Diversity." *Journal of Theoretical Politics*, 15(4): 405–21.

Brender, Adi. 2004. "Ethnic Segregation and the Quality of Local Governments in the Minority's Localities: Local Tax Collection in the Israeli–Arab Municipalities." Unpublished.

Buchanan, James M., and Roger L. Faith. 1987. "Secession and the Limits of Taxation: Toward a Theory of Internal Exit." *American Economic Review*, 77(5): 1023–31.

Burns, Nancy. 1994. *The Formation of American Local Governments: Private Values in Public Institutions.* New York: Oxford University Press.

Calabrese, Stephen, Glenn Cassidy, and Dennis Epple. 2002. "Local Governments, Fiscal Structure, and Metropolitan Consolidation." *Brookings–Wharton Papers on Urban Affairs 2002*: 1–32.

Canning, David, and Marianne Fay. 1993. "The Role of Infrastructures in Economic Growth." Unpublished.

Caselli, Francesco, and Wilbur J. Coleman. 2002. "On the Theory of Ethnic Conflict." Harvard University. Unpublished.

Collier, Paul. 2000. "Ethnicity, Politics, and Economic Performance." *Economics and Politics*, 12(3): 225–45.

Collier, Paul. 2001. "Implications of Ethnic Diversity." *Economic Policy*, 32(16): 127–66.

Collier, Paul, and Jan Willem Gunning. 1999. "Explaining African Economic Performance." *Journal of Economic Literature*, 37(1): 64–111.

Costa, Dora L., and Matthew E. Kahn. 2003a. "Civic Engagement and Community Heterogeneity: An Economist's Perspective." *Perspectives on Politics* 1(1): 103–11.

Costa, Dora L., and Matthew E. Kahn. 2003b. "Understanding the Decline in American Social Capital, 1952–1998." *Kyklos*, 56(1): 17–46.

Dayton-Johnson, Jeff. 2000. "The Determinants of Collective Action on the Local Commons: A Model with Evidence from Mexico." *Journal of Development Economics*, 62(1): 181–208.

Demange, Gabrielle. 2005. "Group Formation: The Interaction of Increasing Returns and Preferences Diversity." In *Group Formation in Economics: Networks, Clubs, and Coalitions.* Gabrielle Demange and Myrna Wooders, eds. Cambridge: Cambridge University Press.

Demange, Gabrielle, and Myrna Wooders, eds. 2005. *Group Formation in Economics: Networks, Clubs, and Coalitions.* Cambridge: Cambridge University Press.

Dudley, Geoff. 1991. "Scale, Aggregation, and the Modifiable Area Unit Problem." *The Operational Geographer* 9(3): 28–33.

Easterly, William. 2001. "Can Institutions Resolve Ethnic Conflict?" *Economic Development and Cultural Change*, 49(4): 687–706.

Easterly, William, and Ross Levine. 1997. "Africa's Growth Tragedy: Policies and Ethnic Divisions." *Quarterly Journal of Economics*, 112(4): 1203–50.

Ellickson, Bryan, Birgit Grodal, Suzanne Scotchmer, and William R. Zame. 1999. "Clubs and the Market." *Econometrica*, 67(5): 1185–1217.

Epple, Dennis, and Thomas Romer. 1991. "Mobility and Redistribution." *Journal of Political Economy*, 99(4): 828–58.

Esteban, Joan, and Debraj Ray. 1994. "On the Measurement of Polarization." *Econometrica*, 62(4): 819–51.

Fafchamps, Marcel. 2000. "Ethnicity and Credit in African Manufacturing." *Journal of Development Economics*, 61(1): 205–35.

Fafchamps, Marcel. 2004. *Market Institutions in Sub-Saharan Africa: Theory and Evidence.* Cambridge: MIT Press.

Fearon, James D. 1998. "Commitment Problems and the Spread of Ethnic Conflict," in *The International Spread of Ethnic Conflict: Fear, Diffusion, and Escalation.* David Lake and Donald Rothschild, eds. Princeton: Princeton University Press, 107–26.

Fearon, James D. 1999. "Why Ethnic Politics and 'Pork' Tend to Go Together." Stanford University. Unpublished.

Fearon, James D. 2002. "Fractionalization and Civil Wars." Stanford University. Unpublished.

Fearon, James D. 2003. "Ethnic and Cultural Diversity by Country." *Journal of Economic Growth* 8(2): 195–222.

Fearon, James D., and David D. Laitin. 1996. "Explaining Interethnic Cooperation." *American Political Science Review*, 90(4): 715–35.

Fearon, James D., and David D. Laitin. 2003. "Ethnicity, Insurgency, and Civil War." *American Political Science Review*, 97(1): 75–90.

Fisman, Raymond J. 1999. "Trade Credit and Productive Efficiency in Developing Economies." Columbia University. Mimeo.

Fisman, Raymond J. 2003. "Ethnic Ties and the Provision of Credit: Relationship-Level Evidence from African Firms." *Advances in Economic Analysis and Policy* 3(1): Article 4.

Florida, Richard. 2002a. "Bohemia and Economic Geography." *Journal of Economic Geography,* 2(1): 55–71.

Florida, Richard. 2002b. "The Economic Geography of Talent." *Annals of the Association of American Geographers*, 92(4): 743–55.

Friedman, David. 1977. "A Theory of the Size and Shape of Nations." *Journal of Political Economy*, 85(1): 59–77.

Garfinkel, Michelle. 2004. "On the Stability of Group Formation: Managing the Conflict Within." *Conflict Management and Peace Science*, 21(1): 43–68.

Ginsburgh, Victor, Ignacio Ortuno-Ortin, and Shlomo Weber. Forthcoming. "Disenfranchisement in Linguistically Diverse Societies: The Case of the European Union." *Journal of the European Economic Association.*

Glaeser, Edward L. 2002. "The Political Economy of Hatred." Harvard University. Unpublished.

Glaeser, Edward L., David Laibson, Jose A. Scheinkman, and Christine L. Soutter. 2000. "Measuring Trust." *Quarterly Journal of Economics*, 115(3): 811–46.

Glaeser, Edward L., Jose A. Scheinkman, and Andrei Shleifer. 1995. "Economic Growth in a Cross-Section of Cities." *Journal of Monetary Economics*, 36(1): 117–43.

Goldin, Claudia, and Lawrence F. Katz. 1999. "Human Capital and Social Capital: The Rise of Secondary School in America, 1910 to 1940." *Journal of Interdisciplinary History*, 29(4): 683–723.

Greif, Avner. 1993. "Contract Enforceability and Economic Institutions in Early Trade: The Maghribi Traders' Coalition." *American Economic Review*, 83(3): 525–48.

Gurr, Ted. 1996. *Minorities at Risk Dataset.* University of Maryland.

Habyarimana, James, Macartan Humphreys, Daniel Posner, and Jeremy Weinstein. 2004. "Ethnic Identifiability: An Experimental Approach." University of California, Los Angeles. Mimeo.

Hong, Lu, and Scott E. Page. 1998. "Diversity and Optimality," Santa Fe Institute Working Paper 98-08-077.

Horowitz, Donald L. 1985. *Ethnic Groups in Conflict.* Berkeley: University of California Press.

Horowitz. Donald L. 2001. *The Deadly Ethnic Riot.* Berkeley: University of California Press.

Humphreys, Macartan, and Habaye ag Mohamed. 2002. "Senegal and Mali: A Comparative Study of Rebellions in West Africa." Paper presented at the World Bank/Center for United Nations Studies Conference, Yale University, 12–15 April.

Humphreys, Macartan, Daniel M. Posner, and Jeremy M. Weinstein. 2002. "Ethnic Identity, Collective Action, and Conflict: An Experimental Approach." Harvard University and UCLA. Unpublished.

Huntington, Samuel P. 1998. *The Clash of Civilizations and the Remaking of the World Order.* New York: Simon and Schuster.

Jackson, Susan E., and Marian N. Ruderman, eds. 1996. *Diversity in Work Teams: Research Paradigms for a Changing Workplace.* Washington, D.C.: American Psychological Association.

Jehiel, Philippe, and Suzanne Scotchmer. 2001. "Constitutional Rules of Exclusion in Jurisdiction Formation." *Review of Economic Studies,* 68(2): 393–413.

Karlan, Dean S. 2003. "Social Capital and Group Banking." Princeton University. Mimeo.

Katzenstein, Peter J. 1985. *Small States in World Markets: Industrial Policy in Europe.* Ithaca: Cornell University Press.

Kaufmann, Chaim D. 1996. "Possible and Impossible Solutions to Ethnic Civil Wars." *International Security,* 20(4): 136–75.

Kaufmann, Chaim D. 1998. "When All Else Fails: Ethnic Population Transfers and Partitions in the Twentieth Century." *International Security,* 23(2): 120–56.

Keefer, Philip, and Stephen Knack. 2000. "Polarization, Politics, and Property Rights: Links between Inequality and Growth," World Bank Policy Research Working Paper 2418.

Khwaja, Asim I. 2000. "Can Good Projects Succeed in Bad Communities? Collective Action in the Himalayas." Harvard University. Mimeo.

Knack, Stephen, and Philip Keefer. 1995. "Institutions and Economic Performance: Cross-Country Tests Using Alternative Institutional Measures," *Economics and Politics,* VII, 207–27.

Kochan, Thomas, Katerina Bezrukova, Robin Ely, Susan Jackson, Aparna Joshi, Karen Jehn, Jonathan Leonard, David Levine, and David Thomas. 2002.

"The Effects of Diversity on Business Performance: Report of the Diversity Research Network." MIT Sloan School of Management. Mimeo.

Kyriacou, Andreas P. 2005. "Rationality, Ethnicity and Institutions: A Survey of Issues and Results." *Journal of Economic Surveys,* 19(1): 23–42.

La Ferrara, Eliana. 2002a. "Inequality and Group Participation: Theory and Evidence from Rural Tanzania." *Journal of Public Economics,* 85(2): 235–73.

La Ferrara, Eliana. 2002b. "Self-Help Groups and Income Generation in the Informal Settlements of Nairobi." *Journal of African Economies,* 11(1): 61–89.

La Ferrara, Eliana. 2003a. "Kin Groups and Reciprocity: A Model of Credit Transactions in Ghana." *American Economic Review,* 93(5): 1730–51.

La Ferrara, Eliana. 2003b. "Solidarity in Heterogeneous Communities," in *Cultural Diversity vs. Economic Solidarity.* Philippe van Parjis, ed. Brussels: DeBoeck University.

La Ferrara, Eliana, and Angelo Mele. 2003. "Racial Segregation and Public School Expenditure." Bocconi University. Mimeo.

La Porta, Rafael, Florencio Lopez-de-Silanes, Andrei Shleifer, and Robert Vishny. 1999. "The Quality of Government." *Journal of Law, Economics, and Organization,* 15(1): 222–79.

Laitin, David D. 1994. "The Tower of Babel as a Coordination Game: Political Linguistics in Ghana." *American Political Science Review,* 88(3): 622–34.

Laitin, David D. 1995. "Marginality: A Microperspective." *Rationality and Society* 7(1): 31–57.

Laitin, David D. 1998. *Identity in Formation: The Russian-Speaking Populations in the Near Abroad.* Ithaca: Cornell University Press.

Laitin, David D. 2000. "What Is a Language Community?" *American Journal of Political Science,* 44(1): 142–54.

Lazear, Edward P. 1999a. "Globalisation and the Market for Team-Mates." *Economic Journal,* 109(454): C15–40.

Lazear, Edward P. 1999b. "Culture and Language." *Journal of Political Economy,* 107(6): S95–126.

Levinson, David. 1998. *Ethnic Groups Worldwide: A Ready Reference Handbook.* Phoenix: Oryx Press.

Lijphart, Arend. 1977. *Democracy in Plural Societies: A Comparative Exploration*. New Haven: Yale University Press.

Lijphart, Arend. 1999. *Patterns of Democracy*. New Haven: Yale University Press.

Luttmer, Erzo F. P. 2001. "Group Loyalty and the Taste for Redistribution." *Journal of Political Economy*, 109(3): 500–528.

Macours, Karen. 2003. "Ethnic Divisions, Interlinkages and Search Costs in the Guatemalan Land Rental Market." Johns Hopkins University. Unpublished.

Madison, James. 1787. "Federalist Papers n. 11."

Massey, Douglas S., and Nancy A. Denton. 1988. "The Dimensions of Racial Segregation." *Social Forces*, 67(2): 281–315.

McMillan, Margaret. 2003. *Paris 1919: Six Months That Changed the World*. New York: Random House.

Miguel, Edward, and Mary Kay Gugerty. Forthcoming. "Ethnic Diversity, Social Sanctions, and Public Goods in Kenya." *Journal of Public Economics*.

Milchtaich, Igal, and Eyal Winter. 2002. "Stability and Segregation in Group Formation." *Games and Economic Behavior*, 38(2): 318–46.

Montalvo, José García, and Martha Reynal-Querol. 2002. "Why Ethnic Fractionalization? Polarization, Ethnic Conflict and Growth." Universitat Pompeu Fabra. Unpublished.

Nopo, Hugo, Jaime Saavedra, and Maximo Torero. 2002. "Ethnicity and Earnings in Urban Peru." GRADE. Mimeo.

Okten, Cagla, and Una Okonkwo Osili. 2004. "Contributions in Heterogeneous Communities: Evidence from Indonesia." *Journal of Population Economics*, 17(4): 603–26.

Olson, Mancur. 1965. *The Logic of Collective Action*. Cambridge: Harvard University Press.

Openshaw, Stan, and Peter J. Taylor. 1979. "A Million or So Correlation Coefficients: Three Experiments on the Modifiable Area Unit Problem," in *Statistical Applications in the Spatial Sciences*. N. Wrigley, ed. London: Pion, 127–44.

O'Reilly, Charles L., Katherine Y. Williams, and Sigal G. Barsade. 1997. "Demography and Group Performance." Unpublished.

Ottaviano, Gianmarco, and Giovanni Peri. 2003. "The Economic Value of Cultural Diversity: Evidence from US Cities." University of California, Davis. Unpublished.

Ottaviano, Gianmarco, and Giovanni Peri. 2004. "Cities and Cultures." Unpublished.

Persson, Torsten, and Guido Tabellini. 2003. *The Economic Effects of Constitutions*. Cambridge: MIT Press.

Posner, Daniel N. 2004a. "Measuring Ethnic Fractionalization in Africa." *American Journal of Political Science*, 48(4): 849–63.

Posner, Daniel N. 2004b. "The Political Salience of Cultural Difference: Why Chewas and Tumbukas Are Allies in Zambia and Adversaries in Malawi." *American Political Science Review*, 98(4): 529–45.

Poterba, James M. 1997. "Demographic Structure and the Political Economy of Public Education." *Journal of Policy Analysis and Management*, 16(1): 48–66.

Prat, Andrea. 2002. "Should a Team Be Homogeneous?" *European Economic Review*, 46(7): 1187–1207.

Rappaport, Jordan. 1999. "Local Growth Empirics." CID Working Paper, Harvard University, No. 23.

Rauch, James E. 2001. "Business and Social Networks in International Trade." *Journal of Economic Literature*, 39(4): 1177–1203.

Rauch, James E., and Alessandra Casella, eds. 2001. *Networks and Markets*. New York: Russell Sage Foundation.

Rauch, James E., and Alessandra Casella. 2003. "Overcoming Informational Barriers to International Resource Allocation: Prices and Ties." *Economic Journal*, 113(484): 21–42.

Ray, Debraj, and Rajiv Vohra. 1999. "A Theory of Endogenous Coalition Structures." *Games and Economic Behavior*, 26(2): 286–336.

Ray, Debraj, and Rajiv Vohra. 2001. "Coalitional Power and Public Goods." *Journal of Political Economy*, 109(6): 1355–84.

Richard, Orlando, Thomas Kochan, and Amy McMillan-Capehart. 2002. "The Impact of Visible Diversity on Organizational Effectiveness: Disclosing the Contents in Pandora's Black Box." *Journal of Business and Management* 8(3): 265–92.

Rogowski, Ronald. 1987. "Trade and the Variety of Democratic Institutions." *International Organization*, 41(2): 203–23.

Sambanis, Nicholas. 2000. "Partition as a Solution to Ethnic War: An Empirical Critique of the Theoretical Literature." *World Politics*, 52(4): 437–83.

Sethi, Rajiv, and Rohini Somanathan. 2004. "Inequality and Segregation." *Journal of Political Economy*, 112(6): 1296–1321.

Spears, Ian S. 2002. "Africa: The Limits of Power Sharing." *Journal of Democracy*, 13(3): 123–36.

Spolaore, Enrico, and Romain T. Wacziarg. 2002. "Borders and Growth." NBER Working Paper 9223.

Srinivas, Mysore Narasimhachar. 1966. *Social Change in Modern India.* Berkeley: University of California Press.

Tajfel, Henri, Michael Billig, Robert P. Bundy, and Claude Flament. 1971. "Social Categorization and Intergroup Behavior." *European Journal of Social Psychology*, 1: 149–78.

Tavares, Jose, and Romain Wacziarg. 2001. "How Democracy Affects Growth." *European Economic Review*, 45(8): 1341–78.

Tiebout, Charles M. 1956. "A Pure Theory of Local Public Expenditure." *Journal of Political Economy*, 64(5): 416–24.

Vigdor, Jacob L. 2004. "Community Composition and Collective Action: Analyzing Initial Mail Response to the 2000 Census." *Review of Economics and Statistics*, 86(1): 303–12.

Weitzman, Martin L. 1992. "On Diversity." *Quarterly Journal of Economics*, 107(2): 363–405.

Wilkinson, Steven. 2002. "Memo on Developing Better Indicators of Ethnic and Non-Ethnic Identities," Paper presented at the LICEP 5th Meeting, Stanford University.

Williams, Katherine Y., and Charles A. O'Reilly, III. 1998. "Demography and Diversity in Organizations: A Review of 40 Years of Research," in *Research in Organizational Behavior: An Annual Series of Analytical Essays and Critical Reviews*, Volume 20. B. M. Staw and L. L. Cummings, eds. Greenwich, Conn.: JAI Press, 77–140.

Kate Baldwin and John D. Huber

ECONOMIC VERSUS CULTURAL DIFFERENCES: FORMS OF ETHNIC DIVERSITY AND PUBLIC GOODS PROVISION

Ethnic diversity is widely held to make governance more difficult. Such diversity is associated with low production of public goods; poor economic growth; and high levels of corruption, violence, and civil conflict. But diversity hardly sentences a country to poor political and economic outcomes. Latvia, for example, has better governance indicators than Brazil, and Zambia has better governance indicators than Nigeria, even though these pairs of countries have similar levels of ethnolinguistic fractionalization (ELF). Why, then, do some countries cope more successfully with ethnic diversity than others?

This article addresses this question by focusing on the nature of substantive differences between groups.

From *American Political Science Review* 104, no. 4 (November 2010), pp. 644–62.

The vast majority of cross-national evidence about ethnic diversity and governance uses the standard measure of ELF (e.g., Alesina et al. 2003; Alesina and La Ferrara 2005; Collier 2000; Easterly and Levine 1997; La Porta et al. 1999). This measure contains information about the identity and size of groups but incorporates no other information about groups' substantive characteristics. Existing arguments about how ethnic diversity affects governance, however, are typically grounded in the assumption that groups differ from each other in substantively important ways, and posit that these differences underlie governance problems in multiethnic societies.

This article examines two important types of differences between groups—cultural and economic. Our goal is to understand the empirical relationship between such differences and public goods provision across countries. Is diversity more problematic for governance in countries when this diversity is based on strong cultural or economic differences between groups? Do standard empirical results about ethnolinguistic fractionalization still hold when controlling for the cultural or economic differences between groups?

The focus on cultural differences has received substantial attention in the literature on ethnic diversity. Scholars argue that such differences make it more difficult for individuals to cooperate across groups. This may be true for a number of reasons, as Habyarimana et al. (2009) describe. One reason is that ethnic similarities make it easier for individuals to communicate with each other (e.g., Bacharach and Gambetta 2001; Deutsch 1966). The shared languages and social networks of ethnically similar individuals allow them to assess each other's intentions and trustworthiness, and to communicate goals and necessary actions. These individuals experience lower transaction costs when cooperating toward common ends. In addition, ethnically similar individuals should find it easier to sanction each other for failing to cooperate (e.g., Fearon and Laitin 1996; Greif 1994; Miguel and Gugerty 2005). Thus, as the cultural differences between groups in a country grow, public goods should be harder to produce. Although these arguments have been subject to lim-

ited cross-national empirical research, a recent paper by Desmet, Ortuño-Ortín, and Weber (2009) shows that redistribution by the government is lower in countries that have higher levels of linguistic diversity, which is a key indicator of cultural differences.

Economic differences between groups have received less attention in the literature, in part because empirical measures of group-based economic differences across countries have not existed. However, there are good reasons to expect that such differences will affect governance. Group-based economic differences can lead to different group needs with respect to public goods, feelings of alienation or discrimination by some groups, different attitudes toward redistribution across groups, and different "class" identities by different groups. The effect of group economic differences on the policy preferences of group members is likely to be particularly important in affecting governance. If the different economic statuses of groups lead them to prioritize different public goods, then it will be difficult for these groups to reach agreement on which public goods to provide (e.g., Alesina, Baqir, and Easterly 1999; Alesina and Drazen 1991; Alesina and Spolaore 1997). Under these circumstances, politicians may try to win reelection by providing private goods for each group, especially when the number of groups is not too large (Fernández and Levy 2008).

This article demonstrates that it is possible to measure differences in the economic well-being of groups using existing cross-national surveys of citizens. Specifically, we use between-group inequality (BGI), which is a weighted average of the differences in mean incomes across groups in a country, as a measure of economic differences between groups. We then argue that between-group inequality can be satisfactorily measured using surveys such as the Afrobarometer, the World Values Survey (WVS), and the Comparative Study of Electoral Systems (CSES). We combine the measure of between-group inequality with existing measures of ELF and with existing measures of cultural differences between groups that are based on language differences (Desmet, Ortuño-Ortín, and Weber 2009; Fearon 2003). The data show that these variables measure different things and that the choice between them has an important impact on our understanding of which countries are most ethnically diverse.

Which measure of ethnic diversity shows the strongest association with public goods provision? We do not find a robust empirical relationship between either the standard ELF measure or measures of cultural difference and public goods provision. However, the tests do reveal that between-group inequality has a large, robust negative relationship with public goods provision. Countries with higher levels of inequality between groups have lower levels of public goods, a finding that has important implications for understanding the pathways by which ethnic diversity creates governance problems.

The article is organized as follows. The next section introduces the measures of ethnic differences—cultural fractionalization (CF) and between-group inequality—that are central to the analysis. Because cross-national measures of between-group inequality do not currently exist, the following section describes how they can be created from cross-national surveys. We then compare the measures of cultural fractionalization, between-group inequality, and ethnolinguistic fractionalization with each other. Our main empirical tests follow. We first treat each country as a unit of analysis and use ordinary least squares (OLS) models to test the relationships between each measure and public goods provision. The results show that only BGI has a robust relationship. Between-group economic differences, however, can be caused by policies related to public goods. We therefore also estimate models [not included here] aimed at exploring whether BGI has a causal effect on public goods provision. The final section concludes the article.

Measures of Cultural and Economic Differences between Groups

The well-known index of ethnolinguistic fractionalization, or *ELF*, measures the probability that two randomly chosen individuals will belong to different groups. It is written as

$$ELF = 1 - \sum_{i=1}^{n} p_i^2,$$

where p_i is the proportion of individuals who belong to group i and n is the number of groups in society.[1] As noted previously, ELF does not include information on the extent of cultural or economic differences across groups. But ELF can be altered to incorporate information about group-based differences.

To measure cultural differences, one approach is to consider language differences between ethnic groups. The importance of language to cultural identity has been emphasized by many scholars (Gellner 1983; Laitin 1994, 1998). Linguistic differences can lead to divergent preferences on linguistic and educational policy; in addition, they make communication between individuals more difficult and are often correlated with social networks (Milroy 1987). As a result, a version of ELF that incorporates information about the extent of linguistic differences between ethnic groups provides a useful measure of the level of cultural differences between groups.

To measure cultural differences, we use a measure first proposed by Greenberg (1956). This measure is a variation on ELF that captures the expected linguistic similarity between two randomly selected individuals in a society, and it has been used by Fearon (2003) to measure cultural fractionalization within societies. * * *

We use Fearon's (2003) measure of linguistic similarity, which he constructed based on the distance between different languages in language trees. Linguists use language trees to classify languages into families, and then within each family, they subclassify languages into different branches. Fearon's measure is based on the premise that the more branches two languages have in common, the more similar the languages are to each other. In Spain, for example, Spanish and Basque are very different because they come from two different language families (Indo-European and Basque). In contrast, Spanish and Catalan are quite similar, only branching apart from each other at the eighth junction in their language tree.[2] * * * If two groups speak the same language, $r_{ij} = l = 1$, and if two groups speak languages from different linguistic trees, $r_{ij} = l = 0$; otherwise, r_{ij} takes a value between 0 and 1 that is increasing in the number of shared branches of the two group's languages. Desmet, Ortuño-Ortín, and Weber (2009) construct a similar measure but give less weight to having large numbers of shared branches within language trees as compared to being part of the same language tree. We are agnostic about which of these measures is more appropriate and thus include both Fearon's and Desmet, Ortuño-Ortín, and Weber's measures.[3]

Although factors other than language may create cultural barriers between groups, focusing on language differences has considerable merit because it employs an objective criterion that can be measured consistently across countries. It is possible to imagine factors unrelated to language that lead to cultural differences in a country; however, it is more difficult to describe such factors in a way that is as amenable to the level of objectivity and cross-national measurement reliability as the linguistic measures. Cultural fractionalization is therefore a good proxy for the underlying level of cultural differences across groups in a society.

Next consider the measurement of group economic differences. A straightforward and easily interpretable measure of group-based income differences is BGI. This measure is based on the familiar Gini index, but instead of calculating inequality based on each individual's income, it assigns each group's mean income to every member of that group. It can be interpreted as the expected difference in the mean income of the ethnic groups of any two randomly selected individuals. * * *

Although not widely familiar to political scientists, between-group inequality has been studied by economists interested in decomposing inequality into its different components.[4] Milanovic (2005) uses the BGI formula as a proxy for global inequality; his second measure of international inequality calculates a Gini in which each country's mean income is weighted by its population. Mancini, Stewart, and Brown 2008 (see also Mancini 2008) advocate the use of BGI as a measure of group differences in their studies of communal violence. The measure is also similar to the grouped version of the Generalized Ethno-linguistic Fractionalization (GELF) measure that Bossert, D'Ambrosio, and La Ferrara (n.d.) developed and applied to the United States.[5]

Both the Gini and BGI have interpretations related to the Lorenz curve. The Lorenz curve is a graphical illustration of the cumulative distribution of a society's income over different ranges of the income distribution. To draw a Lorenz curve based on individual income differences, each person in society is ranked according to their individual income. The points on the Lorenz curve indicate that y percentage of the society's income accrues to the bottom x percentage of people in the income distribution. In a perfectly equal society, where the "bottom" 10% of people control 10% of the society's income, the "bottom" 20% of people control 20% of the society's income, and so on, the Lorenz curve is equal to the 45-degree line. In any society where there is not perfect equality, the Lorenz curve is typically a convex curve below the 45-degree line. The Gini index is equal to two times the area between the Lorenz curve and the 45-degree line.

BGI is based on a ranking of people *not* by their individual income, but by their ethnic group's mean income, and thus ignores information about income differences within groups. Each group member is ranked according to the mean income of their ethnic group. Because BGI is based on the proportion of income held by each group, the Lorenz curve for BGI will be a series of straight lines meeting at points where members of one group end and members of the next group begin. BGI is equal to two times the area between the group-based Lorenz curve and the 45-degree line.

Figure 3.3 illustrates BGI using the Lorenz curve for three hypothetical societies, each divided into three groups—group 1, group 2, and group 3—with 35, 40, and 25 members, respectively. Each society has 100 units of income to distribute among

Figure 3.3 Graphical Illustration of BGI

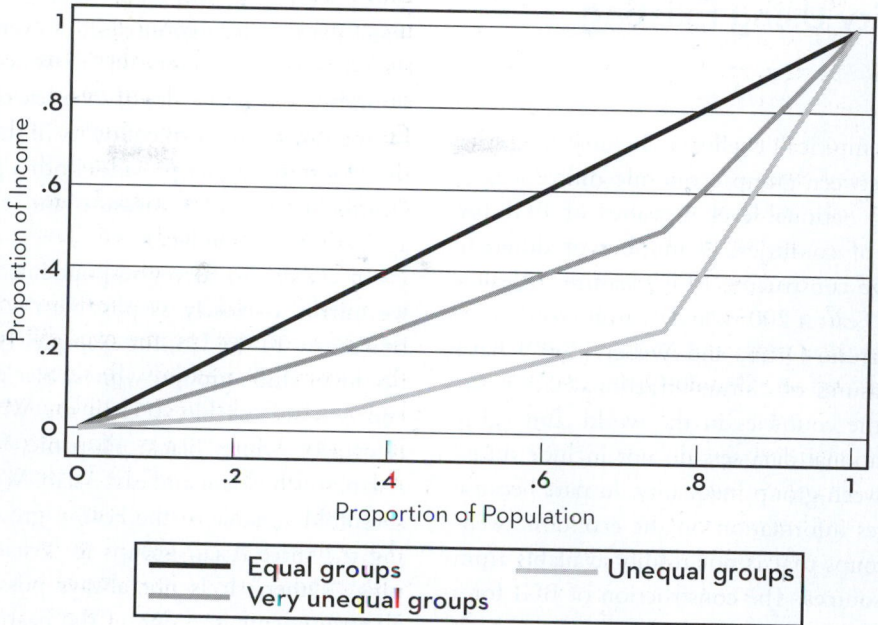

these groups. In a completely equal society, group 1 will receive 35 units of wealth, group 2 will receive 40 units of wealth, and group 3 will receive 25 units of wealth. The Lorenz curve will be a straight line because the group occupying the "bottom" 35% of the income distribution controls 35% of the income, the groups occupying the "bottom" 75% of the income distribution control 75% of the income, and so on. This case is depicted by the solid black line. BGI in this case is 0.

In an unequal society, the wealthiest group will control more income per person than the poorest group. The middle line draws the Lorenz curve if group 1 controls only 20% of the income, group 2 controls only 30% of the income, and group 3 controls 50% of the income. In this case, the group occupying the bottom 35% of the income distribution controls only 20% of the income, and the two groups occupying the bottom 75% of the income distribution control only 50% of the income. The BGI in this case is 0.275. The bottom line depicts the Lorenz curve in an even more unequal society in which

group 1 controls just 5% of the income, group 2 controls 20%, and group 3 controls 75%. In this case, the bottom 75% of the income distribution controls only 25% of the society's income and BGI is 0.55.

Like the Gini, BGI ranges from 0 to 1. It takes on its minimum value of 0 when the average incomes of all groups in society are the same, and it takes on its maximum value of 1 when one infinitely small group controls all the income in society. Put another way, for any level of ELF, BGI will be 0 if all groups have the same mean income. Holding ELF constant, BGI is increasing in the income differences between groups. The effect of income differences across groups on BGI will be largest when ELF is largest. BGI will take its largest values when there are many equally sized groups (as with ELF) and when the income differences between the groups are large. Between-group inequality, then, can be viewed as an extension of the ELF that allows income differences between groups to vary. Conversely, ELF can be viewed as a restriction on between-group inequality that holds differences between all groups constant at 1.

Measuring Between-Group Inequality Using Existing Surveys

The main empirical challenge in analyzing the effects of between-group economic differences is constructing national-level measures of BGI for a large set of countries. A number of different scholars have constructed ELF measures (Alesina et al. 2003; Fearon 2003), and Fearon (2003) and Desmet, Ortuño-Ortín, and Weber (2009) have created measures of cultural fractionalization for almost all the countries in the world. But existing cross-national data sets do not include measures of between-group inequality, in part because BGI requires information on the economic well-being of groups that is not readily available from secondary sources. The construction of BGI for a particular country requires information on both the size of ethnic groups within the country and the economic well-being of these groups. [Fortunately,] existing cross-national surveys—the Afrobarometer, the WVS, and the CSES—can be used to create BGI measures.

The Afrobarometer, WVS, and CSES surveys all contain instruments that make it possible to identify the "ethnicity" of respondents. However, ethnic categories often nest inside broader categories, and as Posner (2004) demonstrates, choices about which groups to include can have a significant impact on the conclusions one draws about the relationship between group diversity and outcomes. A decision rule is therefore necessary to decide which groups are most relevant in a particular country. In this article, we follow the identification of groups made by Fearon (2003) as closely as possible because we believe that Fearon's work is the most careful and theoretically motivated classification of groups that has been completed to date. His seven criteria emphasize groups that are understood as "descent groups" and that are locally viewed as socially or politically consequential. Depending on the country, Fearon's identification

of groups may be based on race (e.g., the US), language (e.g., Belgium), religion (e.g., France), tribe (e.g., many African countries), or even some combination of these factors. He draws on a range of secondary sources to identify the size of each group for the vast majority of countries in the world, and the resulting data set provides both a guide for the creation of the BGI measure and a benchmark against which to judge it.

In classifying survey respondents into groups, we mirror as closely as possible the groups used by Fearon. In the US, for example, Fearon identifies four ethnic groups: whites, blacks, Hispanics, and Asians. Variable x051 in the WVS has seven categories: white, black, Hispanic, other, central Asian, south Asian, and east Asian. We convert this sevenfold variable to the Fearon groups by recoding the three Asian groups to "Asian" and dropping "Other." It is not always possible to place all respondents into one of the Fearon groups. In France, for example, he identifies the groups as French, Muslim, and Bretons. Using the CSES, we cannot identify the Bretons, but we can identify the French and Muslims.

* * * We focus on democracies because dictators have little incentive to provide public goods regardless of the ethnic diversity of their countries (Olson 1993; Sen 1999), and the effect of ELF on governance has been found to differ in democratic and authoritarian countries (Collier 2000). We therefore consider only countries that have a Polity 2 score of 1 or higher. Some countries have more than one survey, and when this occurs, we average BGI scores across the surveys for that country. The resulting 46 countries included in the analysis are listed in Table 3.5.

* * * Is the correlation between the survey data ELF and the Fearon ELF strong? Figure 3.4 plots this relationship for the 46 countries. The survey-based ELF, which takes the average value within countries when there is more than one survey in a country, is obviously very closely related to the Fearon ELF. The Fearon-based measures typically take higher values, particularly at low levels of

Table 3.5 Countries in Study

Survey	Region					
	Western Europe	Other Europe	Asia	Latin America	Africa	Other
WVS only	Belgium Germany Ireland Netherlands Switzerland	Estonia Georgia Latvia Macedonia Moldova	Bangladesh Indonesia India	Colombia Dominican Republic Uruguay Venezuela		
CSES only	Finland France	Bulgaria Czech Republic Hungary Lithuania Romania Russia Slovenia Ukraine				
Both CSES and WVS	Spain			Brazil Mexico		Australia Canada New Zealand US
Afrobarometer					Benin Botswana Kenya Madagascar Malawi Mali Mozambique Namibia Nigeria Senegal South Africa Zambia	
Total countries	8	13	3	6	12	4

CSES, Comparative Study of Electoral Systems: WVS, World Values Survey.

Figure 3.4 Comparing Ethnolinguistic Fractionalizations (ELFs): Fearon Data versus Survey Data

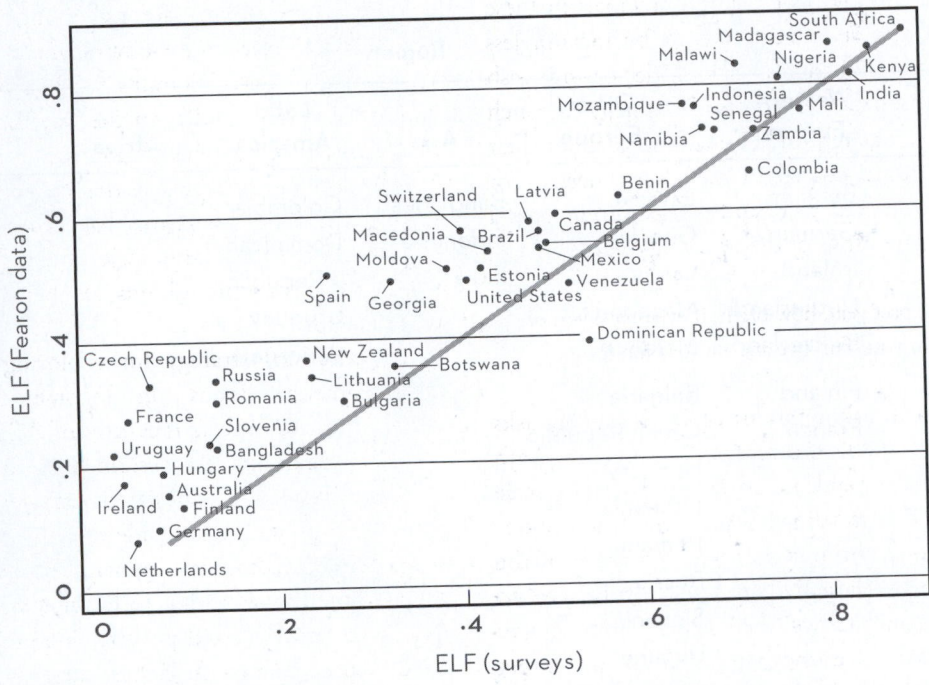

fractionalization, but the overall correlation is an impressive 0.96 [which is higher than the correlation between Fearon's measures of ELF and Alesina et al.'s (2003) measures of ELF].

The next challenge is measuring group economic well-being. Ideally, one would construct the BGI measure using fine-grained, individual-level income or consumption data, aggregated by group. There currently do not exist a large number of multinational surveys that contain this type of data with appropriate information about group identity, but the Afrobarometer, WVS, and CSES surveys contain coarse measures of each respondent's economic well-being that can be used to evaluate the relative well-being of different groups. Even coarse data on group income differences provides information that can be used to measure BGI.

Each survey measures respondents' income or consumption using a different metric. For example, the WVS survey asks the respondent to answer the following question:

> Here is a scale of incomes and we would like to know in what group your household is, counting all wages, salaries, pension, and other incomes that come in. Just give the letter of the group your household falls into, after taxes and other deductions.

The respondent is given a country-specific scale, typically with 8 to 10 categories, created to be meaningful within each country. Each CSES country survey asks a similar question to the WVS, but the CSES reports only the income quintiles of the respondents.

The Afrobarometer survey, like most surveys in developing parts of the world, does not have an income variable. For many individuals in these countries, such a question would be meaningless because the individuals have little or no cash income. Instead, the common strategy in such surveys is to ask respondents questions about their access to things crucial to their basic needs. For the Afrobarometer, each survey asks respondents a number of questions of the following type:

Over the past year, how often, if ever, have you or anyone in your family gone without food?

In addition to asking about food, the survey asks about water, medical care, cooking fuel, and cash income. Each variable is coded on a five-point scale (from 0 to 4) according to how often the respondent has gone without the item. The sum of the responses from these five questions can be used to create an economic well-being metric that ranges from 0 (maximal unmet needs) to 20 (no unmet needs). This index is obviously most useful in distinguishing differences among the least well-off, masking differences that exist among the more well-to-do.

These "income" variables, along with the group identity variables, make it possible to calculate BGI for each survey. In cases where we have multiple surveys for a given country, we average across surveys to create a score for each country.[6][*][*][*] It is reassuring to note that in the survey, whites are richer than Mulattos who are richer than blacks in Brazil; Bulgarians are richer than Turks in Bulgaria; the Flemish are wealthier than the French in Belgium; whites are wealthier than Mestizos and blacks in the Dominican Republic; Muslims are poorer than the "French" in France; and whites are richer than blacks and Hispanics in the US. In the African countries, where the income measures are most limited in that they only distinguish between differences among the poor, the data still capture the fact that whites and people of mixed race background are wealthier than

other ethnic groups in Namibia, the Ibo and Yoruba are richer than the Hausa in Nigeria, and whites, coloureds, and Asians are richer than blacks in South Africa. Thus, in these cases where the income relationships between groups are known, there is considerable face validity in the way that the data rank the relative incomes of groups.

The problem, of course, is that data on between-group economic differences has not been previously collected on a large scale, so little is known about the economic differences between many other groups.

As [another] strategy for exploring how the Afrobarometer's focus on income differences among the poor affects measures of BGI, we conducted simulations. As described in more detail in Appendix 1, the simulated data set contains thousands of societies made up of individuals whose exact income was known. To replicate the Afrobarometer coarsening technique, we assigned all people above a fixed poverty line in the simulated income data to the richest category and then divided the poor into different income levels based on their absolute level of deprivation. We then constructed measures of BGI for each society based on the "true" income variable and the "coarsened" income variable.

Figure 3.5 plots the true BGI (based on the fine-grained income distribution) against the coarsened income data (where income differences exist only at low income levels, as in the Afrobarometer). The dark *xs* represent societies where there are minimal income differences *within* ethnic groups (homogenous groups), the solid gray dots represent societies where there are some income differences *within* ethnic groups (heterogenous groups), and the open gray circles represent societies where there are large income differences *within* ethnic groups (very heterogenous groups). Figure 3.5 also depicts the 45-degree line, making it easy to identify whether "coarsening" leads to overestimates (points above the line) or underestimates (points below the line) of the true BGI. Not surprisingly,

Figure 3.5 *Simulating the Effect of Afrobarometer Data on Estimates of Between-Group Inequality (BGI)*

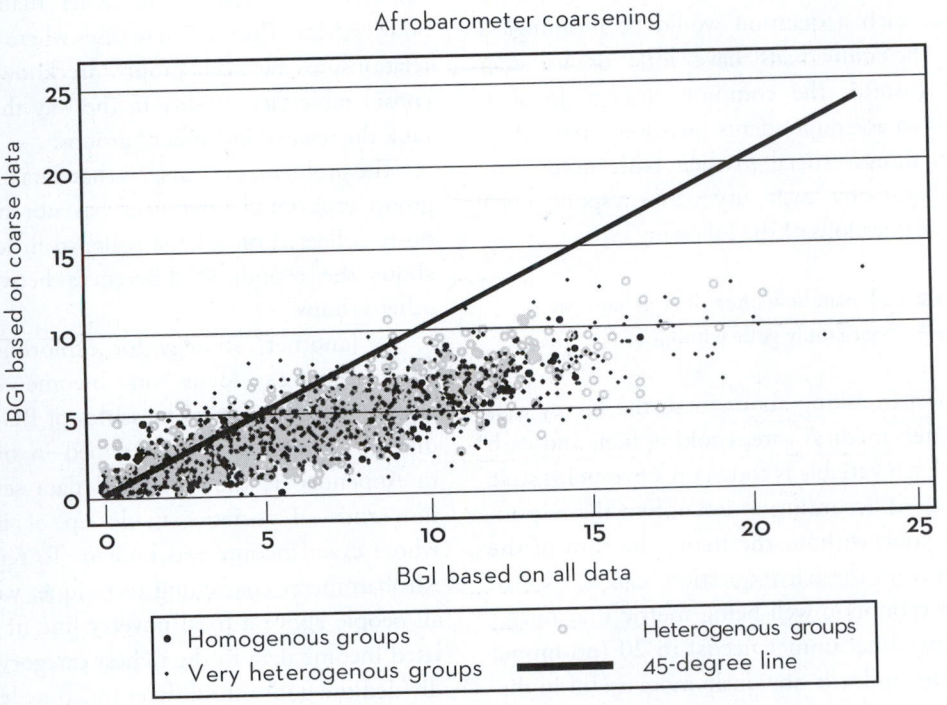

we can see that for any assumption about group income heterogeneity and for any of the three coarsening techniques, on average, the coarsened metrics underestimate the true level of between-group inequality. But we also find that the correlation between the true BGI and the BGI based on the coarsened data is very strong, ranging from 0.76 (when groups are most heterogenous) to 0.87 (when groups are most homogenous).

Thus, despite the fact that the Afrobarometer suppresses information about income differences among the nonpoor, it provides measures of BGI that are highly correlated with finer measures of BGI. Furthermore, the Afrobarometer measures are biased in the "right" direction to the extent that they systematically underestimate the true BGI. This should make it more difficult to find differential results of ELF and BGI on public goods provision.

Comparing Ethnolinguistic Fractionalization, Cultural Fractionalization, and Between-Group Inequality

ELF, CF, and BGI measure theoretically distinct concepts. But are the three measures also empirically distinct? Are the countries with the greatest linguistic differences between ethnic groups different from the countries with the greatest economic differences between groups?

Figure 3.6 depicts the relationships between the three measures of ethnic diversity, with each of the measures standarized to have a mean of 0 and a standard deviation of 1. First, consider the relationship between CF and ELF, which is also discussed in Fearon (2003). For his full set

Figure 3.6 Ethnolinguistic Fractionalization (ELF), Cultural Fractionalization (CF), and Between-Group Inequality (BGI) in 46 Countries

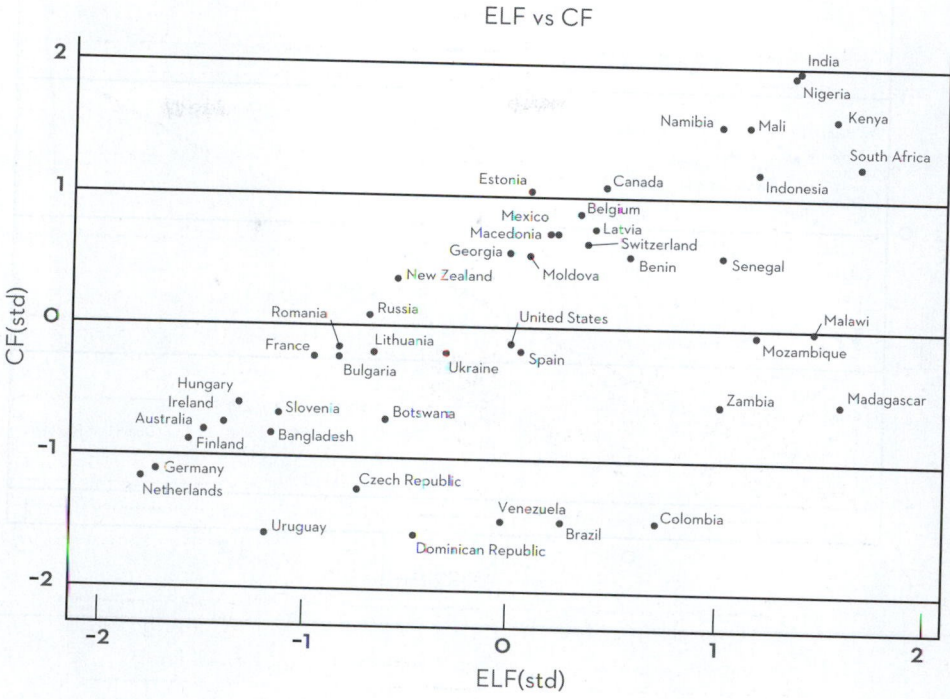

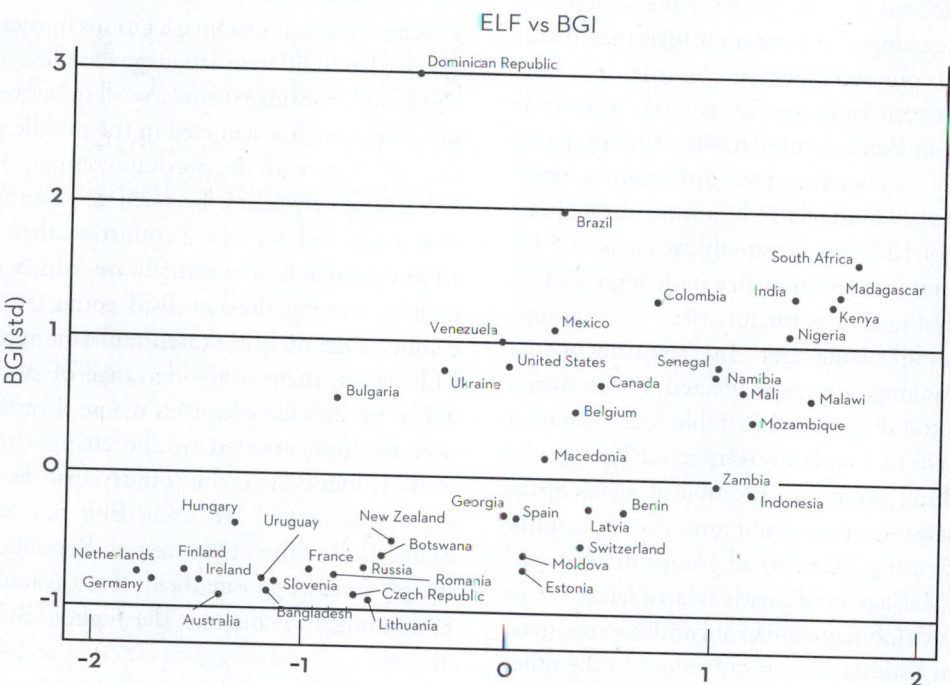

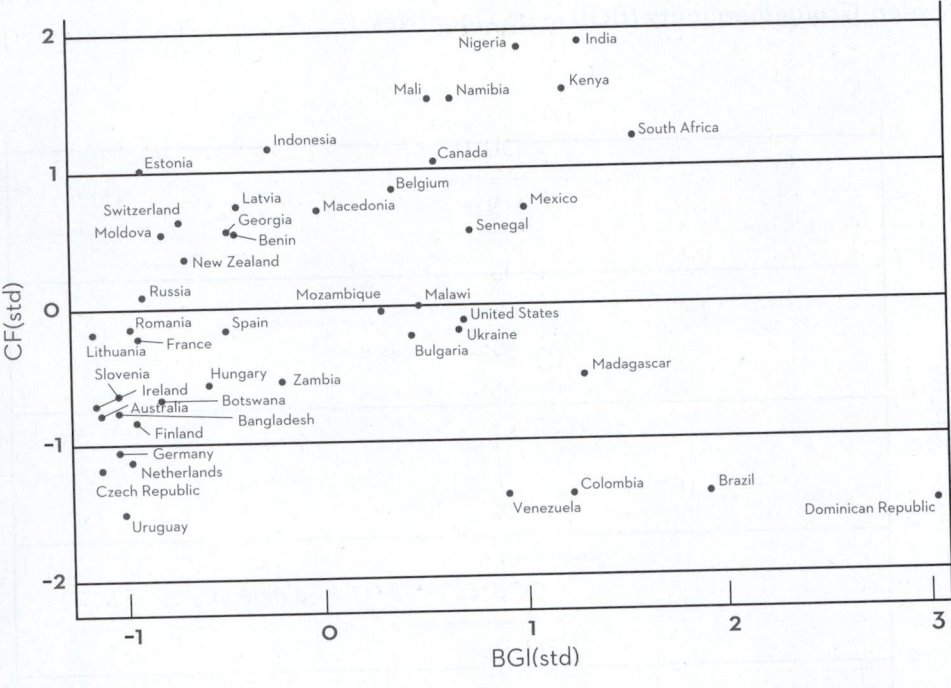

of countries, he found that the two measures are highly correlated ($r = 0.79$), with the largest differences occurring in sub-Saharan Africa and Latin America. In our subset of 46 countries, the correlation between ELF and CF is 0.64, somewhat lower than in Fearon's full data set. The top panel in Figure 3.6 shows that the correlation between the two variables is relatively strong throughout the range of ELF, but definitely weakens as ELF grows. A number of countries with high ELF— particularly those in Latin America—have groups that use similar languages. The countries whose diversity rankings are most affected by the switch from ELF to CF are listed in Table 3.6. Colombia ranks 13th in ELF and only 43rd in CF because the various ethnic groups in Colombia all speak Spanish. Madagascar is the second most diverse country in the data using ELF. But all groups in Madagascar speak Malagasy or a closely related language, so Madagascar's CF score ranks only 30th in the data. Russia and Estonia, in contrast, move in the other

direction, each increasing 13 places in the country rankings when one switches from ELF to CF. This is because the main language groups in these countries are from different language families.

Second, consider the relationship between ELF and BGI, which is depicted in the middle panel of Figure 3.6. As with the previous comparison, there is a strong correlation between the two variables ($r = 0.62$), but for many countries, their relative ranking depends substantially on which measure is used. Among the low BGI countries, there is a wide range of ELF scores, and among the high ELF scores, there is a wide range of BGI scores. Table 3.7 lists the countries whose diversity rankings are most affected by the change from ELF to BGI. Indonesia is the country that declines the most: it is ranked 7th using ELF but only 23rd using BGI. The Dominican Republic moves sharply in the opposite direction: it is ranked only 29th using ELF but has the highest BGI in the data set.

Table 3.6 Countries Whose Diversity Rankings Change Most When Switching from ELF to CF

Country	COUNTRIES WITH LARGEST DECLINE IN RANK		
	ELF Rank	CF Rank	Δ Rank
Colombia	13	43	–30
Madagascar	2	30	–28
Brazil	19	42	–23
Zambia	11	31	–20
Venezuela	27	44	–17
Malawi	4	21	–17
Dominican Republic	29	46	–17

Country	COUNTRIES WITH LARGEST INCREASE IN RANK		
	ELF Rank	CF Rank	Δ Rank
Russia	33	20	13
Estonia	22	9	13
Romania	35	24	11
Georgia	26	15	11
New Zealand	30	19	11

CF, cultural fractionalization; ELF, ethnolinguistic fractionalization.

The bottom panel in Figure 3.6 examines the relationship between CF and BGI. The correlation between these two variables ($r = 0.17$) is quite weak. As is clear in Figure 3.6, a number of countries, particularly in Latin America, have very high levels of between-group inequality but low levels of language difference. Furthermore, there are a number of countries, particularly in eastern and central Europe, where language differences are large, but between-group economic differences are relatively small.

The analysis therefore demonstrates that the three diversity measures, although related, are clearly distinct. The relative rankings of the countries change,

at times dramatically, across the different measures. Incorporating information about cultural fractionalization or the economic well-being of groups therefore alters how we understand the relative ethnic diversity of countries.

Group Differences and Public Goods Provision

Although the three measures differ, do the differences matter for understanding the relationship between diversity and public goods provision? Does

Table 3.7 Countries Whose Diversity Rankings Change Most When Switching from ELF to BGI

	COUNTRIES WITH LARGEST DECLINE IN RANK		
Country	ELF Rank	BGI Rank	Δ Rank
Indonesia	7	23	–16
Lithuania	32	46	–14
Switzerland	17	30	–13
Malawi	4	16	–13
Mozambique	8	20	–12

	COUNTRIES WITH LARGEST INCREASE IN RANK		
Country	ELF Rank	BGI Rank	Δ Rank
Dominican Republic	29	1	28
Bulgaria	36	18	18
Brazil	19	2	17
Venezuela	27	10	17
Ukraine	28	13	15

BGI, between-group inequality; ELF, ethnolinguistic fractionalization.

one of the measures have a stronger relationship with public goods provision than the others, suggesting that it may be the more important factor driving the relationship between ethnic diversity and poor governance outcomes? This section presents results from a series of regression models that analyze the relationship between the measures of diversity and public goods provision.

The models in this section treat a country as the unit of analysis. As noted previously, the survey data used to construct the BGI measures are from the 1996 to 2006 time period. When multiple surveys exist for a given country, we average across the surveys, minimizing measurement error that may be associated with particular surveys. We also average the World Bank's World Development Indicators (WDIs) used to measure public goods over the 1996 to 2006 period, which is important given that the WDIs are often missing in particular years. Because ELF and CF are constant over time, the strategy of using a country as a unit of analysis also facilitates comparison of the correlations between the various measures of diversity and public goods provision.

To measure public goods provision, we rely on ten variables in the World Bank's WDIs, each related to government-provided public goods, such as public health, education, public infrastructure, and the government's taxing capacity. There are a larger number of candidate variables in the WDI data set, but many have large numbers of missing values. We averaged the country values for each variable for the period 1996–2006, and then retained only those variables such that (1) none of the 46 countries had more than 3 missing, and (2) no variable was missing for more than 7 of the 46 countries. The resulting ten variables used in the analysis, with the number of missing countries in brackets, are as follows:

- Expenditure per student, primary (% of GDP per capita) [7]
- Public spending on education, total (% of GDP) [1]
- Immunization, measles (% of children aged 12–23 months) [0]
- Immunization, DPT (% of children aged 12–23 months) [0]
- Improved sanitation facilities (% of population with access) [7]
- Improved water source (% of population with access) [6]
- Roads, paved (% of total roads) [0]
- Procedures to enforce a contract (number) [0]
- Tax revenue (% of GDP) [4]
- Telephone lines (number per 100 people) [0]

Each variable alone is a noisy predictor of the overall level of public goods provision in a country, susceptible to measurement error that is likely idiosyncratic to particular countries. Therefore, rather than choosing one or more specific variables for analysis, we use the information from all ten variables to create a single measure of the overall level of public goods provision. To this end, we conduct a factor analysis on all ten variables. We then use the first dimension of the factor analysis to create the dependent variable, which we call *Public Goods*. The results for the first factor in this factor analysis are shown in Table 3.8. All ten of the variables load strongly on the first factor. The variables with the strongest relationship to the underlying factor, and which therefore receive the greatest weight in the construction of the public goods variable, are immunizations, sanitation, water, and telephone lines, all with factor loadings greater than 0.8. Two

Table 3.8 Factor Analysis of Public Goods Variables

Variable	Factor 1
Primary school spending	0.47
Total public spending on education	0.52
Measles immunizations	0.82
DPT immunizations	0.88
Sanitation facilities	0.91
Water source	0.86
Roads	0.70
Contract enforcement	-0.58
Tax revenue	0.41
Telephone lines	0.85

Eigenvalue of factor 1: 5.21
Proportion of variance explained by factor 1: 0.69

variables have a loading that is less than 0.5—Tax Revenue and Primary School Spending—but each variable still has a relatively strong relationship with the underlying factor. The first factor explains 69% of the variance in these ten variables. Figure 3.7 plots Public Goods against the log of GDP per capita (measured in purchasing power parity). The two variables are obviously strongly correlated, but at any level of economic development, and in particular at lower levels of development, there exists variation in the level of public goods.

We estimate OLS models with robust standard errors using Public Goods as the dependent variable. The models include several controls. One is the level of economic development [*GDP/capita* (*ln*), measured using purchasing power parity], which is known to have a very strong relationship with the level of public goods provision. Scholars have also emphasized the importance of democracy for public goods provision (e.g., Lake and Baum

Figure 3.7 Public Goods Provision and National Wealth

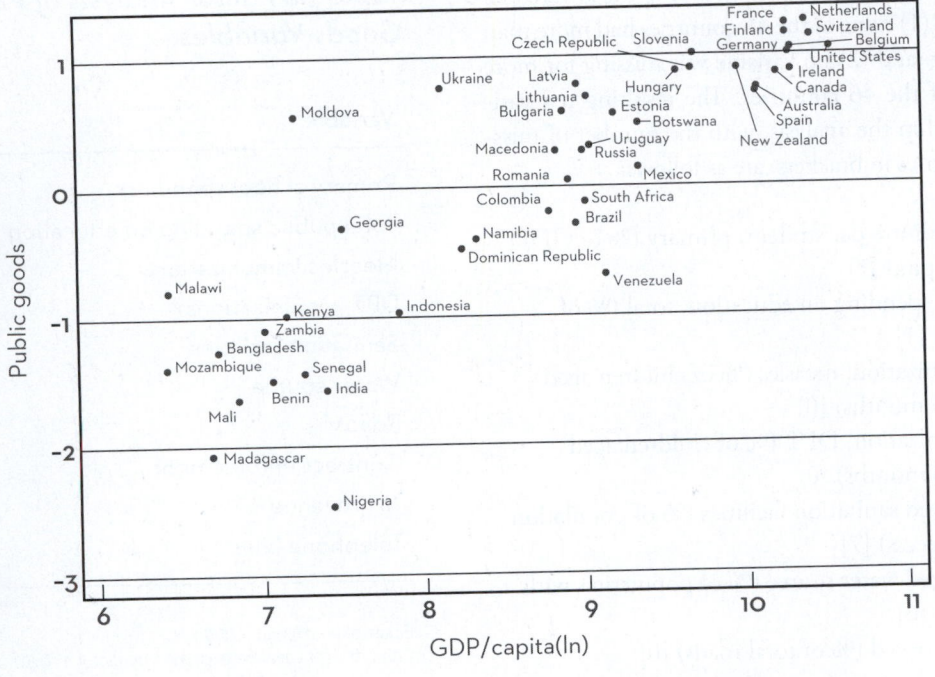

2001), and although we focus on countries that are in some sense democratic (achieving Polity 2 scores of greater than or equal to 1), there is considerable variation within our data set regarding the development of democratic institutions and practices. We therefore include *Polity 2* as a control for the level of democratic institutionalization. It is also important to take into account the population of a country. If there are economies of scale, then public goods provision may be largest in the most populous countries. But if the most populous countries present the most challenges to governance, public goods provision may be negatively correlated with population. In the regression models, we standardize each continuous right-hand-side variable to have a mean of 0 and a standard deviation of 1. This makes it straightforward to compare the size of the effects of the different variables. The parentheses in the tables provide the *p* values for the estimated coefficients.

In Table 3.9, models 1 to 4 include the controls and one of the measures of diversity. Model 1 includes ELF. Consistent with previous research, the coefficient for ELF is in the expected negative direction and is very precisely estimated. Model 2 uses Fearon's cultural fractionalization measure of diversity. The coefficient is in the expected negative direction but is very small and estimated with considerable error. Model 3 uses the Desmet, Ortuño, and Weber measure of cultural fractionalization instead of Fearon's measure. The coefficient has the wrong sign and is also estimated with considerable error. Finally, in model 4, the coefficient for BGI is negative and very precisely estimated. In models including only one measure of ethnic diversity, then, ELF and BGI have a clear relationship to public goods provision, but cultural differences do not.

Next we examine the results when we include measures of each form of diversity in the same model. Model 5 uses the Fearon measure of cultural fractionalization, and model 6 uses the Desmet, Ortuño-Ortín, and Weber measure. In both

Table 3.9 Group Differences and Public Goods Provision I

	(1)	(2)	(3)	(4)	(5)	(6)	(7)
ELF	−0.210	—	—	—	0.009	0.072	0.096
	(0.005)				(0.950)	(0.473)	(0.327)
CF-Fearon	—	−0.007	—	—	0.089	—	—
		(0.928)			(0.383)		
CF-Desmet	—	—	−0.024	—	—	0.069	—
			(0.764)			(0.326)	
BGI	—	—	—	−0.137	−0.133	−0.166	−0.168
				(0.041)	(0.093)	(0.023)	(0.026)
GDP(ln)	0.635	0.733	0.737	0.492	0.474	0.461	0.506
	(0.000)	(0.000)	(0.000)	(0.007)	(0.007)	(0.008)	(0.004)
Population	−0.140	−0.173	−0.168	−0.200	−0.237	−0.240	−0.216
	(0.004)	(0.002)	(0.001)	(0.001)	(0.000)	(0.000)	(0.001)
Polity 2	0.123	0.159	0.149	0.172	0.207	0.224	0.190
	(0.351)	(0.272)	(0.265)	(0.146)	(0.094)	(0.074)	(0.124)
Afrobarometer	—	—	—	−0.620	−0.684	−0.761	−0.676
				(0.038)	(0.038)	(0.025)	(0.036)
WVS	—	—	—	−0.043	−0.015	−0.061	−0.015
				(0.747)	(0.911)	(0.679)	(0.916)
CSES	—	—	—	0.141	0.177	0.145	0.196
				(0.447)	(0.327)	(0.461)	(0.287)
Constant	0.000	0.000	0.000	0.149	0.149	0.192	0.143
	(1.000)	(1.000)	(1.000)	(0.282)	(0.277)	(0.177)	(0.293)
Adj. R squared	0.787	0.761	0.761	0.832	0.829	0.829	0.830
N	46	46	46	46	46	46	46

Notes: P value based on robust standard errors are in parentheses. BGI between-group inequality; CF, cultural fractionalization; CSES, Comparative Study of Electoral Systems; ELF, ethnolinguistic fractionalization; GDP, gross domestic product; WVS, World Values Survey.

models, the coefficient for cultural fractionalization is very imprecisely estimated and has the wrong sign. The models also show that when BGI and ELF are included in the same model, the relationship between ELF and Public Goods disappears. The ELF coefficient now has the wrong sign and is estimated with large error, whereas the coefficient from BGI remains negatively and rather precisely estimated, especially in model 6.

We have estimated a wide range of additional models, and the results for cultural fractionalization are consistently estimated with very large error and often have the wrong sign. Because there is no empirical support for including this variable and it is strongly correlated with ELF, model 7 presents results when only BGI and ELF are included (along with the controls). ELF is positive, although it is estimated with considerable error, and the coefficient for BGI remains negative and precisely estimated. These results from Table 3.9 therefore suggest the possibility that in previous research claiming a correlation between ELF and public goods provision, the relationship was actually being driven by between-group economic differences. * * *

Conclusion

The empirical analysis tells a clear story. First, and most important, we find a strong and robust relationship between the level of public goods provision and between-group inequality. In contrast, neither traditional measures of ELF nor cultural differences between groups (measured using information about the languages groups speak) has such a relationship. Second, although there are clear limits on how hard we can push our data, we have suggestive evidence that between-group economic differences lead to lower public goods provision, particularly in the less established democracies. Third, we find that when controlling for group economic differences, the overall level of inequality itself has no impact on public goods provision. The analysis therefore strongly suggests that paying more attention to group economic

differences will yield strong dividends in efforts to understand the impacts of ethnic diversity and inequality on governance.

Several avenues for future research are worth pursuing. Although the BGI data employed in this article provide useful information about group economic differences, it is important to continue the search for more fine-grained measures of group income to estimate BGI. It is equally important to explore the possibility of measuring cultural differences using factors other than language, such as religion. Additional insight could also be achieved by exploring other definitions of groups in efforts to determine how robust the results are to alternative categorizations of the ethnic groups themselves.

Second, the analysis here assumes that the effect of between-group differences on governance is the same across political systems. But do some institutional forms for governance mitigate or exacerbate the effect of BGI on outcomes? We find, for example, that the negative effect of BGI is largest when the most well-developed democracies are eliminated from the data set, suggesting that there may be an interaction between the level of democracy and BGI. And it may be the case that particular forms of democracy may mediate the effect of BGI. Does federalism, for example, soften the impact of between-group differences on governance by giving groups autonomy to provide the public goods they most value?

Finally, we have provided some evidence that BGI has a causal impact on public goods provision. But as we noted, there are good reasons to suspect that public goods policy also affects between-group inequality. It is certainly possible—perhaps even likely—that these two variables are mutually and negatively reinforcing: low public goods provision exacerbates group economic differences, which impedes public goods provision, which exacerbates group-based inequality, and so forth. We cannot use our data to explore this issue, but it is clear that group-based economic differences do not arise by chance—they are the result of political processes that unfold over time, and that are reinforced or ameliorated by government policy decisions. Between-group inequality might therefore be rightly construed as a measure of group-based discrimination, and the level of such discrimination clearly varies across countries with similar levels of ethnic or cultural fractionalization. Why, then, do some countries have higher levels of group-based inequality than others? And what role does public goods provision play in answering this question? In light of the findings in this study, addressing this question should play a large role in improving our understanding of how between-group economic differences affect policy making.

NOTES

1. The measure of ELF used in this article is from Fearon (2003) and is based on data from the early 1990s. We discuss his system for identifying groups later.

2. Both languages follow these seven branches: Indo-European, Italic, Romance, Italo-Western, Western, Gallo-Iberian, Ibero-Romance. At this point, they diverge in their linguistic classification, with Spanish on the West-Iberian branch and Catalan on the East-Iberian branch.

3. The main difference between these measures is the α they use in calculating cultural fractionalization; however, they also rely on different data to identify ethnic groups. Fearon uses his classification of ethnic groups, based on data from the early 1990s, and Desmet, Ortuño-Ortín, and Weber (2009) use data from the 2005 *Ethnologue*.

4. On the decomposition of the Gini into its between, within, and overlap components, see Pyatt (1976) and Yitzhaki and Lerman (1991).

5. The innovation of the GELF is that it does not *require* one to impose *ex ante* group partitions onto the data. However, in research where scholars are interested in comparing exogenously defined groups, GELF is very similar to BGI. The GELF equivalent of BGI would be based on a "similarity matrix," where individuals from the same ethnic group have the same income and where the similarity between members of any two different ethnic groups is a function of the distance between the

mean incomes of the two ethnic groups (normalized to range from 0 to 1).

6. There are three usable WVS surveys from African countries, each of which also has an Afrobarometer survey. Because the Afrobarometer measure of "income" is quite different than the measure of income from WVS, and because we are taking averages when we have multiple surveys, we do not include these three WVS surveys in our analysis. When these three WVS surveys are included, the results are not affected. For WVS and CSES, we impute missing values for income using standard demographic variables. There are few missing values for the relevant variables in the Afrobarometer surveys.

REFERENCES

Alesina, Alberto, Reza Baqir, and William Easterly. 1999. "Public Goods and Ethnic Divisions." *Quarterly Journal of Economics* 114 (4): 1243–84.

Alesina, Alberto, Arnaud Devleeschauwer, William Easterly, Sergio Kurlat, and Romain Wacziarg. 2003. "Fractionalization." *Journal of Economic Growth* 8 (2): 155–94.

Alesina, Alberto, and Allen Drazen. 1991. "Why Are Stabilizations Delayed?" *American Economic Review* 81 (5): 1170–88.

Alesina, Alberto, and Eliana La Ferrara. 2005. "Ethnic Diversity and Economic Performance." *Journal of Economic Literature* 43 (3): 762–800.

Alesina, Alberto, and Enrico Spolaore. 1997. "On the Number and Size of Nations." *Quarterly Journal of Economics* 112 (4): 1027–56.

Bacharach, Michael, and Diego Gambetta. 2001. "Trust as Type Detection." In *Trust and Deception in Virtual Societies*, eds. Christiano Castelfranchi and Yao-Hua Tan. Norwell, MA: Kluwer Academic, 1–26.

Bardhan, Pranab. 2000. "Irrigation and Cooperation: An Empirical Analysis of 48 Irrigation Communities in South India." *Economic Development and Cultural Change* 48: 847–65.

Bossert, Walter, Conchita D'Ambrosio, and Eliana La Ferrara. n.d. "A Generalized Index of Fractionalization." *Economica*. Forthcoming.

Collier, Paul. 2000. "Ethnicity, Politics and Economic Performance." *Economics and Politics* 12 (3): 222–45.

Dayton-Johnson, Jeff. 2000. "The Determinants of Collective Action on the Local Commons: A Model with Evidence from Mexico." *Journal of Development Economics* 62 (1): 181–208.

Desmet, Klaus, Ignacio Ortuño-Ortín, and Shlomo Weber. 2009. "Linguistic Diversity and Redistribution." *Journal of the European Economic Association* 7 (6): 1291–318.

Deutsch, Karl. 1966. *Nationalism and Social Communication.* Cambridge: MIT Press.

Easterly, William, and Ross Levine. 1997. "Africa's Growth Tragedy: Policies and Ethnic Divisions." *Quarterly Journal of Economics* 112 (4): 1203–50.

Fearon, James. 2003. "Ethnic and Cultural Diversity by Country." *Journal of Economic Growth* 8 (2): 195–222.

Fearon, James, and David Laitin. 1996. "Explaining Interethnic Cooperation." *American Political Science Review* 90 (4): 715–35.

Fernández, Raquel, and Gilat Levy. 2008. "Diversity and Redistribution." *Journal of Public Economics* 92: 925–43.

Gellner, Ernest. 1983. *Nations and Nationalism.* Ithaca, NY: Cornell University Press.

Greenberg, Joseph H. 1956. "The Measurement of Linguistic Diversity." *Language* 32: 109–15.

Greif, Avner. 1994. "Cultural Beliefs and the Organization of Society." *Journal of Political Economy* 102 (5): 912–50.

Habyarimana, James, Macartan Humphreys, Daniel Posner, and Jeremy Weinstein. 2009. *Coethnicity: Diversity and Dilemmas of Collective Action.* New York: Russell Sage Press.

Khwaja, Asim. 2009. "Can Good Projects Succeed in Bad Communities?" *Journal of Public Economics* 93 (7–8): 899–916.

Knack, Stephen, and Philip Keefer. 1997. "Does Social Capital Have an Economic Payoff? A Cross-Country Investigation." *Quarterly Journal of Economics* 112 (4): 1251–88.

Laitin, David. 1994. "The Tower of Babel as a Coordination Game: Political Linguistics in Ghana." *American Political Science Review* 88 (3): 622–34.

Laitin, David. 1998. *Identity in Formation: The Russian-Speaking Population in the Near Abroad.* Ithaca, NY: Cornell University Press.

Lake, David, and Matthew Baum. 2001. "The Invisible Hand of Democracy: Political Control and the Provision of Public Services." *Comparative Political Studies* 34 (6): 587–621.

La Porta, Rafael, Florencio Lopez-de-Silanes, Andrei Shleifer, and Robert W. Vishny. 1999. "The Quality of Government." *The Journal of Law, Economics, and Organization* 15 (1): 22–79.

Mancini, Luca. 2008. "Horizontal Inequality and Communal Violence: Evidence from Indonesian Districts." In *Horizontal Inequalities and Conflict: Understanding Group Violence in Multiethnic Societies*, ed. Frances Stewart. London: Palgrave, 106–35.

Mancini, Luca, Frances Stewart, and Graham K. Brown. 2008. "Approaches to the Measurement of Horizontal Inequalities." In *Horizontal Inequalities and Conflict: Understanding Group Violence in Multiethnic Societies*, ed. Francis Stewart. London: Palgrave McMillan, 85–101.

Massey, Douglas S., and Nancy A. Denton. 1988. "The Dimensions of Residential Segregation." *Social Forces* 67(2): 281–315.

Miguel, Edward, and Mary Kay Gugerty. 2005. "Ethnic Diversity, Social Sanctions, and Public Goods in Kenya." *Journal of Public Economics* 89 (11–12): 2325–68.

Milanovic, Branko. 2005. *Worlds Apart: Measuring International and Global Inequality.* Princeton, NJ: Princeton University Press.

Milroy, Lesley. 1987. *Language and Social Networks.* Oxford: Wiley-Blackwell.

Olson, Mancur. 1993. "Dictatorship, Democracy and Development." *American Political Science Review* 87 (3): 567–76.

Posner, Daniel. 2004. "Measuring Ethnic Fractionalization in Africa." *American Journal of Political Science* 48 (4): 849–63.

Pyatt, Graham. 1976. "On the Interpretation and Disaggregation of Gini Coefficients." *The Economic Journal* 86: 243–55.

Sen, Amartya. 1999. *Development as Freedom.* New York: Anchor Books.

Solt, Frederick. 2009. "Standardizing the World Income Inequality Database." *Social Science Quarterly* 90 (2): 231–42.

Uslaner, Eric M. 2002. *The Moral Foundations of Trust.* New York: Cambridge University Press.

Uslaner, Eric M. 2008. *Corruption, Inequality, and the Rule of Law: The Bulging Pocket Makes the Easy Life.* New York: Cambridge University Press.

Yitzhaki, Shlomo, and Robert Lerman. 1991. "Income Stratification and Income Inequality." *Review of Income and Wealth* 37 (3): 313–29.

Lars-Erik Cederman, Nils B. Weidmann, and Kristian Skrede Gleditsch

HORIZONTAL INEQUALITIES AND ETHNONATIONALIST CIVIL WAR: A GLOBAL COMPARISON

Although logistical and power-related conditions—such as low state-level per capita income, weak state institutions, and peripheral and inaccessible territory—enjoy near-consensus support as explanations of civil war onset, most of the contemporary literature regards explanations rooted in political and economic grievances with suspicion (Blattman and Miguel 2010). In fact, the debate over the status of grievances in such explanations dates back at least to the 1960s, with the introduction of relative deprivation theory. Inspired by psychological theories of conflict, Gurr (1970) and his colleagues argued that economic and other types of inequality increase the risk of internal strife through frustrated expectations. In contrast, today's most influential quantitative studies of civil war give short shrift to grievance-based accounts, based on reports that unequal individual wealth distributions have no statistically distinguishable relationship to internal conflict (e.g., Collier and Hoeffler 2004; Fearon and Laitin 2003).

Yet, despite these alleged nonfindings, the debate over grievances is far from dead. Indeed, inequality continues to occupy a prominent place in the qualitative literature on civil wars and has repeatedly been linked to conflict processes (Sambanis 2005, 323; Stewart 2008; Wood 2003). Moreover, in the last few years, some quantitative studies have started to appear that argue that the current literature's failure to connect distributional asymmetries with conflict behavior may actually be due to inappropriate conceptualization and imperfect measurements, rather than reflecting a fundamental absence of any causal effect (Østby 2008; see also Stewart 2008).

Also relying on quantitative evidence, we join these recent contributions in shifting the explanatory focus from individualist to group-level accounts of inequality and conflict. Because formidable problems of data availability associated with the uneven

From *American Political Science Review* 105, no. 3 (August 2011), pp. 478–95.

coverage and comparability of surveys have stood in the way of assessing such "horizontal inequalities" (HIs), most scholars have had to content themselves with selective case studies or statistical samples restricted to particular world regions.

To overcome these difficulties, we combine our newly geocoded data on politically relevant ethnic groups' settlement areas with Nordhaus's (2006) spatial wealth measures, both with global coverage. Based on this novel strategy, we present the first truly worldwide comparison of horizontal inequality and ethnonationalist civil wars. Controlling for political power access, we show that both advanced and backward ethnic groups are more likely to experience such conflict than groups whose wealth lies closer to the national average. Moreover, in agreement with a broad conception of horizontal inequalities, we find that both political and economic inequalities contribute to civil war.

■ ■ ■

Theorizing Horizontal Inequalities

* * * The starting point of our approach to ethnonationalist warfare is the realization that ethnic groups find themselves in radically different situations for various historical reasons. Whereas some ethnic groups came out on top of the geopolitical game, others were conquered early on, and therefore lost out in the competition for wealth and influence. Moreover, the uneven spread of nationalism delayed mass-level political mobilization in many parts of the world, thus creating differences in both economic and political development that were often exploited by alien rulers (Gellner 1964). As argued by Tilly (1999), nationalism can be thought of as a case of "categorical inequality" because

> it asserts and creates paired and unequal categories, either (a) rival aspirants to nationhood or (b) members of the authentic nation versus others. It involves

claims to prior control over a state, hence to the exclusion of others from that priority. It authorizes agents of the nation to subordinate, segregate, stigmatize, expel, or even exterminate others in the nation's name. (172)

■ ■ ■

* * * We view HIs as structural asymmetries that make ethnonationalist civil war more likely and adopt an indirect research strategy that explains the effect of inequality by postulating a set of causal mechanisms. * * * First, we postulate that objective political and economic asymmetries can be transformed into grievances through a process of group comparison driven by collective emotions. Second, we argue that such grievances trigger violent collective action through a process of group mobilization.

■ ■ ■

What are the observable implications of our analytical framework? The first, and most obvious, hypothesis expects a positive effect of economic HIs on civil war onset. If the causal chain operates as we have postulated, there should be a statistically discernible signal indicating that ethnic groups with GDP per capita far from a country's average have a higher risk of experiencing conflict:

> H1. Economic HIs increase the likelihood of civil war.

However, * * * an uneven wealth distribution is not the only possible type of structural asymmetry. * * * We hypothesize that both economic and political HIs contribute jointly to the outbreak of civil war. Even controlling for political HIs, such as groups' exclusion from political power, income inequalities among ethnic groups should increase the risk of civil war. * * * Our second hypothesis summarizes these theoretical expectations:

> H2. Economic and political HIs both increase the likelihood of civil war.

So far, we have not differentiated between advanced and backward groups' conflict-proneness. As Horowitz (1985) explains, arguments can be advanced for both types of economic HIs leading to a higher risk of conflict. Poorer groups, especially those residing in backward and peripheral regions, often desire to break away from the cores of their countries regardless of the cost, because they perceive themselves to be systematically disadvantaged compared to their wealthier compatriots in terms of economic development and distribution of public goods. Perceptions of disadvantage also characterize members of some relatively wealthy groups, especially if they feel that state-level redistribution denies them the fruits of their success: "Advantaged regions usually generate more income and contribute more revenue to the treasury of the undivided state than they receive. They believe that they are subsidizing poorer regions" (Horowitz 1985, 249–50). Because these groups have more to lose, and are sometimes demographically represented outside their original settlement areas, however, they can be more cost-sensitive as regards secession, but such cases do occur, as illustrated by Slovenia and Croatia (cf. Gourevitch 1979). Nevertheless, there is no reason to assume that the effect of group inequality is perfectly symmetric around relative equality. Remaining agnostic as to the relative frequency of HIs in either direction, we therefore submit these arguments to separate tests by dividing H1 into two subhypotheses:

> H1a. Relatively poor ethnic groups are more likely to experience civil war.
> H1b. Relatively wealthy ethnic groups are more likely to experience civil war.

■ ■ ■

The only broadly available cross-national data source on variation in wealth within countries is the G-Econ data, developed by Nordhaus (2006; see also Nordhaus and Chen 2009).[1] The G-Econ dataset tries to assemble the best available data on local economic activity within countries for geographical grid cells, and convert these to comparable figures in purchasing power parity to allow meaningful comparisons. The resolution of the spatially explicit data set is 1° grid cells. The data are constructed from a variety of sources, including regional gross product data for the lowest available political subdivision, estimates of regional income by industry, and estimates of rural population and agricultural income. The specific methodologies differ by countries and data availability (see Nordhaus 2006 for a detailed discussion). The database has global coverage, but the temporal scope is limited to a single year, 1990.[2] We therefore restrict our analysis to the post–Cold War period, although we present supplementary results extending back to 1946 in the sensitivity analysis that follows. Because it is well known that relative inequality, as opposed to absolute wealth, is characterized by considerable inertia, these assumptions would seem plausible (Stewart and Langer 2008; Tilly 1999).[3]

Despite their relatively broad coverage, there are a number of disadvantages to the Nordhaus data for testing propositions on HIs. Any measure of the value of economic production is strictly speaking a "flow" measure and hence an imperfect proxy for the "stock" of wealth, although this criticism obviously applies with equal force to national-level productivity measures. Because the quality varies considerably across countries, the data are likely to understate the extent of inequality in countries with poor data coverage. Indeed, in some countries the official data may be of such poor quality that the variance is suppressed and accuracies of survey reports may be questionable. We will return to these issues in the section on sensitivity analyses.

Based on the G-Econ data, Buhaug et al. (n.d.) present the first global results on the relationship between spatial inequalities and civil war violence. However, their research design focuses on local measures of inequality across geographic grid cells and the specific locations where conflict first breaks out, and does not capture group-level participation or wealth differences. Another useful approach estimates the wealth of regional subunits of states (Sambanis and Milanovic 2009). A more direct assessment of HIs requires geocoded data on ethnic groups, and in view of H2, also information about their access to executive power. Fortunately, the Ethnic Power Relations dataset (EPR), together with its recent geocoded extension, GeoEPR, fulfills these requirements.

The EPR dataset identifies all politically relevant ethnic groups around the world and measures how access to state power differs among them in all years from 1946 to 2005 (Cederman, Wimmer, and Min 2010). Based on an online expert survey, the sample includes 733 politically relevant ethnic groups in 155 sovereign states.[4] The coding rules define as politically relevant all ethnic groups for which at least one political organization exists that promotes an ethnically oriented agenda in the national political arena, or ethnic groups that are subject to political discrimination. This dataset improves significantly on previous efforts to code ethnic groups' access to power, such as the Minorities at Risk (MAR) dataset (Gurr 1993), which restricts the sample to mobilized and/or discriminated-against minorities and thus largely overlooks the ethnopolitical constellation of power at the center, and Cederman and Girardin (2007), who rely on preliminary, static measures of the political status of ethnic groups and limit their sample to Eurasia and North Africa.

Because the politically relevant groups and their access to political power may change over time, the EPR dataset provides separate coding for subperiods from 1946 to 2005. For each such time period, the demographic size and access to power enjoyed by representatives of an ethnic group are specified. Focusing on executive power only, i.e., representation in the presidency, the cabinet, and senior posts in the administration, including the army, the coding rules categorize all politically relevant ethnic groups according to whether (1) their representatives enjoyed absolute power through monopoly or a dominant position in the executive branch,[5] (2) they shared power with other groups in a junior or senior role,[6] or (3) they were excluded altogether from executive decision making but enjoyed regional or separatist autonomy, or were powerless or discriminated against.[7] In our analysis that follows, we drop category 1, because according to our conflict coding, dominant and monopoly groups cannot by definition stage rebellions against themselves, and base the dummy variable of exclusion on the difference between categories 2 and 3.

To obtain spatial estimates of economic performance for EPR groups based on the Nordhaus grid, we need information on their settlement areas or regions. Because this overlay operation requires data on the precise extent of these regions rather than a simple textual description, existing datasets such as Minorities at Risk (Gurr 1993) are insufficient. We therefore rely on the recently completed GeoEPR dataset, a comprehensive geocoded version of the EPR groups (Wucherpfennig et al. n.d.). GeoEPR provides two types of information about ethnic groups. First, for each group in EPR, the dataset categorizes the type of settlement pattern, distinguishing between regional, urban, and migrant groups (plus mixed categories). For all groups with regional bases, GeoEPR represents the settlement area of a group as a polygon (or a set of polygons, if there is more than one group region in a country). In contrast to earlier geocoding attempts, GeoEPR also tracks major changes in the settlement pattern of a group over time, including those resulting from ethnic cleansing.

Our analysis requires conflict coding at the group level. Because groups as a whole typically do not participate in conflict (e.g., Kalyvas 2006), we use a refined procedure that codes whether a group has links to a rebel organization that was actively involved in fighting. These new data represent an improvement on previous group-level conflict coding used with the EPR data (cf. Cederman, Wimmer, and Min 2010). More precisely, we code our dependent variable as "1" if a rebel organization expresses its political aims (at least partly) in the name of the group *and* a significant number of members of the group were participating in the conflict. For a full sample of rebel groups and their conflict involvement, we rely on the Non-State Actors dataset (Cunningham, Gleditsch, and Salehyan 2009) that identifies the fighting organizations involved in civil wars (according to the Uppsala/PRIO Armed Conflicts Data, see Gleditsch et al. 2002). The link between these organizations and our EPR groups is provided by NSA2EPR, a new conflict resource that identifies organizations fighting for, and recruiting from, particular EPR groups. We provide a list of the conflict onset cases in the article.

Deriving Operational Measures

The G-Econ data allow deriving ethnic group–specific measures of wealth by overlaying polygons indicating group settlement areas with the cells in the Nordhaus data. Dividing the total sum of the economic production in the settlement area by the group's population size enables us to derive group-specific measures of per capita economic production, which can be compared to either the nationwide per capita product or the per capita product of privileged groups.

A visual illustration helps explain the estimation of group GDP from Nordhaus data. Figure 3.8 shows the G-Econ estimates as gray cells; darker shadings indicate wealthier cells. The map shows the spatial variation in wealth across the Yugoslav federation in 1990, based on the CShapes dataset for the historical boundaries (Weidmann, Kuse, and Gleditsch 2010). Relatively wealthy pockets appear primarily in the northwest of the country, in the constituent republics of Slovenia and Croatia. Compared to the other parts of the country, Serbia shows up as a generally poor region.

Together with the settlement areas of GeoEPR, the G-Econ data can now be used to estimate group wealth spatially. Figure 3.8 also shows the settlement regions for the Slovenes and the Albanians. Using techniques similar to those pioneered

in Cederman, Buhaug, and Rød (2009), we derive an indicator of group wealth by summing up the (population-weighted) proportions of the Nordhaus cells covered by a group.[8] For example, as a result of this procedure, the Slovenes get a high score, because their settlement region is located in the rich parts of Yugoslavia. Figure 3.9 shows horizontal inequality for Yugoslavia, measured as the ratio of the group's GDP per capita estimate to the average value for the entire country, depicting wealthier groups in darker shades and poorer ones in brighter shades. Slovenes and Croats receive high scores, but the opposite is true for the Albanians in Kosovo, which are among the poorest groups in the country.

As a further illustration, Figure 3.10 shows the same information for the Sudan. Unsurprisingly, the southern and western groups, the latter including the Fur, emerge as the most impoverished in that state. Extending the comparison to Myanmar, we

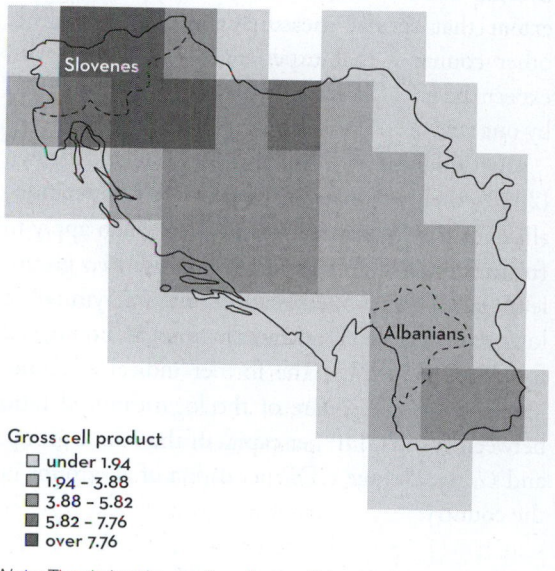

Figure 3.8 G-Econ Cells for Yugoslavia, Overlaid with GeoEPR Group Polygons for Slovenes and Albanians (1990)

Gross cell product
- ☐ under 1.94
- ☐ 1.94 – 3.88
- ☐ 3.88 – 5.82
- ☐ 5.82 – 7.76
- ☐ over 7.76

Note: The darker the shading, the wealthier the cells.

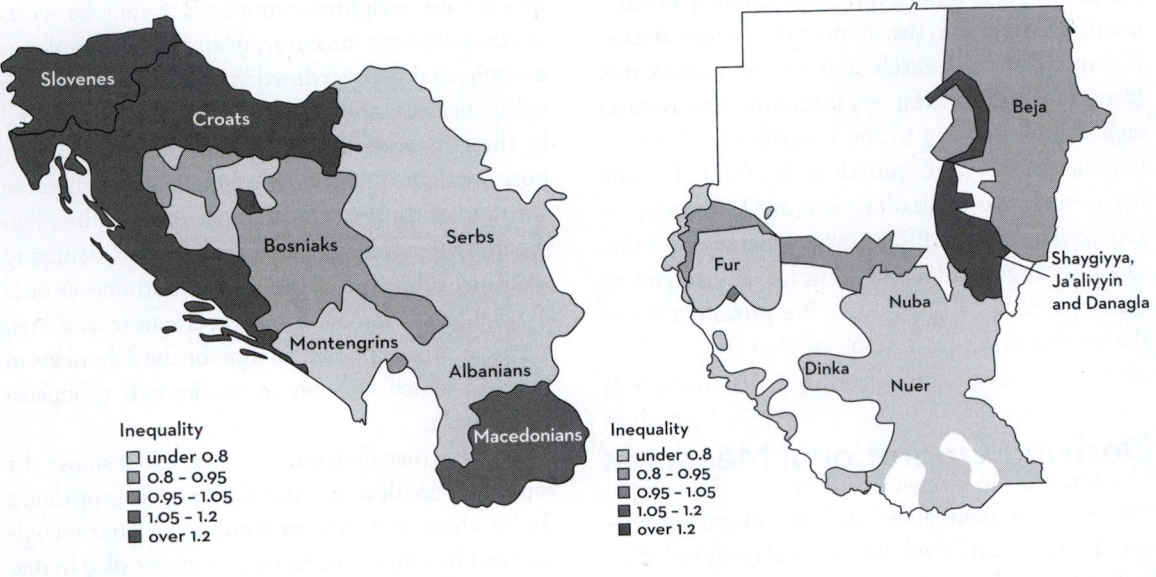

Figure 3.9 Result of Spatial Wealth Estimation for Groups in Yugoslavia

Slovenes
Croats
Bosniaks
Serbs
Montengrins
Albanians
Macedonians

Inequality
- under 0.8
- 0.8 – 0.95
- 0.95 – 1.05
- 1.05 – 1.2
- over 1.2

Figure 3.10 Result of Spatial Wealth Estimation for Groups in the Sudan

Beja
Fur
Nuba
Shaygiyya, Ja'aliyyin and Danagla
Dinka
Nuer

Inequality
- under 0.8
- 0.8 – 0.95
- 0.95 – 1.05
- 1.05 – 1.2
- over 1.2

also illustrate the limitations of our spatial approach (see Figure 3.11). Despite considerable wealth discrepancies between peripheral and central areas, the Nordhaus data exhibit very limited variation, because of underlying data quality issues. To the extent that similar measurement problems afflict other countries that experienced conflict, we can expect the effect of inequality to be underestimated by our study.

As explained by Mancini, Stewart, and Brown (2008), there are many different ways to operationalize horizontal inequalities, most of which apply to entire countries. In this article, we use two group-level measures of inequality, namely a symmetric logged form (see H1) and an asymmetric, nonlogged form (see H1a, 1b). The former indicator defines inequality as the square of the logarithmized ratio between g, the GDP per capita of the ethnic group, and G, the average GDP per capita of all groups in the country:

$$lineq2 = [\log(g/G)]^2.$$

Figure 3.11 Result of Spatial Wealth Estimation for Groups in Myanmar

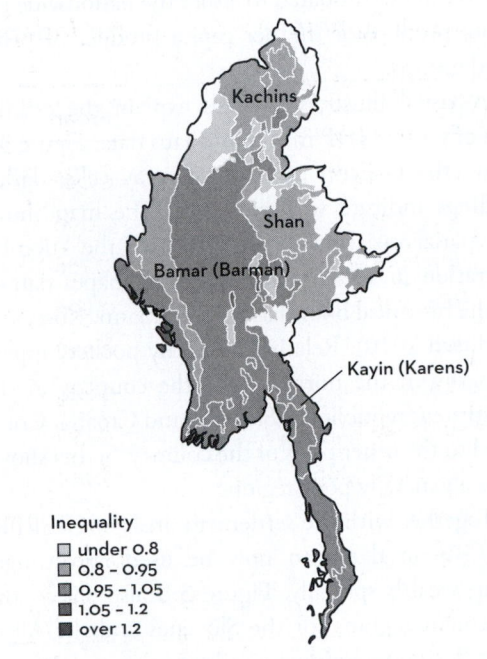

Kachins
Shan
Bamar (Barman)
Kayin (Karens)

Inequality
- under 0.8
- 0.8 – 0.95
- 0.95 – 1.05
- 1.05 – 1.2
- over 1.2

This definition captures deviations from the country average symmetrically and is zero for groups at the country average. As a complement to this symmetric indicator, we also measure inequality asymmetrically with two variables that correspond to groups that are poorer and wealthier than the country average, respectively:

$$low\_ratio = G/g \quad \text{if } g < G,$$
$$0 \quad \text{otherwise;}$$
$$high\_ratio = g/G \quad \text{if } g > G,$$
$$0 \quad \text{otherwise.}$$

This operationalization guarantees that deviations from the country mean are always positive numbers greater than one. For example, a group that is twice as wealthy as the average has $low\_ratio = 0$ and $high\_ratio = 2$, and a group that is three times poorer has $low\_ratio = 3$ and $high\_ratio = 0$. See Table 3.10, which offers descriptive statistics for these indicators and all other independent variables used in the analysis that follows.[9]

We use the nonspatial EPR dataset to derive variables capturing political HIs and group sizes. As we have seen earlier, the EPR dataset provides a time-varying indicator for groups' exclusion from central power. In addition, we measure the group's demographic power balance with the ethnic group(s) in power (EGIP) as its share of the dyadic population.[10] We use a combination of the linear and squared terms to capture the logic of bargaining theory, according to which intermediate power levels are the most conflict-prone, given that weaker groups stand no chance of prevailing in contests, whereas stronger ones do not necessarily have to resort to violence to get concessions (see Wucherpfenning 2011).

At the country level, we control for GDP per capita, based on nonspatial, time-varying statistics drawn from the Penn World Tables and World Bank sources, and num_excl, the total number of excluded groups in the country, as defined by EPR. Both measures should have a negative impact on conflict probability. A large number of studies find a negative

Table 3.10 Summary Statistics for Independent Variables

Variable	Mean	Std. Dev.	Min	Max
Inequality (*lineq*)	−0.067	0.303	−1.799	1.207
Inequality (*lineq2*)	0.096	0.291	0.000	3.238
Ineq. (*low_ratio*)	0.766	0.766	0.000	6.046
Ineq. (*high_ratio*)	0.496	0.614	0.000	3.344
Excluded	0.528	0.499	0.000	1.000
Power balance	0.248	0.262	0.000	1.000
Power balance (sq.)	0.130	0.222	0.000	1.000
GDP per capita (log)	7.944	1.060	5.231	10.494
No. excluded groups	8.405	13.706	0.000	46.000
Year	1998.093	4.300	1991.000	2005.000
Peace years	34.421	18.118	0.000	59.000

association between national GDP per capita and civil war onset (see Hegre and Sambanis 2006). According to Walter's (2006) strategic argument, the *num_excl* variable can be expected to be negatively related to the risk of conflict, because governments facing many ethnic groups fear domino effects and will thus be less willing to make concessions to single groups, as illustrated by Moscow's hard line in dealing with the Chechens' claims. This firmness can be expected to deter other groups from challenging the government. In addition, we also control for the calendar year, because we anticipate a declining trend in terms of conflict probability during the Cold War, thanks to benign effects in the international environment such as peaceful international norms and institutions (Gurr 2000). Finally, the models also contain nonparametric corrections for temporal dependence based on the *peace_years* variable, which measures the number of years a group has lived in peace, as proposed by Beck, Katz, and Tucker (1998).[11]

Empirical Analysis

We are now ready to present the results. Given the limited temporal availability of inequality data, we restrict the sample to group years after the Cold War, from 1991 through 2005. All groups represented in GeoEPR are included, except the dispersed ones that cover their respective countries' entire territory. This leaves us with about 450 groups per year or a total of 6,438 group years, with only 52 conflict onsets * * *. Unless otherwise stated, our analysis therefore relies on rare-events logit models. We compensate for country-level dependencies by estimating clustered standard errors.

Table 3.11 presents the main results. Our starting point is Model 1, which subjects the inequality hypothesis H1 to a first based on the *lineq2* variable. The result is both substantively and statistically significant, suggesting that groups with wealth levels far from the country average are indeed more likely to experience civil war.[12] Moreover, the other variables behave as expected. The coefficients of the variables measuring the demographic power balance point in the right direction, but fail to reach statistical significance. At the country level, both GDP per capita and calendar year have strongly negative effects on the probability of conflict, as theoretically expected. The coefficient for the variable capturing the number of ethnic groups is also negative, but nowhere near statistical significance at conventional levels. Finally, the temporal controls do not seem to make much of a difference, but are retained for comparative purposes.

To improve the precision of our inequality measures, Model 2 discards ethnic groups with a spatially estimated population less than 500,000. Although this censoring limits the number of group-year observations to 3,967 and the conflict onsets to 42, we prefer to rely on this specification.[13] Our spatial method becomes unreliable for small population sizes, primarily because of the low resolution of the G-Econ data and the limited precision of the population estimates for tiny groups.[14] Consequently, the group-size restriction almost triples the inequality coefficient reported in Model 2 without affecting the size of the standard error. Except for this important change, there are few other surprises, except that the coefficient for the *num_excl* variable now becomes significant.

Having considered H1, we now test H2, which postulates that both economic and political HIs increase the risk of internal conflict. Retaining the size restriction of the previous specification, Model 3 introduces a dummy variable for excluded groups that has a strong and statistically discernible impact on onset likelihood. However, this does not undermine the results with regard to economic inequality. This is an important result that strengthens our confidence that different types of grievances operate together and enables us to rule out the possibility that economic inequality could be an artifact of groups' access to executive power (and vice versa). Moreover, it is clear that the addition of the exclusion dummy either preserves or increases the effect of the other variables.[15] We illustrate the effect of inequality in Figure 3.12, which indicates how the

Table 3.11 Explaining Onset of Group-Level Conflict

	Model 1	Model 2	Model 3	Model 4	Model 5
	Group-level variables				
Inequality (*Iineq2*)	0.6661**	1.7463***	1.7342***		
	(0.2402)	(0.2484)	(0.2641)		
Inequality (*smooth*)				1.948***	
Ineq. (*low_ratio*)					1.1255***
					(0.1792)
Ineq. (*high_ratio*)					1.0875***
					(0.2305)
Excluded			1.1680**	1.241**	1.2066**
			(0.3394)	(0.3905)	(0.3702)
Power balance	3.4193	3.0782	5.0982*	5.966*	5.2988*
	(2.4250)	(2.6083)	(2.4433)	(2.789)	(2.4244)
Power balance (sq.)	−4.3510	−4.8846	−6.7212	−8.176*	−7.0736*
	(3.0444)	(3.5827)	(3.5345)	(4.038)	(3.5706)
	Country-level variables				
GDP/capita (log)	−0.4501*	−0.8442***	−0.8639***	−0.9106***	−0.8873***
	(0.1840)	(0.2254)	(0.2237)	(0.2351)	(0.2313)
No. excluded groups	−0.0132	−0.0399*	−0.0524**	−0.0578**	−0.0511**
	(0.0171)	(0.0185)	(0.0158)	(0.2955)	(0.0168)
Year	−0.1772**	−0.2166**	−0.2146***	−0.2213***	−0.2111***
	(0.0568)	(0.0602)	(0.0590)	(0.4816)	(0.0592)
	Group-level conflict history				
Peace years	−0.0190	0.1434	0.1482	0.1601	0.1540
	(0.1071)	(0.1106)	(0.1040)	(0.109)	(0.1038)
Spline 1	0.0007	0.0022	0.0025*	0.0026*	0.0026*
	(0.0010)	(0.0012)	(0.0011)	(0.0011)	(0.0011)
Spline 2	−0.0005	−0.0013	−0.0016*	−0.0017*	−0.0016*
	(0.0007)	(0.0008)	(0.0008)	(−0.0008)	(0.0007)
Spline 3	0.0001	0.0002	0.0003	0.0004	0.0004
	(0.0003)	(0.0003)	(0.0003)	(0.0003)	(0.0003)
Constant	353.3482**	434.7015***	429.9920***	443.7***	422.0450***
	(113.5753)	(120.2728)	(117.9401)	(96.18)	(118.2983)
Observations	6,438	3,967	3,967	3,967	3,967

Notes: Robust, country-clustered standard errors in parentheses.

***$p < .001$. **$p < .01$. *$p < .05$.

Figure 3.12 Predicted Effect of Horizontal Inequality on Probability of Civil War (See Model 3 of Table 3.11)

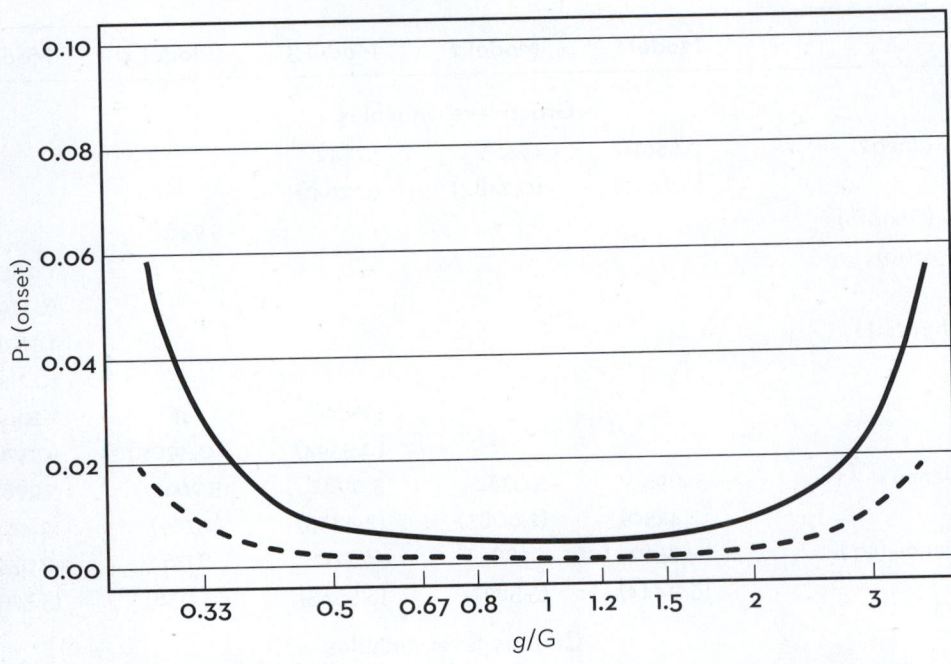

Note: The solid line corresponds to a median profile for excluded groups; the dashed one to the median profile for included groups. The horizontal axis is on a log scale, with tick marks indicating specific values of the *g/G* ratio.

predicted probability of conflict increases as the group's wealth level deviates from the country average in both directions, for a median observation for the post-1990 sample, for excluded and included groups, respectively. The figure reveals that, other things being equal, excluded groups (see the solid curve) are much more likely to experience conflict than included ones (see the dashed curve). However, the increases in risk from greater relative deviations in economic wealth are also substantial, especially for an excluded group, consistent with our argument that both political and economic grievances increase the risk of conflict.

So far we have made the simplifying, but questionable, assumption that the effect of inequality is the same for groups below and above the country's average level of wealth. We therefore need to test

Hypotheses H1a and H1b separately. As a way to do so, Model 4 relaxes the assumption of a parabolic functional form by relying on a smoothed, spline-based local regression specification with three knots. Even if not perfectly symmetric, the estimated functional form shown in Figure 3.13 tells us that both relatively poorer and wealthier groups are more likely to experience civil war, thus confirming both H1a and H1b. The error bands are relatively broad but clearly separate from zero, at least for the poorer groups.[16]

Further increasing our confidence in the separate effects, Model 5 uses the two linear ratio indicators *low_ratio* and *high_ratio* while still controlling for political exclusion. The results are strongly positive for both directions of inequality, lending further support to H1a and H1b. With this model

Figure 3.13 *Effect of Logged Horizontal Inequality on the Probability of Civil War (See Model 4 of Table 3.11)*

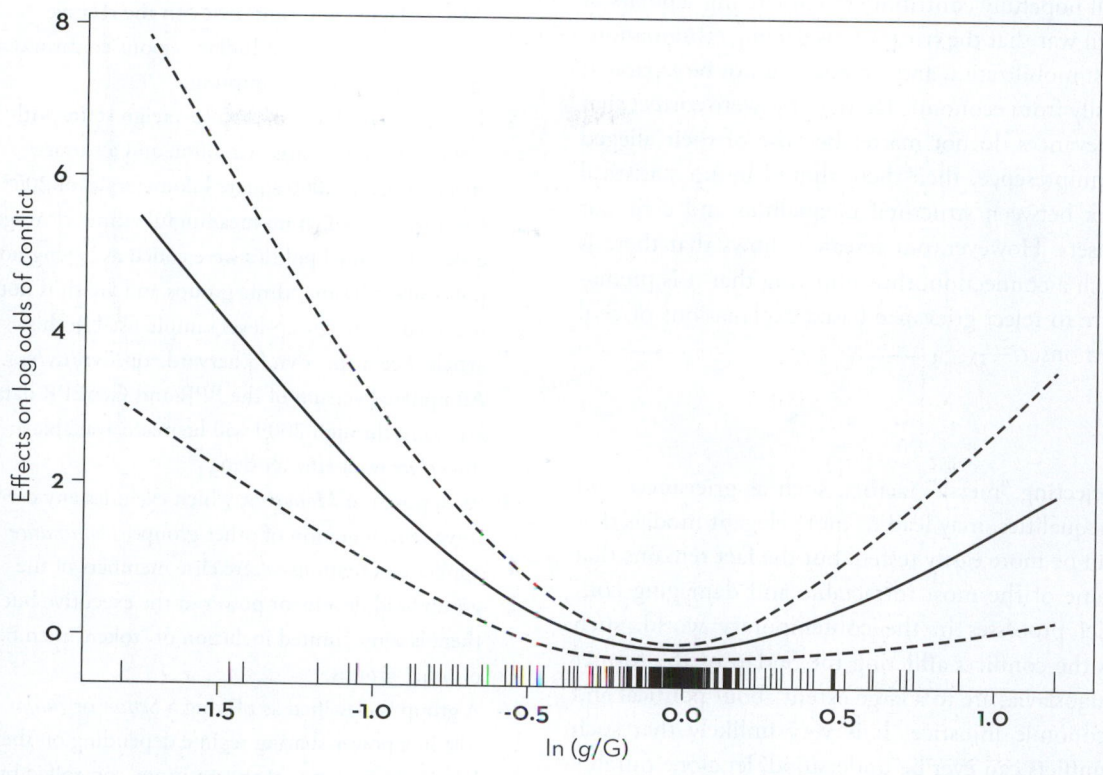

Conclusion

Although there is plenty of room for further data refinement in future research, we believe that the results presented in this article are both of considerable theoretical importance and of direct policy relevance. To our knowledge, this is the first study of civil wars that compares economic horizontal inequality at the global level. Our main result shows that ethnic groups both above and below the country average in terms of per capita income are overrepresented in civil conflict, thus confirming what previous studies have already found within a more limited scope based on case-study research, survey data, and other sources.

In keeping with previous studies, our empirical analysis also detects a strong influence of political horizontal inequality based on measures of ethnic groups' access to central executive power (see, e.g., Cederman, Wimmer, and Min 2010). This effect, which operates along with the influence of economic HIs, confirms Stewart's multidimensional notion of HI and strengthens our confidence in grievance-based explanations of conflict in general.

specification, the demographic measures of power balance also become significant in the expected direction. Furthermore, the impact of the control variables at the country level also becomes stronger compared to Model 3.

■ ■ ■

Although such explanations have partly fallen out of favor in recent civil war research, this finding will hopefully contribute to convincing scholars of civil war that the frustrations driving ethnonationalist mobilization and violence cannot be separated easily from economic factors. If it were correct that grievances do not matter because of their alleged omnipresence, then there should be no statistical link between structural inequalities and civil war onsets. However, our research shows that there is such a connection, thus implying that it is premature to reject grievance-based explanations of civil war onset.

■ ■ ■

Rejecting "messy" factors, such as grievances and inequalities, may lead to more elegant models that can be more easily tested, but the fact remains that some of the most intractable and damaging conflict processes in the contemporary world, such as the conflicts afflicting the Sudan or the former Yugoslavia, are to a large extent about political and economic injustice. It is very unlikely that such conflicts can ever be understood, let alone durably solved, without taking seriously the claims of marginalized populations.

NOTES

1. Another promising avenue is to use light emissions as a proxy for economic activity; see, e.g., Min (2008). Chen and Nordhaus (2010) report that the usefulness of this data source may be mostly limited to cases where official statistics are especially poor.
2. G-Econ 2.2 provides separate estimates for gross cell products in 1995 and 2000. A closer inspection of the documentation (see Chen 2008), however, indicates that these estimates simply adjust the 1990 estimates for updated population figures for 1995 and 2000. As such, the 1995 and 2000 figures contain no independent economic data over the 1990 values.
3. Time-varying data from the Minorities at Risk (MAR) dataset and time series on the relative wealth of Yugoslav and Indian regions confirm that this is a reasonable assumption.
4. The dataset includes all 155 sovereign states with a population of at least 1 million and a surface area of at least 5,000 square kilometers as of 2005. Countries in which no meaningful ethnic cleavage exists in national politics were coded as having no politically relevant ethnic groups and are thus not included in the group-level sample used in this article. See http://dvn.iq.harvard.edu/dvn/dv/epr. An updated version of the EPR and GeoEPR datasets valid through 2009 will be made available at http://www.icr.ethz.ch/data.
5. As opposed to *Monopoly*, which excludes any executive representation of other groups, *Dominance* applies to situations where elite members of the group hold dominant power in the executive but there is some limited inclusion of "token" members of other groups.
6. A group is classified as playing a *Senior* or *Junior* role in a power-sharing regime depending on the relative importance of the positions controlled by group representatives.
7. *Regional Autonomy* applies if the group is excluded but enjoys autonomous power at the regional level granted by the government. In the case of *Separatist Autonomy*, the group has unilaterally declared autonomy in opposition to the center. *Powerless* groups hold no political power at either the national or regional level. *Discriminated*-against groups are not only excluded but also subjected to targeted discrimination with the intent of excluding them from power.
8. This spatial aggregation process retrieves all the G-Econ cells that are covered by a group polygon and computes the total wealth estimate as the sum of the cell values. However, in a number of cases cells do not align perfectly with group polygons, and there is only partial overlap between a cell and

a group polygon. For these cases, only the overlapping area's wealth should enter the group wealth computation. We estimate the wealth of a partial G-Econ cell by distributing its total value as given in the dataset to much finer cells of 2.5 arc-minutes (approximately 5 km, 1/24 of the size of a G-Econ cell). This distribution is population-weighted; i.e., it assumes that wealth is proportional to the number of people in each of the smaller cells. This weighting was done using the *Gridded Population of the World* dataset (Version 3, available at http://sedac.ciesin.columbia.edu/gpw/).

9. We offer summary statistics for the restricted sample as used in Models 2–9. For summary statistics based on the unrestricted sample, see Section 1.6 in the supplemental online Appendix.

10. Formally, denoting the populations of the group and the EGIP as s and S, respectively, the power balance is defined as $s/(s+S)$ if the group is excluded, and as s/S otherwise. Small groups thus have close to a zero share of the dyadic population, whereas those groups that are larger than the EGIP have a power balance greater than 0.5.

11. This method also features three cubic splines.

12. We refrain from including the nonsquared term, because its effect cannot be separated from zero and should be nil according to H1.

13. This sample restriction drops a number of tiny groups, especially in China and Russia, for which no reliable spatial estimate can be computed. See also Section 1.6 in the supplemental online Appendix for further details.

14. Although the lack of comparable group-level data makes it difficult to assess measurement error for the spatial GDP per capita estimates, it is possible to compare the spatial group-size values with those based on the EPR expert survey. By successively increasing the lower size threshold, it can be established that 500,000 is the value where the reduction in the standard deviation between spatial and nonspatial flattens out, thus suggesting that this threshold is appropriate for population estimation.

A further increase of the threshold would lead to serious information loss, thus making it difficult to discern the measured effect.

15. Although both the inequality indicators and the exclusion dummy have a strong, independent effect in this model specification, adding a multiplicative interactive term does not yield a statistically significant coefficient. Inequality and exclusion appear to have additive effects, and the effect of one feature does not depend on the level of the other.

16. Because Model 4 was estimated as a GAM in R without clustered standard errors, these cannot be directly compared with the other models.

REFERENCES

Beck, Nathaniel, Jonathan N. Katz, and Richard Tucker. 1998. "Taking Time Seriously: Time-series–Cross-section Analysis with a Binary Dependent Variable." *American Journal of Political Science* 42 (4): 1260–88.

Blattman, Christopher, and Edward Miguel. 2010. "Civil War" *Journal of Economic Literature* 48 (1): 3–57.

Buhaug, Halvard, Kristian Skrede Gledilsch, Helge Holtermann, Gudrun Østby, and Andreas Forø Tollefsen. N.d. "It's the Local Economy, Stupid! Geographic Wealth Dispersion and Conflict Outbreak Location." *Journal of Conflict Resolution.* Forthcoming.

Cederman, Lars-Erik, Halvard Buhaug, and Jan Ketil Rød. 2009. "Ethno-nationalist Dyads and Civil War: A GIS-based Analysis." *Journal of Conflict Resolution* 53 (4): 496–525.

Cederman, Lars-Erik, and Luc Girardin. 2007. "Beyond Fractionalization: Mapping Ethnicity onto Nationalist Insurgencies." *American Political Science Review* 101 (1): 173–85.

Cederman, Lars-Erik, Andreas Wimmer, and Brian Min. 2010. "Why Do Ethnic Groups Rebel? New Data and Analysis." *World Politics* 62 (1): 87–119.

Chen, Xi. 2008. "Description of Gecon 2.11." Yate University. Typescript. http://gecon.yale.edu/data-and-documentation-gecon-project (accessed April 13, 2011).

Chen, Xi, and William D. Nordhaus. 2010. "The Value of Luminosity Data as a Proxy for Economic Statistics." Working Paper 16317. Cambridge, MA: National Bureau of Economic Research.

Collier, Paul, and Anke Hoeffler. 2004. "Greed and Grievance in Civil Wars." *Oxford Economic Papers* 56 (4): 563–95.

Cunningham, David E., Kristian Skrede Gleditsch, and Idean Salehyan. 2009. "It Takes Two: A Dyadic Analysis of Civil War Duration and Outcome." *Journal of Conflict Resolution* 53 (4): 570–97.

Fearon, James D., and David D. Laitin. 2003. "Ethnicity, Insurgency, and Civil War." *American Political Science Review* 97 (1): 75–90.

Gellner, Ernest. 1964. *Thought and Change.* London: Widenfeld and Nicolson.

Gleditsch, Nils Petter, Peter Wallensteen, Mikael Eriksson, Margareta Sollenberg, and Håvard Strand. 2002. "Armed Conflict 1946–2001: A New Dataset." *Journal of Peace Research* 39 (5): 615–37.

Gourevitch, Peter. 1979. "The Reemergence of 'Peripheral Nationalisms': Some Comparative Speculations on the Spatial Distribution of Political Leadership and Economic Growth." *Comparative Studies in Society and History* 21 (3): 881–912.

Gurr, Ted Robert. 1970. *Why Men Rebel.* Princeton, NJ: Princeton University Press.

Gurr, Ted Robert. 1993. *Minorities at Risk: A Global View of Ethnopolitical Conflicts.* Washington, DC: United States Institute of Peace Press.

Gurr, Ted Robert. 2000. *Peoples versus States: Minorities at Risk in the New Century.* Washington, DC: United States Institute of Peace Press.

Hegre, Håvard, and Nicholas Sambanis. 2006. "Sensitivity Analysis of Empirical Results on Civil War Onset." *Journal of Conflict Resolution* 50 (4): 508–35.

Horowitz, Donald L. 1985. *Ethnic Groups in Conflict.* Berkeley: University of California Press.

Kalyvas, Stathis N. 2006. *The Logic of Violence in Civil War.* Cambridge: Cambridge University Press.

Mancini, Luca, Frances Stewart, and Graham K. Brown. 2008. "Approaches to the Measurement of Horizontal Inequalities." In *Horizontal Inequalities and Conflict: Understanding Group Violence in Multiethnic Societies*, ed. F. Stewart. Houndmills, UK: Palgrave Macmillan, 85–101.

Min, Brian. 2008. "Democracy and Light: Global Evidence on Public Goods Provision from Satellite." University of California, Los Angeles. Typescript. http://bmin.bol.ucla.edu/ (accessed April 13, 2011).

Nordhaus, William D. 2006. "Geography and Macroeconomics: New Data and New Findings." *Proceedings of the National Academy of Sciences* 103 (10): 3510–17.

Nordhaus, William D., and Xi Chen. 2009. "Geography: Graphics and Economics." *B.E. Journal of Economic Analysis and Policy* 9 (2): article 1. http://www.bepress.com/bejeap/vol9/iss2/art1 (accessed April 13, 2011).

Østby, Gudrun. 2008. "Polarization, Horizontal Inequalities, and Violent Civil Conflict." *Journal of Peace Research* 45 (2): 143–62.

Sambanis, Nicholas. 2005. "Conclusion: Using Case Studies to Refine and Expand the Theory of Civil War." In *Understanding Civil War: Evidence and Analysis*, eds. P. Collier and N. Sambanis. Washington, DC: World Bank, 299–330.

Sambanis, Nicholas, and Branko Milanovic. 2009. "Explaining the Demand for Sovereignty." Yale University. Unpublished paper.

Stewart, Frances, ed. 2008. *Horizontal Inequalities and Conflict: Understanding Group Violence in Multiethnic Societies.* Houndmills, UK: Palgrave Macmillan.

Stewart, Frances, and Arnim Langer. 2008. "Horizontal Inequalities: Explaining Persistence and Change." In *Horizontal Inequalities and Conflict: Understanding Group Violence in Multiethnic Societies*, ed. F. Stewart. Houndmills, UK: Palgrave Macmillan, 54–82.

Tilly, Charles. 1999. *Durable Inequality.* Berkeley: University of California Press.

Walter, Barbara F. 2006. "Building Reputation: Why Governments Fight Some Separatists but Not Others." *American Journal of Political Science* 50 (2): 313–30.

Weidmann, Nils B., Doreen Kuse, and Kristian Skrede Gleditsch. 2010. "The Geography of the International System: The CShapes Dataset." *International Interactions* 36 (1): 86–106.

Wood, Elisabeth Jean. 2003. *Insurgent Collective Action and Civil War in El Salvador.* Cambridge: Cambridge University Press.

Wucherpfennig, Julian. 2011. "Bargaining, Power, and Ethnic Conflict." ETH Zürich. Unpublished manuscript.

Wucherpfennig, Julian, Nils B., Weidmann, Luc Girardin, Lars-Erik Cederman, and Andreas Wimmer. N.d. "Politically Relevant Ethnic Groups across Space and Time: Introducing the GeoEPR Dataset." *Conflict Management and Peace Science.* Forthcoming.

4 POLITICAL ECONOMY

Comparative political economy (and its close cousin, international political economy) is among the liveliest areas of research and theorizing in present-day comparative politics. Given the importance and the state of the global economy, that should not surprise us. Among the principal questions this subfield addresses are: (1) what policies and institutions are best for economic growth? (2) how do choices of economic institutions affect the functioning of democracies? and (3) how do changes in the global economy influence political divisions within societies?

Early political economists overwhelmingly favored a minimalist government. Indeed, the field of political economy, the concept of laissez-faire economic liberalism, and the modern discipline of economics are all generally considered to have originated with Adam Smith's *The Wealth of Nations*, published in 1776. Many of Smith's most important ideas, particularly the division and specialization of labor, were already familiar to literate Europeans from earlier works, including Bernard Mandeville's witty and enduring poem *The Fable of the Bees*, first published in 1705, and the French *Encyclopédie* of the 1750s. But it was Smith who, through plain examples and seemingly irrefutable logic, convinced generations of European and American elites that free markets and minimal government would maximize economic growth. The excerpts from *The Wealth of Nations* included in this chapter encapsulate Smith's arguments on the division of labor, the self-regulating nature of capitalism (the "invisible hand"), the advantages of free trade, and the importance of limited but effective government. These ideas remain crucial in understanding what kinds of government policies favor, or impede, economic growth and prosperity.

Perhaps the most fundamental, and certainly the most counterintuitive, argument in political economy is that free international trade (an absence of tariffs, quotas, or other restrictions) benefits all countries, and particularly poorer countries.[1] Virtually every serious student of political economy today, as well as political theorists and practitioners of almost all ideological persuasions—liberals, conservatives, social democrats, and most Marxists[2]—from poor and rich countries alike, believe in free trade and expanding world markets. Mercantilists of the Right and Left—usually xenophobes in the former case and antiglobalization activists in the latter—have constituted, at least until recently, a small and often derided "nut fringe" on the ends of the political spectrum.

If the classical laissez-faire endorsement of free trade remains almost universally accepted, another major tenet—that of the minimalist state—does not. Smith, most nineteenth-century thinkers, and even today's Libertarians emphasize the "dead-weight costs" of government taxation and expenditure and find them justified only to provide collective goods that voluntary or market-based action would undersupply: defense against foreign enemies, enforcement of contracts, maintenance of roads and harbors, and public education.[3] Yet in modern times, government expenditures in advanced economies have grown enormously, apparently at little cost to growth or productivity (see more on this in Chapter 7). Meanwhile, efforts to establish flourishing free-market economies in post-Communist and developing countries have frequently failed, not least because of deficient government institutions.

So how important are institutions? What kinds matter most? And why do so many countries end up with weak or bad institutions? In a pathbreaking 1991 article, "Institutions," the economic historian and Nobel laureate Douglass C. North brought history and logic to bear on these questions: What institutions are most essential to make markets work? Why do they sometimes fail to develop? And to what extent can that failure be reversed? North contended that "path dependence," including a country's colonial experience (for example, the seemingly clear difference between former Spanish and former English colonies in the Americas), played a large role.

Some critics held that geography mattered more than institutions: a tropical climate, or wide distances between major ports and trade routes, would inhibit development no matter how good institutions were. But in fundamental papers by Daron Acemoglu, Simon Johnson, and James Robinson in 2001 and 2002 (summarized here in Acemoglu's "Root Causes," 2003), the geographical argument was rejected, and the sources of institutional difference were clarified. Precisely the regions of the world that were now poorest, they demonstrated, had often been richest around 1500, when the European wave of colonization began. Because Europeans sought to plunder those richer regions, they established predatory institutions (rapacious governments, insecure property rights) that have often survived down to the present day. When Europeans colonized originally poorer and less densely settled regions (Australia, New Zealand, North America), and especially where the climate was more favorable to European survival, they could augment wealth only by attracting settlers, minimizing the burdens of government, and establishing clear property rights. The result had been a "reversal of fortune," in which originally poor regions wound up with good institutions, rapid economic growth, and ultimate wealth, while originally rich regions inherited bad institutions that impoverished them.

Historically, colonization certainly mattered; but, as Ronald Rogowski emphasizes in "Political Cleavages and Changing Exposure to Trade," so did globalization (and reversals of globalization, as happened during and after World War I). Exogenous expansions and contractions of trade, he argues, strongly influence domestic political cleavages, even where these seem to engage other issues. Expanding trade benefits owners of locally abundant factors of production (in the nineteenth-century New World, this factor was land; in Europe in the same period, labor) and harms owners of locally scarce factors. In industrialized countries today, on the other hand, it is their relatively scarce factor, low-skill labor,[4] that suffers (and resists politically), while high-skill labor, capital, and land all benefit. While it obviously cannot explain every aspect of political cleavages in any period (religion, for example, usually matters independently), this simple extension of the famous Stolper–Samuelson Theorem in economics can explain much in periods of rapidly increasing or decreasing globalization.

Increasingly, international institutions and policies matter in economic development and political economy, and the global economic environment matters for domestic politics. While its roots go back at least 250 years, this line of analysis is among the most important in contemporary comparative politics.

NOTES

1. This is not the same thing as saying that every *person* benefits in every country. When the United States trades with China, skilled U.S. workers gain but unskilled U.S. workers lose, whereas in China, at least initially, unskilled workers gain but skilled workers lose. Nonetheless, the gains of skilled U.S. workers far outweigh American unskilled workers' losses, just as the gains of low-skill Chinese workers exceed the losses of skilled Chinese workers. See also note 4.

2. Karl Marx himself was as avid a supporter of free trade as Adam Smith had been, and every early Marxist party in Europe was free-trading. Social Democrats today, in all developed countries, are among the strongest supporters of trade expansion. The late Communist regimes walled themselves off from world markets, but in this—as in many other aspects—they were diametrically opposed to original Marxism.

3. Even Adam Smith endorsed governmental support for education, since the social gain (the overall productivity gain to the economy from a person's acquiring greater skills) exceeds the private return (the increase in the educated person's earnings), meaning that purely private schooling will always undersupply education.

4. It is the ratio that matters in each country: the ratio of low-skill labor to capital, land, etc., is much lower in the advanced economies than, for example, in India or China.

Adam Smith

AN INQUIRY INTO THE NATURE AND CAUSES OF THE WEALTH OF NATIONS

Of the Division of Labour[1]

The greatest improvement[2] in the productive powers of labour, and the greater part of the skill, dexterity, and judgment with which it is any where directed, or applied, seem to have been the effects of the division of labour.

The effects of the division of labour, in the general business of society, will be more easily understood, by considering in what manner it operates in some particular manufactures.

■ ■ ■

To take an example, therefore,[3] from a very trifling manufacture; but one in which the division of labour has been very often taken notice of, the trade of the pin-maker; a workman not educated to this business (which the division of labour has rendered a distinct trade),[4] nor acquainted with the use of the machinery employed in it (to the invention of which the same division of labour has probably given occasion), could scarce, perhaps, with his utmost industry, make one pin in a day, and certainly could not make twenty. But in the way in which this business is now carried on, not only the whole work is a peculiar trade, but it is divided into a number of branches, of which the greater part are likewise peculiar trades. One man draws out the wire, another straights it, a third cuts it, a fourth points it, a fifth grinds it at the top for receiv-

ing the head; to make the head requires two or three distinct operations; to put it on, is a peculiar business, to whiten the pins is another; it is even a trade by itself to put them into the paper; and the important business of making a pin is, in this manner, divided into about eighteen distinct operations, which, in some manufactories, are all performed by distinct hands, though in others the same man will sometimes perform two or three of them.[5] I have seen a small manufactory of this kind where ten men only were employed, and where some of them consequently performed two or three distinct operations. But though they were very poor, and therefore but indifferently accommodated with the necessary machinery, they could, when they exerted themselves, make among them about twelve pounds of pins in a day. There are in a pound upwards of four thousand pins of a middling size. Those ten persons, therefore, could make among them upwards of forty-eight thousand pins in a day. Each person, therefore, making a tenth part of forty-eight thousand pins, might be considered as making four thousand eight hundred pins in a day. But if they had all wrought separately and independently, and without any of them having been educated to this peculiar business, they certainly could not each of them have made twenty, perhaps not one pin in a day; that is, certainly, not the two hundred and fortieth, perhaps not the four thousand eight hundredth part of what they are at present capable of performing, in consequence of a proper division and combination of their different operations.

In every other art and manufacture, the effects of the division of labour are similar to what they are in this very trifling one; though, in many of them, the labour can neither be so much subdivided,

From Edwin Cannan, ed., Adam Smith, *An Inquiry into the Nature and Causes of the Wealth of Nations* (Chicago: University of Chicago Press, 1976. Originally published in 1776.) Book I, pp. 7–19, Book IV, pp. 474–81, 208–9. Some notes have been omitted; those that follow are Cannan's.

nor reduced to so great a simplicity of operation. The division of labour, however, so far as it can be introduced, occasions, in every art, a proportionable increase of the productive powers of labour. The separation of different trades and employments from one another, seems to have taken place, in consequence of this advantage. This separation too is generally carried furthest in those countries which enjoy the highest degree of industry and improvement; what is the work of one man in a rude state of society, being generally that of several in an improved one.

■　■　■

This great increase of the quantity of work which, in consequence of the division of labour, the same number of people are capable of performing,[6] is owing to three different circumstances; first to the increase of dexterity in every particular workman; secondly, to the saving of the time which is commonly lost in passing from one species of work to another; and lastly, to the invention of a great number of machines which facilitate and abridge labour, and enable one man to do the work of many.[7]

■　■　■

It is the great multiplication of the productions of all the different arts, in consequence of the division of labour, which occasions, in a well-governed society, that universal opulence which extends itself to the lowest ranks of the people. Every workman has a great quantity of his own work to dispose of beyond what he himself has occasion for; and every other workman being exactly in the same situation, he is enabled to exchange a great quantity of his own goods for a great quantity, or, what comes to the same thing, for the price of a great quantity of theirs. He supplies them abundantly with what they have occasion for, and they accommodate him as amply with what he has occasion for, and a general plenty diffuses itself through all the different ranks of the society.

■　■　■

Of the Principle Which Gives Occasion to the Division of Labour

This division of labour, from which so many advantages are derived, is not originally the effect of any human wisdom, which foresees and intends that general opulence to which it gives occasion.[8] It is the necessary, though very slow and gradual, consequence of a certain propensity in human nature which has in view no such extensive utility; the propensity to truck, barter, and exchange one thing for another.

* * * [T]his propensity * * * is common to all men, and to be found in no other race of animals, which seem to know neither this nor any other species of contracts. * * *

Nobody ever saw a dog make a fair and deliberate exchange of one bone for another with another dog.[9] Nobody ever saw one animal by its gestures and natural cries signify to another, this is mine, that yours; I am willing to give this for that.

■　■　■

But man has almost constant occasion for the help of his brethren, and it is in vain for him to expect it from their benevolence only. He will be more likely to prevail if he can interest their self-love in his favour, and show them that it is for their own advantage to do for him what he requires of them. Whoever offers to another a bargain of any kind, proposes to do this. Give me that which I want, and you shall have this which you want, is the meaning of every such offer; and it is in this manner that we obtain from one another the far greater part of those good offices which we stand in need of. It is not from the benevolence of the butcher, the brewer, or the baker, that we expect our dinner, but from their regard to their own interest. We address ourselves, not to their humanity but to their self-love, and never talk to them of our own necessities but of their advantages. Nobody but a beggar chuses to depend chiefly upon the benevolence of his fellow-citizens.

■　■　■

As it is by treaty, by barter, and by purchase, that we obtain from one another the greater part of those mutual good offices which we stand in need of, so it is this same trucking disposition which originally gives occasion to the division of labour. In a tribe of hunters or shepherds a particular person makes bows and arrows, for example, with more readiness and dexterity than any other. He frequently exchanges them for cattle or for venison with his companions; and he finds at last that he can in this manner get more cattle and venison, than if he himself went to the field to catch them. From a regard to his own interest, therefore, the making of bows and arrows grows to be his chief business, and he becomes a sort of armourer. Another excels in making the frames and covers of their little huts or moveable houses. He is accustomed to be of use in this way to his neighbours, who reward him in the same manner with cattle and with venison, till at last he finds it his interest to dedicate himself entirely to this employment, and to become a sort of house-carpenter. In the same manner a third becomes a smith or a brazier; a fourth a tanner or dresser of hides or skins, the principal part of the clothing of savages. And thus the certainty of being able to exchange all that surplus part of the produce of his own labour, which is over and above his own consumption, for such parts of the produce of other men's labour as he may have occasion for, encourages every man to apply himself to a particular occupation, and to cultivate and bring to perfection whatever talent or genius he may possess for that particular species of business.[10]

■ ■ ■

Of Restraints upon the Importation from Foreign Countries of Such Goods as Can Be Produced at Home

■ ■ ■

No regulation of commerce can increase the quantity of industry in any society beyond what its capital can maintain. It can only divert a part of it into a direction into which it might not otherwise have gone; and it is by no means certain that this artificial direction is likely to be more advantageous to the society than that into which it would have gone of its own accord.

Every individual is continually exerting himself to find out the most advantageous employment for whatever capital he can command. It is his own advantage, indeed, and not that of the society which he has in view. But the study of his own advantage naturally, or rather necessarily leads him to prefer that employment which is most advantageous to the society.

■ ■ ■

… [E]very individual … necessarily endeavours so to direct that industry, that its produce may be of the greatest possible value.

The produce of industry is what it adds to the subject or materials upon which it is employed. In proportion as the value of this produce is great or small, so will likewise be the profits of the employer. But it is only for the sake of profit that any man employs a capital in the support of industry; and he will always, therefore, endeavour to employ it in the support of that industry of which the produce is likely to be of the greatest value, or to exchange for the greatest quantity either of money or of other goods.

But the annual revenue of every society is always precisely equal to the exchangeable value of the whole annual produce of its industry, or rather is precisely the same thing with that exchangeable value. As every individual, therefore, endeavours as much as he can both to employ his capital in the support of domestic industry, and so to direct that industry that its produce may be of the greatest value; every individual necessarily labours to render the annual revenue of the society as great as he can. He generally, indeed, neither intends to promote the public interest, nor knows how much he is promoting it. By preferring the support of domestic to that of foreign industry, he intends only his own security; and by directing that industry in such a manner as its produce may be of the greatest value, he intends only his own gain, and he is in this, as in many other cases, led by an invisible hand to promote an end which was no part of his intention. Nor is it always the worse for the society that it was no part of it. By pursuing his own interest he frequently promotes that of the society more effectually than when he really intends to promote it. I have never known much good done by those who affected to trade for the public good. It is an affectation, indeed, not very common among merchants, and very few words need be employed in dissuading them from it.

What is the species of domestic industry which his capital can employ, and of which the produce is likely to be of the greatest value, every individual, it is evident, can, in his local situation, judge much better than any statesman or lawgiver can do for him. The statesman, who should attempt to direct private people in what manner they ought to employ their capitals, would not only load himself with a most unnecessary attention, but assume an authority which could safely be trusted, not only to no single person, but to no council or senate whatever, and which would no-where be so dangerous as in the hands of a man who had folly and presumption enough to fancy himself fit to exercise it.

To give the monopoly of the home-market to the produce of domestic industry, in any particular art or manufacture, is in some measure to direct private people in what manner they ought to employ their capitals, and must, in almost all cases, be either a useless or a hurtful regulation. If the produce of domestic can be brought there as cheap as that of foreign industry, the regulation is evidently useless. If it cannot, it must generally be hurtful. It is the maxim of every prudent master of a family, never to attempt to make at home what it will cost him more to make than to buy. The taylor does not attempt to make his own shoes, but buys them of the shoemaker. The shoemaker does not attempt to make his own clothes, but employs a taylor. The farmer attempts to make neither the one nor the other, but employs those different artificers. All of them find it for their interest

to employ their whole industry in a way in which they have some advantage over their neighbours, and to purchase with a part of its produce, or what is the same thing, with the price of a part of it, whatever else they have occasion for.

What is prudence in the conduct of every private family, can scarce be folly in that of a great kingdom. If a foreign country can supply us with a commodity cheaper than we ourselves can make it, better buy it of them with some part of the produce of our own industry, employed in a way in which we have some advantage. The general industry of the country, being always in proportion to the capital which employs it, will not thereby be diminished, no more than that of the above-mentioned artificers; but only left to find out the way in which it can be employed with the greatest advantage. It is certainly not employed to the greatest advantage, when it is thus directed towards an object which it can buy cheaper than it can make. The value of its annual produce is certainly more or less diminished, when it is thus turned away from producing commodities evidently of more value than the commodity which it is directed to produce. According to the supposition, that commodity could be purchased from foreign countries cheaper than it can be made at home. It could, therefore, have been purchased with a part only of the commodities, or what is the same thing, with a part only of the price of the commodities, which the industry employed by an equal capital would have produced at home, had it been left to follow its natural course. The industry of the country, therefore, is thus turned away from a more, to a less advantageous employment, and the exchangeable value of its annual produce, instead of being increased, according to the intention of the lawgiver, must necessarily be diminished by every such regulation.

■   ■   ■

The natural advantages which one country has over another in producing particular commodities are sometimes so great, that it is acknowledged by all the world to be in vain to struggle with them. By means of glasses, hotbeds, and hotwalls, very good grapes can be raised in Scotland, and very good wine too can be made of them at about thirty times the expence for which at least equally good can be brought from foreign countries. Would it be a reasonable law to prohibit the importation of all foreign wines, merely to encourage the making of claret and burgundy in Scotland? But if there would be a manifest absurdity in turning towards any employment, thirty times more of the capital and industry of the country, than would be necessary to purchase from foreign countries an equal quantity of the commodities wanted, there must be an absurdity, though not altogether so glaring, yet exactly of the same kind, in turning towards any such employment a thirtieth, or even a three hundredth part more of either. Whether the advantages which one country has over another, be natural or acquired, is in this respect of no consequence. As long as the one country has those advantages, and the other wants them, it will always be more advantageous for the latter, rather to buy of the former than to make. It is an acquired advantage only, which one artificer has over his neighbour, who exercises another trade; and yet they both find it more advantageous to buy of one another, than to make what does not belong to their particular trades.

■ ■ ■

All systems either of preference or of restraint, therefore, being thus completely taken away, the obvious and simple system of natural liberty establishes itself of its own accord. Every man, as long as he does not violate the laws of justice, is left perfectly free to pursue his own interest his own way, and to bring both his industry and capital into competition with those of any other man, or order of men. The sovereign is completely discharged from a duty, in the attempting to perform which he must always be exposed to innumerable delusions, and for the proper performance of which no human wisdom or knowledge could ever be sufficient; the duty of superintending the industry of private people, and of directing it towards the employments most suitable to the interest of the society. According to the system of natural liberty, the sovereign has only three duties to attend to; three duties of great importance, indeed, but plain and intelligible to common understandings: first, the duty of protecting the society from the violence and invasion of other independent societies; secondly, the duty of protecting, as far as possible, every member of the society from the injustice or oppression of every other member of it, or the duty of establishing an exact administration of justice; and, thirdly, the duty of erecting and maintaining certain public works and certain public institutions, which it can never be for the interest of any individual, or small number of individuals, to erect and maintain; because the profit could never repay the expence to any individual or small number of individuals, though it may frequently do much more than repay it to a great society.

The proper performance of those several duties of the sovereign necessarily supposes a certain expence; and this expence again necessarily requires a certain revenue to support it.

■ ■ ■

NOTES

1. This phrase, if used at all before this time, was not a familiar one. Its presence here is probably due to a passage in Mandeville, *The Fable of the Bees*, pt. ii. (1729), dial. vi., p. 335: 'CLEO. . . . When once men come to be governed by written laws, all the rest comes on apace . . . No number of men, when once they enjoy quiet, and no man needs to fear his neighbour, will be long without learning to divide and subdivide their labour. HOR. I don't understand you. CLEO. Man, as I have hinted before, naturally loves to imitate what he sees others do, which is the reason that savage people all do the same thing: this hinders them from meliorating their condition, though they are always wishing for

it: but if one will wholly apply himself to the making of bows and arrows, whilst another provides food, a third builds huts, a fourth makes garments, and a fifth utensils, they not only become useful to one another, but the callings and employments themselves will, in the same number of years, receive much greater improvements, than if all had been promiscuously followed by every one of the five. HOR. I believe you are perfectly right there; and the truth of what you say is in nothing so conspicuous as it is in watch-making, which is come to a higher degree of perfection than it would have been arrived at yet, if the whole had always remained the employment of one person; and I am persuaded that even the plenty we have of clocks and watches, as well as the exactness and beauty they may be made of, are chiefly owing to the division that has been made of that art into many branches.' The index contains, 'Labour, The usefulness of dividing and subdividing it'. Joseph Harris, *Essay upon Money and Coins*, 1757, pt. i., § 12, treats of the 'usefulness of distinct trades,' or 'the advantages accruing to mankind from their betaking themselves severally to different occupations,' but does not use the phrase 'division of labour'.

2. Ed. 1 reads 'improvements'.

3. Another and perhaps more important reason for taking an example like that which follows is the possibility of exhibiting the advantage, of division of labour in statistical form.

4. This parenthesis would alone be sufficient to show that those are wrong who believe Smith did not include the separation of employments in 'division of labour'.

5. In Adam Smith's *Lectures*, p. 164, the business is, as here, divided into eighteen operations. This number is doubtless taken from the *Encyclopédie*, tom. v. (published in 1755), *s.v.* Épingle. The article is ascribed to M. Delaire, 'qui décrivait la fabrication de l'épingle dans les ateliers même des ouvriers,' p. 807. In some factories the division was carried further. E. Chambers, *Cyclopædia*, vol. ii., 2nd ed.,

1738, and 4th ed., 1741, *s.v.* Pin, makes the number of separate operations twenty-five.

6. Ed. 1 places 'in consequence of the division of labour' here instead of in the line above.

7. 'Pour la célérité du travail et la perfection de l'ouvrage, elles dépendent entièrement de la multitude des ouvriers rassemblés. Lorsqu'une manufacture est nombreuse, chaque opération occupe un homme différent. Tel ouvrier ne fait et ne fera de sa vie qu'une seule et unique chose; tel autre une autre chose: d'où il arrive que chacune s'exécute bien et promptement, et que l'ouvrage le mieux fait est encore celui qu'on a à meilleur marché. D'ailleurs le goût et la façon se perfectionnement nécessairement entre un grand nombre d'ouvriers, parce qu'il est difficile qu'il ne s'en rencontre quelques-uns capables de réfléchir, de combiner, et de trouver enfin le seul moyen qui puisse les mettre audessus de leurs semblables; le moyen ou d'épargner la matière, ou d'allonger le temps, ou de surfaire l'industrie, soit par une machine nouvelle, soit par une manúuvre plus commode.'— *Encyclopédie*, tom i. (1751), p. 717, *s.v.* Art. All three advantages mentioned in the text above are included here.

8. *I.e.*, it is not the effect of any conscious regulation by the state or society, like the 'law of Sesostris,' that every man should follow the employment of his father, referred to in the corresponding passage in *Lectures*, p. 168. The denial that it is the effect of individual wisdom recognising the advantage of exercising special natural talents comes lower down, p. 19.

9. It is by no means clear what object there could be in exchanging one bone for another.

10. This is apparently directed against Harris, *Money and Coins*, pt. i., § II, and is in accordance with the view of Hume, who asks readers to 'consider how nearly equal all men are in their bodily force, and even in their mental powers and faculties, ere cultivated by education'.—'Of the Original Contract,' in *Essays, Moral and Political*, 1748, p. 291.

Douglass C. North
INSTITUTIONS

Institutions are the humanly devised constraints that structure political, economic and social interaction. They consist of both informal constraints (sanctions, taboos, customs, traditions, and codes of conduct) and formal rules (constitutions, laws, property rights). Throughout history, institutions have been devised by human beings to create order and reduce uncertainty in exchange. Together with the standard constraints of economics they define the choice set and therefore determine transaction and production costs and hence the profitability and feasibility of engaging in economic activity. They evolve incrementally, connecting the past with the present and the future; history in consequence is largely a story of institutional evolution in which the historical performance of economies can only be understood as a part of a sequential story. Institutions provide the incentive structure of an economy; as that structure evolves, it shapes the direction of economic change towards growth, stagnation, or decline. In this essay I intend to elaborate on the role of institutions in the performance of economies and illustrate my analysis from economic history.

What makes it necessary to constrain human interaction with institutions? The issue can be most succinctly summarized in a game theoretic context. Wealth-maximizing individuals will usually find it worthwhile to cooperate with other players when the play is repeated, when they possess complete information about the other players' past performance, and when there are small numbers of players. But turn the game upside down. Cooperation is difficult to sustain when the game is not repeated (or there is an endgame), when information on the other players is lacking, and when there are large numbers of players.

These polar extremes reflect contrasting economic settings in real life. There are many examples of simple exchange institutions that permit low cost transacting under the former conditions. But institutions that permit low cost transacting and producing in a world of specialization and division of labor require solving the problems of human cooperation under the latter conditions.

It takes resources to define and enforce exchange agreements. Even if everyone had the same objective function (like maximizing the firm's profits), transacting would take substantial resources; but in the context of individual wealth-maximizing behavior and asymmetric information about the valuable attributes of what is being exchanged (or the performance of agents), transaction costs are a critical determinant of economic performance. Institutions and the effectiveness of enforcement (together with the technology employed) determine the cost of transacting. Effective institutions raise the benefits of cooperative solutions or the costs of defection, to use game theoretic terms. In transaction cost terms, institutions reduce transaction and production costs per exchange so that the potential gains from trade are realizeable. Both political and economic institutions are essential parts of an effective institutional matrix.

The major focus of the literature on institutions and transaction costs has been on institutions as efficient solutions to problems of organization in a competitive framework (Williamson, 1975; 1985). Thus market exchange, franchising, and vertical integration are conceived in this literature as efficient solutions to the complex problems confronting entrepreneurs under various competitive conditions. Valuable as this work has been, such an approach assumes away the central concern of this essay: to explain the varied performance of economies both over time and in the current world.

From *Journal of Economic Perspectives* 5, no. 1 (Winter 1991), pp. 97–112.

How does an economy achieve the efficient, competitive markets assumed in the foregoing approach? The formal economic constraints or property rights are specified and enforced by political institutions, and the literature simply takes those as a given. But economic history is overwhelmingly a story of economies that failed to produce a set of economic rules of the game (with enforcement) that induce sustained economic growth. The central issue of economic history and of economic development is to account for the evolution of political and economic institutions that create an economic environment that induces increasing productivity.

Institutions to Capture the Gains from Trade

Many readers will be at least somewhat familiar with the idea of economic history over time as a series of staged stories. The earliest economies are thought of as local exchange within a village (or even within a simple hunting and gathering society). Gradually, trade expands beyond the village: first to the region, perhaps as a bazaar-like economy; then to longer distances, through particular caravan or shipping routes; and eventually to much of the world. At each stage, the economy involves increasing specialization and division of labor and continuously more productive technology. This story of gradual evolution from local autarky to specialization and division of labor was derived from the German historical school. However, there is no implication in this paper that the real historical evolution of economies necessarily paralleled the sequence of stages of exchange described here.[1]

I begin with local exchange within the village or even the simple exchange of hunting and gathering societies (in which women gathered and men hunted). Specialization in this world is rudimentary and self-sufficiency characterizes most individual households. Small-scale village trade exists within a "dense" social network of informal constraints that facilitates local exchange, and the costs of transacting in this context are low. (Although the basic societal costs of tribal and village organization may be high, they will

not be reflected in additional costs in the process of transacting.) People have an intimate understanding of each other, and the threat of violence is a continuous force for preserving order because of its implications for other members of society.[2]

As trade expands beyond a single village, however, the possibilities for conflict over the exchange grow. The size of the market grows and transaction costs increase sharply because the dense social network is replaced; hence, more resources must be devoted to measurement and enforcement. In the absence of a state that enforced contracts, religious precepts usually imposed standards of conduct on the players. Needless to say, their effectiveness in lowering the costs of transacting varied widely, depending on the degree to which these precepts were held to be binding.

The development of long-distance trade, perhaps through caravans or lengthy ship voyages, requires a sharp break in the characteristics of an economic structure. It entails substantial specialization in exchange by individuals whose livelihood is confined to trading and the development of trading centers, which may be temporary gathering places (as were the early fairs in Europe) or more permanent towns or cities. Some economies of scale—for example, in plantation agriculture—are characteristic of this world. Geographic specialization begins to emerge as a major characteristic and some occupational specialization is occurring as well.

The growth of long-distance trade poses two distinct transaction cost problems. One is a classical problem of agency, which historically was met by use of kin in long-distance trade. That is, a sedentary merchant would send a relative with the cargo to negotiate sale and to obtain a return cargo. The costliness of measuring performance, the strength of kinship ties, and the price of "defection" all determined the outcome of such agreements. As the size and volume of trade grew, agency problems became an increasingly major dilemma.[3] A second problem consisted of contract negotiation and enforcement in alien parts of the world, where there is no easily available way to achieve agreement and enforce contracts. Enforcement means not only such enforcement of agreements but also protection of the goods and services en route from pirates, brigands, and so on.

The problems of enforcement en route were met by armed forces protecting the ship or caravan or by the payment of tolls or protection money to local coercive groups. Negotiation and enforcement in alien parts of the world entailed typically the development of standardized weights and measures, units of account, a medium of exchange, notaries, consuls, merchant law courts, and enclaves of foreign merchants protected by foreign princes in return for revenue. By lowering information costs and providing incentives for contract fulfillment this complex of institutions, organizations, and instruments made possible transacting and engaging in long-distance trade. A mixture of voluntary and semi-coercive bodies, or at least bodies that effectively could cause ostracism of merchants that didn't live up to agreements, enabled long-distance trade to occur.[4]

This expansion of the market entails more specialized producers. Economies of scale result in the beginnings of hierarchical producing organizations, with full-time workers working either in a central place or in a sequential production process. Towns and some central cities are emerging, and occupational distribution of the population now shows, in addition, a substantial increase in the proportion of the labor force engaged in manufacturing and in services, although the traditional preponderance in agriculture continues. These evolving stages also reflect a significant shift towards urbanization of the society.

Such societies need effective, impersonal contract enforcement, because personal ties, voluntaristic constraints, and ostracism are no longer effective as more complex and impersonal forms of exchange emerge. It is not that these personal and social alternatives are unimportant; they are still significant even in today's interdependent world. But in the absence of effective impersonal contracting, the gains from "defection" are great enough to forestall the development of complex exchange. Two illustrations deal with the creation of a capital market and with the interplay between institutions and the technology employed.

A capital market entails security of property rights over time and will simply not evolve where political rulers can arbitrarily seize assets or radically alter their value. Establishing a credible commitment to secure property rights over time requires either a ruler who exercises forebearance and restraint in using coercive force, or the shackling of the ruler's power to prevent arbitrary seizure of assets. The first alternative was seldom successful for very long in the face of the ubiquitous fiscal crises of rulers (largely as a consequence of repeated warfare). The latter entailed a fundamental restructuring of the polity such as occurred in England as a result of the Glorious Revolution of 1688, which resulted in parliamentary supremacy over the crown.[5]

The technology associated with the growth of manufacturing entailed increased fixed capital in plant and equipment, uninterrupted production, a disciplined labor force, and a developed transport network; in short, it required effective factor and product markets. Undergirding such markets are secure property rights, which entail a polity and judicial system to permit low costs contracting, flexible laws permitting a wide latitude of organizational structures, and the creation of complex governance structures to limit the problems of agency in hierarchical organizations.[6]

In the last stage, the one we observe in modern western societies, specialization has increased, agriculture requires a small percentage of the labor force, and markets have become nationwide and worldwide. Economies of scale imply large-scale organization, not only in manufacturing but also in agriculture. Everyone lives by undertaking a specialized function and relying on the vast network of interconnected parts to provide the multitude of goods and services necessary to them. The occupational distribution of the labor force shifts gradually from dominance by manufacturing to dominance, eventually, by what are characterized as services. Society is overwhelmingly urban.

In this final stage, specialization requires increasing percentages of the resources of the society to be engaged in transacting, so that the transaction sector rises to be a large percentage of gross national product. This is so because specialization in trade, finance, banking, insurance, as well as the simple coordination of economic activity, involves an increasing proportion of the labor force.[7] Of necessity, therefore, highly specialized forms of transaction organizations emerge. International specialization and division of labor requires institutions and organizations to safeguard property rights across international boundaries so that capital markets (as well as other kinds of exchange) can take place with credible commitment on the part of the players.

These very schematic stages appear to merge one into another in a smooth story of evolving cooperation. But do they? Does any necessary connection move the players from less complicated to more complicated forms of exchange? At stake in this evolution is not only whether information costs and economies of scale together with the development of improved enforcement of contracts will permit and indeed encourage more complicated forms of exchange, but also whether organizations have the incentive to acquire knowledge and information that will induce them to evolve in more socially productive directions.

In fact, throughout history, there is no necessary reason for this development to occur. Indeed, most of the early forms of organization that I have mentioned in these sections still exist today in parts of the world. There still exist primitive tribal societies; the Suq (bazaar economies engaged in regional trade) still flourishes in many parts of the world; and while the caravan trade has disappeared, its demise (as well as the gradual undermining of the other two forms of "primitive" exchange) has reflected external forces rather than internal evolution. In contrast, the development of European long-distance trade initiated a sequential development of more complex forms of organization.

The remainder of this paper will examine first some seemingly primitive forms of exchange that failed to evolve and then the institutional evolution that occurred in early modern Europe. The concluding section of the paper will attempt to enunciate why some societies and exchange institutions evolve and others do not, and to apply that framework in the context of economic development in the western hemisphere during the 18th and 19th centuries.

When Institutions Do Not Evolve

In every system of exchange, economic actors have an incentive to invest their time, resources, and energy in knowledge and skills that will improve their material status. But in some primitive institutional settings, the kind of knowledge and skills that will pay off will not result in institutional evolution towards more productive economies. To illustrate this argument, I consider three primitive types of exchange—tribal society, a regional economy with bazaar trading, and the long-distance caravan trade—that are unlikely to evolve from within.

As noted earlier, exchange in a tribal society relies on a dense social network. Elizabeth Colson (1974, p. 59) describes the network this way:

> The communities in which all these people live were governed by a delicate balance of power, always endangered and never to be taken for granted: each person was constantly involved in securing his own position in situations where he had to show his good intentions. Usages and customs appear to be flexible and fluid given that judgement on whether or not someone has done rightly varies from case to case. . . . But this is because it is the individual who is being judged and not the crime. Under these conditions, a flouting of generally accepted standards is tantamount to a claim to illegitimate power and becomes part of the evidence against one.

The implication of Colson's analysis as well as that of Richard Posner in his account of primitive institutions (1980) is that deviance and innovation are viewed as threats to group survival.

A second form of exchange that has existed for thousands of years and still exists today in North

Africa and the Middle East is that of the Suq, where widespread and relatively impersonal exchange and relatively high costs of transacting exist.[8] The basic characteristics are a multiplicity of small-scale enterprises with as much as 40 to 50 percent of the town's labor force engaged in this exchange process; low fixed costs in terms of rent and machinery; a very finely drawn division of labor; an enormous number of small transactions, each more or less independent of the next; face to face contacts; and goods and services that are not homogeneous.

There are no institutions devoted to assembling and distributing market information; that is, no price quotations, production reports, employment agencies, consumer guides, and so on. Systems of weights and measures are intricate and incompletely standardized. Exchange skills are very elaborately developed, and are the primary determinant of who prospers in the bazaar and who does not. Haggling over terms with respect to any aspect or condition of exchange is pervasive, strenuous, and unremitting. Buying and selling are virtually undifferentiated, essentially a single activity; trading involves a continual search for specific partners, not the mere offers of goods to the general public. Regulation of disputes involves testimony by reliable witnesses to factual matters, not the weighting of competing, juridical principles. Governmental controls over marketplace activity are marginal, decentralized, and mostly rhetorical.

To summarize, the central features of the Suq are (1) high measurement costs; (2) continuous effort at clientization (the development of repeat-exchange relationships with other partners, however imperfect); and (3) intensive bargaining at every margin. In essence, the name of the game is to raise the costs of transacting to the other party to exchange. One makes money by having better information than one's adversary.

It is easy to understand why innovation would be seen to threaten survival in a tribal society but harder to understand why these "inefficient" forms of bargaining would continue in the Suq. One would anticipate, in the societies with which we are familiar, that voluntary organizations would evolve

to ensure against the hazards and uncertainties of such information asymmetries. But that is precisely the issue. What is missing in the Suq are the fundamental underpinnings of institutions that would make such voluntary organizations viable and profitable. These include an effective legal structure and court system to enforce contracts which in turn depend on the development of political institutions that will create such a framework. In their absence there is no incentive to alter the system.

The third form of exchange, caravan trade, illustrates the informal constraints that made trade possible in a world where protection was essential and no organized state existed. Clifford Geertz (1979, p. 137) provides a description of the caravan trades in Morocco at the turn of the century:

> In the narrow sense, a zettata (from the Berber TAZETTAT, 'a small piece of cloth') is a passage toll, a sum paid to a local power . . . for protection when crossing localities where he is such a power. But in fact it is, or more properly was, rather more than a mere payment. It was part of a whole complex of moral rituals, customs with the force of law and the weight of sanctity—centering around the guest-host, client-patron, petitioner-petitioned, exile-protector, suppliant-divinity relations— all of which are somehow of a package in rural Morocco. Entering the tribal world physically, the outreaching trader (or at least his agents) had also to enter it culturally.
>
> Despite the vast variety of particular forms through which they manifest themselves, the characteristics of protection in the Berber societies of the High and Middle Atlas are clear and constant. Protection is personal, unqualified, explicit, and conceived of as the dressing of one man in the reputation of another. The reputation may be political, moral, spiritual, or even idiosyncratic, or, often enough, all four at once. But the essential transaction is that a man who counts 'stands up and says' (quam wa qal, as the classical tag has it) to those to whom he counts: 'this man is mine; harm him and you insult me;

insult me and you will answer for it.' Benediction (the famous *baraka*), hospitality, sanctuary, and safe passage are alike in this: they rest on the perhaps somewhat paradoxical notion that though personal identity is radically individual in both its roots and its expressions, it is not incapable of being stamped onto the self of someone else.

While tribal chieftains found it profitable to protect merchant caravans they had neither the military muscle nor the political structure to extend, develop, and enforce more permanent property rights.

Institutional Evolution in Early Modern Europe

In contrast to many primitive systems of exchange, long-distance trade in early modern Europe from the 11th to the 16th centuries was a story of sequentially more complex organization that eventually led to the rise of the western world. Let me first briefly describe the innovations and then explore some of their underlying sources.[9]

Innovations that lowered transaction costs consisted of organizational changes, instruments, and specific techniques and enforcement characteristics that lowered the costs of engaging in exchange over long distances. These innovations occurred at three cost margins: (1) those that increased the mobility of capital, (2) those that lowered information costs, and (3) those that spread risk. Obviously, the categories are overlapping, but they provide a useful way to distinguish cost-reducing features of transacting. All of these innovations had their origins in earlier times; most of them were borrowed from medieval Italian city states or Islam or Byzantium and then elaborated upon.

Among the innovations that enhanced the mobility of capital were the techniques and methods evolved to evade usury laws. The variety of ingenious ways by which interest was disguised in loan contracts ranged from "penalties for late payment," to exchange rate manipulation (Lopez and Raymond, 1955, p. 163), to the early form of the mortgage; but all increased the costs of contracting. The costliness of usury laws was not only that they made the writing of contracts to disguise interests complex and cumbersome, but also that enforceability of such contracts became more problematic. As the demand for capital increased and evasion became more general, usury laws gradually broke down and rates of interest were permitted. In consequence, the costs of writing contracts and the costs of enforcing them declined.

A second innovation that improved the mobility of capital, and the one that has received the most attention, was the evolution of the bill of exchange (a dated order to pay, say 120 days after issuance, conventionally drawn by a seller against a purchaser of goods delivered) and particularly the development of techniques and instruments that allowed for its negotiability as well as for the development of discounting methods. Negotiability and discounting in turn depended on the creation of institutions that would permit their use and the development of centers where such events could occur: first in fairs, such as the Champagne fairs that played such a prominent part in economic exchange in 12th and 13th century Europe; then through banks; and finally through financial houses that could specialize in discounting. These developments were a function not only of specific institutions but also of the scale of economic activity. Increasing volume obviously made such institutional developments possible. In addition to the economies of scale necessary for the development of the bills of exchange, improved enforceability of contracts was critical, and the interrelationship between the development of accounting and auditing methods and their use as evidence in the collection of debts and in the enforcement of contracts was an important part of this process (Yamey, 1949; Watts and Zimmerman, 1983).

Still a third innovation affecting the mobility of capital arose from the problems associated with maintaining control of agents involved in long-distance trade. The traditional resolution of this problem in medieval and early modern times was the use of kinship and family ties to bind agents to principals. However, as the size and scope of merchant trading empires grew, the extension of discretionary behavior to others than kin of the principal required the development of more elaborate accounting procedures for monitoring the behavior of agents.

The major developments in the area of information costs were the printing of prices of various commodities, as well as the printing of manuals that provided information on weights, measures, customs, brokerage fees, postal systems, and, particularly, the complex exchange rates between monies in Europe and the trading world. Obviously these developments were primarily a function of the volume of international trade and therefore a consequence of economies of scale.

The final innovation was the transformation of uncertainty into risk. By uncertainty, I mean here a condition wherein one cannot ascertain the probability of an event and therefore cannot arrive at a way of ensuring against such an occurrence. Risk, on the other hand, implies the ability to make an actuarial determination of the likelihood of an event and hence ensure against such an outcome. In the modern world, insurance and portfolio diversification are methods for converting uncertainty into risks and thereby reducing, through the provision of a hedge against variability, the costs of transacting. In the medieval and early modern world, precisely the same conversion occurred. For example, marine insurance evolved from sporadic individual contracts covering partial payments for losses to contracts issued by specialized firms. As F. E. De Roover (1945, p. 198) described:

> By the fifteenth century marine insurance was established on a secure basis. The wording of the policies had already become stereotyped and changed very little during the next three or four hundred years. . . . In the sixteenth century it was already current practice to use printed forms provided with a few blank spaces for the name of the ship, the name of the master, the amount of the insurance, the premium, and a few other items that were apt to change from one contract to another.

Another example of the development of actuarial, ascertainable risk was the business organization that spread risk through either portfolio diversification or institutions that permitted a large number of investors to engage in risky activities. For example, the commenda was a contract employed in long-distance trade between a sedentary partner and an active partner who accompanied the goods. It evolved from its Jewish, Byzantine, and Muslim origins (Udovitch, 1962) through its use at the hands of Italians to the English Regulated Company and finally the Joint Stock Company, thus providing an evolutionary story of the institutionalization of risk.

These specific innovations and particular institutional instruments evolved from interplay between two fundamental economic forces: the economies of scale associated with a growing volume of trade, and the development of improved mechanisms to enforce contracts at lower costs. The causation ran both ways. That is, the increasing volume of long-distance trade raised the rate of return to merchants of devising effective mechanisms for enforcing contracts. In turn, the development of such mechanisms lowered the costs of contracting and made trade more profitable, thereby increasing its volume.

The process of developing new enforcement mechanisms was a long one. While a variety of courts handled commercial disputes, it is the development of enforcement mechanisms by merchants themselves that is significant. Enforceability appears to have had its beginnings in the development of internal codes of conduct in fraternal orders of guild merchants; those who did not live up to them were threatened with ostracism. A further step was the evolution of mercantile law. Merchants carried with them in long-distance trade mercantile codes of conduct, so that Pisan laws passed into the sea codes of Marseilles; Oleron and Lubeck gave laws to the north of Europe, Barcelona to the south of Europe; and from Italy came the legal principle of insurance and bills of exchange (Mitchell, 1969, p. 156).

The development of more sophisticated accounting methods and of notarial records provided evidence for ascertaining facts in disputes. The gradual blending of the voluntaristic structure of enforcement of contracts via internal merchant organizations with enforcement by the state is an important part of the story of increasing the enforceability of contracts. The long evolution of merchant law from its voluntary beginnings and the differences in resolutions that it had with both the common and Roman law are a part of the story.

The state was a major player in this whole process, and there was continuous interplay between the state's fiscal needs and its credibility in its relationships with merchants and the citizenry in general. In particular, the evolution of capital markets was critically influenced by the policies of the state, since to the extent the state was bound by commitments that it would not confiscate assets or use its coercive power to increase uncertainty in exchange, it made possible the evolution of financial institutions and the creation of more efficient capital markets. The shackling of arbitrary behavior of rulers and the development of impersonal rules that successfully bound both the state and voluntary organizations were a key part of this whole process. The development of an institutional process by which government debt could be circulated, become a part of a regular capital market, and be funded by regular sources of taxation was also a key part (Tracy, 1985; North and Weingast, 1989).

It was in the Netherlands, Amsterdam specifically, that these diverse innovations and institutions were combined to create the predecessor of the efficient modern set of markets that make possible the growth of exchange and commerce. An open immigration policy attracted businessmen. Efficient methods of financing long-distance trade were developed, as were capital markets and discounting methods in financial houses that lowered the costs of underwriting this trade. The development of techniques for spreading risk and transforming uncertainty into actuarial, ascertainable risks as well as the creation of large-scale markets that allowed for lowering the costs of information, and the development of negotiable government indebtedness all were a part of this story (Barbour, 1949).

Contrasting Stories of Stability and Change

These contrasting stories of stability and change go to the heart of the puzzle of accounting for changes in the human economic condition. In the former cases, maximizing activity by the actors will not induce increments to knowledge and skills which will modify the institutional framework to induce greater productivity; in the latter case, evolution is a consistent story of incremental change induced by the private gains to be realized by productivity-raising organizational institutional changes.

What distinguished the institutional context of western Europe from the other illustrations? The traditional answer of economic historians has been competition among the fragmented European political units accentuated by changing military technology which forced rulers to seek more revenue (by making bargains with constituents) in order to survive (North and Thomas, 1973; Jones, 1981; Rosenberg and Birdzell, 1986). That is surely part of the answer; political competition for survival in early modern Europe was certainly more acute than in other parts of the world. But it is only a partial answer. Why the contrasting results within western Europe? Why did Spain, the great power of 16th century Europe, decline while the Netherlands and England developed?

To begin to get an answer (and it is only a beginning), we need to dig deeper into two key (and related) parts of the puzzle: the relationship between the basic institutional framework, the consequent organizational structure, and institutional change; and the path dependent nature of economic change that is a consequence of the increasing returns characteristic of an institutional framework.

In the institutional accounts given earlier, the direction and form of economic activity by individuals and organizations reflected the opportunities thrown up by the basic institutional framework of customs, religious precepts, and formal rules (and the effectiveness of enforcement). Whether we examine the organization of trade in the Suq or that in the Champagne Fairs, in each case the trader was constrained by the institutional framework, as well as the traditional constraints common to economic theory.

In each case the trader would invest in acquiring knowledge and skills to increase his wealth. But in the former case, improved knowledge and skills meant getting better information on opportunities and having greater bargaining skills than other traders, since profitable opportunities came from being better informed and being a more skilled bargainer than other traders. Neither activity induced alteration in the basic institutional framework. On the other hand, while a merchant at a medieval European fair would certainly gain from acquiring such information and skills, he would gain also from devising ways to bond fellow merchants, to establish merchant courts, to induce princes to protect goods from brigandage in return for revenue, to devise ways to discount bills of exchange. His investment in knowledge and skills would gradually and incrementally alter the basic institutional framework.

Note that the institutional evolution entailed not only voluntary organizations that expanded trade and made exchange more productive, but also the development of the state to take over protection and enforcement of property rights as impersonal exchange made contract enforcement increasingly costly for voluntary organizations which lacked effective coercive power. Another essential part of the institutional evolution entails a shackling of the arbitrary behavior of the state over economic activity.

Path dependence is more than the incremental process of institutional evolution in which yesterday's institutional framework provides the opportunity set for today's organizations and individual entrepreneurs (political or economic). The institutional matrix consists of an interdependent web of institutions and consequent political and economic organizations that are characterized by massive increasing returns.[10] That is, the organizations owe their existence to the opportunities provided by the institutional framework. Network externalities arise because of the initial setup costs (like the de

novo creation of the U.S. Constitution in 1787), the learning effects described above, coordination effects via contracts with other organizations, and adaptive expectations arising from the prevalence of contracting based on the existing institutions.

When economies do evolve, therefore, nothing about that process assures economic growth. It has commonly been the case that the incentive structure provided by the basic institutional framework creates opportunities for the consequent organizations to evolve, but the direction of their development has not been to promote productivity-raising activities. Rather, private profitability has been enhanced by creating monopolies, by restricting entry and factor mobility, and by political organizations that established property rights that redistributed rather than increased income.

The contrasting histories of the Netherlands and England on the one hand and Spain on the other hand reflected the differing opportunity sets of the actors in each case. To appreciate the pervasive influence of path dependence, let us extend the historical account of Spain and England to the economic history of the New World and the striking contrast in the history of the areas north and south of the Rio Grande.

In the case of North America, the English colonies were formed in the century when the struggle between Parliament and the Crown was coming to a head. Religious and political diversity in the mother country was paralleled in the colonies. The general development in the direction of local political control and the growth of assemblies was unambiguous. Similarly, the colonist carried over free and common socage tenure of land (fee simple ownership rights) and secure property rights in other factor and product markets.

The French and Indian War from 1755 to 1763 is a familiar breaking point in American history. British efforts to impose a very modest tax on colonial subjects, as well as curb westward migration, produced a violent reaction that led via a series of steps, by individuals and organizations, to the Revolution, the Declaration of Independence, the Articles of Confederation, the Northwest Ordinance, and the Constitution, a sequence of institutional expressions that formed a consistent evolutionary pattern despite the precariousness of the process. While the American Revolution created the United States, post-revolutionary history is only intelligible in terms of the continuity of informal and formal institutional constraints carried over from before the Revolution and incrementally modified (Hughes, 1989).

Now turn to the Spanish (and Portuguese) case in Latin America. In the case of the Spanish Indies, conquest came at the precise time that the influence of the Castilian Cortes (parliament) was declining and the monarchy of Castile, which was the seat of power of Spain, was firmly establishing centralized bureaucratic control over Spain and the Spanish Indies.[11] The conquerors imposed a uniform religion and a uniform bureaucratic administration on an already existing agricultural society. The bureaucracy detailed every aspect of political and economic policy. There were recurrent crises over the problem of agency. Wealth-maximizing behavior by organizations and entrepreneurs (political and economic) entailed getting control of, or influence over, the bureaucratic machinery. While the 19th century Wars of Independence in Latin America turned out to be a struggle for control of the bureaucracy and consequent policy as between local colonial control and imperial control, nevertheless the struggle was imbued with the ideological overtones that stemmed from the American and French revolutions. Independence brought U.S.-inspired constitutions, but the results were radically different. In contrast to those of the United States, Latin American federal schemes and efforts at decentralization had one thing in common after the revolutions. None worked. The gradual country-by-country reversion to centralized bureaucratic control characterized Latin America in the 19th century.[12]

The divergent paths established by England and Spain in the New World have not converged despite the mediating factors of common ideological influences. In the former, an institutional framework has evolved that permits complex impersonal exchange necessary to political stability as well as to capture the potential economic benefits of modern technology. In the latter, "personalistic" relationships are still the key to much of the political and economic exchange. They are the consequence of an evolving institutional framework that has produced erratic economic growth in Latin America, but neither political nor economic stability, nor realization of the potential of modern technology.

The foregoing comparative sketch probably raises more questions than it answers about institutions and the role that they play in the performance of economies. Under what conditions does a path get reversed, like the revival of Spain in modern times? What is it about informal constraints that gives them such a pervasive influence upon the long-run character of economies? What is the relationship between formal and informal constraints? How does an economy develop the informal constraints that make individuals constrain their behavior so that they make political and judicial systems effective forces for third party enforcement? Clearly we have a long way to go for complete answers, but the modern study of institutions offers the promise of dramatic new understanding of economic performance and economic change.

NOTES

1. In an article written many years ago (North, 1955), I pointed out that many regional economies evolved from the very beginning as export economies and built their development around the export sector. This is in comparison and in contrast to the old stage theory of history derived from the German historical school, in which the evolution was always from local autarky to gradual evolution of specialization and division of labor. It is this last pattern that is described here, even though it may not characterize the particular evolution that in fact has occurred.

2. For an excellent summary of the anthropological literature dealing with trade in tribal societies, see Elizabeth Colson (1974).

3. Jewish traders in the Mediterranean in the 11th century "solved" the agency problem as a result of close community relationships amongst themselves that lowered information costs and enabled them to act as a group to ostracize and retaliate against agents who violated their commercial code. See Avner Greif (1989).

4. Philip D. Curtin's *Cross-Cultural Trade in World History* (1984) summarizes a good deal of the literature, but is short on analysis and examination of the mechanisms essential to the structure of such trade. *The Cambridge Economic History*, Volume III (1966), has more useful details on the organization of such trade.

5. North and Barry R. Weingast (1989) provide a history and analysis of the political institutions of 17th century England leading up to the Revolution of 1688 and of the consequences for the development of the English capital market.

6. See North (1981), particularly chapter 13, and Chandler (1977). Joseph Stiglitz's (1989) essay "Markets, Market Failures, and Development" details some of the theoretical issues.

7. The transaction sector (that proportion of transaction costs going through the market and therefore measureable) of the U.S. economy was 25 percent of GNP in 1870 and 45 percent of GNP in 1970 (Wallis and North, 1986).

8. There is an extensive literature on the Suq. A sophisticated analysis (on which I have relied) focused on the Suq in Sefrou, Morocco is contained in Geertz, Geertz, and Rosen (1979).

9. For a much more detailed description and analysis of the evolution of European trade see Tracy (forthcoming), particularly Volume II. For a game theoretic analysis of one aspect of this trade revival see P. R. Milgrom, North, and Weingast (1990).

10. The concept of path dependence was developed by W. Brian Arthur (1988, 1989) and Paul David (1985) to explore the path of technological change. I believe the concept has equal explanatory power in helping us understand institutional change. In both cases increasing returns are the key to path dependence, but in the case of institutional change the process is more complex because of the key role of political organizations in the process.

11. The subsequent history of Spanish rise and decline is summarized in North and Thomas (1973).

12. For a summary account of the Latin American experience, see Veliz (1980) or Glade (1969).

REFERENCES

Arthur, W. Brian, "Self-Reinforcing Mechanisms in Economics." In Anderson, Phillip W., Kenneth J. Arrow, and David Pines, eds., *The Economy as an Evolving Complex System.* Reading, MA: Addison-Wesley, 1988.

Arthur, W. Brian, "Competing Technologies, Increasing Returns, and Lock-In by Historical Events," *Economic Journal*, 1989, 99, 116–31.

Barbour, Violet, "Capitalism in Amsterdam in the Seventeenth Century," *Johns Hopkins University Studies in Historical and Political Science*, Volume LXVIII. Baltimore: The Johns Hopkins University Press, 1949.

The Cambridge Economic History. Cambridge: Cambridge University Press, 1966.

Chandler, Alfred, *The Visible Hand.* Cambridge: The Belknap Press, 1977.

Colson, Elizabeth, *Tradition and Contract: The Problem of Order.* Chicago: Adeline Publishing, 1974.

Curtin, Philip D., *Cross-Cultural Trade in World History.* Cambridge: Cambridge University Press, 1984.

David, Paul, "Clio and the Economics of QWERTY," *American Economic Review*, 1985, 75, 332–37.

De Roover F. E., "Early Examples of Marine Insurance," *Journal of Economic History*, November 1945, 5, 172–200.

Geertz, C., H. Geertz, and L. Rosen, *Meaning and Order in Moroccan Society.* Cambridge: Cambridge University Press, 1979.

Glade, W. P., *The Latin American Economies: A Study of Their Institutional Evolution.* New York: American Book, 1969.

Greif, Avner, "Reputation and Economic Institutions in Medieval Trade: Evidences from the Geniza Documents," *Journal of Economic History*, 1989.

Hughes, J. R. T., "A World Elsewhere: The Importance of Starting English." In Thompson, F. M. L., ed., *Essays in Honor of H. J. Habakkuk.* Oxford: Oxford University Press, 1989.

Jones, E. L., *The European Miracle: Environments, Economies, and Geopolitics in the History of Europe and Asia.* Cambridge: Cambridge University Press, 1981.

Kalt, J. P., and M. A. Zupan, "Capture and Ideology in the Economic Theory of Politics," *American Economic Review*, 1984, *74*, 279–300.

Lopez, Robert S., and Irving W. Raymond, *Medieval Trade in the Mediterranean World.* New York: Columbia University Press, 1955.

Milgrom, P. R., D. C. North, and B. R. Weingast, "The Role of Institutions in the Revival of Trade: The Medieval Law Merchant," *Economics and Politics*, March 1990, *II*.

Mitchell, William, *An Essay on the Early History of the Law Merchant.* New York: Burt Franklin Press, 1969.

Nelson, Douglas, and Eugene Silberberg, "Ideology and Legislator Shirking," *Economic Inquiry*, January 1987, *25*, 15–25.

North, Douglass C., "Location Theory and Regional Economic Growth," *Journal of Political Economy*, June 1955, *LXIII*, 243–58.

North, Douglass C., *Structure and Change in Economic History.* New York: Norton, 1981.

North, Douglass C., and Robert Thomas, *The Rise of the Western World: A New Economic History.* Cambridge: Cambridge University Press, 1973.

North, Douglass C., and Barry R. Weingast, "The Evolution of Institutions Governing Public Choice in 17th Century England," *Journal of Economic History*, November 1989, *5*, 172–200.

Posner, Richard, "A Theory of Primitive Society, with Special Reference to the Law," *Journal of Law and Economics*, April 1980, *XXIII*, 1–54.

Rosenberg, Nathan, and L. E. Bridzell, *How the West Grew Rich: The Economic Transformation of the Industrial World.* New York: Basic Books, 1986.

Stiglitz, Joseph, "Markets, Market Failures, and Development," *American Economic Review*, 1989, *79*, 197–203.

Tracy, James, *A Financial Revolution in the Hapsburg Netherlands: Renters and Rentiers in the Country of Holland, 1515–1565.* Berkeley: University of California Press, 1985.

Tracy, James, *The Rise of Merchant Empires.* Cambridge: Cambridge University Press, 1990.

Udovitch, Abraham, "At the Origins of the Western Commenda: Islam, Israel, Byzanteum?" *Speculum*, April 1962, *XXXVII*, 198–207.

Veliz, C., *The Centralist Tradition of Latin America.* Princeton: Princeton University Press, 1980.

Wallis, John J., and Douglass C. North, "Measuring the Transaction Sector in the American Economy, 1870–1970." In Engermann, Stanley, and Robert Gallman, eds., *Income and Wealth: Long-Term Factors in American Economic Growth.* Chicago: University of Chicago Press, 1986.

Watts, R., and J. Zimmerman, "Agency Problems, Auditing, and the Theory of the Firm: Some Evidence," *Journal of Law and Economics*, October 1983, *XXVI*, 613–33.

Williamson, Oliver E., *Markets and Hierarchies: Analysis and Antitrust Implications.* New York: Free Press, 1975.

Williamson, Oliver E., *The Economic Institutions of Capitalism.* New York: Free Press, 1985.

Yamey, B. S., "Scientific Bookkeeping and the Rise of Capitalism," *Economic History Review*, Second Series, 1949, *II*, 99–113.

Daron Acemoglu

ROOT CAUSES: A HISTORICAL APPROACH TO ASSESSING THE ROLE OF INSTITUTIONS IN ECONOMIC DEVELOPMENT

Tremendous differences in incomes and standards of living exist today between the rich and the poor countries of the world. Average per capita income in sub-Saharan Africa, for example, is less than one-twentieth that in the United States. Explanations for why the economic fortunes of countries have diverged so much abound. Poor countries, such as those in sub-Saharan Africa, Central America, or South Asia, often lack functioning markets, their populations are poorly educated, and their machinery and technology are outdated or nonexistent. But these are only *proximate* causes of poverty, begging the question of why these places don't have better markets, better human capital, more investments, and better machinery and technology. There must be some *fundamental* causes leading to these outcomes and, via these channels, to dire poverty.

The two main candidates to explain the fundamental causes of differences in prosperity between countries are geography and institutions. The *geography hypothesis*, which has a large following both in the popular imagination and in academia, maintains that the geography, climate, and ecology of a society shape both its technology and the incentives of its inhabitants. It emphasizes forces of nature as a primary factor in the poverty of nations. The alternative, the *institutions hypothesis*, is about human influences. According to this view, some societies have good institutions that encourage investment in machinery, human capital, and better technologies, and, consequently, these countries achieve economic prosperity.

Good institutions have three key characteristics: enforcement of property rights for a broad cross section of society, so that a variety of individuals have incentives to invest and take part in economic life; constraints on the actions of elites, politicians, and other powerful groups, so that these people cannot expropriate the incomes and investments of others or create a highly uneven playing field; and some degree of equal opportunity for broad segments of society, so that individuals can make investments, especially in human capital, and participate in productive economic activities. These good institutions contrast with conditions in many societies of the world, throughout history and today, where the rule of law is applied selectively; property rights are nonexistent for the vast majority of the population; the elites have unlimited political and economic power, and only a small fraction of citizens have access to education, credit, and production opportunities.

Geography's Influence

If you want to believe that geography is the key, look at a world map. Locate the poorest places in the world where per capita incomes are less than one-twentieth those in the United States. You will find almost all of them close to the equator, in very hot regions that experience periodic torrential rains and where, by definition, tropical diseases are widespread.

However, this evidence does not establish that geography is a primary influence on prosperity. It is true there is a *correlation* between geography and prosperity. But correlation does not prove causation.

From *Finance & Development* (June 2003), pp. 27–30.

Most important, there are often omitted factors driving the associations we observe in the data.

Similarly, if you look around the world, you'll see that almost no wealthy country achieves this position without institutions protecting the property rights of investors and imposing some control over the government and elites. Once again, however, this correlation between institutions and economic development could reflect omitted factors or reverse causality.

To make progress in understanding the relative roles of geographic and institutional factors, we need to find a source of exogenous variation in institutions—in other words, a natural experiment where institutions change for reasons unrelated to potential omitted factors (and geographic factors remain constant, as they almost always do).

The colonization of much of the globe by Europeans starting in the fifteenth century provides such a natural experiment. The colonization experience transformed the institutions in many lands conquered or controlled by Europeans but, by and large, had no effect on their geographies. Therefore, if geography is the key factor determining the economic potential of an area or a country, the places that were rich before the arrival of the Europeans should have remained rich after the colonization experience and, in fact, should still be rich today. In other words, since the key determinant of prosperity remains the same, we should see a high degree of persistence in economic outcomes. If, on the other hand, it is institutions that are central, then those places where good institutions were introduced or developed should be richer than those in which Europeans introduced or maintained extractive institutions to plunder resources or exploit the non-European population.

Historical evidence suggests that Europeans indeed pursued very different colonization strategies, with very different associated institutions, in various colonies. At one extreme, Europeans set up exclusively extractive institutions, exemplified by the Belgian colonization of the Congo, slave plantations in the Caribbean, and forced labor systems in the mines of Central America. These institutions neither protected the property rights of regular citi-

Figure 4.1 Shifting prosperity

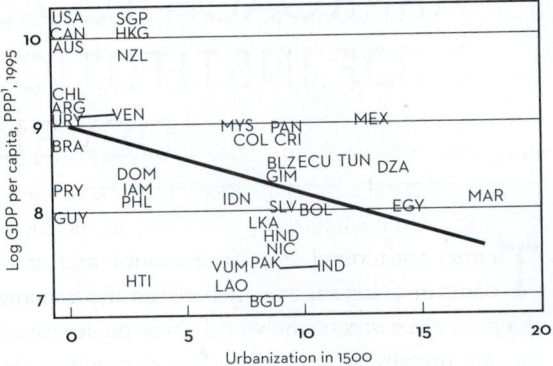

Countries that were rich in 1500 are among the less-well-off societies today.

Source: Author.
Note: ARG = Argentina, AUS = Australia, BGD = Bangladesh, BLZ = Belize, BOL = Bolivia, BRA = Brazil, CAN = Canada, CHL = Chile, COL = Colombia, CRI = Costa Rica, DOM = Dominican Republic, DZA = Albania, ECU = Ecuador, EGY = Egypt, GTM = Guatemala, GUY = Guyana, JAM = Jamaica, HKG = Hong Kong SAR, HND = Honduras, HTI = Haiti, IDN = Idonesia, IND = India, LAO = Lao People's Democratic Republic, LKA = Sri Lanka, MAR = Morocco, MEX = Mexico, MYS = Malaysia, NIC = Nicaragua, NZL = New Zealand, PAK = Pakistan, PAN = Panama, PER = Peru, PHL = Philippines, PRY = Paraguay, SGP = Singapore, SLV = El Salvador, TUN = Tunisia, URY = Uruguay, USA = United States, VEN = Venezuela, VNM = Vietnam
[1]Purchasing power parity.

zens nor constrained the power of elites. At the other extreme, Europeans founded a number of colonies where they created settler societies, replicating—and often improving—the European form of institutions protecting private property. Primary examples of this mode of colonization include Australia, Canada, New Zealand, and the United States. The settlers in these societies also managed to place significant constraints on elites and politicians, even if they had to fight to achieve this objective.

Reversal of Fortune

So what happened to economic development after colonization? Did places that were rich before colonization remain rich, as suggested by the geography hypothesis? Or did economic fortunes change systematically as a result of the changes in institutions?

The historical evidence shows no evidence of the persistence suggested by the geography hypothesis. On the contrary, there is a remarkable *reversal of fortune* in economic prosperity. Societies like the Mughals in India and the Aztecs and the Incas in America that were among the richest civilizations in 1500 are among the poorer societies of today. In contrast, countries occupying the territories of the less developed civilizations in North America, New Zealand, and Australia are now much *richer* than those in the lands of the Mughals, the Aztecs, and the Incas. Moreover, the reversal of fortune is not confined to this comparison. Using various proxies for prosperity before modern times, we can show that the reversal is a much more widespread phenomenon. For example, before industrialization, only relatively developed societies could sustain significant urbanization, so urbanization rates are a relatively good proxy for prosperity before European colonization. The chart here shows a strong negative relationship between urbanization rates in 1500 and income per capita today. That is, the former European colonies that are relatively rich today are those that were poor before the Europeans arrived.

This reversal is *prima facie* evidence against the most standard versions of the geography hypothesis discussed above: it cannot be that the climate, ecology, or disease environments of the tropical areas have condemned these countries to poverty today, because these same areas with the same climate, ecology, and disease environment were richer than the temperate areas 500 years ago. Although it is possible that the reversal may be related to geographic factors whose effects on economic prosperity vary over time—for example, certain characteristics that first cause prosperity, then condemn nations to poverty—there is no evidence of any such factor or any support for sophisticated geography hypotheses of this sort.

Is the reversal of fortune consistent with the institutions hypothesis? The answer is yes. In fact, once we look at the variation in colonization strategies, we see that the reversal of fortune is exactly what the institutions hypothesis predicts. European colonialism made Europeans the most politically powerful group, with the capability to influence institutions more

than any indigenous group was able to at the time. In places where Europeans did not settle and cared little about aggregate output and the welfare of the population, in places where there was a large population that could be coerced and employed cheaply in mines or in agriculture or simply taxed, in places where there were resources to be extracted, Europeans pursued the strategy of setting up extractive institutions or taking over existing extractive institutions and hierarchical structures. In those colonies, there were no constraints on the power of the elites (which were typically the Europeans themselves and their allies) and no civil or property rights for the majority of the population; in fact, many of them were forced into labor or enslaved. Contrasting with this pattern, in colonies where there was little to be extracted, where most of the land was empty, where the disease environment was favorable, Europeans settled in large numbers and developed laws and institutions to ensure that they themselves were protected, in both their political and their economic lives. In these colonies, the institutions were therefore much more conducive to investment and economic growth.

This evidence does not mean that geography does not matter at all, however. Which places were rich and which were poor before Europeans arrived might have been determined by geographic factors. These geographic factors also likely influenced the institutions that Europeans introduced. For example, the climate and soil quality in the Caribbean made it productive to grow sugar there, encouraging the development of a plantation system based on slavery. What the evidence shows instead is that geography neither condemns a nation to poverty nor guarantees its economic success. If you want to understand why a country is poor today, you have to look at its institutions rather than its geography.

No Natural Gravitation

If institutions are so important for economic prosperity, why do some societies choose or end up with bad institutions? Moreover, why do these bad institutions persist long after their disastrous consequences are apparent? Is it an accident of history or the result of misconceptions or mistakes by societies or their policymakers? Recent empirical and theoretical research suggests that the answer is no: there are no compelling reasons to think that societies will naturally gravitate toward good institutions. Institutions not only affect the economic prospects of nations but also are central to the distribution of income among individuals and groups in society—in other words, institutions affect not only the size of the social pie, but also how it is distributed.

This perspective implies that a potential change from dysfunctional and bad institutions toward better ones that will increase the size of the social pie may nonetheless be blocked when such a change significantly reduces the slice that powerful groups receive from the pie and when they cannot be credibly compensated for this loss. That there is no natural gravitation toward good institutions is illustrated by the attitudes of the landed elites and the emperors in Austria-Hungary and in Russia during the nineteenth century. These elite groups blocked industrialization and even the introduction of railways and protected the old regime because they realized capitalist growth and industrialization would reduce their power and their privileges.

Similarly, European colonists did not set up institutions to benefit society as a whole. They chose good institutions when it was in their interests to do so, when they would be the ones living under the umbrella of these institutions, as in much of the New World. In contrast, they introduced or maintained existing extractive institutions when it was in their interest to extract resources from the non-European populations of the colonies, as in much of Africa, Central America, the Caribbean, and South Asia. Furthermore, these extractive institutions showed no sign of evolving into better institutions, either under European control or once these colonies gained independence. In almost all cases, we can link the persistence of extractive institutions to the fact that, even after independence, the elites in these societies had a lot to lose from institutional reform. Their political power and claim to economic rents rested on the existing extractive institutions, as best illustrated by the Caribbean plantation owners whose wealth directly depended on slavery and extractive institutions. Any reform of the system, however beneficial for the country as a whole, would be a direct threat to the owners.

European colonialism is only one part of the story of the institutions of the former colonies, and many countries that never experienced European colonialism nonetheless suffer from institutional problems (while certain other former European colonies have arguably some of the best institutions in the world today). Nevertheless, the perspective developed in this article applies to these cases as well: institutional problems are important in a variety of instances, and, in most of these, the source of institutional problems and the difficulty of institutional reform lie in the fact that any major change creates winners and losers, and the potential losers are often powerful enough to resist change.

The persistence of institutions and potential resistance to reform do not mean that institutions are unchanging. There is often significant institutional evolution, and even highly dysfunctional institutions can be successfully transformed. For example, Botswana managed to build a functioning democracy after its independence from Britain and become the fastest-growing country in the world. Institutional change will happen either when groups that favor change become powerful enough to impose it on the potential losers, or when societies can strike a bargain with potential losers so as to credibly compensate them after the change takes place or, perhaps, shield them from the most adverse consequences of these changes. Recognizing the importance of institutions in economic development and the often formidable barriers to beneficial institutional reform is the first step toward significant progress in jump-starting rapid growth in many areas of the world today.

Ronald Rogowski
POLITICAL CLEAVAGES AND CHANGING EXPOSURE TO TRADE

Why countries have the political cleavages they do and why those cleavages change are among the enduring mysteries of comparative politics. Among the many factors that have been adduced as partial explanations are preexisting cultural and religious divisions, the rapidity and timing of industrialization or of the grant of mass suffrage, the sequence of "crises" of modernization, the electoral system, and—most recently—the product cycle (see, inter alia, Binder et al. 1971; Duverger 1959; Kurth 1979a, 1979b; Lipset and Rokkan 1967; Rokkan 1970, 1981).

Without denying the importance of any of these variables, I want to suggest the relevance of a factor that has, until now, been widely neglected: externally induced changes—in countries with different factor endowments—in exposure to international trade.

To be sure, some studies of individual countries, and even a few comparative inquiries, have argued the significance of changing international trade in particular circumstances: one thinks, in particular, of Abraham 1981, Gerschenkron 1943, Gourevitch 1977 and 1986, Rosenberg 1943, Sunkel and Paz 1973. One author, David R. Cameron (1978), has even suggested a relation, at least in recent decades, between exposure to trade and the rate of growth in state expenditure.

Arguing much more generally, I shall try to show that basic results of the theory of international trade—including, in particular, the well-known Stolper-Samuelson Theorem (Stolper and Samuelson 1941)—imply that increases or decreases in the costs and difficulty of international trade should powerfully affect domestic political cleavages and should do so

differently, but predictably, in countries with different factor endowments. Moreover, I shall suggest that these implications conform surprisingly well with what has been observed about patterns of cleavage and about changes in those patterns in a great variety of countries during four periods of global change in exposure to trade, namely the "long" sixteenth century, the nineteenth century, the Depression of the 1930s, and the years since World War II.

Nonetheless, what I present here remains conjectural and preliminary. The evidence I shall be able to advance is suggestive rather than conclusive. It is principally the clarity of the logical case that seems to me to justify further refinement and testing.

The Stolper-Samuelson Theorem

In 1941 Wolfgang Stolper and Paul Samuelson solved conclusively the old riddle of gains and losses from protection (or, for that matter, from free trade). They showed that in any society protection benefits—and liberalization of trade harms—owners of factors in which that society is *poorly* endowed, relative to the rest of the world, as well as producers who use the scarce factors intensively.[1] Conversely, protection harms—and liberalization benefits—owners of factors the given society holds *abundantly* relative to the rest of the world, and producers who use the abundant factors intensively.[2] Thus, in a society rich in labor but poor in capital, protection would benefit capital and harm labor; and liberalization of trade would benefit labor and harm capital.

So far, the theorem is what it is usually perceived to be: merely a statement, if an important

From *American Political Science Review* 81, no. 4 (December 1987), pp. 1121–37.

and sweeping one, about the effects of tariff policy. The picture is altered, however, when one realizes that exogenous changes can have exactly the same effects as increases or decreases in protection. A cheapening of transport costs, for example, is indistinguishable in its impact from an across-the-board decrease in every affected state's tariffs (Mundell 1957, 330); so is any change in the international regime that decreases the risks or the transaction costs of trade. The converse is of course equally true: when a nation's external transport becomes dearer, or its trade less secure, it is affected exactly as if it had imposed a higher tariff.

The point is of more than academic interest because we know, historically, that major changes in the risks and costs of international trade have occurred: notoriously, the railroads and steamships of the nineteenth century brought drastically cheaper transportation (Landes 1969, 153–54, 196, 201–2; Hobsbawm 1979, Chap. 3); so, in our own generation, did supertankers, cheap oil, and containerization (Rosecrance 1986, 142). According to the familiar argument of Charles Kindleberger (1973) and others, international hegemony decreases both the risks and the transaction costs of international trade; and the decline of hegemonic power makes trade more expensive, perhaps—as, according to this interpretation, in the 1930s—prohibitively so. Analyzing a much earlier period, the Belgian historian Henri Pirenne (1939) attributed much of the final decline of the Roman Empire to the growing insecurity of interregional, and especially of Mediterranean, trade after 600 A.D.[3]

Global changes of these kinds, it follows, should have had global consequences. The "transportation revolutions" of the sixteenth, the nineteenth, and scarcely less of the mid-twentieth century must have benefited, in each affected country, owners and intensive employers of locally abundant factors and must have harmed owners and intensive employers of locally abundant factors. The events of the 1930s should have had exactly the opposite effect. What, however, will have been the *political* consequences of those shifts of wealth and income? To answer that question we require a rudimentary

model of the political process and a somewhat more definite one of the economy.

Simple Models of the Polity and the Economy

I shall assume of domestic political processes only two things: (1) that the beneficiaries of a change will try to continue and accelerate it, while the victims of the same change will endeavor to retard or to halt it; and (2) that those who enjoy a sudden increase in (actual or potential)[4] wealth and income will thereby be enabled to expand their political influence as well (cf. Becker 1983). As regards international trade, (1) implies that the gainers from any exogenous change will seek to continue and to expand free trade, while the losers will seek protection (and, if that fails, imperialism);[5] (2) implies that those who gain, or are positioned to gain, economically from exogenous changes in international trade will increase their political power as well.

Economically, I propose to adopt with minor refinements the traditional three-factor model—land, labor, and capital—and to assume, for now, that the land-labor ratio informs us fully about any country's endowment of those two factors. No country, in other words, can be rich both in land and in labor: a high land-labor ratio implies abundance of land and scarcity of labor; a low ratio signifies the opposite. (I shall later relax this assumption.) Finally, I shall simply define an *advanced* economy as one in which capital is abundant.

This model of factor endowments inevitably oversimplifies reality and will require amendment. Its present simplicity, however, permits us in theory to place any country's economy into one of four cells (see Figure 4.2), according to (1) whether it is advanced or backward and (2) whether its land-labor ratio is high or low. We recognize, in other words, only economies that are (1) capital rich, land rich, and labor poor; (2) capital rich, land poor, and labor rich; (3) capital poor, land rich, and labor poor; or (4) capital poor, land poor, and labor rich.

Political Effects of Increasing Exposure to Trade

I shall now try to demonstrate that the Stolper-Samuelson Theorem, applied to our simple model, implies that increasing exposure to trade must result in *urban-rural conflict* in two kinds of economies and in *class conflict* in the two others.

Consider first the upper right-hand cell of Figure 4.2: the advanced (therefore capital-rich) economy endowed abundantly in labor but poorly in land. Expanding trade must benefit both capitalists and workers; it harms only landowners and the pastoral and agricultural enterprises that use land intensively. Both capitalists and workers—that is to say, almost the entire urban sector—should favor free trade; agriculture should on the whole be protectionist. Moreover, we expect the capitalists and the workers to try, very likely in concert, to expand their political influence. Depending on preexisting circumstances, they may seek concretely an extension of the franchise, a reapportionment of seats, a diminution in the powers of an upper house or of a gentry-based political elite, or a violent "bourgeois" revolution.

Urban-rural conflict should also arise in backward, labor-poor economies (the lower left-hand cell of Figure 4.2) when trade expands, albeit with a complete reversal of fronts. In such "frontier" societies, both capital and labor are scarce: hence both are harmed by expanding trade and will seek protection. Only land is abundant, and therefore only agriculture will gain from free trade. Farmers and pastoralists will try to expand their influence in some movement of a "Populist" and antiurban stripe.

Conversely, in backward economies with low land-labor ratios (the lower right-hand cell of Figure 4.2), land and capital are scarce and labor is abundant. The model therefore predicts *class conflict*: labor will pursue free trade and expanded political power (including, in some circumstances, a workers' revolution); landowners, capitalists, and capital-intensive manufacturers will unite to support protection, imperialism, and a politics of continued exclusion. (Lest the picture of a rising in support of freer markets seem too improbable a priori, I observe at once its general conformity with Popkin's 1979 astute interpretation of the Vietnamese revolution.)

The reverse form of class conflict is expected to arise in the final case, that of an advanced but land-rich economy (the upper left-hand cell of Figure 4.2) under increasing exposure to trade. Because both capital and land are abundant, capitalists,

Figure 4.2 Four Main Types of Factor Endowments

	Land-Labor Ratio	
	High	**Low**
Advanced Economy	Abundant: Capital Land Scarce: Labor	Abundant: Capital Labor Scarce: Land
Backward Economy	Abundant: Land Scarce: Capital Labor	Abundant: Labor Scarce: Capital Land

Figure 4.3 Predicted Effects of Expanding Exposure to Trade

	Land-Labor Ratio	
	High	Low
Advanced Economy	Class cleavage: Land and capital free-trading assertive / Labor defensive, protectionist	Urban-rural cleavage: Capital and land free-trading assertive / Labor defensive, protectionist (Radicalism)
Backward Economy	Urban-rural cleavage: Land free-trading, assertive / Labor and capital defensive, protectionist (U.S. Populism)	Class cleavage: Labor free-trading, assertive / Land and capital defensive, protectionist (Socialism)

capital-intensive industries, and agriculture will all benefit from, and will endorse, free trade; labor being scarce, workers and labor-intensive industries will embrace protection and (if need be) imperialism. The benefited sectors will seek to expand their political power, if not by disfranchisement then by curtailment of workers' economic prerogatives and suppression of their organizations.

These implications of the theory of international trade (summarized in Figure 4.3) seem clear, but do they in any way describe reality? I shall address that question more fully below, but for now it is worth observing how closely the experience of three major countries—Germany, Britain, and the United States—conforms to this analysis in the period of rapidly expanding trade in the last third of the nineteenth century; and how far it can go to explain otherwise puzzling disparities in those states' patterns of political evolution.

Germany and the United States were both still relatively backward, that is, capital-poor, societies: both, in fact, imported considerable amounts of capital in this period (Feis 1965, 24–25 and Chap. 3). Germany, however, was rich in labor and poor in land; the United States, of course, was in exactly the opposite position. Again, the demonstration is easy: the United States imported—and Germany exported

(not least to the United States)—workers.[6] The theory, of course, predicts class conflict in Germany, with labor the "revolutionary" and free-trading element and with land and capital united in support of protection and imperialism. Surely this description will not ring false to any student of German socialism or of Germany's infamous "marriage of iron and rye."[7] For the United States, conversely, the theory predicts—quite accurately, I submit—urban-rural conflict, with the agrarians now assuming the "revolutionary" and free-trading role and with capital and labor uniting in a protectionist and imperialist coalition. E. E. Schattschneider (1960) or Walter Dean Burnham (1970) could hardly have described more succinctly the history of populism and of the election of 1896.[8]

Britain, on the other hand, was already an advanced economy in the later nineteenth century, one in which capital was so abundant that it was exported in vast quantities (Feis 1965, Chap. 1). That it was also rich in labor is demonstrated by its extensive exports of that factor to the United States, Canada, Australia, New Zealand, and Africa.[9] Britain therefore falls into the upper right-hand quadrant of Figure 4.2 and is predicted to exhibit a rural-urban cleavage, with fronts opposite to those found in the United States: capitalists and labor unite in support of free trade and in demands for expanded political power, while landowners and agriculture support protection and imperialism.

While this picture surely obscures important nuances, it illuminates a crucial difference between Britain and, for example, Germany in this period: in Britain, capitalists and labor *did* unite effectively in the Liberal party and forced an expanded suffrage and curtailment of (still principally landowning) aristocratic power; in Germany, with liberalism shattered (Sheehan 1978), the suffrage for the powerful state parliaments was actually contracted, and—far from eroding aristocratic power—the bourgeoisie grew more and more *verjunkert* in style and aspirations.

Political Effects of Declining Exposure to Trade

When declining hegemony or rising costs of transportation substantially constrict external trade, the gainers and losers are simply the reverse of those under increasing exposure to trade: owners of locally scarce factors prosper; owners of locally abundant ones suffer. The latter, however, can invoke no such simple remedy as protection or imperialism; aside from tentative "internationalist" efforts to restore orderly markets (Gourevitch 1986, Chap. 4), they must largely accept their fate. Power and policy, we expect, will shift in each case toward the owners and intensive users of scarce factors.

Let us first consider the situation of the highly *developed* (and therefore, by our earlier definition, capital-rich) economies. In an economy of this kind with a high land-labor ratio (the upper left-hand cell of Figure 4.2), we should expect intense *class* conflict precipitated by a newly aggressive working class. Land and capital are both abundant in such an economy; hence, under declining trade, owners of both factors (and producers who use either factor intensively) lose. Labor being the only scarce resource, workers are well positioned to reap a significant windfall from the protection that dearer or riskier trade affords; and, according to our earlier assumption, like any other

benefited class they will soon try to parlay their greater economic into greater political power. Capitalists and landowners, even if they were previously at odds, will unite to oppose labor's demands.

Quite to the contrary, declining trade in an advanced economy that is labor rich and land poor (the upper right-hand cell of Figure 4.2) will entail *urban-rural* conflict. Capital and labor, being both abundant, are both harmed by the contraction of external trade. Agriculture, as the intense exploiter of the only scarce factor, gains significantly and quickly tries to translate its gain into greater political control.

Urban-rural conflict is also predicted for backward, land-rich countries under declining trade; but here agriculture is on the defensive. Labor and capital being both scarce, both benefit from the contraction of trade; land, as the only locally abundant factor, retreats. The urban sectors unite, in a parallel to the "radical" coalition of labor-rich developed countries under expanding trade, to demand an increased voice in the state.

Finally, in backward economies rich in labor rather than land, class conflict resumes, with labor this time on the defensive. Capital and land, as the locally scarce factors, gain from declining trade; labor, locally abundant, loses economically and is soon threatened politically.

Observe again, as a first test of the plausibility of these results—summarized in Figure 4.4—how they appear to account for some prominent disparities of political response to the last precipitous decline of international trade, the Depression of the 1930s. The U.S. New Deal represented a sharp turn to the left and occasioned a significant increase in organized labor's political power. In Germany, a depression of similar depth (gauged by unemployment rates and declines in industrial production [Landes 1969, 391]) brought to power first Hindenburg's and then Hitler's dictatorship. In both, landowners exercised markedly greater influence than they had under Weimar (Abraham 1981, 85–115 and Chap. 4; Gessner 1977); and indeed a credible case can be made out that the rural sector was the principal early beneficiary of the Nazi regime (see, inter

Figure 4.4 Predicted Effects of Declining Exposure to Trade

Land-Labor Ratio

	High	Low
Advanced Economy	Class cleavage: Labor gains power. Land and capital lose. (U.S. New deal)	Urban-rural cleavage: Land gains power. Labor and capital lose. (Western European Fascism)
Backward Economy	Urban-rural cleavage: Labor and capital gain power. Land loses. (South American Populism)	Class cleavage: Land and capital gain power. Labor loses. (Asian & Eastern European Fascism)

alia, Gerschenkron 1943, 154–63; Gies 1968; Holt 1936, 173–74, 194ff.; Schoenbaum 1966, 156–63).[10] Yet this is exactly the broad difference that the model would lead us to anticipate if we accept that by 1930 both countries were economically advanced—although Germany, after reparations and cessions of industrial territory, was surely less abundant in capital than the United States—but the United States remained rich in land, which in Germany was scarce. Only an obtuse observer would claim that such factors as cultural inheritance and recent defeat in war played no role; but surely it is also important to recognize the sectoral impact of declining trade in the two societies.[11]

As regards the less-developed economies of the time, it may be profitable to contrast the Depression's impact on such South American cases as Argentina and Brazil with its effects in the leading Asian country, Japan. In Argentina and Brazil, it is usually asserted (Cardoso and Faletto 1979, 124–26 and Chap. 5; Skidmore and Smith 1984, 59–60; Sunkel and Paz 1973, 352–54), the Depression gave rise to, or at the least strengthened, "Populist" coalitions that united labor and the urban middle classes in opposition to traditional, landowning elites. In Japan, growing military influence suppressed representative institutions and nascent workers' organizations, ruling in the interest—albeit probably not under the domination—of landowners and capitalists (Kato

1974; Reischauer 1974, 186–87, 195–99). (Similar suppressions of labor occurred in China and Vietnam [Clubb 1972, 135–40; Popkin 1979, xix, 215].)

In considering these contrasting responses, should we not take into account that Argentina and Brazil were rich in land and poor in labor (recall the extent of immigration, especially into Argentina), while in Japan (and, with local exceptions, in Asia generally) labor was abundant and land was scarce (respectively, the lower left- and right-hand cells of Figure 4.4)?

A Preliminary Survey of the Evidence

I want now to undertake a more systematic, if still sketchy, examination of the historical evidence that bears on the hypotheses developed here. This effort will serve principally to suggest directions for further research; it can in no way be described as conclusive.

The "Long" Sixteenth Century

It has long been recognized that improvements in navigation and shipbuilding permitted, from about 1450 on, a previously unimagined expansion of trade, which eventuated in the European "discovery" and colonization of the Americas (Cipolla 1965). Among social scientists, Immanuel Wallerstein (1974) has studied this period most intensively; and it is worth emphasizing that the present analysis conforms with essential aspects, and, indeed, permits some clarification, of his.

Within the context of the age, what Wallerstein calls the *core* economies of the new world system—those, essentially, of northwestern Europe—were defined by their abundance in capital and labor, and by their relative scarcity of land. The *periphery* can be described as the exact inverse: rich in land, poor in both capital and—often leading to the adoption of slavery or serfdom—labor. Under expanding trade, the regimes of the core come to be dominated by a "bourgeois" coalition of capital and skilled labor (the Dutch Republic, the Tudors), and of the manufactures that use both intensively; the older, landed elites lose ground. Conversely, in the periphery, land—in the persons of plantation owners and *Gutsherren*—suppresses both capital and labor and, indeed, almost all urban life.

So far the equation seems apt. Can we, however, not go on to define that Wallersteinian chimera, the *semiperiphery* (Wallerstein 1974, 102–7), as comprising economies that fall into the lower right-hand cell of Figure 4.2, economies poor in capital and land, rich in labor? That would, I suspect, accurately describe most of the southern European economies in this period; and it would correctly predict (see again Figure 4.3) the intense class conflict (including the German Peasants War [Moore 1967, 463–67]) and the wholly retrograde and protectionist policies adopted by a peculiarly united class of landowners and capitalists in many of these regions.[12]

The Nineteenth Century

We can again proceed regionally, generalizing on the sketch of Britain, Germany, and the United States developed earlier for this period. For the period just before the great cheapening of transportation—roughly at the middle of the nineteenth century[13]—Britain can stand as the surrogate for the advanced and labor-rich economies of northwest Europe generally, including Belgium, the Netherlands, and northern France (Hobsbawm 1962, Chap. 9;

Landes 1969, Chap. 3). For this whole region, as for Britain, the model predicts that expanding trade would engender rural-urban conflict: capitalists and workers, united in support of free trade and greater urban influence, oppose a more traditional and protectionist landed sector. It does not seem to me farfetched to see the powerful liberalism and radicalism of this whole region in the later nineteenth century (Carstairs 1980, 50, 62; Cobban 1965, 21–28, 58–67; Daalder 1966, 196–98; Lorwin 1966, 152–55)—or, for that matter, much of the conflict between secularism and clericalism—in this light.

Almost all of the rest of Europe at the dawn of this period can be compared with Germany: poor in capital and in land, rich in labor.[14] (The land-labor ratio seems as a rule to have declined as one moved from north to south within the economically backward regions of Europe [see figures for 1846 in Bowden, Karpovich, and Usher 1937, 3].) As it does for Germany, the model predicts for these other countries, particularly in southern Europe, class conflict as a consequence of increasing exposure to trade: workers (including agricultural wage laborers) press for more open markets and greater influence; capitalists and landowners unite in support of protection and more traditional rule. In its main aspect, this seems to me only a restatement of a central tendency that has long been remarked, namely that class conflict in the nineteenth century came at an earlier phase of industrialization, and more bitterly, to southern and central than to northwestern Europe (e.g., Lipset 1970, 28–30; Macridis 1978, 485–87; cf. Thomson 1962, 375–78); and it seems to me a more credible account of these regions' extremism than Maurice Duverger's (1959, 238) famous invocation of an allegedly more mercurial "Latin" temperament.

The United States, finally, represents the land-rich but labor- and capital-poor "frontier societies" of this period generally: most of both Americas, Australia, New Zealand, even those parts of central and southern Africa that would soon be opened to commercial agriculture. Here, expanding trade benefits and strengthens landowners and farmers against protectionist capitalists and workers (although, as in the United States, the protectionist forces may still prevail); rural-urban conflict ensues, precipitated by demands from the rural sector.

Again, this does not at first glance appear wide of the mark. In many of the Latin American societies, this period cemented landed rule (Skidmore and Smith 1984, 50; Sunkel and Paz 1973, 306–21); in the United States and Canada, it was characterized by conflicts between the industrial East and the agricultural West (Easterbrook and Aitken 1958, 503–4); in almost wholly agricultural Australia, trade precipitated a cleavage between free-trading landowners and increasingly protectionist rural and urban wage labor (Gollan 1955, esp. 162–69; Greenwood 1955, 216–20).

In all of these cases, as I have emphasized before, other factors were surely at work and important aspects are neglected by the present analysis; but it is essential also not to ignore the benefits and costs of expanding trade to the various sectors.

The Depression of the 1930s

Here the fit between theory and reality seems quite strong. Not only the United States but Canada, Australia, and New Zealand were by this time advanced, land-rich economies. Labor, their only scarce factor, gained from the collapse of international trade: workers became more militant; policy shifted to the left. Most Latin American societies remained land-rich but backward; and for them this was quite generally the period of "Populist" coalitions of the two scarce factors, labor and capital. In developed northern Europe, owners and exploiters of the locally scarce factor of land grew more assertive, and generally more powerful, wherever previous developments had not caused them to disappear; capitalists and workers lost ground. Finally, throughout the backward regions of the world economy, where labor was abundant and land was scarce—not only in Asia but in southern and eastern Europe—labor lost to a renascent coalition of the locally scarce factors of land and capital: in Spain, Italy, Rumania, Hungary, and Poland, to name only the most prominent cases (Carsten 1967, Chaps. 2, 5 and pp. 194–204).

After World War II

Under U.S. hegemony, and with new economies in transportation and communication, the West since World War II has experienced one of history's more dramatic expansions of international trade (Organization for Economic Cooperation and Development [OECD] 1982, 62–63).Again, the theory would lead us to expect different regional consequences.

In the developed, labor-rich and land-poor economies—including now not only most of Europe but Japan—the model would predict an "end of ideology," at least as regards issues of class: labor and capital, both beneficiaries of expanding trade, unite to advance it and to oppose any remaining pretensions to rule by the landowning groups.[15] Conversely, in the land-rich and still underdeveloped economies of Latin America, expanding trade displaces the Depression-era "Populist" coalitions of labor and capital and brings renewed influence to the landed sectors. The areas of Asia and of southern Europe that are economically backward and abundant only in labor experience labor militancy and, in not a few cases, revolutionary workers' movements. Finally, and perhaps more as a statement about the future, the few economies rich in both capital and land—principally those of North America, Australia, and New Zealand—should, as they become seriously exposed to international trade, experience class conflict and a considerable suppression of labor. Capital and agriculture will for the most part unite in support of the free trade that benefits them; labor, as the locally scarce factor, will favor protection and imperialism.

Further Implications

To the extent that the model has gained any credibility from the foregoing brief survey, it may be useful to observe some of its other implications for disciplinary riddles and conjectures. Take first Alexander Gerschenkron's (1962) observation, and Albert O. Hirschman's (1968) subsequent challenge and amendment of it, that "latecomers" to economic development tend to assign a stronger role to the state. From the present perspective, what should matter more, at least among labor-rich economies, is whether development *precedes* or *follows* significant exposure to trade. In an economy that has accumulated abundant capital before it is opened to trade, capital and labor will operate in relative harmony, and little state intervention will be required. Where trade precedes development, assertive labor faces—as it did in Imperial Germany—the united opposition of capitalists and landowners. To the extent that labor wins this struggle, it will require a strong state to administer the economy; to the extent that capital and land prevail, a state powerful enough to suppress labor is needed. Either route leads to a stronger state.

Even this generalization, however, applies only to economies where labor is abundant, and land scarce. Hence Hirschman's observation that "latecomers" in Latin America do not behave as Gerschenkron predicts should not surprise us. Where land is abundant, and labor scarce—as has generally been true of the Americas—"late" economic modernization (i.e., one that follows significant exposure to trade) radicalizes owners of *land* rather than owners of labor. In such "frontier" economies, labor and capital again find themselves in the same political camp, this time in support of protection. In the absence of class conflict, no powerful state is required.

This last point, of course, sheds some light on Sombart's old question, Why is there no socialism in the United States? If the model is right, the question is appropriately broadened to, Why is there no socialism in land-rich economies? Simply put, socialism develops most readily where labor is favored by rising exposure to trade and capital is not; labor is then progressive and capital is reactionary. But labor is never favored by rising trade where it is scarce. Powerful socialist movements, the present model suggests, are confined to backward and labor-rich economies under conditions of expanding trade (the less-developed European societies in the later nineteenth century, Asia after World War II).

A third riddle this approach may help resolve is that of the coalitional basis and aims of the North in the U.S. Civil War.[16] As Barrington Moore,

Jr., posed the question in a memorable chapter of *Social Origins of Dictatorship and Democracy* (1967, Chap. 3), What was the connection between *protection* and Free Soil in the platform of the Republican party or of the North more generally, and Why did so broad a coalition support both aims?

If, as seems apparent, labor was scarce in the United States, then the nineteenth century's increasing exposure to trade should have depressed, or at least retarded the advance of, wages. By definition, slaves already received a lower wage than they would voluntarily accept (Else, why coerce them?); and increased trade could reasonably be seen as intensifying, or at least as retarding the demise of, slavery. Conversely, protection in a labor-scarce economy might so raise the general wage level (while, paradoxically, also increasing returns to scarce capital) as to make manumission feasible. Hence to link protection and abolition might seem a wholly sensible strategy. Moreover, because protection in that period would benefit workers and capitalists generally, it could attract the support of a very wide coalition. At least some of the mystery seems dissolved.

Relaxing the Reliance on Land-Labor Ratios

For the sake of logical completeness, and to fill a nagging empirical gap, let us now relax the assumption that the land-labor ratio informs us completely about the relative abundance of these two factors. We admit, in other words, that a country may be rich or poor in *both* land and labor. Four new cases arise in theory if (as I suspect) rarely in practice (see Figure 4.5): economies may be, as before, advanced or backward (i.e., capital rich or capital poor); but they may now be rich in both land and labor or poorly endowed in both factors.

Two cases—that of the advanced economy rich in both factors and of the backward one poor in both—are theoretically improbable[17] and politically uninteresting: if all factors were abundant relative to the rest of the world, the society would unanimously

Figure 4.5 Predicted Effects on Economies That Are Rich or Poor in Both Land and Labor

	Land and Labor Both Abundant	Land and Labor Both Scarce
Advanced Economy	N/A	Expanding trade: 　Capital assertive free-trading 　Land and labor protectionist, defensive Declining trade: 　Land and labor gain power. 　Capital loses.
Backward Economy	Expanding trade: 　Land and labor free-trading assertive 　Capital defensive, protectionist Declining trade: 　Capital gains power. 　Land and labor lose.	N/A

embrace free trade; if all were scarce, it would agree on protection. Let us consider, then, the remaining two possibilities.

In an advanced economy where both land and labor are scarce, expanding trade will benefit only capital. Agriculture and labor—*green* and *red*—will unite in support of protection and, if need be, imperialism; only capitalists will embrace free trade. When trade contracts in such an economy, the scarce factors of land and labor gain, and capital loses, influence; farmers and peasants are likely to seek expanded mass participation in politics and a radical curtailment of capitalist power.

In a backward economy with abundant land and labor (a possibility considered explicitly by Hla Myint [1958, 323]), change in exposure to trade again mobilizes a coalition of red and green, but with diametrically opposed positions. Expanding trade now *benefits* farmers and workers but harms capitalists; and the labor-landowner coalition pursues a wider franchise, free trade, and disempowerment of capital. Contracting trade, however, benefits only the owners of capital and injures both workers and farmers; again intense conflict between capital and the other two factors is predicted, ending in either a capitalist dictatorship or an anti-capitalist revolution.

It is tempting, if speculative in the extreme, to see in the red-green coalitions of Scandinavia in the 1930s (Gourevitch 1986, 131–35; Hancock 1972, 30–31; Rokkan 1966, 84) the natural response to trade contraction of (by then) capital-rich but land- and labor-poor economies; and, conversely, to view modern Russian history, at least until well after World War II, as that of a backward but land- *and* labor-rich economy,[18] which, in a time of expanding trade, indeed forged an anti-capitalist coalition of peasants and workers and, when trade contracted, experienced (as Stalin's enemies alleged at the time) a dictatorship of state capital over both workers and farmers.

Certainly so long as we cling to the view that land can only be abundant where labor is not, and vice-versa, we can offer no trade-based account of red-green coalitions; indeed, changing exposure to trade must drive the two factors apart, for it always helps the one and hurts the other. On the one hand, this reflects reality—coalitions of labor and agriculture have been rare, and have failed even where much seemed to speak for them (e.g., in U.S. populism and on the German left); on the other, it leaves the few actual red-green coalitions, particularly those that arose in circumstances of changing exposure to trade, as standing refutations of the model.

Possible Objections

At least three objections can plausibly be raised to the whole line of analysis that I have advanced here:

First and most fundamentally, it may be argued that the effects sketched out here will not obtain in countries that depend only slightly on trade. A Belgium, where external trade (taken as the sum of exports and imports) roughly equals GDP, can indeed be affected profoundly by changes in the risks or costs of international commerce; but a state like the United States in the 1960s, where trade amounted to scarcely a tenth of GDP, will have remained largely immune (OECD 1982, 62–63).

This view, while superficially plausible, is incorrect. The Stolper-Samuelson result obtains at any margin; and, in fact, holders of scarce factors have been quite as devastated by expanding trade in almost autarkic economies—one need think only of the weavers of capital-poor India or Silesia, exposed in the nineteenth century to the competition of Lancashire mills—as in ones previously more dependent on trade. (Cf. Thomson 1962, 163–64, on the vast dislocations that even slight exposure to trade occasioned in previously isolated areas of nineteenth-century Europe.)

Second, one can ask why the cleavages indicated here should persist. In a world of perfectly mobile factors and rational behavior, people would quickly disinvest from losing factors and enterprises (e.g., farming in Britain after 1880) and move to sectors whose auspices were more favorable. Markets should swiftly clear, and a new, if different, political equilibrium should be achieved.

To this, two answers may be given. First, in some cases trade expands or contracts so rapidly as to frustrate rational expectations. Especially in countries that experience a steady series of such exogenous shocks—Europe, for example, since 1840—divisions based on factor endowments (which ordinarily change only gradually)[19] will be repeatedly revived. Second, often enough some factors' privileged access to political influence makes the extraction of rents and subsidies seem cheaper than adaptation: Prussian *Junker*, familiarly, sought (and, rather easily, won) protection rather than adjustment. In such circumstances, adaptation may be long delayed, sometimes with ultimately disastrous consequences.

Finally, it may be objected that I have said nothing about the outcome of these conflicts. I have not done so for the simple reason that I cannot: history makes it all too plain—as in the cases of nineteenth-century Germany and the United States—that the economic losers from trade may win politically over more than the short run. What I have advanced here is a speculation about *cleavages*, not about outcomes. I have asserted only that those who gain from fluctuations in trade will be strengthened and emboldened politically; nothing guarantees that they will win. Victory or defeat depends, so far as I can see, on precisely those institutional and cultural factors that this perspective so resolutely ignores.

Conclusion

I have not claimed that changes in countries' exposure to trade explain all, or even most, of their varying patterns of political cleavage. It would be foolish to ignore the importance of ancient cultural and religious loyalties, of wars and migrations, or of such historical memories as the French Revolution and the *Kulturkampf*. Neither have I offered anything like a convincing empirical demonstration of the modest hypotheses I have advanced; at most, the empirical regularities that I have noted or have taken over from such authorities as Gerschenkron and Lipset can serve to suggest the plausibility of the model and the value of further refinement and testing of it.

I have presented a theoretical puzzle, a kind of social-scientific "thought-experiment" in Carl G. Hempel's (1965) original sense: a teasing out of unexpected and sometimes counterintuitive implications of theories already widely accepted (Chap. 7). For the Stolper-Samuelson Theorem *is* generally, indeed almost universally, embraced; yet, coupled with a stark and unexceptionable model of the political realm, it plainly implies that changes in exposure to trade must profoundly affect nations' internal political cleavages. Do they do so? If they do not, what is wrong—either with our theories of international trade or with our understanding of politics?

NOTES

1. In fact, the effect flows backward from products and is an extension of the Heckscher-Ohlin theorem: under free trade, countries export products whose manufacture uses locally abundant, and import products whose manufacture uses locally scarce, factors intensively (cf. Leamer 1984, esp. 8–10).

2. Admittedly, this result depends on simplifying assumptions that are never achieved in the real world, among them perfect mobility of factors within national boundaries, a world of only two factors and two goods, and incomplete specialization. Still, as an approximation to reality, it remains highly serviceable (cf. Ethier 1984, esp. 163–64, 181).

3. Later historians have, of course, largely rejected Pirenne's attribution of this insecurity to the rise of Islam and its alleged blockade of Mediterranean commerce (Havighurst 1958). It can hardly be doubted, however, that the decline of Roman power by itself rendered interregional trade far less secure.

4. As transportation costs fall, states may offset the effect by adopting protection. Owners of abundant factors then still have substantial *potential* gains from trade, which they may mortgage to pressure policy toward lower levels of protection.

5. Countries that lack essential resources can only beggar themselves by protection. Ultimately, those in such a society who seek protection from trade must advocate conquest of the missing resources—as indeed occurred in Japan and Germany in the 1930s.

6. Between 1871 and 1890, just under two million Germans emigrated to points outside Europe; in the same years, some seven million immigrants entered the United States (Mitchell 1978, Tbl. A-5; Williams, Current, and Freidel 1969, 158).

7. The Stolper-Samuelson analysis also helps to clear up what had seemed even to the perspicacious Alexander Gerschenkron (1943, 26–27) an insoluble riddle: why the *smallholding* German peasants had quickly become

as protectionist as the *Junker*. Not only landowners, we now see, but all enterprises that *used land intensively*, will have been harmed by free trade. On the other hand—and later the distinction will become crucial—agricultural *wage labor* should have been free trading.

8. That the farmers of the Great Plains were hardly prospering in these years is no refutation of the analysis advanced here. Their *potential* gains were great (see n. 4), and their suffering could plausibly be attributed not to expanded trade but to the obstacles or exploitation laid upon that trade by other sectors. As in Marxist analysis, the older relations of production and of politics could be seen as "fetters."

9. Emigrants from the United Kingdom to areas outside Europe totalled 5.1 million between 1871 and 1890 (see Mitchell 1978, Tbl. A-5).

10. Certainly they had been among its earliest and strongest supporters: virtually every study of late Weimar voting patterns (e.g., Brown 1982; Childers 1983; Lipset 1960, 138–48) has found a large rural-urban difference (controlling for such other variables as religion and class) in support for National Socialism.

11. Historians have, of course, often recognized declining trade's sectoral effects on Weimar's final convulsions; the controversial essay of David Abraham (1981) is only the best-known example. They may, however, have exaggerated agriculture's woes (see Holt 1936; Rogowski 1982).

12. David Sabean (1969, Chap. 3) and Peter Blickle (1981, 76–78) link the Peasants War convincingly to the density and rapid growth of population in the affected areas, i.e., to an increasing abundance of labor.

13. "The world's trade between 1800 and 1840 had not quite doubled. Between 1850 and 1870 it increased by 260 percent" (Hobsbawm 1979, 33).

14. Finer distinctions would require a more precise definition of factor abundance and scarcity. The one commonly accepted for the case of more than two factors stems from Vanek's extension of the Heckscher-Ohlin Theorem (Leamer 1984, 15); it defines a country as abundant (or scarce) in a factor to the extent that its share of world endowment in that factor exceeds (or falls short of) its share of world consumption of all goods and services.

Edward A. Leamer's (1984, App. D) Factor Abundance Profiles are a tentative effort to apply this definition to present-day economies. To do so with any precision for earlier periods hardly seems possible.

15. John Zysman seems to me to have captured the essence of European and Japanese agricultural policy in this period: "The peasantry could be held in place [by subsidies and price supports] even as its economic and social positions were destroyed" (1983, 24).

16. I am grateful to David D'Lugo and Pradeep Chhibber for having raised this issue in seminar discussion.

17. More precisely, they are inconsistent with balanced trade (cf. Leamer 1984, 8–10; Leamer 1987, 14–15).

18. There can be no doubt of Russia's abundance of land: as late as 1960, its population per square kilometer of agricultural land (35.7) was comparable to that of the United States (40.9) or Canada (28.4) and strikingly lower than those of even the more thinly populated nations of western and central Europe (e.g., France, 133; Poland, 146) (World Bank 1983). On the other hand, Myint's (1958, 323–31) insightful analysis suggests how even sparsely populated regions can have great reserves of under-employed labor under conditions of primitive markets and social structures; and he takes episodes of extremely rapid economic growth, such as the USSR exhibited in the 1930s, as putative evidence of such "surplus" labor (Myint 1958, 323–24, 327).

19. The chief exception to this rule arises from extensions of trade to wholly new areas with quite different factor endowments. In 1860, for example, Prussia was abundant in land relative to its trading partners; as soon as the North American plains and the Argentine *pampas* were opened, it ceased to be so. I am grateful to my colleague Arthur Stein for having pointed this out.

REFERENCES

Abraham, David. 1981. *The Collapse of the Weimar Republic.* Princeton: Princeton University Press.

Becker, Gary S. 1983. A Theory of Competition among Pressure Groups for Political Influence. *Quarterly Journal of Economics* 98:371–400.

Binder, Leonard, James S. Coleman, Joseph LaPalombara, Lucian W. Pye, Sidney Verba, and Myron Weiner. 1971. *Crises and Sequences in Political Development.* Princeton: Princeton University Press.

Blickle, Peter. 1981. *The Revolution of 1525: The German Peasants' War From a New Perspective.* Trans. Thomas A. Brady, Jr., and H. C. Erik Midelfort. Baltimore: Johns Hopkins University Press.

Bowden, Witt, Michael Karpovich, and Abbott Payson Usher. 1937. *An Economic History of Europe since 1750.* New York: American Book.

Brown, Courtney. 1982. The Nazi Vote: A National Ecological Study. *American Political Science Review* 76:285–302.

Burnham, Walter Dean. 1970. *Critical Elections and the Mainsprings of American Politics.* New York: W. W. Norton.

Cameron, David R. 1978. The Expansion of the Public Economy: A Comparative Analysis. *American Political Science Review* 72:1243–61.

Cardoso, Fernando Henrique, and Enzo Faletto. 1979. *Dependency and Development in Latin America.* Trans. Marjory Mattingly Urquidi. Berkeley and Los Angeles: University of California Press.

Carstairs, Andrew McLaren. 1980. *A short History of Electoral Systems in Western Europe.* London: George Allen & Unwin.

Carsten, Francis Ludwig. 1967. *The Rise of Fascism.* Berkeley and Los Angeles: University of California Press.

Childers, Thomas. 1983. *The Nazi Voter: The Social Foundations of Fascism in Germany, 1919–1933.* Chapel Hill: University of North Carolina Press.

Cipolla, Carlo M. 1965. *Guns, Sails, and Empires: Technological Innovation and the Early Phases of European Expansion, 1400–1700.* New York: Pantheon Books.

Clubb, Oliver Edmund. 1972. *Twentieth-Century China.* 2d ed. New York: Columbia University Press.

Cobban, Alfred. 1965. *France of the Republics, 1871–1962.* Vol. 3 of *A History of Modern France.* Harmondsworth: Penguin Books.

Daalder, Hans. 1966. The Netherlands: Opposition in a Segmented Society. In *Political Oppositions in Western Democracies,* ed. Robert Dahl. New Haven: Yale University Press.

Duverger, Maurice. 1959. *Political Parties: Their Organization and Activity in the Modern State.* 2d ed. Trans. Barbara and Robert North. New York: John Wiley & Sons.

Easterbrook, William Thomas, and Hugh G. J. Aitken. 1958. *Canadian Economic History.* Toronto: Macmillan of Canada.

Ethier, Wilfred J. 1984. Higher Dimensional Issues in Trade Theory. In *Handbook of International Economics.* Vol. 1, ed. Ronald W. Jones and Peter B. Kenen. Amsterdam: Elsevier Science.

Feis, Herbert. 1965. *Europe, the World's Banker, 1870–1914.* New York: Norton.

Gerschenkron, Alexander. 1943. *Bread and Democracy in Germany.* Berkeley and Los Angeles: University of California Press.

Gerschenkron, Alexander. 1962. *Economic Backwardness in Historical Perspective.* Cambridge, MA: Harvard University Press.

Gessner, Dieter. 1977. *Agrardepression und Präsidialregierungen in Deutschland 1930 bis 1933.* Düsseldorf: Droste Verlag.

Gies, Horst. 1968. Die nationalsozialistische Machtergreifung auf dem agrarpolitischen Sektor. *Zeitschrift für Agrargeschichte und Agrarsoziologie* 16:210–32.

Gollan, Robin A. 1955. Nationalism, the Labour Movement and the Commonwealth, 1880–1900. In *Australia: A Social and Political History*, ed. Gordon Greenwood. London: Angus & Robertson.

Gourevitch, Peter Alexis. 1977. International Trade, Domestic Coalitions, and Liberty: Comparative Responses to the Crisis of 1873–1896. *Journal of Interdisciplinary History* 8:281–313.

Gourevitch, Peter Alexis. 1986. *Politics in Hard Times: Comparative Responses to International Economic Crises.* Ithaca, NY: Cornell University Press.

Greenwood, Gordon. 1955. National Development and Social Experimentation, 1901–1914. In *Australia: A Social and Political History*, ed. author. London: Angus & Robertson.

Hancock, M. Donald. 1972. *Sweden: The Politics of Postindustrial Change.* Hinsdale, IL: Dryden Press.

Havighurst, Alfred F., ed. 1958. *The Pirenne Thesis: Analysis, Criticism, and Revision.* Boston: D. C. Heath.

Hempel, Carl G. 1965. *"Aspects of Scientific Explanation" and Other Essays in the Philosophy of Science.* New York: Free Press.

Hirschman, Albert O. [1968] 1971. The Political Economy of Import-Substituting Industrialization in Latin America. *Quarterly Journal of Economics* 82:2–32. Reprinted in Albert O. Hirschman, *A Bias for Hope: Essays on Development and Latin America.* New Haven: Yale University Press.

Hobsbawm, Eric J. 1962. *The Age of Revolution, 1789–1848.* New York: New American Library.

Hobsbawm, Eric J. 1979. *The Age of Capital, 1848–1875.* New York: New American Library.

Holt, John Bradshaw. 1936. *German Agricultural Policy, 1918–1934: The Development of a National Policy toward Agriculture in Postwar Germany.* Chapel Hill: University of North Carolina Press.

Kato, Shuichi. 1974. Taisho Democracy as the Pre-Stage for Japanese Militarism. In *Japan in Crisis: Essays on Taisho Democracy*, ed. Bernard S. Silberman and H. D. Harootunian. Princeton: Princeton University Press.

Kindleberger, Charles P. 1973. *The World in Depression, 1929–1939.* Berkeley: University of California Press.

Kurth, James R. 1979a. Industrial Change and Political Change: A European Perspective. In *The New Authoritarianism in Latin America*, ed. David Collier. Princeton: Princeton University Press.

Kurth, James R. 1979b. The Political Consequences of the Product Cycle: Industrial History and Political Outcomes. *International Organization* 33:1–34.

Landes, David S. 1969. *The Unbound Prometheus: Technological Change and the Industrial Revolution in Western Europe from 1750 to the Present.* London: Cambridge University Press.

Leamer, Edward A. 1984. *Sources of Comparative Advantage: Theory and Evidence.* Cambridge: MIT Press.

Leamer, Edward A. 1987. Paths of Development in the $3 \times n$ General Equilibrium Model. University of California, Los Angeles. Typescript.

Lipset, Seymour Martin. 1960. *Political Man.* Garden City, NY: Doubleday.

Lipset, Seymour Martin. 1970. Political Cleavages in "Developed" and "Emerging" Politics. In *Mass*

Politics: Studies in Political Sociology, ed. Erik Allardt and Stein Rokkan. New York: Free Press.

Lipset, Seymour Martin, and Stein Rokkan. 1967. *Party Systems and Voter Alignments.* New York: Free Press.

Lorwin, Val R. 1966. Belgium: Religion, Class and Language in National Politics. In *Political Opposition in Western Democracies*, ed. Robert Dahl. New Haven, CT: Yale University Press.

Macridis, Roy C. 1978. *Modern Political Systems: Europe.* 4th ed. Englewood Cliffs, NJ: Prentice-Hall.

Mitchell, Brian R. 1978. *European Historical Statistics, 1750–1970.* Abridged ed. New York: Columbia University Press.

Moore, Barrington, Jr. 1967. *Social Origins of Dictatorship and Democracy: Lord and Peasant in the Making of the Modern World.* Boston: Beacon.

Mundell, Robert A. 1957. International Trade and Factor Mobility. *American Economic Review* 47: 321–35.

Myint, Hla. 1958. The "Classical Theory" of International Trade and the Underdeveloped Countries. *Economic Journal* 68:317–37.

Organization for Economic Cooperation and Development. 1982. *Historical Statistics 1960–1980.* Paris: OECD.

Pirenne, Henri. 1939. *Mohammed and Charlemagne.* London: Allen & Unwin.

Popkin, Samuel. 1979. *The Rational Peasant: The Political Economy of Rural Society in Vietnam.* Berkeley: University of California Press.

Reischauer, Edwin O. 1974. *Japan: The Story of a Nation.* New York: Alfred A. Knopf.

Rogowski, Ronald. 1982. Iron, Rye, and the Authoritarian Coalition in Germany after 1879. Paper delivered at the annual meeting of the American Political Science Association, Denver, CO.

Rokkan, Stein. 1966. Norway: Numerical Democracy and Corporate Pluralism. In *Political Oppositions in Western Democracies*, ed. Robert Dahl. New Haven: Yale University Press.

Rokkan, Stein. 1970. *Citizens, Elections, Parties.* Oslo: Universitetsforlaget.

Rokkan, Stein. 1981. Territories, Nations, Parties: Toward a Geoeconomic-Geopolitical Model for the Explanation of Changes within Western Europe. In *From National Development to Global Community*, ed. Richard L. Merritt and Bruce M. Russett. London: Allen & Unwin.

Rosecrance, Richard. 1986. *The Rise of the Trading State: Commerce and Conquest in the Modern World.* New York: Basic Books.

Rosenberg, Hans. 1943. Political and Social Consequences of the Great Depression in Europe, 1873–1896. *Economic History Review* 13:58–73.

Sabean, David. 1969. The Social Background to the Peasants' War of 1525 in Southern Upper Swabia. Ph.D. diss., University of Wisconsin.

Schattschneider, Elmer E. 1960. *The Semi-Sovereign People: A Realist's View of Democracy in America.* New York: Holt, Rinehart & Winston.

Schoenbaum, David. 1966. *Hitler's Social Revolution: Class and Status in Nazi Germany, 1933–1939.* Garden City, NY: Doubleday.

Sheehan, James J. 1978. *German Liberalism in the Nineteenth Century.* Chicago: University of Chicago Press.

Skidmore, Thomas E., and Peter H. Smith. 1984. *Modern Latin America.* New York: Oxford University Press.

Stolper, Wolfgang Friedrich, and Paul A. Samuelson. 1941. Protection and Real Wages. *Review of Economic Studies* 9:58–73.

Sunkel, Osvaldo, and Pedro Paz. 1973. *El subdesarrollo latinoamericano y la teoria del desarrollo.* 4th ed. Madrid: Siglo veintiuno de España.

Thomson, David. 1962. *Europe since Napoleon.* 2d ed. New York: Alfred A. Knopf.

Wallerstein, Immanuel. 1974. *The Modern World-System: Capitalist Agriculture and the Origins of the European World-Economy in the Sixteenth Century.* New York: Academic.

Williams, Thomas Harry, Richard N. Current, and Frank Freidel. 1969. *A History of the United States since 1865.* 3d ed. Baltimore: Johns Hopkins University Press.

World Bank. 1983. *World Tables.* 3d ed. Vol. 2. Baltimore: Johns Hopkins University Press.

Zysman, John. 1983. *Governments, Markets, and Growth: Financial Systems and the Politics of Industrial Change.* Ithaca, NY: Cornell University Press.

5 DEMOCRATIC REGIMES

If democracy is something positive to strive for, how does it come about, and what are its necessary components? The readings in this chapter try to address these questions by considering the origins and institutions of democracy as well as the dangers that democracy faces. Much of this work has emerged in the past three decades, following the end of the Cold War and the subsequent wave of democratization throughout much of the world.

In their widely cited work "What Democracy Is . . . and Is Not" (1991), Philippe C. Schmitter and Terry Lynn Karl provide an overview of some of democracy's most important elements, among them government accountability, public competition, and the mechanisms of elections and majority rule. Democracy is not just a set of mechanisms, however; it is also a set of agreed-on principles promising that the members of the democracy will abide by the outcomes of competition. But beyond these basic elements is a wide array of democratic types, differing in such areas as how majorities are structured, the nature of executive power, the kinds of checks and balances that will be used to stabilize power, and the way power is decentralized. There is no one necessary mix for democracy, and how these institutions are combined or modified depends on the historical circumstances and the contemporary challenges of the country in question.

However, some scholars do believe that certain kinds of democratic combinations are more stable or responsive than others. Arend Lijphart (1996) investigates two of the most important differences among democracies: presidential versus parliamentary rule, and proportional representation (PR) versus plurality (also known as single-member district plurality or "first past the post") elections. Presidentialism and plurality elections promote majoritarian or a "winner-take-all" form of government; proportional representation tends to generate more consensus in politics. Is one better than the other? Lijphart concludes that in terms of minority rights, participation, and economic equality, the parliamentary PR system is superior to the presidential plurality system of the United States.

What about the centralization of state power? Is unitary or federal government more democratic? This may depend on the diversity of the nation in question. In "The Rise of 'State-Nations'" (2010) Alfred Stepan, Juan J. Linz, and Yogendra Yadav note that in many countries around the world, states and nations do not cohere as neatly as the term *nation-state* implies. Instead, we often find what the authors term "state-nations." In contrast to nation-states, whose dominant national identity is linked to the state, state-nations contain several national groups whose strong identities and competing interests may lead to conflicts that undermine democracy and state integrity. The authors argue that in these cases, stability is possible where such varied identities are embraced by and embodied in state institutions, from religion to multilingualism. Of particular interest is their discussion of asymmetric federalism: the uneven devolution of power among subnational units in order to meet the demands of different ethnic or religious groups. Inclusive and idiosyncratic crafting of state institutions can make multi-nationalism work, and many political scientists cite India as an example of a country that, perhaps against all odds, has made diversity work.

Questions of diversity and identity lead us to the question of how gender figures in the study of comparative politics and the future of democracy itself. Georgina Waylen's "Engendering the 'Crisis of Democracy': Institutions, Representation and Participation" (2015) discusses current challenges to democratic institutions and how they intersect with contemporary gender politics. Waylen notes that the role of women in democratic institutions and in political power has increased over time, though this role has remained often contradictory and circumscribed. At the same time, current conflicts over democratic legitimacy may open new avenues and opportunities for gender equality, through such innovations as electoral quotas and greater roles in policy making. However, Waylen is cautious in her conclusions, noting that a crisis of democratic legitimacy does not necessarily translate into a rethinking of participation and representation along more gender-equitable lines.

While Waylen remains cautious as to improvements in democratic performance, others are much more skeptical, going so far as to question whether democracy is under threat. Roberto Stefan Foa and Yascha Mounk's "The Danger of Deconsolidation" (2016) argues that across developed democracies younger generations are increasingly skeptical of democracy as a value in itself. Worryingly, this also translates into support for authoritarian leaders and perhaps (as research elsewhere indicates) even military rule. It seems hard to imagine that democratic institutions could decline in legitimacy to such an extent, but "illiberal" regimes (see Chapter 6) may be on the rise.

Philippe C. Schmitter and Terry Lynn Karl

WHAT DEMOCRACY IS . . . AND IS NOT

For some time, the word "democracy" has been circulating as a debased currency in the political marketplace. Politicians with a wide range of convictions and practices strove to appropriate the label and attach it to their actions. Scholars, conversely, hesitated to use it—without adding qualifying adjectives—because of the ambiguity that surrounds it. The distinguished American political theorist Robert Dahl even tried to introduce a new term, "polyarchy," in its stead in the (vain) hope of gaining a greater measure of conceptual precision. But for better or worse, we are "stuck" with "democracy" as the catchword of contemporary political discourse. It is the word that resonates in people's minds and springs from their lips as they struggle for freedom and a better way of life; it is the word whose meaning we must discern if it is to be of any use in guiding political analysis and practice.

The wave of transitions away from autocratic rule that began with Portugal's "Revolution of the Carnations" in 1974 and seems to have crested with the collapse of communist regimes across Eastern Europe in 1989 has produced a welcome convergence toward [a] common definition of democracy.[1] Everywhere there has been a silent abandonment of dubious adjectives like "popular," "guided," "bourgeois," and "formal" to modify "democracy." At the same time, a remarkable consensus has emerged concerning the minimal conditions that polities must meet in order to merit the prestigious appellation of "democratic." Moreover, a number of international organizations now monitor how well these standards are met; indeed, some countries even consider them when formulating foreign policy.[2]

From *Journal of Democracy* (Summer 1991), pp. 75–88.

What Democracy Is

Let us begin by broadly defining democracy and the generic *concepts* that distinguish it as a unique system for organizing relations between rulers and the ruled. We will then briefly review *procedures*, the rules and arrangements that are needed if democracy is to endure. Finally, we will discuss two operative *principles* that make democracy work. They are not expressly included among the generic concepts or formal procedures, but the prospect for democracy is grim if their underlying conditioning effects are not present.

One of the major themes of this essay is that democracy does not consist of a single unique set of institutions. There are many types of democracy, and their diverse practices produce a similarly varied set of effects. The specific form democracy takes is contingent upon a country's socioeconomic conditions as well as its entrenched state structures and policy practices.

Modern political democracy is a system of governance in which rulers are held accountable for their actions in the public realm by citizens, acting indirectly through the competition and cooperation of their elected representatives.[3]

A *regime or system of governance* is an ensemble of patterns that determines the methods of access to the principal public offices; the characteristics of the actors admitted to or excluded from such access; the strategies that actors may use to gain access; and the rules that are followed in the making of publicly binding decisions. To work properly, the ensemble must be institutionalized—that is to say, the various patterns must be habitually known, practiced, and accepted by most, if not all, actors. Increasingly, the preferred mechanism of institutionalization is a written body of laws undergirded by a written constitution, though many enduring political norms can have an informal, prudential, or traditional basis.[4]

For the sake of economy and comparison, these forms, characteristics, and rules are usually bundled together and given a generic label. "Democratic" is one; others are "autocratic," "authoritarian," "despotic," "dictatorial," "tyrannical," "totalitarian," "absolutist," "traditional," "monarchic," "oligarchic," "plutocratic," "aristocratic," and "sultanistic."[5] Each of these regime forms may in turn be broken down into subtypes.

Like all regimes, democracies depend upon the presence of *rulers*, persons who occupy specialized authority roles and can give legitimate commands to others. What distinguishes democratic rulers from nondemocratic ones are the norms that condition how the former come to power and the practices that hold them accountable for their actions.

The *public realm* encompasses the making of collective norms and choices that are binding on the society and backed by state coercion. Its content can vary a great deal across democracies, depending upon preexisting distinctions between the public and the private, state and society, legitimate coercion and voluntary exchange, and collective needs and individual preferences. The liberal conception of democracy advocates circumscribing the public realm as narrowly as possible, while the socialist or social-democratic approach would extend that realm through regulation, subsidization, and, in some cases, collective ownership of property. Neither is intrinsically more democratic than the other—just *differently* democratic. This implies that measures aimed at "developing the private sector" are no more democratic than those aimed at "developing the public sector." Both, if carried to extremes, could undermine the practice of democracy, the former by destroying the basis for satisfying collective needs and exercising legitimate authority; the latter by destroying the basis for satisfying individual preferences and controlling illegitimate government actions. Differences of opinion over the optimal mix of the two provide much of the substantive content of political conflict within established democracies.

Citizens are the most distinctive element in democracies. All regimes have rulers and a public realm, but only to the extent that they are democratic do they have citizens. Historically, severe restrictions on citizenship were imposed in most emerging or partial democracies according to criteria of age, gender, class, race, literacy, property ownership, tax-paying status, and so on. Only a small part of the total population was eligible to vote or run for office. Only restricted social categories were allowed to form, join, or support political associations. After protracted struggle—in some cases involving violent domestic upheaval or international war—most of these restrictions were lifted. Today, the criteria for inclusion are fairly standard. All native-born adults are eligible, although somewhat higher age limits may still be imposed upon candidates for certain offices. Unlike the early American and European democracies of the nineteenth century, none of the recent democracies in southern Europe, Latin America, Asia, or Eastern Europe has even attempted to impose formal restrictions on the franchise or eligibility to office. When it comes to informal restrictions on the effective exercise of citizenship rights, however, the story can be quite different. This explains the central importance (discussed below) of procedures.

Competition has not always been considered an essential defining condition of democracy. "Classic" democracies presumed decision making based on direct participation leading to consensus. The assembled citizenry was expected to agree on a common course of action after listening to the alternatives and weighing their respective merits and demerits. A tradition of hostility to "faction," and "particular interests" persists in democratic thought, but at least since *The Federalist Papers* it has become widely accepted that competition among factions is a necessary evil in democracies that operate on a more-than-local scale. Since, as James Madison argued, "the latent causes of faction are sown into the nature of man," and the possible remedies for "the mischief of faction" are worse than the disease, the best course is to recognize them and to attempt to control their effects.[6] Yet while democrats may agree on the inevitability of factions, they tend to disagree about the best forms and rules for governing factional competition. Indeed, differences over the preferred modes and boundaries of competition contribute most to distinguishing one subtype of democracy from another.

The most popular definition of democracy equates it with regular *elections*, fairly conducted and honestly counted. Some even consider the mere fact of elections—even ones from which specific parties or candidates are excluded, or in which substantial portions of the population cannot freely participate—as a sufficient condition for the existence of democracy. This fallacy has been called "electoralism" or "the faith that merely holding elections will channel political action into peaceful contests among elites and accord public legitimacy to the winners"—no matter how they are conducted or what else constrains those who win them.[7] However central to democracy, elections occur intermittently and only allow citizens to choose between the highly aggregated alternatives offered by political parties, which can, especially in the early stages of a democratic transition, proliferate in a bewildering variety. During the intervals between elections, citizens can seek to influence public policy through a wide variety of other intermediaries: interest associations, social movements, locality groupings, clientelistic arrangements, and so forth. *Modern democracy, in other words, offers a variety of competitive processes and channels for the expression of interests and values—associational as well as partisan, functional as well as territorial, collective as well as individual. All are integral to its practice.*

Another commonly accepted image of democracy identifies it with *majority rule*. Any governing body that makes decisions by combining the votes of more than half of those eligible and present is said to be democratic, whether that majority emerges within an electorate, a parliament, a committee, a city council, or a party caucus. For exceptional purposes (e.g., amending the constitution or expelling a member), "qualified majorities" of more than 50 percent may be required, but few would deny that democracy must involve some means of aggregating the equal preferences of individuals.

A problem arises, however, when *numbers* meet *intensities*. What happens when a properly assembled majority (especially a stable, self-perpetuating one) regularly makes decisions that harm some minority (especially a threatened cultural or ethnic group)? In these circumstances, successful democracies tend to qualify the central principle of majority rule in order to protect minority rights. Such qualifications can take the form of constitutional provisions that place certain matters beyond the reach of majorities (bills of rights); requirements for concurrent majorities in several different constituencies (confederalism); guarantees securing the autonomy of local or regional governments against the demands of the central authority (federalism); grand coalition governments that incorporate all parties (consociationalism); or the negotiation of social pacts between major social groups like business and labor (neocorporatism). The most common and effective way of protecting minorities, however, lies in the everyday operation of interest associations and social movements. These reflect (some would say, amplify) the different intensities of preference that exist in the population and bring them to bear on democratically elected decision makers. Another way of putting this intrinsic tension between numbers and intensities would be to say that "in modern democracies, votes may be counted, but influences alone are weighted."

Cooperation has always been a central feature of democracy. Actors must voluntarily make collective decisions binding on the polity as a whole. They must cooperate in order to compete. They must be capable of acting collectively through parties, associations, and movements in order to select candidates, articulate preferences, petition authorities, and influence policies.

But democracy's freedoms should also encourage citizens to deliberate among themselves, to discover their common needs, and to resolve their differences without relying on some supreme central authority.

Classical democracy emphasized these qualities, and they are by no means extinct, despite repeated efforts by contemporary theorists to stress the analogy with behavior in the economic marketplace and to reduce all of democracy's operations to competitive interest maximization. Alexis de Tocqueville best described the importance of independent groups for democracy in his *Democracy in America*, a work which remains a major source of inspiration for all those who persist in viewing democracy as something more than a struggle for election and re-election among competing candidates.[8]

In contemporary political discourse, this phenomenon of cooperation and deliberation via autonomous group activity goes under the rubric of "civil society." The diverse units of social identity and interest, by remaining independent of the state (and perhaps even of parties), not only can restrain the arbitrary actions of rulers, but can also contribute to forming better citizens who are more aware of the preferences of others, more self-confident in their actions, and more civic-minded in their willingness to sacrifice for the common good. At its best, civil society provides an intermediate layer of governance between the individual and the state that is capable of resolving conflicts and controlling the behavior of members without public coercion. Rather than overloading decision makers with increased demands and making the system ungovernable,[9] a viable civil society can mitigate conflicts and improve the quality of citizenship—without relying exclusively on the privatism of the marketplace.

Representatives—whether directly or indirectly elected—do most of the real work in modern democracies. Most are professional politicians who orient their careers around the desire to fill key offices. It is doubtful that any democracy could survive without such people. The central question, therefore, is not whether or not there will be a political elite or even a professional political class, but how these representatives are chosen and then held accountable for their actions.

As noted above, there are many channels of representation in modern democracy. The electoral one, based on territorial constituencies, is the most visible and public. It culminates in a parliament or a presidency that is periodically accountable to the citizenry as a whole. Yet the sheer growth of government (in large part as a byproduct of popular demand) has increased the number, variety, and power of agencies charged with making public decisions and not subject to elections. Around these agencies there has developed a vast apparatus of specialized representation based largely on functional interests, not territorial constituencies. These interest associations, and not political parties, have become the primary expression of civil society in most stable democracies, supplemented by the more sporadic interventions of social movements.

The new and fragile democracies that have sprung up since 1974 must live in "compressed time." They will not resemble the European democracies of the nineteenth and early twentieth centuries, and they cannot expect to acquire the multiple channels of representation in gradual historical progression as did most of their predecessors. A bewildering array of parties, interests, and movements will all simultaneously seek political influence in them, creating challenges to the polity that did not exist in earlier processes of democratization.

Procedures That Make Democracy Possible

The defining components of democracy are necessarily abstract, and may give rise to a considerable variety of institutions and subtypes of democracy. For democracy to thrive, however, specific procedural norms must be followed and civic rights must be respected. Any polity that fails to impose such restrictions upon itself, that fails to follow the "rule of law" with regard to its own procedures, should not be considered democratic. These procedures alone do not define democracy, but their presence is indispensable to its persistence. In essence, they are necessary but not sufficient conditions for its existence.

Robert Dahl has offered the most generally accepted listing of what he terms the "procedural minimal" conditions that must be present for modern political democracy (or as he puts it, "polyarchy") to exist:

1. Control over government decisions about policy is constitutionally vested in elected officials.
2. Elected officials are chosen in frequent and fairly conducted elections in which coercion is comparatively uncommon.
3. Practically all adults have the right to vote in the election of officials.
4. Practically all adults have the right to run for elective offices.
5. Citizens have a right to express themselves without the danger of severe punishment on political matters broadly defined. . . .
6. Citizens have a right to seek out alternative sources of information. Moreover, alternative sources of information exist and are protected by law.
7. . . . Citizens also have the right to form relatively independent associations or organizations, including independent political parties and interest groups.[10]

These seven conditions seem to capture the essence of procedural democracy for many theorists, but we propose to add two others. The first might be thought of as a further refinement of item (1), while the second might be called an implicit prior condition to all seven of the above.

1. Popularly elected officials must be able to exercise their constitutional powers without being subjected to overriding (albeit informal) opposition from unelected officials. Democracy is in jeopardy if military officers, entrenched civil servants, or state managers retain the capacity to act independently of elected civilians or even veto decisions made by the people's representatives. Without this additional caveat, the militarized polities of contemporary Central America, where civilian control over the military does not exist, might be classified by many scholars as democracies, just as they have been (with the exception of Sandinista Nicaragua) by U.S. policy makers. The caveat thus guards against what we earlier called "electoralism"—the tendency to focus on the holding of elections while ignoring other political realities.

2. The polity must be self-governing; it must be able to act independently of constraints imposed by some other overarching political system. Dahl and other contemporary democratic theorists probably took this condition for granted since they referred to formally sovereign nation-states. However, with the development of blocs, alliances, spheres of influence, and a variety of "neocolonial" arrangements, the question of autonomy has been a salient one. Is a system really democratic if its elected officials are unable to make binding decisions without the approval of actors outside their territorial domain? This is significant even if the outsiders are relatively free to alter or even end the encompassing arrangement (as in Puerto Rico), but it becomes especially critical if neither condition [pertains] (as in the Baltic states).

Principles That Make Democracy Feasible

Lists of component processes and procedural norms help us to specify what democracy is, but they do not tell us much about how it actually functions. The simplest answer is "by the consent of the people"; the more complex one is "by the contingent consent of politicians acting under conditions of bounded uncertainty."

In a democracy, representatives must at least informally agree that those who win greater electoral support or influence over policy will not use their temporary superiority to bar the losers from taking office or exerting influence in the future, and that in exchange for this opportunity to keep competing for power and place, momentary losers will respect the winners' right to make binding decisions. Citizens are expected to obey the decisions ensuing from such a process of competition, provided its outcome remains contingent upon their collective preferences as expressed through fair and regular elections or open and repeated negotiations.

The challenge is not so much to find a set of goals that command widespread consensus as to find a set of rules that embody contingent consent. The precise shape of this "democratic bargain," to use Dahl's expression,[11] can vary a good deal from society to society. It depends on social cleavages and such subjective factors as mutual trust, the standard of fairness, and the willingness to compromise. It may even be compatible with a great deal of dissensus on substantive policy issues.

All democracies involve a degree of uncertainty about who will be elected and what policies they will pursue. Even in those polities where one party persists in winning elections or one policy is consistently implemented, the possibility of change through independent collective action still exists, as in Italy, Japan, and the Scandinavian social democracies. If it does not, the system is not democratic, as in Mexico, Senegal, or Indonesia.

But the uncertainty embedded in the core of all democracies is bounded. Not just any actor can get into the competition and raise any issue he or she pleases—there are previously established rules that must be respected. Not just any policy can be adopted—there are conditions that must be met. Democracy institutionalizes "normal," limited political uncertainty. These boundaries vary from country to country. Constitutional guarantees of property, privacy, expression, and other rights are a part of this, but the most effective boundaries are generated by competition among interest groups and co-operation within civil society. Whatever the rhetoric (and some polities appear to offer their citizens more dramatic alternatives than others), once the rules of contingent consent have been agreed upon, the actual variation is likely to stay within a predictable and generally accepted range.

This emphasis on operative guidelines contrasts with a highly persistent but misleading theme in recent literature on democracy—namely, the emphasis upon "civic culture." The principles we have suggested here rest on rules of prudence, not on deeply ingrained habits of tolerance, moderation, mutual respect, fair play, readiness to compromise, or trust in public authorities. Waiting for such habits to sink deep and lasting roots implies a very slow process of regime consolidation—one that takes generations—and it would probably condemn most contemporary experiences *ex hypothesi* to failure. Our assertion is that contingent consent and bounded uncertainty can emerge from the interaction between antagonistic and mutually suspicious actors and that the far more benevolent and ingrained norms of a civic culture are better thought of as a *product* and not a producer of democracy.

How Democracies Differ

Several concepts have been deliberately excluded from our generic definition of democracy, despite the fact that they have been frequently associated with it in both everyday practice and scholarly work. They are, nevertheless, especially important when it comes to distinguishing subtypes of democracy. Since no single set of actual institutions, practices, or values embodies democracy, polities moving away from authoritarian rule can mix different components to produce different democracies. It is important to recognize that these do not define points along a single continuum of improving performance, but a matrix of potential combinations that are *differently* democratic.

1. *Consensus*: All citizens may not agree on the substantive goals of political action or on the role of the state (although if they did, it would certainly make governing democracies much easier).

2. *Participation*: All citizens may not take an active and equal part in politics, although it must be legally possible for them to do so.

3. *Access*: Rulers may not weigh equally the preferences of all who come before them, although citizenship implies that individuals and groups should have an equal opportunity to express their preferences if they choose to do so.

4. *Responsiveness*: Rulers may not always follow the course of action preferred by the citizenry. But when they deviate from such a policy, say on grounds of "reason of state" or "overriding national interest," they must ultimately be held accountable for their actions through regular and fair processes.

5. *Majority rule*: Positions may not be allocated or rules may not be decided solely on the basis of assembling the most votes, although deviations from this principle usually must be explicitly defended and previously approved.

6. *Parliamentary sovereignty*: The legislature may not be the only body that can make rules or even the one with final authority in deciding which laws are binding, although where executive, judicial, or other public bodies make that ultimate choice, they too must be accountable for their actions.

7. *Party government*: Rulers may not be nominated, promoted, and disciplined in their activities by well-organized and programmatically coherent political parties, although where they are not, it may prove more difficult to form an effective government.

8. *Pluralism*: The political process may not be based on a multiplicity of overlapping, voluntaristic, and autonomous private groups. However, where there are monopolies of representation, hierarchies of association, and obligatory memberships, it is likely that the interests involved will be more closely linked to the state and the separation between the public and private spheres of action will be much less distinct.

9. *Federalism*: The territorial division of authority may not involve multiple levels and local autonomies, least of all ones enshrined in a constitutional document, although some dispersal of power across territorial and/or functional units is characteristic of all democracies.

10. *Presidentialism*: The chief executive officer may not be a single person and he or she may not be directly elected by the citizenry as a whole, although some concentration of authority is present in all democracies, even if it is exercised collectively and only held indirectly accountable to the electorate.

11. *Checks and Balances*: It is not necessary that the different branches of government be systematically pitted against one another, although governments by assembly, by executive concentrations, by judicial command, or even by dictatorial fiat (as in time of war) must be ultimately accountable to the citizenry as a whole.

While each of the above has been named as an essential component of democracy, they should instead be seen either as indicators of this or that type of democracy, or else as useful standards for evaluating the performance of particular regimes. To include them as part of the generic definition of democracy itself would be to mistake the American polity for the universal model of democratic governance. Indeed, the parliamentary, consociational, unitary, corporatist, and concentrated arrangements of continental Europe may have some unique virtues for guiding polities through the uncertain transition from autocratic to democratic rule.[12]

What Democracy Is Not

We have attempted to convey the general meaning of modern democracy without identifying it with some particular set of rules and institutions or restricting it to some specific culture or level of development. We have also argued that it cannot be reduced to the regular holding of elections or equated with a particular notion of the role of the state, but we have not said much more about what democracy is not or about what democracy may not be capable of producing.

There is an understandable temptation to load too many expectations on this concept and to imagine that by attaining democracy, a society will have resolved all of its political, social, economic, administrative, and cultural problems. Unfortunately, "all good things do not necessarily go together."

First, democracies are not necessarily more efficient economically than other forms of government. Their rates of aggregate growth, savings, and investment may be no better than those of nondemocracies. This is especially likely during the transition, when propertied groups and administrative elites may respond to real or imagined threats to the "rights" they enjoyed under authoritarian rule by initiating capital flight, disinvestment, or sabotage. In time, depending upon the type of democracy, benevolent long-term effects upon income distribution, aggregate demand, education, productivity, and creativity may eventually combine to improve economic and social performance, but it is certainly too much to expect that these improvements will occur immediately—much less that they will be defining characteristics of democratization.

Second, democracies are not necessarily more efficient administratively. Their capacity to make decisions may even be slower than that of the regimes they replace, if only because more actors must be consulted. The costs of getting things done may be higher, if only because "payoffs" have to be made to a wider and more resourceful set of clients (although one should never underestimate the degree of corruption to be found within autocracies). Popular satisfaction with the new democratic government's performance may not even seem greater, if only because necessary compromises often please no one completely, and because the losers are free to complain.

Third, democracies are not likely to appear more orderly, consensual, stable, or governable than the autocracies they replace. This is partly a byproduct of democratic freedom of expression, but it is also a reflection of the likelihood of continuing disagreement over new rules and institutions. These products of imposition or compromise are often initially quite ambiguous in nature and uncertain in effect until actors have learned how to use them. What is more, they come in the aftermath of serious struggles motivated by high ideals. Groups and individuals with recently acquired autonomy will test certain rules, protest against the actions of certain institutions, and insist on renegotiating their part of the bargain. Thus the presence of antisystem parties should be neither surprising nor seen as a failure of democratic consolidation. What counts is whether such parties are willing, however reluctantly, to play by the general rules of bounded uncertainty and contingent consent.

Governability is a challenge for all regimes, not just democratic ones. Given the political exhaustion and loss of legitimacy that have befallen autocracies from sultanistic Paraguay to totalitarian Albania, it may seem that only democracies can now be expected to govern effectively and legitimately. Experience has shown, however, that democracies too can lose the ability to govern. Mass publics can become disenchanted with their performance. Even more threatening is the temptation for leaders to fiddle with procedures and ultimately undermine the principles of contingent consent and bounded uncertainty. Perhaps the most critical moment comes once the politicians begin to settle into the more predictable roles and relations of a consolidated democracy. Many will find their expectations frustrated; some will discover that the new rules of competition put them at a disadvantage; a few may even feel that their vital interests are threatened by popular majorities.

Finally, democracies will have more open societies and polities than the autocracies they replace, but not necessarily more open economies. Many of today's most successful and well-established democracies have historically resorted to protectionism and closed borders, and have relied extensively upon public institutions to promote economic development. While the long-term compatibility between democracy and capitalism does not seem to be in doubt, despite their continuous tension, it is not clear whether the promotion of such liberal economic goals as the right of individuals to own property and retain profits, the clearing function of markets, the private settlement of disputes, the freedom to produce without government regulation, or the privatization of state-owned enterprises necessarily furthers the consolidation of democracy. After all, democracies do need to levy taxes and regulate certain transactions, especially where private monopolies and oligopolies exist. Citizens or their representatives may decide that it is desirable to protect the rights of collectivities from encroachment by individuals, especially propertied ones, and they may choose to set aside certain forms of property for public or cooperative ownership. In short, notions of economic liberty that are currently put forward in neoliberal economic models are not synonymous with political freedom—and may even impede it.

Democratization will not necessarily bring in its wake economic growth, social peace, administrative efficiency, political harmony, free markets, or "the end of ideology." Least of all will it bring about "the end of history." No doubt some of these qualities could make the consolidation of democracy easier, but they are neither prerequisites for it nor immediate products of it. Instead, what we should be hoping for is the emergence of political institutions that can peacefully compete to form governments and influence public policy, that can channel social and economic conflicts through regular procedures, and that have sufficient linkages to civil society to represent their constituencies and commit them to collective courses of action. Some types of democracies, especially in developing countries, have been unable to fulfill this promise, perhaps due to the circumstances of their transition from authoritarian rule.[13] The democratic wager is that such a regime, once established, will not only persist by reproducing itself within its initial confining conditions, but will eventually expand beyond them.[14]

Unlike authoritarian regimes, democracies have the capacity to modify their rules and institutions consensually in response to changing circumstances. They may not immediately produce all the goods mentioned above, but they stand a better chance of eventually doing so than do autocracies.

NOTES

1. For a comparative analysis of the recent regime changes in southern Europe and Latin America, see Guillermo O'Donnell, Philippe C. Schmitter, and Laurence Whitehead, eds., *Transitions from Authoritarian Rule*, 4 vols. (Baltimore: Johns Hopkins University Press, 1986). For another compilation that adopts a more structural approach see Larry Diamond, Juan Linz, and Seymour Martin Lipset, eds., *Democracy in Developing Countries*, vols. 2, 3, and 4 (Boulder, Colo.: Lynne Rienner, 1989).

2. Numerous attempts have been made to codify and quantify the existence of democracy across political systems. The best known is probably Freedom House's *Freedom in the World: Political Rights and Civil Liberties*, published since 1973 by Greenwood Press and since 1988 by University Press of America. Also see Charles Humana, *World Human Rights Guide* (New York: Facts on File, 1986).

3. The definition most commonly used by American social scientists is that of Joseph Schumpeter: "that institutional arrangement for arriving at political decisions in which individuals acquire the power to decide by means of a competitive struggle for the people's vote." *Capitalism, Socialism, and Democracy* (London: George Allen and Unwin, 1943), 269. We accept certain aspects of the classical procedural approach to modern democracy but differ primarily in our emphasis on the accountability of rulers to citizens and the relevance of mechanisms of competition other than elections.

4. Not only do some countries practice a stable form of democracy without a formal constitution (e.g., Great Britain and Israel), but even more countries have constitutions and legal codes that

offer no guarantee of reliable practice. On paper, Stalin's 1936 constitution for the USSR was a virtual model of democratic rights and entitlements.

5. For the most valiant attempt to make some sense out of this thicket of distinctions, see Juan Linz, "Totalitarian and Authoritarian Regimes," in *Handbook of Political Science*, eds. Fred I. Greenstein and Nelson W. Polsby (Reading, Mass.: Addison Wesley, 1975), 175–411.

6. "Publius" (Alexander Hamilton, John Jay, and James Madison), *The Federalist Papers* (New York: Anchor Books, 1961). The quote is from Number 10.

7. See Terry Karl, "Imposing Consent? Electoralism versus Democratization in El Salvador," in *Elections and Democratization in Latin America, 1980–1985*, eds. Paul Drake and Eduardo Silva (San Diego: Center for Iberian and Latin American Studies, Center for US/Mexican Studies, University of California, San Diego, 1986), 9–36.

8. Alexis de Tocqueville, *Democracy in America*, 2 vols. (New York: Vintage Books, 1945).

9. This fear of overloaded government and the imminent collapse of democracy is well reflected in the work of Samuel P. Huntington during the 1970s. See especially Michel Crozier, Samuel P. Huntington, and Joji Watanuki, *The Crisis of Democracy* (New York: New York University Press, 1975). For Huntington's (revised) thoughts about the prospects for democracy, see his "Will More Countries Become Democratic?," *Political Science Quarterly* 99 (Summer 1984): 193–218.

10. Robert Dahl, *Dilemmas of Pluralist Democracy* (New Haven: Yale University Press, 1982), 11.

11. Robert Dahl, *After the Revolution: Authority in a Good Society* (New Haven: Yale University Press, 1970).

12. See Juan Linz, "The Perils of Presidentialism," *Journal of Democracy* 1 (Winter 1990): 51–69, and the ensuing discussion by Donald Horowitz, Seymour Martin Lipset, and Juan Linz in *Journal of Democracy* 1 (Fall 1990): 73–91.

13. Terry Lynn Karl, "Dilemmas of Democratization in Latin America," *Comparative Politics* 23 (October 1990): 1–23.

14. Otto Kirchheimer, "Confining Conditions and Revolutionary Breakthroughs," *American Political Science Review* 59 (1965): 964–974.

Arend Lijphart

CONSTITUTIONAL CHOICES FOR NEW DEMOCRACIES

Two fundamental choices that confront architects of new democratic constitutions are those between plurality elections and proportional representation (PR) and between parliamentary and presidential forms of government. The merits of presidentialism and parliamentarism were extensively debated by Donald L. Horowitz, Juan J. Linz, and Seymour Martin Lipset in the Fall 1990 issue of the *Journal of Democracy*.[1] I strongly concur with Horowitz's contention that the electoral system is an equally vital element in democratic constitutional design, and therefore that it is of crucial importance to evaluate these two sets of choices in relation with each other. Such an analysis, as I will try to show, indicates that the combination of parliamentarism with proportional representation should be an

From *Journal of Democracy* 2, no. 1 (1991), pp. 72–84.

especially attractive one to newly democratic and democratizing countries.

The comparative study of democracies has shown that the type of electoral system is significantly related to the development of a country's party system, its type of executive (one-party vs. coalition cabinets), and the relationship between its executive and legislature. Countries that use the plurality method of election (almost always applied, at the national level, in single-member districts) are likely to have two-party systems, one-party governments, and executives that are dominant in relation to their legislatures. These are the main characteristics of the Westminster or *majoritarian* model of democracy, in which power is concentrated in the hands of the majority party. Conversely, PR is likely to be associated with multiparty systems, coalition governments (including, in many cases, broad and inclusive coalitions), and more equal executive-legislative power relations. These latter characteristics typify the *consensus* model of democracy, which, instead of relying on pure and concentrated majority rule, tries to limit, divide, separate, and share power in a variety of ways.[2]

Three further points should be made about these two sets of related traits. First, the relationships are mutual. For instance, plurality elections favor the maintenance of a two-party system; but an existing two-party system also favors the maintenance of plurality, which gives the two principal parties great advantages that they are unlikely to abandon. Second, if democratic political engineers desire to promote either the majoritarian cluster of characteristics (plurality, a two-party system, and a dominant, one-party cabinet) or the consensus cluster (PR, multipartism, coalition government, and a stronger legislature), the most practical way to do so is by choosing the appropriate electoral system. Giovanni Sartori has aptly called electoral systems "the most specific manipulative instrument of politics."[3] Third, important variations exist among PR systems. Without going into all the technical details, a useful distinction can be made between *extreme* PR, which poses few barriers to small parties, and

moderate PR. The latter limits the influence of minor parties through such means as applying PR in small districts instead of large districts or nationwide balloting, and requiring parties to receive a minimum percentage of the vote in order to gain representation, such as the 5-percent threshold in Germany. The Dutch, Israeli, and Italian systems exemplify extreme PR and the German and Swedish systems, moderate PR.

The second basic constitutional choice, between parliamentary and presidential forms of government, also affects the majoritarian or consensus character of the political system. Presidentialism yields majoritarian effects on the party system and on the type of executive, but a consensus effect on executive-legislative relations. By formally separating the executive and legislative powers, presidential systems generally promote a rough executive-legislative balance of power. On the other hand, presidentialism tends to foster a two-party system, as the presidency is the biggest political prize to be won, and only the largest parties have a chance to win it. This advantage for the big parties often carries over into legislative elections as well (especially if presidential and legislative elections are held simultaneously), even if the legislative elections are conducted under PR rules. Presidentialism usually produces cabinets composed solely of members of the governing party. In fact, presidential systems concentrate executive power to an even greater degree than does a one-party parliamentary cabinet—not just in a single *party* but in a single *person*.

Explaining Past Choices

My aim is not simply to describe alternative democratic systems and their majoritarian or consensus characteristics, but also to make some practical recommendations for democratic constitutional engineers. What are the main advantages and disadvantages of plurality and PR and of presidentialism and parliamentarism? One way to approach this question is to investigate why contemporary democracies made the constitutional choices they did.

Figure 5.1 Four Basic Types of Democracy

	Presidential	Parliamentary
Plurality Elections	United States Philippines	United Kingdom Old Commonwealth India Malaysia Jamaica
Proportional Representation	Latin America	Western Europe

Figure 5.1 illustrates the four combinations of basic characteristics and the countries and regions where they prevail. The purest examples of the combination of presidentialism and plurality are the United States and democracies heavily influenced by the United States, such as the Philippines and Puerto Rico. Latin American countries have overwhelmingly opted for presidential-PR systems. Parliamentary-plurality systems exist in the United Kingdom and many former British colonies, including India, Malaysia, Jamaica, and the countries of the so-called Old Commonwealth (Canada, Australia, and New Zealand). Finally, parliamentary-PR systems are concentrated in Western Europe. Clearly, the overall pattern is to a large extent determined by geographic, cultural, and colonial factors—a point to which I shall return shortly.

Very few contemporary democracies cannot be accommodated by this classification. The major exceptions are democracies that fall in between the pure presidential and pure parliamentary types (France and Switzerland), and those that use electoral methods other than pure PR or plurality (Ireland, Japan, and, again, France).[4]

Two important factors influenced the adoption of PR in continental Europe. One was the problem of ethnic and religious minorities; PR was designed to provide minority representation and thereby to counteract potential threats to national unity and political stability. "It was no accident," Stein Rokkan writes, "that the earliest moves toward proportional representation (PR) came in the ethnically most heterogeneous countries." The second factor was the dynamic of the democratization process. PR was adopted "through a convergence of pressures from below and from above. The rising working class wanted to lower the thresholds of representation in order to gain access to the legislatures, and the most threatened of the old-established parties demanded PR to protect their position against the new waves of mobilized voters created by universal suffrage."[5] Both factors are relevant for contemporary constitution making, especially for the many countries where there are deep ethnic cleavages or where new democratic forces need to be reconciled with the old antidemocratic groups.

The process of democratization also originally determined whether parliamentary or presidential institutions were adopted. As Douglas V. Verney has pointed out, there were two basic ways in which monarchical power could be democratized: by taking away most of the monarch's personal political prerogatives and making his cabinet responsible to the popularly elected legislature, thus creating a parliamentary system; or by removing the hereditary monarch and substituting a new, democratically elected "monarch," thus creating a presidential system.[6]

Other historical causes have been voluntary imitations of successful democracies and the dominant influence of colonial powers. As Figure 5.1 shows very clearly, Britain's influence as an imperial power has been enormously important. The U.S. presidential model was widely imitated in Latin America in the nineteenth century. And early in the twentieth century, PR spread quickly in continental Europe and Latin America, not only for reasons of partisan accommodation and minority protection, but also because it was widely perceived to be the most democratic method of election and hence the "wave of the democratic future."

This sentiment in favor of PR raises the controversial question of the *quality* of democracy achieved in the four alternative systems. The term "quality" refers to the degree to which a system meets such democratic norms as representativeness, accountability, equality, and participation. The claims and counterclaims are too well-known to require lengthy treatment here, but it is worth emphasizing that the differences between the opposing camps are not as great as is often supposed. First of all, PR and plurality advocates disagree not so much about the respective effects of the two electoral methods as about the weight to be attached to these effects. Both sides agree that PR yields greater proportionality and minority representation and that plurality promotes two-party systems and one-party executives. Partisans disagree on which of these results is preferable, with the plurality side claiming that only in two-party systems can clear accountability for government policy be achieved.

In addition, both sides argue about the *effectiveness* of the two systems. Proportionalists value minority representation not just for its democratic quality but also for its ability to maintain unity and peace in divided societies. Similarly, proponents of plurality favor one-party cabinets not just because of their democratic accountability but also because

of the firm leadership and effective policy making that they allegedly provide. There also appears to be a slight difference in the relative emphasis that the two sides place on quality and effectiveness. Proportionalists tend to attach greater importance to the *representativeness* of government, while plurality advocates view the *capacity to govern* as the more vital consideration.

Finally, while the debate between presidentialists and parliamentarists has not been as fierce, it clearly parallels the debate over electoral systems. Once again, the claims and counterclaims revolve around both quality and effectiveness. Presidentialists regard the direct popular election of the chief executive as a democratic asset, while parliamentarists think of the concentration of executive power in the hands of a single official as less than optimally democratic. But here the question of effectiveness has been the more seriously debated issue, with the president's strong and effective leadership role being emphasized by one side and the danger of executive-legislative conflict and stalemate by the other.

Evaluating Democratic Performance

How can the actual performance of the different types of democracies be evaluated? It is extremely difficult to find quantifiable measures of democratic performance, and therefore political scientists have rarely attempted a systematic assessment. The major exception is G. Bingham Powell Jr.'s pioneering study evaluating the capacity of various democracies to maintain public order (as measured by the incidence of riots and deaths from political violence) and their levels of citizen participation (as measured by electoral turnout).[7] Following Powell's example, I will examine these and other aspects of democratic performance, including democratic representation and responsiveness, economic equality, and macroeconomic management.

Due to the difficulty of finding reliable data outside the OECD countries to measure such aspects of performance, I have limited the analysis to the advanced industrial democracies. In any event, the Latin American democracies, given their lower levels of economic development, cannot be considered comparable cases. This means that one of the four basic alternatives—the presidential-PR form of democracy prevalent only in Latin America—must be omitted from our analysis.

Although this limitation is unfortunate, few observers would seriously argue that a strong case can be made for this particular type of democracy. With the clear exception of Costa Rica and the partial exceptions of Venezuela and Colombia, the political stability and economic performance of Latin American democracies have been far from satisfactory. As Juan Linz has argued, Latin American presidential systems have been particularly prone to executive-legislative deadlock and ineffective leadership.[8] Moreover, Scott Mainwaring has shown persuasively that this problem becomes especially serious when presidents do not have majority support in their legislatures.[9] Thus the Latin American model of presidentialism combined with PR legislative elections remains a particularly unattractive option.

The other three alternatives—presidential-plurality, parliamentary-plurality, and parliamentary-PR systems—are all represented among the firmly established Western democracies. I focus on the 14 cases that unambiguously fit these three categories. The United States is the one example of presidentialism combined with plurality. There are four cases of parliamentarism-plurality (Australia, Canada, New Zealand, and the United Kingdom), and nine democracies of the parliamentary-PR type (Austria, Belgium, Denmark, Finland, Germany, Italy, the Netherlands, Norway, and Sweden). Seven long-term, stable democracies are excluded from the analysis either because they do not fit comfortably into any one of the three categories (France, Ireland, Japan, and Switzerland), or because they are too vulnerable to external factors (Israel, Iceland, and Luxembourg).

Since a major purpose of PR is to facilitate minority representation, one would expect the PR systems to outperform plurality systems in this respect.

There is little doubt that this is indeed the case. For instance, where ethnic minorities have formed ethnic political parties, as in Belgium and Finland, PR has enabled them to gain virtually perfect proportional representation. Because there are so many different kinds of ethnic and religious minorities in the democracies under analysis, it is difficult to measure systematically the *degree* to which PR succeeds in providing more representatives for minorities than does plurality. It is possible, however, to compare the representation of women—a minority in political rather than strictly numerical terms—systematically across countries. The first column of Table 5.1 shows the percentages of female members in the lower (or only) houses of the national legislatures in these 14 democracies during the early 1980s. The 16.4-percent average for the parliamentary-PR systems is about four times higher than the 4.1 percent for the United States or the 4.0-percent average for the parliamentary-plurality countries. To be sure, the higher social standing of women in the four Nordic countries accounts for part of the difference, but the average of 9.4 percent in the five other parliamentary-PR countries remains more than twice as high as in the plurality countries.

Does higher representation of women result in the advancement of their interests? Harold L. Wilensky's careful rating of democracies with regard to the innovativeness and expansiveness of their family policies—a matter of special concern to women—indicates that it does.[10] On a 13-point scale (from a maximum of 12 to a minimum of 0), the scores of these countries range from 11 to 1. The differences among the three groups (as shown in the second column of Table 5.1) are striking: the PR countries have an average score of 7.89, whereas the parliamentary-plurality countries have an average of just 2.50, and the U.S. only a slightly higher score of 3.00. Here again, the Nordic countries have the highest scores, but the 6.80 average of the non-Nordic PR countries is still well above that of the plurality countries.

The last three columns of Table 5.1 show indicators of democratic quality. The third column lists the most reliable figures on electoral participation

Table 5.1 Women's Legislative Representation, Innovative Family Policy, Voting Turnout, Income Inequality, and the Dahl Rating of Democratic Quality

	Women's Repr. 1980–82	Family Policy 1976–80	Voting Turnout 1971–80	Income Top 20% 1985	Dahl Rating 1969
Pres.-Plurality (N=1)	4.1	3.00	54.2%	39.9%	3.0
Parl.-Plurality (N=4)	4.0	2.50	75.3	42.9	4.8
Parl.-PR (N=9)	16.4	7.89	84.5	39.0	2.2

Note: The one presidential-plurality democracy is the United States; the four parliamentary-plurality democracies are Australia, Canada, New Zealand, and the United Kingdom; and the nine parliamentary-PR democracies are Austria, Belgium, Denmark, Finland, Germany, Italy, the Netherlands, Norway, and Sweden.

Sources: Based on Wilma Rule, "Electoral Systems, Contextual Factors and Women's Opportunity for Election to Parliament in Twenty-Three Democracies," *Western Political Quarterly* 40 (September 1987): 483; Harold L. Wilensky, "Common Problems, Divergent Policies: An 18-Nation Study of Family Policy," *Public Affairs Report* 31 (May 1990): 2; personal communication by Harold L. Wilensky to the author, dated 18 October 1990; Robert W. Jackman, "Political Institutions and Voter Turnout in the Industrial Democracies," *American Political Science Review* 81 (June 1987): 420; World Bank, *World Development Report 1989* (New York: Oxford University Press, 1989), 223; Robert A. Dahl, *Polyarchy: Participation and Opposition* (New Haven: Yale University Press, 1971), 232.

(in the 1970s); countries with compulsory voting (Australia, Belgium, and Italy) are not included in the averages. Compared with the extremely low voter turnout of 54.2 percent in the United States, the parliamentary-plurality systems perform a great deal better (about 75 percent). But the average in the parliamentary-PR systems is still higher, at slightly above 84 percent. Since the maximum turnout that is realistically attainable is around 90 percent (as indicated by the turnouts in countries with compulsory voting), the difference between 75 and 84 percent is particularly striking.

Another democratic goal is political equality, which is more likely to prevail in the absence of great economic inequalities. The fourth column of Table 5.1 presents the World Bank's percentages of total income earned by the top 20 percent of households in the mid-1980s.[11] They show a slightly less unequal distribution of income in the parliamentary-PR than in the parliamentary-plurality systems, with the United States in an intermediate position.

Finally, the fifth column reports Robert A. Dahl's ranking of democracies according to ten indicators of democratic quality, such as freedom of the press, freedom of association, competitive party systems, strong parties and interest groups, and effective legislatures.[12] The stable democracies range from a highest rating of 1 to a low of 6. There is a slight pro-PR bias in Dahl's ranking (he includes a number-of-parties variable that rates multiparty systems somewhat higher than two-party systems), but even when we discount this bias we find striking differences between the parliamentary-PR and parliamentary-plurality countries: six of the former are given the highest score, whereas most of the latter receive the next to lowest score of 5.

No such clear differences are apparent when we examine the effect of the type of democracy on the maintenance of public order and peace. Parliamentary-plurality systems had the lowest incidence of riots during the period 1948–77, but the highest incidence of political deaths; the latter

Table 5.2 Economic Growth, Inflation, and Unemployment (in percent)

	Economic Growth 1961–88	Inflation 1961–88	Unemployment 1965–88
Pres.-Plurality (N=1)	3.3	5.1	6.1
Parl.-Plurality (N=4)	3.4	7.5	6.1
Parl.-PR (N=9)	3.5	6.3	4.4

Sources: *OECD Economic Outlook*, No. 26 (December 1979), 131; No. 30 (December 1981), 131, 140, 142; No. 46 (December 1989), 166, 176, 182.

figure, however, derives almost entirely from the high number of political deaths in the United Kingdom, principally as a result of the Northern Ireland problem. A more elaborate statistical analysis shows that societal division is a much more important factor than type of democracy in explaining variation in the incidence of political riots and deaths in the 13 parliamentary countries.[13]

A major argument in favor of plurality systems has been that they favor "strong" one-party governments that can pursue "effective" public policies. One key area of government activity in which this pattern should manifest itself is the management of the economy. Thus advocates of plurality systems received a rude shock in 1987 when the average per capita GDP in Italy (a PR and multiparty democracy with notoriously uncohesive and unstable governments) surpassed that of the United Kingdom, typically regarded as the very model of strong and effective government. If Italy had discovered large amounts of oil in the Mediterranean, we would undoubtedly explain its superior economic performance in terms of this fortuitous factor. But it was not Italy but Britain that discovered the oil!

Economic success is obviously not solely determined by government policy. When we examine economic performance over a long period of time, however, the effects of external influences are minimized, especially if we focus on countries with similar levels of economic development. Table 5.2 presents OECD figures from the 1960s through the 1980s for the three most important aspects of macroeconomic performance—average annual economic growth, inflation, and unemployment rates.

Although Italy's economic growth has indeed been better than that of Britain, the parliamentary-plurality and parliamentary-PR countries as groups do not differ much from each other or from the United States. The slightly higher growth rates in the parliamentary-PR systems cannot be considered significant. With regard to inflation, the United States has the best record, followed by the parliamentary-PR systems. The most sizable differences appear in unemployment levels; here the parliamentary-PR countries perform significantly better than the plurality countries.[14] Comparing the parliamentary-plurality and parliamentary-PR countries on all three indicators, we find that the performance of the latter is uniformly better.

Lessons for Developing Countries

Political scientists tend to think that plurality systems such as the United Kingdom and the United States are superior with regard to democratic quality and governmental effectiveness—a tendency best explained by the fact that political science has always been an Anglo-American-oriented discipline. This prevailing opinion is largely contradicted, however, by the empirical evidence presented above. Wherever significant differences appear, the parliamentary-PR systems almost invariably post the best records, particularly with respect to representation, protection of minority interests, voter participation, and control of unemployment.

This finding contains an important lesson for democratic constitutional engineers: the parliamentary-PR option is one that should be given serious consideration. Yet a word of caution is also in order, since parliamentary-PR democracies differ greatly among themselves. Moderate PR and moderate multipartism, as in Germany and Sweden, offer more attractive models than the extreme PR and multiparty systems of Italy and the Netherlands. As previously noted, though, even Italy has a respectable record of democratic performance.

But are these conclusions relevant to newly democratic and democratizing countries in Asia, Africa, Latin America, and Eastern Europe, which are trying to make democracy work in the face of economic underdevelopment and ethnic divisions? Do not these difficult conditions require strong executive leadership in the form of a powerful president or a Westminster-style, dominant one-party cabinet?

With regard to the problem of deep ethnic cleavages, these doubts can be easily laid to rest. Divided societies, both in the West and elsewhere, need peaceful coexistence among the contending ethnic groups. This requires conciliation and compromise, goals that in turn require the greatest possible inclusion of representatives of these groups in the decision-making process. Such power sharing can be arranged much more easily in parliamentary and PR systems than in presidential and plurality systems. A president almost inevitably belongs to one ethnic group, and hence presidential systems are particularly inimical to ethnic power sharing. And while Westminster-style parliamentary systems feature collegial cabinets, these tend not to be ethnically inclusive, particularly when there is a majority ethnic group. It is significant that the British government, in spite of its strong majoritarian traditions, recognized the need for consensus and power sharing in religiously and ethnically divided Northern Ireland. Since 1973, British policy has been to try to solve the Northern Ireland problem by means of PR elections and an inclusive coalition government.

As Horowitz has pointed out, it may be possible to alleviate the problems of presidentialism by requiring that a president be elected with a stated minimum of support from different groups, as in Nigeria.[15] But this is a palliative that cannot compare with the advantages of a truly collective and inclusive executive. Similarly, the example of Malaysia shows that a parliamentary system can have a broad multiparty and multiethnic coalition cabinet in spite of plurality elections, but this requires elaborate preelection pacts among the parties. These exceptions prove the rule: the ethnic power sharing that has been attainable in Nigeria and Malaysia only on a limited basis and through very special arrangements is a natural and straightforward result of parliamentary-PR forms of democracy.

PR and Economic Policy Making

The question of which form of democracy is most conducive to economic development is more difficult to answer. We simply do not have enough cases of durable Third World democracies representing the different systems (not to mention the lack of reliable economic data) to make an unequivocal evaluation. However, the conventional wisdom that economic development requires the unified and decisive leadership of a strong president or a Westminster-style dominant cabinet is highly suspect. First of all, if an inclusive executive that must do more bargaining and conciliation were less effective at economic policy making than a dominant and exclusive executive, then presumably an authoritarian government free of legislative interference or internal dissent would be optimal. This reasoning—a frequent excuse for the overthrow of democratic governments in the Third World in the 1960s and 1970s—has now been thoroughly discredited. To be sure, we do have a few examples of economic miracles wrought by authoritarian regimes, such as those in South Korea or Taiwan, but these are more than counterbalanced by the sorry economic records of just about all the nondemocratic governments in Africa, Latin America, and Eastern Europe.

Second, many British scholars, notably the eminent political scientist S. E. Finer, have come to the conclusion that economic development requires not so much a *strong* hand as a *steady* one. Reflecting on the poor economic performance of post–World War II Britain, they have argued that each of the governing parties indeed provided reasonably strong leadership in economic policy making but that alternations in governments were too "absolute and abrupt," occurring "between two sharply polarized parties each eager to repeal a large amount of its predecessor's legislation." What is needed, they argue, is "greater stability and continuity" and "greater moderation in policy," which could be provided by a shift to PR and to coalition governments much more likely to be centrist in orientation.[16] This argument would appear to be equally applicable both to developed and developing countries.

Third, the case for strong presidential or Westminster-style governments is most compelling where rapid decision making is essential. This means that in foreign and defense policy parliamentary-PR systems may be at a disadvantage. But in economic policy making speed is not particularly important—quick decisions are not necessarily wise ones.

Why then do we persist in distrusting the economic effectiveness of democratic systems that engage in broad consultation and bargaining aimed at a high degree of consensus? One reason is that multiparty and coalition governments *seem* to be messy, quarrelsome, and inefficient in contrast to the clear authority of strong presidents and strong one-party cabinets. But we should not let ourselves be deceived by these superficial appearances. A closer look at presidential systems reveals that the most successful cases—such as the United States, Costa Rica, and pre-1970 Chile—are at least equally quarrelsome and, in fact, are prone to paralysis and deadlock rather than steady and effective economic policy making. In any case, the argument should not be about governmental aesthetics but about actual performance. The undeniable elegance of the Westminster model is not a valid reason for adopting it.

The widespread skepticism about the economic capability of parliamentary-PR systems stems from confusing governmental strength with effectiveness. In the short run, one-party cabinets or presidents may well be able to formulate economic policy with greater ease and speed. In the long run, however, policies supported by a broad consensus are more likely to be successfully carried out and to remain on course than policies imposed by a "strong" government against the wishes of important interest groups.

To sum up, the parliamentary-PR form of democracy is clearly better than the major alternatives in accommodating ethnic differences, and it has a slight edge in economic policy making as well. The argument that considerations of governmental effectiveness mandate the rejection of parliamentary-PR democracy for developing countries is simply not tenable. Constitution makers in new democracies would do themselves and their countries a great disservice by ignoring this attractive democratic model.

NOTES

1. Donald L. Horowitz, "Comparing Democratic Systems," Seymour Martin Lipset, "The Centrality of Political Culture," and Juan J. Linz, "The Virtues of Parliamentarism," *Journal of Democracy* 1 (Fall 1990): 73–91. A third set of important decisions concerns institutional arrangements that are related to the difference between federal and unitary forms of government: the degree of government centralization, unicameralism or bicameralism, rules for constitutional amendment, and

judicial review. Empirical analysis shows that these factors tend to be related: federal countries are more likely to be decentralized, to have significant bicameralism, and to have "rigid" constitutions that are difficult to amend and protected by judicial review.

2. For a fuller discussion of the differences between majoritarian and consensus government, see Arend Lijphart, *Democracies: Patterns of Majoritarian and Consensus Government in Twenty-One Countries* (New Haven: Yale University Press, 1984).

3. Giovanni Sartori, "Political Development and Political Engineering," in *Public Policy*, vol. 17, eds. John D. Montgomery and Alfred O. Hirschman (Cambridge: Harvard University Press, 1968), 273.

4. The first scholar to emphasize the close connection between culture and these constitutional arrangements was G. Bingham Powell, Jr., in his *Contemporary Democracies Participation, Stability, and Violence* (Cambridge: Harvard University Press, 1982), 67. In my previous writings, I have sometimes classified Finland as a presidential or semipresidential system, but I now agree with Powell (pp. 56–57) that, although the directly elected Finnish president has special authority in foreign policy, Finland operates like a parliamentary system in most other respects. Among the exceptions, Ireland is a doubtful case; I regard its system of the single transferable vote as mainly a PR method, but other authors have classified it as a plurality system. And I include Australia in the parliamentary-plurality group, because its alternative-vote system, while not identical with plurality, operates in a similar fashion.

5. Stein Rokkan, *Citizens, Elections, Parties: Approaches to the Comparative Study of the Processes of Development* (Oslo: Universitetsforlaget, 1970), 157.

6. Douglas V. Verney, *The Analysis of Political Systems* (London: Routledge and Kegan Paul, 1959), 18–23, 42–43.

7. Powell, op. cit., esp. 12–29 and 111–74.

8. Juan J. Linz, "The Perils of Presidentialism," *Journal of Democracy* 1 (Winter 1990), 51–69.

9. Scott Mainwaring, "Presidentialism in Latin America," *Latin American Research Review* 25 (1990), 167–70.

10. Wilensky's ratings are based on a five-point scale (from 4 to 0) "for each of three policy clusters: existence and length of maternity and parental leave, paid and unpaid; availability and accessibility of public daycare programs and government effort to expand daycare; and flexibility of retirement systems. They measure government action to assure care of children and maximize choices in balancing work and family demands for everyone." See Harold L. Wilensky, "Common Problems, Divergent Policies: An 18-Nation Study of Family Policy," *Public Affairs Report* 31 (May 1990), 2.

11. Because of missing data, Austria is not included in the parliamentary-PR average.

12. Robert A. Dahl, *Polyarchy: Participation and Opposition* (New Haven: Yale University Press, 1971), 231–45.

13. This multiple-correlation analysis shows that societal division, as measured by the degree of organizational exclusiveness of ethnic and religious groups, explains 33 percent of the variance in riots and 25 percent of the variance in political deaths. The additional explanation by type of democracy is only 2 percent for riots (with plurality countries slightly more orderly) and 13 percent for deaths (with the PR countries slightly more peaceful).

14. Comparable unemployment data for Austria, Denmark, and New Zealand are not available, and these countries are therefore not included in the unemployment figures in Table 5.2.

15. Horowitz, op. cit., 76–77.

16. S. E. Finer, "Adversary Politics and Electoral Reform," in *Adversary Politics and Electoral Reform*, ed. S. E. Finer (London: Anthony Wigram, 1975), 30–31.

Alfred Stepan, Juan J. Linz, and Yogendra Yadav
THE RISE OF "STATE-NATIONS"

One of the most urgent conceptual, normative, and political tasks of our day is to think anew about how polities that aspire to be democracies can accommodate great sociocultural and even multinational diversity within one state. The need to think anew arises from a mismatch between the political realities of the world we live in and an old political wisdom that we have inherited. The old wisdom holds that the territorial boundaries of a state must coincide with the perceived cultural boundaries of a nation. Thus, this understanding requires that every state must contain within itself one and not more than one culturally homogenous nation, that every state should be a nation, and that every nation should be a state. Given the reality of sociocultural diversity in many of the world's polities, this widespread belief seems to us to be misguided and indeed dangerous since, as we shall argue, many successful democratic states in the world today do not conform to this expectation.

All independent democratic states have a degree of cultural diversity, but for comparative purposes we can say that states may be divided into three broad categories:

1) States that have strong cultural diversity, some of which is territorially based and politically articulated by significant groups with leaders who advance claims of independence in the name of nationalism and self-determination.

2) States that are culturally quite diverse, but whose diversity is nowhere organized by territorially based, politically significant groups that mobilize nationalist demands for independence.

3) States in which a community that is culturally homogeneous enough to consider itself a nation dominates the state, and no other significant group articulates similar claims.

We call countries in the first category "robustly multinational" societies. Canada (owing to Quebec), Spain (especially owing to the Basque Country and Catalonia), and Belgium (owing to Flanders) are all "robustly multinational." India, owing to the Kashmir Valley alone, merits classification in this category. The Sikh-led Khalistan movement in the Punjab, the Mizo independence movement in the northeast, and the Dravidian secessionist movement in southern India strengthen the multinational dimension of the Indian polity.

Switzerland and the United States are both sociologically diverse and multicultural. Yet since neither has significant territorially based groups mobilizing claims for independence, both countries clearly fall into the second and not the first category.

Finally, Japan, Portugal, and most of the Scandinavian countries fall into the third category.

What political implications do these three very different situations have for reconciling democracy with diversity? If a polity has only one significant group which sees itself as a nation, and there exists a relatively common sense of history and religion and a shared language throughout the territory, the building of a nation-state and the building of democracy can reinforce each other.

Yet if competitive elections are inaugurated under conditions that are already "robustly multinational," the logic of nation-state building and the logic of democracy building will come into conflict. This is so because only one of the polity's "nations" will be privileged in the state-building effort, while the other "nations" will go unrecognized and may even be marginalized. But before examining alternatives to the nation-state, we first need to attempt to explain its normative and political power.

The belief that every state should be a nation reflects perhaps the most widely accepted normative

From *Journal of Democracy* 21, no. 3 (July 2010), pp. 50–68.

vision of a modern democratic state—that is, the "nation-state." After the French Revolution, and especially in the latter part of the nineteenth century, France pursued many policies devoted to creating a unitary nation-state in which all French citizens would have only one cultural and political identity. These policies included a package of incentives and disincentives to ensure that French increasingly became the only acceptable language in the state. Political mechanisms to allow the recognition and expression of regional cultural differences were so unacceptable to French nation-state builders that advocacy of federalism was at one time a capital offense. Throughout France, state schools at any given hour were famously teaching the same curriculum with identical syllabi by teachers who had been trained and certified by the same Ministry of Education. Numerous state policies, such as universal military conscription, were designed to create a common French identity and a country that was robustly assimilationist.[1]

Some very successful contemporary democracies such as Sweden, Japan, and Portugal are close to the ideal type of a unitary nation-state. Some federal states such as Germany and Australia have also become nation-states. In our view, if at the time a polity adopts a state-directed program of "nation-state" building sociocultural differences have not acquired political salience, and if most politically aware citizens have a strong sense of shared history, policies designed to build a nation-state should not create problems for the achievement of an inclusive democracy. In fact, the creation of such a national identity and relative homogeneity in the nineteenth century was identified with democratization and was possible in consolidated states.

In the twentieth century, however, attempts to create nation-states via state policies encountered growing difficulties, even in such old states as Spain. Thus if a polity has significant and politically salient cultural or linguistic diversity (as a large number of polities do), then its leaders need to think about, craft, and normatively legitimate a type of polity with the characteristics of a "state-nation."

Identities and Boundaries

Two of the authors of the present essay, Juan Linz and Alfred Stepan, introduced the concept of the state-nation in 1996, but only in a paragraph (and one figure), citing states that "are multicultural, and [which] sometimes even have significant multinational components, [but] which nonetheless still manage to engender strong identification and loyalty from their citizens, an identification and loyalty that proponents of homogeneous nation states perceive that only nation states can engender." They went on to say that neither Switzerland nor India was

> strictly speaking [in the French sense] a nation state, but we believe both can now be called state nations. Under Jawaharlal Nehru, India made significant gains in managing multinational tensions through skillful and consensual usage of numerous consociational practices. Through this process India became in the 1950s and the early 1960s a democratic state-nation.[2]

"Nation-state" policies stand for a political-institutional approach that tries to make the political boundaries of the state and the presumed cultural boundaries of the nation match. Needless to say, the cultural boundaries are far from obvious in most cases. Thus the creation of a nation-state involves privileging *one* sociocultural identity over other potential or actual sociocultural cleavages that can be politically mobilized. "Nation-state" policies have been pursued historically by following a variety of routes that range from relatively soft to downright brutal. These may include: (1) creating or arousing a special kind of allegiance or common cultural identity among those living in a state; (2) encouraging the voluntary assimilation into the nation-state's identity of those who do not share that initial allegiance or cultural identity; (3) various forms of social pressure and coercion to achieve this and to prevent the emergence of alternative cultural identities or to erode them if they exist; and (4) coercion that might, in the more extreme cases, even involve ethnic cleansing.

By contrast, "state-nation" policies stand for a political-institutional approach that respects and protects *multiple but complementary* sociocultural identities. "State-nation" policies recognize the legitimate public and even political expression of active sociocultural cleavages, and they include mechanisms to accommodate competing or conflicting claims without imposing or privileging in a discriminatory way any one claim. "State-nation" policies involve creating a sense of belonging (or "we-feeling") with respect to the statewide political community, while simultaneously creating institutional safeguards for respecting and protecting politically salient sociocultural diversities. The "we-feeling" may take the form of defining a tradition, history, and shared culture in an inclusive manner, with all citizens encouraged to feel a sense of attachment to common symbols of the state and some form of "constitutional patriotism."

In democratic societies, the institutional safeguards constitutive of "state-nation" policies will most likely take the form of federalism, and often specifically *asymmetrical* federalism, possibly combined with consociational practices.[3] Virtually every longstanding and relatively peaceful contemporary democracy with more than one territorially concentrated, politically mobilized, linguistic-cultural group forming a majority in some significant part of its territory is not only federal but "asymmetrically federal" (Belgium, Canada, India) or is a unitary nation-state with a "federacy."[4] As we discuss later, a federacy is a distinct cultural-political unit within an otherwise unitary state that relates to the central government via a set of asymmetrical federal arrangements. This means that such a polity, at a certain point in its history, decided that it could "hold together" within a single democratic system only by constitutionally embedding special cultural and historical prerogatives for some of the member units—prerogatives that respond to those units' distinct linguistic-cultural aspirations, security situations, or historical identities.

We believe that if political leaders in India, Belgium, Spain, and Canada had attempted to force

one language and culture on their respective countries, and had insisted on imposing homogenizing nation-state policies reminiscent of the French Third Republic, the cause of social peace, inclusionary democracy, and individual rights would have been poorly served. For in each of these countries, more than one territorially based, linguistic-cultural cleavage had already been activated. The strategic question, therefore, was whether to attempt to *repress* or to *accommodate* this preexisting, politically activated diversity.

"State-nation" is a term that we introduce to help us think about democratic states that do not—and cannot—fit well into the classic French-style "nation-state" model based on a "we-feeling" resulting from an existing or forged homogeneity. For a summary of the difference between the "nation-state" and "state-nation" as opposing ideal types that shape policies, norms, and institutions for recognizing and accommodating diversity, see Table 5.3 below.

As a diverse polity approximates the state-nation ideal type, we expect it to have the following four empirically verifiable patterns: First, despite multiple cultural identities among its citizens, there will be a high degree of *positive identification* with the state and pride in being citizens of that state. Second, citizens will have *multiple but complementary* political identities and loyalties. Third, there will be a high degree of *institutional trust* in the most important constitutional, legal, and administrative components of the state. Fourth, by world standards, there will be a comparatively high degree of positive support for democracy among all the diverse groups of citizens in the country, and this will include support for the specific statewide democratic institutions through which the polity is governed.

To be sure, these patterns do not simply exist right from the beginning. It all depends on crafting and is very much an outcome of deliberate policies and designs. We turn now to the question of how such "state-nation" behavior and values can be crafted and supported.

Table 5.3 Two Contrasting Ideal Types: "Nation-State" and "State-Nation"

	NATION-STATE	STATE-NATION
Preexisting Conditions		
Sense of belonging or "we-ness"	There is general attachment to one major cultural civilizational tradition. This cultural identity corresponds to existing state boundaries with minor exceptions.	There is attachment to more than one cultural civilizational tradition within the existing boundaries. However, these attachments do not preclude identification with a common state.
State Policy		
Cultural policies	There are homogenizing attempts to foster one core cultural identity, particularly one official language. Multiplicity of cultures is not recognized. The goal is unity in oneness.	There is recognition and support of more than one cultural identity (and more than one official language) within a frame of some common polity-wide symbols. The goal is unity in diversity.
Institutions		
Territorial division of power	The state is unitary or, if a federation, it is mononational and symmetrical.	There is normally a federal system, and it is often asymmetrical. The state can be unitary if aggressive nation-state policies are not pursued and de facto multilingualism is accepted. Federacies are possible.
Politics		
Ethnocultural or territorial cleavages	Such splits are not too salient.	Such splits are salient, but are recognized as such and democratically managed.
Autonomist or secessionist parties	Autonomist parties are normally not "coalitionable." Secessionist parties are outlawed or marginalized in democratic electoral politics.	Autonomist parties can govern in federal units and are "coalitionable" at the center. Nonviolent secessionist parties can sometimes participate in democratic political processes.

Table 5.3 (Continued)

	NATION-STATE	STATE-NATION
	Citizen Orientation	
Political identity	Citizens feel that they belong to the state and to the same cultural nation at the same time.	Many citizens have multiple but complementary identities.
Obedience and loyalty	Citizens believe in obedience to the state and loyalty to the nation.	Citizens feel obedience to the state and identification with its institutions; none of this is based on a single national identity.

State-Nation Policies

On both theoretical and empirical grounds, we contend that there can be a nested set of policy and institutional choices which reinforce each other and help to facilitate the emergence and persistence of a state-nation. This set includes:

1. An asymmetrical, "holding-together" federal state, but *not* a symmetrical, "coming-together" federal state or a unitary state;
2. Both individual rights *and* collective recognition;
3. Parliamentary *instead of* presidential or semi-presidential government;
4. Polity-wide *and* "centric-regional" parties and careers;
5. Politically integrated but *not* culturally assimilated populations;
6. Cultural nationalists in power mobilizing *against* secessionist nationalists;
7. A pattern of multiple *but* complementary identities.

We describe these policies as "nested" because each one tends to depend for its success on the adoption of the ones preceding it. Thus the second policy, "group recognition," is normally nested within the first, federalism (especially asymmetrical federalism). The fourth policy, which has to do with having the kinds of parties and politicians who are ready to form coalitions, is greatly facilitated if the choice of the third policy is parliamentarism because under that form of government the executive is a "shareable good." And the success of the seventh policy, multiple but complementary identities, relies heavily on the prior success of the previous six.

Each of the recommended choices requires some explanation. To begin with, a federal as opposed to a unitary state is appropriate for a state-nation because federal structures will allow a large and territorially concentrated cultural group with serious nationalist aspirations to attain self-governance within that territory. But why do these federal arrangements need to be asymmetrical? In a symmetrical federal system, all units have identical rights and obligations. It is possible, however, that some culturally distinct and territorially concentrated groups might have acquired prerogatives that they wish to retain or reacquire. It is also possible, for example, that some tribal groups controlling large territories (such as the Mizos in India's northeast) would agree to join the federation only if some of their unique land-use laws were respected. Bargains and compromises on these issues, which might be necessary for peace and voluntary membership in the political community, are negotiable in an asymmetrical system, but are normally unacceptable in a symmetrical system.

Second, why does a state-nation need both individual rights and collective recognition? A polity cannot be democratic unless throughout its whole extent the rights of individuals are constitutionally inviolable and protected by the state. This necessary function of central government cannot be devolved. But certain territorially concentrated cultural groups, even nations, may need some collective recognition for rights that go beyond classic liberal rights (or what Michael Walzer calls "Liberalism 2") in order for members of those groups to be able to thrive culturally or even possibly to exercise fully their classic individual liberal rights.[5] Walzer argues that Liberalism 2 "allows for a state committed to the survival and flourishing of . . . a (limited) set of nations, cultures and religions—so long as the basic rights of citizens who have different commitments or no such commitments are protected."[6] There may well be concrete moments in the crafting of a democracy when individuals cannot develop and exercise their full rights until they are active members of a group that struggles and wins some collective goods common to most members of the group. These group rights might be most easily accommodated by a federal system that is asymmetrical. For example, if a large territorially concentrated group speaks a distinct language, some official recognition of the privileged right of that language to be used in government institutions, schools, and the media might be necessary to enable the members of this group to act upon their own individual rights.

If there are territorially concentrated minority religions in the polity, the identification of their practitioners with the center may well be reduced if there is only one established religion throughout the territory. In such cases, identity with the state-nation may be encouraged if, instead, all religions are officially recognized and possibly even financially supported. The financial support of religions, majority and minority, is of course a violation of classic U.S. or French doctrines of separation of church and state, but it is not a violation of any person's individual human rights.[7]

Third, why the need for parliamentarism? In a presidential or semipresidential system, the highest executive office is an "indivisible good"—it can only be held by one person, from one nationality, for a fixed term. A parliamentary system, by contrast, creates the possibility of a "shareable good." That is, there is a possibility that other parties, composed of other nationalities, could help to constitute the ruling coalition. If no single party has a majority, parliamentarism is coalition-requiring. Also, because the government may collapse unless it constantly bargains to retain the support of its coalition partners, parliamentarism often displays coalition-sustaining qualities as well. These "shareable" and "coalition-friendly" aspects of a parliamentary executive might be useful in a robustly multinational society.

If almost all parties draw the vast bulk of their votes from their own respective ethnoterritorial units, the sense of trust in and identification with the center will probably be low. Many analysts would call such parties "regional-secessionist." Yet if there are major polity-wide parties that regularly need allies from regional parties to help form a government at the center, and if the polity-wide parties often help their regional-party allies to form a majority in their own ethnofederal units, then the logic of incentives makes these allegedly "regional-secessionist" parties actually "centric-regional" parties, because they regularly share in rule at the center. This coalitional pattern is possible only if both the polity-wide and the regional parties are "nested" in a system that is both federal and parliamentary.

The importance of "polity-wide careers" can be grasped by considering India as an example. There, English serves as an all-India *lingua franca* that makes it possible for educated members of regional groups who do not speak the majority language (Hindi) to pursue careers in law, communications, business, and the federal civil service. Citizens whose careers are "polity-wide" rather than regional will likely feel strong incentives not to "exit" from the polity-wide networks that such careers open up for them, and upon which their careers in turn depend.[8]

Fifth, it is important that political integration be able to go forward independent of cultural integration. In a state-nation, many cultural and especially ethnonational groups will be educated and self-governing in their own language. They will thus probably never be fully culturally assimilated to the dominant culture in the polity. This is a reality of "state-nations." If the ethnofederal group sees the polity-wide state as having helped to put a "roof of rights" over its head, however, and if the "centric-regional" parties are "coalitionable" with polity-wide parties and regularly help to form the government at the center, and if many individuals from the ethnofederal group enjoy polity-wide careers, then it is a good bet that the ethnofederal group and its members will be politically well-integrated into the state-nation.

Sixth, what do we mean by saying that cultural nationalists in power will mobilize against nationalists who embrace secession? Ernest Gellner forcefully articulated the position of many theorists of the nation-state when he famously asserted: "Nationalism is primarily a political principle, which holds that the political and the national unit should be congruent . . . Nationalist *sentiment* is the feeling of anger aroused by the violation of the principle . . . A nationalist *movement* is one actuated by a sentiment of this kind."[9]

Thus, we are constantly admonished not to advocate state-nation policies because all nationalism inevitably becomes "secessionist nationalism," with eventual demands for independence. Yet there can be a situation in which a "cultural nationalist" movement, nested within an asymmetrically federal and parliamentary system, wins democratic political control of a federal territorial unit; educates the citizens of this territory in the language, culture, and history of their own nation; and also stands ready to join coalitions at the center. If such a cultural nation-

alist group in power is challenged by secessionist nationalists who use force or threaten its use to pursue independence, the ruling nationalist group faces the loss of treasured resources. Under such circumstances, the "cultural nationalists" will likely mobilize the political and security resources under their control to defeat the "secessionist nationalists."[10]

Finally, what do we mean by talking about multiple but complementary identities? In the polity-wide system produced by the six nested policies and norms that we have just discussed, it is possible that citizens could strongly identify with and be loyal to *both* their culturally powerful ethnofederal unit *and* the polity-wide center. They would have these complementary identities because the center has recognized and defended many of their cultural demands and, in addition, has helped to structure and protect their full participation in the larger political life of the country. Such citizens are also likely to have strong trust in the center because they see it (or the institutions historically associated with it) as having helped to deliver some valued collective goods such as independence from a colonial power, security from threatening neighbors, or possibly even a large and growing common market. Thus the pattern of multiple but complementary identities that is likely to obtain is no accident, but an outcome earned by deliberately crafted policies.

The Case of India

India would seem to present one of the most difficult tests for our argument that multiple and complementary identities, as well as democratic state-nation loyalties, are possible even in a polity with robustly multinational dimensions and a plethora of intense linguistic and religious differences. Let us briefly document how extensive these diversities actually are.

One of the greatest points of conflict in multicultural and multinational polities, whether federal or not, is language. When India gained independence in 1947, it had in addition to its most widely spoken single language (Hindi) ten additional languages that were used by at least 13 million people each. Many had their own unique scripts.[11] Added to this linguistic complexity was an enormous diversity of religious beliefs and practices that alone would make the country a case of special interest to students of comparative democratization. India has large communities of almost every world religion, including Hinduism, Buddhism, Sikhism, Christianity, and Islam. In 2009, India's Muslim minority amounted to about 161 million people, the world's third-largest Islamic population, exceeded only by those of Indonesia and Pakistan.[12] At a time when too many scholars and political activists see Islam as being in deep cultural conflict with democracy, it is worth pausing to reflect that the world's largest Islamic community with extensive democratic experience is in multicultural, multinational, federal, and consociational India.

India's longstanding democracy enhances the "scope value" of the state-nation concept by showing that the model can be applied not only to rich but also to very poor countries. Of the world's four long-standing multinational federal democracies—Belgium, Canada, and Spain are the others—only India lacks an advanced industrial economy. To put it in rough terms, in 2008 Belgium, Canada, and Spain all had purchasing-power parity (PPP) per capita Gross National Income of more than US$30,000 per year. The comparable figure for India was a bit less than a tenth of that.[13] Given its extraordinarily deep diversity, India could never have created a French-style democratic nation-state. But it has managed to craft a democratic state-nation, supported by all religions, all socioeconomic groups, and many states that once experienced secessionist movements. In our forthcoming book, we devote the better part of three chapters to showing how Indians imagined, negotiated, and crafted their long-standing democratic state-nation. What follows here is an abbreviated discussion of three key paths followed by India's emerging democratic communities; their long and creative political, ethical, and constitutional search for policy formulas more appropriate

than the classical nation-state model for reconciling deep diversity and democracy; their choice of asymmetrical federalism to help them solve the problem of self-governance in the context of many languages and the special needs of tribal populations; and their creation of a new model of secularism as a way of accommodating India's religious heterogeneity and its great intensity of religious practice.

The building of a state-nation in India was no accident or afterthought. The state-nation model was implicit in the idea of India forged by modern Indian political thinkers, nurtured by the freedom movement, enshrined in the Indian Constitution, sustained by the first generation of postindependence leadership, and institutionalized in competitive politics. In that sense, our "state-nation" model is best seen not only as a new analytic ideal type, but also as a theoretical defense of what political thinkers and practitioners in India knew for more than a century. Here we can only illustrate this with reference to an early episode in India's long and creative search for institutional designs more appropriate than the classical nation-state model for reconciling deep diversity with democracy.

By the mid-1920s, more than two decades before independence, the Indian National Congress (INC) had already begun to look in detail at the question of which political institutions and practices would best serve a self-governing India. The INC rejected the British-drafted Simon Commission Report, and appointed its own committee under the leadership of Motilal Nehru, the father of Jawaharlal Nehru, to outline a constitution for a free India. The Nehru Report, approved by the All Parties Conference in Lucknow in 1928, foreshadowed many provisions of the Indian Constitution of 1950. The definition of citizenship in the Nehru Report was very state-nation—friendly in that it was absolutely inclusive and territorial: "The word 'citizen,' wherever it occurs in this constitution, means every person who was born, or whose father was either born or naturalized, within the territorial limits of the commonwealth" (Article 3). The Nehru Report also laid down that independent India would have parliamentary government (Article 5) and a bicameral, federal system (Articles 8 and 9). All this was incorporated into the Indian Constitution. As we argued above, a parliamentary federal system is the most supportive combination for the emergence of "centric-regional" parties that may be a useful alternative to "exit" for parties with different linguistic majorities.

The radical "state-nation" reconfiguration of India that allowed each large linguistic community to have a state of its own and to govern itself in its local majority language did not fully occur until 1957; however, it was strongly supported at the 1921 INC meeting in Madras and endorsed in the Nehru Report, which held that "the redistribution of provinces should take place on a linguistic basis on the demand of the majority of the population of the area concerned" (Article 86). This formula allowed independent India to respond democratically to the presence within its borders of numerous territorially based linguistic majorities. (At present, 22 languages enjoy "official" constitutional status.) This is a classic feature of the state-nation style of "holding-together" federalism, and by that token unthinkable in a U.S.-style "coming-together" federation. Also supportive of a relatively strong "holding-together" federalism (and again, quite unlike U.S. practice) was the Nehru Committee provision (Article 49) that gave the Supreme Court of the Union "original jurisdiction" in almost all matters. The choice of asymmetrical federalism also allowed for the creation of some small states with tribal majorities, like Mizoram, to preserve tribal cultures by means of special, constitutionally embedded prerogatives that allowed only Mizos to vote in local elections or to buy land. These prerogatives were crucial to the 1986 Mizo Accord that not only helped to end a secessionist war but contributed as well to the building of the "multiple and complementary" identities that our surveys reveal.

On the all-important question of religion, the Nehru Report was also supportive of state-nation policies. Under the section on "Fundamental Rights," it clearly rules out an established religion and supported a religiously impartial state, but unlike the U.S. Constitution, it also implied the admissibility of state aid for religious educational establishments (Article 4). The Indian Constitution duly reflected this spirit. The relationship between religion and the state that the Indian Constituent Assembly crafted later was a highly original creation with strong affinities to our state-nation model. All religious communities were recognized and respected by the state. All religious communities, for example, could run schools, organizations, and charities eligible for state financial support. The norms and practices of this model are now so pervasive that even when the Bharatiya Janata Party (BJP), the party of Hindu nationalism, headed the government coalition, it did not dare break with the tradition of paying extensive state subsidies to help Muslim citizens make the *hajj* (pilgrimage) to Mecca. Every single nation-state in Western Europe has some paid compulsory public holidays for the majority Christian religion (Sweden, Denmark, Norway, and Germany alone have 39) but none of them has a single compulsory public holiday for a non-Christian minority religion. India has five such holidays for the majority Hindu religion, but ten for minority religions, including five for Islam.[14]

Thus, when the Constituent Assembly formally set about its tasks in 1946, there was little doubt that it would adopt provisions for the protection of linguistic, cultural, and religious diversity. The institutional structures and norms that the Constituent Assembly agreed upon facilitated a broad set of policies conducive to the crafting of a robust state-nation on the Indian subcontinent.

India's Experience: Examining the Evidence

Was the "idea of India" described above confined merely to the high traditions of political theory and legal constitutional texts? Or did this idea find resonance among ordinary Indian citizens across different religions, regions, communities, and classes? Fortunately, we can begin to answer this question about ordinary citizens' attitudes because India has been included in all four rounds of the World Values Survey. In addition, the Centre for the Study of Developing Societies (CSDS) in Delhi regularly carries out some of the world's largest social-scientific surveys of political opinions and attitudes. The latest such survey, the National Election Study of 2009, had a nationwide sample of 36,169 people.[15]

In our book, we present in detail and in comparative perspective the Indian evidence on diversity and democracy as seen in the mirror of public opinion. In particular, we look at the four empirical attributes mentioned above that we expect from a successful state-nation: the degree of *positive identification* with the state and pride in being its citizens; the existence of *multiple but complementary* political identities and loyalties; the degree of *institutional trust* in the most important constitutional, legal, and administrative components of the state; and the degree of positive *support for democracy and for polity-wide democratic institutions* among all the diverse groups of citizens in the country.

We do not shy away from many of the continuing problems of India's development that can and must be better addressed: Nearly half of India's women are illiterate, and half its children are underweight; a quarter or more of the population live below the official "poverty line," with this proportion being higher among Muslims. We analyze human-rights violations and the still unresolved secessionist conflicts in Kashmir and Nagaland. We discuss the lethal Hindu-nationalist program that swept the state of Gujarat in 2002, and we consider the Naxalite movement. Notwithstanding these failures on the developmental and human-rights fronts, the evidence regarding the four measures of state-nation success is highly impressive indeed. A large majority of citizens, despite their great linguistic, religious, and cultural diversity, positively identify with and trust the Indian central state while supporting India's democracy.

For example, let us compare the level of national pride in India with the attitudes of the citizens of the other ten long-standing federal democracies

(Argentina, Australia, Austria, Belgium, Brazil, Canada, Germany, Spain, Switzerland, and the United States). The World Values Survey routinely asks citizens whether they feel "great," "some," "little," or "no" pride in being a member of their country. In 2002, 67 percent of Indians expressed "great pride," a figure exceeded only in the United States (71 percent) and Australia (70 percent). Another important state-nation indicator is whether citizens, despite a possible strong sense of identification with an ethnic, linguistic, or cultural minority unit of the federation, nonetheless still trust the central government. Only Switzerland recorded a higher level of trust in the central government (50 percent) than did India (48 percent). It is crucial in a multinational, multilingual, multicultural polity that citizens trust the overall legal system; the three countries in our set of eleven whose citizens were most prone to express trust in the legal system were India (67 percent), Switzerland (65 percent), and Austria (58 percent).[16]

A Few Questions

A classic and frequently used battery of questions concerning democracy asks respondents which of the following three statements is closest to their own opinion: 1) "Democracy is preferable to any other kind of government"; 2) "Under some circumstances, an authoritarian government can be preferable to a democratic one"; or 3) "For people like me, it does not matter whether we have a democratic or a nondemocratic regime." If a respondent opts for the second or third statement, it is coded as an explicitly authoritarianism-accepting response. The percentage of respondents who gave such a response in India (12) is far lower than the comparable figure from five other countries that feature prominently in the democratization literature: Brazil (47), Chile (46), South Korea (38), Uruguay (18), and Spain (17).[17] Using the National Election Study of 2004, which had more than three-thousand Muslim respondents, we were able to evaluate how similar or dissimilar Muslims were from Hindus in this respect. The shares of Indian Muslims and Hindus who chose as their response "Democracy is preferable to any other kind of government" were virtually the same at 87 and 88 percent, respectively.[18]

Some political observers fear that growing religiosity among Hindus and Muslims alike will create new challenges for democracy in India. We tested this by creating a low-medium-high index of "the intensity of religious practice" that we could place alongside an index measuring "support for democracy." We found that for Hindus and Muslims alike, the greater the reported intensity of religious practice, the greater the professed support for democracy.[19] This evidence not only robustly disconfirms the proposition that religious intensity threatens Indian democracy, but also suggests that the Indian state-nation is currently holding its own even in the arena of the greatest contestation of our times, religion.

Let us now shift from surveys and attitudes to policies and outcomes. Let us specifically contrast how India, following state-nation policies, politically integrated its Tamil population in the south, and how nearby Sri Lanka, which pursued nation-state policies toward the Tamil population in its own northeast, barely avoided state disintegration and has just terminated by force a civil war in which approximately a hundred-thousand people were killed.

Sri Lanka provides a counterfactual example that we analyze at length in our book. The main point can be summarized here. India arguably started in a more difficult position in this nearly "matched pair" because the Indian Tamils were involved with the Dravidian movement, which briefly flirted with the idea of secession from India. Indeed, there had been a long series of conflicts between Brahmins and non-Brahmins in what is now the state of Tamil Nadu at India's southern tip. We can thus say that there was a robust multinational dimension to politics in Tamil Nadu, although many Tamils felt great attachment to the polity-wide independence movement led by the INC.[20]

In comparative terms, Sri Lanka actually started in an easier position vis-à-vis its Tamil minority. For a century before independence in 1948, there had been no politically significant riots between Sinhalese, who were largely Buddhists, and the Tamils, who were primarily Hindu. In fact, the first president of the Ceylon Congress Party was a Tamil. Tamils had done well in English-language civil-service exams in Ceylon, and though they were interested in greater power-sharing, it is still true to say that at independence there had been no Tamil demands for devolution or federalism, much less independence. Ceylon also had a much higher per capita income than India, and could have made modest side payments to some Sinhalese groups, especially the Buddhists, who had been marginalized during the period of British colonial rule.

Yet 35 years after independence, the potential issue of Tamil separatism in India had become a nonissue, while the Sri-Lankan nonissue had become a bloody civil war for secession that raged for a quarter of a century. What explains such sharply different outcomes?

Much of the explanation, we believe, is related to the radically differential application of the nested policies that we discussed earlier. Table 5.4 highlights the state-integrating state-nation policies followed by India and the state-disintegrating nation-state policies followed by Sri Lanka.

Extending the Argument

Let us conclude by touching upon three questions that we have not yet addressed. First, can some state-nation policies be of use in unitary states that are not nation-states? We believe that this is quite possible, for we can imagine geopolitical and domestic contexts where *neither* full state-nation policies *nor* full nation-state policies offer plausible ways to manage the multinational dimensions of a polity. Why?

There may be some geopolitical contexts, especially in a country bordering a powerful state that has some irredentist tendencies toward said country,

Table 5.4 Contrasting Strategies of India and Sri Lanka toward Their Respective Tamil Minorities

Policy	India	Sri Lanka
1. An Asymmetrically Federal, but Not a Unitary or Symmetrically Federal State	The constituent assembly creates an asymmetrical federal system that enables state boundaries to be redrawn and eventually allows regional cultural majorities to rule these states in their own languages. A Tamil-speaking state called Tamil Nadu is carved out of Madras State.	No constituent assembly is held, but the parliament approves a constitution that declares Sri Lanka a unitary state. After 1956, the Sinhalese-Buddhist majority increasingly advances majoritarian state policies. No significant devolutionary policies are ever implemented.
2. Individual Rights and Collective Recognition	Language: In 1965, after intense mobilizations and political negotiations, plans for implementing Hindi as the official language of the Indian Union are abandoned. Education becomes the domain of a "three-language" formula. Tamil becomes the official language of Tamil Nadu, and the state is not obliged to use Hindi in its communications with the Union. Religion: All major religions are constitutionally recognized, and minority institutions are eligible for state funds.	Language: In 1956, Sinhalese is made the only official language and English and Tamil are no longer accepted. Religion: Article 9 of the 1978 Constitution assigns Buddhism "the foremost place" among religions. State subsidies favor Buddhists.
3. Parliamentary *instead of* Semipresidential or Presidential Systems	Parliamentarism makes the executive a "shareable good," which allows regional, even potentially secessionist, parties to help form ruling coalitions at the center. Since the late 1970s, the ruling coalition at the center has included one of the Dravidian parties from Tamil Nadu.	In 1978, Sri Lanka creates a semipresidential system in which the president has more powers than in France. From then until now, no northern-based Tamil party joins any coalition at the center.
4. Polity-Wide and "Centric-Regional" Parties (and Careers)	Tamil-centric regional parties, due to their great coalitional ability with polity-wide parties, enjoy substantial presence in the Indian parliament and a disproportionate share of powerful ministries. After the mid-1970s, no significant "regional-separatist" parties exist, and all Tamil parties become "centric regional."	Tamils, especially after 1956, lose virtually all their coalitional ability in polity-wide politics and government formation. No elected Tamil from the north becomes a federal minister after 1957. After the mid-1970s, no major "centric-regional" Tamil parties exist, and all subsequent major Tamil parties are "regional separatist."
5. Politically Integrated but Not Culturally Assimilated Minorities	Tamils integrate politically into the Indian polity but maintain strong pride in Tamil culture. Different governments in Tamil Nadu aggressively take up the promotion of Tamil language and culture, including in state schools and educational curricula.	In 1948, "Indian Tamils" are disenfranchised. In 1983, all members of pro-autonomist Tamil parties must leave parliament. By the mid-1980s, Sri Lanka is "politically multinational" with Tamil guerrilla leaders beyond hope of integration.
6. Cultural Nationalists vs. Territorial Nationalists	Cultural nationalists achieve many of their goals. Territorial nationalists, advocating separatist goals, virtually disappear.	By the late 1970s, violent nationalist guerrillas with explicitly separatist goals become the leaders of the Tamil community in the northeast.
7. *Earned* Pattern of Complementary and Multiple Identities	Strong Tamil identities remain, but polity-wide Indian identity grows. Trust in the central government is higher in the state of Tamil Nadu than it is in the rest of the country.	Marginalized in electoral politics, and facing growing state discrimination and repression, Tamils in the northeast opt for conflict. The ensuing civil war kills 100,000 (most of them Tamils) before ending with the Tamils' defeat in 2009.

in which asymmetrical federalism (or indeed any type of federalism) would present dangers for the nurturing of a new democratic political community via this classic state-nation policy. The safest solution might be a unitary state. At the same time, if the domestic context includes politically significant populations deeply divided over cultural policies (for example, large territorially concentrated parts of the state where most of the populace hews to a distinct language and culture), it would be democratically dangerous and politically implausible to try to impose such classic nation-state policies as a single language. Trouble, even violence, would be the likely result.

If such a combination of geopolitical and domestic factors exists, classic state-nation federal policies will not work. Yet some elements of state-nation policies nonetheless seem a must. But is it possible to follow state-nation policies in a unitary state? We believe that some such policies can be employed. In the hypothetical example above, a key state-nation policy that might be appropriate would be to allow the different cultural or linguistic zones to use their own respective languages at the start of the democratization process.

In our book we analyze the case of Ukraine, which upon its independence from the USSR in 1991 found itself a multinational society, but not a robustly multinational polity. If it had pursued aggressive nation-state policies, such as legally permitting only the Ukrainian language to be used in schools or communications with public officials, Russophones in eastern Ukraine who self-identified as Russians—and especially some of their political leaders—would most likely have become secessionists (much as the Tamils had in Sri Lanka). Some Russians in the east and Crimea could well have requested, and received, Russian military backing for their breakaway efforts.

A second question asks if a democratic, unitary nation-state can use constitutionally embedded federal guarantees in order to respond to the presence of a territorially concentrated minority that has radical cultural differences with the majority population.

We propose a revised theory of *federacy* to tackle this situation. Our new ideal-type definition of a federacy holds it to be a political-administrative unit in an independent unitary state with exclusive power (including some legislative power) in certain areas that is constitutionally or quasi-constitutionally embedded and cannot be changed unilaterally, but whose inhabitants have full citizenship rights in the otherwise unitary state.

In the penultimate chapter of our forthcoming book, we examine how this formula has actually been applied to the democratic management of robustly multinational problems by the otherwise unitary nation-states of Finland (in the case of the Åland Islands) and Denmark (in the cases of both Greenland and the Faroe Islands). We also show that the "scope value" of these kinds of arrangements has extended to the postwar reconstruction of Italy with regard to the once-separatist South Tyrol region (with an 86 percent German-speaking population), as well as to the revolutionary context of 1975 Portugal and its efforts to deal with an emerging secessionist movement in the Azores. The federacy formula also proved useful in negotiating the August 2005 Helsinki Agreement that brought a relatively consensual, peaceful, and inclusionary end to the civil war in Aceh in Indonesia. We also argue that if China ever were to become democratic, a federacy formula could conceivably be of use with regard to Tibet, Hong Kong, and possibly even Taiwan.

Finally, why have we had so little to say about the still-influential federal model presented by the United States? The founders of the United States did not see that country as a multinational polity, and crafted a constitution for what they saw as an emerging nation-state. Indeed, they constitutionally embedded features that make the U.S. model particularly ill-suited to the flexible policy management of robustly multinational societies. Symmetrical U.S.-style federalism would be of no help in managing small, territorially concentrated religious or linguistic minorities such as those found in the Indian state of Mizoram. And U.S.-style presidentialism lacks the coalition-facilitating qualities of parliamentarism, which have often been crucial, as in Tamil Nadu, in helping to promote the evolution of regional-separatist parties into "centric-regional" parties that can join polity-wide coalitions.

Symmetrical federalism and presidentialism have been enormously successful in maintaining stable democratic rule in the United States, a country that, although composed of immigrants from many lands, is not robustly multinational: For all its diversity, the United States does not contain territorially based, politically significant groups mobilizing nationalist demands for independence. But many of the world's democracies are unavoidably confronted with the task of governing robustly multinational societies, and these countries have much more to learn from the experience of India than from that of the United States.

NOTES

1. See the classic account of these policies in Eugen Weber, *Peasants into Frenchmen: The Modernization of Rural France, 1870–1914* (Stanford: Stanford University Press, 1976). Most nineteenth-century progressives and democrats, particularly those associated with the French Revolution, were profoundly opposed to federalism.
2. See the chapter titled "Stateness, Nationalism, and Democratization," in Juan J. Linz and Alfred Stepan, *Problems of Democratic Transition and Consolidation: Southern Europe, South America, and Post-Communist Europe* (Baltimore: Johns Hopkins University Press, 1996), 34, as well as Figure 2.1.
3. We accept Robert A. Dahl's definition of federalism as "a system in which some matters are exclusively *within* the competence of certain local units—cantons, states, provinces—and are constitutionally *beyond* the scope of the authority of the national government; and where certain other matters are constitutionally outside the scope of the authority of the smaller units." Robert A. Dahl, "Federalism and the Democratic Process," in *Democracy, Liberty, and Equality* (Oslo: Norwegian University Press, 1986), 114.
4. For more details on "asymmetrical" and "holding-together" federalism, see Alfred Stepan, "Federalism and Democracy: Beyond the U.S. Model," *Journal of Democracy* 10 (October 1999): 19–34.
5. See Charles Taylor, "The Politics of Recognition," in Amy Gutmann, ed., *Multiculturalism: Examining the Politics of Recognition* (Princeton: Princeton University Press, 1994).
6. The quote from Michael Walzer is from Gutmann, *Multiculturalism*, 99.
7. See Alfred Stepan, "The World's Religious Systems and Democracy: Crafting the 'Twin Tolerations'?" in his *Arguing Comparative Politics* (Oxford: Oxford University Press, 2001), 213–54.
8. However, the systematic effort by an ethnocultural group to monopolize access to careers, even in their own ethnofederal unit, runs counter to the nurturing and preservation of a state-nation.
9. All quotes are from the influential opening paragraphs of Ernest Gellner's *Nations and Nationalism* (Ithaca: Cornell University Press, 1983), 1. Emphasis in the original.
10. At the same time, a convergence between cultural and secessionist nationalists on some issues cannot be ruled out if the secessionists come into conflict with the central state over the use of force.
11. For an analytic discussion of these figures, see Jyotirindra Das Gupta, *Language Conflict and National Development: Group Politics and National Language Policy in India* (Berkeley: University of California Press, 1970), 31–68.
12. Pew Forum on Religion in Public Life, "Mapping the Global Muslim Population: A Report on the Size and Distribution of the World's Muslim Population," 7 October 2009, 14. Available at *http://pewforum.org/docs/?DocID=450*.
13. See the World Bank's World Development Indicators Database.
14. For the Indian model in comparative perspective and the question of paid holidays, see Alfred Stepan, "Multiple Secularisms of Modern Democratic and Non-Democratic Regimes," in Craig Calhoun

and Mark Juergensmeyer, eds., *Rethinking Secularism* (New York: Oxford University Press, 2010).

15. Survey archives at the CSDS go back to 1965. Yogendra Yadav, one of the authors, has been involved with directing, designing, and analyzing these surveys, including the National Election Study series. Since 2003, the other two authors have worked with the CSDS team to design some questions for the surveys. For an overview of the CSDS tradition of survey research, see Lokniti Team, "National Election Study 2004: An Introduction," *Economic and Political Weekly*, 18 December 2004, 5373–82.

16. All the data for these 11 long-standing federal democracies come from various rounds of the World Values Survey coordinated by Ronald Inglehart and his colleagues at the Inter-University Consortium for Political and Social Research, University of Michigan.

17. Data on Latin America come from the 2008 Latinobarómetro, on Spain from the 1992

Eurobarometer, on Korea from the 2004 Korea Democracy Barometer, and on India from the previously cited 2004 National Election Study.

18. According to a Pearson's chi-square test, the findings for all religious communities are statistically significant (p-value < .001). Thus, the probability of this occurring by chance is less than one in a thousand.

19. Full methodological details will appear in the forthcoming book from which the present essay is adapted. Our regression indicates that a one-unit increase in the index of religiosity (controlling for other factors) predicts approximately a 3.5 percent increase in the probability of support for democracy.

20. For excellent discussions of some secessionist tendencies in what is now Tamil Nadu, see Narendra Subramanian, *Ethnicity and Populist Mobilization: Political Parties, Citizens and Democracy in South India* (Oxford: Oxford University Press, 1999).

Georgina Waylen

ENGENDERING THE "CRISIS OF DEMOCRACY": INSTITUTIONS, REPRESENTATION AND PARTICIPATION

Many democracies have been undergoing significant changes in the last few decades and are widely perceived to be suffering a serious crisis of representation, participation and legitimacy. As evidence that something has gone badly wrong with democracy, *The Economist* (2014) claims that first, democracy has not proved as easy to 'transplant' as expected (as shown by the experience of Iraq and recently democratized countries such as South Africa), and second, the dysfunctional elements of

long-standing democracies such as gridlock in the US, disillusionment in the EU together with the impact of globalization, the power of the banks and international financial institutions (IFIs) have led to voter disengagement and lack of trust in politicians, in combination with important changes in party and party systems. Academics argue that many of these trends are visible as ongoing dealignment, the development of catch-all parties and personalization of politics, providing further evidence of problems in contemporary representative democracies (Dalton 2004). But while there may be some consensus on

From *Government and Opposition* 50, no. 3 (2015), pp. 495–520.

the symptoms, there is far less agreement about the causes and potential solutions to any crisis of participation and representation in political institutions. *The Economist* (2014) argues for minimizing the role of the central state, enhancing local democracy and updating institutions (for example, with open primaries and reforms to party financing), while young protestors on the streets in countries such as Chile and Brazil demand greater equality and more state spending on social welfare, health and education.

As part of this perceived crisis, the male domination of democracy—in terms of both the nature of its institutions and who participates—has been identified as both problematic, and in many ways emblematic, of the more generalized democratic crisis (and for some, emblematic of a crisis of capitalism too) (Campbell 2014). By the same token, replacing the 'male, pale and stale' with more women at the highest level in key institutions has also been seen as a potential solution to various contemporary political and economic problems. This is either because women are supposedly less corrupt and more risk averse than men (for example, the benefits of 'Lehmann Sisters' versus 'Lehmann Brothers' touted in the financial sphere) or because their presence can embody and symbolize a new and fresh style of politics (Agerberg et al. 2014; Prugl 2012). But I am not suggesting in this article that male dominance is responsible or that more women is the solution; rather I am exploring the gender dynamics of the perceived 'crisis of democracy'.[1]

The gendered aspects of the 'crisis' are notable in two ways. First there is a paradox. On the one hand, it is incontrovertible that democracy still plays out multiple ways to privilege predominantly white, elite, heterosexual men and to reinforce male dominance in a range of contexts (Waylen et al. 2013). At the end of 2014 on average only 22 per cent of legislators in lower houses globally were women (IPU 2014). Very few countries have parity or gender-balanced cabinets and, despite prominent exceptions such as Angela Merkel (the chancellor of Germany) and Christine Lagarde (at the International Monetary Fund), few women head national

executives or prominent international bodies. On the other hand, there has been a sharp increase in the numbers of women participating in democratic institutions over the last two decades, leading some gender scholars to claim that the 'male monopoly' over many political systems and institutions has ended (Dahlerup and Leyenaar 2013). So we are seeing the widespread discussion of women's underrepresentation, at the same time as some women appear to be making significant headway within electoral institutions. Second, it raises the possibility that the 'crisis of democracy' may provide some significant opportunities to further enhance women's participation in electoral politics because the demands of those in favour of greater gender equality in the public sphere and those looking for solutions to the 'crisis' appear to coincide in the current conjuncture.[2]

How should we understand these developments? In order to assess both the extent to which the male domination of politics is an important facet of the contemporary 'crisis of democracy' and to explore whether the crisis offers opportunities to lessen male dominance, we need to do two things. First we have to examine how far contemporary democracies remain male dominated and assess the gendered significance of the changes associated with the crisis of democracy that we have seen in recent years. Is it still 'business as usual' in gender terms? Second, we need to analyse the different measures that have been advocated and implemented to reduce male dominance in democracies and assess their effectiveness. We will then be in a better position to speculate about whether the 'crisis' could offer opportunities to reduce the male domination of politics.

To facilitate this, the main body of the article will explore both how democracy in theory and now democracy in practice are gendered, tracing through a 'gender audit' of both the descriptive and substantive representation of women within democratic institutions, and the extent to which contemporary democracies have moved away from the original conceptions underlying democratic theory. It will then be possible to analyse whether the contemporary 'crisis of democracy', often perceived as a crisis of representation, participation and legitimacy, is gendered in ways that are new or unexpected. We can then discuss the effectiveness of some measures that have been advocated to undermine the male dominance of politics in contemporary democracies.

The empirical examples used in this article are drawn from both long-standing and newer democracies (both parliamentary and presidential) and particularly from Europe and Latin America. The article uses a fairly narrow (mid-range) definition of democracy—that is, with a formal/procedural emphasis—and looks at both the formal and informal institutions/rules/norms of democracy. The focus is therefore on democratic institutions rather than on women's movements/civil society outside those institutions, or on a wider more deliberative notion of democracy. The article will not directly address the political economy of the current perceived crisis of representative democracy but will touch briefly on the impact of economic crisis as exacerbating some of the trends identified as part of the 'crisis of democracy'.

The article argues that, despite the increased descriptive representation of women, democratic institutions remain deeply shaped by the same elements that informed early liberal theory. Therefore, to engender democracy in a more egalitarian way, we need to do more than just ensure that even greater numbers of women of all races and classes—not just elite white women—are involved as actors at all levels of politics. We also need to change the institutions, both formal and informal, that are associated with democracy in order to promulgate democracies with enhanced levels of participation, representation and legitimacy. Thus, although it is possible to envisage women's greater descriptive representation resulting from some of the measures implemented as part of efforts to ameliorate the 'crisis of democracy', the more fundamental changes to the institutions of democracy that are necessary both to ensure a better democracy for women, as well as other underrepresented groups and minorities, and as a result a better democracy for all are harder to imagine.

Democracy in Theory and Practice

Democracy in Theory

There is now a huge literature on the complex relationship between gender and democracy showing that it is gendered in multiple and sometimes contradictory ways. Challenging the gender blindness of political theory, feminist scholars first drew attention to the exclusionary ways in which democracy has been both theorized and operationalized, with the result that women and men were incorporated differently into democratic polities.[3] Pioneering early work undertaken in the 1980s interrogated how the founding principles of liberal democracy were fundamentally masculinist (Elshtain 1981; Pateman 1983a, 1983b, 1989). It showed that as a consequence of its theoretical roots, the ways in which democracies operated in practice were unlikely to offer women political equality and would have difficulty in dealing with notions of difference. As a result, even when women had achieved formal equality within liberal democracies, these polities could still exclude women in practice. We will look in turn at each of the three interlinked themes running through various conceptions of liberal democracy focused on by feminist political theorists: the relationship between the public and private spheres, the notion of the individual and the construction of citizenship.

For a long time, the theoretical underpinnings of liberal democracy depended on a separation of the public and private spheres based on hugely gendered assumptions. As a result, liberal political theory, while appearing gender neutral, by maintaining a division between the public and the private as central to liberal democracy, maintained a division between men and women, where only men could be abstract individuals in the public sphere (Pateman 1983a, 1983b, 1989). Feminist political theorists such as Carole Pateman (1983a, 1983b, 1989) demonstrated the crucial role played in this by seventeenth-century social contract theorists such as Locke. She and others highlighted and challenged the notion dominant within much liberal political theory of the public sphere as a sphere of male citizens enjoying rights from which women were excluded, and they exposed the ways in which women were analytically relegated to the private sphere lying outside the domain of the political. Liberal democratic theory defined the political as masculine in a very profound sense that made it hard to incorporate women on the same terms as men and excluded many activities in which women are involved as not being political.

Feminist political theorists, however, also highlighted how the public and private have never been completely separate and distinct; nor has the boundary between the two been fixed. Women have never been entirely outside the public sphere even though they have been analytically relegated to the private sphere. But the roles ascribed to women in the private sphere affected and still affect their roles in public sphere (Elshtain 1981). For example, even today the sexual division of labour in the private sphere and the household affects the sexual division of labour in the public sphere, where women and men often undertake different forms of employment with 'women's jobs' often based on women's supposed caring capabilities and roles in the private sphere. Because the private sphere was positioned outside the jurisdiction of the state in liberal theory, feminists also politicized 'private' issues such as marital rape and domestic violence. And, as part of the challenge to dominant understandings of what constitutes the public sphere, they also tried to widen definitions of what counts as 'political' and get women seen as political beings.

Second, and linked to this, feminist political theory exposed and challenged the dominant conceptualization of the individual contained within liberal political theory and liberal democracy. The liberal notion of the individual has been an implicitly masculine one. It was a 'he' who was the head of household and entered the public sphere to enjoy its rights and privileges. Women were therefore not individuals and relegated to their roles in the private sphere. This liberal democratic notion of the individual is also contained in the 'rational autonomous individual' who enters the market that underlies much liberal economic theory (and more recently game theory). Feminist economists (among others) have critiqued the rational economic actor, arguing that individuals do not act in the ways predicted by liberal theory.

Finally the relationship between individuals and the state and polity has also been theorized through the concept of citizenship. Although citizenship, couched in terms of the individual, can be seen as gender neutral, feminists have argued very trenchantly that citizenship remains and always has been gendered (Siim 2013). At worst women were excluded from full citizenship and at best incorporated into citizenship in different ways to men. Initially citizenship was restricted to men (but for long periods also excluding working-class men and men of different races such as black slaves in the US); men were incorporated as soldiers and then as wage earners—that is, through their activities in the public sphere. Only later were women incorporated as citizens, often on the basis of their activities in the private sphere as mothers, rather than as workers or soldiers. The legacy of this differential incorporation affected a range of spheres and its impact remains today. Welfare states, for example, were often created using a model of social rights and citizenship that saw men as breadwinners responsible for a dependent wife and children and as such women experience social rights very differently to men (Waylen 1998: 13).

Feminist political theorists such as Anne Phillips (1991, 1993) detailed the impact of these factors on the operation of liberal democracies in practice. For example, the roles played by women in the public and private spheres as well as the ways in which they have been incorporated into citizenship resulted historically in significantly lower rates of participation by women in many democratic processes. Indeed, liberal democracy has found the empowerment of many disadvantaged and minority groups difficult to accommodate within its frameworks, because of its emphasis on the individual as the basic unit in political life (Young 1990). Yet at the same time Philips (1992: 82) has been loath to give up on liberal democracy, arguing that feminism can be used to inspire a more substantial version of liberal democracy.

Indeed, feminist political scientists in turn have considered whether democracies are more likely to implement gender equality policies than other types of political system. Tripp (2013a: 516) argues that 'simple cross-national bivariate regressions between regime type and broader measures of women's status reveal a strong correlation between democracy and women's status even controlling for economic growth'. Htun and Weldon (2010) have also investigated whether regime type matters in the adoption of gender equality policies. Although they found that there is considerable variation between the implementation of different forms of gender equality policies and that regime type is not always a predictor for this, the degree of democracy is one variable that predicts the effectiveness of the advocates advancing women's rights (alongside factors such as state capacity and policy legacies), as democracies tend to have more developed civil societies, which allows women's organizations to have greater influence. Scholars have also examined the extent to which transitions to democracy and post-conflict settlements can offer opportunities for the enhancement of women's representation and gender equality policies, such as through the creation of new institutions and constitutions (Tripp 2013b; Waylen 1994, 2007, 2014a). Tripp, for example, has found that post-conflict states in Africa have higher rates of women's representation than other African states that have not experienced conflict. Furthermore, in a similar vein to Tripp's (2013a) arguments about regime type and gender equality, Oscar Encarnación (2014) argues that 'political regime is a better predictor of gay rights than either economic development or cultural factors such as religion'. Over the last decade, gay rights have deepened considerably in democracies—in contrast to many non-democracies—because of several mechanisms,

including the presence of vibrant civil societies, the protection of citizenship, respect for the rule of law and a socially tolerant living environment.

Therefore, while on the one hand historically excluding women, liberal democracies' open civil societies and cultures of rights and citizenship can provide opportunities that do not exist in other political systems.

Democracy in Practice

Having explored liberal democracy's complex theoretical underpinnings, we are now in a position to conduct a 'gender audit' of contemporary democracies to assess the extent of change, looking at how far men and women now participate and are represented (both descriptively and substantively) differently, and also at the ways in which political institutions such as legislatures and political parties are gendered. This will enable us to determine how far the legacies of early liberal democratic thinking—notions of the individual and the 'political' as profoundly masculine, the division between the public and private, and the gendered nature of citizenship—remain. Despite some important contextual differences between them, it is possible to detect trends that are common to both in recent and more long-standing democracies and which were first identified by pioneering feminist political scientists 20 to 30 years ago (Randall 1982).

At a time when political participation (measured, for example, by voter turnout) has been declining and trust in politicians and political institutions has also been falling, women's numerical presence in electoral institutions ('descriptive' representation) has increased. However, it is a mixed picture. Globally the trend has been away from male monopoly, and now only 19 per cent of polities (including many non- or semi-democracies but also Brazil and Japan) have fewer than 10 per cent women in their representative bodies. The vast majority of democracies still exhibit 'male dominance', with between 10 and 40 per cent female representation. In 46 per cent of polities (including the UK and US), women are in a small minority (10–25 per cent), and in nearly 30 per cent—predominantly in Europe and Latin America—women are in a large minority (25–40 per cent). But only around 5 per cent of states are gender balanced with 40–60 per cent female representation, most notably the Nordic states (an average of 42.3 per cent) and some African countries, such as South Africa and Rwanda. Furthermore, although the legitimacy of all-male executives is often questioned, the 'acceptable minimum' number of women in an executive varies and can still be as low as only one woman minister (Dahlerup and Leyenaar 2013).

Men therefore remain much more likely to become politicians than women. And in both newer and older democracies, it is elite women (in terms of class and race) who predominate among female representatives, with many other groups of women (and men) still under-represented. The factors that explain levels of women's representation have sometimes been couched in terms of supply and demand (Norris 1991). The supply of male and female candidates differs, with more men coming forward, as women's roles in the public sphere are still affected by their perceived roles in the private sphere—for example, caring responsibilities, experience and ambition (Lawless and Fox 2010). And on the demand side, electoral rules also impact on the numbers of women who become legislators. In the absence of effective electoral quotas, first past the post (FPTP) systems tend to have lower levels of female representation than more proportional (PR) electoral systems as parties are more likely to choose balanced/diverse electoral lists in proportional representation systems than single candidates in a first past the post system; other factors such as district magnitude, rates of incumbency and the presence of open or closed electoral lists also play a part.

Political parties too, despite a perceived decline in their strength and influence, still play a central role. Long identified as key gatekeepers, they have affected women's participation and representation by determining candidate selection procedures and often displaying a preference for men (Lovenduski

and Norris 1993). Women have faced difficulties in getting selected or were put into unwinnable seats or low down on party lists for legislative elections (Lovenduski and Norris 1993). A range of characteristics, such as party ideology, levels of institutionalization and centralization and the presence of women activists within all levels of party hierarchies, have been found to affect the numbers of women selected. In her study of European political parties in the 1990s, Caul (1999) found that left-wing parties tended to field more women candidates, as did parties with larger numbers of women in party executives. But over the last two decades, increased pressure to select women—whether from women activists within parties, demonstration effects, or because parties feel that it might increase their support from women voters—has contributed to the improvement in women's descriptive representation. However, evidence that many different types of party still discriminate against women remains (Fortin-Rittberger and Rittberger 2014; Schwindt-Bayer and Wiesehemeier 2014).

Although gender scholars initially tended to focus primarily on legislatures and candidate selection, in recent years they have become more interested in executives and party leadership positions (Jalalzai 2013; Krook and O'Brien 2012). The change is first because in most polities the locus of power sits with the executive rather than the legislature. Second, it is because there has been a real world increase in the numbers of women in executives. The number of women leaders has doubled over the last decade (Alexander and Jalalzai 2014). Latin America, for example, has recently seen a swathe of female presidents in Brazil, Argentina, Chile and Costa Rica, and more generally there has been a move away from female leaders with connections to political families (which has been particularly true in Asia—for example Indira Gandhi, Benazir Bhutto, Corazon Aquino) to greater numbers of 'self-made' women politicians such as Dilma Rousseff (Brazil), Angela Merkel (Germany) and Michelle Bachelet (Chile). And we have even seen a small number of 'parity' or gender-balanced cabinets, for example, during Zapatero's socialist government in Spain, at the beginning of Bachelet's first term of office in Chile in 2006 and more recently in Italy, Sweden and Scotland (Franceschet and Thomas 2011). Finally, it became evident that larger numbers of women in legislatures (high descriptive representation) do not necessarily lead to the kinds of changes desired by some feminists.

Although research in this area is still at a relatively early stage, some of the complexities of the gendering of contemporary executive office and political leadership are emerging. A number of, somewhat contradictory, trends have been noted. In their study of female cabinet ministers in five presidential democracies, Escobar and Taylor Robinson (2014) found that, except for appointments to economic posts, the political capital resources and effectiveness of the women are not significantly different to their male colleagues. There is also some evidence that women leaders' pathways to office do not differ hugely from men's (Mueller-Rommel et al. [2014] found this in their study of prime ministers in Europe). However, although there are increasing numbers of women now being appointed to more non-traditional 'hard' ministries such as defence, interior and even foreign affairs or finance, the long-recognized tendency for female cabinet ministers to be appointed to 'soft' positions such as education, health and women's ministries continues (again resonating with women's perceived roles in the private sphere). And a study of the cabinet careers of ministers in Westminster democracies found that, on average, women ministers started in more lowly positions and were less likely to be promoted to high-status jobs than male ministers (Curtin et al. 2014).

At the same time, analyses of the gender of party leadership (often a stepping-stone to becoming prime minister in parliamentary democracies) show first that women are more likely to stand for party leader in low-competition situations—namely, when few men are putting themselves forward (Beckwith 2014)—and furthermore, that women are not only more likely to succeed in becoming party leaders when the political party is doing badly, but they are also more likely than a male leader to be removed if their party is doing badly (O'Brien 2014).

Gender scholars have not only looked at women's 'presence' and their descriptive representation but for some time they have also looked at substantive representation and the relationship between the two. Substantive representation, according to Childs and Lovenduski (2013), is the extent to which representatives advance a group's policy preferences and interests. However, the concept of 'women's interests' has long been a contested one, with many gender scholars disputing the extent to which there can be common interests shared by all women regardless of differences (for example, in terms of class, race and sexuality). As a result, others argue that substantive representation should be understood in terms of 'voice' and 'claims making' by representatives on behalf of particular groups (thereby raising the issue of who judges the veracity of claims to represent particular groups) (Childs and Lovenduski 2013).

Notwithstanding these conceptual issues, recent analyses of the substantive representation of women within liberal democracies have focused on two main themes. First, studies have looked at the extent to which female representatives, for example in legislatures, 'act for' women, measured in terms of advancing or voting for legislation or policy change that is seen to be in women's interests—whether this is around equality issues, reproductive rights or more traditional welfare concerns (Schwindt-Bayer 2010). The empirical evidence is somewhat mixed. It does seem that on the whole women legislators are more likely to promote and support measures that are identified with 'women's interests' than men, but this varies considerably according to the issue as well as party strength, party discipline and the party's position on that issue (Swers 2002, 2013). For example, women legislators of different parties are more likely to act together around less contentious issues such as child maintenance payments and domestic violence than more contentious ones like reproductive rights and abortion rights in particular (Franceschet and Piscopo 2008; Waylen 2000). As part of the scepticism about the relationship between descriptive and substantive representation, attention also shifted from notions of a 'critical mass'—the number of female representatives (often seen as 30 per cent) needed to make a significant difference—to a focus on 'critical actors', that is, examining the roles of key women (and men) who seek to represent women substantively as a group (Childs and Krook 2009).

Second, state bureaucracies and policy-making processes are another important area for feminist scholars thinking about how women's interests (however defined) might fare within governance structures. Building on long-standing feminist analyses of the state which see it not as a homogeneous entity but as a complex collection of institutions and contested power relations, state structures are not considered neutral but gendered, and as a result policy outputs may have a differential impact on men and women, often with a detrimental effect on women (Waylen 1998). Some feminist scholars have also focused on efforts to create gender equality policies and women's policy agencies within the state (so-called 'state feminism') (Stetson and Mazur 1995). Other feminists have subjected ostensibly gender-neutral policies to gendered analysis. Recently attention has turned to the austerity policies implemented in many developed economies as a response to the economic crisis beginning in 2007/8. Although male unemployment initially rose more than female unemployment, subsequent cuts in state employment and the state provision of welfare services have had a negative impact on many women. It is particularly poor, often ethnic minority and migrant, women—who make up a substantial part of the paid providers of welfare services and low-paid state employees and who are often the largest recipients of the welfare payments and services—that have been hardest hit. In the UK, retrenchment has also been accompanied by a hardening of public attitudes towards welfare recipients, migrants and equality policies.

We can see that, even if these have narrowed over recent decades, gender differences in participation and representation remain in liberal democracies.

But one dimension we have yet to explore explicitly as part of our gender audit is the role of political institutions *qua* institutions in the gendering of democracy. Following an 'institutionalist turn' in much of political science, many gender scholars—who share an understanding of institutions as gendered rules, norms and practices (with both formal and informal dimensions) that shape actors' strategies and preferences—have started looking at political institutions in terms of both the formal rules and also the informal norms and practices (Krook and Mackay 2011). We have seen that the formal rules of most political systems are now ostensibly gender neutral (with the exception of quotas). There are few political systems that have not extended full suffrage to women and men, and women formally complete as candidates on the same terms. But at the same time we saw that the operation of different electoral rules—for example, first past the post and proportional representation systems—does contribute to different levels of male and female representation. And, as we will see, formal rule change such as the introduction of quotas and changes to constitutions to enhance rights and equality can have a huge impact if they are well designed, appropriate and enforced. However, this does not undermine the notion that political institutions are gendered nominally and substantively—nominally through gender capture and substantively through numerous mechanisms, like social norms based on accepted ideas about masculinity and femininity that equate masculinity with rationality, power, boundary setting and control and femininity with its opposite: passivity, care, emotion and irrationality, that result in gender bias (Chappell and Waylen 2013). Of course, masculinity and femininity come in plural forms, with some forms of masculinity operating hegemonically in some settings—for example, in the military.

The gendered nature of the informal institutions—the informal rules, norms and practices—is therefore one dimension of political systems that requires more attention. However, as a number of political scientists have pointed out, informal institutions are often harder to discern than formal ones as their rules and sanctions are not explicit (generally unwritten and communicated through channels that are not official according to Helmke and Levitsky (2004)) and as a result they are often even harder to change. Informal rules, norms and practices can act to prevent women's political participation and effectiveness. In her study of Scotland, Kenny (2013) has shown how informal norms affect selection procedures, informing assumptions about what constitutes a good candidate. Informal networks (often termed 'old boy' networks) can act to exclude women. Elin Bjarnegård (2013), for example, has identified the importance of 'homosocial capital', whereby male-dominated informal networks influence candidate selection processes in political parties in Thailand. Within political institutions, these informal practices can continue to work in gendered ways. The heckling that is commonplace and largely tolerated in the UK Parliament can be extremely gendered, with female MPs forced to endure misogynistic comments (Chappell and Waylen 2013). The persistence of informal norms and rules can sometimes undermine attempts to change or reform existing formal rules or impact on newly created institutions such as the Scottish Parliament or the International Criminal Court, ensuring that their 'newness' remains 'nested' in old practices that continue to be 'remembered' while the new is 'forgotten' (Chappell 2014; Mackay 2014). It is also possible for new informal norms to develop that can undermine a new institution. For example, the French quota system has been routinely sabotaged by a new informal norm that it is acceptable for (larger and wealthier) parties to ignore the quota rules and pay the fine (Waylen 2014a).

Gendering the 'Crisis of Democracy'

In this section, we explore in more depth how recent changes in participation, representation and legitimacy associated with the 'crisis of democracy' are gendered, before considering how male dominance

in contemporary democracies could be lessened. Two interlinked trends associated with the 'crisis of democracy' are important to our analysis: first, changes to parties and party systems; and, second, an increased focus on leadership, the personalization of politics and the changed role of the media. Dahlerup and Leyenaar (2013) argue that these have both positive and negative effects on women's participation and representation within electoral politics.

Widespread dealignment—with declining levels of party membership and voting—accompanied by declining levels of trust in politicians and interest in politics are symptomatic of the changes in party systems. As mass parties disappear, some rank-and-file organizations such as women's sections have been abolished, and the 'new-look' parties, comprising a small core of professionalized politicians and advisers, remain open to accusations of continuing male domination. But, increasingly, 'catch-all' parties, less differentiated by ideology, try to appeal to different groups of voters. As part of this, women voters are often targeted in specific (and more 'modern') ways. Policy proposals, such as promises to increase the availability of childcare, are often aimed at women. Throughout the Scottish independence referendum campaign in 2014, for example, the gender gap in support for independence was identified as a key motivation for the childcare pledges of the SNP (Scottish National Party). One poll conducted in August 2014 put the gender gap at 12 per cent, with women's support for independence running at only 27 per cent, with men's at 39 per cent. However, the gap was estimated to have narrowed to only 3 per cent in the referendum in mid-September 2014, with 47 per cent of men and 44 per cent of women voting for independence (Ashcroft 2014).

To broaden their appeal, parties also try to present a less male-dominated image, hoping that women will provide 'fresh faces' or make parties appear more modern. For example, in part to counter the perception that it is dominated by a male public school clique, the UK coalition government of 2010–15 positioned women MPs prominently in the television coverage of parliamentary debates (particularly Prime Minister's Question Time) and very publicly appointed more women MPs to cabinet posts in the reshuffle of July 2014. Parties also attempt to select and field more women candidates (seen as part of the motivation for Michelle Bachelet's selection in 2005 as presidential candidate by the increasingly tired ruling Concertación coalition in Chile (Staab and Waylen 2014).

However, some of the new selection procedures widely touted as part of measures to revitalize politics and counteract falling party memberships can have negative effects on women's representation. There is some evidence, for example, that selection through primaries can result in fewer women candidates and make it harder to enforce mechanisms aimed at increasing numbers of underrepresented groups. Magda Hinojosa (2012) found in her analysis of candidate selection in Latin America that primaries disadvantage women candidates. Party fragmentation and the rise of 'anti-politics' parties, on both the left and the right, can also affect women's representation in a number of ways. An increasing number of parties can sometimes reduce the number of women elected as more small parties often each have fewer women representatives on the top of their lists (Dahlerup and Leyenaar 2013). Some (but not all) right-wing populist parties, often anti-migrant and xenophobic, also have few women representatives, but parties at the other end of the political spectrum—such as Green parties—often have higher than average numbers of women in senior positions, including as leader.[4] Dahlerup and Leyenaar (2013) argue that, on balance, the overall effect of these changes on women's representation has been positive in the European countries they studied.

Accompanying the decline in political parties and party systems has been an increased emphasis on leadership and a personalization of politics. As such, the personal characteristics of leaders become more important, with a differential effect on women and men. On the one hand women's performance (such as that of Julia Gillard in Australia) is often judged differently (and often more harshly) than men's, but at the same time women can be more likely to achieve leadership positions if they are seen as 'new brooms' or as part of a revitalization of politics (Beckwith 2014; O'Brien 2014). Now that increased numbers of women have reached leadership positions, more research is needed on whether men and women exercise (or are seen to exercise) leadership in different ways. Franceschet et al. (2013), for example, argue that female leaders in Latin America use four different strategic frames to justify their political careers: the traditional supermadre, the technocratic caretaker, the macho minimizer and the difference denier. And given the new prominence of devices, such as leaders' debates, in parliamentary as well as presidential elections, it would be useful to know more about their gendered dimensions.

The increased role of the media, and social media in particular, also has a mixed impact on women's political activity. It is clear that the ways that politicians and leaders are treated by the media continue to be very gendered, and there is some argument that female politicians in particular are increasingly subjected to the kind of scrutiny more often afforded to celebrities. For example, the appearance, dress and behaviour of female politicians are much more widely commented on than their male colleagues' (O'Brien and Savigny 2014). On 16 July 2014 the *Daily Mail*, a UK newspaper, used the headline 'Thigh Flashing Esther, and the Battle of the Downing Street Catwalk' to report the increased number of female politicians appointed to David Cameron's cabinet in the reshuffle of July 2014, illustrating it with catwalk-style pictures of all the new female ministers. At the same time Angela Merkel was widely reported (positively in the German media but less positively elsewhere) as having worn the same tunic on at least three public occasions since 1998.

However, new forms of grassroots participation can also be facilitated by social media, allowing campaigns a prominence that would have been hard to achieve otherwise. But conversely social media can also facilitate the harassment and denigration of women campaigners and politicians, as the campaigners (including a female MP) to get a woman on the UK currency found in 2013 when they received misogynistic abuse, including rape threats, via Twitter. This phenomenon has been identified by Krook and Restrepo-Sanis (2014) as part of more generalized violence against women in politics. Indeed, some commentators have speculated that the (new and old) media treatment of female politicians increasingly acts to discourage women from putting themselves forward for office. The 'crisis of democracy' therefore appears to have some contradictory effects, intensifying some existing trends which are resulting in increasing descriptive representation for women, at the same time as subjecting female politicians to greater pressures.

What More Can Be Done to Undermine Male Dominance in Politics?

If there is now additional momentum to reduce male dominance as a result of the 'crisis of democracy', it is useful to analyse the strategies on offer. These have been framed in terms of improving women's descriptive and substantive representation as well as promoting institutional change. Increasing women's descriptive representation, and particularly of under-represented groups such as poor, working-class, LGBT, disabled and ethnic minority women, is advocated for all formal institutions, including executives and judiciaries as well as parliaments and other international governance organizations, and at all levels from the local to the international for both symbolic and justice reasons. Having more women in the supply pipeline will also increase the pool of eligible candidates for executive positions, particularly in parliamentary democracies where cabinets are drawn primarily from elected representatives.

There are a number of strategies to increase both supply and demand that vary in their effectiveness. Several measures to encourage more women to put themselves forward and to support potential women

candidates exist. 'Soft' measures range from the provision of funding (such as EMILY's list in the US) to the leadership training courses and mentoring programmes undertaken by political parties, universities, women's policy agencies and non-governmental organizations. On their own, these will have only a limited effect, as many parties still display a reluctance to select female candidates. It is also essential to increase the demand for female candidates. New formal rules are one of the most important ways to ensure that women are selected by parties. The best-known and most effective measure to increase the demand for women candidates and therefore levels of women's representation is gender quotas. These have been very widely adopted all over world and, if they are well designed, appropriate and enforced (which does not always happen), are a 'fast track' way to increase in women's representation (Dahlerup 2006; Franceschet et al. 2012; Krook 2009). Indeed, more than 50 per cent of electoral polities now have a form of quota, whether in the form of electoral quotas, party quotas or reserved seats (Dahlerup and Norris 2014).

Despite their potential and proven efficacy, quotas have been controversial, with critics arguing that they undermine merit and result in women politicians who are less qualified than their male peers (reminiscent of the 'milk maid' syndrome in the ex-Soviet bloc). But there is no evidence that 'quota women' are different from other women politicians. Allen et al.'s (2014) analysis of Labour women elected from all-women shortlists in 1997 in the UK shows that 'quota women' are as well qualified as their non-quota colleagues and are treated the same both by voters and by the gatekeepers of executive office. It is also argued that gender quotas can improve the quality of male politicians. Besley et al. (2013) examined the data on candidates in Swedish municipalities over seven elections and claim that the 'zipper quota' implemented by the Social Democratic Party actually increased the competence of male politicians. As a result of all these factors, Murray (2014) argues that gender quotas should be reframed; rather than being seen as applying only to women candidates, they should be seen as quotas for men in order to undermine men's dominance over the talent pool and reduce the suspicion and security that women politicians are subjected to.[5] However, as Franceschet and Piscopo (2008) argue, using the case of Argentina, quotas may increase the number of women, but they do not necessarily disturb the underlying male hierarchies or exclusionary male networks.

A number of measures have also been implemented to improve the substantive representation of women and ensure 'gender-friendly' policy-making. Among the best-known formal mechanisms are state women's machineries/women's policy agencies. These have had mixed success, depending on their location within the state, their levels of funding, support from government, technical expertise and capacity to initiate or deliver policy—many have been peripheral, underfunded and powerless in the face of resistance both inside and outside the state (Waylen 2000). Some have also been criticized by feminist activists outside the state for ignoring their claims-making and failing to represent their interests or voices. In part as a response to the critique that gender concerns are marginalized within these separate, often ineffectual bodies, gender has been 'mainstreamed' within national and international organizations, trying to ensure that the gendered implications of all policy are considered at every stage, from design to implementation (Waylen 2008). Again, the verdict on the effectiveness of gender mainstreaming is mixed. Some believe that it can make a difference (and even be transformatory) if there is institutional commitment and it is implemented and monitored by trained staff, but others argue that gender mainstreaming can never be any more than a technocratic tool with limited possibilities for profound change. But, although limited in its potential, gender mainstreaming can uncover the ways in which many policies (such as austerity policies and welfare cuts discussed earlier) are highly differentiated in their impact on women and men in ways not immediately recognized by policymakers.

It is clear from the preceding discussion that achieving gender-equitable democracy and under-mining the male dominance of political systems require more than an increase in the numbers of women and the introduction of mechanisms such as gender mainstreaming into policy-making to enhance substantive representation. Indeed, presence is sometimes over-emphasized—it may be necessary but it is also limited in what it can achieve (Waylen 2014b). More profound institutional change is necessary to enable critical actors to be more effective and challenge male dominance. Institutional change can take various forms—either via the creation of new institutions (for example, as a result of a transition to democracy or the design of a new constitution) or more commonly via the reform or redesign of existing institutions such as legislatures and parties. But it is also clear from the preceding analysis that changing formal institutions is often not enough. Informal institutions also need to be modified as pre-existing informal institutions can undermine efforts to create more gender-equitable outcomes or the absence of 'completing' informal institutions makes the success of formal rule change less likely. However, changing informal institutions—such as the often widely accepted gendered norms and practices that contribute to a sense of politics as a masculine business and undermine women's effectiveness, making it harder for women to progress through politics and for certain gender measures to become law—presents a big challenge, as we saw from our discussion of 'nested newness'. But changing both the formal and informal institutions, creating more open and transparent political systems in place of closed and male-dominated ones, makes it more likely that women will come forward.

Conclusions

Contemporary democracies remain male dominated, despite the changes that have taken place over the last couple of decades that have brought a significant increase in the numbers of women in positions of power. We have also seen how democracies have not escaped their rootedness in liberal theory. The analytical separation of the public and the private and the construction of notions of the 'political' and the individual as masculine still mean that women and men are incorporated into politics in different ways. Therefore, although politics in contemporary democracies is no longer 'business as usual', it certainly has not been transformed.

We have also seen that the 'crisis of democracy', often seen as a crisis of representation, participation and legitimacy, has had a somewhat contradictory impact in gender terms. On the one hand, it has increased the opportunities as well as intensified the pressure for an increase in the numbers of women in electoral politics. Measures to raise the levels of women's descriptive representation by increasing the demand for women politicians, such as quotas, now have widespread acceptability and there is a greater sense of urgency surrounding their implementation in many contexts. Increasing the representation of women also offers some potential to revitalize democratic politics. There is evidence, for example, that the presence of women leaders increases women's levels of political activity and voting (Alexander and Jalalzai 2014; Reyes-Householder and Schwindt-Bayer 2014).

In this sense, the 'crisis of democracy' has itself contributed to the reduction in the male dominance of politics. And one of its perceived solutions—raising the numbers of women—could help to ameliorate some of the widely perceived symptoms of the crisis, such as declining levels of participation and a sense of the increasing aloofness of politicians from 'ordinary people'. However, it is necessary to go further than this to ensure the greater participation and representation of, not just some women, but all currently under-represented groups and minorities. This is fundamental to ensuring a secure future for liberal democracy. Replacing white, privately and Oxbridge-educated male MPs and cabinet ministers with white, privately and Oxbridge-educated female MPs in the UK Houses of Parliament is not necessarily a significant improvement.

At the same time the 'crisis of democracy' has intensified some of the trends that make politics a difficult place for many women and can also lead to policy outcomes that are not necessarily gender friendly. As we have seen, the increased presence of women (descriptive representation) in the political sphere does not necessarily lead to their increased substantive representation. Women legislators cannot necessarily be relied upon to support progressive gender agendas, for example around equality and reproductive rights. And measures to increase women's substantive representation, such as gender mainstreaming and women's policy agencies, have had mixed effectiveness (one consequence of both the political and economic crisis has been to lessen support for equalities policies in many polities, even if this has been maintained in others, like Chile). Many of these measures have therefore been subject to increased contestation, retrenchment and backlash in recent years. And while new forms of participation, such as citizens' juries, can afford new opportunities for exercising voice, facilitated by social media like Twitter, the new (and old) media can also provide new forms of accentuating gender difference in ways that have negative repercussions for many women.

For the future of democracy to be one where the participation of and representation of all groups is enhanced, and the decline in the legitimacy of political institutions is reversed, more profound institutional change than simply increasing the participation of (some) women in politics is required. This alone cannot provide a solution to the 'crisis of democracy' or end male dominance in politics. We need change to the formal as well as the informal rules, norms and practices that shape political life and democracy to help to enable everyone to participate fully, regardless of race, class, gender, disability or sexuality.

NOTES

1. For example, even countries such as Sweden—long seen as a beacon for high levels of women's representation—are also perceived as experiencing a 'crisis of democracy'.

2. A similar phenomenon has long been noted in less institutionalized democracies in the context of political crisis (as well as some transitions to democracy).

3. The definitions of democracy operationalized in much of the political science literature are also gendered in significant ways. For example, although the conceptual definitions generally stress the importance of the representation of all adults, which clearly includes women, as Pamela Paxton (2000) demonstrates, when some mid-range scholars operationalize their definitions of democracy, the requirement that women are enfranchised somehow disappears from view. As a result, some polities that formally excluded women have been defined as democratic even though at least 50 per cent of the adult population could not participate. Rueschemeyer et al. (1992), for example, consider that Switzerland became democratic in 1848 and France in 1877, when in fact women could only vote from 1971 and 1944, respectively. If the incorporation of women as equals into a political system was made a fundamental criterion, the commonly accepted typologies of when countries became democratic, such as Huntington's (1991) waves of democracy, would look very different (Paxton 2000).

4. However, there is some concern that radical anti-austerity parties like Syriza in Greece (and also Podemos in Spain) have few women in top leadership positions. The Syriza government appointed in January 2015 contained no women in ministerial positions and only six in subministerial and alternative positions.

5. Murray (2014) argues that the debate about quotas should be widened to one that focuses on increasing the quality of representation overall through a greater diversity of representatives (not just more women) that draws on wider talent pools.

REFERENCES

Agerberg, M., Sundstrom, A. and Wangnerud, L. (2014), 'Why Regime Type Affects the Link between Gender and Corruption', paper presented at the IPSA Congress, Montreal, July.

Alexander, A. and Jalalzai, F. (2014), 'The Symbolic Effects of Female Heads of State and Government', paper presented to the APSA Annual Meeting, Washington, August.

Allen, P., Cutts, D. and Campbell, R. (2014), 'Measuring the Quality of Politicians Elected by Gender Quotas—Are They Any Different?', *Political Studies*, published early online, September, doi:10.1111/1467-9248.12161.

Ashcroft, P. (2014), 'Post-Referendum Scotland Poll', Lord Ashcroft Polls, 18–19 September, www.lordashcroftpolls.com.

Beckwith, K. (2014), 'From Party Leader to Prime Minister?: Gender and Leadership Contests in Western Europe', paper presented at ECPR Joint Sessions, Salamanca, Spain, April.

Besley, T., Folke, O., Persson, T. and Rickne, J. (2013), 'Gender Quotas and the Crisis of the Mediocre Man: Theory and Evidence from Sweden', unpublished manuscript.

Bjarnegård, E. (2013), *Gender, Informal Institutions and Political Recruitment* (Basingstoke: Palgrave).

Campbell, B. (2014), *End of Equality* (London: Seagull Books).

Caul, M. (1999), 'Women's Representation in Parliament: The Role of Political Parties', *Party Politics*, 5(1): 79–98.

Chappell, L. (2014), 'Newness, Oldness and Gender Justice Outcomes: A View from the International Criminal Court', *Politics and Gender*, 10(4): 572–94.

—— and Waylen, G. (2013), 'Gender and the Hidden Life of Institutions', *Public Administration*, 91(3): 599–615.

Childs, S. and Krook, M.L. (2009), 'Analysing Women's Substantive Representation: From Critical Mass to Critical Actors', *Government and Opposition*, 44(2): 125–45.

—— and Lovenduski, J. (2013), 'Political Representation', in G. Waylen, K. Celis, J. Kantola and L. Weldon (eds), *Oxford Handbook on Gender and Politics* (Oxford: Oxford University Press): 489–513.

Curtin, J., Kerby, M. and Dowding, K. (2014), 'Gender and Promotion in the Executive: Cabinet Careers in the World of Westminster', paper presented at ECPR Joint Sessions, Salamanca, Spain, April.

Dahlerup, D. (2006) (ed.), *Women, Quotas and Politics* (London: Routledge).

—— and Leyenaar, M. (2013), *Breaking Male Dominance in Old Democracies* (Oxford: Oxford University Press).

—— and Norris, P. (2014), 'On the Fast Track: Why Gender Quota Laws Spread around the World', paper presented to the APSA Annual Meeting, Washington, August.

Dalton, R. (2004), *Democratic Challenges. Democratic Choices: The Erosion of Political Support in Advanced Industrial Democracies* (Oxford: Oxford University Press).

The Economist (2014), 'What's Gone Wrong with Democracy', *The Economist*, 1 March.

Elshtain, J. (1981), *Public Man, Private Woman: Women in Social and Political Thought* (Princeton: Princeton University Press).

Encarnación, O. (2014), 'Gay Rights: Why Democracy Matters', *Journal of Democracy*, 25(3): 90–103.

Escobar, M. and Taylor Robinson, M. (2014), 'It's All in the Resume: Comparing the Credentials and Political Capital Resources of Men and Women in Presidential Cabinets', paper presented at ECPR Joint Sessions, Salamanca, Spain, April.

Fortin-Rittberger, J. and Rittberger, B. (2014), 'Descriptive Representation in the European Parliament', paper presented to the APSA Annual Meeting, Washington, August.

Franceschet, S., Krook, M.L. and Piscopo, J. (2012) (eds), *The Impact of Gender Quotas: Women's Descriptive, Substantive and Symbolic Representation* (Oxford: Oxford University Press).

—— and Piscopo, J.M. (2008), 'Gender Quotas and Women's Substantive Representation: Lessons from Argentina', *Politics and Gender*, 4(3): 393–425.

——, Piscopo, J. and Thomas, G. (2013), 'Super Madres', paper presented to the APSA Annual Meeting, Chicago, August.

——, and Thomas, G. (2011), 'Gender and Executive Office: Analysing Parity Cabinets in Chile and Spain', paper presented to ECPR General Conference, Reykjavik.

Helmke, G. and Levitsky, S. (2004), 'Informal Institutions and Comparative Politics: A Research Agenda', *Perspectives on Politics*, 2(4): 725–40.

Hinojosa, M. (2012), *Selecting Women, Electing Women: Political Representation and Candidate Selection in Latin America* (Philadelphia, PA: Temple University Press).

Htun, M. and Weldon, L. (2010), 'When Do Governments Promote Women's Rights? A Framework for the Comparative Analysis of Sex Equality Policy', *Perspectives on Politics*, 8(1): 207–16.

Huntington, S. (1991), *The Third Wave: Democratization in the Late Twentieth Century* (Norman: University of Oklahoma Press).

Inter-Parliamentary Union (IPU) (2014), 'Women in National Parliaments Database', 1 December, www.ipu.org/wmn-e/world.htm.

Jalalzai, F. (2013), *Shattered, Cracked or Firmly Intact? Women and the Executive Glass Ceiling Worldwide* (Oxford: Oxford University Press).

Kenny, M. (2013), *Gender and Political Recruitment: Theorizing Institutional Change* (Basingstoke: Palgrave).

Krook, M.L. (2009), *Quotas for Women in Politics* (Oxford: Oxford University Press).

—— and Mackay, F. (2011) (eds), *Gender, Politics, and Institutions: Toward a Feminist Institutionalism* (Basingstoke: Palgrave).

—— and O'Brien, D. (2012), 'All the President's Men? The Appointment of Female Cabinet Ministers Worldwide', *Journal of Politics*, 74(3): 840–55.

—— and Restrepo-Sanis, J. (2014), 'Violence against Women in Politics: Concepts and Policy Solutions', paper presented to the APSA Annual Meeting, Washington, August.

Lawless, J. and Fox, R. (2010), *It Still Takes a Candidate: Why Women Don't Run for Office* (Cambridge: Cambridge University Press).

Lovenduski, J. and Norris, P. (1993) (eds), *Gender and Party Politics* (London: Sage).

Mackay, F. (2014), 'Remembering the Old, Forgetting the New: "Nested Newness" and the Limits of Gendered Institutional Change', *Politics and Gender*, 10(4): 459–71.

Mueller-Rommel, F., Kubbe, I. and Vercesi, M. (2014), 'How Women Become Prime Minister in Europe', paper presented at ECPR Joint Sessions, Salamanca, Spain, April.

Murray, R. (2014), 'Quotas for Men: Reframing Gender Quotas as a Means of Improving Representation for All', *American Political Science Review*, 108(3): 520–32.

Norris, P. (1991), 'Gender Differences in Political Participation in Britain: Traditional, Radical and Revisionist Models', *Government and Opposition*, 26(1): 56–74.

O'Brien, D. (2014), 'Rising to the Top: Gender, Political Performance, and Party Leadership in Parliamentary Democracies', paper presented at ECPR Joint Sessions, Salamanca, Spain, April.

—— and Savigny, H. (2014), 'Female Politicians in the British Press', *Journalism Education*, 3(1): 6–27.

Pateman, C. (1983a), 'Feminism and Democracy', in G. Duncan (ed.), *Democratic Theory and Practice* (Cambridge: Cambridge University Press): 204–17.

—— (1983b), Feminist Critiques of the Public/Private Dichotomy', in S. Benn and G. Gaus (eds), *The Public and Private in Social Life* (London: Croom Helm): 281–303.

—— (1989), *The Sexual Contract* (Stanford, CA: Stanford University Press).

Paxton, P. (2000), 'Women's Suffrage in the Measurement of Democracy: Problems of Operationalization', *Studies in Comparative International Development*, 35: 92–111.

Phillips, A. (1991), *Engendering Democracy* (Cambridge: Polity Press).

—— (1992), 'Must Feminists Give Up on Liberal Democracy', *Political Studies*, 40(1): 68–82.

—— (1993), *Democracy and Difference* (Cambridge: Polity Press).

Prugl, E. (2012), '"If Lehmann Brothers Had Been Lehmann Sisters . . ." Gender and Myth in the Aftermath of the Financial Crisis', *International Political Sociology*, 6: 21–35.

Randall, V. (1982), *Women and Politics* (Basingstoke: Macmillan).

Reyes-Householder, C. and Schwindt-Bayer, L. (2014), 'The Presence of *Presidentas*: Consequences for Political Attitudes and Participation', paper presented to the APSA Annual Meeting, Washington, August.

Rueschmeyer, D., Stephens, E.H. and Stephens, J.D. (1992), *Capitalist Development and Democracy* (Cambridge: Cambridge University Press).

Schwindt-Bayer, L. (2010), *Political Power and Women's Representation in Latin America* (Oxford: Oxford University Press).

—— and Wiesehemeier, N. (2014), 'Selecting and Electing Women in Spain', paper presented to the APSA Annual Meeting, Washington, August.

Siim, B. (2013), 'Citizenship', in G. Waylen, K. Celis, J. Kantola and L. Weldon (eds), *Oxford Handbook on Gender and Politics* (Oxford: Oxford University Press): 756–80.

Staab, S. and Waylen, G. (2014), 'Gender, Politics and Institutions in Bachelet's Chile', paper presented at ECPR Joint Sessions, Salamanca, April.

Stetson, D., and Mazur, A. (1995) (eds), *Comparative State Feminism* (Thousand Oaks, CA: Sage).

Swers, M. (2002), *The Difference Women Make: The Policy Impact of Women in Congress* (Chicago: University of Chicago Press).

—— (2013), *Women in the Club: Gender and Policy Making in the Senate* (Chicago: University of Chicago Press).

Tripp, A.M. (2013a), Political Systems and Gender', in G. Waylen, K. Celis, J. Kantola and L. Weldon (eds), *Oxford Handbook on Gender and Politics* (Oxford: Oxford University Press): 514–35.

—— (2013b), 'Women's Movements and Constitution Making after Civil War and Violent Upheaval in Africa', paper presented at Gendering New Institutions Workshop, Manchester, November.

Waylen, G. (1994), 'Women and Democratization: Conceptualizing Gender Relations in Transition Politics', *World Politics*, 46(3): 327–54.

—— (1998), 'Gender, Feminism and the State', in V. Randall and G. Waylen (eds), *Gender, Politics and the State* (London: Routledge): 1–17.

—— (2000), 'Gender and Democratic Politics: A Comparative Analysis of Argentina and Chile', *Journal of Latin American Studies*, 32(3): 765–93.

—— (2007), *Engendering Transitions: Women's Mobilization, Institutions and Gender Outcomes* (Oxford: Oxford University Press).

—— (2008), 'Transforming Global Governance: Challenges and Opportunities', in S. Rai and G. Waylen (eds), *Global Governance: Feminist Perspectives* (Basingstoke: Palgrave): 254–75.

—— (2014a), Informal Institutions, Institutional Change and Gender Equality', *Political Research Quarterly*, 67(1): 212–23.

—— (2014b), 'A Seat at the Table—Is It Enough? Gender and Multiparty Negotiations in South Africa and Northern Ireland', *Politics and Gender*, 10(4): 495–523.

——, Celis, K., Kantola, J. and Weldon, L. (2013) (eds), *Oxford Handbook on Gender and Politics* (Oxford: Oxford University Press).

Young, I.M. (1990), *Justice and the Politics of Difference* (Princeton: Princeton University Press).

Roberto Stefan Foa and Yascha Mounk

THE DANGER OF DECONSOLIDATION

For four decades, *Die Welt*, one of West Germany's leading newspapers, refused to acknowledge the existence of an East German state. Since the paper's editors expected the communist regime to collapse within a matter of years, they put scare quotes around its initials whenever they discussed the German Democratic Republic (GDR). While other papers reported about the policies pursued by the GDR, *Die Welt* unfailingly wrote about the "GDR."

Sometime in the summer of 1989, the paper's leadership finally decided to give up on the pretense that the East German regime was on the verge of collapse. The communists had been in power for so long, and seemed so well-entrenched, that the scare quotes had become an embarrassing denial of reality. On 2 August 1989, reporters were allowed to drop the scare quotes when writing about the GDR for the first time in the paper's history. Three months later, the Berlin Wall fell. On 3 October 1990, the GDR ceased to exist.

The editors of *Die Welt* radically misjudged the signs of the times. At precisely the moment when they should have realized that support for the communist regime was dwindling, they finally reconciled themselves to its durability. They were hardly alone. The collective failure of social scientists, policy makers, and journalists to take seriously the possibility that the Soviet bloc might collapse should serve as a warning. Even the best-trained and most methodologically rigorous scholars are liable to assume that the recent past is a reliable guide to the future, and that extreme events are not going to happen.

Three decades ago, most scholars simply assumed that the Soviet Union would remain stable. This assumption was suddenly proven false. Today, we have even greater confidence in the durability of the world's affluent, consolidated democracies. But do we have good grounds for our democratic self-confidence? At first sight, there would seem to be some reason for concern. Over the last three decades, trust in political institutions such as parliaments or the courts has precipitously declined across the established democracies of North America and Western Europe. So has voter turnout. As party identification has weakened and party membership has declined, citizens have become less willing to stick with establishment parties. Instead, voters increasingly endorse single-issue movements, vote for populist candidates, or support "antisystem" parties that define themselves in opposition to the status quo. Even in some of the richest and most politically stable regions of the world, it seems as though democracy is in a state of serious disrepair.

Most political scientists, however, have steadfastly declined to view these trends as an indication of structural problems in the functioning of liberal

From *Journal of Democracy* 27, no. 3 (July 2016), pp. 5–17.

democracy, much less as a threat to its very existence. A wide range of leading scholars, including Ronald Inglehart, Pippa Norris, Christian Welzel, and Russell J. Dalton, have generally interpreted these trends as benign indications of the increasing political sophistication of younger generations of "critical" citizens who are less willing to defer to traditional elites. Keeping with a distinction made by David Easton in 1975, many scholars acknowledge that "government legitimacy," or support for particular governments, has declined. But they also insist that "regime legitimacy," or support for democracy as a system of government, remains robust. Thus people may increasingly feel that democracy is not working well in their country or that the government of the day is doing a poor job, but this only makes them all the more appreciative of the fact that liberal democracy allows them to protest the government or vote it out of office. According to this view, democracies such as France, Sweden, and the United States remain as consolidated and stable today as they ever have been.

In our view, however, this optimistic interpretation may no longer be tenable. Drawing on data from Waves 3 through 6 of the World Values Surveys (1995–2014), we look at four important types of measures that are clear indicators of regime legitimacy as opposed to government legitimacy: citizens' express support for the system as a whole; the degree to which they support key institutions of liberal democracy, such as civil rights; their willingness to advance their political causes within the existing political system; and their openness to authoritarian alternatives such as military rule.

What we find is deeply concerning. Citizens in a number of supposedly consolidated democracies in North America and Western Europe have not only grown more critical of their political leaders. Rather, they have also become more cynical about the value of democracy as a political system, less hopeful that anything they do might influence public policy, and more willing to express support for authoritarian alternatives. The crisis of democratic legitimacy extends across a much wider set of indicators than previously appreciated.

How much importance do citizens of developed countries ascribe to living in a democracy? Among older generations, the devotion to democracy is about as fervent and widespread as one might expect: In the United States, for example, people born during the interwar period consider democratic governance an almost sacred value. When asked to rate on a scale of 1 to 10 how "essential" it is for them "to live in a democracy," 72 percent of those born before World War II check "10," the highest value. So do 55 percent of the same cohort in the Netherlands. But, as Figure 5.2 shows, the millennial generation (those born since 1980) has grown much more indifferent. Only one in three Dutch millennials accords maximal importance to living in a democracy; in the United States, that number is slightly lower, around 30 percent.[1]

The decline in support for democracy is not just a story of the young being more critical than the old; it is, in the language of survey research, owed to a "cohort" effect rather than an "age" effect. Back in 1995, for example, only 16 percent of Americans born in the 1970s (then in their late teens or early twenties) believed that democracy was a "bad" political system for their country. Twenty years later, the number of "antidemocrats" in this same generational cohort had increased by around 4 percentage points, to 20 percent. The next cohort—comprising those born in the 1980s—is even more antidemocratic: In 2011, 24 percent of U.S. millennials (then in their late teens or early twenties) considered democracy to be a "bad" or "very bad" way of running the country. Although this trend was somewhat more moderate in Europe, it was nonetheless significant: In 2011, 13 percent of European youth (aged 16 to 24) expressed such a view, up from 8 percent among the same age group in the mid-1990s (see Figure 5.3).

Public-opinion data thus suggest a significant generational reversal. Not so long ago, young people were much more enthusiastic than older people about democratic values: In the first waves of the World Values Survey, in 1981–84 and 1990–93, young respondents were much keener than their elders on protecting freedom of speech and

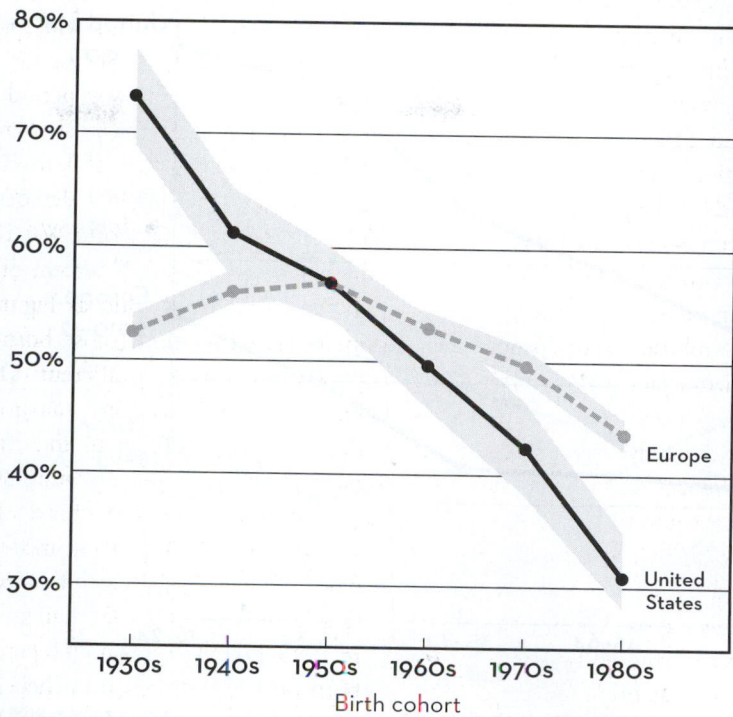

Figure 5.2 *Percent of Respondents Rating It "Essential" to "Live in a Country That Is Governed Democratically," by Age Cohort (Decade of Birth)*

Source: World Values Surveys, Waves 5 and 6 (2005–14). Data pooled from EU member states. Valid responses: United States, 3,398; European Union, 25,789. Bootstrap 95 percent confidence intervals are shown in gray.

significantly less likely to embrace political radicalism. Today, the roles have reversed: On the whole, support for political radicalism in North America and Western Europe is higher among the young, and support for freedom of speech lower.[2]

Withdrawal from Democratic Institutions

People can have an abstract allegiance to "democracy" while simultaneously rejecting many key norms and institutions that have traditionally been regarded as necessary ingredients of democratic governance. Therefore, if we are to understand why levels of support for democracy have changed, we must study the ways in which people's conception of democracy, as well as their degree of engagement with democratic institutions, have changed.[3] Beyond support for regular elections, which are essential even according to the most minimal interpretation of democracy, full-fledged support for democracy should also entail a commitment to liberal values such as the protection of key rights and civil liberties, as well as a willingness to use the institutions of liberal democracy to effect political change.[4] So how have political participation and support for liberal democracy fared in the recent past?

A battery of questions on interpretations of democracy was not fielded in the World Values Survey until 2005, so there is not enough time-series data to measure directly how citizens' understanding

Figure 5.3 Percent Responding That "Having a Democratic Political System" Is a "Bad" or "Very Bad" Way to "Run This Country," by Age Group

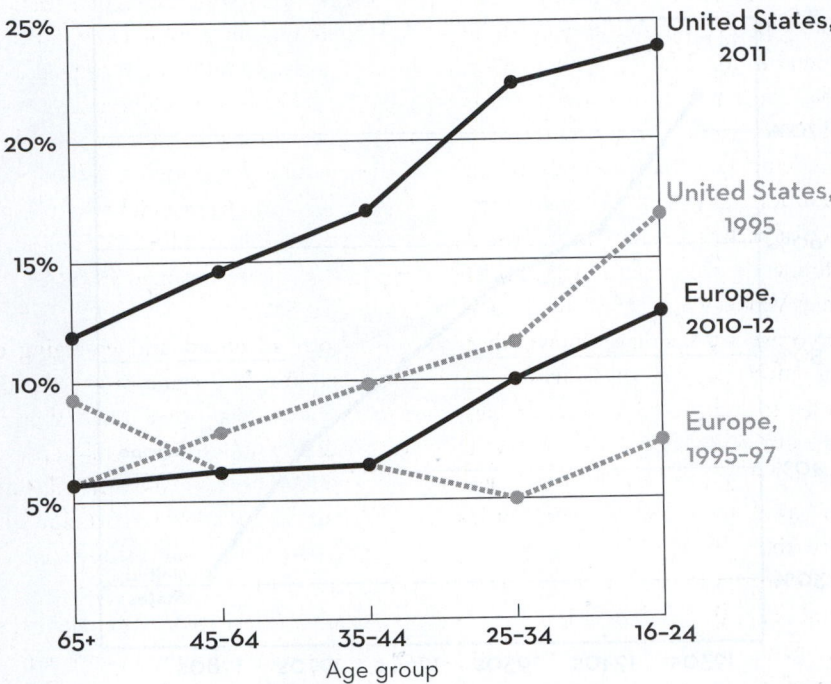

Source: World Values Surveys, Waves 3 to 6 (1995–2014). Data for Europe include a constant country sample in both waves: Germany, Sweden, Spain, the Netherlands, Romania, Poland, and the United Kingdom. Valid responses: United States, 1995: 1,452; United States, 2011: 2,164; European countries, 1995–97: 6,052; European countries, 2010–12: 8,197.

of democracy has evolved over time. It is possible, however, to analyze differences between generational cohorts as a proxy. Taking the pooled data from Europe and the United States, we find that attitudes toward liberal institutions do not differ radically among different generations. But a liberal conception of democracy is somewhat less entrenched among millenials (born since the 1980s) than their baby-boomer parents (born during the first two decades after the Second World War). In the United States, for example, 41 percent of those born during the interwar and initial postwar decades state that it is "absolutely essential" in a democracy that "civil rights protect people's liberty." Among millennials, this share falls to 32 percent. In the European Union, these figures are 45 and 39 percent, respectively.

Any minimally liberal understanding of representative democracy needs to encompass the notion that elections should be free and fair. So it is disquieting that in mature democracies such an interpretation of democracy, though still endorsed by a clear majority of the population, is weaker among younger voters. In the United States, for example, only 10 percent of citizens born in the interwar years and 14 percent of baby-boomers say that it is "unimportant" in a democracy for people to "choose their leaders in free elections" (with "unimportant" defined as 1 to 5 on a 10-point scale of importance). Among millennials, this figure rises to 26 percent. In Europe, there is a similar, though less dramatic, pattern, with 9 percent of the interwar and baby-boomer generations versus 13 percent of millennials responding that free and fair elections are unimportant. (Since we lack time-series data on these measures, these findings are preliminary and will have to be confirmed by future surveys.) Moreover, there is no broad reason to assume that young people should, in general, be prone to a less liberal interpretation of democracy, as the opposite pattern is found in places such as China, India, and sub-Saharan Africa.

The health of a democracy depends not only on support for key political values such as civil rights, but also on the active participation of an informed citizenry. Indeed, following in the tradition of Gabriel Almond and Sidney Verba's classic 1963 work, *The Civic Culture*, successive studies have shown that civic engagement affects democracy's ability to deliver public goods, to hold officials accountable, and to provide effective government. This makes it all the more troubling that there has been a long-documented withdrawal from formal democratic participation: Since the 1960s, voter turnout has fallen and political-party membership has plummeted in virtually all established democracies.

Just as younger generations are less committed to the importance of democracy, so too are they less likely to be politically engaged. In fact, in both Western Europe and North America, interest in politics has rapidly and markedly declined among the young. At the same time, it has either remained stable or even increased among older cohorts. As a result, overall levels of engagement have remained steady at around 60 percent in the United States and about 50 percent in Europe. In other words, the aggregate figure, important as it is in its own right, masks the most striking part of the story: the quickly widening generational gap in political apathy.

In 1990, both a majority of young Americans (those between the ages of 16 and 35) and a majority of older Americans (36 years and older) reported being "fairly interested" or "very interested" in politics—53 and 63 percent, respectively. By 2010, the share of young Americans professing an interest in politics had dropped by more than 12 percentage points and the share of older Americans had risen by 4 percentage points. As a result, the generation gap had widened from 10 percentage points to 26 percentage points. Among European respondents, who on the whole report less interest in politics than do their American counterparts, this phenomenon is even starker: The gap between young and old more than tripled between 1990 and 2010, from 4 to 14 percentage points. This is attributable almost solely to a rapid loss of interest among young respondents. Whereas the share of Europeans aged 36 or older who were interested in politics remained stable at 52 percent, among the young that figure dropped from 48 to 38 percent (see Figure 5.4).

In both advanced and emerging democracies, the generation that came of age during the 1960s withdrew from traditional forms of political engagement, such as joining political parties and voting. This trend has continued, with millennials even less likely than their parents to participate in the democratic system via formal institutions. Most scholars have resisted the conclusion that young people are worryingly disengaged from democratic politics by arguing that a decline in conventional forms of political participation has been compensated for by a rise in "nonconventional" forms of activism, such as membership in new social movements or participation in protests and boycotts.[5] Recent data from Wave 5 (2005–2009) and Wave 6 (2010–14) of the World Values Survey, however, suggest that this no longer holds true: The baby-boomer generation has not managed to transfer its proclivity to engage in non-conventional forms of activism to its children and grandchildren. As a result, more recent generations are not just disengaged from the formal institutions of liberal democracy; they are also less likely to participate in nonconventional political activities, such as joining new social movements or participating in political protest.

Historically, citizens have been more likely to engage in protests when they are young. So it is striking that, in the United States, one in eleven baby-boomers has joined a demonstration in the past twelve months, but only one in fifteen millennials has done so. In Europe, the picture is a little more mixed: Young respondents are more likely than older ones

Figure 5.4 The Widening "Political Apathy Gap"

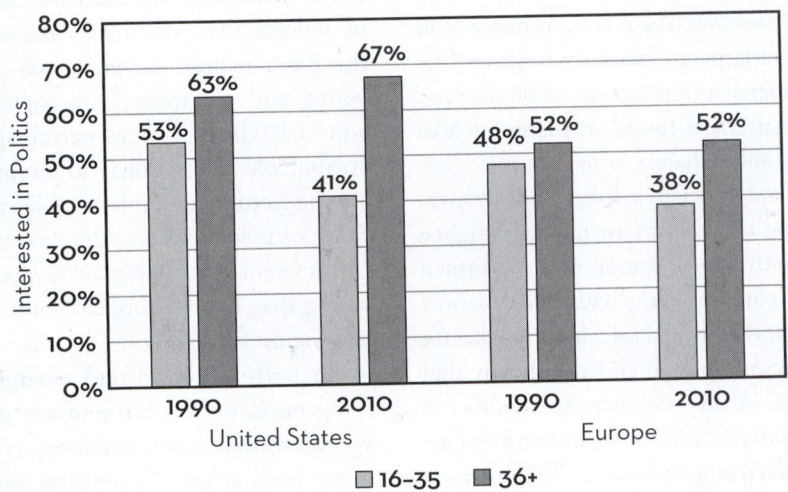

Note: We compared the shares of U.S. and European respondents who reported being "fairly interested" or "very interested" in politics across two age cohorts: those 16 to 35 years old and those 36 or older. European countries included in both waves (constant sample) are Germany, the Netherlands, Poland, Romania, Spain, and Sweden. Number of valid responses: United States, 1990: 1,812; United States, 2011: 2,210; Europe, 1990–93: 13,588; Europe, 2010–12: 8,771.
Source: World Values Surveys, Waves 2 (1990–94) and 6 (2010–14).

to have attended protests in the course of the past twelve months, but they do so at lower levels than previous cohorts did at the same age. This decline in political engagement is even more marked for such measures as active membership in new social movements. Participation in humanitarian and human-rights organizations, for example, is about half as high among the young as among older age cohorts. Thus we find that millennials across Western Europe and North America are less engaged than their elders, both in traditional forms of political participation and in oppositional civic activity.

Rising Support for Authoritarian Alternatives

It is clear that citizens today express less of an attachment to liberal democracy, interpret the nature of democracy in a less liberal way, and have less hope of affecting public policy through active participation

in the political process than they once did. What is not clear is how serious a warning sign this is for democratic politics and institutions. Dwindling support for, and engagement with, political institutions might simply reflect the fact that liberal democracy no longer faces any serious competition from alternative regime forms. Perhaps the real reason that citizens who came of age after the end of the Cold War do not express the same fervor in supporting liberal democracy is not that they are indifferent toward their system of government, but simply that they have never experienced a real threat to it. Although this optimistic reading may at first seem plausible, it does not square with the fact that explicit support for authoritarian regime forms is also on the rise.

In the past three decades, the share of U.S. citizens who think that it would be a "good" or "very good" thing for the "army to rule"—a patently undemocratic stance—has steadily risen. In 1995, just one in sixteen respondents agreed with that position; today, one in six agree. While those who hold this view remain in the minority, they can no longer be dismissed as a small fringe, especially since there have been similar increases in the number of those who favor a "strong leader who doesn't have to bother with parliament and elections" and those who want experts rather than the government to "take decisions" for the country. Nor is the United States the only country to exhibit this trend. The proportion agreeing that it would be better to have the army rule has risen in most mature democracies, including Germany, Sweden, and the United Kingdom.

Similarly, while 43 percent of older Americans, including those born between the world wars and their baby-boomer children, do not believe that it is legitimate in a democracy for the military to take over when the government is incompetent or failing to do its job, the figure among millennials is much lower at 19 percent. In Europe, the generation gap is somewhat less stark but equally clear, with 53 percent of older Europeans and only 36 percent of millennials strongly rejecting the notion that a government's incompetence can justify having the army "take over."

Strikingly, such undemocratic sentiments have risen especially quickly among the wealthy. In 1995, the "rich" (defined as deciles 8 to 10 on a ten-point income scale) were the most *opposed* to undemocratic viewpoints, such as the suggestion that their country would be better off if the "army" ruled. Lower-income respondents (defined as deciles 1 to 5) were most in favor of such a proposition. Since then, relative support for undemocratic institutions has reversed. In almost every region, the rich are now more likely than the poor to express approval for "having the army rule." In the United States, for example, only 5 percent of upper-income citizens thought that army rule was a "good" or "very good" idea in the mid-1990s. That figure has since risen to 16 percent. By way of comparison, in Latin America in the mid-1990s, a decade after the return to civilian rule, 21 percent of upper-income respondents still supported military rule. That figure now stands at 33 percent.

The idea that support for military rule has markedly increased among wealthy citizens of long-established liberal democracies is so counter-intuitive that it naturally invites skepticism. Yet it is consistent with similar survey items that measure citizens' openness to other authoritarian alternatives. In the United States, among all age cohorts, the share of citizens who believe that it would be better to have a "strong leader" who does not have to "bother with parliament and elections" has also risen over time: In 1995, 24 percent of respondents held this view; by 2011, that figure had increased to 32 percent. Meanwhile, the proportion of citizens who approve of "having experts, not government, make decisions according to what they think is best for the country" has grown from 36 to 49 percent. One reason for these changes is that whereas two decades ago affluent citizens were much more likely than people of lower income groups to defend democratic institutions, the wealthy are now moderately more likely than others to favor a strong leader who can ignore democratic institutions (see Figure 5.5).

Remarkably, the trend toward openness to non-democratic alternatives is especially strong among citizens who are both young *and* rich. Returning to the question of approval for military rule, in 1995 only 6 percent of rich young Americans (those born since 1970) believed that it would be a "good" thing for the army to take over; today, this view is held by 35 percent of rich young Americans. Nor is the United States an outlier among mature democracies. In Europe in 1995, 6 percent of high-income earners born since 1970 favored the possibility of "army rule"; today, 17 percent of young upper-income Europeans favor it. This is a striking finding: Rising support for illiberal politics is driven not only by the disempowered, middle-aged, and underemployed. Its vocal supporters can also be found among the young, wealthy, and privileged.

While support for military rule among the young and the wealthy may seem like an aberration, their embrace of nondemocratic practices and institutions should not come as a surprise. If we widen the historical lens, we see that, with the exception of a brief period in the late twentieth century, democracy has usually been associated with redistributive demands by the poor and therefore regarded with

Figure 5.5 Support for Authoritarianism by Income in the U.S.

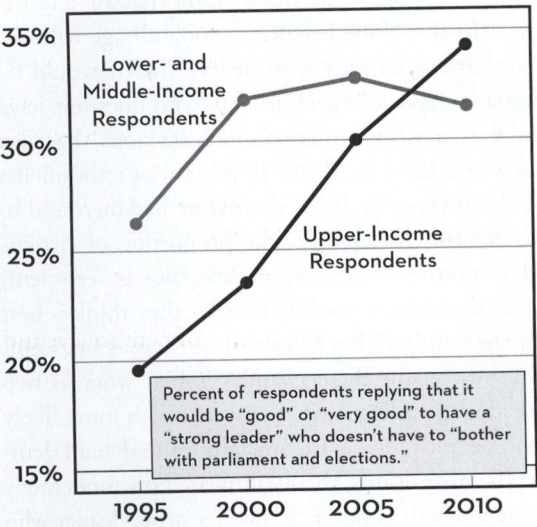

Source: World Values Surveys, Waves 3 through 6 (1995–2014). Data from the U.S. sample only. Upper income defined as the top three income deciles (8–10 on a 10-point scale). Lower and middle income defined as the bottom seven deciles (1–7 on a 10-point income scale). Sample size: upper-income respondents (1,172); lower- and middle-income respondents (4,659).

skepticism by elites. The newfound aversion to democratic institutions among rich citizens in the West may be no more than a return to the historical norm.[6]

Is Democracy Deconsolidating?

One of the key findings of comparative politics is the astonishing stability of wealthy consolidated democracies. In the first years of their existence, both poor and wealthy democracies are vulnerable to regime change. Poor democracies remain in danger even when they have been democratic for a number of years and have successfully changed governments through elections. Democracies that are both wealthy and consolidated, however, appear to be safe: As Adam Przeworski and Fernando Limongi have shown, no consolidated democracy with a

GDP per capita of over $6,000 in 1985 international prices has ever collapsed.[7]

This key finding has underwritten an important body of literature on democratization and regime stability, but it has simultaneously occluded an entire area of study. Apparently secure in the knowledge that wealthy consolidated democracies will not experience regime breakdown, political scientists have abstained from pursuing questions that would seem to be among the most fundamental for the discipline: What can empirical indicators tell us about whether rich consolidated democracies are as stable as they were in the past? Do empirical indicators give us reason to believe that seemingly stable democracies may be in trouble? And what might happen if wealthy democracies do eventually start to experience occasional breakdown, as have virtually all other political-regime types in the history of mankind?

In the famous formulation of Juan Linz and Alfred Stepan, democracies are consolidated when they are the "only game in town."[8] This metaphor is as elusive as it is evocative. What does it mean, in concrete terms, for democracy to be the only game in town? In our view, the degree to which a democracy is consolidated depends on three key characteristics: the degree of popular support for democracy as a system of government; the degree to which antisystem parties and movements are weak or nonexistent; and the degree to which the democratic rules are accepted.

This empirical understanding of democratic consolidation opens up conceptual space for the possibility of "democratic deconsolidation." In theory, it is possible that, even in the seemingly consolidated democracies of North America and Western Europe, democracy may one day cease to be the "only game in town": Citizens who once accepted democracy as the only legitimate form of government could become more open to authoritarian alternatives. Stable party systems in which all major forces were once united in support of democracy could enter into phases of extreme instability or witness the meteoric rise of antisystem parties. Finally, rules that were once respected by all important political players could suddenly come under attack by politicians jostling for partisan advantage.

It is at least plausible to think that such a process of democratic deconsolidation may already be underway in a number of established democracies in North America and Western Europe. In the United States, citizens have rapidly lost faith in the political system; in early March 2016, for example, public approval of Congress stood at a mere 13 percent. Wealthy businessman and television personality Donald Trump, having attracted fervent and surprisingly broad support by railing against the political system and promising policies that would openly violate the rights of ethnic and religious minorities, appears to have won the Republican nomination for the presidency of the United States. Meanwhile, even mainstream political actors are increasingly willing to violate the informal rules for the sake of partisan advantage: To name but one example of the resulting gridlock and constitutional dysfunction, the U.S. Senate has refused even to consider President Barack Obama's nominee for a vacant seat on the Supreme Court.

In Europe, too, there have been many signs of democratic deconsolidation in recent years. Approval ratings for the continent's leading politicians stand at record lows, and citizens have grown deeply mistrustful of their political institutions. Far-right populist parties, such as France's National Front or the Sweden Democrats, have risen from obscurity to transform the party system of virtually every Western European country. Meanwhile, parts of Central and Eastern Europe bear witness to the institutional and ideological transformations that might be afoot: In Poland and Hungary, populist strongmen have begun to put pressure on critical media, to violate minority rights, and to undermine key institutions such as independent courts.

To answer the question of whether democracy is deconsolidating in these countries in a rigorous manner would require a research program of considerable breadth that is beyond the scope of a single essay focusing on public-opinion data. But before

such a project can get off the ground, an important empirical puzzle needs to be identified and a set of coherent explanatory goals formulated.

If we take the number of people who claim to endorse democracy at face value, no regime type in the history of mankind has held such universal and global appeal as democracy does today. Yet the reality of contemporary democracies looks rather less triumphant than this fact might suggest. Citizens of democracies are less and less content with their institutions; they are more and more willing to jettison institutions and norms that have traditionally been regarded as central components of democracy; and they are increasingly attracted to alternative regime forms.

Far from showing that citizens have merely become more willing to criticize particular governments because their expectations of democracy have grown, this indicates a deep tension at the heart of contemporary politics: Even as democracy has come to be the only form of government widely viewed as legitimate, it has lost the trust of many citizens who no longer believe that democracy can deliver on their most pressing needs and preferences. The optimistic view that this decline in confidence merely represents a temporary downturn is no more than a pleasing assumption, based in part on a reluctance to call into question the vaunted stability of affluent democracies.

Democracies do not die overnight, nor do democracies that have begun to deconsolidate necessarily fail. But we suspect that the degree of democratic consolidation is one of the most important factors in determining the likelihood of democratic breakdown. In a world where most citizens fervently support democracy, where antisystem parties are marginal or nonexistent, and where major political forces respect the rules of the political game, democratic breakdown is extremely unlikely. It is no longer certain, however, that this is the world we live in.

Even if subsequent research should show that democratic deconsolidation really is underway, this would not mean that any particular democracy would soon collapse. Nor is it obvious that the democracy that had deconsolidated the most would be the first to fail. Regime change is always a matter of accident as well as intention, of historical circumstances as well as structural preconditions. But if democratic deconsolidation were proven to be in progress, it would mean that what was once unthinkable should no longer be considered outside the realm of possibility. As democracies deconsolidate, the prospect of democratic breakdown becomes increasingly likely—even in parts of the world that have long been spared such instability. If political scientists are to avoid being blindsided by the demise of established democracies in the coming decades, as they were by the fall of communism a few decades ago, they need to find out whether democratic deconsolidation is happening; to explain the possible causes of this development; to delineate its likely consequences (present and future); and to ponder the potential remedies.

NOTES

1. These gaps remain consistent at other points in the spectrum. If we take responses of 9 or 10, then the rate declines from 85 percent among Americans born in the 1930s to 43 percent among those born since the 1980s, and from 68 percent of Europeans born in the 1930s to 59 percent born since the 1980s. At the other end of the spectrum, the share of respondents expressing no clear importance to living in a democracy (1 to 5 on the scale) constitutes only 4 percent of Americans born in the 1930s, but 21 percent of millennials, and 6 percent of Europeans born in the 1930s, but 11 percent of millennials.

2. Support for radicalism is measured by responses to a left-right political scale, with "1" as radical left and "10" as radical right. In both Europe and North America, self-reported political radicalism is higher among the youngest age cohort (born since 1980) than any previous generation in any previous survey.

3. Andreas Schedler and Rodolfo Sarsfield, "Democrats with Adjectives: Linking Direct and Indirect Measures of Democratic Support," *European Journal of Political Research* 46 (August 2007): 637–59, and Michael Bratton and Robert Mattes, "How People View Democracy: Africans' Surprising Universalism," *Journal of Democracy* (January 2001): 107–21.

4. See Robert A. Dahl, Ian Shapiro, and José Antônio Cheibub, eds., *The Democracy Sourcebook* (Cambridge: MIT Press, 2003); and Alejandro Moreno and Christian Welzel, "Enlightening People: The Spark of Emancipative Values," in Russell J. Dalton and Christian Welzel, eds., *The Civic Culture Transformed: From Allegiant to Assertive Citizens* (New York: Cambridge University Press, 2013).

5. Christian Welzel, *Freedom Rising: Human Empowerment and the Quest for Emancipation* (New York: Cambridge University Press, 2013) and Pippa Norris, *Democratic Deficit: Critical Citizens Revisited* (New York: Cambridge University Press, 2011).

6. Two recent contributions to this argument are Carles Boix, *Democracy and Redistribution* (New York: Cambridge University Press, 2003) and Daron Acemoglu and James A. Robinson, *Economic Origins of Dictatorship and Democracy* (New York: Cambridge University Press, 2006).

7. Adam Przeworski et al., *Democracy and Development: Political Institutions and Well-Being in the World, 1950–1990* (New York: Cambridge University Press, 2000).

8. Juan J. Linz and Alfred Stepan, *Problems of Democratic Transition and Consolidation* (Baltimore: Johns Hopkins University Press, 1996).

6 NONDEMOCRATIC REGIMES

When we think about different kinds of regimes around the world, we tend to think only in terms of democracy or authoritarianism. In democratic societies, authoritarianism is often viewed as something of a temporary aberration until a subject people is able to throw off its fetters and join the free world. Thus, it might seem less important to understand the complexities of authoritarianism than to concentrate on how countries make the transition from there to democracy. But authoritarianism is a much more diverse and entrenched form of politics. Remember that democracy is the newcomer to political life, having been established relatively recently in human history.

The selection from Juan J. Linz and Alfred Stepan in this chapter is in many ways a culmination of research these two scholars have been conducting since the 1960s. For them, to understand how countries become democratic it is important to understand the regime type that precedes democracy. Linz and Stepan lay out a comprehensive analysis of the difference between totalitarianism and authoritarianism and describe how each has an impact on the most basic facets of nondemocratic rule. Why does this matter? Linz and Stepan argue that the type of authoritarian or totalitarian regime strongly affects how and if democracy will replace it. The institutions of nondemocratic rule will shape the path to democracy in the future. This kind of analysis, sometimes called "path dependent," has grown in recent years within the study of comparative politics and is consistent with a greater focus on institutions as actors in their own right. Stepan and Linz, with Yogendra Yadav, also authored "The Rise of State-Nations," which we covered in Chapter 5. In that work they observe that their discussion of state-nations was first broached in this article, as they considered how the interaction of regime type and social institutions can shape the prospects for political change.

Stepan and Linz's work reflects much of the literature from the 1980s and 1990s, which has been described as belonging to a "transition paradigm." In other words, this scholarship emphasized paths of change from authoritarianism and the institutional or other factors that shape how those changes come about. In the 2000s, however, political scientists grew more skeptical of their emphasis on this type of research, when many authoritarian regimes failed to give way or seemingly democratizing states instead developed new, hybrid forms of nondemocratic rule. Accordingly, scholars turned their attention to these semidemocratic or illiberal systems as regimes in their own right rather than simply transitions to democracy that had not yet come to fruition. Steven Levitsky and Lucan A. Way's "The Rise of Competitive Authoritarianism" (2002) provides a succinct overview of the practices of hybrid regimes, which combine formal participatory mechanisms (such as elections) with institutions and policies designed to hinder challenges to power. This can include biased media coverage, harassment of opposition candidates, weak legislatures, and corrupt judiciaries. Competitive authoritarianism may be a more tenacious form of nondemocratic rule, given its ostensibly democratic mechanisms, meant to channel and divide opposition. However, the authors note the inherent tension in such systems, in which participatory mechanisms, even when largely powerless, create the spaces in which challenges to those in power may emerge. Finally, the argument regarding hybrid regimes also notes that democracies themselves can slowly erode into illiberalism, with participatory institutions losing power as that power is concentrated into the hands of an elite.

Many of the discussions noted above are rooted in experiences in Latin America, Eastern Europe, and the former Soviet Union. But of course, they have applications elsewhere. Larry Diamond's "The Rule of Law versus the Big Man" (2008) builds on many of the above ideas as they relate to Africa. There, many competitive authoritarian systems rely on particular highly centralized presidencies and clientelism—a patron-client relationship based on personal connections and benefits. Such a system generates a highly personal, corrupt, and largely unaccountable form of rule. In Africa, these systems are often dominated by a so-called "big man," who solidifies his power with this network of patronage. Following Levitsky and Way, we might conclude that such regimes, though unstable, are not easily dislodged and simply transfer from one big man to another. However, Diamond is more optimistic, suggesting that in Africa civil society presents a growing challenge to competitive authoritarianism. Moreover, he emphasizes that international actors can play an important role in bolstering society while holding authoritarian rulers accountable, a point also made by Levitsky and Way.

With the general decline of military rule in Africa and Latin America, it may seem unnecessary to include a reading on this type of regime. However, as we noted in Chapter 5, support for the military remains in politics and is perhaps even growing in some developed democracies as other institutions lose their legitimacy. In "Military Rule" (2014), Barbara Geddes, Erica Frantz, and Joseph G. Wright note that not all forms of military rule are alike, distinguishing between a "military strongman" unfettered by other officers and rule by a group of officers who may constrain a dictator. The difference is important; while both are inclined toward human rights abuses, strongmen are more inclined toward war and pose a greater barrier to democratization.

The first selections in this chapter do not focus on one nondemocratic regime that looms large: China. Gary King, Jennifer Pan, and Margaret E. Roberts's "How Censorship in China Allows Government Criticism but Silences Collective Expression" (2013) looks at the ways in which technology can create new paths to perpetuate authoritarian rule. In the recent past it has frequently been argued that the

Internet and social media would undermine nondemocratic rule by empowering citizens with control over information. In contrast, these authors find that, in the case of China, governmental Internet control is both powerful and subtle. Censorship is not focused on stopping discussions over sensitive topics, unless those discussions have the potential to generate collective action—in other words, the ability to mobilize the public. More sophisticated means of information control can lead nondemocratic regimes to channel, rather than suppress, public discontent. Nondemocratic regimes with technical prowess may have found a new way to perpetuate their rule.

Juan J. Linz and Alfred Stepan
MODERN NONDEMOCRATIC REGIMES

Democratic transition and consolidation involve the movement from a nondemocratic to a democratic regime. However, specific polities may vary immensely in the *paths* available for transition and the unfinished *tasks* the new democracy must face before it is consolidated. Our central endeavor in the next two chapters is to show how and why much—though of course not all—of such variation can be explained by prior regime type.

For over a quarter of a century the dominant conceptual framework among analysts interested in classifying the different political systems in the world has been the tripartite distinction between democratic, authoritarian, and totalitarian regimes. New paradigms emerge because they help analysts see commonalities and implications they had previously overlooked. When Juan Linz wrote his 1964 article "An Authoritarian Regime: The Case of Spain," he wanted to call attention to the fact that between what then were seen as the two major stable political poles—the democratic pole and the totalitarian pole—there existed a form of polity that had its own internal logic and was a steady regime type. Though this type was nondemocratic, Linz argued that it was

fundamentally different from a totalitarian regime on four key dimensions—pluralism, ideology, leadership, and mobilization. This was of course what he termed an *authoritarian regime*. He defined them as: "political systems with limited, not responsible, political pluralism, without elaborate and guiding ideology, but with distinctive mentalities, without extensive nor intensive political mobilization, except at some points in their development, and in which a leader or occasionally a small group exercises power within formally ill-defined limits but actually quite predictable ones."[1]

In the 1960s, as analysts attempted to construct categories with which to compare and contrast all the systems in the world, the authoritarian category proved useful. As the new paradigm took hold among comparativists, two somewhat surprising conclusions emerged. First, it became increasingly apparent that more regimes were "authoritarian" than were "totalitarian" or "democratic" combined. Authoritarian regimes were thus the modal category of regime type in the modern world. Second, authoritarian regimes were not necessarily in transition to a different type of regime. As Linz's studies of Spain in the 1950s and early 1960s showed, the four distinctive dimensions of an authoritarian regime—limited pluralism, mentality, somewhat constrained leadership, and weak mobilization—could cohere for a long period as a reinforcing and integrated system that was relatively stable.

From *Problems of Democratic Transition and Consolidation: Southern Europe, South America, and Post-Communist Europe* (Baltimore: Johns Hopkins University Press, 1996), pp. 38–54. Some of the authors' notes have been omitted.

Typologies rise or fall according to their analytic usefulness to researchers. In our judgment, the existing tripartite regime classification has not only become less useful to democratic theorists and practitioners than it once was, it has also become an obstacle. Part of the case for typology change proceeds from the implications of the empirical universe we need to analyze. Very roughly, if we were looking at the world of the mid-1980s, how many countries could conceivably be called "democracies" of ten years' duration? And how many countries were very close to the totalitarian pole for that entire period?

Answers have, of course, an inherently subjective dimension, particularly as regards the evaluation of the evidence used to classify countries along the different criteria used in the typology. Fortunately, however, two independently organized studies attempt to measure most of the countries in the world as to their political rights and civil liberties. The criteria used in the studies are explicit, and there is a very high degree of agreement in the results. If we use these studies and the traditional tripartite regime type distinction, it turns out that more than 90 percent of modern nondemocratic regimes would have to share the same typological space—"authoritarian."[2] Obviously, with so many heterogenous countries sharing the same typological "starting place," this typology of regime type cannot tell us much about the extremely significant range of variation in possible transition paths and consolidation tasks that we believe in fact exists. Our purpose in the rest of this chapter is to reformulate the tripartite paradigm of regime type so as to make it more helpful in the analysis of *transition paths* and *consolidation tasks*. We propose therefore a revised typology, consisting of "democratic," "authoritarian," "totalitarian," "post-totalitarian," and "sultanistic" regimes.

Democracy

To start with the democratic type of regime, there are of course significant variations within democracy. However, we believe that such important categories

as "consociational democracy" and "majoritarian democracy" are subtypes of democracy and not different regime types. Democracy as a regime type seems to us to be of sufficient value to be retained and not to need further elaboration at this point in the book.

Totalitarianism

We also believe that the concept of a totalitarian regime as an ideal type, with some close historical approximations, has enduring value. If a regime has eliminated almost all pre-existing political, economic, and social pluralism, has a unified, articulated, guiding, utopian ideology, has intensive and extensive mobilization, and has a leadership that rules, often charismatically, with undefined limits and great unpredictability and vulnerability for elites and nonelites alike, then it seems to us that it still makes historical and conceptual sense to call this a regime with strong totalitarian tendencies.

If we accept the continued conceptual utility of the democratic and totalitarian regime types, the area in which further typological revision is needed concerns the regimes that are clearly neither democratic nor totalitarian. By the early 1980s, the number of countries that were clearly totalitarian or were attempting to create such regimes had in fact been declining for some time. As many Soviet-type regimes began to change after Stalin's death in 1953, they no longer conformed to the totalitarian model, as research showed. This change created conceptual confusion. Some scholars argued that the totalitarian category itself was wrong. Others wanted to call post-Stalinist regimes authoritarian. Neither of these approaches seems to us fully satisfactory. Empirically, of course, most of the Soviet-type systems in the 1980s were not totalitarian. However, the "Soviet-type" regimes, with the exception of Poland * * *, could not be understood in their distinctiveness by including them in the category of an authoritarian regime.

The literature on Soviet-type regimes correctly drew attention to regime characteristics that were no longer totalitarian and opened up promising new studies of policy-making. One of these perspectives was "institutional pluralism." However, in our judgment, to call these post-Stalinist polities *pluralistic* missed some extremely important features that could hardly be called pluralistic. Pluralist democratic theory, especially the "group theory" variant explored by such writers as Arthur Bentley and David Truman, starts with *individuals in civil society* who enter into numerous freely formed interest groups that are relatively autonomous and often criss-crossing. The many groups in civil society attempt to aggregate their interests and compete against each other in political society to influence state policies. However, the "institutional pluralism" that some writers discerned in the Soviet Union was radically different, in that almost all the pluralistic conflict occurred in *regime-created organizations within the party-state* itself. Conceptually, therefore, this form of competition and conflict is actually closer to what political theorists call *bureaucratic politics* than it is to *pluralistic politics*.

Rather than forcing these Soviet-type regimes into the existing typology of totalitarian, authoritarian, and democratic regimes, we believe we should expand that typology by explicating a distinctive regime type that we will call *post-totalitarian*.[3] Methodologically, we believe this category is justified because on each of the four dimensions of regime type—pluralism, ideology, leadership, and mobilization—there can be a post-totalitarian ideal type that is different from a totalitarian, authoritarian, or democratic ideal type. Later in this chapter we will also rearticulate the argument for considering sultanism as a separate ideal-type regime.

To state our argument in bold terms, we first present a schematic presentation of how the five ideal-type regimes we propose—democratic, totalitarian, post-totalitarian, authoritarian, and sultanistic—differ from each other on each one of the four constituent characteristics of regime type (Table 6.1). In the following chapter we make explicit what we believe are the implications of each regime type for democratic transition paths and the tasks of democratic consolidation.

Post-totalitarianism

Our task here is to explore how, on each of the four dimensions of regime type, post-totalitarianism is different from totalitarianism, as well as different from authoritarianism. Where appropriate we will also call attention to some under-theorized characteristics of both totalitarian and post-totalitarian regimes that produce dynamic pressures for out-of-type change. We do not subscribe to the view that either type is static.

Post-totalitarianism, as Table 6.1 implies, can encompass a continuum varying from "early post-totalitarianism," to "frozen post-totalitarianism," to "mature post-totalitarianism." Early post-totalitarianism is very close to the totalitarian ideal type but differs from it on at least one key dimension, normally some constraints on the leader. There can be frozen post-totalitarianism in which, despite the persistent tolerance of some civil society critics of the regime, almost all the other control mechanisms of the party-state stay in place for a long period and do not evolve (e.g., Czechoslovakia, from 1977 to 1989). Or there can be mature post-totalitarianism in which there has been significant change in all the dimensions of the post-totalitarian regime except that politically the leading role of the official party is still sacrosanct (e.g., Hungary from 1982 to 1988, which eventually evolved by late 1988 very close to an out-of-type change).

Concerning *pluralism*, the defining characteristic of totalitarianism is that there is no political, economic, or social pluralism in the polity and that pre-existing sources of pluralism have been uprooted or systematically repressed. In an authoritarian regime there is some limited political pluralism and often quite extensive economic and social pluralism. In an authoritarian regime, many of the manifestations of the limited political pluralism and the more extensive social and economic pluralism predate the authoritarian regime. How does pluralism in post-totalitarian regimes contrast with the near absence of pluralism in totalitarian regimes and the limited pluralism of authoritarian regimes?

Table 6.1 Major Modern Regime Ideal Types and Their Defining Characteristics

Characteristic	Democracy	Authoritarianism	Totalitarianism	Post-totalitarianism	Sultanism
Pluralism	Responsible political pluralism reinforced by extensive areas of pluralist autonomy in economy, society, and internal life of organizations. Legally protected pluralism consistent with "societal corporatism" but not "state corporatism."	Political system with limited, not responsible political pluralism. Often quite extensive social and economic pluralism. In authoritarian regimes most of pluralism had roots in society before the establishment of the regime. Often some space for semiopposition.	No significant economic, social, or political pluralism. Official party has *de jure* and *de facto* monopoly of power. Party has eliminated almost all pretotalitarian pluralism. No space for second economy or parallel society.	Limited, but not responsible social, economic, and institutional pluralism. Almost no political pluralism because party still formally has monopoly of power. May have "second economy," but state still the overwhelming presence. Most manifestations of pluralism in "flattened polity" grew out of tolerated state structures or dissident groups consciously formed in opposition to totalitarian regime. In mature post-totalitarianism opposition often creates "second culture" or "parallel society."	Economic and social pluralism does not disappear but is subject to unpredictable and despotic intervention. No group or individual in civil society, political society, or the state is free from sultan's exercise of despotic power. No rule of law. Low institutionalization. High fusion of private and public.
Ideology	Extensive intellectual commitment to citizenship and procedural rules of contestation. Not teleological. Respect for rights of minorities, state of law, and value of individualism.	Political system without elaborate and guiding ideology but with distinctive mentalities.	Elaborate and guiding ideology that articulates a reachable utopia. Leaders, individuals, and groups derive most of their sense of mission, legitimation, and often specific policies from their commitment to some holistic conception of humanity and society.	Guiding ideology still officially exists and is part of the social reality. But weakened commitment to or faith in utopia. Shift of emphasis from ideology to programmatic consensus that presumably is based on rational decision-making and limited debate without too much reference to ideology.	Highly arbitrary manipulation of symbols. Extreme glorification of ruler. No elaborate or guiding ideology or even distinctive mentalities outside of despotic personalism. No attempt to justify major initiatives on the basis of ideology. Pseudo-ideology not believed by staff, subjects, or outside world.

Characteristic	Democracy	Authoritarianism	Totalitarianism	Post-totalitarianism	Sultanism
Mobilization	Participation via autonomously generated organization of civil society and competing parties of political society guaranteed by a system of law. Value is on low regime mobilization but high citizen participation. Diffuse effort by regime to induce good citizenship and patriotism. Toleration of peaceful and orderly opposition.	Political system without extensive or intensive political mobilization except at some points in their development.	Extensive mobilization into a vast array of regime-created obligatory organizations. Emphasis on activism of cadres and militants. Effort at mobilization of enthusiasm. Private life is decried.	Progressive loss of interest by leaders and nonleaders involved in organizing mobilization. Routine mobilization of population within state-sponsored organizations to achieve a minimum degree of conformity and compliance. Many "cadres" and "militants" are mere careerists and opportunists. Boredom, withdrawal, and ultimately privatization of population's values become an accepted fact.	Low but occasional manipulative mobilization of a ceremonial type by coercive or clientelistic methods without permanent organization. Periodic mobilization of parastate groups who use violence against groups targeted by sultan.
Leadership	Top leadership produced by free elections and must be exercised within constitutional limits and state of law. Leadership must be periodically subjected to and produced by free elections.	Political system in which a leader or occasionally a small group exercises power within formally ill-defined but actually quite predictable norms. Effort at co-optation of old elite groups. Some autonomy in state careers and in military.	Totalitarian leadership rules with undefined limits and great unpredictability for members and nonmembers. Often charismatic. Recruitment to top leadership highly dependent on success and commitment in party organization.	Growing emphasis by post-totalitarian political elite on personal security. Checks on top leadership via party structures, procedures, and "internal democracy." Top leaders are seldom charismatic. Recruitment to top leadership restricted to official party but less dependent upon building a career within party's organization. Top leaders can come from party technocrats in state apparatus.	Highly personalistic and arbitrary. No rational-legal constraints. Strong dynastic tendency. No autonomy in state careers. Leader unencumbered by ideology. Compliance to leaders based on intense fear and personal rewards. Staff of leader drawn from members of his family, friends, business associates, or men directly involved in use of violence to sustain the regime. Staff's position derives from their purely personal submission to the ruler.

In mature post-totalitarianism, there is a much more important and complex play of institutional pluralism within the state than in totalitarianism. Also, in contrast to totalitarianism, post-totalitarianism normally has a much more significant degree of social pluralism, and in mature post-totalitarianism there is often discussion of a "second culture" or a "parallel culture." Evidence of this is found in such things as a robust underground *samizdat* literature with multi-issue journals of the sort not possible under totalitarianism.[4] This growing pluralism is simultaneously a dynamic source of vulnerability for the post-totalitarian regime and a dynamic source of strength for an emerging democratic opposition. For example, this "second culture" can be sufficiently powerful that, even though leaders of the second culture will frequently be imprisoned, in a mature post-totalitarian regime opposition leaders can generate substantial followings and create enduring oppositional organizations in civil society. At moments of crisis, therefore, a mature post-totalitarian regime can have a cadre of a democratic opposition based in civil society with much greater potential to form a democratic political opposition than would be available in a totalitarian regime. A mature post-totalitarian regime can also feature the coexistence of a state-planned economy with extensive partial market experiments in the state sector that can generate a "red bourgeoisie" of state sector managers and a growing but subordinate private sector, especially in agriculture, commerce and services.

However, in a post-totalitarian regime this social and economic pluralism is different in degree and kind from that found in an authoritarian regime. It is different in degree because there is normally more social and economic pluralism in an authoritarian regime (in particular there is normally a more autonomous private sector, somewhat greater religious freedom, and a greater amount of aboveground cultural production). The difference in kind is typologically even more important. In a post-totalitarian society, the historical reference for both the power holders of the regime and the opposition is the previous totalitarian regime. By definition, the existence of a previous totalitarian regime means that most of the pre-existing sources of responsible and organized pluralism have been eliminated or repressed and a totalitarian order has been established. There is therefore an active effort at "detotalitarianization" on the part of oppositional currents in civil society. Much of the emotional and organizational drive of the opposition in civil society is thus consciously crafted to forge alternatives to the political, economic, and social structures created by the totalitarian regime, structures that still play a major role in the post-totalitarian society. Much of the second culture therefore is not traditional in form but is found in new movements that arise out of the totalitarian experience. There can also be a state-led detotalitarianization in which the regime itself begins to eliminate some of the most extreme features of the monist experience. Thus, if there is growing "institutional pluralism," or a growing respect for procedure and law, or a newly tolerated private sector, it should be understood as a kind of pluralism that emerges *out of* the previous totalitarian regime.

However, it is typologically and politically important to stress that there are significant limits to pluralism in post-totalitarian societies. In contrast to an authoritarian regime, there is *no* limited and relatively autonomous pluralism in the explicitly political realm. The official party in all post-totalitarian regimes is still legally accorded the leading role in the polity. The institutional pluralism of a post-totalitarian regime should not be confused with political pluralism; rather, institutional pluralism is exercised within the party-state or within the newly tolerated second economy or parallel culture. The pluralism of the parallel culture or the second culture should be seen as a *social* pluralism that may have political implications. But we must insist that the party and the regime leaders in post-totalitarian regimes, unless they experience out-of-type change, accord *no* legitimacy or responsibility to nonofficial political pluralism.[5] Even the formal pluralism of satellite parties becomes politically relevant only in the final stages of the regime after the transition is in progress.

When we turn to the dimension of *leadership*, we also see central tendencies that distinguish totalitarian from authoritarian leadership. Totalitarian leadership is unconstrained by laws and procedures and is often charismatic. The leadership can come from the revolutionary party or movement, but members of this core are as vulnerable to the sharp policy and ideological changes enunciated by the leader (even more so in terms of the possibility of losing their lives) as the rest of the population. By contrast, in the Linzian scheme, authoritarian leadership is characterized by a political system in which a leader or occasionally a small group exercises power within formally ill-defined but actually quite predictable norms. There are often extensive efforts to co-opt old elite groups into leadership roles, and there is some autonomy in state careers and in the military.

As in a totalitarian regime, post-totalitarian leadership is still exclusively restricted to the revolutionary party or movement. However, in contrast to a totalitarian regime, post-totalitarian leaders tend to be more bureaucratic and state technocratic than charismatic. The central core of a post-totalitarian regime normally strives successfully to enhance its security and lessen its fear by reducing the range of arbitrary discretion allowed to the top leadership.

In contrast to those who say that the totalitarian regime concept is static, we believe that, when an opportunity presents itself (such as the death of the maximum leader), the top elite's desire to reduce the future leader's absolute discretion is predictably a dynamic source of pressure for out-of-type regime change from totalitarianism to post-totalitarianism. The post-totalitarian leadership is thus typologically closer in this respect to authoritarian leadership, in that the leader rules within unspecified but in reality reasonably predictable limits. However, the leadership in these two regime types still differs fundamentally. Post-totalitarian leadership is exclusively recruited from party members who develop their careers in the party organization itself, the bureaucracy, or the technocratic apparatus of the

state. They all are thus recruited from the structures created by the regime. In sharp contrast, in most authoritarian regimes, the norm is for the regime to co-opt much of the leadership from groups that have some power, presence, and legitimacy that does not derive directly from the regime itself. Indeed, the authoritarian regime has often been captured by powerful fragments of the pre-existing society. In some authoritarian regimes, even access to top positions can be established not by political loyalties as much as by some degree of professional and technical expertise and some degree of competition through examinations that are open to the society as a whole. In mature post-totalitarian regimes, technical competence becomes increasingly important, but we should remember that the original access to professional training was controlled by political criteria. Also, the competences that are accepted or recognized in post-totalitarian systems are technical or managerial but do not include skills developed in a broader range of fields such as the law, religious organizations, or independent business or labor.

The limited party-bureaucratic-technocratic pluralism under post-totalitarianism does not give the regime the flexibility for change within the regime that co-optation of nonregime elites can give to many authoritarian regimes. The desire to resist the personalized leadership of the First Secretary–ideologue can be a source of change from totalitarian to post-totalitarian, but it can also lead eventually to the oligarchic leadership of aging men supported by the nomenklatura. Attempts at rejuvenation at the top by including or co-opting new men and women from the outside are normally very limited. In extreme cases (i.e., the GDR and post-1968 Czechoslovakia), frozen post-totalitarianism shows geriatric tendencies. Under crisis circumstances, the inability to renovate leadership, not so paradoxically, is a potential source of dynamic change in that a frozen post-totalitarian regime, with its old and narrow leadership base, has a very limited capacity to negotiate. Such a leadership structure, if it is not able to repress opponents in a crisis, is particularly vulnerable to *collapse*. One of the reasons why midlevel cadres in the once all-powerful coercive apparatus might, in time of crisis, let the regime collapse rather than fire upon the democratic opposition has to do with the role of ideology in post-totalitarianism.

The contrast between the role of *ideology* in a totalitarian system and in a post-totalitarian system is sharp, but it is more one of behavior and belief than one of official canon. In the area of ideology, the dynamic potential for change from a totalitarian to a post-totalitarian regime, both on the part of the cadres and on the part of the society, is the growing empirical disjunction between official ideological claims and reality. This disjunction produces lessened ideological commitment on the part of the cadres and growing criticism of the regime by groups in civil society. In fact, many of the new critics in civil society emerge out of the ranks of former true believers, who argue that the regime does not—or, worse, cannot—advance its own goals. The pressures created by this tension between doctrine and reality often contribute to an out-of-type shift from a totalitarian regime effort to mobilize enthusiasm to a post-totalitarian effort to maintain acquiescence. In the post-totalitarian phase, the elaborate and guiding ideology created under the totalitarian regime still exists as the official state canon, but among many leaders there is a weakened commitment to and faith in utopia. Among much of the population, the official canon is seen as an obligatory ritual, and among groups in the "parallel society" or "second culture," there is constant reference to the first culture as a "living lie." This is another source of weakness, of the "hollowing out" of the post-totalitarian regime's apparent strength.

The role of ideology in a post-totalitarian regime is thus diminished from its role under totalitarianism, but it is still quite different from the role of ideology in an authoritarian regime. Most authoritarian regimes have diffuse nondemocratic mentalities, but they do not have highly articulated ideologies concerning the leading role of the party, interest groups, religion, and many other aspects of civil society, political society, the economy, and the state that still exist in a regime we would call

post-totalitarian. Therefore, a fundamental contrast between a post-totalitarian and authoritarian regime is that in a post-totalitarian regime there is an important ideological legacy that cannot be ignored and that cannot be questioned officially. The state-sanctioned ideology has a *social presence* in the organizational life of the post-totalitarian polity. Whether it expresses itself in the extensive array of state-sponsored organizations or in the domain of incipient but still officially controlled organizations, ideology is part of the social reality of a post-totalitarian regime to a greater degree than in most authoritarian regimes.

The relative de-ideologization of post-totalitarian regimes and the weakening of the belief in utopia as a foundation of legitimacy mean that, as in many authoritarian regimes, there is a growing effort in a post-totalitarian polity to legitimate the regime on the basis of performance criteria. The gap between the original utopian elements of the ideology and the increasing legitimation efforts on the basis of efficacy, particularly when the latter fails, is one of the sources of weakness in post-totalitarian regimes. Since democracies base their claim to obedience on the procedural foundations of democratic citizenship, as well as performance, they have a layer of insulation against weak performance not available to most post-totalitarian or authoritarian regimes. The weakening of utopian ideology that is a characteristic of post-totalitarianism thus opens up a new dynamic of regime vulnerabilities—or, from the perspective of democratic transition, new opportunities—that can be exploited by the democratic opposition. For example, the discrepancy between the constant reiteration of the importance of ideology and the ideology's growing irrelevance to policymaking or, worse, its transparent contradiction with social reality contribute to undermining the commitment and faith of the middle and lower cadres in the regime. Such a situation can help contribute to the rapid collapse of the regime if mid-level functionaries of the coercive apparatus have grave doubts about their right to shoot citizens who are protesting against the regime and its ideology, as we shall see when we discuss events in 1989 in East Germany and Czechoslovakia.

The final typological difference we need to explore concerns *mobilization*. Most authoritarian regimes never develop complex, all-inclusive networks of association whose purpose is the mobilization of the population. They may have brief periods of intensive mobilization, but these are normally less intensive than in a totalitarian regime and less extensive than in a post-totalitarian regime. In totalitarian regimes, however, there is extensive and intensive mobilization of society into a vast array of regime-created organizations and activities. Because utopian goals are intrinsic to the regime, there is a great effort to mobilize enthusiasm to activate cadres, and most leaders emerge out of these cadres. In the totalitarian system, "privatized" bourgeois individuals at home with their family and friends and enjoying life in the small circle of their own choosing are decried.

In post-totalitarian regimes, the extensive array of institutions of regime-created mobilization vehicles still dominates associational life. However, they have lost their intensity. Membership is still generalized and obligatory but tends to generate more boredom than enthusiasm. State-technocratic employment is an alternative to cadre activism as a successful career path, as long as there is "correct" participation in official organizations. Instead of the mobilization of enthusiasm that can be so functional in a totalitarian regime, the networks of ritualized mobilization in a post-totalitarian regime can produce a "cost" of time away from technocratic tasks for professionals and a cost of boredom and flight into private life by many other people. When there is no structural crisis and especially when there is no perception of an available alternative, such privatization is not necessarily a problem for a post-totalitarian regime. Thus, Kadar's famous saying, "Those who are not against us are for us," is a saying that is conceivable only in a post-totalitarian regime, not in a totalitarian one. However, if the performance of a post-totalitarian as opposed to a totalitarian regime is so poor that the personal rewards of private life are eroded, then privatization and apathy may contribute to a

new dynamic—especially if alternatives are seen as possible—of crises of "exit," "voice," and "loyalty."[6]

Let us conclude our discussion of post-totalitarianism with a summary of its political and ideological weaknesses. We do this to help enrich the discussion of why these regimes collapsed so rapidly once they entered into prolonged stagnation and the USSR withdrew its extensive coercive support.

Totalitarianism, democracy, and even many authoritarian regimes begin with "genetic" legitimacy among their core supporters, given the historical circumstances that led to the establishment of these regimes. By contrast, post-totalitarianism regimes do not have such a founding genetic legitimacy because they emerge out of the routinization, decay, or elite fears of the totalitarian regime. Post-totalitarian regimes, because of coercive resources they inherit and the related weaknesses of organized opposition, can give the appearance of as much or more stability than authoritarian regimes; if external support is withdrawn, however, their inner loss of purpose and commitment makes them vulnerable to collapse.

Post-totalitarian politics was a result in part of the moving away from Stalinism, but also of social changes in Communist societies. Post-totalitarian regimes did away with the worst aspects of repression but at the same time maintained most mechanisms of control. Although less bloody than under Stalinism, the presence of security services—like the Stasi in the GDR—sometimes became more pervasive. Post-totalitarianism could have led to moderate reforms in the economy, like those discussed at the time of the Prague Spring, but the Brezhnev restoration stopped dynamic adaptation in the USSR and in most other Soviet-type systems, except for Hungary and Poland.

Post-totalitarianism had probably less legitimacy for the ruling elites and above all the middle-level cadres than had a more totalitarian system. The loss of the utopian component of the ideology and the greater reliance on performance (which after some initial success did not continue) left the regimes vulnerable and ultimately made the use of massive repression less justifiable. Passive compliance and careerism opened the door to withdrawal into private life, weakening the regime so that the opposition could ultimately force it to negotiate or to collapse when it could not rely on coercion.

The weakness of post-totalitarian regimes has not yet been fully analyzed and explained but probably can be understood only by keeping in mind the enormous hopes and energies initially associated with Marxism-Leninism that in the past explained the emergence of totalitarianism and its appeal.[7] Many distinguished and influential Western intellectuals admired or excused Leninism and in the 1930s even Stalinism, but few Western intellectuals on the left could muster enthusiasm for post-totalitarianism in the USSR or even for perestroika and glasnost.

The emergence and evolution of post-totalitarianism can be the result of three distinct but often interconnected processes: (1) deliberate policies of the rulers to soften or reform the totalitarian system (detotalitarianism by choice), (2) the internal "hollowing out" of the totalitarian regimes' structures and an internal erosion of the cadres' ideological belief in the system (detotalitarianism by decay), and (3) the creation of social, cultural, and even economic spaces that resist or escape totalitarian control (detotalitarianism by societal conquest).

"Sultanism"

A large group of polities, such as Haiti under the Duvaliers, the Dominican Republic under Trujillo, the Central African Republic under Bokassa, the Philippines under Marcos, Iran under the Shah, Romania under Ceaușescu, and North Korea under Kim Il Sung, have had strong tendencies toward an extreme form of patrimonialism that Weber called *sultanism*. For Weber,

> *patrimonialism* and, in the extreme case, *sultanism* tend to arise whenever traditional domination develops an administration and a military force which are purely personal instruments of the master. . . . Where domination . . . operates primarily on the basis of discretion, it will be called *sultanism* . . . The non-traditional element is not, however, rationalized in impersonal terms, but consists only in the extreme development of the ruler's discretion. It is this which distinguishes it from every form of rational authority.[8]

Weber did not intend the word *sultanism* to imply religious claims to obedience. In fact, under Ottoman rule, the ruler held two distinct offices and titles, that of sultan and that of caliph. Initially, the Ottoman ruler was a sultan, and only after the conquest of Damascus did he assume the title of caliph, which entailed religious authority. After the defeat of Turkey in World War I and the proclamation of the republic, the former ruler lost his title of sultan but retained his religious title of caliph until Atatürk eventually forced him to relinquish even that title. Our point is that the secular and religious dimensions of his authority were conceptually and historically distinguished. Furthermore, the term *sultan* should not be analytically bound to the Middle East. Just as there are mandarins in New Delhi and Paris as well as in Peking and there is a macho style of politics in the Pentagon as well as in Buenos Aires, there are sultanistic rulers in Africa and the Caribbean as well as in the Middle East. What we do want the term *sultanism* to connote is a generic style of domination and regime rulership that is, as Weber says, an extreme form of patrimonialism. In sultanism, the private and the public are fused, there is a strong tendency toward familial power and dynastic succession, there is no distinction between a state career and personal service to the ruler, there is a lack of rationalized impersonal ideology, economic success depends on a personal relationship to the ruler, and, most of all, the ruler acts only according to his own unchecked discretion, with no larger, impersonal goals.

Table 6.1 gives substantial details on what a sultanistic type is in relation to pluralism, ideology, mobilization, and leadership. In this section we attempt to highlight differences between sultanism, totalitarianism, and authoritarianism because, while we believe they are distinct ideal types, in any concrete case a specific polity could have a mix of some sultanistic and some authoritarian tendencies (a combination that might open up a variety of transition options) or a mix of sultanistic and totalitarian tendencies (a combination that would tend to eliminate numerous transition options).

In his long essay "Totalitarian and Authoritarian Regimes," Juan Linz discussed the special features that make sultanism a distinctive type of nondemocratic regime.[9] Since the sultanistic regime type has not been widely accepted in the literature, we believe it will be useful for us to highlight systematically its distinctive qualities so as to make more clear the implications of this type of regime for the patterns of democratic resistance and the problems of democratic consolidation.

In sultanism, there is a high fusion by the ruler of the private and the public. The sultanistic polity becomes the personal domain of the sultan. In this domain there is no rule of law and there is low institutionalization. In sultanism there may be extensive social and economic pluralism, but almost never political pluralism, because political power is so directly related to the ruler's person. However, the essential reality in a sultanistic regime is that all individuals, groups, and institutions are permanently subject to the unpredictable and despotic intervention of the sultan, and thus all pluralism is precarious.

In authoritarianism there may or may not be a rule of law, space for a semi-opposition, or space for regime moderates who might establish links with opposition moderates, and there are normally extensive social and economic activities that function within a secure framework of relative autonomy. Under sultanism, however, there is no rule of law, no space for a semiopposition, no space for regime moderates who might negotiate with democratic moderates, and no sphere of the economy or civil society that is not subject to the despotic exercise of the sultan's will. As we demonstrate in the next chapter, this critical difference between pluralism in authoritarian and sultanistic regimes has immense implications for the types of transition that are *available* in an authoritarian regime but *unavailable* in a sultanistic regime.

There is also a sharp contrast in the function and consequences of ideology between totalitarian and sultanistic regimes. In a totalitarian regime not only is there an elaborate and guiding ideology, but ideology has the function of legitimating the regime, and rulers are often somewhat constrained by their own value system and ideology. They or their followers, or both, believe in that ideology as a point of reference and justification for their actions. In contrast, a sultanistic ruler characteristically has no elaborate and guiding ideology. There may be highly personalistic statements with pretensions of being an ideology, often named after the sultan, but this ideology is elaborated after the ruler has assumed power, is subject to extreme manipulation, and, most importantly, is not believed to be constraining on the ruler and is relevant only as long as he practices it. Thus, there could be questions raised as to whether Stalin's practices and statements were consistent with Marxism-Leninism, but there would be no reason for anyone to debate whether Trujillo's statements were consistent with Trujilloism. The contrast between authoritarian and sultanistic regimes is less stark over ideology; however, the distinctive mentalities that are a part of most authoritarian alliances are normally more constraining on rulers than is the sultan's idiosyncratic and personal ideology.

The extensive and intensive mobilization that is a feature of totalitarianism is seldom found in a sultanistic regime because of its low degree of institutionalization and its low commitment to an overarching ideology. The low degree of organization means that any mobilization that does occur is uneven and sporadic. Probably the biggest difference between sultanistic mobilization and authoritarian mobilization is the tendency within sultanism (most dramatic in the case of the Duvaliers' Tonton Macoutes in Haiti) to use para-state groups linked to the sultan to wield violence and terror against anyone who opposes the ruler's will. These para-state groups are not modern bureaucracies with generalized norms and procedures; rather, they are direct extensions of the sultan's will. They have no significant institutional autonomy. As Weber stressed, they are purely "personal treatments of the master."

Finally, how does leadership differ in sultanism, totalitarianism, and authoritarianism? The essence of sultanism is *unrestrained personal rulership*. This personal rulership is, as we have seen, unconstrained by ideology, rational-legal norms, or any balance of power. "Support is based not on a coincidence of interest between preexisting privileged social groups and the ruler but on interests created by his rule, rewards he offers for loyalty, and the fear of his vengeance."[10]

In one key respect leadership under sultanism and totalitarianism is similar. In both regimes the leader rules with undefined limits on his power and there is great unpredictability for elites and nonelites alike. In this respect, a Stalin and a Somoza are alike. However, there are important differences. The elaborate ideology, with its sense of nonpersonal and public mission, is meant to play an important legitimating function in totalitarian regimes. The ideological pronouncements of a totalitarian leader are taken seriously not only by his followers and cadres, but also by the society and intellectuals, including—in the cases of Leninism, Stalinism, and Marxism (and even fascism)—by intellectuals outside the state in which the leader exercises control. This places a degree of organizational, social, and ideological constraint on totalitarian leadership that is not present in sultanistic leadership. Most importantly, the intense degree to which rulership is personal in sultanism makes the *dynastic* dimension of rulership normatively acceptable and empirically common, whereas the public claims of totalitarianism make dynastic ambition, if not unprecedented, at least aberrant.

The leadership dimension shows an even stronger contrast between authoritarianism and sultanism. As Linz stated in his discussion of authoritarianism, leadership is exercised in an authoritarian regime "with formally ill-defined but actually quite predictable" norms.[11] In most authoritarian regimes some bureaucratic entities play an important part. These bureaucratic entities often retain or generate their own norms, which imply that there are procedural and normative limits on what leaders can ask them to do in their capacity as, for example, military officers, judges, tax officials, or police officers. However, a sultanistic leader simply "demands unconditional administrative compliance, for the official's loyalty to his office is not an impersonal commitment to impersonal tasks that define the extent and content of his office, but rather a servant's loyalty based on a strictly personal relationship to the ruler and an obligation that in principle permits no limitation."[12]

We have now spelled our the central tendencies of five ideal-type regimes in the modern world, four of which are nondemocratic. We are ready for the next step, which is to explore why and how the *type* of prior nondemocratic regime has an important effect on the democratic transition paths available and the tasks to be addressed before democracy can be consolidated.

NOTES

1. Juan J. Linz, "An Authoritarian Regime: The Case of Spain," in Erik Allardt and Yrjö Littunen, eds., *Cleavages, Ideologies and Party Systems* (Helsinki: Transactions of the Westermarck Society, 1964), 291–342. Reprinted in Erik Allardt and Stein Rokkan, eds., *Mass Politics: Studies in Political Sociology* (New York: Free Press, 1970). The definition is found on 255.

2. We arrive at this conclusion in the following fashion. The annual survey coordinated by Raymond D. Gastil employs a 7-point scale of the political rights and civil liberties dimensions of democracy. With the help of a panel of scholars, Gastil, from 1978 to 1987, classified annually 167 countries on this scale. For our purposes if we call the universe of democracies those countries that from 1978 to 1987 never received a score of lower than 2 on the Gastil scale for political rights and 3 for civil liberty, we come up with 42 countries. This is very close to the number of countries that

Coppedge and Reinicke classify as "full polyarchies" in their independent study of the year 1985. Since our interest is in how countries become democracies we will exclude those 42 countries from our universe of analysis. This would leave us with 125 countries in the universe we want to explore. If we then decide to call long-standing "totalitarian" regimes those regimes that received the lowest possible score on political rights and civil liberties on the Gastil scale for each year in the 1978–1987 period, we would have a total of nine countries that fall into the totalitarian classification. Thus, if one used the traditional typology, the Gastil scale would imply that 116 of 125 countries, or 92.8 percent of the universe under analysis, would have to be placed in the same typological space. See Raymond D. Gastil, ed., *Freedom in the World: Political Rights and Civil Liberties*, 1987–1988 (New York: Freedom House, 1990), 54–65.

3. Juan Linz, in his "Totalitarian and Authoritarian Regimes," in Fred I. Greenstein and Nelson W. Polsby, eds., *Handbook of Political Science* (Reading, Mass.: Addison-Wesley Publishing Co., 1975), 3:175–411, analyzed what he called "post-totalitarian authoritarian regimes," see 336–50. Here, with our focus on the available paths to democratic transition and the tasks of democratic consolidation, it seems to both of us that it is more useful to treat post-totalitarian regimes not as a subtype of authoritarianism, but as an ideal type in its own right.

4. For example, in mature post-totalitarian Hungary the most influential *samizdat* publication, *Beszélö*, was issued from 1982 to 1989, was issued as a quarterly with publication runs of 20,000. Information supplied to Alfred Stepan by the publisher and editorial board member, Miklós Haraszti. Budapest, August 1994.

5. Hungary in 1988–89 represents a mature post-totalitarian regime which, by engaging in extensive detotalitarianization and by increasingly recognizing the legitimacy of other parties, had experienced significant out-of-type changes even before the Communist Party lost power. * * *

6. The reference, of course, is to Albert Hirschman, *Exit, Voice and Loyalty* (Cambridge: Harvard University Press, 1970), 59. For a fascinating discussion of this dynamic in relation to the collapse of the GDR, see Hirschman, "Exit, Voice and the Fate of the German Democratic Republic: An Essay on Conceptual History," *World Politics* 45:2 (January 1993): 173–202.

7. On the ideological and moral attractiveness of revolutionary Marxist-Leninism as a total system and the "vacuum" left in the wake of its collapse, see Ernest Gellner, "Homeland of the Unrevolution," *Daedalus* (Summer 1993): 141–54.

8. Max Weber, *Economy and Society: An Outline of Interpretive Sociology*, ed. Guenther Roth and Claus Wittich (Berkeley: University of California Press, 1978), 1:231, 232. Italics in the original.

9. Linz, "Totalitarian and Authoritarian Regimes," 259–63.

10. Ibid., 260.

11. Ibid., 255.

12. Ibid., 260.

Steven Levitsky and Lucan A. Way
THE RISE OF COMPETITIVE AUTHORITARIANISM

The post–Cold War world has been marked by the proliferation of hybrid political regimes. In different ways, and to varying degrees, polities across much of Africa (Ghana, Kenya, Mozambique, Zambia, Zimbabwe), postcommunist Eurasia (Albania, Croatia, Russia. Serbia, Ukraine), Asia (Malaysia, Taiwan), and Latin America (Haiti, Mexico, Paraguay, Peru) combined democratic rules with authoritarian governance during the 1990s. Scholars often treated these regimes as incomplete or transitional forms of democracy. Yet in many cases these expectations (or hopes) proved overly optimistic. Particularly in Africa and the former Soviet Union, many regimes have either remained hybrid or moved in an authoritarian direction. It may therefore be time to stop thinking of these cases in terms of transitions to democracy and to begin thinking about the specific types of regimes they actually are.

In recent years, many scholars have pointed to the importance of hybrid regimes. Indeed, recent academic writings have produced a variety of labels for mixed cases, including not only "hybrid regime" but also "semidemocracy," "virtual democracy," "electoral democracy," "pseudodemocracy," "illiberal democracy," "semi-authoritarianism," "soft authoritarianism," "electoral authoritarianism," and Freedom House's "Partly Free."[1] Yet much of this literature suffers from two important weaknesses. First, many studies are characterized by a democratizing bias. Analyses frequently treat mixed regimes as partial or "diminished" forms of democracy,[2] or as undergoing prolonged transitions to democracy. Such characterizations imply that these cases are moving in a democratic direction. Yet as both Jeffrey Herbst and Thomas Carothers have recently argued, this is often not the case.[3] Although some hybrid regimes (Mexico, Senegal, Taiwan) underwent democratic transitions in the 1990s, others (Azerbaijan, Belarus) moved in a distinctly authoritarian direction. Still others either remained stable or moved in multiple directions (Malaysia, Russia, Ukraine, Zambia, Zimbabwe), making the unidirectional implications of the word "transitional" misleading.

Second, terms like "semidemocratic," "semiauthoritarian," and "Partly Free" are often used as residual categories and tend to gloss over important differences among regime types. For example, El Salvador, Latvia, and Ukraine were all hybrid regimes in the early 1990s, and each received a combined political rights and civil liberties score of six—or "Partly Free"—from Freedom House in 1992–93. Yet these regimes differed in fundamental ways. Whereas in Latvia the principal undemocratic feature was the absence of citizenship rights for people of Russian descent, in El Salvador the main undemocratic features included substantial human rights violations and the absence of civilian control over the military. Ukraine possessed both universal citizenship rights and a civilian-controlled military, but civil liberties were frequently violated and incumbents routinely abused or manipulated democratic procedures. Hence, although each of these cases could be categorized as "hybrid," "semidemocratic," or "partly free," such labels obscure crucial differences—differences that may have important causal implications. Different mixes of authoritarian and democratic features have distinct historical roots, and they may have different implications for economic performance, human rights, and the prospects for democracy.

From *Journal of Democracy* 13, no. 2 (April 2002), pp. 51–65.

Defining Competitive Authoritarianism

This article examines one particular type of "hybrid" regime: *competitive authoritarianism.* In competitive authoritarian regimes, formal democratic institutions are widely viewed as the principal means of obtaining and exercising political authority. Incumbents violate those rules so often and to such an extent, however, that the regime fails to meet conventional minimum standards for democracy. Examples include Croatia under Franjo Tudjman, Serbia under Slobodan Milošević, Russia under Vladimir Putin, Ukraine under Leonid Kravchuk and Leonid Kuchma, Peru under Alberto Fujimori, and post-1995 Haiti, as well as Albania, Armenia, Ghana, Kenya, Malaysia, Mexico, and Zambia through much of the 1990s. Although scholars have characterized many of these regimes as partial or "diminished" forms of democracy, we agree with Juan Linz that they may be better described as a (diminished) form of authoritarianism.[4]

Competitive authoritarianism must be distinguished from democracy on the one hand and full-scale authoritarianism on the other. Modern democratic regimes all meet four minimum criteria: (1) Executives and legislatures are chosen through elections that are open, free, and fair; (2) virtually all adults possess the right to vote; (3) political rights and civil liberties, including freedom of the press, freedom of association, and freedom to criticize the government without reprisal, are broadly protected; and (4) elected authorities possess real authority to govern, in that they are not subject to the tutelary control of military or clerical leaders.[5] Although even fully democratic regimes may at times violate one or more of these criteria, such violations are not broad or systematic enough to seriously impede democratic challenges to incumbent governments. In other words, they do not fundamentally alter the playing field between government and opposition.[6]

In competitive authoritarian regimes, by contrast, violations of these criteria are both frequent enough and serious enough to create an uneven playing field between government and opposition. Although elections are regularly held and are generally free of massive fraud, incumbents routinely abuse state resources, deny the opposition adequate media coverage, harass opposition candidates and their supporters, and in some cases manipulate electoral results. Journalists, opposition politicians, and other government critics may be spied on, threatened, harassed, or arrested. Members of the opposition may be jailed, exiled, or—less frequently—even assaulted or murdered. Regimes characterized by such abuses cannot be called democratic.

Competitive authoritarianism must therefore be distinguished from unstable, ineffective, or otherwise flawed types of regimes that nevertheless meet basic standards of democracy, and this includes what Guillermo O'Donnell has called "delegative democracies."[7] According to O'Donnell, delegative democracies are characterized by low levels of horizontal accountability (checks and balances) and therefore exhibit powerful, plebiscitarian, and occasionally abusive executives. Yet such regimes meet minimum standards for democracy. Delegative democracy thus applies to such cases as Argentina and Brazil in the early 1990s, but not to Peru after Fujimori's 1992 presidential self-coup.

Yet if competitive authoritarian regimes fall short of democracy, they also fall short of full-scale authoritarianism. Although incumbents in competitive authoritarian regimes may routinely manipulate formal democratic rules, they are unable to eliminate them or reduce them to a mere façade. Rather than openly violating democratic rules (for example, by banning or repressing the opposition and the media), incumbents are more likely to use bribery, co-optation, and more subtle forms of persecution, such as the use of tax authorities, compliant judiciaries, and other state agencies to "legally" harass, persecute, or extort cooperative behavior from critics. Yet even if the cards are stacked in favor of autocratic incumbents, the persistence of meaningful democratic institutions creates arenas through which opposition forces may—and frequently do—pose significant challenges. As a result, even though democratic institutions may be badly flawed, both authoritarian incumbents and their opponents must take them seriously.

In this sense, competitive authoritarianism is distinct from what might be called "façade" electoral regimes—that is, regimes in which electoral institutions exist but yield no meaningful contestation for power (such as Egypt, Singapore, and Uzbekistan in the 1990s). Such regimes have been called "pseudodemocracies," "virtual democracies," and "electoral authoritarian" regimes. In our view, they are cases of full-scale authoritarianism.[8] The line between this type of regime and competitive authoritarianism can be hard to draw, and noncompetitive electoral institutions may one day become competitive (as occurred in Mexico). It is essential, however, to distinguish regimes in which democratic institutions offer an important channel through which the opposition may seek power from those regimes in which democratic rules simply serve as to legitimate an existing autocratic leadership.

Finally, competitive authoritarianism must be distinguished from other types of hybrid regimes. Regimes may mix authoritarian and democratic features in a variety of ways, and competitive authoritarianism should not be viewed as encompassing all of these regime forms. Other hybrid regime types include "exclusive republics"[9] (regimes with strong democratic institutions but highly restrictive citizenship laws) and "tutelary" or "guided" democracies—competitive regimes in which nondemocratic actors such as military or religious authorities wield veto power.

Four Arenas of Democratic Contestation

Due to the persistence of meaningful democratic institutions in competitive authoritarian regimes, arenas of contestation exist through which opposition forces may periodically challenge, weaken, and occasionally even defeat autocratic incumbents. Four such arenas are of particular importance:

(1) the electoral arena; (2) the legislative arena; (3) the judiciary arena; and (4) the media.

(1) The electoral arena. The first and most important arena of contestation is the electoral arena. In authoritarian regimes, elections either do not exist or are not seriously contested. Electoral competition is eliminated either de jure, as in Cuba and China, or de facto, as in Kazakhstan and Uzbekistan. In the latter, opposition parties are routinely banned or disqualified from electoral competition, and opposition leaders are often jailed. In addition, independent or outside observers are prevented from verifying results via parallel vote counts, which creates widespread opportunities for vote stealing. As a result, opposition forces do not present a serious electoral threat to incumbents, and elections are, for all intents and purposes, noncompetitive. Thus Kazakhstani president Nursultan Nazarbayev was reelected in 1999 with 80 percent of the vote, and in Uzbekistan, President Islam Karimov was reelected in 2000 with 92 percent of the vote. (As a rule of thumb, regimes in which presidents are reelected with more than 70 percent of the vote can generally be considered noncompetitive.) In such cases, the death or violent overthrow of the president is often viewed as a more likely means of succession than his electoral defeat.

In competitive authoritarian regimes, by contrast, elections are often bitterly fought. Although the electoral process may be characterized by large-scale abuses of state power, biased media coverage, (often violent) harassment of opposition candidates and activists,[10] and an overall lack of transparency, elections are regularly held, competitive (in that major opposition parties and candidates usually participate), and generally free of massive fraud. In many cases, the presence of international observers or the existence of parallel vote-counting procedures limits the capacity of incumbents to engage in large-scale fraud. As a result, elections may generate considerable uncertainty, and autocratic incumbents must therefore take them seriously. For example, Russian president Boris Yeltsin in 1996 and Ukrainian president Leonid Kuchma in 1999 faced strong electoral challenges from former communist parties. Despite concerted efforts to use blackmail and other techniques to secure votes,[11] Kuchma won only 35 percent of the vote in the first round of the 1999 presidential elections and 56 percent in the second round. In Kenya, longtime autocrat Daniel arap Moi won reelection with bare pluralities in 1992 and 1997, and in Zimbabwe, the opposition Movement for Democratic Change nearly won the 2000 parliamentary elections. In several cases, opposition forces have managed to defeat autocratic incumbents or their hand-picked candidates, as occurred in Nicaragua in 1990, Zambia in 1991, Malawi and Ukraine in 1994, Albania in 1997, and Ghana in 2000.

Although incumbents may manipulate election results, this often costs them dearly and can even bring them down. In Peru, for example, Fujimori was able to gain reelection in 2000 but was forced to resign amid scandal months later. Similarly, efforts by Milošević to falsify Serbian election results in 2000 led to a regime crisis and the president's removal. Regime crises resulting from electoral fraud also occurred in Mexico in 1988 and Armenia in 1996.

(2) The legislative arena. A second arena of contestation is the legislature. In most full-scale authoritarian regimes, legislatures either do not exist or are so thoroughly controlled by the ruling party that conflict between the legislature and the executive branch is virtually unthinkable. In competitive authoritarian regimes, legislatures tend to be relatively weak, but they occasionally become focal points of opposition activity. This is particularly likely in cases in which incumbents lack strong majority parties. In both Ukraine and Russia in the 1990s, for example, presidents were faced with recalcitrant parliaments dominated by former communist and other left-wing parties. The Ukrainian parliament repeatedly blocked or watered down economic reform legislation proposed by President Kuchma, and in 2000–2001, despite Kuchma's threats to

take "'appropriate" measures if it did not cooperate, parliament blocked the president's effort to call a referendum aimed at reducing the powers of the legislature. Although incumbents may attempt to circumvent or even shut down the legislature (as in Peru in 1992 and Russia in 1993), such actions tend to be costly, particularly in the international arena. Thus both Fujimori and Yeltsin held new legislative elections within three years of their "self-coups," and Yeltsin continued to face opposition from the post-1993-coup parliament.

Even where incumbent executives enjoy large legislative majorities, opposition forces may use the legislature as a place for meeting and organizing and (to the extent that an independent media exists) as a public platform from which to denounce the regime. In Peru, despite the fact that opposition parties exerted little influence over the legislative process between 1995 and 2000, anti-Fujimori legislators used congress (and media coverage of it) as a place to air their views. In Ukraine in November 2000, opposition deputy Aleksandr Moroz used parliament to accuse the president of murder and to distribute damaging tapes of the president to the press.

(3) The judicial arena. A third arena of potential contestation is the judiciary. Governments in competitive authoritarian regimes routinely attempt to subordinate the judiciary, often via impeachment, or, more subtly, through bribery, extortion, and other mechanisms of co-optation, In Peru, for example, scores of judges—including several Supreme Court justices—were entwined in the web of patronage, corruption, and blackmail constructed by Fujimori's intelligence chief, Vladimiro Montesinos. In Russia, when the Constitutional Court declared Yeltsin's 1993 decree disbanding parliament to be unconstitutional, Yeltsin cut off the Court's phone lines and took away its guards. In some cases, governments resort to threats and violence. In Zimbabwe, after the Supreme Court ruled that occupations of white-owned farmland—part of the Mugabe government's land-redistribution policy—were illegal, independent justices received a wave of violent threats from pro-government "war veterans." Four justices, in-

cluding Chief Justice Anthony Gubbay, opted for early retirement in 2001 and were replaced by justices with closer ties to the government.

Yet the combination of formal judicial independence and incomplete control by the executive can give maverick judges an opening. In Ukraine, for example, the Constitutional Court stipulated that President Kuchma's referendum to reduce the powers of the legislature was not binding. In Slovakia, the Constitutional Court prevented Vladimír Mečiar's government from denying the opposition seats in parliament in 1994, and in Serbia, the courts legitimized local opposition electoral victories in 1996. Courts have also protected media and opposition figures from state persecution. In Croatia, the courts acquitted an opposition weekly that had been charged with falsely accusing President Tudjman of being a devotee of Spain's Francisco Franco. Similarly, in Malaysia in 2001, a High Court judge released two dissidents who had been jailed under the regime's Internal Security Act and publicly questioned the need for such a draconian law.[12]

Although competitive authoritarian governments may subsequently punish judges who rule against them, such acts against formally independent judiciaries may generate important costs in terms of domestic and international legitimacy. In Peru, for example, the pro-Fujimori congress sacked three members of the Constitutional Tribunal in 1997 after they attempted to block Fujimori's constitutionally dubious bid for a third presidential term. The move generated sharp criticism both domestically and abroad, however, and the case remained a thorn in the regime's side for the rest of the decade.

(4) The media. Finally, the media are often a central point of contention in competitive authoritarian regimes. In most full-blown autocracies, the media are entirely state-owned, heavily censored, or systematically repressed. Leading television and radio stations are controlled by the government (or its close allies), and major independent newspapers and magazines are either prohibited by law (as in Cuba) or de facto eliminated (as in Uzbekistan and

Turkmenistan). Journalists who provoke the ire of the government risk arrest, deportation, and even assassination. In competitive authoritarian regimes, by contrast, independent media outlets are not only legal but often quite influential, and journalists—though frequently threatened and periodically attacked—often emerge as important opposition figures. In Peru, for example, independent newspapers such as *La República* and *El Comercio* and weekly magazines such as *Sí* and *Caretas* operated freely throughout the 1990s. In Ukraine, newspapers such as *Zerkalo nedeli, Den,* and, more recently, *Vicherni visti* functioned as important sources of independent views on the Kuchma government.

Independent media outlets often play a critical watchdog role by investigating and exposing government malfeasance. The Peruvian media uncovered a range of government abuses, including the 1992 massacre of students at La Cantuta University and the forgery of the signatures needed for Fujimori's party to qualify for the 2000 elections. In Russia, Vladimir Gusinsky's Independent TV was an important source of criticism of the Yeltsin government, particularly with respect to its actions in Chechnya. In Zimbabwe, the *Daily News* played an important role in exposing the abuses of the Mugabe government. Media outlets may also serve as mouthpieces for opposition forces. In Serbia, the Belgrade radio station B-92 served as a key center of opposition to Milošević in the second half of the 1990s. Newspapers played an important role in supporting opposition forces in Panama and Nicaragua in the late 1980s.

Executives in competitive authoritarian regimes often actively seek to suppress the independent media, using more subtle mechanisms of repression than their counterparts in authoritarian regimes. These methods often include bribery, the selective allocation of state advertising, the manipulation of debts and taxes owed by media outlets, the fomentation of conflicts among stockholders, and restrictive press laws that facilitate the prosecution of independent and opposition journalists. In Russia, the government took advantage of Independent TV's debts to the main gas company, Gazprom, to engineer a takeover by government-friendly forces. In Peru, the Fujimori government gained de facto control over all of the country's privately owned television stations through a combination of bribery and legal shenanigans, such as the invalidation of Channel 2 owner Baruch Ivcher's citizenship. Governments also make extensive use of libel laws to harass or persecute independent newspapers "legally." In Ghana, for example, the Jerry Rawlings government used colonial-era libel statutes to imprison several newspaper editors and columnists in the 1990s, and in Croatia, the Open Society Institute reported in 1997 that major independent newspapers had been hit by more than 230 libel suits. Similarly, Armenia's government used libel suits to quiet press criticism after the country's controversial 1996 elections.[13]

Yet efforts to repress the media may be costly to incumbents in competitive authoritarian regimes. For example, when in 1996 the Tudjman government in Croatia tried to revoke the license of Radio 101, a popular independent station in the capital, the massive protests that broke out both galvanized the opposition and temporarily split the ruling party. In Ukraine in 2000, charges that President Kuchma had sought the killing of an opposition journalist led to large domestic protests and partial isolation from the West. In Peru, the persecution and exiling of Ivcher provoked substantial protest at home and became a focal point of criticism abroad.

Inherent Tensions

Authoritarian governments may coexist indefinitely with meaningful democratic institutions. As long as incumbents avoid egregious (and well-publicized) rights abuses and do not cancel or openly steal elections, the contradictions inherent in competitive authoritarianism may be manageable. Using bribery, co-optation, and various forms of "legal" persecution, governments may limit opposition challenges without provoking massive protest or international repudiation.

Yet the coexistence of democratic rules and autocratic methods aimed at keeping incumbents in power creates an inherent source of instability. The presence of elections, legislatures, courts, and an independent media creates periodic opportunities for challenges by opposition forces. Such challenges create a serious dilemma for autocratic incumbents. On the one hand, repressing them is costly, largely because the challenges tend to be both formally legal and widely perceived (domestically and internationally) as legitimate. On the other hand, incumbents could lose power if they let democratic challenges run their course.[14] Periods of serious democratic contestation thus bring out the contradictions inherent in competitive authoritarianism, forcing autocratic incumbents to choose between egregiously violating democratic rules, at the cost of international isolation and domestic conflict, and allowing the challenge to proceed, at the cost of possible defeat. The result is often some kind of regime crisis, as occurred in Mexico in 1988; Nicaragua in 1990; Zambia in 1991; Russia in 1993; Armenia in 1996; Albania in 1997; Ghana, Peru, Serbia, and Ukraine in 2000; and Zambia (again) in 2001. A similar crisis appears likely to emerge in Zimbabwe surrounding the March 2002 presidential election.

In some cases, such as those of Kenya, Malaysia, Russia, and Ukraine, autocratic incumbents weathered the storm. In several of these countries, the regime cracked down and dug in deeper. In other cases, such as Nicaragua in 1990, Zambia in 1991, and Ghana and Mexico in 2000, competitive authoritarian governments failed to crack down and lost power. In still other cases, including Peru and Serbia, autocrats attempted to crack down but, in doing so, were badly weakened and eventually fell.

But succession is not democratization. Although in many cases (Croatia, Nicaragua, Peru, Slovakia, Serbia) incumbent turnover resulted in democratic transitions, in other cases, including Albania, Zambia, Ukraine, and Belarus, newly elected leaders continued or even intensified many of the authoritarian practices of their predecessors. Hence, while the removal of autocratic elites creates an important *opportunity* for regime change and even democratization, it does not ensure such an outcome.

Although it is beyond the scope of this article to explain variations in the capacity of competitive authoritarian regimes to survive crises brought about by episodes of democratic contestation, one pattern is worth noting.[15] In regions with closer ties to the West, particularly Latin America and Central Europe, the removal of autocratic incumbents has generally resulted in democratization in the post–Cold War period. In Latin America, for example, four out of five competitive authoritarian regimes democratized after 1990 (the Dominican Republic, Mexico, Nicaragua, and Peru, but not Haiti). Similarly, during the same period four out of five competitive authoritarian regimes in Central Europe democratized (Croatia, Serbia, Slovakia, and Romania, but not Albania). By contrast, the record of competitive authoritarian regimes in Africa and the former Soviet Union is strikingly different. Among former Soviet republics, only one competitive authoritarian regime (Moldova) democratized in the 1990s.

This evidence suggests that proximity to the West may have been an important factor shaping the trajectory of competitive authoritarian regimes in the 1990s. Linkages to the West—in the form of cultural and media influence, elite networks, demonstration effects, and direct pressure from Western governments—appear to have raised the costs of authoritarian entrenchment, making the democratization of competitive authoritarian regimes more likely. Where Western linkages were weaker, or where alternative, nondemocratic hegemons (such as Russia or China) exerted substantial influence, competitive authoritarian regimes were more likely either to persist or to move in a more authoritarian direction.

Paths to Competitive Authoritarianism

Although competitive authoritarian regimes are not a new phenomenon (historical examples include parts of East Central Europe in the 1920s and Argentina under Perón from 1946 to 1955), they have clearly proliferated in recent years. Competitive authoritarianism emerged out of three different regime paths during the 1990s. One path was the decay of a full-blown authoritarian regime. In these cases, established authoritarian regimes were compelled—often by a combination of domestic and international pressure—either to adopt formal democratic institutions or to adhere seriously to what had previously been façade democratic institutions. Yet due to the weakness of opposition movements, transitions fell short of democracy, and incumbents proved adept at manipulating or selectively adhering to the new democratic rules. Transitions of this type occurred across much of sub-Saharan Africa, where economic crisis and international pressure compelled established autocrats to call multiparty elections, but where many transitions fell short of democratization and many autocrats retained power.

A second path to competitive authoritarianism was the collapse of an authoritarian regime, followed by the emergence of a new, competitive authoritarian regime. In these cases, weak electoral regimes emerged, more or less by default, in the wake of an authoritarian breakdown. Although the absence of democratic traditions and weak civil societies created opportunities for elected governments to rule autocratically, these governments lacked the capacity to consolidate authoritarian rule. This path was followed by such postcommunist countries as Armenia, Croatia, Romania, Russia, Serbia, and Ukraine, as well as by Haiti after 1994.

A third path to competitive authoritarianism was the decay of a democratic regime. In these cases, deep and often long-standing political and economic crises created conditions under which freely elected governments undermined democratic institutions—either via a presidential "self-coup" or through selective, incremental abuses—but lacked the will or capacity to eliminate them entirely. Examples of such transitions include Peru in the early 1990s and perhaps contemporary Venezuela.

The roots of this recent proliferation lie in the difficulties associated with consolidating both democratic *and* authoritarian regimes in the immediate post–Cold War period. Notwithstanding the global advance of democracy in the 1990s (and the democratic optimism that it inspired among scholars), in much of the world democratic regimes remained difficult to establish or sustain. A large number of transitions took place in countries with high levels of poverty, inequality, and illiteracy; weak states and civil societies; institutional instability; contested national borders; and—in parts of the former communist world—continued domination by the state of the economy, major religious institutions, and other areas of social activity.

Yet if the prospects for full-scale democratization remained bleak in much of the post–Cold War world, so too were the prospects for building and sustaining full-scale authoritarian regimes.[16] In large part, this change was a product of the post–Cold War international environment. Western liberalism's triumph and the Soviet collapse undermined the legitimacy of alternative regime models and created strong incentives for peripheral states to adopt formal democratic institutions. As Andrew Janos has argued, periods of liberal hegemony place a "web of constraints" on nondemocratic governments that seek to maintain international respectability and viability. Thus, during the brief period of liberal hegemony that followed World War I, relatively authoritarian governments in Central Europe faced strong pressure to tolerate a semi-free press, regular scrutiny from opposition members of parliament, and a quasi-independent judiciary.[17] When Western liberal states are challenged by authoritarian counter-hegemonic powers, however, these "webs of constraints" tend to disappear. Counter-hegemonic powers provide alternative sources of legitimacy and military and economic assistance, thereby weakening the incentive for governing elites to maintain formal democratic institutions. Thus the emergence of Nazi Germany and Soviet Russia as regional powers contributed to the collapse of Central European hybrid regimes in the 1930s, and the strength of the Soviet Union facilitated the establishment of Leninist dictatorships across much of the Third World

during the Cold War. When Western powers face a challenger to their hegemony, they are more likely to tolerate autocracies that can present themselves as buffers against their rivals.

The 1990s marked a period of Western liberal hegemony similar to that of the 1920s but much broader in scope. International influences took many forms, including demonstration effects, conditionality (as in the case of European Union membership), direct state-to-state pressure (in the form of sanctions, behind-the-scenes diplomacy, and even direct military intervention), and the activities of emerging transnational actors and institutions. In this new context, the liberal democratic model gained unprecedented acceptance among postcommunist and Third World elites. Perhaps more importantly, the absence of alternative sources of military and economic aid increased the importance of being on good terms with Western governments and institutions. Although the effect of international pressure varied considerably across regions (and even across countries), for most governments in most poorer and middle-income countries, the benefits of adopting formal democratic institutions—and the costs of maintaining overtly authoritarian ones—rose considerably in the 1990s.

Emerging and potential autocrats also confronted important domestic impediments to the consolidation of authoritarian regimes. To consolidate a fully closed regime, authoritarian elites must eliminate all major sources of contestation through the systematic repression or co-optation of potential opponents. Such action requires both elite cohesion and a minimally effective—and financially solvent—state apparatus. Resource scarcity has made it more difficult for leaders to sustain the patronage networks that previously undergirded authoritarian state structures. In addition, uncertain hierarchical control over repressive organs, while heightening the risk of civil war, has also increased the difficulty of consolidating authoritarian rule. Finally, in many postcommunist regimes the dispersal of control over different state and economic resources among different groups made it difficult for any single leader to establish complete control, resulting in a kind of pluralism by default.

A substantial number of regimes *were* able to overcome the domestic and international obstacles to authoritarian rule in the 1990s. Some benefited from pockets of permissiveness in the international system, due in large part to economic or security issues that trumped democracy promotion on Western foreign policy agendas. Others benefited from state control over revenues from valuable commodities (such as oil), which undermined the development of an autonomous civil society and gave rulers the means to co-opt potential opponents, and still others took advantage of quasi-traditional elite networks that facilitated the establishment of neopatrimonial regimes (as in Central Asia).

Yet in much of Africa, Latin America, and postcommunist Eurasia in the 1990s, emerging or potential autocrats lacked these advantages. Due to a combination of international pressure, state weakness, and elite fragmentation, many incumbents found the cost of co-opting or repressing opponents to be prohibitively high. As a result, even some highly autocratic leaders were unable to eliminate important arenas of contestation. The sources of authoritarian weakness varied across cases. In Albania and Haiti, for example, international factors were probably decisive in preventing full-scale authoritarian rule. In Africa, a contraction of resources caused by the end of Cold War sponsorship and the conditionality imposed by international financial institutions left some governments too weak to co-opt or repress even relatively feeble opposition challenges.[18] In post-Soviet countries such as Moldova, Russia, and Ukraine, the fragmentation of control over state and economic resources generated political competition even where civil society remained weak. What is common to virtually all of these cases, however, is that pluralism and democratic contestation persisted less because elites wanted them than because elites simply could not get rid of them.

In the 1990s, then, competitive authoritarian regimes were most likely to emerge where conditions were unfavorable to the consolidation of either democratic or authoritarian regimes. It must be noted, of course, that such conditions do not necessarily result in competitive authoritarianism. In some cases, including El Salvador, Mali, and Mongolia, democracy may take hold in spite of highly unfavorable conditions. In other cases, the breakdown of authoritarian rule may result in state collapse and civil war, as occurred in Liberia, Sierra Leone, and Somalia.

Conceptualizing Nondemocracies

We conclude by echoing Thomas Carothers' call to move beyond what he calls the "transition paradigm."[19] It is now clear that early hopes for democratization in much of the world were overly optimistic. Many authoritarian regimes have survived the "third wave" of democratization. In other cases, the collapse of one kind of authoritarianism yielded not democracy but a new form of nondemocratic rule. Indeed, a decade after the collapse of the Soviet Union, the majority of the world's independent states remained nondemocratic. Yet whereas an extensive literature has emerged concerning the causes and consequences of democratization, emerging types of democracy, and issues of democratic consolidation, remarkably little research has been undertaken on the emergence or persistence of nondemocratic regimes.

The post–Cold War Western liberal hegemony, global economic change, developments in media and communications technologies, and the growth of international networks aimed at promoting democracy and human rights all have contributed to reshaping the opportunities and constraints facing authoritarian elites. As a result, some forms of authoritarianism, such as totalitarianism and bureaucratic authoritarianism, have become more difficult to sustain. At the same time, however, several new (or partially new) nondemocratic regime types took on greater importance in the 1990s, including competitive authoritarianism. A range of other nondemocratic outcomes also gained in importance, including other types of hybrid regimes, postcommunist patrimonial dictatorships, and cases of sustained state collapse ("chaosocracy").[20] Research on these nondemocratic outcomes is critical to gaining a better understanding of the full (rather than hoped for) set of alternatives open to post–Cold War transitional regimes.

NOTES

The authors thank Jason Brownlee, Timothy Colton, Michael Coppedge, Keith Darden, Jorge Domínguez, Steve Hanson, Marc Morjé Howard, Rory MacFarquhar, Mitch Orenstein, Maria Popova, Andreas Schedler, Oxana Shevel, and Richard Snyder for their comments on earlier drafts of this article.

1. Terry Lynn Karl, "The Hybrid Regimes of Central America," *Journal of Democracy* 6 (July 1995): 72–87; William Case, "Can the 'Halfway House' Stand? Semidemocracy and Elite Theory in Three Southeast Asian Countries," *Comparative Politics* 28 (July 1996): 437–64; Richard A. Joseph, "Africa, 1990–1997: From *Abertura* to Closure," *Journal of Democracy* 9 (April 1998): 3–17; Larry Diamond, *Developing Democracy: Toward Consolidation* (Baltimore: Johns Hopkins University Press, 1999); Fareed Zakaria, "The Rise of Illiberal Democracy," *Foreign Affairs* 76 (November–December 1997): 22–41; Thomas Carothers, *Aiding Democracy Abroad: The Learning Curve* (Washington, D.C.: Carnegie Endowment for International Peace, 1999); Gordon P. Means, "Soft Authoritarianism in Malaysia and Singapore," *Journal of Democracy* 7 (October 1996): 103–17; Andreas Schedler, "Mexico's Victory: The Democratic Revelation," *Journal of Democracy* 11 (October 2000): 5–19; and M. Steven Fish, "Authoritarianism despite Elections: Russia in Light of Democratic Theory and Practice," paper prepared for delivery at the 2001 Annual Meeting of the American Political Science Association, San Francisco, 30 August–2 September 2001.

2. See David Collier and Steven Levitsky, "Democracy with Adjectives: Conceptual Innovation in Comparative Research," *World Politics* 49 (April 1997): 430–51.

3. See Jeffrey Herbst, "Political Liberalization in Africa after Ten Years," *Comparative Politics* 33 (April 2001): 357–75; Thomas Carothers, "The End of the Transition Paradigm," *Journal of Democracy* 13 (January 2002): 5–21.

4. Juan J. Linz, *Totalitarian and Authoritarian Regimes* (Boulder, Colo.: Lynne Rienner, 2000), 34.

5. See Scott Mainwaring, Daniel Brinks, and Aníbal Pérez Linan, "Classifying Political Regimes in Latin America, 1945–1999," *Studies in Comparative International Development* 36 (Spring 2001). This definition is consistent with what Larry Diamond calls "mid-range" conceptions of democracy (Larry Diamond, *Developing Democracy*, 13–15).

6. Obviously, the exact point at which violations of civil and political rights begin to fundamentally alter the playing field is difficult to discern and will always be open to debate. However, the problem of scoring borderline cases is common to all regime conceptualizations.

7. Guillermo O'Donnell, "Delegative Democracy," *Journal of Democracy* 5 (January 1994): 55–69.

8. Larry Diamond, *Developing Democracy*, 15–16; Richard A. Joseph, "Africa, 1990–1997"; Jason Brownlee, "Double Edged Institutions: Electoral Authoritarianism in Egypt and Iran," paper presented at the 2001 Annual Meeting of the American Political Science Association, San Francisco, 30 August–2 September 2001.

9. Philip G. Roeder, "Varieties of Post-Soviet Authoritarian Regimes," *Post-Soviet Affairs* 10 (January–March 1994): 61–101.

10. In Kenya, government-backed death squads were responsible for large-scale violence, particularly in ethnic minority areas. See Joel Barkan and Njuguna Ng'ethe, "Kenya Tries Again," in Larry Diamond and Marc F. Planner, eds., *Democratization in Africa* (Baltimore: Johns Hopkins University Press, 1999), 185. Substantial violence against opposition forces was also seen in Serbia and Zimbabwe in the 1990s.

11. See Keith Darden, "Blackmail as a Tool of State Domination: Ukraine under Kuchma," *East European Constitutional Review* 10 (Spring–Summer 2001): 67–71.

12. *The Economist*, 14 July 2001, 37.

13. H. Kwasi Prempeh, "A New Jurisprudence for Africa," *Journal of Democracy* 10 (July 1999): 138; Nebojsa Bjelakovic and Sava Tatic, "Croatia: Another Year of Bleak Continuities," *Transitions-on-Line*, http://archive.tol.cz/countries/croar97.html (1997); Mikhail Diloyen, "Journalists Fall through the Legal Cracks in Armenia," *Eurasia Insight* (June 2000).

14. These dilemmas are presented in an insightful way in Andreas Schedler, "The Nested Game of Democratization by Elections," *International Political Science Review* 23 (January 2002).

15. For a more developed explanation, see Steven Levitsky and Lucan A. Way, "Competitive Authoritarianism: Hybrid Regime Change in Peru and Ukraine in Comparative Perspective," Studies in Public Policy Working Paper No. 355 (Glasgow: University of Strathclyde Center for the Study of Public Policy, 2001).

16. On obstacles to authoritarianism in the former Soviet Union, see Philip G. Roeder, "The Rejection of Authoritarianism," in Richard Anderson, M. Stephen Fish, Stephen E. Hanson, and Philip G. Roeder, *Postcommunism and the Theory of Democracy* (Princeton: Princeton University Press, 2001).

17. Andrew Janos, *East Central Europe in the Modern World: The Politics of Borderlands from Pre- to Postcommunism* (Stanford, Calif.: Stanford University Press, 2000), 97–99.

18. Michael Bratton and Nicolas van de Walle, *Democratic Experiments in Africa: Regime Transitions in Comparative Perspective* (New York: Cambridge University Press, 1997), 100.

19. Thomas Carothers, "The End of the Transition Paradigm."

20. See Richard Snyder, "Does Lootable Wealth Breed Disorder? States, Regimes, and the Political Economy of Extraction," paper presented at the 2001 Annual Meeting of the American Political Science Association, San Francisco, 30 August–2 September 2001. See also Juan J. Linz, *Totalitarian and Authoritarian Regimes*, 37.

Larry Diamond

THE RULE OF LAW VERSUS THE BIG MAN

As the articles in this cluster make clear, governance in Africa is in a state of transition or, some would say, suspension. Two powerful trends vie for dominance. One is the long-standing organization of African politics and states around autocratic personal rulers; highly centralized and overpowering presidencies; and steeply hierarchical, informal networks of patron-client relations that draw their symbolic and emotional glue from ethnic bonds. The other is the surge since 1990 of democratic impulses, principles, and institutions. Of course, the formal institutions of democracy—including free, fair, and competitive elections—can coexist with the informal practices of clientelism, corruption, ethnic mobilization, and personal rule by largely unchecked presidents. Indeed, much of the story of African politics over the last two decades has been the contest between these two approaches to power—even in countries that are formally democratic. But slowly, democracy, with its norms of freedom, participation, accountability, and trans-

From *Journal of Democracy* 19, no. 2 (April 2008), pp. 138–49.

parency, is giving rise to new and more vigorous horizontal forms of organization, in both the state and civil society.

According to Freedom House, fully half the 48 states of sub-Saharan Africa (hereafter "Africa") are democracies today, but analysts will inevitably differ on whether the glass is half-full or half-empty. I am more worried than Richard Joseph that democratization is starting to lose momentum in Africa. Certainly Kenya's calamitous December 2007 election, which triggered horrific violence and ethnic cleansing that few analysts fully anticipated, shows that nothing can be taken for granted. As Joseph and Kwasi Prempeh note, even the high-profile democracies in South Africa and Ghana are showing worrisome trends. Moreover, it is possible to argue that a number of the African countries Freedom House classifies as electoral democracies are really better scored as "competitive authoritarian states."[1]

Nevertheless, even if some of Africa's "democracies" hover in a gray zone between democracy and pseudodemocracy, the larger picture still represents historic progress. In the half-century since decolonization began, there have never been so many democracies and so much public pressure on democracy's behalf. Civil society has never been stronger, mass publics have never been so questioning and vigilant, and the natural impulse toward the reassertion of predatory personal rule has never faced so many constraints. Prempeh is right that these constraints remain weak relative to their counterparts in Europe and now parts of Asia and Latin America that are much more economically developed and better educated. Yet if we take Africa's history of abusive government as our measure, significant progress is evident.

Part of this progress is taking place at the level of specific democratic institutions. As Joel Barkan notes in his comparative analysis of six African legislatures, under certain circumstances, we see (even in Uganda's nondemocracy) the emergence of legislative coalitions for reform. These comprise legislators who (for varying motives) want to enhance their own branch's power relative to that of the executive. Doing so, he writes, entails institutional (and even constitutional)

changes to give African legislatures significantly more resources, and more financial independence. The same is true for African judiciaries and other institutions of horizontal accountability, such as ombudsmen and anticorruption commissions. When these bodies have serious leaders, significant resources, and independent legal authority, they can begin to cut away at seemingly impregnable dynamics of predatory corruption and abuse of power. With leadership, resources, and authority, Joseph notes, the Economic and Financial Crimes Commission of Nigeria made unprecedented progress in prosecuting venal governors and other prominent public officials—until the country's new president reassigned the Commission's chairman in late 2007.

When Africa's "second liberation" began in 1990, the continent was home to just three countries that could be called democracies (Botswana, Mauritius, and the Gambia) with a total population of only about three million. Between that year and 2008, more than twenty African countries made transitions to democracy or something near it.[2] Today, of the 24 African countries that Freedom House rates as democracies, eight are relatively "liberal," meaning that they score no worse than a 2 on FH's scales of political rights and civil liberties (where 1 is the most free and 7 the most repressive).

Between 2001 and 2007, twenty-two African countries experienced a net improvement in their freedom scores (though some were by a small margin from a very authoritarian starting point), while only nine countries suffered declines. In 2007 itself, however, eight African countries declined in freedom while only four gained. The most recent trend is moving slightly downward, then, but over the last six years African countries have continued improving in their levels of freedom and democracy, more than a decade after the onset of this democratic wave.

The picture looks worse, however, if we focus on Africa's biggest countries, the seven with populations above thirty million. South Africa is still a liberal democracy. None of the other six—Congo (Kinshasa), Ethiopia, Kenya, Nigeria, Sudan, and Tanzania—can be said to be a democracy at all.

Still, the general transformation of African politics has been extraordinary. Many of the electoral democracies that emerged after 1990—such as those in Benin, Mali, and South Africa—have persisted for more than a decade. Following two decades of rule under coupmaker Jerry Rawlings, Ghana has emerged as one of Africa's most liberal and vibrant democracies, reclaiming a leading position like that of its early postindependence years.

The positive trend is all the more remarkable when one looks at the many unlikely democratizers. They include four of the six poorest countries on the Human Development Index (Mali, Mozambique, Niger, and Sierra Leone) and several others in the bottom twenty (such as Benin, Burundi, Malawi, and Zambia), as well as four countries (Burundi, Liberia, Mozambique, and Sierra Leone) where democratization followed murderous civil conflicts, including the one in Burundi that left 200,000 dead.

Across Africa, the formal constitutional rules governing how leaders acquire and leave power are coming to matter more than ever before. As Daniel Posner and Daniel Young have shown in these pages, Africa's politics have grown less violent and more institutionalized since 1990.[3] Between that year and 2005, six presidents, including Uganda's Yoweri Museveni, succeeded in eviscerating term limits. But these cases were the minority. Powerful presidents such as Ghana's Rawlings and Kenya's Daniel Arap Moi, joined eventually by ten others, ran into term-limit provisions that forced them to step down. After more than two decades in power, Rawlings and Moi were tempted to hang on, but yielded to domestic and international pressure. Three African leaders—including President Olusegun Obasanjo in Nigeria—tried hard and failed to extend their presidencies. Further, from the 1960s through the 1980s, more than two-thirds of African leaders left power violently—usually, as a result of a coup or assassination. During the 1990s, Posner and Young find, peaceful exits—principally as a result of electoral defeat or voluntary resignation—became the norm. Between 2000 and 2005, roughly four out of five African leaders were replaced this way.

Even more decisive than the rise of democracy has been the end of the one-party state. Since the 1990s, African elections have become increasingly regular and frequent, and almost all of them have been contested. As has been the case in Nigeria—and in Ethiopia, the Gambia, Kenya, Uganda, and Zimbabwe, among others—many of these elections have been brutally fought and outrageously rigged. But the sight of a ruling party or a "big man" losing is no longer quite so odd. Whereas only one African president was defeated at the polls between 1960 and 1990, incumbent presidents lost one out of every seven tries at reelection between 1990 and 2005.[4] Moreover, electoral alternation has significant positive effects on public support for and confidence in democracy.[5]

Why do African presidents feel more constrained now? Posner and Young advance two intriguing explanations. One is greater sensitivity to international pressure. The median level of foreign aid (relative to the overall economy) in countries where presidents did not attempt to secure third terms was almost twice as high as in those countries where the presidents did (and often succeeded). The other explanation points to public opinion. The nine African presidents who declined to seek a third term had narrower electoral mandates than the nine who did, suggesting a greater sensitivity to public opinion.

Building from the Bottom Up

This points to another positive trend in Africa, with potentially lasting consequences: the growth of civil society.[6] As wide varieties of associations independent of ruling parties have begun to engage in political dialogue and advocacy, demands for increased political accountability gain force, challenging and at times even preempting presidents inclined to flirt with the idea of staying in power. Some of these organizations—including many student associations, trade unions, religious bodies, and interest groups based on commercial, professional, and ethnic solidarities—date back to colonial days or the era just after independence. Yet active as well is a new generation of groups devoted explicitly to promoting democracy and good governance: think tanks, bar associations, human rights organizations, women's and civic-education groups, election-monitoring networks, and local as well as national-level development organizations.

More than ever, the building of democracy in Africa is a bottom-up affair. Nongovernmental organizations are teaching people their rights and duties as citizens, giving them the skills and confidence to demand answers from their rulers, to expose and challenge corruption, to resolve conflicts peacefully, to promote accommodation among ethnic and religious groups, to monitor government budgets and spending, to promote community development, and to recruit and train new political leaders. Civic groups and think tanks are also working at the national level to monitor elections, government budgets, and parliamentary deliberations; to expose waste, fraud, and abuses of power; and to lobby for legal reforms and institutional innovations to control corruption and improve the quality and transparency of governance.

These organizations draw strength not only from the funding and advice that international foundations and donors give them, but more importantly from their increasingly dense interactions with one another. The African Democracy Forum now links dozens of organizations from thirty countries on the basis of a common desire to advance the related causes of democracy and good governance.[7] Some African civil society organizations, most notably the Institute for Democracy in South Africa (IDASA), have reached a point of institutional maturity where they are now assisting democratic development elsewhere on the continent.

Also significant has been the growth of independent media and new information and communication technologies in Africa. The long tradition of independent daily newspapers has been enriched by a proliferation of newsweeklies and community and cross-border radio stations. Many of the community stations focus on local-development and health issues, from agriculture to HIV/AIDS, but they also address political issues and compensate for their low-wattage signals with high-voltage independence. And some broadcast from exile as the last sources of credible information about the deplorable conditions in their own home countries. One of the best is SW Radio Africa. Accurately self-billed as the "Independent Voice of Zimbabwe," it left the air when the Mugabe regime succeeded in suppressing its signal with Chinese-provided jamming gear. Undaunted, the station then turned to live streaming and posting on the Internet.

Perhaps most revolutionary are the ways that digital technology is being used in Africa, even where few computers (not to mention broadband Internet access) can be found. One nonprofit organization, kiwanja.net, is making available free software—FrontlineSMS—that can be used by charities and NGOs to facilitate text-messaging via short-message service (SMS) on everything from crop, weather, and road conditions to health news and politics. "Originally developed for conservationists to keep in touch with communities in National Parks in South Africa, the system allows mass-messaging to mobile phones and crucially the ability [for recipients] to reply to a central computer."[8]

Then there is the mobile phone, whose beauty is its versatility and astonishingly rapid empowerment of even poor individuals. Today, more than 30 million Nigerians (nearly one in every four) own a mobile phone. In Africa as a whole, the number of mobile users is believed to be approaching 300 million.[9] This rapid spread has enabled quantum leaps forward in election monitoring. In Nigeria in April 2007, millions of ordinary citizens instantly became election monitors by reporting what they saw (much of it bad, unfortunately) at the polls. The profusion of evidence did not stop massive rigging, but it may be helping to provide the legal basis for court challenges to overturn some of the cheating's effects.

The abovementioned FrontlineSMS technology is the brainchild of intrepid British anthropologist and programmer Ken Banks. Now being revised with support from the MacArthur Foundation, FrontlineSMS has also served to facilitate feedback to community radio programs in South Africa, to monitor voting in the Philippines, to send "security alerts to fieldworkers in Afghanistan [and] market prices to smallholder farmers in Aceh, and to circumvent government restrictions in countries including Zimbabwe and Pakistan."[10] Increasingly in Africa, and around the world, text-messaging will give citizens, NGOs, and community radio stations a powerful tool not only to extend their reach and connect people in ways that enhance development, but to monitor what governments do, document human rights abuses as they happen, and facilitate civic organization and demonstrations.

As text-messaging gains momentum in Africa, it will probably encounter a technological challenge from its biggest global nemesis, the communist regime in China. The rulers of the People's Republic are continually and desperately looking for ways to contain and disrupt any uncontrolled citizen activity that takes on a political edge. African dictatorships can be expected to call on Beijing for help in fighting this new tool for promoting democratic mobilization. African civil societies, meanwhile, can be expected to look for ways around the control mechanisms—one hopes with plenty of technical support from sympathetic actors in international civil society.

Coinciding with the flowering of civil society has been a visible public demand for and appreciation of democracy. When surveyed by the Afrobarometer in 2005 and 2006, an average of 62 percent of the public in eighteen countries said that "democracy is preferable to any other kind of government."[11] Levels of support for democracy ran as high as 75 percent in Ghana, Kenya, and Senegal, and reached 65 percent or higher in ten of the countries surveyed. In fact, in only a few African countries can one find much of an avowed appetite for any specific form of authoritarian rule, and never does it rise above a fifth of the population. Moreover, this is not just an abstract commitment to democracy in general. Four out of five Africans surveyed believe that "regular, open, and honest elections" are the only way to choose their country's leaders, and two-thirds agree that elected assemblies (not the president) should make the laws in the country, even if the president dis-

agrees with them.[12] Only about one in six Africans, on average, expresses a positive preference for an authoritarian option such as military or one-party rule. And a slight majority (52 percent) actively rejects all three authoritarian options offered.

Africans' support for democracy seems to flow from something other than a naïve sense that democracy must spell quick economic progress. When asked to define what democracy means to them, "a majority of Africans interviewed (54 percent) regard it in procedural terms by referring to the protection of civil liberties, participation in decision making, voting in elections, and governance reforms."[13] And when asked whether they felt that their system of electoral democracy "should be given more time to deal with inherited problems" or instead, if it "cannot produce results soon, we should try another form of government," 56 percent of Africans in 2005–2006 chose to give democracy more time. This represents a significant increase in patience with democracy since 2000.

Michael Bratton notes that while the demand for democracy is proving fairly resilient in Africa, the perceived supply is more questionable. For example, while 81 percent of Africans want free and fair elections that can remove incumbents, only 47 percent think they are getting this in their countries. Two-thirds of Africans want their president to be subject to the rule of law, but barely a third (36 percent) thinks that he is.[14] Clearly, Africans value and demand democracy—but African parties and politicians are not meeting citizens' aspirations.

Consequently, disillusionment is rising. Between 2000 and 2005, satisfaction with the way democracy works declined an average of 13 percentage points (from 58 to 45 percent) across the countries surveyed. While satisfaction rose in a few relatively well-functioning democracies such as Ghana and South Africa, it declined in eight of the twelve countries surveyed both times. Nevertheless, even on the supply side there are cautious grounds for optimism. The perception that one's own country is a democracy has held constant at around 50 percent, and 54 percent think it is likely that their country will remain a democracy.[15] Nor are the problematic numbers set in stone. On the contrary, there is evidence that actually delivering democracy can dramatically improve citizen attitudes and perceptions. Analyzing the 2005 data, Bratton found that respondents' perception of the most recent national election as free and fair was the most powerful predictor of their readiness to agree that their countries were democracies. In other words, the ruler's performance is no longer enough to satisfy the public—formal institutions are starting to matter more than informal ones.[16]

The Deadening Hand of Personal Rule

These trends, hopeful as they are, nonetheless tell only part of the story. Countries such as Cameroon, Eritrea, Ethiopia, Gabon, Sudan, and Togo remained trapped in longstanding patterns of authoritarian rule. Nigeria, Uganda under the increasingly corrupt Museveni, and now Kenya have been slipping backwards. And in Zimbabwe, deepening repression is morphing into a psychosis of authoritarian misrule under an aging dictator, Robert Mugabe, who seems increasingly detached from reality as his country's economy collapses amid hyperinflation that his policies have bred.

No less worrisome are the poor governance, persistent corruption, and stubborn personalism that so often continue to beset Africa's democracies. Of the six measures that the World Bank Institute uses to gauge the quality of governance in a country, the one known as "voice and accountability" (which includes freedom of expression and citizen participation in selecting the government) is a rough and partial surrogate for democracy. The others measure political stability and the absence of violence; the effectiveness of public services and administration; whether or not public regulations "permit and promote private sector development"; the rule of law (including the quality of policing and the courts); and control of corruption.

Africa does poorly on all these measures. On average, it ranks in the thirtieth percentile—a little better on the political measures of accountability and stability, but slightly worse on the measures of rule of law, corruption control, regulatory quality, and governmental effectiveness. On these latter four measures, which I collect together as a gauge of "state quality," Africa's mean percentile ranking, twenty-eighth, trails well behind Eastern Europe (fifty-ninth), Latin America and East Asia (forty-seventh), the Middle East (forty-second), and even South Asia (thirty-sixth).

Save for South Africa, the other six largest countries in Africa rank very low in their quality of governance. Five of the six have worse governance than the continent as a whole, and three of them dismally so. Across all six measures, Nigeria ranks in the thirteenth percentile. On rule of law plus control of corruption and political stability plus control of violence, only 5 percent of countries score worse. Ethiopia ranks in the eighteenth percentile, Sudan in the fifth, Congo (Kinshasa) in the third. Kenya and Tanzania do better, at the twenty-sixth and thirty-sixth percentiles, respectively, but Kenya still scores below the African average.

Underlying these painful figures is the continuing neopatrimonial character of politics in Africa. Experts call postcolonial African states *neo*patrimonial because they combine the forms of a modern bureaucratic state—constrained in theory by laws, constitutions, and other impersonal rules and standards—with the informal reality of personalized, unaccountable power and pervasive patron-client ties. These ties radiate out and down from the biggest "big man"—the autocratic president—to his lieutenants and allies, who in turn serve as patrons to lower-level power brokers, and down to the fragmented mass of ordinary citizens, who are trapped by their dependence on local political patrons.

In such systems, the informal always trumps the formal. Subordinates owe loyalty to their personal patrons, not to laws and institutions. Presidents and their minions use state resources as a personal slush fund to maintain political dominance, giving their clients state offices, jobs, licenses, contracts, vehicles, bribes, and other access to illicit rents, while getting unconditional support in return.[17] State offices at every level become permits to loot, for either an individual or a somewhat wider network of family members, ethnic kin, political clients, and business cronies.[18] Corruption, clientelism, and personal rule thus seep into the culture, making the system even more resilient. In Africa, contending patron-client networks organize along ethnic or subethnic lines, and the president sees his ethnic kin as the most reliable loyalists in the struggle for power. This makes the system particularly unstable, as conflicts over pelf, power, and identity mix in a volatile, even explosive brew.[19] The typical African pattern of concentrating extreme power in the presidency makes politics even more of a tense, zero-sum game. This helps to explain how a single rigged election can ignite the paroxysms of violence and ethnic cleansing that a horrified world has been watching lately in Kenya, where ethnic groups that have been shut out of the presidency ever since independence nurse deep anger.

The fundamental purpose of neopatrimonial governments is not to produce *public* goods—roads, bridges, markets, irrigation, education, health care, public sanitation, clean drinking water, effective legal systems—that increase productivity, improve human capital, stimulate investment, and generate development. The point of neopatrimonialism, rather, is to produce *private* goods for those with access to power. Contracts are granted not on the basis of who can deliver the best service for the lowest price, but rather on who will pay the biggest bribe. Budgets are steered to projects that can readily generate bribes. Government funds disappear into the overseas accounts of officeholders. Public payrolls are swollen with the ranks of phantom workers and soldiers whose pay goes into the pockets of higher-ups.

One thing that can arrest the decay and refresh the system is a change in leadership. But a key feature of the neopatrimonial system is the way the "king of the hill" hangs on and on. In 2005, Uganda's President Museveni, whose original claim to his office was being the top general of the strongest private army in his conflict-wracked homeland, "openly bribed members of parliament, blackmailed and intimidated others to amend the constitution and remove term limits on the presidency so that he can run again, and again, and again."[20] In the run-up to the February 2006 election, he stepped up his harassment of the independent media and those elements of civil society that he had not already coopted. Then he jailed the main opposition presidential candidate, before finally claiming a highly suspect first-round victory through apparent manipulation of the vote count.[21]

Museveni's two decades in power hardly make him Africa's longest-serving president, however. Omar Bongo of small but oil-rich Gabon in West Africa has ruled for nearly four decades. Robert Mugabe's merciless reign in Zimbabwe has stretched past a quarter-century. In Angola, Cameroon, and Guinea, presidents have also ruled for well over twenty years, and in Burkina Faso for nearly that. Sudan's Hassan al-Bashir has held power for eighteen years, and Meles Zenawi in Ethiopia and Yahya Jammeh in the Gambia for more than a decade each. None of them shows any sign of surrendering office. Of course, such prolonged personal reigns are hardly new in Africa—witness the late Mobutu Sese Seko's 32 years in power in Zaire, now Congo (Kinshasa)—but they have always been associated with national decline, if not disaster.

If Africa is now suspended between democracy and personal rule, what can tip it toward democracy? The deciding factor will not be economic development. For probably decades to come, much of Africa will remain well below the high level of development that seems to assure democratic survival. Steady economic growth can help to give people more confidence in democracy, building up its long-term legitimacy. But sustainable development has been stymied by the same factor that has undermined democracy itself: bad governance. If both democracy and development are to have a future in Africa, the core priority must be to improve the quality of governance.

Social scientists often lament their lack of adequate understanding of the policy challenges of our time, calling for more research. We do need to understand better how winning coalitions can be generated and sustained for the kinds of institutional reforms that will gain traction on Africa's core problem of bad, corrupt, abusive governance. But broadly, we know where the answers lie. Countervailing institutions of power—the judiciary, the legislature, and the whole apparatus of countercorruption, audit, human rights, and other oversight bodies that are sometimes called a "fourth branch of government"—must be greatly strengthened in their political autonomy, statutory authority, and financial and human resources. Power and resources must be decentralized down to elected lower levels of government, ideally (in any large country) through a federal system (the one saving grace that has held Nigeria together). Political parties must themselves be democratized internally and made more effective as organizations, independent of ethnicity or personal ties. Elections must be truly free and fair, and thus electoral administrations must be made up of career civil-service professionals who, as in India, have the training, resources, autonomy, and *esprit de corps* to resist partisan pressures. State economic ownership and control must be diminished, but the state must be strengthened in its capacity to deliver its essential mission of managing the economy and generating the public goods (such as schools, roads, courts, markets, and other infrastructure) needed for development. And citizens must have the freedom to monitor and report on what government does, and to organize to challenge it and pursue their interests.

It is not difficult to find, in African civil societies and in the state itself, numerous actors ready to rise to the challenge. The problem is that African leaders are not generally to be found among these coalitions for reform, because they calculate that their own interests lie not in reform, but in building or reinforcing monopolies of power and wealth. Of course, in the absence of democracy, it is always the monopolists who triumph. But democracy in itself is no guarantee against the resurgence of many bad practices.

For much of the last half-century (and well before that of course, under colonial rule), the missing link has been the international community,

which has been only too happy to embrace any African despot in the quest for resources and strategic advantage. Idealists, by contrast, have thought that the answer lies in "foreign aid," which is supposed to make up for the vast shortages of financial resources needed to deliver health, education, and roads. About US$600 billion later, we know (or at least we *should* know) that pouring more aid unconditionally on bad governments is like pouring gasoline on a fire. In the circumstances of predatory rule in Africa, aid functions like the revenue that gushes in from oil exports—it is just another source of external rents that enables rulers to float on a cushion above their societies, controlling the state without having to answer to their own people.

Certainly Richard Joseph is correct that the entry of China into the "great game" of aid, investment, and resources in Africa creates a new context, in some ways akin to the superpower competition of the Cold War. And the "new cold war" against international terrorism has not helped. Both developments have given African authoritarian regimes new alternatives and new forms of leverage against Western pressure for democratic reform. But this is not the 1960s or 1970s. African societies are informed and autonomously organized as never before. Africans are aware of their political rights and demanding of democracy as never before. And together, Europe and the United States still provide the vast bulk of aid and investment in Africa.

Most of all, principled pressure is needed from international actors, tying substantial flows of development assistance to concrete institutional improvements in governance. Donors can also provide generous financial and technical assistance to the institutions of governance—African legislatures, judiciaries, countercorruption commissions, and other agencies of horizontal accountability—that must work well if the balance is to tip from autocracy to democracy. It is the very fluidity of things on the continent today—so powerfully evoked by Joseph's concept of "frontier Africa"—that makes so much possible. From the experience of a small but growing number of better-functioning African democracies, we know that the continent is not condemned to perpetual misrule. The challenge now is for the international donors to join with Africans in demanding that their governments be truly accountable.

NOTES

1. Steven Levitsky and Lucan Way, *Competitive Authoritarianism: International Linkage. Organizational Power, and the Fate of Hybrid Regimes* (Cambridge University Press, forthcoming). They classify countries on the basis of their respective regimes during the period 1990–95, and then track their evolution. On this basis, they classify Benin, Malawi, Mozambique, and Zambia all as competitive authoritarian regimes, whereas other analyses (including that of Freedom House) often have considered them democracies. I exclude the Central African Republic because of its very poor freedom score, average 5 on the two seven-point scales of Freedom House.

2. The Gambia, whose politics had been dominated for almost thirty years by one leader and his party, slipped entirely from democratic ranks after a military coup in 1994. Retrospectively, some analysts have questioned just how democratic the Gambia was at that point.

3. Daniel Posner and Daniel Young, "The Institutionalization of Political Power in Africa," *Journal of Democracy* 18 (July 2007): 126–40.

4. Posner and Young, "Institutionalization of Political Power in Africa," 131.

5. Michael Bratton, "The 'Alternation Effect' in Africa," *Journal of Democracy* 15 (October 2004): 147–58.

6. The evidence and arguments here are developed at greater length in Larry Diamond, *Developing Democracy: Toward Consolidation* (Baltimore: Johns Hopkins University Press, 1999), ch. 6.

7. See *www.africandemocracyforum.org*.

8. "Texts Monitor Nigerian Elections," BBC News, 20 April 2007. Available at *http://news.bbc.co.uk/2/hi/technology/6570919.stm*.

9. This would probably represent something like 30 percent of the roughly 750 million people in sub-Saharan Africa, even allowing for some people owning multiple devices.

10. From *http://frontlinesms.kiwanja.net*.

11. Most of the data presented here from the Afrobarometer is available in the publications of the project, at *www.afrobarometer.org/publications.html*. See in particular, "The Status of Democracy, 2005–2006: Findings from Afrobarometer Round 3 for 18 Countries," Afrobarometer Briefing Paper no. 40, June 2006.

12. Michael Bratton, "Formal vs. Informal Institutions in Africa," *Journal of Democracy* 18 (July 2007): 96–110.

13. Michael Bratton, Robert Mattes, and E. Gyimah-Boadi, *Public Opinion, Democracy, and Market Reform in Africa* (Cambridge: Cambridge University Press, 2005), 69–70.

14. Bratton, "Formal vs. Informal Institutions," Figure 2, 106.

15. Bratton, "Formal vs. Informal Institutions," 102.

16. Bratton, "Formal vs. Informal Institutions," Table 2, 107.

17. Michael Bratton and Nicolas van de Walle, *Democratic Experiments in Africa: Regime Transitions in Comparative Perspective* (Cambridge: Cambridge University Press, 1997), 61–68; Robert H. Jackson and Carl G. Rosberg, *Personal Rule in Black Africa: Prince, Autocrat, Prophet, Tyrant* (Berkeley: University of California Press, 1982), 38–42.

18. Drawing on Max Weber, Joseph has called such systems "prebendal." Richard A. Joseph, *Democracy and Prebendal Politics in Nigeria: The Rise and Fall of the Second Republic* (Cambridge: Cambridge University Press, 1987), 6; see also 55–68 for elaboration of the concept and its relationship to clientelism.

19. Joseph, *Democracy and Prebendal Politics in Nigeria*, 8. This work develops these themes at length,

20. Andew Mwenda, "Please Stop Helping Us," paper presented to the Novartis Foundation, 12 August 2006, 3.

21. Andrew Mwenda, "Personalizing Power in Uganda," *Journal of Democracy* 18 (July 2007): 23–37.

Barbara Geddes, Erica Frantz, and Joseph G. Wright
MILITARY RULE

Military Rule

To defend against foreign and domestic enemies, governments organize military forces supplied with weapons and trained to use them. The concentration of weapons and training in militaries makes them potentially dangerous to those who pay their salaries. Since World War II, military officers have overthrown many civilian governments. Occasionally, they return power to civilians after a few days, but often they do not. Instead, they establish military rule, led by either a single military strongman or a junta representing the officer corps. Although military rule has become less common during the past two decades, the military still governed 19% of the world's countries in the first decade of the twenty-first century.[1]

Military rule entails governance by men who specialize in armed force and maintaining order rather than in political affairs. They are more accustomed to hierarchy and obedience than to bargaining. Because their training and experience differ from those of civilian politicians, military rulers sometimes make different policy choices than would civilian autocrats. The areas in which choices differ include war, response to opposition, and whether to end their own intervention in politics.

Despite their specialization in the use of force, military-led regimes are surprisingly fragile. When officers seize control of governments, they of course retain control over weapons and the men who use them. It thus seems that they would have special advantages in coercive capacity relative to other ruling groups: the abilities to deter opposition through threat of force and to use force to defeat opposition (Debs 2010, Svolik 2013). These apparent advantages, however, do not help military rulers to maintain power. Paradoxically, military regimes survive less long than democracies or other kinds of autocracy (Geddes 1999).

The fragility of military rule seems counterintuitive not only because of military regimes' advantage in coercion but also because military institutions have highly coherent, disciplined internal organization that might be expected to impede challenges from within, while coercion deters challenges from outside. As Finer (1976, pp. 5–9) noted long ago, military institutions are more intensively organized than parties. All individuals in the military go through training, and incentives to enforce the obedience of subordinates to superiors are built into every aspect of military institutions. If intensive hierarchical organization and enforced discipline help maintain communist party rule, as is often thought, then it would seem that military regimes should also benefit from these advantages. And yet, the empirical study of military rule shows that these incentives do not prevent the ultimate disobedience: rebellion against the regime's most senior officer. Leader ouster occurs more frequently in military regimes than in other forms of autocracy, and other officers carry out most of these ousters (Frantz & Ezrow 2011; Gandhi 2008, pp. 176–77). The frequency of both leader ouster and regime breakdown in military regimes indicates their frailty.

The behavior of military rulers challenges expectations in other ways as well. We might expect military dictators to use force against threats to their rule (Davenport 2007a). Yet, military regimes faced with economic crisis or active popular opposition often negotiate a return to the barracks instead

From *Annual Review of Political Science* 17 (2014), pp. 147–62.

(Geddes 1999). Prominent theories of dictatorship see autocratic political actors as agents of the rich (Acemoglu & Robinson 2006, Boix 2003), but military leaders do not routinely represent the rich or indeed the other societal interests that may ally with them (Nordlinger 1977).[2] The relative autonomy of some military rulers from powerful societal interests and their ability to redistribute economic resources both within and between classes are inconsistent with models of autocracy as systems for maintaining the wealth of the currently rich. If military rulers have some autonomy from societal interests and pursue their own interests just as other political actors do, then theories of autocratic rule should take into account the distinctive interests of military actors. Even where they do not rule, the military is an important faction in authoritarian ruling alliances, as the Arab Spring makes apparent. Currently, most theories of autocracy ignore this gorilla in the room.

The main reason to examine military rule as a distinct subset of autocracies is that empirical studies show that officers who lead nations behave somewhat differently than nonofficers. This article summarizes what is currently known, thought, and theorized about military rule, how it ends, and how it affects the likelihood of democratization. We begin with a review of some foundational studies of military rule before turning to a definition and some basic distinctions. Different scholars have defined military rule in different ways, often without making the definition explicit, and these alternative definitions lead to contrasting conclusions in empirical studies. We show that definitional differences reconcile some of the apparently contradictory findings.

Subsequent sections review theories about what happens during military rule and the evidence available to support them, factors that contribute to the breakdown of military rule, and what happens after officers return to the barracks. Our review suggests that military rulers are more likely than civilian dictators to abuse their citizens and more likely to embroil them in civil war. Military strongmen, described more fully below, are more belligerent than either governments ruled by the military institution or civil-ian autocrats. Despite their propensity for using force against opponents, regimes led by the military institution tend to collapse peacefully and to be followed by democratization. Other forms of autocracy, including military strongmen, are more likely to be overthrown by force and followed by a new dictatorship.

Foundational Studies of Military Rule

scholars began to analyze military rule as newly independent governments fell to military intervention, especially in the 1960s. The upsurge in military interventions in the richer South American countries with little prior history of military rule also increased academic interest in the phenomenon. Much of the early literature focused on the reasons for military intervention in politics, but some analysts also attempted to generalize about the military's typical strengths and weaknesses in governance, as well as the effect of military rule on economic development, the creation of national identity in new nations, and the spread of modern values and skills.

The intuition that rule by military officers should differ from rule by civilians motivates many of the early studies, but scholars have different ideas about how and why they would differ. Initially, analysts investigated the class and educational backgrounds of officers to see if they explain their policy choices. Studies of officers in many different developing countries find that they usually come from middle- and lower-middle-class families, often from rural areas or small towns. Some officer corps include many sons of peasants, but none seem dominated by sons of the upper classes (Janowitz 1977, pp. 79–91; Nordlinger 1977, pp. 32–34). The policies implemented vary from one case to the next. Officers from the same kinds of backgrounds follow conservative policies benefiting landowners in some settings and leftist policies that expropriate the property of landowners in others.

Whether military rulers serve the interests of the rich seems to depend on local circumstances and specific officers' ideology. Officers are seldom rich when they seize power, although in some settings they become rich after the seizure (Johnson 1962, pp. 105–13; Nordlinger 1977, pp. 32–43). After seizing power, some military governments defend the economic status quo, yet others destroy traditional elites and nationalize large parts of their countries' economies. Even those who defend the capitalist economic status quo may not serve as agents of existing economic interests, however. General Augusto Pinochet, for example, certainly a defender of capitalism, initiated policies opposed by most Chilean business owners at the time. Only a very abstract account of economic policy making during the Pinochet government would call it an agent of groups it neither consulted nor cared about (Biglaiser 2002, Remmer 1989). Many businesses failed during the Pinochet years, and new businesses were created in response to drastic changes in the policy rules of the game. Pinochet can be seen as an agent of capitalism in the abstract, but not as an agent of the particular capitalists who dominated the Chilean economy in the first years of military rule. In general, scholars of military rule have failed to reach a consensus about whose interests the military serves besides its own. Those who work on some countries see military rulers as allies of the rich, whereas those who work on other countries see them as representatives of the lower middle class or agents of redistribution and change.

In many of the newly independent nations, military forces inherited from the colonial era overrepresented ethnic groups living in less developed areas, but most new governments attempted to recruit nationally. This change in the ethnicity of recruits tended to exacerbate the conflict between senior and junior officers that can motivate the ouster of one military leader by another. Ethnic grievances have motivated many coups, especially when one ethnicity dominated the first government but another the army. Case studies of military intervention in Africa often emphasize ethnicity (e.g., Bebler 1973, Decalo 1976, Luckham 1971), although it has received less systematic attention from comparativists than class background.

Some early observers believed that military governments would help unify ethnically divided societies because of the military's emphasis on internal unity and national identity. As Nordlinger (1977) notes, however, ethnic antagonisms often permeate the militaries in new nations despite such training. He concludes that far from its having a special capacity to foster national unity, the military's coercive response to ethnic grievances leads to much more disastrous outcomes than would muddling along by civilians. He points to the bloody civil wars in Pakistan/Bangladesh, Nigeria, and Sudan as evidence of the consequences of intransigent military responses to ethnic demands.

Despite ethnic rivalries in some countries, studies find that officers tend to share interests arising from their military careers (Janowitz 1977, Nordlinger 1977). Some of these interests are mundane: the desire for higher pay and better living conditions; demand for more rapid promotion; and resentment about the politicization of promotions. Other concerns center on the military's potential efficacy as a fighting force: officers value the military's monopolization of the use of force and resent the creation by political leaders of other armed forces, such as party militias and presidential bodyguards. Officers place a high value on discipline and oppose any effort by politicians to unionize enlisted men or introduce dual structures of command in the form of political commissars. Low pay, political interference with promotions, efforts to unionize enlisted men, the creation of workers' militias, and the nicer uniforms of members of the presidential guard have been cited as reasons for military coups (Bebler 1973, Nordlinger 1977, Stepan 1971). Officers also value the unity of the armed forces, an essential feature of an effective fighting organization. The concern about unity can deter coups when plotters fear that their attempt to seize power would divide the army, and it can motivate officers to negotiate a return to the barracks when political factionalism threatens unity after they have taken power (Nordlinger 1977, Potash 1996).

Much of the early literature also emphasizes the military's inherent inability to govern countries with modern economies or to handle the negotiation among groups needed to maintain a stable government (Finer 1976, pp. 12–14; Janowitz 1977, pp. 154–56). Finer highlights the need for cooperation with the pre-existing state bureaucracy, and Janowitz (pp. 160–68) the need but likely inability to develop civilian support bases in order to survive in power. Clapham & Philip (1985) argue that military regime stability "depends on its capacity to acquire civilian allies who are willing to accept subordination to military leadership in exchange for some share in running the state and especially some share in the benefits which it provides" (pp. 12–13). With hindsight, these insights seem prescient. Many studies have noted the military's collaboration with civilian administrators and technocrats. Some authors describe military officers as having a special affinity for bureaucrats or as being "armed bureaucrats" themselves (e.g., Feit 1973). Military leaders who organize civilian support bases have indeed survived longer, but officers have proved more adept at organizing civilian support than many early analysts expected. Dictators who seized power through armed force (most often by coup) later created a civilian support party or allied themselves with a pre-existing party about 60% of the time. Regimes established by military leaders who later created a party survive on average three times longer than those in which military rulers lack a civilian party, as Janowitz would have expected (Geddes 2011).

Most early analysts made no distinctions among dictatorships led by officers, but the surprising establishment of military rule in some of the most industrialized developing countries and the apparent economic success and political robustness of some of these regimes led to a partial reevaluation. Stepan's (1971) very detailed empirical investigation of the changes that occurred in the Brazilian military before the 1964 intervention, along with his analysis of the centrality of the military's professional interests in their decisions, laid the groundwork for the development of new theories. These theories emphasize differences between the rule of juntas representing the officer corps, labeled "rule by the military

as an institution," and one-man rule by an officer. O' Donnell (1973), responding to the same military regime in Brazil as well as the contemporaneous one in Argentina, embeds the idea of rule by the military as an institution in a theory about why democracy could tend to break down in more industrialized developing countries. He ties this somewhat collegial form of military rule to a theory about conflict between, on the one hand, the increasing mobilization of ordinary citizens into politics as economies industrialized and, on the other hand, elite interest in policies to favor investors. He thus defines what he labels bureaucratic-authoritarianism not only as rule by the military as an institution but also as dictatorship committed to (*a*) conservative economic ideology facilitated by the delegation of economic policy to technocrats and (*b*) an understanding of national security focused on the challenges of leftist internal subversion rather than external enemies.

Subsequent research, however, has delinked rule by the military institution from the socio-economic conditions and ideological commitments of the cases in which it was first identified. Remmer (1989) shows that collegial forms of military rule have occurred in Latin America at all levels of economic development and have occurred in regimes committed to reformist policies and the greater inclusion of the poor in the benefits of development (e.g., Peru 1968-1980), as well as in those committed to conservative economic policies and exclusion.

In distinguishing one-man rule from more collegial military rule, Remmer emphasizes the dictator's personal control of the security forces as an indicator of his concentration of power. Such control allows the dictator to threaten and coerce fellow officers. She also notes that Pinochet's active-duty status gave him control over promotions and retirements in the army for 16 years, allowing him to craft a highly loyal instrument within a few years (see also Arriagada 1988). In contrast, security services are more likely to remain within the regular military chain of command during collegial military rule, and other officers often insist that the general who becomes dictator retire from active duty in order to limit his control over their own futures. Remmer's (1989) conclusions are drawn from an examination of all autocracies led by officers in Latin America.

Geddes' (1999, 2003) theorization of elite rivalry in autocracies builds on the ideas of Nordlinger (1977), O'Donnell (1973), Remmer (1989), and others. She distinguishes "military regimes," by which she means rule by an officer constrained by other officers (rule by the military institution), from one-man rule, which she labels personalist. She does not distinguish military-led personalist regimes from those led by civilians. She defines personalist regimes as autocracies in which discretion over policy and personnel is concentrated in the hands of one man, although in the real world that discretion is often maintained by balancing the interests of multiple competing groups within the dictator's support coalition; the military, or the faction of it that supports the dictator, is one of the groups balanced. An important aspect of the concentration of power is control of the security apparatus, as noted by Remmer (1989). An implication of Geddes' stylized depiction of elite rivalries in different forms of autocracy is that more collegial forms of military rule are less likely to survive crises and differences of opinion within the ruling group than are other kinds of autocracy, an expectation that has been confirmed empirically (Brownlee 2009, Geddes 2003, Smith 2005, Wright & Escribà-Folch 2012).

Contemporary Definitions of Military Rule

The different meanings of the term military rule in different studies can create confusion, and theoretical expectations vary depending on the analyst's understanding of military rule. This section describes the three commonly used meanings of the term in order to disentangle apparently contradictory findings. Different definitions of military rule guided the data collection for different datasets used to identify military rule, so the datasets are not interchangeable and the choice of dataset can determine

the results. Which dataset should be used depends on the definition of military rule embedded in the theory being tested.

The most inclusive definition of military rule refers to dictatorship led by a military officer, regardless of the make-up and influence of the rest of the leadership group. The second usage, building on O'Donnell (1973) and Remmer (1989), limits the term military regime to dictatorships led by somewhat collegial bodies representing the officer corps (rule by the military institution), in which multiple officers influence decision making. The third usage, sometimes called military strongman rule, refers to the subset of dictatorships in which power is concentrated in the hands of a single military officer.

For clarity, in this article our label for autocratic rule by a member of the military, regardless of the nature of the rest of the leadership, is "military-led autocracy." Military-led autocracy encompasses two distinctive forms of rule: domination of decision making by a group of officers representing the military institution, which we label a "military regime"; and dictatorship controlled by a single officer absent elite constraints, which we call "military strongman" rule.

Examples of military-led autocracy include Idi Amin's tyranny in Uganda; the Egyptian dictatorship initiated by the Free Officers in 1952, which ended with the ouster of Hosni Mubarak in 2011; and the Brazilian dictatorship from 1964 to 1985. In each case, the leadership post was always held by a current or former military officer. Here, the career of the dictator before the seizure of power determines the regime label. No additional information about the autocracy is taken into account.

In the second usage, autocracies are only labeled military regimes if the dictator consults with other high-ranking officers and can be constrained by them. This definition emphasizes the difference between somewhat collegial forms of military leadership and more narrowly based dictatorships such as those led by General Amin in Uganda or General Trujillo in the Dominican Republic. Amin and Trujillo were also military officers (and their governments would be considered military according to the first definition), but the military did not rule "as an institution" because the dictator had concentrated so much power in his own hands that he did not usually need to bargain with other officers. Of the dictatorships mentioned in the paragraph above, only the Brazilian would be considered a military regime. In contrast to the other examples, the Brazilian dictatorship was initiated via a coup supported by the great majority of officers; consultation among them remained important through the many years of military control, most visibly during negotiations over planned presidential successions every few years (Stepan 1971). Rule by the military institution implies not only that a man in uniform occupies the top leadership post but also that other officers have some political influence. The strongest indicator of influence is the ability of the officer corps to enforce term limits and manage succession.

In contrast, Amin, who had many other officers murdered, is classified as a military strongman. Other officers held some key positions in the dictatorship, but they had little influence on basic political decisions. Military strongmen are made, not born, in a process that usually occurs after seizures of power. Immediately after seizures of power, most military governments are unstructured and somewhat chaotic. How decisions will be made and enforced is unclear even to participants. Leadership within the junta or other governing entity tends to be collegial. Hierarchies and routines for making and implementing decisions are not yet established; personnel within the junta may change rapidly; and citizens, especially those with personal links to members of the governing group, often have considerable ability to influence decisions (Geddes 2006).

The transition from unstructured military rule to strongman rule results from bargaining and conflict among high-ranking officers after the seizure of power. The man initially chosen to lead a military dictatorship needs the continued cooperation of other officers in order to retain his post because any officer with control over a few hundred troops could potentially oust him. To retain that support, he must make credible commitments to share spoils and policy influence with other officers in return for their commitment to refrain from overthrowing him. A military dictator can take a number of actions to make his own commitment more credible; for example, he can retire from active duty in order to limit his ability to control other officers' careers and postings, and delegate ministries and control over security services to other officers. The ability of other junta members to commit their subordinates to refrain from ousting the dictator, however, is more problematic. In a disciplined, unified military, high-ranking officers can credibly bargain on behalf of their subordinates, who can be expected to follow orders. Such bargains stabilize collegial military regimes.

In factionalized militaries riven by ethnic or personal rivalries, however, junta members cannot guarantee the behavior of subordinate officers. In that situation, leaders may try sharing spoils and influence more broadly by creating larger military command committees to rule rather than small juntas. Leaders who cannot trust lower-ranked officers to obey their superiors' orders also have strong incentives to organize a civilian support base to counterbalance potential military opposition. An organized civilian support network, a party, partially liberates the military leader from dependence on other officers and creates the opportunity for the dictator to play the factions in his alliance off against each other.[3] Strongmen are the dictators who prove especially adept at the manipulation of factions within the ruling alliance, leading to the gradual marginalization of other officers from decision making.

Analysts define military rule in particular ways because they expect specific features of the definition to have behavioral consequences and thus to affect what happens after a military dictator takes power. Many assume that officers play a large enough role in actual governance and policy making for their special competences and disabilities to affect political outcomes. Janowitz (1977), for example, describes officers' competence in administering many specific tasks but emphasizes their lack of experience and training to oversee a complicated national economy or other tasks that require arbitration among competing goals. From this he infers that military dictatorships will not improve growth rates after seizing power. He thus assumes that officers will be making basic economic policy decisions, or at any rate interfering in them, rather than delegating economic policy to civilian experts. Some theorizing about military rule explicitly assumes decision making through bargaining among a group of top officers, rather than one-man rule. Geddes' (1999) depiction of bargaining among military factions as similar to a battle-of-the-sexes game, for example, only makes sense if we assume consultation among officers about important decisions. The suggestion that military dictators can use the military as the institutional basis for organizing government (Gandhi 2008, pp. 25–28, 93) or implementing policies also seems to imply rule by the military as a whole rather than by one man who has marginalized other officers from most decision making. These analysts all seem to have in mind military regimes.

The designation "military strongman" implies that the dictator is relatively unconstrained by the need to consult with other officers. The lack of constraint implies that military strongmen's decisions depend on their own preferences and expectations about their personal futures. Debs & Goemans' (2010) argument that dictators' fear of imprisonment or assassination after ouster may motivate them to initiate diversionary wars suggests individual decision making, as would be expected under strongman rule, rather than collegial.

In contrast to both strongman rule and rule by the military institution, the concept of military-led autocracy implies that the analyst believes the distinction between constrained and unconstrained military dictators will not affect the behavior under study. One might hypothesize, for example, that any military-led autocracy, regardless of the dictator's relationship with fellow officers, would be likely to use more coercion against protestors than would a civilian-led dictatorship. More generally, some characteristics of the military, such as hierarchy, discipline, and a propensity to use force, can be expected to influence the behavior of all military-led autocracies because the dictator and other officers share these traits.

The analyst's understanding of military rule or the understanding implied by the argument being investigated determines which data should be used for testing. Currently, three regime-type datasets identify periods of military rule. Cheibub et al.'s (2010) update (hereafter CGV) of the Democracy/Dictatorship dataset identifies country-years as democratic or not and identifies individual dictators as civilians, military officers, or monarchs. These authors code political leaders as military if they wear or have ever worn a uniform (with an exception for participation in World War II). Leaders whose only military experience was in an insurgency are coded as civilian. Spans of country-years that are both non-democratic and ruled by a military leader are treated as periods of military-led autocracy.

Hadenius & Teorell's (2007) dataset (hereafter HT) also identifies military dictatorships.[4] They classify autocracies as "pure military" if Banks & Wilson (2012) code the executive as military and the legislature as nonexistent or ineffective.[5] "Rebel" regimes, that is, regimes that achieved control via insurgency, are included in the military category. Military hybrids, as coded by HT, have military executives but "effective" legislatures. Using these data, analysts can also identify military-led autocracies by combining spans of country-years ruled by pure military and military hybrid dictatorships.

Emphasis on rule by the military institution underpins the identification of military rule in the dataset created by Geddes et al. (2013) (GWF). In these data, a number of coding rules are used to distinguish collegial military rule from strongman rule (described in Geddes 2003). Because this dataset relies on a more restrictive definition of military rule, it identifies significantly fewer periods of dictatorship as military. CGV identify 1,737 country-years between 1946 and 2008 as military, whereas GWF identify only 575.[6] The GWF data capture periods in which autocracies are governed by "military regimes."[7] The CGV and GWF datasets could be combined to create a measure of autocratic rule by military strongmen. This would entail identifying the consecutive country-years coded both as personalist by GWF and as military by CGV.[8]

For the purpose of investigating arguments about how the military as an organization or institution affects decision making or autocratic breakdown, the GWF dataset is more appropriate because it limits the regimes coded as military to those in which multiple high-ranking officers influence decision making. If, however, one wants to know whether the dictator's training and past career in the military affect his decision making, longevity, or likelihood of starting wars, the CGV or HT dataset is appropriate. If instead one seeks to compare the behavior of military autocrats constrained by other members of the military with the behavior of those who are not thus constrained, or to evaluate whether civilian strongmen differ from their military counterparts, the CGV and GWF datasets combined, as described above, are appropriate. Readers should note which data were used when deciding how to interpret analysts' empirical results.

With these differences in mind, we now discuss some of the central findings of studies of military rule. We interpret them in light of the definition of military rule implied by the dataset(s) used.

Military Rule and Violence

It seems that, because militaries have professional expertise in the use of force, military governments would use more violence against domestic opponents than autocrats not from the military (Debs 2010, Svolik 2013). As Davenport (1995) summarizes this idea, repression "can easily be applied because armies are prepared to use force at all times" (p. 120).

But the relationship between military rule and repression is not completely straightforward. Policzer's (2009) case study of repression during the Pinochet dictatorship in Chile, for example, provides insight into why a dictator might prefer to avoid using regular military forces to repress opposition. During the first months after the 1973 coup, the responsibilities of officers who were assigned to administer subnational areas included dealing with domestic "enemies." In some regions, extremist commanding officers killed many civilians thought to be leftists, sometimes after a perfunctory military trial. In others, however, commanding officers enforced preexisting democratic legal norms and treated political prisoners humanely. Some even had the courage to resist the Arellano mission, Pinochet's effort to impose a hard line on local commanders. The Chilean junta's decision to remove control of internal subversion from the military's hands and create a specialized and centralized internal security service arose from its inability to control the implementation of repression under the existing arrangement and the threat to military unity posed by deep disagreements within the officer corps over how regime opponents should be treated (Policzer 2009, pp. 56–85). Janowitz (1977) and Nordlinger (1977) both stress the deep reluctance of most regular military officers to carry out domestic repression. In short, although the hypothesis that military-led autocracies are especially repressive is plausible, the story may be more complicated.

The empirical record so far is mixed. Poe et al. (1999) find that military rule increases human rights violations relative to civilian government. Their measure of military control identifies governments that achieved power via coup and either were led by a military executive or had mixed military and civilian cabinets with an officer apparently controlling the government from behind the scenes (Poe & Tate 1994, p. 858). They thus include most of the governments that would be labeled "military-led autocracy" in the CGV data. Davenport (2007b) investigates the effect of different types of autocracy on civil liberties as well as personal integrity violations (torture, execution, incarceration, and disappearance) using a very early version of the GWF data. He finds that military regimes and dominant-party regimes are less likely to repress civil liberties than personalist regimes (which in the GWF data include both military strongmen and civilian despots). Dominant-party regimes are also less likely to violate personal integrity, but military regimes exhibit the same level of human rights violations as other autocracies (Davenport 2007b). Neither Davenport (2007b) nor Poe et al. (1999) cover a very long period of time, and they could be challenged in other ways, but together they suggest that more physical integrity violations are committed in military-led autocracies than under civilian-led ones. Davenport's research indicates, however, that the opposite is true for repression of civil liberties. Gandhi (2008) also shows, using CGV data, that military-led autocracies are less likely than civilian dictatorships to repress speech or workers' rights, though more likely to interfere with media freedom.

Although military governments commit human rights violations, regular officers and soldiers may not carry out most atrocities. This responsibility often lies in the hands of internal security services and the national police instead. Indeed, the case-study literature notes that dictators often use internal security services to spy on and to counterbalance the regular military.[9] Officers from the regular military may head internal security agencies, but the agencies are often not subsumed within the regular military chain of command or staffed by regular soldiers. Janowitz (1977, p. 46) observes "again and again . . . the conscious effort made by military officials to remove their regular units from the distasteful task of internal security. "Besides distaste, officers fear that their subordinates will disobey orders to fire on civilians."

Soldiers have resisted using arms against fellow citizens at crucial historical junctures. The Serbian military's unwillingness to shoot anti-Milošević protesters, for example, contributed to the dictator's ouster after fraudulent elections in 2000 (Binnendijk & Marovic 2006). The first military interventions in some African countries occurred when civilian dictators ordered the army to repress opposition demonstrations; officers ousted dictators rather than firing on fellow citizens (Decalo 1976, Englebert 1998). Arguably the Egyptian military ousted Mubarak in 2011 because it was faced with the same choice (Barany 2011). These experiences highlight the military's ambivalent approach to the

domestic use of force. Military leaders are, as Debs (2010), Nordlinger (1977), and Svolik (2013) suggest, likely to turn to force sooner than civilian dictators, but they usually use specialized security agencies to implement repression because they do not trust regular officers and soldiers to follow orders about repressing fellow citizens.[10] In short, the propensity of military dictators to use violence seems to arise from their training, or perhaps lack of training in bargaining, rather than their control of a reliable instrument of coercion in the army.

Military regimes are also more likely than single-party autocracies to become involved in civil wars (Fjelde 2010). Nordlinger (1977) argues that officers' attitudes and training hinder their ability to compromise and lead to kneejerk violent responses to challenges, especially challenges to national integrity. He describes events leading to civil war in Nigeria, Pakistan/Bangladesh, and Sudan to illustrate his argument. Fjelde's (2010) discussion of the usefulness of parties for coopting opposition complements and extends Nordlinger's argument. Fjelde tests her ideas using two different measures of military rule, the HT dataset and an early version of GWF. Her specification also goes some way toward showing that military rule increases the likelihood of civil war rather than vice versa. She uses an interaction between regime type and time in power to show that civil war becomes more likely over time as the military remains in power. This result makes it unlikely that the correlation between military rule and civil war is caused by the tendency of military leaders to seize power during the conflicts leading up to civil wars. Using HT data, Fjelde finds that civil wars are more likely to start during military-led autocracies and electoral autocracies (dictatorships with multiparty legislative elections) than during single-party dictatorships or monarchies. Using GWF data, she finds that civil wars are more likely in military regimes, personalist dictatorships, and monarchies than in dominant-party regimes. Military regimes are somewhat more prone to civil war than the other types coded by GWF, but the differences among military, personalist, and monarchic regimes are small relative to the difference between these types and dominant-party regimes.[11] In short, military-led autocracies seem to be less skilled at avoiding the escalation of grievances into civil war than other kinds of autocracy, a finding that holds even when the definition of military rule is restricted to military regimes.

Evidence also suggests that military strongmen engage in more belligerent international behavior than other dictators. Lai & Slater (2006) find that military-led autocracies are more likely to initiate conflict than are party-based autocracies. They argue that the military's uncertain hold on power leads it to initiate diversionary wars to shore up domestic support. Lai & Slater use an earlier version of Banks & Wilson's (2012) dataset to identify military-led autocracies and Polity scores to capture constraints on the executive by civilian actors. They interpret unconstrained military executives as military strongmen and find no difference between the behavior of these dictators and that of military executives who share formal powers with civilian elites. This finding suggests that civilians with formal powers to constrain military partners cannot really do so.

In contrast, other officers do seem able to constrain some military dictators. Using data that distinguish military juntas from unconstrained military strongmen, Weeks (2012) finds significant differences in conflict propensity between strongmen and regimes led by the military institution. Consistent with earlier research (Frantz & Ezrow 2011, Peceny & Beer 2003, Peceny et al. 2002, Peceny & Butler 2004), Weeks argues that personalist dictatorships start more wars than other autocracies or democracies because they face little domestic accountability. She departs from earlier research, however, in arguing that the preferences of leaders with military backgrounds make them more prone to using arms to achieve their ends than are civilian personalists. To test these ideas, she combines some of the components used by Geddes (2003) to classify regime types with other variables to distinguish military juntas (i.e., rule by a group of officers) from military strongmen. Juntas thus largely overlap with military regimes as defined in the GWF data, but Weeks distinguishes military strongmen from civilian personalist dictators, which is not possible using GWF data alone. Her data analysis shows that military strongmen are more likely to initiate war than are juntas or civilian personalist rulers, who are in turn more belligerent than dominant-party regimes and democracies. Weeks' findings thus challenge Lai & Slater's (2006, p. 114) argument that military regimes start more wars because they lack parties "to help manage elite factionalism and curb mass dissent." Although she does not make this point, most military strongmen—who are the most likely to start wars—are supported by parties created after their accession to power, whereas most juntas are not.

Another strand of research on the causes of war notes that dictators who face a high probability of death, imprisonment, or exile after ouster should be more tempted to start diversionary wars in order to avoid ouster by rallying domestic support (Chiozza & Goemans 2011, Debs & Goemans 2010, Goemans 2000). Evidence is mixed, however, on the type of autocrat most likely to suffer a terrible fate following ouster. Debs & Goemans (2010), using CGV data, show that military dictators are more likely to face costly fates, whereas Escribà-Folch (2013) and Geddes et al. (2014), using GWF data, show that leaders of personalist regimes are. The difference in datasets explains the difference in findings. Men who once wore uniforms lead a little over half of personalist regimes. Although these military strongmen are coded personalist in the GWF dataset, they are considered military in the CGV dataset and make up about half of military-led autocracies.[12] Taken together, these findings suggest that military strongmen are more likely to face bad fates after ouster than are leaders of military regimes. Such an interpretation is consistent with Weeks (2012), who finds military strongmen more belligerent than military juntas. Her study is unique in comparing different types of military rule.

How Military Rule Ends

Although the literature on diversionary war emphasizes dictators' efforts to cling to power at all costs, other observers have noted that some coups against military rulers are motivated by the desire to return power to civilians and that military regimes often negotiate their extrications rather than being forced out. Factionalism within military regimes can lead to decisions to return to the barracks because officers often care more about the unity of the fighting force than they do about remaining in power (Geddes 1999, Nordlinger 1977). Because officers usually return to the barracks without being forced out, they tend to negotiate their extrication and thus are less likely to be violently removed. Between 1946 and 2010, only about 43% of military regimes fell to insurgency, popular uprising, or invasion compared to 64% of dominant-party regimes and more than 90% of personalist dictatorships, as shown in Figure 6.1 (Geddes et al. 2014). Nearly all nonviolent breakdowns of military regimes resulted in democratization.

Usually military regimes extricate themselves from power by overseeing an election among civilian contenders. In contrast to dominant-party and personalist regimes, outgoing members of military regimes do not typically run in transitional elections. Military incumbents have participated in transitional elections only 19% of the time, whereas incumbents from dominant-party regimes ran in 83% of transitional elections and personalist ran in 78%. Incumbent participation in transitional elections is the strongest predictor of government harassment of the opposition in transitional elections (Ofosu 2013).[13] This finding helps to explain why military regimes are more likely to end in democratization than are other kinds of autocracy (see Figure 6.2). Nearly 62% of military regimes democratize, whereas less than 45% of dominant-party regimes and 36% of personalist dictatorships do (Geddes et al. 2014)

The expectation that splits within the military ruling group lead to decisions to return to the barracks depends on the existence of a ruling group able to constrain the dictator. Consequently, the same results should not be expected if CGV or other data that combine military regimes with military strongmen in a single category are used.

Conclusion

We have highlighted the theoretical development of different understandings of military rule and the consequences of those differences for empirical studies. Most of the early comparative literature on mili-

---

Figure 6.1 Coerced Regime Collapses Sorted by Incumbent Autocratic Regime Type

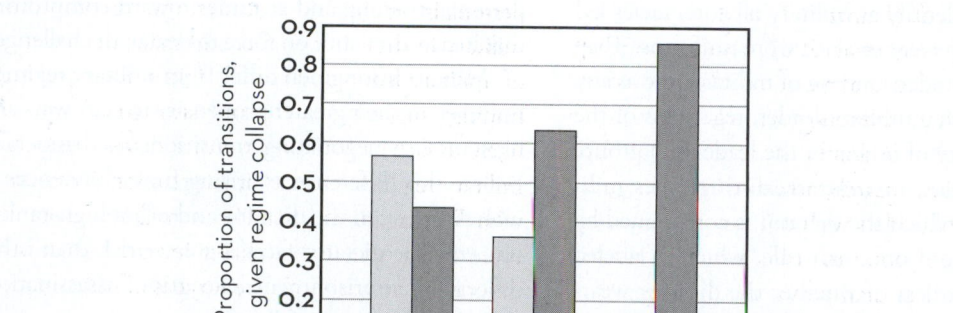

Coerced transitions (*dark gray*) include foreign invasions, coups, uprisings, and ouster by insurgents; noncoerced transitions (*light gray*) include elections and rule changes made by regime insiders.

Figure 6.2 Autocratic Regime Type and Democratization

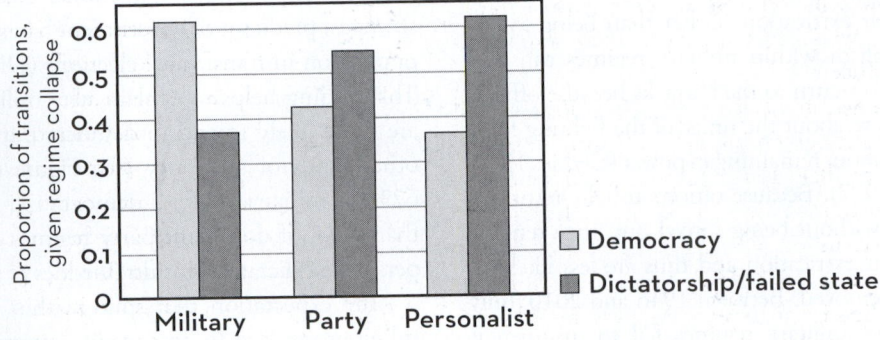

Light gray bars show the proportion of regime breakdowns that ended in democratization for military regimes, dominant-party regimes, and personalist dictatorships.

tary rule built on the expectation or observation that military dictators behave differently than other political leaders and did not distinguish between military strongmen and military dictators constrained by a junta (Finer 1976, Janowitz 1977, Nordlinger 1977). Scholars motivated by military seizures of power in most of the richest countries of Latin America, however, emphasized the distinction between dictatorships led by the military institution and rule by military strongmen (O'Donnell 1973, Remmer 1989).

Each of these understandings of military rule is associated with a dataset. The CGV and HT datasets (and their precursor, earlier versions of Banks & Wilson 2012) identify as military all autocracies led by dictators who wear or once wore uniforms. They thus reflect the understanding of military rule as any dictatorship with a military leader, regardless of the power or identity of others in the leadership group. The GWF dataset, in contrast, distinguishes military regimes in which the dictator is constrained by other officers from one-man rule, which is labeled personalist regardless of whether the dictator wears a uniform. The difference in the country-years identified as "military" across these datasets is substantial. The GWF dataset, identifies as military fewer than half of the country-years that the CGV dataset identifies as military. Consequently, studies using different datasets can reach apparently contradic-

tory conclusions, most of which can be reconciled by keeping in mind how the definition of military rule implied by the author's choice of data affects the interpretation of results.

The second part of this article summarized the results of important recent empirical studies of military rule. Preliminary results suggest that military-led autocracies are responsible for more human rights violations and wind up embroiled in more civil wars than nonmilitary regimes. The distinction between military strongmen and military regimes may not affect the propensity to use violence against opponents, since both the dictator and his military allies share the training and attitudes toward compromise that increase reliance on force to deal with challenges.

Military strongmen differ from military regimes, however, in their greater propensity to start wars and resistance to negotiating transitions to democracy. We see this difference as arising from differences of interest between the dictator and other high-ranked officers. The dictator faces a greater risk than other officers of imprisonment, execution, assassination, or exile if the regime falls. Consequently, he may be more willing to start a diversionary war or to refuse to negotiate a return to the barracks, even in the face of mobilized popular opposition and possible violent ouster. Military dictators who face little constraint on their actions, that is, military strongmen, are more free to start wars and resist negotiating with domestic opponents than are leaders of military regimes, who must negotiate their responses with fellow officers.

The findings about war and transitions show that military strongmen behave differently in some policy domains than do military rulers whose decisions are constrained by other officers. In all the areas examined, military dictatorships behave differently than civilian-led dictatorships. These findings suggest that theories of authoritarianism should take the military and its distinctive interests into account.

NOTES

1. This figure comes from merging the Geddes et al. (2013) (GWF) and Cheibub et al. (2010) (CGV) datasets. Twenty-one of 150 countries have been ruled by autocracies labeled as military in the GWF and/or CGV datasets from 2000 to 2010. We discuss these datasets in more later.

2. For examples of redistribution by military-led dictatorships, see case studies of Myanmar post-1952, Egypt post-1952, Peru 1968–1980, and Burkina Faso 1982-1987. Other military-led governments have of course protected the status quo.

3. See Geddes (2011) for a more detailed statement of this argument and some evidence to support it. For a description of the transition from collegial military rule to strongman rule under General Barrientos in Bolivia, see Corbett (1972, pp. 408–16) and Wagner (1989); under Captain Sankara in Burkina Faso, see Britain (1985, pp. 43–45) and Englebert (1998, pp. 54–65); under Colonel Saleh in Yemen, see Burroughs (1987, pp. 92–131).

4. See Wahman et al. (2013) for additional information about this dataset.

5. Other scholars also use Banks & Wilson's codings (or earlier versions by Banks) to identify military control, including Lai & Slater (2006), Poe & Tate (1994), and Poe et al. (1999).

6. The GWF figure combines pure military regimes, indirect military regimes, and military-personalist regimes. Figures mentioned later rely on the same combination.

7. The GWF dataset also identifies beginning and end dates for regimes, defined in terms of the (often informal) rules that determine membership in the regime's leadership group, how policy decisions are made, and how leaders are selected, rather than leaving analysts to infer regime changes from certain kinds of leadership changes (as in the CGV dataset). In the HT dataset, changes in the number of legal parties are recorded as regime changes, regardless of whether the identity of the dictator and other regime insiders has changed. These different implicit or explicit understandings of the concept "regime" also affect which dataset an analyst should use for different purposes.

8. See the coding rules on the GWF data website, http://dictators.la.psu.edu, for information about how these two datasets relate to each other. Because CGV is coded as of December 31 and GWF as of January 1, an adjustment is necessary to align the years of the two datasets.

9. See, for example, Policzer (2009) on Pinochet's strategic use of the security service to monitor the military, and Burggraaff (1972) on the similar use of security forces by Pérez Jiménez in Venezuela.

10. The Argentine military regime (1976–1983) is an exception. It spread the responsibility for fighting internal subversion across many military units and individual officers (Buchanan 1987).

11. Wilson (2013) revisits Fjelde's work in an attempt to better understand how the specific measure of military rule influences her empirical results. He shows that although similar results emerge from an earlier version of GWF and the HT data, results differ substantially if CGV's coding of military dictatorship is used. His study lends further weight to the claim that the data used to capture military rule can affect the answers obtained.

12. Fifty-four percent of country-years between 1946 and 2008 coded by GWF as personalist dictatorship are coded as military-led by CGV.

13. Calculated from GWF data. Transitional elections were identified using Hyde & Marinov's (2012) Nelda dataset.

LITERATURE CITED

Acemoglu D, Robinson J. 2006. *The Economic Origins of Dictatorship and Democracy.* Cambridge, MA: Cambridge Univ. Press

Arriagada G. 1988. *Pinochet: The Politics of Power,* transl. N Morris. Boston: Allen & Unwin. From Spanish

Banks AS, Wilson KA. 2012. *Cross-National Time-Series Data Archive.* Jerusalem: Databanks Intl.

Barany Z. 2011. The role of the military. *J. Dem.* 22(4):24–35

Bebler A. 1973. *Military Rule in Africa: Dahomey, Ghana, Sierra Leone, and Mali.* New York: Praeger

Biglaiser G. 2002. *Guardians of the Nation? Economists, Generals, and Economic Reform in Latin America.* Notre Dame, IN: Univ. Notre Dame Press

Binnendijk AL, Marovic I. 2006. Power and persuasion: Nonviolent strategies to influence state security forces in Serbia 2000 and Ukraine 2004. *Communist Post-Communist Stud.* 39:411–29

Boix C. 2003. *Democracy and Redistribution.* Cambridge, MA: Cambridge Univ. Press

Britain V. 1985. Introduction to Sankara & Burkina Faso. *Rev. Afr. Polit. Econ.* 32:39–47

Brownlee J. 2009. Portents of pluralism: How hybrid regimes affect democratic transitions. *Am. J. Polit. Sci.* 53(3):515–32

Buchanan PG. 1987. The varied faces of domination: State terror, economic policy, and social rupture during the Argentine "Proceso," 1976–81. *Am. J. Polit. Sci.* 31(2):336–82

Burggraaff WJ. 1972. *The Venezuelan Armed Forces in Politics, 1935–1959.* Columbia: Univ. Missouri Press

Burroughs RD. 1987. *The Yemen Arab Republic: The Politics of Development, 1962–1986.* Boulder and London: Westview and Croom Helm

Cheibub JA, Gandhi J, Vreeland JR. 2010. *Democracy and dictatorship data set.* https://netfiles.uiuc.edu/cheibub/www/DDpage.html

Chiozza G, Goemans H. 2011. *Leaders and International Conflict.* New York: Cambridge Univ. Press

Clapham C, Philip G. 1985. The political dilemmas of military regimes. In *The Political Dilemmas of Military Regimes,* ed. C Clapham, G Philip, pp. 1–26. London: Croom Helm

Corbett CD. 1972. Military institutional development and sociopolitical change: The Bolivian case. *J. Interam. Stud. World Aff.* 14(4):399–435

Davenport C. 1995. Assessing the military's influence on political repression. *J. Polit. Mil. Soc.* 23(Summer): 119–44

Davenport C. 2007a. State repression and political order. *Annu. Rev. Polit. Sci.* 10:1–23

Davenport C. 2007b. State repression and tyrannical peace. *J. Peace Res.* 44(4):485–504

Debs A. 2010. *Living by the sword and dying by the sword? Leadership transitions in and out of dictatorships.* Presented at Annu. Meet. Midwest Polit. Sci. Assoc., Chicago, IL

Debs A, Goemans H. 2010. Regime type, the fate of leaders and war. *Am. Polit. Sci. Rev.* 104(3):430–46

Decalo S. 1976. *Coups and Army Rule in Africa: Studies in Military Style.* New Haven, CT: Yale Univ. Press

Englebert P. 1998. *Burkina Faso: Unsteady Statehood in West Africa.* Boulder, CO: Westview

Escribà-Folch A. 2013. Accountable for what? Regime types, performance, and the fate of outgoing dictators, 1946–2004. *Democratization* 20(1): 160–85

Feit E. 1973. *The Armed Bureaucrats: Military-Administrative Regimes and Political Development.* Boston: Houton Mifflin

Finer SE. 1976. *The Man on Horseback: The Role of the Military in Politics.* Harmondsworth, UK: Penguin. 2nd ed.

Fjelde H. 2010. Generals, dictators, and kings. *Confl. Manag. Peace Sci.* 27(3):195–218

Frantz E, Ezrow N. 2011. *The Politics of Dictatorship: Institutions and Outcomes in Authoritarian Regimes.* Boulder, CO: Lynne Rienner

Gandhi J. 2008. *Political Institutions under Dictatorship.* Cambridge, MA: Cambridge Univ. Press

Geddes B. 1999. What do we know about democratization after twenty years? *Annu. Rev. Polit. Sci.* 2:115–44

Geddes B. 2003. *Paradigms and Sand Castles: Theory Building and Research Design in Comparative Politics.* Ann Arbor: Univ. Mich. Press

Geddes B. 2006. Stages of development in authoritarian regimes. In *World Order after Leninism*, ed. V Tismaneanu, MM Howard, R Sil, pp. 149–70. Seattle: Univ. Washington Press

Geddes B. 2011. *How the military shapes "democratic" institutions in dictatorships.* Presented at How Autocracies Work: Beyond the Electoral Paradigm, Univ. Mich.

Geddes B, Wright JG, Frantz E. 2013. *Authoritarian regimes data set.* http://dictators.la.psu.edu

Geddes B, Wright JG, Frantz E. 2014. Autocratic breakdown and regime transitions: A new data set. *Perspect. Polit.* 12: In press

Goemans H. 2000. Fighting for survival: The fate of leaders and the duration of war. *J. Confl. Resolut.* 44(5):555–79

Hadenius A, Teorell J. 2007. Pathways from authoritarianism. *J. Democracy* 18(1):143–57

Hyde S, Marinov N. 2012. Which elections can be lost? *Polit. Analysis* 20(2):191–210

Janowitz M. 1977. *Military Institutions and Coercion in the Developing Nations.* Chicago: Univ. Chicago Press

Johnson JL. 1962. The Latin-American military as a politically competing group in transitional society. In *The Role of the Military in Underdeveloped Countries*, ed. JL Johnson, pp. 91–129. Princeton, NJ: Princeton Univ. Press

Lai B, Slater D. 2006. Institutions of the offensive: Domestic sources of dispute initiation in authoritarian regimes, 1950–1992. *Am. F. Polit. Sci.* 50(1):113–26

Luckham R. 1971. *The Nigerian Military: A Sociological Analysis of Authority and Revolt 1960–67.* Cambridge, MA: Cambridge Univ. Press

Nordlinger E. 1977. *Soldiers in Politics: Military Coups and Governments.* Englewood Cliffs, NJ: Prentice-Hall

O'Donnell G. 1973. *Modernization and Bureaucratic Authoritarianism.* Berkeley: Univ. Calif. Inst. Intl. Stud.

Ofosu G. 2013. *Explaining variation in the fairness of transitional election across authoritarian regime types.* Unpublished manuscript, Dep. Polit. Sci., Univ. Calif. Los Angeles

Peceny M, Beer CC. 2003. Peaceful parties and puzzling personalists. *Am. Polit. Sci. Rev.* 97(2):339–42

Peceny M, Beer CC, Sanchez-Terry S. 2002. Dictatorial peace? *Am. Polit. Sci. Rev.* 96(1):15–26

Peceny M, Butler CK. 2004. The conflict behavior of authoritarian regimes. *Int. Polit.* 41(4):565–81

Poe SC, Tate CN. 1994. Repression of human rights to personal integrity in the 1980s: A global analysis. *Am. Polit. Sci. Rev.* 88(4):853–72

Poe SC, Tate CN, Keith LC. 1999. Repression of the human right to personal integrity revisited: A global cross-national study covering the years 1976–1993. *Int. Stud. Q.* 43(2):291–313

Policzer P. 2009. *The Rise and Fall of Repression in Chile.* Notre Dame, IN: Univ. Notre Dame Press

Potash RA. 1996. *The Army and Politics in Argentina, 1962–1973: From Frondizi's Fall to the Peronist Restoration.* Stanford, CA: Stanford Univ. Press

Remmer K. 1989. *Military Rule in Latin America.* New York: Unwin Hymen

Smith B. 2005. Life of the party: The origins of regime breakdown and persistence under single-party rule. *World Polit.* 57(3):421–51

Stepan A. 1971. *The Military in Politics: Changing Patterns in Brazil.* Princeton, NJ: Princeton Univ. Press

Svolik MW. 2013. Contracting on violence: The moral hazard in authoritarian repression and military intervention in politics. *J. Confl. Resolut.* 57:765–94

Wagner ML. 1989. Chapter 1—Historical setting. In *A Country Study: Bolivia*, ed. RA Hudson, DM Hanratty. Washington, DC: Fed. Res. Div., Libr. Congr. http://lcweb2.loc.gov/frd/cs/botoc.html

Wahman M, Teorell J, Hadenius A. 2013. Authoritarian regime types revisited: Updated data in comparative perspective. *Comp. Polit.* 19(1):19–34

Weeks JL. 2012. Strongmen and straw men: Authoritarian regimes and the initiation of international conflict. *Am. Polit. Sci. Rev.* 106(2):326–47

Wilson MC. 2013. A discreet critique of discrete regime type data. *Comp. Polit. Stud.* doi: 10.1177/0010414013488546

Wright JG, Escribà-Folch A. 2012. Authoritarian institutions and regime survival: Transitions to democracy and subsequent autocracy. *Br. J. Polit. Sci.* 42(2):283–309

Gary King, Jennifer Pan, and
Margaret E. Roberts

HOW CENSORSHIP IN CHINA ALLOWS GOVERNMENT CRITICISM BUT SILENCES COLLECTIVE EXPRESSION

Introduction

The size and sophistication of the Chinese government's program to selectively censor the expressed views of the Chinese people is unprecedented in recorded world history. Unlike in the U.S., where social media is centralized through a few providers, in China it is fractured across hundreds of local sites. Much of the responsibility for censorship is devolved to these Internet content providers, who may be fined or shut down if they fail to comply with government censorship guidelines. To comply with government, each individual site privately employs up to 1,000 censors. Additionally, approximately 20,000–50,000 Internet police (*wang jing*) and Internet monitors (*wang guanban*) as well as an estimated 250,000–300,000 "50 cent party members" (*wumao dang*) at all levels of government—central, provincial, and local—participate in this huge effort (Chen and Ang 2011, and our interviews with informants, granted anonymity). China overall is tied with Burma at 187th of 197 countries on a scale of press freedom (Freedom House 2012), but the Chinese censorship effort is by far the largest.

In this article, we show that this program, designed to *limit* freedom of speech of the Chinese people, paradoxically also *exposes* an extraordinarily rich source of information about the Chinese government's interests, intentions, and goals—a subject of long-standing interest to the scholarly and policy communities. The information we unearth is available in continuous time, rather than the usual sporadic media reports of the leaders' sometimes visible actions. We use this new information to develop a theory of the overall purpose of the censorship program, and thus to reveal some of the most basic goals of the Chinese leadership that until now have been the subject of intense speculation but necessarily little empirical analysis. This information is also a treasure trove that can be used for many other scholarly (and practical) purposes.

Our central theoretical finding is that, contrary to much research and commentary, the purpose of the censorship program is *not* to suppress criticism of the state or the Communist Party. Indeed, despite widespread censorship of social media, we find that when the Chinese people write scathing criticisms of their government and its leaders, the probability that their post will be censored does not increase. Instead, we find that the purpose of the censorship program is to reduce the probability of collective action by clipping social ties whenever any collective movements are in evidence or expected. We demonstrate these points and then discuss their far-reaching implications for many research areas within the study of Chinese politics and comparative politics.

In the section below, we begin by defining two theories of Chinese censorship. We then describe our unique data source and the unusual challenges involved in gathering it. We then lay out our strategy for analysis, give our results, and conclude.

From *American Political Science Review* (May 2013), pp. 326–43.

Government Intentions and the Purpose of Censorship

Previous Indicators of Government Intent

Deciphering the opaque intentions and goals of the leaders of the Chinese regime was once the central focus of scholarly research on elite politics in China, where Western researchers used Kremlinology—or Pekingology—as a methodological strategy (Chang 1983; Charles 1966; Hinton 1955; MacFarquhar 1974, 1983; Schurmann 1966; Teiwes 1979). With the Cultural Revolution and with China's economic opening, more sources of data became available to researchers, and scholars shifted their focus to areas where information was more accessible. Studies of China today rely on government statistics, public opinion surveys, interviews with local officials, as well as measures of the visible actions of government officials and the government as a whole (Guo 2009; Kung and Chen 2011; Shih 2008; Tsai 2007a, b). These sources are well suited to answer other important political science questions, but in gauging government intent, they are widely known to be indirect, very sparsely sampled, and often of dubious value. For example, government statistics, such as the number of "mass incidents", could offer a view of government interests, but only if we could somehow separate true numbers from government manipulation. Similarly, sample surveys can be informative, but the government obviously keeps information from ordinary citizens, and even when respondents have the information researchers are seeking they may not be willing to express themselves freely. In situations where direct interviews with officials are possible, researchers are in the position of having to read tea leaves to ascertain what their informants really believe.

Measuring intent is all the more difficult with the sparse information coming from existing methods because the Chinese government is not a monolithic entity. In fact, in those instances when different agencies, leaders, or levels of government work at cross purposes, even the concept of a unitary intent or motivation may be difficult to define, much less measure. We cannot solve all these problems, but by providing more information about the state's revealed preferences through its censorship behavior, we may be somewhat better able to produce useful measures of intent.

Theories of Censorship

We attempt to complement the important work on how censorship is conducted, and how the Internet may increase the space for public discourse (Duan 2007; Edmond 2012; Egorov, Guriev, and Sonin 2009; Esarey and Xiao 2008, 2011; Herold 2011; Lindtner and Szablewicz 2011; MacKinnon 2012; Xiao 2011; Yang 2009), by beginning to build an empirically documented theory of why the government censors and what it is trying to achieve through this extensive program. While current scholarship draws the reasonable but broad conclusion that Chinese government censorship is aimed at maintaining the status quo for the current regime, we focus on what specifically the government believes is critical, and what actions it takes, to accomplish this goal.

To do this, we distinguish two theories of what constitutes the goals of the Chinese regime as implemented in their censorship program, each reflecting a different perspective on what threatens the stability of the regime. First is a *state critique* theory, which posits that the goal of the Chinese leadership is to suppress dissent, and to prune human expression that finds fault with elements of the Chinese state, its policies, or its leaders. The result is to make the sum total of available public expression more favorable to those in power. Many types of state critique are included in this idea, such as poor government performance.

Second is what we call the theory of *collective action potential*: the target of censorship is people who join together to express themselves collectively, stimulated by someone other than the government, and seem to have the potential to generate collective action. In this view, collective expression—many people communicating on social media on the same subject—regarding actual collective action, such as protests, as well as those about events that seem likely to generate collective action but have not yet done so, are likely to be censored. Whether social media posts with collective action potential find fault with or assign praise to the state, or are about subjects unrelated to the state, is unrelated to this theory.

An alternative way to describe what we call "collective action potential" is the apparent perspective of the Chinese government, where collective expression organized outside of governmental control equals factionalism and ultimately chaos and disorder. For example, on the eve of the Communist Party's 90th birthday, the state-run Xinhua news agency issued an opinion that western-style parliamentary democracy would lead to a repetition of the turbulent factionalism of China's Cultural Revolution (http://j.mp/McRDXk). Similarly, at the Fourth Session of the 11th National People's Congress in March of 2011, Wu Bangguo, member of the Politburo Standing Committee and Chairman of the Standing Committee of the National People's Congress, said that "On the basis of China's conditions . . . we'll not employ a system of multiple parties holding office in rotation" in order to avoid "an abyss of internal disorder" (http://j.mp/Ldhp25). China observers have often noted the emphasis placed by the Chinese government on maintaining stability (Shirk 2007; Whyte 2010; Zhang et al. 2002), as well as the government's desire to limit collective action by clipping social ties (Perry 2002, 2008). The Chinese regime encounters a great deal of contention and collective action; according to Sun Liping, a professor of Sociology at Tsinghua University, China experienced 180,000 "mass incidents" in 2010 (http://j.mp/McQeji). Because the government encounters collective action frequently, it influences the actions and perceptions of the regime. The stated perspective of the Chinese government is that limitations on horizontal communications is a legitimate and effective action designed to protect its people (Perry 2010)—in other words, a paternalistic strategy to avoid chaos and disorder, given the conditions of Chinese society.

Current scholarship has not been able to differentiate empirically between the two theories we offer. Marolt (2011) writes that online postings are censored when they "either criticize China's party state and its policies directly or advocate collective political action." MacKinnon (2012) argues that during the Wenzhou high speed rail crash, Internet content providers were asked to "track and censor critical postings." Esarey and Xiao (2008) find that Chinese bloggers use satire to convey criticism of the state in order to avoid harsh repression. Esarey and Xiao (2011) write that party leaders are most fearful of "Concerted efforts by influential netizens to pressure the government to change policy," but identify these pressures as criticism of the state. Shirk (2011) argues that the aim of censorship is to constrain the mobilization of political opposition, but her examples suggest that critical viewpoints are those that are suppressed.

Collective action in the form of protests is often thought to be the death knell of authoritarian regimes. Protests in East Germany, Eastern Europe, and most recently the Middle East have all preceded regime change (Ash 2002; Lohmann 1994; Przeworski et al. 2000). A great deal of scholarship on China has focused on what leads people to protest and their tactics (Blecher 2002; Cai 2002; Chen 2000; Lee 2007; O'Brien and Li 2006; Perry 2002, 2008). The Chinese state seems focused on preventing protest at all costs—and, indeed, the prevalence of collective action is part of the formal evaluation criteria for local officials (Edin 2003). However, several recent works argue that authoritarian regimes may expect and welcome substantively narrow protests as a way of enhancing regime stability by identifying, and then dealing with, discontented communities (Chen 2012; Dimitrov 2008; Lorentzen 2010). Chen (2012) argues that small, isolated protests have a long tradition in China and are an expected part of government.

Outline of Results

The nature of the two theories means that either or both could be correct or incorrect. Here, we offer evidence that, with few exceptions, the answer is simple: state critique theory is incorrect and the theory of collective action potential is correct. Our data show that the Chinese censorship program allows for a wide variety of criticisms of the Chinese government, its officials, and its policies. As it turns out, censorship is primarily aimed at restricting the spread of information that may lead to collective action, regardless of whether or not the expression is in direct opposition to the state and whether or not it is related to government policies. Large increases in online volume are good predictors of censorship when these increases are associated with events related to collective action, e.g., protests on the ground. In addition, we measure sentiment within each of these events and show that during these events, the government censors views that are both supportive and critical of the state. These results reveal that the Chinese regime believes suppressing social media posts with collective action potential, rather than suppression of criticism, is crucial to maintaining power.

Data

We describe here the challenges involved in collecting large quantities of detailed information that the Chinese government does not want anyone to see and goes to great lengths to prevent anyone from accessing. We discuss the types of censorship we study, our data collection process, the limitations of this study, and ways we organize the data for subsequent analyses.

Types of Censorship

Human expression is censored in Chinese social media in at least three ways, the last of which is the focus of our study. First is "The Great Firewall of China," which disallows certain entire Web sites from operating in the country. The Great Firewall is an obvious problem for foreign Internet firms, and for the Chinese people interacting with others outside of China on these services, but it does little to limit the expressive power of Chinese people who

can find other sites to express themselves in similar ways. For example, Facebook is blocked in China but RenRen is a close substitute; similarly Sina Weibo is a popular Chinese clone of Twitter, which is also unavailable.

Second is "keyword blocking" which stops a user from posting text that contain banned words or phrases. This has limited effect on freedom of speech, since netizens do not find it difficult to outwit automated programs. To do so, they use analogies, metaphors, satire, and other evasions. The Chinese language offers novel evasions, such as substituting characters for those banned with others that have unrelated meanings but sound alike ("homophones") or look similar ("homographs"). An example of a homograph is 目田, which has the nonsensical literal meaning of "eye field" but is used by World of Warcraft players to substitute for the banned but similarly shaped 自由 which means freedom. As an example of a homophone, the sound "hexie" is often written as 河蟹, which means "river crab," but is used to refer to 和谐, which is the official state policy of a "harmonious society."

Once past the first two barriers to freedom of speech, the text gets posted on the Web and the censors read and remove those they find objectionable. As nearly as we can tell from the literature, observers, private conversations with those inside several governments, and an examination of the data, content filtering is in large part a manual effort—censors read posts by hand. Automated methods appear to be an auxiliary part of this effort. Unlike The Great Firewall and keyword blocking, hand censoring cannot be evaded by clever phrasing. Thus, it is this last and most extensive form of censoring that we focus on in this article.

Collection

We begin with social media blogs in which it is at least possible for writers to express themselves fully, prior to possible censorship, and leaving to other research social media services that constrain authors to very short Twitter-like (*weibo*) posts (e.g., Bamman, O'Connor, and Smith 2012). In many countries, such as the U.S., almost all blog posts appear on a few large sites (Facebook, Google's blogspot, Tumblr, etc.); China does have some big sites such as sina.com, but a large portion of its social media landscape is finely distributed over numerous individual sites, e.g., local bbs forums. This difference poses a considerable logistical challenge for data collection—with different Web addresses, different software interfaces, different companies and local authorities monitoring those accessing the sites, different network reliabilities, access speeds, terms of use, and censorship modalities, and different ways of potentially hindering or stopping our data collection. Fortunately, the structure of Chinese social media also turns out to pose a special opportunity for studying localized control of collective expression, since the numerous local sites provide considerable information about the geolocation of posts, much more than is available even in the U.S.

The most complicated engineering challenges in our data collection process involve locating, accessing, and downloading posts from many Web sites before Internet content providers or the government reads and censors those that are deemed by authorities as objectionable;[1] revisiting each post frequently enough to learn if and when it was censored; and proceeding with data collection in so many places in China without affecting the system we were studying or being prevented from studying it. The reason we are able to accomplish this is because our data collection methods are highly automated whereas Chinese censorship entails manual effort. Our extensive engineering effort, which we do not detail here for obvious reasons, is executed at many locations around the world, including inside China.

Ultimately, we were able to locate, obtain access to, and download social media posts from 1,382 Chinese Web sites during the first half of 2011. The most striking feature of the structure of Chinese social media is its extremely long (power-law like) tail. * * * The largest sources of posts include blog. sina (with 59% of posts), hi.baidu, bbs.voc, bbs.m4, and tianya, but the tail keeps going.[2]

Social media posts cover such a huge range of topics that a random sampling strategy attempting to cover everything is rarely informative about any individual topic of interest. Thus, we begin with a stratified random sampling design, organized hierarchically. We first choose eighty-five separate topic areas within three categories of hypothesized political sensitivity, ranging from "high" (such as Ai Weiwei) to "medium" (such as the one child policy) to "low" (such as a popular online video game). We chose the specific topics within these categories by reviewing prior literature, consulting with China specialists, and studying current events. * * * Then, within each topic area, defined by a set of keywords, we collected all social media posts over a six-month period. We examined the posts in each area, removed spam, and explored the content with the tool for computer-assisted reading (Crosas et al. 2012; Grimmer and King 2011). With this procedure we collected 3,674,698 posts, with 127,283 randomly selected for further analysis. (We repeated this procedure for other time periods, and in some cases in more depth for some issue areas, and overall collected and analyzed 11,382,221 posts.) All posts originating from sites in China were written in Chinese, and excluded those from Hong Kong and Taiwan.[3] For each post, we examined its content, placed it on a timeline according to topic area, and revisited the Web site from which it came repeatedly thereafter to determine whether it was censored. We supplemented this information with other specific data collections as needed.

The censors are not shy, and so we found it straightforward to distinguish (intentional) censorship from sporadic outages or transient time-out errors. The censored Web sites include notes such as "Sorry, the host you were looking for does not exist, has been deleted, or is being investigated" and are sometimes even adorned with pictures of Jingjing and Chacha, Internet police cartoon characters.

Although our methods are faster than the Chinese censors, the censors nevertheless appear highly expert at their task. We illustrate this with analyses of random samples of posts surrounding the 9/27/2011 Shanghai Subway crash, and posts collected between 4/10/2012 and 4/12/2012 about Bo Xilai, a recently deposed member of the Chinese elite, and a separate collection of posts about his wife, Gu Kailai, who was accused and convicted of murder. We monitored each of the posts in these three areas continuously in near real time for nine days. (Censorship in other areas follow the same basic pattern.) Histograms of the time until censorship appear in Figure 6.3 For all three, the vast majority of censorship activity occurs within 24 hours of the original posting, although a few deletions occur longer than five days later. This is a remarkable organizational accomplishment, requiring large scale military-like precision: The many leaders at different levels of government and at different Internet content providers first need to come to a decision (by agreement, direct order, or compromise) about what to censor in each situation; they need to communicate it to tens or hundreds of thousands of individuals; and then they must all complete execution of the plan within roughly 24 hours. As Edmond (2012) points out, the proliferation of information sources on social media makes information more difficult to control; however, the Chinese government has overcome these obstacles on a national scale. Given the normal human difficulties of coming to agreement with many others, and the usual difficulty of achieving high levels of intercoder reliability on interpreting text (e.g., Hopkins and King 2010),

the effort the government puts into its censorship program is large, and highly professional. We have found some evidence of disagreements within this large and multifarious bureaucracy, such as at different levels of government, but we have not yet studied these differences in detail.

Limitations

As we show below, our methodology reveals a great deal about the goals of the Chinese leadership, but it misses self-censorship and censorship that may occur before we are able to obtain the post in the first place; it also does not quantify the direct effects of The Great Firewall, keyword blocking, or search filtering in finding what others say. We have also not studied the effect of physical violence, such as the arrest of bloggers, or threats of the same. Although many officials and levels of government have a hand in the decisions about what and when to censor, our data only sometimes enable us to distinguish among these sources.

We are of course unable to determine the consequences of these limitations, although it is reasonable to expect that the most important of these are physical violence, threats, and the resulting self-censorship. Although the social media data we analyze include expressions by millions of Chinese and cover an extremely wide range of topics and speech behavior, the presumably much smaller number of

Figure 6.3 The Speed of Censorship, Monitored in Real Time

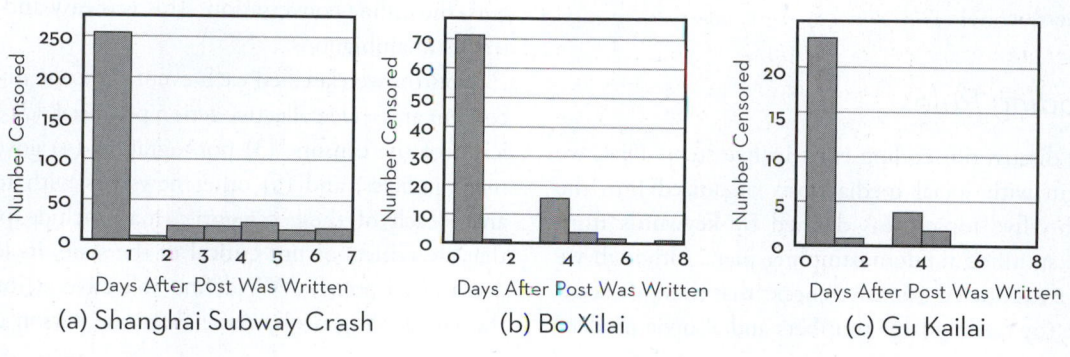

(a) Shanghai Subway Crash (b) Bo Xilai (c) Gu Kailai

discussions we cannot observe are likely to be those of the most (or most urgent) interest to the Chinese government.

Finally, in the past, studies of Internet behavior were judged based on how well their measures approximated "real world" behavior; subsequently, online behavior has become such a large and important part of human life that the expressions observed in social media are now important in their own right, regardless of whether it is a good measure of non-Internet freedoms and behaviors. But either way, we offer little evidence here of connections between what we learn in social media and press freedom or other types of human expression in China.

Analysis Strategy

Overall, an average of approximately 13% of all social media posts are censored. This average level is quite stable over time when aggregating over all posts in all areas, but masks enormous changes in volume of posts and censorship efforts. Our first hint of what might (not) be driving censorship rates is a surprisingly low correlation between our ex ante measure of political sensitivity and censorship: Censorship behavior in the low and medium categories was essentially the same (16% and 17%, respectively) and only marginally lower than the high category (24%).[4] Clearly something else is going on. To convey what this is, we now discuss our coding rules, our central hypothesis, and the exact operational procedures the Chinese government may use to censor.

Coding Rules

We discuss our coding rules in five steps. First, we begin with social media posts organized into the eighty-five topic areas defined by keywords from our stratified random sampling plan. Although we have conducted extensive checks that these are accurate (by reading large numbers and also via modern computer-assisted reading technology), our topic areas will inevitably (with any machine or human classification technology) include some posts that do not belong. We take the conservative approach of first drawing conclusions even when affected by this error. Afterward, we then do numerous checks (via the same techniques) after the fact to ensure we are not missing anything important. We report below the few patterns that could be construed as a systematic error; each one turns out to strengthen our conclusions.

Second, conversation in social media in almost all topic areas (and countries) is well known to be highly "bursty," that is, with periods of stability punctuated by occasional sharp spikes in volume around specific subjects (Ratkiewicz et al. 2010). We also found that with only two exceptions—pornography and criticisms of the censors, described below—censorship effort is often especially intense within *volume bursts*. Thus, we organize our data around these volume bursts. We think of each of the eighty-five topic areas as a six-month time series of daily volume and detect bursts using the weights calculated from robust regression techniques to identify outlying observations from the rest of the time series (Huber 1964; Rousseeuw and Leroy 1987). In our data, this sophisticated burst detection algorithm is almost identical to using time periods with volume more than three standard deviations greater than the rest of the six-month period. With this procedure, we detected eighty-seven distinct volume bursts within sixty-seven of the eighty-five topic areas.[5]

Third, we examined the posts in each volume burst and identified the real-world *event* associated with the online conversation. This was easy and the results unambiguous.

Fourth, we classified each event into one of five content areas: (1) collective action potential, (2) criticism of the censors, (3) pornography, (4) government policies, and (5) other news. As with topic areas, each of these categories may include posts that are critical or not critical of the state, its leaders, and its policies. We define collective action as the pursuit of goals by more than one person controlled or spurred by actors other than government officials or their agents. Our theoretical category of "collective action potential" involves any event that has the potential to cause collective action, but to be conservative, and to ensure clear and replicable coding rules, we limit this category to events which (a) involve protest or organized crowd formation outside the Internet; (b) relate to individuals who have organized or incited collective action on the ground in the past; or (c) relate to nationalism or nationalist sentiment that has incited protest or collective action in the past. (Nationalism is treated separately because of its frequently demonstrated high potential to generate collective action and also to constrain foreign policy, an area which has long been viewed as a special prerogative of the government; Reilly 2012.)

Events are categorized as criticism of censors if they pertain to government or nongovernment entities with control over censorship, including individuals and firms. Pornography includes advertisements and news about movies, Web sites, and other media containing pornographic or explicitly sexual content. Policies refer to government statements or reports of government activities pertaining to domestic or foreign policy. And "other news" refers to reporting on events, other than those which fall into one of the other four categories.

Finally, we conducted a study to verify the reliability of our event coding rules. To do this, we gave our rules above to two people familiar with Chinese politics and asked them to code each of the eighty-seven events (each associated with a volume burst) into one of the five categories. The coders worked independently and classified each of the events on their own. Decisions by the two coders agreed in 98.9% (i.e., eighty-six of eighty-seven) of the events. The only event with divergent codes was the pelting of Fang Binxing (the architect of China's Great Firewall) with shoes and eggs. This event included criticism of the censors and to some extent collective action because several people were working together to throw things at Fang. We broke the tie by counting this event as an example

of criticism of the censors, but however this event is coded does not affect our results since we predict both will be censored.

Central Hypothesis

Our central hypothesis is that the government censors *all* posts in topic areas during volume bursts that discuss events with collective action potential. That is, the censors do not judge whether individual posts have collective action potential, perhaps in part because rates of intercoder reliability would likely be very low. In fact, Kuran (1989) and Lohmann (2002) show that it is information about a collective action event that propels collective action and so distinguishing this from explicit calls for collective action would be difficult if not impossible. Instead, we hypothesize that the censors make the much easier judgment, about whether the posts are on topics associated with events that have collective action potential, and they do it regardless of whether or not the posts criticize the state.

The censors also attempt to censor all posts in the categories of pornography and criticism of the censors, but not posts within event categories of government policies and news.

The Government's Operational Procedures

The exact operational procedures by which the Chinese government censors are of course not observed. But based on conversations with individuals within and close to the Chinese censorship apparatus, we believe our coding rules can be viewed as an approximation to them. (In fact, after a draft of our article was written and made public, we received communications confirming our story.) We define topic areas by hand, sort social media posts into topic areas by keywords, and detect volume bursts automatically via statistical methods for time series data on post volume. (These steps might be combined by the government to detect topics automatically based on spikes in posts with high similarity, but this would likely involve considerable error given inadequacies in known fully automated clustering technologies.) In some cases, identifying the real-world event might occur before the burst, such as if the censors are secretly warned about an upcoming event (such as the imminent arrest of a dissident) that could spark collective action. Identifying events from bursts that were observed first would need to be implemented at least mostly by hand, perhaps with some help from algorithms that identify statistically improbable phrases. Finally, the actual decision to censor an individual post—which, according to our hypothesis, involves checking whether it is associated with a particular event—is almost surely accomplished largely by hand, since no known statistical or machine learning technology can achieve a level of accuracy anywhere near that which we observe in the Chinese censorship program. Here, censors may begin with keyword searches on the event identified, but will need to manually read through the resulting posts to censor those which are related to the triggering event. For example, when censors identified protests in Zengcheng as precipitating online discussion, they may have conducted a keyword search among posts for Zengcheng, but they would have had to read through these posts by hand to separate posts about protests from posts talking about Zengcheng in other contexts, say Zengcheng's lychee harvest.

Results

We now offer three increasingly specific tests of our hypotheses. These tests are based on (1) post volume, (2) the nature of the event generating each volume burst, and (3) the specific content of the censored posts.* * *

Post Volume

If the goal of censorship is to stop discussions with collective action potential, then we would expect more censorship during volume bursts than at other times. We also expect some bursts—those with collective action potential—to have much higher levels of censorship.

To begin to study this pattern, we define *censorship magnitude* for a topic area as the percent censored within a volume burst minus the percent censored outside all bursts. (The base rates, which vary very little across issue areas and which we present in detail in graphs below, do not impose empirically relevant ceiling or floor effects on this measure.) This is a stringent measure of the interests of the Chinese government because censoring during a volume burst is obviously more difficult owing to there being more posts to evaluate, less time to do it in, and little or no warning of when the event will take place.

Panel (a) in Figure 6.4 gives a histogram with results that appear to support our hypotheses. The results show that the bulk of volume bursts have a censorship magnitude centered around zero, but with an exceptionally long right tail (and no corresponding long left tail). Clearly volume bursts are often associated with dramatically higher levels of censorship even compared to the baseline during the rest of the six months for which we observe a topic area.

The Nature of Events Generating Volume Bursts

We now show that volume bursts generated by events pertaining to collective action, criticism of censors, and pornography are censored, albeit as we show in different ways, while post volume generated by discussion of government policy and other news is not. We discuss the state critique hypothesis in the next subsection. Here, we offer three separate, and increasingly detailed, views of our present results.

First, consider panel (b) of Figure 6.4, which takes the same distribution of censorship magnitude as in panel (a) and displays it by event type. The result is dramatic: events related to collective action, criticism of the censors, and pornography fall largely

Figure 6.4 "Censorship Magnitude," the Percent of Posts Censored inside a Volume Burst minus outside Volume Bursts

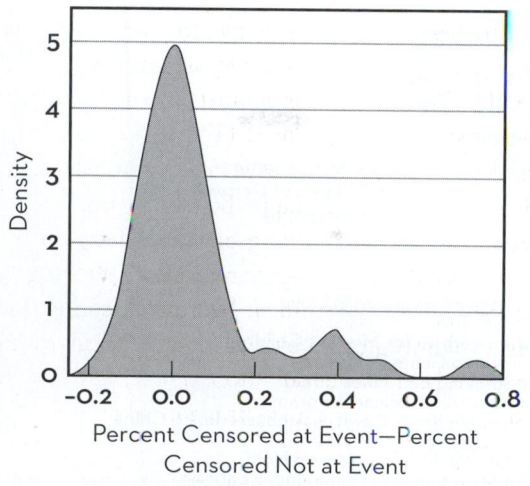

(a) Distribution of Censorship Magnitude

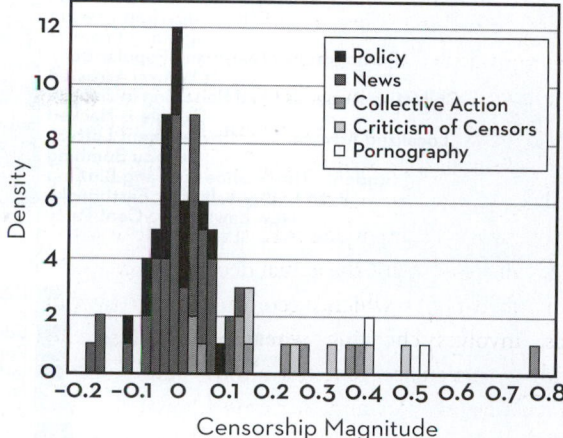

(b) Censorship Magnitude by Event Type

to the right, indicating high levels of censorship magnitude, while events related to policies and news fall to the left. On average, censorship magnitude is 27% for collective action, but −1% and −4% for policy and news.[6]

Second, we list the specific events with the highest and lowest levels of censorship magnitude. These appear, using the same color scheme, in Figure 6.5. The events with the highest collective action potential include protests in Inner Mongolia precipitated by the death of an ethnic Mongol herder by a coal truck driver, riots in Zengcheng by migrant workers over an altercation between a pregnant woman and security personnel, the arrest of artist/political dissident Ai Weiwei, and the bombings over land claims in Fuzhou. Notably, one of the highest "collective action potential" events was not political at all: following the Japanese earthquake and subsequent meltdown of the nuclear plant in Fukushima, a rumor spread through Zhejiang Province that the iodine in salt would protect people from radiation exposure, and a mad rush to buy salt ensued. The rumor was biologically false, and had nothing to do with the state one way or the other, but it was highly censored; the reason appears to be because of the localized control of collective expression by actors other than the government. Indeed, we find that salt rumors on local Web sites are much more likely to be censored than salt rumors on national Web sites.[7]

Consistent with our theory of collective action potential, some of the most highly censored events are not criticisms or even discussions of national policies, but rather highly localized collective expressions that represent or threaten group formation. One such example is posts on a local Wenzhou Web site expressing support for Chen Fei, a environmental activist who supported an environmental lottery to help local environmental protection. Even though Chen Fei is *supported* by the central government, all posts supporting him on the local Web site are censored, likely because of his record of organizing collective action. In the mid-2000s, Chen founded an environmental NGO with more than 400 registered members who created China's first "no-plastic-bag village," which eventually led to legislation on use of plastic bags. Another example is a heavily censored group of posts expressing collective anger about lead

Figure 6.5 Events with Highest and Lowest Censorship Magnitude

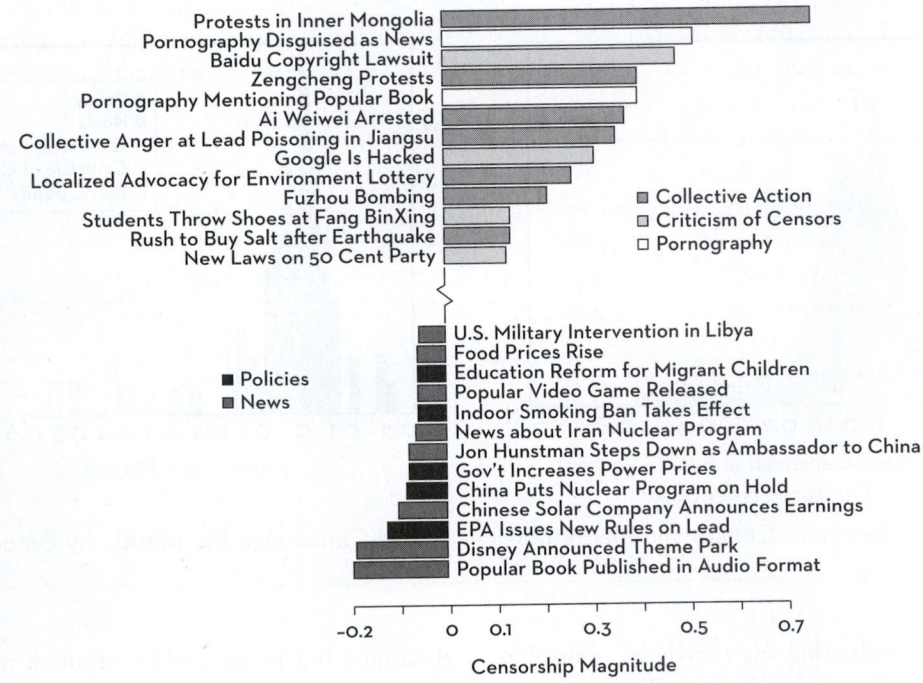

poisoning in Jiangsu Province's Suyang County from battery factories. These posts talk about children sickened by pollution from lead acid battery factories in Zhejiang Province belonging to the Tianneng Group, and report that hospitals refused to release results of lead tests to patients. In January 2011, villagers from Suyang gathered at the factory to demand answers. Such collective organization is not tolerated by the censors, regardless of whether it supports the government or criticizes it.

In *all* events categorized as having collective action potential, censorship within the event is more frequent than censorship outside the event. In addition, these events are, on average, considerably more censored than other types of events. These facts are consistent with our theory that the censors are intentionally searching for and taking down posts related to events with collective action potential. However, we add to these tests one based on an examination of what might lead to different

levels of censorship among events within this category: Although we have developed a quantitative measure, some of the events in this category clearly have more collective action potential than others. By studying the specific events, it is easy to see that events with the lowest levels of censorship magnitude generally have less collective action potential than the very highly censored cases, as consistent with our theory.

To see this, consider the few events classified as collective action potential with the lowest levels of censorship magnitude. These include a volume burst associated with protests about ethnic stereotypes in the animated children's movie *Kungfu Panda 2*, which was properly classified as a collective action event, but its potential for future protests is obviously highly limited. Another example is Qian Yunhui, a village leader in Zhejiang, who led villagers to petition local governments for compensation for land seized and was then (supposedly accidentally) crushed to death by a truck. These two events involving Qian had high collective action potential, but both were before our observation period. In our period, there was an event that led to a volume burst around the much narrower and far less incendiary issue of how much money his family was given as a reparation payment for his death.

Finally, we give some more detailed information of a few examples of three types of events, each based on a random sample of posts in one topic area. First, Figure 6.6 gives four time series plots that ini-

tially involve low levels of censorship, followed by a volume spike during which we witness very high levels of censorship. Censorship in these examples is high in terms of the absolute number of censored posts and the percent of posts that are censored. The pattern in all four graphs (and others we do not show) is evident: the Chinese authorities disproportionately focus considerable censorship efforts during volume bursts.

We also went further and analyzed (by hand and via computer-assisted methods described in

Figure 6.6 High Censorship during Collective Action Events (in 2011)

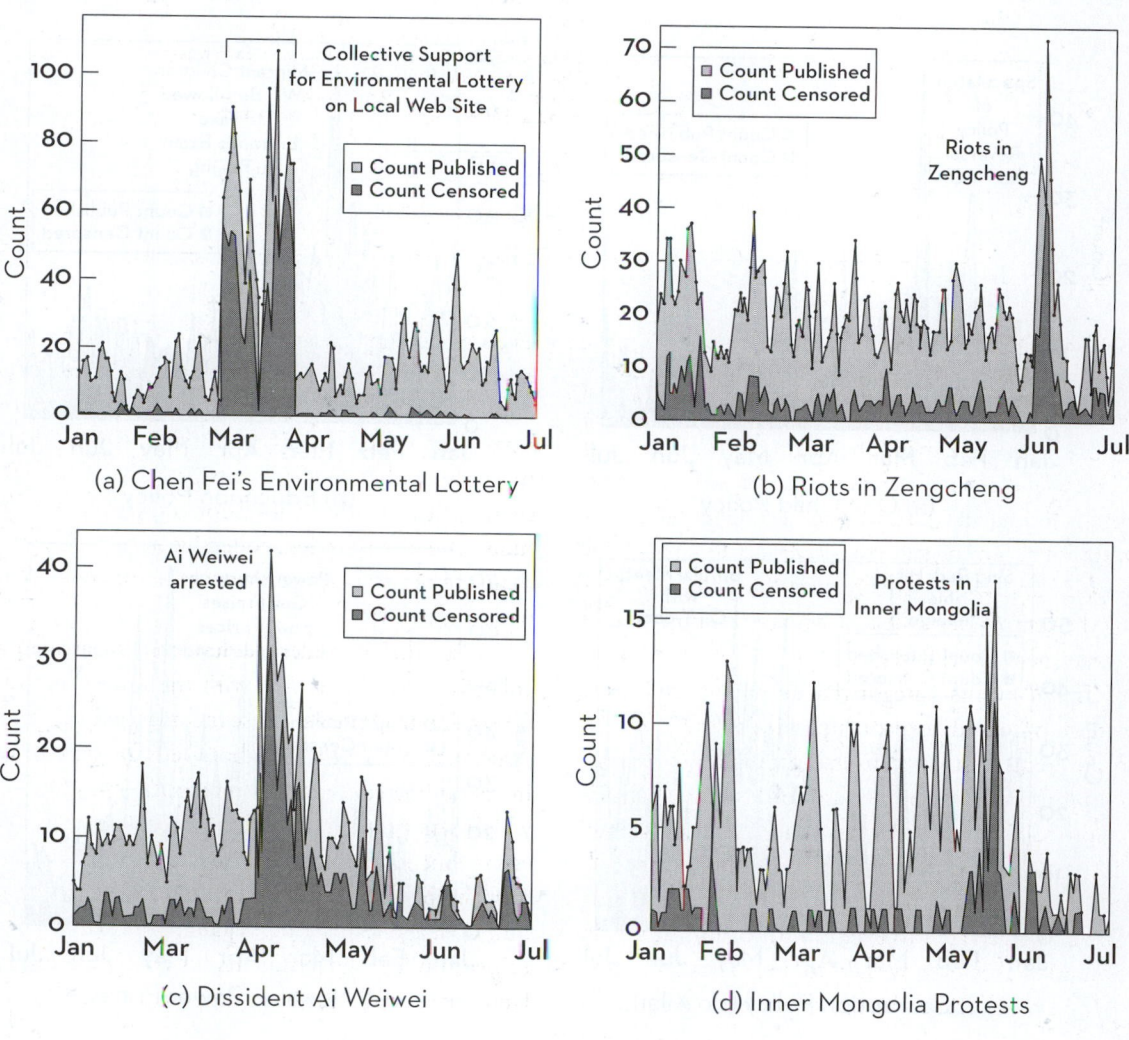

(a) Chen Fei's Environmental Lottery

(b) Riots in Zengcheng

(c) Dissident Ai Weiwei

(d) Inner Mongolia Protests

Grimmer and King 2011) the smaller number of uncensored posts during volume bursts associated with events that have collective action potential, such as in panel (a) of Figure 6.6 where the dark gray area does not entirely cover the light gray during the volume burst. In this event, and the vast majority of cases like this one, uncensored posts are not about the event, but just happen to have the keywords we used to identify the topic area. Again we find that the censors are highly accurate and aimed at increasing censorship magnitude. Automated methods of individual classification are not capable of this high a level of accuracy.

Second, we offer four time-series plots of random samples of posts in Figure 6.7 which illustrate topic areas with one or more volume bursts but without censorship. These cover important, controversial, and potentially incendiary topics—including policies involving the one child policy, education policy, and corruption, as well as news about power prices—but none of the volume bursts were associated with any localized collective

Figure 6.7 Low Censorship on News and Policy Events (in 2011)

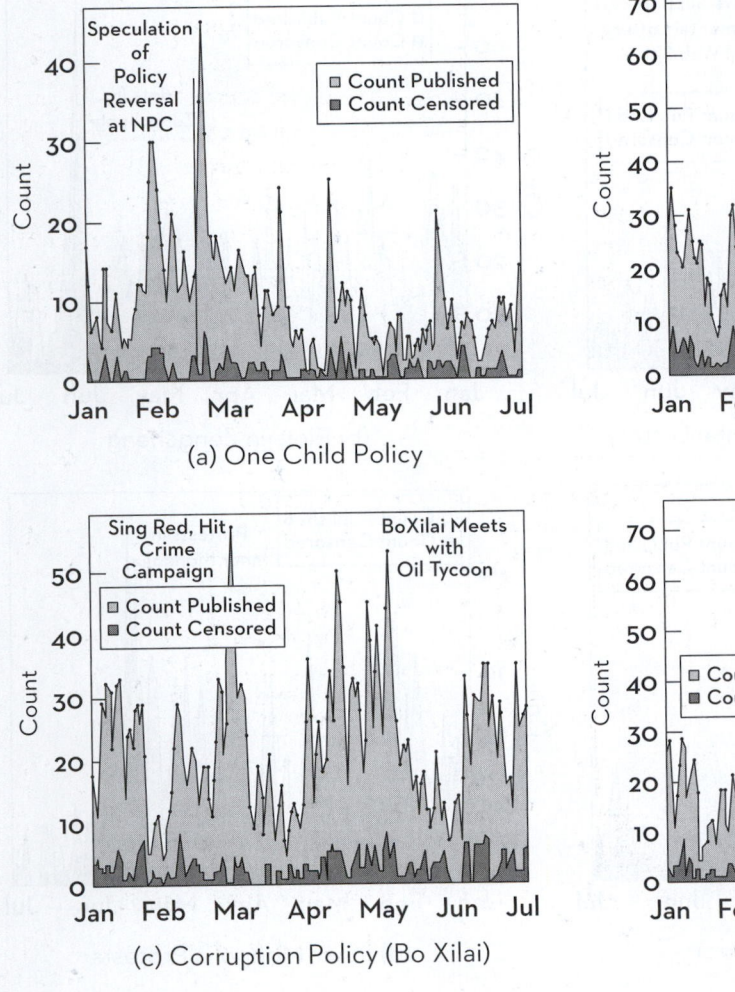
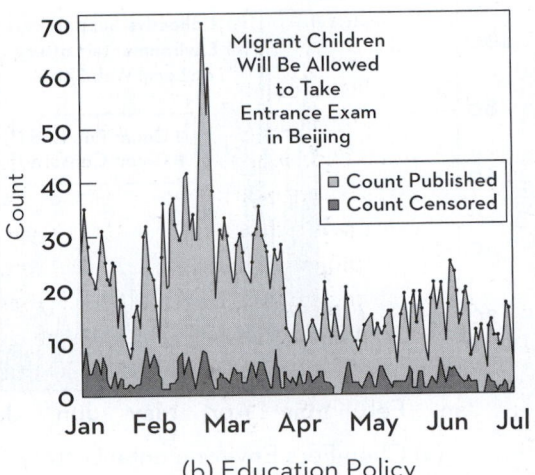
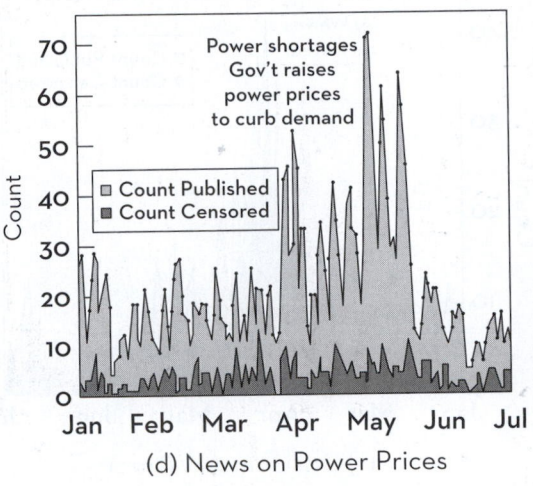

(a) One Child Policy

(b) Education Policy

(c) Corruption Policy (Bo Xilai)

(d) News on Power Prices

expression, and so censorship remains consistently low.

Finally, we found that almost all of the topic areas exhibit censorship patterns portrayed by Figures 6.6 and 6.7. The two with divergent patterns can be seen in Figure 6.8. These topics involve analyses of random samples of posts in the areas of pornography (panel [a]) and criticism of the censors (panel [b]). What is distinctive about these topics compared to the remaining we studied is that censorship levels remain high consistently in the entire six-month period and, consequently, do not increase further during volume bursts. Similar to American politicians who talk about pornography as undercutting the "moral fiber" of the country, Chinese leaders describe it as violating public morality and damaging the health of young people, as well as promoting disorder and chaos; regardless, censorship in one form or another is often the consequence.

More striking is an oddly "inappropriate" behavior of the censors: They offer freedom to the Chinese people to criticize every political leader except for themselves, every policy except the one they implement, and every program except the one they run. Even within the strained logic the Chinese state uses to justify censorship, Figure 6.8 (panel [b])—which reveals consistently high levels of censored posts that involve criticisms of the censors—is remarkable.

Content of Censored and Uncensored Posts

Our final test involves comparing the content of censored and uncensored posts. State critique theory predicts that posts critical of the state are those censored, regardless of their collective action potential. In contrast, the theory of collective action potential predicts that posts related to collective action events will be censored regardless of whether they criticize or praise the state, with both critical and supportive posts uncensored when events have no collective action potential.

To conduct this test in a very large number of posts, we need a method of automated text analysis that can accurately estimate the percentage of posts in each category of any given categorization scheme. We thus adapt to the Chinese language the methodology introduced in the English language by Hopkins and King (2010). This method does not require (inevitably error prone) machine translation, individual classification algorithms, or identification of a list of keywords associated with each category; instead, it requires a small number of posts read and categorized in the original Chinese. We conducted a series of rigorous validation tests and obtain highly accurate results—as accurate as if it were possible to read and code all the posts by hand, which of course is not feasible.* * *

Figure 6.8 Two Topics with Continuous High Censorship Levels (in 2011)

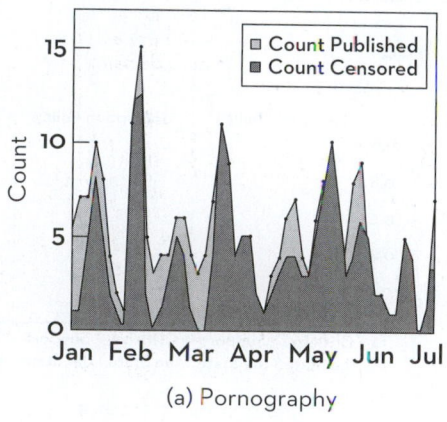

(a) Pornography

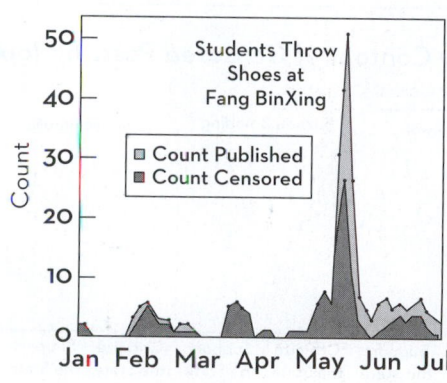

(b) Criticism of the Censors

For our analyses, we use categories of posts that are (1) critical of the state, (2) supportive of the state, or (3) irrelevant or factual reports about the events. However, we are not interested in the percent of posts in each of these categories, which would be the usual output of the Hopkins and King procedure. We are also not interested in the percent of posts in each category among those posts which were censored and among those which were not censored, which would result from running the Hopkins-King procedure once on each set of data. Instead, we need to estimate and compare the percent of posts censored in each of the three categories. We thus develop a Bayesian procedure * * * to extend the Hopkins-King methodology to estimate our quantities of interest.

We first analyze specific events and then turn to a broader analysis of a random sample of posts from all of our events. For collective action events we choose those which unambiguously fit our definition—the arrest of the dissident Ai Weiwei, protests in Inner Mongolia, and bombings in reaction to the state's demolition of housing in Fuzhou City. Panel (a) of Figure 6.9 reports the percent of posts that are censored for each event, among those that criticize the state and those which support the state; vertical bars are 95% confidence intervals. As is clear, regardless of whether the posts support or criticize the state, they are all censored at a high level, about 80% on average. Despite the conventional wisdom that

the censorship program is designed to prune the Internet of posts critical of the state, a hypothesis test indicates that the percent censorship for posts that criticize the state is not larger than the percent censorship of posts that support the state, for each event. This clearly shows support for the collective action potential theory and against the state critique theory of censorship.

We also conduct a parallel analysis for three topics, taken from the analysis in Figure 6.7, that cover highly visible and apparently sensitive policies associated with events that had no collective action potential—one child policy, corruption policy, and news of increasing food prices. In this situation, we again get the empirical result that is consistent with our theory, in both analyses: Categories critical and supportive of the state both fall at about the same, low level of censorship, about 10% on average.

To validate that these results hold across all events, we randomly draw posts from all volume bursts with and without collective action potential. Figure 6.10 presents the results in parallel to those in Figure 6.9. Here, we see that categories critical and supportive of the state again fall at the same, high level of censorship for collective action potential events, while categories critical and supportive of the state fall at the same, low level of censorship for news and policy events. Again, there is no significant difference between the percent censored among those

Figure 6.9 Content of Censored Posts by Topic Area

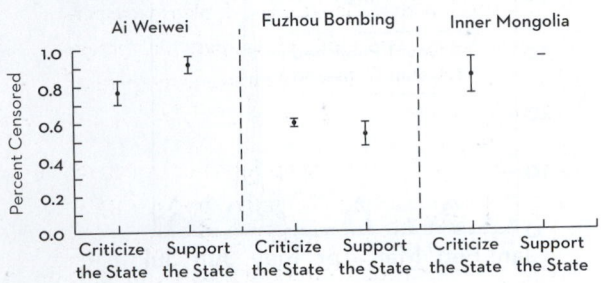
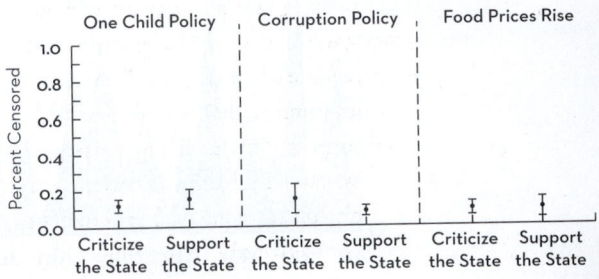

Figure 6.10 Content of All Censored Posts (Regardless of Topic Area)

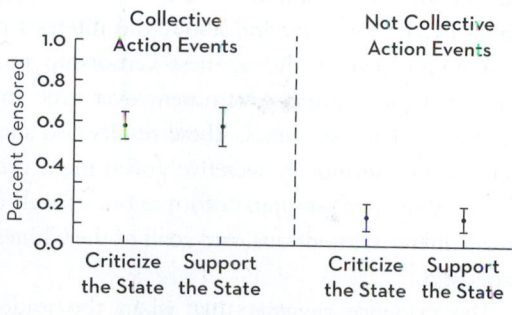

which criticize and support the state, but a large and significant difference between the percent censored among collective action potential and noncollective action potential events.

The results are unambiguous: posts are censored if they are in a topic area with collective action potential and not otherwise. Whether or not the posts are in favor of the government, its leaders, and its policies has no measurable effect on the probability of censorship.

Finally, we conclude this section with some examples of posts to give some of the flavor of exactly what is going on in Chinese social media. First we offer two examples, not associated with collective action potential events, of posts not censored even though they are unambiguously against the state and its leaders. For example, consider this highly personal attack, naming the relevant locality:

> This is a city government [Yulin City, Shaanxi] that treats life with contempt, this is government officials run amuck, a city government without justice, a city government that delights in that which is vulgar, a place where officials all have mistresses, a city government that is shameless with greed, a government that trades dignity for power, a government without humanity, a government that has no limits on immorality, a government that goes back on its word, a government that

treats kindness with ingratitude, a government that cares nothing for posterity. . . .

Another blogger wrote a scathing critique of China's one child policy, also without being censored:

> The [government] could promote voluntary birth control, not coercive birth control that deprives people of descendants. People have already been made to suffer for 30 years. This cannot become path dependent, prolonging an ill-devised temporary, emergency measure. . . . Without any exaggeration, the one child policy is the brutal policy that farmers hated the most. This "necessary evil" is rare in human history, attracting widespread condemnation around the world. It is not something we should be proud of.

Finally in a blog castigating the CCP (Chinese Communist Party) for its broken promise of democratic, constitutional government while, with reference to the Tiananmen square incident, another wrote, the following state critique, again without being censored:

> I have always thought China's modern history to be full of progress and revolution. At the end of the Qing, advances were seen in all areas, but after the Wuchang uprising, everything was lost. The Chinese Communist Party made a promise of democratic, constitutional government at the beginning of the war of resistance against Japan. But after 60 years that promise is yet to be honored. China today lacks integrity, and accountability should be traced to Mao. In the 1980s, Deng introduced structural political reforms, but after Tiananmen, all plans were permanently put on hold . . . intra-party democracy espoused today is just an excuse to perpetuate one party rule.

These posts are neither exceptions nor unusual: We have thousands more. Negative posts, including those about "sensitive" topics such as Tiananmen square or reform of China's one-party system, do not accidentally slip through a leaky or imperfect system. The evidence indicates that the censors have no intention of stopping them. Instead, they are focused on removing posts that have collective action potential, regardless of whether or not they cast the Chinese leadership and their policies in a favorable light. To emphasize this point, we now highlight the obverse condition by giving examples of two posts related to events with collective action potential that support the state but which nevertheless were quickly censored. During the bombings in Fuzhou, the government censored this post, which unambiguously condemns the actions of Qian Mingqi, the bomber, and explicitly praises the government's work on the issues of housing demolition, which precipitated the bombings:

> The bombing led not only to the tragedy of his death but the death of many government workers. Even if we can verify what Qian Mingqi said on Weibo that the building demolition caused a great deal of personal damage, we should still condemn his extreme act of retribution. . . . The government has continually put forth measures and laws to protect the interests of citizens in building demolition. And the media has called attention to the plight of those experiencing housing demolition. The rate at which compensation for housing demolition has increased exceeds inflation. In many places, this comensation can change the fate of an entire family.

Another example is the following censored post supporting the state. It accuses the local leader Ran Jianxin, whose death in police custody triggered protests in Lichuan, of corruption:

> According to news from the Badong county propaganda department web site, when Ran Jianxin was party secretary in Lichuan, he exploited his position for personal gain in land requisition, building demolition, capital construction projects, etc. He accepted bribes, and is suspected of other criminal acts.

Concluding Remarks

The new data and methods we offer seem to reveal highly detailed information about the interests of the Chinese people, the Chinese censorship program, and the Chinese government over time and within different issue areas. These results also shed light on an enormously secretive government program designed to suppress information, as well as on the interests, intentions, and goals of the Chinese leadership.

The evidence suggests that when the leadership allowed social media to flourish in the country, they also allowed the full range of expression of negative and positive comments about the state, its policies, and its leaders. As a result, government policies sometimes look as bad, and leaders can be as embarrassed, as is often the case with elected politicians in democratic countries, but, as they seem to recognize, looking bad does not threaten their hold on power so long as they manage to eliminate discussions associated with events that have collective action potential—where a locus of power and control, other than the government, influences the behaviors of masses of Chinese people. With respect to this type of speech, the Chinese people are individually free but collectively in chains.

Much research could be conducted on the implications of this government strategy; as a spur to this research, we offer some initial speculations here. For one, so long as collective action is prevented, social media can be an excellent way to obtain effective measures of the views of the populace about specific public policies and experiences with the many parts of Chinese government and the performance of public officials. As such, this "loosening" up on the constraints on public expression may, at the same time, be an effective governmental tool in learning how to satisfy, and ultimately mollify, the masses. From this perspective, the surprising empirical patterns we discover may well be a theoretically optimal strategy for a regime to use social media to maintain a hold on power. For example, Dimitrov (2008) argues that regimes collapse when their people stop bringing grievances to the state, since it is an indicator that the state is no longer regarded as legitimate. Similarly, Egorov, Guriev, and Sonin (2009) argue that dictators with low natural resource endowments allow freer media in order to improve bureaucratic performance. By extension, this suggests that allowing criticism, as we found the Chinese leadership does, may legitimize the state and help the regime maintain power. Indeed, Lorentzen (2012) develops a formal model in which authoritarian regimes balance media openness with regime censorship in order to minimize local corruption while maintaining regime stability. Perhaps the formal theory community will find ways of improving their theories after conditioning on our empirical results.

More generally, beyond the findings of this article, the data collected represent a new way to study China and different dimensions of Chinese politics, as well as facets of comparative politics more broadly. For the study of China, our approach sheds light on authoritarian resilience, center-local relations, subnational politics, international relations, and Chinese foreign policy. By examining what events are censored at the national level versus a subnational level, our approach indicates some areas where local governments can act autonomously. Additionally, by clearly revealing government intent, our approach allows an examination of the differences between the priorities of various subnational units of government. Because we can analyze social media and censorship in the content of real-world events, this approach is able to reveal insights into China's international relations and foreign policy. For example, do displays of nationalism constrain the government's foreign policy options and activities? Finally, China's censorship apparatus can be thought of as one of the input institutions. Nathan (2003) identifies as an important source of authoritarian resilience, and the effectiveness and capabilities of the censorship apparatus may shed light on the CCP's regime institutionalization and longevity.

In the context of comparative politics, our work could directly reveal information about state capacity as well as shed light on the durability of authori-

tarian regimes and regime change. Recent work on the role of Internet and social media in the Arab spring (Ada et al. 2012; Bellin 2012) debate the exact role played by these technologies in organizing collective action and motivating regional diffusion, but consistently highlight the relevance of these technological innovations on the longevity of authoritarian regimes worldwide. Edmond (2012) models how the increase in information sources (e.g., Internet, social media) will be bad for a regime unless the regime has economies of scale in controlling information sources. While Internet and social media in general have smaller economies of scale, because of how China devolves the bulk of censorship responsibility to Internet content providers, the regime maintains large economies of scale in the face of new technologies. China, as a relatively rich and resilient authoritarian regime, with a sophisticated and effective censorship apparatus, is probably being watched closely by autocrats from around the world.

Beyond learning the broad aims of the Chinese censorship program, we seem to have unearthed a valuable source of continuous time information on the interests of the Chinese people and the intentions and goals of the Chinese government. Although we illustrated this with time series in 85 different topic areas, the effort could be expanded to many other areas chosen ex ante or even discovered as online communities form around new subjects over time. The censorship behavior we observe may be predictive of future actions outside the Internet * * *, is informative even when the traditional media is silent, and would likely serve a variety of other scholarly and practical uses in government policy and business relations.

Along the way, we also developed methods of computer-assisted text analysis that we demonstrate work well in the Chinese language and adapted it to this application. These methods would seem to be of use far beyond our specific application. We also conjecture that our data collection procedures, text analysis methods, engineering infrastructure, theories, and overall analytic and empirical strategies might be applicable in other parts of the world that suppress freedom of the press.

NOTES

1. See MacKinnon (2012) for additional information on the censorship process.
2. See http://blog.sina.com.cn/, http://hi.baidu.com/, http://voc.com.cn/, http://bbs.m4.cn/, and http://tianya.cn/.
3. We identified posts as originating from mainland China by sending out a DNS query using the root url of the post and identifying the host IP.
4. That all three figures are higher than the average level of 13% reflects the fact that the topic areas we picked *ex ante* had generated at least some public discussion and included posts about events with collective action potential.
5. We attempted to identify duplicate posts, the Chinese equivalent of "retweets," sblogs (spam blogs), and the like. Excluding these posts had no noticeable effect on our results.
6. The baseline (the percent censorship outside of volume bursts) is typically very small, 3-5% and varies relatively little across topic areas.
7. As in the two relevant events in Figure 6.5, pornography often appears in social media in association with the discussion of some other popular news or discussion, to attract viewers.

REFERENCES

Ada, Sean, Henry Farrell, Marc Lync, John Sides, and Deen Freelon. 2012. "Blogs and Bullets: New Media and Conflict after the Arab Spring." http://j.mp/WviJPK.

Ash, Timothy Garton. 2002. *The Polish Revolution: Solidarity.* New Haven: Yale University Press.

Bamman, D., B. O'Connor, and N. Smith. 2012. "Censorship and Deletion Practices in Chinese Social Media." *First Monday* 17: 3–5.

Bellin, Eva. 2012. "Reconsidering the Robustness of Authoritarianism in the Middle East: Lessons from the Arab Spring." *Comparative Politics* 44 (2): 127–49.

Blecher, Marc. 2002. "Hegemony and Workers' Politics in China." *The China Quarterly* 170: 283–303.

Branigan, Tania. 2012. "Chinese Politician Bo Xilai's Wife Suspected of Murdering Neil Heywood." *The Guardian* April 10. http://j.mp/K189ce.

Cai, Yongshun. 2002. "Resistance of Chinese Laid-off Workers in the Reform Period." *The China Quarterly* 170: 327–44.

Chang, Parris. 1983. *Elite Conflict in the Post-Mao China.* New York: Occasional Papers Reprints.

Charles, David. 1966. "The Dismissal of Marshal P'eng Teh-huai." In *China under Mao: Politics Takes Command*, ed. Roderick MacFarquhar. Cambridge: MIT University Press, 20–33.

Chen, Feng. 2000. "Subsistence Crises, Managerial Corruption and Labour Protests in China." *The China Journal* 44: 41–63.

Chen, Xi. 2012. *Social Protest and Contentious Authoritarianism in China.* New York: Cambridge University Press.

Chen, Xiaoyan, and Peng Hwa Ang. 2011. "Internet Police in China: Regulation, Scope and Myths." In *Online Society in China: Creating, Celebrating, and Instrumentalising the Online Carnival*, eds. David Herold and Peter Marolt. New York: Routledge, 40–52.

Crosas, Merce, Justin Grimmer, Gary King, Brandon Stewart, and the Consilience Development Team. 2012. "Consilience: Software for Understanding Large Volumes of Unstructured Text."

Dimitrov, Martin. 2008. "The Resilient Authoritarians." *Current History* 107 (705): 24–29.

Duan, Qing. 2007. *China's IT Leadership.* Vdm Verlag Saarbrücken, Germany.

Economy, Elizabeth. 2012. "The Bigger Issues behind China's Bo Xilai Scandal." *The Atlantic* April 11. http://j.mp/JQBBbv.

Edin, Maria. 2003. "State Capacity and Local Agent Control in China: CPP Cadre Management from a Township Perspective." *China Quarterly* 173 (March): 35–52.

Edmond, Chris. 2012. "Information, Manipulation, Coordination, and Regime Change." http://j.mp/WviWlz.

Egorov, Georgy, Sergei Guriev, and Konstantin Sonin. 2009. "Why Resource-poor Dictators Allow Freer Media: A Theory and Evidence from Panel Data." *American Political Science Review* 103 (4): 645–68.

Esarey, Ashley, and Qiang Xiao. 2008. "Political Expression in the Chinese Blogosphere: Below the Radar." *Asian Survey* 48 (5): 752–72.

Esarey, Ashley, and Qiang Xiao. 2011. "Digital Communication and Political Change in China." *International Journal of Communication* 5: 298–C319.

Freedom House. 2012. "Freedom of the Press, 2012." www.freedomhouse.org.

Grimmer, Justin, and Gary King. 2011. "General Purpose Computer-Assisted Clustering and Conceptualization." *Proceedings of the National Academy of Sciences* 108 (7): 2643–50. http://gking.harvard.edu/files/abs/discov-abs.shtml.

Guo, Gang. 2009. "China's Local Political Budget Cycles." *American Journal of Political Science* 53 (3): 621–32.

Herold, David. 2011. "Human Flesh Search Engine: Carnivalesque Riots as Components of a 'Chinese Democracy.'" In *Online Society in China: Creating, Celebrating, and Instrumentalising the Online Carnival*, eds. David Herold and Peter Marolt. New York: Routledge, 127–45.

Hinton, Harold. 1955. *The "Unprincipled Dispute" within Chinese Communist Top Leadership*. Washington, DC: U.S. Information Agency.

Hopkins, Daniel, and Gary King. 2010. "A Method of Automated Nonparametric Content Analysis for Social Science." *American Journal of Political Science* 54 (1): 229–47.

Huber, Peter J. 1964. "Robust Estimation of a Location Parameter." *Annals of Mathematical Statistics* 35: 73–101.

King, Gary, and Langche Zeng. 2001. "Logistic Regression in Rare Events Data." *Political Analysis* 9 (2, Spring): 137–63. http://gking.harvard.edu/files/abs/0s-abs.shtml.

Kung, James, and Shuo Chen. 2011. "The Tragedy of the Nomenklatura: Career Incentives and Political Radicalism during China's Great Leap Famine." *American Political Science Review* 105: 27–45.

Kuran, Timur. 1989. "Sparks and Prairie Fires: A Theory of Unanticipated Political Revolution." *Public Choice* 61 (1): 41–74.

Lee, Ching-Kwan. 2007. *Against the Law: Labor Protests in China's Rustbelt and Sunbelt*. Berkeley, CA: University of California Press.

Lindtner, Silvia, and Marcella Szablewicz. 2011. "China's Many Internets: Participation and Digital Game Play across a Changing Technology Landscape." In *Online Society in China: Creating, Celebrating, and Instrumentalising the Online Carnival*, eds. David Herold and Peter Marolt. New York: Routledge, 89–105.

Lohmann, Susanne. 1994. "The Dynamics of Informational Cascades: The Monday Demonstrations in Leipzig, East Germany, 1989–1991." *World Politics* 47 (1): 42–101.

Lohmann, Susanne. 2002. "Collective Action Cascades: An Informational Rationale for the Power in Numbers." *Journal of Economic Surveys* 14 (5): 654–84.

Lorentzen, Peter. 2010. "Regularizing Rioting: Permitting Protest in an Authoritarian Regime." Working Paper.

Lorentzen, Peter. 2012. "Strategic Censorship." *SSRN*. http://j.mp/Wvj3xx.

MacFarquhar, Roderick. 1974. *The Origins of the Cultural Revolution, Volume 1: Contradictions among the People 1956–1957*. New York: Columbia University Press.

MacFarquhar, Roderick. 1983. *The Origins of the Cultural Revolution, Volume 2: The Great Leap Forward 1958–1960*. New York: Columbia University Press.

MacKinnon, Rebecca. 2012. *Consent of the Networked: The Worldwide Struggle for Internet Freedom*. New York: Basic Books.

Marolt, Peter. 2011. Grassroots Agency in a Civil Sphere? Rethinking Internet Control in China. In *Online Society in China: Creating, Celebrating, and Instrumentalising the Online Carnival*, eds. David Herold and Peter Marolt. New York: Routledge, 53–68.

Nathan, Andrew. 2003. "Authoritarian Resilience." *Journal of Democracy* 14 (1): 6–17.

O'Brien, Kevin, and Lianjiang Li. 2006. *Rightful Resistance in Rural China*. New York: Cambridge University Press.

Perry, Elizabeth. 2002. *Challenging the Mandate of Heaven: Social Protest and State Power in China.* Armork, NY: M. E. Sharpe.

Perry, Elizabeth. 2008. "Permanent Revolution? Continuities and Discontinuities in Chinese Protest." In *Popular Protest in China*, ed. Kevin O'Brien. Cambridge, MA: Harvard University Press, 205–16.

Perry, Elizabeth. 2010. "Popular Protest: Playing by the Rules." In *China Today, China Tomorrow: Domestic Politics, Economy, and Society*, ed. Joseph Fewsmith. Plymouth, UK: Rowman and Littlefield, 11–28.

Przeworski, Adam, Michael E. Alvarez, Jose Antonio Cheibub, and Fernando Limongi. 2000. *Democracy and Development: Political Institutions and Wellbeing in the World, 1950–1990.* New York: Cambridge University Press.

Ratkiewicz, J., F. Menczer, S. Fortunato, A. Flammini, and A. Vespignani. 2010. "Traffic in Social Media II: Modeling Bursty Popularity." In *Social Computing, 2010 IEEE Second International Conference.* Minneapolis, MN IEEE, 393–400.

Reilly, James. 2012. *Strong Society, Smart State: The Rise of Public Opinion in China's Japan Policy.* New York: Columbia University Press.

Rousseeuw, Peter J., and Annick Leroy. 1987. *Robust Regression and Outlier Detection.* New York: Wiley.

Schurmann, Franz. 1966. *Ideology and Organization in Communist China.* Berkeley, CA: University of California Press.

Shih, Victor. 2008. *Factions and Finance in China: Elite Conflict and Inflation.* Cambridge: Cambridge University Press.

Shirk, Susan. 2007. *China: Fragile Superpower: How China's Internal Politics Could Derail Its Peaceful Rise.* New York: Oxford University Press.

Shirk, Susan L. 2011. *Changing Media, Changing China.* New York: Oxford University Press.

Teiwes, Frederick. 1979. *Politics and Purges in China: Retification and the Decline of Party Norms.* Armork, NY: M. E. Sharpe.

Tsai, Kellee. 2007a. *Capitalism without Democracy: The Private Sector in Contemporary China.* Ithaca, NY: Cornell University Press.

Tsai, Lily. 2007b. *Accountability without Democracy: Solidary Groups and Public Goods Provision in Rural China.* Cambridge: Cambridge University Press.

Whyte, Martin. 2010. *Myth of the Social Volcano: Perceptions of Inequality and Distributive Injustice in Contemporary China.* Stanford, CA: Stanford University Press.

Xiao, Qiang. 2011. "The Rise of Online Public Opinion and Its Political Impact." In *Changing Media, Changing China*, ed. Susan Shirk. New York: Oxford University Press, 202–24.

Yang, Guobin. 2009. *The Power of the Internet in China: Citizen Activism Online.* New York: Columbia University Press.

Zhang, Liang, Andrew Nathan, Perry Link, and Orville Schell. 2002. *The Tiananmen Papers.* New York: Public Affairs.

7

POLITICAL VIOLENCE

In this chapter we look at violence against states and peoples that is not carried out by states themselves. Recall from Chapter 2 that the state is commonly defined as the organization that maintains a monopoly of violence over a territory. States use this force at the domestic level, through such institutions as the law and police, to generate stability. At the international level, armies and diplomacy help generate peace. But at times, the monopoly of force may escape state control, as in the case of revolutions and terrorism.

In some circumstances, the public may seek to overthrow the current regime through revolution. Theda Skocpol transformed political science and the study of revolutionary events with her piece "France, Russia, China: A Structural Analysis of Social Revolutions" (1976). Expanded in her 1979 book, *States and Social Revolutions*, Skocpol's thinking on revolution contributed to political science by returning our attention to the state, and *States and Social Revolutions* went on to become one of the most cited works in the field. Why do revolutions, sweeping transformations in existing regime and state institutions, occur? In each case, Skocpol believes that a particular set of conditions in the state and society is necessary to set revolutions in motion. Her analysis, influenced by Marx, is structural—that is, institutions are central (if not decisive) in shaping the likelihood of dramatic political change.

Whereas Skocpol considers the central factors surrounding revolution, related work tackles the puzzle of what causes terrorism. Some scholars and observers have assumed that terrorism is primarily a result of institutional factors, such as authoritarianism or poverty. However, the research tends not to support such arguments. Martha Crenshaw's classic piece, "The Causes of Terrorism" (1981), focuses more on individual motivations that lead people to resort to terrorist acts. Crenshaw notes that certain structural preconditions can foster terrorism but also makes the striking comment that "In their intense commitment, separation from the outside world, and intolerance of internal dissent, terrorist groups resemble religious sects or cults." Given that her work long predates the current wave of terrorism, her observation about terrorism as a religion (as opposed to religion leading to terrorism) is worth noting.

Crenshaw's findings dovetail with Scott Atran and Robert Axelrod's piece "Reframing Sacred Values" (2008). Focused on the Israeli–Palestinian conflict, they find an important role for values such as religion, honor, and justice in explanations for political violence—things that transcend "rational" goals such as statehood or a change in regime. Ending political violence often requires acknowledging the importance of key moral values of the other side. This a difficult task when one assumes the other side is disingenuous, simply using such arguments to rationalize its violence. But Atran and Axelrod's work is consistent with James I. Walsh and James A. Piazza's "Why Respecting Physical Integrity Rights Reduces Terrorism" (2010). The authors believe that violating human rights, particularly what they call "physical integrity," through such strategies as torture undermines widely shared norms. This attack on dignity—a source of humiliation, which is central to the idea of sacred values—alienates some members of society who are then more likely to turn to violence.

Theda Skocpol

FRANCE, RUSSIA, CHINA: A STRUCTURAL ANALYSIS OF SOCIAL REVOLUTIONS

"A revolution," writes Samuel P. Huntington in *Political Order in Changing Societies*, "is a rapid, fundamental, and violent domestic change in the dominant values and myths of a society, in its political institutions, social structure, leadership, and government activities and policies."[1] In *The Two Tactics of Social Democracy in the Democratic Revolution*, Lenin provides a different, but complementary perspective: "Revolutions," he says, "are the festivals of the oppressed and the exploited. At no other time are the masses of the people in a position to come forward so actively as creators of a new social order."[2]

Together these two quotes delineate the distinctive features of *social revolutions*. As Huntington points out, social revolutions are rapid, basic transformations of socio-economic and political institutions, and—as Lenin so vividly reminds us—social revolutions are accompanied and in part effectuated through class upheavals from below. It is this combination of thoroughgoing structural transformation and massive class upheavals that sets social revolutions apart from coups, rebellions, and even political revolutions and national independence movements.

If one adopts such a specific definition, then clearly only a handful of successful social revolutions have ever occurred. France, 1789, Russia, 1917, and China, 1911–49, are the most dramatic and clear-cut instances. Yet these momentous upheavals have helped shape the fate of the majority of mankind, and their causes, consequences, and potentials have preoccupied many thoughtful people since the late eighteenth century.

Nevertheless, recently, social scientists have evidenced little interest in the study of social revolutions

From *Comparative Studies in Society and History* 18, no. 2 (April 1976), pp. 175–210. Some of the author's notes have been omitted.

as such. They have submerged revolutions within more general categories—such as "political violence," "collective behavior," "internal war," or "deviance"—shorn of historical specificity and concern with large-scale social change.[3] The focus has been mostly on styles of behavior common to wide ranges of collective incidents (ranging from riots to coups to revolutions, from panics to hostile outbursts to "value-oriented movements," and from ideological sects to revolutionary parties), any of which might occur in any type of society at any time or place. Revolutions tend increasingly to be viewed not as "locomotives of history," but as extreme forms of one or another sort of behavior that social scientists, along with established authorities everywhere, find problematic and perturbing.

Why this avoidance by social science of the specific problem of social revolution? Ideological bias might be invoked as an explanation, but even if it were involved, it would not suffice. An earlier generation of American social scientists, certainly no more politically radical than the present generation, employed the "natural history" approach to analyze handfuls of cases of great revolutions.[4] In large part, present preoccupation with broader categories can be understood as a reaction against this natural history approach, deemed by its critics too "historical" and "a-theoretical."

In the "Introduction" to a 1964 book entitled *Internal War*, Harry Eckstein defines "a theoretical subject" as a "set of phenomena about which one can develop informative, testable generalizations that hold for all instances of the subject, and some of which apply to those instances alone."[5] He goes on to assert that while "a statement about two or three cases is certainly a generalization in the dictionary sense, a generalization in the methodological sense must usually be based on more; it ought to cover a number of cases large enough for certain rigorous testing procedures like statistical analysis to be used."[6] Even many social scientists who are not statistically oriented would agree with the spirit of this statement: theory in social science should concern itself only with general

phenomena; the "unique" should be relegated to "narrative historians."

Apparently it directly follows that no theory specific to social revolution is possible, that the *explanandum* of any theory which sheds light on social revolutions must be something more general than social revolution itself. Hence the efforts to conceptualize revolution as an extreme instance of patterns of belief or behavior which are also present in other situations or events.

This approach, however, allows considerations of technique to define away substantive problems. Revolutions are not just extreme forms of individual or collective behavior. They are distinctive conjunctures of socio-historical structures and processes. One must comprehend them as complex wholes—however few the cases—or not at all.

Fortunately social science is not devoid of a way of confronting this kind of problem. Social revolutions *can* be treated as a "theoretical subject." To test hypotheses about them, one may employ the comparative method, with national historical trajectories as the units of comparison. As many students of society have noted, the comparative method is nothing but that mode of multivariate analysis to which sociologists necessarily resort when experimental manipulations are not possible and when there are "too many variables and not enough cases"—that is, not enough cases for statistical testing of hypotheses.[7] According to this method, one looks for concomitant variations, contrasting cases where the phenomena in which one is interested are present with cases where they are absent, controlling in the process for as many sources of variation as one can, by contrasting positive and negative instances which otherwise are as similar as possible.

Thus, in my inquiry into the conditions for the occurrence and short-term outcomes of the great historical social revolutions in France, Russia and China, I have employed the comparative historical method, specifically contrasting the positive cases with (a) instances of non–social revolutionary modernization, such as occurred in Japan, Germany and Russia (up to 1904), and with (b) instances of abortive social revolutions, in particular Russia in 1905 and Prussia/Germany in 1848. These comparisons have helped me to understand those aspects of events and of structures and processes which distinctively rendered the French, Chinese and Russian Revolutions successful social revolutions. In turn, the absence of conditions identified as positively crucial in France, Russia and China constitutes equally well an explanation of why social revolutions have not occurred, or have failed, in other societies. In this way, hypotheses developed, refined, and tested in the comparative historical analysis of a handful of cases achieve a potentially general significance.

Explaining the Historical Cases: Revolution in Modernizing Agrarian Bureaucracies

Social revolutions in France, Russia and China occurred, during the earlier world-historical phases of modernization, in agrarian bureaucratic societies situated within, or newly incorporated into, international fields dominated by more economically modern nations abroad. In each case, social revolution was a conjuncture of three developments: (1) the collapse or incapacitation of central administrative and military machineries; (2) widespread peasant rebellions; and (3) marginal elite political movements. What each social revolution minimally "accomplished" was the extreme rationalization and centralization of state institutions, the removal of a traditional landed upper class from intermediate (regional and local) quasi-political supervision of the peasantry, and the elimination or diminution of the economic power of a landed upper class.

In the pages that follow, I shall attempt to explain the three great historical social revolutions, first, by discussing the institutional characteristics of agrarian states, and their special vulnerabilities and potentialities during the earlier world-historical phases of modernization, and second, by pointing to the peculiar characteristics of old regimes in France, Russia and China, which made them uniquely vulnerable among the earlier modernizing agrarian states to social-revolutionary transformations. Finally, I shall suggest reasons for similarities and differences in the outcomes of the great historical social revolutions.

An agrarian bureaucracy is an agricultural society in which social control rests on a division of labor and a coordination of effort between a semi-bureaucratic state and a landed upper class.[8] The landed upper class typically retains, as an adjunct to its landed property, considerable (though varying in different cases) undifferentiated local and regional authority over the peasant majority of the population. The partially bureaucratic central state extracts taxes and labor from peasants either indirectly through landlord intermediaries or else directly, but with (at least minimal) reliance upon cooperation from individuals of the landed upper class. In turn, the landed upper class relies upon the backing of a coercive state to extract rents and/or dues from the peasantry. At the political center, autocrat, bureaucracy, and army monopolize decisions, yet (in varying degrees and modes) accommodate the regional and local power of the landed upper class and (again, to varying degrees) recruit individual members of this class into leading positions in the state system.

Agrarian bureaucracies are inherently vulnerable to peasant rebellions. Subject to claims on their surpluses, and perhaps their labor, by landlords and state agents, peasants chronically resent both. To the extent that the agrarian economy is commercialized, merchants are also targets of peasant hostility. In all agrarian bureaucracies at all times, and in France, Russia and China in non-revolutionary times, peasants have had grievances enough to warrant, and recurrently spur, rebellions. Economic crises (which are endemic in semi-commercial agrarian economies anyway) and/or increased demands from above for rents or taxes might substantially enhance the likelihood of rebellions at particular times. But such events ought to be treated as short-term precipitants of peasant unrest, not fundamental underlying causes.

Modernization is best conceived not only as an *intra*societal process of economic development accompanied by lagging or leading changes in non-economic institutional spheres, but also as a world-historic *inter*societal phenomenon. Thus,

> a necessary condition of a society's modernization is its incorporation into the historically unique network of societies that arose first in Western Europe in early modern times and today encompasses enough of the globe's population for the world to be viewed for some purposes as if it consisted of a single network of societies.[9]

Of course, societies have always interacted. What was special about the modernizing intersocietal network that arose in early modern Europe was, first, that it was based upon trade in commodities and manufactures, as well as upon strategic politico-military competition between independent states,[10] and, second, that it incubated the "first (self-propelling) industrialization" of England after she had gained commercial hegemony within the Western European–centered world market.[11]

In the wake of that first commercial-industrial breakthrough, modernizing pressures have reverberated throughout the world. In the first phase of world modernization, England's thoroughgoing commercialization, capture of world market hegemony, and expansion of manufactures (both before and after the technological Industrial Revolution which began in the 1780s), transformed means and stakes in the traditional rivalries of European states and put immediate pressure for reforms, if only to facilitate the financing of competitive armies and navies, upon the other European states and especially upon the ones with less efficient fiscal machineries.[12] In the second phase, as Europe modernized and further expanded its influence around the globe, similar militarily compelling pressures were brought to bear on those non-European societies which escaped immediate colonization, usually the

ones with pre-existing differentiated and centralized state institutions.

During these phases of global modernization, independent responses to the dilemmas posed by incorporation into a modernizing world were possible and (in some sense) necessary for governmental elites in agrarian bureaucracies. Demands for more and more efficiently collected taxes; for better and more generously and continuously financed militaries; and for "guided" national economic development, imitating the available foreign models, were voiced within these societies especially by bureaucrats and the educated middle strata. The demands were made compelling by international military competition and threats. At the same time, governmental leaders did have administrative machineries, however rudimentary, at their disposal for the implementation of whatever modernizing reforms seemed necessary and feasible (at given moments in world history). And their countries had not been incorporated into dependent economic and political positions in a world stratification system dominated by a few fully industrialized giants.

But agrarian bureaucracies faced enormous difficulties in meeting the crises of modernization. Governmental leaders' realm of autonomous action tended to be severely limited, because few fiscal or economic reforms could be undertaken which did not encroach upon the advantages of the traditional landed upper classes which constituted the major social base of support for the authority and functions of the state in agrarian bureaucracies. Only so much revenue could be squeezed out of the peasantry, and yet landed upper classes could often raise formidable obstacles to rationalization of tax systems. Economic development might mean more tax revenues and enhanced military prowess, yet it channelled wealth and manpower away from the agrarian sector. Finally, the mobilization of mass popular support for war tended to undermine the traditional, local authority of landlords or landed bureaucrats upon which agrarian bureaucratic societies partly relied for the social control of the peasantry.

Agrarian bureaucracies could not indefinitely "ignore" the very specific crises, in particular fiscal and martial, that grew out of involvement with a modernizing world, yet they could not adapt without undergoing fundamental structural changes. Social revolution helped accomplish "necessary" changes in some but was averted by reform or "revolution from above" in others. Relative stagnation, accompanied by subincorporation into international power spheres, was still another possibility (e.g., Portugal, Spain?). Social revolution was never deliberately "chosen." Societies only "backed into" social revolutions.

All modernizing agrarian bureaucracies have peasants with grievances and face the unavoidable challenges posed by modernization abroad. So, in some sense, potential for social revolution has been built into all modernizing agrarian bureaucracies. Yet, only a handful have succumbed. Why? A major part of the answer, I believe, lies in the insight that "not oppression, but weakness, breeds revolution."[13] It is the breakdown of a societal mode of social control which allows and prompts social revolution to unfold. In the historical cases of France, Russia and China, the unfolding of social revolution depended upon the emergence of revolutionary crises occasioned by the incapacitation of administrative and military organizations. That incapacitation, in turn, is best explained not as a function of mass discontent and mobilization, but as a function of a combination of pressures on state institutions from more modernized countries abroad, and (in two cases out of three) built-in structural incapacities to mobilize increased resources in response to those pressures. France, Russia and China were also special among all agrarian bureaucracies in that their agrarian institutions afforded peasants not only the usual grievances against landlords and state agents but also "structural space" for autonomous collective insurrection. Finally, once administrative/military breakdown occurred in agrarian bureaucracies with such especially insurrection-prone peasantries, then, and only then, could organized revolutionary

leaderships have great impact upon their societies' development—though not necessarily in the ways they originally envisaged.

Breakdown of Societal Controls: Foreign Pressures and Administrative/Military Collapse

If a fundamental cause and the crucial trigger for the historical social revolutions was the incapacitation of administrative and military machineries in modernizing agrarian bureaucracies, then how and why did this occur in France, Russia and China? What differentiated these agrarian bureaucracies which succumbed to social revolution from others which managed to respond to modernizing pressures with reforms from above? Many writers attribute differences in response to qualities of will or ability in governmental leaders. From a sociological point of view, a more satisfying approach might focus on the interaction between (a) the magnitude of foreign pressures brought to bear on a modernizing agrarian bureaucracy, and (b) the particular structural characteristics of such societies that underlay contrasting performances by leaders responding to foreign pressures and internal unrest.

Overwhelming foreign pressures on an agrarian bureaucracy could cut short even a generally successful government program of reforms and industrialization "from above." Russia is the obvious case in point. From at least the 1890s onward, the Czarist regime was committed to rapid industrialization, initially government-financed out of resources squeezed from the peasantry, as the only means of rendering Russia militarily competitive with Western nations. Alexander Gerschenkron argues that initial government programs to promote heavy industry had succeeded in the 1890s to such an extent that, when the government was forced to reduce its direct financial and administrative role after 1904, Russia's industrial sector was nevertheless capable of autonomously generating further growth (with the aid of foreign capital investments).[14] Decisive steps to modernize agriculture and free peasant labor for permanent urban migration were taken after the unsuccessful Revolution of 1905.[15] Had she been able to sit out World War I, Russia might have recapitulated the German experience of industrialization facilitated by bureaucratic guidance.

But participation in World War I forced Russia to fully mobilize her population including her restive peasantry. Army officers and men were subjected to years of costly fighting, and civilians to mounting economic privations—all for nought. For, given Russia's "industrial backwardness . . . enhanced by the fact that Russia was very largely blockaded . . . ," plus the "inferiority of the Russian military machine to the German in everything but sheer numbers . . . , military defeat, with all of its inevitable consequences for the internal condition of the country, was very nearly a foregone conclusion."[16] The result was administrative demoralization and paralysis, and the disintegration of the army. Urban insurrections which brought first middle-strata moderates and then the Bolsheviks to power could not be suppressed, owing to the newly-recruited character and war weariness of the urban garrisons.[17] Peasant grievances were enhanced, young peasant men were politicized through military experiences, and, in consequence, spreading peasant insurrections from the spring of 1917 on could not be controlled.

It is instructive to compare 1917 to the Revolution of 1905. Trotsky called 1905 a "dress rehearsal" for 1917, and, indeed, many of the same social forces with the same grievances and similar political programs took part in each revolutionary drama. *What accounts for the failure of the Revolution of 1905 was the Czarist regime's ultimate ability to rely upon the army to repress popular disturbances.* Skillful tactics were involved: the regime bought time to organize repression and assure military loyalty with well-timed liberal concessions embodied in the October Manifesto of 1905 (and later largely retracted). Yet, it was of crucial importance that the futile 1904–05 war with Japan was, in comparison

with the World War I morass, circumscribed, geographically peripheral, less demanding of resources and manpower, and quickly concluded once defeat was apparent.[18] The peace treaty was signed by late 1905, leaving the Czarist government free to bring military reinforcements back from the Far East into European Russia.

The Russian Revolution occurred in 1917 because Russia was too inextricably entangled with foreign powers, friend and foe, economically and militarily more powerful than she. Foreign entanglement must be considered to explain not only the administrative and military incapacitation of 1917, but also entry into World War I. That involvement cannot be considered "accidental." Nor was it "voluntary" in the same sense as Russia's entry into the 1904 war with Japan.[19] Whatever leadership "blunders" were involved, the fact remains that in 1914 both the Russian state and the Russian economy depended heavily on Western loans and capital. Moreover, Russia was an established part of the European state system and could not remain neutral in a conflict that engulfed the whole of that system.[20]

Foreign pressures and involvements so inescapable and overwhelming as those that faced Russia in 1917 constitute an extreme case for the earlier modernizing agrarian bureaucracies we are considering here. For France and China the pressures were surely no more compelling than those faced by agrarian bureaucracies such as Japan, Germany and Russia (1858–1914) which successfully adapted through reforms from above that facilitated the extraordinary mobilization of resources for economic and military development. Why were the Bourbon and Manchu regimes unable to adapt? Were there structural blocks to effective response? First, let me discuss some general characteristics of all agrarian states, and then point to a peculiar structural characteristic shared by Bourbon France and Manchu China which I believe explains these regimes' inability to meet snow-balling crises of modernization until at last their feeble attempts triggered administrative and military disintegration, hence revolutionary crises.

Weber's ideal type of bureaucracy may be taken as an imaginary model of what might logically be the most effective means of purposively organizing social power. According to the ideal type, fully developed bureaucracy involves the existence of a hierarchically arrayed officialdom, where officials are oriented to superior authority in a disciplined manner because they are dependent for jobs, livelihood, status and career-advancement on resources and decisions channeled through that superior authority. But in preindustrial states, monarchs found it difficult to channel sufficient resources through the "center" to pay simultaneously for wars, culture and court life on the one hand, and a fully bureaucratic officialdom on the other. Consequently, they often had to make do with "officials" recruited from wealthy backgrounds, frequently, in practice, landlords. In addition, central state jurisdiction rarely touched local peasants or communities directly; governmental functions were often delegated to landlords in their "private" capacities, or else to non-bureaucratic authoritative organizations run by local landlords.

Inherent in all agrarian bureaucratic regimes were tensions between, on the one hand, state elites interested in preserving, using, and extending the powers of armies and administrative organizations and, on the other hand, landed upper classes interested in defending locally and regionally based social networks, influence over peasants, and powers and privileges associated with the control of land and agrarian surpluses. Such tensions were likely to be exacerbated once the agrarian bureaucracy was forced to adapt to modernization abroad because foreign military pressures gave cause, while foreign economic development offered incentives and models, for state elites to attempt reforms which went counter to the class interests of traditional, landed upper strata. Yet there were important variations in the ability of semi-bureaucratic agrarian states to respond to modernizing pressures with reforms which sharply and quickly increased resources at the disposal of central authorities. What can account for the differences in response?

■ ■ ■

The Manchu Dynasty proved unable to mobilize resources sufficient to meet credibly the challenges posed by involvement in the modernizing world. "[T]he problem was not merely the very real one of the inadequate resources of the Chinese economy as a whole. In large measure the financial straits in which the Peking government found itself were due to . . . [inability to] command such financial capacity as there was in its empire."[21] Part of the explanation for this inability lay in a characteristic which the Chinese state shared with other agrarian states: lower and middle level officials were recruited from the landed gentry, paid insufficient salaries, and allowed to engage in a certain amount of "normal" corruption, withholding revenues collected as taxes from higher authorities.[22] Yet, if the Manchu Dynasty had encountered the forces of modernization at the height of its powers (say in the early eighteenth century) rather than during its declining phase, it might have controlled or been able to mobilize sufficient resources to finance modern industries and equip a centrally controlled modern army. In that case, officials would never have been allowed to serve in their home provinces, and thus local and regional groups of gentry would have lacked institutional support for concerted opposition against central initiatives. But, as it happened, the Manchu Dynasty was forced to try to cope with wave after wave of imperialist intrusions, engineered by foreign industrial or industrializing nations anxious to tap Chinese markets and finances, immediately after a series of massive mid-nineteenth-century peasant rebellions. The Dynasty had been unable to put down the Taiping Rebellion on its own, and the task had fallen instead to local, gentry-led, self-defense associations and to regional armies led by complexly interrelated gentry who had access to village resources and recruits. In consequence of the gentry's role in putting down rebellion, governmental powers formerly accruing to central authorities or their bureaucratic agents, including, crucially, rights to collect and allocate various taxes, devolved upon local, gentry-dominated, sub-district governing associations and upon provincial armies and officials increasingly aligned with the provincial gentry against the center.[23]

Unable to force resources from local and regional authorities, it was all Peking could do simply to meet foreign indebtedness, and after 1895 even that proved impossible.

> Throughout the period from 1874 to 1894, the ministry [of Revenue in Peking] was engaged in a series of largely unsuccessful efforts to raise funds in order to meet a continuing series of crises—the dispute over Ili with Russia, the Sino-French War [1885], floods and famines, the Sino-Japanese War [1895]. . . . After 1895 the triple pressure of indemnity payments, servicing foreign loans, and military expenditures totally wrecked the rough balance between income and outlay which Peking had maintained [with the aid of foreign loans] until that time.[24]

The Boxer Rebellion of 1900, and subsequent foreign military intervention, only further exacerbated an already desperate situation.

Attempts by dynastic authorities to remedy matters through a series of "reforms" implemented after 1900—abolishing the Confucian educational system and encouraging modern schools;[25] organizing the so-called "New Armies" (which actually formed around the nuclei of the old provincial armies);[26] transferring local governmental functions to provincial bureaus;[27] and creating a series of local and provincial gentry-dominated representative assemblies[28]—only exacerbated the sorry situation, right up to the 1911 breaking point. "Reform destroyed the reforming government."[29] With each reform, dynastic elites thought to create powers to counterbalance entrenched obstructive forces, but new officials and functions were repeatedly absorbed into pre-existing local and (especially) regional cliques of gentry.[30] The last series of reforms, those that created representative assemblies, ironically provided cliques of gentry with legitimate representative organs from which to launch the liberal, decentralizing "Constitutionalist movement" against the Manchus.

What ultimately precipitated the "revolution of 1911" was a final attempt at reform by the central government, one that directly threatened the financial interests of the gentry power groups for the purpose of strengthening central government finances and control over national economic development:

> The specific incident that precipitated the Revolution of 1911 was the central government's decision to buy up a [railroad] line in Szechwan in which the local gentry had invested heavily. . . . The Szechwan uprising, led by the moderate constitutionalists of the Railway Protection League, sparked widespread disturbances that often had no connection with the railway issue. . . .[31]

Conspiratorial groups affiliated with Sun Yat Sen's T'eng Meng Hui, and mainly composed of Western-educated students and middle-rank New Army officers, joined the fray to produce a series of military uprisings. Finally,

> . . . the lead in declaring the independence of one province after another was taken by two principal elements: the military governors who commanded the New Army forces and the gentry-official-merchant leaders of the provincial assemblies. These elements had more power and were more conservative than the youthful revolutionarists of the T'eng Meng Hui.[32]

The Chinese "Revolution of 1911" irremediably destroyed the integument of civilian elite ties—traditionally maintained by the operation of Confucian educational institutions and the central bureaucracy's policies for recruiting and deploying educated officials so as to strengthen "cosmopolitan" orientations at the expense of local loyalties—which had until that time provided at least the semblance of unified governance for China. "Warlord" rivalries ensued as gentry interests attached themselves to regional military machines, and this condition of intra-elite disunity and rivalry (only imperfectly and temporarily overcome by Chiang Kai-Shek's regime between 1927 and 1937)[33] condemned China to incessant turmoils and provided openings (as well as cause) for lower-class, especially peasant, rebellions and for Communist attempts to organize and channel popular unrest.

Peasant Insurrections

If administrative and military breakdown in a modernizing agrarian bureaucracy were to inaugurate social revolutionary transformations, rather than merely an interregnum of intra-elite squabbling, then widespread popular revolts had to coincide with and take advantage of the hiatus of governmental supervision and sanctions. Urban insurrections provided indispensable support during revolutionary interregnums to radical political elites vying against other elites for state power: witness the Parisian *sans culottes'* support for the Jacobins;[34] the Chinese workers' support for the Communists (between 1920 and 1927);[35] and the Russian industrial workers' support for the Bolsheviks. But fundamentally more important in determining final outcomes were the peasant insurrections which in France, Russia and China constituted irreversible attacks on the powers and privileges of the traditional landed upper classes.

Agrarian bureaucracy has been the only historical variety of complex society with differentiated, centralized government that has, in certain instances, incubated a lower-class stratum that was *simultaneously strategic* in the society's economy and polity (as surplus producer, payer of rents and taxes, and as provider of corvée and military manpower), and yet *organizationally autonomous* enough to allow the "will" and "tactical space" for collective insurrection against basic structural arrangements.

How have certain agrarian bureaucracies exemplified such special propensity to peasant rebellion? As Eric Wolf has pointed out, "ultimately, the decisive factor in making a peasant rebellion possible lies in the relation of the peasantry to the field of power which surrounds it. A rebellion cannot start from a situation of complete impotence. . . ."[36] If they are to act upon, rather than silently suffer, their omnipresent grievances, peasants must have "internal leverage" or "tactical mobility." They have this to varying degrees according to their position in the total agrarian social structure. Institutional patterns which relate peasants to landlords and peasants to each other seem to be the co-determinants of degrees of peasant "tactical mobility." Sheer amounts of property held by peasants gain significance only within institutional contexts. If peasants are to be capable of self-initiated rebellion against landlords and state officials, they must have (a) some institutionally based collective solidarity, and (b) autonomy from direct, day-to-day supervision and control by landlords in their work and leisure activities. Agricultural regimes featuring large estates worked by serfs or laborers tend to be inimical to peasant rebellion—witness the East Elbian Junker regime[37]—but the reason is not that serfs and landless laborers are economically poor, rather that they are subject to close and constant supervision and discipline by landlords or their agents. If large-estate agriculture is lacking, an agrarian bureaucracy may still be relatively immune to widespread peasant rebellion if landlords control sanctioning machineries,[38] such as militias and poor relief agencies, at local levels. On the other hand, landlords as a class, and the "system" as a whole, will be relatively vulnerable to peasant rebellion if: (a) sanctioning machineries are centralized; (b) agricultural work and peasant social life are controlled by peasant families and communities themselves. These conditions prevailed in France and Russia and meant that, with the incapacitation of central administrative and military bureaucracies, these societies became susceptible to the spread and intensification of peasant revolts which in more normal circumstances could have been contained and repressed.

It is worth emphasizing that peasant actions in revolutions are not intrinsically different from peasant actions in "mere" rebellions or riots. When peasants "rose" during historical social revolutionary crises, they did so in highly traditional rebellious patterns: bread riots, "defense" of communal lands or customary rights, riots against "hoarding" merchants or landlords, "social banditry." Peasants initially drew upon traditional cultural themes to justify rebellion. Far from becoming revolutionaries through adoption of a radical vision of a desired new society, "revolutionary" peasants have typically been "backward-looking" rebels incorporated by circumstances beyond their control into political processes occurring independently of them, at the societal "center."[39]

∎ ∎ ∎

Historians agree that the Russian Emancipation of the serfs in 1861, intended by the Czar as a measure to stabilize the agrarian situation, actually enhanced the rebellious potential of the ex-serfs. Heavy redemption payments and inadequate land allotments fuelled peasant discontent. More important, legal reinforcement of the *obshchina's* (peasant commune's) authority over families and individuals fettered ever-increasing numbers of peasants to the inadequate lands, reinforced collective solidarity, retarded the internal class differentiation of the peasantry, and left communes largely free to run their own affairs subject only to the collective fulfillment of financial obligations to the state.[40] Estate owners were deprived of most direct authority over peasant communities.[41]

Not surprisingly, given this agrarian situation, widespread peasant rebellions erupted in Russia in 1905, when the Czarist regime simultaneously confronted defeat abroad and an anti-autocratic movement of the middle classes, the liberal gentry, and the working classes at home. "Economic hardship created a need for change; peasant tradition, as well as revolutionary propaganda, suggested the remedy [i.e., attacks on landlords and land seizures]; official preoccupation and indecisiveness invited the storm; and soon the greatest disturbance since the days of Pugachev was under way."[42]

In the wake of the unsuccessful Revolution of 1905, the Czarist regime abandoned its policy of shoring up the peasant commune. It undertook the break-up of repartitional lands into private holdings and implemented measures to facilitate land sales by poorer peasants and purchases by richer ones.[43] Between 1905 and 1917, these measures, in tandem with general economic developments, did something to alleviate agrarian stagnation, promote permanent rural migration to urban industrial areas, and increase class differentiation and individualism in the countryside.[44] However, by 1917, little enough had been accomplished—only one-tenth of all peasant families had been resettled on individual holdings[45]—that peasant communities engaged in solidary actions against both landlords and any rich peasant "separators" who did not join their struggle.

"Any shrewd observer of Russian conditions who weighed the lessons of the agrarian disorders of 1905 could have foreseen that a breakdown of central power and authority was almost certain to bring an even greater upheaval in its train."[46] And, indeed, between the spring and the autumn of 1917, "side by side with the mutiny of the Russian army marched a second great social revolutionary movement: the seizure of the landed estates by the peasantry."[47]

The peasant movement of 1917 was primarily a drive of the peasantry against the *pomyeschik* class. Among the cases of agrarian disturbance, violent and peaceful, 4,954, overwhelmingly the largest number, were directed against landlords, as against 324 against the more well-to-do peasants, 235 against the Government and 211 against the clergy.[48]

The broad general result of the wholesale peasant land seizure of 1917 was a sweeping levelling in Russian agriculture. The big latifundia, even the small estate, ceased to exist. On the other hand landless or nearly landless peasants obtained larger allotments.[49]

For the peasants simply applied traditional communal repartitional procedures to lands seized from the landlords. Their revolt, together with the Bolsheviks' victory, " . . . sealed forever the doom of the old landed aristocracy."[50]

The Chinese case presents decisive contrasts with France and Russia but nevertheless confirms our general insight about the importance of structurally conditioned "tactical space" for peasant insurrection as a crucial factor in the translation of administrative/military breakdown into social revolution.

Except in infertile and marginal highland areas, Chinese peasants, though mostly family smallholders or tenants,[51] did not live in their own village communities clearly apart from landlords.

> The Chinese peasant . . . was a member of two communities: his village and the marketing system to which his village belonged ["typically including fifteen to twenty-five villages . . ." dependent on one of 45,000 market towns]. An important feature of the larger marketing community was its elaborate system of stratification. . . . Those who provided *de facto* leadership within the marketing community *qua* political system and those who gave it collective representation at its interface with larger polities were gentrymen— landed, leisured, and literate. . . . It was artisans, merchants, and other full-time economic specialists, not peasants, who sustained the heartbeat of periodic marketing that kept the community alive. It was priests backed by gentry temple managers . . . who gave religious meaning to peasants' local world.[52]

Voluntary associations, and clans where they flourished, were likewise contained within marketing communities, headed and economically sustained by gentry. Thus kinship, associational and clientage ties cut across class distinctions between peasants and landlords in traditional China. Gentry controlled at local levels a variety of sanctioning machineries, including militias and other organizations which functioned *de facto* as channels of poor relief.[53]

Not surprisingly, therefore, settled Chinese peasant agriculturalists did not initiate class-based revolts against landlords, either in pre-modern or in revolutionary (1911–49) times. Instead, peasant rebellion manifested itself in the form of accelerating rural violence and social banditry, spreading outward from the mountainous "border areas" at the edges of the empire or at the intersections of provincial boundaries. Social banditry invariably blossomed during periods of central administrative weakness or collapse and economic deflation and catastrophe. Precisely because normal traditional Chinese agrarian-class relations were significantly commercialized, local prosperity depended upon overall administrative stability, and peasants were not cushioned against economic dislocations by kin or village communal ties. During periods of dynastic decline, local (marketing) communities "closed in" upon themselves normatively, economically, and coercively,[54] and poorer peasants, especially in communities without well-to-do local landed elites, lost property and livelihood, and were forced to migrate. Such impoverished migrants often congregated as bandits or smugglers operating out of "border area" bases and raiding settled communities. Ultimately they might provide (individual or group) recruits for rebel armies led by marginal elites vying for imperial power.[55]

The nineteenth and the first half of the twentieth centuries constituted a period of dynastic decline and interregnum in China, complicated in quite novel ways by Western and Japanese economic and military intrusions. Peasant impoverishment, local community closure, spreading social banditry and military conflicts among local militias, bandit groups, and warlord and/or "ideological" armies characterized the entire time span, and peaked during the mid-nineteenth and mid-twentieth centuries.

The Communist movement originated as a political tendency among a tiny fraction of China's nationalist and pro-modern intellectual stratum and created its first mass base among Chinese industrial workers concentrated in the treaty ports and to a lesser degree among students and southeast Chinese peasants. But after 1927, the Chinese Communists were forced out of China's cities and wealthier agrarian regions by Kuomintang military and police repression. Would-be imitators of the Bolsheviks were thus forced to come to terms with the Chinese agrarian situation. This they did initially (between 1927 and 1942) by recapitulating the experiences and tactics of traditional rebel elite contenders for imperial power in China. Scattered, disorganized and disoriented Communist leaders, along with military units (which had split off from KMT or warlord armies) of varying degrees of loyalty, retreated to mountainous border areas, there often to ally with already existing bandit groups.[56] Gradually the fruits of raiding expeditions, plus the division and weakness of opposing armies, allowed the "Communist" base areas to expand into administrative regions.

Only after a secure and stable administrative region had finally been established in Northwest China (after 1937) could the Communists finally turn to the intra-market-area and intra-village political organizing that ultimately bypassed and then eliminated the gentry, and so made their drive for power unique in China's history. Before roughly 1940, ideological appeals, whether "Communist" or "Nationalist," played little role in mediating Communist elites' relations to peasants, and spontaneous class struggle, fuelled from below, played virtually no role in achieving whatever (minimal) changes in agrarian class *relations* were accomplished in Communist base areas.[57] To be sure, ideology was important in integrating the Party, an elite organization, and in mediating its relationship with the Red Army. But until Party and Army established relatively secure and stable military and administrative control over a region, Communist cadres were not in a position to penetrate local communities in order to provide organization, leadership, and encouragement for peasants themselves to expropriate land. This finally occurred in North China in

the 1940s.[58] Once provided with military and organizational protection from landlord sanctions and influence, peasants often reacted against landlords with a fury that exceeded even what Party policy desired. Perhaps Communist ideological appeals were partially responsible for peasant insurrection. More likely, even at this stage, the Communist organizations' important input to local situations was not a sense of grievances, or their ideological articulation, but rather simply *protection* from traditional social controls: William Hinton's classic *Fanshen: A Documentary of Revolution in a Chinese Village* vividly supports such an interpretation.[59]

Even to gain the military strength they needed to defeat the Kuomintang, the Chinese Communists had to shove aside—or encourage and allow peasants to shove aside—the traditional landed upper class and establish a more direct link to the Chinese peasantry than had ever before been established between an extra-local Chinese rebel movement and local communities.[60] The Chinese Communists also established more direct links to peasants than did radical elites in Russia or France. The Chinese Revolution, at least in its closing stages, thus has more of the aspect of an elite/mass movement than the other great historical social revolutions. Yet the reasons for this peasant mass-mobilizing aspect have little to do with revolutionary ideology (except in retrospect) and everything to do with the "peculiarities" (from a European perspective) of the Chinese agrarian social structure. That structure did not afford settled Chinese peasants institutional autonomy and solidarity against landlords, yet it did, in periods of political-economic crisis, generate marginal poor-peasant outcasts whose activities exacerbated the crises and whose existence provided potential bases of support for oppositional elite-led rebellions or, in the twentieth-century world context, a revolutionary movement. Thus Chinese Communist activities after 1927 and ultimate triumph in 1949 depended directly upon *both* the insurrectionary potentials and the blocks to peasant insurrection built into the traditional Chinese social structure.

Radical Political Movements and Centralizing Outcomes

Although peasant insurrections played a decisive role in each of the great historical social revolutions, nevertheless an exclusive focus on peasants—or on the peasant situation in agrarian bureaucracies—cannot provide a complete explanation for the occurrence of social revolutions. Russia and China were recurrently rocked by massive peasant rebellions,[61] yet peasant uprisings did not fuel structural transformations until the late eighteenth century and after. Obviously agrarian bureaucracies were exposed to additional and unique strains and possibilities once English and then European commercialization-industrialization became a factor in world history and development. The stage was set for the entry of marginal elites animated by radical nationalist goals.

Who were these marginal elites? What sectors of society provided the social bases for nationalist radicalisms? *Not* the bourgeoisie proper: merchants, financiers and industrialists. These groups have had surprisingly little *direct* effect upon the politics of modernization in any developing nation, from England to the countries of the Third World today. Instead, their activities, commerce and manufacturing, have created and continuously transformed, indeed revolutionized, the national and international *contexts* within which bureaucrats, professionals, politicians, landlords, peasants, and proletarians have engaged in the decisive political struggles. To be sure, in certain times and places, the "bourgeois" commercial or industrial context has been pervasive enough virtually to determine political outcomes, even without the overt political participation of bourgeois actors. But such was not the case in the earlier modernizing agrarian bureaucracies, including France, Russia and China.

Instead, nationalist radicals tended to "precipitate out" of the ranks of those who possessed specialized skills and were oriented to state activities or employments, but either lacked traditionally prestigious attributes such as nobility, landed wealth, or general humanist education, or else found themselves in situations where such attributes were no longer personally or nationally functional. Their situations in political and social life were such as to make them, especially in times of political crises, willing to call for such radical reforms as equalization of mobility opportunities, political democracy, and (anyway, before the revolution) extension of civil liberties. Yet the primary orientation of these marginal elites was toward a broad goal that they shared with all those, including traditionally prestigious bureaucrats, whose careers, livelihoods, and identities were intertwined with state activities: the goal of extension and rationalization of state powers in the name of national welfare and prestige.

■　■　■

In Russia, by 1917, the revolutionary sects, such as the Bolsheviks and the Left Social Revolutionaries, constituted the surviving politically organized representatives of what had earlier been an out-look much more widespread among university-educated Russians: extreme alienation, disgust at Russia's backwardness, preoccupation with public events and yet refusal to become involved in the round of civil life.[62] As Russia underwent rapid industrialization after 1890, opportunities for university education were extended beyond the nobility—a circumstance which helped to ensure that universities would be hotbeds of political radicalism—yet, before long, opportunities for professional and other highly skilled employments also expanded. Especially in the wake of the abortive 1905 Revolution, Russia's university-educated moved toward professional employments and liberal politics.[63] Yet when events overtook Russia in 1917, organized radical leadership was still to be found among the alienated intelligentsia.

In China, as in Russia, radical nationalist modernizers came from the early student generations of university-educated Chinese.[64] Especially at first, most were the children of traditionally wealthy and prestigious families, but urban and "rich peasant" backgrounds, respectively, came to be overrepresented in the (pre-1927) Kuomintang and the Communist elites.[65] With the abolition of the Confucian educational system in 1904, and the collapse of the imperial government in 1911, even traditionally prestigious attributes and connections lost their meaning and usefulness. At the same time, neither warlord regimes nor the Nationalist government after 1927 offered much scope for modern skills or credentials; advancement in these regimes went only to those with independent wealth or personal ties to military commanders. Gradually, the bulk of China's modern-educated, and especially the young, came to support the Communist movement, some through active commitment in Yenan, others through passive political support in the cities.[66]

Two considerations help to account for the fact that radical leadership in social revolutions came specifically from the ranks of skilled and/or university-educated marginal elites oriented to state employments and activities. First, agrarian bureaucracies are "statist" societies. Even before the era of modernization official employments in these societies constituted both an important route for social mobility and a means for validating traditional status and supplementing landed fortunes. Second, with the advent of economic modernization in the world, state activities acquired greater-than-ever objective import in the agrarian bureaucratic societies which were forced to adapt to modernization abroad. For the concrete effects of modernization abroad first impinged upon the state's sphere, in the form of sharply and suddenly stepped up military competition or threats from more developed nations abroad. And the cultural effects of modernization abroad first impinged upon the relatively highly educated in agrarian bureaucracies, that is upon those who were mostly either employed by the state or else connected or oriented to its activities.

■ ■ ■

The earlier modernizing agrarian bureaucracies that (to varying degrees) successfully adapted to challenges from abroad did so either through revolution, or basic reforms "from above" or social revolution "from below." Either traditional bureaucrats successfully promoted requisite reforms or else their attempts precipitated splits within the upper class which could, if the peasantry were structurally insurrection-prone, open the door to social revolution. In the context of administrative/military disorganization and spreading peasant rebellions, tiny, organized radical elites that never could have created revolutionary crises on their own gained their moments in history. As peasant insurrections undermined the traditional landed upper classes, and the old regime officials and structures tied to them, radical elites occupied center stage, competing among themselves to see who could seize and build upon the foundations of central state power.

"A complete revolution," writes Samuel Huntington, " . . . involves . . . the creation and institutionalization of a new political order."[67] A social revolution was consummated when one political elite succeeded in creating or capturing political organizations—a revolutionary army, or a revolutionary party controlling an army—capable of restoring minimal order and incorporating the revolutionary masses, especially the peasantry, into national life. No political elite not able or willing to accept the peasants' revolutionary economic gains could hope to emerge victorious from the intra-elite or inter-party conflicts that marked revolutionary interregnums. Elites with close social or politico-military ties to traditional forms of landed upper-class institutional power (i.e., the privileged rentier bourgeoisie of France, the Kerensky regime in Russia, the [post-1927] Kuomintang in China) invariably lost out.

The historical social revolutions did not culminate in more liberal political arrangements. At opening stages of the French, Russian (1905) and Chinese revolutions, landed upper-class/middle-strata political coalitions espoused "parliamentary liberal" programs.[68] But events pushed these groups and programs aside, for the organized elites who provided the ultimately successful leadership in all social revolutions ended up responding to popular turmoil—counterrevolutionary threats at home and abroad, peasant anarchist tendencies, and the international crises faced by their societies—by creating *more* highly centralized, bureaucratized and rationalized state institutions than those that existed prior to the revolutions. This response, moreover, was entirely in character for elites adhering to world views which gave consistent primacy to organized political action in human affairs.[69]

■ ■ ■

Let me sum up what this essay has attempted to do. To explain the great historical social revolutions, I have, first, conceptualized a certain type of society, the agrarian bureaucracy, in which social control of the lower strata (mainly peasants) rests with institutions locally and regionally controlled by landed upper classes, together with administrative and military machineries centrally controlled; and second, I have discussed differences between agrarian bureaucracies which did and those which did not experience social revolutions in terms of (a) institutional structures which mediate landed upper-class relations to state apparatuses and peasant relations to landed upper classes and (b) types and amounts of international political and economic pressures (especially originating with more developed nations) impinging upon agrarian bureaucracies newly incorporated into the modernizing world. According to my analysis, social revolutions occurred in those modernizing agrarian bureaucracies—France, Russia and China—which *both* incubated peasantries structurally prone to autonomous insurrection *and* experienced severe administrative and military disorganization due to the direct or indirect effects of military competition or threats from more modern nations abroad.

In the process of elucidating this basic argument, I have at one point or another alluded to evidence concerning Prussia (Germany), Japan (and Turkey), and Russia in 1905. Obviously the coverage of these and other "negative" cases has been far

from complete. Yet partial explanations have been offered for the avoidance of social revolution by Prussia/Germany, Japan and Russia through 1916. Japan and Russia escaped administrative/military collapse in the face of moderate challenges from abroad because their traditional governmental elites were significantly differentiated from landed upper classes. Prussia lacked a structurally autonomous, insurrection-prone peasantry, and therefore when, in 1848, the King hesitated for a year to use his armies to repress popular disturbances, the Junker-led army, manned by peasants from the estates east of the Elbe, remained loyal and intact until it was finally used to crush the German Revolutions during 1849–50.

This comparative historical analysis has been meant to render plausible a theoretical approach to explaining revolutions which breaks with certain long-established sociological proclivities. While existing theories of revolution focus on discontent, and its articulation by oppositional programs or ideologies, as the fundamental cause of revolutions, I have emphasized mechanisms and dynamics of societal social control through political and class domination. Moreover, while other theories view the impact of modernization (as a cause of revolution) in terms of the effects of processes of economic development on class structures, "system equilibrium," or societal members' levels of satisfaction, my approach focuses on the effects of modernization—viewed also as an intersocietal politico-strategic process—upon adaptive capacities of the agrarian bureaucratic states and upon the opportunities open to political elites who triumph in revolutions.

Obviously, thorough testing of these ideas will require more precise delineation of concepts and the extension of hypotheses derived from this analysis to new cases. But I have made a start. And I hope that especially those who disagree with my conclusions will themselves turn to historical evidence to argue their cases. Social science can best grow through the interplay of theory and historical investigation, and comparative historical analysis represents one indispensable tool for achieving this.

NOTES

1. Samuel P. Huntington, *Political Order in Changing Societies* (New Haven: Yale University Press, 1968), p. 264.

2. Stephan T. Possony, ed., *The Lenin Reader* (Chicago: Henry Regnery Company, 1966), p. 349.

3. For important examples see: Ted Robert Gurr, *Why Men Rebel* (Princeton, N.J.: Princeton University Press, 1970); Neil J. Smelser, *Theory of Collective Behavior* (New York: The Free Press of Glencoe, 1963); and Harry Eckstein, "On the Etiology of Internal Wars," *History and Theory* 4(2) (1965).

4. Crane Brinton, *The Anatomy of Revolution* (New York: Vintage Books, 1965; original edition, 1938); Lyford P. Edwards, *The Natural History of Revolution* (Chicago: University of Chicago Press, 1971; originally published in 1927); George Sawyer Petee, *The Process of Revolution* (New York: Harper and Brothers, 1938); and Rex D. Hopper, "The Revolutionary Process," *Social Forces* 28 (March, 1950): 270–79.

5. Harry Eckstein, ed., *Internal War* (New York: The Free Press, 1964), p. 8.

6. *Ibid.*, p. 10.

7. See: Ernest Nagel, ed., *John Stuart Mill's Philosophy of Scientific Method* (New York: Hafner Publishing Co., 1950); Marc Bloch, "Toward a Comparative History of European Societies," in Frederic C. Lane and Jelle C. Riemersma, eds., *Enterprise and Secular Change* (Homewood, Ill.: The Dorsey Press, 1953), pp. 494–521; William H. Sewell, Jr., "Marc Bloch and the Logic of Comparative History," *History and Theory* 6(2) (1967): 208–18; Neil J. Smelser, "The Methodology of Comparative Analysis" (unpublished draft); and S. M. Lipset, *Revolution and Counterrevolution* (New York: Anchor Books, 1970), part I.

8. In formulating the "agrarian bureaucracy" societal type concept, I have drawn especially upon the work and ideas of S. N. Eisenstadt in *The Political Systems of Empires* (New York: The Free Press, 1963); Barrington Moore, Jr., in *Social Origins of Dictatorship and Democracy* (Boston: Beacon Press, 1967); and Morton H. Fried, "On the Evolution of Social Stratification and the State," pp. 713–31 in Stanley Diamond, ed., *Culture in History* (New York: Columbia University Press, 1960). The label "agrarian bureaucracy" is pilfered from Moore. Clear-cut instances of agrarian bureaucratic societies were China, Russia, France, Prussia, Austria, Spain, Japan, Turkey.

9. Terence K. Hopkins and Immanuel Wallerstein, "The Comparative Study of National Societies," *Social Science Information* 6 (1967), 39.

10. See Immanuel Wallerstein, *The Modern World System: Capitalist Agriculture and the Origins of the European World-Economy in the Sixteenth Century* (New York and London: Academic Press, 1974).

11. E. J. Hobsbawm, *Industry and Empire* (Baltimore, Md.: Penguin Books, 1969).

12. See Walter L. Dorn, *Competition for Empire, 1740–1763* (New York: Harper and Row, 1963; originally, 1940).

13. Christopher Lasch, *The New Radicalism in America* (New York: Vintage Books, 1967), p. 141.

14. Alexander Gerschenkron, "Problems and Patterns of Russian Economic Development," pp. 42–72 in Cyril E. Black, ed., *The Transformation of Russian Society* (Cambridge, Mass.: Harvard University Press, 1960).

15. Geroid Tanquary Robinson, *Rural Russia under the Old Regime* (Berkeley and Los Angeles: University of California Press, 1969; originally published in 1932), Chap. 11.

16. William Henry Chamberlin, *The Russian Revolution*, Volume I (New York: Grosset and Dunlap, 1963; originally published in 1935), pp. 64–65.

17. Katharine Chorley, *Armies and the Art of Revolution* (London: Faber and Faber, 1943), Chap. 6.

18. *Ibid.*, pp. 118–19.

19. In 1904, "[t]he Minister of Interior, von Plehve, saw a desirable outlet from the [turbulent domestic] situation in a 'little victorious war'" (Chamberlin, *op. cit.*, p. 47).

20. See: Leon Trotsky, *The Russian Revolution* (selected and edited by F. W. Dupee) (New York: Anchor Books, 1959; originally published in 1932),

Volume I, Chap. 2; and Roderick E. McGrew, "Some Imperatives of Russian Foreign Policy," pp. 202–29 in Theofanis George Stavrou, ed., *Russia under the Last Tsar* (Minneapolis: University of Minnesota Press, 1969).

21. Albert Feuerwerker, *China's Early Industrialization* (New York: Atheneum, 1970; originally published in 1958), p. 41.

22. Chung-li Chang, *The Chinese Gentry* (Seattle: University of Washington Press, 1955); Ping-ti Ho, *The Ladder of Success in Imperial China* (New York: Columbia University, Press, 1962); and Franz Michael, "State and Society in Nineteenth Century China," *World Politics* 7 (April, 1955): 419–33.

23. Philip Kuhn, *Rebellion and Its Enemies in Late Imperial China* (Cambridge, Mass.: Harvard University Press, 1970).

24. Feuerwerker, *op. cit.*, pp. 40–41.

25. Mary C. Wright, ed., *China in Revolution: The First Phase, 1900–1913* (New Haven: Yale University Press, 1968), pp. 24–26.

26. Yoshiro Hatano, "The New Armies," pp. 365–82 in Wright, ed., *op. cit.*; and John Gittings, "The Chinese Army," pp. 187–224 in Jack Gray, ed., *Modern China's Search for a Political Form* (London: Oxford University Press, 1969).

27. John Fincher, "Political Provincialism and the National Revolution," in Wright, ed., *op. cit.*, p. 202.

28. Fincher, *op. cit.*; and P'eng-yuan Chang, "The Constitutionalists," in Wright, ed., *op. cit.*

29. Wright, ed., *op. cit.*, p. 50.

30. Fincher, *op. cit.*

31. Wright, ed., *loc. cit.*

32. John King Fairbank, *The United States and China* (third edition) (Cambridge, Mass.: Harvard University Press, 1971), p. 132.

33. Martin C. Wilbur, "Military Separatism and the Process of Reunification under the Nationalist Regime, 1922–1937," pp. 203–63 in Ping-ti Ho and Tang Tsou, eds., *China in Crisis*, Volume I, Book I (Chicago: University of Chicago Press, 1968).

34. Albert Soboul, *The Sans Culottes* (New York: Anchor Books, 1972; originally published in French in 1968); and George Rudé, *The Crowd in the French Revolution* (London: Oxford University Press, 1959).

35. Jean Chesneaux, *The Chinese Labor Movement, 1919–1927* (Stanford: Stanford University Press, 1968).

36. Eric R. Wolf, *Peasant Wars of the Twentieth Century* (New York: Harper and Row, 1969), p. 290.

37. In 1848 the East Elbian region of "Germany" escaped general peasant insurrection, and the Prussian armies that crushed the German Revolutions of 1848 were recruited from the East Elbian estates, officers and rank-and-file alike. See: Theodore Hamerow, *Restoration, Revolution, Recreation* (Princeton, N.J.: Princeton University Press, 1958); and Hajo Holborn, *A History of Modern Germany: 1648–1840* (New York: Alfred A. Knopf, 1963).

38. "Sanctioning machineries" are organizations which control forceful or remunerative sanctions. "Social control" also involves normative pressures, but to be truly binding, especially in hierarchical situations, these must typically be "backed up" by application or credible threat of application of force or manipulation of needed remuneration.

39. See Wolf, *op. cit.*, "Conclusion"; and Moore, *op. cit.*, Chap. 9 and "Epilogue."

40. Terence Emmons, "The Peasant and the Emancipation," and Francis M. Watters, "The Peasant and the Village Commune," both in Wayne S. Vucinich, ed., *The Peasant in Nineteenth-Century Russia* (Stanford: Stanford University Press, 1968); and Robinson, *op. cit.*

41. Jerome Blum, *Lord and Peasant in Russia* (Princeton, N.J.: Princeton University Press, 1961), pp. 598–9; and Robinson, *op. cit.*, pp. 78–79.

42. Robinson, *op. cit.*, p. 155.

43. *Ibid.*, pp. 188–207.

44. Gerschenkron, *op. cit.*, pp. 42–72.

45. Robinson, *op. cit.*, pp. 225–6.

46. Chamberlin, *op. cit.*, p. 257.

47. *Ibid.*, p. 242.

48. *Ibid.*, p. 252.

49. *Ibid.*, p. 256.

50. *Ibid.*, p. 256.

51. R. H. Tawney, *Land and Labour in China* (Boston: Beacon Press, 1966; originally published in 1932), Chap. 2.

52. G. William Skinner, "Chinese Peasants and the Closed Community: An Open and Shut Case," *Comparative Studies in Society and History* 13(3) (July 1971), pp. 272–73.

53. Kuhn, *op. cit., passim.*

54. Skinner, *op. cit.*, 278ff.

55. See: Skinner, *op. cit.*, Kuhn, *op. cit.*; and George E. Taylor, "The Taiping Rebellion: Its Economic Background and Social Theory," *Chinese Social and Political Science Review* 16 (1933): 545–614.

56. See: Mark Selden, *The Yenan Way in Revolutionary China* (Cambridge, Mass.: Harvard University Press, 1971), Chaps. 1–2; Dick Wilson, *The Long March 1935* (New York: Avon Books, 1971); and Agnes Smedly, *The Great Road: The Life and Times of Chu Teh* (New York: Monthly Review Press, 1956).

57. Selden, op. cit.; Franz Schurmann, *Ideology and Organization in Communist China* (second edition) (Berkeley and Los Angeles: University of California Press, 1968), pp. 412–37; Ilpyong J. Kim, "Mass Mobilization Policies and Techniques Developed in the Period of the Chinese Soviet Republic," pp. 78–98 in A. Doak Barnett, ed., *Chinese Communist Politics in Action* (Seattle: University of Washington Press, 1969).

58. Selden, *op. cit.*; and Schurmann, *op. cit.*

59. William Hinton, *Fanshen: A Documentary of Revolution in a Chinese Village* (New York: Vintage Books, 1968; first published in 1966).

60. Schurmann, *op. cit.*, pp. 425–31.

61. See, for example, Roland Mousnier, *Peasant Uprisings in the Seventeenth Century: France, Russia and China* (New York: Harper and Row, 1972; originally published in French, 1967).

62. George Fischer, "The Intelligentsia and Russia," pp. 253–73 in Black, ed., *op. cit.*

63. George Fischer, "The Russian Intelligentsia and Liberalism," pp. 317–36 in Hugh McLean, Martin Malia and George Fischer, eds., *Russian Thought and Politics—Harvard Slavic Studies*, Volume IV (Cambridge, Mass.: Harvard University Press, 1957); and Donald W. Treadgold, "Russian Radical Thought, 1894–1917," pp. 69–86 in Stavrou, ed., *op. cit.*

64. John Israel, "Reflections on the Modern Chinese Student Movement," *Daedalus* (Winter 1968): 229–53; and Robert C. North and Ithiel de Sola Pool, "Kuomintang and Chinese Communist Elites," pp. 319–455 in Harold D. Lasswell and Daniel Lerner, eds., *World Revolutionary Elites* (Cambridge, Mass.: The M.I.T. Press, 1966).

65. North and Pool, *op. cit.*

66. John Israel, *Student Nationalism in China: 1927–1937* (Stanford: Hoover Institute Publications, 1966).

67. Huntington, *op. cit.*, p. 266.

68. See: Norman Hampson, *A Social History of the French Revolution* (Toronto: University of Toronto Press, 1963), Chap. 2; Sidney Harcave, *The Russian Revolution of 1905* (London: Collier Books, 1970; first published in 1964); and P'eng-yuan Chang, "The Constitutionalists," pp. 143–83 in Wright, ed., *op. cit.*

69. On the Bolsheviks, see Robert V. Daniels, "Lenin and the Russian Revolutionary Tradition," pp. 339–54 in McLean, Malia and Fischer, eds., *op. cit.* Daniels argues that "the more autocratic societies like pre-revolutionary Russia . . . prompted historical theories which put a premium on individual will, power and ideas . . . ," p. 352.

Martha Crenshaw
THE CAUSES OF TERRORISM

Terrorism occurs both in the context of violent resistance to the state as well as in the service of state interests. If we focus on terrorism directed against governments for purposes of political change, we are considering the premeditated use or threat of symbolic, low-level violence by conspiratorial organizations. Terrorist violence communicates a political message; its ends go beyond damaging an enemy's material resources.[1] The victims or objects of terrorist attack have little intrinsic value to the terrorist group but represent a larger human audience whose reaction the terrorists seek. Violence characterized by spontaneity, mass participation, or a primary intent of physical destruction can therefore be excluded from our investigation.

The study of terrorism can be organized around three questions: why terrorism occurs, how the process of terrorism works, and what its social and political effects are. Here the objective is to outline an approach to the analysis of the causes of terrorism, based on comparison of different cases of terrorism, in order to distinguish a common pattern of causation from the historically unique.

The subject of terrorism has inspired a voluminous literature in recent years. However, nowhere among the highly varied treatments does one find a general theoretical analysis of the causes of terrorism. This may be because terrorism has often been approached from historical perspectives, which, if we take Walter Laqueur's work as an example, dismiss explanations that try to take into account more than a single case as "exceedingly vague or altogether wrong."[2] Certainly existing general accounts are often based on assumptions that are neither explicit nor factually demonstrable. We find judgments centering on social factors such as the permissiveness and affluence in which

Western youth are raised or the imitation of dramatic models encouraged by television. Alternatively, we encounter political explanations that blame revolutionary ideologies, Marxism-Leninism or nationalism, governmental weakness in giving in to terrorist demands, or conversely government oppression, and the weakness of the regime's opponents. Individual psychopathology is often cited as a culprit.

Even the most persuasive of statements about terrorism are not cast in the form of testable propositions, nor are they broadly comparative in origin or intent. Many are partial analyses, limited in scope to revolutionary terrorism from the Left, not terrorism that is a form of protest or a reaction to political or social change. A narrow historical or geographical focus is also common; the majority of explanations concern modern phenomena. Some focus usefully on terrorism against the Western democracies.[3] In general, propositions about terrorism lack logical comparability, specification of the relationship of variables to each other, and a rank-ordering of variables in terms of explanatory power.

We would not wish to claim that a general explanation of the sources of terrorism is a simple task, but it is possible to make a useful beginning by establishing a theoretical order for different types and levels of causes. We approach terrorism as a form of political behavior resulting from the deliberate choice of a basically rational actor, the terrorist organization. A comprehensive explanation, however, must also take into account the environment in which terrorism occurs and address the question of whether broad political, social, and economic conditions make terrorism more likely in some contexts than in others. What sort of circumstances lead to the formation of a terrorist group? On the other hand, only a few of the people who experience a given situation practice terrorism. Not even all individuals who share the

From *Comparative Politics* 13, no. 4 (July 1981), pp. 379–99.

goals of a terrorist organization agree that terrorism is the best means. It is essential to consider the psychological variables that may encourage or inhibit individual participation in terrorist actions. The analysis of these three levels of causation will center first on situational variables, then on the strategy of the terrorist organization, and last on the problem of individual participation.

This paper represents only a preliminary set of ideas about the problem of causation; historical cases of terrorism are used as illustrations, not as demonstrations of hypotheses. The historical examples referred to here are significant terrorist campaigns since the French Revolution of 1789; terrorism is considered as a facet of secular modern politics, principally associated with the rise of nationalism, anarchism, and revolutionary socialism.[4] The term *terrorism* was coined to describe the systematic inducement of fear and anxiety to control and direct a civilian population, and the phenomenon of terrorism as a challenge to the authority of the state grew from the difficulties revolutionaries experienced in trying to re-create the mass uprisings of the French Revolution. Most references provided here are drawn from the best-known and most-documented examples: Narodnaya Volya and the Combat Organization of the Socialist-Revolutionary party in Russia, from 1878 to 1913; anarchist terrorism of the 1890s in Europe, primarily France; the Irish Republican Army (IRA) and its predecessors and successors from 1919 to the present; the Irgun Zwai Leumi in Mandate Palestine from 1937 to 1947; the Front de Libération Nationale (FLN) in Algeria from 1954 to 1962; the Popular Front for the Liberation of Palestine from 1968 to the present; the Rote Armee Fraktion (RAF) and the 2nd June Movement in West Germany since 1968; and the Tupamaros of Uruguay, 1968–1974.

The Setting for Terrorism

An initial obstacle to identification of propitious circumstances for terrorism is the absence of significant empirical studies of relevant cross-national factors. There are a number of quantitative analyses of collective violence, assassination, civil strife, and crime,[5] but none of these phenomena is identical to a campaign of terrorism. Little internal agreement exists among such studies, and the consensus one finds is not particularly useful for the study of terrorism.[6] For example, Ted Robert Gurr found that "modern" states are less violent than developing countries and that legitimacy of the regime inhibits violence. Yet, Western Europe experiences high levels of terrorism. Surprisingly, in the 1961–1970 period, out of 87 countries, the United States was ranked as having the highest number of terrorist campaigns.[7] Although it is impractical to borrow entire theoretical structures from the literature on political and criminal violence, some propositions can be adapted to the analysis of terrorism.

To develop a framework for the analysis of likely settings for terrorism, we must establish conceptual distinctions among different types of factors. First, a significant difference exists between *preconditions*, factors that set the stage for terrorism over the long run, and *precipitants*, specific events that immediately precede the occurrence of terrorism. Second, a further classification divides preconditions into enabling or permissive factors, which provide opportunities for terrorism to happen, and situations that directly inspire and motivate terrorist campaigns. Precipitants are similar to the direct causes of terrorism.[8] Furthermore, no factor is neatly compartmentalized in a single nation-state; each has a transnational dimension that complicates the analysis.

First, modernization produces an interrelated set of factors that is a significant permissive cause of terrorism, as increased complexity on all levels of society and economy creates opportunities and vulnerabilities. Sophisticated networks of transportation and communication offer mobility and the means of publicity for terrorists. The terrorists of Narodnaya Volya would have been unable to operate without Russia's newly established rail system, and the Popular Front for the Liberation of Palestine could not indulge in hijacking without the jet aircraft. In Algeria, the FLN only adopted a strategy of urban bombings when they were able to acquire plastic explosives. In 1907, the Combat Organization of the Socialist-Revolutionary party paid 20,000 rubles to an inventor who was working on an aircraft in the futile hope of bombing the Russian imperial palaces from the air.[9] Today we fear that terrorists will exploit the potential of nuclear power, but it was in 1867 that Nobel's invention of dynamite made bombings a convenient terrorist tactic.

Urbanization is part of the modern trend toward aggregation and complexity, which increases the number and accessibility of targets and methods. The popular concept of terrorism as "urban guerilla warfare" grew out of the Latin American experience of the late 1960s.[10] Yet, as E. J. Hobsbawn has pointed out, cities became the arena for terrorism after the urban renewal projects of the late nineteenth century, such as the boulevards constructed by Baron Haussman in Paris, made them unsuitable for a strategy based on riots and the defense of barricades.[11] In preventing popular insurrections, governments have exposed themselves to terrorism. P. N. Grabosky has recently argued that cities are a significant cause of terrorism in that they provide an opportunity (a multitude of targets, mobility, communications, anonymity, and audiences) and a recruiting ground among the politicized and volatile inhabitants.[12]

Social "facilitation," which Gurr found to be extremely powerful in bringing about civil strife in general, is also an important permissive factor. This concept refers to social habits and historical traditions that sanction the use of violence against the government, making it morally and politically justifiable, and even dictating an appropriate form, such as demonstrations, coups, or terrorism. Social myths, traditions, and habits permit the development of terrorism as an established political custom. An excellent example of such a tradition is the case of Ireland, where the tradition of physical force dates from the eighteenth century, and the legend of Michael Collins in 1919–21 still inspires and

partially excuses the much less discriminate and less effective terrorism of the contemporary Provisional IRA in Northern Ireland.

Moreover, broad attitudes and beliefs that condone terrorism are communicated transnationally. Revolutionary ideologies have always crossed borders with ease. In the nineteenth and early twentieth centuries, such ideas were primarily a European preserve, stemming from the French and Bolshevik Revolutions. Since the Second World War, Third World War revolutions—China, Cuba, Algeria—and intellectuals such as Frantz Fanon and Carlos Marighela[13] have significantly influenced terrorist movements in the developed West by promoting the development of terrorism as routine behavior.

The most salient political factor in the category of permissive causes is a government's inability or unwillingness to prevent terrorism. The absence of adequate prevention by police and intelligence services permits the spread of conspiracy. However, since terrorist organizatons are small and clandestine, the majority of states can be placed in the permissive category. Inefficiency or leniency can be found in a broad range of all but the most brutally efficient dictatorships, including incompetent authoritarian states such as tsarist Russia on the eve of the emergence of Narodnaya Volya as well as modern liberal democratic states whose desire to protect civil liberties constrains security measures. The absence of effective security measures is a necessary cause, since our limited information on the subject indicates that terrorism does not occur in the communist dictatorships; and certainly repressive military regimes in Uruguay, Brazil, and Argentina have crushed terrorist organizations. For many governments, however, the cost of disallowing terrorism is too high.

Turning now to a consideration of the direct causes of terrorism, we focus on background conditions that positively encourage resistance to the state. These instigating circumstances go beyond merely creating an environment in which terrorism is possible; they provide motivation and direction for the terrorist movement. We are dealing here with reasons rather than opportunities.

The first condition that can be considered a direct cause of terrorism is the existence of concrete grievances among an identifiable subgroup of a larger population, such as an ethnic minority discriminated against by the majority. A social movement develops in order to redress these grievances and to gain either equal rights or a separate state; terrorism is then the resort of an extremist faction of this broader movement. In practice, terrorism has frequently arisen in such situations: in modern states, separatist nationalism among Basques, Bretons, and Québeçois has motivated terrorism. In the colonial era, nationalist movements commonly turned to terrorism.

This is not to say, however, that the existence of a dissatisfied minority or majority is a necessary or a sufficient cause of terrorism. Not all those who are discriminated against turn to terrorism, nor does terrorism always reflect objective social or economic deprivation. In West Germany, Japan, and Italy, for example, terrorism has been the chosen method of the privileged, not the downtrodden. Some theoretical studies have suggested that the essential ingredient that must be added to real deprivation is the perception on the part of the deprived that this condition is not what they deserve or expect, in short, that discrimination is unjust. An attitude study, for example, found that "the idea of justice or fairness may be more centrally related to attitudes toward violence than are feelings of deprivation. It is the perceived injustice underlying the deprivation that gives rise to anger or frustration."[14] The intervening variables, as we have argued, lie in the terrorists' perceptions. Moreover, it seems likely that for terrorism to occur the government must be singled out to blame for popular suffering.

The second condition that creates motivations for terrorism is the lack of opportunity for political participation. Regimes that deny access to power and persecute dissenters create dissatisfaction. In this case, grievances are primarily political, without social or economic overtones. Discrimination is not directed against any ethnic, religious, or racial subgroup of the population. The terrorist organization is not necessarily part of a broader social movement; indeed, the population may be largely apathetic. In situations where paths to the legal expression of opposition are blocked, but where the regime's repression is inefficient, revolutionary terrorism is doubly likely, as permissive and direct causes coincide. An example of this situation is tsarist Russia in the 1870s.

Context is especially significant as a direct cause of terrorism when it affects an elite, not the mass population. Terrorism is essentially the result of elite disaffection; it represents the strategy of a minority, who may act on behalf of a wider popular constituency who have not been consulted about, and do not necessarily approve of, the terrorists' aims or methods. There is remarkable relevance in E. J. Hobsbawm's comments on the political conspirators of post-Napoleonic Europe: "All revolutionaries regarded themselves, with some justification, as small elites of the emancipated and progressive operating among, and for the eventual benefit of, a vast and inert mass of the ignorant and misled common people, which would no doubt welcome liberation when it came, but could not be expected to take much part in preparing it."[15] Many terrorists today are young, well-educated, and middle class in background. Such students or young professionals, with prior political experience, are disillusioned with the prospects of changing society and see little chance of access to the system despite their privileged status. Much terrorism has grown out of student unrest; this was the case in nineteenth century Russia as well as post–World War II West Germany, Italy, the United States, Japan, and Uruguay.

Perhaps terrorism is most likely to occur precisely where mass passivity and elite dissatisfaction coincide. Discontent is not generalized or severe enough to provoke the majority of the populace to action against the regime, yet a small minority, without access to the bases of power that would permit overthrow of the government through coup d'état or subversion, seeks radical change. Terrorism may thus be a sign of a stable society rather than a symptom of fragility and impending collapse. Terrorism is the resort of an elite when conditions are not revolutionary. Luigi Bonanate has blamed terrorism on a "blocked society" that is strong enough to preserve itself (presumably through popular inertia) yet resistant to innovation. Such self-perpetuating "immobilisme" invites terrorism.[16]

The last category of situational factors involves the concept of a precipitating event that immediately precedes outbreaks of terrorism. Although it is generally thought that precipitants are the most unpredictable of causes, there does seem to be a common pattern of government actions that act as catalysts for terrorism. Government use of unexpected and unusual force in response to protest or reform attempts often compels terrorist retaliation. The development of such an action-reaction syndrome then establishes the structure of the conflict between the regime and its challengers. There are numerous historical examples of a campaign of terrorism precipitated by a government's reliance on excessive force to quell protest or squash dissent. The tsarist regime's severity in dealing with the populist movement was a factor in the development of Narodaya Volya as a terrorist organization in 1879. The French government's persecution of anarchists was a factor in subsequent anarchist terrorism in the 1890s. The British government's execution of the heros [sic] of the Easter Rising set the stage for Michael Collins and the IRA. The Protestant violence that met the Catholic civil rights movement in Northern Ireland in 1969 pushed the Provisional IRA to retaliate. In West Germany, the death of Beno Ohnesorg at the hands of the police in a demonstration against the Shah of Iran in 1968 contributed to the emergence of the RAF.

This analysis of the background conditions for terrorism indicates that we must look at the terrorist organization's perception and interpretation of the situation. Terrorists view the context as permissive, making terrorism a viable option. In a material sense, the means are placed at their disposal by the environment. Circumstances also provide the terrorists with compelling reasons for seeking political change. Finally, an event occurs that snaps the terrorists' patience with the regime. Government action is now seen as intolerably unjust, and terrorism becomes not only a possible decision but a morally acceptable one. The regime has forfeited its status as the standard of legitimacy. For the terrorist, the end may now excuse the means.

The Reasons for Terrorism

Significant campaigns of terrorism depend on rational political choice. As purposeful activity, terrorism is the result of an organization's decision that it is a politically useful means to oppose a government. The argument that terrorist behavior should be analyzed as "rational" is based on the assumption that terrorist organizations possess internally consistent sets of values, beliefs, and images of the environment. Terrorism is seen collectively as a logical means to advance desired ends. The terrorist organization engages in decision-making calculations that an analyst can approximate. In short, the terrorist group's reasons for resorting to terrorism constitute an important factor in the process of causation.[17]

Terrorism serves a variety of goals, both revolutionary and subrevolutionary. Terrorists may be revolutionaries (such as the Combat Organization of the Socialist-Revolutionary Party in the nineteenth century or the Tupamaros of the twentieth); nationalists fighting against foreign occupiers (the Algerian FLN, the IRA of 1919–21, or the Irgun); minority separatists combatting indigenous regimes (such as the Corsican, Breton, and Basque movements, and the Provisional IRA); reformists (the bombing of nuclear construction sites, for example, is meant to halt nuclear power, not to overthrow governments); anarchists or millenarians (such as the original anarchist movement of the nineteenth century and modern millenarian groups such as the Red Army faction in West Germany, the Italian Red Brigades, and the Japanese Red Army); or reactionaries acting to prevent change from the top (such as the Secret Army Organization during the Algerian war or the contemporary Ulster Defence Association in Northern Ireland).[18]

Saying that extremist groups resort to terrorism in order to acquire political influence does not mean that all groups have equally precise objectives or that the relationship between means and ends is perfectly clear to an outside observer. Some groups are less realistic about the logic of means and ends than others. The leaders of Narodnaya Volya, for example, lacked a detailed conception of how the assassination of the tsar would force his successor to permit the liberalization they sought. Other terrorist groups are more pragmatic: the IRA of 1919–21 and the Irgun, for instance, shrewdly foresaw the utility of a war of attrition against the British. Menachem Begin, in particular, planned his campaign to take advantage of the "glass house" that Britain operated in.[19] The degree of skill in relating means to ends seems to have little to do with the overall sophistication of the terrorist ideology. The French anarchists of the 1890s, for example, acted in light of a well-developed philosophical doctrine but were much less certain of how violence against the bourgeoisie would bring about freedom. It is possible that anarchist or millenarian terrorists are so preoccupied with the splendor of the future that they lose sight of the present. Less theoretical nationalists who concentrate on the short run have simpler aims but sharper plans.

However diverse the long-run goals of terrorist groups, there is a common pattern of proximate or short-run objectives of a terrorist strategy. Proximate objectives are defined in terms of the reactions that terrorists want to achieve in their different audiences.[20] The most basic reason for terrorism is to gain recognition or attention—what Thomas P. Thornton called advertisement of the cause. Violence and bloodshed always excite human curiosity, and the theatricality, suspense, and threat of danger inherent in terrorism enhance its attention-getting qualities. In fact, publicity may be the highest goal of some groups. For example, terrorists who are fundamentally protesters might be satisfied with airing their grievances before the world. Today, in an interdependent world, the need for international recognition encourages transnational terrorist activities, with escalation to ever more destructive and spectacular violence. As the audience grows larger, more diverse, and more accustomed to terrorism, terrorists must go to extreme lengths to shock.

Terrorism is also often designed to disrupt and discredit the processes of government, by weakening it administratively and impairing normal operations. Terrorism as a direct attack on the regime aims at the insecurity and demoralization of government officials, independent of any impact on public opinion. An excellent example of this strategy is Michael Collins's campaign against the British intelligence system in Ireland in 1919–21. This form of terrorism often accompanies rural guerrilla warfare, as the insurgents try to weaken the government's control over its territory.

Terrorism also affects public attitudes in both a positive and a negative sense, aiming at creating either sympathy in a potential constituency or fear and hostility in an audience identified as the "enemy." These two functions are interrelated, since intimidating the "enemy" impresses both sympathizers and the uncommitted. At the same time, terrorism may be used to enforce obedience in an audience from whom the terrorists demand allegiance. The FLN in Algeria, for example, claimed more Algerian than French victims. Fear and respect were not incompatible with solidarity against the French.[21] When terrorism is part of a struggle between incumbents and challengers, polarization of public opinion undermines the government's legitimacy.

Terrorism may also be intended to provoke a counterreaction from the government, to increase publicity for the terrorists' cause and to demonstrate to the people that their charges against the regime are well founded. The terrorists mean to force the state to show its true repressive face, thereby driving the people into the arms of the challengers. For example, Carlos Marighela argued that the way to win popular support was to provoke the regime to measures of greater repression and persecution.[22] Provocative terrorism is designed to bring about revolutionary conditions rather than to exploit them.

The FLN against the French, the Palestinians against Israel, and the RAF against the Federal Republic all appear to have used terrorism as provocation.

In addition, terrorism may serve internal organizational functions of control, discipline, and morale building within the terrorist group and even become an instrument of rivalry among factions in a resistance movement. For example, factional terrorism has frequently characterized the Palestinian resistance movement. Rival groups have competed in a vicious game where the victims are Israeli civilians or anonymous airline passengers, but where the immediate goal is influence within the resistance movement rather than the intimidation of the Israeli public or international recognition of the Palestinian cause.

Terrorism is a logical choice when oppositions have such goals and when the power ratio of government to challenger is high. The observation that terrorism is a weapon of the weak is hackneyed but apt. At least when initially adopted, terrorism is the strategy of a minority that by its own judgment lacks other means. When the group perceives its options as limited, terrorism is attractive because it is a relatively inexpensive and simple alternative, and because its potential reward is high.

Weakness and consequent restriction of choice can stem from different sources. On the one hand, weakness may result from the regime's suppression of opposition. Resistance organizations who lack the means of mounting more extensive violence may then turn to terrorism because legitimate expression of dissent is denied. Lack of popular support at the outset of a conflict does not mean that the terrorists' aims lack general appeal. Even though they cannot immediately mobilize widespread and active support, over the course of the conflict they may acquire the allegiance of the population. For example, the Algerian FLN used terrorism as a significant means of mobilizing mass support.[23]

On the other hand, it is wrong to assume that where there is terrorism there is oppression. Weakness may mean that an extremist organization deliberately rejects nonviolent methods of opposition

open to them in a liberal state. Challengers then adopt terrorism because they are impatient with time-consuming legal methods of eliciting support or advertising their cause, because they distrust the regime, or because they are not capable of, or interested in, mobilizing majority support. Most terrorist groups operating in Western Europe and Japan in the past decade illustrate this phenomenon. The new millenarians lack a readily identifiable constituency and espouse causes devoid of mass appeal. Similarly, separatist movements represent at best only a minority of the total population of the state.

Thus, some groups are weak because weakness is imposed on them by the political system they operate in, others because of unpopularity. We are therefore making value judgments about the potential legitimacy of terrorist organizations. In some cases resistance groups are genuinely desperate, in others they have alternatives to violence. Nor do we want to forget that nonviolent resistance has been chosen in other circumstances, for example, by Gandhi and by Martin Luther King. Terrorists may argue that they had no choice, but their perceptions may be flawed.[24]

In addition to weakness, an important rationale in the decision to adopt a strategy of terrorism is impatience. Action becomes imperative. For a variety of reasons, the challenge to the state cannot be left to the future. Given a perception of limited means, the group often sees the choice as between action as survival and inaction as the death of resistance.

One reason for haste is external: the historical moment seems to present a unique chance. For example, the resistance group facing a colonial power recently weakened by a foreign war exploits a temporary vulnerability: the IRA against Britain after World War I, the Irgun against Britain after World War II, and the FLN against France after the Indochina war. We might even suggest that the stalemate between the United States and North Vietnam stimulated the post-1968 wave of anti-imperialist terrorism, especially in Latin America. There may be other pressures or catalysts provided by the regime, such as the violent precipitants discussed earlier or the British decision to introduce conscription in Ireland during World War I.

A sense of urgency may also develop when similar resistance groups have apparently succeeded with terrorism and created a momentum. The contagion effect of terrorism is partially based on an image of success that recommends terrorism to groups who identify with the innovator. The Algerian FLN, for example, was pressured to keep up with nationalists in Tunisia and Morocco, whose violent agitation brought about independence in 1956. Terrorism spread rapidly through Latin America in the post-1968 period as revolutionary groups worked in terms of a continental solidarity.

Dramatic failure of alternative means of obtaining one's ends may also fuel a drive toward terrorism. The Arab defeat in the 1967 war with Israel led Palestinians to realize that they could no longer depend on the Arab states to further their goals. In retrospect, their extreme weakness and the historical tradition of violence in the Middle East made it likely that militant nationalists should turn to terrorism. Since international recognition of the Palestinian cause was a primary aim (given the influence of outside powers in the region) and since attacks on Israeli territory were difficult, terrorism developed into a transnational phenomenon.

These external pressures to act are often intensified by internal politics. Leaders of resistance groups act under constraints imposed by their followers. They are forced to justify the organization's existence, to quell restlessness among the cadres, to satisfy demands for revenge, to prevent splintering of the movement, and to maintain control. Pressures may also come from the terrorists' constituency.

In conclusion, we see that terrorism is an attractive strategy to groups of different ideological persuasions who challenge the state's authority. Groups who want to dramatize a cause, to demoralize the government, to gain popular support, to provoke regime violence, to inspire followers, or to dominate a wider resistance movement, who are weak vis-à-vis the regime, and who are impatient to act, often find terrorism a reasonable choice. This is especially so when conditions are favorable, providing opportunities and making terrorism a simple and rapid option, with immediate and visible payoff.

Individual Motivation and Participation

Terrorism is neither an automatic reaction to conditions nor a purely calculated strategy. What psychological factors motivate the terrorist and influence his or her perceptions and interpretations of reality? Terrorists are only a small minority of people with similar personal backgrounds, experiencing the same conditions, who might thus be expected to reach identical conclusions based on logical reasoning about the utility of terrorism as a technique of political influence.

The relationship between personality and politics is complex and imperfectly understood.[25] Why individuals engage in political violence is a complicated problem, and the question why they engage in terrorism is still more difficult.[26] As most simply and frequently posed, the question of a psychological explanation of terrorism is whether or not there is a "terrorist personality," similar to the authoritarian personality, whose emotional traits we can specify with some exactitude.[27] An identifiable pattern of attitudes and behavior in the terrorism-prone individual would result from a combination of ego-defensive needs, cognitive processes, and socialization, in interaction with a specific situation. In pursuing this line of inquiry, it is important to avoid stereotyping the terrorist or oversimplifying the sources of terrorist actions. No single motivation or personality can be valid for all circumstances.

What limited data we have on individual terrorists (and knowledge must be gleaned from disparate sources that usually neither focus on psychology nor use a comparative approach) suggest that the outstanding common characteristic of terrorists is their normality. Terrorism often seems to be the connecting link among widely varying personalities. Franco Venturi, concentrating on the terrorists of a single small group, observed that "the policy of terrorism united many very different characters and mentalities" and that agreement on using terrorism was the cement that bound the members of Narodnaya Volya together.[28] The West German psychiatrist who conducted a pretrial examination of four members of the RAF concluded that they were "intelligent," even "humorous," and showed no symptoms of psychosis or neurosis and "no particular personality type."[29] Psychoanalysis might penetrate beneath superficial normality to expose some unifying or pathological trait, but this is scarcely a workable research method, even if the likelihood of the existence of such a characteristic could be demonstrated.

Peter Merkl, in his study of the pre-1933 Nazi movement—a study based on much more data than we have on terrorists—abandoned any attempt to classify personality types and instead focused on factors like the level of political understanding.[30] An unbiased examination of conscious attitudes might be more revealing than a study of subconscious predispositions or personalities. For example, if terrorists perceive the state as unjust, morally corrupt, and violent, then terrorism may seem legitimate and justified. For example, Monica D. Blumenthal and her coauthors found that "the stronger the perception of an act as violence, the more violence is thought to be an appropriate response."[31] The evidence also indicates that many terrorists are activists with prior political experience in nonviolent opposition to the state. How do these experiences in participation influence later attitudes? Furthermore, how do terrorists view their victims? Do we find extreme devaluation, depersonalization, or stereotyping? Is there "us versus them" polarization or ethnic or religious prejudice that might sanction or prompt violence toward an out-group? How do terrorists justify and rationalize violence? Is remorse a theme?

The questions of attitudes toward victims and justifications for terrorism are especially important because different forms of terrorism involve various degrees of selectivity in the choice of victims. Some acts of terrorism are extremely discriminate,

while others are broadly indiscriminate. Also, some terrorist acts require more intimate contact between terrorist and victim than others. Thus, the form of terrorism practiced—how selective it is and how much personal domination of the victim it involves—would determine the relevance of different questions.

Analyzing these issues involves serious methodological problems. As the Blumenthal study emphasizes, there are two ways of analyzing the relationship between attitudes and political behavior.[32] If our interest is in identifying potential terrorists by predicting behavior from the existence of certain consciously held attitudes and beliefs, then the best method would be to survey a young age group in a society determined to be susceptible. If terrorism subsequently occurred, we could then see which types of individuals became terrorists. (A problem is that the preconditions would change over time and that precipitants are unpredictable.) The more common and easier way of investigating the attitudes-behavior connection is to select people who have engaged in a particular behavior and ask them questions about their opinions. Yet attitudes may be adopted subsequent, rather than prior, to behavior, and they may serve as rationalizations for behavior engaged in for different reasons, not as genuine motivations. These problems would seem to be particularly acute when the individuals concerned have engaged in illegal forms of political behavior.

Another problem facing the researcher interested in predispositions or attitudes is that terrorists are recruited in different ways. Assuming that people who are in some way personally attracted to terrorism actually engage in such behavior supposes that potential terrorists are presented with an appropriate opportunity, which is a factor over which they have little control.[33] Moreover, terrorist groups often discourage or reject potential recruits who are openly seeking excitement or danger for personal motives. For instance, William Mackey Lomasney, a member of the Clan na Gael or American Fenians in the nineteenth century (who was killed in 1884 in an attempt to blow up London Bridge), condemned the "disgraceful" activities of the hotheaded and impulsive Jeremiah O'Donovan Rossa:

> Were it not that O'Donovan Rossa has openly and unblushingly boasted that he is responsible for those ridiculous and futile efforts . . . we might hesitate to even suspect that any sane man, least of all one professedly friendly to the cause, would for any consideration or desire for notoriety take upon himself such a fearful responsibility, and, that having done so, he could engage men so utterly incapable of carrying out his insane designs.[34]

Lomasney complained that the would-be terrorists were:

> such stupid blundering fools that they make our cause appear imbecile and farcical. When the fact becomes known that those half-idiotic attempts have been made by men professing to be patriotic Irishmen what will the world think but that Irish revolutionists are a lot of fools and ignoramuses, men who do not understand the first principles of the art of war, the elements of chemistry or even the amount of explosive material necessary to remove or destroy an ordinary brick or stone wall. Think of the utter madness of men who have no idea of accumulative and destructive forces undertaking with common blasting powder to scare and shatter the Empire.[35]

Not only do serious terrorists scorn the ineptitude of the more excitable, but they find them a serious security risk. Rossa, for example, could not be trusted not to give away the Clan na Gael's plans for terrorism in his New York newspaper articles. In a similar vein, Boris Savinkov, head of the Combat Organization of the Socialist-Revolutionary party in Russia, tried to discourage an aspirant whom he suspected of being drawn to the adventure of terrorism:

> I explained to him that terrorist activity did not consist only of throwing bombs; that it was much more minute, difficult and tedious than might be imagined; that a terrorist is called upon to live a rather dull existence for months at a time, eschewing meeting his own comrades and doing most difficult and unpleasant work—the work of systematic observation.[36]

Similar problems in analyzing the connection between attitudes and behavior are due to the fact that there are role differentiations between leaders and followers. The degree of formal organization varies from the paramilitary hierarchies of the Irgun or the IRA to the semi-autonomous coexistence of small groups in contemporary West Germany or Italy or even to the rejection of central direction in the nineteenth century anarchist movement in France. Yet even Narodnaya Volya, a self-consciously democratic group, observed distinctions based on authority. There are thus likely to be psychological or background differences between leaders and cadres. For example, a survey of contemporary terrorist movements found that leaders are usually older than their followers, which is not historically unusual.[37] In general, data are scant on individual terrorist leaders, their exercise of authority, the basis for it, and their interactions with their followers.[38] Furthermore, if there is a predisposition to terrorism, the terrorism-prone individual who obtains psychic gratification from the experience is likely to be a follower, not a leader who commands but does not perform the act.

An alternative approach to analyzing the psychology of terrorism is to use a deductive method based on what we know about terrorism as an activity, rather than an inductive method yielding general propositions from statements of the particular. What sort of characteristics would make an individual suited for terrorism? What are the role requirements of the terrorist?

One of the most salient attributes of terrorist activity is that it involves significant personal danger.[39] Furthermore, since terrorism involves premediated, not impulsive, violence, the terrorist's awareness of the risks is maximized. Thus, although terrorists may simply be people who enjoy or disregard risk,[40] it is more likely that they are people who tolerate high risk because of intense commitment to a cause. Their commitment is strong enough to make the risk of personal harm acceptable and perhaps to outweigh the cost of society's rejection, although defiance of the majority may be a reward in itself. In either case, the violent activity is not gratifying per se.

It is perhaps even more significant that terrorism is a group activity, involving intimate relationships among a small number of people. Interactions among members of the group may be more important in determining behavior than the psychological predispositions of individual members. Terrorists live and make decisions under conditions of extreme stress. As a clandestine minority, the members of a terrorist group are isolated from society, even if they live in what Menachem Begin called the "open underground."[41]

Terrorists can confide in and trust only each other. The nature of their commitment cuts them off from society; they inhabit a closed community that is forsaken only at great cost. Isolation and the perception of a hostile environment intensify shared belief and commitment and make faith in the cause imperative. A pattern of mutual reassurance, solidarity, and comradeship develops, in which the members of the group reinforce each other's self-righteousness, image of a hostile world, and sense of mission. Because of the real danger terrorists confront, the strain they live under, and the moral conflicts they undergo, they value solidarity highly.[42] Terrorists are not necessarily people who seek "belonging" or personal integration through ideological commitment, but once embarked on the path of terrorism, they desperately need the group and the cause. Isolation and internal consensus explain how the beliefs and values of a terrorist group can be so drastically at odds with those of society at large. An example of such a divorce from social and political reality is the idea of the RAF that terrorism would lead to a resurgence of Nazism in West Germany that would in turn spark a workers' revolt.[43]

In their intense commitment, separation from the outside world, and intolerance of internal dissent, terrorist groups resemble religious sects or cults. Michael Barkun has explained the continued commitment of members of millenarian movements, a conviction frequently expressed in proselytizing in order to validate beliefs, in terms of the reinforcement and reassurance of rightness that the individual receives from other members of the organization. He also notes the frequent practice of initiation rites that involve violations of taboos, or "bridge-burning acts," that create guilt and prevent the convert's return to society. Thus the millenarian, like the terrorist group, constitutes "a community of common guilt."[44] J. Bowyer Bell has commented on the religious qualities of dedication and moral fervor characterizing the IRA: "In the Republican Movement, the two seemingly opposing traditions, one of the revolution and physical force, and the other of pious and puritanical service, combine into a secular vocation."[45]

If there is a single common emotion that drives the individual to become a terrorist, it is vengeance on behalf of comrades or even the constituency the terrorist aspires to represent. (At the same time, the demand for retribution serves as public justification or excuse.) A regime thus encourages terrorism when it creates martyrs to be avenged. Anger at what is perceived as unjust persecution inspires demands for revenge, and as the regime responds to terrorism with greater force, violence escalates out of control.

There are numerous historical demonstrations of the central role vengeance plays as motivation for terrorism. It is seen as one of the principal causes of anarchist terrorism in France in the 1890s. The infamous Ravachol acted to avenge the "martyrs of Clichy," two possibly innocent anarchists who were beaten by the police and sentenced to prison. Subsequent bombings and assassinations, for instance that of President Carnot, were intended to avenge Ravachol's execution.[46] The cruelty of the sentences imposed for minor offenses at the "Trial of the 193," the hanging of eleven southern revolutionaries after Soloviev's unsuccessful attack on the tsar in 1879, and the "Trial of the 16" in 1880 deeply affected the members of Narodnaya Volya. Kravchinski (S. Stepniak) explained that personal resentment felt after the Trial of the 193 led to killing police spies; it then seemed unreasonable to spare their employers, who were actually responsible for the repression. Thus, intellectually the logic first inspired by resentment compelled them to escalate terrorism by degrees.[47] During the Algerian war, the French execution of FLN prisoners; in Northern Ireland, British troops firing on civil rights demonstrators; in West Germany, the death of a demonstrator at the hands of the police—all served to precipitate terrorism as militants sought to avenge their comrades.

The terrorists' willingness to accept high risks may also be related to the belief that one's death will be avenged. The prospect of retribution gives the act of terrorism and the death of the terrorist meaning and continuity, even fame and immortality. Vengeance may be a function not only of anger but of a desire for transcendence.

Shared guilt is surely a strong force in binding members of the terrorist group together. Almost all terrorists seem compelled to justify their behavior, and this anxiety cannot be explained solely by reference to their desire to create a public image of virtuous sincerity. Terrorists usually show acute concern for morality, especially for sexual purity, and believe that they act in terms of a higher good. Justifications usually focus on past suffering, on the glorious future to be created, and on the regime's illegitimacy and violence, to which terrorism is the only available response. Shared guilt and anxiety increase the group's interdependence and mutual commitment and may also make followers more dependent on leaders and on the common ideology as sources of moral authority.

Guilt may also lead terrorists to seek punishment and danger rather than avoid it. The motive of self-sacrifice notably influenced many Russian terrorists of the nineteenth century. Kaliayev, for example, felt that only his death could atone for the murder he committed. Even to Camus, the risk of death for the terrorist is a form of personal absolution.[48] In other cases of terrorism, individuals much more pragmatic than Kaliayev, admittedly a religious mystic, seemed to welcome capture because it brought release from the

strains of underground existence and a sense of content and fulfillment. For example, Ya'acov Meridor, a member of the Irgun High Command, felt "high spirits" and "satisfaction" when arrested by the British because he now shared the suffering that all fighters had to experience. He almost welcomed the opportunity to prove that he was prepared to sacrifice himself for the cause. In fact, until his arrest he had felt "morally uncomfortable," whereas afterwards he felt "exalted."[49] Menachem Begin expressed similar feelings. Once, waiting as the British searched the hotel where he was staying, he admitted anxiety and fear, but when he knew there was "no way out," his "anxious thoughts evaporated." He "felt a peculiar serenity mixed with incomprehensible happiness" and waited "composedly," but the police passed him by.[50]

Vera Figner, a leader of the Narodnaya Volya, insisted on physically assisting in acts of terrorism, even though her comrades accused her of seeking personal satisfaction instead of allowing the organization to make the best use of her talents. She found it intolerable to bear a moral responsibility for acts that endangered her comrades. She could not encourage others to commit acts she would not herself commit; anything less than full acceptance of the consequences of her decisions would be cowardice.[51]

It is possible that the willingness to face risk is related to what Robert J. Lifton has termed "survivor-guilt" as well as to feelings of group solidarity or of guilt at harming victims.[52] Sometimes individuals who survive disaster or escape punishment when others have suffered feel guilty and may seek relief by courting a similar fate. This guilt may also explain why terrorists often take enormous risks to rescue imprisoned comrades, as well as why they accept danger or arrest with equanimity or even satisfaction.

It is clear that once a terrorist group embarks on a strategy of terrorism, whatever its purpose and whatever its successes or failures, psychological factors make it very difficult to halt. Terrorism as a process gathers its own momentum, independent of external events.

Conclusions

Terrorism per se is not usually a reflection of mass discontent or deep cleavages in society. More often it represents the disaffection of a fragment of the elite, who may take it upon themselves to act on the behalf of a majority unaware of its plight, unwilling to take action to remedy grievances, or unable to express dissent. This discontent, however subjective in origin or minor in scope, is blamed on the government and its supporters. Since the sources of terrorism are manifold, any society or polity that permits opportunities for terrorism is vulnerable. Government reactions that are inconsistent, wavering between tolerance and repression, seem most likely to encourage terrorism.

Given some source of disaffection—and in the centralized modern state with its faceless bureaucracies, lack of responsiveness to demands is ubiquitous—terrorism is an attractive strategy for small organizations of diverse ideological persuasions who want to attract attention for their cause, provoke the government, intimidate opponents, appeal for sympathy, impress an audience, or promote the adherence of the faithful. Terrorists perceive an absence of choice. Whether unable or unwilling to perceive a choice between terrorist and nonterrorist action, whether unpopular or prohibited by the government, the terrorist group reasons that there is no alternative. The ease, simplicity, and rapidity with which terrorism can be implemented and the prominence of models of terrorism strengthen its appeal, especially since terrorist groups are impatient to act. Long-standing social traditions that sanction terrorism against the state, as in Ireland, further enhance its attractiveness.

There are two fundamental questions about the psychological basis of terrorism. The first is why the individual takes the first step and chooses to engage in terrorism: Why join? Does the terrorist possess specific psychological predispositions, identifiable in advance, that suit him or her for terrorism? That terrorists are people capable of intense commitment tells us little, and the motivations for terrorism vary immensely. Many individuals are potential terrorists, but few actually make that commitment. To explain why terrorism happens, another question is more appropriate: Why does involvement continue? What are the psychological mechanisms of group interaction? We are not dealing with a situation in which certain types of personalities suddenly turn to terrorism in answer to some inner call. Terrorism is the result of a gradual growth of commitment and opposition, a group development that furthermore depends on government action. The psychological relationships within the terrorist group—the interplay of commitment, risk, solidarity, loyalty, guilt, revenge, and isolation—discourage terrorists from changing the direction they have taken. This may explain why—even if objective circumstances change when, for example, grievances are satisfied, or if the logic of the situation changes when, for example, the terrorists are offered other alternatives for the expression of opposition—terrorism may endure until the terrorist group is physically destroyed.

NOTES

1. For discussions of the meaning of the concept of terrorism, see Thomas P. Thornton, "Terror as a Weapon of Political Agitation," in Harry Eckstein, ed. *Internal War: Problems and Approaches* (New York: Free Press of Glencoe, 1964), pp. 71–99; Martha Crenshaw Hutchinson, "The Concept of Revolutionary Terrorism," *Revolutionary Terrorism: The FLN in Algeria, 1954–1962* (Stanford: The Hoover Institution Press, 1978), chap. 2; and E. Victor Walter, *Terror and Resistance: A Study of Political Violence, with Case Studies of Some Primitive African Communities* (New York: Oxford University Press, 1969).

2. Walter Laqueur, "Interpretations of Terrorism—Fact, Fiction and Political Science," *Journal of Contemporary History*, 12 (January 1977), 1–42. See also his major work *Terrorism* (London: Weidenfeld and Nicolson, 1977).

3. See, for example, Paul Wilkinson, *Terrorism and the Liberal State* (London: Macmillan, 1977), or J. Bowyer Bell, *A Time of Terror: How*

Democratic Societies Respond to Revolutionary Violence (New York: Basic Books, 1978).

4. This is not to deny that some modern terrorist groups, such as those in West Germany, resemble premodern millenarian movements. See specifically Conor Cruise O'Brien, "Liberty and Terrorism," *International Security*, 2 (1977), 56–67. In general, see Norman Cohn, *The Pursuit of the Millennium* (London: Secker and Warburg, 1957), and E. J. Hobsbawm, *Primitive Rebels: Studies in Archaic Forms of Social Movement in the 19th and 20th Centuries* (Manchester: Manchester University Press, 1971).

5. A sampling would include Douglas Hibbs, Jr., *Mass Political Violence: A Cross-National Causal Analysis* (New York: J. Wiley, 1973); William J. Crotty, ed. *Assassinations and the Political Order* (New York: Harper & Row, 1971); Ted Robert Gurr, *Why Men Rebel* (Princeton: Princeton University Press, 1971), and Gurr, Peter N. Grabosky, and Richard C. Hula, *The Politics of Crime and Conflict* (Beverly Hills: Sage, 1977).

6. For a summary of these findings, see T. R. Gurr, "The Calculus of Civil Conflict," *Journal of Social Issues*, 28 (1972), 27–47.

7. Ted Robert Gurr, "Some Characteristics of Political Terrorism in the 1960s," in Michael Stohl, ed., *The Politics of Terrorism* (New York: M. Decker, 1979), pp. 23–50 and 46–47.

8. A distinction between preconditions and precipitants is found in Harry Eckstein, "On the Etiology of Internal Wars," *History and Theory*, 4 (1965), 133–62. Kenneth N. Waltz also differentiates between the framework for action as a permissive or underlying cause and special reasons as immediate or efficient causes. In some cases we can say of terrorism, as he says of war, that it occurs because there is nothing to prevent it. See *Man, the State and War* (New York: Columbia University Press, 1959), p. 232.

9. Boris Savinkov, *Memoirs of a Terrorist*, trans. Joseph Shaplen (New York: A. & C. Boni, 1931), pp. 286–87.

10. The major theoreticians of the transition from the rural to the urban guerrilla are Carlos Marighela, *For the Liberation of Brazil* (Harmondsworth: Penguin Books, 1971), and Abraham Guillen,

Philosophy of the Urban Guerrilla: The Revolutionary Writings of Abraham Guillen, trans. and edited by Donald C. Hodges (New York: Morrow, 1973).

11. E. J. Hobsbawm, *Revolutionaries: Contemporary Essays* (New York: Meridian, 1973), pp. 226–27.

12. P. N. Grabosky, "The Urban Context of Political Terrorism," in Stohl, ed., pp. 51–76.

13. See Amy Sands Redlick, "The Transnational Flow of Information as a Cause of Terrorism," in Yonah Alexander, David Carlton, and Paul Wilkinson, eds., *Terrorism: Theory and Practice* (Boulder: Westview Press, 1979), pp. 73–95. See also Manus I. Midlarsky, Martha Crenshaw, and Fumihiko Yoshida, "Why Violence Spreads: The Contagion of International Terrorism," *International Studies Quarterly*, 24 (June 1980), 262–98.

14. Monica D. Blumenthal, et al., *More about Justifying Violence: Methodological Studies of Attitudes and Behavior* (Ann Arbor: Survey Research Center, Institute for Social Research, University of Michigan, 1975), p. 108. Similarly, Peter Lupsha, "Explanation of Political Violence: Some Psychological Theories versus Indignation," *Politics and Society*, 2 (1971), 89–104, contrasts the concept of "indignation" with Gurr's theory of relative deprivation, which holds that expectations exceed rewards (see *Why Men Rebel*, esp. pp. 24–30).

15. Hobsbawm, *Revolutionaries*, p. 143.

16. Luigi Bonanate, "Some Unanticipated Consequences of Terrorism," *Journal of Peace Research*, 16 (1979), 197–211. If this theory is valid, we then need to identify such blocked societies.

17. See Barbara Salert's critique of the rational choice model of revolutionary participation in *Revolutions and Revolutionaries: Four Theories* (New York: Elsevier, 1976). In addition, Abraham Kaplan discusses the distinction between reasons and causes in "The Psychodynamics of Terrorism," *Terrorism—an International Journal*, 1, 3 and 4 (1978), 237–54.

18. For a typology of terrorist organizations, see Paul Wilkinson, *Political Terrorism* (New York: Wiley, 1975). These classes are not mutually exclusive, and they depend on an outside assessment of goals. For example, the Basque ETA would consider itself revolutionary as well as separatist. The RAF

considered itself a classic national liberation movement, and the Provisional IRA insists that it is combatting a foreign oppressor, not an indigenous regime.

19. J. Bowyer Bell presents a succinct analysis of Irgun strategy in "The Palestinian Archetype: Irgun and the Strategy of Leverage," in *On Revolt: Strategies of National Liberation* (Cambridge [Ma.]: Harvard University Press, 1976), chap. 3.

20. See Thornton's analysis of proximate goals in "Terror as a Weapon of Political Agitation," in Eckstein, ed., pp. 82–88.

21. Walter's discussion of the concept of "forced choice" explains how direct audiences, from whom the victims are drawn, may accept terrorism as legitimate; see *Terror and Resistance*, pp. 285–89.

22. See Marighela, *For the Liberation of Brazil*, pp. 94–95. The West German RAF apparently adopted the idea of provocation as part of a general national liberation strategy borrowed from the Third World.

23. See Hutchinson, *Revolutionary Terrorism*, chap. 3, pp. 40–60.

24. See Michael Walzer's analysis of the morality of terrorism in *Just and Unjust Wars: A Moral Argument with Historical Illustrations* (New York: Basic Books, 1977), pp. 197–206. See also Bernard Avishai, "In Cold Blood," *The New York Review of Books*, March 8, 1979, pp. 41–44, for a critical appraisal of the failure of recent works on terrorism to discuss moral issues. The question of the availability of alternatives to terrorism is related to the problem of discrimination in the selection of victims. Where victims are clearly responsible for a regime's denial of opportunity, terrorism is more justifiable than where they are not.

25. See Fred I. Greenstein, *Personality and Politics: Problems of Evidence, Inference, and Conceptualization* (Chicago: Markham, 1969).

26. See Jeffrey Goldstein, *Aggression and Crimes of Violence* (New York: Oxford University Press, 1975).

27. A study of the West German New Left, for example, concludes that social psychological models of authoritarianism do help explain the dynamics of radicalism and even the transformation from protest to terrorism. See S. Robert Lichter, "A Psychopolitical Study of West German Male

Radical Students," *Comparative Politics*, 12 (October 1979), pp. 27–48.

28. Franco Venturi, *Roots of Revolution: A History of the Populist and Socialist Movements in Nineteenth Century Russia* (London: Weidenfeld and Nicolson, 1960), p. 647.

29. Quoted in *Science*, 203, 5 January 1979, p. 34, as part of an account of the proceedings of the International Scientific Conference on Terrorism held in Berlin, December 1978. Advocates of the "terrorist personality" theory, however, argued that terrorists suffer from faulty vestibular functions in the middle ear or from inconsistent mothering resulting in dysphoria. For another description see John Wykert, "Psychiatry and Terrorism," *Psychiatric News*, 14 (February 2, 1979), 1 and 12–14. A psychologist's study of a single group, the Front de Libération du Québec, is Gustav Morf, *Terror in Quebec: Case Studies of the FLQ* (Toronto: Clarke, Irvin, and Co., 1970).

30. Peter Merkl, *Political Violence under the Swastika: 581 Early Nazis* (Princeton: Princeton University, 1974), 33–34.

31. Blumenthal, et al., *More about Justifying Violence*, p. 182.

32. Ibid., p. 12. Lichter also recognizes this problem.

33. Ibid., pp. 12–13.

34. William O'Brien and Desmond Ryan, eds., *Devoy's Post Bag*, vol. II (Dublin: C. J. Fallon, Ltd., 1953), p. 51.

35. Ibid., p. 52.

36. Savinkov, *Memoirs*, p. 147.

37. Charles A. Russell and Bowman H. Miller, "Profile of a Terrorist," *Terrorism—an International Journal*, 1 (1977), reprinted in John D. Elliott and Leslie K. Gibson, eds., *Contemporary Terrorism: Selected Readings* (Gaithersburg, Md.: International Association of Chiefs of Police, 1978), pp. 81–95.

38. See Philip Pomper's analysis of the influence of Nechaev over his band of followers: "The People's Revenge," *Sergei Nechaev* (New Brunswick [N.J.]: Rutgers University Press, 1979), chap. 4.

39. A Rand Corporation study of kidnappings and barricade-and-hostage incidents concluded that such tactics are not necessarily perilous, while

admitting that drawing statistical inferences from a small number of cases in a limited time period (August 1968 to June 1975) is hazardous. See Brian Jenkins, Janera Johnson, and David Ronfeldt, *Numbered Lives: Some Statistical Observations from 77 International Hostage Episodes*, Rand Paper P-5905 (Santa Monica: The Rand Corporation, 1977).

40. Psychiatrist Frederick J. Hacker, for example, argues that terrorists are by nature indifferent to risk; see *Crusaders, Criminals, Crazies: Terror and Terrorism in Our Time* (New York: Norton, 1976), p. 13.

41. Menachem Begin, *The Revolt* (London: W. H. Allen, 1951).

42. J. Glenn Gray, "The Enduring Appeals of Battle," *The Warriors: Reflections on Men in Battle* (New York: Harper & Row, 1970), chap. 2, describes similar experiences among soldiers in combat.

43. Statements of the beliefs of the leaders of the RAF can be found in *Textes des prisonniers de la Fraction armée rouge et dernières lettres d'Ulrike Meinhof* (Paris: Maspéro, 1977).

44. Michael Barkun, *Disaster and the Millennium* (New Haven: Yale University Press, 1974), pp. 14–16. See also Leon Festinger, et al., *When Prophecy Fails: A Social and Psychological Study of a Modern Group That Predicted the Destruction of the World* (New York: Harper Torchbooks, 1964).

45. J. Bowyer Bell, *The Secret Army* (London: Anthony Blond, 1970), p. 379.

46. Jean Maitron, *Histoire du mouvement anarchiste en France (1880–1914)* (Paris: Societé universitaire d'éditions et de librairie, 1955), pp. 242–43.

47. S. Stepniak (pseudonym for Kravchimski), *Underground Russia: Revolutionary Profiles and Sketches from Life* (London: Smith, Elder, and Co., 1882), pp. 36–37; see also Venturi, *Roots of Revolution*, pp. 639 and 707–8.

48. See Albert Camus, "Les meurtriers délicats," in *L'Homme Révolté* (Paris: Gallimard, 1965), pp. 571–79.

49. Ya'acov Meridor, *Long is the Road to Freedom* (Tujunga [Ca.]: Barak Publications, 1961), pp. 6 and 9.

50. Begin, *The Revolt*, p. 111.

51. Vera Figner, *Mémoires d'une révolutionnaire*, trans. Victor Serge (Paris: Gallimard, 1930), pp. 131 and 257–62.

52. Such an argument is applied to Japanese Red Army terrorist Kozo Okamoto by Patricia Steinhof in "Portrait of a Terrorist," *Asian Survey*, 16 (1976), 830–45.

Scott Atran and Robert Axelrod
REFRAMING SACRED VALUES

Conflicts That Appear Intractable

Sacred values differ from material or instrumental values in that they incorporate moral beliefs that drive action in ways that seem dissociated from prospects for success. Across the world, people believe that devotion to essential or core values—such as the welfare of their family and country, or their commitment to religion, honor, and justice—are, or ought to be, absolute and inviolable. Such deeper "cultural" values that are bound up with people's identities often trump trade-offs with other values, particularly economic ones (Carmichael et al. 1994).

In this essay, we focus on questions related to the current Israeli-Palestinian conflict but also employ a wide range of historical examples from international politics. Our intended audience is those scholars and practitioners who are interested in understanding and resolving conflicts that involve, or seem to involve, inviolable values. We hope our

From *Negotiation Journal* 24, no. 3 (July 2008), pp. 221–46.

findings will be useful to negotiation practitioners of all kinds including mediators, diplomats, third-party neutrals, as well as the leaders and the publics directly involved. We also hope that researchers who seek a deeper understanding of the problems and possibilities for resolving seemingly intractable conflicts will find our research useful.

Our analysis begins with the interest-based approach pioneered by Roger Fisher and William Ury (1981).[1] While the importance of framing is well recognized in the negotiation literature, surprisingly little has been written on how the process actually works.[2] With this essay, we seek to fill that gap by analyzing how one frame can displace another. While we discuss a wide variety of historical cases, we also draw on experimental evidence from random samples of three stakeholder publics deeply engaged in the same conflict, namely, the contemporary conflict between Israel and Palestine. The process of randomly surveying these three publics contrasts with the more common practice of relying on self-recruited American college students (e.g., Baron and Spranca 1997; Tetlock, Kristel, and Elson 2000). In addition, we interviewed leaders involved in this conflict to see how their responses compared to the responses of their constituencies. Most important, our study of framing and reframing suggests a number of ways to overcome barriers to conflict resolution when sacred values are engaged.

Differences in sacred values are an important part of many fundamental political disputes and tend to make disputes much harder to resolve (Bazerman, Tebrunsel, and Wade-Benzoni 2008; Susskind et al. 2005). Counterintuitively, understanding an opponent's sacred values, we believe, offers surprising opportunities for breakthroughs to peace. Because of people's emotional unwillingness to negotiate sacred values, conventional wisdom suggests that negotiators either should leave sacred values for last in political negotiations or should try to bypass them with sufficient material incentives. Our empirical findings and historical analysis suggest that conventional wisdom is wrong. In fact, offering to provide material benefits in exchange for giving up a sacred value actually makes settlement more difficult because people see the offering as an insult rather than a compromise. And leaving issues related to sacred values for last only blocks compromise on otherwise mundane and material matters.

Seemingly intractable political conflicts—in the Middle East, the Balkans, Kashmir, Sri Lanka, and beyond—and the extreme behaviors often associated with these conflicts, such as suicide bombings, are often motivated by sacred values. Consider, for example, the view of martyrdom as a sacred duty expressed to us by Sheikh Hamed Al Betawi, a judge of the *Shari'a* Court of Palestine and a former preacher at Al Aqsa' Mosque (the Jerusalem mosque that represents the third-holiest site in Islam): "A martyr fights and dies for dignity, nation, religion, and *Al 'Aqsa.*' In the Koran, the book of *Al-Tauba*, verse 111, tells us that Allah brings souls to Paradise killing the enemy and getting killed—that is the sacred principle of *jihad*" (Al Betawi 2004).

Nevertheless, there have also been significant historical instances in which sacred values have motivated peacemaking, which Egypt's Anwar Sadat expressed in his autobiography, *In Search of Identity* (1977). He recounts that the October 1973 War allowed Egypt to recover "pride and self-confidence," which freed him to think about the "psychological barrier" that was a "huge wall of suspicion, fear, hate and misunderstanding that has for so long existed between Israel and the Arabs." Based on his own experience in jail, he felt that "change should take place first at the deeper and perhaps more subtle level than the conscious level. . . . We had been accustomed . . . to regard Israel as 'taboo,' an entity whose emotional associations simply prevented anyone from approaching it." He ultimately decided on a personal visit to the Al Aqsa mosque in Jerusalem and to the Israeli Knesset "in fulfillment of my claim that I would be willing to go anywhere in search of peace. . . . I regarded my mission in Israel as truly sacred" (Sadat 1977: 304).

Appeals to sacred values, then, can motivate both war and peace. The issue for conflict resolvers is to determine how sacred values appeal to war and how they can be reframed to appeal to peace.

In this time of great uncertainty in the Middle East, we went to the area to conduct a scientific study on the values underpinning political conflict. We based our questioning of senior Israeli and Palestinian leaders on a recent series of surveys with hundreds of Palestinians and Israelis that dealt with some hypothetical trade-offs for peace that have been discussed or proposed in negotiations. Our research findings and discussions with leaders indicate that violent opposition to compromise over issues that people consider sacred actually *increases* when material incentives to compromise are offered. Support for violence *decreases*, however, when an adversary makes symbolic gestures that show recognition of the other's core values (Atran, Axelrod, and Davis 2007b; Ginges et al. 2007). Symbolic gestures may then allow and facilitate political negotiations that also involve material trade-offs.

Here we take a deeper look at the issues at stake, informed by analysis of the recent history of political conflicts both in the Middle East and in other areas of the world. The role of *sacred values* in political conflict is often seriously misunderstood. Sacred values are certainly critical to the maintenance of seemingly intractable rivalries. Our approach suggests that a creative reframing of these values may often allow symbolic concessions that can help resolve long-standing disputes, be they religious, ethnic, or cultural.

Rational versus Devoted Actors

Ever since the end of the Second World War, *"rational actor"* models have dominated strategic thinking at all levels of government policy (Gaddis 1995) and military planning (Allison 1971). Rational actor models have always had serious deficiencies as general models of human reasoning and decision making because human behavior can never be reduced purely to rational calculation. But in a confrontation between states, and especially during the Cold War, these models were arguably useful in anticipating a wide array of challenges and formulating policies to prevent nuclear war. Now, however,

we are witnessing the rise of *"devoted actors,"* such as suicide terrorists (Atran 2003), who are willing to make extreme sacrifices that are independent of, or seem all out of proportion to, likely prospects of success.[3] This is most evident for the most tenacious conflicts that are grounded in cultural and religious opposition rather than those based primarily on political competition for resources. Nowhere is this issue more pressing than in the Israeli-Palestinian dispute, which people across the world consistently view as one of the greatest dangers to world peace (Pew Research Center 2006).

Efforts to resolve political conflicts or counter political violence are still often based on the assumption that adversaries make rational choices. Such assumptions are prevalent in risk assessment and modeling by foreign aid and international development projects, and by American diplomatic, military, and intelligence services. For example, the membership and performance of the principal forum for U.S. foreign policy, the National Security Council (NSC), which includes close policy coordination with the National Economic Council, demonstrates that policy decisions should result from instrumental choices by goal-oriented political and economic actors. The U.S. National Security Strategy statement (U.S.NSC 2006) explicitly states a commitment to "results-oriented planning" that focuses on "actions and results rather than legislation or rule-making." It embodies a clear focus on practical consequences rather than on moral principles whose consequences may be indeterminate.

"Look at the NSC's composition, which determines the direction of U.S. foreign policy," says Richard Davis (2007), a former director of terrorism prevention at the White House Homeland Security Council. "It is institutionally structured within a narrow intellectual frame weighted to consideration of practical costs and benefits in terms of our national economy, intelligence, military, and law enforcement. There is limited provision for missions of health, education, or human services that represent our values." An apparent exception to lack of concern with matters related directly to human welfare is NSC monitoring of the United States Agency for International Development (USAID). But even here, the NSC is most concerned with USAID programs that have strict budgetary cycles and are often considered as tactical means for advancing strategic interests.

"We can't afford to wait for tsunamis to demonstrate that the U.S. does not always act in its own self interest," Davis noted. Indeed, unscheduled U.S aid to Indonesian tsunami victims in early 2005 may represent the only event since the invasion of Iraq that dramatically increased favorable opinion of the U.S. in a major Muslim country, as well as the perception that combating terrorism was not a uniquely U.S. problem. The implications of the Pew survey, as suggested in the summary report by Pew, was that through tsunami relief in Indonesia's Aceh province, the United States demonstrated to the Indonesian public that America could act in ways that were not exclusively in its own self-interest. Indonesians became more willing to see U.S. actions against terrorism in the region as not necessarily only a matter of promoting U.S. interests. People began to dissociate U.S. interests from terrorism and to consider terrorism a problem in its own right (Pew Research Center 2005).

Here, one might be tempted to argue that U.S. policy is not sufficiently rational, that the provision of health, education, and human services foreign aid has nothing to do with promoting values as such but is simply another way to "buy" peace. Nevertheless, the more that one side perceives another's initiatives to be strongly motivated by self-interest, the less likely it is that those initiatives will succeed in gaining trust in highly charged cultural conflicts. For example, following the massive earthquake in Azad Kashmir on October 5, 2005, the United States began providing humanitarian aid to victims. When we interviewed villagers about this aid in May 2006, however, many pointed to Apache helicopters that parachuted in supplies and ubiquitous USAID signs as evidence that the United States was trying to buy their support without engaging them personally. In contrast, Kashmiris praised the many

hundreds of Cuban doctors who tended patients in remote villages for their "selfless" devotion to others, noting that the Cubans came and left with no self-promoting speeches or signs (Kashmir 2006).

Many conflicts cannot be treated exclusively in terms of *realpolitik* or the marketplace. To most of us, the thought of selling or endangering one's children or betraying one's country for money (or for almost anything else we can imagine) is morally abhorrent, and most of us would be outraged and disgusted by someone willing to offer such a trade-off for our children, our country, or anything else we may value as "sacred." As we have seen, when people are asked to trade sacred values for material rewards they tend to react with outrage and anger (Baron and Spranca 1997; Tetlock 2003). Nevertheless they are sometimes able to accept privileging one sacred value for another, such as devotion to religion versus devotion to family.

Sacred Values

Sacred values are moral imperatives that seem to drive behavior independently of any concrete material goal. They often have their basis in religion, but such transcendent core secular values as a belief in the importance of individual morality, fairness, reciprocity, and collective identity (i.e., "justice for my people") can also be sacred values. These values will often trump economic thinking or considerations of *realpolitik*.

For example, the U.S. Senate recently raised the bounty offered for information leading to the capture of Al Qaeda leader Osama Bin Laden to fifty million dollars (Anonymous 2007). It is doubtful, however, that this new increase will have greater sway than previous increases among the people living along the Afghan-Pakistan frontier who may know his whereabouts. Even the poorest Pashtun tribesman in the area will defend to the death an ancient code of honor known as *pashtunwali*. Its third tenet, *melmastiya*, refers to hospitality as a sacred duty and requires protecting valued guests at the risk of one's own life. Violating this code means repudiating tribal identity for one's self and one's family.

Devotion to some core values may represent universal responses to long-term evolutionary strategies that go beyond short-term individual calculations of self-interest but that advance individual interests in the aggregate and long run (Lim and Baron 1997). This may include devotion to children (Hamilton 1964), to community (Durkheim 1912/1995), or even to a sense of fairness (Hauser 2006). Other such values are clearly specific to particular societies and historical contingencies, such as the sacred status of cows in Hindu culture or the sacred status of Jerusalem in Judaism, Christianity, and Islam.[4] Sometimes, as with sacred cows (Harris 1966) or sacred forests (Atran, Medin, and Ross 2005), what is seen as inherently sacred in the present may have a more materialistic origin, representing the accumulated material wisdom of generations who resisted individual urges to gain an immediate advantage of meat or firewood for the long-term benefits of renewable sources of energy and sustenance.

Political leaders often appeal to sacred values as a way of mobilizing their constituents to action (Varshney 2003) and as a least-cost method of enforcing policy goals (Goodin 1980). Political leaders also invoke sacred values as a least-cost method of discrediting adversaries, for example, when U.S. politicians accuse one another of disregard for "the sanctity of marriage" or of usurping "God's gift of life." What works as sacred in one society is often entirely ineffective and mundane in another. When Iranian President Mahmoud Ahmadinejad publicly embraced and kissed on the hand an elderly woman who used to be his schoolteacher, Iran's ultraconservative *Hezbollah* newspaper intoned: "This type of indecency progressively has grave consequences, like violating religious and sacred values" (ABC Online 2007). Contrast the Iranian example with the kissing expected of American candidates on campaign tours. A rallying cry to protect sacred values in one culture can be utterly innocuous in another.

Many policy makers, however, argue that all so-called sacred values are only "pseudo-sacred" because in a world of scarce resources there is always room for trade-offs (Hoffman et al. 1999): people cannot really devote all of their time, energy, and life to upholding any one such value. Even apparently "irrational" behaviors arguably reflect "rational" calculations of the holdout's long-term interests, however incomprehensible those interests appear to others. Consider the angry resistance of the impoverished Lakota Sioux to offers of hundreds of millions of dollars in compensation for the Black Hills that the U.S. government has claimed ownership of since 1877 (Lazarus 1999). The Sioux say that claims on their land are claims to their identity as a people. Another example is Adolph Hitler's "principled" refusal to maximize material benefits for war. To uphold the scientifically baseless but sacred value of "racial purity," Hitler vehemently refused the equivalent of hundreds of millions dollars in payoffs to racially reclassify a relatively few Austrian Jews (Eidinow and Edmonds 2001).

In these and other examples, the actors may be described as "holding out" for greater benefits, such as eternal glory over worldly greed, where, for them, glory is a more rewarding and hence more rational outcome. But such interpretations only obscure the issue by giving post hoc interpretations of any seemingly irrational behavior (in the sense of immunity to material trade-offs) so as to fit a rational actor model. No explanatory or predictive power is thereby gained.

Given these interpretations of apparently irrational behavior, one might be tempted to think of protected values, including sacred values, as self-serving "posturing" or part of some strategy for longer-term economic or psychological benefits (Baron and Spranca 1997). It is true that sacred values are sometimes exploited by politicians for their own material interests or some greater future gain, such as enhanced personal reputation, prestige, and votes. Nevertheless, the seeming intractability of certain political conflicts and the reality of violence associated with these conflicts, such as suicide bombings, compels negotiation scholars and researchers to pay greater attention to the nature and depth of people's commitment to sacred values.[5]

Apparently Irrational Conflict

One reason resource-deficient revolutionary movements can compete with much larger armies and police forces is the willingness of members of these movements to delay gratification and sacrifice themselves for a greater cause. Consider the founding of the United States: without calculating the probability of success, a few poorly equipped rebels knowingly took on the mightiest empire in the world (Dickinson 1768).[6] The Declaration of Independence concluded with the words: "And for the support of this Declaration, with a firm reliance on the protection of Divine Providence, we mutually pledge to each other our Lives, our Fortunes and our sacred Honor."

Matters of principle, or "sacred honor," are enforced to a degree far out of proportion to any individual or immediate material payoff when they are seen as defining "who we are." Revenge, "even if it kills me," between whole communities that mobilize to redress insult or shame to a single member goes far beyond individual "tit-for-tat" (Axelrod and Hamilton 1981) and may become the most important duties in life. This is because such behavior defines and defends what it means to be, say, a Southern gentleman (Nisbett and Cohen 1996), a Solomon Islander (Havemeyer 1929), or an Arab tribesman (Peters 1967). The Israeli army has risked the lives of many soldiers to save one or a few as a matter of "sacred duty," as have certain elite U.S. military units (Bowden 2000).

Of course, sincere displays of willingness to avenge at all costs can have the long-term payoff of thwarting aggressive actions by stronger but less committed foes. Likewise, a willingness to sacrifice for buddies can help create greater *esprit du corps* that may lead to a more formidable fighting force. But these acts far exceed the effort required for any short-term payoff and offer no immediate guarantee for long-term success.

To study possible trade-offs between sacred values and material rewards, in 2005 we talked with families and supporters of Palestinian suicide bombers. We asked about the amount of compensation that their society should give to the family of a suicide bomber. We found that willingness to allow compensation decreased as the amount offered increased: one hundred thousand dinars is significantly less acceptable than ten thousand dinars, and one million dinars is much less acceptable (Atran 2007a). Follow-up interviews clearly point to a willingness to accept minimal compensation for loss of a family member (who may be a helper or wage earner) and one's home (Israeli retaliation often includes destruction of the bomber's house). Nevertheless, Palestinians see more substantial payments to families as unacceptable, even disgusting, because they would create the impression that the martyr had acted as a materially calculating actor rather than as a martyr devoted to a moral cause.

In conjunction with Israeli psychologist Jeremy Ginges and Palestinian political scientist Khalil Shikaki, our team surveyed more than twelve hundred Palestinians in the West Bank and Gaza and found differences between those Palestinians who refuse political compromise because they believe it violates sacred values versus those Palestinians who do not (Ginges et al. 2007). Both groups overwhelmingly support suicide bombings that may include the killing of civilians. Each group was given a hypothetical choice to delay a suicide bombing to save the lives of an entire Palestinian family or to delay a suicide bombing to save only the sick father.[7] Palestinians who do not consider political compromise to violate sacred values expressed the rational preference of trading off an obligation for the sake of the entire family rather than for the father alone. By contrast, the sacred values group was more likely to express willingness to delay a suicide bombing if only the sick father would benefit rather than to save the lives of an entire family, including the father (Atran 2007b).

These examples also highlight what we call moral framing. When considering delaying a martyrdom mission in order to help a sick father, the trade-off is allowed within an overarching moral frame of social duties and (material) attempts to balance duties. But when considering delaying a mission to save one's own family from retaliation, only the bombing mission itself falls within the moral frame of duty, and avoidance of retaliation is considered a cowardly and immoral act. In this case, the higher the costs, the less likely there is willingness to compromise in the performance of duty.

Consider another example of insensitivity to quantity or material balance. Recently, a group of Holocaust survivors traveled to Maidenak Death Camp in Poland on what they considered a sacred mission to search for mementos of those killed by the Nazis. "We've spent a million dollars so far to find rings worth maybe $100 retail," said an organizer of the expedition. "But the objects tell a powerful story. There is no way that a modern person can understand the experience, but looking at an object. . . . Its rescue gives us all an opportunity to connect with the people here and their sacrifice" (Roberts 2005).[8]

It is the "who we are" identity aspect that is often so hard for members of one culture to understand regarding another. Nevertheless, understanding and acknowledging other peoples' values may help to avoid or resolve even long-standing and deep-seated conflicts. Consider, for example, the pacification of postwar Japan. Many in the wartime U.S. administration and military considered the Japanese Emperor a war criminal who should be executed. But wartime advisors such as anthropologists Ruth Benedict and Margaret Mead, as well as psychological-warfare specialists in General Douglas MacArthur's command (Dower 1999), argued that preserving, and even signaling respect for, the Emperor might lessen the likelihood that the Japanese, who regarded him with religious awe, would fight to the death to save him. Moreover, his symbolic weight could, and would, be used by the occupation government to bolster moderate and pro-American factions in postwar Japan.

Consider as well, in this regard, the case of "ping-pong" diplomacy between the United States and China. As expected, the Chinese won match after match against the visiting American table tennis team in 1971. In the United States, Ping-Pong is considered a "basement sport" so there was little at stake. In contrast, table tennis is a sport of national prestige to China (Eckstein 1993). So, at little cost

to itself, the United States was able to provide something of great symbolic value for the other side. This exchange contributed to a historic breakthrough in Sino-American relations during the Cold War.[9]

Sometimes the symbolic value of a gesture that is weighty to the parties directly involved may seem trivial to an outside party. If France allowed Muslim students to wear headscarves in public schools, which is now prohibited, beneficial effects could reverberate throughout the Muslim world. For most Americans and their political leaders, this would not be a significant concession—Muslim and Jewish headgear in public schools is commonplace and uncontroversial in the United States. The problem, however, is that in France, unlike in the United States, signs of physical and religious distinction in school are considered to be an affront to the symbolically defining value of French political culture ever since the French Revolution, namely, a universal and uniform sense of social equality (however lacking in practice). "The only community is the nation," declared former French Prime Minister Dominique de Villepin (Anonymous 2005)—an uninterrupted national sentiment that dates to Jean-Jacques Rousseau's *Social Contract* (1762). Indeed, the American ideal of cultural diversity is perceived by a broad political spectrum in France as an attempt to force an alien notion of community and identity between the only two moral entities that are widely recognized in France: the individual and the state (Roy 2004). This example shows that recognizing one another's sacred values is not a transparent process, even for allies and for members of societies that seem similar in so many other ways. More importantly, it illustrates that recognizing and showing respect for another's core values is easy or even possible only if doing so does not entail compromising one's own core values.

Symbolic Concessions

When we brief policy makers around the world on our research, they often readily acknowledge their own values as sacred yet fail to appreciate adequately the sacred values of others. We are often surprised to hear, after the briefing is finished, that "of course it's all about [sacred] values." And despite the institutional preference for rational choice thinking, we find that ordinary people in surveys around the world also tell us that sacred values are important to them.

To measure emotional outrage and propensity for violence, our research team asked about various peace deals involving compromises over issues integral to the Israeli-Palestinian conflict. For this analysis we used three samples from the West Bank and Gaza. The first was a sample of 535 Palestinian refugees, the second was a sample of 719 Palestinian students, and the third was a sample of 601 Jewish adult settlers residing in the West Bank and Gaza (Ginges et al. 2007).[10] The proposed compromises were exchanging land for peace (asked of settlers), sovereignty over Jerusalem (asked of students), the right of Palestinian refugees to return to their former lands and homes inside Israel (asked of refugees), and recognition of the validity of the adversary's own sacred values (asked of all three groups). We proposed material incentives, such as significant payments to individual families, credible offers to relocate or rebuild destroyed infrastructure, and so forth. We found that such material offers to promote the peaceful resolution of political and cultural conflicts backfire when adversaries consider contested issues to reflect sacred values. Material offers to make concessions that were seen as violations of sacred values were perceived as insults. But we also found that symbolic concessions of no apparent material benefit might open the way to resolving seemingly irresolvable conflicts.

One senior member of the National Security Council responded recently to our latest briefing in this way: "This seems right. On the settlers [who were to be removed from Gaza], [Israeli Prime Minister Ariel] Sharon realized too late that he shouldn't have berated them about wasting Israel's money and endangering soldier's lives. Sharon told me that he realized only afterwards that he should have made a symbolic concession and called them Zionist heroes making yet another sacrifice" (Atran, Axelrod, and Davis 2007b).

A further illustration of how sacred values can lie at the heart of deep-seated political disputes comes from Isaac Ben Israel, a former Air Force general and current Knesset member in Israel's ruling coalition: "Israel recognizes that the [Hamas-led] Palestinian government is still completely focused on what it considers to be its essential principles. . . . For Hamas, a refusal to utter the simple words 'We recognize Israel's right to exist' is clearly an essential part of their core values. Why else would they suffer the international boycott . . . and let their own government workers go without pay, their people go hungry, and their leaders risk assassination?" Hamas's Ghazi Hamad, then spokesman for the Palestinian government, told us: "In principle we have no problem with a Palestinian state encompassing all of our lands within the 1967 borders. But let Israel apologize for our tragedy in 1948, and then we can talk about negotiating over our right of return to historic Palestine." In rational-choice models of decision making, that something as intangible as an apology should stand in the way of peace does not readily compute.

A closer look at apologies in political conflicts indicates that such concessions may not be so much deal makers in themselves, as means of facilitating political compromise that may also involve significant material transactions. One telling example concerns the negotiations between Israel and the Federal Republic of Germany in 1951, before Germany began reparations payments and before diplomatic relations were established between the two countries (Lustick 2006). In 1948, the newly established State of Israel was in dire economic straits. But Israel and the World Jewish Congress refused to demand direct compensation from Germany for the property of murdered European Jews. Any official recognition or contact with Germany was morally anathema, no matter how actively opposed then–German chancellor Konrad Adenauer and others in his government had been to the previous Nazi regime, and no matter how desperate the need for the money to help consolidate the Jewish state.

With the West's acceptance of the Federal Republic, Jewish insistence on a world boycott of Germany seemed politically untenable. Despite recognizing the political weakness of its international position, Israel insisted that before any amount of money could be considered, Germany must publicly declare contrition for the murder and suffering of Jews at German hands. On September 27, 1951, Adenauer delivered a much anticipated speech at the Bundestag, the German national parliament, acknowledging that "the Federal Republic and with it the great majority of the German people are aware of the immeasurable suffering that was brought upon the Jews of Germany and the occupied territories during the time of National Socialism. The overwhelming majority of the German people abominated the crimes committed against the Jews and did not participate in them." Although this symbolic concession to Jewish sensibilities was only half-hearted—because, in fact, the majority of wartime Germans at least acquiesced to Nazi actions—it was enough to start the reconciliation process between Israel and Germany.

Of course, recognition of scared values will not lessen tensions if the recognition is perceived as not merely half-hearted but actually insincere. Take, for example, the U.S. administration's apology for the abuse of detainees at Abu Ghraib prison in Iraq. In May 2004, then–Secretary of Defense Donald Rumsfeld offered "my deepest apology" to "those Iraqis who were mistreated" (Garamone 2004). He then went on to claim that mistreatment was not the fault of U.S. policy, purpose, or principle, but of a few wayward soldiers whose behavior was "inconsistent with the values of our nation, inconsistent with the teachings of the military, and it was fundamentally un-American." As historian Elazar Barkan notes, this hedging of regret at the abuse of the prisoners with regret of Arab misunderstanding of American culture "did not quell the critics." The apology was angrily dismissed as insincere by large segments of the Arab and Muslim world (Barkan 2006).

Mustafa Zahrani, an Iranian scholar and former top diplomat, told us recently that "symbolic statements are important if sincere and without reservation. It was important to us that the United States show consideration and respect for our culture. But in 2000, I was with the mullahs in Mecca when [then–Secretary of State Madeleine] Albright seemed to apologize to Iran for past offenses but then said [in a memorandum] 'despite the trend towards democracy, control over the military, judiciary, courts and police remains in unelected hands.' Our leadership interpreted this as a call for a coup inside our country" (Atran, Axelrod, and Davis 2007b).[11]

Symbolic gestures do not always stand alone, unhinged from all material considerations. Rather, they often help to recast a moral frame that determines the scope and limits of possible material transactions and negotiations. Consider, in this regard, attempts by Israeli and Palestinian negotiators to reach agreement following the 2000 Camp David Summit. Then–Israeli Prime Minister Ehud Barak had expressed readiness to state regret for the suffering of Palestinian refugees who fled or were expelled during what Israel calls its "War of Independence" and what Palestinians call "the Catastrophe" (al-Nakba) and to perhaps accept shared responsibility, but not primary responsibility (as Palestinian leaders insisted). U.S. President Bill Clinton was further prepared to declare publicly the need to compensate and resettle refugees, without requiring Israel to accept refugees into its own territory or to acknowledge responsibility for their sorrow (Gresh 2001).

At Taba in January 2001, the Palestinian delegation formally continued to insist on Israel recognizing "its moral and legal responsibility for the forced displacement and dispossession of the Palestinian civilian population during the 1948 war and for preventing the refugees from returning to their homes." Palestinian negotiators downplayed this insistence when Israel acknowledged willingness to express some responsibility for Palestinian suffering in the wake of Israel's creation and to allow for a symbolic return of a limited number of 1948 refugees into Israel itself (Lustick 2006). Unfortunately, the timing was wrong. Clinton was handing over power to George W. Bush, and Ehud Barak was about to be replaced by Ariel Sharon. The new leaders wanted to revise the decisions of their political rivals.[12]

With these historical considerations about failed negotiations and our previous experimental findings about sacred barriers to conflict resolution in mind, the members of our team went to the Middle East to compare the responses of leaders to the responses of their publics. From February to March 2007 we talked to leaders of Hamas in Damascus and Gaza, Fateh in Ramallah, and Israel in Jerusalem and Tel Aviv (Atran, Axelrod, and Davis 2007c). We probed directly issues of material trade-offs and symbolic concessions. Leaders responded in the same way as their publics, except that for leaders the symbolic concession was not enough in itself but only a necessary condition to opening serious negotiations involving material issues as well. For example, Musa Abu Marzouk, the former chairman and current deputy chairman of Hamas, said "No" to a trade-off for peace without granting a right of return, a more emphatic "No, we do not sell ourselves for any amount" when offered a trade-off with a substantial material incentive (credible offering of substantial U.S. aid for the rebuilding of Palestinian infrastructure), but "Yes, an apology is important, but only as a beginning. It's not enough because our houses and land were taken away from us and something has to be done about that" (Abu Marzouk 2007).

In a parallel line of questioning, we asked Binyamin Netanyahu, a former Israeli Prime Minister and the current opposition leader in parliament, "Would you seriously consider accepting a two-state solution following the 1967 borders if all major Palestinian factions, including Hamas, were to recognize the right of the Jewish people to an independent state in the region?" Referring to symbolic concessions as well as security benefits, he answered, "OK, but the Palestinians would have to show that they sincerely mean it, change their textbooks and anti-Semitic characterizations, and then allow some border adjustments so that Ben Gurion [Airport] would be out of range of shoulder-fired missiles" (Netanyahu 2007).

As Ariel Merari, Israel's former chief hostage negotiator, told us: "Trusting the adversary's intentions is critical to negotiations, which have no chance unless both sides believe the other's willingness to recognize its existential concerns" (2007). Indeed, recognition of some "existential values" may change other existential values into material concerns, "since the PLO's recognition of Israel, most Israelis no longer see rule over the West Bank as existential."

Overcoming Sacred Barriers

Sacred values provide the moral frame that delimits which agreements are possible. For the most part, members of a moral community—be it a family, ethnic group, religious congregation, or nation—implicitly share their community's sacred values. Thus, there is usually no need to refer to these values or even to be conscious of them when pursuing trade-offs or negotiations within a community. Sacred values usually become highly relevant and salient only when challenged, much as food takes on overwhelming value in people's lives only when it is denied. Direct threats to a community's sacred values are most apparent when different moral communities come into conflict.

Conflict becomes so intense as to appear irresolvable when different communities frame values in ways that make them seem incompatible with each other. But what often makes values incompatible is the way they are applied to the here and now. While values can be held firmly, their application depends a good deal on how they are understood, and what they are taken to imply, and these interpretations and applications of sacred values are not always fixed and inflexible. Indeed, sacred values that seem incompatible within certain frames may actually become compatible when reframed.

In what follows, we offer some advice for reframing sacred values in order to overcome barriers to conflict resolution. We base this advice on our empirical findings and historical analyses.

Refine Sacred Values to Exclude Outmoded Claims

Article 32 of the Hamas Covenant (1988) highlights "Zionist scheming . . . laid out in *The Protocols of the Elders of Zion.*" *The Protocols* is a notorious anti-Semitic tract forged by Russian Czarist police. In private, Hamas leaders grant that *The Protocols* may not be a statement of fact. By explicitly renouncing its endorsement of *The Protocols*, Hamas could demonstrate that it no longer wants others to see it as anti-Semitic. Likewise, Israel could distance itself from the old Zionist slogan that Palestine was, "A Land without People for a People without Land."[13]

Our talks with leaders on both sides indicate awareness that their current positions involve outmoded and historically inaccurate claims. They also acknowledge that were the other side to renounce such blatant falsehoods, this could lead to a psychological breakthrough. Overcoming historical precedents and emotional barriers to renouncing even patently false claims, however, may require neutral mediation by those who understand both sides. Even then, it takes time. According to Lord John Alderdice, a principal mediator in the Northern Ireland conflict, it took nine years of back-and-forth for this to happen in Northern Ireland (Alderdice 2007a and 2007b).[14]

Exploit the Inevitable Ambiguity of Sacred Values

Reframing values may require creative ambiguity and involve asymmetry in the way each side perceives the reframing. For example, during World War II the U.S. government promised the American people and its allies that it would accept nothing less than "unconditional surrender." But the government and people of Japan were adamant that the Emperor must be preserved. Realizing this, the United States reframed the meaning of "unconditional surrender" by making clear that it would graciously allow the Emperor of Japan to retain his title and liberty.

People often apply the "same" sacred values in different ways, which facilitates creative use of ambiguity. Many Americans consider "equality" to be a core value, a gift from God, and a self-evident truth as stated in the Declaration of Independence and codified under the law in the Fourteenth Amendment to the U.S. Constitution. Historically, though, popular and legal notions of equality have varied considerably and continue to do so: from voting privileges only for property-holding white males to "universal suffrage," and from "separate but equal" education for whites and blacks to "equal opportunity" for all men and women.

Religious values are particularly open-textured in this way (Atran 2002), however much people believe their interpretation to be the only literal or right one. In Judaism, the religious commandment to "Keep the Sabbath Holy," whose violation in biblical times was punishable by death, continues to undergo radical reinterpretation: in today's Jerusalem, a chief dispute between Orthodox versus Reform Jews is whether God allows driving on Saturdays. Or, take the biblical commandment "Thou Shalt Not Kill"— many U.S. conservatives believe it warrants both an antiabortion agenda and capital punishment, whereas many U.S. liberals consider this commandment to warrant abolition of capital punishment and a pro–abortion rights agenda. American political leaders who seek election or to govern from the center must learn to finesse seemingly contrary interpretations of sacred values in creative ways.

For both Israelis and Palestinians, "The Land" is sacred, with Jerusalem at its center. Israelis simply refer to their country as "The Land" (*Ha-Aretz*), whereas for Palestinians "Land and Honor" (*Ard wal 'Ard*) are one. Israeli political leaders creatively reinterpreted the historical scope of "The Land," first to justify claims on Gaza and then to justify leaving it. If Palestinians, who simply refer to Jerusalem as "The Holy" (*Al Quds*), can reframe their idea of the city to include only its Arab suburbs and part of the Temple Mount (*Haram Al-Sharif*), then Israel might be willing to accept the Palestinian capital there. Constructively reframing the issue of Jerusalem in this way need not call into question "the strength of attachment" to the sacred value of Jerusalem.

For Muslims, the meaning of *jihad*, or "Holy War," can be interpreted in radically different ways, whether as an inner mental struggle for the preservation of faith or as physical combat against external enemies who threaten Islam. For supporters of militant Islamist groups whom we have surveyed, including members of Hamas and Indonesia's *Jemaah Islamiyah, jihad* is the "Sixth Pillar" of Islam, which trumps four of the five traditional pillars (almsgiving, pilgrimage, fasting, and prayer); only the pillar expressing faith in God stands up to *jihad*. For many other Muslims, there is no such "Sixth Pillar," and professed belief in it may be heretical and blasphemous. Given the popular and political division of Palestinian society today, Palestinian leaders must carefully navigate meanings of *jihad* without alienating major segments of Palestinian society or the outside world.

This issue of reframing *jihad* is currently an important consideration in Saudi Arabia's counterterrorism efforts. As one senior Saudi official (2008) recently told us:

> During the Afghanistan war [with the Soviets] we praised the *mujahedin* and Bin Laden in our newspapers everyday. He was the leader of the Arab heroes. *Mujahedin* entered our vocabulary in a positive frame. Then we said he was bad. The people were confused. Before a hero and overnight a bad man. We had to reframe *jihad* to distinguish "moral *jihad*" from the *Takfiri* ideology [a "rejectionist" view of Islam, including rejection of *Wahabi* and *Salafi* ideology which prohibits sowing discord, or *fitna*, among Muslims; *takfir* means "excommunication" and preaches that those who do not follow jihad are *kuffar*, or "infidels," including Muslims who are excommunicated and so can be killed]. The mujahedin had been heroes for us, and for you [America] in Afghanistan and now they were terrorists . . . and we had to have a way of reframing *jihad* in order to show that the Takfiri way of *jihad* was different, their training, ideology, tactics.

Shift the Context

One way leaders can navigate through the muddle of meanings that attend sacred values is to shift the context so that one sacred value becomes more relevant than others in a specific context. At West Point for example, cadets acculturate to two competing "honor codes." There is a formal one, which requires telling the truth and obeying the orders of hierarchical superiors, and an informal one, which entails loyalty to peers. Army leaders understand that at times they must carefully balance vertical loyalty to commanders against horizontal loyalties to comrades, for example, by not punishing cadets who refuse to snitch on their buddies.

We spoke with Sheikh Hassan Yousef, a West Bank Hamas leader currently detained in Israel's Ketziot prison, about suicide bombers. "Suffering and humiliation make it understandable, even animals defend themselves to the death," he told us. "But God created people to live, not to die. We have to find an exit. We need a dialogue of civilizations, not a clash of civilizations. No mother wants her child to die" (Atran 2004). Then–Palestinian Prime Minister Ismail Haniya expressed a similar sentiment to us (Atran 2006). These Hamas leaders clearly mean here to appeal to our common understanding of humanity as being equal to, or greater than, Islamist calls for martyrdom. Of course, on other occasions and in other circumstances these same leaders may reverse priorities, for example, when they feel possible windows of opportunity for a breakthrough to the outside, such as international recognition or aid, are closed to them. Such changing appeals do not necessarily represent either "flip flops" in thinking or hypocrisy but a fluid and changing appreciation of values according to how circumstances can be framed in terms of them. That is part of the paradoxical nature of sacred values, "eternal" and morally absolute, yet widely open to interpretation.

One way to shift context is to change a value's scope from the here and now to an indefinite time in the future. In the 1920s, for example, the Soviet leader Joseph Stalin moved the goal of a world victory for communism to an indefinite future when he declared communism in one country to have priority, contradicting Lenin's views that the imperial powers were about to destroy themselves in historical time.

Ami Ayalon, former head of Shin Beit, Israel's counter-terrorism and internal security agency, expressed to us his view that Hamas's proposals for a *hudna*, or provisional armistice, could be moving in this direction (see Atran, Axelrod, and Davis 2007a). Consider that the first *hudna* was the eighth-century Treaty of Hudaibiyyah, a nonaggression pact between Mohammed and the Quraish tribe. The founder of Hamas, Sheikh Ahmed Yasin, originally offered a ten-year *hudna* in return for complete withdrawal from all territories captured in the Six Day War and the establishment of a Palestinian state in the West Bank and Gaza. At various times, Yasin stated that a *hudna* was renewable for thirty, forty, or one hundred years, although it would never signal recognition of Israel. Ahmed Yousef, political adviser to then–Palestinian Prime Minister Ismail Haniya, told us that there is no limit in principle to how many times a *hudna* might be renewed. He compared Hamas's practical willingness to live alongside Israel to the Irish Republican Army's (IRA) willingness to accept a permanent armistice with Great Britain while still refusing to recognize British sovereignty over Northern Ireland. Of course, the IRA never refused to recognize Britain's existence, and many Israelis believe that Hamas's refusal of recognition and permanent peace indicates that any *hudna* will just be a smoke screen to allow military preparation for an eventual attack on Israel. For Ahmed Yousef, an indefinite *hudna* in no way contradicts Hamas's refusal to recognize Israel. But for Ami Ayalon (who recently lost the vote for leadership of Israel's Labor Party to Ehud Barak), a *hudna* that disallows military preparation for an attack on Israel and does not *explicitly* rule out some future form of recognition can allow dialogue.

Provisionally Prioritize Values

Fulfilling one sacred value may require delay in achieving others. To save the American Union,

President Abraham Lincoln was willing to postpone emancipation. Similarly, Israeli leader David Ben Gurion was willing to accept a partition of Palestine that left Israel without control over historical Judea or Jerusalem in order to attain statehood. Lincoln and Ben Gurion both wanted the delay to be only provisional. Nevertheless, in later life Ben Gurion argued against settlement in the West Bank and Gaza. This example suggests that prioritization of current values may allow for a change in the scope of values over time.

Yasser Arafat, who headed the Palestine Liberation Organization (PLO), steered that organization to officially recognize Israel. But Fateh, the PLO's largest contingent, also headed by Arafat, has never renounced its guiding principles and goals. These include, in Article 12 of Fateh's constitution, the "complete liberation of Palestine, and eradication of Zionist economic, political, military, and cultural existence" (Fateh 1964). In a related vein, Hamas's Ghazi Hamad noted that although Hamas may continue to call for an end to Israel, a Hamas-led government could officially acknowledge Israel if a majority of Palestinians expressed this desire through a popular referendum. "There is a difference between a political party's principles and obligations of a government," he told us. "After all, not everything in the Republican Party platform is United States government policy."

Previous Israeli governments were never entirely convinced that Arafat's commitment to the PLO position on recognition of Israel trumped the Fateh Constitution's prohibition of recognition. The current Israeli government rejected the idea that the Hamas-led government would possibly "allow" recognition of Israel as a Hamas ploy to mask its real intentions to destroy Israel. But several senior members of the present Israeli government and opposition to whom we spoke consider Palestinian president and current Fateh leader Mahmoud Abbas to be sincere in recognizing Israel's right to exist and in wanting peace, despite the persistence of nonrecognition clauses in Fateh's constitution. This suggests, again, that pragmatic prioritization of one value over another, however provisional to begin with, may facilitate a more permanent realignment of values.

Demonstrate Respect Where Possible

One way to demonstrate respect for the other side's sacred values is to avoid insulting the other side with offers to buy off their core values with money. As we have seen, offering material trade-offs for core values can backfire and actually increase moral outrage, disgust, and propensity for violence.

Another relatively low-cost way to show respect for other's values is to find things that mean much to the other side but little to one's own side. In the case of "ping-pong diplomacy" that we discussed earlier, the United States demonstrated respect for Chinese sensitivity about receiving equal treatment on the world stage by demonstrating that America does not always have to better China in matters that the Chinese care for.

As an example of a relatively small symbolic step that may have big implications, consider the recent approval by the Israeli education ministry of a textbook for Arab third graders in Israel that for the first time describes Israel's 1948 War of Independence as a "catastrophe" for many Palestinians and their society. In a recent op-ed in the *International Herald Tribune*, Rami Khouri, director of the Issam Fares Institute at the American University of Beirut and editor-at-large of the Beirut-based *Daily Star*, echoed a growing sentiment that

> this may be the first tangible sign that the Zionist Israeli establishment is prepared to move in the direction of acknowledging what happened to Palestinians in 1948, which is a vital Palestinian demand for any serious peace-making effort to succeed. Israelis in turn would expect a reciprocal Palestinian acknowledgement of Israel's core narrative (Khouri 2007).

It is noteworthy that the revised textbooks are only for Arab children, not Jewish children, which is why, above, we characterized this symbolic step as "relatively small." If Jewish children also learned this revised history it would better signal a sincere concession. But such a concession, though still relatively easy to implement, carries increased risk for undermining part of Zionism's moral narrative among the next generation. Undertaking the added risk may require an offsetting symbolic gesture from the other side. As Binyamin Netanyahu intimated, a change in Palestinian textbooks that omitted reference to Jewish perfidy since the time of Mohammed could reciprocally signal a sincere change of heart.

Still another way to demonstrate respect for the "who we are" aspect of a sacred value is to use the other side's preferred name: for example, the People's Republic of China rather than "red China," Israel rather than "the Jewish entity," or the Palestinian people rather than "Palestinian Arabs."

Apologize for What You Sincerely Regret

An apology should be consistent with one's own core values while simultaneously demonstrating sensitivity to the values of others. Unfortunately, an apology that is viewed as insincere can make matters worse. A good example is Japan's repeated apologies for atrocities committed in World War Two. China dismissed Japan's apologies and practically froze relations between the two countries when Japanese Prime Minister Junishiro Koizumi visited the Yasukuni Shrine, a shrine that honors Japan's 2.5 million war dead but also includes fourteen convicted Class-A war criminals (Onishi 2007; People's Daily Online 2006).[15]

Likewise, a qualified apology can be seen as worse than none at all. We have seen this in the case of the abuse of detainees at Abu Ghraib. When the United States apologized only for the acts of a few wayward soldiers, the result was angry dismissal by many in the Arab and Muslim world (Barkan 2006).

Without the acceptance of responsibility, apologies may not work. For Palestinians, Israel's continued settlement activity has been inconsistent with steps made toward recognition of Palestinian rights, including acknowledgment of some responsibility for the 1948 "catastrophe" and recognition of the plight of Palestinian refugees. For Israelis, in turn, the Palestinian Authority's failure to prevent armed attacks on Israeli civilians has been inconsistent with Palestinian overtures of recognition of the right of the Jewish people to an independent state in the region. The result is distrust of the other's sincerity by both sides. Symbolic gestures provide openings only if consistent actions follow.

One way to assess whether or not an apology might work is to float it through back channels or try it out in private. As we have seen, the Federal Republic of Germany's apology to the Jewish people took serious negotiation before finally reaching a text acceptable to Germany and sufficient for Israel.

Reframe Responsibility

In the winter of 2008, Israel was unable to prevent numerous rocket attacks coming from the Gaza Strip. The continuing attacks were a challenge to Israel's sovereignty and honor. The Israeli government had a choice about whom to hold responsible. It chose to hold responsible Fateh as well as its rival, Hamas, even though Hamas had control of the Gaza Strip. In other words, Israel chose a frame that held Palestine as a whole responsible for what any of their factions did. Framing the situation this way had the advantage for Israel of putting pressure on Hamas not only directly, but also indirectly through Fateh. But if Fateh had little leverage on the actions of Hamas, then holding Fateh as well as Hamas responsible would not be effective. Indeed, holding Fateh responsible would risk undermining Fateh's policy of restraint toward Israel.

Alternatively, Israel could have reframed the situation so as to hold only Hamas (and its allies in Gaza) responsible for the rocket attacks. Reframing the situation this way would have forgone whatever leverage Fateh might have had over Hamas but would have the advantage of sustaining the understandings with Fateh that have led to a relatively

low level of attack from the West Bank. Which frame would best serve Israel's interest in the long run would depend on whether Fateh had effective capacity to pressure Hamas *or* could get such capacity if pushed hard enough. In general, the choice of how to frame responsibility for an action from the other side is implicitly a matter of strategic analysis even more than a question about which frame is more accurate as a description of who caused the action to be taken.[16] Of course, Israel was not completely free to choose any frame it wished. In particular, holding only Hamas responsible would not have been tolerated by those Israelis who refused to make any distinctions among Palestinian factions as long as Israel's sovereignty and honor were being challenged.

A Possible Key to Impossible Conflicts

Reframing sacred values presents special difficulties and opportunities for overcoming barriers to seemingly intractable conflicts. The difficulty in reframing issues that involve sacred values lies in the people's general unwillingness to concede that they will ever abandon, or even significantly change, their attachment to a sacred value. Doing so would likely be seen as tantamount to abandoning or altering core social identity. The opportunities for reframing issues that involve sacred values arise from the fact that their propositional content is generally open-textured, somewhat the way metaphors are. This is particularly true of religious values, which survive in time and spread in space because they are readily reinterpretable in ways that are sensitive to changing contexts (Atran and Norenzayan 2004).

In sum, our empirical findings from the Middle East and our historical examples suggest an approach to seemingly intractable political conflicts that differs from received wisdom about "business-like" negotiations. Asking the other side to compromise a sacred value by offering material concessions can make matters worse, not better. Our evidence shows that both the public and its leaders may interpret such material offers as an insult. Surprisingly, however, our survey results and discussions with leaders indicate that even materially intangible symbolic gestures that show respect for the other side and its core values may open the door to dialogue in the worst of conflicts.

Finding ways to reframe core values so as to overcome psychological barriers to symbolic offerings is a daunting challenge. But meeting this challenge may offer greater opportunities for breakthroughs to peace than hitherto realized. The difficulty in creatively reframing sacred values may provide a key to unlocking the most deep-seated conflicts.

NOTES

This research was supported by the National Science Foundation, the U.S. Air Force Office of Scientific Research, and France's Center National de la Recherche Scientifique. For their helpful comments we thank Lydia Chen, John Chin, Robert Mnookin, James Sebenius, Valerie Roth, and Amy Saldinger.

1. In particular, rather than focus on positions, we focus on the parties' underlying interests, including the protection of sacred values, and rather than bargaining over positions, we focus on recognizing and acknowledging the sacred values involved in order to invent options for mutual gain.

2. Graham Allison (1971) shows how bureaucratic interests can affect the "face of an issue." Kingdon (1984) shows how "policy entrepreneurs" can get an issue on the national agenda by advocating particular problem definitions and proposals.

3. We do not wish to imply that devoted actors are irrational. Devoted actors use the logic of appropriateness (I choose something because I think it is appropriate for perceived rules and/or to what I consider to be my identity) rather than the logic of consequences (I choose something because of its anticipated consequences) (March and Olsen 1989). Of course, to protect an important value, a consequentialist might wish to appear to be using the logic of appropriateness (Schelling 1960).

4. For work on overcoming cultural barriers in negotiation see Bazerman, Tebrunsel, and Wade-Benzoni (2008), Grove and Carter (1999), and Lederach (1995).

5. A useful website on intractable conflicts is at http://www.beyondintractability.org/index.jsp?nid=1, accessed March 19, 2008.

6. In the aftermath of opposition to the 1765 Stamp Act, which many colonists saw as a violation of the "rights of free men" to the principal of no taxation without representation, England's Parliament continued to insist on the principal of taxing its colonies but tried to mollify opposition by imposing only moderate duties. The supposedly innocuous nature of the taxes, argued John Dickinson in *Letters from a Farmer in Pennsylvania* in 1768, masked their true perniciousness: "Nothing is wanted at home but a PRECEDENT, the force of which shall be established by the tacit submission of the colonies . . . IF Parliament succeeds in this attempt, other statutes will impose sums of money as they choose to take, *without any other* LIMITATION *than their* PLEASURE."

7. The results are based on two surveys of Palestinians in the West Bank and Gaza. Both were conducted in person. One was a sample of 535 refugees interviewed in December 2005. The other was a random sample of 719 Palestinian students surveyed individually in fourteen Palestinian university campuses throughout the West Bank and Gaza in May–June 2006, a month before the Israeli re-entry into Gaza. The student sample consisted of approximately equal numbers of students who self-identified as Islamists (50.1 percent) and nationalists (49.9 percent), of males (49.9 percent) and females (50.1 percent).

8. In experiments in which psychologist Douglas Medin offers people an exact material replication of their wedding ring, as well as a significant cash bonus, they generally do not accept the bargain. Those who trade are usually in the process of getting a divorce or are foreign spouses of Americans from cultures in which rings are not symbols of the sanctity of marriage.

9. Note that cricket matches between India and Pakistan are not likely to have such an effect because cricket has more or less equal value for both countries, so that game becomes zero-sum, with only a loser and a winner.

10. For details of the first two surveys see endnote 7. The third survey sampled 601 Jewish adults residing in the West Bank and Gaza (settlers). This sample was selected via random digit dialing procedures in which all telephone numbers had an equal probability of selection. This population consists primarily of people who moved to the West Bank and Gaza after the 1967 war for economic benefits or religious/ideological beliefs and who occupy significant tracts of land that would make up a Palestinian State and who generally refuse to leave. The survey was carried out in August 2005, a few days before the Israeli withdrawal from Gaza.

11. See also Pollack (2004) and World Federation of Scientists (2007). On January 7, 1998, the new "reformist" Iranian president Mohamed Khatami stated in an interview with CNN: "I do know that the feelings of the great American people have been hurt, and of course I regret it." He reiterated Iranian grievances against the United States but went on to compare in a very positive vein the current process of nation building in Iran with the heroic age of American nation building in the eighteenth and nineteenth centuries. On April 12, 1999, at a formal dinner at the White House President Bill Clinton stated with pointed reference to Iran: "I think sometimes it's quite important to tell people, look, you have a right to be angry at something my country or my culture did to you fifty or sixty or one-hundred or one-hundred-fifty years ago. But that is different from saying that I am outside the faith, and you are God's chosen."

12. An important question here is whether the very act of apology was partly responsible for the loss of support for Barak (and Khatami; see endnote 11). Public support on the issue may first have to be sounded out or prepared.

13. This expression was coined by Israel Zangwill a century ago. The point Zangwill was making was that the Arab population of Palestine was not a distinct nationality.

14. On issues related to framing in the Northern Ireland case see also Byrne (2001), Grove and Carter (1999), and Stephenson, Condor, and Abell (2007).

15. Another telling example of a failed apology concerns Japan's attempts to compensate the aging victims of its wartime sexual slavery. In 1995, Japan set up the Asian Women's Fund to pay out money to former "comfort women" in South Korea, Thailand, and the Philippines. But the Japanese government stressed that the money came from "citizens" and not from the government itself, arguing that postwar treaties absolve it from all individual claims related to World War Two. The governments of Taiwan and South Korea rejected payments from the fund, accusing Japan of failing to clearly take moral responsibility in "atoning" for its treatment of the women. For general advice on apologies, see Goldberg, Green, and Sander (1987). On the conditions for success of an apology in health care disputes, see Robbennolt (2005).

16. This analysis applies the idea of rewarding positive acts as well as punishing hostile acts. For a sophisticated treatment of the long-run effects of alternative frames, see Dennett (2003).

REFERENCES

ABC Online. 2007. Ahmadinejad under fire for embracing his teacher. Available from http://www.abc.net.au/News/Newsitems/200705/s1912815.htm.

Abu Marzouk, M. 2007. Interview with S. Atran, Syria, February 23.

Al Betawi, H. 2004. Interview with S. Atran, Nablus, West Bank, September 8.

Alderdice, J. 2007a. Interview with Scott Atran at Fifth Meeting, Permanent Monitoring Panel on Terrorism, World Federation of Scientists, Erice, Italy, May 1.

———. 2007b. Remarks made at Fifth Meeting, Permanent Monitoring Panel on Terrorism, World Federation of Scientists, Erice, Italy, May 18.

Allison, G. 1971. *Essence of decision: Explaining the Cuban missile crisis.* New York: HarperCollins.

Anonymous. 2005. Interview with Dominique de Villepin: Il n'y a de communauté que nationale. *La Vie*, February 24.

———. 2007. U.S. doubles Bin Laden bounty to 50 million. *Agence France Presse wire*, July 13.

Atran, S. 2002. *In gods we trust: The evolutionary landscape of religion.* New York: Oxford University Press.

———. 2003. Genesis of suicide terrorism. *Science* 299: 1534–1539.

———. 2004. Hamas may give peace a chance. *New York Times*, December 18.

———. 2006. Is Hamas ready to deal? *New York Times*, August 17.

———. 2007a. Sacred values, terrorism and the limits of rational choice. In *In the same light as slavery: Building a global antiterrorist consensus*, edited by J. McMillan. Washington, DC: Institute for National Strategic Studies, National Defense University Press.

———. 2007b. Terrorism and radicalization: What to do, what not to do. Presentation to U.S. Department of State and U.K. House of Lords, October-November. Available from http://www.edge.org/3rd_culture/Atran07/index.html.

Atran, S., R. Axelrod, and R. Davis. 2007a. Give Palestine's unity government a chance. *The Huffington Post*, March 7. Available from http://www.huffingtonpost.com/scott-atran-robert-axelrod-and-richard-davis/give-palestines-unity-go_b_42882.html.

———. 2007b. Sacred barriers to conflict resolution. *Science* 317: 1039–1040.

———. 2007c. Synopsis of briefing to National Security Council staff, The White House, March 28. Available from http://www.sitemaker.umich.edu/satran/files/synopsis_atran-sageman_nsc_brief_28_march_2007.pdf.

Atran, S., D. Medin, and N. Ross. 2005. The cultural mind: Environmental decision making and cultural modeling within and across populations. *Psychological Review* 112: 744–776.

Atran, S. and A. Norenzayan. 2004. Religion's evolutionary landscape. *Behavioral and Brain Sciences* 27: 713–770.

Axelrod, R. and W. Hamilton. 1981. The evolution of cooperation. *Science* 211: 1390–1396.

Barkan, E. 2006. The worst is yet to come: Abu Ghraib and the politics of not apologizing. In *Taking wrongs seriously: Apologies and reconciliation*, edited by E. Barkan and A. Karn. Stanford, CA: Stanford University Press.

Baron, J. and M. Spranca. 1997. Protected values. *Organizational Behavioral and Human Decision Processes* 70: 1–16.

Bazerman, H., A. Tebrunsel, and K. Wade-Benzoni. 2008. When sacred issues are at stake. *Negotiation Journal* 24(1): 113–117.

Bowden, M. 2000. *Black Hawk down: A study of modern war.* London: Penguin.

Byrne, S. 2001. Consociational and civic society approaches to peacebuilding in Northern Ireland. *Journal of Peace Research* 38(3): 327–352.

Carmichael, D., J. Hubert, B. Reeves, and A. Schanche (eds). 1994. *Sacred sites, sacred places.* London: Routledge.

Davis, R. 2007. Interview with S. Atran, Washington, DC, March 28.

Dennett, D. 2003. *Freedom evolves.* New York: Viking.

Dickinson, J. 1768. *Letters from a farmer in Pennsylvania.* Dublin: Printed for J. Sheppard.

Dower, J. 1999. *Embracing defeat: Japan in the wake of World War II.* New York: W. W. Norton.

Durkheim, E. 1995. *The elementary forms of religious life.* New York: Macmillan. First published in 1912.

Eckstein, R. 1993. Ping pong diplomacy: A view from behind the scenes. *The Journal of American–East Asian Relations* 2: 327–340.

Eidinow, J. and D. Edmonds. 2001. *Wittgenstein's poker.* New York: Ecco.

Fateh, C. 1964. Constitution. Available from http://web.archive.org/web/20070607150221/www.fateh.net/e_public/constitution.html.

Fisher, R. and W. Ury. 1981. *Getting to yes: Negotiating agreement without giving in.* New York: Houghton Mifflin.

Gaddis, J. 1995. *Strategies of containment: A critical appraisal of postwar national security*, rev. edn. New York: Oxford University Press.

Garamone, J. 2004. Rumsfeld accepts responsibility for Abu Ghraib. *American Foreign Press Service*, May 7.

Ginges, J., S. Atran, D. Medin, and K. Shikaki. 2007. Sacred bounds on rational resolution of violent political conflict. *Proceedings of the National Academy of Sciences* 104: 7357–7360.

Goldberg, S., E. Green, and F. Sander. 1987. Saying you're sorry. *Negotiation Journal*: 221–224.

Goodin, R. 1980. Making moral incentives pay. *Policy Sciences* 12: 131–145.

Gresh, A. 2001. The Middle East: How the peace was lost. *Le Monde diplomatique*, English langage edition, September. Available from http://mondediplo .com/2001/09/01middleeastleader.

Grove, A. and N. Carter. 1999. Not all blarney is cast in stone: International cultural conflict in Northern Ireland. *Political Psychology* 20(4): 725–765.

Hamas. 1988. Covenant. Available from http://www .yale.edu/lawweb/avalon/mideast/hamas.htm.

Hamilton, W. 1964. The genetical evolution of social behavior. *Journal of Theoretical Biology* 7: 1–52.

Harris, M. 1966. Cultural ecology of India's sacred cattle. *Current Anthropology* 7: 261–276.

Hauser, M. 2006. *Moral minds: How nature designed our universal sense of right and wrong.* New York: Ecco.

Havemeyer, L. 1929. *Ethnography.* Boston: Ginn & Co.

Hoffman, A., J. Gillespie, D. Moore, K. Wade-Benzoni, L. Thompson, and M. Bazerman. 1999. A mixed-motive perspective on the economics versus environmental debate. *American Behavioral Scientist* 42: 1254–1276.

Kashmir, A. 2006, Interviews with S. Atran, Pakistan, April–May.

Khouri, R., 2007. A different history lesson. *International Herald Tribune*, August 3.

Kingdon, J. W. 1984. *Agendas, alternatives and public policies.* Boston: Little, Brown.

Lazarus, E. 1999. *Black Hills, white justice: The Sioux Nation versus the United States, 1775 to the present.* Lincoln: University of Nebraska Press.

Lederach, J. P. 1995. *Preparing for peace: Conflict transformation across cultures: Syracuse.* New York: Syracuse University Press.

———. 1997. *Building peace: Conflict sustainable reconciliation in divided societies.* Washington, DC: United States Institute of Peace Press.

Lim, C. S. and J. Baron. 1997. Protected Values in Malaysia, Singapore and the United States. Department of Psychology, University of Pennsylvania. Available from http://www.sas.upenn.edu/-baron /lim.htm.

Lustick, I. 2006. Negotiating truth: The Holocaust, Lehavdil, and al-Nakba. *Journal of International Affairs* 60: 51–80.

March, J. and J. Olsen. 1989. *Rediscovering institutions: The organizational basis of politics.* New York: Free Press.

Merari, A. 2007. Interview with S. Atran, Erice, Italy, May 19.

Netanyahu, B. 2007. Interview with S. Atran. The Knesset, Jerusalem, February 27.

Nisbett, R. and D. Cohen. 1996. *The culture of honor.* Boulder, CO: Westview Press.

Onishi, N. 2007. Japan's "atonement" to former sex slaves stirs anger. *New York Times*, April 25.

People's Daily Online. 2006. Japan PM's shrine visit sparks anger in China. August 16.

Peters, E. 1967. Some structural aspects of the feud among the camel herding Bedouin of Cyrenaica. *Africa* 37: 261–262.

Pew Research Center. 2005. U.S. image up slightly, but still negative. Available from http://pewglobal.org /reports/display.php?ReportID=247.

———. 2006. America's image slips, but allies share U.S. concerns over Iran, Hamas. Available from http://pewglobal.org/reports/display .php?ReportID=252.

Pollack, K. 2004. *The Persian puzzle: The conflict between Iran and America.* New York: Random House.

Robbennolt, J. 2005. What we know and don't know about the role of apologies in resolving health care disputes. *Georgia State University Law Review* 21: 10009–10027.

Roberts, S. 2005. Revisiting a killing field in Poland. *New York Times*, November 4.

Roy, O. 2004. *Globalized Islam.* New York: Columbia University Press.

Sadat, A. 1977. *In search of identity: An autobiography.* New York: Harper & Row.

Schelling, T. 1960. *The strategy of conflict.* Cambridge, MA: Harvard University Press.

Senior Saudi Official (unnamed). 2008. Interviewed by S. Atran. Security Forces Officers Club, Riyadh, February 23.

Stephenson, C., S. Condor, and J. Abell. 2007. The minority-majority conundrum in Northern Ireland. *Political Psychology* 28(1): 105–125.

Susskind, L., H. Levine, G. Aran, S. Kaniel, Y. Sheleg, and M. Halbertal. 2005. Religious and ideological dimensions of the Israeli settlements issue: Reframing the narrative? *Negotiation Journal* 21: 177–191.

Tetlock, P. 2003. Thinking the unthinkable: Sacred values and taboo cognitions. *Trends in Cognitive Science* 7: 320–324.

Tetlock, P. E., O. V. Kristel, and B. Elson. 2000. The psychology of the unthinkable: Taboo trade-offs, forbidden base rates, and heretical counterfactuals. *Journal of Personality and Social Psychology* 78: 853–70.

U.S. National Security Council. 2006. National security strategy. Available from http://www.whitehouse.gov/nsc/nss/2006/nss2006.pdf.

Varshney, A. 2003. Nationalism, ethnic conflict and rationality. *Perspectives on Politics* 1: 85–99.

World Federation of Scientists. 2007. Conference at Erice, Italy, May 18.

James I. Walsh and James A. Piazza

WHY RESPECTING PHYSICAL INTEGRITY RIGHTS REDUCES TERRORISM

What is the relationship between respect for human rights and the incidence of terrorism? One line of thinking holds that there is an inverse relationship between these variables. Governments must restrict rights if they wish to reduce terrorist attacks (Dreher et al., in press; Gearty, 2007; Hoffman, 2004). States that seek to preserve human rights and political freedoms are limited in their ability to monitor and detain terrorism suspects, are prohibited from making broad police sweeps to catch terrorist perpetrators and their sympathizers, limit coercive interrogation of suspects, and must afford suspected terrorists access to a lawyer and a public trial. Freedom of assembly and of the press allows terrorists and their supporters to publicize their grievances. Sometimes law enforcement and intelligence agencies are legally prohibited from sharing information on terrorist activity (Pape, 2003; Schmid, 1992). The implication is that states that protect human rights are more vulnerable to terrorist attacks. This seems to be borne out by studies indicating that democracies experience more terrorism (Eubank & Weinberg, 2001; Piazza, 2008; Schmid, 1992; Wade & Reiter, 2007) and more nuanced studies that find that new democracies (Eyerman, 1998) and states with constrained executives (Li, 2005) are more frequently targeted by terrorists.

An alterative line of thinking holds that abuse of human rights actually encourages terrorism. This view is outlined in a statement by U.K. Prime Minister Gordon Brown to a summer 2007 meeting of the Labour Party: "We cannot win this [war on terror] militarily or by policing or intelligence alone. We need to engage people so that we can win the battle of hearts and minds" (Branigan, 2007, p. 1). The statement suggests that governments that respect human rights can outmaneuver terrorists by winning the support of the population, depriving the terrorists of the logistical support they require. If this is the case, then respect for human rights is a "win–win" scenario—governments that secure such

From *Comparative Political Studies* 43, no. 5 (2010), pp. 551–77.

rights not only comply with their normative obligations but also experience fewer terrorist attacks.

This article explores the argument that protecting human rights reduces terrorism. We first develop the theoretical underpinnings of the argument that violation of human rights promotes terrorism. We focus on a critical subclass of human rights, physical integrity rights, which protect individuals from extrajudicial murder, disappearance, torture, or political imprisonment by the authorities. We describe physical integrity rights as critical because their violation offends the most widely shared norms of appropriate government conduct. Abuse of physical integrity rights increases terrorism, we hypothesize, through three mechanisms—by alienating the government from members of the population that could provide it with intelligence about terrorist groups, by causing conflicts with other political forces in the country thereby damaging the efficacy of government counterterrorism policy, and by reducing international willingness to cooperate with the government. In our analysis, we subject our hypothesis to a series of tests using a sample of 195 countries over a multiyear period. Although much research in this area uses data only on transnational terrorism, we develop a new data set that also includes information on attacks by domestic terrorist groups. Our findings consistently show that respect for physical integrity rights does substantially reduce terrorism. This conclusion is consistent across specifications using different measures of terrorism and diverse model specifications and including numerous control variables.

The findings have important implications for scholarship and for counterterrorism policy that we briefly discuss in the conclusion. The contention that human rights violations increase terrorism has not been empirically substantiated in previous studies, nor has it been theoretically articulated in the terrorism literature. The relevant literature has instead focused on how democratic institutions influence the probability that a state will experience terrorist attacks. This focus on institutional arrangements has produced valuable insights but overlooks how government behavior in the form of respect for human rights might be related to vulnerability to terrorism. Furthermore, the empirical terrorism literature tests only predictors of transnational terrorism, failing to also consider domestic terrorism, as our article does. Finally, our results suggest that rather than centering global counterterrorism policy on democracy promotion, priority should be given to promoting respect for physical integrity rights abroad as a means of reducing terrorist attacks.

Human Rights and Terrorism

Does government respect for human rights increase or reduce terrorism? Three bodies of work address this question directly or indirectly. A handful of recent articles directly investigate the effects of rights on terrorist attacks. They reach different conclusions. Abadie (2006) and Kurrild-Klitgaard, Justesen, and Klemmensen (2006) find a curvilinear relationship between terrorism and rights that allow individuals to participate in the political process. Abrahms (2007) concludes that civil liberties that permit freedom of expression, association, and personal autonomy reduce terrorism. Kurrild-Klitgaard et al. find no relationship at all between this measure and transnational terrorist attacks. These works differ from each other and from the present article in their measurement of terrorism and expectations about which rights influence terrorism. Kurrild-Klitgaard et al. utilize the International Terrorism: Attributes of Terrorist Events (ITERATE) terrorism data set, which includes only transnational attacks but covers a rather long time series. Abadie and Abrahms use measures that include both transnational and domestic terrorism, but only for a single year. In our empirical analysis, we utilize a new, more comprehensive data set that allows us to assess the causal influence of human rights on terrorist attacks by both transnational and domestic groups over a number of years. We also develop the argument that a different type of human rights—those to physical integrity—is more closely tied to terrorism than are rights protecting civil liberties and political participation, the rights examined in previous studies.

There is also a substantial literature exploring if and how democracy influences terrorism. Democratic regimes allow individuals rights of speech, movement, legal protection, and organization. This literature may thus be said to indirectly address the connection between rights and terrorism. Most of this work concludes that democracies experience more terrorism than do nondemocracies (Eubank & Weinberg, 2001; Ivanova & Sandler, 2006; Li & Schaub, 2004; Piazza, 2008; Schmid, 1992; Wade & Reiter, 2007). The rights necessary for democratic participation also provide terrorist groups with more freedom to publicize their grievances, recruit members and supporters, and plan attacks. Other work has added nuance to these general findings by analyzing how different features of democracy encourage or retard transnational terrorism. Eyerman (1998), for example, finds that newly established democracies are more likely to experience terrorism than are nondemocracies or older democracies. The most sophisticated study in this vein is Li (2005), which makes two important advances. First, Li disaggregates democracy into two basic characteristics—democratic participation and constraints on the actions of the executive. He argues that these characteristics should influence terrorism in different ways. Political groups are less likely to resort to terrorism when participation is greater because this allows them to redress their grievances through legitimate political channels. More constraints on the executive branch increase attacks by limiting the government's ability to take aggressive action against terrorist groups. Second, he argues that any relationship between human rights and terrorism is spurious, and the true causal factor is the extent to which the executive is constrained by other branches of government. Such institutional checks on an elected government keep it from engaging in systematic human rights violations. These checks and balances preserve human rights and civil liberties, which in turn promotes terrorist activity.

All of these studies, including Li's, draw attention to the relationship between terrorism and democratic institutions, or the quality of these institutions, rather than considering the role played by the behavior of governments. Separating the influence of institutional structures from the government's behavior is a promising research avenue for two reasons. First, other research demonstrates that democracies vary in their respect for human rights. B. Bueno de Mesquita, Cherif, Downs, and Smith (2005) and Davenport and Armstrong (2004) show that only countries with the highest levels of democratic rule consistently protect a wide range of human rights. This would seem to call into question the assumption of Li (2005) that protection of human rights is solely a consequence of constraints on the executive. Second, Li's article suggests that institutional constraints prevent the government from abusing rights that allow wide participation in the political process. He does not analyze the effect of conceptually distinct physical integrity rights. Below we make the case that it is these rights that have most substantial influence on terrorism.

A third body of work finds that abuses of these physical integrity rights are significant predictors of political dissent and of insurgency, though sometimes in a curvilinear manner in which states employing intermediate levels of repression experienced the most acute violence. We draw on this research in developing our theory of how abuse fuels terrorism. A great deal of theoretical and historical work suggests that repressing human rights promotes large-scale, organized insurgency. Joes (2004) summarizes and extends this line of analysis, arguing that the key difference between successful and failed counterinsurgency campaigns is a policy of "rectitude" rather than repression. In cases where state and military officials offered rectitude—for example, generous treatment of civilian populations in which insurgents are lodged and humane treatment of captured insurgents—counterinsurgency efforts were successful. Counterinsurgency failed where officials employed harsh repression and in particular collective punishment of civilians. State brutality assists insurgents in recruitment efforts and eases their campaigns to maintain and even widen their popular support within society (Joes, 2004, pp. 156–170; Rice, 1988). Hashim (2006, pp. 299–318) underscores the need of states confronting insurgencies to create and support "legitimate coercive state apparatuses" to delegitimize, and eventually disarm, nongovernment groups and to foster support within the local population for counterinsurgency activities. Legitimacy is built on respect for rule of law, proper treatment of local populations, and use of restraint when engaged in military and policing efforts. Merom (2003) argues that more powerful democracies lose counterinsurgency campaigns when the educated middle classes become alienated by the government's use of violence. This forces the government into crisis as it attempts to both defeat militants and quell metropolitan dissent. Others analyze the relationships between dissent and repression. This literature addresses a broad set of important questions including the sources of popular and elite dissent, how and why governments engage in repression, and the relationships between these two causal processes. The branch of this research that is most relevant for our purposes examines how repression leads to subsequent dissent and has produced inconsistent findings. Different authors argue that repression effectively quells dissent (Hibbs, 1973), that it prompts dissent (Francisco, 1996), that the relationship is curvilinear (Mueller & Weede, 1990), or that there is no relationship between these variables (Gurr & Moore, 1997). One reason for these varied findings may be that the sheer breadth of the scope of inquiry has led to inconsistent operationalization of key concepts such as dissent and repression. This adds further support to our decision to limit our study to the subset of repressive policies that involve threats to physical integrity and the subset of dissent that qualifies as terrorism. In the next section, though, we hold that many of the theoretical expectations regarding the influence of repression on dissent are quite likely to hold for terrorism and physical integrity rights.

Why Respect for Physical Integrity Rights Reduces Terrorism

Our central hypothesis is that government violations of a certain class of human rights, those to physical integrity, promote terrorism. Governments violate physical integrity rights when they inflict arbitrary physical harm on individuals. Specific actions that constitute physical integrity violations are extrajudicial killings, torture, disappearances, and political imprisonment (Cingranelli & Richards, 1999). One can imagine a wide range of government counterterrorism actions that might promote terrorism, but we expect that violations of physical integrity rights should have a particularly powerful influence on terrorism because those rights resonate with universal ideas about human dignity. Keck and Sikkink (1998) argue that norms about protecting the bodily integrity of members of vulnerable or innocent groups are among the most widely shared across countries and cultures. Cultures and polities vary widely in the respect they accord other types of human rights, such as those allowing political expression and participation or economic and social equality, but nearly all include norms against violations of the physical integrity of innocents (also see Cingranelli & Richards, 1999). We take this observation as the starting point for our analysis. Governments require support from the population, domestic political movements, and from the international community to mount an effective counterterrorism policy. Violating the widely shared norms of protecting physical integrity rights, we argue, alienates at least some members of all three of these groups. The precise mechanism through which human rights abuses reduce political support for or otherwise hinder the government's counterterrorism efforts varies across these audiences in ways we detail below.

Garnering Community Support

Countries experience less terrorism when the government has the support, or at least the passive acceptance, of the constituent communities of the terrorist groups. Governments derive their legitimacy in part from the perception that they treat individuals similarly and equitably (Dahl, 1971). Widespread violations of physical integrity rights undermine this legitimacy in the eyes of the public, making them less willing to support the authorities' counterterror efforts and more willing to support those of the terrorists (Abrahms, 2007). Public support is critical to the survival of terrorist groups. These groups have fewer political, economic, and military resources than the states they oppose. Terrorists rely instead on political, financial, and logistical support from networks of noncombatant supporters drawn from the populations in which they operate or on whose behalf they claim to launch attacks. The success of terrorist groups thus depends, in large part, on their ability to maintain the loyalty and support of some fraction of the constituent population. States that are able to win the support of all or a critical segment of that constituent population can deprive terrorists of important capabilities. This is why competitions between a government and terrorists are often described as a "battle for the hearts and minds" of the populace. Abuse of physical integrity rights makes it more difficult for the government to win this battle for two reasons.

As Hoffman and McCormick (2004) explain, an important goal of most terrorist organizations is to draw attention to their grievances. They plan attacks in ways that maximize popular and media attention. State violation of human rights augments these grievances and makes terrorist appeals for support more effective. Abuse of the physical integrity rights of members of the constituency on whose behalf the terrorists claim to act will alienate at least some from the authorities enough to either actively support or turn a blind eye to terrorist activities. Under some conditions, such abuses may increase the number and quality of potential recruits and allow terrorist groups to grow in size and in terms of the education and abilities of their members (E. Bueno de Mesquita, 2005). Terrorist propaganda can undercut the government by drawing attention to how

such abuses violate global norms of rights to physical integrity (Finnemore & Sikkink, 1998, p. 32) as well as norms particular to the local culture that reflect this concern. Brutal treatment of noncombatants by the state can facilitate communitarian mobilization efforts of militants, assisting them in radicalizing formerly passive populations (Holsti, 2000). State repression can foster conditions under which ethnic, religious, or social groups experience communal discrimination, constructing what is referred to in the internal conflict literature as "collective grievances" against the state or political status quo. These collective grievances are ripe for exploitation by terrorist groups, thus enhancing popular support for antisystem political violence (Wimmer, 1997). Security forces may seek to avoid this political reaction by directing their use of force against only suspected terrorists and argue that such targeted violence does not violate the norm of protecting the bodily integrity of noncombatants. But the authorities typically find it very difficult to restrict the infliction of such violence on known terrorists. It is expensive and time-consuming to obtain the information needed to reliably distinguish terrorists from nonterrorists. Indiscriminate violence is much cheaper and easier to implement. But it will also victimize many nonterrorists and turn some of them against the government, especially when there is an active and organized group that can provide them with some promise of retribution against the government's actions (Kalyvas, 2004).

Abusing physical integrity rights thus drives at least some to support terrorists. As important, it drives others to refrain from supporting the government. Informants in the civilian population can provide the authorities with important information about terrorist groups' activities. Terrorist groups rely on gaps in intelligence and law enforcement information and their ability to blend into local populations to evade capture by state authorities. Governments respond by seeking information about terrorist groups' activities from members of the constituent population. States that commit human rights abuses alienate civilians who might be willing to provide the authorities with such intelligence. Governments also seek to cultivate moderate political forces among the noncombatants in the terrorist groups' constituent population. Government abuse of physical integrity rights marginalizes and delegitimizes these moderates, who can be described by the terrorists as stooges of the authorities and as ineffective in preventing or moderating repression.

Because government abuse of physical integrity rights encourages the population to tilt toward the terrorists, might they not act in ways that deliberately provoke such repression? It is not difficult to find examples of such behavior (see, e.g., Neumann, Lawrence, & Smith, 2007, pp. 66-68), but we suspect it does not characterize all or even most terrorist groups. Although we lack systematic studies of the issue, few works identify the desire to *deliberately* provoke repression as a key motive for terrorist groups to launch attacks. There is not much evidence pointing in the direction of the conclusion that it is clearly more important than objectives such as publicizing grievances, attracting supporters, and impressing those who already back the terrorist movement (Crenshaw, 1991). Nonetheless, we take seriously the possibility that there is an endogenous relationship between terrorist attacks and the protection of rights and seek to control for such a possibility in the empirical analysis below.

Maintaining Domestic Political Support

Counterterrorism is also more effective, and terrorist attacks are reduced, when the government maintains its support among powerful political actors. Governments that abuse physical integrity rights expose themselves to criticism by rival domestic political actors such as political parties in democracies or internal factions and dissidents in nondemocracies. Governments facing such challenges need to spend political capital defending their policies, which reduces the resources they can devote to counterterrorism. This type of political pressure may also lead the authorities to change policies midstream

with the objective of dampening criticism, which may also reduce the effectiveness of their counterterror efforts. Many counterterrorism policies, such as the monitoring of communications and financial exchanges or the surveillance or secret detention of suspected terrorists, are less effective if the targets of these measures are aware of their use. Investigations of physical integrity rights violations may lead to the deliberate or inadvertent publication of information about these measures. All of these distract governments from the issue at hand and jeopardize the consistency and coherence of counterterrorism programs, leaving terrorists freer to organize and to commit attacks.

Two historical cases and one contemporary one guide our thinking on this point. In each case, physical integrity violations committed in campaigns against terrorists bred political opposition that placed the government on the defensive, provoked scrutiny of counterterrorism policy, and eventually propelled the government into political crisis, damaging the coherence of its counterterrorism policy and, often, its very ability to maintain power. Use of torture and extrajudicial killings by French security forces in Algeria to combat FLN terrorists during the 1956 Battle of Algiers, when publicized by journalists and public intellectuals, provided political fodder for leftist politicians seeking to weaken the governing coalition of the Fourth Republic while also provoking a backlash, and coup attempt, by right-wing politicians and members of the military. The crisis in Algeria, and the revelation of French counterterrorism actions in the face of the FLN campaign, forced the already unstable government of Edgar Faure on the defensive in the face of contradictory demands by the French Left and Right to abandon repression in Algeria versus adopting a harder line on Algerian terrorists. Between 1956 and 1958, the consistency of French counterterrorism policy deteriorated as France experienced five governments before being forced to allow Algerian independence and witnessing the collapse of the Fourth Republic itself (Horne, 1979). A similar phenomenon occurred in Israel in the wake of its 1982 invasion of Lebanon to root out PLO terrorists. Although the incursion initially enjoyed widespread support among the political parties in Israel, extrajudicial killings in Palestinian refugee camps out of which the PLO operated in southern Lebanon sparked public protest in Israel and eventually led to the withdrawal of the Israeli Labor Party's support for government counterterrorism efforts in Lebanon and an official inquiry. Opposition tied the hands of Israeli Prime Minister Menachim Begin, leading him to scale back efforts to pursue PLO leaders. Outrage over abuses eventually forced Begin into retirement from political life in 1983 while compelling Israeli forces to withdraw to a narrow security perimeter on the southern border of Lebanon, allowing new terrorist movements such as Amal and Hezbollah to further develop (Merom, 2003).

Maintaining International Support

Finally, governments that resort to physical integrity violations when fighting terrorism risk losing international support for their efforts. Because terrorism is frequently a transnational phenomenon—meaning that terrorist groups often cross borders to commit attacks, attack foreign targets either at home or abroad, or maintain fund-raising, recruiting, training, and communications capacities in more than one country—it requires international cooperation to successfully combat it. Foreign governments can provide intelligence on the activities of terrorist groups within their territory and use their law enforcement and security agencies to restrict the actions of these groups. Governments and international organizations can forge multinational policing regimes and monitoring and information sharing agreements and can cooperate to track down and neutralize financial assets of terrorist groups. However, flagrant human rights abuses by countries fighting terrorism can damage international cooperation and assistance (Hoffman, 2004). Governments and international organizations that attach importance to respect for human rights, or are bound by international human rights treaties,

may become less willing to provide support for the counterterrorism programs of states that violate human rights, fearing the domestic and international consequences of collaborating with a notorious regime (Abrahms, 2007, p. 244; Cingranelli & Richards, 1999).

Perhaps the most clear-cut example of this pitfall can be found in the contemporary strain placed on transatlantic counterterrorism cooperation by allegations of detainee abuse and the practice of rendering terror suspects to "black sites" by U.S. security officials where they are subject to torture. Revelations of abuse of prisoners and terrorist suspects in Guantánamo Bay in Cuba and in Abu Ghraib prison in Iraq in the spring of 2004 and of the rendition of suspects by the U.S. Central Intelligence Agency, possibly with the clandestine assistance of European governments, to secret detention centers in Europe and the Middle East for torture inflamed European public opinion, leading to demands for independent investigations. In 2007, German and Italian courts issued warrants for the arrest of CIA personnel believed to have been involved in the rendition and subsequent torture of Khalid al-Masri, a German citizen of Lebanese descent erroneously linked to Islamic terrorist networks, and Hasan Mustapha Osama Nasr, an Egyptian-born Muslim cleric residing in Milan. Though these cases have not progressed because the U.S. Justice Department refuses to honor demands by Interpol that the agents, now pulled from field operations, be surrendered to European authorities, they did prompt the Council of Europe to issue a resolution in June 2007 demanding a review of all U.S.-EU bilateral military basing agreements with an eye to instituting human rights clauses. These cases also spurred the European Parliament in February of the same year to call for the closure of Guantánamo Bay and all European terrorism detention sites used by the Americans, a call for investigations by individual European governments of CIA use of stopover sites in Europe, and an immediate ban on all CIA officials or aircraft suspected to have been involved in rendition operations in Europe. Perceptions that the United States has permitted human rights violations to creep into its counterterrorism efforts have raised the ire of European politicians, human rights organizations, and publics, whereas allegations that European governments have been complicit in abuses have made them wary of further cooperation with U.S. intelligence agencies (Walsh, 2010, p. 129).

Method and Data

In our analysis we examine whether or not countries with poor records of protecting physical integrity rights experience more terrorism than those that preserve such rights. We measure our dependent variable, the incidence of terrorism, as the number of terrorist attacks recorded for each country in our data set for each year for which data are available. We draw on two sources of data. The first is the ITERATE data set, compiled and coded by Edward Mickolus (2006). This data set is used in many of the studies of terrorism cited earlier (i.e., Eyerman, 1998; Li, 2005; Li & Schaub, 2004) and in our analysis is examined for the period from 1981—when the time series on our key independent variable, physical integrity rights, begins—until 2003. ITERATE includes information only on transnational attacks: attacks where the perpetrator and victims are of different nationalities. Because we have no reason to believe that respect for physical integrity rights should influence only transnational terrorism, we also coded attacks from the RAND-MIPT (Memorial Institute for the Prevention of Terrorism) Terrorism Knowledge Base, a database of terrorist incidents built using open-source materials.[1] The MIPT database includes *both* domestic and transnational terrorist attacks for the period from 1998 to 2004, the last year for which we have data for many of our independent variables. We used the MIPT database to determine for each country-year the number of (a) domestic terrorist attacks, (b) transnational terrorist attacks, and (c) total terrorist attacks, where total attacks is the sum of domestic and transnational attacks.* * *

We examine independent variables that fall into three categories: the government's respect for physical integrity rights, measures of democracy, and the state's counterterrorism capacity. The Cingranelli and Richards (CIRI) Human Rights data set's physical integrity index is our key independent variable. This covers 195 countries from 1981 to 2004 (Cingranelli & Richards, 2004). The CIRI data set measures government respect for four physical integrity rights: the extent to which the government engages in disappearances, extrajudicial killings, holding political prisoners, and torture. Each of these measures ranges in values from 0, indicating the least respect for the right in question, to a maximum value of 2. The physical integrity index combines these evaluations of individual rights into an overall measure of the authorities' respect for physical integrity rights. Therefore, the index itself ranges in value from 0, indicating least respect for these rights, to a maximum value of 8.

As discussed earlier, scholars have used three measures of democracy in the study of transnational terrorism: constraints on the executive, participation, and the durability of the regime.* * *

A number of articles find that the government's capacity to implement an effective counterterrorist policy reduces attacks (Lai, 2007; Li, 2005; Li & Schaub, 2004). The logic here is straightforward. Terrorism is a risky business for the perpetrators because terrorist groups are weaker than the states they target. Governments that can identify the members, supporters, and plans of a group can neutralize terrorists quickly and deter the formation of new terrorist groups. The leaders of terrorist groups realize that they face the risk of interdiction and disruption and consider the targeted state's capacity to mount an effective counterterrorist policy when deciding if they should launch attacks. Our operationalization follows Lai's (2007) study, which has the most extended discussion of this issue. Lai operationalizes state capacity with four variables: government involvement in an international war, government involvement in a civil war, the natural log of the state's population, and the number of telephone lines per 1,000 residents. We use the first three of these measures and drop the measure of telephone lines, which Lai did not find to be statistically significant in most of his models.* * *

Results

Table 7.1 summarizes the main results. Table 7.1 reports the results for four regression models. The models all include the same independent variables.

Table 7.1 Physical Integrity Rights and Terrorism

Dependent Variable	MIPT Domestic Attacks	MIPT Transnational Attacks	MIPT All Attacks	ITERATE Attacks
Physical Integrity	−0.227**	−0.271*	−0.228**	−0.116***
	(−2.79)	(−2.41)	(−3.04)	(−3.80)
Participation	0.003	0.006	−0.001	0.005
	(0.35)	(0.67)	(−0.09)	(1.04)
Executive Constraints	0.163	−0.039	0.129	0.026
	(1.6)	(−0.42)	(1.52)	(0.52)
Durable	0.646**	0.870***	0.724***	−0.133
	(2.74)	(3.62)	(3.57)	(−0.58)
International War	−0.239	−0.332	−0.309	0.458**
	(−0.50)	(−0.79)	(−0.68)	(3.02)
Civil War	0.733*	0.871**	0.833**	0.721***
	(2.28)	(3.09)	(3.14)	(4.34)
Population (ln)	0.296**	0.124	0.255**	0.222***
	(3.04)	(0.91)	(2.9)	(4.96)
GDP per Capita (ln)	0.148	0.524*	0.274	0.285***
	(0.95)	(2.19)	(1.93)	(5.83)
Constant	−2.349*	−5.018***	−2.658**	−1.812***
	(−2.14)	(−3.51)	(−2.64)	(−4.30)
Delta (ln)	4.246***	1.755***	4.075***	1.986***
Log Likelihood	−1334	−771	−1526	−4166
Countries	153	153	153	142
Observations	774	774	774	2,547
Years	1998–2004	1998–2004	1998–2004	1981–2003

Note: Robust z statistics clustered on countries in parentheses.
*p < .05. **p < .01. ***p < .001.

The key independent variable of interest, government respect for physical integrity rights, is lagged one period to account for possible endogeneity with terrorist attacks, an issue we also address in greater detail below. The four models in Table 7.1 have different dependent variables—the number of domestic attacks according to MIPT, the number of transnational attacks according to MIPT, the total number of terrorist attacks according to MIPT, and the number of transnational attacks recorded in the ITERATE data set.

Government respect for physical integrity rights is statistically significant at the 5% level or less and signed in the expected negative direction in all four models. Greater respect for physical integrity rights consistently reduces the number of terrorist attacks regardless of the type of terrorism—domestic or transnational—and the source of the measure of terrorism (MIPT or ITERATE). Of the measures of democratic political institutions, only durable is consistently statistically significant across the models, reaching the 1% level of significance in the three models based on MIPT data. Participation and executive constraints are not significant in any of the models.[2] This is an important difference from the results reported in Li (2005) and other articles that analyze the relationship between democratic rule and terrorist attacks. Recall that Li finds that both of these variables are statistically significant and signed in the expected directions across specifications. Li does not include a measure of physical integrity rights or a dependent variable that counts domestic terrorist attacks, which might account for this difference.[3] Among the control variables, population is significant in three of the models and GDP per capita is significant in two. Civil war is significant in all of the models. This is broadly consistent with the findings of Lai (2007). However, and in contrast to Lai's findings, international war is a statistically significant independent variable only in the model using ITERATE to measure terrorism.

Figure 7.1 reports simulation results from the CLARIFY utility developed by King et al. (2000) to evaluate the substantive influence of changes in the value of respect for physical integrity rights on levels of change of the dependent variables. For these simulations, we set all of the other independent variables to their mean except for the dummy variables civil war and international war (both set to 0, indicating the absence of such conflicts) and the dummy variable durable (set to 0, indicting that the country is not a democracy or has been a democracy for less than 15 years).[4] Figure 7.1 depicts the percentage decrease in the expected number of terrorist attacks a country will experience when government respect for physical integrity rights is increased by one unit. Changes in government respect for physical integrity rights have a noticeable negative influence on all the measures of terrorism. The effect is particularly large for improvements in physical integrity rights from low levels. Raising respect for physical integrity rights from its lowest level of 0 by only one unit reduces the expected number of terrorist attacks by between 17% and 40%, depending on the measure of terrorism. Smaller but still substantial reductions in terrorism result from further improvements in physical integrity rights. These marginal changes diminish in size at higher levels of initial government respect for physical integrity.

The conclusion we draw from these baseline models is that physical integrity rights have a statistically significant and substantively large influence on the number of terrorist attacks.

■　■　■

Conclusions and Implications

The evidence presented here provides support for our hypothesis that abuse of physical integrity rights promotes terrorism. This relationship is robust across a range of measures of terrorism and model specifications and the inclusion of control variables including civil war, democracy, other human rights, and measures of government counterterrorism capacity. This finding has important implications for how we study the origins of terrorism and for counterterrorism policy.

Figure 7.1 Percentage Decrease in Expected Number of Terrorist Attacks for One-Unit Increases in Physical Integrity Index

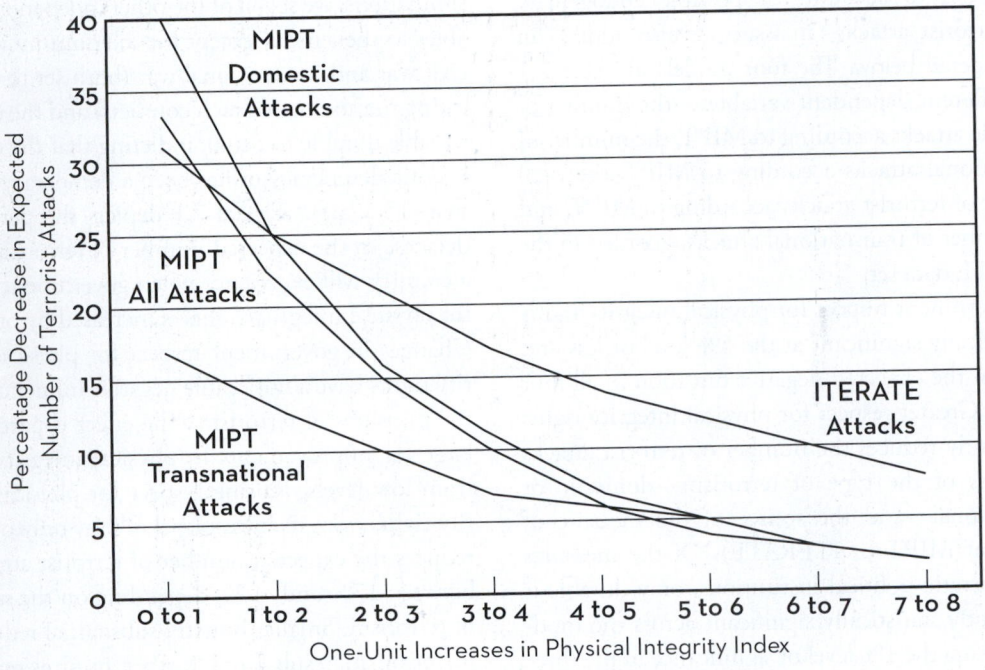

Our theory and findings differ from existing scholarly research on the causes of terrorism. Much of this work has drawn attention to the relationships between institutions of democratic governance and terrorism. Less attention has been paid to how the actual behavior of the government, such as its degree of respect for human rights, itself influences the incidence of terrorist attack the state exposes itself to. The relationships between institutional measures of democratic rule and terrorism largely disappear when one considers government behavior in the form of respect for physical integrity rights. It appears, then, that how governments exercise their power, rather than how they are structured, is the decisive political factor determining a society's vulnerability to terrorism. The fact that the empirical relationships between physical integrity rights and terrorism are quite robust suggests that human rights should be taken more seriously by those interested in understanding the causes of terrorism. Future research could seek to build on this insight in a number of ways. The release to researchers of more and better data on terrorism would allow future researchers to address the possibility of an endogenous relationship between terror and physical integrity rights with more sophisticated statistical techniques. Researchers might also use process tracing of carefully selected cases to address these concerns about endogeneity (for an example of this approach in a different context, see You, 2005). Other research could investigate how repression of physical integrity rights influences the decision making of specific terrorist groups. Is repression an important motive for the formation of terrorist groups? Do terrorist groups persuade potential supporters to join by drawing attention to government abuse of physical integrity rights? Does an increase in such abuse make terrorist groups more effective in enlisting recruits, raising funds, gathering intelligence on targets and on the government's counterterrorism efforts, and garnering shelter and logistical support from their constituent population? Our article suggests that the answers to all of these questions are yes, but the research design we employ does not allow us to investigate decision-making dynamics of terrorist groups and leaders or how important physical integrity abuses are compared to other factors. The basic hypothesis we advance here could be made considerably richer and more nuanced by sophisticated qualitative or case study research on how human rights abuses influence the activities of terrorist groups.

The findings of this article also lead to two suggestions about how governments might craft more effective counterterrorism policy. First, governments that prioritize counterterrorism should carefully protect physical integrity rights. For example, our findings lend support to the contention that the American government's violation of physical integrity rights—in the form of extrajudicial detention, the use of "harsh interrogation techniques" by American personnel, and the rendering of suspected terrorists to countries that torture them—is counterproductive. Such abuses empower terrorists by giving them the opportunity to accuse the United States of brutality, to downplay the atrocity of the violence they themselves commit, to demonstrate their willingness to stand up to a powerful state, to seek the sympathy of potential supporters, to damage sympathy for the United States within the international community, and to discourage multinational cooperation in the war on terror. More scrupulous adherence to the rule of law and basic human rights standards would allow the United States to prevent its terrorist opponents from effectively deploying these arguments. This suggestion has particular force for regimes that engage in widespread abuses of physical integrity rights. Our results suggest that the governments that abuse the most have the most to gain in terms of counterterrorism from reducing repression by even small degrees. Recall from Figure 7.1 that countries with the lowest levels of respect for physical integrity rights see the largest drop in terrorism when their human rights records improve even slightly. We recognize that

this advice to avoid physical integrity abuses may impose political costs on some governments. Some autocratic regimes engage in such abuses as a way to maintain their hold on power. Political forces in democracies may seek to weaken legal protections for human rights in a misguided attempt to counter terrorism or to demonstrate their "toughness" to constituents. Authorities who act on these pressures need to recognize that doing so likely will fuel rather than dampen support for terrorism.

Second, powerful states such as the United States use their diplomatic, military, and economic resources to counter terrorism that originates overseas. Our research suggests that the most effective way to achieve this objective over the long run is by promoting the protection of human rights in countries that experience much terrorism. Again, the gains from this would be, on average, largest in countries that engage in widespread abuses of human rights. It is often argued that powerful countries can best reduce terrorism in the rest of the world by promoting democracy or by encouraging economic development. These are certainly worthwhile goals. But our data analysis leads us to conclude that their influence on terrorism is at best uncertain. We found little evidence that democratic institutions or economic development alone reduces terrorism when one also accounts for the government's human rights behavior. This suggests that the United States and the European Union might find that a more effective way to reduce terrorism would be to use their political and economic leverage to convince other governments to refrain from abusing physical integrity rights. An additional advantage of this proposal is that small or moderate changes in physical integrity rights are easier to achieve than is full-scale democratization or economic development. Successful democratization, for example, requires wide-ranging changes to political institutions, including the conduct of free and fair elections, the creation of multiple political parties, the effective separation of powers among the executive and legislative, and a legal system able to institute the rule of law in at least minimal ways. Improvements in physical integrity rights involve fewer changes to the structure of the political system and thus are easier for even authoritarian governments to implement while still retaining power.

NOTES

1. When the analysis was conducted, the Memorial Institute for the Prevention of Terrorism (MIPT) database was made available to the public online. Since the end of 2007, MIPT has been removed and is in the process of being integrated into the Global Terrorism Database compiled by the National Consortium for Study of Terrorism and Responses to Terrorism (http://www.start.umd.edu/gtd/).

2. Multicollinearity among independent variables does not appear to be a problem in these models. We calculated the mean variance inflation factor for the models reported in Table 7.1 using the collin command in Stata. The mean variance inflation factor for the International Terrorism: Attributes of Terrorist Events (ITERATE) model was 1.76, and those for the MIPT models were all under 2.5.

3. We re-estimated the model using ITERATE data as the dependent variable but did not include the physical integrity measure as an independent variable. This specification is similar to that reported in Li (2005). All of the independent variables except durable and participation were statistically significant at the 1% level and signed in the expected direction. Participation had a p score of .19. We suspect that this last difference from the results reported in Li is because of the fact that our data cover only the period since 1981, whereas Li's data begin in 1968.

4. Results were similar to those reported in this paragraph when the value of durable was set to 1.

REFERENCES

Abadie, Alberto. (2006). Poverty, political freedom, and the roots of terrorism. *American Economic Review, 96*, 50–56.

Abrahms, Max. (2007). Why democracies make superior counterterrorists. *Security Studies, 16*, 223–253.

Branigan, Tania. (2007, June 8). Brown sets out tougher plans in anti-terror battle. *The Guardian*, p. 1.

Bueno de Mesquita, Bruce, Cherif, Feryal Marie, Downs, George W., & Smith, Alastair. (2005). Thinking inside the box: A closer look at democracy and human rights. *International Studies Quarterly, 49*, 439–458.

Bueno de Mesquita, Ethan. (2005). The quality of terror. *American Journal of Political Science, 49*, 515–530.

Cingranelli, David L., & Richards, David L. (1999). Measuring the level, pattern, and sequence of government respect for physical integrity rights. *International Studies Quarterly, 43*, 407–417.

Cingranelli, David L., & Richards, David L. (2004). *The Cingranelli-Richards (CIRI) human rights dataset.* Retrieved December 2, 2009, from http://www.humanrights data.org.

Crenshaw, Martha. (1991). How terrorism declines. *Terrorism and Political Violence, 3*, 379–399.

Dahl, Robert. (1971). *Polyarchy: Participation and opposition.* New Haven, CT: Yale University Press.

Davenport, Christian, & Armstrong, David A. (2004). Democracy and the violation of human rights. *American Journal of Political Science, 48*, 538–554.

Dreher, Axel, Gasebner, Martin, & Siemers, Lars-H.R. (in press). Does terror threaten human rights? Evidence from panel data. *Journal of Law and Economics.*

Eubank, William, & Weinberg, Leonard. (2001). Terrorism and democracy: Perpetrators and victims. *Terrorism and Political Violence, 13,* 155–164.

Eyerman, Joe. (1998). Terrorism and democratic states: Soft targets or accessible systems. *International Interactions, 24*, 151–170.

Finnemore, Martha, & Sikkink, Kathryn. (1998). International norm dynamics and political change. *International Organization, 52*, 887–917.

Francisco, Ronald. (1996). Coercion and protest: An empirical test in two democratic states. *American Journal of Political Science, 40*, 1179–1204.

Gearty, Connor. (2007). Terrorism and human rights. *Government and Opposition, 42*, 340-362.

Gurr, Ted, & Moore, Will. (1997). Ethnopolitical rebellion: A cross-sectional analysis of the 1980s with risk assessments for the 1990s. *American Journal of Political Science, 41,* 1079–1103.

Hashim, Ahmed S. (2006). *Insurgency and counterinsurgency in Iraq.* Ithaca, NY: Cornell University Press.

Hibbs, Douglas A. (1973). *Mass political violence: A cross-national causal analysis.* New York: John Wiley.

Hoffman, Bruce, & McCormick, Gordon. (2004). Terrorism, signaling and suicide attack. *Studies in Conflict and Terrorism, 27,* 243–281.

Hoffman, Paul. (2004). Human rights and terrorism. *Human Rights Quarterly, 26,* 932–955.

Holsti, Kalevi J. (2000). Political causes of humanitarian emergencies. In Wayne Nafziger, Frances Stewart, & Raimo Vayrynen (Eds.), *War, hunger and displacement: The origins of humanitarian emergencies* (pp. 239–282). Oxford, UK: Oxford University Press.

Horne, Alistair. (1979). *Savage war of peace: Algeria 1954–1962.* New York: Viking.

Ivanova, K., & Sandler, T. (2006). CBRN incidents: Political regimes, perpetrators, and targets. *Terrorism and Political Violence, 18,* 423–448.

Joes, Anthony James. (2004). *Resisting rebellion: The history and politics of counterinsurgency.* Lexington: University of Kentucky Press.

Kalyvas, Stathis. (2004). The paradox of terrorism in civil war. *Journal of Ethics, 8,* 97–138.

Keck, Margaret, & Sikkink, Kathryn. (1998). *Activists beyond borders: Advocacy networks in international politics.* Ithaca, NY: Cornell University Press.

King, Gary, Tomz, Michael, & Wittenberg, Jason. (2000). Making the most of statistical analyses: Improving interpretation and presentation. *American Journal of Political Science, 44,* 341–355.

Kurrild-Klitgaard, Peter, Justesen, Mogens, & Klemmensen, Robert. (2006). The political economy of freedom, democracy and transnational terrorism. *Public Choice, 128,* 289–315.

Lai, Brian. (2007). Draining the swamp: An empirical examination of the production of international terrorism, 1968–1998. *Conflict Management and Peace Science, 24,* 297–310.

Li, Quan. (2005). Does democracy promote or reduce transnational terrorist events? *Journal of Conflict Resolution, 49,* 278–297.

Li, Quan, & Schaub, Drew. (2004). Economic globalization and transnational terrorist incidents: A pooled time series analysis. *Journal of Conflict Resolution, 48,* 230–258.

Merom, Gil. (2003). *How democracies lose small wars.* Cambridge, UK: Cambridge University Press.

Mickolus, Edward F. (2006). *International terrorism: Attributes of terrorist events* [Computer file]. Dunn Loring, VA: Vinyard Software.

Mueller, Edward N., & Weede, Erich. (1990). Cross-national variation in political violence: A rational action approach. *Journal of Conflict Resolution, 34,* 624–651.

Neumann, Peter R., Lawrence, Michael, & Smith, Rowan. (2007). *The strategy of terrorism: How it works, and why it fails.* London: Routledge.

Pape, Robert A. (2003). The strategic logic of suicide terrorism. *American Political Science Review, 97,* 343–361.

Piazza, James A. (2008). Do democracy and free markets protect us from terrorism? *International Politics, 45,* 72–91.

Rice, Edward. (1988). *Wars of the third kind: Conflict in underdeveloped countries.* Berkeley: University of California Press.

Schmid, Alex. (1992). Terrorism and democracy. *Terrorism and Political Violence, 4,*14–25.

Wade, Sara Jackson, & Reiter, Dan. (2007). Does democracy matter? Regime type and suicide terrorism. *Journal of Conflict Resolution, 51,* 329–348.

Walsh, James Igoe. (2010). *The international politics of intelligence sharing.* New York: Columbia University Press.

Wimmer, Andreas. (1997). Who owns the state? Understanding ethnic conflict in post-colonial societies. *Nations and Nationalism, 3,* 631–665.

You, Jong-Sung. (2005, September). *Embedded autonomy or crony capitalism?* Paper prepared for the annual meeting of the American Political Science Association, Washington, DC.

8 DEVELOPED DEMOCRACIES

This chapter explores some of the aspects and challenges of developed democracies, countries that have stable democratic regimes, a high level of economic development, and extensive civil rights and liberties. It focuses specifically on three questions:

1. What enables developed democracies to emerge and thrive?
2. How do institutional differences among developed democracies affect their politics and policies?
3. Can developed democracies continue to promote equality—for example, through generous welfare states—in the twenty-first century?

By many measures, the United States was the first developed democracy. Universal male suffrage—albeit almost always restricted to free white males—had been enacted by the 1830s in almost all U.S. states, whereas in Britain even the 1832 Reform Act extended the franchise to only about one in five adult males. Institutionalization in the United States was advanced, and per capita income (according to the economic historian Angus Maddison) already exceeded that of contemporary France. The liberal French nobleman, intellectual, and politician Alexis de Tocqueville visited the United States in 1831 and set out to explain to his European compatriots why and how American democracy worked. He came to two firm conclusions, well set out in the introduction to his 1835 classic, *Democracy in America*: (1) social equality led inevitably to democracy; and (2) equality, at least in Europe and America, was everywhere increasing.

Tocqueville saw economic growth and prosperity as but one of the causes of social equalization, and thus of democracy. However, the sociologist and political scientist Seymour Martin Lipset, in his classic *Political Man* (1960), first perceived what is now taken as a commonplace: that although other factors still matter, richer countries are highly likely to be both more equal and more democratic. Wealth alone, through a series of processes that Lipset explored, leads normally to democracy.

Lipset's theory thus predicted that, as countries become richer, they also become more democratic. That picture came to seem simplistic, and some (most notably Przeworski and Limongi [1997]) argued that, at most, wealthy societies were less likely to relapse to authoritarian rule once they had democratized. In the 2003 article excerpted here, Carles Boix and Susan C. Stokes found that, once one excluded the Soviet satellites and the oil-rich countries, wealth did seem to lead almost inevitably to democratization: democratization, in this sense, seemed still to be "endogenous" (having an internal cause). Subjecting that hypothesis to a yet stricter test, however—did *increases* in wealth correlate with *increases* in democracy?—Daron Acemoglu and his associates contended in "Income and Democracy" (2008) that such a correlation held only in the very long run. The cross-sectional, or "snapshot," correlation between wealth and democracy, while true, was (they held) spurious: both wealth and democracy seem to be caused by some other factor, most likely (these authors argue) better institutions and property rights.

Tocqueville's even more basic premise was that economic equality fostered democracy. Like Thomas Jefferson, he held that unequal societies could not become (or remain) democratic. More recent students, including Boix, have held the same. In their 2014 book, *Inequality and Democratization*, Ben W. Ansell and David J. Samuels draw on a variety of historical data to argue that just the opposite is true: democratizing societies usually exhibit high and increasing levels of economic inequality, at least as measured by the standard Gini index of inequality (where an index of zero indicates that everyone obtains the same income, while an index of one would mean that only one person receives all of society's income). Extremely poor societies, even where a small upper class is very wealthy, display low Gini indices; only as a new middle class, produced by commerce or industrialization, becomes wealthy does the Gini index rise; and the newly wealthy, fearing depredation by the traditional elites more than expropriation by the masses, often press for democratization as a better guarantee of the rule of law.

As we saw in Chapter 5, democracies in general divide between "majoritarian" and "proportional" (PR) electoral systems. Developed democracies also differ on this dimension: the United States, the United Kingdom, Canada, Australia, France, and Japan are majoritarian (or mostly so), whereas most of the other developed democracies (including virtually all of the smaller ones) use PR. An interesting sidelight is that several of the developed democracies have recently changed their electoral systems: France used PR for one election in 1986, then reverted to a majoritarian system; in the early 1990s Italy and Japan changed from mostly proportional systems to mostly majoritarian ones. At almost the same time, New Zealand replaced a "first-past-the-post" majoritarian system with PR, and Italy has since shifted back to a mostly PR system.

What are countries actually choosing when they adopt (or retain) one electoral system or another? As Chapter 5 emphasized, a majoritarian system normally (as in the United States) allows only two major parties to survive, whereas PR encourages a multiplicity of parties. This regularity is so powerful and has such strong causal properties that it is called, after its discoverer, Duverger's Law—one of the very few causal laws in political science. Maurice Duverger's original 1951 explanation of it has never really been surpassed, and its essence is presented in this chapter. Note particularly how Duverger shows that, in a majoritarian system, the rise of a new "third" party (e.g., Labour in Britain between 1900 and 1930) normally dooms the old "second" party (in that case, the Liberals) to insignificance, and how the introduction of PR has often allowed the declining second party to survive, albeit much diminished.

Since Duverger, numerous studies have shown PR to have one other very important effect, this one on policy: PR is associated with much higher levels of welfare spending, greater redistribution of income, and hence greater equality. But why? Perhaps voters in PR countries just happen to prefer higher levels of welfare spending. As early as 2002, the comparativist Bingham Powell showed that this was unlikely to be true: rather, given identical voter preferences, majoritarian systems were likely to produce more right-wing (i.e., less redistributionist) policies, whereas PR would more reliably produce the policy that voters (or, more precisely, the median voter) actually wanted, which generally entailed greater redistribution and welfare spending. In a yet more fundamental contribution, reproduced here in abridged form, Torben Iversen and David Soskice (2006) advanced powerful logic and evidence about how exactly this result came about: given identical voter preferences, a PR system was far likelier to produce a "center-left" coalition, a majoritarian one a "center-right" government, with the latter adopting far less redistributionist policies and lower levels of welfare expenditure. As they note, fully three-quarters of the governments chosen under PR systems in the postwar period have been center-left, whereas three-quarters of those elected under majoritarian systems have been center-right.[1]

We commonly imagine that generous welfare states curb incentives and slow economic growth. But, as their leading student Peter Lindert has shown, welfare states seem to be almost "a free lunch": they are *not* associated with slower growth or less efficiency.[2] A deeper reason that welfare states work, and may even make their societies *more* competitive, is suggested by Margarita Estévez-Abe and her coauthors in their contribution to the seminal *Varieties of Capitalism* (2001). Many of the most globally competitive economies, they suggest, depend on high-quality, specialized production that requires well-trained workers with firm- or sector-specific skills. They contend that workers will invest in acquiring those skills only if generous policies of social insurance buffer them against transient market downturns or permanent obsolescence. Hence generous welfare states (such as Sweden) tend to have workers with highly specialized skills, whereas less generous ones (such as the United States) have workforces with more general, transferable skills. As logical side effects, the generous welfare states are economically more equal and encourage greater achievement by less talented youth; paradoxically, the less redistributionist countries encourage greater gender equality.

NOTES

1. The Stanford political scientist Jonathan Rodden has developed an elegant theory and much supporting evidence to explain this phenomenon: supporters of Left parties, in almost all countries, are heavily concentrated in industrial districts. Hence, even seemingly neutral drawing of district lines leaves Left parties with overwhelming majorities

in relatively few districts, whereas parties of the Right win slimmer majorities in many districts. Hence the Left typically wins a smaller share of seats in majoritarian systems than it does of votes, whereas in PR systems its share of seats must closely reflect its share of the vote.

2. Peter Lindert, *Growing Public: Social Spending and Economic Growth since the Eighteenth Century*, 2 vols. (Cambridge: Cambridge University Press, 2004).

Alexis de Tocqueville
AUTHOR'S INTRODUCTION

Among the novel objects that attracted my attention during my stay in the United States, nothing struck me more forcibly than the general equality of condition among the people. I readily discovered the prodigious influence that this primary fact exercises on the whole course of society; it gives a peculiar direction to public opinion and a peculiar tenor to the laws; it imparts new maxims to the governing authorities and peculiar habits to the governed.

I soon perceived that the influence of this fact extends far beyond the political character and the laws of the country, and that it has no less effect on civil society than on the government; it creates opinions, gives birth to new sentiments, founds novel customs, and modifies whatever it does not produce. The more I advanced in the study of American society, the more I perceived that this equality of condition is the fundamental fact from which all others seem to be derived and the central point at which all my observations constantly terminated.

I then turned my thoughts to our own hemisphere, and thought that I discerned there something analogous to the spectacle which the New World presented to me. I observed that equality of condition, though it has not there reached the extreme limit which it seems to have attained in the United States, is constantly approaching it; and that the democracy which governs the American communities appears to be rapidly rising into power in Europe.

Hence I conceived the idea of the book that is now before the reader.

It is evident to all alike that a great democratic revolution is going on among us, but all do not look at it in the same light. To some it appears to be novel but accidental, and, as such, they hope it may still be checked; to others it seems irresistible, because it is the most uniform, the most ancient, and the most permanent tendency that is to be found in history.

I look back for a moment on the situation of France seven hundred years ago, when the territory was divided among a small number of families, who were the owners of the soil and the rulers of the inhabitants; the right of governing descended with the family inheritance from generation to generation; force was the only means by which man could act on man; and landed property was the sole source of power.

Soon, however, the political power of the clergy was founded and began to increase: the clergy opened their ranks to all classes, to the poor and the rich, the commoner and the noble; through the church, equality penetrated into the government, and he who as a serf must have vegetated in perpetual bondage took his place as a priest in the midst of nobles, and not infrequently above the heads of kings.

From *Democracy in America* (New York: A. A. Knopf, 1945), pp. 3–16. Author's notes have been omitted.

The different relations of men with one another became more complicated and numerous as society gradually became more stable and civilized. Hence the want of civil laws was felt; and the ministers of law soon rose from the obscurity of the tribunals and their dusty chambers to appear at the court of the monarch, by the side of the feudal barons clothed in their ermine and their mail.

While the kings were ruining themselves by their great enterprises, and the nobles exhausting their resources by private wars, the lower orders were enriching themselves by commerce. The influence of money began to be perceptible in state affairs. The transactions of business opened a new road to power, and the financier rose to a station of political influence in which he was at once flattered and despised.

Gradually enlightenment spread, a reawakening of taste for literature and the arts became evident; intellect and will contributed to success; knowledge became an attribute of government, intelligence a social force; the educated man took part in affairs of state.

The value attached to high birth declined just as fast as new avenues to power were discovered. In the eleventh century, nobility was beyond all price; in the thirteenth, it might be purchased. Nobility was first conferred by gift in 1270, and equality was thus introduced into the government by the aristocracy itself.

In the course of these seven hundred years it sometimes happened that the nobles, in order to resist the authority of the crown or to diminish the power of their rivals, granted some political power to the common people. Or, more frequently, the king permitted the lower orders to have a share in the government, with the intention of limiting the power of the aristocracy.

In France the kings have always been the most active and the most constant of levelers. When they were strong and ambitious, they spared no pains to raise the people to the level of the nobles; when they were temperate and feeble, they allowed the people to rise above themselves. Some assisted democracy by their talents, others by their vices. Louis XI and Louis XIV reduced all ranks beneath the throne to the same degree of subjection; and finally Louis XV descended, himself and all his court, into the dust.

As soon as land began to be held on any other than a feudal tenure, and personal property could in its turn confer influence and power, every discovery in the arts, every improvement in commerce of manufactures, created so many new elements of equality among men. Henceforward every new invention, every new want which it occasioned, and every new desire which craved satisfaction were steps towards a general leveling. The taste for luxury, the love of war, the rule of fashion, and the most superficial as well as the deepest passions of the human heart seemed to cooperate to enrich the poor and to impoverish the rich.

From the time when the exercise of the intellect became a source of strength and of wealth, we see that every addition to science, every fresh truth, and every new idea became a germ of power placed within the reach of the people. Poetry, eloquence, and memory, the graces of the mind, the fire of imagination, depth of thought, and all the gifts which Heaven scatters at a venture turned to the advantage of democracy; and even when they were in the possession of its adversaries, they still served its cause by throwing into bold relief the natural greatness of man. Its conquests spread, therefore, with those of civilization and knowledge; and literature became an arsenal open to all, where the poor and the weak daily resorted for arms.

In running over the pages of our history, we shall scarcely find a single great event of the last seven hundred years that has not promoted equality of condition.

The Crusades and the English wars decimated the nobles and divided their possessions: the municipal corporations introduced democratic liberty into the bosom of feudal monarchy; the invention of firearms equalized the vassal and the noble on the field of battle; the art of printing opened the same resources to the minds of all classes; the post brought knowledge alike to the door of the cottage and to the gate of the palace; and Protestantism proclaimed that all men are equally able to find the road to heaven. The discovery of America opened a thousand new paths to fortune and led obscure adventurers to wealth and power.

If, beginning with the eleventh century, we examine what has happened in France from one half-century to another, we shall not fail to perceive that at the end of each of these periods a twofold revolution has taken place in the state of society. The noble has gone down the social ladder, and the commoner has gone up; the one descends as the other rises. Every half-century brings them nearer to each other, and they will soon meet.

Nor is this peculiar to France. Wherever we look, we perceive the same revolution going on throughout the Christian world.

The various occurrences of national existence have everywhere turned to the advantage of democracy: all men have aided it by their exertions, both those who have intentionally labored in its cause and those who have served it unwittingly; those who have fought for it and even those who have declared themselves its opponents have all been driven along in the same direction, have all labored to one end; some unknowingly and some despite themselves, all have been blind instruments in the hands of God.

The gradual development of the principle of equality is, therefore, a providential fact. It has all the chief characteristics of such a fact: it is universal, it is lasting, it constantly eludes all human interference, and all events as well as all men contribute to its progress.

Would it, then, be wise to imagine that a social movement the causes of which lie so far back can be checked by the efforts of one generation? Can it be believed that the democracy which has overthrown the feudal system and vanquished kings will retreat before tradesmen and capitalists? Will it stop now that it has grown so strong and its adversaries so weak?

Whither, then, are we tending? No one can say, for terms of comparison already fail us. There is greater equality of condition in Christian countries at the present day than there has been at any previous time, in any part of the world, so that the magnitude of what already has been done prevents us from foreseeing what is yet to be accomplished.

The whole book that is here offered to the public has been written under the influence of a kind of religious awe produced in the author's mind by the view of that irresistible revolution which has advanced for centuries in spite of every obstacle and which is still advancing in the midst of the ruins it has caused.

It is not necessary that God himself should speak in order that we may discover the unquestionable signs of his will. It is enough to ascertain what is the habitual course of nature and the constant tendency of events. I know, without special revelation, that the planets move in the orbits traced by the Creator's hand.

If the men of our time should be convinced, by attentive observation and sincere reflection, that the gradual and progressive development of social equality is at once the past and the future of their history, this discovery alone would confer upon the change the sacred character of a divine decree. To attempt to check democracy would be in that case to resist the will of God; and the nations would then be constrained to make the best of the social lot awarded to them by Providence.

The Christian nations of our day seem to me to present a most alarming spectacle; the movement which impels them is already so strong that it cannot be stopped, but it is not yet so rapid that it cannot be guided. Their fate is still in their own hands; but very soon they may lose control.

The first of the duties that are at this time imposed upon those who direct our affairs is to educate democracy, to reawaken, if possible, its religious beliefs; to purify its morals; to mold its actions; to substitute a knowledge of statecraft for its inexperience, and an awareness of its true interest for its blind instincts, to adapt its government to time and place, and to modify it according to men and to conditions. A new science of politics is needed for a new world.

This, however, is what we think of least; placed in the middle of a rapid stream, we obstinately fix our eyes on the ruins that may still be descried upon the shore we have left, while the current hurries us away and drags us backward towards the abyss.

In no country in Europe has the great social revolution that I have just described made such rapid progress as in France; but it has always advanced without guidance. The heads of the state have made no preparation for it, and it has advanced without their consent or without their knowledge. The most powerful, the most intelligent, and the most moral classes of the nation have never attempted to control it in order to guide it. Democracy has consequently been abandoned to its wild instincts, and it has grown up like those children who have no parental guidance, who receive their education in the public streets, and who are acquainted only with the vices and wretchedness of society. Its existence was seemingly unknown when suddenly it acquired supreme power. All then servilely submitted to its caprices; it was worshipped as the idol of strength; and when afterwards it was enfeebled by its own excesses, the legislator conceived the rash project of destroying it, instead of instructing it and correcting its vices. No attempt was made to fit it to govern, but all were bent on excluding it from the government.

The result has been that the democratic revolution has taken place in the body of society without that concomitant change in the laws, ideas, customs, and morals which was necessary to render such a revolution beneficial. Thus we have a democracy without anything to lessen its vices and bring out its natural advantages; and although we already perceive the evils it brings, we are ignorant of the benefits it may confer.

While the power of the crown, supported by the aristocracy, peaceably governed the nations of Europe, society, in the midst of its wretchedness, had several sources of happiness which can now scarcely be conceived or appreciated. The power of a few of his subjects was an insurmountable barrier to the tyranny of the prince; and the monarch, who felt the almost divine character which he enjoyed in the eyes of the multitude, derived a motive for the just use of his power from the respect which he inspired. The nobles, placed high as they were above the people, could take that calm and benevolent interest in their fate which the shepherd feels towards his flock; and without acknowledging the poor as their equals, they watched over the destiny of those whose welfare Providence had entrusted to their care. The people, never having conceived the idea of a social condition different from their own, and never expecting to become equal to their leaders, received benefits from them without discussing their rights. They became attached to them when they were clement and just and submitted to their exactions without resistance or servility, as to the inevitable visitations of the Deity. Custom and usage, moreover, had established certain limits to oppression and founded a sort of law in the very midst of violence.

As the noble never suspected that anyone would attempt to deprive him of the privileges which he believed to be legitimate, and as the serf looked upon his own inferiority as a consequence of the immutable order of nature, it is easy to imagine that some mutual exchange of goodwill took place between two classes so differently endowed by fate. Inequality and wretchedness were then to be found in society, but the souls of neither rank of men were degraded.

Men are not corrupted by the exercise of power or debased by the habit of obedience, but by the exercise of a power which they believe to be illegitimate, and by obedience to a rule which they consider to be usurped and oppressive.

On the one side were wealth, strength, and leisure, accompanied by the pursuit of luxury, the refinements of taste, the pleasures of wit, and the cultivation of the arts; on the other were labor, clownishness, and ignorance. But in the midst of this coarse and ignorant multitude it was not uncommon to meet with energetic passions, generous sentiments, profound religious convictions, and wild virtues.

The social state thus organized might boast of its stability, its power, and, above all, its glory.

But the scene is now changed. Gradually the distinctions of rank are done away with; the barriers that once severed mankind are falling; property is divided, power is shared by many, the light of intelligence spreads, and the capacities of all classes tend towards equality. Society becomes democratic, and the empire of democracy is slowly and peaceably introduced into institutions and customs.

I can conceive of a society in which all men would feel an equal love and respect for the laws of which they consider themselves the authors; in which the authority of the government would be respected as necessary, and not divine; and in which the loyalty of the subject to the chief magistrate would not be a passion, but a quiet and rational persuasion. With every individual in the possession of rights which he is sure to retain, a kind of manly confidence and reciprocal courtesy would arise between all classes, removed alike from pride and servility. The people, well acquainted with their own true interests, would understand that, in order to profit from the advantages of the state, it is necessary to satisfy its requirements. The voluntary association of the citizens might then take the place of the individual authority of the nobles, and the community would be protected from tyranny and license.

I admit that, in a democratic state thus constituted, society would not be stationary. But the impulses of the social body might there be regulated and made progressive. If there were less splendor than in an aristocracy, misery would also be less prevalent; the pleasures of enjoyment might be less excessive, but those of comfort would be more general; the sciences might be less perfectly cultivated, but ignorance would be less common; the ardor of the feelings would be constrained, and the habits of the nation softened; there would be more vices and fewer crimes.

In the absence of enthusiasm and ardent faith, great sacrifices may be obtained from the members of a commonwealth by an appeal to their understanding and their experience; each individual will feel the same necessity of union with his fellows to protect his own weakness; and as he knows that he can obtain their help only on condition of helping them, he will readily perceive that his personal interest is identified with the interests of the whole community. The nation, taken as a whole, will be less brilliant, less glorious, and perhaps less strong; but the majority of the citizens will enjoy a greater degree of prosperity, and the people will remain peaceable, not because they despair of a change for the better, but because they are conscious that they are well off already.

If all the consequences of this state of things were not good or useful, society would at least have appropriated all such as were useful and good; and having once and forever renounced the social advantages of aristocracy, mankind would enter into possession of all the benefits that democracy can offer.

But here it may be asked what we have adopted in the place of those institutions, those ideas, and those customs of our forefathers which we have abandoned.

The spell of royalty is broken, but it has not been succeeded by the majesty of the laws. The people have learned to despise all authority, but they still fear it; and fear now extorts more than was formerly paid from reverence and love.

I perceive that we have destroyed those individual powers which were able, single-handed, to cope with tyranny; but it is the government alone that has inherited all the privileges of which families, guilds, and individuals have been deprived; to the power of a small number of persons, which if it was sometimes oppressive was often conservative, has succeeded the weakness of the whole community.

The division of property has lessened the distance which separated the rich from the poor; but it would seem that, the nearer they draw to each other, the greater is their mutual hatred and the more vehement the envy and the dread with which they resist each other's claims to power; the idea of right does not exist for either party, and force affords to both the only argument for the present and the only guarantee for the future.

The poor man retains the prejudices of his forefathers without their faith, and their ignorance without their virtues; he has adopted the doctrine of self-interest as the rule of his actions without understanding the science that puts it to use; and his selfishness is no less blind than was formerly his devotion to others.

If society is tranquil, it is not because it is conscious of its strength and its well-being, but because it fears its weakness and its infirmities; a single effort may cost it its life. Everybody feels the evil, but no one has courage or energy enough to seek the cure. The desires, the repinings, the sorrows, and the joys of the present time lead to nothing visible or permanent, like the passions of old men, which terminate in impotence.

We have, then, abandoned whatever advantages the old state of things afforded, without receiving any compensation from our present condition; we have destroyed an aristocracy, and we seem inclined to survey its ruins with complacency and to accept them.

The phenomena which the intellectual world presents are not less deplorable. The democracy of France, hampered in its course or abandoned to its lawless passions, has overthrown whatever crossed its path and has shaken all that it has not destroyed. Its empire has not been gradually introduced or peaceably established, but it has constantly advanced in the midst of the disorders and the agitations of a conflict. In the heat of the struggle each partisan is hurried beyond the natural limits of his opinions by the doctrines and the excesses of his opponents, until he loses sight of the end of his exertions, and holds forth in a way which does not correspond to his real sentiments or secret instincts. Hence arises the strange confusion that we are compelled to witness.

I can recall nothing in history more worthy of sorrow and pity than the scenes which are passing before our eyes. It is as if the natural bond that unites the opinions of man to his tastes, and his actions to his principles, was now broken; the harmony that has always been observed between the feelings and the ideas of mankind appears to be dissolved and all the laws of moral analogy to be abolished.

Zealous Christians are still found among us, whose minds are nurtured on the thoughts that pertain to a future life, and who readily espouse the cause of human liberty as the source of all moral greatness. Christianity, which has declared that all men are equal in the sight of God, will not refuse to acknowledge that all citizens are equal in the eye of the law. But, by a strange coincidence of events, religion has been for a time entangled with those institutions which democracy destroys; and it is not infrequently brought to reject the equality which it loves, and to curse as a foe that cause of liberty whose efforts it might hallow by its alliance.

By the side of these religious men I discern others whose thoughts are turned to earth rather than to heaven. These are the partisans of liberty, not only as the source of the noblest virtues, but more especially as the root of all solid advantages; and they sincerely desire to secure its authority, and to impart its blessings to mankind. It is natural that they should hasten to invoke the assistance of religion, for they must know that liberty cannot be established without morality, nor morality without faith. But they have seen religion in the ranks of their adversaries, and they inquire no further; some of them attack it openly, and the rest are afraid to defend it.

In former ages slavery was advocated by the venal and slavish-minded, while the independent and the warm-hearted were struggling without hope to save the liberties of mankind. But men of high and generous character are now to be met with, whose opinions are directly at variance with their inclinations, and who praise that servility and meanness which they have themselves never known. Others, on the contrary, speak of liberty as if they were able to feel its sanctity and its majesty, and loudly claim for humanity those rights which they have always refused to acknowledge.

There are virtuous and peaceful individuals whose pure morality, quiet habits, opulence, and talents fit them to be the leaders of their fellow men. Their love of country is sincere, and they are ready to make the greatest sacrifices for its welfare. But civilization often finds them among its opponents; they confound its abuses with its benefits, and the idea of evil is inseparable in their minds from that of novelty.

Near these I find others whose object is to materialize mankind, to hit upon what is expedient without heeding what is just, to acquire knowledge without faith, and prosperity apart from virtue; claiming to be the champions of modern civilization, they place themselves arrogantly at its head, usurping a place which is abandoned to them, and of which they are wholly unworthy.

Where are we, then?

The religionists are the enemies of liberty, and the friends of liberty attack religion; the high-minded and the noble advocate bondage, and the meanest and most servile preach independence; honest and enlightened citizens are opposed to all progress, while men without patriotism and without principle put themselves forward as the apostles of civilization and intelligence.

Has such been the fate of the centuries which have preceded our own? and has man always inhabited a world like the present, where all things are not in their proper relationships, where virtue is without genius, and genius without honor; where the love of order is confused with a taste for oppression, and the holy cult of freedom with a contempt of law; where the light thrown by conscience on human actions is dim, and where nothing seems to be any longer forbidden or allowed, honorable or shameful, false or true?

I cannot believe that the Creator made man to leave him in an endless struggle with the intellectual wretchedness that surrounds us. God destines a calmer and a more certain future to the communities of Europe. I am ignorant of his designs, but I shall not cease to believe in them because I cannot fathom them, and I had rather mistrust my own capacity than his justice.

There is one country in the world where the great social revolution that I am speaking of seems to have nearly reached its natural limits. It has been effected with ease and simplicity; say rather that this country is reaping the fruits of the democratic revolution which we are undergoing, without having had the revolution itself.

The emigrants who colonized the shores of America in the beginning of the seventeenth century somehow separated the democratic principle from all the principles that it had to contend with in the old communities of Europe, and transplanted it alone to the New World. It has there been able to spread in perfect freedom and peaceably to determine the character of the laws by influencing the manners of the country.

It appears to me beyond a doubt that, sooner or later, we shall arrive, like the Americans, at an almost complete equality of condition. But I do not conclude from this that we shall ever be necessarily led to draw the same political consequences which the Americans have derived from a similar social organization. I am far from supposing that they have chosen the only form of government which a democracy may adopt; but as the generating cause of laws and manners in the two countries is the same, it is of immense interest for us to know what it has produced in each of them.

It is not, then, merely to satisfy a curiosity, however legitimate, that I have examined America; my wish has been to find there instruction by which we may ourselves profit. Whoever should imagine that I have intended to write a panegyric would be strangely mistaken, and on reading this book he will perceive that such was not my design; nor has it been my object to advocate any form of government in particular, for I am of the opinion that absolute perfection is rarely to be found in any system of laws. I have not even pretended to judge whether the social revolution, which I believe to be irresistible, is advantageous or prejudicial to mankind. I have acknowledged this revolution as a fact already accomplished, or on the eve of its accomplishment; and I have selected the nation, from among those which have undergone it, in which its development has been the most peaceful and the most complete, in order to discern its natural consequences and to find out, if possible, the means of rendering it profitable to mankind. I confess that in America I saw more than America; I sought there the image of democracy itself, with its inclinations, its character, its prejudices, and its passions, in order to learn what we have to fear or to hope from its progress.

In the first part of this work I have attempted to show the distinction that democracy, dedicated to its inclinations and tendencies and abandoned almost without restraint to its instincts, gave to the laws the course it impressed on the government, and in general the control which it exercised over affairs of state. I have sought to discover the evils and the advantages which it brings. I have examined the safeguards used by the Americans to direct it, as well as those that they have not adopted, and I have undertaken to point out the factors which enable it to govern society.

My object was to portray, in a second part, the influence which the equality of conditions and democratic government in America exercised on civil society, on habits, ideas, and customs; but I grew less enthusiastic about carrying out this plan. Before I could have completed the task which I set for myself, my work would have become purposeless. Someone else would before long set forth to the public the principal traits of the American character and, delicately cloaking a serious picture, lend to the truth a charm which I should not have been able to equal.

I do not know whether I have succeeded in making known what I saw in America, but I am certain that such has been my sincere desire, and that I have never, knowingly, molded facts to ideas, instead of ideas to facts.

Whenever a point could be established by the aid of written documents, I have had recourse to the original text, and to the most authentic and reputable works. I have cited my authorities in the notes, and anyone may verify them. Whenever opinions, political customs, or remarks on the manners of the country were concerned, I have endeavored to consult the most informed men I met with. If the point in question was important or doubtful, I was not satisfied with one witness, but I formed my opinion on the evidence of several witnesses. Here the reader must necessarily rely upon my word. I could frequently have cited names which either are known to him or deserve to be so in support of my assertions; but I have carefully abstained from this practice. A stranger frequently hears important truths at the fireside of his host, which the latter would perhaps conceal from the ear of friendship; he consoles himself with his guest for the silence to which he is restricted, and the shortness of the traveler's stay takes away all fear of an indiscretion. I carefully noted every conversation of this nature as soon as it occurred, but these notes will never leave my writing-case. I had rather injure the success of my statements than add my name to the list of those strangers who repay generous hospitality they have received by subsequent chagrin and annoyance.

■ ■ ■

Carles Boix and Susan C. Stokes

ENDOGENOUS DEMOCRATIZATION

Introduction

Are rich dictatorships more likely than poor dictatorships to collapse and be replaced by democracies? Consider, for example, Chile, which in 1985 had a per capita gross domestic product (GDP) of $3,400 and was under dictatorship, and Benin, which in the same year had a per capita income of about one-third of Chile's, $1,108, and was also under dictatorship. Setting aside other differences between these countries, did their relative levels of development make a transition to democracy more likely in Chile than in Benin?

Anyone who has followed recent scholarship would be likely to answer no. This is the answer that would follow from Adam Przeworski and Fernando Limongi's "Modernization: Theories and Facts," a study that hit the field of political development like a bolt of lightning and immediately changed the landscape.[1] In it they reconsider the classic proposition that economic development favors democracy, identifying an ambiguity in this proposition. Why do we observe a higher proportion of democracies among rich countries than among poor countries? Is it because development increases the likelihood that poor countries will undergo a transition to democracy? They call this an "endogenous" theory. Or is it because development makes democracies, once established, less likely to fall to dictatorships? They call this an "exogenous" theory. The conceptual distinction is brilliant, and Przeworski and Limongi offer evidence that the exogenous theory holds and the endogenous one fails.

Their conclusion has been deeply influential among social scientists and policy analysts. In a review of Przeworski and Limongi's later book (coauthored with Michael E. Alvarez and José Antonio Cheibub), which restates the rejection of endogenous democrati-

tization, David Brown writes: "In a convincing fashion, the authors argue that modernization theory (at least its endogenous variant) has no empirical basis. Put simply, the probability that any given country will become democratic does not change as its level of income rises."[2] Arguing that the U.S. should continue its embargo against Cuba, Juan López dismisses the counter-argument that trade will promote economic development, which in turn will help Cuba democratize. Citing Przeworski and Limongi, López writes: "Countries under dictatorial regimes are not more likely to experience a transition to democracy as they reach higher levels of economic development."[3]

We challenge Przeworski and Limongi's refutation of endogenous democratization on both theoretical and empirical grounds. First we show that to sustain the conceptual distinction between endogenous and exogenous democratization, one would need a theory in which development induces actors in democracies to sustain that system but does not induce actors in a dictatorship to change to democracy. Przeworski and Limongi fail to provide a persuasive theory linking development to democracy only under the condition of a preexisting democracy.

Having challenged Przeworski and Limongi on theoretical grounds, we then reconsider their empirical case against endogenous democratization. In their 1997 article they estimate the probability at discrete income levels that a dictatorship will collapse and become a democracy. Finding that these probabilities fail to increase monotonically as income rises, they conclude that they have refuted endogenous democratization. In the later study with Alvarez and Cheibub, they use econometric tools on observations pooled across their full data set to estimate the effect of income on the probability of transitions to and from democracy.[4] Their analysis

From *World Politics* 55 (July 2003), pp. 517–49.

reveals a small but significant endogenous effect: at higher levels of income, a transition to democracy becomes more likely. Seemingly reluctant to embrace this result, however, they focus instead on the probabilities disaggregated by income levels.

We successfully replicate these results and then examine their robustness in three ways. First, we show that in the sample Przeworski and his colleagues analyze, development in poor and middle-income countries increases the probability of democracy for both endogenous and exogenous reasons: development increases both the probability of the transition to democracy and the probability that an existing democracy will sustain itself. The endogenous effect of development is attenuated at high levels of income. This attenuation does not argue against the endogenous model but merely reflects the small sample size and the accumulated effects of development at lower levels. Second, we correct a problem of sample selection by extending the statistical analysis to a larger sample of observations that starts in the mid-nineteenth century. This reanalysis reveals a large endogenous effect, associated with the earlier wave of democratization in Western Europe. By restricting their analysis to post-1950 cases, Przeworski, Limongi, and their associates underestimate the endogenous effect of development on transitions to democracy. Third, we estimate a model with additional theoretically appropriate controls. These controls reveal that economic development has a strong endogenous effect on democratization.

The Theory

Although Przeworski and Limongi's article is unabashedly empirical and conceptual, it includes a brief theoretical discussion about the relationship between democracy and development.[5] We quote their "intuitive story" in full:

> Suppose that the political forces competing over the distribution of income choose between complying with the verdicts of democratic com-

petition, in which case each can expect to get some share of total income, or risking a fight over dictatorship, which is costly but which gives the victor all of the income. Now suppose that the marginal utility of consumption is lower at higher levels of consumption. Thus the gain from winning the struggle for dictatorship is smaller. In turn, if the production function has diminishing marginal returns in capital stock, the "catch-up" from destroying a part of it during the war for dictatorship is faster at lower levels of wealth. Hence, in poor countries the value of becoming a dictator is greater and the accumulated cost of destroying capital stock is lower. In wealthy countries, by contrast, the gain from getting all rather than a part of total income is smaller and the recuperation from destruction is slower. Hence, struggle for dictatorship is more attractive in poor countries.[6]

If we are to sustain theoretically the empirical finding that development makes already-existing democracies more stable but does not make dictatorships more likely to democratize, then the initial regime condition of our theoretical model matters a lot. At the beginning of Przeworski and Limongi's story, the regime in place appears to be a poorly institutionalized democracy, one in danger of reverting to dictatorship. But they need two stories. The first would assume a democracy and would have to show that the actors become increasingly likely to stick with democracy as the economy grows. The second would assume a dictatorship and would have to show that actors are not more likely to choose democracy as the economy grows.

Graphically, this theory would have to support the functional forms displayed in Figure 8.1, which depicts per capita income on the horizontal axis and the probability of regime transition on the vertical axis. Whereas the probability of a democratic breakdown (P_{DA}) is negatively correlated with per capita income, the probability of a transition to democracy (P_{AD}) is independent of the level of development.

We formalize both stories in the appendix. In one the status quo is dictatorship; in the other the

Figure 8.1 The Exogenous Theory of Regime Change

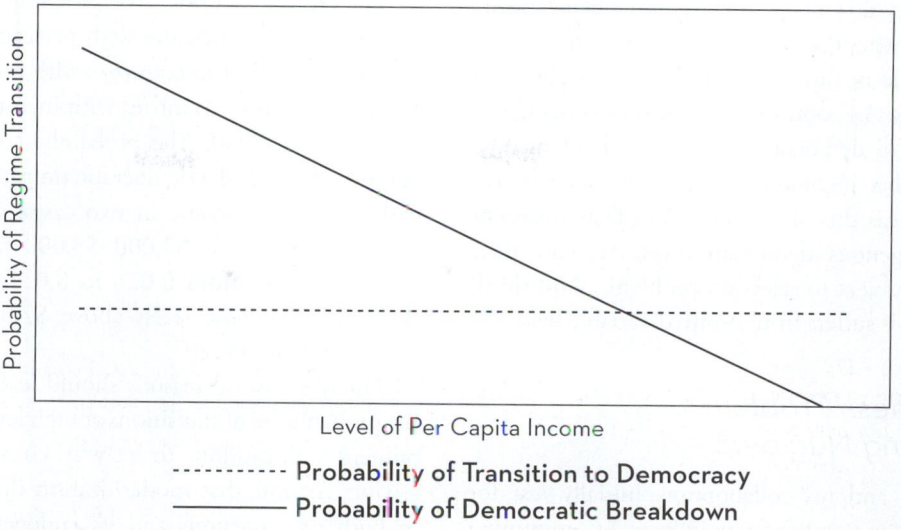

status quo is democracy. In the former case, the dictator decides whether to hold elections or continue under dictatorship. If the dictator chooses not to democratize, then the opposing faction must decide whether to acquiesce to the dictator's rule or fight to take over the dictatorship. When the status quo is democracy, the ruling party decides whether to hold a new round of elections or fight for dictatorial powers. Either choice sets off a struggle, either to win elections or to win the fight for dictatorial powers. Following Przeworski and Limongi's intuitions, we assume that the fight for dictatorship is costly to both sides and that the utility they derive from income declines as income grows.[7]

We find that when the status quo is democracy, income growth does increase the stability of democracy (or at least it does so under certain assumptions about the likely outcomes of each type of struggle—whether by elections or by war—and about how the pie is divided between the winners and losers of elections). But when the status quo is dictatorship, the results are the same. Economic growth increases the incentives for the ruling faction to democratize (under the same conditions that apply to the first

game). Hence, Przeworski and Limongi's intuitive story fails to produce the theoretical underpinnings for the idea that development favors democracy exogenously but not endogenously.

Having suggested that Przeworski and Limongi's intuitive story actually predicts that development will cause democracy under initial conditions of both democracy and dictatorship, we show in the next section that the facts accord with this theoretical prediction. Development is both an endogenous and an exogenous cause of democracy.

The Facts

To review Przeworski and Limongi's conclusions: "[There] are no grounds to believe that economic development breeds democracies." The higher frequency of democracy among high-income countries is fully explained by the fact that "once established, democracies are likely to die in poor countries and certain to survive in wealthy ones."[8] Przeworski et al.'s version of this conclusion is equally emphatic: "[T]he reason [why wealth and democracy go together] is not that democracies are more likely to emerge when countries develop under authoritarianism, but that, however they do emerge, they are more likely to survive in countries that are already developed."[9]

We argue in this section that their findings fail on three tests of robustness. First, they observe few transitions to democracy at high levels of income and infer that income does not cause such transitions, whereas this observation is in fact consistent with endogenous democratization. Second, their sample is subject to selection problems. And third, their analysis suffers from omitted variable bias.

Robustness Problem 1: Dwindling Numbers

Przeworski and his collaborators initially test for exogenous and endogenous effects by examining the probabilities of transitions from democracy to authoritarianism and from authoritarianism to democracy at discrete levels of per capita GDP.[10] Figure 8.2 is a graphic representation of data taken from *Democracy and Development*.[11] The table and figure indicate that the probability of a democratic breakdown falls with development, from 0.12

when per capita income is below $1,000 to 0 when income exceeds $7,000.[12] The probability of a democratic transition increases with per capita income, from less than 0.01 in countries with income below $1,000, to 0.06 in countries with incomes between $6,000 and $7,000. The probability of a dictatorial breakdown and a democratic transition declines with per capita income in two cases: when countries move from the $2,000–$3,000 range to the $3,000–$4,000 (from 0.026 to 0.015) and, more abruptly, at income levels above $7,000 (from a peak of 0.06 to 0.029).

Purely statistical reasons should lead us to treat the probabilities of transitions at high levels of development with caution. To see why, consider the following. Assume that modernization theory is right in both its exogenous and its endogenous forms. Development happens, countries get richer, and, as a result, dictatorships undergo transitions to democracy. And as countries get richer, democracy is more likely to stick. In this happy scenario the world gets increasingly rich and increasingly democratic. By the time the world becomes quite rich, the number of remaining dictatorships would be small. Because

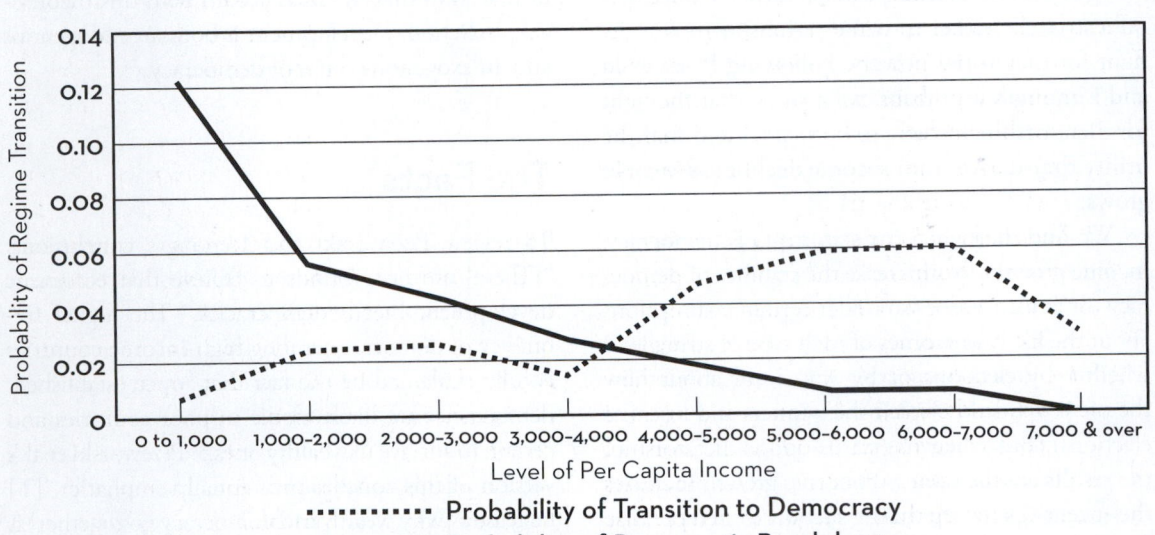

Figure 8.2 Probability of Regime Transitions by Income Intervals, 1950–90

it is small, the possible number of transitions from dictatorship to democracy is also small. Therefore we would be ill advised to draw inferences about the probability that a dictatorship would fall: small variations in the number of transition events would cause large changes in our probability estimates. At the limit, consider that the year is 2050, there is one dictatorship left in the world, it rules a country whose per capita income is $10,000, and all other dictatorships have fallen before achieving such a high income. If our one remaining dictatorship collapses at this level, we would infer that the probability of a dictatorship falling at $10,000 is 1. If it doesn't, we would infer that the probability of a dictatorship falling at $10,000 is 0. A changed outcome in just one case would lead us to one or the other extreme of the distribution of probabilities.

Along these same lines, Przeworski and his associates claim that few dictatorships become wealthy and then undergo a transition to democracy. They write: "The hypothesis implied by [modernization] theory is that *if* a country develops over a longer period under dictatorship, so that all the modernizing consequences have time to accumulate, then it will embrace democracy. But for most dictatorships this premise is vacuous: only 19 dictatorships—to remind, out of 123—did develop over longer periods of time and reached 'modernity.'?"[13] More specifically, only nineteen dictatorships achieved a per capita income of $4,115, the level at which, by their calculations, the probability of being a democracy is 0.5.[14] Of the nineteen, some never fell, others fell not at the moment they surpassed the 0.5 threshold but later, and a few fell on time.

Yet Przeworski and Limongi may be drawing the wrong inference from the fact that few developing dictatorships became wealthy and then turned into democracies. Assume, again, that both endogenous and exogenous mechanisms are at work. Then there may be few dictatorships left at a high level of income precisely *because* development at lower levels of income already helped turn them into democracies and then helped keep them democratic. The premise of endogenous modernization is only "vacuous" if

one accepts the proposition that countries can be considered to undergo development only when they achieve a high level of income. Przeworski and Limongi count as countries "that developed under authoritarianism and became 'modern'" only ones that achieved a per capita income of $4,115. But it is not obvious to us why countries that move from a per capita income of $1,000 to $2,000, or from $2,000 to $3,000, and so on are failing to undergo development. If they are developing, and if dictatorships collapse and are replaced by democracies as they achieve development at these lower levels, then their absence from the pool of dictatorships at higher levels of income does not refute endogenous modernization but instead supports it. Indeed, from this perspective the anomaly is not that the number of dictatorships that became rich and then democratized is small, but that some dictatorships survived at all, despite earlier development.

This dynamic is visible in the sample under analysis. Table 8.1 reproduces the number of annual observations by income bracket and type of regime.[15] Notice that the number of country-years above $7,000 is about 16 percent of the total sample and that within this subset only 5 percent were not democratic. Simply put, at a per capita income of $7,000, the effects of development on political regime have already taken place: countries that were going to develop and democratize had already done so before reaching the range of the very rich.

To test whether this may be the case we proceed as follows. We reexamine the analysis undertaken in *Democracy and Development* to ascertain the relationship between development and regime type. We then subject these results to several tests of robustness. To assess the impact of development on democracy, Przeworski and his coauthors simultaneously examine the effect of per capita income on the yearly probability of democratic transitions and democratic breakdowns through a dynamic probit analysis. We have reestimated their central model, which includes per capita income as well as a full set of control variables: the growth rate; the rate of turnover of chief executives (calculated as the

Table 8.1 Annual Observations by Income Level and Type of Regime (1950-90)

	Total	Authoritarian Regimes	Democratic Regimes	Percent Democracies
0–$2,000	2,016	1,690	326	16.2
$2,001–$4,000	842	511	331	39.3
$4,001–$6,000	431	212	219	50.8
$6,001–$7,000	158	33	125	79.1
$7,001–	679	35	644	94.8

Source: Data taken from Przeworski et al. (n. 4), Table 2.3.

number of changes of chief executive during the life of a political regime divided by the number of years of that political regime); the index of religious fragmentation (calculated as a Hirsch-Herfindhal index of fractionalization of religious groups); the percentage of Catholics, Protestants, and Muslims; whether the country was a former colony or not; the number of democratic breakdowns suffered by the country in previous years; and the proportion of democracies in the world each year.[16]

We reproduce our reestimation in Table 8.2. Our results are practically identical to theirs. (The small differences we find may be due to the fact that we do not impose any restrictions on the sample by excluding oil exporters.) The analysis reports two coefficients: the beta coefficient, which indicates the probability of a transition from democracy to authoritarianism, and the alpha coefficient, which, summed with the beta coefficient, indicates the probability that an authoritarian regime will remain in place. Notice that both coefficients for per capita income are statistically significant. The beta coefficient is negative: the probability of a democratic breakdown declines with per capita income. The sum of the alpha and beta coefficients is also negative and significant: although it is small, its negative sign indicates that the stability of authoritarianism

also declines with per capita income. In short, development increases the probability of a transition to democracy.[17]

Figure 8.3 simulates the results in Table 8.2. Holding all other variables constant at their means, it plots the probability of regime transition as per capita income changes. The probability of a democratic breakdown declines steeply with income. The probability of a democratic transition rises moderately from 0.01 to about 0.06 percent per year.

Robustness Problem 2: Sample Selection

To understand the relationship between democracy and development, we need to look more closely at the sample under investigation. Table 8.3 classifies countries depending on whether they entered the sample as authoritarian systems (upper panel) or as democratic regimes (lower panel). Within each category, it further divides countries by their level of per capita income according to when they first entered the sample and according to the last year we observed them. Finally, the table indicates which countries had the same regime at the beginning and the end of the period and which of them changed.

Table 8.2 Estimation of Regime Transitions (1950–90)

Dependent Variable: (1) Probability of Transition to Dictatorship: Beta Coefficient
(2) Probability of Stable Dictatorship: Sum of Alpha and Beta Coefficients

Independent Variables	ALL COUNTRIES	
	Beta	Alpha
Constant	0.065**	3.305**
	(0.898)	(1.045)
Per capita income[a] (in thousand $)	−0.546***	0.514***
	(0.122)	(0.130)
Growth rate	−0.022	0.040**
	(0.017)	(0.020)
Rate of turnover of chief executives[b]	0.976***	−1.504***
	(0.280)	(0.341)
Religious fragmentation[c]	2.561***	−2.665***
	(0.990)	(1.091)
Percentage of Catholics	−0.011	0.010
	(0.005)	(0.006)
Percentage of Protestants	−0.024	0.027
	(0.016)	(0.016)
Percentage of Muslims	0.000	0.000
	(0.005)	(0.006)
Former colony	−0.012	0.446
	(0.450)	(0.496)
Number of previous democratic breakdowns	0.896***	−1.258***
	(0.121)	(0.139)
British colony	−0.842**	0.677
	(0.424)	(0.471)
Proportion democracies in the world	−3.600*	0.683
	(1.861)	(2.207)
Log-likelihood	−291.89	
Prob > Chi²	0.0000	
Pseudo R^2	0.8913	
Number of observations	3991	

***$p < 0.01$; **$p < 0.05$; *$p < 0.10$; standard errors in parentheses

a. Real per capita income (in constant dollars, Chain Index, expressed in international prices, base 1985), taken from Summers and Heston (n. 21).
b. Number of changes of chief executives during the life of a political regime divided by the number of years of that political regime.
c. Level of religious fractionalization, measured as a Hirsch-Herfindhal index of fractionalization. Estimation: Dynamic probit model.

Figure 8.3 Simulated Probabilities of Regime Transition by Income, 1950–90

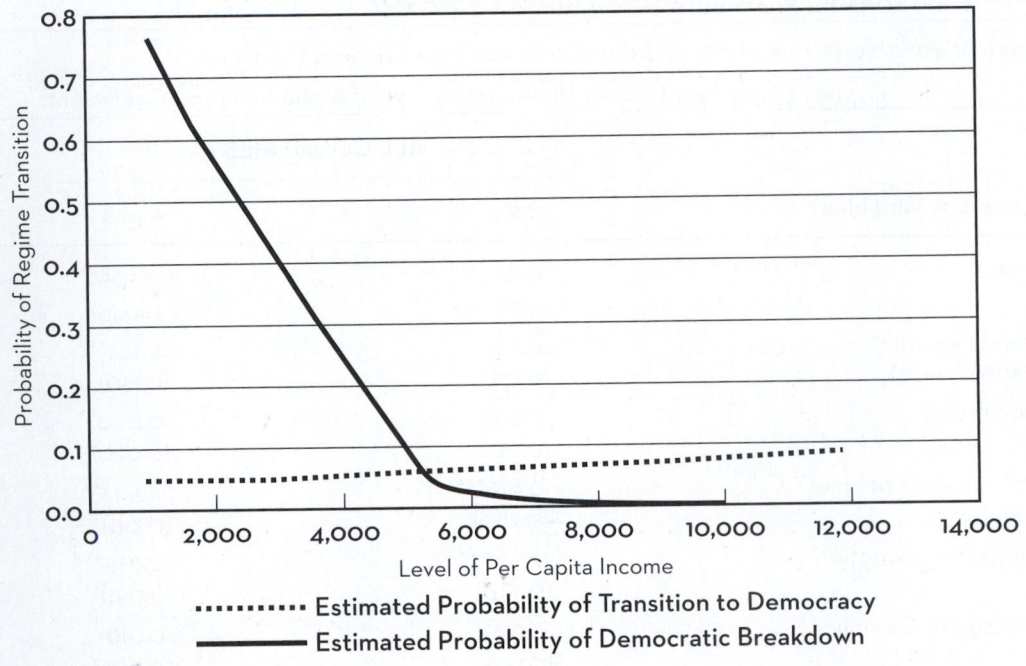

Two points relevant for the study of political transitions are worth underlining. First, at the outset, in 1950, the distribution of regimes was not random but highly correlated with per capita income. Among countries entering the sample at less than $2,000 per capita, seventy-two out of ninety were dictatorships. By contrast, among those with over $4,000 per capita income, seventeen out of twenty countries were democratic. In light of this distribution, a complete theory of democratization cannot be drawn without exploring the dynamics that led to this skewed distribution and without accounting for the democratization dynamics of the high-income countries. That is, we need to push our sample back in time to the point where no democracies existed and then observe what generated the process of democratization.

Second, growth patterns are not randomly distributed either. Out of 135 countries, 57 started and ended with less than $2,000 and 89 with less than $4,000. We know that before 1800 per capita

income was uniformly low across all countries.[18] It was only after the early nineteenth century and the industrial takeoff of several nations that there was selective economic development and overall divergence across the globe. To refute the endogenous theory of democratization we must therefore show that democratization did not follow development among those nations that took off in the nineteenth century. Here, too, we must gather observations from a point in time when differential development was just beginning.

To do so we combine Przeworski et al.'s data set for the period 1950–90 with Carles Boix and Sebastian Rosato's data set on political regimes from 1800 to 1949.[19] The new data set codes countries as democracies if they meet three conditions: elections are free and competitive; the executive is accountable to citizens (either through elections in presidential systems or to the legislative power in parliamentary regimes); and at least 50 percent of the male electorate

Table 8.3 Income and Political Mobility across Time and Countries in the Postwar Period

A. Countries That Started as Dictatorships

Per Capita Income at Entry Point		Per Capita Income at Exit Point				Total
		0–2,000	2,001–4,000	4,001–6,000	6,000–	
0–2000	Authoritarian	43	14	1	2	72
	Democratic	5	4	1	2	
2,001–4,000	Authoritarian	0	3	3	1	10
	Democratic	0	1	1	1	
4,001–	Authoritarian	0	0	0	1	3
	Democratic	0	0	0	2	
Total		48	22	6	9	

B. Countries That Started as Democracies

Per Capita Income at Entry Point		Per Capita Income at Exit Point				Total
		0–2,000	2,001–4,000	4,001–6,000	6,000–	
0–2000	Democratic	5	6	1	3	21
	Authoritarian	4	2	0	0	
2,001–4,000	Democratic	0	2	2	8	12
	Authoritarian	0	0	0	0	
4,001–	Democratic	0	0	2	15	17
	Authoritarian	0	0	0	0	
Total		9	10	5	26	

is enfranchised.[20] To measure per capita income, we have merged the previous data from Robert Summers and Alan Heston with per capita income data reported by Angus Maddison, adjusting the Maddison data to make it comparable with the Summers-Heston data set.[21] The combination of all these data gives us a panel of over 6,500 country-year observations for the period 1850 to 1990.

To underline the fact that democracy was especially endogenous to development before World War II, we first report the results of dynamic probit estimations for two separate periods: 1950–90 and 1850–1949 (Table 8.4 models 1 and 2). We do not have the full set of controls employed in Table 8.2 for the period before 1950 and therefore only estimate the model with per capita income. In these estimations democracy is coded as 1 (Przeworski and associates code it as 0). The substantive results for the postwar period in model 1 are very similar to the estimates for per capita income obtained in

Table 8.2: per capita income slightly increases the probability of democratization and substantially reduces the chances of a democratic breakdown. But in the period from the mid-nineteenth century until World War II, the reverse is true. In this period per capita income has a strong positive and statistically significant effect on transitions to democracy (beta coefficient in Table 8.4, model 2). By contrast, income growth does not reduce the probability of a democratic breakdown—the alpha coefficient is not statistically significant (although it is in a joint test with the beta coefficient, that is, with the unconditional effect).

To determine more precisely how development affects regime dynamics in different periods and to avoid any bias from truncated samples, we report in model 3 an estimation for the whole sample where we distinguish between three periods: the first democratization wave, which ended in 1924, when the number of democracies peaked at twenty-eight (or two-fifths of all sovereign nations); the period from 1925 to World War II, when the number of democracies declined by more than half; and the period after 1945.[22]

Figure 8.4a–b simulates the results in Table 8.4, model 3. The probability of democratic transition for the three periods is represented in Figure 8.4a. The probability of a democratic breakdown is depicted in Figure 8.4b. Whereas in the postwar period development increases the likelihood of democratic transitions only modestly, before 1925 development contributed powerfully to democratization. In the earlier period the annual probability of a transition to democracy was negligible—less than 5 percent per year—for a country with a per capita income of $1,000. But it increased very quickly to reach an annual probability of more than 20 percent at $3,500. By contrast, although democratic breakdowns were dampened by a higher level of development, the effect of per capita income was much smaller than in the postwar period; see Figure 8.4b.

In short, democratization is a process endogenous to development. But this fact is less salient when we look only at a post-1950 sample. Countries that were economically developed by 1950 were already democratic by that time. And most countries that were not developed by 1950 either did not develop enough to make their way into democracy in the following decades or were prevented from democratizing by some exogenous variable (such as Soviet domination).

A second look at Figure 8.2 shows some evidence that the probability of regime change, and particularly the probability of democratic transitions, may vary with the level of per capita income. Drawing on the extended sample from 1850 to 1990, Table 8.5 reports a spline function in which we estimate how transition dynamics change at low, medium, and high levels of development—below $3,000, between $3,000 and $6,000, and above $6,000 respectively.[23] Two results are worth noting. First, although more development always increases the probability that a transition to democracy will occur, the rate at which development increases the probability of a democratic transition declines with income—in other words, the impact of development on democratization exhibits diminishing returns. A simulation of the results shows that for low and medium levels of development, the probability of a transition to democracy grows by about 2 percent for each $1,000 increase in per capita income. For high levels of development, the probability of a democratic transition still goes up with income, but only by about 0.5 percent for each additional $1,000. Second, the same effect of diminishing returns actually takes place for the impact with which development stabilizes democracies. Whereas the probability of democratic breakdowns declines rapidly as income goes up at low and middle levels of development, the marginal impact of additional wealth at high levels of development is very light.

Robustness Problem 3: Omitted Variables

In this section we probe the robustness of Przeworski and his associates' rejection of endogenous democratization by introducing theoretically plausible

Table 8.4 Estimation of Regime Transitions (1850–90)

Dependent Variable: (1) Probability of Transition to Democracy: Beta Coefficient
(2) Probability of Stable Democracy: Sum of Alpha and Beta

Independent Variables	Model 1 1950–1990		Model 2 1850–1949		Model 3 1850–1990	
	Beta	Alpha	Beta	Alpha	Beta	Alpha
Constant	−2.035*** (0.067)	3.173*** (0.147)	−2.709*** (0.277)	4.171*** (0.436)	−2.445*** (0.468)	3.461*** (0.612)
Per capita income (in thousand $)	0.023 (0.017)	0.215*** (0.048)	0.294*** (0.125)	−0.056 (0.180)		
1850–1924					−1.948** (0.969)	2.762* (1.470)
1945–90					0.418 (0.473)	−0.294 (0.629)
Per capita income (in thousand $) in 1850–1924					1.067*** (0.348)	−0.635 (0.588)
Per capita income (in thousand $) in 1925–44					0.067 (0.245)	0.250 (0.281)
Per capita income (in thousand $) in 1945–90					0.022 (0.017)	0.222*** (0.049)
Log-likelihood	−463.82		−116.09		−568.37	
Prob > Chi²	0.0000		0.0000		0.0000	
Pseudo R^2	0.8413		0.9037		0.8645	
Number of observations	4404		1739		6143	

***$p < 0.01$; **$p < 0.05$; *$p < 0.10$; standard errors in parentheses
Estimation: dynamic probit model

independent variables that they have omitted from their analysis.

Przeworski and Limongi write: "[If] modernization theory is to have any predictive power, there must be some level of income at which one can be relatively sure that the country will throw off the dictatorship. One is hard put to find this level."[24] This is in contrast to the probability that democracies will collapse and become dictatorships, which falls to 0 when a country's per capita income goes above about $6,000. They show that some dictatorships survive beyond the point at

Figure 8.4 *Probability of Democratic Transition and Breakdown*

a) Annual Probability of Democratic Transition by Historical Periods

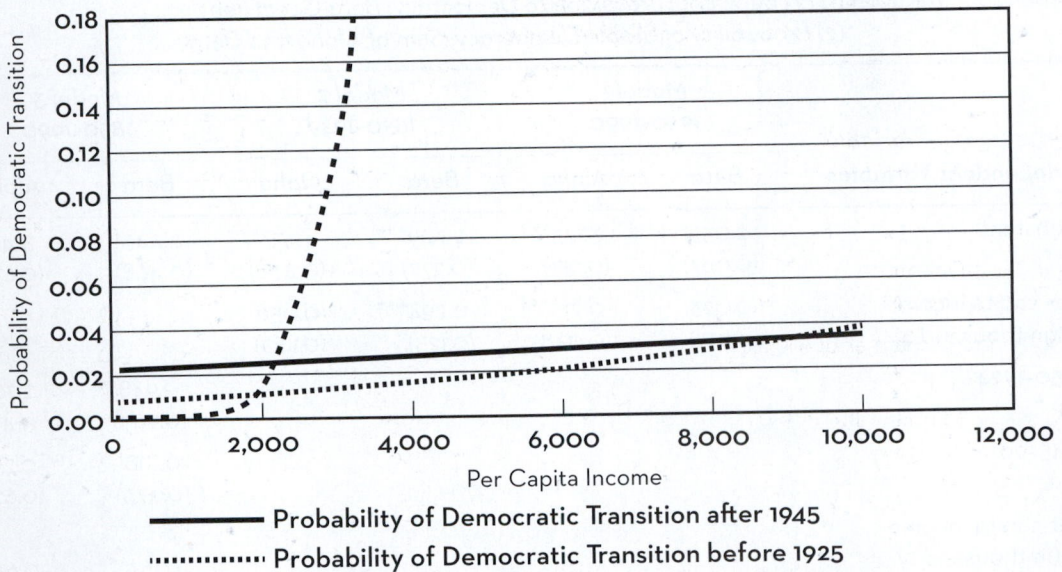

— Probability of Democratic Transition after 1945

·············· Probability of Democratic Transition before 1925

- - - - - Probability of Democratic Transition between 1925 and 1940

b) Annual Probability of Democratic Breakdown by Historical Periods

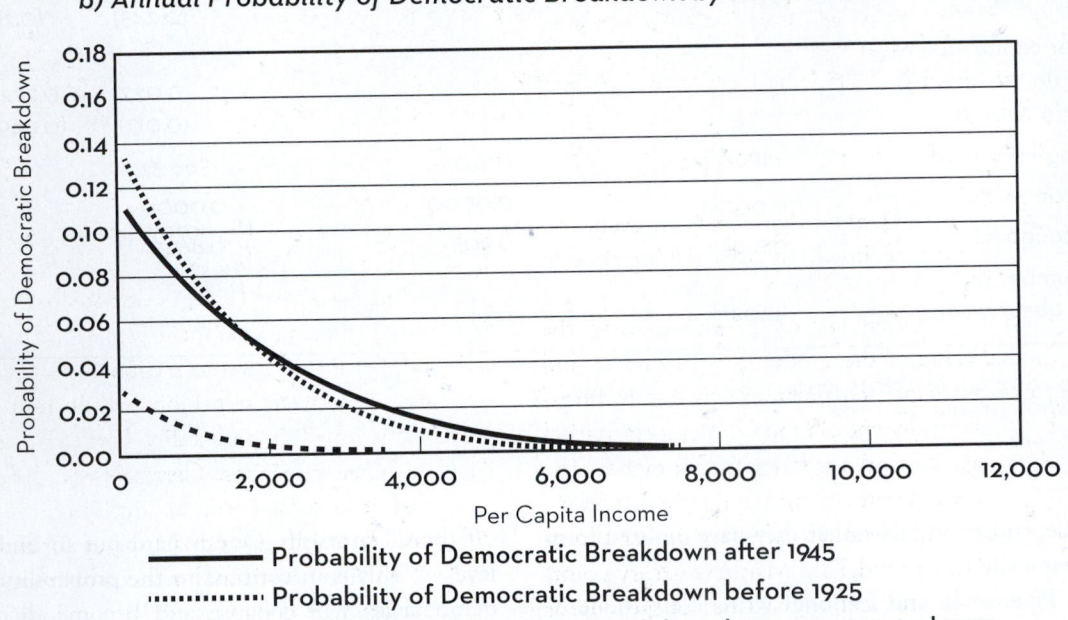

— Probability of Democratic Breakdown after 1945

·············· Probability of Democratic Breakdown before 1925

- - - - - Probability of Democratic Breakdown between 1925 and 1940

Table 8.5 The Impact of Development on Regime Transitions by Level of Development

Dependent Variable: (1) Probability of Transition to Democracy: Beta Coefficient
(2) Probability of Stable Democracy: Sum of Alpha and Beta

Independent Variables	Model 1	
	Beta	Alpha
Constant	−2.471***	3.493***
	(0.123)	(0.226)
Per capita income (in thousand $)	0.282***	0.123^^^
	(0.072)	(0.128)
Per capita income above $3,000 (in thousand $)	−0.119**	−0.020^^^
	(0.055)	(0.091)
Per capita income above $6,000 (in thousand $)	−0.136***	0.093^^^
	(0.037)	(0.07)
Log-likelihood	−578.82	
Prob > Chi^2	0.0000	
Pseudo R^2	0.8620	
Number of observations	6143	

***$p < 0.01$; **$p < 0.05$; *$p < 0.10$; standard errors in parentheses
Estimation: dynamic probit model
^^^ $p < 0.01$ in joint test of all alpha coefficients of per capita income

which the odds of being a democracy are even, and that some dictatorships have lasted a long time in rich countries.

Yet from a purely statistical point of view, the predictive value of the model may be greater and the persistence of rich dictatorships less inconsistent with the endogenous model of democratization than Przeworski and his associates contend. The existence of measurement error and of omitted variables should lead anyone to expect a number of outliers in the fitted model. As Matthew Cleary points out in this same context, outliers are not the same as logical contradictions.[25] And in this case the number of outliers is not so large. Returning to Przeworski and Limongi's list, of the nineteen countries that developed above $4,115 income per capita, two of them, Chile and Czechoslovakia, had dictatorships that fell the exact year (1989) when the probability of the country being a democracy, given its income, went to 0.5.[26] Of the seventeen countries remaining, five more underwent transitions within four years of breaking the 0.5 probability barrier.[27] Income data are missing for East Germany and Bulgaria, which leaves only ten true anomalies, fewer than 10 percent of the observations. Only if our expectations were deterministic and monocausal should we reject endogenous democratization in light of these exceptions.

Assume, again, that endogenous and exogenous democratization are both at work but that wealth is one of several factors that determine whether a dictatorship falls and whether a democracy lasts. If multiple causes jointly determine whether a dictatorship falls, then the survival of some rich dictatorships is less surprising.

Heeding Boix, perhaps another factor is the mobility of capital.[28] Even though on average capital becomes more mobile as countries develop, there may be some rich countries where it remains fixed, say, oil producers.[29] Let us imagine, hypothetically, that the following equation captures the relationship between income, fixed assets, and the probability of a transition to democracy:

$$P(t|a) = \alpha + \beta_1 X_1 + \beta_2 X_2 + \varepsilon|a$$

$P(t|a)$ is the probability of a transition to democracy given that a country is a dictatorship, X_1 is the per capita income of the country, and X_2 is a measure of the immobility of its capital assets. In some set of countries, X_2 is so large that it will swamp the effect of per capita income, even when the country becomes very rich. All the countries where X_2 is small have already become democracies, and their increasing wealth has—happily—gotten them stuck under a democratic regime. Under these assumptions we would expect development to have the impact that we have shown it to have: most countries develop and then become democracies, but a few remain dictatorships despite considerable wealth.[30]

International forces that Przeworski and his associates omit from their estimations may also help explain the persistence of some relatively wealthy dictatorships. During the cold war the United States and the Soviet Union exerted powerful pressures on the internal politics of countries within their respective spheres of domination. Whereas U.S. preferences for democracy or dictatorship in Latin America and the Caribbean shifted with political events and with U.S. administrations, the Soviet Union exerted uniform pressure against democratization in Eastern Europe and did so consistently through almost the entire period covered by the Przeworski data set. We would expect this influence, then, to constitute a countervailing pressure against democratization, even as these countries developed economically.

In Table 8.6 we estimate the same dynamic probit model we reproduced in Table 8.2 excluding all countries under Soviet control (model 2) and Soviet-dominated and oil-rich countries (model 3).[31] The sum of alpha and beta coefficients gives us the effect of each independent variable on the estimated probability that a dictatorship will remain stable. Comparing this sum in the model that includes all countries with the sum in the model that excludes countries under Soviet influence, the latter sum remains a negative number but has a larger absolute value (−.063 versus −0.032). This means that, once we control for the exogenous factors of international politics and factor endowments, economic development makes democratization more likely.

The magnitude of the effect of development on democratic transitions can be seen in Figure 8.5, which simulates the effect of economic growth on the probability of transitions to democracy in the postwar period, among the full sample of countries and among non-Soviet-dominated and non-oil-producing countries. For all countries in the sample, the probability of a transition more than doubles when one moves from the poorest to the wealthiest income level (from $1,000 to $12,000). For countries outside of the immediate zone of Soviet domination, the same rise in income is associated with a 300 percent increase in the probability of a transition to democracy, from 0.07 to 0.21. If one removes from the sample both Soviet-dominated and oil-producing countries, the corresponding increase in probabilities of a transition is from 0.06 to 0.33, which means a non-oil-producing, non-Soviet country that had somehow remained a dictatorship up to the highest income level would be expected to democratize in three years after reaching a per capita income of $12,000. Far from being nonexistent, for many countries the endogenous effect of development on democracy is profound.[32]

Table 8.6 Estimation of Regime Transitions with and without Soviet-Dominated and Oil-Rich Countries

Dependent Variable: (1) Probability of Transition to Dictatorship: Beta Coefficient
(2) Probability of Stable Dictatorship: Sum of Alpha and Beta Coefficients

Independent Variables	All Countries		No Soviet Countries		Neither Soviet nor Oil Country	
	Beta	Alpha	Beta	Alpha	Beta	Alpha
Constant	0.065**	3.305**	0.065	3.233***	-0.046	3.476***
	(0.898)	(1.045)	(0.898)	(1.045)	(0.917)	(1.078)
Per capita income[a] (in thousand $)	-0.546***	0.514***	-0.546***	0.483***	-0.492***	0.389***
	(0.122)	(0.130)	(0.122)	(0.130)	(0.119)	(0.129)
Growth rate	-0.022	0.040**	-0.022	0.038**	-0.024	0.042**
	(0.017)	(0.020)	(0.017)	(0.020)	(0.017)	(0.020)
Rate of turnover of chief executives[b]	0.976***	-1.504***	0.976***	-1.477***	0.957***	-1.414***
	(0.280)	(0.341)	(0.280)	(0.342)	(0.280)	(0.342)
Religious fragmentation[c]	2.561***	-2.665***	2.561***	-3.030***	2.298***	-2.695**
	(0.990)	(1.091)	(0.990)	(1.107)	(1.024)	(1.142)
Percentage of Catholics	-0.011	0.010	-0.011**	0.011*	-0.011**	0.010*
	(0.005)	(0.006)	(0.005)	(0.006)	(0.005)	(0.006)
Percentage of Protestants	-0.024	0.027	-0.024	0.030*	-0.021	0.026
	(0.016)	(0.016)	(0.016)	(0.017)	(0.016)	(0.017)
Percentage of Muslims	0.000	0.000	0.000	0.001	0.001	-0.002
	(0.005)	(0.006)	(0.005)	(0.006)	(0.005)	(0.006)
Former colony	-0.012	0.446	-0.012	0.559	-0.111	0.696
	(0.451)	(0.496)	(0.450)	(0.498)	(0.483)	(0.533)
Number of previous democratic breakdowns	0.896***	-1.258***	0.896***	-1.229***	0.859***	-1.139***
	(0.121)	(0.139)	(0.121)	(0.140)	(0.120)	(0.142)
British colony	-0.842**	0.677	-0.842**	0.719	-0.681	0.561
	(0.424)	(0.471)	(0.424)	(0.470)	(0.467)	(0.516)
Proportion democracies in the world	-3.600*	0.683	-3.600*	0.780	-3.458*	0.380
	(1.861)	(2.207)	(1.861)	(2.209)	(1.877)	(2.259)
Log-likelihood	-291.89		-287.40		-264.08	
Prob > Chi²	0.0000		0.0000		0.0000	
Pseudo R²	0.8913		0.8899		0.8881	
Number of observations	3991		3847		3447	

***$p < 0.01$; **$p < 0.05$; *$p < 0.10$; standard errors in parentheses

Estimation: dynamic probit model

a. Real per capita income (in constant dollars, Chain Index, expressed in international prices, base 1985), taken from Summers and Heston (n. 21).

b. Number of changes of chief executives during the life of a political regime divided by the number of years of that political regime.

c. Level of religious fractionalization, measured as a Hirsch-Herfindhal index of fractionalization.

Figure 8.5 Simulated Probabilities of Regime Transition by Income (1950-90)

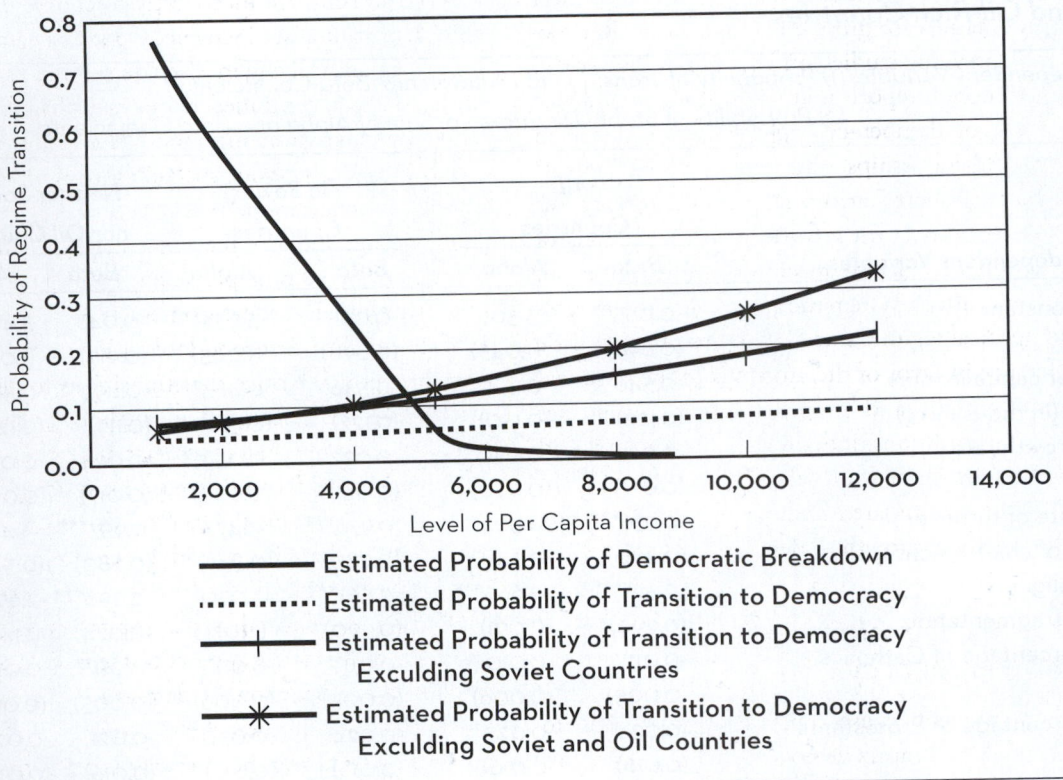

Estimated Probability of Democratic Breakdown

Estimated Probability of Transition to Democracy

Estimated Probability of Transition to Democracy Exculding Soviet Countries

Estimated Probability of Transition to Democracy Exculding Soviet and Oil Countries

Endogenous Growth

Development itself may be endogenous to the type of political regime, that is, it may partly depend on the presence of democratic institutions. If that were the case, we would observe higher proportions of democracies among developed countries precisely because the introduction of democratic procedures caused development in the first place. If this were true, estimates of the impact of per capita income on regime dynamics would be biased by the endogeneity of economic growth to regime type. More specifically, if democracies led to more growth than authoritarian regimes, this would mean that our models (estimated in Tables 8.2, 8.4, and 8.6) overstate the impact of income on maintaining democracies in power. Still, that potential effect of democracies on growth would not diminish the

proposition that democratic transitions are fostered by economic development.

The theoretical literature on the impact of democratic institutions on growth is split on the issue. In the nineteenth century liberal and socialist thinkers agreed that democracy, based on universal suffrage, threatened property and therefore capitalism. In the postwar period several scholars argued that dictatorships were more effective at increasing saving and investment rates and at insulating political elites from rent seeking and particularistic interests.[33] Yet a wide set of arguments have also been forwarded claiming that democracies lead to higher growth rates. Democracies constrain the confiscatory temptations of rulers and thereby secure property rights. They increase political accountability and reduce corruption and waste. They are more likely to provide public goods essential to development. From an empirical point of view, the evidence that the type of political regime matters for growth is rather scant. Reviewing all previous studies on that issue, Przeworski and Limongi report that eight found evidence in favor of democracy, eight found evidence in favor of dictatorships, and five discovered no difference.[34] Robert Barro finds that democracy has a positive impact on growth at medium levels of development.[35] More recently, Przeworski et al. conclude, after a systematic analysis of growth rates and political regimes since 1950, that "there is little difference in favor of dictatorships in the observed rates of growth" and "even that difference vanishes once the conditions under which dictatorships and democracies existed are taken into account."[36] In short, these cumulated findings cast doubt on any endogeneity of growth to democracy.[37]

Equality, Development, and Democracy

If development causes dictatorships to fall to democracy and causes democracy to last, why is this so? Boix offers an explanation of the connection between development and democracy. As countries develop, incomes become more equally distributed.[38] Income equality means that the redistributive scheme that would win democratic support (the one supported by the median voter) would deprive the rich of less income than the one the median voter would support if income distribution were highly unequal. Hence the rich find a democratic tax structure to be less expensive for them as their country gets wealthier, and they are more willing to countenance democratization.

As Boix makes clear, this model explains how development reduces the incentives actors face to choose dictatorship, whether the status quo is dictatorship or democracy. Even though the choice of a democratic (or nondemocratic) government precedes the actual process of voting about the distribution of assets, it is informed by the outcomes each political agent anticipates will take place under each alternative political regime. Capitalists living in a rich dictatorship are more likely to choose democracy than capitalists living in a poor dictatorship, just as capitalists living in a rich democracy are more likely to favor continued democracy than capitalists living in a poor democracy. Hence Boix's theory is simultaneously about sustaining democracy and about democratization.[39]

Our data support the idea that democracy is caused not by income per se but by other changes that accompany development, in particular, income equality. A second look at Figure 8.4a supports the point. Notice that transitions to democracy before 1949 occurred at much lower levels of per capita income than those that came after 1950. If the level of per capita income strictly speaking caused political transitions, then the shape of the transition probability would be the same across periods.

Further evidence that per capita income is a proxy for other causes appears in Figure 8.6, which displays the proportion of democratic regimes by per capita income after 1950, before 1950, and before 1900. During the postwar period 50 percent of countries with a per capita income above $4,000 were democracies. Before 1950, about 90 percent of the countries with a per capita above $4,000 were democratic. The threshold above which the odds of being a democracy were at least even was about $2,500. Again, if per capita income per se caused democracy, we would not expect these differences in threshold.

Boix examines the economic variables that shape democratic transitions and stability in a data set spanning the period 1850 to 1980, that is, in a universe that includes the political transitions of the second half of the nineteenth century and the first half of the twentieth century.[40] We summarize his results here to clarify the relationship between development and democratization. Since data on income inequality are practically nonexistent for any country before World War II, Boix relies on two indicators that predict the extent of economic inequality considerably well: the distribution of

Figure 8.6 Distribution of Democracies

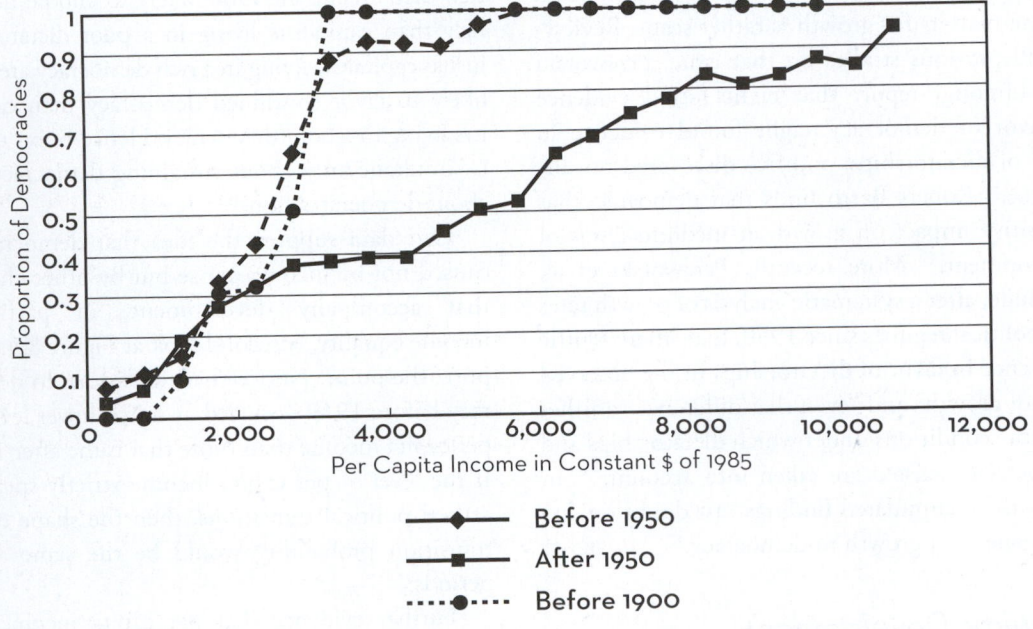

Legend:
— ◆ — Before 1950
— ■ — After 1950
····● ···· Before 1900

X-axis: Per Capita Income in Constant $ of 1985
Y-axis: Proportion of Democracies

agricultural property[41] and the quality of human capital.[42] For the period after 1950 the correlation coefficient between the Gini index of economic inequality (excluding socialist economies) and the percentage of family farms is –0.66.[43] For countries with a per capita income below $2,000 the correlation coefficient is –0.75. The coefficient of correlation of the index of education and the Gini index reported by Klaus Deininger and Lyn Squire for the period 1950–90 is –0.59.

These data produce a panel of over 6,100 country-year observations just with per capita income and between 4,400 and 3,300 observations once we introduce the other variables. The results of the estimations (again using a dynamic probit model) are reproduced in Table 8.7. To investigate the behavior and sensitivity of per capita income to these additional variables, Table 8.7 reports four models. Model 1 estimates the effects of the per capita income alone on democratic transitions and stability for the whole period from 1850 to 1990.

Model 2 adds the proportion of family farms. Model 3 includes as well the extent of human capital. Model 4 incorporates the degree of occupational diversification on regime transitions. This variable, also developed by Tatu Vanhanen, is the average percentage of the nonagricultural population and the percentage of urban population. The urban population is defined as people living in cities of twenty thousand or more inhabitants.

Per capita income, which is significant from both a statistical and a substantive point of view in model 1, progressively loses strength in successive estimations. The statistical significance of per capita income (both its alpha and beta coefficients) is strongly eroded by the introduction of the index of education. From a substantive point of view, the introduction of education cuts the impact of per capita income on democratic stability (the sum of the alpha and beta coefficients) by half. This finding seems to indicate that per capita income, as employed in the modernization literature in postwar

Table 8.7 Estimating the Probability of Political Transition from 1850 to 1980

Dependent Variable: (1) Probability of Transition to Democracy: Beta coefficient

(2) Probability of Stable Democracy: Sum of Alpha and Beta coefficients

Independent Variables	Model 1		Model 2		Model 3		Model 4	
	Beta	Alpha	Beta	Alpha	Beta	Alpha	Beta	Alpha
Constant	−2.086***	3.329***	−2.2382***	3.1132***	−2.3789***	3.1472***	−2,447***	3.0080***
	(0.061)	(0.142)	(0.1377)	(0.2325)	(0.1541)	(0.2651)	(0.2375)	(0.3586)
Per capita income	0.0297*	0.2308***	0.1004***	0.1268**	0.0579^^^	0.1212^^^	−0.0085^^^	0.1267^^^
(in thousands)[a]	(0.0157)	(0.0499)	(0.0342)	(0.0668)	(0.0435)	(0.0857)	(0.0968)	(0.1484)
Percentage of family farms[b]			−0.0017^^^	0.0143***	−0.0031^^^	0.0145***	−0.0060^^^	0.0195***
			(0.0036)	(0.0053)	(0.0036)	(0.0054)	(0.0051)	(0.0074)
Index of education[c]					0.0087***	−0.0022	0.0066^^^	0.0010^^^
					(0.0036)	(0.0078)	(0.0065)	(0.0114)
Index of occupational[d] diversification							0.0110^^^	−0.0024^^^
							(0.0096)	(0.0145)
Log-likelihood	−589.19		−385.84		−382.38		−281.66	
p > Chi²	0.0000		0.0000		0.0000		0.0000	
Pseudo R^2	0.8595		0.8683		0.8695		0.8759	
Number of observations	6143		4267		4267		3275	

***p < 0.01; **p < 0.05; *p < 0.10; standard errors in parentheses

Estimation: dynamic probit model

^^^p < 0.01 in joint test of interactive terms and its components; ^^p < 0.05 in joint test of interactive terms and its components; ^p < 0.10 in joint test of interactive terms and its components

Sources: per capita income—Summers-Heston (n. 21) and Maddison (n. 18); family farms—Vanhanen (n. 41); education—(n. 41); occupational diversification—Vanhanen (n. 41) Democratic Institutions: own code (Boix and Rosato, n. 19) for 1850–1949 and Przeworski et al. (n. 4) for 1950–90.

a. Per capita income. Log of per capita GDP in $ in 1985 constant prices.

b. Area of family farms as a percentage of the total area of holdings.

c. Arithmetic mean of the percentage of literates in the adult population and the "level of students." The level of students is the number of students per 100,000 inhabitants normalized so that 1,000 students per 100,000 inhabitants corresponds to a level of 100 percent.

d. Arithmetic mean of percentage of nonagricultural population and percentage of urban population. Urban population is defined as population living in cities of 20,000 or more inhabitants.

samples, behaves mostly as a proxy for other more fundamental factors.[44]

In contrast to per capita income, economic equality (measured in the countryside in farm ownership and in general in literacy rates) increases both the chances of a democratic transition and the stability of democratic regimes. Still, the mechanisms through which countries become democratic and the cause of democratic breakdowns are partly different. Whereas the distribution of rural property has a small effect on democratization, the chances of a transition to democracy increase considerably as the economy becomes more diversified: the yearly probability of a democratic transition goes from less than 1 percent when less than a quarter of the economy is urbanized and industrialized to about 10 percent when more than three-quarters is urbanized and industrialized.

In turn, both the economic structure and asset specificity determine the robustness of democracies. The probability of a democratic breakdown in any given year reaches 20 percent in highly unequal and underdeveloped countries. As either rural equality or industrialization increases, the authoritarian threat disappears. In an agrarian economy the probability of a democratic breakdown falls to 0 as one moves from concentrated land ownership (as in countries such as Russia before the Stolypin reforms and the Soviet Revolution, Spain for most of the twentieth century, and most Latin American nations) to the highly fragmented property systems (as in countries such as Norway, the United States, and Canada, where at the turn of the twentieth century family farms represented between three-fifths and four-fifths of all land). Even when the distribution of property remains highly unequal, the chances of an authoritarian backlash disappear as the economy industrializes.

To sum up, per capita incomes rise in countries where incomes are becoming more equal. Not higher income but income equality causes countries to democratize and to sustain democracy. If early-industrializing countries achieved income equality at lower levels of per capita income than did

later-industrializing ones, this would explain why the endogenous democratizing effect was powerful before 1950 and weaker after 1950.[45]

Conclusions

The work of Przeworski and Limongi, as well as their work with Alvarez and Cheibub, has been agenda setting. They have put facts on the table and asked for some explanations. Among their many important contributions is to warn us that the dynamics of achieving democracy and of sustaining it may not be the same. But we must be sure that all of the questions they pose are the right ones. We hope we have shown that the right question is not why development fails to increase the chances of a transition to democracy, even though it does increase the chances that an already-existing democracy will last. Instead, the right questions are the following. First, given that economic development predicts both transitions to democracy and the stability of democratic regimes, why did the income threshold for democratization rise in the period after 1950? In other words, why in effect could a country "buy" democracy more cheaply—for a lower level of per capita income—in late-nineteenth-century England or Norway than in late-twentieth-century Chile or Benin? Second, why were early-industrializing despots more vulnerable to economic development—more at risk of being replaced by elected regimes—than were their late-industrializing counterparts? Why in the century leading up to World War II was the main contribution of economic growth to bring democracy about, whereas its main contribution after World War II was to protect democracy once it already existed?

We began this article by asking whether Chile's relatively higher per capita income in 1985 made it more likely to democratize than Benin, which that same year had roughly one-third of Chile's per capita income. The answer is yes. We have shown that economic development both causes democracy and sustains it. Yet a full answer to why this is so requires

Figure 8.7 A Game of Regime Choice (Status Quo Democracy)

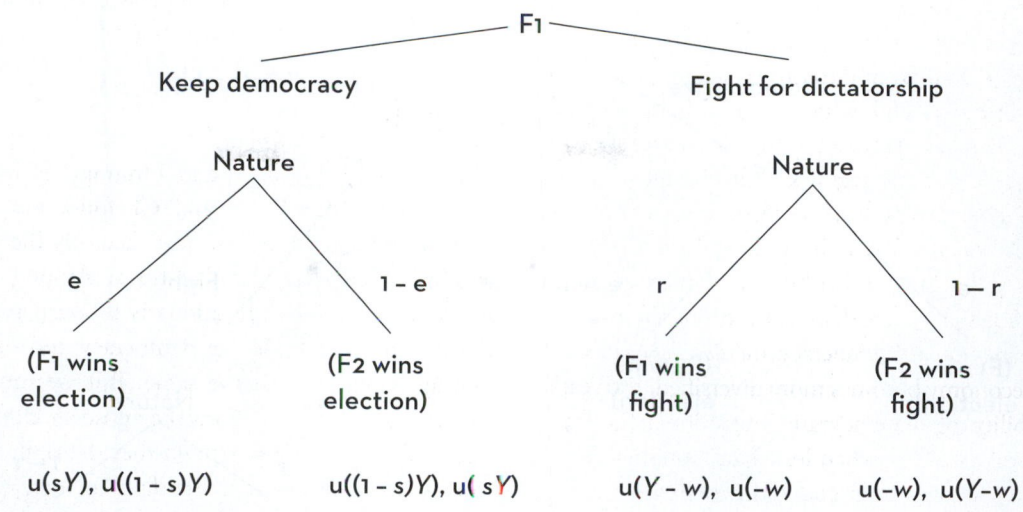

us to understand the hidden mechanisms and consequences of economic development.

Appendix: Transition Games

Game 1: Status Quo Democracy

Consider first the situation in which two factions compete in a democracy. The incumbent ($F1$) decides whether to hold elections or undertake the "fight for dictatorship." If $F1$ holds elections, it wins with probability e or loses with probability $1-e$. If $F1$ decides to fight, it wins with probability r or loses with probability $1-r$. If there's a fight, both $F1$ and $F2$ pay a cost of war (w); the winner of the fight for dictatorship takes all the income (Y), the loser gets nothing. If an election is held, the winner takes a larger portion (s) of the income, the loser a smaller portion ($1-s$). The expected payoffs are listed at the bottom of Figure 8.7:

Following Przeworski and Limongi, we assume declining marginal utility of income; specifically, we assume utility equals the square root of income. $F1$ chooses democracy iff

$$r(u(Y-w)) + (1-r)(u(-w)) - e(u(sY)) - (1-e)$$
$$(u((1-s))Y) < 0 \qquad (1)$$

Taking the first-order derivative of u with respect to Y tells us the effect of development on democracy. Development causes democracy when

$$\tfrac{1}{2}\,[r(Y-w)^{-1/2}] - \tfrac{1}{2}[e(Y)^{-1/2}\,s^{1/2}] - \tfrac{1}{2}[(1-e)\,(Y)^{-1/2}$$
$$(1-s)^{1/2}] < 0$$

which simplifies to

$$r(Y-w)^{-1/2} - Y^{-1/2}\,[e(s)^{1/2} + (1-e)(1-s)^{1/2}] < 0 \qquad (2)$$

Focusing on the denominators $(Y-w)^{-1/2}$ and $Y^{1/2}$ on the left-hand side of inequality 2, we see that, ceteris paribus, development increases the magnitude of the second expression in relation to the first and hence the probability of democracy.

Naturally, the choice of strategy is affected by other parameters: on one side, by the probability (r) that the ruling faction would win a war for dictatorship; on the other, by the relative probabilities that the ruling faction or the opposition wins the election (e, $1-e$), and by the shares of income going to the winner and the loser of elections (s, $1-s$). Holding everything else constant, the chances of democracy decrease with a larger r yet increase with e and s. Still, the conditional effects of higher economic development on e and s are more

Figure 8.8 A Game of Regime Choice (Status Quo Dictatorship)

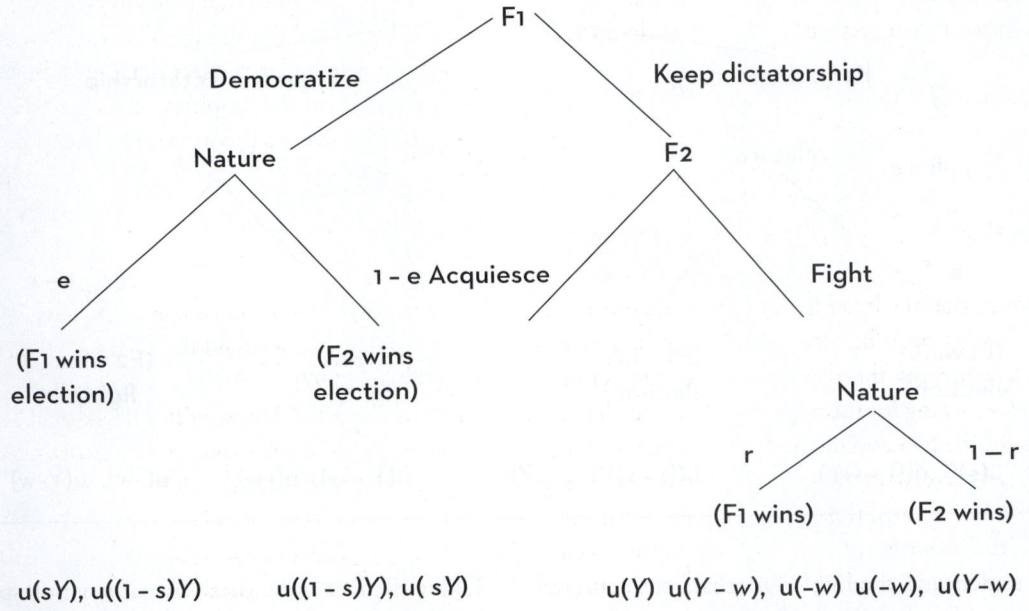

ambiguous: perhaps counterintuitively, the greater the incumbent's probability of winning elections and the greater his share of income if he wins, the less economic development generates democracy. This, however, remains a marginal effect generally trumped by the direct boost democracy gets from development.

Game 2: Status Quo Dictatorship

Now consider that faction *F1* is a dictator and must decide whether to remain as a dictator or undertake a transition to democracy, in which case (as before) *F1* wins with probability *e* and takes portion *s* of income *Y* or loses with probability $1 - e$ and takes a smaller portion $1 - s$ of income. If *F1* decides against a transition, *F2* must decide whether to acquiesce or to fight to take over the dictatorship. If it acquiesces, it gets no income and *F1* gets it all. If *F2* fights, it gets all the income minus the cost of war (*w*) with probability $1 - r$, or just pays the cost of war with probability *r*. See Figure 8.8.

By backward induction, faced with the choice of whether to acquiesce or fight the dictatorship, *F2* will always fight unless the condition specified in inequality 3 holds:

$$r(u(-w)) + (1 - r)(u(Y-w)) < 0 \qquad (3)$$

If this inequality holds, *F2* would always acquiesce and—anticipating his acquiescence—*F1* would never democratize.

This inequality leads us to consider the utility loss to the loser of fighting and losing, weighted by the probability of the dictator winning, compared to the utility of fighting and winning, weighted by the probability that those currently out of power win. If the latter weighted utility is larger than the former, democracy never happens.

Assuming inequality 3 does not hold, at the first decision node *F1* will democratize iff

$$r(u(Y-w)) + (1 - r)(u(-w)) - e(u(sY)) - (1 - e)$$
$$(u((1-s))Y) < u(0)$$

Taking the first-order derivative of u with respect to Y (assuming $u(y) = Y^{1/2}$) again tells us the effect of development (marginal changes in Y) on democracy:

$$\tfrac{1}{2}[r(Y-w)^{-1/2}] - \tfrac{1}{2}[e(s)^{1/2} + (1-e)(1-s)^{1/2}(Y)^{-1/2}] < 0$$

which simplifies to

$$r(Y-w)^{-1/2} - Y^{-1/2}[e(s)^{1/2} + (1-e)(1-s)^{1/2}] < 0$$

Notice that the latter is the same inequality as (2) in the first game. When inequality 2 holds, development encourages the dictatorship to democratize. Again bracketing for the moment all but the denominators of the first and second terms, it seems unambiguous that development encourages democracy. This means, in turn, that the same mechanisms that reduce the incentive of a staging a coup (the declining marginal utility of income) apply to explain the cases in which $F1$ should acquiesce to democracy. The growth of per capita income predicts both a fall in the likelihood of democratic breakdowns and a rise in the likelihood of democratic transitions. In sum, employing the parameters of Przeworski and Limongi, endogenous democratization theory still holds: dictatorships will democratize under the stimulus of economic development.

In several senses, these games are not particularly successful. Some of the comparative statics they yield fail to conform to intuition. As in the first game, there are some values of r (the probability of the dictator winning a fight for continued dictatorship), $e/(1 - e)$ (the ratio of the dictator's and opponent's probabilities of winning elections), and $s/(1 - s)$ (the relative share of the national income going to winners and losers of elections) for which growing development marginally reduces the probability of democracy. A more compelling theoretical model of the relation between economic growth and democracy might less ambiguously predict that growth would cause democracy. But our central point is that these models do not sustain the claim that development causes democratic stability but not transitions to democracy. If it were empirically true that development was related to democracy exogenously but not endogenously, then we would need a theoretical foundation that is different from the games sketched here. Our main goal, however, is to cast doubt on the empirical claim and hence on the need to provide a theory to sustain that position.

NOTES

1. Adam Przeworski and Fernando Limongi, "Modernization: Theories and Facts," *World Politics* 49 (January 1997).
2. David Brown, "Review of Przeworski et al.'s *Democracy and Development,*" *Comparative Political Studies* 34 (June 2001), 576.
3. Juan López, "Sanctions on Cuba Are Good, but Not Enough," *Orbis* 44 (Summer 2000), 349.
4. Adam Przeworski, Micheal E. Alvarez, José Antonio Cheibub, and Fernando Limongi, *Democracy and Development: Political Institutions and Well-Being in the World, 1950–1990* (New York: Cambridge University Press, 2000).
5. Przeworski and Limongi (n. 1); the version appearing in Przeworski et al. (n. 4) drops the theoretical discussion altogether (chap. 2).
6. Przeworski and Limongi (n. 1), 166. See also Adam Przeworski, "Why Democracies Survive in Affluent Countries" (Manuscript, Department of Politics, New York University, New York, 1996).
7. According to Przeworski and Limongi, the second mechanism that reduces the likelihood of a democratic breakdown in rich countries concerns the way in which capital stock recovers from a war, since capital stock goes back to its steady state at a faster rate in a poor country than in a rich country. Although this reasoning fits squarely with the predictions of the classical Solowian growth model, which is based on a standard production function with diminishing returns, their conclusion that a faster catch-up rate should increase the value of being a dictator in a poor country is unwarranted. What should matter is not the rate at which the economy returns to its steady state but rather total

national output, which determines the return (income flow) that the expropriator will obtain. Accordingly, the value of being a dictator is much higher in a wealthy country (ignoring any possible effect of a declining marginal utility of income).

8. Przeworski and Limongi (n. 1), 167.

9. Przeworski et al. (n. 4), 106. Summarizing the results of a multivariate dynamic probit analysis of transitions, Przeworski and his associates acknowledge "the impact of per capita income . . . is apparent for both regimes, but it is orders of magnitude larger for democracies" (p. 123). But, as the quote cited above suggests, they seem reluctant to embrace the finding that income growth causes democratization.

10. In this article we follow Przeworski and his coauthors' terminology in equating "development" with growth of per capita income. Yet our discussion below implies that other aspects of development, especially growing income equality, are probably more relevant dimensions of development for political change than are growing incomes. We also follow these authors in using the terms "dictatorship" and "authoritarianism" as synonyms and in treating both as equivalent to nondemocracy. "Nondemocracy" becomes the more accurate term as we shift our analysis back in time, when regimes at risk of democratization included monarchies and parliamentary regimes with limited franchises, neither of which would fit today's concept of dictatorship.

11. Przeworski et al. (n. 4), 93, Table 2.3.

12. All figures are international prices of 1985.

13. Przeworski et al. (n. 4), 160.

14. In Przeworski et al. (n. 4) the number of dictatorships rises to twenty.

15. Data are from Przeworski et al. (n. 4), 93, Table 2.3.

16. Their estimation appears in Przeworski et al. (n. 4), 124, Table 2.17.

17. In Table 2.17 in Przeworski et al. (n. 4), the authors report the coefficients in two columns: beta (the coefficient of transition to dictatorship) in the first one; and beta plus alpha (the latter being the coefficient of remaining authoritarian conditional on being authoritarian in the previous period). We have opted, instead, to report beta and alpha in separate columns.

18. Paul Bairoch, *Economics and World History: Myths and Paradoxes* (Chicago: University of Chicago Press, 1993), chap. 9; Angus Maddison, *Monitoring the World Economy, 1820–1992* (Paris: Organization for Economic Co-operation and Development, 1995).

19. Carles Boix and Sebastian Rosato, "A Complete Data Set of Political Regimes, 1800–1999" (Department of Political Science, University of Chicago, Chicago, 2001).

20. Boix and Rosato (n. 19) report both a full discussion of the coding and the data set.

21. Maddison (n. 18); Robert Summers and Alan Heston, "The Penn World Table (Mark 5): An Expanded Set of International Comparisons, 1950–1988," *Quarterly Journal of Economics* 106 (May 1991). Although the two data sets employ different definitions of per capita income, their observations are extremely well correlated. For the period 1950–90 the Summers-Heston data and the Maddison data on per capita income have a correlation coefficient of 0.987.

22. Running the same regression with different periods does not alter the main results of Table 8.4, model 3. The dummy for the interwar period has been dropped from model 3 to avoid collinearity.

23. The income variables are defined as the corresponding per capita income above a given threshold and zero below. To choose the thresholds for this estimation, we have first examined the variation in our coefficient for different per capita segments through separate functions.

24. Przeworski and Limongi (n. 1), 163.

25. Matthew Cleary, "Testing Endogenous and Exogenous Modernization Theory" (Paper presented at the annual meeting of the American Political Science Association, Atlanta, September 2–5, 1999).

26. As Przeworski and Limongi note, Chile broke through the $4,115 threshold twice but underwent a transition only on the second breakthrough.

27. The list, with the year they achieved $4,115 first and the year of the transition second, is Brazil (1980, 1978), South Korea (1985, 1988), Greece

(1970, 1974), Poland (1985, 1989), and Portugal (1973, 1975). Poland also achieved the threshold income in 1974, without democratizing.

28. Carles Boix, *Democracy and Redistribution* (New York: Cambridge University Press, 2003).

29. When we extend our analysis back to the mid-nineteenth century, other fixed assets suggest themselves. Yet what is critical is not just that an asset is fixed and that it plays a large role in a country's exports, but also that it accounts for a large portion of the country's GDP. Britain's coal industry in the nineteenth century, for example, would not fit these criteria.

30. For evidence on the negative impact of oil on democratic transitions, see Boix (n. 28), chap. 3.

31. We exclude all the Soviet-dominated countries (rather than employ a dummy variable for these cases) because the variable gauging its conditional effect on regime transition is perfectly collinear with the variable democracy and drops out of the estimation.

32. We do not pretend here to exhaust the list of omitted variables that might reduce the number of democratic transitions among a subset of wealthy nations. A third possibility would be that there are different types of dictatorships with differential probability rates of breakdown. For example, military governments may be less resilient than civilian juntas to development effects. We thank Adam Przeworski for suggesting this possibility to us.

33. For the literature on the effect on savings and investment, see Walter Galenson, "Introduction," in Galenson, ed., *Labor and Economic Development* (New York: Wiley, 1959); Karl de Schweinitz, Jr., "Industrialization, Labor Controls and Democracy," *Economic Development and Cultural Change* 7 (July 1959); Samuel P. Huntington, *Political Order in Changing Societies* (New Haven: Yale University Press, 1968). For the literature on insulated elites, see Stephan Haggard, *Pathways from the Periphery: The Politics of Growth in the Newly Industrializing Countries* (Ithaca, N.Y.: Cornell University Press, 1990).

34. Adam Przeworski and Fernando Limongi, "Political Regimes and Economic Growth," *Journal of Economic Perspectives* 7 (Summer 1993).

35. Robert Barro, *Determinants of Economic Growth* (Cambridge: MIT Press, 1997).

36. Przeworski et al. (n. 4), 178.

37. Although democracies may not affect growth too much, we do not deny that particular constitutional structures matter for growth, for example, having some form of liberal structure with an independent legislature. Indeed, there seems to be growing evidence that a constrained executive leads to higher levels of development. Douglass North, *Institutions, Institutional Change and Economic Performance* (Cambridge: Cambridge University Press, 1990); Bradford J. DeLong and Andrei Shleifer, "Princes and Merchants: European City Growth before the Industrial Revolution," *Journal of Law and Economics* 36 (October 1993); Daron Acemoglu, Simon Johnson, and James A. Robinson, "The Colonial Origins of Comparative Development: An Empirical Investigation," *American Economic Review* 91 (December 2001). It is difficult to claim, however, that the introduction of democracy, understood as competitive elections and universal suffrage, was at the root of the industrial takeoff of the West. A more plausible argument, and one that we partly pursue in the following section, is that once certain liberal institutions, sustained by a social and economic balance of power, led to growth, this generated particular conditions, such as growing income equality, which in turn opened the door to democratic constitutions.

38. Boix (n. 28). Recent data collected by Deininger and Squire on income inequality, consisting of 692 comparable observations (587 of them with Gini coefficients), show that, at low levels of economic development, the degree of inequality is highly variable across countries. For economies under a per capita income of $5,000, the mean Gini index is 42.5 with the values ranging from 20.9 to 66.9 and a standard deviation of 10.4. At higher levels of economic development, the occurrence of inequality diminishes. In economies with a per capita income of more than $10,000 (constant prices of 1985), the average Gini index is 34.2 with a standard deviation of 3.6. Klaus Deininger and Lyn Squire, "A New Data Set Measuring Income Inequality,"

World Bank Economic Review 19 (September 1996). Boix's fuller discussion also examines the effect of economic development on capital mobility and of capital mobility on democratization.

39. The long-term trend toward income equality as economies develop suggests other plausible mechanisms linking development with democratization. For example, assume as a starting point a dictatorship in which poor people are excluded from participation. As the country develops, incomes become more equal. If the desire to participate grows among the poor and middle class as their incomes begin to catch up to the those of the wealthy (as Lipset long ago claimed it would) and if their organizational capacity also grows, then the costs of repression will rise as a function of economic development. In this case even if—contra Przeworski and Limongi—the marginal returns of capital remain stable, development would cause transitions to democracy.

40. Boix (n. 28).

41. The distribution of agricultural property is measured by the area of family farms as a percentage of the total area of holdings. This measure, gathered and reported by Vanhanen, defines family farms as those "that provide employment for not more than four people, including family members . . . that are cultivated by the holder family itself and . . . that are owned by the cultivator family or held in ownerlike possession"; Tatu Vanhanen, *Prospects of Democracy: A Study of 172 Countries* (London: Routledge, 1997), 48. This definition, which aims at distinguishing family farms from large farms cultivated mainly by hired workers, is not dependent on the actual size of the farm—the size of the farm varies with the type of product and the agricultural technology used. The percentage of family farms captures the degree of concentration and therefore inequality in the ownership of land. The data set, reported in averages for each decade, covers the period from 1850 to 1979. It varies from countries with 0 percent of family farms to nations where 94 percent of the agricultural land is owned in family farms; the mean of the sample is 30 percent with a standard deviation of 23 percent. An extensive literature has related the unequal distribution of land to an unbalanced distribution of income.

42. To measure the level of human capital, Boix (n. 28) relies on Vanhanen's "index of knowledge distribution," which consists in the arithmetic mean of the percentage of literates in the adult population and the "level of students." The level of students is the number of students per 100,000 inhabitants, normalized so that 1,000 students per 100,000 inhabitants corresponds to a level of 100 percent. The Vanhanen index of education, which also covers the period 1850–1979, varies from 0.5 to 99 percent with a mean of 29.2 and a standard deviation of 22.7.

43. The Gini index is taken from Deininger and Squire (n. 38).

44. The introduction of the index of occupational diversification (without the variables of family farms and education) only reduces the statistical significance of the beta coefficient of per capita income. This estimation is not displayed in Table 8.7.

45. Data on income inequality are too scarce before 1950 to test this hypothesis. However, if we look at its proxies, such as education and the distribution of agrarian property, inequality seems to have been less acute in advanced countries than in developing countries for similar levels of per capita income. For example, taking our country-year observations with per capita income lower than $2,000, the mean literacy index is around 40 percent of the population in developed countries and 20 percent in developing nations. For observations with a per capita income between $2,000 and $4,000, the average literacy index is 50 percent in advanced countries and 41 percent in developing countries. The average percentage of family farms is 39 percent and 28 percent in developed and developing countries for per capita incomes lower than $2,000. The difference gets larger for per capita incomes between $2,000 and $4,000: the average percentage of family farms is 42 percent in advanced countries and 25 percent in the rest. The universe of advanced countries includes North America, Western Europe, Japan, Australia, and New Zealand.

Daron Acemoglu, Simon Johnson, James A. Robinson, and Pierre Yared

INCOME AND DEMOCRACY

One of the most notable empirical regularities in political economy is the relationship between income per capita and democracy. Today, all OECD countries are democratic, while many of the non-democracies are in the poor parts of the world, for example sub-Saharan Africa and Southeast Asia. The positive cross-country relationship between income and democracy in the 1990s is depicted in Figure 8.9, which shows the association between the Freedom House measure of democracy and log income per capita in the 1990s.[1] This relationship is not confined solely to a cross-country comparison. Most countries were nondemocratic before the modern growth process took off at the beginning of the nineteenth century. Democratization came together with growth. Robert J. Barro (1999, 160), for example, summarizes this as follows: "Increases in various measures of the standard of living forecast a gradual rise in democracy. In contrast, democracies that arise without prior economic development . . . tend not to last."[2]

This statistical association between income and democracy is the cornerstone of the influential modernization theory. Lipset (1959) suggested that democracy was both created and consolidated by a broad process of "modernization" which involved changes in "the factors of industrialization, urbanization, wealth, and education [which] are so closely interrelated as to form one common factor. And the factors subsumed under economic development carry with it the political correlate of democracy" (80). The central tenet of the modernization theory, that higher income per capita causes a country to be democratic, is also reproduced in most major

works on democracy (e.g., Robert A. Dahl 1971; Samuel P. Huntington 1991; Dietrich Rueschemeyer, John D. Stephens, and Evelyn H. Stephens 1992).

In this paper, we revisit the relationship between income per capita and democracy. Our starting point is that existing work, which is based on cross-country relationships, does not establish causation. First, there is the issue of reverse causality; perhaps democracy causes income rather than the other way around. Second, and more important, there is the potential for omitted variable bias. Some other factor may determine both the nature of the political regime and the potential for economic growth.

We utilize two strategies to investigate the causal effect of income on democracy. Our first strategy is to control for country-specific factors affecting both income and democracy by including country fixed effects. While fixed effect regressions are not a panacea for omitted variable biases,[3] they are well suited to the investigation of the relationship between income and democracy, especially in the postwar era. The major source of potential bias in a regression of democracy on income per capita is country-specific, historical factors influencing both political and economic development. If these omitted characteristics are, to a first approximation, time-invariant, the inclusion of fixed effects will remove them and this source of bias. Consider, for example, the comparison of the United States and Colombia. The United States is both richer and more democratic, so a simple cross-country comparison, as well as the existing empirical strategies in the literature, which do not control for fixed country effects, would suggest that higher per capita income causes democracy. The idea of fixed effects is to move beyond this comparison and

From *American Economic Review* 98, no. 3 (2008), pp. 808–42.

Figure 8.9 Democracy and Income, 1990s

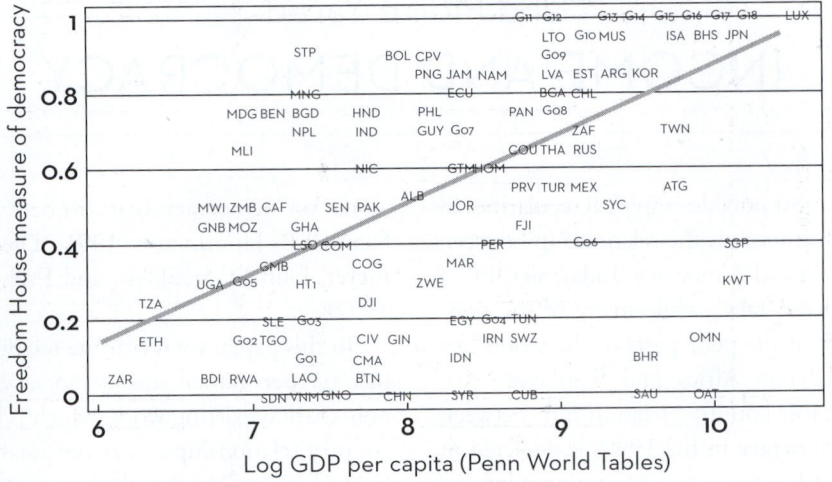

investigate the "within-country variation," that is, to ask whether Colombia is more likely to *become* (relatively) democratic as it *becomes* (relatively) richer. In addition to improving inference on the causal effect of income on democracy, this approach is more closely related to modernization theory as articulated by Lipset (1959), which emphasizes that individual countries should become more democratic if they are richer, not simply that rich countries should be democratic.

Our first result is that once fixed effects are introduced, the positive relationship between income per capita and various measures of democracy disappears. Figures 8.10 and 8.11 show this diagrammatically by plotting changes in our two measures of democracy, the Freedom House and Polity scores, for each country between 1970 and 1995 against the change in GDP per capita over the same period. These figures confirm that there is no relationship between *changes* in income per capita and *changes* in democracy.

This basic finding is robust to using various different indicators for democracy, to different econometric specifications and estimation techniques, in different subsamples, and to the inclusion of additional covariates. The absence of a significant relationship between income and democracy is *not* driven by large standard errors. On the contrary, the relationship between income and democracy is estimated relatively precisely. In many cases, two-standard-error bands include only very small effects of income on democracy and often exclude the OLS estimates. These results, therefore, shed considerable doubt on the claim that there is a strong causal effect of income on democracy.[4]

While the fixed effects estimation is useful in removing the influence of long-run determinants of both democracy and income, it does not necessarily estimate the causal effect of income on democracy. Our second strategy is to use instrumental-variables (IV) regressions to estimate the impact of income on democracy.[5] We experiment with two potential

Figure 8.10 Change in Democracy and Income [Freedom House Scores], 1970–1995

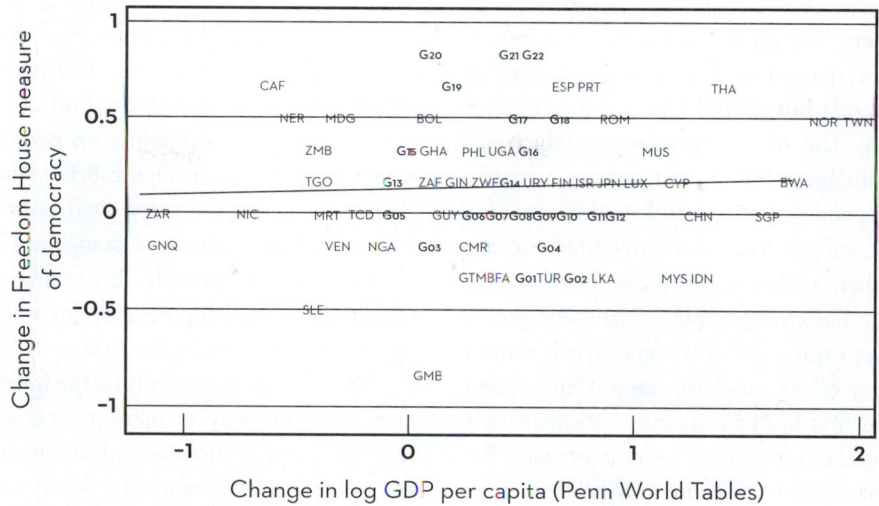

Notes: Changes are total difference between 1970 and 1995. Countries are included if they were independent by 1970. Start and end dates are chosen to maximize the number of countries in the cross section. The regression represented by the fitted line yields a coefficient of 0.032 (standard error = 0.058), $N = 102$, $R^2 = 0.00$. The "G" prefix corresponds to the average for groups of countries. G01 is FJI and KEN; G02 is COL and IND; G03 is IRN, JAM, and SLV; G04 is CHL and DOM; G05 is CIV and RWA; G06 is CHE, CRI, and NZL; G07 is DZA and SWE; G08 is AUS, DNK, MAR, and NLD; G09 is BEL, CAN, FRA, and GBR; G10 is AUT, EGY, ISL, ITA, PRY, and USA; G11 is BRB, NOR, and TUN; G12 is IRL and SYR; G13 is BDI and TZA; G14 is GAB, MEX, and TTO; G15 is PER and SEN; G16 is HTI and JOR; G17 is LSO and NPL; G18 is BRA and COG; G19 is ARG and HND; G20 is BEN and MLI; G21 is GRC, MWI, and PAN; and G22 is ECU and HUN.

Figure 8.11 Change in Democracy and Income [Polity Scores], 1970–1995

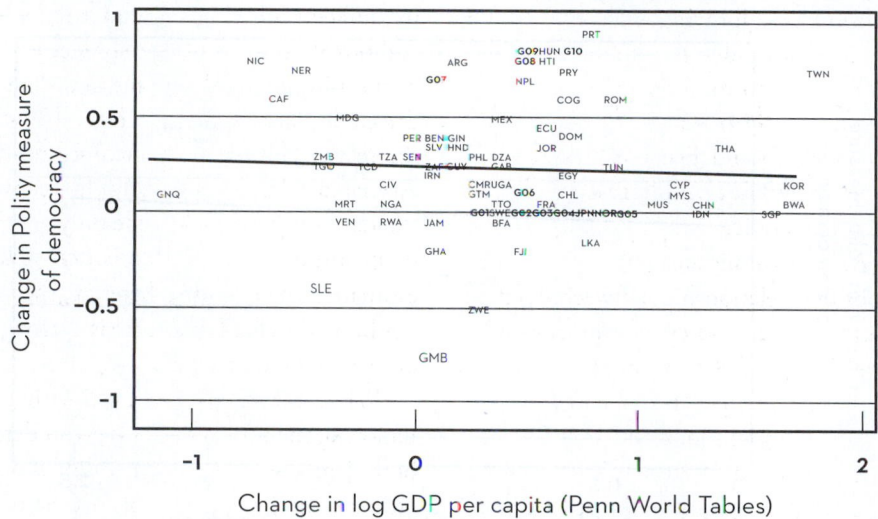

Notes: See notes to Figure 8.10. The regression represented by the fitted line yields a coefficient of –0.024 (standard error = 0.063), $N = 98$, $R^2 = 0.00$. G01 is CHE, CRI, and NZL; G02 is AUS, DNK, and NLD; G03 is BEL, CAN, FIN, GBR, and TUR; G04 is AUT, COL, IND, ISL, ISR, ITA, and USA; G05 is IRL and SYR; G06 is KEN, MAR, and URY; G07 is BOL and MLI; G08 is MWI and PAN; G09 is GRC and LSO; and G10 is BRA and ESP.

instruments. The first is to use past savings rates, and the second is to use changes in the incomes of trading partners. The argument for the first instrument is that variations in past savings rates affect income per capita but should have no direct effect on democracy. The second instrument, which we believe is of independent interest, creates a matrix of trade shares and constructs predicted income for each country using a trade-share-weighted average income of other countries. We show that this predicted income has considerable explanatory power for income per capita. We also argue that it should have no direct effect on democracy. Our second major result is that both IV strategies show no evidence of a causal effect of income on democracy. We recognize that neither instrument is perfect, since there are reasonable scenarios in which our exclusion restrictions could be violated (e.g., saving rates might be correlated with future anticipated regime changes; or democracy scores of a country's trading partners, which are correlated with their income levels, might have a direct effect on its democracy). To alleviate these concerns, we show that the most likely

sources of correlation between our instruments and the error term in the second stage are not present.

We also look at the relationship between income and democracy over the past 100 years using fixed effects regressions and again find no evidence of a positive impact of income on democracy. These results are depicted in Figure 8.12, which plots the change in Polity score for each country between 1900 and 2000 against the change in GDP per capita over the same period. This figure confirms that there is no relationship between income and democracy conditional on fixed effects.

These results naturally raise the following important question: why is there a cross-sectional correlation between income and democracy? In other words, why are rich countries democratic today? At a statistical level, the answer is clear: even though there is no relationship between changes in income and democracy in the postwar era or over the past 100 years or so, there is a positive association over the past 500 years. Most societies were nondemocratic 500 years ago and had broadly similar income levels. The positive cross-sectional relationship

Figure 8.12 Change in Democracy and Income, 1900-2000

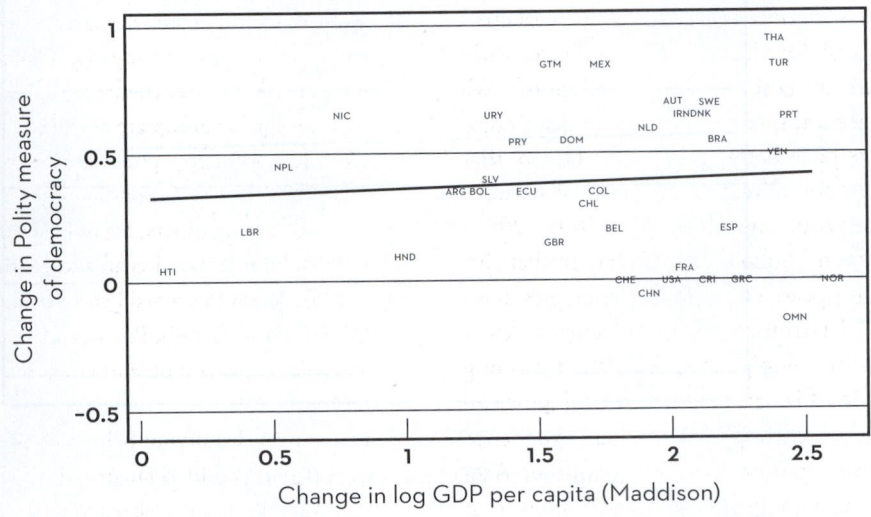

Change in log GDP per capita (Maddison)

Notes: Log GDP per capita is from Angus Maddison (2003) Changes are total difference between 1900 and 2000. The regression represented by the fitted line yields a coefficient of 0.035 (standard error = 0.049), *N* = 37, R² = 0.00.

reflects the fact that those that have become more democratic over this time span are also those that have grown faster. One possible explanation for the positive cross-sectional correlation is, therefore, that there is a causal effect of income on democracy, but it works at *much* longer horizons than the existing literature has posited. Although the lack of a relationship over 50 or 100 years sheds some doubt on this explanation, this is a logical possibility.

We favor another explanation for this pattern. Even in the absence of a simple causal link from income to democracy, political and economic development paths are interlinked and are jointly affected by various factors. Societies may embark on *divergent political-economic development paths*, some leading to relative prosperity and democracy, others to relative poverty and dictatorship. Our hypothesis is that the positive cross-sectional relationship and the 500-year correlation between changes in income and democracy are caused by the fact that countries have embarked on divergent development paths at some *critical junctures* during the past 500 years.[6]

We provide support for this hypothesis by documenting that the positive association between changes in income and democracy over the past 500 years is largely accounted for by a range of historical variables. In particular, for the whole world sample, the positive association is considerably weakened when we control for date of independence, early constraints on the executive, and religion.[7] We then turn to the sample of former European colonies, where we have better proxies for factors that have influenced the development paths of nations. Acemoglu, Johnson, and Robinson (2001, 2002) and Engerman and Sokoloff (1997) argue that differences in European colonization strategies have been a major determinant of the divergent development paths of colonial societies. This reasoning suggests that in this sample, the critical juncture for most societies corresponds to their experience under European colonization. Furthermore, Acemoglu, Johnson, and Robinson (2002) show that the density of indigenous populations at the time of colonization has been a particularly important vari-

able in shaping colonization strategies, and provide estimates of population densities in the year 1500 (before the advent of colonization). When we use information on population density, as well as on independence year and early constraints on the executive, the 500-year relationship between changes in income and democracy in the former colonies sample disappears. This pattern is consistent with the hypothesis that the positive cross-sectional relationship between income and democracy today is the result of societies embarking on divergent development paths at certain critical junctures during the past 500 years (although other hypotheses might account for these patterns).

A related question is whether income has a separate causal effect on transitions to, and away from, democracy. * * * Using both linear regression models and double-hazard models that simultaneously estimate the process of entry into, and exit from, democracy, we find no evidence that income has a causal effect on the transitions either to or from democracy.

NOTES

1. All figures use the three-letter World Bank country codes to identify countries, except when multiple countries are clustered together. When such clustering happens, countries are grouped together, the averages for the group are plotted in the figure, and the countries in each group are identified in the footnote to the corresponding figure.

2. See also, among others, Seymour Martin Lipset (1959), John B. Londregan and Keith T. Poole (1996), Adam Przeworski and Fernando Limongi (1997), Barro (1997), Przeworski et al. (2000), and Elias Papaioannou and Gregorios Siourounis (2006).

3. Fixed effects would not help inference if there are time-varying omitted factors affecting the dependent variable and correlated with the right-hand-side variables (see the discussion below). They may, in fact, make problems of measurement error

worse because they remove a significant portion of the variation in the right-hand-side variables. Consequently, fixed effects are certainly no substitute for instrumental-variables or structural estimation with valid exclusion restrictions.

4. It remains true that over time there is a general tendency toward greater incomes and greater democracy throughout the world. In our regressions, time effects capture these general (world-level) tendencies. Our estimates suggest that these world-level movements in democracy are unlikely to be driven by the causal effect of income on democracy.

5. A recent creative attempt is by Edward Miguel, Shankar Satyanath, and Ernest Sergenti (2004), who use weather conditions as an instrument for income in Africa to investigate the impact of income on civil wars. Unfortunately, weather conditions are a good instrument only for relatively short-run changes in income, thus not ideal to study the relationship between income and democracy.

6. See, among others, Douglass C. North and Robert P. Thomas (1973), North (1981), Eric L. Jones (1981), Stanley L. Engerman and Kenneth L. Sokoloff (1997), and Acemoglu, Johnson, and Robinson (2001, 2002) for theories that emphasize the impact of certain historical factors on development processes during critical junctures, such as the collapse of feudalism, the age of industrialization, or the process of colonization.

7. See Max Weber (1930), Huntington (1991), and Steven M. Fish (2002) for the hypothesis that religion might have an important effect on economic and political development.

REFERENCES

Acemoglu, Daron, Simon Johnson, and James A. Robinson. 2001. "The Colonial Origins of Comparative Development: An Empirical Investigation." *American Economic Review,* 91(5): 1369–1401.

Acemoglu, Daron, Simon Johnson, and James A. Robinson. 2002. "Reversal of Fortune: Geography and Institutions in the Making of the Modern World Income Distribution." *Quarterly Journal of Economics,* 117(4): 1231–94.

Barro, Robert J. 1997. *Determinants of Economic Growth: A Cross-Country Empirical Study.* Cambridge, MA: MIT Press.

Barro, Robert J. 1999. "Determinants of Democracy." *Journal of Political Economy,* 107(6): S158–83.

Dahl, Robert A. 1971. *Polyarchy: Participation and Opposition.* New Haven, CT: Yale University Press.

Engerman, Stanley L., and Kenneth L. Sokoloff. 1997. "Factor Endowments, Institutions, and Differential Paths of Growth among New World Economies: A View from Economic Historians of the United States." In *How Latin America Fell Behind: Essays on the Economic Histories of Brazil and Mexico, 1800–1914,* ed. Stephen Haber, 60–304. Stanford, CA: Stanford University Press.

Fish, Steven M. 2002. "Islam and Authoritarianism." *World Politics,* 55(1): 4–37.

Huntington, Samuel P. 1991. *The Third Wave: Democratization in the Late Twentieth Century.* Norman: University of Oklahoma Press.

Jones, Eric L. 1981. *The European Miracle: Environments, Economies, and Geopolitics in the History of Europe and Asia.* New York: Cambridge University Press.

Lipset, Seymour M. 1959. "Some Social Requisites of Democracy: Economic Development and Political Legitimacy." *American Political Science Review,* 53(1): 69–105.

Londregan, John B. and Keith T. Poole. 1996. "Does High Income Promote Democracy?" *World Politics,* 49(1): 1–30.

Maddison, Angus. 2003. *The World Economy: Historical Statistics.* Paris: Organisation for Economic Co-operation and Development.

Miguel, Edward, Shanker Satyanath, and Ernest Sergenti. 2004. "Economic Shocks and Civil Conflict: An Instrumental Variables Approach." *Journal of Political Economy,* 112(4): 725–53.

North, Douglass C. 1981. *Structure and Change in Economic History,* New York: W.W. Norton & Co.

North, Douglass C., and Robert P. Thomas. 1973. *The Rise of the Western World: A New Economic History.* Cambridge, UK: Cambridge University Press.

Papaioannou, Elias, and Gregorios Siourounis. 2006. "Economic and Social Factors Driving the Third Wave of Democratization." Unpublished.

Przeworski, Adam, Michael Alvarez, José A. Cheibub, and Fernando Limongi. 2000. *Democracy and Development: Political Institutions and Material Well-being in the World, 1950–1990*. New York: Cambridge University Press.

Przeworski, Adam and Fernando Limongi. 1997. "Modernization: Theory and Facts." *World Politics,* 49(2): 155–83.

Rueschemeyer, Dietrich, Evelyne Huber Stephens, and John D. Stephens. 1992. *Capitalist Development and Democracy.* Chicago: University of Chicago Press.

Weber, Max. 1930. *The Protestant Ethic and the Spirit of Capitalism.* London: Allen and Unwin.

Ben W. Ansell and David J. Samuels

FROM *INEQUALITY AND DEMOCRATIZATION:* AN ELITE-COMPETITION APPROACH

Why Democracy?

What explains the emergence of democracy? Why did some countries democratize in the nineteenth century, while others never have? Which social groups are relatively more or less important proponents of regime change? Does economic growth promote democracy, and if so, how?

Debate about answers to these questions continues. In recent years, scholars have turned away from the question of whether economic development per se fosters regime change, and begun to explore the question of whether the *distributional consequences* of economic development help explain patterns of democracy and dictatorship.

In particular, a set of papers and two influential books by Daron Acemoglu and James Robinson (henceforth "A&R": 2001; 2006) and Carles Boix (2003) have propelled research in this new direction. These books offer what we call *redistributivist* theories of regime change, in that they focus on how economic inequality—the relative distribution of income or assets—impacts voters' demand for redistribution. All else equal, redistributivist arguments suggest that inequality harms democracy's prospects because, in intensifying voters' desire for redistribution of autocratic elites' wealth, it generates a similarly intense reaction by those same elites, who will dig in their heels to maintain the political status quo. In an equal society, demand for redistribution would be weaker—as would elite opposition to liberalization.

In reinvigorating research on the "economic origins of dictatorship and democracy" (the title of Acemoglu and Robinson's book), redistributivist approaches implicitly adopt the fundamental tenet of Modernization Theory—that political change can follow economic change. Yet they add an important new twist, in drawing our attention to the fact that economic development can have very different political consequences, depending on how the growing economic pie is divided up. Such arguments begin with an apparently straightforward contrast between autocracies, which restrict the franchise, and democracies, which allow the poor greater voice and vote. Logically, because there are always more poor people

From *Inequality and Democratization: An Elite-Competition Approach* (New York: Cambridge University Press, 2014), Chapter 1.

than rich people, franchise extensions lower the average voter's income, which should increase demand for redistribution. When such redistributive pressures are high, economic elites will—out of self-interest—resist granting the poor the vote.

We challenge this purported syllogism between democracy and redistribution, and the concomitant assumption that a natural tension exists between democracy and property. Indeed, it is likely that the tension between *autocracy* and property, due to lack of voice and accountability, is far greater than any threat to property under democracy. We also argue that the threat from the median voter that drives redistributivist approaches is a chimera, and that political-economy theories built on such fear lead scholars down an unfruitful path. Democracy does not emerge when redistributive threats to elite interests are low. Instead, it is more likely when rising yet politically disenfranchised groups demand greater voice in government affairs because *they* have more to lose. Democracy is about fear of the autocratic state, not fear of the poor.

Democracy or Property? The Redistributivist Thesis

The notion of "democracy as Robin Hood"—that the poor would use the vote to soak the rich—enjoys an exalted status in contemporary political-economy research. And perhaps for good reason, for it draws on deep and well-known philosophical roots. One can find fear of the depredations of majority rule in Aristotle's *Politics* (Book III, Ch. 10, 14–18), while modern political philosophers as different as Rousseau, Adam Smith, and Tocqueville also all implied in one way or another that democracy and property are incompatible.

Given its philosophical pedigree, the notion that economic equality would inevitably follow political equality has "dominated the hopes and fears attached to democracy" since the earliest days of representative government (Przeworski 2009, 301). Indeed, an intellectual strange bedfellows coalition spanning the political spectrum has long buttressed the redistrib-

utivist logic: those on the left have hoped the poor would remain unsatisfied with the mere acquisition of *de jure* political equality, while those on the right have feared universal suffrage would threaten property.

Both sides have had powerful incentives to advance the notion that democracy and property are in tension not just in theory, but in fact. On the left, we find this claim in Marx and Engels, who both believed democracy should precede communism because universal suffrage would undermine property and exacerbate class struggle. Marx emphasized this theme in the *18th Brumaire* and in *Class Struggles in France*, for example. And not surprisingly, the quest for "distributive justice" has long served as the core principle mobilizing leftist political movements.

On the right, one sees the alleged syllogism between democracy and redistribution in a prominent strand of conservative-libertarian thought, which also assumes that politics is driven by a clash between rich and poor. Democracy is a vehicle for the "legalized plunder," in the words of Frédéric Bastiat (1850), of the property and income of the rich through taxation and redistribution. Fear of redistribution, demands for lower taxes, and calls for economic liberty rather than equality have long mobilized conservative movements.

According to Przeworski (1999, 40), the logic of the supposed tension between democracy and property is so intuitively obvious that by 1850 the idea that democracy would inevitably bring about socioeconomic equality was universally accepted. To this day, Przeworski suggests that intelligent observers have a hard time reconciling universal suffrage and economic inequality, believing that under democracy the poor will naturally soak the rich (Przeworski 2010, 85). Hope on the left and fear on the right—and the clashing calls for economic equality or economic liberty—still drive political debate.

The notion of a tension between democracy and property also figures in prominent accounts of regime change. For example, in engaging and critiquing Barrington Moore, Rueschemeyer, Stephens, and Stephens (1992, 6) (RSS) suggest that democracy emerges due to demands for both political *and* economic equality. RSS drew on Marx in suggesting that the working class would be democracy's 'most frequent proponent' (42) precisely because democracy creates opportunities for redistribution.

In recent years redistributivist arguments with intellectual roots on the other side of the political spectrum have gained traction. In 1981, Allan Meltzer and Scott Richard—who can fairly be classified as "free-market" economists—distilled the alleged incompatibility of democracy and property into a simple formal-theoretic rational-expectations argument about electoral politics. Since there are always more poor people than rich people, universal suffrage means that a majority of voters—and most importantly the median voter under majority rule—earn less than average income. Because everyone with below average income should want to raise taxes on everyone with above average income, democracy should always produce pressure for redistribution—and such pressure should increase with inequality, because as the rich get richer the poorer median voter would gain more by continuing to raise taxes.

Meltzer and Richard's model has had enormous impact on the study of political economy. Many have explored its intended application, relating the degree of inequality to variation in redistributive social-welfare spending. Boix and A&R derived their arguments about regime change from Meltzer and Richard's assumption that everyone, from the incumbent dictator down to the lowliest peasant, knows that in a democracy the poor will soak the rich—and that the larger the gap between rich and poor, the worse will be the soaking.

Boix assumes that political regimes aggregate preferences about redistribution from among those who have the right to participate (p.10). Given this, low levels of inequality under autocracy enhance the chances of democratization because redistributive pressure from the poor is low. Acemoglu and Robinson begin similarly, stating, "Democracy is usually not given by the elite because its values have changed. It is demanded by the disenfranchised as a way to obtain political power and thus secure a larger share of the economic benefits of the system" (p. 29).

Although these books differ in their arguments and conclusions to some degree, they begin from and apply similar theoretical principles—that outcomes of political conflict are a function of the preferences of the median voter, who would like high taxes and substantial redistribution to poor people like themselves (see Acemoglu and Robinson 2006, 103–4; Boix 2003, 23–4). The rich, meanwhile, seek the opposite: no taxes and no redistribution. All redistributivist arguments—whether about social-welfare spending or regime change—focus on elites' fear of the relatively poor median voter, highlighting the similarity between conservative fears and leftist hopes that democracy and redistribution go hand in hand.

Puzzles for the Redistributivist Approach

In our view, the redistributivist thesis offers a misleading understanding of the relationship between inequality and democratization. Our motivation for developing an alternative explanation of this relationship starts with a question: Is democracy more likely to emerge from an autocracy with a Gini coefficient of income inequality of .24, or one with a Gini of .51?

In principle, Gini coefficients can range from 0 (perfect equality—everyone has the same amount) to 1 (perfect inequality—one person has everything, while everyone else has nothing), but .24 is among the lowest Ginis ever recorded. In contrast, .51 is a highly unequal society, at approximately the 80th percentile of historical estimates. Given this, Boix's answer embodies the conventional wisdom: democracy is more likely to emerge in the equal country. In turn, A&R might suggest that democracy is unlikely in either country, because they predict that regime change is only likely when inequality is at a "middling" level.[1]

Now consider a different question: Which country was more likely to democratize: China in 1880, or the UK in 1867? Everyone knows the answer to this question, but what not everyone knows is that the Gini coefficient in China in 1880 was .24, while in the UK in 1867 it was .51.[2] Even if these estimates are somewhat imprecise, no one questions these two countries' levels of inequality relative to each other. This generates a conundrum: all else equal, if Boix's argument were correct, China should have democratized long ago, while the UK might still be an autocracy. For their part, A&R argued that democratization was likely in the nineteenth-century UK, but only because they also suggested that inequality was moderate at that time. However, Victorian Britain's Dickensian chasm between rich and poor suggests that the case does not comfortably fit their argument.

As we will confirm, these cases are not outliers. Many recent examples of regime change—Brazil and South Africa most notoriously perhaps—occurred as income inequality was peaking. Holding all else equal for the moment, the juxtaposition of the UK against China, as well as cases of recent transitions in high-inequality countries, raise questions about the empirical accuracy of redistributivist hypotheses, simply because such examples confound the claim that regime change should occur when the threat of redistribution from the poor is relatively low.

We are hardly the first to question the utility of the median-voter model. Meltzer and Richard offered a seductively parsimonious explanation of redistributive politics, yet empirical support for their argument remains notably weak. Even though the decades since the article's publication have brought better measures of democracy, inequality, and redistribution, scholars have been confounded in their efforts to confirm a relationship between these three variables. Instead, findings have consistently and repeatedly called into question the notions that democracies redistribute more than autocracies and that inequality is correlated with pressures for redistribution.[3] In fact, results have repeatedly found that democracies redistribute less than they "should," and some scholars have even found that redistribution *declines* as inequality increases (e.g., Moene and Wallerstein 2001, 2003; Shelton 2007).

The lack of firm support for the MR thesis has caused endless scholarly head-scratching and has generated a cottage industry of research seeking to salvage the belief that a tension exists between democracy and property. Some suggest the thesis would hold if other factors didn't dilute the impact of voters' natural demand for redistribution, such as elites' ability and willingness to tilt the playing field by flooding politics with money;[4] elites' ability to shape the poor's political beliefs, particularly through ownership of mass media;[5] or the fact that as the salience of noneconomic issues such as ethnicity or religion increases, demand for redistribution declines.[6]

All efforts to explain the MR model's shortcomings accept its basic premise, that voters' desire for redistribution increases as their incomes decline. However, other attempts to account for the model's weak empirical performance dispense with this assumption. Perhaps relatively poor voters oppose redistributive schemes and believe instead that (1) the market system is fair and the rich should be respected, not envied; (2) structural constraints either do not exist or do not shape one's life chances; (3) people generally get what they deserve in life and shouldn't ask for a handout; (4) expropriating the rich might have unintended and undesirable consequences; or (5) even though they are poor in the present, they might be rich in the future (Alesina and La Ferrara 2005; Benabou and Ok 2001). For any or all of these reasons, most voters might prefer policies that equalize economic opportunity, but not outcomes (see e.g., Hochschild 1996).

No consensus exists as to why democracies redistribute less than they "should," but the empirical point remains: insisting on portraying democracy as Robin Hood makes little social-scientific sense. Still, scholars have been unwilling to abandon their faith in the redistributive model, leading Przeworski to sardonically call it "political economists' favorite toy" (2010, 85). Models that explain a lot using only a little are rare gems—things of great beauty and value, at least to social scientists. Simplicity is seductive, and parsimonious models often become the conventional wisdom. Yet simplicity is not always a virtue, because Ockham's razor can sometimes shave off too much, eliminating vital information.

We call attention to the Meltzer-Richard model's inability to explain redistribution in existing democracies because if it cannot accomplish what it was designed to do, we have little reason to expect it to explain regime change, especially based on expectations actors have about redistribution in *hypothetical future* democracies. The model's empirical and theoretical weaknesses need to be brought front and center in the study of regime change, because the lack of a clear relationship between democracy and redistribution implies that median-voter models lead scholars down an intellectually unprofitable path.

Democracy and Property?

Our elite-competition approach offers a new theoretical explanation of the process of "endogenous" democratization—of the relationship between economic growth, inequality, and regime change. We start by turning the Meltzer-Richard model on its head. We assume that an elective affinity exists between property and democracy, rather than tension, and that a causal arrow runs from the former to the latter. In our view, regime change does not emerge from autocratic elites' fear that the poor would expropriate their wealth under democracy. It instead results when politically disenfranchised yet rising economic groups seek to rein in the power of autocratic elites to expropriate *their* income and assets.

We will argue and demonstrate empirically that the threat from the median voter under democracy is largely irrelevant to the story of regime change. Instead, we presume that elites who control the autocratic government represent the far greater threat—to the property of those who lack political rights. Typically, economic development brings about the rise of new economic groups, whose members are wealthier than average and who have growing economic interests to protect, but who lack political rights. Given their precarious political position, these rising elites will invest in changing the political regime, in an effort to rein in its expropriative authority.

The roots of this argument lie in Enlightenment liberalism, which connects the rise of commercial society with demands to rein in arbitrary government authority over individual rights, particularly over property. In recent decades, just as Meltzer and Richard were translating the "democracy *or* property" thesis for modern social science, scholars such as Douglass North (1986) were doing the same for the "democracy *and* property" antithesis. Perhaps the best-known modern statement linking greater demand for property rights to greater demand for limited government is North and Weingast's (1989) explanation of the emergence of limits on state authority during England's Glorious Revolution. The emergence of democracy takes a back seat in this tale, which focuses on explaining the sources of economic growth, but the authors' emphasis on the importance of secure contract and property rights is clearly rooted in Enlightenment liberalism (see also Weingast 1997).

Scholars of regime change have largely ignored the implications of these ideas. Indeed, Przeworski (2007, 6) has gone so far as to suggest that North and Weingast's argument would "bewilder" nineteenth-century observers. This view is erroneous, as is the more relevant notion that it was consensus opinion at that time that the poor would, if given the opportunity, use the vote to soak the rich. In fact, nineteenth-century observers would readily recognize the influence of John Locke, who not coincidentally published his *Two Treatises* the year of the Glorious Revolution, in North and Weingast. More importantly, contemporary scholars who write in the spirit of North's "neoclassical theory of the state" build on a well-known intellectual tradition that draws on elements of Enlightenment liberalism—a body of thought hardly unknown in the early nineteenth century.

Enlightenment liberalism was not exclusively concerned with property, but material interests were always central—and Locke's emphasis on individuals' material interests and the threat that control over government poses to life, liberty and property proved intellectually and politically influential.[7] Adam Smith, for example, drew this connection out explicitly, stating that although some government involvement in the economy was necessary, oppressive government was an obstacle to economic development and was best prevented by parliamentary sovereignty and taxation by representative consent. Malthus agreed, believing the greatest threat to liberty was the growth of executive power, and that both small landholders and emerging urban middle classes offered a necessary counterbalance (Jones 1990).

Emerging theories of limited government did not focus on protecting the rich from the poor, but on protecting property holders from arbitrary and tyrannical government authority. Utilitarians later built on these ideas. For example, echoing Hobbes and Madison, in his *Essay on Government* (1820), Jeremy Bentham's disciple James Mill (father of John Stuart) argued that to guarantee individuals' security of property, protection against the government was more important than protection against each other (Krouse 1982, 513). James Mill harbored a deep suspicion of power held by a narrow elite, and like Bentham and Montesquieu sought to articulate a theory of the "protective" functions of government. Mill and his Utilitarian contemporaries believed that autocracy allowed narrow private interests to hijack the public interest (Collini, Winch, and Burrow 1983, 109)—and the narrower the suffrage, the greater the influence of private interests.

Deriving "democratic conclusions from Hobbesian premises" (ibid., 108), Mill concluded that suffrage equaled protection against tyranny—and that logically, the wider the suffrage, the greater the protection. Democracy and property were compatible for Mill because a broad franchise would remove wealthy voters' ability to exploit non-voters (Dunn 1979, 24). Although Mill had little love for the masses, he "hated the few more than he loved the many" (Thomas 1969, 255) and believed like Bentham (and later, Gramsci) that the poor posed no danger to the rich because they were ideologically dominated by the (conservative) middle classes, and tended to respect property (Collini, Winch, and Burrow 1983, 104; Dunn 1979, 24n).

Mill's argument extended Locke's notion of the protective functions of government, and other prominent liberals shared his views. For example,

Malthus' and Mill's friend David Ricardo, a strong advocate of laissez-faire capitalism, free trade, and minimal taxation, also passionately defended politically liberal causes, including parliamentary reform (Peach 2008). Although he is sometimes mistakenly cited as advocating suffrage limited to property holders (e.g., Collini, Winch, and Burrow 1983, 107; Przeworski 2010, 82), Ricardo also agreed with Mill and other liberals that the poor would not vote to overturn property, stating that fear of the poor was a "bugbear by which the corrupt always endeavor to rally those who have property to lose around them" to oppose suffrage expansion (Ricardo [1824] 1888, 555). He demurred about the benefits of *universal* suffrage but argued that expanding the electorate would nonetheless "substantially secure to the people the good government they wish for" by reducing corruption and rent-seeking (ibid.).

Unlike his father, James, John Stuart Mill emphasized government's educative over its protective functions, a more elitist view. However, contrary to what RSS (2) imply, J.S. Mill did not believe democracy and property were incompatible. Instead, he hewed to the liberal notion that the primary purpose of government was "the provision of a legal framework for making and enforcing contracts, and to defending the liberty, rights, and life of persons and property" (Gibbons 1990, 101), and in his *Considerations on Representative Government* he repeated his father's argument that individual security would be maximized under democracy, because autocracy offers opportunities for the ruling class to exploit its narrow interests at everyone else's expense (Krouse 1982, 528).

Ever since Hobbes, political theorists have highlighted the necessity of the state to discourage predation by one private party against another. Yet these same scholars also understood that Leviathan could become the predator; this fear that a government powerful enough to control citizens could also threaten their liberties rests at the very core of Enlightenment political thought. Resolving this tension remains one of liberalism's central concerns. Locke argued that government's primary purpose was to protect individual rights—to life, liberty, and property. And for liberals like Malthus, Smith, Ricardo, and both Mills, democracy offered relatively greater protection than autocracy. Such theories of limited government were comparatively unconcerned with protecting the rich from the poor, and focused instead on protecting property holders from abuse of government authority.

Democracy, Property, and Elite Competition

The long appeal of the notion that democracy and property are in tension can be traced to its roots in both radical and conservative political thought. Yet the intellectual origins of Modernization Theory—and of the notion of "endogenous" democratization—actually lie with the antithetical notion that democracy and property are fully compatible. Building on Enlightenment liberal ideas and more recent neo-institutionalist research, we draw attention away from demands for redistribution, and toward demands for protection of property rights—to the connection between taxation and (the demand for) representation.

Contemporary neo-institutional theories—such as those of North and Weingast (1989), Douglass North's (1990) "neoclassical theory of the state," Mancur Olson's (1993) conception of the state as a "stationary bandit," and Margaret Levi's (1989) theory of "predatory rule"—all begin from a similar premise: all else equal, property rights are likely to be relatively more secure under democracy.[8]

Given this, although economic exchange typically occurs within the existing political rules, North suggests that regime change can occur when citizens "find it worthwhile to devote resources to altering the more basic structure of the polity, to reassign rights" North (1990, 47). In particular, citizens may seek to extend third-party enforcement of contracts and property rights in order to "eliminate rulers' capricious capacity to confiscate wealth" (North 1990, 51). Bates and Lien (1985) argued similarly

that limited government follows from actors' efforts to "wrest control over public policy from revenue-seeking monarchs" (53).

What sorts of political actors will seek to broaden suffrage and impose limits on government authority? And under what conditions will such actors gain sufficient resources to become politically effective? Our understanding of the relationship between economic development, inequality, and regime change differs in two important ways from arguments that focus on the threat from the median voter: (1) in terms of which social actors drive regime transitions and (2) in terms of the nature and political impact of economic inequality.

First, redistributivist arguments focus on elites' relative fear of the median voter—and thus on the mobilizational capacity of everyone who earns less than the median voter. However, redistributivist arguments have ignored the fact that the median voter is typically quite poor, particularly in developing autocracies. That is, one cannot assume that the median voter is—in sociological, cultural, or political terms—a member of the "middle" class. Individuals with incomes and social status we consider middle class are * * * typically found in the upper quartile—or even the upper decile—of the income distribution. Often, even members of the working classes earn more than the median income.

To the extent that the actors social scientists typically highlight as driving regime change—the bourgeoisie and/or the working class, for example—are located far above the median voter, and to the extent that the median voter in an autocracy is relatively poor, we have good reason to question the empirical accuracy and the theoretical utility of the core redistributivist assumption. After all, Mancur Olson's (1965) theory of collective action suggests that the poor are numerous, possess few resources, have diffuse and diverse interests, and tend to lack self-awareness of their status as politically oppressed—much less have any idea of how to remedy the supposed fact of their oppression.

We offer a more empirically plausible hypothesis about who will organize to promote regime change: political transitions result from the emergence of intra-elite conflict, between a group that controls the state and other relatively wealthy groups that do not. Individuals are far more likely to mobilize when they constitute smaller, wealthier groups with more homogenous and concrete interests—traits we find among both incumbent and disenfranchised economic elites. Intra-elite conflict under autocracy is more likely to emerge when societies experience an imbalance between political and economic power. More specifically, we expect intra-elite political conflict not just when new economic groups emerge that have a growing fear of expropriation, but when their growing numbers and wealth make them a more credible political threat and too costly to repress or co-opt.

Following Dahl (1971) and Knight (1992), the outcome of such conflict will depend on actors' relative bargaining strength, which is in turn a function of the nature and extent of economic development. For example, with modernization, landed elites may find themselves losing ground to new economic groups such as an industrial and/or financial bourgeoisie, a middle class, or the urban working classes, all of whom earn more than the median voter. Such rising groups will demand political concessions and an end to expropriative taxation, in an effort to translate their newfound economic gains into political influence (Bates and Lien 1985; Herb 2003; Levi 1989; Ross 2004).

Focusing on political contestation between economic groups near the top of the income distribution, rather than on conflict between rich and poor, draws attention to the second key distinction between our approach and redistributivist arguments: in terms of the way we conceptualize economic inequality and its political consequences. Unlike redistributivist arguments, we account for the political impact of economic growth across different sectors, distinguishing between inequality in land (historically, predominantly owned by the incumbent autocratic elite) and inequality produced by growing sectors in industry and finance (more likely to be dominated by rising yet disenfranchised groups).

Distinguishing among economic sectors has important ramifications for how we understand regime change. Most importantly, it opens up the possibility that the political impact of land inequality could differ from the political impact of income inequality—as for example when a rising urban financial bourgeoisie lacks political voice relative to a stagnating yet politically entrenched landed elite.

In terms of the relative distribution of land, our empirical prediction is conventional: inequality supports autocracy, while equality fosters democracy. However, our causal mechanism differs: High land inequality does not primarily signify elites' fear that the rural poor would vote to expropriate land under a future democracy, or support a government that would do so. It proxies for the relative strength of a conservative landowning elite unwilling to share political power with representatives of rising and competing economic groups.

High land inequality signifies that a relatively small and cohesive group controls agricultural policy and rural labor mobility. In such a context, landed elites prefer autocracy because they need the state's coercive authority to repress wage demands and keep labor in place, working the land. In contrast, low land inequality signifies a relatively greater proportion of smallholders. In such a situation the key theoretical issue is not the relatively lower redistributive threat from landless peasants, but the greater likelihood of economic (and thus political) divisions within the agrarian sector, the relatively weaker political position of large landowners vis-à-vis control over agricultural policy, and the relatively lower political demand for coercive control over rural labor mobility.

Turning to income inequality, our prediction is counterintuitive. We suggest that democracy is more likely to emerge when rising disenfranchised groups accumulate a growing share of national income. Yet because such groups are found near the top of the income distribution—not near the middle—democratization will occur when income inequality is relatively *high*. This claim rests on the following fact * * *: historically, the process of economic development that has led to the emergence of growing but politically disenfranchised economic groups has also been associated with a pronounced *increase* in income equality. To the extent that this is true, land *equality* and income *inequality* will be associated with democratization; other combinations of these variables will be less likely to lead to regime change.

Our argument uses land and income inequality as measures of the relative balance of economic power, and suggests that political and economic change will co-evolve. We recognize that land and income are not, in the real world, perfectly separable goods. Yet for purposes of thinking about the relative fruitfulness of different theories of the relationship between democracy, development, and inequality, it will become clear how important it is to distinguish these two factors. Tables 8.8a and 8.8b set out our baseline expectations for the relative impacts of land and income inequality on the probability of democratization, along with examples of countries that might be considered "ideal types" for thinking through the connection between inequality and regime change.

In short, in our approach the key actors differ from redistributivist approaches, as does our understanding of the nature and political impact of inequality. We also take the fiscal consequences of control of the state's expropriative capacity more seriously. Median voter models stress the elites' fear that the masses will tax them, but ignore the far more plausible reverse dynamic, that incumbent elites will engage in regressive taxation and impose fiscal burdens on anyone who lacks political rights. Elites who control the state represent a greater threat to the median voter than vice versa because they are more cohesive, have greater resources, and control more effective means of coercion.[9]

Democratization is not about whether the median voter is going to soak the rich; it is about whether all citizens—but particularly rising economic groups who lack political representation—can obtain impartial protection against arbitrary violations of contracts and property rights. Regime change comes about due to divisions within the elite—between those who control the state and those who fear those who control the state. Land inequality may very well retard democracy, but economic development under autocracy has typically meant that while many remain mired in poverty, some proportion of the population is growing wealthy, producing an increase in income inequality. The newly wealthy will be more eager, willing and able to fight to protect

Table 8.8a Income and Land Inequality: Probability of Democratization

	Low Land Inequality	High Land Inequality
Low Income Inequality	Moderate	Low
High Income Inequality	High	Moderate

Table 8.8b Income and Land Inequality: Example Cases

	Low Land Inequality	High Land Inequality
Low Income Inequality	Korea 1970	Germany 1900, China 1880
High Income Inequality	UK 1900, Sweden 1900, China 2010	Brazil 1985

their economic interests. In contrast, lower levels of income inequality will be associated with less intense demands for political change. This book elaborates on this argument, providing the basis for a new understanding of the historical relationship between economic and political change.

■ ■ ■

The puzzle of democracy's emergence has bedeviled social scientists for centuries, and there are few political questions more important in the world today than whether democracy, "the last best hope of earth," in Abraham Lincoln's famous words, can emerge and thrive. What are the conditions that support government that can preserve individual liberties and prevent tyranny? As he would later argue at length (Olson 1982), Olson's *Logic of Collective Action* reminds us that the problem John Locke and James Mill both identified—that a small minority in control of government have both the means and the motive to impose their interests upon the disenfranchised majority—is central to the question of regime change. Democracy does not emerge because of threats from the poor, but because relatively wealthy yet relatively disenfranchised groups want to live free from fear of state predation. The conditions under which relative economic elites will invest their own livelihoods—and lives, often—in an effort to rein in state authority remains a pressing issue for investigation.

NOTES

1. In an earlier paper, Acemoglu and Robinson (2001) suggested that the probability of regime change increases monotonically with inequality, but they abandoned this hypothesis in their book.

2. The former estimate comes from Milanovic, Lindert, and Williamson (2011). The latter comes from Bourguignon and Morrisson (2002).

3. See, for example, Aidt, Daunton, and Dutta (2010); Aidt, Dutta, and Loukoianova (2006);

Aidt and Jensen (2011); Banerjee and Duflo (2003); Benabou (1996); Cheibub (1998); Cutright (1965); Dincecco and Prado (2010); Easterly and Rebelo (1993); Haggard and Kaufman (2012); Jackman (1974); Kenworthy and McCall (2008); Lott and Kenny (1999); Pampel and Williamson (1992); Perotti (1996); Putterman (1996); Rodrigiuez (1999); Scheve and Stasavage (2009); Shelton (2007); Tullock (1983). Reviews of the literature include Harms and Zink (2003); Mueller (2003); Roemer (1998).

4. Critics of democracy have long suggested that elites' informal influence under democracy, which derives from their material wealth and privileged access to those who hold power, overwhelms the masses' numerical advantage. This argument can be traced to Pareto and Mosca, is found in the work of Roberto Michels, C. Wright Mills, and E.E. Schattschneider, and continues—perhaps less as critique of democracy per se than as a call for reform—to hold a prominent place in discussions of American (e.g., Bartels 2010; Gilens 2012; Schlozman, Verba, and Brady 2012) and comparative politics (e.g., Winters 2011). Political economists agree—witness the well-known efforts seeking to explain why most government spending tends to favor the wealthy (e.g., Benabou 1996, 2000; Benabou and Ok 2001; Grossman and Helpman 2002; Justman and Gradstein 1999; Lizzeri and Persico 2004; Ross 2006; Stigler 1970).

5. One need not be an acolyte of Gramsci to appreciate this point; after all, utilitarianism's avatar J.S. Mill suggested that political equality per se would never drive public spending because most voters lack the necessary self-understanding to cast a vote in their own interest.

6. See Alesina and Glaeser (2005); Gilens (2000); Grossmann (2003); Huber and Stanig (2009); Lee and Roemer (1998); Roemer (1998, 2005).

7. A cogent summary of the origins and influence of the liberal idea of "protective democracy" can be found in Held (1987, Chapter 2).

8. Counter-examples exist, but are historically rare. For example, Barro (1991, 284) found only three modern dictatorships that were not hostile to

private property, only one of which has not since democratized (Singapore) (see also e.g., Leblang 1996; Rodrik 2000). Recent work on autocratic regimes has not questioned this view (see e.g., Gehlbach and Keefer 2011).

9. And in any case, the median voter is not a tax collector—so even if preferences exist for redistribution, it is ultimately the state, vulnerable as it is to capture by the rich, that does the taxing and spending. (We owe this last point to Dan Slater, whose work [Slater 2010] elaborates in great detail on the role of the state in autocratic regimes; see also Albertus and Menaldo 2012; Slater and Smith 2012; Smith 2007).

BIBLIOGRAPHY

Acemoglu, D. and J.A. Robinson. 2000. "Why Did the West Extend the Franchise? Democracy, Inequality, and Growth in Historical Perspective." *The Quarterly Journal of Economics* 115 (4):1167–1199.

——. 2001. "A Theory of Political Transitions." *American Economic Review* 91 (4):938–963.

——. 2006. *Economic Origins of Dictatorship and Democracy.* New York: Cambridge University Press.

Aidt, T.S., M. Daunton, and J. Dutta. 2010. "The Retrenchment Hypothesis and the Extension of the Franchise in England and Wales." *The Economic Journal* 120 (547):990–1020.

Aidt, T.S., J. Dutta, and E. Loukoianova. 2006. "Democracy Comes to Europe: Franchise Extension and Fiscal Outcomes 1830–1938." *European Economic Review* 50 (2):249–283.

Aidt, T.S. and P.S. Jensen. 2011. "Workers of the World, Unite! Franchise Extensions and the Threat of Revolution in Europe, 1820–1938." *Discussion Papers of Business and Economics.*

Albertus, M. and V. Menaldo. 2012. "If You're against Them You're with Us: The Effect of Expropriation on Autocratic Survival." *Comparative Political Studies* 45 (8), 973–1003.

Alesina, A. and E.L. Glaeser. 2005. *Fighting Poverty in the US and Europe: A World of Difference.* New York: Oxford University Press.

Alesina, A. and E. La Ferrara. 2005. "Preferences for Redistribution in the Land of Opportunities." *Journal of Public Economics* 89 (5):897–931.

Banerjee, A.V. and E. Duflo. 2003. "Inequality and Growth: What Can the Data Say?" *Journal of Economic Growth* 8 (3):267–299.

Barro, R.J. 1991. "A Cross-country Study of Growth, Saving, and Government." In B.D. Bernheim and J.D. Shoven (eds.), *National Saving and Economic Performance.* Chicago: University of Chicago Press, 271–304.

Bartels, L.M. 2010. *Unequal Democracy: The Political Economy of the New Gilded Age.* Princeton, NJ: Princeton University Press.

Bastiat, Frédéric. 1850. *La Loi.* Ludwig von Mises Institute. Auburn, Alabama. 2007.

Bates, R.H. and D.H. Lien. 1985. "A Note on Taxation, Development, and Representative Government." *Politics & Society* 14 (1):53.

Benabou, Roland. 1996. "Inequality and Growth." In *NBER Macroeconomics Annual Volume 11.* Cambridge, MA: MIT Press, 11–92.

——. 2000. "Unequal Societies: Income Distribution and the Social Contract." *The American Economic Review* 90 (1):96–129.

Benabou, R. and E.A. Ok. 2001. "Social Mobility and the Demand for Redistribution: The POUM Hypothesis." *Quarterly Journal of Economics* 116 (2):447–487.

Boix, Carles. 2003. *Democracy and Redistribution.* New York: Cambridge University Press.

——. 2011. "Democracy, Development, and the International System." *American Political Science Review* 105 (4):809–828.

Bourguignon, François and Christian Morrisson. 2002. "Inequality among World Citizens: 1820–1992." *The American Economic Review* 92 (4):727–744.

Cheibub, J.A. 1998. "Political Regimes and the Extractive Capacity of Governments: Taxation in Democracies and Dictatorships." *World Politics* 50:349–376.

Collini, Stefan, Donald Winch, and John Burrow. 1983. *That Noble Science of Politics: A Study in Nineteenth-Century Intellectual History.* Cambridge, UK: Cambridge University Press.

Coppedge, Michael. 2012. *Democratization and Research Methods: Strategies for Social Inquiry.* New York: Cambridge University Press.

Cutright, Phillips. 1965. "Political Structure, Economic Development, and National Social Security Programs." *American Journal of Sociology*:537–550.

Dahl, R.A. 1971. *Polyarchy: Participation and Opposition.* New Haven, CT: Yale University Press.

Dincecco, Mark and Mauricio Prado. 2010. "War, Democracy, and Government Size over the Long Run: A Structural Breaks Analysis." Unpublished. IMT Luca Institute for Advanced Studies.

Dunn, John. 1979. *Western Political Theory in the Face of the Future.* Cambridge, UK: Cambridge University Press.

Easterly, W. and S. Rebelo. 1993. "Fiscal Policy and Economic Growth." *Journal of Monetary Economics* 32 (3):417–458.

Gehlbach, Scott and Philip Keefer. 2011. "Investment without Democracy: Ruling-party Institutionalization and Credible Commitment in Autocracies." *Journal of Comparative Economics* 39 (2): 123–139.

Gibbons, John. 1990. "J. S. Mill, Liberalism, and Progress." In Richard Bellamy (ed.), *Victorian Liberalism: Nineteenth Century Political Thought and Practice.* London: Routledge.

Gilens, M. 2000. *Why Americans Hate Welfare: Race, Media, and the Politics of Antipoverty Policy.* Chicago, IL: University of Chicago Press.

———. 2012. *Affluence and Influence: Economic Inequality and Political Power in America.* Princeton, NJ: Princeton University Press.

Grossman, Gene and Elhanan Helpman. 2002. *Special Interest Politics.* Cambridge, MA: MIT Press.

Grossman, V. 2003. "Income Inequality, Voting over the Size of Public Consumption, and Growth." *European Journal of Political Economy* 19 (2):265–287.

Haggard, S. and R.R. Kaufman. 2012. "Inequality and Regime Change: Democratic Transitions and the Stability of Democratic Rule." *American Political Science Review* 106 (3):495–516.

Harms, P. and S. Zink. 2003. "Limits to Redistribution in a Democracy: A Survey." *European Journal of Political Economy* 19 (4):651–668.

Held, David. 1987. *Models of Democracy.* Cambridge, UK: Polity Press.

Herb, M. 2003. "Taxation and Representation." *Studies in Comparative International Development* 38 (3):3–31.

Hochschild, J.L. 1996. *Facing up to the American Dream: Race, Class, and the Soul of the Nation.* Princeton, NJ: Princeton University Press.

Huber, J. and P. Stanig. 2009. "Individual Income and Voting for Redistribution across Democracies." Unpublished. Columbia University.

Jackman, R. 1974. "Political Democracy and Social Inequality." *American Sociological Review* 39 (1):29–45.

Jones, H. Stuart. 1990. *Victorian Political Thought.* New York: St. Martin's.

Justman, M. and M. Gradstein. 1999. "The Industrial Revolution, Political Transition, and the Subsequent Decline in Inequality in 19th-century Britain." *Explorations in Economic History* 36 (2):109–127.

Kenworthy, L. and L. McCall. 2008. "Inequality, Public Opinion and Redistribution." *Socio-Economic Review* 6 (1):35–68.

Knight, J. 1992. *Institutions and Social Conflict.* New York: Cambridge University Press.

Krouse, Richard. 1982. "Two Concepts of Democratic Representation: James and John Stuart Mill." *Journal of Politics* 44 (2):509–537.

Kuznets, S. 1955. "Economic Growth and Income Inequality." *The American Economic Review* 45 (1):1–28.

Leblang, D.A. 1996. "Property Rights, Democracy and Economic Growth." *Political Research Quarterly* 49 (1):5–26.

Lee, W. and J.E. Roemer. 1998. "Income Distribution, Redistributive Politics, and Economic Growth." *Journal of Economic Growth* 3 (3):217–240.

Levi, M. 1989. *Of Rule and Revenue.* Berkeley: University of California Press.

Lindert, P.H. 2004. *Growing Public: Social Spending and Economic Growth since the Eighteenth Century.* New York: Cambridge University Press.

Lipset, S.M. 1959. "Some Social Requisites of Democracy: Economic Development and Political Legitimacy." *American Political Science Review* 53 (1):69–105.

Lizzeri, A. and N. Persico, 2004. "Why Did the Elites Extend the Suffrage? Democracy and the Scope of Government, with an Application to Britain's Age of Reform." *Quarterly Journal of Economics* 119 (2):707–765.

Lott, J.R., Jr and L.W. Kenny. 1999. "Did Women's Suffrage Change the Size and Scope of Government?" *Journal of Political Economy* 107 (6):1163–1198.

Meltzer, A.H. and S.F. Richard. 1981. "A Rational Theory of the Size of Government." *Journal of Political Economy* 89 (5):914–927.

Milanovic, Branko, Peter Lindert, and Jeffrey Williamson. 2011. "Pre-Industrial Inequality." *The Economic Journal* 121 (551): 255–272.

Mill, James. [1820] 1992. "An Essay on Government." Reprinted in Terence Ball (ed.), *James Mill: Political Writings.* Avon, UK: The Bath Press, 1–42.

Moene, K.O. and M. Wallerstein. 2001. "Inequality, Social Insurance, and Redistribution." In *American Political Science Review* 95:859–874.

Mueller, D.C. 2003. *Public Choice III.* New York: Cambridge University Press.

North, Douglass. 1986. *Structure and Change in Economic History.* New York: W.W. Norton.

——. 1990. *Institutions, Institutional Change, and Economic Performance.* New York: Cambridge University Press.

North, Douglass and Barry Weingast. 1989. "Constitutions and Commitment: The Evolution of Institutions Governing Public Choice in Seventeenth-century England." *The Journal of Economic History* 49 (04):803–832.

Olson, Mancur. 1965. *The Logic of Collective Action.* Cambridge, MA: Harvard University Press.

——. 1982. *The Rise and Decline of Nations.* New Haven, CT: Yale University Press.

——. 1993. "Dictatorship, Democracy, and Development." *American Political Science Review* 87 (3):567–576.

Pampel, F.C. and J.B. Williamson. 1992. *Age, Class, Politics, and the Welfare State.* New York: Cambridge University Press.

Peach, Terry. 2008. "Ricardo, David (1772–1823)." In *The New Palgrave Dictionary of Economics.* New York: Palgrave.

Perotti, R. 1996. "Growth, Income Distribution, and Democracy: What the Data Say." *Journal of Economic Growth* 1 (2):149–187.

Przeworski, Adam. 1999. "Minimalist Democracy: A Defense." In Ian Shapiro and Casiano Hacker-Cordón (eds.), *Democracy's Value.* New York: Cambridge University Press, 23–55.

——. 2007. "Political Rights, Property Rights, and Economic Development." Presented at the Weatherhead Center for International Affairs, Harvard University.

——. 2009. "Democracy, Equality and Redistribution." In R. Bourke and R. Geuss (eds.), *Political Judgment: Essays for John Dunn.* New York: Cambridge University Press, 281–312.

——. 2010. *Democracy and the Limits of Self-government.* New York: Cambridge University Press.

Putterman, L. 1996. "Why Have the Rabble Not Redistributed the Wealth? On the Stability of Democracy and Unequal Property." In *IEA Conference Volume Series*, vol. 115. New York: The Macmillan Press Ltd, 359–389.

Ricardo, David. [1824] 1888. "Observations on Parliamentary Reform." In *The Works of David Ricardo* 5. London: John Murray, 495–503.

Rodrigiuez, F.C. 1999. "Does Distributional Skewness Lead to Redistribution? Evidence from the United States." *Economics & Politics* 11 (2):171–199.

Rodrik, D. 2000. "Institutions for High-quality Growth: What They Are and How to Acquire Them." *Studies in Comparative International Development* 35 (3):3–31.

Roemer, J.E. 1998. "Why the Poor Do Not Expropriate the Rich: An Old Argument in New Garb." *Journal of Public Economics* 70 (3):399–424.

——. 2005. "Will Democracy Engender Equality?" *Economic Theory* 25 (1):217–234.

Ross, M. 2006. "Is Democracy Good for the Poor?" *American Journal of Political Science* 50 (4):860–874.

Ross, M. 2004. "Does Taxation Lead to Representation?" *British Journal of Political Science* 34 (2):229–249.

Rueschemeyer, D., E.H. Stephens, and J. Stephens. 1992. *Capitalist Development and Democracy.* Chicago: University of Chicago Press.

Scheve, K. and D. Stasavage. 2006. "Religion and Preferences for Social Insurance." *Quarterly Journal of Political Science* 1 (3):255–286.

Schlozman, K.L., S. Verba, and H.E. Brady. 2012. *The Unheavenly Chorus: Unequal Political Voice and the Broken Promise of American Democracy.* Princeton, NJ: Princeton University Press.

Shelton, C.A. 2007. "The Size and Composition of Government Expenditure." *Journal of Public Economics* 91 (11-12):2230–2260.

Slater, D. 2010. *Ordering Power: Contentious Politics and Authoritarian Leviathans in Southeast Asia.* New York: Cambridge University Press.

Slater, Dan and Ben Smith. 2012. "Economic Origins of Democratic Breakdown? Contrary Evidence from Southeast Asia and Beyond." Unpublished. University of Chicago.

Smith, B.B. 2007. *Hard Times in the Lands of Plenty: Oil Politics in Iran and Indonesia.* New York: Cornell University Press.

Stigler, G.J. 1970. "Director's Law of Public Income Redistribution." *Journal of Law and Economics* 13 (1):1–10.

Thomas, W. 1969. "James Mill's Politics: The 'Essay on Government' and the Movement for Reform." *Historical Journal* 12:249–294.

Tullock, G. 1983. "Further Tests of a Rational Theory of the Size of Government." *Public Choice* 41 (3):419–421.

Weingast, Barry. 1997. "The Political Foundations of Democracy and the Rule of Law." *American Political Science Review* 91 (2):245–263.

Winters, J.A. 2011. *Oligarchy.* New York: Cambridge University Press.

Maurice Duverger

THE NUMBER OF PARTIES

Only individual investigation of the circumstances in each country can determine the real origins of the two-party system. The influence of such national factors is certainly very considerable; but we must not in their *favour* underestimate the importance of one general factor of a technical kind, the electoral system. Its effect can be expressed in the following formula: *the simple-majority single-ballot system favours the two-party system.* Of all the hypotheses that have been defined in this book, this approaches the most nearly perhaps to a true sociological law. An almost complete correlation is observable between the simple-majority single-ballot system and the two-party system: dualist countries use the simple-majority vote and simple-majority vote countries are dualist. The exceptions are very rare and can generally be explained as the result of special conditions.

We must give a few details about this coexistence of the simple-majority and the two-party systems. First let us cite the example of Great Britain and the Dominions: the simple-majority system with a single ballot is in operation in all; the two-party system operates in all, with a Conservative-Labour antagonism tending to replace the Conservative-Liberal

From *Political Parties: Their Organization and Activity in the Modern State* (New York: Wiley, 1954), pp. 217–28.

antagonism. It will be seen later that Canada, which appears to present an exception, in fact conforms to the general rule.[1] Although it is more recent and more restricted in time the case of Turkey is perhaps more impressive. In this country, which had been subjected for twenty years to the rule of a single party, divergent tendencies were manifest as early as 1946; the secession of the Nationalist party, which broke away from the opposition Democratic party in 1948, might have been expected to give rise to a multi-party system. On the contrary, at the 1950 elections the simple-majority single-ballot system, based on the British pattern (and intensified by list-voting), gave birth to a two-party system: of 487 deputies in the Great National Assembly only ten (i.e., 2.07%) did not belong to one or the other of the two major parties, Democrats and Popular Republicans. Nine were Independents and one belonged to the Nationalist party. In the United States the traditional two-party system also coexists with the simple-majority single-ballot system. The American electoral system is, of course, very special, and the present-day development of primaries introduces into it a kind of double poll, but the attempt sometimes made to identify this technique with the "second ballot" is quite mistaken. The nomination of candidates by an internal vote inside each party is quite a different thing from the real election. The fact that the nomination is open makes no difference: the primaries are a feature of party organization and not of the electoral system.

The American procedure corresponds to the usual machinery of the simple-majority single-ballot system. The absence of a second ballot and of further polls, particularly in the presidential election, constitutes in fact one of the historical reasons for the emergence and the maintenance of the two-party system. In the few local elections in which proportional representation has from time to time been tried it shattered the two-party system: for example in New York between 1936 and 1947, where there were represented on the City Council 5 parties in 1937 (13 Democrats, 3 Republicans, 5 American Labor, 3 City Fusionists, 2 dissident Democrats), 6 parties in 1941 (by the addition of 1 Communist), and 7 parties in 1947 (as a result of an internal split in the American Labor party supported by the Garment Trade Unions).

■ ■ ■

Elimination [of third parties] is itself the result of two factors working together: a mechanical and a psychological factor. The mechanical factor consists in the "under-representation" of the third, i.e., the weakest party, its percentage of seats being inferior to its percentage of the poll. Of course in a simple-majority system with two parties the vanquished is always under-represented by comparison with the victor, as we shall see below, but in cases where there is a third party it is under-represented to an even greater extent than the less favoured of the other two. The example of Britain is very striking: before 1922, the Labour party was under-represented by comparison with the Liberal party; thereafter the converse regularly occurred (with the one exception of 1931, which can be explained by the serious internal crisis in the Labour party and the crushing victory of the Conservatives); in this way the third party finds the electoral system mechanically unfair to it (Fig. 8.13). So long as a new party which aims at competing with the two old parties still remains weak the system works against it, raising a barrier against its progress. If, however, it succeeds in outstripping one of its forerunners, then the latter takes its place as third party and the process of elimination is transferred.

The psychological factor is ambiguous in the same way. In cases where there are three parties operating under the simple-majority single-ballot system the electors soon realize that their votes are wasted if they continue to give them to the third party: whence their natural tendency to transfer their vote to the less evil of its two adversaries in order to prevent the success of the greater evil. This "polarization" effect works to the detriment of a new party so long as it is the weakest party but is turned against the less favoured of its older rivals as soon as the new party outstrips it. It operates in fact in the same way as "under-representation." The reversal of the two effects does not always

Figure 8.13 Disparity between Percentage of Votes and Percentage of Seats in Great Britain

I Gross disparity

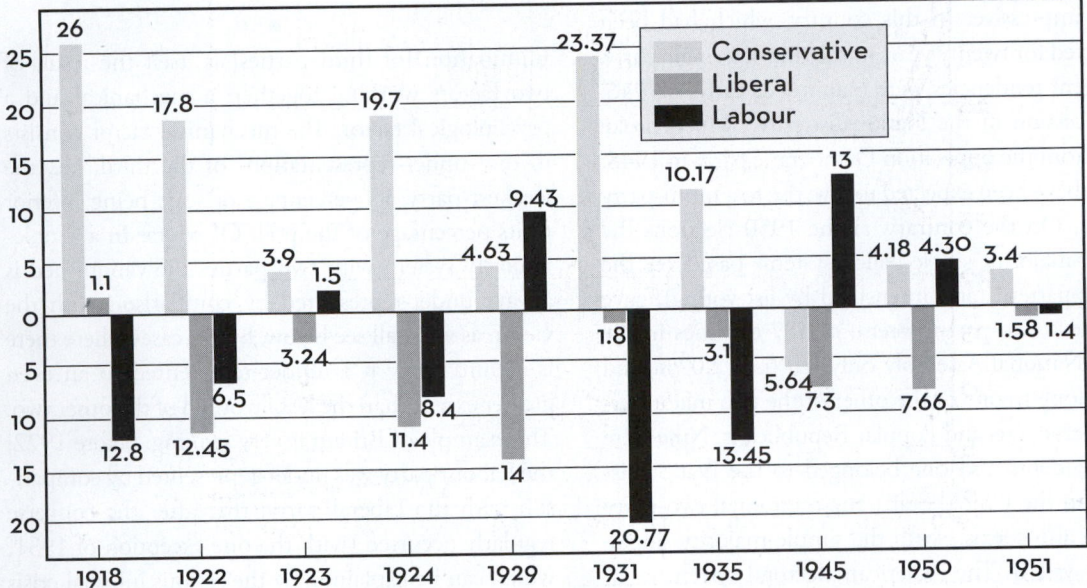

II Net disparity (related to percentage of votes)

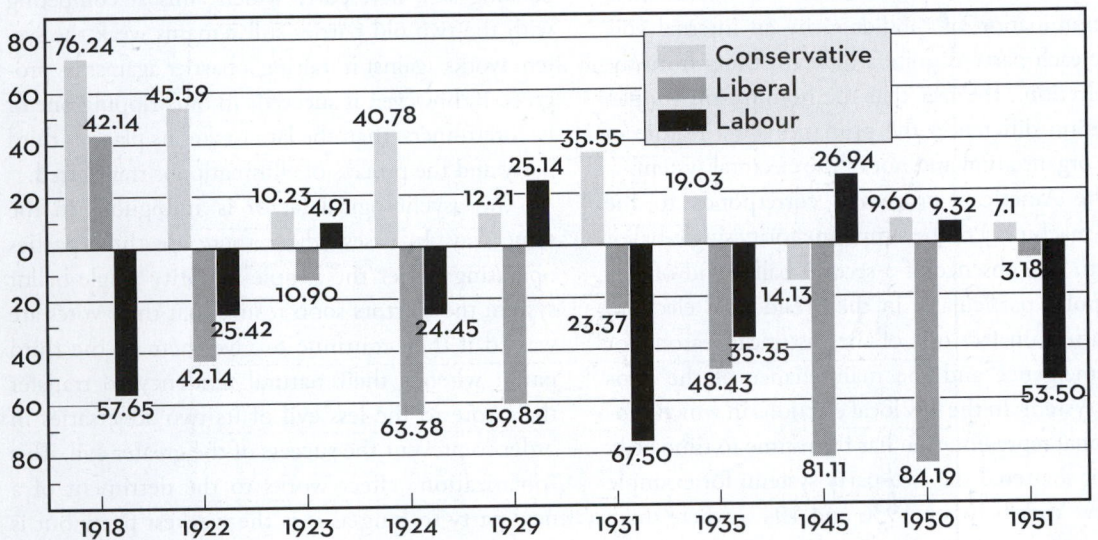

Figure 8.14 Elimination of Liberal Party in Great Britain

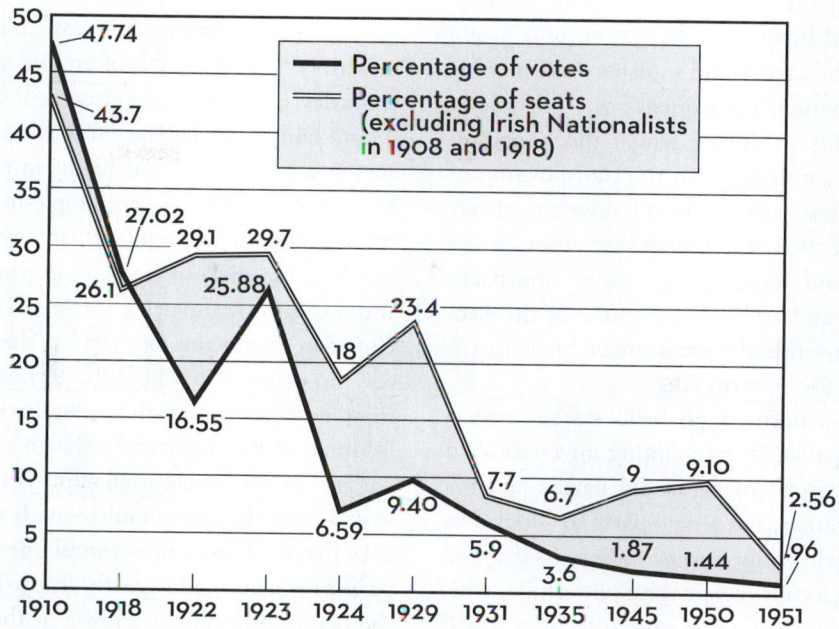

Figure 8.15 "Rescue" of Belgian Liberal Party by P.R. (No. of Seats in Chamber of Deputies)

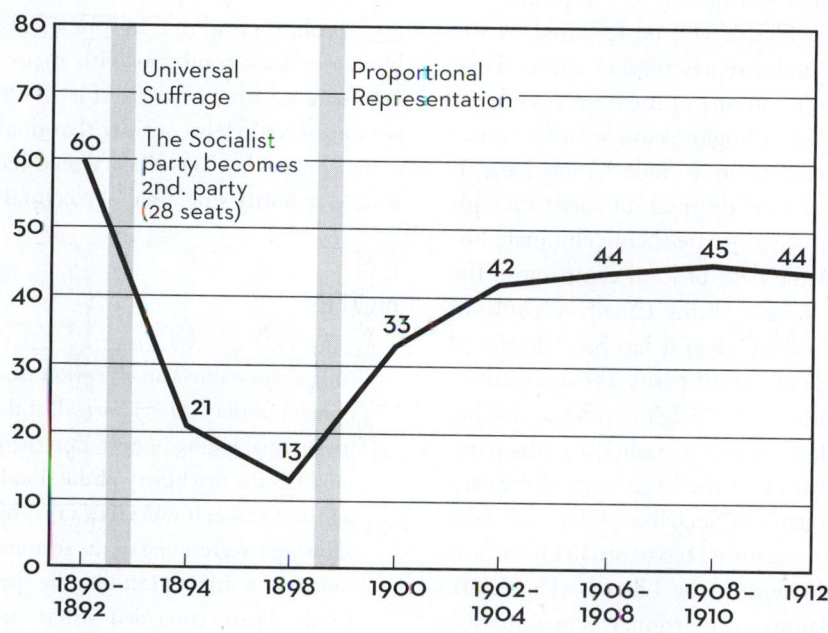

occur at the same moment, under-representation generally being the earlier, for a certain lapse of time is required before the electors become aware of the decline of a party and transfer their votes to another. The natural consequence is a fairly long period of confusion during which the hesitation of the electors combines with the transposition of the "under-representation" effect to give an entirely false picture of the balance of power amongst the parties: England experienced such drawbacks between 1923 and 1935. The impulse of the electoral system towards the creation of bipartism is therefore only a long-term effect.

The simple-majority single-ballot system appears then to be capable of maintaining an established dualism in spite of schisms in old parties and the birth of new parties. For a new party to succeed in establishing itself firmly it must have at its disposal strong backing locally or great and powerful organization nationally. In the first case, moreover, it will remain circumscribed within the geographical area of its origin and will only emerge from it slowly and painfully, as the example of Canada demonstrates. Only in the second case can it hope for a speedy development which will raise it to the position of second party, in which it will be favoured by the polarization and under-representation effects. Here perhaps we touch upon one of the deep-seated reasons which have led all Anglo-Saxon Socialist parties to organize themselves on a Trade Union basis; it alone could put at their disposal sufficient strength for the "take-off," small parties being eliminated or driven back into the field of local campaigns. The simple-majority system seems equally capable of re-establishing dualism when it has been destroyed by the appearance of a third party. The comparison between Great Britain and Belgium offers a striking contrast: in both countries a traditional two-party system was broken up at the beginning of the century by the emergence of Socialism. Fifty years later the majority system restored bipartism in Great Britain by the elimination of the Liberals (Fig. 8.14), whereas in Belgium proportional representation saved the Liberal party and later made possible the

birth of the Communist party, without counting a few other parties between the wars (Fig. 8.15).

Can we go further and say that the simple-majority system is capable of producing bipartism in countries where it has never existed? If they already show a fairly clear tendency towards two parties, the answer would unquestionably be in the affirmative. The establishment of the simple-majority single-ballot system in Western Germany would undoubtedly have the effect of gradually destroying the small and medium-sized parties, leaving the Socialists and Christian Democrats face to face; there is undoubtedly no country in which the technical conditions more nearly approach those required for the establishment of a parliamentary system after the British pattern. In Italy an electoral reform of the same kind would have the same results—with the sole difference that the Communists would be one of the two parties, which would greatly imperil the future of the democratic system. However, the brutal application of the single-ballot system in a country in which multipartism has taken deep root, as in France, would not produce the same results, except after a very long delay. The electoral system works in the direction of bipartism; it does not necessarily and absolutely lead to it in spite of all obstacles. The basic tendency combines with many others which attenuate it, check it, or arrest it. With these reserves we can nevertheless consider that dualism of parties is the "brazen law" (as Marx would have said) of the simple-majority single-ballot electoral system.

NOTE

1. Australia too offers an exception since the development of the *Country party*. But the system of preferential voting in operation there profoundly modifies the machinery of the simple-majority poll and makes it more like a two-ballot system by allowing a regrouping of the scattered votes. It is moreover a striking fact that the appearance of the Country party coincided with the introduction of the preferential vote.

Torben Iversen and David Soskice

ELECTORAL INSTITUTIONS AND THE POLITICS OF COALITIONS: WHY SOME DEMOCRACIES REDISTRIBUTE MORE THAN OTHERS

Why do some countries redistribute more than others? Most work on the politics of redistribution starts from the premise that democratic institutions empower those who stand to benefit from redistribution. The basic logic is succinctly captured in the Meltzer–Richard (1981) model, where the voter with the median income is also the decisive voter. With a typical right-skewed distribution of income, the median voter will push for redistributive spending up to the point where the benefit of such spending to the median voter is outweighed by the efficiency costs of distortionary taxation.

This argument implies that redistribution is much greater in democracies than in nondemocracies (at least of the right-authoritarian variety), and that, among the latter, inegalitarian societies redistribute more than egalitarian ones. There is some evidence to support the first implication, although it is disputed (see Ross 2005), but most of the variance in redistribution is probably within the same regime type. According to data from the Luxembourg Income Study, for example, the reduction in the poverty rate in United States as a result of taxation and transfers was 13% in 1994, whereas the comparable figure for Sweden was 82% (the poverty rate is the percentage of households below 50% of the median income). To explain this variance, we have to look at political and economic differences among democracies, but the second implication—that inegalitarian societies redistribute more—turns

out to be of little help. In fact the empirical relationship between inequality and redistribution is the opposite of the predicted one (see Bénabou 1996; Moene and Wallerstein 2001; Perotti 1996). Sweden not only redistributes more than the United States, but also is a much more egalitarian society. So the explanation for why some democracies redistribute more than others would seem to lie more or less wholly outside the standard framework in political economy to explain democratic redistribution.

One possibility is that the power of the working class and left political parties varies across countries (see, e.g., Korpi 1983, 1989; Hicks and Swank 1992; Huber and Stephens 2001). Because it is plausible that redistribution is a function of government policies, and such policies reflect the preferences of those who govern, looking for differences in government partisanship is a promising avenue. Furthermore, if left governments not only redistribute more but also reduce inequality of earnings by, say, investing heavily in public education, partisanship may also explain why equality and redistribution tend to co-vary. Indeed, there is much evidence to the effect that government partisanship helps explain cross-national differences in redistribution (Boix 1998; Bradley et al. 2003; Kwon and Pontusson 2003), and our findings corroborate this evidence. But it raises another puzzle: why are some democracies dominated by left governments, whereas others are dominated by right governments?

Although government partisanship is often assumed to reflect the level of working-class mobilization, we argue that it is in fact mainly determined

From *American Political Science Review* 100, no. 2 (May 2006), pp. 165–81.

by differences in coalitional dynamics associated with particular electoral systems. Table 8.9 shows the strong empirical relationship using a new dataset on parties and legislatures (see Cusack and Engelhardt 2002; Cusack and Fuchs 2002). The figures are the total number of years with right and left governments in 17 advanced democracies between 1945 and 1998, organized by type of electoral system. Mirroring a similar finding by Powell (2002), about three fourths of governments in majoritarian systems were center-*right*, whereas three fourths of governments under PR were center-*left* (excluding here "pure" center governments). The numbers in parentheses convey a sense of the evidence at the level of countries, classifying countries according to whether they have an overweight (more than 50%) of center-left or center-right governments during the 1945–98 period. We discuss the data (and the one outlier) in detail next.

Our explanation for the association of Table 8.9 builds on an emerging literature on the effects of electoral formulae on economic policies and outcomes (see, e.g., Persson and Tabellini 1999, 2000, 2003; Rogowski and Kayser 2002; Austen-Smith 2000). In particular, we argue that the electoral formula affects coalition behavior and leads to systematic differences in the partisan composition of governments—hence, to different distributive outcomes. The model we propose assumes that parties represent classes, or coalition of classes, and that it is difficult for parties to commit credibly to electoral platforms that deviate from the preferences of their constituents. We also make a critical departure from standard models based on Meltzer–Richard (1981) by allowing taxes and transfers to vary across classes, thereby transforming redistributive politics into a multidimensional game. In particular, we move away from a simple rich-poor model to one in which the middle class will fear taxation by the poor, even as it faces an incentive to ally with the poor to take from the rich. The only constraint is that the rich cannot "soak" the middle class and poor under democracy—a condition that can be justified on empirical, normative, and institutional grounds.

Based on these very general assumptions we show that in a two-party majoritarian system the center-right party is more likely to win government power, and redistribute less, than in a multi-party PR system where the center party is more likely to ally with parties to its left. The intuition is that in a majoritarian system where parties cannot fully commit, the median voter faces low taxes if a center-right party deviates to the right if elected, but faces high taxes and redistribution to low-income groups if a

Table 8.9 Electoral System and the Number of Years with Left and Right Governments (1945–98)

| | | GOVERNMENT PARTISANSHIP | | Proportion of Right Governments |
		Left	Right	
Electoral system	Proportional	342	120	0. 26
		(8)	(1)	
	Majoritarian	86	256	0. 75
		(0)	(8)	

Note: Excludes centrist governments (see text for details).

center-left party in government deviates to the left. With PR, on the other hand, the middle-class party has an incentive to form a coalition with the left party because they can together "exploit" the rich. No such exploitation of the poor is feasible under realistic assumptions. Remarkably, therefore, the same set of assumptions about redistributive policies leads to opposite predictions about government partisanship depending on the electoral system. We test the model on postwar data for redistribution and government partisanship for advanced democracies since the Second World War.

The Evidence

We test our argument in two parts. In the first part, we use partisanship and electoral system as explanatory variables to account for differences in the level of redistribution. In the second part, we use partisanship as the dependent variable, testing the proposition that the electoral system shapes coalition behavior and therefore the composition of governments.

Data

We base our analysis of redistribution on the Luxembourg Income Study (LIS), which has been compiling a large database on pre- and post-tax and transfer income inequality during the past three decades. The LIS data used for this study cover 14 countries from the late 1960s (the first observation is 1967) to the late 1990s (the last observation is 1997). All 14 countries have been democracies since the Second World War. There are a total of 61 observations, with the number of observations for each country ranging from 2 to 7. About one-fifth of the observations are from the 1970s and late 1960s, about 40% from the 1980s, and the remainder from the 1990s. The data are based on separate national surveys, but considerable effort has gone into harmonizing (or "Lissifying") them to ensure comparability across countries and time. The LIS

data are widely considered to be of high quality and the best available for the purposes of studying distribution and redistribution (see Brady 2003; OECD 1995).

As noted previously, we use the data specifically to explore the determinants of redistribution as measured by the percentage reduction in the Gini coefficient from before to after taxes and transfers. The Gini coefficient is perhaps the best summary measure of inequality, and varies from 0 (when there is a perfectly even distribution of income) to 1 (when all income goes to the top decile). Using an adjusted version of the LIS data—constructed by Huber, Stephens, and their associates (Bradley et al. 2003)[1]—we include only working age families, primarily because generous public pension systems (especially in Scandinavia) discourage private savings and therefore exaggerate the degree of redistribution among older people. Furthermore, because data are only available at the household level, income is adjusted for household size using a standard square root divisor (see OECD 1995).

On the independent side, the key variables for explaining redistribution are government partisanship and electoral system. The first is an index of the partisan left-right "center of gravity" of the cabinet based on (1) the average of three expert classifications of government parties' placement on a left-right scale, weighted by (2) their decimal share of cabinet portfolios. The index goes from left to right and is standardized to vary between 0 and 1. The measure was conceived by Gross and Sigelman (1984) and has been applied to OECD countries by Cusack in a new comprehensive data set on parties and partisanship (see Cusack and Fuchs 2002 and Cusack and Engelhardt 2002 for details). The expert codings are from Castles and Mair (1984), Laver and Hunt (1992), and Huber and Inglehart (1995).

One issue raised by this measure is how we can be sure that partisan effects are due to differences in "who governs" as opposed to differences in voter preferences. Our argument is that the electoral system affects the party composition of governments, and hence government policies—*not* that electorates in different countries want different governments and policies (although that might of course also be the case). One way of making sure is to use the difference between the ideological center of gravity of the government and the ideological position of the median voter. Because the position of each party represented in the legislature is known, we can use the position of the party with the median legislator as a proxy for the median voter preference. Hence, we also test our model using this relative center of gravity measure. In cases with single-party majority governments (such as the current British Labour government)—where the government party controls the median legislator by definition—we use the *mean* position of the legislative parties weighted by the parties' seat shares (so that the Labour government would be recorded as being left of center).[2]

Turning to measurement of electoral system, the theoretical distinction between majoritarian two-party systems and proportional multiparty systems is roughly matched by differences in actual electoral systems (see Table 8.10). With the partial exception of Austria (because of the strong position of the two main parties), all PR systems tend to have multiple parties and coalition governments, whereas the non-PR systems have few parties and frequent single-party majority governments (although Australia and Ireland *have* experienced several instances of coalition governments).[3] This is indicated in the third column of Table 8.10 using Laasko and Taagepera's (1979) measure of the effective number of parties in parliament.[4] France is somewhat of an outlier among the majoritarian cases, but the second round of voting in the French runoff system usually involves candidates from only two parties.

The division of countries into two electoral systems is bolstered by the quantitative proportionality measure in the last column. This is a composite index based on Lijphart's measure of the effective threshold of representation and Gallagher's measure of the disproportionality between votes and seats (data are from Lijphart 1994). Note that the index is consistent with the division into a majoritarian and a proportional group: there are no cases that should

be "switched" based on their value on the index. All our results go through if we use this index instead of the PR-majoritarian dichotomy.

We also controlled for variables that are commonly assumed to affect redistribution and/or partisanship. These variables, with definitions, sources, as well as a short discussion of causal logic, are listed next.

PRETAX AND TRANSFER INEQUALITY

This variable is included to capture the Meltzer–Richard logic that more inequality leads to more redistribution. It is measured as the earnings of a worker in the 90th percentile of the earnings distribution as a share of the earnings of the worker with a median income. We are using earnings data, despite their limitations, because the Meltzer–Richard model applies to individuals, not households. The data are from OECD's wage dispersion data set (unpublished electronic data).

CONSTITUTIONAL VETO POINTS

Composite measure of federalism, presidentialism, bicameralism, and the frequency of referenda, based on Huber, Ragin, and Stephens (1993). The more independent decision nodes, the more veto points. The left in countries with many veto points may have found it harder to overcome opposition to redistributive spending.

UNIONIZATION

According to power resource theory, high union density should lead to more political pressure for redistribution and a stronger left, whereas simultaneously reducing primary income inequality. The data are from Visser (1989, 1996).

VOTER TURNOUT

Lijphart (1997) argues that there is much evidence to the effect that voter nonturnout is concentrated among the poor. Higher turnout may therefore be associated with less redistribution. The turnout data are from annual records in Mackie and Rose (1991) and in International Institute for Democracy and Electoral Assistance (1997).

Table 8.10 Key Indicators of Party and Electoral Systems

	Electoral System	Effective Number of Legislative Parties	Proportionality of Electoral System
Majoritarian			
Australia	Majority[a]	2.5	0.19
Canada	SMP	2.2	0.13
France	Runoff[b]	3.8	0.16
Ireland	STV[c]	2.8	0.70
Japan	SNTV[d]	2.7	0.61
New Zealand	SMP	2.0	0.00
UK	SMP	2.1	0.16
USA	SMP	1.9	0.39
Average		2.5	0.30
Proportional			
Austria	PR	2.4	0.89
Belgium	PR	5.2	0.86
Denmark	PR	4.4	0.96
Finland	PR	5.1	0.87
Germany	PR	2.6	0.91
Italy	PR	4.0	0.91
Netherlands	PR	4.6	1.00
Norway	PR	3.3	0.76
Sweden	PR	3.3	0.90
Average		3.9	0.90

a. The use of the single transferable vote in single-member constituencies makes the Australian electoral system a majority rather than plurality system.
b. The two-round runoff system has been in place for most of the postwar period with short interruptions of PR (1945 until early 1950s and 1986–88).
c. The Irish single transferable vote system (STV) is unique. Although it is sometimes classified as a PR system, the low constituency size (five or less) and the strong centripetal incentives for parties in the system makes it similar to a median-voter-dominated SMP system.
d. The single nontransferable voting (SNTV) in Japan (until 1994) deviates from SMP in that more than one candidate is elected from each district, but small district size and nontransferability make it clearly distinct from PR list systems.

UNEMPLOYMENT

Because the unemployed receive no wage income, they are typically poor in the absence of transfers. Because all countries have public unemployment insurance, higher unemployment will therefore "automatically" be linked to more redistribution. We use standardized rates from OECD, *Labour Force Statistics* (Paris: OECD, various years).

REAL PER CAPITA INCOME

This is a standard control to capture "Wagner's Law," which says that demand for social insurance is income elastic. The data are expressed in constant 1985 dollars and are from the World Bank's Global Development Network Growth Database (http://www.worldbank.org/research/growth/GDNdata.htm)—itself based on Penn World Table 5.6, Global Development Finance and World Development Indicators.

FEMALE LABOR FORCE PARTICIPATION

Women's participation in the labor market is likely to affect redistributive spending because it entitles some women to benefits (unemployment insurance, health insurance, etc.) for which they would otherwise be ineligible. Because women tend to be lower paid it may also increase support for the left and for redistributive policies. The measure is female labor force participation as a percentage of the working age population and is taken from OECD, *Labour Force Statistics* (Paris: OECD, various years).

■ ■ ■

Findings

REDISTRIBUTION

We begin our presentation with the results from estimating a simple baseline model with economic variables only (column 1 in Table 8.11). As expected, female labor force participation and unemployment are associated with more redistribution. Contrary to Wagner's Law, higher per capita income slightly reduces redistribution, although the result is not statistically significant across model specifications.

As in other studies, we also find that inequality of pretax and transfer earnings has a *negative* effect on redistribution, contrary to the Meltzer-Richard model expectation. This negative effect is statistically significant at a .01 level, and the substantive impact is strong: a 1 SD increase in inequality is associated with a .3 standard deviation reduction in redistribution.

Yet the effect of inequality *reverses* (though the positive effect is not significant) when we include controls for the political-institutional variables (columns 2–4). One likely reason for this change is that left governments, as well as strong unions and PR, not only cause an increase in redistribution but also reduce inequality. Ansell (2005), for example, has found strong evidence that left governments spend more on primary education, which is likely to increase the equality of the wage structure. If so, excluding partisanship produces an omitted variable bias on the coefficient for inequality.

The most important result in Table 8.11 is that right partisanship has a strong and statistically significant negative effect on redistribution, regardless of whether we use the absolute (column 2) or the relative (column 3) measure of partisanship. A 1 SD shift to the right reduces redistribution by about 1/3 SD. This confirms previous research, especially that of Bradley et al. (2003), and it adds the finding that partisanship matters *even* when measured relative to the ideological center of the legislature. This is important to our story because it implies that political parties, and the coalitions they form, matter for redistribution—not just differences in the preferences of electorates.

The results also suggest that multiple veto points, as expected, reduce redistribution, and that PR has a direct (positive) effect on redistribution. The latter effect holds regardless of which measure of electoral system in Table 8.10 that we use. Our model suggests one possible reason for this because if the probability of left deviation from a median voter platform is not too high, center-left governments will always redistribute more to the poor under PR than under majoritarian rules. To test this, we ran the same model using the percentage reduction in the poverty rate instead of reduction in the gini coefficient as the dependent

Table 8.11 Regression Results for Reduction in Inequality (Standard Errors in Parentheses)

	(1)	(2)	(3)
Inequality	−16.75***	13.17	12.48
	(5.68)	(9.36)	(8.96)
Political–institutional variables			
Government partisanship (right)	−	−2.38***	−
		(0.73)	
Government partisanship relative to median legislator	−	−	−2.93***
			(0.75)
Voter turnout	−	0.01	−0.06
		(0.10)	(0.10)
Unionization	−	0.16*	0.15*
		(0.09)	(0.09)
Number of veto points	−	−1.57**	−1.79***
		(0.62)	(0.59)
Electoral system (PR)	−	5.00**	4.44**
Controls			
		(2.15)	(2.06)
Per capita income	−0.001***	−0.001	−0.001
	(0.00)	(0.00)	(0.000)
Female labor force participation	0.73***	0.36	0.45***
	(0.11)	(0.20)	(0.20)
Unemployment	0.81***	0.99***	1.08***
	(0.27)	(0.27)	(0.26)
ρ	.4	.7	.7
R-squared	0.648	0.746	0.765
N	47	47	47

Note: Significance levels: ***<. 01; **<. 05; *<. 10 (two-tailed tests). All independent variables are measures of the cumulative effect of these variables between observations on the dependent variable. See regression equation and text for details.

variable. Consistent with this proposition it turns out that whereas the effect of partisanship is about the same, the direct effect of PR is notably stronger.[5]

There may also be effects of electoral systems that we have not modeled. Persson and Tabellini (2003), for example, have argued that single-member plurality systems incentivize politicians to target spending on geographically concentrated constituencies, whereas PR, with ideally only one electoral district, encourages politicians to spend more on universalistic benefit programs. Because universalistic programs are likely to be more redistributive than geographically targeted programs, this would mean that PR has a direct effect on redistribution. But our focus is on the effect of electoral system on partisanship, to which we now turn.

PARTISANSHIP

Whereas both government partisanship and electoral system are important in explaining redistribution, partisanship itself is shaped by the distinct coalitional politics associated with different electoral systems. A key implication of our argument is that center-left governments tend to dominate over long periods of time under PR, whereas center-right governments tend to dominate under majoritarian institutions. Although the electoral system has a direct effect on redistribution, we argue that partisanship is one of the key mechanisms through which it exerts an effect on redistribution. * * *

Conclusion

The details of actual tax-and-spend policies for the purpose of redistribution are complex, but the explanation for redistribution in advanced democracies is arguably fairly simple. We propose here that to a very considerable extent, redistribution is the result of electoral systems and the class coalitions they engender. The contribution of this paper is to provide a very general model that explains the electoral system effect, and to empirically test this model.

To explain redistributive policies under democracy, it is essential to understand that policies are multidimensional and that groups have to form partisan coalitions to govern. Both features of redistributive politics are assumed away in standard political economy models that follow the setup in Meltzer and Richard (1981). In our model, by contrast, there is nothing that prevents the poor from taking from the middle class, or the middle class taking from the rich. This means that the middle class, which tends to decide who governs, has an incentive to ally with the poor to exploit the rich, but also an incentive to support the rich to avoid being exploited by the poor. In a majoritarian two-party system, the latter motive dominates because the middle class cannot be sure that the poor will not set policies in a center-left leadership party. In a PR system with three representative parties, on the other hand, the first motive dominates because the middle-class party *can* make sure that a coalition with the left party will not deviate from pursuing their common interest in taxing and redistributing from the rich. The center-right governments therefore tend to dominate in majoritarian systems, whereas the center-left governments tend to dominate in PR systems.

NOTES

1. We are grateful to the authors for letting us use their data.
2. We did the same in a small number of cases where the government position is equivalent to the median legislator, but where it is not a single-party majority government.
3. Ireland is perhaps the most ambiguous case, but it is not part of the redistribution regression, and the results for partisanship are not sensitive to the particular electoral system measure we use or whether Ireland is included or excluded.
4. The effective number of parties is defined as one divided by the sum of the square root of the shares of seats held by different parties (or one divided by the Hilferding index).
5. The effect of going from a majoritarian system to a PR system is to increase redistribution to the poor by .7 SD whereas the effect on the gini coefficient is .5 SD.

REFERENCES

Ansell, Ben. 2005. "From the Ballot to the Blackboard? Partisan and Institutional Effects on Human Capital Policy in the OECD. Department of Government." Harvard University. Typescript.

Austen-Smith, David. 2000. "Redistributing Income under Proportional Representation." *Journal of Political Economy* 108 (6): 1235–69.

Bénabou, Roland. 1996. "Inequality and Growth." In *National Bureau of Economic Research Macro Annual*, ed. Ben S. Bernanke and Julio J. Rotemberg, Cambridge: MIT Press, Vol. 11, pp. 11–74.

Boix, Carles. 1998. *Political Parties, Growth and Equality.* New York: Cambridge University Press.

Bradley David, Evelyne Huber, Stephanie Moller, François Nielsen, and John Stephens. 2003. "Distribution and Redistribution in Postindustrial Democracies." *World Politics* 55 (2): 193–228.

Brady, David. 2003. "Rethinking the Sociological Measure of Poverty." *Social Forces* 81 (3): 715–52.

Castles, Francis, and Peter Mair. 1984. "Left-Right Political Scales: Some Expert Judgments." *European Journal of Political Research* 12: 73–88.

Cusack, Thomas R., and Lutz Engelhardt. 2002. "The PGL File Collection: File Structures and Procedures." Wissenschaftszentrum Berlin für Sozialforschung.

Cusack, Thomas R., and Susanne Fuchs. 2002. "Documentation Notes for Parties, Governments, and Legislatures Data Set." Wissenschaftszentrum Berlin für Sozialforschung.

Gross, Donald A., and Lee Sigelman. 1984. "Comparing Party Systems: A Multidimensional Approach." *Comparative Politics* 16: 463–79.

Hicks, Alexander, and Duane Swank. 1992. "Politics, Institutions, and Welfare Spending in Industrialized Democracies, 1960–82." *American Political Science Review* 86 (3): 649–74.

Huber, Evelyne, Charles Ragin, and John Stephens. 1993. "Social Democracy, Christian Democracy, Constitutional Structure and the Welfare State." *American Journal of Sociology* 99 (3): 711–49.

Huber, Evelyne, and John D. Stephens. 2001. *Development and Crisis of the Welfare State: Parties and Policies in Global Markets.* Chicago: University of Chicago Press.

Huber, John D., and Ronald Inglehart. 1995. "Expert Interpretations of Party Space and Party Locations in 42 Societies." *Party Politics* 1: 73–111.

International Institute for Democracy and Electoral Assistance. 1997. *Voter Turnout from 1945 to 1997: A Global Report on Political Participation.* Stockholm: IDEA Information Services.

Korpi, Walter. 1983. *The Democratic Class Struggle.* London: Routledge & Kegan Paul.

Korpi, Walter. 1989. "Power, Politics and State Autonomy in the Development of Social Citizenship—Social Rights during Sickness in 18 OECD Countries since 1930." *American Sociological Review* 54 (3): 309–28.

Kwon, Hyeok Yong, and Jonas Pontusson. 2003. "The Zone of Partisanship, Parties, Unions and Welfare Spending on OECD Countries, 1962–99." Unpublished Manuscript, Department of Political Science, Cornell University.

Laasko, Markku, and Rein Taagepera. 1979. "Effective Number of Parties: A Measure with Applications to Western Europe." *Comparative Political Studies* 12 (3): 3–27.

Laver, Michael, and W. Ben Hunt. 1992. *Policy and Party Competition.* New York: Routledge.

Lijphart, Arend. 1994. *Electoral Systems and Party Systems: A Study of Twenty-Seven Democracies, 1945–90.* New York: Oxford University Press.

Lijphart, Arend. 1997. "Unequal Participation: Democracy's Unresolved Dilemma." *American Political Science Review* 91: 1–14.

Mackie, Thomas T., and Richard Rose. 1991. *The International Almanac of Electoral History*, 3rd edition. London: Macmillan.

Meltzer, Allan H., and Scott F. Richard. 1981. "A Rational Theory of the Size of Government." *Journal of Political Economy* 89: 914–27.

Moene, Karl Ove, and Michael Wallerstein. 2001. "Inequality, Social Insurance and Redistribution." *American Political Science Review* 95 (4): 859–74.

OECD. 1995. "Income Distribution in OECD Countries: Evidence from the Luxembourg Income Study." *Social Policy Studies* No. 18.

Perotti, Roberto. 1996. "Growth, Income Distribution and Democracy: What the Data Say." *Journal of Economic Growth* 1 (2): 149–87.

Persson, Torsten, and Guido Tabellini. 1999. "The Size and Scope of Government: Comparative Politics with Rational Politicians." *European Economic Review* 43: 699–735.

Persson, Torsten, and Guido Tabellini. 2000. *Political Economics: Explaining Economic Policy.* Cambridge: MIT Press.

Persson, Torsten, and Guido Tabellini. 2003. *The Economic Effects of Constitutions.* MIT Press.

Powell, Bingham. 2002. "PR, the Median Voter, and Economic Policy: An Exploration." Paper presented at the 2002 Meetings of the American Political Science Association, Boston.

Rogowski, Ronald, and Mark Andreas Kayser. 2002. "Majoritarian Electoral Systems and Consumer Power: Price-level Evidence from the OECD Countries." *American Journal of Political Science* 46 (3): 526–39.

Ross, Michael. 2005. "Does Democracy Reduce Infant Mortality?" Paper presented in Workshop on Democratic Institutions and Economic Performance. Duke University. April 1–2, 2005.

Visser, Jelle. 1989. *European Trade Unions in Figures.* Deventer/Netherlands: Kluwer Law and Taxation Publishers.

Visser, Jelle. 1996. "Unionization Trends Revisited." Mimeo. University of Amsterdam.

Margarita Estévez-Abe, Torben Iversen, and David Soskice

SOCIAL PROTECTION AND THE FORMATION OF SKILLS: A REINTERPRETATION OF THE WELFARE STATE

Introduction

Social protection rescues the market from itself by preventing market failures. More specifically, * * * social protection * * * [helps] economic actors overcome market failures in skill formation. We show, in this chapter, that different types of social protection are complementary to different skill equilibria. * * *

Young people are less likely to invest in specific skills if the risk of loss of employment opportunities that require those specific skills is high. Employers who rely on specific skills to compete effectively in international markets therefore need to institutionalize some sort of guarantee to insure workers against potential risks. Without implicit agreements for long-term employment and real wage stability, their specific skills will be under-supplied. Employers' promises are not, however, sufficiently credible by themselves. This is why social protection as governmental policy becomes critical. * * *

Institutional differences that safeguard returns on specific skills explain why workers and employers invest more in specific skills. The absence of such

From Peter A. Hall and David Soskice, eds., *Varieties of Capitalism: The Institutional Foundations of Comparative Advantage* (New York: Oxford University Press, 2001), pp. 145–83.

institutions, in countries such as the USA and UK, gives workers a strong incentive to invest in transferable skills. In such an environment, it then also makes more economic sense for firms to pursue product market strategies that use these transferable skills intensely. * * *

The model of micro-level links between skills and social protection we develop in this chapter has important policy implications. First, our model predicts what types of political alliance are likely to emerge in support of a particular type of social protection. For example, in economies where companies engage in product market strategies that require a combination of firm- and industry-specific skills, and where a large number of workers invest in such skills, a strong alliance between skilled workers and their employers in favor of social protection advantageous to them is likely to emerge—even if this means reducing job opportunities for low-skilled workers. By contrast, where business has no common interest in the promotion of specific skills, it will have no interest in defending * * * social protection. Second, we show that different systems of social protection have deeper ramifications for inequality than commonly assumed. Some skill equilibria—sustained by different systems of social protection—produce more inequalities based on the academic background of workers, while others produce more inequalities based on gender.

■ ■ ■

Product Market Strategies, Skill Types, and the Welfare State

■ ■ ■

Skills and Product Market Strategies

[We distinguish] three types of skills associated with different product market strategies: (i) firm-specific skills; (ii) industry-specific skills; and (iii) general skills.[1] These skills differ significantly in terms of their asset specificity (i.e., portability). Firm-specific skills are acquired through on-the-job training, and are least portable. They are valuable to the employer who carried out the training but not to other employers. Industry-specific skills are acquired through apprenticeship and vocational schools. These skills, especially when authoritatively certified, are recognized by any employer within a specific trade. General skills, recognized by all employers, carry a value that is independent of the type of firm or industry. Of course, any actual production system will involve all three types of skills to some degree. Nonetheless, we can characterize distinctive product market strategies based upon the "skill profile" they require.

* * * [M]ass production of standardized goods does not require a highly trained workforce. Production work is broken into a narrow range of standardized tasks that only require semi-skilled workers. Traditional US manufacturing industries such as automobile and other consumer durables fall into this category. There is, however, a variant of mass production called diversified mass production (DMP). The DMP strategy, in contrast, aims at producing a varied range of products in large volumes. Japanese auto-makers and domestic electronic appliances industry are good examples. This production strategy depends on workers capable of performing a wide range of tasks to enable frequent product changes in the line (Koike 1981). Workers are also expected to solve problems that emerge in the production line themselves to minimize downtime (Shibata 1999). The tasks these workers perform involve high levels of knowledge about their company products and machineries in use, and hence are highly firm-specific.

There are product market strategies that do not mass produce. One strategy is a high-quality product niche market strategy. It requires a highly trained workforce with industry-specific craft skills. The prototype of this production strategy does not involve any scale merit, and the process tends to involve highly craft-intensive workshops. Custom-made clothing, jewelry, and fine porcelain may be examples of such production. Another strategy is a hybrid. It pursues high-quality product lines, but takes the production out of small-scale craft shops in order to increase the volume of production. Streeck (1992b) calls this diversified quality production. This production strategy requires firm-specific skills in addition to high levels of craft skills. Germany is a prototype of this type of production.

All the above strategies require firm-specific and industry-specific skills to varying degrees. It is important, however, to note that relative abundance of high levels of general skills (i.e., university and postgraduate qualifications) brings comparative advantages in radical product innovation. Let us take the example of the USA to illustrate this point. For example, start-up software companies in the USA take advantage of a highly flexible labor market with university-educated people combining excellent general skills with valuable knowledge about the industry acquired from switching from one job to another. Another example would be American financial institutions, which have taken advantage of an abundant supply of math Ph.D.'s to develop new products such as derivatives. Complex systems development (for e-commerce, for example), biotechnology, segments of the telecommunications industry, and advanced consulting services are other examples that fall into this class of industries.

The Welfare-Skill Formation Nexus

We make the three following assumptions about workers' economic behavior:

(i) *People calculate overall return to their educational/training investment before deciding to commit themselves. (The investment cost of further training and education can be conceptualized in terms of wages forgone during the period of training and education, in addition to any tuition or training fees incurred.)*

(ii) *People choose to invest in those skills that generate higher expected returns, provided that the riskiness of the investments is identical.*

(iii) Ceteris paribus, *people refrain from investing in skills that have more uncertain future returns (i.e., people are risk averse).*

From these assumptions, it follows that a rational worker must consider three factors in making skill investment decisions: (i) the initial cost of acquiring the skills as, for instance, when a worker receives a reduced wage during the period of training; (ii) the future wage premium of specific skills; and (iii) the risks of losing the current job and the associated wage premium.

The core skills required by an industry are critical for this analysis because they vary in the degree to which they expose workers to the risk of future income losses. Highly portable skills are less risky than highly specific skills because in the former case the market value of the skill is not tied to a particular firm or industry. Faced with future job insecurity, a rational worker will not invest his or her time and money in skills that have no remunerative value outside the firm or industry. In other words, in the absence of institutional interventions into workers' payoff structure, general rather than asset-specific skill acquisition represents the utility-maximizing strategy.

Let us now examine what types of institutions are necessary in order to protect investments in asset-specific skills. We can distinguish three different types of protection, which might be called *employment protection, unemployment protection,* and *wage protection. Employment protection* refers to institutionalized employment security. The higher the employment protection, the less likely that a worker will be laid off even during economic downturns. *Unemployment protection* means protection from income reduction due to unemployment, and can thus reduce the uncertainty over the wage level throughout one's career. *Wage protection,* finally, is an institutional mechanism that protects wage levels from market fluctuations. In this section, we first contrast the significance of *employment protection* and *unemployment protection* for firm-specific and industry-specific skills. We will discuss wage protection in a separate section, because it is generally not considered to be part of the welfare system.

Firm-specific skills are, *ex hypothesi*, worthless outside that specific firm, and they therefore require a high level of *employment protection* in order to convince workers to invest in such skills (Aoki 1988). Since workers will only be paid the value of their non-firm-specific skills in the external market, the greater their investment in specific skills the greater the discrepancy between current wages and the wages they could fetch in the external market. In order to invest heavily in firm-specific skills, workers therefore need assurances that they can remain in the company for a long enough period to reap the returns on such investments (see Lazear and Freeman 1996; Osterman 1987; Schettkat 1993). If not, the expenditures of training must be commensurably lower, and/or the premium on future wages higher. In either case, the cost of training for the firm goes up, and it will offer less training.

Because rational workers weigh higher expected income later in their career against the risks of losing their current job, the only way to encourage workers to carry a substantial part of the costs of firm-specific training is to increase job security and/or reduce the insecurity of job loss. Hence we can interpret institutionalized lifetime employment, or subsidies to keep redundant workers within the firm, as safeguarding mechanisms for firm-specific skill investment.

∎ ∎ ∎

For firms pursuing product market strategies which depend heavily on firm- and industry-specific skills, promise of employment and unemployment security can thus provide a cost-effective path to improving the firms' competitive position in international markets (cf. Ohashi and Tachibanaki 1998; Koike 1994). Contrary to conventional neoclassical theory, which sees efforts to increase protection against job loss as an interference with the efficient operation of labor markets, measures to reduce future uncertainty over employment status—hence uncertainty over future wage premiums—can significantly improve firms' cost effectiveness (Schettkat 1993). And the more successful these firms are, the greater their demand for specific skills. We are in a specific skills equilibrium.

If there is little protection built into either the employment or the unemployment system, the best insurance against labor market risks for the worker is to invest in general, or portable, skills that are highly valued in the external labor market. If general skills are what firms need for pursuing their product market strategies successfully, low employment protection can thus give these firms a competitive edge. Indeed, if most firms are pursuing general skills strategies, then higher protection will undermine workers' incentives to invest in these skills, *without* significantly increasing their appropriation of specific skills (because there is little demand for such skills). In this general skills equilibrium the neoclassical efficiency argument for little protection is more valid.[2]

The predictions of the argument are summarized in Fig. 8.16, which identifies the four main welfare production regimes and gives an empirical example of each (discussed below).

∎ ∎ ∎

Figure 8.16 Social Protection and Predicted Skill Profiles

		Employment protection	
		Low	High
Unemployment protection	High	Industry-specific skills Example: Denmark	Industry-specific, firm-specific skill mix Example: Germany
	Low	General skills Example: United States	Firm-specific skills Example: Japan

Self-Reinforcing Inequalities and Political Preferences

So far the discussion has focused on the efficiency aspects of social protection. In this section we extend the core argument to unravel two sets of previously neglected logics by which welfare production regimes perpetuate inequalities. First, we point out that general skill systems are more likely to create a "poverty trap." Second, we cast light upon the gender inequality consequences of different product market strategies. Finally, we discuss how these distributive implications of different welfare state regimes are reproduced and perpetuated through distinct patterns of political support for social protection.

Distribution, Poverty Traps, and Product Market Strategies

Our argument has far-reaching implications for equality and labor market stratification, some of which are poorly understood in the existing welfare state literature. Product market strategies that rely on high levels of industry-specific and firm-specific skills are likely to create more egalitarian societies than product market strategies based on general skills. They therefore help us understand large and persistent cross-national differences in the distribution of wages and incomes. The existing literature can only account for these differences in so far as they are caused by redistributive state policies. This is far too narrow an approach. We contend that most inequalities result from particular welfare production regimes (i.e., combinations of product market strategies, skill profiles, and the political-institutional framework that supports them).

The basic logic of our argument is straightforward. We argue that different skill systems and accompanying training systems have important economic implications for those who are academically weak and strong respectively. For the bottom one-third, or so, of the academic ability distribution, a highly developed vocational training system offers the best opportunities for students to acquire skills that are valued by employers. When entry into vocational training is competitive, these students have an incentive to be as good as they can academically in order to get into the best training programs with the most promising career prospects (Soskice 1994). Therefore, countries with well-developed (and competitive) vocational training systems provide a stable economic future even to those students who are not academically strong. General education systems, in contrast, offer these students relatively few opportunities for improving their labor market value outside of the school system. As a result, there are fewer incentives for them to work hard inside the school system.

In firm-specific skill-training systems, employers develop strong stakes in overseeing the quality of potential employees (i.e., trainees) and developing clear job entry patterns.[3] Since employers are committed to make significant initial human capital investment in new job entrants, they will be interested in monitoring the quality of the pool of the new school leavers. As a result, they are likely to establish a working relationship with various schools for systematic hiring of new school leavers. Since employers in a firm-specific skill system carry out initial job training, new school graduates have a chance of building careers as skilled workers. This gives young schoolgoers a strong incentive to work hard in school. The "from-school-to-work" transition is likely to be more institutionalized (Dore and Sako 1989). Similarly, in the case of industry-specific skills where employers are involved, employers take an interest in ensuring the quality of vocational training and the certification of skills (Finegold and Soskice 1988). In these systems, education-work transition is also relatively institutionalized (Blossfeld and Mayer 1988; Ni Cheallaigh 1995).

In general skill regimes, in contrast, the "from-school-to-work" transition is less institutionalized (see Allmendinger 1989). Hiring is more flexible. Employers hire new job entrants with different educational backgrounds. Promotion and opportunities for further skill training are themselves contingent upon the job performance of the worker. There is not so much initial human capital investment by employers as there is in firm-specific skill systems. Because of the absence of a clear vocational track, systems based on general skills therefore tend to disadvantage those who are not academically inclined. Regardless of the presence or absence of vocational schools and apprenticeship programs, for employers who emphasize general skills a certificate from a vocational school does not add much value to the worker. Potential workers therefore have to demonstrate their competence in terms of general scholarly achievement, and getting a tertiary degree becomes an essential component. Because there is a hierarchy of post-secondary schools, if the student thinks there is a possibility of making it into the tertiary educational system, he or she has a strong incentive to work hard. For those who are not academically inclined, by contrast, the system produces the unintended consequence of undermining the incentive to work hard in school. In the absence of a specialized vocational track, unless a student believes that he or she can make the cut into college, there is not much gained by being a good student.

In short, in general skill systems, since the completion of elementary and secondary school does not qualify them for a vocational certificate that leads to secure jobs, academically weak students face lower returns from their educational investment. Since the opportunity for vocational training—both on the job and off the job—for these students will remain low, it creates an impoverished labor pool. In contrast, at the top end of the ability distribution, a general education system offers the largest returns to those with advanced graduate and postgraduate degrees. These returns tend to be more modest in specific skills systems because a large number of companies depend more on industry-specific and firm-specific skills than professional degrees or broad academic qualifications. General skill systems, therefore, reward those students who are academically talented in terms of labor market entry. Distribution of academic aptitude thus translates into distribution of skills, and consequently into a very skewed distribution of earnings. As a consequence, academically weak students in general skill regimes are worse

off than their counterparts elsewhere: they are more likely to be trapped in low-paid unskilled jobs.

Gender Equality and Skill Types

Compared to men, women face an additional set of issues when making skill investment choices (see Estévez-Abe 1999). In addition to the probability of layoff, women have to take into consideration the likelihood of career interruption due to their role as mothers (see Daly 1994; Rubery et al. 1996). For a woman to invest in specific skills, she has to be assured that potential career interruptions will not (i) lead to dismissal; or (ii) reduce her wage level in the long run. A high probability of dismissal reduces the incentives to acquire firm-specific skills. A high probability of reduction in wages after becoming a mother—because of time off due to childbirth and -rearing—reduces the incentives to invest in either firm-specific or industry-specific skills.

For women, therefore, employment protection necessarily involves two factors in addition to the employment and unemployment protection discussed earlier. These two factors are (i) protection against dismissal, such as maternity, parental, and family leave policies; and (ii) income maintenance during leaves and guarantees of reinstatement to the same job at the same wage level upon return to work.

As for industry-specific skill investments, leave programs and generous income maintenance during the leave function in the same way as unemployment protection for male skilled workers. A higher wage replacement ratio thus encourages specific skill investment. Firm-specific and industry-specific skills again require slightly different institutional guarantees. While income maintenance during leave is sufficient for industry-specific skills, firm-specific skill investment by women faces another issue. In firm-specific skill regimes, reinstatement to the original job after the leave means that women fall behind their male cohort in skill formation and promotion. This means that despite generous income replacement during the leave, time off due to childbirth and -rearing reduces women's overall earnings. The very fact that the child-rearing years for women coincide with the critical early years of employment compounds the problem. Therefore, for women to invest in firm-specific skills, affordable childcare is more important than a family leave policy. In short, compared to men, it takes more institutional support to encourage women to make specific skill investments. This means that employers' incentives differ significantly from the earlier descriptions of employment and unemployment protection. From the employers' perspective, it costs more to provide incentives for women to invest in specific skills than it does for men (Spencer 1973). Not only do additional income maintenance and childcare create a greater financial burden, but they come with the organizational cost of hiring replacement workers during regular workers' maternal and childcare leaves. And not only is it expensive to hire highly skilled workers as replacement workers, but it is also very difficult to seek those skills in the external labor market—especially in the case of firm-specific skills.

Given these additional financial and organizational costs, employers are unlikely to support family leave or childcare programs except under two circumstances: (i) when someone other than the employer covers the program expenses; or (ii) when there is an acute shortage of men willing to invest in the skills they need.

From a woman's perspective, this means that it does not pay to invest in skills for which there is an abundant supply of males. Even if a woman invests to acquire a specific skill, as far as there is an abundant supply of male skilled workers, her skill investment will not be protected to the same degree as men's. Given this situation, women are more likely than men to invest in general skills. Furthermore, even women who are willing to invest in skill training will rationally choose trades and professions where there are few men. Hence a vicious cycle of occupational segregation of women arises. In countries where there is an established vocational training system, women's enrollment choices will reflect women's tendency to avoid "male jobs."

In short, product market strategies that rely on firm-specific and industry-specific skills are more gender segregating than product market strategies based on general skills. As we argued, general skills provide more flexibility without penalizing career interruptions, precisely because they do not require any external guarantee and reinforcement. We can thus predict that economies with a large presence of companies with specific skill strategies demonstrate high occupational gender segregation, while general skill systems are more gender neutral.

■ ■ ■

Comparative Patterns

Our argument implies a tight coupling between employment protection, unemployment protection, and skill formation. The dominant mode of firm structure, as well as circumstances in the historical development of different welfare production regimes, have led some countries to emphasize *employment protection* over *unemployment protection*, or vice versa. As we noted in the theoretical discussion, political opposition to strong *employment protection* legislation will be greater in countries with a high proportion of small firms.

The predictions of our model are summarized in Fig. 8.16.

When *neither* employment *nor* unemployment protection is high, workers have a strong incentive to protect themselves against labor market insecurities by investing heavily in highly portable skills. Since workers are reluctant to take on specific skills in this scenario—or at least unlikely to share much of the cost of training such skills—firms have an incentive to use technologies that rely least on specific skills. This, in turn, increases demand for general skills, and availability of general skill jobs makes general education more attractive for workers, thus creating a self-reinforcing dynamic. In this case we expect skill profiles to be heavily tilted toward general and broad occupational skills, with a weak or absent vocational training system.

When employment and unemployment protection are both high, on the other hand, workers will find it more attractive to invest in firm- and industry-specific skills. In turn, this makes it more cost-efficient for firms to engage in production that requires large inputs of labor with specific skills. As firms specialize in this type of production, the job market for general skills shrinks. Note here that a standard trade argument supports the idea of self-reinforcing dynamics in both types of systems: institutional comparative advantage makes an intensive use of relatively more abundant skills an efficient production strategy. Yet, not all countries necessarily conform to these two ideal types. Where companies can offer very high levels of job protection and a large and attractive internal labor market, firm-specific skill formation can flourish in the absence of strong unemployment protection (represented by the south-east corner of Fig. 8.16). If career opportunities are extensive within the firm, and if the firm makes credible commitments to job security, the external labor market will be small and workers will have an incentive to take advantage of internal career opportunities by investing in company-specific skills. This, essentially, is the Japanese situation (see Aoki 1988; Koike 1981). In most other cases, firms have neither the size nor the resources and institutional capacity to commit credibly to lifetime employment. It is for this reason that we would *ordinarily* expect the development of firm-specific skills to be coupled with generous protection against unemployment.

On the flip side of the Japanese system, we find welfare production regimes with extensive unemployment protection, but low or only modest employment protection. Especially in economies dominated by small firms, with small internal labor markets and little organizational capacity to adapt to business cycles, employment protection is a costly and unattractive option for employers. Denmark is an archetypal example of an economy with a small-firm industrial structure. Yet, generous unemployment protection for skilled workers is still a requisite for workers to invest in industry-specific skills in these cases, much the same way as employment protection is a requisite for investment in firm-specific skills. In effect, unemployment protection increases employment security *within the industry* as opposed to security within a particular firm. At a high level of abstraction, therefore, the *industry* in a country with high unemployment and low employment protection becomes functionally equivalent to the *firm* in a country with low unemployment and high employment protection.

■   ■   ■

Putting the Pieces Together

Fig. 8.17 plots the eighteen OECD countries on the employment and unemployment protection indexes [that we have adopted]. Countries are distributed along a primary axis, corresponding to the south-west–north-east diagonal in Fig. 8.16, with some countries further divided along a secondary axis, corresponding to the north-west–south-east diagonal in Fig. 8.16. The main axis separates countries into two distinct welfare production regimes: one combining weak employment and unemployment protection with a general skills profile, represented by the Anglo-Saxon countries and Ireland; and one combining high protection on at least one of the two social protection dimensions with firm- and/or industry-specific skills, represented by the continental European countries and Japan. The secondary axis divides the latter group into one with greater emphasis on employment protection and the creation of firm-specific skills, exemplified primarily by Japan and Italy,[4] and one with greater emphasis on unemployment protection and the production of industry-specific skills, exemplified by Denmark, the Netherlands, and Switzerland.

The data on skills * * * have been summarized in the form of averages for each cluster of countries (only tenure rates are relevant for the division along the secondary axis). The high protection countries are also those with the most developed vocational training systems, and tenure rates decline with

Figure 8.17 Social Protection and Skill Profiles

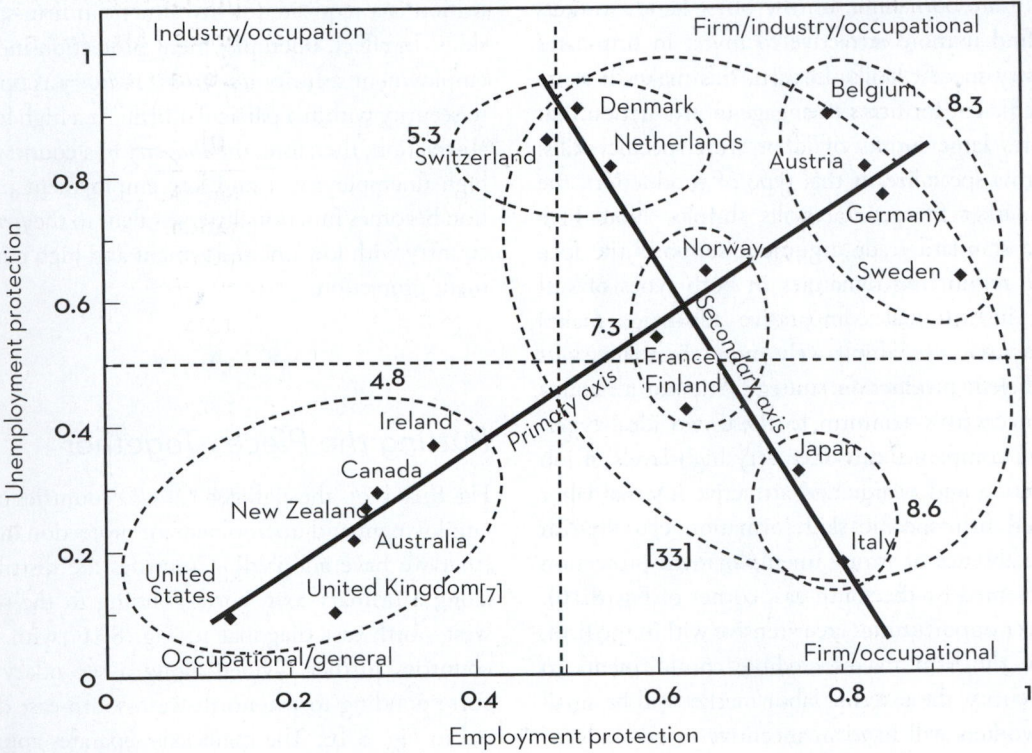

Source: OECD, *Database on Unemployment Benefit Entitlements and Replacement Rates* (undated); Huber, Ragin, Stephens (1997); OECD Economic Outlook (Paris: OECD, various years); OECD, *Labour Force Statistics* (Paris: OECD, various years); European Commission, *Unemployment in Europe* (various years); and national sources; Income Data Services, *Industrial Relations and Collective Bargaining*. (London, Institute of Personnel and Development, 1996).

employment protection. Clearly, the empirical patterns we observe correspond rather closely to our main theoretical thesis, namely that skill formation is closely linked to social protection.

The coupling of social protection and skill systems helps us understand the product market strategies of companies and the creation of comparative advantages in the global economy. Thus, where there is a large pool of workers with advanced and highly portable skills, and where social protection is low, companies enjoy considerable flexibility in attracting new workers, laying off old ones, or starting new production lines. This flexibility allows for high responsiveness to new business opportunities, and facilitates the use of rapid product innovation strate-

gies. In economies with a combination of firm- and industry-specific skills, such strategies are hampered by the difficulty of quickly adapting skills to new types of production, and by restrictions in the ability of firms to hire and fire workers. On the other hand, these welfare-production regimes advantage companies that seek to develop deep competencies within established technologies, and to continuously upgrade and diversify existing product lines ("diversified quality production" in the terminology of Streeck 1991).

There is considerable case-oriented research to support these propositions (see especially Hollingsworth and Boyer 1997 and Soskice 1999), and they can be bolstered by quantitative evidence constructed by Thomas Cusack from U.S. Patent Office data. Breaking them into thirty technology classes, Cusack counted the number of references to scientific articles for patents in each technology class and country, and then divided this number by the world number of scientific citations per technology class.[5] The idea is that the number of scientific citations, as opposed to citations to previous patents and non-scientific sources, is a good proxy for the extent to which national firms are engaged in radical innovation strategies. The results are shown in the first column of Table 8.11, with countries ranked by the average ratio of scientific citations for patents secured by national firms. As it turns out, the Anglo-Saxon countries and Ireland all have ratios that are significantly higher than in the specific skills countries of continental Europe and Japan. Precisely as we would expect.

At the low-tech end of product markets, we have to rely on a different type of data to detect cross-national differences. In column (2) of Table 8.12 we used the proportion of the working-age population employed in private social and personal services as a proxy. As argued by Esping-Andersen (1990: ch. 8) and Iversen and Wren (1998), firms that rely heavily on low-skilled and low-paid labor for profitability tend to be concentrated in these industries. Although we only have data for a sub-set of countries, the numbers display a rather clear cross-national pattern. Producers of standardized and low-productivity services thrive in general skills countries such as Australia and the United States because they can hire from a large pool of unskilled workers who are afforded much job protection and whose wages are held down by low unemployment protection. By contrast, firms trying to compete in this space in specific skills countries such as Germany and Sweden are inhibited by higher labor costs and lower flexibility in hiring and firing. These differences have magnified during the 1980s and 1990s, and Britain is now closer to the mean for the general skills countries.

In an open international trading system, differences in product market strategies will tend to be

Table 8.12 Scientific Citation Rates and Low-Wage Service Employment in Eighteen OECD Countries

	(1) Scientific citation ratio[a]	(2) Private service employment[b]
Ireland	1.514	—
United States	1.310	23
New Zealand	1.267	—
Canada	1.032	20
United Kingdom	0.837	16
Australia	0.804	26
Sweden	0.757	14
The Netherlands	0.754	14
Norway	0.690	17
Switzerland	0.639	—
France	0.601	11
Belgium	0.598	13
Germany	0.592	14
Japan	0.586	—
Austria	0.575	—
Finland	0.552	11
Denmark	0.536	11
Italy	0.491	9

a. The average number of scientific citations per patent by national firms in each of thirty technology classes as a proportion of the average number of citations in each class for the entire world.
b. The number of people employed in wholesale, retail trade, restaurants and hotels, and in community, social and personal services, 1982–91, as a percentage of the working-age population.
Source: Col. 1: United States Patent Office Data. Col. 2: OECD (1996).

perpetuated, which in turn feed back into organized support for existing social protection regimes. Contrary to the popular notion of a "race to the bottom" in social policies, differences across countries persist and are even attenuated through open trade. Correspondingly, from the 1970s to the 1980s and 1990s, unemployment benefits remained stable or rose in most continental European countries, but they were cut in Ireland and all the Anglo-Saxo countries with the exception of Australia.[6] Moreover, whereas labor markets have become even more deregulated in the latter countries, employment protection has remained high in the former. Although some countries have seen a notable relaxation in the protection of temporary employment, there is no reduction in the level of protection for regular employment (*OECD Employment Outlook* 1999). This evidence, and the theoretical explanation we provide for it, seriously challenge the notion, popular in much

of the economic literature, that social protection is simply inefficient forms of labor market "rigidities." Social protection can provide important competitive advantages. By the same token we question the prevalent approach in the sociological and political science literature, which understands social protection solely in terms of its redistributive effects.

Implications for Labor Market Stratification

That said, we are not implying that welfare production regimes are irrelevant for distributive outcomes. To the contrary, our argument has important implications for equality and labor market stratification, and it helps account for the political divisions over the welfare state. Partly these effects are direct consequences of particular product market strategies and their associated skill profiles; partly they

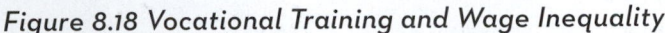

Figure 8.18 Vocational Training and Wage Inequality

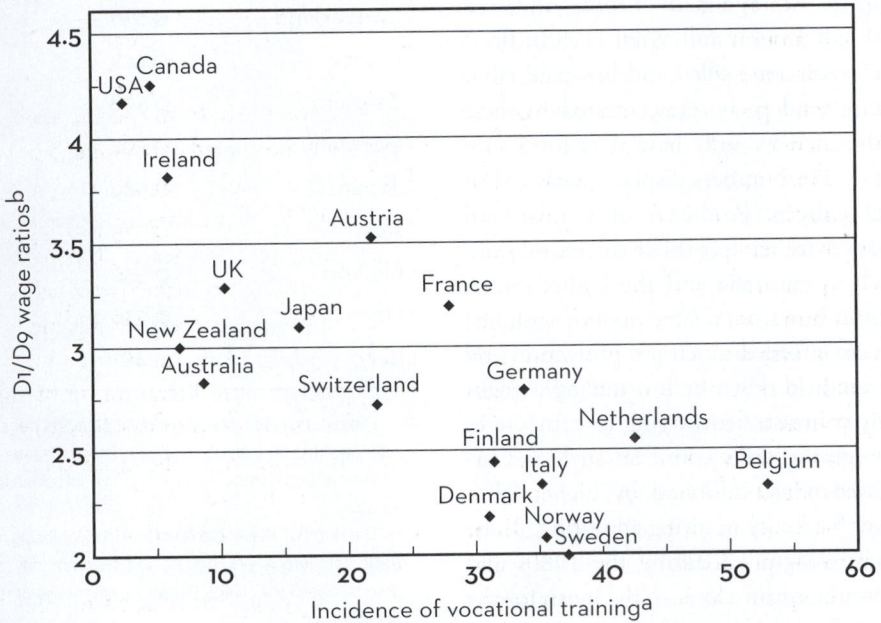

a. The share of an age cohort in either secondary or post-secondary (ISCED5) vocational training. *Source:* UNESCO (1999).
b. The earnings of worker in the top decile of the earnings distribution relative to a worker in the bottom decile of the earnings distribution.
Sources: D1/D9 wage ratios: UNESCO (1999). Incidence of vocational training: OECD, *Electronic Data Based on Wage Dispersion* (undated).

reflect the effects of the collective wage-bargaining system that is itself an important component of the wage protection system.

With respect to wage protection, the most important issue is what we have previously referred to as wage protection for the unemployed. Such protection implies that workers with similar skills are paid the same amount across firms and industries, and in practice this is accomplished through collective wage-bargaining at the industry level or at higher levels. It is striking, though not surprising, that all countries with a strong emphasis on industry-specific skills have developed effective wage coordination at the industry level. Conversely, general skills countries, and countries with a strong emphasis on firm-specific skills (Japan in particular), lack such coordination.

Very extensive evidence has now been accumulated that demonstrates the importance of the structure of the wage-bargaining system for the wage structure (see especially Rowthorn 1992; Rueda and Pontusson 2000; and Wallerstein 1999), but we believe the skill system is equally important. Fig. 8.18, which uses the incidence of vocational training as the indicator for skill system, clearly shows the empirical association between skills and earnings equality, and there is a good reason. Because specific skills systems generate high demand for workers with good vocational training, young people who are not academically inclined have career opportunities that are largely missing in general skills systems. Whereas a large proportion of early school leavers in the former acquire valuable skills through the vocational training system, in the latter most early school leavers end up as low-paid unskilled workers for most or all of their working lives.

In combination, the wage-bargaining system—i.e., whether it is industry coordinated or not—and the skill system—i.e., whether it is specific skills or general skills biased—provides a powerful explanation of earnings inequality as we have illustrated in Fig. 8.19. The figure shows earnings and income inequality for each combination of bargaining and skill system. The big drop in earnings equality

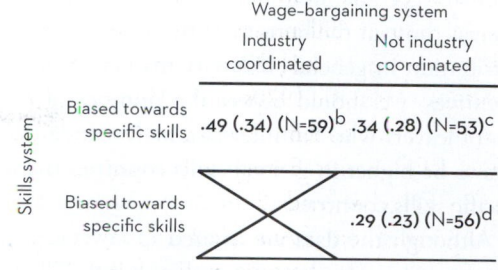

Figure 8.19 Skills, the Bargaining System, and Equality[a]

	Wage-bargaining system	
	Industry coordinated	Not industry coordinated
Biased towards specific skills	.49 (.34) (N=59)[b]	.34 (.28) (N=53)[c]
Biased towards specific skills		.29 (.23) (N=56)[d]

a. Numbers are D9/D1 earnings ratios based on gross earnings (including all employer contributions for pensions, social security, etc.) of a worker at the bottom decile of the earnings distribution relative to the worker at the top decile. Figures are averages for the period 1977–1993. Numbers in parentheses are D9/D1 income ratios based on disposable income of a person at the bottom decile of the earnings distribution relative to a person at the top decile. Most figures are from the early 1990s, with a few from the 1980s.
b. Austria, Belgium, Denmark, Finland, Germany, Netherlands, Norway, Sweden, Switzerland
c. France, Italy, Japan
d. Australia, Canada, Ireland, New Zealand, UK, US
Sources: Skills: see Table 8.8. Bargaining system: see Iversen (1999a: ch. 3). Inequality measures: see *OECD Employment Outlook* (1991, 1996); Gottschalk and Smeeding (2000: fig. 2).

occurs as we move from specific skills systems with industry-coordinated bargaining to general skills systems where industry-coordinated wage-bargaining is lacking. By themselves this pair of dichotomous variables account for nearly 70 percent of the cross-national variance in income inequality.[7] Yet, despite their importance for explaining inequality, neither variable is accorded much attention in the established welfare state literature, notwithstanding the focus on distribution in this literature. In our theoretical framework, on the other hand, they are integral parts of the story, even though we have focused on micro mechanisms that emphasize the importance of efficiency.

The hypothesized relationship between product market strategies, skill composition, and equality points to another, and quite different, source of evidence: academic test scores. Because specific skills systems create strong incentives among young schoolgoers to do as well as they can in school in order to get the best vocational training spots, whereas those at the bottom of the academic ability distribution in general skills systems have few such incentives, we should expect the number of early school leavers who fail internationally standardized tests to be higher in general skills countries than in specific skills countries.

Although the data are limited in coverage, this is in fact what we observe (see Fig. 8.20). Whereas the percentage failing the test varies between 15 and 22 percent in the Anglo-Saxon countries, it is only between 8 and 14 in the countries emphasizing more specific skills for which we have data. Although these differences could be due to the overall quality of the educational system, it is not the case that the Anglo-Saxon countries spend less money on primary education, and there is no systematic dif-

ference in average scorers. This points to the importance of incentives outside the school system, which vary systematically according to the dominant product market strategies of firms and their associated demand for particular skills.

But general skills systems are not necessarily bad for all types of inequality. They perform better in terms of gender equality at work (Estévez-Abe 1999). When we compare degrees of occupational segregation, specific skills systems fare worse than general skills systems. Specific skills systems segregate women into "female occupations" such as low-rank clerical and service jobs. Table 8.13 shows the occupational breakdown of women employed expressed in terms of a percentage of women over total workforce within the same category. While the data are not conclusive, it nonetheless shows that countries (see Germany and Sweden in Table 8.13) that adopt high-quality product market strategies—

Figure 8.20 The Failure of Early School Leavers to Pass Standardized Tests in Eleven OECD Countries

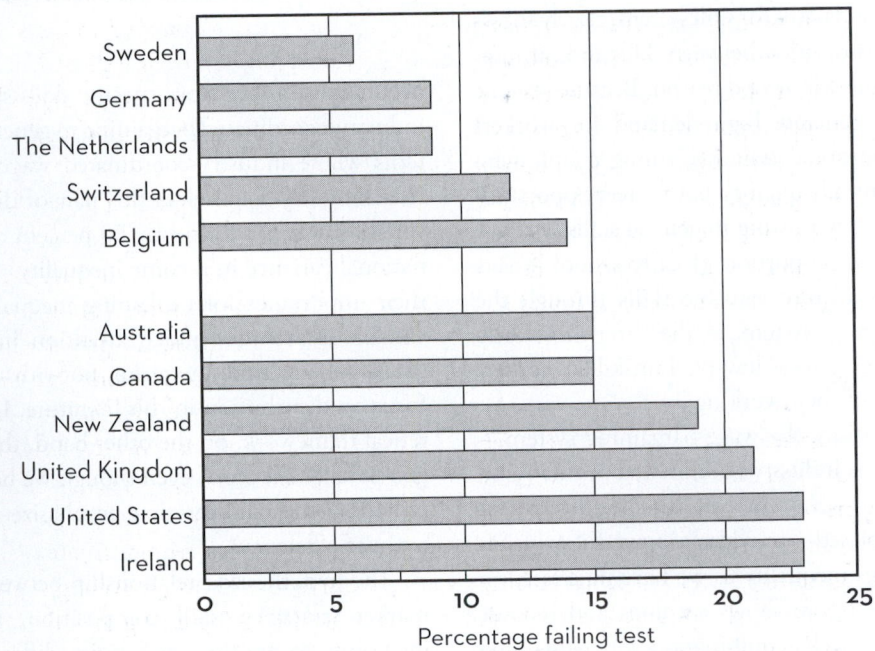

Percentage failing test

Source: OECD (2000).

Table 8.13 Share of Women by Occupation (%)[a]

	(1) Professional, technical, and related workers	(2) Administrative and managerial workers	(3) Clerical and related workers	(4) Sales workers	(5) Service workers	(6) Production and related workers
USA (1989)	22	26	70	33	30	30
Japan (1988)	10	7	58	11	40	39[b]
Germany (1986)	15	11	59	52	67	21
The Netherlands (1993)	14	0	55	32	45	12
Sweden (1989)	15		57	25	72	24
Australia (1987)	8	18	20	43	76	31

a. Percentages represent the ratio of women over the total of men and women employed within each occupational category.
b. The female ratio for occupational category (6) in Japan is exceptionally high due to a demographically shrinking pool of young male workers (Estévez-Abe 1999).
Source: ILO (1989–90).

thus dependent on high industry-specific skills—employ women for production jobs to a lesser degree. The USA, the archetypal general skills system, shows significantly higher ratios of women in technical and managerial positions when compared to specific skills systems. Our findings support Esping-Andersen's argument about the US employment system being more gender equal than that found in Germany and Sweden (Esping-Andersen 1999). Our explanation, however, differs from his.

Conclusion

Protection of employment and income is widely seen in the welfare state literature as reducing workers' dependence on the market and employers ("decommodification" in Esping-Andersen's terminology). In turn, this is argued to reflect a particular balance of power between labor and capital. We reject both theses. Although strong unions and left governments undoubtedly affect distributive outcomes, we have argued that employment and income protection can be seen as efforts to *increase* workers' dependence on particular employers, as well as their exposure to labor market risks. Moreover, social protection often stems from the strength rather than the weakness of employers.

The key to our argument is the link between social protection and the level and composition of skills. In a modern economy, skills are essential for firms to compete in international markets, and depending on the particular product market strategy of firms, they rely on a workforce with a certain combination of firm-specific, industry-specific, and general skills. To be cost-effective firms need workers who are willing to make personal investments in these skills. And if firms want to be competitive in product markets that require an abundance of specific skills, workers must be willing to acquire these skills at the cost of increasing their dependence on a particular employer or group of employers. Because investment in specific skills increases workers' exposure to risks, only by insuring against such risks can firms satisfy their need for specific skills.

The particular combination of employment protection and unemployment protection determines the profile of skills that is likely to emerge in an economy. Thus employment protection increases the propensity of workers to invest in firm-specific skills, whereas unemployment protection facilitates investment in industry-specific skills. The absence of both gives people strong incentives to invest in general skills. These predictors are borne out by the comparative data, which show that most countries combine either low protection with general skills, or high protection with specific skills.

Two factors contribute to the distinctiveness and resilience of particular welfare production regimes. The first is that such regimes tend to be reinforced by institutions—collective wage-bargaining systems, business organizations, employee representation, and financial systems—that facilitate the credible commitment of actors to particular strategies, such as wage restraint and long-term employment, that are necessary to sustain cooperation in the provision of specific skills. The second is that those workers and employers who are being most advantaged by these institutional complementaries also tend to be in strong political positions, in terms of both economic clout and sheer numbers. For example, the more a welfare production system emphasizes the creation of specific skills, the more likely it is that the median voter will be someone with considerable investments in specific skills, and the more likely it is that employers' interest organizations will be dominated by firms pursuing specific skills strategies. Both will contribute to perpetuating institutions and policies that advantage firms and workers with heavy investments in specific skills.

Our argument has broader implications for our understanding of the welfare state that reach well beyond the immediate effects of employment and income protection. In particular, earnings dispersion, by far the most important determinant of the overall distribution of income, is closely related to particular skill systems as well as the wage-bargaining institutions that tend to go with these systems. Similarly, the combination of particular product market strategies and skills has distinct effects on the career opportunities of particular groups, especially women. Thus, our theory implies that gender-based segmentation of the labor market varies systematically across welfare production systems.

■ ■ ■

NOTES

1. Our framework builds upon Gary Becker's distinction between general and specific skills (1964: ch. 3). In Becker's definition, firm-specific training increases productivity only in the firm where training takes place. General training, in contrast, raises productivity equally in all firms. In an analogous manner, industry-specific training can be defined as training that raises productivity in all firms in the industry, but not in other industries. Firm-, industry-, and general skills are skills acquired through firm-specific, industry-specific, and general training.

2. Since the general skills are portable, there is no risk associated with separation from current employer. See Gary Becker (1964). This does not mean that high turnover in countries with more general skills does not produce negative welfare consequences from the economy-wide efficiency perspective. For an interesting elaboration on this issue, see Chang and Wang (1995).

3. It is worth noting that monitoring the quality of the general education system becomes important where a lot of human capital investment takes place beyond the general education system, because poor general education increases the cost of training workers in industry-specific and firm-specific skills.

4. Although the position of Italy is probably exaggerated by the failure to account for semipublic unemployment insurance arrangements, as noted above.

5. The data are coded into references to previous patents and others, where many of the latter are references to scientific articles. To get a good estimate for the number of scientific articles in the "other" category, the proportion of scientific references to other references was calculated for a random sample (6,000) for each country and technology class. These factors were then used to correct the overall dataset so as to get a better measure of scientific citations.

6. Based on gross unemployment replacement rates published in OECD's *Database on Unemployment Benefit Entitlements and Replacement Rates* (undated).

7. The estimated regression equation is: Income equality = 0.23 + 0.048 × Specific skills + 0.055 × Industry coordination, where $R^2 = 0.69$.

REFERENCES

Allmendinger, Jutta. 1989. "Educational Systems and Labor Market Outcomes." *European Sociological Review* 5 (3): 231–50.

Aoki, Masahiko. 1988. *Information, Incentives and Bargaining in the Japanese Economy.* Cambridge: Cambridge University Press.

Becker, Gary. 1964. *Human Capital: A Theoretical and Empirical Analysis, with Special Reference to Education.* New York: Columbia University Press.

Blossfeld, Hans-Peter, and Karl Ulrich Mayer. 1988. "Labor Market Segmentation in the Federal Republic of Germany: An Empirical Study of Segmentation Theories from a Life Course Perspective." *European Sociologic Review* 4 (2): 123–40.

Chang, Chun, and Yijiang Wang. 1995. "A Framework for Understanding Differences in Labor Turnover and Human Capital Investment." *Journal of Economic Behavior and Organization* 28(1): 91–105.

Daly, Mary. 1994. "A Matter of Dependency? The Gender Dimension of British Income-Maintenance Provision." *Sociology* 28 (3): 779–97.

Dore, Ronald. and Mari Sako. 1989. *How the Japanese Learn to Work.* London: Routledge.

Esping-Andersen, Gøsta. 1990. *Three Worlds of Welfare Capitalism.* Princeton: Princeton University Press.

———. 1999. *Social Foundations of Postindustrial Economies.* Oxford: Oxford University Press.

Estévez-Abe, Margarita. 1999. "Comparative Political Economy of Female Labor Force Participation." Paper presented at the meeting of the American Political Science Association, Atlanta, 2–5 September.

Finegold, David, and David Soskice. 1988. "The Failure of Training in Britain: Analysis and Prescription." *Oxford Review of Economic Policy* 4 (3): 21–53.

Gottschalk, Peter, and T. M. Smeeding. 2000. "Empirical Evidence on Income Inequality in Industrialized Countries." In *The Handbook of Income Distribution,* ed. A. B. Atkinson and F. Bourguignon. London: North Holland Press.

Hollingsworth, J. Rogers, and Robert Boyers, eds. 1997. *Contemporary Capitalism: The Embeddedness of Institutions.* Cambridge: Cambridge University Press.

Huber, Evelyne, John D. Stephens, Charles Ragin, and John Stephens. 1993. "Social Democracy, Christian Democracy, Constitutional Structure and the Welfare State." *American Journal of Sociology* 99 (3): 711–49.

ILO. 1989–90. *Yearbook of Labour Statistics.* Geneva: ILO.

Income Data Services. 1996. *Industrial Relations and Collective Bargaining.* London: Institute of Personnel and Development.

Iversen, Torben. 1999. *Contested Economic Institutions: The Politics of Macroeconomics and Wage Bargaining in Advanced Democracies.* New York: Cambridge University Press.

———, and Anne Wren. 1998. "Equality, Employment, and Budgetary Restraint: The Trilemma of the Service Economy." *World Politics* 50 (July): 507–46.

Koike, Kazuo. 1981. *Nihon no Jukuren: Sugureta Jinzai Keisei Shisutemu* [Skills in Japan: An Effective Human Capital Formation System]. Tokyo: Yuhikaku.

———. 1994. "Learning and Incentive Systems in Japanese Industry." In *The Japanese Firm,* ed. Masahiko Aoki and Ronald Dore. Oxford: Clarendon Press: 41–65.

Lazear, Edward, and Richard Freeman. 1996. "Relational Investing: The Workers' Perspective." NBER Working Paper 5346.

Ni Cheallaigh, Martina. 1995. *Apprenticeship in the EU Member States: A Comparison.* Berlin: European Center for the Development of Vocational Training.

OECD. 1991. "Unemployment Benefit Rules and Labour Market Policy." *OECD Employment Outlook.* Paris: OECD: 199–236.

———. 1996. *OECD International Sectoral Data Base.* Paris: OECD.

———. 1999. *OECD Education Database.* Paris: OECD.

———. *Labour Force Statistics.* Paris: OECD (various years).

———. *OECD Employment Outlook.* Paris: OECD (various years).

Ohashi, Isao, and Toshiaki Tachibanaki, eds. 1998. *Internal Labor Markets, Incentives and Employment.* New York: St Martin's Press.

Osterman, Peter. 1987. "Choice of Employment Systems in Internal Labour Markets." *Industrial Relations* 26 (1): 46–67.

Rowthorn, Robert. 1992. "Corporatism and Labour Market Performance." In *Social Corporatism: A Superior Economic System?*, ed. Jukka Pekkarinen, Matti Pohjola, and Bob Rowthorn. Oxford: Clarendon Press: 44–81.

Rubery, Jill, Colette Fagan, and Friederike Maier. 1996. "Occupational Segregation, Discrimination and Equal Opportunity." In *International Handbook of Labour Market Policy and Evaluation*, ed. Gunther Schmid, Jacqueline O'Reilly, and Klaus Schomann. Cheltenham: Edward Elgar: 431–61.

Rueda, David, and Jonas Pontusson. 2000. "Wage Inequality and Varieties of Capitalism." *World Politics* 52 (April): 350–83.

Schettkat, Ronald. 1993. "Compensating Differentials? Wage Differentials and Employment Stability in the U.S. and German Economies." *Journal of Economic Issues* 27 (1): 153–70.

Shibata, Hiromichi. 1999. "Comparison of American and Japanese Work Practices: Skill Formation, Communications and Conflict Resolution." *Industrial Relations* 38 (2): 192–214.

Soskice, David. 1994. "Reconciling Markets and Institutions: The German Apprenticeship System." In *Training and the Private Sector: International Comparisons*, ed. Lisa M. Lynch. Chicago: Chicago University Press: 25–60.

———. 1999. "Divergent Production Regimes: Coordinated and Uncoordinated Market Economies in the 1980s and 1990s." In *Continuity and Change in Contemporary Capitalism*, ed. Herbert Kitschelt et al. Cambridge: Cambridge University Press: 101–34.

Spencer, Michael. 1973. "Job Market Signaling." *Quarterly Journal of Economics* 87 (3): 355–74.

Streeck, Wolfgang. 1991. "On the Institutional Conditions of Diversified Quality Production." In *Beyond Keynesianism: The Socioeconomics of Production and Full Employment*, ed. Egon Matzner and Wolfgang Streeck. Aldershot: Elgar: 21–61.

———. 1992. *Social Institutions and Economic Performance: Studies on Industrial Relations in Advanced European Capitalist Countries.* London: Sage.

UNESCO. 1999. *UNESCO Statistical Yearbook.* New York: UNESCO.

Wallerstein, Michael. 1999. "Wage-Setting Institutions and Pay Inequality in Advanced Industrial Societies." *American Journal of Political Science* 43 (3): 649–80.

9 COMMUNISM AND POSTCOMMUNISM

This section traces the concept of communism: its limitations, collapse, and future prospects. We begin with the most commonly read work of Karl Marx and Friedrich Engels, *Manifesto of the Communist Party* (1848), in which they lay out their understanding of human history and its dynamics, and the inevitability of the communist revolution to come. For Marx and Engels, economic relations are the driving force of all human relations, and it is changes in these economic relations that drive history. History is a succession of revolutions by those who are exploited against those who exploit them. At the midpoint of the nineteenth century, with the Industrial Revolution well under way, the authors predicted that capitalism's own limitations would soon bring about its overthrow and replacement by a communist system in which resources and wealth would be shared equally. Marx and Engels thus combined research with activism. Their ideas would go on to spark communist movements across the globe and revolutions in such places as Russia in 1917 and China in 1949.

But communism in practice was more challenging than Marx or Engels anticipated. Implementing the idea of eliminating private property and market forces led to an economy administered by the state and backed by authoritarian rule. In addition to denying democratic freedoms, communism also grew increasingly unable to provide for material needs and economic growth. By the 1980s, attempts to reform this ossified structure in the Soviet Union and Eastern Europe quickly led to its undoing.

This does not mean, however, that the result has been a complete or successful transition to liberal democracy across the region. While democratic regimes quickly emerged in much of Eastern Europe, where communist rule was relatively short, these regimes now appear to be under strain. In the former Soviet Union, democracy has been the exception rather than the rule. Why?

Grzegorz Ekiert's piece "The Illiberal Challenge in Post-Communist Europe" (2012) addresses this puzzle with regard to Eastern Europe. While certainly there has been a rise in illiberal, populist, and even authoritarian individuals and values in the region, Ekiert challenges the skeptical interpretations that have gained currency and argues that in fact these forces pose relatively little threat to democracy and the market economy. Economic difficulties in the region may have given credence to illiberalism, but by and large public support for democracy remains strong.

He does acknowledge, however, that it remains unclear whether ongoing economic problems will eventually erode this support.

These fears of the failure of democratization and economic transition can be seen in the case of former Soviet states. Henry E. Hale's "25 Years after the USSR: What's Gone Wrong?" (2016) picks up from Ekiert's discussion of liberalism, citing Russia as an example of where democratization clearly failed. Working through a number of contending explanations, his view is that patrimonialism (what he calls "patronalism") is the key explanation for the persistence of authoritarianism in Russia and other former Soviet states after the collapse of communism. Hale argues that across the former Soviet Union, post-communist political power was quickly reconsolidated within small personal networks, rather than invested in political values that included a respect for the rule of law. Yet this still begs the question of why this became the norm across the former Soviet Union as opposed to Eastern Europe. Part may be a function of history, as Hale notes that patrimonial rule had been prevalent across the countries of the former Soviet Union for centuries, long before communism itself. Moreover, the construction of strong presidential rule after communism (which was not the case in Eastern Europe) enabled leaders to consolidate power and build patrimonial networks that could hang on to power. Finally, Hale argues that the European Union (EU) was an important force, compelling Eastern European states to reject patrimonialism in favor of norms that would enable them to join the EU. These factors all suggest that patrimonialism across the former Soviet Union is unlikely to be rolled back in the near future.

Our readings in this chapter and in Chapter 6 have addressed the resilience of authoritarianism in both Russia and China. One remaining puzzle is the difference between the two countries in economic performance. Both undertook economic reform and sought to improve their relationships with traditional adversaries such as the United States. Yet despite the fact that Russia has benefited from a more developed economy, better educated population, and stronger infrastructure, China's growth has been dramatic while Russia has stagnated. One obvious factor is Russia's reliance on natural resources, which helps to reinforce the patrimonialism discussed above. However, Harley Balzer's article "Russia and China in the Global Economy" (2008) argues that another important consideration is the very different views that both regimes have had toward globalization. In China, the relative weakness of the economy and the fragmentation of the Communist Party following years of political turmoil created an opening for a new elite who saw globalization as a way to overcome this tumult and catch up with the outside world. In contrast, the high degree of centralization of the Communist Party in the Soviet Union created a deeply institutionalized regime that saw international integration as a form of weakness, a view that continues to this day. This complicated relationship to globalization—whether it weakens or strengthens sovereignty and economic prosperity—is not limited to communist or postcommunist regimes, as we well know. We will consider this question again in Chapter 11.

Karl Marx and Friedrich Engels
MANIFESTO OF THE COMMUNIST PARTY

A spectre is haunting Europe—the spectre of communism. All the powers of old Europe have entered into a holy alliance to exorcise this spectre: Pope and Tsar, Metternich and Guizot, French Radicals and German police-spies.

Where is the party in opposition that has not been decried as communistic by its opponents in power? Where is the opposition that has not hurled back the branding reproach of communism, against the more advanced opposition parties, as well as against its reactionary adversaries?

Two things result from this fact:

I. Communism is already acknowledged by all European powers to be itself a power.
II. It is high time that Communists should openly, in the face of the whole world, publish their views, their aims, their tendencies, and meet this nursery tale of the spectre of communism with a manifesto of the party itself.

To this end, Communists of various nationalities have assembled in London and sketched the following manifesto, to be published in the English, French, German, Italian, Flemish and Danish languages.

I—Bourgeois and Proletarians

The history of all hitherto existing society is the history of class struggles.

Freeman and slave, patrician and plebian, lord and serf, guild-master and journeyman, in a word, oppressor and oppressed, stood in constant opposition to one another, carried on an uninterrupted, now hidden, now open fight, a fight that each time ended, either in a revolutionary reconstitution of society at large, or in the common ruin of the contending classes.

In the earlier epochs of history, we find almost everywhere a complicated arrangement of society into various orders, a manifold gradation of social rank. In ancient Rome we have patricians, knights, plebians, slaves; in the Middle Ages, feudal lords, vassals, guild-masters, journeymen, apprentices, serfs; in almost all of these classes, again, subordinate gradations.

The modern bourgeois society that has sprouted from the ruins of feudal society has not done away with class antagonisms. It has but established new classes, new conditions of oppression, new forms of struggle in place of the old ones.

Our epoch, the epoch of the bourgeoisie, possesses, however, this distinct feature: it has simplified class antagonisms. Society as a whole is more and more splitting up into two great hostile camps, into two great classes directly facing each other—bourgeoisie and proletariat.

From the serfs of the Middle Ages sprang the chartered burghers of the earliest towns. From these burgesses the first elements of the bourgeoisie were developed.

The discovery of America, the rounding of the Cape, opened up fresh ground for the rising bourgeoisie. The East-Indian and Chinese markets, the colonisation of America, trade with the colonies, the increase in the means of exchange and in commodities generally, gave to commerce, to navigation, to industry, an impulse never before known, and thereby, to the revolutionary element in the tottering feudal society, a rapid development.

From *The Marx-Engels Reader*, Second Edition (New York: W. W. Norton, 1978) pp. 473–77.

The feudal system of industry, in which industrial production was monopolized by closed guilds, now no longer suffices for the growing wants of the new markets. The manufacturing system took its place. The guild-masters were pushed aside by the manufacturing middle class; division of labor between the different corporate guilds vanished in the face of division of labor in each single workshop.

Meantime, the markets kept ever growing, the demand ever rising. Even manufacturers no longer sufficed. Thereupon, steam and machinery revolutionized industrial production. The place of manufacture was taken by the giant, MODERN INDUSTRY; the place of the industrial middle class by industrial millionaires, the leaders of the whole industrial armies, the modern bourgeois.

Modern industry has established the world market, for which the discovery of America paved the way. This market has given an immense development to commerce, to navigation, to communication by land. This development has, in turn, reacted on the extension of industry; and in proportion as industry, commerce, navigation, railways extended, in the same proportion the bourgeoisie developed, increased its capital, and pushed into the background every class handed down from the Middle Ages.

We see, therefore, how the modern bourgeoisie is itself the product of a long course of development, of a series of revolutions in the modes of production and of exchange.

Each step in the development of the bourgeoisie was accompanied by a corresponding political advance in that class. An oppressed class under the sway of the feudal nobility, an armed and self-governing association of medieval commune: here independent urban republic (as in Italy and Germany); there taxable "third estate" of the monarchy (as in France); afterward, in the period of manufacturing proper, serving either the semi-feudal or the absolute monarchy as a counterpoise against the nobility, and, in fact, cornerstone of the great monarchies in general—the bourgeoisie has at last, since the establishment of Modern Industry and of the world market, conquered for itself, in the modern representative state, exclusive political sway. The executive of the modern state is but a committee for managing the common affairs of the whole bourgeoisie.

The bourgeoisie, historically, has played a most revolutionary part.

The bourgeoisie, wherever it has got the upper hand, has put an end to all feudal, patriarchal, idyllic relations. It has pitilessly torn asunder the motley feudal ties that bound man to his "natural superiors," and has left no other nexus between people than naked self-interest, than callous "cash payment." It has drowned out the most heavenly ecstasies of religious fervor, of chivalrous enthusiasm, of philistine sentimentalism, in the icy water of egotistical calculation. It has resolved personal worth into exchange value, and in place of the numberless indefeasible chartered freedoms, has set up that single, unconscionable freedom—Free Trade. In one word, for exploitation, veiled by religious and political illusions, it has substituted naked, shameless, direct, brutal exploitation.

The bourgeoisie has stripped of its halo every occupation hitherto honored and looked up to with reverent awe. It has converted the physician, the lawyer, the priest, the poet, the man of science, into its paid wage laborers.

The bourgeoisie has torn away from the family its sentimental veil, and has reduced the family relation into a mere money relation.

The bourgeoisie has disclosed how it came to pass that the brutal display of vigor in the Middle Ages, which reactionaries so much admire, found its fitting complement in the most slothful indolence. It has been the first to show what man's activity can bring about. It has accomplished wonders far surpassing Egyptian pyramids, Roman aqueducts, and Gothic cathedrals; it has conducted expeditions that put in the shade all former exoduses of nations and crusades.

The bourgeoisie cannot exist without constantly revolutionizing the instruments of production, and thereby the relations of production, and with them the whole relations of society. Conservation of the old modes of production in unaltered form, was, on the contrary, the first condition of existence for all earlier industrial classes. Constant revolutionizing of production, uninterrupted disturbance of all social conditions, everlasting uncertainty and agitation distinguish the bourgeois epoch from all earlier ones. All fixed, fast frozen relations, with their train of ancient and venerable prejudices and opinions, are swept away, all new-formed ones become antiquated before they can ossify. All that is solid melts into air, all that is holy is profaned, and man is at last compelled to face with sober senses his real condition of life and his relations with his kind.

The need of a constantly expanding market for its products chases the bourgeoisie over the entire surface of the globe. It must nestle everywhere, settle everywhere, establish connections everywhere.

The bourgeoisie has, through its exploitation of the world market, given a cosmopolitan character to production and consumption in every country. To the great chagrin of reactionaries, it has drawn from under the feet of industry the national ground on which it stood. All old-established national industries have been destroyed or are daily being destroyed. They are dislodged by new industries, whose introduction becomes a life and death question for all civilized nations, by industries that no longer work up indigenous raw material, but raw material drawn from the remotest zones; industries whose products are consumed, not only at home, but in every quarter of the globe. In place of the old wants, satisfied by the production of the country, we find new wants, requiring for their satisfaction the products of distant lands and climes. In place of the old local and national seclusion and self-sufficiency, we have intercourse in every direction, universal interdependence of nations. And as in material, so also in intellectual production. The intellectual creations of individual nations become common property. National one-sidedness and narrow-mindedness become more and more impossible, and from the numerous national and local literatures, there arises a world literature.

The bourgeoisie, by the rapid improvement of all instruments of production, by the immensely facilitated means of communication, draws all, even the most barbarian, nations into civilization. The cheap prices of commodities are the heavy artillery with which it forces the barbarians' intensely obstinate hatred of foreigners to capitulate. It compels all nations, on pain of extinction, to adopt the bourgeois mode of production; it compels them to introduce what it calls civilization into their midst, i.e., to become bourgeois themselves. In one word, it creates a world after its own image.

The bourgeoisie has subjected the country to the rule of the towns. It has created enormous cities, has greatly increased the urban population as compared with the rural, and has thus rescued a considerable part of the population from the idiocy of rural life. Just as it has made the country dependent on the towns, so it has made barbarian and semi-barbarian countries dependent on the civilized ones, nations of peasants on nations of bourgeois, the East on the West.

The bourgeoisie keeps more and more doing away with the scattered state of the population, of the means of production, and of property. It has agglomerated population, centralized the means of production, and has concentrated property in a few hands. The necessary consequence of this was political centralization. Independent, or but loosely connected provinces, with separate interests, laws, governments, and systems of taxation, became lumped together into one nation, with one government, one code of laws, one national class interest, one frontier, and one customs tariff.

The bourgeoisie, during its rule of scarce one hundred years, has created more massive and more colossal productive forces than have all preceding generations together. Subjection of nature's forces to man, machinery, application of chemistry to industry and agriculture, steam navigation, railways, electric telegraphs, clearing of whole continents for cultivation, canalization or rivers, whole populations conjured out of the ground—what earlier century had even a presentiment that such productive forces slumbered in the lap of social labor?

We see then: the means of production and of exchange, on whose foundation the bourgeoisie built itself up, were generated in feudal society. At a certain stage in the development of these means of production and of exchange, the conditions under which feudal society produced and exchanged, the feudal organization of agriculture and manufacturing industry, in one word, the feudal relations of property became no longer compatible with the already developed productive forces; they became so many fetters. They had to be burst asunder; they were burst asunder.

Into their place stepped free competition, accompanied by a social and political constitution adapted in it, and the economic and political sway of the bourgeois class.

A similar movement is going on before our own eyes. Modern bourgeois society, with its relations of production, of exchange and of property, a society that has conjured up such gigantic means of production and of exchange, is like the sorcerer who is no longer able to control the powers of the nether world whom he has called up by his spells. For many a decade past, the history of industry and commerce is but the history of the revolt of modern productive forces against modern conditions of production, against the property relations that are the conditions for the existence of the bourgeois and of its rule. It is enough to mention the commercial crises that, by their periodical return, put the existence of the entire bourgeois society on its trial, each time more threateningly. In these crises, a great part not only of the existing products, but also of the previously created productive forces, are periodically destroyed. In these crises, there breaks out an epidemic that, in all earlier epochs, would have seemed an absurdity— the epidemic of over-production. Society suddenly finds itself put back into a state of momentary barbarism; it appears as if a famine, a universal war of devastation, had cut off the supply of every means of subsistence; industry and commerce seem to be destroyed. And why? Because there is too much civilization, too much means of subsistence, too much industry, too much commerce. The produc-

tive forces at the disposal of society no longer tend to further the development of the conditions of bourgeois property; on the contrary, they have become too powerful for these conditions, by which they are fettered, and so soon as they overcome these fetters, they bring disorder into the whole of bourgeois society, endanger the existence of bourgeois property. The conditions of bourgeois society are too narrow to comprise the wealth created by them. And how does the bourgeoisie get over these crises? On the one hand, by enforced destruction of a mass of productive forces; on the other, by the conquest of new markets, and by the more thorough exploitation of the old ones. That is to say, by paving the way for more extensive and more destructive crises, and by diminishing the means whereby crises are prevented.

The weapons with which the bourgeoisie felled feudalism to the ground are now turned against the bourgeoisie itself.

But not only has the bourgeoisie forged the weapons that bring death to itself; it has also called into existence the men who are to wield those weapons— the modern working class—the proletarians.

In proportion as the bourgeoisie, i.e., capital, is developed, in the same proportion is the proletariat, the modern working class, developed—a class of laborers, who live only so long as they find work, and who find work only so long as their labor increases capital. These laborers, who must sell themselves piecemeal, are a commodity, like every other article of commerce, and are consequently exposed to all the vicissitudes of competition, to all the fluctuations of the market.

Owing to the extensive use of machinery, and to the division of labor, the work of the proletarians has lost all individual character, and, consequently, all charm for the workman. He becomes an appendage of the machine, and it is only the most simple, most monotonous, and most easily acquired knack, that is required of him. Hence, the cost of production of a workman is restricted, almost entirely, to the means of subsistence that he requires for maintenance, and for the propagation of his race. But the price of a commodity, and therefore also of labor, is equal to its cost of production. In proportion, therefore, as the repulsiveness of the work increases, the wage decreases. What is more, in proportion as the use of machinery and division of labor increases, in the same proportion the burden of toil also increases, whether by prolongation of the working hours, by the increase of the work exacted in a given time, or by increased speed of machinery, etc.

Modern Industry has converted the little workshop of the patriarchal master into the great factory of the industrial capitalist. Masses of laborers, crowded into the factory, are organized like soldiers. As privates of the industrial army, they are placed under the command of a perfect hierarchy of officers and sergeants. Not only are they slaves of the bourgeois class, and of the bourgeois state; they are daily and hourly enslaved by the machine, by the overlooker, and, above all, in the individual bourgeois manufacturer himself. The more openly this despotism proclaims gain to be its end and aim, the more petty, the more hateful and the more embittering it is.

The less the skill and exertion of strength implied in manual labor, in other words, the more modern industry becomes developed, the more is the labor of men superseded by that of women. Differences of age and sex have no longer any distinctive social validity for the working class. All are instruments of labor, more or less expensive to use, according to their age and sex.

No sooner is the exploitation of the laborer by the manufacturer, so far at an end, that he receives his wages in cash, than he is set upon by the other portion of the bourgeoisie, the landlord, the shopkeeper, the pawnbroker, etc.

The lower strata of the middle class—the small tradespeople, shopkeepers, and retired tradesmen generally, the handicraftsmen and peasants—all these sink gradually into the proletariat, partly because their diminutive capital does not suffice for the scale on which Modern Industry is carried on, and is swamped in the competition with the large capitalists, partly because their specialized skill is rendered worthless by new methods of production.

Thus, the proletariat is recruited from all classes of the population.

The proletariat goes through various stages of development. With its birth begins its struggle with the bourgeoisie. At first, the contest is carried on by individual laborers, then by the work of people of a factory, then by the operative of one trade, in one locality, against the individual bourgeois who directly exploits them. They direct their attacks not against the bourgeois condition of production, but against the instruments of production themselves; they destroy imported wares that compete with their labor, they smash to pieces machinery, they set factories ablaze, they seek to restore by force the vanished status of the workman of the Middle Ages.

At this stage, the laborers still form an incoherent mass scattered over the whole country, and broken up by their mutual competition. If anywhere they unite to form more compact bodies, this is not yet the consequence of their own active union, but of the union of the bourgeoisie, which class, in order to attain its own political ends, is compelled to set the whole proletariat in motion, and is moreover yet, for a time, able to do so. At this stage, therefore, the proletarians do not fight their enemies, but the enemies of their enemies, the remnants of absolute monarchy, the landowners, the non-industrial bourgeois, the petty bourgeois. Thus, the whole historical movement is concentrated in the hands of the bourgeoisie; every victory so obtained is a victory for the bourgeoisie.

But with the development of industry, the proletariat not only increases in number; it becomes concentrated in greater masses, its strength grows, and it feels that strength more. The various interests and conditions of life within the ranks of the proletariat are more and more equalized, in proportion as machinery obliterates all distinctions of labor, and nearly everywhere reduces wages to the same low level. The growing competition among the bourgeois, and the resulting commercial crises, make the wages of the workers ever more fluctuating. The increasing improvement of machinery, ever more rapidly developing, makes their livelihood more and more precarious; the collisions between individual workmen and individual bourgeois take more and more the character of collisions between two classes. Thereupon, the workers begin to form combinations (trade unions) against the bourgeois; they club together in order to keep up the rate of wages; they found permanent associations in order to make provision beforehand for these occasional revolts. Here and there, the contest breaks out into riots.

Now and then the workers are victorious, but only for a time. The real fruit of their battles lie not in the immediate result, but in the ever expanding union of the workers. This union is helped on by the improved means of communication that are created by Modern Industry, and that place the workers of different localities in contact with one another. It was just this contact that was needed to centralize the numerous local struggles, all of the same character, into one national struggle between classes. But every class struggle is a political struggle. And that union, to attain which the burghers of the Middle Ages, with their miserable highways, required centuries, the modern proletarian, thanks to railways, achieve in a few years.

This organization of the proletarians into a class, and, consequently, into a political party, is continually being upset again by the competition between the workers themselves. But it ever rises up again, stronger, firmer, mightier. It compels legislative recognition of particular interests of the workers, by taking advantage of the divisions among the bourgeoisie itself. Thus, the Ten-Hours Bill in England was carried.

Altogether, collisions between the classes of the old society further in many ways the course of development of the proletariat. The bourgeoisie finds itself involved in a constant battle. At first with the aristocracy; later on, with those portions of the bourgeoisie itself, whose interests have become antagonistic to the progress of industry; at all time with the bourgeoisie of foreign countries. In all these battles, it sees itself compelled to appeal to the proletariat, to ask for help, and thus to drag it into the political arena. The bourgeoisie itself, therefore, supplies the proletariat with its own elements of political and general education, in other words, it furnishes the proletariat with weapons for fighting the bourgeoisie.

Further, as we have already seen, entire sections of the ruling class are, by the advance of industry, precipitated into the proletariat, or are at least threatened in their conditions of existence. These also supply the proletariat with fresh elements of enlightenment and progress.

Finally, in times when the class struggle nears the decisive hour, the progress of dissolution going on within the ruling class, in fact within the whole range of old society, assumes such a violent, glaring character, that a small section of the ruling class cuts itself adrift, and joins the revolutionary class, the class that holds the future in its hands. Just as, therefore, at an earlier period, a section of the nobility went over to the bourgeoisie, so now a portion of the bourgeoisie goes over to the proletariat, and in particular, a portion of the bourgeois ideologists, who have raised themselves to the level of comprehending theoretically the historical movement as a whole.

Of all the classes that stand face to face with the bourgeoisie today, the proletariat alone is a genuinely revolutionary class. The other classes decay and finally disappear in the face of Modern Industry; the proletariat is its special and essential product.

The lower middle class, the small manufacturer, the shopkeeper, the artisan, the peasant, all these fight against the bourgeoisie, to save from extinction their existence as fractions of the middle class. They are therefore not revolutionary, but conservative. Nay, more, they are reactionary, for they try to roll back the wheel of history. If, by chance, they are revolutionary, they are only so in view of their impending transfer into the proletariat; they thus defend not their present, but their future interests; they desert their own standpoint to place themselves at that of the proletariat.

The "dangerous class," the social scum, that passively rotting mass thrown off by the lowest layers of the old society, may, here and there, be swept into the movement by a proletarian revolution; its conditions of life, however, prepare it far more for the part of a bribed tool of reactionary intrigue.

In the condition of the proletariat, those of old society at large are already virtually swamped. The proletarian is without property; his relation to his wife and children has no longer anything in common with the bourgeois family relations; modern industry labor, modern subjection to capital, the same in England as in France, in America as in Germany, has stripped him of every trace of national character. Law, morality, religion, are to him so many bourgeois prejudices, behind which lurk in ambush just as many bourgeois interests.

All the preceding classes that got the upper hand sought to fortify their already acquired status by subjecting society at large to their conditions of appropriation. The proletarians cannot become masters of the productive forces of society, except by abolishing their own previous mode of appropriation, and thereby also every other previous mode of appropriation. They have nothing of their own to secure and to fortify; their mission is to destroy all previous securities for, and insurances of, individual property.

All previous historical movements were movements of minorities, or in the interest of minorities. The proletarian movement is the self-conscious, independent movement of the immense majority, in the interest of the immense majority. The proletariat, the lowest stratum of our present society, cannot stir, cannot raise itself up, without the whole superincumbent strata of official society being sprung into the air.

Though not in substance, yet in form, the struggle of the proletariat with the bourgeoisie is at first a national struggle. The proletariat of each country must, of course, first of all settle matters with its own bourgeoisie.

In depicting the most general phases of the development of the proletariat, we traced the more

or less veiled civil war, raging within existing society, up to the point where that war breaks out into open revolution, and where the violent overthrow of the bourgeoisie lays the foundation for the sway of the proletariat.

Hitherto, every form of society has been based, as we have already seen, on the antagonism of oppressing and oppressed classes. But in order to oppress a class, certain conditions must be assured to it under which it can, at least, continue its slavish existence. The serf, in the period of serfdom, raised himself to membership in the commune, just as the petty bourgeois, under the yoke of the feudal absolutism, managed to develop into a bourgeois. The modern laborer, on the contrary, instead of rising with the process of industry, sinks deeper and deeper below the conditions of existence of his own class. He becomes a pauper, and pauperism develops more rapidly than population and wealth. And here it becomes evident that the bourgeoisie is unfit any longer to be the ruling class in society, and to impose its conditions of existence upon society as an overriding law. It is unfit to rule because it is incompetent to assure an existence to its slave within his slavery, because it cannot help letting him sink into such a state, that it has to feed him, instead of being fed by him. Society can no longer live under this bourgeoisie, in other words, its existence is no longer compatible with society.

The essential conditions for the existence and for the sway of the bourgeois class is the formation and augmentation of capital; the condition for capital is wage labor. Wage labor rests exclusively on competition between the laborers. The advance of industry, whose involuntary promoter is the bourgeoisie, replaces the isolation of the laborers, due to competition, by the revolutionary combination, due to association. The development of Modern Industry, therefore, cuts from under its feet the very foundation on which the bourgeoisie produces and appropriates products. What the bourgeoisie therefore produces, above all, are its own grave-diggers. Its fall and the victory of the proletariat are equally inevitable.

II—Proletarians and Communists

In what relation do the Communists stand to the proletarians as a whole? The Communists do not form a separate party opposed to the other working-class parties.

They have no interests separate and apart from those of the proletariat as a whole.

They do not set up any sectarian principles of their own, by which to shape and mold the proletarian movement.

The Communists are distinguished from the other working-class parties by this only:

1. In the national struggles of the proletarians of the different countries, they point out and bring to the front the common interests of the entire proletariat, independently of all nationality.
2. In the various stages of development which the struggle of the working class against the bourgeoisie has to pass through, they always and everywhere represent the interests of the movement as a whole.

The Communists, therefore, are on the one hand practically, the most advanced and resolute section of the working-class parties of every country, that section which pushes forward all others; on the other hand, theoretically, they have over the great mass of the proletariat the advantage of clearly understanding the lines of march, the conditions, and the ultimate general results of the proletarian movement.

The immediate aim of the Communists is the same as that of all other proletarian parties: Formation of the proletariat into a class, overthrow of the bourgeois supremacy, conquest of political power by the proletariat.

The theoretical conclusions of the Communists are in no way based on ideas or principles that have been invented, or discovered, by this or that would-be universal reformer.

They merely express, in general terms, actual relations springing from an existing class struggle, from a historical movement going on under our very eyes. The abolition of existing property relations is not at all a distinctive feature of communism.

All property relations in the past have continually been subject to historical change consequent upon the change in historical conditions.

The French Revolution, for example, abolished feudal property in favor of bourgeois property.

The distinguishing feature of communism is not the abolition of property generally, but the abolition of bourgeois property. But modern bourgeois private property is the final and most complete expression of the system of producing and appropriating products that is based on class antagonisms, on the exploitation of the many by the few.

In this sense, the theory of the Communists may be summed up in the single sentence: Abolition of private property.

We Communists have been reproached with the desire of abolishing the right of personally acquiring property as the fruit of a man's own labor, which property is alleged to be the groundwork of all personal freedom, activity and independence.

Hard-won, self-acquired, self-earned property! Do you mean the property of petty artisan and of the small peasant, a form of property that preceded the bourgeois form? There is no need to abolish that; the development of industry has to a great extent already destroyed it, and is still destroying it daily.

Or do you mean the modern bourgeois private property?

But does wage labor create any property for the laborer? Not a bit. It creates capital, i.e., that kind of property which exploits wage labor, and which cannot increase except upon conditions of begetting a new supply of wage labor for fresh exploitation. Property, in its present form, is based on the antagonism of capital and wage labor. Let us examine both sides of this antagonism.

To be a capitalist, is to have not only a purely personal, but a social STATUS in production. Capital is a collective product, and only by the united action of many members, nay, in the last resort, only by the united action of all members of society, can it be set in motion.

Capital is therefore not only personal; it is a social power.

When, therefore, capital is converted into common property, into the property of all members of society, personal property is not thereby transformed into social property. It is only the social character of the property that is changed. It loses its class character.

Let us now take wage labor.

The average price of wage labor is the minimum wage, i.e., that quantum of the means of subsistence which is absolutely requisite to keep the laborer in bare existence as a laborer. What, therefore, the wage laborer appropriates by means of his labor merely suffices to prolong and reproduce a bare existence. We by no means intend to abolish this personal appropriation of the products of labor, an appropriation that is made for the maintenance and reproduction of human life, and that leaves no surplus wherewith to command the labor of others. All that we want to do away with is the miserable character of this appropriation, under which the laborer lives merely to increase capital, and is allowed to live only in so far as the interest of the ruling class requires it.

In bourgeois society, living labor is but a means to increase accumulated labor. In communist society, accumulated labor is but a means to widen, to enrich, to promote the existence of the laborer.

In bourgeois society, therefore, the past dominates the present; in communist society, the present dominates the past. In bourgeois society, capital is independent and has individuality, while the living person is dependent and has no individuality.

And the abolition of this state of things is called by the bourgeois, abolition of individuality and freedom! And rightly so. The abolition of bourgeois individuality, bourgeois independence, and bourgeois freedom is undoubtedly aimed at.

By freedom is meant, under the present bourgeois conditions of production, free trade, free selling and buying.

But if selling and buying disappears, free selling and buying disappears also. This talk about free selling and buying, and all the other "brave words" of our bourgeois about freedom in general, have a meaning, if any, only in contrast with restricted selling and buying, with the fettered traders of the Middle Ages, but have no meaning when opposed to the communist abolition of buying and selling, or the bourgeois conditions of production, and of the bourgeoisie itself.

You are horrified at our intending to do away with private property. But in your existing society, private property is already done away with for nine-tenths of the population; its existence for the few is solely due to its non-existence in the hands of those nine-tenths. You reproach us, therefore, with intending to do away with a form of property, the necessary condition for whose existence is the non-existence of any property for the immense majority of society.

In one word, you reproach us with intending to do away with your property. Precisely so; that is just what we intend.

From the moment when labor can no longer be converted into capital, money, or rent, into a social power capable of being monopolized, i.e., from the moment when individual property can no longer be transformed into bourgeois property, into capital, from that moment, you say, individuality vanishes.

You must, therefore, confess that by "individual" you mean no other person than the bourgeois, than the middle-class owner of property. This person must, indeed, be swept out of the way, and made impossible.

Communism deprives no man of the power to appropriate the products of society; all that it does is to deprive him of the power to subjugate the labor of others by means of such appropriations.

It has been objected that upon the abolition of private property, all work will cease, and universal laziness will overtake us.

According to this, bourgeois society ought long ago to have gone to the dogs through sheer idleness; for those who acquire anything, do not work. The whole of this objection is but another expression of the tautology: There can no longer be any wage labor when there is no longer any capital.

All objections urged against the communistic mode of producing and appropriating material products, have, in the same way, been urged against the communistic mode of producing and appropriating intellectual products. Just as to the bourgeois, the disappearance of class property is the disappearance of production itself, so the disappearance of class culture is to him identical with the disappearance of all culture.

That culture, the loss of which he laments, is, for the enormous majority, a mere training to act as a machine.

But don't wrangle with us so long as you apply, to our intended abolition of bourgeois property, the standard of your bourgeois notions of freedom, culture, law, etc. Your very ideas are but the outgrowth of the conditions of your bourgeois production and bourgeois property, just as your jurisprudence is but the will of your class made into a law for all, a will whose essential character and direction are determined by the economical conditions of existence of your class.

The selfish misconception that induces you to transform into eternal laws of nature and of reason the social forms stringing from your present mode of production and form of property—historical relations that rise and disappear in the progress of production—this misconception you share with every ruling class that has preceded you. What you see clearly in the case of ancient property, what you admit in the case of feudal property, you are of course forbidden to admit in the case of your own bourgeois form of property.

Abolition of the family! Even the most radical flare up at this infamous proposal of the Communists.

On what foundation is the present family, the bourgeois family, based? On capital, on private gain. In its completely developed form, this family exists only among the bourgeoisie. But this state of things finds its complement in the practical absence of the family among proletarians, and in public prostitution.

The bourgeois family will vanish as a matter of course when its complement vanishes, and both will vanish with the vanishing of capital.

Do you charge us with wanting to stop the exploitation of children by their parents? To this crime we plead guilty.

But, you say, we destroy the most hallowed of relations, when we replace home education by social.

And your education! Is not that also social, and determined by the social conditions under which you educate, by the intervention direct or indirect, of society, by means of schools, etc.? The Communists have not intended the intervention of society in education; they do but seek to alter the character of that intervention, and to rescue education from the influence of the ruling class.

The bourgeois claptrap about the family and education, about the hallowed correlation of parents and child, becomes all the more disgusting, the more, by the action of Modern Industry, all the family ties among the proletarians are torn asunder, and their children transformed into simple articles of commerce and instruments of labor.

But you Communists would introduce community of women, screams the bourgeoisie in chorus.

The bourgeois sees his wife a mere instrument of production. He hears that the instruments of production are to be exploited in common, and, naturally, can come to no other conclusion that the lot of being common to all will likewise fall to the women.

He has not even a suspicion that the real point aimed at is to do away with the status of women as mere instruments of production.

For the rest, nothing is more ridiculous than the virtuous indignation of our bourgeois at the community of women which, they pretend, is to be openly and officially established by the Communists. The Communists have no need to introduce free love; it has existed almost from time immemorial.

Our bourgeois, not content with having wives and daughters of their proletarians at their disposal, not to speak of common prostitutes, take the greatest pleasure in seducing each other's wives. (Ah, those were the days!)

Bourgeois marriage is, in reality, a system of wives in common and thus, at the most, what the Communists might possibly be reproached with is that they desire to introduce, in substitution for a hypocritically concealed, an openly legalized system of free love. For the rest, it is self-evident that the abolition of the present system of production must bring with it the abolition of free love springing from that system, i.e., of prostitution both public and private.

The Communists are further reproached with desiring to abolish countries and nationality.

The workers have no country. We cannot take from them what they have not got. Since the proletariat must first of all acquire political supremacy, must rise to be the leading class of the nation, must constitute itself *the* nation, it is, so far, itself national, though not in the bourgeois sense of the word.

National differences and antagonism between peoples are daily more and more vanishing, owing to the development of the bourgeoisie, to freedom of commerce, to the world market, to uniformity in the mode of production and in the conditions of life corresponding thereto.

The supremacy of the proletariat will cause them to vanish still faster. United action of the leading civilized countries at least is one of the first conditions for the emancipation of the proletariat.

In proportion as the exploitation of one individual by another will also be put an end to, the exploitation of one nation by another will also be put an end to. In proportion as the antagonism between classes within the nation vanishes, the hostility of one nation to another will come to an end.

The charges against communism made from a religious, a philosophical and, generally, from an ideological standpoint, are not deserving of serious examination.

Does it require deep intuition to comprehend that man's ideas, views, and conception, in one word, man's consciousness, changes with every change in the conditions of his material existence, in his social relations and in his social life?

What else does the history of ideas prove, than that intellectual production changes its character in proportion as material production is changed? The ruling ideas of each age have ever been the ideas of its ruling class.

When people speak of the ideas that revolutionize society, they do but express that fact that within the old society the elements of a new one have been created, and that the dissolution of the old ideas keeps even pace with the dissolution of the old conditions of existence.

When the ancient world was in its last throes, the ancient religions were overcome by Christianity. When Christian ideas succumbed in the eighteenth century to rationalist ideas, feudal society fought its death battle with the then revolutionary bourgeoisie. The ideas of religious liberty and freedom of conscience merely gave expression to the sway of free competition within the domain of knowledge.

"Undoubtedly," it will be said, "religious, moral, philosophical, and juridicial ideas have been modified in the course of historical development. But religion, morality, philosophy, political science, and law, constantly survived this change."

"There are, besides, eternal truths, such as Freedom, Justice, etc., that are common to all states of society. But communism abolishes eternal truths, it abolishes all religion, and all morality, instead of constituting them on a new basis; it therefore acts in contradiction to all past historical experience."

What does this accusation reduce itself to? The history of all past society has consisted in the development of class antagonisms, antagonisms that assumed different forms at different epochs.

But whatever form they may have taken, one fact is common to all past ages, viz., the exploitation of one part of society by the other. No wonder, then, that the social consciousness of past ages, despite all the multiplicity and variety it displays, moves within certain common forms, or general ideas, which cannot completely vanish except with the total disappearance of class antagonisms.

The communist revolution is the most radical rupture with traditional relations; no wonder that its development involved the most radical rupture with traditional ideas.

But let us have done with the bourgeois objections to communism.

We have seen above that the first step in the revolution by the working class is to raise the proletariat to the position of ruling class to win the battle of democracy.

The proletariat will use its political supremacy to wrest, by degree, all capital from the bourgeoisie, to centralize all instruments of production in the hands of the state, i.e., of the proletariat organized as the ruling class; and to increase the total productive forces as rapidly as possible.

Of course, in the beginning, this cannot be effected except by means of despotic inroads on the rights of property, and on the conditions of bourgeois production; by means of measures, therefore, which appear economically insufficient and untenable, but which, in the course of the movement, outstrip themselves, necessitate further inroads upon the old social order, and are unavoidable as a means of entirely revolutionizing the mode of production.

These measures will, of course, be different in different countries.

Nevertheless, in most advanced countries, the following will be pretty generally applicable.

1. Abolition of property in land and application of all rents of land to public purposes.
2. A heavy progressive or graduated income tax.
3. Abolition of all rights of inheritance.
4. Confiscation of the property of all emigrants and rebels.
5. Centralization of credit in the banks of the state, by means of a national bank with state capital and an exclusive monopoly.
6. Centralization of the means of communication and transport in the hands of the state.
7. Extension of factories and instruments of production owned by the state; the bringing into cultivation of waste lands, and the improvement of the soil generally in accordance with a common plan.
8. Equal obligation of all to work. Establishment of industrial armies, especially for agriculture.
9. Combination of agriculture with manufacturing industries; gradual abolition of all the distinction between town and country by a more equable distribution of the populace over the country.
10. Free education for all children in public schools. Abolition of children's factory labor in its present form. Combination of education with industrial production, etc.

When, in the course of development, class distinctions have disappeared, and all production has been concentrated in the hands of a vast association of the whole nation, the public power will lose its political character. Political power, properly so called, is merely the organized power of one class for oppressing another. If the proletariat during its contest with the bourgeoisie is compelled, by the force of circumstances, to organize itself as a class; if, by means of a revolution, it makes itself the ruling class, and, as such, sweeps away by force the old conditions of production, then it will, along with these conditions, have swept away the conditions for the existence of class antagonisms and of classes generally, and will thereby have abolished its own supremacy as a class.

In place of the old bourgeois society, with its classes and class antagonisms, we shall have an association in which the free development of each is the condition for the free development of all.

■　■　■

IV—Position of the Communists in Relation to the Various Existing Opposition Parties

Section II has made clear the relations of the Communists to the existing working-class parties, such as the Chartists in England and the Agrarian Reformers in America.

The Communists fight for the attainment of the immediate aims, for the enforcement of the momentary interests of the working class; but in the movement of the present, they also represent and take care of the future of that movement. In France, the Communists ally with the Social Democrats against the conservative and radical bourgeoisie, reserving, however, the right to take up a critical position in regard to phases and illusions traditionally handed down from the Great Revolution.

In Switzerland, they support the Radicals, without losing sight of the fact that this party consists of antagonistic elements, partly of Democratic Socialists, in the French sense, partly of radical bourgeois.

In Poland, they support the party that insists on an agrarian revolution as the prime condition for national emancipation, that party which fomented the insurrection of Krakow in 1846.

In Germany, they fight with the bourgeoisie whenever it acts in a revolutionary way, against the absolute monarchy, the feudal squirearchy, and the petty-bourgeoisie.

But they never cease, for a single instant, to instill into the working class the clearest possible recognition of the hostile antagonism between bourgeoisie and proletariat, in order that the German workers may straightway use, as so many weapons against the bourgeoisie, the social and political conditions that the bourgeoisie must necessarily introduce along with its supremacy, and in order that, after the fall of the reactionary classes in Germany, the fight against the bourgeoisie itself may immediately begin.

The Communists turn their attention chiefly to Germany, because that country is on the eve of a bourgeois revolution that is bound to be carried out under more advanced conditions of European civilization and with a much more developed proletariat than that of England was in the seventeenth, and France in the eighteenth century, and because the bourgeois revolution in Germany will be but the prelude to an immediately following proletarian revolution.

In short, the Communists everywhere support every revolutionary movement against the existing social and political order of things.

In all these movements, they bring to the front, as the leading question in each, the property question, no matter what its degree of development at the time.

Finally, they labor everywhere for the union and agreement of the democratic parties of all countries.

The Communists disdain to conceal their views and aims. They openly declare that their ends can be attained only by the forcible overthrow of all existing social conditions. Let the ruling classes tremble at a communist revolution. The proletarians have nothing to lose but their chains. They have a world to win.

Proletarians of all countries, unite!

Grzegorz Ekiert

THE ILLIBERAL CHALLENGE IN POST-COMMUNIST EUROPE

Two decades of political, economic, and social transformations in Eastern and Central Europe resulted in outcomes that initially were hardly expected. Despite general pessimism about the prospect of liberal democracy in the region, several post-communist countries have developed consolidated democratic systems and working market economies. Other countries, however, either have returned to authoritarianism, albeit of a different sort, or have

From *Taiwan Journal of Democracy* 8, no. 2 (December 2012), pp. 63–77.

persisted in a semireformed and unconsolidated state, dashing the initial hopes of a democratic future for the entire region. Today, ten formerly communist countries are members of the European Union, while others are still either in a waiting room with increasingly uncertain prospects for full membership or destined to remain the neighbors of the EU for the foreseeable future. Finally, the current financial and sovereign debt crisis in Europe has had varied impacts on countries of the region. Some have experienced severe economic problems (the Baltic Republics, Hungary, Bulgaria, and Romania), while others have weathered the crisis so far with few difficulties (e.g., Poland, Slovakia). Some recovered quickly (e.g., Estonia, Lithuania), while others are suffering a prolonged crisis (e.g., Hungary, Croatia, Slovenia). Thus, former Eastern Europe has moved from drab communist uniformity to diversity, displaying a surprising range of contrasting political and economic outcomes.

Among the many challenges of transition, the task of rebuilding a civil society able to provide underpinnings for working democracy was considered especially difficult. Yet, despite well-founded doubts about whether civil societies would be able to recover from decades of communist suppression, we have seen significant gains across the region and in many countries vibrant and well-organized civil societies have emerged. Even in countries that experienced authoritarian reversals, civil societies appear to be well-institutionalized, connected to international NGO networks, and grudgingly tolerated by the state. Despite clear efforts in countries like Russia and others, there is no obvious case of civil society capture by the authoritarian state. Finally, there are also very few instances of significant grass-roots extremist movements or civil-society actors mobilized in support of illiberal values and policies.

There have been, however, persistent doubts about the nature and normative orientations of these newly reconstituted civil societies. Early in the transitions, Przeworski predicted inevitable erosion of support for democracy.[1] Ost warned that "the danger of new dictatorship in Eastern Europe comes from the bottom, not from the top."[2] Others envisioned escalating mass protests, an upsurge in nationalism, ethnic violence, racism, and xenophobia, as well as the emergence of reactionary, populist, and authoritarian movements, fueled by angry publics and representing marginalized sectors of society. While initial fears about popular revolts against neo-liberal economic reforms implemented after 1989 and against growing inequalities faded away after the first decade of transformations, warnings of the populist backlash fueled by illiberal political entrepreneurs feeding on popular discontent, religious fundamentalism, nationalism, and xenophobia have been a constant element in the commentaries on the region. In 2007, Krastev claimed that "the liberal era that began in Central Europe in 1989 has come to an end. Populism and illiberalism are tearing the region apart."[3] Similarly, Rupnik argued that "the recent populist backlash is a direct challenge to the liberal paradigm that has prevailed in the region for a decade and a half."[4]

While not denying the obvious presence of illiberal political orientations as well as xenophobia, rabid nationalism, and extremist movements in many countries of the region,[5] it is striking how little success populist politicians have had so far in stirring grass-roots movements of rage and manipulating such sentiments. If one considers the social cost and disruptiveness of the post-communist dual (political and economic) transformations, it is surprising that the extremism of both right and left has been relatively marginal and that populist and illiberal parties (with few exceptions) have not been more successful. The response of the populations to dramatic economic and social dislocations and declining living standards both during the initial economic transformations and during the current financial and economic crisis has been surprisingly subdued. There have been no widespread IMF riots in the region, despite rising unemployment, inequality, and often crippling austerity measures introduced by various states. As Greskovits once noted, post-communist societies have been surprisingly patient.[6]

In fact, all significant cases of mass popular mobilization across the region were not movements of rage against the neo-liberal reforms or democracy and capitalism. Instead, these were movements against transgressions from the path of reforms, best epitomized by the so-called colored revolutions. Civil-society groups sought to challenge ruling elites and their efforts to subvert democratic institutions and the rule of law. They rejected corrupt economic practices and called for more freedom, both political and economic, and for more transparency. Finally, while recent public opinion polls suggest a decline in support of liberal values among the new member states of the EU, support for liberal values has been growing in authoritarian and semiauthoritarian countries of the former Soviet bloc.[7] In short, the often-predicted mass protest movement against post-communist reforms and against neo-liberal economic policies has never materialized. Populism and extremist views come more often from the fringes of the political elite than from civil society and grass-roots movements. Moreover, populist elite actors have had little success in mobilizing angry masses and building organized bases of support for illiberal causes within new civil societies.

In this essay, I am going to discuss, briefly, three issues. First, I will comment on the diversity of transformation outcomes. Second, I will discuss the reconstitution of civil societies in the region. Finally, I will evaluate the strength of liberal ideas and support for democracy in the context of costly post-communist economic and social transformations and in response to the current financial crisis. I argue that given the cost of the neo-liberal reforms and reoccurring economic downturns—as well as efforts by new autocrats to control and use civil society for their own ends—it is surprising how little support there is for illiberal ideas and various alternatives to democracy, the rule of law, and a market economy.

Post-Communist Societies: A Surprising Diversity of Outcomes

Initially, post-communism was considered, with some good reasons, to be the most unfriendly environment in which to build liberal political and economic orders. Liberal outcomes were hardly expected, and scholars predicted the return to rule of "demagogues, priests and colonels,"[8] or the emergence of "low-performing, institutionally mixed market economies and incomplete, elitist, and exclusionary democracies."[9] Moving away from communism, all these countries faced four formidable challenges: establishing a working democratic regime, transforming the state-controlled economy into a free-market economy, establishing an efficient state based on the rule of law, and reconstituting a vibrant civil society that would provide underpinning for both working democracy and a market economy.

Yet, despite similar challenges, common declared goals, a democracy-friendly and supportive international environment, and generally similar policy designs, former communist countries have moved along increasingly divergent trajectories during the last two decades. The common communist legacy seems to not matter much for the outcomes of transformations. While East Central Europe has seen successful democratization and relatively fast convergence with the old EU-15 countries, especially in the quality of democracy and welfare policies, and Southeast Europe has made considerable progress in building democracy and market economies, other subregions have endured political stagnation, corrupt state capitalism, and authoritarian reversals. Moreover, the distance on almost every empirical indicator among traditional subregions of the former Soviet bloc remains surprisingly and stubbornly stable.[10] Figure 9.1 below, depicting the Freedom House ratings of civil rights and political liberties for four subregions of the former communist world, shows the significantly divergent trajectories of political development. Trajectories of economic developments, state reforms, and welfare policies show similar patterns. These diverging patterns of post-communist transformations have been extensively debated by social scientists. Various authors invoke different explanatory factors, including historical legacies and initial social and economic conditions, types of democratic breakthroughs, choice

Figure 9.1 Freedom House: Political Rights and Civil Liberties, 1981–2010

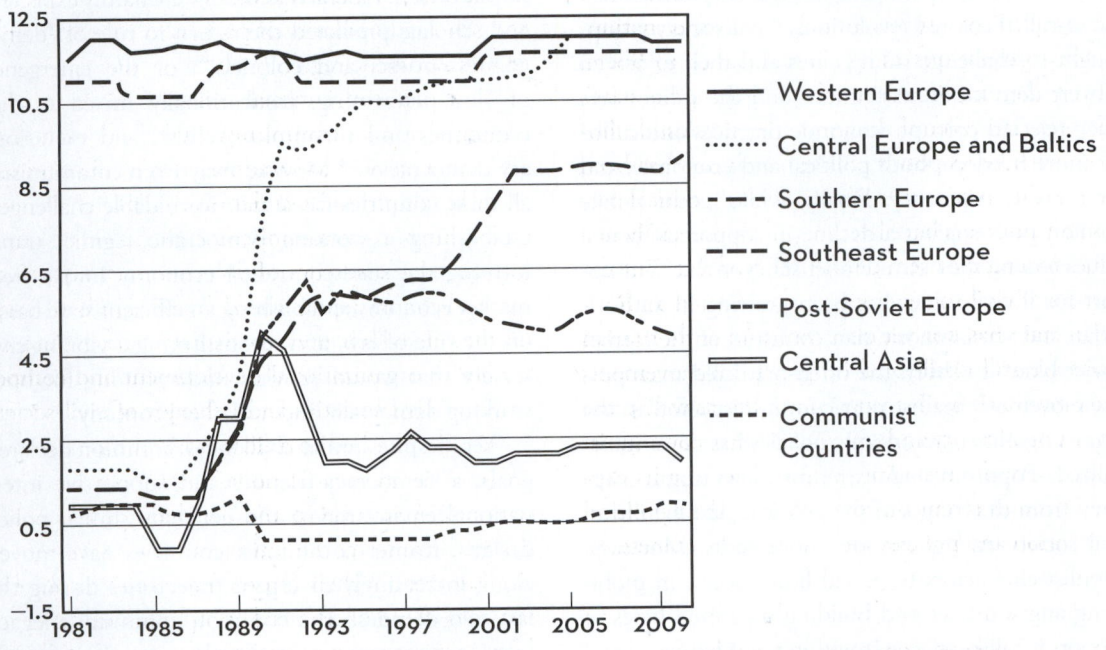

- —— Western Europe
- ········ Central Europe and Baltics
- – – – Southern Europe
- — — Southeast Europe
- – – – Post-Soviet Europe
- —— Central Asia
- - - - Communist Countries

of democratic institutions, dominant features of domestic political competition, proximity to the West, and the influence of powerful international actors in support of democratic consolidation, as exemplified by the EU accession process.[11]

Thus, post-communist states today are remarkably different, face different challenges, and their commitment to liberal political and economic institutions is uneven. New EU member states and candidate countries seem to be firmly anchored in the European liberal tradition and attendant political practices, while other countries are moving in an illiberal direction. Russian-style "Putinism" not only has become an established political practice but also has increasingly become a coherent political program (managed democracy plus state capitalism) to be emulated by other leaders with authoritarian ambitions. The sovereign debt crisis in the European Union is likely not only to end any further enlargement of the EU but also to make the Western liberal model increasingly unattractive to countries balancing between authoritarianism and democracy.

Authoritarian rulers are likely to embrace illiberal policies as a sensible alternative to what they perceive as the Western malaise. In short, illiberal political and economic practices may sound like credible and legitimate alternatives for struggling countries of the former Soviet bloc, and the resurgence of antiliberal regimes following Russia's lead may be inevitable not only in countries outside the EU but also for some new EU members. Recent political developments in Hungary may provide a good example of such shift of political commitments.

Disenchantment with the Western political and economic models may result in illiberalism from above, with antiliberal regimes consistently supporting antiliberal forces and organizations within civil society. In fact, the strongest antiliberal, right-wing movements and organizations exist today in countries with antiliberal parties in power—be it in democratic Hungary or in authoritarian Russia. Similarly, the post-2005 Kaczynski government in Poland supported the resurgence of populism and right-wing illiberal movements and organizations within Polish civil society. An increasingly polarized civil society seems to be emerging in Russia, with the government supporting illiberal and nationalistic organizations as a counterbalance to liberal movements and organizations challenging the state's authoritarian reversal. In short, the successful illiberal challenge in post-communist Europe has been seen, so far, in countries where illiberal political parties and autocrats have been in power, especially in a nondemocratic or semidemocratic context. But the capture of civil society by the consolidated authoritarian state has not yet occurred, and authoritarian rulers are still challenged by proliberal movements and organizations. Transnational links, as well as the surprising diversity and resilience of post-communist civil society, are instrumental in preventing its capture by states intent on reconfiguring their political orientation and policies away from liberal tenets.

Post-Communism and the Surprising Revival of Civil Society

During the last two decades, scholars and experts on the region have argued that civil society is weak in post-communist countries. Early studies of "social capital" conducted in the 1990s found lower levels of social trust, community engagement, and confidence in social and political institutions across Central and Eastern Europe.[12] More recent analyses have shown low levels of voluntary associational membership and weak unconventional political participation.[13] The picture of even the most successful post-communist countries that arises from the literature is one of "democracies without citizens," in which elites have succeeded in protecting basic civic rights and implementing democratic procedures, the rule of law, and multiparty competition, but failed to counter the paucity of voluntarism at the grass-roots level and weak participation in the institutions of representative governance. Since democracies need strong civil societies, many authors have

pointed to the declining legitimacy of democratic institutions, disenchantment with liberal values, and the growing popularity of populist and radical-right parties across the region.[14]

Yet, this conventional wisdom regarding the weakness of post-communist civil society seems to generate a number of paradoxes and is built on questionable empirical foundations.[15] Studies of civil society in post-communist Europe have tended to rely on simple surveys of voluntary activity asking respondents to report the different kinds of associations in which they participate, rather than on studies of organizational development and composition of civil societies and behavior of civil-society actors. This has led to a little-noticed inconsistency in the data on organizational membership in post-communist states. On the one hand, comparative survey data from the European Social Survey or the European Values Survey have shown a consistently low level of reported group membership, with little or no change over time. On the other hand, official registries from within individual countries show a phenomenal growth of listed groups and organizations.[16]

In Poland, for example, the number of registered NGOs grew by 400 percent from 1989 to 1994. While the growth leveled after that point, it has remained strong in subsequent years, with an average addition of some four thousand new NGOs and five hundred foundations every year, across all types of organizations, in all regions of the country. This development of civil-society organizations has not been restricted to major urban centers or specific groups or classes within society. And this picture is not unique to Poland. By pursuing a multidimensional strategy for analyzing the constitution of civil society and the behavior of civil-society organizations, Ekiert and Foa have been able to present a picture of post-communist civil society that is more complex and more robust than has been commonly assumed. Thus, we should abandon any simplistic generalizations regarding the "weakness" of post-communist civil society or its "demobilization" following democratic transition. At the same time, we still know little about actual behavior and normative orientations of civil-society actors in various post-communist countries. While public opinion surveys suggest that commitment to democracy and trust in civil-society organizations has improved across the region (see Figure 9.2), research on civil-society actors may generate a different picture.

Moreover, the conditions for civil society development and activities have been favorable in most of the countries in the region. In East Central Europe, the quality of public space, legal protections, and resources available to civil-society actors are similar today to those in established Western democracies. Countries of Southeastern Europe have made considerable progress in improving the quality of public space as well. While other subregions either did not make any progress (Central Asia) or registered significant decline after initial improvement (the remaining part of the former Soviet Union, except the Baltic republics) during the last decade or so, there still is more freedom to organize and pursue diverse interests than under the old regimes. In fact, even in countries with authoritarian regimes in place such as Russia, significant segments of civil society have been growing undisturbed.[17]

In sum, civil societies in post-communist countries can be described as surprisingly strong and diverse. Civil-society organizations, from trade unions to professional organizations to business associations, were also supportive of the general direction of political and economic transformations in the initial years of transition. As Ekiert and Kubik documented, during the most difficult initial years of economic and political transformation, civil-society organizations rarely questioned democratic or market reforms, even if they were involved in intense contentious activities.[18] They termed this normative orientation of civil-society actors "contentious reformism." Moreover, in the second decade of transformations, civil societies in many laggard countries mobilized to bring about the renewal of liberal commitments and policies. Angry masses proved not to be a threat to liberalism in the region. This does not mean, however,

that civil-society organizations cannot be enlisted in the task of building an illiberal political system or mobilized for nationalistic causes. Yet, until now, post-communist civil-society organizations have tended to support liberal causes and major cases of popular mobilization (such as the so-called colored revolutions or recent mass protests in Russia against electoral fraud and in Hungary against constitution changes and restriction of media freedoms) and were almost exclusively in support of liberal principles. This is clearly a surprising development, given initial expectations. Across post-communist Europe, relatively strong civil societies tend to support liberal freedoms and values and strive to make the ruling elites accountable.

Post-Communist Contention: The Surprising Strength of Liberal Ideas

Since the fall of communist regimes, experts on the region constantly have worried about the depth of support for democracy and the viability of liberal ideas. After all, this part of Europe had a dark past and was home to right- and left-wing extremism, virulent nationalism, and shocking atrocities. The violent collapse of the former Yugoslavia served as a reminder that hideous pasts can easily be revived. Similarly, the treatment of minorities, from the Chechens to the Roma, has not inspired much confidence.

Likewise, analysts frequently predicted imminent popular revolts in response to the staggering cost of economic transformations, growing unemployment, disappointment with falling living standards, and the dismantling of the old, familiar systems of protections and privileges. It was widely expected that dashed expectations and the absence of significant improvements in living conditions would spawn political extremism and turn populations against democracy and market reforms. And, indeed, the economic data show the staggering depth of the transitory recession in the early years of the transformations, the inability of many countries to improve their economic conditions and living standards, and the vulnerability of even the most successful reformers to international economic crises. The current financial crisis has hit many countries of the region hard. For example, Latvia's GDP fell by 25 percent in 2009 and unemployment went up from 7 to 23 percent in the span of two years. Austerity policies followed with deep cuts to employment in the civil service, salaries, pensions, and benefits.

Such predictions have been supported by public opinion data showing that support for new political and economic regimes and trust in public authorities have fallen from the heights registered shortly after the collapse of communism. Also, nostalgia for the old system has been rising, especially in less successful countries. Another indication of the disenchantment with the outcomes of transformation has been the growing strength of popular support for nationalistic and populist parties and movements. As Rupnik noted in 2007, "the recent populist backlash is a direct challenge to the liberal paradigm that had prevailed in the region for a decade and a half."[19] In the view of many commentators, the global financial crisis and the EU sovereign debt crisis have further undermined the attraction and credibility of the Western model and, by extension, support for liberal democracy and welfare capitalism. Is it true that liberal ideas are in retreat in the post-communist world? Are the countries of the region turning their backs on the West and searching for alternative political and economic models? Is illiberal civil society on the march in the region?

There is no doubt that the normative preferences of civil-society actors matter greatly in determining the political outcomes of their activities. Berman provides a notable example of strong civil society that turned against liberal values and democracy and facilitated the rise of the totalitarian Nazi state in Germany during the intrawar period.[20] In the Weimar Republic, dense and vibrant civil society ultimately supported extremist political options and fueled opposition to the democratic regime. In addition, values and preferences may determine whether civil society develops along normative or clientelistic lines. That is, whether civil-society organizations exist to defend citizen rights, work for public good, and advance the rule of law and the democratic process, or simply to serve as a means of extracting material rents for their leaders and members of the state and local administration.

One of the traditional indicators of the liberal commitment of civil-society actors is the degree to which citizens express a normative commitment to democracy.[21] Public opinion surveys often ask whether democracy is a "good" or "bad" way to run the country, and these trends, based on the World Value Survey data, are shown for the four clusters of post-communist societies below (Figure 9.2). The normative commitment to democracy is the weakest among the post-Soviet states, yet it stands almost as high in Southeastern Europe as in Southern and Western Europe. Central Europe, meanwhile, fits somewhere between the two. In terms of change over time, between 1990 and 2005, effective support for democracy has consolidated. However, more recent surveys[22] show that while support for democracy declined slightly in democratic countries in the region (EU members), it increased in other countries. Thus, there is no massive defection from democracy and market capitalism as a result of the current economic crisis and subsequent austerity policies. There is, however, a detectable impact of the Euro-zone crisis on the support for liberal democracy among new member states. This suggests that economic fortune alone may not drive political preferences, and that the rise of antiliberal sentiments may depend on the credibility of liberal projects of which European integration is the most important one.

Post-communist civil societies also fare well with regard to the extent to which they are normative rather than clientelistic in function. As one indicator that may detect the extent to which civic movements serve to advance the interests of citizens rather than their own private interests, we can take the degree of

Figure 9.2 Normative Commitment to Democracy

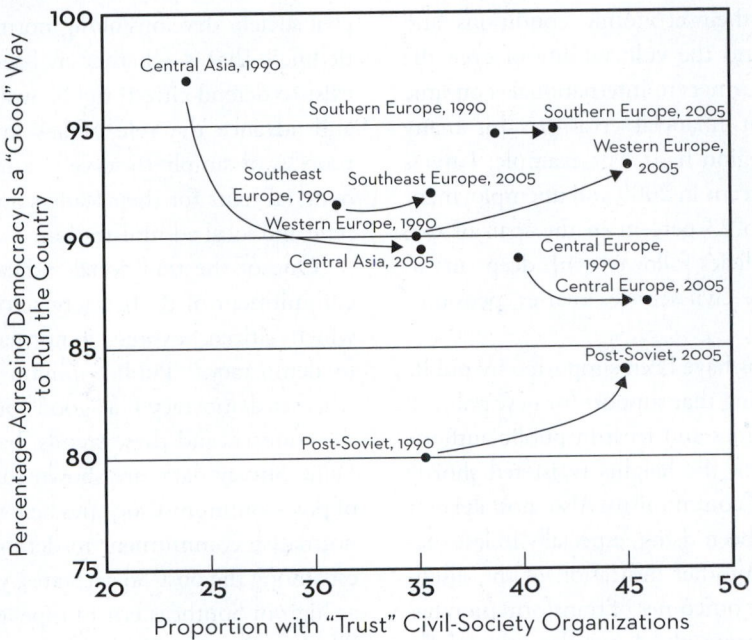

Source: Attitudinal items are from the World Values Surveys, waves 2-5 (1990–2005).

Country coding: Czech Republic, Estonia, Hungary, Latvia, Lithuania, Poland, Slovak Republic, Slovenia (Central Europe and Baltics); Albania, Bosnia-Herzegovina, Bulgaria, Croatia, Macedonia, Romania, Serbia (Southeast Europe); Azerbaijan, Kyrgyz Republic, Uzbekistan (Central Asia); Armenia, Belarus, Georgia, Moldova, Russia, Ukraine (Post-Soviet Europe); Greece, Portugal, Spain (Southern Europe); Austria, Belgium, Denmark, Finland, France, Germany, Ireland, Italy, Luxembourg, Netherlands, Sweden, United Kingdom (Western Europe).

trust that survey respondents express to have in the civil-society organizations of their country. In East Central Europe and post-Soviet Europe, the public's evaluation of voluntary associations and NGOs is comparable to that found in Southern and Western Europe; only in the Balkans and Central Asia does this confidence lag behind, possibly reflecting a greater degree of clientelism and cooptation. Also charted is the trend over time of trust in civil-society organizations since 1990 (see Figure 9.2). These trends clearly suggest a consolidation of public trust in the civic sector, for public trust in nongovernment organizations has grown across all post-communist societies since 1990.

Yet, the picture emerging from public opinion polls is not consistent. Some evidence against the consolidation of liberal preferences can be found in the left-right polarization of respondents. Since the seminal work of Bell,[23] it has been argued that ideological differences narrow as countries develop economically, and empirical evidence suggests this has indeed occurred across Western democracies.[24] However, in the new democracies of Central and Eastern Europe, the concern has often been expressed that far from converging on the median, ideological divisions have widened with the growing popularity of populist and radical-right parties, in particular. Table 9.1 shows the left-right placement of respondents in a sample of West and East European countries in 1990 at the start of transition, and more recently in 2005, using the World Values Survey item for left-right placement on a ten-point scale. Respondents at the extremes ("1" and "10") are classified as extreme left and right, respectively,

Table 9.1 Ideological Polarization among Survey Respondents (1990–1992 and 2005–2007)

	Year	Extreme Left	Center	Extreme Right
France	1990	5.1	93.2	1.8
	2005	9.1	88.1	2.8
Italy	1990	8.5	88.8	2.8
	2005	4.9	91.9	3.2
Netherlands	1990	2.5	95.0	2.5
	2005	2.7	95.2	2.1
Sweden	1990	1.2	94.8	4.1
	2005	2.7	94.1	3.2
Great Britain	1990	3.1	93.5	3.4
	2005	3.8	93.8	2.5
West Germany	1990	0.9	97.5	1.7
	2005	3.1	95.6	1.3
Western Europe Average	1990	3.5	93.8	2.7
	2005	4.4	93.1	2.5
Poland	1990	3.6	88.6	7.9
	2005	4.5	85.7	9.9
Romania	1990	1.7	95.6	2.8
	2005	6.0	85.4	8.6
Slovenia	1990	2.5	94.9	2.6
	2005	6.8	86.8	6.4
East Germany	1990	2.2	96.2	1.6
	2005	6.5	92.2	1.4
Eastern Europe Average	1990	2.5	93.8	3.7
	2005	5.9	87.5	6.6

Source: World Values Surveys, waves 2 (1990–1992) and 5 (2005–2007).

while those in between are classified as centrist. It can be seen that, while levels of ideological polarization in Western Europe have remained low and stable, radicalization has increased in this sample of Eastern European countries. Yet, the overall level remains relatively low, both as an overall propor-tion of the population and by broader international comparison. While 6.6 percent of Eastern Europe-ans in this country sample position themselves on the radical right ("10" on a ten-point left-to-right scale) in 2005, the equivalent figures are 13 percent in India, 19 percent in Indonesia, and 25 percent in Colombia. As recent election results and polls suggest, the Euro crisis resulted in the increase of support for illiberal political options in some countries of the region (e.g., Hungary) but not in others (e.g., Poland). Thus, extremism in Eastern European politics may appear worrying from the Western European perspective, but is relatively mild in comparison with other emerging democracies.

Moreover, this rise of extremist attitudes has not manifested itself in mass radical movements or organized civil-society activities. As Greskovits noted, "domestically, it is not the marginalized masses who appear to be the immediate problem—most of them have simply withdrawn from politics and do not even vote—but rather various elite and middle-class groups that for different reasons have chosen to rally behind radical economic and political agendas."[25] As long as the radical agenda is not supported by a state that actively seeks to mobilize popular support for the departure from liberal policies, extremist attitudes may well remain marginalized.

Finally, it should be emphasized that, over the last decade, the most significant popular mobilizations were in defense of human rights, liberal values, and democratic principles. They not only were more numerous, but also they were much larger and more significant than any mobilizations in support of illiberal causes and policies. From the phenomenon of the colored revolutions in Ukraine, Georgia, or Serbia to recent demonstrations in Russia and Hungary, there is solid evidence of liberal commitments in post-communist societies.[26] Although the recent European Bank for Reconstruction and Development survey documents the decline of support for democracy and a market economy in the most successful countries of East Central Europe, it also registers an increase in support for liberal policies in countries of the former Soviet Union and in the Balkans. In short, the growth and consolidation of new civil societies in the region has not generated significant populist and extremist movements. These new civil societies tend to support liberal causes and mobilize when the states and autocratic leaders violate democratic principles. They indeed pose a liberal challenge to government that follows authoritarian temptations.

Conclusions

The three vignettes presented in this essay offer two different and somehow inconsistent messages. First, despite initial expectations, the collapse of communist regimes resulted in the emergence of a number of consolidated liberal democracies securely anchored in European political and economic structures and in a significant expansion of civil society across the region. Moreover, despite severe economic difficulties and the costs of economic reforms, both at the beginning of transition and during the current financial crisis, support for democracy and commitment to economic reforms and market economy remains relatively high both among the elites and populations. Even in countries that failed to consolidate democracy, there is growing popular support for liberal principles manifested in significant civil-society mobilizations to challenge authoritarian practices. In addition, there is no marked increase across the region in radical political movements either on the right or on the left, while civil societies are becoming stronger and better organized even in places where they face unfriendly governments. In short, this is an optimistic message pointing to the viability of liberal ideas and a commitment to democratic practices among East European populations and organized civil-society actors.

Yet, strong civil society can be a blessing or a curse depending on specific circumstances. While democracy has been consolidated in many post-communist countries, competitive authoritarianism has been consolidated in others.[27] The new authoritarian states in the region are eager to colonize public spaces with organizations that support their policies and can be mobilized against proliberal forces and movements. Moreover, the sovereign debt crisis in Europe is having pernicious effects on peripheral European economies. Not only is the economic crisis exported from the center to the periphery but also the viability and attraction of the European liberal model is being increasingly questioned.

It is almost certain that countries in the region will face years of slow economic growth, high unemployment, and repeated austerity measures to reduce their deficits and public debt. Economic problems of the EU may also affect the size of its budget and its structural funds. Greskovits may be right in pointing to the exhaustion of some stabilizing mechanisms that, during the first two decades of transformations, eased the cost of reforms (such as high welfare spending, expanding black and gray markets, and labor migrations in search of employment in more developed European economies).[28] Moreover, countries outside of the Euro-zone may be relegated to the position of second-class citizens within the EU and those outside of the EU may be permanently excluded from it. Further enlargements may not be forthcoming, weakening the position of the EU as a hegemonic political and economic model. Such combination of economic and political factors is likely to affect the preferences of both political elites and popular actors who may, after all, turn their backs on Western ideas and search for alternatives to liberal democracy and welfare capitalism. As a result, post-communist countries may face significant illiberal challenges from below in coming years, especially in countries where illiberal elites and parties dominate politics and in places where authoritarian states expand their basis of support by colonizing the civil-society domain.

NOTES

1. Adam Przeworski, *Democracy and the Market: Political and Economic Reforms in Eastern Europe and Latin America* (Cambridge, England: Cambridge University Press, 1991).

2. David Ost et al., "Is Latin American the Future of Eastern Europe?" *Problems of Communism* (May–June 1992): 49.

3. Ivan Krastev, "The Strange Death of the Liberal Consensus," *Journal of Democracy* 18, no. 4 (2007): 56.

4. Jacques Rupnik, "From Democratic Fatigue to Populist Backlash," *Journal of Democracy* 18, no. 4 (2007): 19.

5. See, for example, Petr Kopecky and Cas Mudde, *Uncivil Society: Contentious Politics in Post-Communist Eastern Europe* (London: Routledge, 2003), and Sabrina Ramet, *The Radical Right in Central and Eastern Europe since 1989* (University Park: Penn State Press, 1999).

6. Béla Greskovits, *The Political Economy of Protest and Patience* (Budapest: Central European University, 1998).

7. European Bank for Reconstruction and Development, "Crisis in Transition: The People's Perspective," Transition Report, 2011.

8. Kenneth Jowitt, *New World Disorder: The Leninist Extinction* (Berkeley: Berkeley University of California Press, 1992), 220.

9. Béla Greskovits, *The Political Economy of Protest and Patience: East European and Latin American Transformations Compared* (Budapest: Central European University Press, 2007), 184.

10. Jacques Rupnik, "The Postcommunist Divide," *Journal of Democracy* 10, no. 1 (1999): 57–62, and Grzegorz Ekiert, Jan Kubik, and Milada Vachudova, "Democracy in Postcommunist World: An Unending Quest," *East European Politics and Societies* 21, no. 1 (2007): 1–24.

11. Grzegorz Ekiert and Stephen Hanson, *Capitalism and Democracy in Central and Eastern Europe* (Cambridge, England: Cambridge University Press, 2003); Milada Vachudova, *Europe Undivided: Democracy, Leverage and Integration after Communism* (Oxford: Oxford University Press, 2005); Frank Schimmelfennig, *The EU, NATO and the Integration of Europe: Rules and Rhetoric* (Cambridge, England: Cambridge University Press, 2003).

12. Richard Rose, "What Does Social Capital Add to Individual Welfare? An Empirical Analysis in Russia," SCI Working Paper, no. 15 (Washington, DC: World Bank, 1999), and Richard Rose, William Mishler, and Christian Haerpfer, "Getting Real: Social Capital in Post-Communist Societies," Conference on the Erosion of Confidence in Advanced Democracies, Brussels, November 7–9, 1996.

13. Mark Howard, *The Weakness of Civil Society in Postcommunist Europe* (Cambridge, England: Cambridge University Press, 2002), and Michael Bernhard and Ekrem Karakoc, "Civil Society and Legacies of Dictatorship," *World Politics* 59 (2007): 539–567.

14. Ramet, *The Radical Right in Central and Eastern Europe since 1989*; Michael Minkenberg, "The Radical Right in Post-Socialist Central and Eastern Europe: Comparative Observations and Interpretations," *East European Politics and Societies* 16, no. 2 (2002): 335–362; Kopecky and Mudde, *Uncivil Society*; and Rupnik, "From Democratic Fatigue to Populist Backlash."

15. See Grzegorz Ekiert and Roberto Foa, "The Weakness of Civil Society Reassessed," Center for European Studies Open Forum Working Papers, no. 11 (Cambridge, MA: Harvard University, September 2012).

16. Renata Nagy and Istvan Sebesteny, "Methodological Practice and Practical Methodology: Fifteen Years in Non-profit Statistics," *Hungarian Statistical Review*, Special Number (2008): 12; Zdenka Mansfeldova et al., "Civil Society in Transition: Civic Engagement and Nonprofit Organizations in Central and Eastern Europe after 1989," in *Future of Civil Society: Making Central European Nonprofit-Organizations Work*, ed. Annette Zimmer and Eckhard Priller (Wisbaden: VS Verlag für Sozialwissenschaften, 2004), 99–121; and Eva Kuti, "Policy Initiatives towards the Third Sector under the Conditions of Ambiguity–the Case of Hungary," in *Policy Initiatives towards the Third Sector in an International Perspective*, ed. Ben Gidron and Michal Bar (Heidelberg: Springer, 2010), 127–158.

17. Debra Javelin and Sarah Lindemann-Komarowa, "A Balanced Assessment of Russian Civil Society," *Journal of International Affairs* 63, no. 2 (Spring/Summer 2010):171–188.

18. Grzegorz Ekiert and Jan Kubik, "Contentious Politics in New Democracies," *World Politics* 50, no. 4 (1998): 547–581, and Grzegorz Ekiert and Jan Kubik, *Rebellious Civil Society* (Ann Arbor: Michigan University Press, 1999).

19. Rupnik, "From Democratic Fatigue to Populist Backlash," 19.

20. Sheri Berman, "Civil Society and the Collapse of the Weimar Republic," *World Politics* 49, no. 3 (April 1997): 401–429.

21. See Gabriel Almond and Sidney Verba, *The Civic Culture* (Boston: Little, Brown, 1963).

22. European Bank for Reconstruction and Development, "Crisis in Transition: The People's Perspective."

23. Daniel Bell, *The End of Ideology: On the Exhaustion of Political Ideas in the Fifties* (Glencoe, IL: Free Press, 1960).

24. Russell Dalton, "Social Modernization and the End of Ideology Debate: Patterns of Ideological Polarization," *Japanese Journal of Political Science* 7, no. 1 (2006): 1–22.

25. Greskovits, *The Political Economy of Protest and Patience*, 41.

26. Taras Kuzio, "Civil Society, Youth and Societal Mobilization in Democratic Revolutions," *Communist and Post-Communist Studies* 39, no. 3 (September 2006): 365–386; Henry Hale, "Democracy or Autocracy on the March? The Colored Revolutions as Normal Dynamics of Patronal Presidentialism," *Communist and Post-Communist Studies* 39, no. 3 (September 2006): 305–329; and Valerie J. Bunce and Sharon L. Wolchik, "International Diffusion and Postcommunist Electoral Revolutions," *Communist and Post-Communist Studies* 39, no. 3 (2006): 283–304.

27. Stephen Levitsky and Lucan Way, *Competitive Authoritarianism: Hybrid Regimes after the Cold War* (Cambridge, England: Cambridge University Press, 2010).

28. Béla Greskovits, "Economic Woes and Political Disaffection," *Journal of Democracy* 18, no. 4 (2007): 40–45.

488   CHAPTER NINE ▪ COMMUNISM AND POSTCOMMUNISM

Henry E. Hale

25 YEARS AFTER THE USSR: WHAT'S GONE WRONG?

After a quarter-century, the 1991 breakup of the Soviet Union looks like a de-democratizing event. Leading up to that fateful year, Mikhail Gorbachev had been one of the world's great democratizers. In just six years after rising to the top post in one of history's most repressive regimes, he had almost completely freed the media, launched competitive elections, and ended the Communist Party's political monopoly. But this trend stopped in its tracks and even went into reverse when the Soviet Union broke apart into fifteen newly independent states in late 1991. In fact, if we take Freedom House measures and leave aside the three Baltic states, which were generally not recognized as being part of the USSR and soon joined the EU, there has not been a single year when the post-Soviet space on average has enjoyed the level of "political rights" (to use Freedom House's term) that was achieved under Gorbachev.[1] What accounts for this depressing reality?

There is no shortage of theories—most with at least some element of truth—but the best known all leave major puzzles unresolved. In recent years, it has become fashionable among Russia-watchers to blame that country's democratic woes on its strongman president, Vladimir Putin. But this fails to explain why so many other post-Soviet countries have similar or greater levels of authoritarian rule. Some see Russia as exporting autocracy to its neighbors, but the post-Soviet political systems that most resemble Russia's today actually appeared far earlier, years before anyone outside of St. Petersburg had heard of a midlevel city official and former KGB lieutenant-colonel named Putin.

And Russia, which has from time to time destabilized leaders whom it dislikes, has often failed spectacularly to keep friendly but unpopular client regimes in power. This has been true not only in Ukraine—a big country with a significant nationalist tradition—but even in tiny South Ossetia, a de facto Russian vassal state.

Perhaps post-Soviet Eurasia's nondemocratic rulers have simply learned on their own how to organize their repressive machines more effectively, but this too raises questions: Why have some authoritarians proved apter pupils than others? Why have some been able to act on their knowledge while others have failed to do so? And why have democracy's advocates failed to learn and apply counterlessons of their own as effectively as research on other parts of the world suggests they should?[2] Is it just a sad coincidence that Eurasia has had so many competent illiberal presidents at the same time?

A closer look shows that even presidents who were at first widely seen as democrats wound up using authoritarian methods. They include Eduard Shevardnadze of Georgia, who as Gorbachev's foreign minister took part in ending the Cold War and then resigned to warn of the Soviet hardliners' coup that came in 1991. They also include Armenia's President Levon Ter-Petrossian, a former dissident, and President Askar Akayev of Kyrgyzstan, an academic who had made his career outside the Communist Party apparatus and was initially viewed as his country's great democratic hope. That leaders of such diverse backgrounds ended up ruling in the same nondemocratic way hints at something deeper.

Many "deeper" explanations, however, fare little better. If weak civil society across the region is to

From *Journal of Democracy* 27, no. 3 (July 2016), pp. 24–35.

blame, how to account for the massive outbursts of collective action and public spirit that we periodically witness there? If the problem is a "resource curse," why are resource-poor Belarus and Tajikistan as durably authoritarian as petrochemical-rich Russia and Kazakhstan? Is an authoritarian culture to blame? Many current democracies (Germany, for example) were once characterized in this way, and studies have found that support for competitive elections and political pluralism is strong even in Russia.[3]

If weak economic development is the trouble, why has authoritarianism grown in step with post-Soviet economic growth? And why are some of the region's poorer countries (Georgia, Kyrgyzstan, Moldova, and Ukraine) also among its more democratic? Corruption is a logical suspect, though that leads to other puzzles: Why is corruption so stubbornly pervasive in Eurasia? And why have vigorous even if imperfect democracies been able to flourish in other places vexed by corruption, such as India? A stronger case can be made that the decades-long communist experience is to blame, but scholars disagree about exactly which aspects of the communist legacy had this effect, and some research even finds that certain aspects belong to a "usable past" that can support democracy.[4]

Without denying some role for these other factors, I locate the main source of Eurasia's democratic disappointment in a different kind of historical legacy, one that is older than communism and that has interacted in an unfortunate way with institutions that have worked well in other (especially Western) contexts. This legacy has done the most damage to democratic prospects, ironically, where leaders have had the broadest popular support. In some times and places, certain international forces and institutional designs have mitigated its effects, which helps to explain some of the partial exceptions to nondemocratic rule seen across Eurasia.

What is the malign legacy behind Eurasia's sorry silver jubilee? It is a combination of patronalism and presidentialism that would be even more damaging to democratic prospects were it not for the pull of the EU and the happenstance of nonpresidentialist constitutions in a few post-Soviet countries.

A Pattern of Regime Cycling

According to the widely used metrics of Freedom House, the sole post-Soviet country aside from the Baltic states *ever* to have earned an annual rating of Free is Ukraine. And that was only between 2005 and 2010, after the Orange Revolution. Although the net regional trend since 1991 has been bad enough, it could be worse: The new authoritarianism of Eurasia is not that of today's China or even Saudi Arabia, and is certainly not as harsh and bloody as the dictatorships found in the pre-Gorbachev USSR or Pinochet's Chile.

Of course, things could always get worse. Turkmenistan and Uzbekistan have long had highly repressive governments, and maybe their model will spread. Occasional political killings are believed with varying degrees of evidence to have taken place in most post-Soviet countries. Ramzan Kadyrov, the Russian-sponsored strongman who keeps Chechnya in line for Moscow, is a brutal character. But to date, a sober look at Eurasia mainly reveals heavy-handed manipulations of the media and the political system (buttressed by corrupt cooptation) rather than mass killings or jailings.

In fact, trends in the average Freedom House political-rights score for the entire non-Baltic post-Soviet region reveal that the *net* movement toward authoritarianism has been slight and anything but steady. As Figure 9.3 illustrates, things were no worse, freedom-wise, in 2015 than they were in 2004 or 2010, and indeed they were worse still in 2008, 2009, and 2011. And the net change between the democratic high point of 1992 and 2016 is still less than a single point on this 7-point scale where 7 is least free. Over a quarter-century, that is not much: Gorbachev's reforms across the same swath of the world map moved the Freedom House needle in a positive direction by three full points in just the few short years between 1987 and 1991.

Figure 9.3 Freedom House Political-Rights Scores for the Non-Baltic, Post-Soviet Region (Average for 1991–2015)

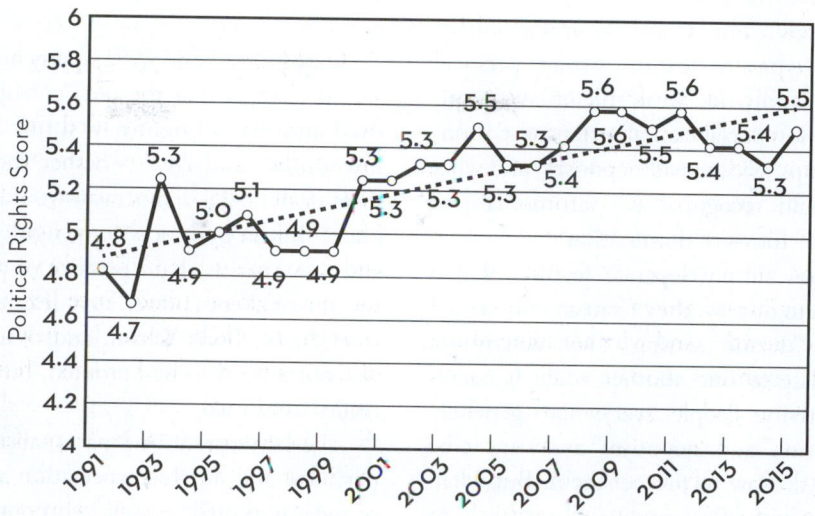

Note: Freedom House assigns countries a Political Rights score between 1 and 7, with a rating of 1 representing the most-free conditions and a rating of 7 the least-free.

The non-Baltic post-Soviet states are Armenia, Azerbaijan, Belarus, Georgia, Kazakhstan, Kyrgyzstan, Moldova, Russia, Tajikistan, Turkmenistan, Ukraine, and Uzbekistan.

If we were to look even more closely, what we would see would be a pattern of *cycling* or oscillation as regimes waver back and forth between the autocratic and democratic ends of the political-rights spectrum. The figure records no fewer than *eleven* reversals of direction in Eurasia's net regime dynamics since the USSR dissolved. Plotting the paths of individual countries over the same period on a single chart (as I once tried to do) would yield a confusing, hard-to-read tangle of lines. For there is no lockstep movement to be shown. Instead, the twelve non-Baltic regimes in the old Soviet space have moved with great dynamism—each in its own way, and none fully in step with the others. The very thoroughness with which their ups and downs have offset one another is why the average regional level of political closure has only inched upward, in fits and starts.

Although regime cycling with only a slight overall trend to authoritarianism has been the regional norm since the Soviet collapse, it is possible to dis-

cern one set of countries with worse political closure (Russia plus Armenia, Azerbaijan, Belarus, and the five Central Asian states) and another that shows more openness (Ukraine plus Moldova and Georgia). Even within these clusters, however, substantial movements in both directions still occur. Thus it is wise to avoid treating regimes as if the most recent year's "snapshot" is everything. Instead, it is the dynamic oscillation itself—and not this or that movement in one direction or the other—that is the thing to be explained. The cycling between movement away from and movement toward authoritarianism is mainly the product of one of this region's strongest legacies: patronalism.

Patronalism is "a social equilibrium in which individuals organize their political and economic pursuits primarily around the personalized exchange of concrete rewards and punishments, and not primarily around abstract, impersonal principles such as ideological belief or categorizations that include many people one has not actually met in person."[5] In short, highly patronalistic societies are those in which connections not only matter (as they do just about everywhere), but matter overwhelmingly. Such societies typically feature strong personal friendships and family ties, weak rule of law, pervasive corruption, low social capital, extensive patron-client relationships, widespread nepotism, and what sociologists would recognize as "patrimonial" or "neopatrimonial" forms of domination.

These are not simply separate features that a society happens to display; they form an entrenched *equilibrium*, a "default setting" that determines how people relate to one another when it comes to political activity. People everywhere generally oppose "corruption" and "nepotism" and want to be able to rely on the law to protect them. But when they expect that virtually everyone else is likely to practice corruption and nepotism, and believe that they cannot rely on others to obey or enforce the law, then they face potent incentives to engage in the very same practices themselves if they want to get anything done, even good things. For example, a mayor who completely rejects any palm-greasing, favor-currying, and under-the-table connection-leveraging will in all likelihood be running a city that loses investment, businesses, and jobs to rival towns where the mayors "know how the game is played." What might seem like "clean government" heroism in Western eyes may look to locals more like naïve incompetence, even as these locals sincerely rail against rampant corruption. In short, if others are ignoring the rules, playing by them puts you at a competitive disadvantage and makes you honest but unproductive.

This helps to explain why patronalism has been so tenacious in Eurasia—and elsewhere. Arguably, patronalism is as old as the first human communities: They were small so everyone knew each other, and the most natural way to govern was through personal connections. Patronalism has been the rule of world history, not the exception.[6] It is not an artifact of Bolshevik rule: Even a cursory look at precommunist Russia, Ukraine, Central Asia, and the Caucasus makes clear that patronalist practices, including pervasive patron-client relations, were the dominant way of life for centuries before the Russian Revolution.[7]

In both 1917 and 1991, many hoped that things would change, that the old "corrupt" politics was dead and that a bright new future based on ideas, institutions, and laws (whether those of communism or of liberal democracy) would arise to take its place. But on both occasions, figures soon emerged who saw that the hard practice of patronal politics was their ticket to power, or at least to keeping it. To Josef Stalin, Boris Yeltsin, and others, patronalism was not a weed to be uprooted, but a resource and reality to be used.

The key to reducing patronalism is to create a pervasive and durable expectation across the whole of society (though especially among the elites) that people will no longer engage in the same practices as before. This belief must be sustained beyond a revolutionary moment and into the formative stages of a new regime, when disillusionment can gather force and a leader can be tempted by the patronalist path to keeping power. This is extraordinarily difficult, and while some countries in the West and elsewhere have largely escaped it over the course of many generations, failures to overcome patronalism fill the pages of history. Few leaders anywhere have even tried to defeat patronalism as this would be to cut off the branch upon which they sit. Fewer still have succeeded. Only in Georgia after the Rose Revolution did a post-Soviet leader try seriously to curtail patronalism's reach within society. But most now agree that President Mikheil Saakashvili, despite certain impressive reforms, including the cleanup of his small country's notoriously corrupt traffic police, always ran a (somewhat cloaked) patronal regime. World history has served up very few Lee Kwan Yews.

Liberal democracy requires a full-scale assault on patronalism. The former demands, at the very least, a strong rule of law, low corruption, and a robust civil society based on impersonal principles. Patronalism's tenacity thus goes a long way toward explaining why there is so little liberal democracy in the post-Soviet space. The great exception, the three small Baltic countries, began with lower levels of patronalism and benefited from strong EU-membership prospects after 1991.[8]

In the post-Soviet space, the patronal legacy has meant that politics is first and foremost a *struggle among extended networks of personal acquaintances,* not among formal institutions such as "parties," "parliament," "firms," or even "the presidency" or "the state." Such networks often have roots in a particular formal entity—such as the Soviet-era KGB and its successor agencies—but the most powerful ones typically have their people in all major spheres that can affect politics, including state officialdom, business, the NGO world, the media, and an array of ideologically diverse political parties. And competing networks can share common roots, as with the bitter rivalries among former KGB officials in Russia today. Putin's network is now the most powerful in Russia and clearly has this kind of reach, though before Putin turned against billionaire Mikhail Khodorkovsky and his Yukos corporation in 2003, the latter's network too had connections across virtually the whole spectrum of Russia's formal entities. So did many others that still exist but have made their peace with the dominant patron.

Because competing political-economic networks cannot rely on courts and the rule of law to protect them if they lose power, they need *direct, personal* access to power. This creates an imperative to avoid being on the losing side of any struggle for supreme power. Thus while networks, their chief patrons, and their rank-and-file members can have varying policy preferences and interests just as do people in the West, these are routinely trumped by raw political considerations flowing from the extreme dangers that losing brings. Finally, because each network's choice of allies affects each potential partner's own prospects of being on the winning side, and because all networks must make such choices at the same time, *coordination* is central to patronal politics.

Political pluralism tends to emerge when networks fail to coordinate their political activities around a single recognized patron, with at least two

"sides" having the support of roughly equal coalitions, a circumstance that creates space for opposition politics. Thus in Ukraine during its time as non-Baltic Eurasia's only country ranked Free, political pluralism was the byproduct of a highly corrupt power struggle among three roughly equal networks (those of Viktor Yushchenko, Viktor Yanukovych, and Yulia Tymoshenko). Similar conditions obtained in Russia before Putin; in Moldova after the Communist Party's July 2009 ouster; in Georgia after Saakashvili's political departure in 2013; and in Kyrgyzstan after its 2010 revolution.

Conversely, political closure tends to result when a country's most powerful networks successfully coordinate their political activities around a single patron or manage to defeat those who failed to strike a deal with the winning side in time. Even when the country's chief patron does not ban opposition forces, their activists typically find it hard to raise funds, obtain media access, and even locate venues in which to meet: Nobody wants to risk alienating the chief patron. Competition continues, but morphs into a contest for the president's favor and a higher place in the president's "power pyramid." Tensions run high as the president's closest associates (family members, old friends) try to elbow aside those who are merely "partners" in the regime.

The most effective presidents are those who can keep all the different networks on board and more or less pulling on the same oar. This can be delicate, painstaking work: A too-hasty presidential action (or, conversely, a failure to act) can spark a revolt. The sheer amount of time and energy that it takes to coordinate and referee among multiple networks explains why post-Soviet authoritarianism has been such a creeping affair. The smart course is to dial up the heat slowly, bringing the proverbial frog in a pot to a boil before it realizes what has happened. Putin, Belarus's Alyaksandr Lukashenka, Tajikistan's Emomili Rahmon, Azerbaijan's Heydar and Ilham Aliyev (father and son), and Kazakhstan's Nursultan Nazarbayev all work (or worked) this way.

Should the "consensus" patron's will or ability to remain as patron ever come into doubt, coordination will break down and a new accommodation will need to be forged. Some rulers may groom successors with an eye toward keeping the old deal intact, but coalition members may not find this credible. Putin eventually turned against some of the networks that had aided his rise, and Ilham Aliyev jailed some of his late father's key partners soon after taking power. The longer a new accommodation takes to nail down, the better chance political pluralism has to emerge. So post-Yanukovych Ukraine maintains a corrupt but vibrant pluralism, while Turkmenistan had no opening whatsoever as the death of its president in 2006 was followed by swift elite agreement on a new supreme patron.

All this has several implications for regime dynamics in the former USSR. First, patronalism has fed a baseline public dissatisfaction with corrupt politics. Even where leaders are highly popular, as in today's Russia and Kazakhstan, people know from experience that corruption persists and they remain unhappy that their leaders have done little to fight it. They see the "necessary evil" side of this corruption, but still dislike it. Their distaste is dry tinder that a spark can ignite into the wildfire of mass protest. The clash of elite networks—over succession, for instance—can strike such sparks (consider the color revolutions). So can regime blunders such as Putin's clumsy fraud in the 2011 Russian parliamentary elections or Yanukovych's backfiring assaults on the EuroMaidan rallies in late 2013 and early 2014. The result, at least where somewhat contested elections remain the norm, is a pattern of regime cycling, a steady closure of the political space punctuated by periods of protest and competitive politics—even revolution—until the country's most important power networks coordinate again around a single patron.

Why Not Patronal Democracy?

The general difficulty of achieving liberal democracy in highly patronalist societies, however, cannot explain why Russian-style political closure remains more common than the patronal democracy that characterized Ukraine after the Orange Revolution. This was genuine democracy, just highly corrupt with political competition anchored more by a balance of power among political machines than by any rule of law. In the post-Soviet context, the prevalence of heavily presidentialist constitutions is a big part of the answer. Absent other constraints, such constitutions facilitate the coordination of networks' legal *and illegal* behavior around a single patron by making whoever is president the focal point of such coordination and by signaling that the president's network is in all likelihood the strongest one (its head is president, after all).

As the various network chieftains who play this complex coordination game see things, therefore, presidentialist constitutions give whatever networks control the presidency an edge that can be used either to recruit other networks or to crush them. But a presidentialist constitution—especially one that sets term limits—also opens the door to the predictable power struggles known as regular elections. So networks must always look ahead, and calibrate their loyalty to the incumbent president as chief patron by asking if a new president is likely, and who that might be.

These calculations can be observed across post-Soviet history, and appear in even the most authoritarian cases. Post-Soviet presidentialism is mostly a product of the late Gorbachev era, when the USSR's leader created his own (not directly elected) presidency in a bid to retain political control while he dismantled the Communist Party. Each of the fifteen Soviet Socialist Republics had an incentive to acquire a president of its own in order to bargain with Gorbachev for a better deal within (or outright independence from) the Soviet Union.

By the early 2000s, every non-Baltic post-Soviet state but Moldova had a directly elected president who had consolidated power by taming parliament and building a potent reelection machine. Political closure increased as the new century dawned. But when a presidential turnover approached or arrived, network coordination broke down here or there, and a time of relative openness ensued, only to give way to a new bout of closure once the patronal networks recoordinated themselves. And so the cycling of regimes went round and round, out of sync across the former Soviet space.

In 2015, the only three non-Baltic post-Soviet countries that were less closed than Gorbachev's 1991 USSR—Georgia, Moldova, and Ukraine—each had a nonpresidential constitution. Kyrgyzstan, the only other country with a nonpresidential constitution as of 2015, was among the most democratic of the rest, and was markedly more so than its Central Asian neighbors. Moreover, presidentialist constitutions in Georgia, Kyrgyzstan, and Ukraine had coincided with growing political closure, punctuated by the periodic but temporary openings that presidentialism brings. The nonpresidentialist constitutions in these countries emerged either during revolutions as explicit efforts to avoid the future concentration of power (as in Ukraine and Kyrgyzstan) or as the president was in his constitutionally final term and sought to weaken his successor or to reemerge as a strong prime minister (as in Georgia). The general trend in the nonpresidentialist countries has not been toward closure, in stark contrast with the presidentialist countries.

Perhaps surprisingly, another part of the answer has been strong popular support for post-Soviet leaders. Patrons with mass publics behind them are less likely to face popular unrest, and also will meet less resistance to closure from within regime ranks because challengers cannot count on popular support. Popularity was crucial to the emerging authoritarianism of Putin and Lukashenka. Even in nonpresidentialist countries where elections are generally free and fair, networks whose leaders enjoy the highest popularity stand the best chance of capturing all major posts and setting regime closure in motion. The Communist Party of Moldova did this in that nonpresidentialist country during the 2000s. Yanukovych did something similar in Ukraine after he won the 2010 presidential election there, using his "honeymoon period" to convince parliament to elect his man prime minister, setting the stage to restore a presidentialist constitution.

Of course, a leader's popularity may be to some extent a product of political closure, which prevents criticism and stifles positive coverage of the opposition. But in the post-Soviet world, the popularity of leaders such as Putin, Lukashenka, Nazarbayev, and Heydar Aliyev largely *preceded* the establishment of their political machines and media monopolies. Media monopolies *sustained* popularity in these cases, but did not cause it to emerge. And even the sustaining must be based on at least *something*. In the post-Soviet space, the most popular leaders have benefited from an appealing personal leadership style (a strong suit for Putin, Lukashenka, and Nazarbayev); a credible claim to have brought "stability" after the tumultuous 1990s (especially in Azerbaijan and Tajikistan); and good economic performance (the commodities boom of the 2000s helped).

A final factor, international "linkage and leverage," helps to distinguish the post-Soviet experience from that of other world regions where patronal presidents are common. A strong case has been made that linkage and leverage underlie democratization in Latin America and Africa, where economies are vulnerable enough or ties to the West are dense enough for liberalizing pressure to complicate the lives of patronal presidents. But strong linkage and leverage have been little in evidence outside the Baltic States.[9] The EU and the prospect of joining its exclusive club showed a real ability to discourage antidemocratic practices in Central and Eastern Europe's most patronalistic countries (including presidentialist Romania) in the 1990s and 2000s. But in the former USSR, only the Baltics have been allowed to join (they were admitted in 2004), while the other states have not even been treated as credible candidates.

Disrupting Patronalism

The core problem is less that post-Soviet Eurasia is "not ready" than that "EU prospects" are something of a self-fulfilling prophecy. The EU appears to be one of the few forces anywhere capable of systematically transforming the kind of expectations both elites and citizens have about "how things work" in their countries, and ensuring that this change endures beyond a tumultuous transition period. And as noted above, transforming such expectations could potentially not only disrupt the coordination of a country's power networks around a single patron but could also even undermine the patronalist equilibrium in which these societies find themselves. In this light, the EU's inability to see promise in post-Soviet countries has itself done a lot to make this pessimistic assessment true. That said, recent trends in countries such as Hungary and Poland make clear that the EU is hardly a panacea.

If all this is right, post-Soviet authoritarianism is at once more deeply rooted and more contingent—even fragile—than is often realized. The deep, pre-Soviet historical legacy of patronalism raises huge obstacles to liberal democracy. Yet the region's particular authoritarian systems are often vulnerable and may even suddenly collapse if anything disrupts the political-economic network coordination on which they depend. Disruptors can include succession crises and major missteps by leaders, among other things.

But the disruptions are often temporary while the practice of networking is remarkably resilient. Thus periods of open political and even electoral competition tend to fade once a winner emerges and power networks coordinate themselves around the new patron, a process strongly encouraged by presidentialist constitutions. And ironically, leaders initially elected in the most democratic fashion with the strongest popular support are actually in the best position to effect political closure rapidly.

None of this is to say that nonpresidential constitutions are the solution. They help, but they too can be designed in ways that either promote or complicate the coordination of networks around a single patron, and they can sometimes be overpowered. But if designed in the right way, they can at least make longer-lasting periods of pluralism more likely, as has been the case with all of today's most democratic post-Soviet countries.

Indeed, patronal democracy is possible. It is even common in other parts of the world, especially where underpinned by nonpresidentialist constitutions or strong international linkage and leverage. But as in India and Romania today, it comes freighted with a massive load of corruption and other problems that favorite Western nostrums such as "leadership training" find hard to eradicate. International democracy promoters no doubt feel frustrated when their advice to post-Soviet party leaders about how to win votes in a democracy is ignored, but the problem is less the stupidity, greed, or power lust of these politicians than the whole different set of political incentives with which they must contend.

While the near-term outlook for full, liberal democracy in post-Soviet Eurasia is grim, there are slender rays of hope. Constitutions that appear designed to disrupt network coordination around a single patron have been appearing in a rising number of Eurasian countries. Accordingly, Georgia, Kyrgyzstan, and Ukraine all have avoided new authoritarian turns for several years now, though their politics remain rough affairs at best. In addition, Georgia's reforms (including its traffic-policing overhaul) have made a strong-enough impression both at home and across the region that they might catch on elsewhere, maybe even in enhanced form.

In the longer term, perhaps the "economic development always spurs democratization" school of thought will be proved correct.[10] From the vantage of 2016, however, that "longer term" appears long indeed. Many more of these mordant "anniversary celebrations" will likely have to pass before the former Soviet states regain even the level of political openness that they could boast when Gorbachev became the USSR's last leader in 1991.

NOTES

1. Freedom House rates countries for "political rights" on a scale of 1 to 7, with 1 being most free and 7 being least free. When Gorbachev came to power in 1985, the USSR was a 7. By 1991, it had improved to a 4. The mean score of all non-Baltic

post-Soviet states in 1992, their first full year of independence, was 4.67, which proved to be the best average score for the whole post-Soviet period.

2. Staffan I. Lindberg, *Democracy and Elections in Africa* (Baltimore: Johns Hopkins University Press, 2006).

3. Henry E. Hale, "The Myth of Mass Russian Support for Autocracy: The Public Opinion Foundations of a Hybrid Regime," *Europe-Asia Studies* 63 (October 2011): 1357–75.

4. Anna M. Grzymala-Busse, *Redeeming the Communist Past: The Regeneration of Communist Parties in East Central Europe* (New York: Cambridge University Press, 2002).

5. Henry E. Hale, *Patronal Politics: Eurasian Regime Dynamics in Comparative Perspective* (New York: Cambridge University Press, 2015), 20.

6. Douglass C. North, John Joseph Wallis, and Barry R. Weingast, *Violence and Social Orders: A Conceptual Framework for Interpreting Recorded Human History* (New York: Cambridge University Press, 2009).

7. For example, David L. Ransel, "Character and Style of Patron-Client Relations in Russia," in Antoni Maczak, ed., *Klientelsysteme im Europa der Frühen Neuzeit* (Munich: Oldenbourg, 1988), 211–31.

8. For example, Herbert Kitschelt and his coauthors, in *Post-Communist Party Systems: Competition, Representation and Inter-Party Cooperation* (New York: Cambridge University Press, 1999), code these countries as having experienced a lower degree of "patrimonial" communist rule during the Soviet period, while all other post-Soviet countries are found to have a highly patrimonial legacy.

9. Steven Levitsky and Lucan A. Way, *Competitive Authoritarianism: Hybrid Regimes after the Cold War* (New York: Cambridge University Press, 2010).

10. In particular, see Daniel Treisman, "Income, Democracy, and Leader Turnover," *American Journal of Political Science* 59 (October 2015): 927–42.

Harley Balzer

RUSSIA AND CHINA IN THE GLOBAL ECONOMY

In mid-December 2004, Baikal Finanz, a previously unheard-of Russian firm with no offices and no known officers, won a nontransparent auction to buy Yuganskneftegaz, the major oil production asset of Yukos, Russia's most efficient oil company. The same week Lenovo, a computer firm established twenty years earlier as a venture of the Chinese Academy of Sciences, purchased IBM's personal computer division. Most people looking at Russia and China when Mao died in 1976 assumed that Russia[1] was better positioned to become a major player in global technology industries. The Soviet Union was participating in the Apollo-Soyuz joint space missions and enjoying the benefits of détente and stability (not yet visible stagnation) under Brezhnev. The USSR was a superpower with many of the "requisites" for development. In literacy levels and numbers of scientific, technical, and other specialists with advanced education, Russia was far ahead of China's overwhelmingly peasant society just emerging from the chaos of the Cultural Revolution and accompanying isolation.

Since Mao's death China has generated high economic growth rates for three decades, fostering internationally competitive industries and lifting a significant number of people out of poverty. Beginning in the late 1980s, Russia experienced severe economic dislocations, and economic growth

From *Demokratizatsiya* 16, no. 1 (2008), pp. 37–48.

resumed only after a fall in living standards and the 1998 financial crisis. Most of the growth in Russia since August 1998 is attributable to the ruble devaluation and increased oil prices, raising questions about its sustainability. Despite windfall oil revenues, Russia's growth rate since Vladimir Putin became president has been among the lowest in former USSR countries.

Growth based on industry has helped China overtake Russia on a range of human capital and development indicators. Internet and cell phone use among China's *urban* population is now roughly equivalent to that of Russia's city dwellers. Spending for education and research and development as a proportion of national budgets is at least equal. China is an important global player in a growing number of technology industries and in the international economic system, things Russian leaders merely talk about.

What accounts for an outcome that contradicts most people's expectations? My argument emphasizes differing approaches to integration with the international economy. China has embraced economic globalization and integration on a scale surpassing many other Asian countries, while Russia remains wary and peripheral. Russia's economy is open, but selling natural resources and arms generates few linkages leading to higher value-added production. Russia's economic integration is "thin." China's integration is "thick," involving participation in technology chains and participation in entire product cycles. China vastly overperforms in producing value-added products given its level of development; Russia markedly underperforms relative to the industrial base, educational system, and research and development potential inherited from the Soviet era. China joined the WTO in 2001; Russia has been a year or two away from membership since 1993.

These differences increasingly influence politics: China's thick integration has fostered regional, sectoral, and institutional interests that defended and expanded the policies of reform and openness; Russia's thin integration generates few countervailing

forces to contest renewed administrative domination of the economy.

Conventional Wisdom Explanations for China's Rise

Prevailing explanations for China's economic success emphasize initial conditions and/or specific policies. Initial advantages include an abundant supply of low-cost labor not covered by the welfare system; the decision to begin reforms with agriculture; shorter duration of communist rule; less complete Communist Party penetration of society; qualitative differences in leadership; and communities of co-ethnics willing to provide investment capital. These explanations do not hold up when examined in a comparative perspective. Analyses emphasizing specific policies commonly stress a gradual and experimental approach to reform carried out in the stable environment provided by authoritarian leadership. Such accounts misread the contentious story of China's development.

The large supply of agricultural workers available to provide low-wage labor in export-oriented industries is frequently cited as the key factor in China's success. China's rural population was outside the state welfare system, so peasants made redundant by improved agricultural production following decollectivization were forced to seek employment in Township and Village Enterprises (TVEs) or the new industrial zones. Most Chinese were quickly subjected to hard budget constraints. In Russia, welfare and other alternatives persisted.[2] Arguments based on cheap labor and welfare systems, however, fail to explain why other Asian or Latin American countries with large numbers of potential low-wage workers unprotected by welfare systems have not emulated China's success. Central European and Baltic countries have performed better than Russia despite inheriting comparable Soviet welfare systems and demographic profiles.

Other initial conditions cited to explain China's rise include investment by overseas Chinese, an "agriculture first" approach, and China's shorter period under communism. Comparison challenges these explanations. Diasporas with capital to invest are hardly unique to China. Why did India lag? In the United States, people of Russian descent constitute the heritage group with the highest proportion of millionaires per capita.[3] Clearly, diasporas invest only when conditions are conducive. Decades of agricultural reform did not produce economic miracles in Latin America. Some countries where communism was a post–World War II phenomenon have performed relatively well economically (Estonia, Slovenia, Slovakia), but others have not (Moldova, Serbia).

Some authors attribute the different outcomes in Russia and China to the leadership's character during the communist system's formative period, focusing on the dominant leader's personality (summed up as "Mao was no Stalin") or on weaker Communist Party penetration in China. Chang and Halliday's one-sided but revealing biography of Mao would lead to the conclusion that Stalin was no Mao, while Walder argues that China's was the most "neo-traditional" of Communist systems, with the greatest degree of party penetration.[4] The Soviet economy misallocated resources, imposing an enormous cost on efforts to establish a market system. Yet China's economy was arguably more uneven and more severely misallocated, with the "Third Line" swallowing vast resources that a poor nation could ill afford. It is difficult to determine whether Stalin or Mao wreaked greater environmental havoc.

In the debate between "gradualists" and proponents of rapid reform, China's approach is portrayed as a case of successful gradual reform allowing trial-and-error approaches with mid-course corrections. Russian analysts have been particularly enamored of an "enlightened authoritarian" explanation for China's success. Official Chinese accounts understandably embrace these claims. But attributing China's economic success to guided gradualism misreads the story. If government tutelage was responsible for China's economic development, we should expect

state-owned enterprises (SOEs) to be a success story rather than an anchor on the economy. China's initial "reform" was less a matter of administered policy than a series of experiments that spread rapidly and escaped government control.[5] Some authors argue that the Chinese state retained capacity that the Soviet state lost.[6] However, substantial evidence demonstrates that it was precisely in the realms where the Chinese state *partially lost* control that China's reforms have been most successful. Vivienne Shue goes even further, suggesting that China's leaders have taken credit for simply getting out of the way.[7]

Once Deng chose "reform and openness," the key to China's success was largely what the government did *not* do: it did not prevent local entrepreneurship or create obstacles that stifled development. The Chinese government followed this course not out of an enlightened sense of developmental responsibility, but rather because a combination of self-interest and strong pressure from groups benefiting from the changes compelled it to do so.[8] During the 1980s, policy oscillated between support for and limitations on the openings. Economic retrenchment was repeatedly abandoned despite political repression, including after the Tiananmen Square violence in 1989, because economic forces benefiting from the reforms pushed back, helping pro-reform leaders to prevail.

A conundrum for those who emphasize China's nondemocratic path is that despite China's lack of democracy, local officials, entrepreneurs, and investors appear to have exerted a greater influence on some aspects of economic policy in Communist Party–ruled China than in ostensibly democratic Russia. Chinese leaders encouraged both outreach by TVEs and efforts to attract foreign direct investment (FDI). Subsequent development stimulated local initiative and intense competition, generating forces that initially circumvented and eventually began to influence government policy. The government's goals of stimulating production and providing employment were overfulfilled, but hardly in the ways originally intended.

Whether this arrangement can continue to sustain growth despite serious social strains, environmental disaster, and a proliferation of corruption is *the* question for China in the twenty-first century. Whatever the future trajectory, the key to China's economic success thus far has been openness and thick international integration, which provided resources, stimulated competition, encouraged high-value exports, and fostered coalitions to defend the opening. China's flexible approach to reform and openness was possible because Chinese leaders and elites embraced globalization. In this respect, the difference between China and Russia is striking.

Attitudes toward Globalization

Chinese discourse on globalization views it as their great opportunity to overcome centuries of relative backwardness. China's leaders are convinced that they are coping with and guiding China's integration into the international economy. While many Russian observers also view China in this way, Russian elite attitudes toward Russia's relationship with the global economy are profoundly ambivalent. As a former imperial power that derived its status from military and ideological, rather than economic, sources, Russia has found it far more difficult to embrace an environment that accords so little weight to its comparative advantages.

Internationalization has been a major theme of China's reforms from the outset. Deng advocated openness and integration almost immediately after Mao's death. In the 1990s, China's leaders embraced economic internationalization as the way to develop the economy and establish China's place in the world.[9] By the end of the 1990s, not only the leadership but also most ordinary Chinese had come to accept globalization as an "inevitable stage in China's modernization as well as an opportunity to catch up with the developed countries."[10]

Russian commentators generally suggest that they have a choice about participating in globalization, and many would prefer to not exercise the option. Russians tend to equate globalization with Americanization, viewing it as a major threat to Russia's future. Some argue that Russia must protect itself from harmful influences until the leadership develops a strategic plan for coping with the global economy. Extreme nationalists such as Aleksandr Dugin pose a choice between shunning globalization or Russia ceasing to exist.

What accounts for Chinese elites embracing economic globalization while Russians question it? The answer is the mutually reinforcing interaction of historical legacy with political and economic conditions. Length of time spent under communism is less important than the timing of when communism was established and dismantled. Deng's policy of openness followed immediately after the Cultural Revolution. China was economically weak and Mao's heirs were on the defensive. In contrast, the Soviet cultural revolution of 1928–31 created a new elite that remained in power until the 1970s and bequeathed economic autarky and superpower myths to the next generation. A key segment of Russia's elites are the heirs of a Stalinist party faction that explicitly rejected the West and internationalism. Their heroic period came in the years 1927–45, encompassing the first five-year plans and the "Great Patriotic War." This period fell between the two modern eras of globalization (roughly 1870–1912 and since 1960), when autarky was a plausible strategy. When Gorbachev initiated perestroika, Russia viewed itself a co-equal superpower. The problem is less that Russians have ambivalent attitudes toward the West than that many Russians believe the West has little to teach them.

China began its reforms after Mao's death with neither a self-confident ruling elite nor a horde of policy intellectuals invested in the old system. The Communist Party remained in power even as it accepted new economic approaches, and increasingly has been forced to adjust policies toward greater openness and competition, a change reflected in its membership.[11] In China, a consensus has developed in support of international integration, with debates focusing on the modes and consequences of integration rather than the process itself. Thickening international integration has induced China's leaders to accept the policies that have generated consistent economic growth. Russia's thinner integration has brought less benefit, whether measured as sustainable economic growth or improved living standards. Russia's new wealth remains hostage to global commodity prices; poverty reduction has been slow, and the growth of the middle class has not kept pace with the rising cost of entry.[12] The relative benefits of thick integration are evident from a comparison of leading economic sectors, regional development, human capital, and corruption.

Leading Sectors

Leading sectors in an economy impact the quality of interaction with the international economy profoundly. Although both China and Russia have become major exporters, the nature of their exports differs markedly. China is a global manufacturing center; Russia is a petrostate.

Learning the practices and engaging in the competition required for success in the international economy is rarely a first choice. Both countries' communist leaders were schooled in similar principles of autarkic self-reliance. China's industrial development has encouraged significant reorientation. In Russia, the commodity economy would certainly benefit from greater internationalization, but rising prices in the early 2000s made it possible for economic and political interests to severely restrict the scope of internationalization.

China's industrial development is stunning in both quantity and quality. Often the data on sheer volume of production obscure the large share of value-added products in the mix. Movement up the production chains in turn helps explain China's thickening integration. China's evolving economic relationship with Taiwan demonstrates the key role leading sectors played in advancing openness. While national-level leaders in Beijing were initially ambivalent about business engagement with

Taiwan, some local leaders were far less reticent. Over time, attitudes at the top changed. The story is not entirely edifying. Shared norms, a common linguistic and cultural environment, and familiar management practices that did not always conform to international standards or enhance transparency facilitated the relationship with Taiwan. The shared business culture includes a "common understanding of local bookkeeping, inventory management, and gift-giving practices."[13]

In contrast to China's robust manufacturing sectors, finished goods represent less than 10 percent of Russian exports. Hydrocarbons and other natural resources account for an overwhelming share of both exports and state revenues. The character and political implications of economies based on commodities and on petroleum in particular are well understood. Although natural resources are not always negative, it requires unusual circumstances to embed them in a knowledge economy leading to balanced growth.

Resource-based economies frequently have a negative impact on human capital, encouraging private supply of education and health care rather than creating demand for public goods. High returns from resource sales divert investment away from productive or science-based industries. Energy firms' "pocket" banks, which have little interest in business-development lending, tend to dominate the banking system. Income disparities resulting from both the high returns to energy sector elites and extensive corruption stunt the development of a middle class that might demand public goods, transparency, or democracy.

Russia's vast natural-resource endowment is being used simultaneously to support the economy, underpin the projection of Russian power, and serve the interests of individuals in a position to reap enormous financial windfalls. Contradictions and corruption are inevitable, while the international linkages that are created do little to foster growth in other industrial sectors. Minimal success in diversifying the economy is clear from the character of regional development.[14]

Regional Development

Power devolved to regions in both China and Russia in the 1980s and 1990s. In some areas of China, this resulted in rapid economic development. David Zweig characterizes the processes in China as "segmented deregulation."[15] Restrictions were removed in specific sectors of the economy and in discrete geographic locales not through the enlightened administration by a developmental state but because of fierce competition ("fevers") to take advantage of openings perceived as having uncertain time horizons. Regions and enterprises competed for FDI and workers competed for jobs. Rather than an "East Asian model" of enlightened bureaucrats overseeing development, China is a case where success derives from competition. Differences in degree of integration with the international economy now largely explain regional disparities in China.[16]

Russia's "thinner" economic integration generated few incentives to overcome deep and long-standing separation from international economic relationships. When regions were given the opportunity to establish free economic zones in the 1990s, it produced a flurry of special commercial privileges, tax evasion, and black market schemes rather than industrial development zones. Many regional leaders interpreted Yeltsin's "take all the sovereignty you can swallow" as carte blanche to loot their locality. Appointed by the president and using the threat of ethnic or regional separatism to enhance their autonomy, they had minimal accountability. When Yeltsin instituted a system of elections for regional leaders, it began to reward leaders who pursued successful economic policies and defeat those who did not.

The essential feature of successful federalism is a *division* of powers. Unfettered local power can lead to anarchy and unrestrained corruption. Unchecked central power raises equally serious problems of credible commitment. Russian and Chinese leaders now are reasserting central control. Attempts to concentrate power in the center are hardly unusual given Russia's resource wealth. By neutering the Federation Council, achieving a pliant Duma, and abolishing gubernatorial elections, Putin has eliminated countervailing forces. Most seriously, he has undermined the regions' capacity to generate wealth through their own development projects. The central government controls natural resources, while regional integration with the international economy remains subject to Kremlin approval. Hu's attempts to rein in regional independence have been less damaging to the economy than Putin's because China's thicker international linkages created countervailing forces supporting continued integration. These forces include not only economic interests but also China's educational and scientific institutions.

Human Capital

Russia's thin international linkages and reliance on commodities have contributed to a very different human capital trajectory from that in China. There is no more striking example of China's relative improvement in development indicators than its advances in education, science, and technology. Starting from a much lower base in 1977, with perhaps 50 percent literacy and 1 percent of the population receiving higher education, China has generated substantial gains across the entire range of education and science and technology indicators. In contrast, Russia lost ground for more than a decade. The one significant Russian achievement, doubling the proportion of young people in higher education, was accomplished largely by adding fee-paying students, exacerbating corruption. Russia's increased tertiary enrollments coincided with reduced coverage at the secondary, primary, and preschool levels, and the current enrollments will not be sustainable as the school-age population declines in the coming decade. While aging and brain drain have severely affected both the Russian and Chinese scientific communities, they have responded quite differently.

At China's National Conference on Science in 1978, Deng proclaimed "Backwardness must be recognized before it can be changed. One must learn from those who are most advanced before one can catch up with and surpass them."[17] This underscores a crucial difference with Russia: no Russian political leader could make such a speech and survive. Russians remain convinced that they have the best schools and best scientists in the world, and everyone else should learn from them.

Individuals took advantage of the opportunities Deng created and diverted the opening in directions different from what political leaders intended. Overseas Chinese wishing to aide relatives quickly expanded the programs' scope, while commodification of international exchanges gave bureaucrats incentives to support and intensify the process. In contrast to Russia, where foreign degrees and time spent on professional exchanges abroad can hinder professionals' career advancement, Chinese with foreign doctorates (*yangboshi*) frequently are given preferential treatment compared with those with Chinese degrees (*tuboshi*). Many Chinese research facilities still experience severe funding and housing problems; going abroad qualifies scientists for special housing and research funds when they return. Four of China's top universities now hire almost exclusively from among Chinese with foreign PhDs; Russian universities refuse to recognize foreign credentials.

In contrast to China's increasing integration, many Russians continue to insist on following a "unique" path in science and education. At a time when internationalization and globalization are major items on the agendas of most national education systems, vested interests and path dependence constrain Russian leaders. The leadership of the Academy of Sciences remains intent on restoring its Soviet-era position and reversing the limited progress made in shifting to competitive peer-reviewed funding during the 1990s.

One feature common to both the Russian and Chinese education systems is increasing corruption in access to education and in evaluating performance. In this realm the education systems reflect a more general problem infesting both societies.

Corruption

Economic systems depend on governments to provide crucial public goods, but government involvement inevitably creates opportunities for cronyism and rent seeking. While no government has eliminated corruption, most seek ways to limit its extent and minimize the damage it causes. Analysis of corruption typically focuses on measuring its extent and finding ways to reduce its prevalence. Less attention has been devoted to exploring differences in its effects—in what might be called the *quality* of corruption.

Corruption levels in Russia and China as measured by available indices do not appear markedly different. But while corruption is a serious problem in both Russia and China, it has been perceived to be more damaging in Russia.[18] Russian bureaucrats manifest a proclivity for slaughtering golden (or diamond or hydrocarbon) geese rather than encouraging egg production. In China, the goose is frequently all they have and they tend to be more solicitous, in part because without the goose, foreigners have little interest in investing.

China might have grown faster with less corruption, but even with markedly increased corruption since 1992, China's economic growth shows no signs of slowing down. In Russia, natural-resource development and the "National Projects" are not transparent and are riddled with rent seeking. The cost of bribing government officials has increased with the commodities boom, hindering business development.[19] So we are left with a dilemma: similarly high levels of corruption may coincide with quite different economic performance and trajectories.

The differences in economic performance and the effects of corruption lead to two questions. First, why did Chinese "development coalitions" focus on productive activity rather than (or along with) rent seeking and theft? Second, is the focus on productive activity what makes corruption in China less damaging to economic development? Russia certainly offered greater opportunities for rents and nonproductive activity. Natural resources are the paradigmatic source of rents, and hydrocarbons in particular invite abuse.

China created new industries; Russia redistributed the existing ones. Chinese industrial development was based on TVEs and special economic zones (SEZs). The TVEs were built from the bottom up, and this could be done only by attracting investors and reinvesting profits. China's SEZs provided havens for dubious deals, but they had to attract investment and produce marketable products. China did not touch the SOEs for nearly two decades. Russia privatized most state enterprises quite rapidly, resulting in asset stripping by agents in control of unprofitable enterprises.

Much of the corruption in China's early reform years depended on creating public goods or developing private industry. There were few opportunities to divert resource exports or expropriate property. Value had to be created before it could be stolen. Network capital undermined central control through informal relationships with local governments. In many instances these activities could be called "dual benefit": less good for the economy than honest activity, but not solely destructive.

Corruption should be viewed along a continuum between relatively productive and entirely parasitic. Key questions involve whether proceeds from corruption stay in country or flee, whether they are invested or consumed, and whether the amounts are so large as to seriously damage the economy. We need to examine how officials extract the funds, what they do with the funds, and the effects of corruption on public policy. David Kang's comparative study of corruption similarly suggests that the crucial issue is not the extent of corruption but its quality. Both Korea and the Philippines experienced extensive corruption, but the two cases differed in social organization, constraints, and incentives. Korean state officials supplied public goods and supported investment, even if this was not their primary goal. Kang's contrast of Indonesia and Taiwan has particular resonance for the Russian case:

Indonesia was able to experience moderate economic growth because of the fortunate happenstance of hav-

ing large oil reserves. Oil revenues provided the means for economic growth and allowed a semblance of order for more than twenty-five years. However, the growth was never deep enough to become self-sustaining.[20]

It is crucial to focus on both the character and the extent of corruption. Boris Yeltsin got it right in June 1996 when he fired Korzhakov, Barsukov, and Soskovets, saying that they "Took too much and gave too little."[21] The Russian and Chinese experience suggests that international integration strongly influences the character and scale of corruption.

Conclusion

China's embrace of globalization and the resulting thick international economic integration have been the key to its emergence as a commercial and manufacturing power. Russian resistance to integration makes it less able to overcome resource dependence. When Russian leaders suggest that they need to emulate China's policies, they emphasize policies based on strong governmental control, rather than the diverse and independent local and regional economic activity that accounts for China's early success.

China has neither solved all its problems nor discovered an optimal development model. Challenges and weaknesses are easily identified, particularly problems stemming from uneven development, environmental damage, growing corruption, social unrest, and demographic shifts. Minxin Pei now characterizes China as a case of "trapped transition," fostering local mafia states.[22] Many analysts point out that China must eventually confront the issue of genuine property rights. Foreign firms still resist moving software development and high-end IT operations to China because of inadequate protections against copyright infringement. All of these weaknesses could limit China's future development.

Despite the accumulated problems, China's industrial growth is something post-Soviet Russia has been unable to emulate. A few countries (Norway, Canada, Australia, and, more recently, Chile, Peru, and Brazil) have managed to embed their natural resources in knowledge economies. If any hydrocarbon producer had the scientific and educational potential to join this group, it was Russia, thanks to the human capital inherited from the Soviet era. That Russia's scientific and educational endowment is being squandered is hardly surprising, though this makes it no less tragic. The surprise is the success China has achieved in developing human capital and science and technology infrastructure. Both China's achievements and Russia's decline reflect the differing qualit of their international integration.

China's current path may prove to be unsustainable, but the results of three decades of integration are not easily discounted. In contrast, Russian elites show enormous resistance to thicker integration, instead calling for a fundamental restructuring of existing international economic institutions. Outsiders have few sources of leverage. Neighbors need Russia's hydrocarbons. The leading (natural resource) sectors of the Russian economy are not permitted to accept levels of foreign investment that would compel greater transparency or restructuring. Terrorist threats make it easier for the government to pursue nationalist and isolationist policies at home while the international community focuses on cooperation to promote security (including energy security) rather than encouraging Russian leaders to alter their policies.

The character of integration with the international economy explains why China and not Russia is becoming a commercial and industrial power, and has profound implications for their future development trajectories. Both countries need greater societal involvement in political life to address daunting problems. By generating diverse economic interests that affect policy, China's thick international integration has created the potential for continued influence. Russia's thinner integration places fewer constraints on leaders who appear to be "dizzy with petroleum."

NOTES

1. The Russian Republic was the largest component of the Soviet Union until its dissolution in December 1991. For simplicity and continuity, I refer to "Russia" throughout this article, meaning the Russian Republic through 1991 and the Russian Federation thereafter.

2. Jeffrey D. Sachs and Wing Thye Woo, "Reform in China and Russia," *Economic Policy* 18 (1994): 101–45. Sachs and Woo cite "three interrelated flaws" in the Soviet economy: overbuilt heavy industry but too little light industry and services; almost all workers in state-subsidized jobs; and the entire population covered by the welfare system. Characterizing the welfare system as a "flaw" contradicts statements Sachs makes elsewhere about the importance of safety nets during transition.

3. Thomas J. Stanley and William D. Danko, *The Millionaire Next Door: The Surprising Secrets of America's Wealth* (New York: Pocket Books, 1996), 19. The "poster children" for returning Russians are Boris Jordan, who was manipulated into helping disguise the Kremlin takeover of NTV, and Paul Khlebnikov, the *Forbes* journalist who was murdered in 2004.

4. Jung Chang and Jon Halliday, *Mao: The Unknown Story* (New York: Alfred A. Knopf, 2005); Andrew Walder, *Communist Neo-Traditionalism: Work and Authority in Chinese Industry* (Berkeley: University of California Press, 1988).

5. Jude Howell, *China Opens Its Doors: The Politics of Economic Transition* (Boulder, CO: Lynne Reiner, 1993); Minxin Pei, *From Reform to Revolution: The Demise of Communism in China and the Soviet Union* (Cambridge, MA: Harvard University Press, 1994); David Zweig, *Internationalizing China: Domestic Interests and Global Linkages* (Ithaca, NY: Cornell University Press, 2002).

6. Yan Sun, "Reform, State and Corruption: Is Corruption Less Destructive in China than in Russia?" *Comparative Politics*, October 1999, 1–20; Steven Lee Solnick, "The Breakdown of Hierarchies in the Soviet Union and China: A Neoinstitutional Perspective," *World Politics*, 48

(January 1996): 209–38; Andrei Shleifer, "Federalism with and without Political Centralization: China versus Russia," in Shleifer, *A Normal Country, Russia after Communism* (Cambridge, MA: Harvard University Press, 2005), 147–55; Barry Naughton, "Chinese Economic Success: Effective Reform Policies or Unique Conditons?" in *The Evolutionary Transition to Capitalism*, ed. Kazimierz Z. Poznanski, 135–53 (Boulder, CO: Westview, 1995).

7. Vivienne Shue, "Legitimacy Crisis in China?," in *State and Society in 21st-century China: Crisis, Contention and Legitimation*, ed. Peter Hays Gries and Stanley Rosen, 24–49 (New York: Routledge, 2004).

8. My discussion here draws on the works by Howell, Pei, and Zweig cited in note 5; Mary Gallagher, "Reform and Openness: Why China's Economic Reforms Have Delayed Democracy," *World Politics* 54, no. 3 (2002): 338–72; and Yongnian Zheng, *Globalization and State Transformation in China* (New York: Cambridge University Press, 2004). For a different perspective see Dali L. Yang, *Remaking the Chinese Leviathan: Market Transition and the Politics of Governance in China* (Stanford, CA: Stanford University Press, 2004).

9. Thomas G. Moore, "China and Globalization," in *East Asia and Globalization*, ed. Samuel S. Kim, 105–32 (Lanham, MD: Rowman and Littlefield, 2000); Lee Branstetter and Nicholas Lardy, "China's Embrace of Globalization" (National Bureau of Economic Research Working Paper 12373, July 2006).

10. Yunxiang Yan, "Managed Globalization: State Power and Cultural Transition in China," in *Many Globalizations: Cultural Diversity in the Contemporary World*, ed. Peter L. Berger and Samuel P. Huntington, 19–47, quoted passage 20 (Oxford, UK: Oxford University Press, 2002).

11. David Shambaugh, *China's Communist Party: Atrophy and Adaptation* (Berkeley: University of California Press, 2008, forthcoming).

12. Most of the growth of the middle class from 1995 to 1998 was a result of trickle-down from oil revenues. See Thane Gustafson, *Capitalism Russian-Style* (Cambridge: Cambridge University Press, 1999). It is likely that the increase in oil prices during 2000–6 has produced a similar situation, though we will know for certain only when prices fall. A recent study by the Russian Academy of Sciences found that the middle class shrank from 25 percent to 22 percent of the population between 2003 and 2006. Half of the Russians included in the middle class by this study worked for the government.

13. Merritt T. Cooke, "The Politics of Greater China's Integration into the Global Info Tech (IT) Supply Chain," *Journal of Contemporary China* 13, no. 40 (2004): 491–506, quoted passage 497.

14. I. P. Gurova, E. V. Zykova, and E. B. Skliarova, "Diversifikatsiia rossiiskogo eksporta [Diversification of Russian exports]," *EKO* no. 9 (2007): 29–42.

15. Zweig, *Internationalizing China.*

16. Sylvie Démurger, Jeffrey D. Sachs, Wing Thye Woo, Shuming Bao, Gene Chang, and Andrew Mellinger, "Geography, Economic Policy, and Regional Development in China" (National Bureau of Economic Research, Working Paper 8897, April 2002); Becky P. Y. Loo, "Export Expansion in the People's Republic of China since 1978: A Case Study of the Pearl River Delta," *The China Quarterly* 177 (March 2004): 133–54.

17. Quoted in Zweig, *Internationalizing China*, 165.

18. Sun, "Reform, State and Corruption"; Solnick, "The Breakdown of Hierarchies."

19. World Bank, *Anticorruption in Transition 3: Who is Succeeding . . . and Why?* (Washington, DC: IBRD/World Bank, 2006), 38; INDEM, "Vo skol'ko raz uvelichilas' korruptsiia za 4 goda: Rezul'taty novogo issledovaniia Fonda INDEM [By how many times has corruption increased in 4 years: Results of new research by the INDEM Fund]" (Moscow: INDEM, 2005), 3–4.

20. David C. Kang, *Crony Capitalism: Corruption and Development in South Korea and the Philippines* (Cambridge: Cambridge University Press, 2002), 190, emphasis added.

21. Russian television broadcasts on ORT and NTV, June 20, 1996.

22. Minxin Pei, *China's Trapped Transition: The Limits of Developmental Autocracy* (Cambridge, MA: Harvard University Press, 2006).

10 DEVELOPING COUNTRIES

Few people in any developed country can imagine the grinding burden of poverty, and the horrible moral dilemmas it brings, that people experience in typical "developing" countries. Do famine-stricken parents, themselves the only means of support for several children, feed themselves or their children first? Do they sell or abandon some children to keep the others alive? We recoil at even contemplating such choices. William Easterly, a World Development Bank economist, confronts us directly with such images in the opening chapter of his important book *The Elusive Quest for Growth* (2001).

The intellectual puzzle of developing world poverty is that according to all our standard economic models, it should not persist. Investment in poor countries should earn much higher returns than in rich ones—a phenomenon known technically as "declining marginal productivity of capital." Hence, investment rates and economic growth should also be much higher. This standard result of economic theory is usually called the theory of *convergence*. It holds that initially poor countries should grow so much faster than rich ones that their growth rates (and, allowing for random variation, their levels of wealth) should very quickly "converge" on those of rich countries. In short, all poor countries should be duplicating the experience of the Asian "tigers." Korea, Taiwan, and China should be the rule, not the exception. More shocking, perhaps, rapid growth and rapid convergence should occur especially where poorer countries are open to foreign investment (because foreign investors will want those higher returns) and even more under imperialism (because it opens countries to foreign investment and guarantees foreign investors' property rights).

It seems at first self-evident that nothing like this has happened in the real world. Indeed, until the seventeenth century no society seems to have remained wealthy for any significant period of time. As Gregory Clark shows in his "Sixteen-Page Economic History of the World" (2007), through all previous millennia even the best-organized and most progressive societies (ancient China, ancient Greece and Rome) failed to escape the "Malthusian trap": greater wealth only incentivized people to have more children, population growth exceeded economic growth, and the rich societies became poor once again—unless some catastrophe (typically war or disease) so thinned the population as to raise the land–labor and capital–labor ratios back to a level that assured the lucky survivors higher incomes. Only the seemingly miraculous technological breakthroughs of the early modern period and the Industrial Revolution allowed a few societies (but not most) to escape this "trap." And even now, much of the world's population has not experienced economic growth or improvement in living standards.

So how pessimistic should we be? Lant Pritchett, a development economist at the World Bank, argued forcefully in his influential article "Divergence, Big-Time" (1997) that virtually all of the predictions of convergence theory had been wrong over the previous century and more: countries had diverged, not converged, in their rates of growth and levels of wealth. But that turns out to be true only if we weigh all countries, big and small, equally. As Branko Milanovic, the lead economist in the World Bank's research department, showed in his 2005 book, *Worlds Apart*, population-weighted, between-nation inequality has been trending almost uniformly downward since the 1960s. This is due chiefly to the very rapid economic growth of China, and, to a lesser extent, that of India, both with huge populations. Thus, convergence has been happening, in one important sense, at the world level; but this does not resolve the mystery of why so many smaller nations have remained impoverished.

The region that failed most notably to grow, at least until quite recently, is sub-Saharan Africa. Indeed, a significant number of African countries are poorer today than they were when they gained their independence from imperial powers. Thus, Paul Collier (another World Bank economist) and Jan Willem Gunning (an Oxford University economist who specializes in Africa) ask simply, "Why Has Africa Grown Slowly?" and weigh the major competing explanations: "policy" versus "destiny," and external versus internal factors (1999). They conclude that policy—rather than the longer-term factors emphasized by such scholars as Daron Acemoglu (see Chapter 4)—is mostly to blame. In the past, this largely meant external policies, that is, the intrusive policies of richer and more powerful countries. More recently, internal policies have played a larger role.

Our inherited view of developing world poverty includes ideas of rampant disease, low life expectancy, and (in part as a result of high child mortality rates) a propensity to have many children and to invest little in the education of any one of them. As Daron Acemoglu and Simon Johnson note at the outset of "Disease and Development" (2007), this picture is woefully outdated. Amazing improvements in public health (better sanitation, almost universal immunization) have led to much lower death rates (particularly among infants and children) and much higher life expectancies. As demographers would expect, those improvements have in turn lowered fertility rates (the number of children born to each woman) and increased incentives to educate each child. Whereas as recently as the 1960s the average couple in a poor country gave birth to six children, in the 1990s this rate was only three children per couple. Worries about the "population explosion" are exaggerated. Indeed, both in the advanced economies and in some of the rapidly growing ones (such as China), the bigger problem will be an aging and declining population—too few young people, with the average couple giving birth to fewer than two children, thus failing to replace themselves fully in the next generation. And although we might assume that higher life expectancy would lead to higher per capita production, Acemoglu and Johnson show that this seems not to be the case. A lower death rate does not, by itself, translate into more rapid economic growth—although, over the long run, the greater propensity to invest in human capital (education) should have that effect.

To summarize bluntly: the quest for growth indeed remains elusive. Although the great success stories, particularly that of China, hold out hope, and although improvements in public health have greatly increased quality of life in even the poorest countries, comparativists remain baffled about why so many nations remain mired in poverty, and especially about why long-term growth in productivity seems so hard to achieve. The issue has more than moral implications, for the growing gap between rich and poor countries raises incentives to migrate: if citizens of Chad, Afghanistan, Guatemala, or North Korea are doomed to poverty, they will be willing to risk and spend a lot to get to higher wages in Europe, North America, or (in the case of North Korea) China. Thus, the richer or more rapidly growing countries have a strong self-interest in solving the riddle of self-perpetuating poverty.

William Easterly
TO HELP THE POOR

When I see another child eating, I watch him, and if he doesn't give me something I think I'm going to die of hunger.

—A TEN-YEAR-OLD CHILD IN GABON, 1997

I am in Lahore, a city of 6 million people in Pakistan, on a World Bank trip as I write this chapter. Last weekend I went with a guide to the village of Gulvera, not far outside Lahore. We entered the village on an impossibly narrow paved road, which the driver drove at top speed except on the frequent occasions that cattle were crossing the road. We continued as the road turned into a dirt track, where there was barely enough space between the village houses for the car. Then the road seemed to dead-end. But although I could not detect any road, the guide pointed out to the driver how he could make

a sharp right across an open field, then regain a sort of a road—flat dirt anyway. I hated to think what would happen to these dirt roads in rainy season.

The "road" brought us to the community center for the village, where a number of young and old men were hanging out (no women, on which more in a moment). The village smelled of manure. The men were expecting us and were extremely hospitable, welcoming us in to the brick-and-mortar community center, everyone grasping each of our right hands with their two hands and seating us on some rattan benches. They provided pillows for us to lean on or with which to otherwise make ourselves comfortable. They served us a drink of lassi, a sort of yogurt-milk mixture. The lassi pitcher was thickly covered with flies, but I drank my lassi anyway.

The men said that during the week, they worked all day in the fields, then came to the community center in the evenings to play cards and talk. The women couldn't come, they said, because they still had work to do in the evenings. Flocks of flies hummed everywhere, and some of the men had open sores on their

From *The Elusive Quest for Growth: Economists' Adventures and Misadventures in the Tropics* (Cambridge, MA.: MIT Press, 2001), pp. 5–19. Author's notes have been omitted.

legs. There was one youngish but dignified man nicknamed Deenu to whom everyone seemed to defer. Most of the men were barefoot, wearing long dusty robes. A crowd of children hung around the entrance watching us—only boys, no girls.

I asked Deenu what the main problems of Gulvera village were. Deenu said they were glad to have gotten electricity just six months before. Imagine getting electricity after generations spent in darkness. They were glad to have a boys' elementary school. However, they still lacked many things: a girls' elementary school, a doctor, drainage or sewerage (everything was dumped into a pool of rancid water outside the community center), telephone connections, paved roads. The poor sanitary conditions and lack of access to medical care in villages like Gulvera may help explain why a hundred out of every thousand babies die before their first birthday in Pakistan.

I asked Deenu if we could see a house. He walked with us over to his brother's house. It was an adobe-walled dirt-floor compound, which had two small rooms where they lived, stalls for the cattle, an outside dung-fired oven built into a wall, piles of cattle dung stacked up to dry, and a hand pump hooked up to a well. Children were everywhere, including a few girls finally, staring curiously at us. Deenu said his brother had seven children. Deenu himself had six brothers and seven sisters. The brothers all lived in the village; the sisters had married into other villages. The women in the household hung back near the two small rooms. We were not introduced to them.

Women's rights have not yet come to rural Pakistan, a fact reflected in some grim statistics: there are 108 men for every 100 women in Pakistan. In rich countries, women slightly outnumber men because of their greater longevity. In Pakistan, there are what Nobel Prize winner Amartya Sen called "missing women," reflecting some combination of discrimination against girls in nutrition, medical care, or even female infanticide. Oppression of women sometimes takes an even more violent turn. There was a story in the Lahore newspaper of a brother who had killed his sister to preserve the family honor; he had suspected her of an illicit affair.

Violence in the countryside is widespread in Pakistan, despite the peaceful appearance of Gulvera. Another story in the Lahore paper described a village feud in which one family killed seven members of another family. Bandits and kidnappers prey on travelers in parts of the countryside in Pakistan.

We walked back to the community center, passing a group of boys playing a game, where they threw four walnuts on the ground and then tried to hit one of the walnuts with another one. Deenu asked us if we would like to stay for lunch, but we politely declined (I didn't want to take any of their scarce food), said our good-byes, and drove away. One of the villagers rode away with us, just to have an adventure. He told us that they had arranged for two cooks to prepare our lunch. I felt bad about having declined the lunch invitation.

We drove across the fields to where four brothers had grouped their compounds into a sort of a village and went through the same routine: the men greeting us warmly with two hands and seating us on rattan benches outside. No women were to be seen. The children were even more numerous and uninhibited than in Gulvera; they were mostly boys but this time also a few girls. They crowded around us watching everything we did, frequently breaking into laughter at some unknown faux pas by one of us. The men served us some very good milky sweet tea. I saw a woman peeking out from inside the house, but when I looked in her direction, she pulled back out of sight.

We walked into one of the brothers' compounds. Many women stood at the doors into their rooms, hanging back but watching us. The men showed us a churn that they used to make butter and yogurt. One of the men tried to show us how to use it, but he himself didn't know; this was woman's work. The children nearly passed out from laughing. The men brought us some butter to taste. They said they melted the butter to make ghee—clarified butter—which was an important ingredient in their cooking. They said if you ate a lot of ghee, it made you stronger. Then they gave us some ghee to taste. Most of their food seemed to consist of dairy products.

I asked what problems they faced. They had gotten electricity just one month before. They otherwise had the same unfulfilled needs as Gulvera: no telephone, no running water, no doctor, no sewerage, no roads. This was only a kilometer off the main road just outside Lahore, so we weren't in the middle of nowhere. They were poor, but these were relatively well-off villagers compared to more remote villages in Pakistan. The road leading to their mini-village was a half-lane track constructed of bricks that they had made themselves.

The majority of people in Pakistan are poor: 85 percent live on less than two dollars a day and 31 percent live in extreme poverty at less than one dollar a day. The majority of the world's people live in poor nations like Pakistan, where people live in isolated poverty even close to a major city. The majority of the world's people live in poor nations where women are oppressed, far too many babies die, and far too many people don't have enough to eat. We care about economic growth for the poor nations because it makes the lives of poor people like those in Gulvera better. Economic growth frees the poor from hunger and disease. Economy-wide GDP growth per capita translates into rising incomes for the poorest of the poor, lifting them out of poverty.

The Deaths of the Innocents

The typical rate of infant mortality in the richest fifth of countries is 4 out of every 1,000 births; in the poorest fifth of countries, it is 200 out of every 1,000 births. Parents in the poorest countries are fifty times more likely than in the richest countries to know grief rather than joy from the birth of a child. Researchers have found that a 10 percent decrease in income is associated with about a 6 percent higher infant mortality rate.

The higher rates of babies dying in the poorest countries reflect in part the higher rates of communicable and often easily preventable diseases such as tuberculosis, syphilis, diarrhea, polio, measles, tetanus, meningitis, hepatitis, sleeping sickness, schistosomiasis, river blindness, leprosy, trachoma, intestinal worms, and lower respiratory infections. At low incomes, disease is more dangerous because of lower medical knowledge, lower nutrition, and lower access to medical care.

Two million children die every year of dehydration from diarrhea. Another 2 million children die annually from pertussis, polio, diphtheria, tetanus, and measles.

Three million children die annually from bacterial pneumonia. Overcrowding of housing and indoor wood or cigarette smoke make pneumonia among children more likely. Malnourished children are also more likely to develop pneumonia than well-fed children. Bacterial pneumonia can be cured by a five-day course of antibiotics, like cotrimoxazole, that costs about twenty-five cents.

Between 170 million and 400 million children annually are infected with intestinal parasites like hookworm and roundworm, which impair cognition and cause anemia and failure to thrive.

Deficiency of iodine causes goiters—swelling of the thyroid gland at the throat—and lowered mental capacity. About 120,000 children born each year suffer from mental retardation and physical paralysis caused by iodine deficiency. About 10 percent of the world's population, adults and children both, suffer from goiter.

Vitamin A deficiency causes blindness in about half a million children and contributes to the deaths of about 8 million children each year. It is not independent of the other diseases discussed here; it makes death more likely from diarrhea, measles, and pneumonia.

Medicines that would alleviate these diseases are sometimes surprisingly inexpensive, a fact that UNICEF often uses to dramatize the depths of poverty of these suffering people. Oral rehydration therapy, at a cost of less than ten cents for each dose, can alleviate dehydration. Vaccination against pertussis, polio, diphtheria, measles, and tetanus costs about fifteen dollars per child. Vitamin A can be added to diets through processing of salt or sugar or administered directly through vitamin A capsules every six months. Vitamin A capsules cost about two cents each. Iodizing salt supplies, which costs about five cents per affected person per year, alleviates iodine deficiency. Intestinal parasites can be cured with inexpensive drugs like albendazole and praziquantel.

Wealthier and Healthier

Lant Pritchett, from Harvard's Kennedy School of Government, and Larry Summers, the former U.S. secretary of the treasury, found a strong association between economic growth and changes in infant mortality. They pointed out that a third factor that was unchanging over time for each country, like "culture" or "institutions," could not be explaining the simultaneous change in income and change in infant mortality. Going further, they argued that the rise in income was causing the fall in mortality rather than the other way around. They used a statistical argument that we will see more of later in this book. They observed some income increases that were probably unrelated to mortality, like income increases due to rises in a country's export prices. They traced through the effect of such an income increase, finding that it still did result in a fall in infant mortality. If an income increase that has nothing to do with mortality changes is still associated with a fall in mortality, this suggests that income increases are causing reduced mortality.

Pritchett and Summers's findings, if we can take them literally, imply huge effects of income growth on the death of children. The deaths of about half a million children in 1990 would have been averted if Africa's growth in the 1980s had been 1.5 percentage points higher.

The Poorest of the Poor

The statistics presented so far are national averages. Behind the averages of even the poorest nation, there is still regional variation. Mali is one of the poorest nations on earth. The countryside along the Niger River around the city of Tombouctou (Timbuktu) is one of the poorest regions in Mali and thus one of the poorest places on earth. At the time of a survey in 1987, over a third of the children under age five had had diarrhea in the preceding two weeks. Very few of them were on simple and cheap oral rehydration therapy. None had been vaccinated for diphtheria, pertussis, or typhoid. Forty-one percent of children born do not live to the age of five, three times the mortality rate in the capital of Bamako and one of the highest child mortality rates ever recorded.

As in Tomboctou, there are some regions or peoples at the very bottom of the economic pyramid, despised even by other poor. "In Egypt they were *madfoun*—the buried or buried alive; in Ghana, *ohiabrubro*—the miserably poor, with no work, sick with no one to care for them; in Indonesia, *endek arak tadah*; in Brazil, *miseraveis*—the deprived; in Russia, *bomzhi*—the homeless; in Bangladesh *ghrino gorib*—the despised/hated poor." In Zambia the *balandana sana* or *bapina* were described in these terms: "Lack food, eat once or twice; poor hygiene, flies fall over them, cannot afford school and health costs, lead miserable lives, poor dirty clothing, poor sanitation, access to water, look like mad people, live on vegetables and sweet potatoes." In Malawi, the bottom poor were *osaukitsitsa*, "mainly households headed by the aged, the sick, disabled, orphans and widows." Some were described as *onyentchera*, "the stunted poor, with thin bodies, short stature and thin hairs, bodies that did not shine even after bathing, and who experience frequent illnesses and a severe lack of food."

Eating

High mortality in the poorest countries also reflects the continuing problem of hunger. Daily calorie intake is one-third lower in the poorest fifth of countries than in the richest fifth.

A quarter of the poorest countries had famines in the past three decades; none of the richest countries faced a famine. In the poorest nations like Burundi, Madagascar, and Uganda, nearly half of all children under the age of three are abnormally short because of nutritional deficiency.

An Indian family housed in a thatched hut seldom "could have two square meals a day. The lunch would be finished munching some sugarcane. Once in a while they would taste 'sattu' (made of flour), pulses [dried beans], potatoes etc. but for occasions only."

In Malawi, the poorest families "stay without food for 2–3 days or even the whole week . . . and may simply cook vegetables for a meal . . . some households literally eat bitter maize bran (*gaga/deya owawa*) and *gmelina* sawdust mixed with a little maize flour especially during the hunger months of January and February."

Oppression of the Poor

Poor societies sometimes have some form of debt bondage. To take one example, observers of India report "a vicious cycle of indebtedness in which a debtor may work in a moneylender's house as a servant, on his farm as a laborer. . . . The debt may accumulate substantially due to high interest rates, absence due to illness, and expenses incurred for food or accommodations."

Ethnic minorities are particularly prone to oppression. In Pakistan in 1993, the Bengali community of Rehmanabad in Karachi "had been subject to evictions and bulldozing, and on returning to the settlement and constructing temporary housing of reeds and sacks, have faced on-going harassment by land speculators, the police and political movements."

Poor children are particularly vulnerable to oppression. Forty-two percent of children aged ten to fourteen are workers in the poorest countries. Less than 2 percent of children aged ten to fourteen are workers in the richest countries. Although most countries have laws forbidding child labor, the U.S. State Department classifies many countries as not enforcing these laws. Eighty-eight percent of the poorest countries are in this no-enforcement category; none of the richest countries is. For example, we have this

story of Pachawak in western Orissa state in India: "Pachawak dropped out of class 3 when one day his teacher caned him severely. Since then he has been working as child labor with a number of rich households. Pachawak's father owns 1.5 acres of land and works as a laborer. His younger brother of 11-years-old also became a bonded laborer when the family had to take a loan for the marriage of the eldest son. The system is closely linked to credit, as many families take loans from landlords, who in lieu of that obligation keep the children as 'kuthia.' Pachawak worked as a cattle grazer from 6 A.M. to 6 P.M. and got paid two to four sacks of paddy a year, two meals a day, and one lungi [wrap-around clothing]."

One particularly unsavory kind of child labor is prostitution. In Benin, for example, "the girls have no choice but to prostitute themselves, starting at 14, even at 12. They do it for 50 francs, or just for dinner."

Another occupation in which children work in poor countries is particularly dangerous: war. As many as 200,000 child soldiers from the ages of six to sixteen fought wars in poor countries like Myanmar, Angola, Somalia, Liberia, Uganda, and Mozambique.

Women are also vulnerable to oppression in poor countries. Over four-fifths of the richest fifth of countries have social and economic equality for women most of the time, according to the *World Human Rights Guide* by Charles Humana. None of the poorest fifth of countries has social and economic equality for women. In Cameroon, "Women in some regions require a husband's, father's, or brother's permission to go out. In addition, a woman's husband or brother has access to her bank accounts, but not vice versa." A 1997 survey in Jamaica found that "in all communities, wife-beating was perceived as a common experience in daily life." In Georgia in the Caucasus, "women confessed that frequent household arguments resulted in being beaten." In Uganda in 1998, when women were asked, "What kind of work do men in your area do?" they laughed and said, "Eat and sleep then wake up and go drinking again."

Growth and Poverty

My World Bank colleagues Martin Ravallion and Shaohua Chen collected data on spells of economic growth and changes in poverty covering the years 1981 to 1999. They get their data from national surveys of household income or expenditure. They require that the methodology of the survey be unchanged over the period that they are examining so as to exclude spurious changes due to changing definitions. They found 154 periods of change in 65 developing countries with data that met this requirement.

Ravallion and Chen defined poverty as an absolute concept within each country: the poor were defined as the part of the population that had incomes below $1 a day at the beginning of each period they were examining. Ravallion and Chen keep this poverty line fixed within each country during the period they analyze. So the question was, How did aggregate economic growth change the share of people below this poverty line?

The answer was quite clear: fast growth went with fast poverty reduction, and overall economic contraction went with increased poverty. Here I summarize Ravallion and Chen's data by dividing the number of episodes into four equally sized groups from the fastest growing to the fastest declining. I compare the change in poverty in countries with the fastest growth to the poverty change in countries with the fastest decline [see Table 10.1 below].

The increases in poverty were extremely acute in the economies with severe economic declines—most of them in Eastern Europe and Central Asia. These were economies that declined with the death of the old communist system and kept declining while awaiting the birth of a new system. Several of these poverty-increasing declines also occurred in Africa. Poverty shot up during severe recessions in Zambia, Mali, and Côte d'Ivoire, for example.

Countries with positive income growth had a decline in the proportion of people below the poverty line. The fastest average growth was associated with the fastest poverty reductions. Growth was reaching the poor in Indonesia, for example, which had average income growth of 76 percent from 1984 to 1996. The proportion of Indonesians beneath the poverty line in 1993 was one-quarter of what it was in 1984. (A bad reversal came with Indonesia's crisis over 1997–1999, with average income falling by 12 percent and the poverty rate shooting up 65 percent, again confirming that income and poverty move together.)

All of this in retrospect seems unsurprising. For poverty to get worse with economic growth, the distribution of income would have to get much more

Table 10.1

	Percentage change in average incomes per year	Percent change in poverty rate per year
Strong contraction	−9.8	23.9
Moderate contraction	−1.9	1.5
Moderate expansion	1.6	−0.6
Strong expansion	8.2	−6.1

unequal as incomes increased. There is no evidence for such disastrous deteriorations in income inequality as income rises. In Ravallion and Chen's data set, for example, measures of inequality show no tendency to get either better or worse with economic growth. If the degree of inequality stays about the same, then income of the poor and the rich must be rising together or falling together.

This is indeed what my World Bank colleagues David Dollar and Aart Kraay have found. A 1 percent increase in average income of the society translates one for one into a 1 percent increase in the incomes of the poorest 20 percent of the population. Again using statistical techniques to isolate direction of causation, they found that an additional one percentage point per capita growth *causes* a 1 percent rise in the poor's incomes.

There are two ways the poor could become better off: income could be redistributed from the rich to the poor, and the income of both the poor and the rich could rise with overall economic growth. Ravallion and Chen's and Dollar and Kraay's findings suggest that on average, growth has been much more of a lifesaver to the poor than redistribution.

To Begin the Quest

The improvement in hunger, mortality, and poverty as GDP per capita rises over time motivates us on our quest for growth. Poverty is not just low GDP; it is dying babies, starving children, and oppression of women and the downtrodden. The well-being of the next generation in poor countries depends on whether our quest to make poor countries rich is successful. I think again back to the woman I saw peering out at me from a house in a village in Pakistan. To that unknown woman I dedicate the elusive quest for growth as we economists, from rich countries and from poor countries, trek the tropics trying to make poor countries rich.

■ ■ ■

Gregory Clark

THE SIXTEEN-PAGE ECONOMIC HISTORY OF THE WORLD

He may therefore be justly numbered among the benefactors of mankind, who contracts the great rules of life into short sentences, that may be easily impressed on the memory, and taught by frequent recollection to recur habitually to the mind.

—Samuel Johnson, Rambler No. 175 (November 19, 1751)

The basic outline of world economic history is surprisingly simple. Indeed it can be summarized in one diagram: Figure 10.1. Before 1800

income per person—the food, clothing, heat, light, and housing available per head—varied across societies and epochs. But there was no upward trend. A simple but powerful mechanism explained in this book, the *Malthusian Trap*, ensured that short-term gains in income through technological advances were inevitably lost through population growth.

Thus the average person in the world of 1800 was no better off than the average person of 100,000 BC. Indeed in 1800 the bulk of the world's population was poorer than their remote ancestors. The lucky denizens of wealthy societies such as eighteenth-century England or the Netherlands managed a material lifestyle equivalent to that of the

From *A Farewell to Alms: A Brief Economic History of the World* (Princeton, NJ: Princeton University Press, 2007), Chapter 1.

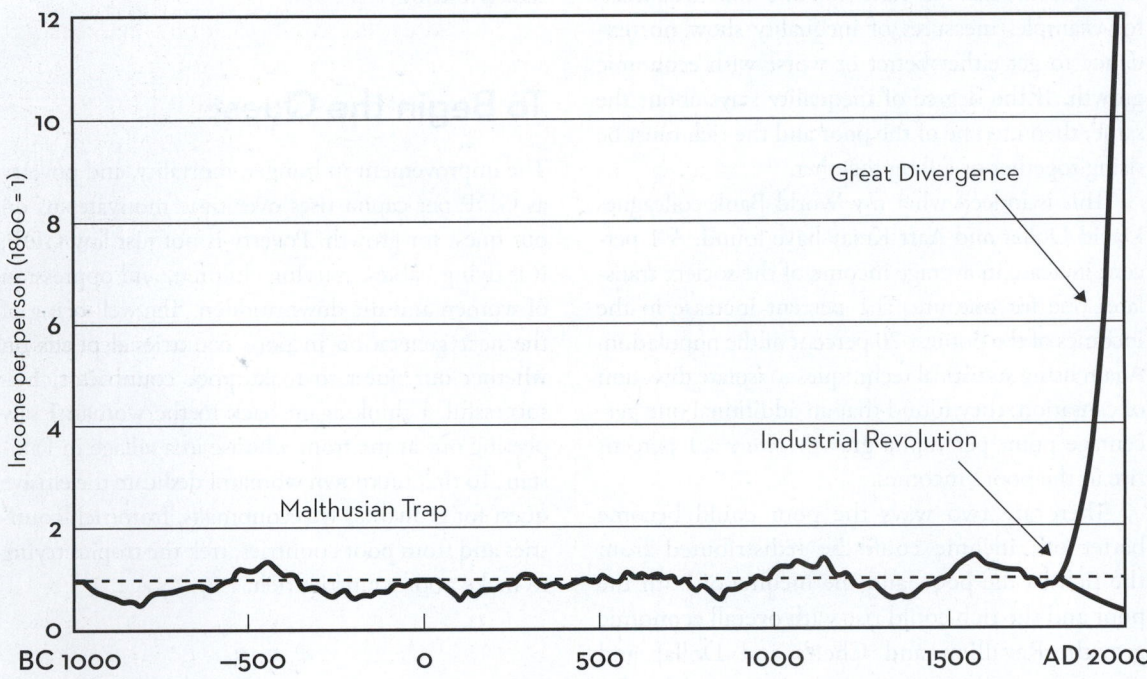

Figure 10.1 World Economic History in One Picture. Incomes Rose Sharply in Many Countries after 1800 but Declined in Others.

Stone Age. But the vast swath of humanity in East and South Asia, particularly in China and Japan, eked out a living under conditions probably significantly poorer than those of cavemen.

The quality of life also failed to improve on any other observable dimension. Life expectancy was no higher in 1800 than for hunter-gatherers: thirty to thirty-five years. Stature, a measure both of the quality of diet and of children's exposure to disease, was higher in the Stone Age than in 1800. And while foragers satisfy their material wants with small amounts of work, the modest comforts of the English in 1800 were purchased only through a life of unrelenting drudgery. Nor did the variety of material consumption improve. The average forager had a diet, and a work life, much more varied than the typical English worker of 1800, even though the English table by then included such exotics as tea, pepper, and sugar.

And hunter-gatherer societies are egalitarian. Material consumption varies little across the mem-

bers. In contrast, inequality was pervasive in the agrarian economies that dominated the world in 1800. The riches of a few dwarfed the pinched allocations of the masses. Jane Austen may have written about refined conversations over tea served in china cups. But for the majority of the English as late as 1813 conditions were no better than for their naked ancestors of the African savannah. The Darcys were few, the poor plentiful.

So, even according to the broadest measures of material life, average welfare, if anything, declined from the Stone Age to 1800. The poor of 1800, those who lived by their unskilled labor alone, would have been better off if transferred to a hunter-gatherer band.

The Industrial Revolution, a mere two hundred years ago, changed forever the possibilities for material consumption. Incomes per person began to undergo sustained growth in a favored group of countries. The richest modern economies are now ten to twenty times wealthier than the 1800 average. Moreover the biggest beneficiary of the Industrial Revolution has so far been the unskilled. There have been benefits aplenty for the typically wealthy owners of land or capital, and for the educated. But industrialized economies saved their best gifts for the poorest.

Prosperity, however, has not come to all societies. Material consumption in some countries, mainly in sub-Saharan Africa, is now well below the preindustrial norm. Countries such as Malawi or Tanzania would be better off in material terms had they never had contact with the industrialized world and instead continued in their preindustrial state. Modern medicine, airplanes, gasoline, computers—the whole technological cornucopia of the past two hundred years—have succeeded there in producing among the lowest material living standards ever experienced. These African societies have remained trapped in the Malthusian era, where technological advances merely produce more people and living standards are driven down to subsistence. But modern medicine has reduced the material minimum required for subsistence to a level far below that of the Stone Age. Just as the Industrial Revolution reduced income inequalities *within* societies, it has increased them *between* societies, in a process recently labeled the *Great Divergence*.[1] The gap in incomes between countries is of the order of 50:1. There walk the earth now both the richest people who ever lived and the poorest.

Thus world economic history poses three interconnected problems: Why did the Malthusian Trap persist for so long? Why did the initial escape from that trap in the Industrial Revolution occur on one tiny island, England, in 1800? Why was there the consequent Great Divergence?* * * The explanation for both the timing and the nature of the Industrial Revolution, and at least in part for the Great Divergence, lies in processes that began thousands of years ago, deep in the Malthusian era. The dead hand of the past still exerts a powerful grip on the economies of the present.

The focus on material conditions in this history will strike some as too narrow, too incidental to vast social changes over the millennia. Surely our material riches reflect but a tiny fraction of what makes industrialized societies modern?

On the contrary, there is ample evidence that wealth—and wealth alone—is the crucial determinant of lifestyles, both within and between societies. Income growth changes consumption and lifestyles in highly predictable ways. The recent demise first of the American farmer and then of the manufacturing worker were already preordained when income began its upward march during the Industrial Revolution. Had we been more clear-sighted, we could have foreseen in 1800 our world of walk-in closets, his-and-her bathrooms, caramel macchiatos, balsamic reductions, boutique wines, liberal arts colleges, personal trainers, and $50 entrees.

There are surely many surprises ahead for mankind in the centuries to come, but for the most part the economic future is not an alien and exotic land. We already see how the rich live, and their current lifestyle predicts powerfully how we will all eventually live if economic growth continues.[2] Anyone who has visited the British Museum or the Sistine Chapel, for example, has had a foretaste of the relentless tide of tourism set to be unleashed on the world by another few decades of strong economic growth.[3] Even the high-income demand for unique and individualized travel and dining experiences is now catered to on an industrial scale.

Just as we can see the future through the lives of the rich, so the small wealthy elite of the preindustrial world led lives that prefigured our own. The delight of the modern American suburbanite in his or her first SUV echoes precisely that of Samuel Pepys, the wealthy London civil servant, on acquiring his first coach in 1668.[4] A walk through the reconstructed villas of Pompeii and Herculaneum, frozen in time on the day of the eruption of Vesuvius in AD 79, reveals homes that suburban Americans would happily move into: "Charming home with high ceilings, central courtyard, great room, finely detailed mosaics, and garden water feature—unobstructed Vesuvian views."

Thus I make no apologies for focusing on income. Over the long run income is more powerful than any ideology or religion in shaping lives. No God has commanded worshippers to their pious duties more forcefully than income as it subtly directs the fabric of our lives.

The Malthusian Trap: Economic Life to 1800

■   ■   ■

The crucial factor was the rate of technological advance. As long as technology improved slowly, material conditions could not permanently improve, even while there was cumulatively significant gain in the technologies. The rate of technological advance in Malthusian economies can be inferred from population growth. The typical rate of technological advance before 1800 was well below 0.05 percent per year, about a thirtieth of the modern rate.

* * * The economy of humans in the years before 1800 turns out to be just the *natural* economy of all animal species, with the same kinds of factors determining the living conditions of animals and humans. It is called the Malthusian Trap because the vital insight underlying the model was that of the Reverend Thomas Robert Malthus, who in 1798 in *An Essay on the Principle of Population* took the initial steps toward understanding the logic of this economy.

In the Malthusian economy before 1800 economic policy was turned on its head: vice now was virtue then, and virtue vice. Those scourges of failed modern states—war, violence, disorder, harvest failures, collapsed public infrastructures, bad sanitation—were the friends of mankind before 1800. They reduced population pressures and increased material living standards. In contrast policies beloved of the World Bank and the United Nations today—peace, stability, order, public health, transfers to the poor—were the enemies of prosperity. They generated the population growth that impoverished societies.

At first sight the claim of no material advance before 1800 seems absurd.* * * How is it possible to claim that material living conditions were on average the same across all * * * societies?

But the logic of the Malthusian model matches the empirical evidence for the preindustrial world. While even long before the Industrial Revolution small elites had an opulent lifestyle, the average person in 1800 was no better off than his or her ancestors of the Paleolithic or Neolithic.

The Malthusian logic developed in this book also reveals the crucial importance of fertility control to material conditions before 1800. All preindustrial societies for which we have sufficient records to reveal fertility levels experienced some limitation on fertility, though the mechanisms varied widely. Most societies before 1800 consequently lived well above the bare subsistence limit. That is why there has been plenty of room for African living standards to fall in the years since the Industrial Revolution.

Mortality conditions also mattered, and here Europeans were lucky to be a filthy people who squatted happily above their own feces, stored in basement cesspits, in cities such as London. Poor hygiene, combined with high urbanization rates with their attendant health issues, meant incomes had to be high to maintain the population in eighteenth-century England and the Netherlands. The Japanese, with a more highly developed sense of cleanliness, could maintain the level of population at miserable levels of material comforts, and they were accordingly condemned to subsist on a much more limited income.

Since the economic laws governing human society were those that govern all animal societies, mankind was subject to natural selection throughout the Malthusian era, even after the arrival of settled agrarian societies with the Neolithic Revolution of 8000 BC, which transformed hunters into settled agriculturalists. The Darwinian struggle that shaped human nature did not end with the Neolithic Revolution but continued right up until the Industrial Revolution.

For England we will see compelling evidence of differential survival of types in the years 1250–1800. In particular, economic success translated powerfully into reproductive success. The richest men had twice as many surviving children at death as the poorest. The poorest individuals in Malthusian England had so few surviving children that their families were dying out. Preindustrial England was thus a world of constant downward mobility. Given the static nature of the Malthusian economy, the superabundant children of the rich had to, on average, move down the social hierarchy in order to find work. Craftsmen's sons became laborers, merchants' sons petty traders, large landowners' sons smallholders. The attributes that would ensure later economic dynamism—patience, hard work, ingenuity, innovativeness, education—were thus spreading biologically throughout the population.

Just as people were shaping economies, the economy of the preindustrial era was shaping people, at least culturally and perhaps also genetically.[5] The Neolithic Revolution created agrarian societies that were just as capital intensive as the modern world. At least in England, the emergence of such an institutionally stable, capital-intensive economic system created a society that rewarded middle-class values with reproductive success, generation after generation. This selection process was accompanied by changes in the characteristics of the preindustrial economy, due largely to the population's adoption of more middle-class preferences. Interest rates fell, murder rates declined, work hours increased, the taste for violence declined, and numeracy and literacy spread even to the lower reaches of society.

The Industrial Revolution

The stasis of the preindustrial world, which occupied most of the history of mankind, was shattered by two seemingly unprecedented events in European society in the years 1760–1900. The first was the Industrial Revolution, the appearance for the first time of rapid economic growth fueled by increasing production efficiency made possible by advances in knowledge. The second was the demographic transition, a decline in fertility which started with the upper classes and gradually encompassed all of society. The demographic transition allowed the efficiency advance of the Industrial Revolution to translate not into an endless supply of impoverished people but into the astonishing rise of income per person that we have seen since 1800.* * *

The Industrial Revolution and the associated demographic transition constitute the great questions of economic history. Why was technological advance so slow in all preindustrial societies? Why did the rate of advance increase so greatly after 1800? Why was one by-product of this technological advance a decline in fertility? And, finally, why have all societies not been able to share in the ample fruits of the Industrial Revolution?

There are only three established approaches to these puzzles. The first locates the Industrial Revolution in events outside the economic system, such as changes in political institutions, in particular the introduction of modern democracies. The second argues that preindustrial society was caught in a stable, but stagnant, economic equilibrium. Some shock set forces in motion that moved society to a new, dynamic equilibrium. The last approach argues that the Industrial Revolution was the product of a gradual evolution of social conditions in the Malthusian era: growth was endogenous. According to the first two theories the Industrial Revolution might never have occurred, or could have been delayed thousands of years. Only the third approach suggests that there was any inevitability to it.

The classic description of the Industrial Revolution has suggested that it was an abrupt transition between economic regimes, as portrayed in Figure 10.1, with a change within fifty years from preindustrial productivity growth rates to modern rates. If this is correct then only theories that emphasize an external shock or a switch between equilibria could possibly explain the Industrial Revolution.

The classic description has also suggested that significant technological advances across disparate sectors of the economy contributed to growth during the Industrial Revolution, again pointing toward some economywide institutional change or equilibrium shift. This implies that we should be able to find the preconditions for an Industrial Revolution by looking at changes in institutional and economic conditions in England in the years just before 1800. And waves of economists and economic historians have thrown themselves at the problem with just such an explanation in mind—with spectacular lack of success.

The conventional picture of the Industrial Revolution as a sudden fissure in economic life is not sustainable. There is good evidence that the productivity growth rate did not experience a clean upward break in England, but instead fluctuated irregularly over time all the way back to 1200. Arguments can be made for 1600, for 1800, or even for 1860 as the true break between the Malthusian and modern economies.

When we try to connect advances in efficiency to the underlying rate of accumulation of knowledge in England, the link turns out to depend on many accidental factors of demand, trade, and resources. In crucial ways the classic Industrial Revolution in England in 1760–1860 was a blip, an accident, superimposed on a longer-running upward sweep in the rate of knowledge accumulation that had its origins in the Middle Ages or even earlier.

Thus, though an Industrial Revolution of some kind certainly occurred between 1200 and 1860 in Europe, though mankind crossed a clear divide, a materialist's Jordan at the gates of the Promised Land, there is still plenty of room for debate about its precise time and place, and hence debate about the conditions which led to it. An evolutionary account of gradual changes is a much more plausible explanation than has previously been appreciated.

Despite the dominant role that institutions and institutional analysis have played in economics and economic history since the time of Adam Smith, institutions play at best a minor direct role in the story of the Industrial Revolution told here, and in

the account of economic performance since then. By 1200 societies such as England already had all the institutional prerequisites for economic growth emphasized today by the World Bank and the International Monetary Fund. These were indeed societies more highly incentivized than modern high-income economies: medieval citizens had more to gain from work and investment than their modern counterparts. Approached from the Smithian perspective, the puzzle is not why medieval England had no growth, but why today's northern European countries, with their high tax rates and heavy social spending, do not suffer economic collapse. The institutions necessary for growth existed long before growth itself began.

These institutions did create the conditions for growth, but only slowly and indirectly over centuries and perhaps even millennia. Here the book argues that the Neolithic Revolution, which established a settled agrarian society with massive stocks of capital, changed the nature of the selective pressures operating on human culture and genes. Ancient Babylonia in 2000 BC superficially possessed an economy remarkably similar to that of England in 1800. But the intervening years had profoundly shaped the culture, and maybe even the genes, of the members of agrarian societies. It was these changes that created the possibility of an Industrial Revolution only in AD 1800, not in 2000 BC.

Why an Industrial Revolution in England? Why not China, India, or Japan?[6] The answer hazarded here is that England's advantages were not coal, not colonies, not the Protestant Reformation, not the Enlightenment, but the accidents of institutional stability and demography: in particular the extraordinary stability of England back to at least 1200, the slow growth of English population between 1300 and 1760, and the extraordinary fecundity of the rich and economically successful. The embedding of bourgeois values into the culture, and perhaps even the genetics, was for these reasons the most advanced in England.

Both China and Japan were headed in the same direction as England in 1600–1800: toward a society embodying the bourgeois values of hard work, patience, honesty, rationality, curiosity, and learning. They too enjoyed long periods of institutional stability and private property rights. But they were headed there more slowly than England. David Landes is correct in observing that the Europeans had a culture more conducive to economic growth.[7]

China and Japan did not move as rapidly along the path as England simply because the members of their upper social strata were only modestly more fecund than the mass of the population. Thus there was not the same cascade of children from the educated classes down the social scale.

The samurai in Japan in the Tokugawa era (1603–1868), for example, were ex-warriors given ample hereditary revenues through positions in the state bureaucracy. Despite their wealth they produced on average little more than one son per father. Their children were thus mainly accommodated within the state bureaucracy, despite the fixed number of positions. The Qing imperial lineage was the royal family of China from 1644 to 1911. They too were wealthy through the entitlements that fell to persons of their status. They produced more children than the average Chinese, but only modestly so.

Thus, just as accidents of social custom triumphed over hygiene, marriage, and reproduction to make Europeans richer than Asians in the Malthusian era, they also seem to have given Europe a greater cultural dynamic.

Whatever its cause, the Industrial Revolution has had profound social effects. As a result of two forces—the nature of technological advance and the demographic transition—growth in capitalist economies since the Industrial Revolution strongly promoted greater equality. Despite fears that machines would swallow up men, the greatest beneficiaries of the Industrial Revolution so far have been unskilled workers.

Thus, while in preindustrial agrarian societies half or more of the national income typically went to the owners of land and capital, in modern industrialized societies their share is normally less than a quarter. Technological advance might have been expected to dramatically reduce unskilled wages. After all, there was a class of workers in the preindustrial economy who, offering only brute strength, were quickly swept aside by machinery. By 1914 most horses had disappeared from the British economy, swept aside by steam and internal combustion engines, even though a million had been at work in the early nineteenth century. When their value in production fell below their maintenance costs they were condemned to the knacker's yard.

Similarly there was no reason why the owners of capital or land need not have increased their shares of income. The redistribution of income toward unskilled labor has had profound social consequences. But there is nothing in the happy developments so far that ensures that modern economic growth will continue to be so benign in its effects.

The Great Divergence

* * * Why [has] the Industrial Revolution, while tending to equalize incomes within successful economies,* * * at the same time led to a Great Divergence in national economic fortunes[?] How did we end up in a world where a minority of countries has unprecedented riches while a significant group has seen declining incomes since the Industrial Revolution? This disparity is reflected in ever-widening gaps in hourly labor costs across countries. In 2002, for example, apparel workers in India cost $0.38 per hour, compared to $9 in the United States* * *. As the World Trade Organization labors to gradually dissolve remaining trade barriers, does this imply the end of all basic manufacturing activity in advanced economies? Do we face a future dystopia for rich societies in which the wages of the unskilled plummet to Third World levels?

The technological, organizational, and political changes spawned by the Industrial Revolution in the nineteenth century all seemed to predict that it would soon transform most of the world in the way it was changing England, the United States, and northwestern Europe. By 1900, for example, cities such as Alexandria in Egypt, Bombay in India, and

Shanghai in China were all, in terms of transport costs, capital markets, and institutional structures, fully integrated into the British economy. Yet the growth in a favored few nations was followed haltingly in others, leading to an ever-widening income gap between societies.

This divergence in incomes is an intellectual puzzle on a par with that of the Industrial Revolution itself. And it provides a further severe test of theories of the Industrial Revolution. Can these theories be reconciled with the increasing divergence within the world economy?

A detailed examination of the cotton industry, one of the few found from the earliest years in both rich and poor countries, shows that the anatomy of the Great Divergence is complex and unexpected, and again hard to reconcile with economists' favorite explanations—bad institutions, bad equilibria, and bad development paths. In fact workers in poorly performing economies simply supply very little actual labor input on the job. Workers in modern cotton textile factories in India, for example, are actually working for as little as fifteen minutes of each hour they are at the workplace. Thus the disparity in hourly labor costs across the world is actually much less than it would appear from the differences in wage rates between rich and poor countries. Labor may cost $0.38 per hour in India, but its true cost per unit of work delivered is much higher. The threat to the living standards of unskilled workers in the United States from free trade with the Third World is less acute than hourly labor costs suggest. The new technologies of the Industrial Revolution could easily be transferred to most of the world, and the inputs for production obtained cheaply across the globe. But the one thing that could not be replicated so easily or so widely was the *social environment* that underpinned the cooperation of people in production in those countries where the technologies were first developed.

One reason why the social environment could not be replicated seems to be the comparatively long histories of various societies. In *Guns, Germs, and Steel* Jared Diamond suggested that geography, botany, and zoology were destiny.[8] Europe and Asia pressed ahead economically, and remained ahead to the present day, because of accidents of geography. They had the kinds of animals that could be domesticated, and the orientation of the Eurasian land mass allowed domesticated plants and animals to spread easily between societies. But there is a gaping lacuna in his argument. In a modern world in which the path to riches lies through industrialization, why are bad-tempered zebras and hippos the barrier to economic growth in sub-Saharan Africa? Why didn't the Industrial Revolution free Africa, New Guinea, and South America from their old geographic disadvantages, rather than accentuate their backwardness? And why did the takeover of Australia by the British propel a part of the world that had not developed settled agriculture by 1800 into the first rank among developed economies?

The selection mechanisms discussed earlier can help explain how an initial advantage in establishing settled agrarian societies in Europe, China, and Japan, possibly from geography, was translated into a persistent cultural advantage in later economic competition. Societies without such a long experience of settled, pacific agrarian society cannot instantly adopt the institutions and technologies of the more advanced economies, because they have not yet culturally adapted to the demands of productive capitalism.

But history also teaches us that, even within societies of the same tradition and history, there can be regions and periods of economic energy and regions and periods of economic torpor. The economic fortunes of the north and south of England reversed after World War I; Ireland has become as rich as England after being significantly poorer for at least two hundred years; southern Germany has overtaken northern Germany.

These variations in the economic vitality of societies existed across the Malthusian era, and they continue to exist to this day. But in the Malthusian era the effects of these variations were dampened by the economic system. They mainly determined population densities. Polish farm workers in the early nineteenth century, for example, were allegedly slovenly, idle, and drunken compared to their British counterparts.[9] Yet living standards were little higher in England than in Poland. Instead Poland was very lightly populated. Since the Industrial Revolution such differences in the economic environment show up as variations in income levels.

Shifts in the nature of production technologies have further widened international income gaps. While Polish workers had low hourly outputs in farm tasks compared to workers in preindustrial England and the United States, the quality of their output was not markedly inferior. Polish wheat could still, after rescreening, be retailed at full price on the British market. When the majority of the tasks in agriculture consisted of such things as digging drainage ditches, spreading manure, and beating straw with a stick to extract the grain, the attitudes of the workers were not particularly important.

However, modern production technologies, developed in rich countries, are designed for labor forces that are disciplined, conscientious, and engaged. Products flow through many sets of hands, each one capable of destroying most of the value of the final output. Error rates by individual workers must be kept low to allow such processes to succeed.[10] The introduction of such techniques in nineteenth-century England was accompanied by greater attention to worker discipline. When workers in poor countries lack these qualities of discipline and engagement, modern production systems are feasible only when little is demanded of each worker, to keep error rates as low as possible. This concept helps explain the dramatically lower observed work efforts of textile mill workers in such poor countries as India. It is cheaper to have frequently idle workers than idle machinery or defective output.

The Rise of Wealth and the Decline of Economics

Economics as a discipline arose in the dying decades of the Malthusian era. Classical economics was a brilliantly successful description of this world. But the torrent of goods unleashed by the Industrial Revolution not only created extremes of wealth and poverty across nations; it also undermined the ability of economic theory to explain these differences.

Thus there is a great irony in economic history. In most areas of inquiry—astronomy, archaeology, paleontology, biology, history—knowledge declines as we move away from our time, our planet, our society. In the distant mists lurk the strange objects: quasars, dwarf human species, hydrogen sulfide–fueled bacteria. But in economics the Malthusian era, however odd, is the known world. Preindustrial living standards are predictable based on knowledge of disease and environment. Differences in social energy across societies were muted by the Malthusian constraints. They had minimal impacts on living conditions. Since the Industrial Revolution, however, we have entered a strange new world in which economic theory is of little use in understanding differences in income across societies, or the future income in any specific society. Wealth and poverty are a matter of differences in local social interactions that are magnified, not dampened, by the economic system, to produce feast or famine.

The final great surprise that economic history offers—which was revealed only within the past thirty years—is that material affluence, the decline in child mortality, the extension of adult life spans, and reduced inequality have not made us any happier than our hunter-gatherer forebears. High incomes profoundly shape lifestyles in the modern developed world. But wealth has not brought happiness. Another foundational assumption of economics is incorrect.

Within any society the rich are happier than the poor. But, as was first observed by Richard Easterlin in 1974, rapidly rising incomes for everyone in the successful economies since 1950 have not produced greater happiness.[11] In Japan, for example, from 1958 to 2004 income per person rose nearly sevenfold, while self-reported happiness, instead of rising, declined modestly. It is evident that our happiness depends not on our absolute well-being but instead on how we are doing relative to our reference group. Each individual—by acquiring more income, by buying a larger house, by driving a more elegant car—can make herself happier, but happier only at the expense of those with less income, meaner housing, and junkier cars. Money does buy happiness, but that happiness is transferred from someone else, not added to the common pool.

That is why, despite the enormous income gap between rich and poor societies today, reported happiness is only modestly lower in the poorest societies. And this despite the fact that the citizens of poor nations, through the medium of television, can witness almost firsthand the riches of successful economies. It thus might be that there is no absolute effect of income on happiness, even at the lowest income levels. The people of the world of 1800, in which all societies were relatively poor and communities were much more local in scope, were likely just as happy as the wealthiest nations of the world today, such as the United States.

Since we are for the most part the descendants of the strivers of the preindustrial world, those driven to achieve greater economic success than their peers, perhaps these findings reflect another cultural or biological heritage from the Malthusian era. The contented may well have lost out in the Darwinian struggle that defined the world before 1800. Those who were successful in the economy of the Malthusian era could well have been driven by a need to have more than their peers in order to be happy. Modern man might not be designed for contentment. The envious have inherited the earth.

NOTES

1. Pomeranz, 2000.
2. Thus when Bill and Melinda Gates were expecting a third child in 2002 they expanded their house, in light of their greater space needs, to its current 50,000 square feet.
3. The major export of New Zealand, for example, is now tourism services.
4. Pepys, 2000, November 28, 1668.
5. I first became interested in this idea in 1989. Clark and McGinley, 1989, argued through a simulation exercise that the logic of the Malthusian era implied that people evolved after the Neolithic Revolution toward greater patience and lower fertility. At the time these ideas seemed to conflict with the historical record and biological possibilities. My interest was reignited by a theoretical paper, making the same argument, by Oded Galor and Omar Moav; Galor and Moav, 2002.
6. Landes, 1998; Pomeranz, 2000; Mokyr, 2005.
7. Landes, 1998.
8. Diamond, 1997.
9. Jacob, 1826, 30, 65, 79–80.
10. Kremer, 1993.
11. Easterlin, 1974; Blanchflower and Oswald, 2004.

REFERENCES

Blanchflower, David G., and Andrew J. Oswald. 2004. "Well-Being over Time in Britain and the USA." *Journal of Public Economics* 88(7–8): 1359–1386.

Clark, Gregory, and Alan McGinley. 1989. "Selective Pressure and Economic History: Economics in the Very Long Run." Paper presented to the Berkeley-Stanford Economic History Seminar, May 25.

Diamond, Jared M. 1997. *Guns, Germs, and Steel: The Fates of Human Societies.* New York: W. W. Norton.

Easterlin, Richard A. 1974. "Does Economic Growth Improve the Human Lot? Some Empirical Evidence." In *Nations and Households in Economic Growth: Essays in Honour of Moses Abramowitz,* ed. Paul A. David and Melvin W. Reder. New York: Academic Press.

Galor, Oded, and Omer Moav. 2002. "Natural Selection and the Origin of Economic Growth." *Quarterly Journal of Economics* 117: 1133–1191.

Jacob, William. 1826. *Report on the Trade in Foreign Corn and on the Agriculture of the North of Europe.* London: James Ridgeway.

Kremer, Michael. 1993. "The O-Ring Theory of Development." *Quarterly Journal of Economics* 108(3): 551–575.

Landes, David, 1998. *The Wealth and Poverty of Nations. Why Some Are So Rich and Some So Poor.* London: Little, Brown.

Mokyr, Joel. 2005. "The Intellectual Origins of Modern Economic Growth." *Journal of Economic History* 65(2): 285–351.

Pepys, Samuel. 2000. *The Diary of Samuel Pepys*, ed. Robert Latham and William Matthews. Berkeley: University of California Press.

Pomeranz, Kenneth. 2000. *The Great Divergence: China, Europe, and the Making of the Modern World Economy.* Princeton, N.J.: Princeton University Press.

Paul Collier and Jan Willem Gunning
WHY HAS AFRICA GROWN SLOWLY?

In the 1960s, Africa's future looked bright. On the basis of Maddison's (1995) estimates of per capita GDP for a sample of countries, during the first half of the century Africa had grown considerably more rapidly than Asia; by 1950, the African sample had overtaken the Asian sample. In the 1950s there were uncertainties of political transition, but after 1960 Africa was increasingly free of colonialism, with the potential for governments that would be more responsive to domestic needs. During the period 1960–73, growth in Africa was more rapid than in the first half of the century. Indeed, for this period, African growth and its composition were indistinguishable from the geographically very different circumstances of south Asia (Collins and Bosworth, 1996). Political self-determination in Africa and economic growth seemed to be proceeding hand-in-hand.

However, during the 1970s both political and economic matters in Africa deteriorated. The leadership of many African nations hardened into autocracy and dictatorship. Africa's economies first faltered and then started to decline. While Africa experienced a growth collapse, nations of south Asia modestly improved their economic performance. A good example of this divergence is the comparison of Nigeria and Indonesia. Until around 1970, the economic performance of Nigeria was broadly superior to that of Indonesia, but over the next quarter-century outcomes diverged markedly, despite the common experience for both countries of an oil boom in a predominantly agricultural economy. Since 1980, aggregate per capita GDP in sub-Saharan Africa has declined at almost 1 percent per annum. The decline has been widespread: 32 countries are poorer now than in 1980. Today, sub-Saharan Africa is the lowest-income region in the world. Map 10.1 and Table 10.2, taken together, offer a snapshot of Africa today. Map 10.1 is a map of the continent. Table 10.2 gives some basic information on population, GDP, standard of living, and growth rates for countries of sub-Saharan Africa. We focus on the sub-Saharan countries, setting aside the north African countries of Algeria, Egypt, Libya, Morocco and Tunisia. This is conventional for the studies of this area, since the north African countries are part of a different regional economy—the Middle East—with its own distinctive set of economic issues. It is clear that Africa has suffered a chronic failure of economic growth. The problem for analysis is to determine its causes.

The debate on the causes of slow African growth has offered many different explanations. These can be usefully grouped into a two-by-two matrix, distinguishing on the one hand between policy and exogenous "destiny" and, on the other, between

From *Journal of Economic Perspectives* 13, no. 3 (Summer 1999), pp. 3–22.

Map 10.1 The Political Geography of Africa

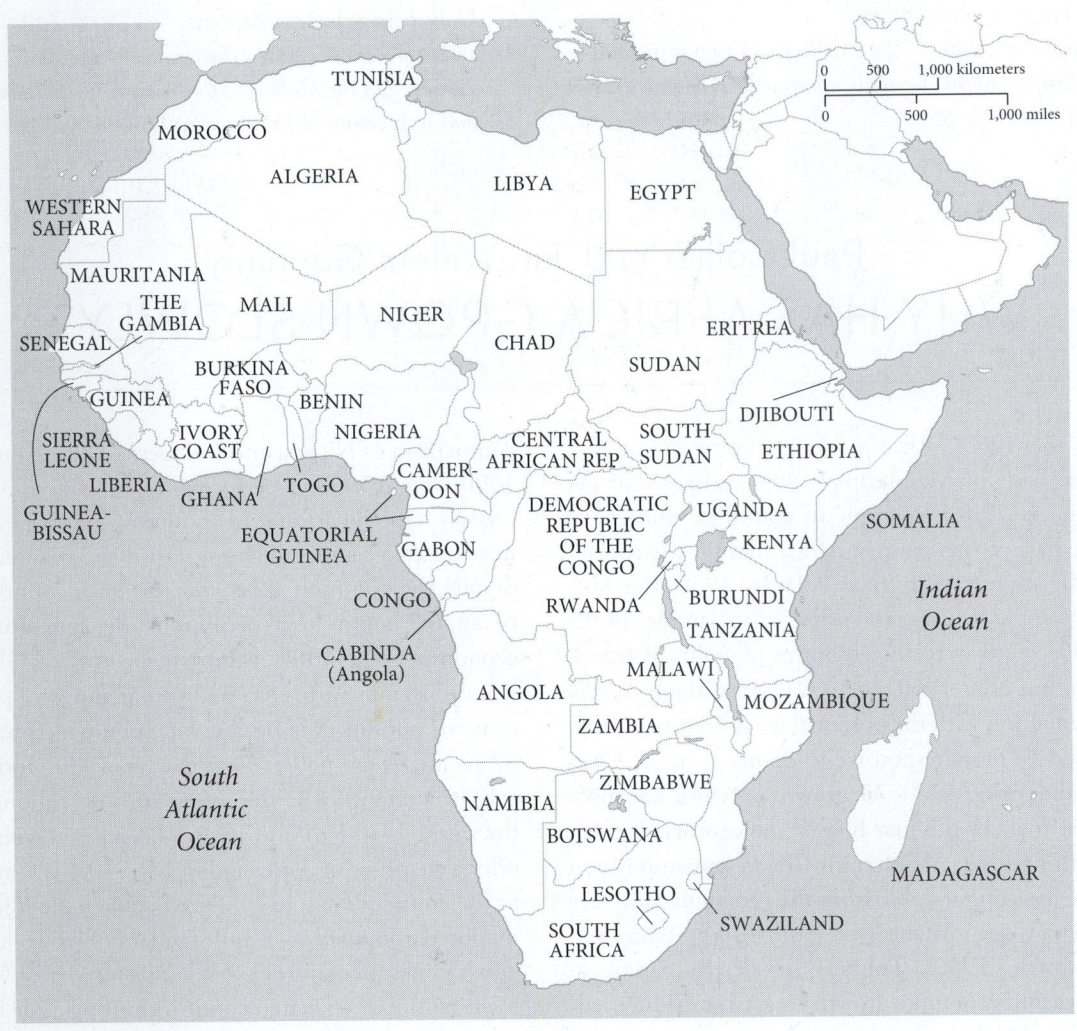

domestic and external factors. Table 10.3 compares Africa to other developing regions, using this grouping. Until recently it has largely been accepted that the main causes of Africa's slow growth were external, with the debate focusing upon whether external problems were policy-induced or exogenous. Especially during the 1980s, the World Bank, the International Monetary Fund and bilateral donors came to identify exchange rate and trade policies as the primary causes of slow growth in Africa. Table 10.3 offers some evidence that official exchange rates in sub-Saharan Africa have been more overvalued relative to (often illegal) market rates than is common for other less developed economies of Asia and Latin America. Tariffs and quantitative trade restrictions have also been higher in Africa than elsewhere. The rival thesis, often favored by African governments, was that the crisis was due to deteriorating and volatile terms of trade, and as Table 10.3 shows, terms of trade have indeed been more volatile for Africa than for other less developed economies. Jeffrey Sachs and his co-authors have emphasized a further

Table 10.2 The Economies of Sub-Saharan Africa

Country	Population (Millions) 1997	GDP US$m at 1990 Prices 1997	GNP per Capita (PPP $) 1997	GNP Average Annual % Growth Per Capita 1965–97	Life Expectancy at Birth (Years) 1995	% of Population below $1 a Day (Early 1990s)	Trade as % of GDP (in PPP) 1997
Angola	11.6	9,886	728	. . .	48	. . .	77
Benin	5.7	2,540	1,240		48	. . .	17
Botswana	1.5	4,458	7,440	7.7	66	33	. . .
Burkina Faso	11.1	3,643	936	0.9	47		7
Burundi	6.4	939	661	1.1	51	. . .	5
Cameroon	13.9	11,254	1,739	1.4	57	. . .	13
Cape Verde	0.4	393	. . .	. . .	66		. . .
Central African Republic	3.4	1,420	1,254	–1.2	50	. . .	10
Chad	6.7	1,492	978	0.1	49	. . .	4
Comoros	0.7	251	. . .	. . .	57	. . .	. . .
Congo	2.7	2,433	1,275	1.7	53	. . .	80
Congo, Dem. Rep.	48.0	6,094	698	–3.7	. . .	. . .	7
Côte d'Ivoire	14.3	13,320	1,676	–0.9	50	18	30
Djibouti	0.4	384	. . .		49	. . .	. . .
Equatorial Guinea	0.4	541	. . .	. . .	49	. . .	. . .
Eritrea	3.4	1,010	990	. . .	52	. . .	. . .
Ethiopia	60.1	11,327	493	–0.5	49	46	7
Gabon	1.1	7,280	6,480	0.4	55	. . .	58
Gambia	1.0	332	1,372	0.5	46	. . .	30
Ghana	18.3	7,892	1,492	–0.9	57	. . .	19
Guinea	7.6	3,699	1,763	. . .	46	26	14
Guinea-Bissau	1.1	306	1,041	0.1	45	88	13

(Continued)

Table 10.2 The Economies of Sub-Saharan Africa (Continued)

Country	Population (Millions) 1997	GDP US$m at 1990 Prices 1997	GNP per Capita (PPP $) 1997	GNP Average Annual % Growth Per Capita 1965–97	Life Expectancy at Birth (Years) 1995	% of Population below $1 a Day (Early 1990s)	Trade as % of GDP (in PPP) 1997
Kenya	28.4	9,879	1,150	1.3	55	50	16
Lesotho	2.1	998	2,422	3.2	62	49	...
Liberia	2.5	...	...	...	57	...	...
Madagascar	15.8	3,187	892	–1.9	58	72	11
Malawi	10.1	2,480	688	0.5	45	...	21
Mali	11.5	3,132	715	0.5	47	...	19
Mauritania	2.4	1,346	1,654	–0.2	53	31	28
Mauritius	1.1	3,755	9,147	3.8	71	...	37
Mozambique	18.3	2,144	541	–0.1	47	...	15
Namibia	1.6	3,141	4,999	0.7	60	...	...
Niger	9.8	2,776	824	–2.5	48	62	9
Nigeria	118.4	34,418	854	0.0	51	31	23
Rwanda	5.9	1,979	643	0.1	47	46	9
São Tomé & Principe	0.1	56	...	...	...	...	...
Senegal	8.8	6,708	1,670	–0.5	50	54	11
Seychelles	0.1	435	...	...	...	...	...
Sierra Leone	4.4	...	401	–1.4	40	...	24
Somalia	10.4	...	...	...	48	...	...
South Africa	43.3	117,089	7,152	0.1	64	24	23
Sudan	27.9	13,119	...	–0.2	54	...	...
Swaziland	0.9	1,031	...	...	59	...	...
Tanzania	31.5	4,956	608	...	52	11	14
Togo	4.3	1,726	1,408	–0.6	56	...	24
Uganda	20.8	6,822	1,131	...	44	69	6
Zambia	8.5	3,564	900	–2.0	48	85	26
Zimbabwe	11.7	7,904	2,207	0.5	52	41	21

Sources: *African Development Report* (1998); and *World Development Indicators* (1999).

Table 10.3 Africa Compared with Other Developing Regions

(figures are unweighted country averages)	Sub-Saharan Africa	Other LDCs
Domestic-Destiny		
Life expectancy in 1970 (years)	45.2	57.3
Income in 1960 (1985 $ PPP-adjusted)	835.5	1855.2
Ethnic Fractionalization	67.6	32.7
Domestic-Policy		
Political Rights, 1973–90	6.0	4.0
Bureaucracy	1.38	1.72
External-Destiny		
Population <100 km from the sea or river (%)	21.0	52.0
Terms of trade volatility	16.4	12.8
External-Policy		
Parallel market exchange rate premium	40.0	26.0
Average tariffs 1996–98 (%)	21.0	13.0
Quantitative Restrictions, 1988–90 (%)	46.0	21.0
Endogenous		
Growth of GDP per capita, 1965–90	0.5	1.7
Investment rate in 1997 (%)	18.0	25.0
Population growth rate, 1980–97 (%)	2.8	1.8
Capital flight/private wealth, 1990 (%)	39.0	14.0

Sources: Life expectancy, *World Development Indicators* (1998). Income and growth: Penn World Tables 5.6. The index of ethno-linguistic diversity is on the scale 0–100 with 0 being homogenous (Mauro, 1995). The Gastil index of political rights is on the range 1–7 with 1 being fully democratic.

The index of bureaucracy is on the scale 0–6 with high score indicating better quality (Knack and Keefer, 1995). Population living less than 100 km from the sea or a navigable river, from Bloom and Sachs (1998), Table 2 (other LDCs is the weighted average for Asia and Latin America). Terms of trade volatility is the standard deviation of annual log changes 1965–92, (Collins and Bosworth, 1996). Parallel exchange rate premium (%), (Easterly and Levine, 1997).

Average tariff: simple average, computed by IMF, we would like to thank Robert Sharer for these numbers. QRs: weighted average incidence of non-tariff measures over product lines; other LDCs is simple average of Latin America and East Asia; from Rodrik (1999, Table 12).

Investment rate and population growth rate, *World Development Indicators* (1999). Capital flight/private wealth as of 1990 (Collier and Pattillo, 1999).

adverse external "destiny" factor: Africa's population is atypically landlocked. As shown in Table 10.3, a high proportion of the population is remote from the coast or navigable waters.

Recently, attention has shifted to possible domestic causes of slow growth within African nations, but the debate as to the relative importance of policy-induced and exogenous problems has continued. Sachs and his co-authors have attributed slow growth to "the curse of the tropics." Africa's adverse climate causes poor health, and so reduces life expectancy below that in other regions, which puts it at a disadvantage in development. The adverse climate also leads to leached soils and unreliable rainfall, which constrains African agriculture. African nations also appear to have more ethnic diversity than other poor nations of the world, which may make it harder to develop an interconnected economy. In contrast to the domestic destiny argument, Collier and Gunning (1999) have emphasized domestic policy factors such as poor public service delivery. African governments have typically been less democratic and more bureaucratic than their Asian and Latin American counterparts.

Of course, once the conditions for slow growth are established by any combination of these reasons, they can become self-reinforcing in an endogenous process. Weak economic growth helps explain a lower saving rate and a higher proportion of flight capital for Africa compared to the less developed nations of Asia and Africa. Richer countries tend to see their population growth rates drop off, so the poverty of Africa has helped to keep its birth rates high, even as compared to the world's other less developed economies. Similarly, poverty may have increased the incidence of Africa's numerous civil wars, as well as being a consequence of them.

In the discussion that follows, we assess the policy/destiny and domestic/external distinctions in various combinations. During the mid-1990s, African performance started to improve, with a few countries growing quite rapidly. We conclude by assessing these different explanations as guides to whether this improvement is likely to be transient or persistent.

Four Types of Explanation
Domestic-Destiny

Africa has several geographic and demographic characteristics which may predispose it to slow growth. First, much of the continent is tropical and this may handicap the economy, partly due to diseases such as malaria and partly due to hostile conditions for livestock and agriculture. Life expectancy has historically been low, with the population in a high-fertility, high-infant-mortality equilibrium. With the advent of basic public health measures, population growth became very high. In particular, Africa has not been through the demographic transition whereby fertility rates decline which occurred in Asia and Latin America over the past 40 years. On one estimate, Africa's low life expectancy and high population growth account for almost all of Africa's slow growth (Bloom and Sachs, 1998). The argument is not clear-cut, however. Low life expectancy and high fertility are consequences of low income as well as causes, so the estimates are likely to be biased upwards. The household-level evidence suggests that the effects of poor health on income are small, although these in turn will be biased downwards by the omission of large-scale changes in economic activity which cannot be detected at the household level.

Whether or not Africa's past demographic characteristics have contributed to its slow growth, some African countries seem certain to go through a distinctive and disastrous demographic transition during the next two decades. As a result of AIDS, adult mortality rates will rise dramatically. In Africa, AIDS is a heterosexual disease. During the 1980s in parts of Africa it spread rapidly across the population before the risks became apparent, with up to 20–25 percent of adults now HIV-positive in some countries (World Bank, 1997). This human tragedy will have substantial economic effects during the next decade, especially since infection rates appear to be higher among the more educated, but it does not account for historically slow growth.

A second key characteristic of Africa which may predispose it to slow growth is that soil quality is poor and much of the continent is semi-arid, with rainfall subject to long cycles and unpredictable failure. Soils derive disproportionately from a very old type of rock ("Basement Complex"), which is low in micronutrients and varies considerably between localities. The application of additional macronutrients, which is the fertilizer package associated with the Green Revolution, is generally ineffective with low levels of micronutrients. Africa probably has scope for its own agricultural revolution, but it will depend upon locality-specific packages of micronutrients (Voortman et al., 1999). Since the 1960s, the semi-arid areas of Africa have been in a phase of declining rainfall (Grove, 1991). While there are no estimates of the output consequences of this decline, it may be significant, since agriculture is typically about one-quarter of GDP in this region. Given the lack of irrigation, the unpredictability of rainfall implies high risks in agriculture. With incomplete insurance and a high rate of time preference, households have to use assets for purposes of consumption-smoothing rather than investment. Households can thus become trapped in low-income, high-liquidity equilibria (Dercon, 1997).

A third relevant characteristic of Africa's economies, which can be seen as a result of these semi-arid conditions, is that the continent has very low population density. One by-product is high costs of transport which in turn have added to risk: poor market integration has hampered the use of trade for risk sharing. Another consequence of low population density is that Africa has relatively high natural resource endowments per capita (Wood and Mayer, 1998). High levels of natural resources can cause several problems. High levels of exported natural resources may lead to an appreciation of the exchange rate, which in turn makes manufacturing less competitive. Yet manufacturing may offer larger growth externalities, such as learning, than natural resource extraction. Natural resources may also increase "loot-seeking" activities. Collier and Hoeffler (1998) find that a dependence on natural resources strongly increases the risk of civil war, which has been a widespread phenomenon in Africa.

A further consequence of low population density is that African countries have much higher ethnolinguistic diversity than other regions; when groups come together less, there is less mingling and merging. Easterly and Levine (1997) find that this high level of diversity is the most important single cause of Africa's slow growth. There are various interpretations of this result. A common perception is that Africa's high ethnic diversity accounts for its high incidence of civil war. This turns out to be false: high levels of ethnic and religious diversity actually make societies significantly safer (Collier and Hoeffler, 1999). The effects of ethnic diversity on growth turn out to be contingent upon the political system; diversity has deleterious effects only when it occurs in the context of governments which are undemocratic. Collier (1999) finds that in democratic societies, ethnic diversity has no effect on either growth or the quality of public projects, but that in dictatorships, high levels of diversity reduce growth rates by 3 percentage points and double the rate of project failure relative to homogeneity. Dictatorships tend not to transcend the ethnic group of the dictator, so that the more ethnically fragmented the society, the more narrowly based a dictatorship will be, whereas democratic governments in such societies must be ethnically cross-cutting. In turn, the more narrowly based the government, the greater the payoff to predation relative to the inducement of generalized growth. Africa's problem was thus not its ethnic diversity but its lack of democracy in the context of diversity.

A fourth characteristic of Africa that may hinder its growth prospects is that because of its colonial heritage, Africa has much smaller countries in terms of population than other regions. Sub-Saharan Africa has a population about half that of India, divided into 48 states. These many states, combined with low levels of income, make Africa's national economies radically smaller than those of other regions. Very small states might be economically disadvantaged for several reasons. If government has some fixed costs, either in its administrative role or as a provider of services, then it may be hard for a small state to perform at minimum cost. Moreover, the society may forfeit much more extensive scale economies if it combines small scale with isolation. Some domestic markets will be too small even for the minimum efficient scale of production of a single producer; all domestic markets taken alone will be less competitive than in larger economies. Small economies are also perceived by investors as significantly more risky (Collier and Dollar, 1999b). Finally, they may have a slower rate of technological innovation; Kremer (1993) argues the incidence of discoveries may be broadly proportional to the population, so that if discoveries cannot readily spread between societies, low-population societies will have less innovation. However, in aggregate these effects cannot be large, because growth regressions generally find that state size does not affect a nation's rate of economic growth.

Domestic-Policy

For much of the post-colonial period, most African governments have been undemocratic. The median African government during the 1970s and 1980s was close to autocracy, and far less democratic than the median non-African developing country (as measured by the Gastil scale of political rights shown in Table 10.3). A typical pattern was that governments were captured by the educated, urban-resident population, with few agricultural or commercial interests. They expanded the public sector while imposing wide-ranging controls on private activity. These choices have been economically costly.

Public employment was expanded, often as an end in itself. For example, in Ghana by the late 1970s the public sector accounted for three-quarters of formal wage employment (Ghana Central Bureau of Statistics, 1988), and even in a more market-oriented economy like Kenya, the figure was 50 percent as of 1990 (Kenya Central Bureau of Statistics, 1996). Indeed, economic decline may have increased pressure for public sector employment. The large number of public sector employees

was reconciled with limited tax revenue by reducing wage rates and non-wage expenditures. The ratio of wage to non-wage expenditures in African governments is double that in Asia, and this has lowered the quality of public services; for example, in education, teaching materials are often lacking. The large, ill-paid public sector became the arena in which ethnic groups struggled for resources. For example, in the Ghanaian public sector, the locally dominant ethnic group received a wage premium of 25 percent over other groups after controlling for worker characteristics, and cognitive skills were completely unrewarded (Collier and Garg, 1999). The combination of low wage levels and payment structures, which rewarded social connections rather than skill, made it difficult for managers to motivate staff, and the difficulties of service delivery were compounded by the low ratio of non-wage to wage expenditures.

Since public sector employment was the main priority, managers were not under severe pressure for actual delivery of services from their political masters. Because of the lack of democracy, neither were they accountable to the broader public. As a result, Africa experienced a paradox of poor public services despite relatively high public expenditure (Pradhan, 1996). Poor service delivery handicapped firms through unreliable transport and power, inadequate telecommunications networks, and unreliable courts. For example, manufacturing firms in Zimbabwe need to hold high levels of inventories, despite high interest rates, due to unreliable delivery of inputs tied to poor transportation infrastructure (Fafchamps et al., 1998). A survey of Ugandan firms found that shortage of electricity was identified as the single most important constraint upon firm growth; indeed, the provision of electricity by firms for their own use was almost as large as the public supply of electricity (Reinikka and Svensson, 1998). A study in Nigeria found that their own generators accounted for three-quarters of the capital equipment of small manufacturers (Lee and Anas, 1991). The poor state of African telecommunications was estimated to reduce African growth rates by 1 percentage point, according to Easterly and Levine (1997). (However, since telecommunications was the main infrastructure variable which they could quantify, and since lack of different kinds of infrastructure is probably highly correlated, their estimate is probably a proxy for a wider range of infrastructural deficiencies.) African commercial courts are more corrupt than those in other regions (Widner, 1999). As a result, firms face greater problems of contract enforcement. Some firms can overcome these by relying upon their social networks to screen potential clients, but it is common to restrict business to long-standing clients (Bigsten et al., 1999). Ethnic minorities, such as Asians in East Africa and Lebanese in West Africa, tend to have more specialized social networks and so are better able than African firms to screen new clients (Biggs et al., 1996). The problem of contract enforcement thus makes markets less competitive and reduces the potential gains from trade, while tending to perpetuate the dominant position of minorities in business.

Poor public service delivery also handicapped households through inefficient education, health and extension services. A survey of primary education expenditures in Uganda found that, of the non-wage money released by the Ministry of Finance, on average, less than 30 percent actually reached the schools (Ablo and Reinikka, 1998). The expansion of the public sector has reduced private initiative. Since major areas of economic activity were reserved for the public sector—often including transport, marketing and banking—and African elites looked to the public sector rather than the private sector for advancement, Africa was slow to develop indigenous entrepreneurs.

African governments built various economic control regimes. A few nations, such as Ethiopia, Angola and Tanzania, had wide-ranging price controls under which private agents had an incentive to reduce production—at least officially marketed production. These governments often attempted to counterbalance these incentives with coercive production targets, but the net effect was usually dramatic declines in economic activity. More commonly, firms were subject to considerable regulation. For example, for many years manufacturing firms wishing to set up in Kenya had to acquire letters of no objection from existing producers, which resulted in a predictably low level of competition. In Uganda, when the government removed the requirement that coffee could only be transported by rail, the market for road haulage expanded sufficiently to induce new entry, which in turn broke an existing cartel, nearly halving haulage rates. Similarly, in Tanzania during the long period when agricultural marketing was heavily regulated, marketing margins for grain were double what they were both before regulation and after deregulation (Bevan et al., 1993). In this period, food prices became much more volatile: between 1964 and 1980 the coefficient of variation (that is, the ratio of the standard deviation to the mean) of maize prices at regional centers doubled, falling again sharply when markets were liberalized.

Government interventions undermined the functioning of product markets in many countries. Private trading, which was often associated with ethnic minorities such as the Indians in East Africa and the Lebanese in West Africa, was sometimes banned. A particularly damaging intervention, practiced even in relatively market-friendly economies such as Kenya, was to ban private inter-district trade in food. Where government marketing monopolies were focused on ensuring the food supply to urban areas, this provision discouraged farmers from specializing in non-food export crops, since they could not rely on being able to buy food locally.

Since the political base of governments was urban, agriculture was heavily taxed and the public agronomic research needed to promote an African green revolution, based on locally specific packages of micronutrients, was neglected. The main source of agricultural growth has been the gradual adoption of cash crops by smallholders, a process slowed down by government pricing policies (Bevan et al., 1993). While governments favored manufacturing, the basis for industrial growth in this area was also undermined, since trade and exchange rate policies induced industrial firms to produce under uncompetitive conditions and only for small and captive domestic markets.

The same urban bias initially led governments to favor the urban wage labor force. In the immediate post-colonial period, minimum wages rose and unions acquired influence, so that wages increased substantially. However, post-independence inflation has usually eroded minimum wages, so that in most of Africa wage rigidities in the labor market are not currently a significant impediment to the growth process. The exceptions are South Africa, where the labor market may just be going through such a real wage adjustment now, and the low inflation environments of Ethiopia and the countries in the "franc zone," the 13 former colonies of France in west and central Africa which had currencies pegged to the French franc. While high wage levels are not normally a hindrance to African economies, the job matching process appears to be inefficient, so that job mobility offers unusually high returns (Mengistae, 1998). This is an instance of the high costs of market information; for example, newspapers are expensive and have low circulation.

Financial markets were heavily regulated, with bank lending directed to the government, public enterprises or "strategic" sectors, very limited financial intermediation and virtually no competition between financial institutions. A common proxy for the extent of financial intermediation, known as "financial depth," is the broad money supply, M2, relative to GDP. But although Africa has even less financial depth than other developing areas, currently available evidence suggests that this may have had only a modest impact on its growth. For example, Easterly and Levine (1997) estimate that lack of financial depth reduced the annual growth rate by only 0.3 percentage points. Similarly, microeconomic survey evidence on manufacturing firms indicates that the lack of external finance is not currently the binding constraint on industrial investment (Bigsten et al., 1999).

External-Destiny

Africa is better located than Asia for most developed economy markets. However, most Africans live much farther from the coast or navigable rivers than in other regions and so face intrinsically higher transport costs for exports (as shown in Table 10.3). Further, much of the population lives in countries which are landlocked, so that problems of distance are compounded by political barriers. Even a relatively open border like the one between Canada and the United States appears to be a substantial impediment to trade, in the sense that trade across Canadian provinces or across the United States is far greater than trade of equal distance between Canada and the United States (McCallum, 1995). Landlocked countries face national borders on all sides, which may constitute an irreducible barrier to trade even if they have good relations with their neighbors. Typically, growth regressions find that being landlocked reduces a nation's annual growth rate by around half of 1 percent.

A further aspect of external destiny is that Africa's exports are concentrated in a narrow range of commodities, with volatile prices that have declined since the 1960s. The deterioration in the terms of trade for such commodities has undoubtedly contributed to Africa's growth slowdown. However, there is controversy over whether its atypical exposure to terms of trade volatility has been damaging. Deaton and Miller (1996) find little evidence of detrimental effects in the short run. However, case study evidence suggests that shocks have often had longer-run deleterious effects. Investment has been concertinaed into short periods, during which construction booms have raised the unit cost of capital, and government budgets have been destabilized, with spending rising during booms but being difficult to reduce subsequently (Collier and Gunning, 1999b; Schuknecht, 1999).

Africa has attracted much more aid per capita than other regions. Donor allocation rules have typically favored countries which have small populations and low incomes, and were recent colonies—and African countries met all three criteria. There has been a long debate as to whether aid has been detrimental or beneficial for the growth process (for recent overviews, see Gwin and Nelson, 1997; World Bank, 1998). Early critics claimed that aid reduced the incentive for good governance (for example, Bauer, 1982). Since the 1980s, the World Bank and the International Monetary Fund have attempted to make policy improvement a condition for the receipt of aid. Econometric work does not find that aid has had a significant effect on policy: to the extent that aid encourages or discourages policy changes, the two effects apparently offset each other. However, the effect of aid on growth has been shown to be policy-dependent. Where policies are good, aid substantially raises growth rates; where they are poor, diminishing returns rapidly set in so that aid cannot significantly contribute to growth. This result holds whether the measure of policy is objective indicators of the fiscal and exchange rate stance (Burnside and Dollar, 1997), or subjective but standardized ratings of a broader range of policies done by the World Bank (Collier and Dollar, 1999a). Until recently, many African policy environments were not good enough for aid to raise growth substantially. Hence, the evidence does not support Bauer's (1982) claim that Africa's large aid receipts were a cause of its slow growth, but does suggest that Africa largely missed the opportunity for enhanced growth which aid provided.

Excluding South Africa and the oil exporters (whose terms of trade have improved), the net aid inflows since 1970 have been around 50 percent greater than the income losses from terms of trade deterioration. The combination was thus somewhat analogous to an increase in export taxation: the terms of trade losses taking money from exporters, while the aid provided money to governments.

External-Policy

In recent decades, African governments adopted exchange rate and trade policies which were atypically anti-export and accumulated large foreign debts. On a range of indicators, Africa has had much higher trade barriers and more misaligned exchange rates than other regions (Dollar, 1992; Sachs and Warner, 1997). Exchange rates were commonly highly overvalued, reflecting the interest of the political elite in cheap imports. Tariffs and export taxes were higher in Africa than in other regions of the world, partly because of the lack of other sources of tax revenue to finance the expansion of the public sector. Exports were sharply reduced as a result of export crop taxation. For example, Dercon (1993) shows that Tanzanian cotton exports would have been 50 percent higher in the absence of taxation. Quantitative restrictions on imports were also used much more extensively, despite yielding no revenue. They often arose because of the difficulties of fine-tuning import demand in a situation where government was attempting to keep exchange rates fixed with few reserves. They probably persisted because they generated large opportunities for corruption, since someone could often be bribed to circumvent the quantitative limits.

The international growth literature has reached a consensus that exchange rate overvaluation and tight trade restrictions are damaging, but controversy continues over the effects of more moderate trade restrictions (Rodrik, 1999). However, there are reasons why Africa's poor export performance may have been particularly damaging. Since 1980, African export revenue per capita has sharply declined, which in turn has induced severe import compression of both capital goods and intermediate inputs. Moreover, because African economies are so much smaller than other economies, external barriers of a given height have been significantly more damaging (Collier and Gunning, 1999).

By the 1990s, several African economies had accumulated unsustainable international debts, largely from public agencies. Clearly, this is one way in which poor decisions of the past become embedded in the present. There is a good theoretical argument that high indebtedness discourages private investment due to the fear of the future tax liability. There is some supporting evidence for this claim, although since poor policies lower GDP, using high debt/GDP as an explanatory variable may simply be a proxy for poor policies more broadly (Elbadawi et al., 1997).

Policy or Destiny?

The dichotomy between policy and destiny is of course an oversimplification: some apparently exogenous features of Africa have often been induced by policy, and conversely, African policies may reflect exogenous factors.

Consider, first, some of the "exogenous" factors that we have discussed under destiny. For example, the claim by Sachs and Warner (1997) that geography and demography almost fully account for Africa's slow growth rests largely upon the lack of a demographic transition to lower fertility rates in Africa, as has happened in most of Latin America and Asia. However, it is more plausible to regard these continuing high fertility rates as a consequence of slow growth than a cause. The lack of employment opportunities for young women has prevented the opportunity cost of children from rising, and the low returns to education in an environment where many of the "good" jobs are allocated by political criteria have reduced the incentive for parents to educate their children.

Similarly, the argument that the concentration of Africa's population in the interior is an external force holding down growth can also be seen as an endogenous outcome; specifically, the population has remained in the interior because of the failure of Africa's coastal cities to grow. In turn, this is partly because the failure to industrialize has slowed urbanization, and partly because policy has often been biased against coastal cities; for example, in both Nigeria and Tanzania the capital was relocated from the coast to the interior. Where policy was less biased, as in the Côte d'Ivoire during the 1970s, the coastal population grew so rapidly that it supported massive emigration from the landlocked economy of Burkina Faso: at its peak, around 40 percent of the Ivorien population were immigrants.

Further, being landlocked need not be an economic disadvantage. Developed landlocked economies, such as Switzerland, have atypically low international transport costs because they have oriented their trade towards their neighbors. By contrast, Africa's landlocked economies trade with Europe, so that neighboring countries are an obstacle rather than a market. These patterns of trade are partly a legacy of the colonial economy, but they also reflect the high trade barriers within Africa erected by postindependence governments, and the slow rate of growth. Ultimately, landlocked economies were faced with neighboring markets that were both inaccessible and unattractive, which did not make it desirable to reorient the economy to trade with them. Finally, Africa's continued export concentration in a narrow range of primary commodities, which we discussed earlier as reflecting the destiny of resource endowments, probably also reflects a number of public policy decisions. Other export activities have been handicapped either directly through overvalued exchange rates, or indirectly, through high transactions costs. Poor policy has given Africa a comparative disadvantage in "transaction-intensive" activities such as manufacturing.

Now consider the reverse situation; that is, how some of the dysfunctional policies that we have discussed can also be considered the outcome of exogenous forces. The anti-export policies which we argue hindered growth can be viewed as a consequence of the fact that most of the population lives far from the coast (Gallup and Sachs, 1999). In such societies, it might be argued that the elasticity of growth with respect to openness is lower and so the incentive for openness is reduced. However, at present Africa offers little evidence for this hypothesis. According to the World Bank's standardized ratings of policy (currently confidential), all five of the worst-rated countries on the continent are coastal whereas many of the best-rated countries are landlocked. As another example, it is possible that restrictive import policies are adopted, at least initially, in response to trade shocks like those created by an external dependence on commodity exports

(Collier and Gunning, 1999b). The prevalence of natural resources may bring forth a variety of other policy errors, as well. For example, it may worsen policy by turning politics into a contest for rents or, through crowding out manufactured exports, prevent the emergence of potentially the most potent lobby for openness.

Along with being endogenous to fixed effects like geography, policies are also affected by experience. Societies which have experienced high levels of economic risk may place a higher priority on income-sharing arrangements such as expanded opportunities of public employment, rather than focusing on income generation. Societies also learn from past failure. The African nations which have recently implemented the strongest economic reforms, such as Ghana and Uganda, tended to be those which had earlier experienced the worst economic crises. However, African countries facing the challenge of reversing economic failure have lacked significant role models within the continent. In east Asia, Hong Kong, Singapore, Taiwan and Korea provided early role models, as did Chile since the late 1970s in Latin America. Within-continent models may be important because the information is both closer to hand and more evidently pertinent. Once Africa develops examples of success, the scope for societal learning across the continent will make it unlikely that Africa is "destined" to poor policies by its geography: although its geographic characteristics may have given it some weak tendencies towards poor policies in the initial post-independence period.

Sorting out the policy effects from the destiny effects is a difficult econometric problem. In the ordinary least squares regressions common in the analysis of African growth, the dependent variable is typically the average growth rate over a long period, and a variety of policy and destiny variables enter as the explanatory variables. Depending upon the specification, either policy or destiny can appear important.

An alternative approach is to consider the extent to which African slow growth has been persistent, to take advantage of the insight that policies have varied, whereas destiny-like geographic disadvantages remain constant over time. Along these lines, Diamond (1998) provides a convincing explanation from a historical perspective of why geographic reasons, such as the north-south axis of the continent, caused African agriculture to develop only slowly prior to European colonization, due to a combination of technological isolation and small scale. However, since colonization gradually relaxed some of these constraints (while introducing others), pre–20th century experience is of limited pertinence for explaining patterns of growth in the last few decades.

More recent experience tends to argue that destiny plays less of a role than policy. After all, the economies of Africa did grow relatively quickly through the first half of the 20th century, and up until the early 1970s, which tends to argue that they were not obviously destined for lower growth. The arrival of slow economic growth in the 1970s coincides with a phase in which African economic policy became both statist and biased against exports. Moreover, the main exception to African economic collapse, Botswana, experienced the most rapid growth in the world despite the seeming exogenous disadvantages of being landlocked and having very low population density.

The most sophisticated econometric test of whether something about Africa seems intrinsically connected to slow growth is the study by Hoeffler (1999). She searches for a continental fixed effect using panel regressions of five-year periods over 1965–90. She first estimates a simple growth model in which the explanatory variables are initial income, investment, population growth, and schooling. She then uses the coefficients on these variables to compute the residuals, and regresses the residuals on regional dummies. The Africa dummy is small and insignificant; that is, there is no continental fixed effect to explain. However, she does find that both being landlocked and being tropical significantly reduce growth, and these are indeed locational characteristics of much of Africa. Between them they would reduce the African growth rate by around

0.4 percentage points relative to that of other developing regions.

Whereas in the distant past the economies of Africa may well have been intrinsically disadvantaged by factors like less easy access to water transportation or the geography of the continent, the thesis that this has persisted into recent decades is less plausible. Remember that by 1950 Africa had a higher per capita income than south Asia and its subsequent performance was indistinguishable from that region until the mid-1970s. Coastal Africa is not intrinsically markedly worse-endowed in any geographical sense than much of coastal Asia or Brazil, although its soil types pose distinct challenges for agronomic research.

By contrast, it is easy to point to policies which until very recently have been dysfunctional. Even as of 1998, Africa had the worst policy environment in the world according to the World Bank ratings. Microeconomic evidence shows how these policies damaged the growth of firms. Poor infrastructure, poor contract enforcement and volatile policies all make the supply of inputs unreliable. Firms have responded to this risky environment partly by reducing risks: they hold large inventories, invest in electricity generators, and restrict their business relations to known enterprises. They have also responded by reducing investment. A striking implication is the conjunction of a high marginal return on capital and a very low rate of investment, even for firms that are not liquidity constrained. In Africa, the elasticity of investment with respect to profits may be as low as 0.07 (Bigsten et al., 1999). Some of the effects of poor policy are highly persistent. Most notably, the colonial governments of Africa provided little education, especially at the secondary level. Although independent governments rapidly changed these priorities, for the past 30 years Africa has had a markedly lower stock of human capital than other continents. The rapid growth in education has, however, gradually narrowed the gap with other regions.

Even if one disagrees with this view that policy is more important in explaining Africa's slow rate of growth and finds the "destiny" explanations more persuasive, this by no means condemns Africa to growing more slowly than other regions. Some of the economic disadvantages of being tropical may be overcome, for example, by the discovery of vaccines or new strains of crops. Moreover, Africa has two potential growth advantages over other regions which should offset against any locational disadvantage. It has lower per capita income and so could benefit from a convergence effect with richer countries, and it has higher aid inflows and so could benefit from aid-induced growth. If public policies were as good as in other regions, aid and convergence should enable even those countries which are land-locked and tropical to grow more rapidly than other developing regions for several decades. Although the growth regressions would imply that in the long term such countries would converge on a lower steady-state income than more favorably located countries, even this is doubtful. If the coastal African nations grew, then being landlocked would cease to be disadvantageous, since the gains from trading with close neighbors would expand.

Domestic or External?

Until recently, there was broad agreement that Africa's problems were predominantly associated with its external relations, although some analysts emphasized the policy-induced lack of openness and markets, while others attributed poor performance to over-dependence on a few commodities, the prices of which were declining and volatile. In our view, the argument that Africa's poor performance originates in its overdependence on commodities has looked weaker in recent years: Africa has lost global market share in its major exports, often spectacularly. The focus of the discussion has consequently shifted to underlying reasons for poor domestic performance, and in turn to domestic factors. The domestic factors, as we have argued, can be divided into those that smack of destiny, like the fact that much of Africa has a tropical climate, and those that are related to policy. Indeed, we believe that domestic policies largely unrelated to trade may now be the main obstacles to growth in much of Africa.

To illustrate our argument, we focus on Africa's failure to industrialize. It might appear that Africa is intrinsically uncompetitive in manufactures because its high natural resource endowments give it a comparative advantage in that area (Wood and Mayer, 1998). But while Africa may have a comparative advantage in natural resources in the long run, at present African wages are often so low that were African manufacturing to have similar levels of productivity to other regions, it would be competitive. Hence, it is low productivity which needs to be explained.

African manufacturing has been in a low-productivity trap. Because African firms are oriented to small domestic markets, they are not able to exploit economies of scale, nor are they exposed to significant competition, and their technology gap with the rest of the world is unusually wide—yielding large opportunities for learning. This suggests that African manufacturing might have atypically large potential to raise productivity through exporting. However, most African firms fail to step onto this productivity escalator. This is because they face high costs for other reasons. As discussed already, transactions costs are unusually high. With transport unreliable, firms typically need to carry very large stocks of inputs to maintain continuity of production, despite higher interest rates than elsewhere. Telecommunications are much worse than other regions. Malfunctioning of the courts makes contract enforcement unreliable, so that firms are reluctant to enter into deals with new partners, in turn making markets less competitive.

These high transactions costs have a relatively large impact on manufacturing. Compared with natural resource extraction, manufacturing tends to have a high share of intermediate inputs and a low share of value-added to final price. Consequently, transactions costs tend to be much larger relative to value-added. Africa's intrinsic comparative advantage in natural resource exports may thus have been reinforced by public policies which have made manufacturing uncompetitive relative to resource extraction. African policies may have given the region a comparative disadvantage in transactions-intensive activities.

Conclusion: Will Africa Grow?

During the mid-1990s, average African growth accelerated and performance became more dispersed. A few countries such as Uganda, Côte d'Ivoire, Ethiopia and Mozambique started to grow very fast, whereas others such as the Democratic Republic of the Congo and Sierra Leone descended into social disorder. "Africa" became less meaningful as a category. Both the improvement in the average performance and the greater dispersion among countries were consistent with what had happened to policy. During the 1990s many of the most egregious exchange rate, fiscal and trade policies were improved. By 1998, although Africa still ranked as the region with the worst policies on the World Bank ratings, it was also the region with by far the greatest policy dispersion.

However, the faster growth coincided not only with better policies but with improvements in the terms of trade. Further, investment in Africa as a share of GDP is currently only 18 percent. This is much lower than other regions: for example, 23 percent in South Asia and 29 percent on average in lower middle-income countries. Even these figures may understate Africa's true investment shortfall. Capital goods are more expensive in Africa than the international average, so that once the investment share is recalculated at international relative prices it approximately halves. Although it is not possible to disaggregate investment into its public and private components with complete accuracy, estimates suggest that the shortfall in African investment is due to low private investment. Thus, growth may be unsustainable unless there is a substantial increase in private investment.

On an optimistic interpretation of the evidence, Africa's slow growth from the early 1970s into the 1990s has been due to policies which reduced its openness to foreign trade. Since these policies have largely been reversed during the last decade, if this is correct then Africa should be well-placed for continued growth.

The pessimistic interpretation is that Africa's problems are intrinsic, often rooted in geography. This view implies that economic progress in Africa will be dependent upon international efforts to make its environment more favorable, such as research to eradicate tropical diseases, and finance to create transport arteries from the coast to the interior. The thesis that Africa's economic problems are caused by ethno-linguistic fractionalization has similarly intractable implications.

Our own interpretation lies between these extremes. We suggest that while the binding constraint upon Africa's growth may have been externally-oriented policies in the past, those policies have now been softened. Today, the chief problem is those policies which are ostensibly domestically-oriented, notably poor delivery of public services. These problems are much more difficult to correct than exchange rate and trade policies, and so the policy reform effort needs to be intensified. However, even widespread policy reforms in this area might not be sufficient to induce a recovery in private investment, since recent economic reforms are never fully credible. Investment rating services list Africa as the riskiest region in the world. Indeed, there is some evidence that Africa suffers from being perceived by investors as a "bad neighborhood." Analysis of the global risk ratings shows that while they are largely explicable in terms of economic fundamentals, Africa as a whole is rated as significantly more risky than is warranted by these fundamentals (Haque et al., 1999). Similarly, private investment appears to be significantly lower in Africa than is explicable in terms of economic fundamentals (Jaspersen et al., 1999). "Africa" thus seems to be treated as a meaningful category by investors.

The perception of high risk for investing in Africa may partly be corrected by the passage of time, but reforming African governments can also take certain steps to commit themselves to defend economic reforms. Internationally, governments may increasingly make use of rules within the World Trade Organization, and shift their economic relations with the European Union from unreciprocated trade preferences to a wider range of reciprocated commitments. Domestically, there is a trend to freedom of the press, and the creation of independent centers of authority in central banks and revenue authorities, all of which should generally help to reinforce a climate of openness and democracy, which is likely to be supportive of economic reform.

REFERENCES

Ablo, Emanuel and Ritva Reinikka. 1998. "Do Budgets Really Matter? Evidence from Public Spending on Education and Health in Uganda." Policy Research Working Paper No. 1926, World Bank.

African Development Bank. 1998. *African Development Report.* Oxford: Oxford University Press.

Bates, Robert, H. 1983. *Essays in the Political Economy of Rural Africa.* Cambridge: Cambridge University Press.

Bauer, Peter T. 1982. "The Effects of Aid." *Encounter.* November.

Bevan, David L., Paul Collier and Jan Willem Gunning. 1993. *Agriculture and the Policy Environment: Tanzania and Kenya.* Paris: OECD.

Biggs, T., M. Raturi and P. Srivastava. 1996. "Enforcement of Contracts in an African Credit Market: Working Capital Financing in Kenyan Manufacturing." RPED Discussion Paper, Africa Region, World Bank.

Bigsten, Arne, P. Collier, S. Dercon, B. Gauthier, J. W. Gunning, A. Isaksson, A. Oduro, R. Oostendorp, C. Pattillo, M. Soderbom, M. Sylvain, F. Teal and A. Zeufack. 1999, forthcoming. "Investment by Manufacturing Firms in Africa: A Four-Country

Panel Data Analysis." *Oxford Bulletin of Economics and Statistics*.

Bloom, John and Jeffrey Sachs. 1998. "Geography, Demography and Economic Growth in Africa." *Brookings Papers in Economic Activity*, 2, 207–95.

Burnside, Craig and David Dollar. 1997. "Aid, Policies and Growth." Policy Research Working Paper No. 1777, World Bank.

Collier, Paul. 1999. "The Political Economy of Ethnicity," in *Proceedings of the Annual Bank Conference on Development Economics.* Pleskovic, Boris and Joseph E. Stiglitz, eds. Washington, DC: World Bank.

Collier, Paul and David Dollar. 1999a. "Aid Allocation and Poverty Reduction." Policy Research Working Paper 2041, World Bank, Washington, DC.

Collier, Paul and David Dollar. 1999b. "Aid, Risk and the Special Concerns of Small States." Mimeo, Policy Research Department, World Bank, Washington, DC.

Collier, Paul and Ashish Garg. 1999, forthcoming. "On Kin Groups and Wages in the Ghanaian Labour Market." *Oxford Bulletin of Economics and Statistics*, 61:2, 131–51.

Collier, P. and J. W. Gunning. 1999. "Explaining African Economic Performance." *Journal of Economic Literature.* March, 37:1, 64–111.

Collier, P. and J.W. Gunning. 1999a, forthcoming. "The IMF's Role in Structural Adjustment." *Economic Journal.* World Bank, Washington, DC.

Collier, P. and J. W. Gunning with associates. 1999b. *Trade Shocks in Developing Countries: Theory and Evidence.* Oxford: Oxford University Press (Clarendon).

Collier, Paul and Anke Hoeffler. 1998. "On the Economic Causes of Civil War." *Oxford Economic Papers.* 50, 563–73.

Collier, Paul and Anke Hoeffler. 1999. "Loot-Seeking and Justice-Seeking in Civil War." Mimeo, Development Research Department, World Bank, Washington, DC.

Collier, Paul and Catherine Pattillo, eds. 1999. *Investment and Risk in Africa.* Macmillan: London.

Collins, S. and B. P. Bosworth. 1996. "Economic Growth in East Asia: Accumulation versus Assimilation." *Brookings Papers in Economic Activity*, 2, 135–203.

Deaton, A. and R. Miller. 1996. "International Commodity Prices, Macroeconomic Performance and Politics in Sub-Saharan Africa." *Journal of African Economies*, 5 (Supp.), 99–191.

Dercon, Stefan. 1993. "Peasant Supply Response and Macroeconomic Policies: Cotton in Tanzania." *Journal of African Economies*, 2, 157–94.

Dercon, Stefan. 1997. "Wealth, Risk and Activity Choice: Cattle in Western Tanzania." *Journal of Development Economics,* 55:1, 1–42.

Diamond, Jared. 1998. *Guns, Germs, and Steel: The Fates of Human Societies.* New York: W. W. Norton & Co.

Dollar, David. 1992. "Outward-Oriented Developing Economies Really Do Grow More Rapidly: Evidence from 95 LDCs 1976–85." *Economic Development and Cultural Change,* 40, 523–44.

Easterly, William and Ross Levine. 1997. "Africa's Growth Tragedy: Policies and Ethnic Divisions." *Quarterly Journal of Economics,* CXII, 1203–50.

Elbadawi, Ibrahim A., Benno J. Ndulu, and Njuguna Ndung'u. 1997. "Debt Overhang and Economic Growth in Sub-Saharan Africa," in *External Finance for Low-Income Countries.* Iqbal, Zubair and Ravi Kanbur, eds. Washington, DC: IMF Institute.

Fafchamps, Marcel, Jan Willem Gunning and Remco Oostendorp. 1998. "Inventories, Liquidity and Contractual Risk in African Manufacturing." Department of Economics, Stanford University, mimeo.

Gallup, John L. and Jeffrey D. Sachs. 1999. "Geography and Economic Growth," in *Proceedings of the Annual World Bank Conference on Development Economics.* Pleskovic, Boris and Joseph E. Stiglitz, eds. Washington, DC: World Bank.

Ghana Central Bureau of Statistics. 1988. *Quarterly Digest of Statistics.* Accra.

Grove, A. T. 1991. "The African Environment," in *Africa 30 Years On.* Rimmer, Douglas, ed. London: James Currey.

Gwin, Catherine and Joan Nelson. 1997. *Perspectives on Aid and Development.* Washington, DC: Johns Hopkins for Overseas Development Council.

Haque, Nadeem U., Nelson Mark and Donald J. Mathieson. 1999. "Risk in Africa: Its Causes and Its Effects on Investment," in *Investment and Risk in Africa.* Collier, Paul and Catherine Pattillo, eds. London: Macmillan.

Hoeffler, Anke A. 1999. "Econometric Studies of Growth, Convergence and Conflicts." D. Phil. Thesis, Oxford University.

Jaspersen, Frederick, Anthony H. Aylward and A. David Cox. 1999. "Risk and Private Investment: Africa Compared with Other Developing Areas," in *Investment and Risk in Africa.* Collier, Paul and Catherine Pattillo, eds. London: Macmillan.

Kenya Central Bureau of Statistics. 1996. *Statistical Abstract.* Nairobi.

Knack, Stephen and Phillip Keefer. 1995. Institutions and Economic Performance: Cross-Country Tests Using Alternative Institutional Measures." *Economics and Politics,* 7:3, 207–28.

Kremer, Michael. 1993. "Population Growth and Technological Change: One Million B.C. to 1990." *Quarterly Journal of Economics*, 108:3, 681–716.

Lee, K. S. and A. Anas. 1991. "Manufacturers' Responses to Infrastructure Deficiencies in Nigeria: Private Alternatives and Policy Options," in *Economic Reform in Africa.* Chibber, A. and S. Fischer, eds. Washington, DC: World Bank.

Maddison, Angus. 1995. *Monitoring the World Economy.* Paris: OECD.

Mauro, P. 1995. "Corruption and Growth." *Quarterly Journal of Economics,* 110, 681–712.

McCallum, J. 1995. "National Borders Matter: Canada-U.S. Regional Trade Patterns." *American Economic Review,* 85, 615–23.

Mengistae, Taye. 1998. "Ethiopia's Urban Economy: Empirical Essays on Enterprise Development and the Labour Market." D.Phil. Thesis, University of Oxford.

Pradhan, Sanjay. 1996. "Evaluating Public Spending." Discussion Paper 323. Washington, DC.: World Bank.

Reinikka, Ritva and Jakob Svensson. 1998. "Investment Response to Structural Reforms and Remaining Constraints: Firm Survey Evidence from Uganda." Mimeo, Africa Region, World Bank.

Rodrik, Dani. 1999. *Making Openness Work: The New Global Economy and the Developing Countries.* Washington, DC: Overseas Development Council.

Sachs, J. D. and Mark Warner. 1997. "Sources of Slow Growth in African Economies." *Journal of African Economies,* 6, 335–76.

Schuknecht, Ludger. 1999. "Tying Governments' Hands in Commodity Taxation." *Journal of African Economies,* 8:2, 152–81.

Voortman, R. L., B. G. J. S. Sonneveld and M. A. Keyzer. 1999. "African Land Ecology: Opportunities and Constraints for Agricultural Development." Mimeo, Centre for World Food Studies, Free University, Amsterdam.

Widner, Jennifer, A. 1999. "The Courts as Restraints," in *Investment and Risk in Africa.* Collier, Paul and Catherine Pattillo, eds. London: Macmillan.

Wood, Adrian and J. Mayer. 1998. "Africa's Export Structure in a Comparative Perspective," Study No. 4 of the UNCTAD series *Economic Development and Regional Dynamics in Africa: Lessons from the East Asian Experience.*

World Bank. 1997. *Confronting Aids*, Policy Research Report. Oxford University Press.

World Bank. 1998. *Assessing Aid: What Works, What Doesn't, and Why*, Policy Research Report. Oxford University Press.

World Bank. 1999. *World Development Indicators.* Washington, DC: Development Data Center.

Daron Acemoglu and Simon Johnson

DISEASE AND DEVELOPMENT: THE EFFECT OF LIFE EXPECTANCY ON ECONOMIC GROWTH

Introduction

Improving health around the world today is an important social objective, which has obvious direct payoffs in terms of longer and better lives for millions. There is also a growing consensus that improving health can have equally large indirect payoffs through accelerating economic growth (see, e.g., Bloom and Sachs 1998; Gallup and Sachs 2001; WHO 2001; Alleyne and Cohen 2002; Bloom and Canning 2005; Lorentzen, McMillan, and Wacziarg 2005). For example, Gallup and Sachs (2001, 91) argue that wiping out malaria in sub-Saharan Africa could increase that continent's per capita growth rate by as much as 2.6 percent a year, and a recent report by the World Health Organization states that "in today's world, poor health has particularly pernicious effects on economic development in sub-Saharan Africa, South Asia, and pockets of high disease and intense poverty elsewhere" (WHO 2001, 24) and "extending the coverage of crucial health services . . . to the world's poor could save millions of lives each year, reduce poverty, spur economic development and promote global security" (i).

The evidence supporting this recent consensus is not yet conclusive, however. Although cross-country regression studies show a strong correlation between measures of health (e.g., life expectancy) and both the level of economic development and recent economic growth, these studies have not established a causal effect of health and disease on economic growth. Since countries suffering from short life expectancy and ill health are also disadvantaged in other ways (and often this is the reason for their poor health outcomes), such macro studies may be capturing the negative effects of these other, often omitted, disadvantages. While a range of micro studies demonstrate the importance of health for individual productivity,[1] these studies do not resolve the question of whether health differences are at the root of the large income differences we observe because they do not incorporate general equilibrium effects. The most important general equilibrium effect arises because of diminishing returns to effective units of labor, for example, because land and/or physical capital are supplied inelastically. In the presence of such diminishing returns, micro estimates may exaggerate the aggregate productivity benefits from improved health, particularly when health improvements are accompanied by population increases.

This article investigates the effect of general health conditions, proxied by life expectancy at birth, on economic growth. We exploit the large improvements in life expectancy driven by international health interventions, more effective public health measures, and the introduction of new chemicals and drugs starting in the 1940s. This episode, which we refer to as the *international epidemiological transition*, led to an unprecedented improvement in life expectancy in a large number of countries.[2] Figure 10.2 shows this by plotting life expectancy in countries that were initially (circa 1940) poor, middle-income, and rich. It illustrates that while in the 1930s life expectancy was low in many poor and middle-income contries, this transition brought their levels of life expectancy close to those prevailing in richer parts of the world.[3] As a consequence,

From *Journal of Political Economy* 115, no. 6 (2007), pp. 925–30, 975–76.

Figure 10.2 Log Life Expectancy at Birth for Initially Rich, Middle-Income, and Poor Countries in the Base Sample

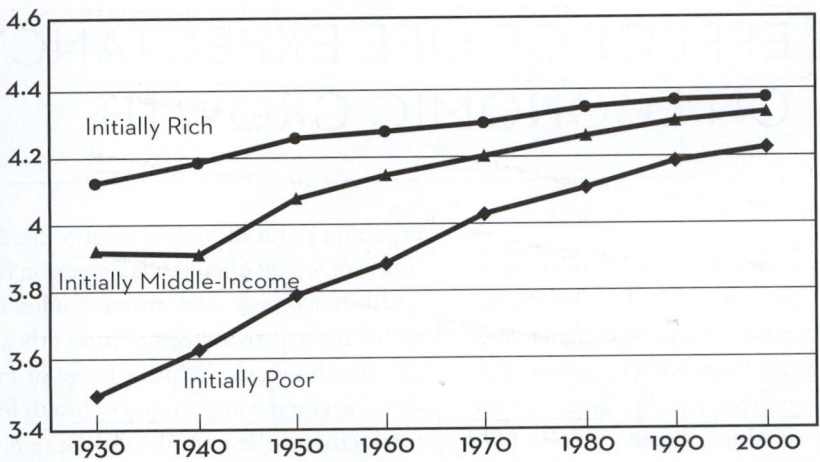

health conditions in many poor countries today, though still in dire need of improvement, are significantly better than the corresponding health conditions were in the West at the same stage of development.[4]

The international epidemiological transition provides us with an empirical strategy to isolate potentially exogenous changes in health conditions. The effects of the international epidemiological transition on a country's life expectancy were related to the extent to which its population was initially (circa 1940) affected by various specific diseases, for example, tuberculosis, malaria, and pneumonia, and to the timing of the various health interventions.

The early data on mortality by disease are available from standard international sources, though they have not been widely used in the* * * literature. These data allow us to create an instrument for changes in life expectancy based on the preintervention distribution of mortality from various diseases around the world and the dates of global intervention (e.g., discovery and mass production of penicillin and streptomycin, or the discovery and widespread use of DDT against mosquito vectors).* * * We document that there were large

declines in disease-specific mortality following these global interventions. More important, we show that the predicted mortality instrument has a large and robust effect on changes in life expectancy starting in 1940, but has no effect on changes in life expectancy prior to this date (i.e., before the key interventions).

The instrumented changes in life expectancy have a fairly large effect on population: a 1 percent increase in life expectancy is related to an approximately 1.7–2 percent increase in population over a 40–60–year horizon. The magnitude of this estimate indicates that the decline in fertility rates was insufficient to compensate for increased life expectancy, a result that we directly confirm by looking at the relationship between life expectancy and total births.

However, we find no statistically significant effect on total GDP* * *. More important, GDP per capita and GDP per working age population show relative declines in countries experiencing large increases in life expectancy. In fact, our estimates exclude any positive effects of life expectancy on GDP per capita within 40- or 60-year horizons. This is consistent with the overall pattern in Figure 10.3, which, in contrast to Figure 10.2, shows no convergence in

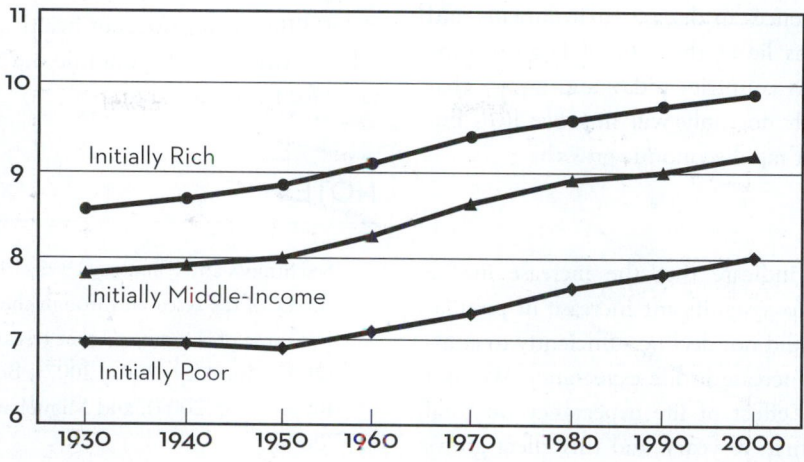

income per capita between initially poor, middle-income, and rich countries. We document that these results are robust to a range of specification checks and to the inclusion of various controls. We also document that our results are not driven by life expectancy at very early ages. The predicted mortality instrument has a large, statistically significant and robust effect on life expectancy at 20 (and at other ages), and using life expectancy at 20 instead of life expectancy at birth as our measure of general health conditions leads to very similar results.

The most natural interpretation of our results comes from neoclassical growth theory. Increased life expectancy raises population, which initially reduces capital-to-labor and land-to-labor ratios, thus depressing income per capita. This initial decline is later compensated by higher output as more people enter the labor force and as more capital is accumulated. This compensation can be complete and may even exceed the initial level of income per capita if there are significant productivity benefits from longer life expectancy. Yet, the compensation may also be incomplete if the benefits from higher life expectancy are limited and if some factors of production, for example, land, are supplied inelastically.

Our findings do not imply that improved health has not been a great benefit to less developed nations during the postwar era. The accounting approach of Becker, Philipson, and Soares (2005), which incorporates information on longevity and health as well as standards of living, would suggest that these interventions have considerably improved "overall welfare" in these countries. What these interventions have not done, and in fact were not intended to do, is increase output per capita in these countries.

Our article is most closely related to two recent contributions: Weil (2007) and Young (2005). Weil calibrates the effects of health using a range of micro estimates and finds that these effects could be quite important in the aggregate.[5] * * * Young evaluates the effect of the recent HIV/AIDS epidemic in Africa. Using micro estimates and calibration of the neoclassical growth model, he shows that the decline in population resulting from HIV/AIDS may increase income per capita despite significant disruptions and human suffering caused by the disease.[6]

■ ■ ■

Concluding Remarks

A recent consensus in academic and policy circles holds that differences in disease environments and health conditions lie at the root of large income differences across countries today and argues that improving health not only will improve lives but will by itself spur rapid economic growth.

■ ■ ■

Our results indicate that the increase in life expectancy led to a significant increase in population; birth rates did not decline sufficiently to compensate for the increase in life expectancy. We find a small positive effect of life expectancy on total GDP over the first 40 years, and this effect grows somewhat over the next 20 years, but not enough to compensate for the increase in population. Overall, the increases in life expectancy (and the associated increases in population) appear to have reduced income per capita. There is no evidence that the increase in life expectancy led to faster growth of income per capita or output per worker. This evidence casts doubt on the view that health has a first-order impact on economic growth.

Considerable caution is necessary in interpreting our results for at least two reasons. The most important limitation is that because our approach exploits the international epidemiological transition around the 1940s, the results may not be directly applicable to today's world; the international epidemiological transition was a unique event, and perhaps similar changes in life expectancy today would not lead to an increase in population and the impact on GDP per capita may be more positive. Second, the diseases that take many lives in the poorer parts of the world today are not the same ones as those 60 years ago; most notably HIV/AIDS is a major killer today but was not so in 1940. Many of the diseases we focus on had serious impacts on children (with the notable exception of tuberculosis), whereas HIV/AIDS affects individuals at the peak of their labor productivity and could have a larger negative impact on growth. Further study of the effects of the HIV/AIDS epidemic on economic outcomes as well as more detailed analysis of different measures of health on human capital investments and economic outcomes are major areas for future research.

NOTES

1. See Strauss and Thomas (1998) for an excellent survey of the research through the late 1990s. For some of the more recent research, see Schultz (2002), Bleakley (2003, 2007), Behrman and Rosenzweig (2004), and Miguel and Kremer (2004).

2. The term "epidemiological transition" was coined by demographers and refers to the process of falling mortality rates after about 1850, associated with the switch from infectious to degenerative disease as the major cause of death (Omran 1971). Some authors prefer the term "health transition," since this includes the changing nature of ill health more generally (e.g., Riley 2001). We focus on the rapid decline in mortality (and improvement in health) in poorer countries after 1940, most of which was driven by the fast spread of new technologies and practices around the world (hence the adjective "international"). The seminal works on this episode include Stolnitz (1955), Omran (1971), and Preston (1975).

3. In this figure and throughout the article, rich countries are those with income per capita in 1940 above the level of Argentina (the richest Latin American country at that time, according to Maddison's [2003] data, in our base sample).

4. For example, life expectancy at birth in India in 1999 was 60 compared to 40 in Britain in 1820, when income per capita was approximately the same level as in India today (Maddison 2001, 30). According to Maddison (264), income per capita in Britain in 1820 was $1,707, whereas it stood at $1,746 in India in 1998 (all figures in 1990 international dollars).

5. Weil's baseline estimate uses the return to the age of menarche from Knaul's (2000) work on Mexico as a general indicator of "overall return to health." Using Behrman and Rosenzweig's (2004) estimates from returns to birth weight differences in monozygotic twins, he finds smaller effects.

6. For more pessimistic views on the economic consequences of HIV/AIDS, see Arndt and Lewis (2000), Bell, Devarajan, and Gersbach (2003), Forston (2006), and Kalemli-Ozcan (2006).

REFERENCES

Alleyne, George A. O., and Daniel Cohen. 2002. "The Report of Working Group I of the Commission on Macroeconomics and Health." WHO Comm. on Macroeconomics and Health, Geneva.

Arndt, Channing, and Jeffrey D. Lewis. 2000. "The Macro Implications of HIV/AIDS in South Africa: A Preliminary Assessment." *South African J. Econ.* 68 (December): 380–92.

Becker, Gary S., Tomas J. Philipson, and Rodrigo R. Soares. 2005. "The Quantity and Quality of Life and the Evolution of World Inequality." *A.E.R.* 95 (March): 277–91.

Behrman, Jere R., and Mark R. Rosenzweig. 2004. "Returns to Birthweight." *Rev. Econ. and Statis.* 86 (May): 586–601.

Bell, Clive, Shantanyanan Devarajan, and Hans Gersbach. 2003. "The Long-Run Economic Costs of AIDS: Theory and an Application to South Africa." Policy Research Paper no. 3152 (October), World Bank, Washington, DC.

Bleakley, Hoyt. 2003. "Disease and Development: Evidence from the American South." *J. European Econ. Assoc.* 1 (April–May): 376–86.

———. 2007. "Disease and Development: Evidence from Hookworm Eradication in the American South." *Q.J.E.* 122 (February): 73–117.

Bloom, David E., and David Canning. 2005. "Health and Economic Growth: Reconciling the Micro and Macro Evidence." Working Paper no. 42 (February), Center Democracy, Development, and Rule

of Law, Stanford Inst. Internat. Studies, Stanford, CA. http://cddrl.stanford.edu.

Bloom, David E., and Jeffrey D. Sachs. 1998. "Geography, Demography, and Economic Growth in Africa." *Brookings Papers Econ. Activity*, no. 2: 207–73.

Forston, Jane. 2006. "Mortality Risks in Human Capital Investment: The Impact of HIV AIDS in Sub-Saharan Africa." Manuscript, Princeton Univ.

Gallup, John Luke, and Jeffrey D. Sachs. 2001. "The Economic Burden of Malaria." *American J. Tropical Medicine and Hygiene* 64, suppl. 1 (January): 85–96.

Kalemli-Ozcan, Sebnem. 2006. "AIDS, Reversal of the Demographic Transition and Economic Development: Evidence from Africa." Manuscript, Univ. Houston.

Knaul, Felicia Marie. 2000. "Health, Nutrition and Wages: Age at Menarche and Earnings in Mexico." In *Wealth from Health: Linking Social Investments to Earnings in Latin America*, edited by William D. Savedoff and T. Paul Schultz, Washington, DC: Inter-American Development Bank.

Lorentzen, Peter, John McMillan, and Romain Wacziarg. 2005. "Death and Development." Working paper no. 11620 (September), NBER, Cambridge, MA.

Maddison, Angus. 2001. *The World Economy: A Millennial Perspective.* Paris: OECD, Development Centre.

———. 2003. *The World Economy: Historical Statistics.* Paris: OECD, Development Centre.

Miguel, Edward, and Michael Kremer. 2004. "Worms: Identifying Impacts on Education and Health in the Presence of Treatment Externalities." *Econometrica* 72 (January): 159–217.

Omran, Abdel R. 1971. "The Epidemiologic Transition: A Theory of the Epidemiology of Population Change." *Milbank Memorial Fund Q.* 49, no. 4, pt. 1 (October): 509–38.

Preston, Samuel H. 1975. "The Changing Relation between Mortality and Level of Economic Development." *Population Studies* 29 (July): 231–48.

Riley, James C. 2001. *Rising Life Expectancy: A Global History.* Cambridge: Cambridge Univ. Press.

Schultz, T. Paul. 2002. "Wage Gains Associated with Height as a Form of Health Human Capital." *A.E.R Papers and Proc.* 92 (May): 349–53.

Stolnitz, George J. 1955. "A Century of International Mortality Trends: I." *Population Studies* 9, no. 1 (July): 24–55.

Strauss, John, and Duncan Thomas. 1998. "Health, Nutrition, and Economic Development." *J. Econ. Literature* 36 (June): 766–817.

Weil, David N. 2007. "Accounting for the Effect of Health on Economic Growth." *Q.J.E.* 122 (August): 1265–1306.

WHO (World Health Organization). 2001. *Macroeconomics and Health: Investing in Health for Economic Development.* http://www3.who.int /whosis/cmh.

Young, Alwyn. 2005. "The Gift of the Dying: The Tragedy of AIDS and the Welfare of Future African Generations." *Q.J.E.* 120 (May): 423–66.

11 GLOBALIZATION

We conclude this reader with selections that relate to globalization. Evocative and rather vague, this term can be incorporated into discussion of just about any kind of politics that has some "global" aspect to it. However, here we refer specifically to the extensive and intensive connections between political, societal, and economic institutions among countries. To political scientists, *globalization* describes the modern intersection between comparative politics (the study of domestic politics across countries) and international relations (the study of foreign relations between countries). As a result, scholars of both international relations and comparative politics have been drawn to this contentious topic. Just as globalization blurs the lines between the domestic and the international, it also blurs the lines between comparative politics and international relations.

The 2008–09 economic recession has helped bring attention to scholars who are more broadly critical of globalization, among them the economist Dani Rodrik. In his 2011 book, *The Globalization Paradox*, he returns to his frequent argument that globalization, sovereignty, and democracy are essentially incompatible. In the selection included in this chapter, he asks whether the problems caused by globalization can be managed by institutions of global governance that would transcend the nation-state. Rodrik is skeptical, looking at the European Union as an example of the limits of such institutions. Beyond his discussion of the technical difficulties in creating global governance, Rodrik points out that the desire for globalization can be found primarily among an elite of well-educated and highly mobile citizens. For the majority of people in the world, however, globalization entails more risk than reward, as economic security and political authority move beyond their control. For this majority, the nation-state remains an important institution of sovereignty, and Rodrik suggests that states and societies must remain active in managing and limiting globalization.

In line with Rodrik's argument that certain groups of people benefit from globalization while others suffer, François Bourguignon's "Inequality and Globalization" (2016) lays bare further contradictions (and promises) of globalization. We might imagine that globalization has led to greater poverty around the world, yet this is not the case. China's economic reforms and those of India have resulted in a dramatic drop in global poverty and a *narrowing* of inequality between rich and poor countries. Yet within countries themselves, inequality has risen as the benefits of globalization have been spread unevenly (as Rodrik notes). A decline in inequality between countries is a positive development, but if it comes at the price of greater in-country inequality, this may engender a backlash. Indeed, historian Niall

Ferguson, in his piece "Populism as a Backlash against Globalization: Historical Perspectives" (2016), worries that economic difficulties in the developed democracies empower populist leaders who advance policies that will undermine growth and international stability. For him, the lessons of an earlier wave of globalization in the nineteenth and early twentieth centuries, which ended in isolationism and economic nationalism, are not comforting.

Lest we end on such a pessimistic note, John S. Dryzek's "Global Civil Society: The Progress of Post-Westphalian Politics" (2012) moves away from an economy-centric focus to consider the growth and impact of global civil society (organized life, whether political or otherwise, that exists outside of the state) on domestic and international politics. If we use the frameworks constructed to evaluate civil society at the domestic level, global civil society may be found wanting, lacking the power to shape international policy. The travails of international climate change agreements may be a good example here. However, Dryzek argues that growing international civil society does have the power to change international norms, if not necessary directly influence policy. As he concludes, "global civil society can be both an agent and an arena," suggesting that solutions to the challenges of globalization may lie not only with states but also with engaged and interconnected societies that can help change the way in which we think about the proper goals of political activity.

Dani Rodrik

IS GLOBAL GOVERNANCE FEASIBLE? IS IT DESIRABLE?

The nation state is passé. Borders have disappeared. Distance is dead. The earth is flat. Our identities are no longer bound by our places of birth. Domestic politics is being superseded by newer, more fluid forms of representation that transcend national boundaries. Authority is moving from domestic rule-makers to transnational networks of regulators. Political power is shifting to a new wave of activists organized around international non-governmental organizations. The decisions that shape our economic lives are made by large multinational companies and faceless international bureaucrats.

How many times have we heard these or similar statements, heralding or decrying the dawn of a new era of global governance?

And yet look at the way events have unfolded in the recent crisis of 2007–08. Who bailed out the global banks to prevent the financial crisis from becoming even more cataclysmic? Who pumped in the liquidity needed to soothe international credit markets? Who stimulated the global economy through fiscal expansion? Who provided unemployment compensation and other safety nets for the workers who lost their jobs? Who is setting the new rules on compensation, capital adequacy, and liquidity for large banks? Who gets the lion's share of the blame for everything that went wrong before, during, and after?

From *The Globalization Paradox: Democracy and the Future of the World Economy* (New York: W. W. Norton, 2011), pp. 207–32.

The answer to each one of these questions is the same: *national governments*. We may think we live in a world whose governance has been radically transformed by globalization, but the buck still stops with domestic policy makers. The hype that surrounds the decline of the nation state is just that: hype. Our world economy may be populated by a veritable alphabet soup of international agencies—everything from ADB to WTO[1]—but democratic decision making remains firmly lodged within nation states. "Global governance" has a nice ring to it, but don't go looking for it anytime soon. Our complex and variegated world allows only a very thin veneer of global governance—and for very good reasons, too.

Overcoming the Tyranny of Nation States

It's no longer just cranks and wide-eyed utopians who entertain the idea of global government. Many economists, sociologists, political scientists, legal scholars, and philosophers have joined the search for new forms of governance that leave the nation state behind. Of course, few of these analysts advocate a truly global version of the nation state; a global legislature or council of ministers is too much of a fantasy. The solutions they propose rely instead on new conceptions of political community, representation, and accountability. The hope is that these innovations can replicate many of constitutional democracy's essential functions at the global level.

The crudest form of such global governance envisages straightforward delegation of national powers to international technocrats. It involves autonomous regulatory agencies charged with solving what are essentially regarded as "technical" problems arising from uncoordinated decision making in the global economy. For obvious reasons, economists are particularly enamored of such arrangements. For example, when the European economics network VoxEU.org solicited advice from leading economists on how to address the frailties of the global financial system in the wake of the 2008 crisis, the proposed solutions often took the form of tighter international rules administered by some kind of technocracy: an international bankruptcy court, a world financial organization, an international bank charter, an international lender of last resort, and so on.[2] Jeffrey Garten, undersecretary of commerce for international trade in the Clinton administration, has long called for the establishment of a global central bank.[3] Economists Carmen Reinhart and Ken Rogoff have proposed an international financial regulator.

These proposals may seem like the naive ruminations of economists who don't understand politics, but in fact they are often based on an explicit political motive. When Reinhart and Rogoff argue for an international financial regulator, their goal is as much to fix a political failure as it is to address economic spillovers across nations; perhaps the political motive even takes precedence over the economic one. They hope to end political meddling at the national level that they perceive has emasculated domestic regulations. They write: "a well-endowed, professionally staffed international financial regulator—operating without layers of political hacks—would offer a badly needed counterweight to the powerful domestic financial service sector."[4] The political theory that underpins this approach holds that delegating regulatory powers to an insulated and autonomous global technocracy leads to better governance, both global and national.

In the real world, delegation requires legislators to give up their prerogative to make the rules and reduces their ability to respond to their constituents. As such, it typically takes place under a narrow set of conditions. In the United States, for example, Congress delegates rulemaking powers to executive agencies only when its political preferences are quite similar to the president's and when the issues under consideration are highly technical.[5] Even then, delegation remains partial and comes with elaborate accountability mechanisms. Delegation is a *political* act. Hence, many preconditions have to be satisfied before delegation to supranational bodies can become widespread and sustainable. We would need to create a "global body politic" of some sort, with common norms, a transnational political community, and new mechanisms of accountability suited to the global arena.

Economists don't pay much attention to these prerequisites, but other scholars do. Many among them see evidence that new models of global governance are indeed emerging. Anne-Marie Slaughter, a scholar of international relations at Princeton, has focused on transnational networks populated by regulators, judges, and even legislators. These networks can perform governance functions even when they are not constituted as intergovernmental organizations or formally institutionalized. Such networks, Slaughter argues, extend the reach of formal governance mechanisms, allow persuasion and information sharing across national borders, contribute to the formation of global norms, and can generate the capacity to implement international norms and agreements in nations where the domestic capacity to do so is weak.[6]

The governance of financial markets is in fact the arena where such networks have advanced the furthest and which provides Slaughter's most telling illustrations. The International Organization of Securities Commissions (IOSCO) brings together the world's securities regulators and issues global principles. The Basel Committee on Banking Supervision performs the same role for banking regulators. These networks have small secretariats (if any at all) and no enforcement power. Yet they certainly exert influence through their standard-setting powers and legitimacy—at least in the eyes of regulators. Their deliberations often become a reference point in domestic discussions. They may not entirely substitute for nation states, but they end up creating internationally intertwined networks of policy makers.

To achieve legitimacy, global governance must transcend exclusive clubs of regulators and technocrats. Can these networks go beyond narrowly technical areas and encompass broader social purposes? Yes, says John Ruggie, the Harvard scholar who coined the term "embedded liberalism" to describe the Bretton Woods regime. Ruggie agrees that transnational networks have undermined the traditional model of governance based on nation states. To right this imbalance, he argues, we need greater emphasis on corporate social responsibility at the global level. An updated version of embedded liberalism would move beyond a state-centered multilateralism to "a multilateralism that actively embraces the potential contributions to global social organization by civil society and corporate actors." These actors can advance new global norms—on human rights, labor practices, health, anti-corruption, and environmental stewardship—and then enshrine them in the operations of large international corporations and policies of national governments. Multinational corporations' funding of HIV/AIDS treatment programs in poor nations represents one prominent example.

The United Nation's Global Compact, which Ruggie had a big hand in shaping, embodies this agenda. The Compact aims to transform international corporations into vehicles for the advancement of social and economic goals. Such a transformation would benefit the communities in which these corporations and their affiliates operate. But, as Ruggie explains, there would be additional advantages. Improving large corporations' social and environmental performance would spur emulation by other, smaller firms. It would alleviate the widespread concern that international competition creates a race to the bottom in labor and environmental standards at the expense of social inclusion at home. And it would allow the private sector to shoulder some of the functions that states are finding increasingly difficult to finance and carry out, as in public health and environmental protection, narrowing the governance gap between international markets and national governments.[7]

Arguments on behalf of new forms of global governance—whether of the delegation, network, or corporate social responsibility type—raise troubling questions. To whom are these mechanisms supposed to be accountable? From where do these global clubs of regulators, international non-governmental organizations, or large firms get their mandates? Who empowers and polices them? What ensures that the voice and interests of those who are less globally networked are also heard? The Achilles' heel of global governance is lack of clear accountability relationships. In a nation state, the electorate is the ultimate source of political mandates and elections the ultimate vehicle for accountability. If you do not respond to your constituencies' expectations and aspirations, you are voted out. Global electoral accountability of this sort is too far-fetched a notion. We would need different mechanisms.[8]

Probably the best argument for an alternative *global* conception of accountability comes from two distinguished political scientists, Joshua Cohen and Charles Sabel. These scholars begin by arguing that the problems global governance aims to solve don't lend themselves to traditional notions of accountability. In the traditional model, a constituency with well-defined interests empowers its representative to act on behalf on those interests. Global regulation presents challenges that are new, often highly technical, and subject to rapidly evolving circumstances. The global "public" typically has only a hazy notion of what problems need solving and how to solve them.

In this setting, accountability hinges on the international regulator's ability to provide "a good explanation" for what she chooses to do. "Questions are decided by argument about the best way to address problems," write Cohen and Sabel, "not [by] simply exertions of power, expressions of interest, or bargaining from power positions on the basis of interest."[9] There is no presumption here that the solutions will be "technocratic" ones. Even when values and interests diverge and disagreement prevails, the hope is that the process of transnational deliberation will generate the explanations that all or most can acknowledge as legitimate. Global rule-making becomes accountable to the extent that the reasoning behind the rules is found to be compelling by those to whom the rules would apply.

Cohen and Sabel's scheme provides room, at least in principle, for variation in institutional practices across nation states within an overall frame-

work of global cooperation and coordination. A country and its policy makers are free to experiment and implement different solutions as long as they can explain to their peers—policy makers in the other countries—why they have arrived at those solutions. They must justify their choices publicly and place them in the context of comparable choices made by others. A skeptic may wonder, however, if such mechanisms will not lead instead to widespread hypocrisy as policy makers continue with business-as-usual while rationalizing their actions in loftier terms.

Ultimately, Cohen and Sabel hope that these deliberative processes would feed into the development of a global political community, in which "dispersed peoples might come to share a new identity as common members of an organized global populace."[10] It is difficult to see how their conception of global governance would work in the absence of such a transformation in political identities. At the end of the day, global governance requires individuals who feel that they are global citizens.

Maybe we are not too far from that state of affairs. The Princeton ethicist Peter Singer has written powerfully about the development of a new global ethic that follows from globalization. "If . . . the revolution in communications has created a global audience," he writes, "then we might need to justify our behavior to the whole world."[11] The economist and philosopher Amartya Sen has argued that it is quite misleading to think of ourselves as bound by a single, unchanging identity—ethnic, religious, or national—with which we are born. Each one of us has multiple identities, based on our profession, gender, occupation, class, political leanings, hobbies and interests, sports teams we support, and so on.[12] These identities do not come at the expense of each other, and we freely choose how much weight we put on them. Many identities cross national boundaries, allowing us to form transnational associations and define our "interests" across a broad geography. This flexibility and multiplicity creates room, in principle, for the establishment of a truly global political community.

There is much that is attractive in these ideas about the potential for global governance. As Sen puts it, "there is something of a tyranny of ideas in seeing the political divisions of states (primarily, national states) as being, in some way, fundamental, and in seeing them not only as practical constraints to be addressed, but as divisions of basic significance in ethics and political philosophy."[13] Furthermore, political identity and community have been continuously redefined over time in ever more expansive terms. Human associations have moved from the tribal and local to city states and then on to nation states. Shouldn't a global community be next?

The proof of the pudding is in the eating. How far can these emergent forms of global governance go and how much globalization can they support? A good place to start is the European Union, which has traveled further along the road of transnational governance than any other collection of nation states.

European Union: The Exception That Tests the Rule

When Cohen and Sabel were developing their ideas on global governance through deliberation, they had one concrete example in mind: the European Union. The European experiment shows both the potential and the limitations of these ideas.

European nations have achieved an extraordinary amount of economic integration among themselves. Nowhere is there a better approximation of deep integration or hyperglobalization, albeit at the regional level. Underneath Europe's single market lies an enormous institutional artifice devoted to removing transaction costs and harmonizing regulations. EU members have renounced barriers on the movement of goods, capital, and labor. But beyond that they have signed on to 100,000-plus pages of EU-wide regulations—on everything from science policy to consumer protections—that lay out common standards and expectations. They have set up a European Court of Justice that assiduously enforces these regulations. They have empowered an administrative arm in the form of the European Commission to propose new laws and implement common policies in external trade, agriculture, competition, regional assistance, and many other areas. They have established a number of programs to provide financial assistance to lagging regions of the Union and foster economic convergence. Sixteen of the members have adopted a common currency (the euro) and succumbed to a common monetary policy administered by the European Central Bank. In addition to all this, the EU has many specialized agencies that are too numerous to list here.

The EU's democratic institutions are less well developed. The directly elected European Parliament operates mostly as a talking shop rather than as a source of legislative initiative or oversight. Real power lies with the Council of Ministers, which is a collection of ministers from national governments. How to establish and maintain democratic legitimacy and accountability for Europe's extensive supranational setup has long been a thorny question. Critics from the right blame EU institutions for overreaching while critics from the left complain about a "democratic deficit."

European leaders have made significant efforts in recent years to boost the *political* infrastructure of the European Union, but it has been a bumpy and arduous road. An ambitious effort to ratify a European Constitution failed after voters in France and The Netherlands rejected it in 2005. In the wake of this failure came the Lisbon Treaty, which entered into force in December 2009—but only after the United Kingdom, Poland, Ireland, and the Czech Republic secured exclusions from some of the requirements of the treaty. The treaty reforms the voting rules in the Council of Ministers, gives more power to the European Parliament, renders the European Union's human rights charter legally binding, and establishes a new executive position in the form of the president of the European Council.

As the opt-outs received by Britain and others suggest, there remain significant differences among member states on the desirability of turning Europe into a true political federation. Britain zealously guards its distinctive constitution and legal system from the encroachment of EU rules or institutions. In many areas such as financial regulation and monetary policy, it has little interest in bringing its practices in line with those of the others. Britain's interest in Europe remains primarily economic. Its minimalist approach to European institution building contrasts sharply with France's and Germany's occasionally more ambitious federalist goals.

As important as these broad debates over the European Union's constitutional architecture may be, much of the organization's real work gets done under an informal, evolving set of practices that Charles Sabel calls "experimentalist governance." The member states and the higher-level EU institutions decide on the goals to be accomplished. These could be as ambitious and ill-defined as "social inclusion" or as narrow as "a unified energy grid." National regulatory agencies are given freedom to advance these goals in the ways they see fit, but the quid pro quo is that they must report their actions and results in what are variably called forums, networked agencies, councils of regulators, or open methods of coordination. Peer review allows national regulators to compare their approaches to those of others and revise them as necessary. Over time, the goals themselves are updated and altered in light of the learning that takes place in these deliberations.[14]

Experimentalist governance helps create Europe-wide norms and contributes to building transnational consensus around common approaches. They need not necessarily result in complete homogenization. Where differences continue to exist, they do so in the context of mutual understanding and accountability, so that they are much less likely to turn into sources of friction. The requirement that national practices be justified renders national differences easier to accommodate.

The members of the European Union may seem like a diverse bunch, but compared to the nations that make up the world economy they are a model of concord. These twenty-seven nations are bound

together by a common geography, culture, religion, and history. Excluding Luxembourg, where measured income per head is very high, the richest among them (Ireland, in 2008) is only 3.3 times wealthier than the poorest (Bulgaria), compared to a multiple of almost 190 across the world. EU members are driven by a strong sense of strategic purpose that extends considerably beyond economic integration. European unity in fact looms larger as a political goal than it does as an economic one.

Despite all these comparative advantages, the European Union's institutional evolution has progressed slowly and large differences remain among the member states. Most telling is the well recognized tension between deepening the Union and expanding it to incorporate new members. Consider the long-simmering debate over Turkey. French and German opposition to Turkey's entrance into the European Union derives in part from cultural and religious reasons. But the fear that Turkey's divergent political traditions and institutions would greatly hamper European political integration also plays a large role. Britain, on the other hand, welcomes anything that would temper French and German ambitions for a *political* Europe, and for that reason supports eventual membership for Turkey. Everyone understands that the deepening of Europe's political integration becomes more problematic as the number of members increases and the European Union's composition becomes more diverse.

Europe's own dilemma is no different from that faced by the world economy as a whole. As we saw in previous chapters, deep economic integration requires erecting an extensive transnational governance structure to support it. Ultimately, the European Union will either bite the political bullet or resign itself to a more limited economic union. Those who push for a political Europe stand a greater chance of achieving a truly single European market than those who want to limit the conversation to the economic level. But political advocates have yet to win the argument. They face great opposition both from their national electorates and from other political leaders with differing visions.

Thus Europe has become a halfway house—economically more integrated than any other region of the world, but with a governance structure that remains a work in progress. It has the potential to turn itself into a true economic union, but it is not there yet. When European economies come under stress, the responses are overwhelmingly national.

The governance gaps became particularly obvious during the crisis of 2008 and its aftermath. Europe's banks are supervised by national regulators. When they started going bust, there was practically no coordination among EU governments. Bailouts of banks and other firms were carried out separately by individual governments, often in ways that harmed other EU members. There was also no coordination in the design of recovery plans and fiscal stimulus programs, even though there are clear spillovers (German firms benefit from a French fiscal stimulus almost as much as French firms do, given how intertwined the two economies are). When European leaders finally approved a "common" framework for financial oversight in December 2009, Britain's finance minister underscored the limited nature of the agreement by emphasizing that "responsibility lies with national regulators."[15]

The poorer and worse-hit members of the European Union could count on only grudging support from Brussels. Latvia, Hungary, and Greece were forced to turn to the IMF for financial assistance as a condition for getting loans from richer EU governments.[16] (Imagine what it would look like if Washington were to require California to submit to IMF monitoring in order to benefit from Federal Recovery Funds.) Others dealing with crushing economic problems were left to fend for themselves (Spain and Portugal). In effect, these countries had the worst of both worlds: economic union prevented their resort to currency devaluation for a quick boost to their competitiveness, while the lack of political union precluded their receiving much support from the rest of Europe.

In light of all this it would be easy to write off the European Union, but that would be too harsh a judgment. Membership in the Union did make

a difference to the willingness of smaller countries to live by hyperglobalization rules. Consider Latvia, the small Baltic country, which found itself experiencing economic difficulties similar to those Argentina had lived through a decade earlier. Latvia had grown rapidly since joining the European Union in 2004 on the back of large amounts of borrowing from European banks and a domestic property bubble. It had run up huge current account deficits and foreign debts (20 percent and 125 percent of GDP, respectively, by 2007). Predictably, the global economic crisis and the reversal in capital flows in 2008 left the Latvian economy in dire straits. As lending and property prices collapsed, unemployment rose to 20 percent and GDP declined by 18 percent in 2009. In January 2009, the country had its worst riots since the collapse of the Soviet Union.

Latvia had a fixed exchange rate and free capital flows, just like Argentina. Its currency had been pegged to the euro since 2005. Unlike Argentina, however, the country's politicians managed to tough it out without devaluing the currency and introducing capital controls (the latter would have explicitly broken EU rules). By early 2010, it looked as if the Latvian economy had begun to stabilize.[17] The difference with Argentina was that Latvia's membership in a larger political community changed the balance of costs and benefits of going it alone. The right to free circulation of labor within the European Union allowed many Latvian workers to emigrate, serving as a safety valve for an economy under duress. Brussels prevailed on European banks to support their subsidiaries in Latvia. Most important, the prospect of adopting the euro as the domestic currency and joining the Eurozone compelled Latvian policy makers to foreclose any options—such as devaluation—that would endanger that objective, despite the very high short-term economic costs.

For all its teething problems, Europe should be viewed as a great success considering its progress down the path of institution building. For the rest of the world, however, it remains a cautionary tale. The European Union demonstrates the difficulties of achieving a political union robust enough to underpin deep economic integration even among a comparatively small number of like-minded countries. At best, it is the exception that tests the rule. The European Union proves that transnational democratic governance is workable, but its experience also lays bare the demanding requirements of such governance. Anyone who thinks global governance is a plausible path for the world economy at large would do well to consider Europe's experience.

Would Global Governance Solve Our Problems?

Let's give global governance enthusiasts the benefit of the doubt and ask how the mechanisms they propose would resolve the tensions that hyperglobalization generates.

Consider how we should deal with the following three challenges:

1. Chinese exports of toys to the United States are found to contain unsafe levels of lead.
2. The subprime mortgage crisis in the United States spreads to the rest of the world as many of the securities issued by U.S. banks and marketed in foreign countries turn out to be "toxic."
3. Some of the goods exported from Indonesia to the United States and Europe are manufactured using child labor.

In all three cases, a country exports a good, service, or asset that causes problems for the importing country. Chinese exports of lead-tainted toys endanger the health of American children; U.S. exports of mispriced mortgage-based assets endanger financial stability in the rest of the world, and Indonesian exports of child-labor services threaten labor standards and values in the United States and Western Europe. Prevailing international rules do not provide clear-cut solutions for these challenges, so we need to think our way through them. Can we address them

through markets alone? Do we need specific rules, and if so, should they be national or global? Might the answers differ across these three areas?

Consider the similarities between these problems, even though they are drawn from quite different domains of the world economy. At the core of each is a dispute about standards, with respect to lead content, rating of financial securities, and child labor. In all three cases there are differences in the standards applied (or desired) by the exporting and importing countries. Exporters may have lower standards and therefore possess a competitive advantage in the markets of the importing countries. However, purchasers in the importing country cannot directly observe the standard under which the exported good or service has been produced. A consumer cannot tell easily whether the toy contains lead paint or has been manufactured using child labor under exploitative conditions; nor can a lender fully identify the risk characteristics of the bundled assets it holds. Everything else held constant, importers are less likely to buy the good or the service in question if it contains lead paint, has been made by children, or is likely to cause financial havoc.

At the same time, consumers' preferences vary. Each one of us probably places somewhat different weights on upholding the standard versus obtaining other benefits, such as a low price. You may be willing to pay an extra $2 for a T-shirt certified as child-labor-free, but I may want to pay no more than $1. You may be willing to trade off some extra risk for additional yield on a security, while I am more conservative in my investment philosophy. Some may be willing to purchase lead-tainted toys if it makes a big enough difference to the price, while others would consider it abhorrent. For this reason, any standard creates gainers and losers when applied uniformly.

How do we respond to these three challenges? The default option is to neglect them until they loom too large to ignore. We may choose this option for several reasons. First, we may trust the standard applied in the exporting country. The credit rating agencies in the United States are supposedly the best in the world, so why would any country worry about buying triple-A-rated U.S. mortgage securities? Chinese lead regulations are, on paper, more stringent than those in the United States, so why get concerned about the health hazards of Chinese toys? Second, we may think standards and regulations in foreign countries are none of our business. Buyers simply beware. Third, we may actually think that differences in regulatory standards are a source of comparative advantage—and hence of gains from trade—just like differences in productivity or skills across nations. If lax labor standards enable Indonesia to sell us cheaper goods, this is just another manifestation of the benefits of globalization.

These shortsighted arguments undercut the efficiency of the global economy and ultimately undermine its legitimacy. The challenges presented raise legitimate concerns and deserve serious responses. Consider therefore some of the possibilities.

Global standards

We may be tempted to seek global standards by which all countries would have to abide. We might require compliance with core labor standards of all producers, a common set of banking regulations, and uniform product safety codes. This is the global governance solution par excellence. In many areas we are gravitating toward this kind of approach, as we have seen, but obvious limitations remain. Nations are unlikely to agree on the appropriate standards and often for very good reasons.

Labor standards offer the easiest example. The argument that rich countries' restrictions on child labor may be a poor fit for developing countries has long prevented a global consensus from emerging. Child labor of the type that activists in rich nations object to is often an unavoidable consequence of poverty. Preventing young children from working in factories may end up doing more harm than good if the most likely alternative for the children is not going to school but employment in domestic trades that are even more odious (prostitution is an oft-mentioned illustration). This argument against homogenization applies to other labor regulations too, such as maximum hours of work or minimum wages. More

broadly, as long as basic human rights such as non-discrimination and freedom of association are not violated, nations ought to be free to choose the labor standards that best fit their own circumstances and social preferences. Common standards are costly, even if they may facilitate acceptance of certain kinds of imports in the rich countries.

This is also true in the area of financial regulation. What is "safe" for the United States may not be "safe enough" for France or Germany. The United States may accept happily a bit more risk than the other two countries as the price of financial innovation. On the other hand, the U.S. may want its banks to have higher capital requirements as a cushion against risk taking than French or German policy makers think necessary. In each case, neither position is necessarily right and the other wrong. Nations have different views because they have different preferences and circumstances.

Product safety rules seem the easiest to organize around a common standard, but even here there are important constraints. Note first that Chinese lead paint standards are in fact quite stringent. The problem arises not from differences in standards as written, but from differences in standards as practiced. As in most developing countries, the Chinese government has trouble enforcing and monitoring product standards. These difficulties often arise not from lack of willingness, but from lack of ability stemming from administrative, human resource, and financial constraints. No global standard can change this underlying reality. Perhaps, as Slaughter suggests, participation in global networks can help Chinese regulators improve by enabling information sharing and transfer of "best practices." Don't hold your breath. Improving domestic institutions is a long, drawn-out process over which foreigners typically have a very limited influence.

Even if nations were to agree on global standards, they may end up converging on the wrong set of regulations. Global finance provides an apt illustration. The Basel Committee on Banking Supervision, the global club of bank regulators, has been widely hailed as the apogee of international financial cooperation, but has produced largely inadequate agreements.[18] The first set of recommendations (Basel I) encouraged risky short-term borrowing and may have played a role in precipitating the Asian financial crisis. The second (Basel II) relied on credit rating agencies and banks' own models to generate risk weights for capital requirements, and is now widely viewed as inappropriate in light of the recent financial crisis. By neglecting the fact that the risks created by an individual bank's actions depend on the liquidity of the system as a whole, the Basel Committee's standards have, if anything, magnified systemic risks. In light of the great uncertainty about the merits of different regulatory approaches, it may be better to let a variety of regulatory models flourish side by side.

Market-based solutions

There is a more market-friendly alternative. Instead of mandating adherence to global standards, it entails mandating provision of *information*. If we enhance the information available to importers about the standards under which goods and services have been produced, every buyer can then make the decision that best fits his or her circumstances.

Consider child labor. We can imagine a system of certification and labeling that lets consumers in the advanced nations distinguish between imported goods that have been produced by children and those that have not. There are already many such labeling schemes in operation. RugMark, for example, is an international non-governmental organization that certifies that no child labor has been used in carpets from India and Nepal. Presumably, child-labor-free products cost more to produce and are more expensive. Consumers can express their preferences through the products they want to buy. Those who oppose the use of child labor can pay extra and buy the appropriately labeled goods while others remain free to consume the cheaper product. An attractive feature of labeling is that it doesn't impose a common standard on everyone in the importing country. I don't have to pay for your high standard if a lower one is good enough for me.

This would seem like a good solution, especially since it makes limited demands on global governance. And there may be certain areas where it makes a lot of sense. But as a generic solution, it falls far short.

Until the recent financial crisis we would have pointed to credit rating agencies as a successful instance of labeling. These agencies functioned, in principle, in the way that labeling is supposed to work. If you were risk-averse, you could restrict yourself to triple-A-rated, low-yield securities. If you wanted more yield, at the expense of higher risk, you could invest in lower-rated securities instead. These ratings allowed investors, again in principle, to decide where they wanted to be on the risk spectrum. The government did not need to micromanage portfolio decisions.

We have learned since that the information conveyed by credit ratings was not nearly as meaningful as it appeared at the time. For a variety of reasons, not least that the credit rating agencies were paid by the very firms whose securities they were evaluating, toxic assets received top ratings. Too many investors got burned because they took the ratings seriously. The market for information worked quite poorly.

The costs of faulty ratings were borne not just by the investors in those securities but by society at large. This is the problem of systemic risk: when large, highly leveraged institutions go bust, they threaten to take the entire financial system with them. The failure of credit rating agencies had consequences well beyond those who purchased the toxic securities.

Every system of labeling in fact raises a higher-order governance question: To whom are the certifiers accountable, or who certifies the certifiers? Credit rating worked poorly in financial markets because credit rating agencies maximized their income and neglected their fiduciary duties to society. A complicated governance problem was "solved" by handing it over to private profit-seeking entities whose incentives weren't properly aligned with society's.

The problem with labeling is no less serious in the case of labor or environmental standards, where diverse coalitions of non-governmental organizations and private corporations have taken the lead in the face of governmental deadlock. All of the participants have their own agenda, with the result that the meaning the labels convey can become quite ambiguous. For example, "fair trade" labels denote products such as coffee, chocolates, or bananas that are grown in an environmentally sustainable manner and which pay the farmers a certain minimum price. This seems like a win-win. Consumers can sip their coffee knowing that they are contributing to alleviating poverty and safeguarding the environment. But does the consumer really know or understand what the "fair trade" label on her coffee means?

We have very little reliable information on how labeling efforts such as "fair trade" work out in practice. One of the few academic studies on the subject looked at coffee in Guatemala and Costa Rica and found very little interest on the part of growers in fair trade certification. This is quite surprising in light of the apparent advantages, most notably in terms of better prices. In reality, the price premium the growers received seems to have been low compared to what they could get from growing specialty coffees. Often, the price was not high enough to cover the investments necessary to fit the requirements for certification. Moreover, the benefits did not necessarily flow to the poorest farmers, who are the landless indigenous growers.[19] Other reports suggest that only a tiny share of the price premium for fair trade coffee finds its way to the growers.[20]

Fair trade or other labeling programs like Rug-Mark may be doing some good on the whole, but we should be skeptical about how informative these labels are and the likely magnitude of their effects. And what is true of NGO-led efforts is all the more true of corporate social responsibility. Corporations, after all, are motivated by the bottom line. They may be willing to invest in social and environmental projects if doing so buys them customers' goodwill. Yet we shouldn't assume their motives align closely with those of society at large, or exaggerate their willingness to advance societal agendas.

The most fundamental objection to labeling and other market-based approaches is that they overlook the *social* dimension of standard-setting. For example, the conventional approach to dealing with health and safety hazards calls for standards, not labeling. If labeling works so well, why don't we deal with these issues in the same way, by letting individuals decide how much risk they want to take? As far as I know, not even libertarian economists have proposed that the best way to deal with the problem of lead-tainted Chinese toys is to *label* Chinese-made toys as having uncertain or high lead content and let consumers choose according to their own preferences and health-hazard/price trade-offs. Instead, our natural instinct is to push for more regulation and better enforcement of existing standards. Even the U.S. toy industry has asked the federal government to impose mandatory safety-testing standards for all toys sold in the United States.[21]

We prefer uniform, government-mandated standards in these cases for several reasons. We may be skeptical that consumers will have enough information to make the right choices or the capacity to process the information they have. We may believe in the importance of social goals and norms in addition to individual preferences. Even though a few people in our midst may be willing to sign on as indentured servants for a price, we are unlikely as a society to allow them to do so. Finally, individuals acting in their own best interest may create problems for the rest of society and as a consequence their freedom to choose may need to be restricted. Think again of the mess that the banks that invested in toxic assets created for the rest of us or how sweatshops can undermine employment conditions for others in the economy.

These reasons apply as much to social and economic issues as they do to health and safety risks. They suggest that labeling and certification will play only a limited role in addressing the governance challenges of the global economy.

The limits of global governance

Global governance offers little help in solving these challenges we have considered. We are dealing with problems rooted in deep divisions among different societies in terms of preferences, circumstances, and capabilities. Technical fixes don't help. Neither do networks of regulators, market-based solutions, corporate social responsibility, or transnational deliberation. At best, these new forms of governance provide a kind of global governance-light. They simply cannot carry the weight of a hyperglobalized world economy. The world is too diverse to be shoehorned into a single political community.

In the case of lead-tainted toys, most people would agree that the obvious and correct solution is to let the domestic standard prevail. The United States should determine its own health and safety standards, and allow only toys that satisfy those standards to be imported. If other countries want to have different standards, or are unable to match U.S. standards for practical reasons, they would be similarly entitled to their own variants. But they cannot expect to export their products freely to the United States unless they meet the U.S. standards. This approach enables countries to uphold their own regulations, even if it comes at the cost of barriers at the border.

Can we not apply the same principle to financial regulation labor standards, or other areas of conflict arising from differences in national standards? We can, and we should.

Globalization and Identity Redux

In Nick Hornby's comic novel *Juliet, Naked* (2009), one of the main characters, Duncan, obsesses over an obscure and reclusive American rock musician named Tucker Crowe. Duncan's life revolves around Crowe: he lectures on him, organizes meetings and conventions, and has written an unpublished book on the great man. Initially, Duncan has few people nearby with whom he can share his passion. The nearest Tucker Crowe fan lives sixty miles away and Duncan can meet up with him only once or twice a year. Then the Internet comes along. Duncan sets up a Web site and makes contact with hundreds of equally passionate Tucker Crowe aficionados scattered around the world. As Hornby writes, "now the nearest fans lived in Duncan's laptop," and he could talk to them all the time.[22]

New information and communication technologies are bringing ordinary people like Duncan together around shared interests in ways that scholars including Peter Singer and Amartya Sen hope will shrink the world. Thanks to these global links, local attachments are becoming less important as transnational moral and political communities loom ever larger. Or are they?

Even though Duncan's story sounds familiar—we've all had similar transformations in our own lives thanks to the Internet—it doesn't tell us the full story. Do our global interactions really erode our local and national identities? Evidence from the real world presents a very different and quite surprising picture. Consider the case of Netville.

In the mid-1990s, a new housing development in one of the suburbs of Toronto engaged in an interesting experiment. The houses in this Canadian residential community were built from the ground up with the latest broadband telecommunications infrastructure and came with a host of new Internet technologies. Residents of Netville (a pseudonym) had access to high-speed Internet, a videophone, an online jukebox, online health services, discussion forums, and a suite of entertainment and educational applications.[23]

These new technologies made the town an ideal setting for nurturing global citizens. The people of Netville were freed from the tyranny of distance. They could communicate with anyone in the world as easily as they could with a neighbor, forge their own global links, and join virtual communities in cyberspace. They would begin, observers expected, to define their identities and interests increasingly in global, rather than local, terms.

What actually transpired was quite different. Glitches experienced by the telecom provider left some homes without a link to the broadband network. This allowed researchers to compare across wired and non-wired households and reach some conclusions about the consequences of being wired. Far from letting local links erode, wired people actually strengthened their existing local social ties. Compared to non-wired residents, they recognized more of their neighbors, talked to them more often, visited them more frequently, made many more local phone calls. They were more likely to organize local events and mobilize the community around common problems. They used their computer network to facilitate a range of social activities—from organizing barbecues to helping local children with their homework. Netville exhibited, as one resident put it, "a closeness that you don't see in many communities." What was supposed to have unleashed global engagement and networks had instead strengthened local social ties.

As powerful as information and communication technologies are, we should not assume that they will lead us down the path of global consciousness or transnational political communities. Distance matters. Our local attachments largely still define us and our interests.

The World Values Survey periodically polls random samples of individuals around the world on their attitudes and attachments. A recent round of surveys asked people in fifty-five countries about the strength of their local, national, and global identities. The results were similar across the world—and quite instructive. They reveal that attachment to the nation state overwhelms all other forms of identity. People see themselves primarily as citizens of their nation, next as members of their local community, and only last as "global citizens." The sole exceptions, where people identified more with the world than with their nation, were violence-ridden Colombia and tiny Andorra.[24]

These surveys uncover an important divide between elites and the rest of society. A strong sense of global citizenship tends to be confined, where it exists, to wealthy individuals and those with the highest levels of educational attainment. Conversely, attachment to the nation state is generally much stronger (and global identities correspondingly weaker) among individuals from lower social classes. This cleavage is perhaps not that surprising. Skilled professionals and investors can benefit from global opportunities wherever they may arise. The nation state and what it does matters a lot less to these people than it does to less mobile workers and others with fewer skills who have to make do with what's nearby. This opportunity gap reveals a certain dark side to the clamor for global governance. The construction of transnational political communities is a project of globalized elites attuned largely to their needs.

If Not Global Governance, Then What?

The new forms of global governance are intriguing and deserve further development, but ultimately they run up against some fundamental limits: political identities and attachments still revolve around nation states; political communities are organized domestically rather than globally; truly global norms have emerged only in a narrow range of issues; and there remain substantial differences across the world on desirable institutional arrangements. These new transnational mechanisms can take the edge off some contentious issues, but they are no substitute for real governance. They are insufficient to underpin extensive economic globalization.

We need to accept the reality of a divided world polity and make some tough choices. We have to be explicit about where one nation's rights and responsibilities end and another nation's begin. We cannot fudge the role of nation states and proceed on the assumption that we are witnessing the birth of a global political community. We must acknowledge and accept the restraints on globalization that a divided global polity entails. *The scope of workable global regulation limits the scope of desirable globaliza-*

tion. Hyper-globalization cannot be achieved, and we should not pretend that it can.

Ultimately, this reality check can lead us to a healthier, more sustainable world order.

NOTES

1. African Development Bank and World Tourism (not Trade) Organization, respectively.
2. See http://voxeu.org/index.php?q=node/2544.
3. See Jeffrey Garten, "The Case for a Global Central Bank," Yale School of Management, posted online, September 21, 2009, at http://ba.yale.edu /news_events/CMS/Articles/6958.shtml.
4. Carmen Reinhart and Kenneth Rogoff, "Regulation Should Be International," *Financial Times*, November 18, 2008 (http://www.ft.com/cms /s/0/983724fc-b589-11dd-ab71-0000779fd18c .html?nclick_check=1).
5. David Epstein and Sharyn O'Halloran, *Delegating Powers: A Transaction Cost Politics Approach to Policy Making under Separate Powers* (Cambridge and New York: Cambridge University Press, 1999).
6. Anne-Marie Slaughter. *A New World Order* (Princeton and Oxford: Princeton University Press, 2004).
7. John G. Ruggie, "Reconstituting the Global Public Domain—Issues, Actors, and Practices," *European Journal of International Relations*, 10 (2004), pp. 499–531.
8. There is a parallel debate in international law on whether it is possible to institute effective legal norms and practices at the global level in the absence of global government. See, e.g., Jeffrey L. Dunoff and Joel P. Trachtman, eds., *Ruling the World?: Constitutionalism, International Law, and Global Governance* (Cambridge and New York: Cambridge University Press, 2009), and Eric Posner, *The Perils of Global Legalism* (Chicago: University of Chicago Press, 2009), in addition to the work of Anne-Marie Slaughter already cited. The case against "global legalism" is stated succinctly by Posner, who argues that without legal institutions—legislators, enforcers, and courts— law cannot control behavior.
9. Joshua Cohen and Charles F. Sabel, "Global Democracy?" *International Law and Politics*, 37 (2005), p. 779.
10. Ibid., p. 796.
11. Peter Singer, *One World: The Ethics of Globalization* (New Haven: Yale University Press, 2002), p. 12.
12. Amartya Sen, *Identity and Violence: The Illusion of Destiny* (New York: W. W. Norton, 2006).
13. Amartya Sen, *The Idea of Justice* (Cambridge, MA: Harvard University Press, 2009), p. 143.
14. See Cohen and Sabel, "Global Democracy?" and Charles F. Sabel and Jonathan Zeitlin, "Learning from Difference: The New Architecture of Experimentalist Governance in the EU," *European Law Journal*, vol. 14, no. 3 (May 2008), pp. 271–327.
15. Stephen Castle, "Compromise with Britain Paves Way to Finance Rules in Europe," *New York Times*, December 2, 2009 (http://www.nytimes .com/2009/12/03/business/global/03eubank.html? _r=1& sudsredirect=true).
16. The decision to send Greece to the IMF caused a certain amount of controversy within the European Union since, unlike the other two countries, Greece is a member of not only the European Union but also the Eurozone. Ultimately, insistence on this score by German chancellor Angela Merkel overcame opposition from French president Nicolas Sarkozy and the European Central Bank president Jean-Claude Trichet.
17. See "After Severe Recession, Stabilization in Latvia," IMF Survey online, February 18, 2010, http://www.imf.org/external/pubs/ft/survey /so/2010/CAR021810A.htm.
18. The national regulators that negotiate these international agreements have their own interests, of course, and they enter into agreements in part as a counterweight to domestic political pressures. See David Andrew Singer, *Regulating Capital: Setting Standards for the International Financial System* (Ithaca, NY: Cornell University Press, 2007).

19. Colleen E. H. Berndt, "Is Fair Trade in Coffee Production Fair and Useful? Evidence from Costa Rica and Guatemala and Implications for Policy," Mercatus Policy Series, Policy Comment No. 11, George Mason University, June 2007.

20. Andrew Chambers, "Not So Fair Trade," *The Guardian*, December 12, 2009 (http://www.guardian.co.uk/commentisfree/cif-green/2009/ dec/12 /fair-trade-fairtrade-kitkat-farmers).

21. See "Toy Makers Seek Standards for U.S. Safety," *New York Times*, September 7, 2007 (http://www .nytimes.com/2007/09/07/business/07toys.html?_r=2).

22. Nick Hornby, *Juliet, Naked* (New York: Penguin, 2009).

23. This account is based on Keith Hampton, "Netville: Community On and Offline in a Wired Suburb," in Stephen Graham, ed., *The Cybercities Reader* (London: Routledge, 2004), pp. 256–62. I owe the reference to this study to Nicholas A. Christakis and James H. Fowler, *Connected: The Surprising Power of Our Social Networks and How They Shape Our Lives* (New York: Little, Brown, 2009).

24. The data that I summarize here come from the World Values Survey databank at http://www .worldvaluessurvey.org/services/index.html.

François Bourguignon

INEQUALITY AND GLOBALIZATION

When it comes to wealth and income, people tend to compare themselves to the people they see around them rather than to those who live on the other side of the world. The average Frenchman, for example, probably does not care how many Chinese exceed his own standard of living, but that Frenchman surely would pay attention if he started lagging behind his fellow citizens. Yet when thinking about inequality, it also makes sense to approach the world as a single community: accounting, for example, not only for the differences in living standards within France but also for those between rich French people and poor Chinese (and poor French and rich Chinese).

When looking at the world through this lens, some notable trends stand out. The first is that global inequality greatly exceeds inequality within any individual country. This observation should come as no surprise, since global inequality reflects the enormous differences in wealth between the world's richest and the world's poorest countries, not just the differences within them. Much more striking is the fact that, in a dramatic reversal of the trend that prevailed for most of the twentieth century, global inequality has declined markedly since 2000 (following a slower decline during the 1990s). This trend has been due in large part to the rising fortunes of the developing world, particularly China and India. And as the economies of these countries continue to converge with those of the developed world, global inequality will continue to fall for some time.

Even as global inequality has declined, however, inequality within individual countries has crept upward. There is some disagreement about the size of this increase among economists, largely owing to the underrepresentation of wealthy people in national income surveys. But whatever its extent, increased inequality within individual countries has partially offset the decline in inequality among countries. To counteract this trend, states should pursue policies aimed at redistributing income, strengthen the regulation of the labor and financial markets, and

From *Foreign Affairs* (January/February 2016), pp. 11–15.

develop international arrangements that prevent firms from avoiding taxes by shifting their assets or operations overseas.

The Great Substitution

Economists typically measure income inequality using the Gini coefficient, which ranges from zero in cases of perfect equality (a theoretical country in which everyone earns the same income) to one in cases of perfect inequality (a state in which a single individual earns all the income and everyone else gets nothing). In continental Europe, Gini coefficients tend to fall between 0.25 and 0.30. In the United States, the figure is around 0.40. And in the world's most unequal countries, such as South Africa, it exceeds 0.60. When considering the world's population as a whole, the Gini coefficient comes to 0.70—a figure so high that no country is known to have ever reached it.

Determining the Gini coefficient for global inequality requires making a number of simplifications and assumptions. Economists must accommodate gaps in domestic data—in Mexico, an extreme case, surveys of income and expenditures miss about half of all households. They need to come up with estimates for years in which national surveys are not available. They need to convert local incomes into a common currency, usually the U.S. dollar, and correct for differences in purchasing power. And they need to adjust for discrepancies in data collection among countries, such as those that arise when one state measures living standards by income and another by consumption per person or when a state does not collect data at all.

Such inexactitudes and the different ways of compensating for them explain why estimates of just how much global inequality has declined over the past two-plus decades tend to vary—from around two percentage points to up to five, depending on the study. No matter how steep this decline, however, economists generally agree that the end result has been a global Gini coefficient of around 0.70 in the years between 2008 and 2010.

The decline in global inequality is largely the product of the convergence of the economies of developing countries, particularly China and India, with those of the developed world. In the first decade of this century, booming economies in Latin America and sub-Saharan Africa also helped accelerate this trend. Remarkably, this decline followed a nearly uninterrupted rise in inequality from the advent of the Industrial Revolution in the early nineteenth century until the 1970s. What is more, the decline has been large enough to erase a substantial part of the inequality that built up over that century and a half.

Even as inequality among countries has decreased, however, inequality within individual countries has increased, gaining, on average, more than two percentage points in terms of the Gini coefficient between 1990 and 2010. The countries with the biggest economies are especially responsible for this trend—particularly the United States, where the Gini coefficient rose by five percentage points between 1990 and 2013, but also China and India and, to a lesser extent, most European countries, among them Germany and the Scandinavian states. Still, inequality within countries is not rising fast enough to offset the rapid decline in inequality among countries.

The good news is that the current decline in global inequality will probably persist. Despite the current global slowdown, China and India have such huge domestic markets that they retain an enormous amount of potential for growth. And even if their growth rates decline significantly in the next decade, so long as they remain higher than those of the advanced industrial economies, as is likely, global inequality will continue to fall. The prospects for growth are less favorable for the smaller economies in Latin America and sub-Saharan Africa that depend primarily on commodity exports, since world commodity prices may remain low for some time. All told, then, global inequality will likely keep falling in the coming decades—but probably at the slow pace seen during the 1990s rather than the rapid one enjoyed during the following decade.

The bad news, however, is that economists might have underestimated inequality within individual countries and the extent to which it has increased since the 1990s, because national surveys tend to underrepresent the wealthy and underreport income derived from property, which disproportionately accrues to the rich. Indeed, tax data from many developed states suggest that national surveys fail to account for a substantial portion of the incomes of the very highest earners.

According to the most drastic corrections for such underreporting, as calculated by the economists Sudhir Anand and Paul Segal, global inequality could have remained more or less constant between 1988 and 2005. Most likely, however, this conclusion is too extreme, and the increase in national inequality has been too small to cancel out the decline in inequality among countries. Yet it still points to a disheartening trend: increased inequality within countries has offset the drop in inequality among countries. In other words, the gap between average Americans and average Chinese is being partly replaced by larger gaps between rich and poor Americans and between rich and poor Chinese.

Interconnected and Unequal

The same factor that can be credited for the decline in inequality among countries can also be blamed for the increase in inequality within them: globalization. As firms from the developed world moved production overseas during the 1990s, emerging Asian economies, particularly China, started to converge with those of the developed world. The resulting boom triggered faster growth in Africa and Latin America as demand for commodities increased. In the developed world, meanwhile, as manufacturing firms outsourced some of their production, corporate profits rose but real wages for unskilled labor fell.

Economic liberalization also played an important role in this process. In China, the market reforms initiated by Deng Xiaoping in the 1980s contributed just as much to rapid growth as did the country's opening to foreign investment and trade, and the same is true of the reforms India undertook in the early 1990s. As with globalization, such reforms didn't just enable developing countries to get closer to the developed world; they also created a new elite within those countries while leaving many citizens behind, thus increasing domestic inequality.

The same drive toward economic liberalization has contributed to increasing inequality in the developed world. Reductions in income tax rates, cuts to welfare, and financial deregulation have also helped make the rich richer and, in some instances, the poor poorer. The increase in the international mobility of firms, wealth, and workers over the past two decades has compounded these problems by making it harder for governments to combat inequality: for example, companies and wealthy people have become increasingly able to shift capital to countries with low tax rates or to tax havens, allowing them to avoid paying more redistributive taxes in their home countries. And in both developed and developing countries, technological progress has exacerbated these trends by favoring skilled workers over unskilled ones and creating economies of scale that disproportionately favor corporate managers.

Maintaining Momentum

In the near future, the greatest potential for further reductions in global inequality will lie in Africa—the region that has arguably benefited the least from the past few decades of globalization, and the one where global poverty will likely concentrate in the coming decades as countries such as India leap ahead. Perhaps most important, the population of Africa is expected to double over the next 35 years, reaching some 25 percent of the world's population, and so the extent of global inequality will increasingly depend on the extent of African growth. Assuming that the economies of sub-Saharan Africa sustain the modest growth rates they have seen in recent years, then inequality among countries should keep declining, although not as fast as it did in the first decade of this century.

To maintain the momentum behind declining global inequality, all countries will need to work harder to reduce inequality within their borders, or at least prevent it from growing further. In the world's major economies, failing to do so could cause disenchanted citizens to misguidedly resist further attempts to integrate the world's economies—a process that, if properly managed, can in fact benefit everyone.

In practice, then, states should seek to equalize living standards among their populations by elimi-

nating all types of ethnic, gender, and social discrimination; regulating the financial and labor markets; and implementing progressive taxation and welfare policies. Because the mobility of capital dulls the effectiveness of progressive taxation policies, governments also need to push for international measures that improve the transparency of the financial system, such as those the G-20 and the Organization for Economic Cooperation and Development have endorsed to share information among states in order to clamp down on tax avoidance. Practical steps such as these should remind policymakers that even though global inequality and domestic inequality have moved in opposite directions for the past few decades, they need not do so forever.

Niall Ferguson

POPULISM AS A BACKLASH AGAINST GLOBALIZATION: HISTORICAL PERSPECTIVES

The headline of Andrew Sullivan's coruscating May 2016 article in *New York* magazine was "America Has Never Been So Ripe for Tyranny." Just a few weeks before, *The Boston Globe* had published a spoof front page, dated April 9th, 2017. Purporting to report on the first hundred days of Donald Trump's presidency, the headlines were as follows:

"DEPORTATIONS TO BEGIN"

"President Trump Calls for Tripling of ICE Force; Riots Continue"

"Markets Sink as Trade War Looms"

"U.S. Soldiers Refuse Orders to Kill ISIS Families"

"New Libel Law Targets 'Absolute Scum' in Press"

Anyone who has read Philip Roth's brilliant counterfactual novel, *The Plot against America* (2004), will already have felt a shudder of panic at the prospect of a Republican victory in the coming U.S. elections. In Roth's story, a candidate campaigning with the slogan "America First" wins the 1940 presidential election, defeating Franklin D. Roosevelt, and proceeds to lead the United States down the path to fascist hell.

Such comparisons between the United States today and Germany in the 1930s are becoming

From *Horizons—Journal of International Relations and Sustainable Development* 8 (Autumn 2016), pp. 12–21.

commonplace. As a professional historian, I would like to offer what seems to me a better analogy.

Our Tranquil Times

Journalists are fond of saying that we are living in a time of "unprecedented" instability. In reality, as numerous studies have shown, our time is a period of remarkable stability in terms of conflict. In fact, viewed globally, there has been a small uptick in organized lethal violence since the misnamed Arab Spring. But even allowing for the horrors of the Syrian civil war, the world is an order of magnitude less dangerous than it was in the 1970s and 1980s, and a haven of peace and tranquility compared with the period between 1914 and 1945.

This point matters because the defining feature of interwar fascism was its militarism. Fascists wore uniforms. They marched in enormous and well-drilled parades and they planned wars. That is not what we see today.

So why do so many commentators feel that we are living through "unprecedented instability"? The answer, aside from plain ignorance of history, is that political populism has become a global phenomenon, and established politicians and political parties are struggling even to understand it, much less resist it. Yet populism is not such a mysterious thing, if one only has some historical knowledge. The important point is not to make the mistake of confusing it with fascism, which it resembles in only a few respects.

Rather like a television chef, I shall describe a recipe for populism, based on historical experience. It is a simple recipe, with just five ingredients.

Five Ingredients for a Populist Backlash

The first of these ingredients is a rise in immigration. In the past 45 years, the percentage of the population of the United States that is foreign-born has risen

Figure 11.1 Foreign-Born Population as a Percentage of Total U.S. Population, 1900–2014

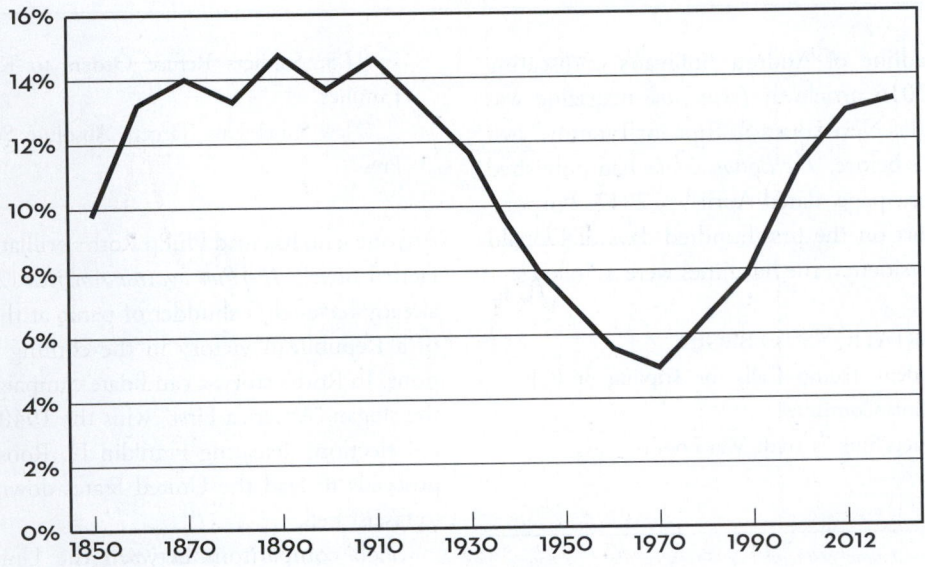

Graph: Courtesy of Niall Ferguson

from below 5 percent in 1970 to over 13 percent in 2014—almost as high as the rates achieved between 1860 and 1910, which ranged between 13 percent and an all-time high of 14.7 percent in 1890.

So when people say, as they often do, that "the United States is a land based on immigration," they are indulging in selective recollection. There was a period, between 1910 and 1970, when immigration drastically declined. It is only in relatively recent times that we have seen immigration reach levels comparable with those of a century ago, in what has justly been called the first age of globalization.

Ingredient number two is an increase in inequality. Drawing on the work done on income distribution by Thomas Piketty and Emmanuel Saez, we can see that we have recently regained the heights of inequality that were last seen in the pre–World War I period.

The share of income going to the top 1 percent of earners is back up from below 8 percent of total income in 1970 to above 20 percent of total income. The peak before the financial crisis, in 2007, was almost exactly the same as the peak on the eve of the Great Depression in 1928.

Ingredient number three is the perception of corruption. For populism to thrive, people have to start believing that the political establishment is no longer clean. Recent Gallup data on public approval of institutions in the United States show, among other things, notable drops in the standing of all institutions save the military and small businesses.

Just 9 percent of Americans have "a great deal" or "quite a lot" of confidence in the U.S. Congress—a remarkable figure. It is striking to see which other institutions are down near the bottom of the league. Big business is second-lowest, with just 21 percent of the public expressing confidence in it. Newspapers, television news, and the criminal justice system fare only slightly better. What is even more remarkable is the list of institutions that have fallen furthest in recent times: the U.S. Supreme Court now has just a 36 percent approval rating, down from a historical average of 44 percent, while the Presidency has dropped from 43 percent to 36 percent approval.

The financial crisis appears to have convinced many Americans—and not without good reason—that there is an unhealthy and likely corrupt

Figure 11.2 The Top 1% Income Share in the United States since 1913

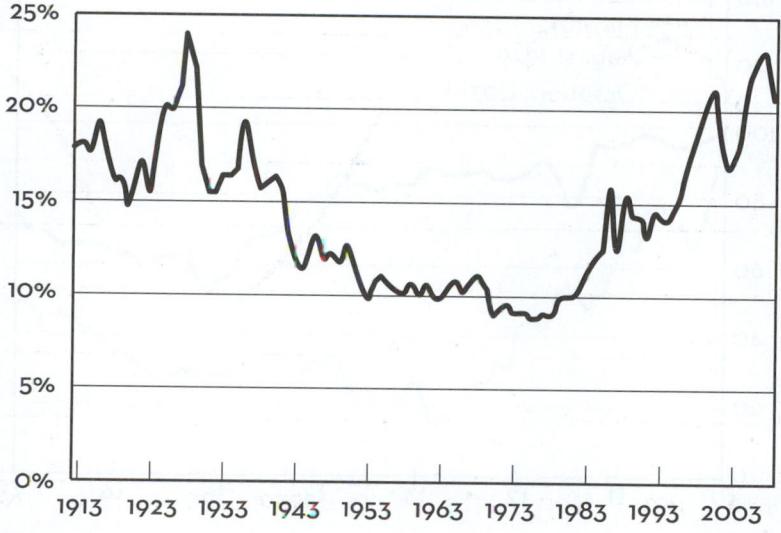

Graph: Courtesy of Niall Ferguson

relationship between political institutions, big business, and the media.

The fourth ingredient necessary for a populist backlash is a major financial crisis. The three biggest financial crises in modern history—if one uses the U.S. equity market index as the measure—were the crises of 1873, 1929, and 2008. Each was followed by a prolonged period of depressed economic performance, though these varied in their depth and duration.

In the most recent of these crises, the peak of the U.S. stock market was October 2007. With the onset of the financial crisis, we essentially replayed for about a year the events of 1929 and 1930. However, beginning in mid- to late 2009, we bounced out of the crisis, thanks to a combination of monetary, fiscal, and Chinese stimulus, whereas the Great Depression was characterized by a deep and prolonged decline in stock prices, as well as much higher unemployment rates and lower growth.

The first of these historical crises is the least known: the post-1873 "great depression," as contemporaries called it. What happened after 1873 was nothing as dramatic as 1929; it was more of a slow burn. The United States and, indeed, the world economy went from a financial crisis—which was driven by excessively loose monetary policy and real estate speculation, amongst other things—into a protracted period of deflation. Economic activity was much less impaired than in the 1930s. Yet the sustained decline in prices inflicted considerable pain, especially on indebted farmers, who complained (in reference to the then prevailing gold standard) that they were being "crucified on a cross of gold."

We have come a long way since those days; gold is no longer a key component of the monetary base, and farmers are no longer a major part of the workforce. Nevertheless, in my view, the period after 1873 is much more like our own time, both economically and politically, than the period after 1929.

There is still one missing ingredient to be added. If one were cooking, this would be the moment when flames would leap from the pan. The flammable ingredient is, of course, the demagogue, for populist demagogues react vituperatively and explosively against all of the aforementioned four ingredients.

Figure 11.3 United States Equity Indices in Three Depressions (Peak=100)

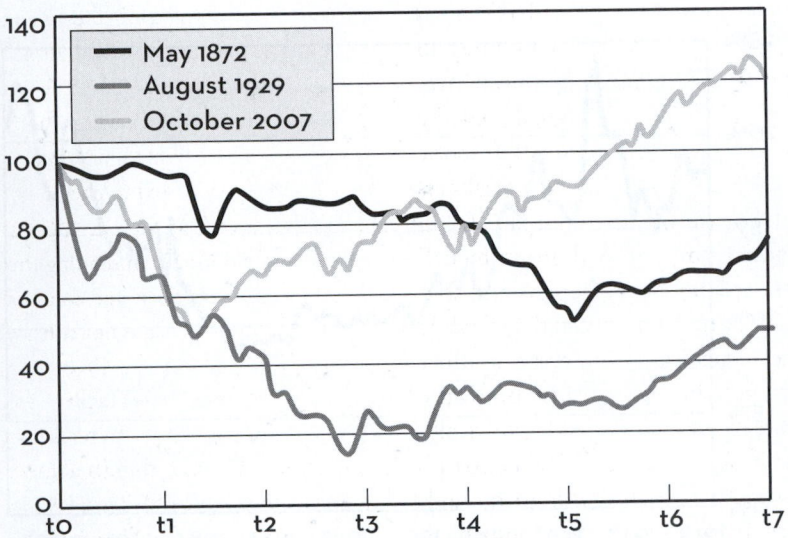

Graph: Courtesy of Niall Ferguson

Kearney's Cause

Now, my argument is not intended to dismiss or downplay those elements of Donald Trump's campaign for President of the United States that have been implicitly, if not explicitly, racist. Nor do I treat lightly the various signals he has given of indifference to, or at least ignorance of, the U.S. Constitution. My point is that these demerits do not by themselves qualify Trump for comparison with Mussolini, much less with Hitler.

Rather, I want to argue that Trump has much more in common with the demagogues of the earlier, lesser depression of the late nineteenth century, and that it is to that period that we should look for historical analogies and insights.

The best illustration of my case is the now forgotten figure of Denis Kearney, leader of the Workingmen's Party of California and the author of the slogan "The Chinese Must Go!" Himself an Irish immigrant to the United States—as opposed to the son of a Scottish immigrant and grandson of a German, which is what Donald Trump is—Kearney was part of a movement of nativist parties and "Anti-Coolie" clubs that sought to end Chinese immigration into the United States.

The report of the Joint Special Committee to Investigate Chinese Immigration in 1877 gives a flavor of the times. "The Pacific coast must in time become either Mongolian or American" was the committee's view. The report argued that the Chinese brought with them the habits of despotic government, a tendency to lie in court, a weakness for tax evasion and "insufficient brainspace [. . .] to furnish [the] motive power for self-government." Moreover, Chinese women were "bought and sold for prostitution and treated worse than dogs," while the Chinese were "cruel and indifferent to their sick." Giving such inferior beings citizenship, the committee's report declared, "would practically destroy republican institutions on the Pacific coast."

The realities were, it scarcely needs to be said, very different. According to the "Six Companies" of Chinese in San Francisco—corporate bodies that represented the Chinese population of the city—there was compelling evidence that Chinese immigration was a boon to California. Not only did the Chinese provide labor for the state's rapidly developing railroads and farms; they also tended to improve the neighborhoods in which they settled. Moreover, there was no evidence of a disproportionate Chinese role in gambling and prostitution. In fact, statistics showed that the Irish were more of a charge on the city's hospital and almshouse than the Chinese.

Nevertheless, a powerful coalition of "laboring men and artisans," small businessmen and "grangers" (the term used to describe those who aimed to shift the burden of taxation onto big business and the rich), rallied to Kearney's cause. As one shrewd contemporary observer noted, part of his appeal was that he was attacking not just the Chinese, but also the big steamship and railroad companies that profited from employing Chinese labor, not to mention the corrupt two-party establishment that ran San Francisco politics:

> Neither Democrats nor Republicans had done, nor seemed likely to do, anything to remove these evils or to improve the lot of the people. They were only seeking (so men thought) places or the chance of jobs for themselves, and could always be bought by a powerful corporation. Working men must help themselves; there must be new methods and a new departure [. . .] The old parties, though both denouncing Chinese immigration in every convention they held, and professing to legislate against it, had failed to check it [. . .] Everything, in short, was ripe for a demagogue. Fate was kind to the Californians in sending them a demagogue of a mean type, noisy and confident, but with neither political foresight nor constructive talent.

Kearney may have lacked foresight and "constructive talent," but there is no gainsaying what he and his ilk were able to achieve. Beginning with the Page Law (1875) prohibiting the immigration of Asian women for "lewd or immoral purposes," American legislators scarcely rested until Chinese immigration to the United States had been stopped altogether. The Chinese Exclusion Act (1882) suspended immigration of Chinese for 10 years, introduced "certificates of registration" for departing laborers (effectively re-entry permits), required Chinese officials to vet travelers from Asia, and, for the first time in American history, created an offense of illegal immigration, with the possibility of deportation as a part of the penalty. The Foran Act (1885) banned all contract laborers from immigrating to America. Legislation passed in the Scott Act (1888) banned all Chinese from travel to the United States except "teachers, students, merchants, or travelers for pleasure." In all, between 1875 and 1924 more than a dozen pieces of legislation served to restrict and finally end altogether Chinese immigration.

No one should therefore underestimate the power of populism. For all his coarseness and bombast, Denis Kearney and his allies effectively sealed the American border along the Pacific coast of the United States; indeed, one cartoon of the time depicted them constructing a wall across the San Francisco harbor. In the 1850s and 1860s, as many as 40 percent of all Chinese emigrants had travelled beyond Asia, though the numbers arriving in the United States had in fact been relatively small (between 1870 and 1880, a total of 138,941 Chinese immigrants came, just 4.3 percent of the total, a share dwarfed by the vast European exodus across the Atlantic in the same period). What exclusion did ensure in the late nineteenth century was that Chinese immigration would not grow, as it surely would have, but instead dwindled and then ceased.

Ironies

Populism, then, is not just a form of political entertainment. One sometimes hears it said of Donald Trump: "Ah, he says wild things on the campaign trail, but when he is president it will be fine." History suggests otherwise. It suggests that men who threaten to restrict immigration—as well as to impose tariffs and to discourage capital export, as populists generally do—mean what they say.

Indeed, populists are under a special compulsion to enact what they pledge on the campaign trail, for their followers are fickle to begin with. In the case of Trump, most have already defected from the Republican Party establishment. If he fails to deliver, they can defect from him, too.

Of course, populists are bound eventually to disappoint their supporters. For populism is a toxic brew as well as an intoxicating one. Populists nearly always make life miserable for whichever minorities they chose to scapegoat, but they seldom make life much better for the people whose ire they whip up.

Whatever the demagogues may promise—and they always promise "jam today"—populism tends to have significantly more economic costs than benefits. Restricting immigration, imposing tariffs on imported goods, penalizing firms for investing abroad: such measures, if adopted by an American government in 2017, would be almost certain to reduce growth and employment, rather than the reverse. That has certainly been the Latin American experience—and few regions of the world have run the populist experiment more often.

The foreign dimension brings us to a final irony. Despite their habitual insistence on narrow national self-interest, populists are nearly always part of a global phenomenon. Globalization had been making enormous strides prior to 1873, with world trade, migration, and international capital flows growing at unprecedented rates. But the crisis of that year generated a populist backlash against globalization that was itself global in its scope.

Then, just as now, the principal targets of the demagogues were immigration, free trade, and high finance. Just as the United States excluded immigrants and raised tariffs, so did European countries by adopting similar discriminatory measures. In Bismarck's Germany, populism was often antisemitic—as it was in the France of the Dreyfus Affair—while in late Victorian Britain it was anti-Irish. Tariffs went up almost everywhere except in Britain.

Populism today has a similarly global quality. In June, the British vote to leave the European Union was hailed by populists right across the European continent as well as by Donald Trump in the United States and, implicitly, by Vladimir Putin in Russia.

Yielding to the Complicators

Let me conclude with a note of qualified optimism. Because populism is not fascism, populist victories should not be construed as harbingers of war—if anything, the opposite is true. In the 1870s and 1880s, populists did achieve significant reductions in globalization: not only immigration restrictions, but also higher tariffs. But they did not form many national governments, and they did not subvert any constitutions. Nor were populists much interested in starting wars; if anything, they lent towards isolationism and viewed imperialism as just another big business racket.

In most countries, the populist high tide was in the 1880s. What came next—in many ways as a reaction to populism, but also as an alternative set of policy solutions to the same public grievances—was Progressivism in the United States and socialism in Europe.

Perhaps something similar will also happen in our time. Perhaps that is something to look forward to. Nevertheless, we would do well to remember that World War I broke out during the progressive not the populist era.

The world today is, as I observed at the outset, in much less turmoil than one might infer from television news. Nevertheless, the economic and social consequences of globalization and the most recent financial crisis sowed the seeds for the populist backlash that we now see.

Populists are not fascists. They prefer trade wars to actual wars; administrative border walls to more defensible fortifications. The maladies they seek to cure are not imaginary: uncontrolled rising immigration, widening inequality, free trade with "unfree" countries, and political cronyism are all things that a substantial section of the electorate have some reason to dislike. The problem with populism is that its remedies are wrong and, in fact, counterproductive.

What we most have to fear—as was true of Brexit—is not therefore Armageddon, but something more prosaic: an attempt to reverse certain aspects of globalization, followed by disappointment when the snake oil does not really cure the patient's ills, followed by the emergence of a new and ostensibly more progressive set of remedies for our current malaise. The "terrible simplifiers" may have their day then. But they will end up yielding power to well-intentioned complicators, those more congenial to educated elites, but probably every a bit as dangerous, if not more so.

John S. Dryzek

GLOBAL CIVIL SOCIETY: THE PROGRESS OF POST-WESTPHALIAN POLITICS

Introduction

The 1648 Treaty of Westphalia is usually credited with establishing the system of sovereign states, making politics within states a categorically differ-

From *Annual Review of Political Science* 15 (2012), pp. 101–19.

ent activity from that between them. Whether going to war or establishing treaties or facilitating trade, politics beyond the borders of the state was solely a matter for the government of the state. Although the world was never quite like this (sovereignty never meant much for those at the mercy of colonial powers), Westphalian imagery long remained powerful for those who analyzed or acted within the global order. Global civil society brings a broader set of actors and kinds of relationships to bear in politics that is transnational rather than international.

The roots of global civil society can be traced back a century or even two, but its challenge to Westphalian imagery has since World War II gathered pace, especially during the past two decades or so. Global civil society is today a popular concept among academics and political actors alike, and it has changed the terms of discourse about and within global politics (Chandhoke 2002, p. 52). Yet what global civil society really means, the degree to which it mixes civility and activism, the extent to which it is actually global rather than merely transnational, and exactly who belongs in it remain cloaked in ambiguity (Corry 2006, pp. 305–7). The enthusiasm with which the rise of global civil society was celebrated among those keenly aware of the pathologies of the system of sovereign states has since been tempered by conceptual questioning, doubts about the standing of those claiming to act in and on behalf of civil society, and elucidation of some decidedly uncritical roles and relationships.

In light of enthusiasm, critique, and sober assessment, this review tries to sort out where the post-Westphalian politics of global civil society now stands, especially in terms of its potential contributions to accountability, freedom, and democracy in world politics. As befits an article in a political science journal, I stress the more clearly political activities of civil society, involving activism and advocacy that can range from confrontational to supportive in relation to other power centers. This means downplaying activities such as service provision, emergency relief, development aid, commercial standardization, information exchange, and mutual support. However, I do not ignore the latter, particularly when (on some accounts) they play a political role in rendering global society governable. Particular organizations can combine (for example) advocacy and aid—think of Oxfam and Save the Children on development and relief issues. My rela-

tive emphasis on the different kinds of activity is in keeping with that found in the literature.

Beyond the Shadow of the State

Conceptual discussions of global civil society often begin with a history of the idea and associated practice of civil society within nation-states, before tracing the expansion of the concept beyond the boundaries of specific states (for example, Kaldor 2003, pp. 7–8). In such accounts, eighteenth-century Europe yields the beginnings of commercial societies in which civil society emerges as a peaceful realm of social life protected from the arbitrary power of rulers, but still needing a state to enforce laws. Civil society could also be said to include the economy (explicitly in the later treatment of Hegel), though more recently it has become conventional to exclude economic transactions. It has also become common to stress the politicized aspects of civil society, as home to social movements of various sorts (Cohen & Arato 1992).

Although some might think that the ambiguity rampant in the concept of global civil society could be ameliorated through greater attention to what civil society actually does within states (e.g., Bartelson 2006), it may actually be liberating to let go of the idea that we should use state-connected politics as the necessary touchstone for any analysis of global civil society. There are several reasons for this.

First, global civil society has quite a long history of its own. As Keane (2003, p. 201) points out, eighteenth-century thinkers such as Emmerich de Vattel and Immanuel Kant envisaged an international order that was a civil society (without war), although states were essential components of that society. The idea of global civil society can indeed be thought of as a realm of civility, in which war, terrorism, draconian antiterror policies and discourse, aggressive nationalism, assertions of empire and military power, and submission to the imperatives of the capitalist market have no place. Today, though, global civil society is increasingly thought of not just as a realm of civility, but as home to a particular kind of political activity for which states may be the targets but are not otherwise full participants. In this light, the membership of global civil society can consist of social movements, the producers and consumers of old and new media, foundations, academics, individual activists and publicists, networks defined by common values or beliefs, and nongovernmental organizations (NGOs). The latter can be defined by a normative commitment (such as human rights or poverty alleviation), shared material interest (business and labor groups), religion, ethnicity, or profession. For the most part activities are civil, but they can also be disruptive and involve protests, demonstrations, and ridicule of actual or perceived power holders. This activist role is itself of long standing (Keck & Sikkink 1998, pp. 39–78), reaching back to antislavery movements in the nineteenth century, the Women's International League for Peace and Freedom after World War I (Cochran 2008), and the activists who pushed for the Universal Declaration of Human Rights in 1948.

Second, global civil society in its recent incarnations may really not be an outgrowth of state-ordered civil society, but rather a response to globalization (for empirical support from a case study of biotechnology regulation, see Coleman & Wayland 2006). "The appearance of global civil society before the appearance of a global state and a global rule of law in effect reverses the sequence of civic development in the West" (Chambers & Kopstein 2006, p. 378). As such, it may demand analysis and understanding in terms and categories somewhat different from those established in the old state-associated civil society tradition (Corry 2006).

Third, civil society now has much more inspirational force within the global arena than within states. There are many people for whom being a part of global civil society is an important part of their identity, and a way to legitimate demands to be heard by international governmental organizations. Some of these organizations too have used the language of global civil society in efforts to consult more broadly beyond the states that set them up. For example, Japan designated an "Ambassador in Charge of Civil Society" for G-8 negotiations it was hosting (Keane 2003, p. 25).

Such inspirational force is hard to find within states. It did play a part in oppositions against the decidedly uncivil states of the Soviet bloc leading up to the revolutions of 1989; indeed, these events could be described as revolutions of civil society (Arato 1993). But that inspiration quickly yielded to laments about the weak capacity of any civil society to check the power of postcommunist governments that, though elected, were otherwise reluctant to accept any limits on what they could do (Bernhard 1996). Old habits of nonassociation learned under communism proved hard to break, and the concept of civil society came to name only what was missing. Within developed liberal democracies, the supportive role of what was once called civil society seems now to be discussed mostly under the heading of "social capital," a concept not easily transposed to any transnational context, where dense face-to-face interaction is less feasible (though see Smith 1998). Initiatives such as President George H.W. Bush's "Thousand Points of Light" and British Prime Minister David Cameron's "Big Society" seek to induce private organizations to take on public functions, but they do not actually use the language of civil society. And in both these cases, the initiative and the terminology came from government leadership—not from what we might call civil society itself.

Paradoxically, taking global civil society out from under the shadow of the state can draw support from those who believe that civil society as a concept *only* makes sense when paired with a state. For Brown (2000, pp. 21–22), "civil society is the fragile achievement of a small number of Western societies. . . . For this reason, and because of the absence of an international counterpart to the domestic state, to apply the notion of civil society to developments globally is a mistake." Similarly, Bowden (2006) observes that the global level has no state-analogue to regulate civil society in the way that is so important within states; the state is the guarantor for civil society, which can then take shape as a source of inputs to, interlocutor with, critic of, and supporter of the state. Goodhart (2005) argues that democratic civil society exists in symbiosis with a state within a defined territory, and that even anti-authoritarian civil society (as once found in Latin America and Eastern Europe) only makes sense in terms of the state it targets and wants to transform. These authors all conclude that global civil society cannot therefore rightfully be said to exist. But it would be equally valid to conclude that all the practices currently grouped under this heading really stand in need of a new name. Yet it is too late to seek a new name that would confirm this difference; "global civil society" it must be, however different that really is from the domestic entity that bears a similar name.

Treating global civil society as much more than just a transplant from state to globe does not preclude the possibility that states still matter: Chambers & Kopstein (2006, p. 378) point out that "global civil society still cannot do without the state and the nation state at that. The vast majority of organizations, associations, and movements that make up global civil society have their homes and headquarters in countries that offer them the protection and predictability of an established liberal legal order." But what is protected can operate globally in terms very different from civil society as it was conceptualized within states.

The Rise of Global Civil Society

Although international civil society does, as we have seen, possess roots going back several centuries, global civil society seems to have taken a very rapid upswing in recent decades in terms of the amount of political and intellectual attention it receives, as well as in terms of crude indicators such as the number of international NGOs, social movement protests, gatherings of activists (such as the annual World Social Forum, which began in 2001 in Porto Alegre, Brazil), and media with an intentionally transnational reach. Keane (2003, p. 92) identifies a number of contributory factors, including economic globalization, advances in communications technology (the internet in particular), the deliberate choices of governments in establishing NGOs, and the increasing incidence of multilateral negotiations between states that inspire NGOs and activists to shadow them. Smith & Wiest (2005) find that the incidence of a state's citizens' participation in transnational civil society organizations is explained not by the state's degree of integration in the global economy, but rather by the extent of its involvement in international institutions. This finding should give pause to those who argue that participation in global civil society simply reflects and reinforces economic advantage.

Civil society activity may increase in response to the perceived failure of existing governance mechanisms to confront problems effectively or to recognize key values and interests. With domestic politics in mind, Jänicke (1996) defines civil society in functional terms as public action in response to failure in the state or the economy. Such failures are ubiquitous in global politics, applying to public authority in general (such as that exercised by international governmental organizations), not just states and markets. Sometimes this failure leads NGOs to take on a substantial operational role in delivering aid and relief.

Failure motivates political action too. For example, Lipschutz & Mayer (1996) point to evident limitations in global government and relying on the market in environmental affairs, suggesting that joint action grounded in local communities but seeking transnational connection can often do a better job. Here, whether such action can actually do better is less important in explaining activity than the belief of activists that they can do better. A failure of global governance is clearly evident in the case of climate change, where years of multilateral negotiations have failed to yield effective agreement. Climate change correspondingly has long featured a very high level of global civil society activity (Newell 2000). Activists and NGOs turn up in massive numbers at the annual Conference of the Parties to the United Nations Framework Convention on Climate Change, and increasingly involve themselves in networked governance alternatives to multilateral negotiations (Bäckstrand 2008), such as the Clean Technology Fund. In contrast, the global governance of economic affairs is much more effective in both producing decisive outcomes and restricting civil society influence—although the limited neoliberal terms in which those outcomes are produced, emphasizing economic growth rather than social justice, lead to its own kind of failure and consequent activist response.

States have various mechanisms for authorizing representatives and making government accountable to the public (for example, election, selection on the basis of merit, loyalty to the party, mandated consultation process). These mechanisms are either weak or nonexistent at the global level. In taking on these functions, global civil society becomes the locus of demands for legitimacy and accountability that now pervade global governance (Scholte 2007, Grant & Keohane 2005). So if we did want to persist with tired comparisons to domestic politics, the proper counterpart would be elections and other kinds of representation and accountability mechanisms, not rule-governed social civility. Within states, accountability has come to be associated strongly with the possibility of sanctioning representatives—especially through voting against them. Given the absence of elections and weakness of other sanctioning mechanisms in global affairs, accountability therein may have to mean something different. At any rate, global civil society takes on meaning through reference to its engagement with, not just its separation from, public authority. This engagement is spurred by emerging demands for the democratization of global politics (Scholte 2002), meaning global civil society plays a large part in the thinking of political theorists when they turn their attention to the possibilities for global democracy. Many of the values that animate enthusiasts for civil society are democratic values. Later in this article I return to what

democratic theorists make of these developments, and how they think about what accountability in global politics can mean.

The Enthusiasts

The more enthusiastic supporters of global civil society see in it possibilities not just for enhanced representation and accountability within the existing world order, but for thoroughly transforming that order in ways that would counteract its domination by large corporations, powerful states, low-visibility financial networks, and bureaucratic international organizations. Global civil society promises everything that established centers of power lack: openness, publicity, civility, inclusiveness, a broad variety of values, a potentially wide range of participants, contestation, and reflexivity. These hopes are not necessarily fully consistent with each other. For example, civility and contestation can pull in different directions, if contestation turns to ridicule (think of the "fossil of the day" awards given out by the Climate Action Network at multilateral climate negotiations, designed to shame their recipients).

Maximally, then, global civil society represents the hope for an entirely different global order. For example, Lipschutz (1992) sees in the rise of global civil society a major challenge to the problematic states system. Falk (1998) sees "globalization from below." Kaldor (2003) subtitles her book "An Answer to War," seeing in global civil society the emergence of ways to resolve conflicts and establish relationships in nonviolent fashion. The fact that shooting wars between states are increasingly rare might seem to imply there is less for civil society to do in this respect, though of course global politics remains pervaded by other kinds of violence, including civil conflicts that themselves involve transnational networks (what Kaldor 2007 calls "new wars").

Is there any evidence for the kind of transformative role for global civil society that the enthusiasts see? The litany of successes for global civil society might begin with the Universal Declaration of

Human Rights in 1948—although the hopes for a transformed global order that attended the founding of the United Nations were soon checked by the reality of the Cold War. More recent successes can be found with the campaign against land mines culminating in the 1997 Ottawa Convention (Price 1998) and the establishment of the International Criminal Court in 1998 (Glasius 2009). Stiglitz (2002, p. 20) credits the antiglobalization/global justice movement that began in 1999 with changing ways of thinking and practices in national governments and international institutions, including the World Bank (see also Schlemmer-Schulte 2001 on World Bank consultation with civil society organizations). There have been other occasions when civil society organizations and activists have been very visible, although the outcomes have been more ambiguous. On February 15, 2003, 11 million people in 700 cities in 60 countries marched against the invasion of Iraq (they were described the next day in the *New York Times* as "a new superpower"). The invasion of course happened anyway, but the scale of the protests did perhaps indicate the increased political costs that would attend any similar kind of military action in future. The "Make Poverty History" campaign led by celebrities such as Bono managed to get a massive commitment from the states participating in the G8 summit at Gleneagles in 2005 to increase aid to developing countries—though delivering on that commitment was another matter entirely.

Simply enumerating success stories is no proof of transformation; it would be equally possible to enumerate failures (such as the resurgence of neoliberalism in the wake of the Global Financial Crisis of 2008 that briefly looked to have buried it), unchecked by civil society activity. Effectiveness in influencing collective outcomes on particular high-profile occasions is, however, not the only valid measure of success or reason for being positive about the role of civil society. Global civil society also offers hope for new forms of living and acting together. Keane (2003, p. 141) believes that we can find in global civil society "oases of freedom in a vast desert of localised injustice and resistance." Given the vastness of the desert, global civil society is for Keane something that always has to be struggled for.

The Critics

Nobody Elected Civil Society

Civil society can be home to some unsavory people and organizations (Heins 2004, Chambers & Kopstein 2001), such as racist militias and populist demagogues, but this is probably less true globally than within states, given the civilizing force of engagement in transnational activity. The dominant theme in criticisms of global civil society is actually unrepresentativeness. As Anderson & Rieff (2005, p. 29) put it, "Citizens do not vote for this or that civil society organization as their representatives because, in the end, NGOs exist to reflect their own principles, not to represent a constituency to whose interests and desires they must respond." NGOs are often responsive to wealthy donors rather than any body of citizens (Jordan & van Tuijl 2006). Heins (2005) sees global civil society as composed of self-appointed representatives, coming mostly from wealthy countries, and so helping to constitute a global elite, not a counterweight to established power. For the critics, it is easy to condemn even apparently successful interventions such as the banning of landmines as just another episode in the development of global elites (Anderson 2000). In an odd way the critics actually validate the democratic aspirations of global civil society but simply believe it falls far short of any such aspirations.

A first response to charges of unrepresentativeness might be that the charge is overdrawn. To begin, various accountability mechanisms do check the leaders of organizations, although these mechanisms involve members, contributors, governments, and other organizations and activists in networks rather than ordinary people (Wapner 2002) or aid recipients dependent on operational NGOs. Networked or peer accountability is institutionalized in associations that NGOs themselves sometimes establish to monitor their own activities. For example, a number of development NGOs consent to certification of their activities from Social Accountability International (Brown 2007, p. 27). Elitism and unrepresentativeness are themselves contested within global civil society. For example, Third World activists started the campaign of "Not About Us Without Us" as a counterpart to the "Make Poverty History Campaign" dominated by wealthy activists (Brassett & Smith 2010, p. 426). At the seventh annual meeting of the World Social Forum in Nairobi in 2007, Kenyan poor peoples' movements protested against the claims of well-organized NGOs to represent Africa.

A better response to the charge is to ask: Unrepresentative compared to what? Compared to some ideal model of egalitarian democracy, global civil society may do badly. Compared to other realities in a global order dominated by large corporations, hegemonic states, neoliberal market thinking, secretive and unresponsive international organizations, low-visibility financial networks, and military might, global civil society does rather well. The criticisms of unrepresentativeness do not do justice to what is possible and what is not in global politics. The egalitarian democracy in whose name the criticisms are made has never existed in global politics, and there are good reasons for that.

The critics might respond that there are better ways of realizing democratic aspirations in global politics, but to date no compelling argument has been made for any such alternative. One prominent alternative involves pushing the United Nations General Assembly in the direction of an elected body, as advocated by the Campaign for a United Nations Parliamentary Assembly (http://www.unpacampaign.org; see also Falk & Strauss 2001). But global elections are a truly distant prospect, and the miserable experience of elections to the European Parliament hardly inspires optimism (these low-turnout elections are not fought on European issues, and mainly provide an opportunity for a small number of voters to vent anger at their national governments).

Evaluating the activities of global civil society in terms of some implicit ideal model of democracy is ultimately a pointless exercise. It is more useful to think of the contribution of global civil society to processes of democratization. Democratization means expanding the scope of issues subject to collective control, the effective number of people who can exercise influence over the content of collective decisions, and the competence with which such influence and control is exercised. On all three dimensions, global politics is surely better off with the activities of global civil society than without.

In light of recent developments in the theory of representation, the critics look a bit unsophisticated. Conventional theories of representation (Pitkin 1967), to which the critics are mostly wedded, stress tests of authorization and accountability. Representatives in global civil society are mostly self-authorized. Yet their representation claim can still be tested and justified. Montanero (2008) proposes tests of whether or not the representative facilitates the empowerment of those he/she claims to represent, is accountable to them, considers public reputation, and is acceptable to peers. Saward (2009) believes we should ask how connected the representative is within the political system, whether there is a constituency to validate a representation claim, whether the representative is independent from strategic advantage, and whether the representative is independent from the structural imperatives of any state (see also Saward 2010). In light of Keane's (2009) view that contemporary democracy is mostly "monitory democracy" [corresponding to what Pettit (2006) calls the "editorial" aspect of democracy, whereby collective decisions can be contested], we might also ask whether the representative is effective in scrutinizing policies, proposals, and actions in light of the concerns of the constituency he or she claims to represent.

Global Governmentality

A second criticism cuts more deeply than any worries about representation, seeing the whole ensemble of global civil society (including, perhaps especially, its nonadvocacy aspects such as aid, relief, and information exchange) as a force that bolsters rather than challenges the established global order. In this light, participation in civil society often means socialization into this order (Comor 2001). Thus these critics contend that, far from pointing to a changed world order, civil society helps make the existing world governable (Amoore & Langley 2004).

A subtle way to ponder the complicity of civil society in established power deploys the idea of governmentality associated with Michel Foucault and his followers. For Foucault, governmentality is the shaping of compliant subjects by dominant discourses, especially liberalism, such that society can be rendered governable. Individuals therefore have the illusion of freedom but are disciplined to exercise that freedom in ways that support the established political-economic order. In this light, global civil society could contribute to global governmentality through its very "civil" qualities: it channels putative discontent into activities that do not upset the status quo. Jaeger (2007) argues in these terms that global civil society is actually complicit in depoliticization and fails to offer any substantial challenge to the neoliberal status quo. For Jaeger, there may be a global public sphere, but it is put in service as a subsystem of the global political system rather than contesting the structural status quo of the global political economy. Jaeger's evidence comes from an examination of United Nations governance discourse about civil society, so it is hardly surprising that his evidence confirms his claim, because that is not where more contestatory activities are going to be validated.

For Bartelson (2006), global civil society follows its domestic counterpart in making society governable and legitimating governance; as such, it has no emancipatory potential (see also Amoore & Langley 2004). Similarly, Sending & Neumann (2006) take on the "governance without government" literature to argue that civil society is not an alternative to state-based power but simply another means through which power is exercised. Thus, civil society does not challenge the power of states but rather joins in the task of governing: "nonstate actors are enrolled to perform governance functions by virtue of their technical expertise, advocacy and capacity for will-formation" (Sending & Neumann 2006, p. 664). But the Sending & Neumann analysis is not convincing because they look only for evidence from cases that proves their point, especially the degree to which NGOs operate in conjunction with the (highly atypical) Norwegian government in international affairs. They do not look for, still less recognize, contestatory possibilities in global civil society.

Global civil society can indeed also feature protest and contestation. The empirical study of networks by Katz (2006) concludes that sometimes NGOs do seem to serve the established order but that sometimes they can constitute a "counter-hegemonic bloc." In this light, governmentality analysis, however one-sided it typically proves, simply drives home the need to retain and cultivate such contestation. As Lipschutz (2005) puts it, working within a governmentality framework himself, civil society needs to contest the "constitutive politics" of the way the world is organized, rather than take its place within the "distributive politics" of the status quo. Irrespective of the validity of such a distinction, or indeed of the finer points of governmentality analysis, contestation and its attendant reflexivity are essential in responding to pitfalls highlighted by the global governmentality critique (Munck 2006). But should civil society actors *always* choose contestation and radical opposition over more cooperative engagement with centers of power such as states, international organizations, and other forms of governance? Is the choice necessarily so stark?

Terms of Engagement: Global Governance or Public Spheres?

Most definitions of civil society see it as somehow separate or at least different from formally constituted public authority. Yet such separation does not sit well in a world moving in the direction of networked governance (Rhodes 1997) that blurs distinctions between public and private, between governmental and nongovernmental roles. This is perhaps why Keane believes the currently popular notion of "governance without government" in world politics (Rosenau & Czempiel 1992) "issues a direct challenge to the whole theory of global civil society" (Keane 2003, p. 96). Keane prefers to speak of a global "cosmocracy" in which civil society organizations enter into relationships with governments and international governmental organizations that can vary from integration to cooperation to distance to confrontation. Keane thinks the difference between global governance and cosmocracy matters a lot, but really the distinction is very fine, because both can involve civil society organizations playing a part in governing.

The involvement of nongovernmental organizations in government has a long history within states. For example, the corporatist states of Northern Europe have long granted a formal share in policy making to business and labor federations, and, in their more expansive moments, to representatives of women's and environmentalist organizations. Although the kind of tight relationship that corporatism connotes is hard to envisage in global politics, some authors have advocated a formalized role for civil society in association with international governmental organizations. Willetts (2006) sees insidious corporatist ideas at work in the 2004 report of the UN-sponsored Panel of Eminent Persons on United Nations–Civil Society Relations. Saif Gadafy's (2008) notorious Ph.D. thesis from the London School of Economics and Political Science advocates such a role, eventually leading to the cosmopolitan irony of an advocate of greater civil society involvement in international organizations being the subject of an arrest warrant from one such organization that was set up largely in response to pressure from civil society—the International Criminal Court.

Civil society participation in transnational networked governance was very evident in connection with the 2002 World Summit on Sustainable Development in Johannesburg (Carr & Norman 2008).

One of the main activities at the summit was the establishment of numerous partnerships involving NGOs, developing country governments, and corporations—what von Frantzius (2004, p. 469) refers to as "the privatization of sustainable development," though really it is just a blurring of public and private.

The alternative to thinking about civil society as a component of governance is to conceptualize its proper place as constituting a public sphere at some degree of critical distance from government and governance alike. The public sphere is usually defined in terms of its orientation to public affairs, while not seeking a formal share of public authority. Matters can be a bit more complicated at transnational and global levels because government officials—especially from disadvantaged countries—can sometimes play a prominent role in the public sphere. Bolivian President Evo Morales has encouraged transnational social movements on climate change, hosting the World People's Conference on Climate Change and the Rights of Mother Earth in 2010, though that summit constructed "the people" in a particular and partial way (Stevenson 2011).

Public spheres can be constituted in clearly oppositional terms, though they do not have to be; and the less oppositional, the more vulnerable they are to the governmentality critique. Sometimes opposition is very evident, as in the antiglobalization protests that began in 1999 in Seattle and have accompanied numerous international gatherings of powerful states and international organizations ever since. The invasion of Iraq organized by the United States in 2003 brought 11 million protesters into the streets on the same day (though some governments of powerful states such as France and Germany also opposed the invasion). The Arab world has featured a very lively transnational (but obviously not global) public sphere featuring old and new media, facilitated of course by a common language, that has long stood in contrast to the moribund state of politics within most Arab states. The transnational Arab public sphere could generate news and information with far greater credibility than state-controlled newspapers, radio, and television in the region, and in 2011 its opposition to the authoritarian regimes of the Arab world became very visible.

Global civil society can, then, feature anything from very close engagement with governance to clear opposition to established power. Can global civil society prosper in its integration with policy-making bodies, or should it keep a critical distance?

Certainly the temptations of integration are obvious for activists frustrated by a long history of exclusion from the corridors of power. But we know from the history of states that the inclusion of organized interests in the state is sometimes beneficial to those interests, sometimes a matter of cooptation and neutralization that saps both energy and, eventually, membership from the group in question—because groups with a close relationship with government are often also funded by government, so there is little incentive for group leaders to seek funding elsewhere or to deal with a potentially troublesome membership (Dryzek et al. 2003). Much turns on the particular configuration of movement aims and governmental priorities; if movements cannot attach their defining concern to a core imperative of government, they are better off keeping their distance. Can we apply this sort of analysis to the choices of global civil society if and when its members are invited to share in policy making, be it in formal consultation with international governmental organizations, cooperation with states, or participation in consequential governance networks?

Sometimes there will be little choice here. For example, if a development or emergency relief NGO wants to work in a developing country, it may have to get approval from the host government, which may have laws regulating NGO activity (for example, requiring employment of locals). In such cases it is the operational rather than advocacy role of the NGO that requires cooperation with the host government.

When a civil society organization is contemplating whether or not to work with a government of any kind or level, including international governmental organizations, if the organization's defining concerns cannot be aligned with the core priority of the governmental organization then the organization may be better off keeping its distance. For example, the World Trade Organization (WTO) and International Monetary Fund have core priorities consistent with the neoliberal market economics that underpins the global political economy. Organizations with a social justice or environmental agenda should therefore be wary of engaging too closely with them, and treat with skepticism any claims that (for example) the WTO is being "greened" (as suggested by Weinstein & Charnovitz 2001). Whatever its record in the past, the World Bank's commitment to neoliberal economics is less fixed, and so engagement may be less hazardous. The United Nations Environment Program (UNEP) has core priorities that are quite consistent with the defining interest of (some) green social movement organizations, and so engagement is not especially hazardous—though UNEP is not an especially powerful organization, even on environmental issues.

There is plenty of scope for judgment here on the part of groups as they think about the terms of engagement with established power. Murkier still are choices about participation in governance networks of the sort so central to a post-Westphalian world. The core priorities of networks are harder to identify than those of formal organizations such as states or international governmental organizations. Here it may be beneficial to examine the kind of discourse that a network features. If the network is dominated by a particular uncongenial discourse—as for example global financial networks are dominated by neoliberalism and attendant assumptions about efficient markets—then a group that does not accept the core tenets of that discourse should think long and hard about the terms on which it engages.

The Search for Conceptual Clarity

Global civil society evokes enthusiasm and skepticism, hopes and fears, new ways of thinking about the world, a continuation of deep traditions, and much more besides. Its vast literature helps reinforce the idea in world politics that global civil society matters. At one level global civil society seems to presage a different world. At another level the real content and importance of that change remain obscure. The amelioration of obscurity might seem to begin with some conceptual clarification that would in turn facilitate the generation of a progressive (if not cumulative) body of social scientific work on the real nature and impact of global civil society in world politics.

There have been numerous empirical studies of particular NGOs, episodes of activism, processes leading up to global agreements, and networks of actors (several of which I have cited). These studies, though, lack unifying conceptual order. The development of global civil society as a concept has been influenced by political actors more than social scientists. So it should come as no surprise that it is not a concept that is especially tractable in (social) scientific terms. It is full of ambiguities concerning how to classify its membership and what kinds of actions belong under its umbrella, and it is often invoked for rhetorical purposes (Amoore & Langley 2004). This constitutive role could conceivably cause trouble for social scientific analysis, because if people who invoke the term start to mean something different by it, any timeless and cross-contextual validity of the concept may be imperiled. If it follows the course of concepts such as democracy and sustainable development, we may well find its meaning changes with time as a result of the intervention of key actors. Sustainable development, for example, has with time become increasingly reconciled to conventional notions of economic growth as a result of engagement with the concept by large corporations on the global stage.

Should we devote the effort to force global civil society into a conceptually precise shape that would improve the prospects for social scientific analysis? Or should we just map the variety of meanings and use each when appropriate (Anheier 2007)? Those who have studied democracy in all its varieties have taken the latter tack. What this means is that sub-

specializations in political science work with different definitions of democracy and are largely oblivious to competing definitions (see Coppedge & Gerring 2011 for an attempt to produce a new, disaggregated conceptualization that all could use). Omelicheva (2009, p. 110) believes that global civil society "is currently lacking an intelligible conceptual apparatus and empirical theory to support rigorous empirical research," while acknowledging, "For some, this might not be a problem since multiple meanings of GCS can provide a space for dialogue." Omelicheva then takes a moderate position, seeking some shared points of reference while allowing continued dispute on details (p. 111). She recognizes that "there is nothing wrong with empirical work inspired by ideas from political philosophy" (p. 121) but then says "the field is still in need of a clear conception of GCS as an observable phenomenon and an analytical category devoid of liberal-democratic qualities or other imputed normative values" (p. 122).

However laudable such an aim might be in social scientific terms, it is going to be problematic if global civil society is an *essentially* contested concept in Gallie's (1956) terms: that is, no contestation, no concept. It may well be the case that contestation of the meaning of civil society is integral to the very nature of the concept. That still allows boundaries around this contestation: civil society is not war, it is not empire, it is not coercive diplomacy, it is not chaos, it is not (just) the market. But treating civil society as an essentially contested concept means that the kinds of empirical methods appropriate to its study are likely to be ethnography, in-depth interviewing, and discourse analysis, rather than causal hypothesis testing (Taylor 2002). These sorts of analyses will yield appreciation of the variety of meanings that global civil society can take, rather than convergence on any single meaning.

For better or for worse, empirical analysis of global civil society is tied up with normative agendas and associated contests over the meaning and significance of particular practices and ideas, including the idea of global civil society itself. Rather than seek to banish normative agendas in the name of social science, we might perhaps call on political theory to clarify the content of these agendas and meanings.

The Political Theory of Global Civil Society

Given that global civil society sits firmly in the defining territory of international relations (on some accounts threatening to change the character of international relations completely), the obvious place to take this next step in the search for clarity would be in international relations theory. But whereas for its enthusiasts global civil society changes everything, for large areas of international relations scholarship it apparently changes nothing. Now, articles on global civil society do occasionally appear in mainstream international relations journals (see the reference list). But those operating in the theoretical core of international relations scholarship appear largely unmoved. If we consult the index of the recent authoritative 44-chapter *Oxford Handbook of International Relations* (Reus-Smit & Snidal 2008), we find only five entries for civil society, four of which are inconsequential and in passing. Related concepts such as nonstate actors (5), NGOs (1), international NGOs (1), and transnational social movements (2) fare little better. There are actually only three paragraphs in the 732 pages of the *Handbook* that say anything substantive about civil society, and then only to warn that "civil society is inherently opposed to the centralizing and homogenizing force of American 'Empire' but is always vulnerable to being subverted or manipulated"—for example "to become an instrument for the penetration of 'Empire' into Eastern Europe and Central Asia" (Cox 2008, p. 91). Global civil society's contribution to hopes for global democracy is absent entirely—remarkably, there is not a single entry for "democracy" in the index of the *Handbook*.

International relations theory is perhaps too distracted by its interminable battles between realism, liberalism, and constructivism to be able to devote sustained attention to a substantive topic such as global civil society. However, constructivists allow civil society actors a role in the construction of global norms (Price 1998; Finnemore & Sikkink 2001, p. 400; Payne 2001; Khagram et al. 2002). They are particularly interested in challenges to the norm of sovereignty that privileges the agency of states. Still, many of the prominent works on global civil society are by people who are not international relations scholars; as such, they are inflected with particular enthusiasms (or skepticisms) and are not easy to order conceptually. In the absence of much help from international relations theory, is there any political theory that can do better?

Political theory is still largely Westphalian in that it works with the image of a sovereign state as the locus of public authority. (This led to an easy division of labor with international relations theory, inasmuch as the latter concerns itself with relations between sovereign states, though why the two kinds of theory eventually stopped talking to each other very much is another puzzle.) Emerging post-Westphalian political theory needs to come to grips with networked governance in particular. There is a massive literature on governance networks, most of it empirical. Some of this work stresses networks operating within national boundaries in the shadow of a state (Bell & Hindmoor 2009), but for much of it networks extend rather easily across boundaries. As we have already seen, Keane (2003, p. 96) fears losing global civil society to "governance without government" of the sort found in networks, but whether or not such a loss really matters turns on the conditions of governance—and networked governance in particular. Networked governance can indeed involve low-visibility interaction producing outcomes with no publicity and no accountability, dominated by a single hegemonic discourse. Global financial affairs have often been organized on this kind of basis, with civil society organizations and activists generally conspicuous by their absence from consequential networks. More defensibly, networks can also feature what Braithwaite (2007) calls "nodes of contestation," with a place for civil society activism. It is easy to identify contestation that stands outside networks, easy to identify cases of civil society organizations fully integrated in networks, much harder to identify the semi-integrated condition that any node of contestation would represent, and harder still (perhaps impossible) to locate such nodes that would be immune from Foucauldian charges of complicity in governmentality. No ready examples come to mind, meaning some close empirical study in these terms is called for.

Contestation in the context of networked governance requires political freedom. For some activists, freedom may be secured in liberal terms by the state they inhabit (see Chambers & Kopstein 2006, p. 378), which can guarantee individual rights against coercion (including coercion from the state itself). But for those venturing into global civil society without such guarantees, a different concept of freedom is appropriate. For republicans such as Pettit (1997), freedom is primarily a matter of nondomination: people are free to the extent nobody has the capacity to dominate them. In these terms, formal liberal rights are empty in the face of extreme material inequality. Republican ideas of freedom as nondomination travel much more easily to governance networks than do liberal ideas about rights guaranteed by and in a state, so republican freedom can facilitate post-Westphalian reconceptualization of politics more generally. Networks can be evaluated according to how well they secure nondomination (it is the capacity for domination that republicans worry about, not its observed practice). Indeed, we can use freedom as nondomination as a test for civil society organizations worried about their engagement with a particular network. Nondomination cannot be guaranteed for them by laws of the kind that liberals favor (because networks operate without formal laws), but it can exist to greater or lesser degree in the operations of a network. For Bohman (2007, pp. 65–66), freedom as nondomination is actually a test to distinguish between good and bad civil society: good civil society exists only when it promotes nondomination. For Braithwaite (2007, p. 167), in a networked context, "Deliberative democracy is the ideal that can most fruitfully be deployed to enrich freedom as nondomination" because "giving direct democratic voice to people affected by a decision is the best way to respect the autonomy and empower the public reason of citizens." This consideration resonates with all those who engage global civil society with the language of democracy, so let us now see what democratic theory can say about global civil society.

The Democratic Theory of Global Civil Society

Thinking in thoroughly post-Westphalian terms enables us to take more seriously the possibility that global civil society is central to meaningful global democratization, rather than an ersatz substitute for elections or a supportive waystation on the road to cosmopolitan institutions (as advocated by Held 1995 and other cosmopolitan democrats), or indeed something whose contribution to global democracy has to be ruled out because it cannot play the same role that it does within states (Goodhart 2005). Becoming post-Westphalian in a deep ontological sense means letting go not only of the idea of the sovereign state, but also of the individualistic basis for the establishment of sovereign authority formalized by Thomas Hobbes at the same time as the Treaty of Westphalia (his *Leviathan* appeared in 1651 but he wrote it in the 1640s). This move is actually consistent with Kaldor's (2003) take on global civil society as "an answer to war," at least in the sense both Westphalia and *Leviathan* were in their different ways also "answers to war" (respectively, wars of religion and civil war).

A post-Westphalian ontology can stress discourses and informal networks as well as individuals and formal organizations. In this light, the engagement and contestation of discourses in the public sphere are essential aspects of democracy (Dryzek 2006). Discourses in global politics are likely to be especially consequential inasmuch as they can take on some of the coordinating functions that the formal organization of the state undertakes in domestic politics (for example, global environmental affairs have in recent decades been coordinated largely by the discourse of sustainable development, global financial affairs by neoliberalism). Prominent discourses in global civil society include human rights, sustainable development, poverty alleviation, transparency, climate justice, green radicalism, and human security. These discourses can take their place on the global stage alongside others either ingrained in the global polity or advanced and reinforced by the actions of states, such as neoliberalism, neoconservatism, a realist discourse of anarchy in security affairs, counterterror, and various "civilizational" discourses of the sort we can read into Huntington's (1996) clash of civilizations (Asian values, liberal-democratic triumphalism, Islamic radicalism). Some discourses are of course advanced by both state and civil society actors. Particular discursive contests might involve human rights versus counterterror; a three-cornered contest between neoliberalism, sustainable development, and green radicalism; the alleged clash of civilizations; and human rights versus Asian values (at least as characterized by former Singapore Prime Minister Lee Kwan Yew).

In this light, global civil society is essentially a pattern of discursive representation (Keck 2003, Dryzek & Niemeyer 2008). Activists and organizations can be seen as representing particular discourses as they interact with each other and with centers of public authority such as states and international governmental organizations. So Bono represents antipoverty or a discourse of Africa, Transparency International represents transparency and anticorruption, Sea Shepherd represents green radicalism, Amnesty International represents human rights. Any claim to be representing global civil society itself (Amoore & Langley 2004) is in part an invocation of a cosmopolitan discourse. Interpreting representation in discursive terms enables us to rethink the question of accountability that is central to democratic representation. Accountability can mean so much more than the potential for sanctioning a representative. Discursive accountability means continuing to communicate in terms that make sense within the discourse being represented, even as the representative encounters representatives of other discourses, and even as he or she reflects on his or her positions in light of such encounters (Dryzek & Niemeyer 2008, p. 490). In this sense, it is akin to what Mansbridge (2009, p. 384) calls "narrative accountability," though the latter requires a specific audience defined in conventional terms to which an account is given. The narrative may, however, be constructed within the frame provided by a particular discourse—for example, environmental NGOs will normally draw on a green or sustainability discourse. For Mansbridge, deliberative accountability is more demanding than narrative in that it involves two-way interchange between the representative and those being represented. If it is a discourse that is thought of as being represented, rather than persons, deliberative accountability may be harder to locate.

Accountability is just one aspect of representation, and representation just one aspect of democracy. We can speak of discursive representation, but what about discursive democracy? Discursive democracy can be said to exist to the extent of dispersed and competent control over the collectively consequential engagement of discourses in the global public sphere. Again it is important to think in terms of degrees: the key democratic question when it comes to evaluating the role of global civil society is the *degree* to which its activities can subject global decisions to dispersed and competent control, not whether it measures up to some ideal of political equality and popular control. And if collective decisions have to be justified in terms of discourses beyond narrowly administrative or economistic terms, that is a democratic advance—however far we may remain from any ideal. Decentralized control is only a force for democracy to the extent it features communicative action by people acting as citizens (whether individually or collectively) rather than as economic actors; and this is exactly what global civil society promises.

When it comes to critical competence in discursive contests in the world system, civil society actors have one important advantage over states and corporations, which is their greater freedom to act on a reflexive basis (Dryzek 2006, pp. 121–23). Reflexivity here means the ability to contemplate the constellation of discourses operative on a particular issue and to figure out how any action will affect that constellation. States are heavily constrained by their imperatives to ensure their own security, maintain legitimacy in the eyes of their own populations, and maximize economic growth. An extreme example of antireflexive state action in world politics can be found in the George W. Bush administration in the United States, whose actions on the global stage, even if they made sense in narrowly instrumental terms, reconfigured the global constellation of discourses in ways detrimental to U.S. interests (including raising the standing of a discourse of international anarchy). Corporations are even more constrained than states because of their need to maximize profits. So however disadvantaged they are when it comes to material resources, civil society actors are privileged in terms of the freedom to act reflexively. Reflexive action is not, however, the preserve of the materially disadvantaged or those opposed to dominant discourses. For example, the World Business Council for Sustainable Development has helped shift the meaning of sustainable development in a direction friendly to economic growth, free trade, and corporate involvement.

The opportunity for reflexive action is not always grasped by civil society actors, who do not necessarily think about what they are doing in these terms. But civil society actions that are condemned as instrumentally irresponsible or ineffective can turn out to make sense in reflexive terms. Consider for example the way initially inchoate antiglobalization protests led eventually to the construction of a coherent counterdiscourse to neoliberal globalization, or how the Climate Action Network's shaming of particular countries and delegates at multilateral negotiations risks alienating the country in question but keeps a more serious environmental discourse alive in the discursive field surrounding negotiations. (For an extended analysis of another environmental incident in these terms, see Dryzek 2006, pp. 116–17, 122–23.) Recognizing reflexivity in terms of influence over the constellation of discourses in the global system enables reassessment of civil society effectiveness. Activities such as protests against the invasion of Iraq in 2003 may look ineffective in direct instrumental terms, yet still have profound effects in reordering the global balance of discourses. Speaking of "norms" rather than "discourses" enables a link to the interest of constructivist international relations scholars in norm change, though this connection is currently undeveloped.

Brassett & Smith (2010) warn that thinking of its contribution to global democratization in discursive terms still risks seeing global civil society as simply an agent with too circumscribed a role within deliberative global governance, as too tightly connected to providing inputs for, and so ultimately legitimating, global governance. This warning resonates with the governmentality critique discussed above. They stress the importance of maintaining the vitality of civil society as an "affective arena" of endless contestation, critique, performance, and identity formation. Those concerned with expanding real influence (be it in conventional instrumental terms or the reflexive terms just established) over the production of collective outcomes might balk at such a suggestion. But the answer is surely that global civil society can be both an agent and an arena; there is no need to force it into either role to the exclusion of the other.

Conclusion

Critics notwithstanding, global civil society is here to stay, and the actors and activities that can be categorized under its umbrella continue to expand. When examined through reference to frameworks developed within and about the politics of states, global civil society may look as though it fails to measure up, whether in terms of the very idea of a civil society, or any contribution it might make to freedom and democracy. Global civil society only comes into its own once we question these points of reference in the politics of the sovereign state. This reframing does not mean its puzzles and problems thereby disappear. But it does set the scene for their analysis in more productive terms. There remains plenty of room for dispute about what the best terms might be, but in this respect global civil society is no different from venerable concepts such as democracy: it is a work that is always in progress, both practically and conceptually.

LITERATURE CITED

Amoore L, Langley P. 2004. Ambiguities of global civil society. *Rev. Int. Stud.* 30:89–110

Anderson K. 2000. The Ottawa Convention banning landmines, the role of international non-governmental organizations and the idea of international civil society. *Eur. J. Int. Law* 11(1):91–120

Anderson K, Rieff D. 2005. "Global civil society": A sceptical view. In *Global Civil Society 2004/2005*, ed. H Anheier, M Glasius, M Kaldor, pp. 26–39. London: Sage

Anheier HK. 2007. Reflections on the concept and measurement of global civil society. *Voluntas* 18:1–15

Arato A. 1993. Interpreting 1989. *Soc. Res.* 60:609–46

Bäckstrand K. 2008. Accountability of networked climate governance: The rise of transnational climate partnerships. *Glob. Env. Polit.* 8(3):74–102

Bartelson J. 2006. Making sense of global civil society. *Eur. J. Int. Relat.* 12(3):371–95

Bell S, Hindmoor A. 2009. *Rethinking Governance: The Centrality of the State in Modern Society.* Cambridge, UK: Cambridge Univ. Press

Bernhard M. 1996. Civil society after the first transition: Dilemmas of post-communist democratization in Poland and beyond. *Communist Post-Communist Stud.* 29(3):309–30

Bohman J. 2007. *Democracy across Borders: From Dêmos to Dêmoi.* Cambridge, MA: MIT Press

Bowden B. 2006. Civil society, the state, and the limits to global civil society. *Glob. Soc.* 20(2):155–78

Braithwaite J. 2007. Contestatory citizenship, deliberative denizenship. In *Common Minds*, ed. G Brennan, F Jackson, R Goodin, M Smith, pp. 161–81. Oxford, UK: Oxford Univ. Press

Brassett J, Smith W. 2010. Deliberation and global civil society: Agency, arena, affect. *Rev. Int. Stud.* 36:413–30

Brown C. 2000. Cosmopolitan world citizenship and global civil society. *Crit. Rev. Int. Soc. Polit. Phil.* 3(1):7–26

Brown LD. 2007. *Civil society legitimacy and accountability: Issues and challenges.* Work. Pap. No. 32, Hauser Cent. Int. Dev., Harvard Univ.

Carr DL, Norman S. 2008. Global civil society? The Johannesburg World Summit on Sustainable Development. *Geoforum* 39:358–71

Chambers S, Kopstein J. 2001. Bad civil society. *Polit. Theory* 29:837–65

Chambers S, Kopstein J. 2006. Civil society and the state. In *The Oxford Handbook of Political Theory*, ed. JS Dryzek, B Honig, A Phillips, pp. 363–81. Oxford, UK: Oxford Univ. Press

Chandhoke N. 2002. The limits of global civil society. In *Global Civil Society 2002*, ed. H Anheier, M Glasius, M Kaldor, pp. 35–53. Oxford, UK: Oxford Univ. Press

Cochran M. 2008. *International public spheres, deliberation and normative power: The case of the Women's International League for Peace and Freedom.* Presented at Annu. Meet. Am. Polit. Sci. Assoc., 104th, Boston, Aug. 28–31

Cohen J, Arato A. 1992. *Civil Society and Political Theory.* Cambridge, MA: MIT Press

Coleman WD, Wayland S. 2006. The origins of global civil society and nonterritorial governance: Some empirical reflections. *Glob. Governance* 12:241–61

Comor E. 2001. The role of communication in global civil society: Forces, processes, prospects. *Int. Stud. Q.* 45:389–408

Coppedge M, Gerring J. 2011. Conceptualizing and measuring democracy: A new approach. *Perspect. Polit.* 9(2):247–67

Corry TO. 2006. Global civil society and its discontents. *Voluntas* 17(4):303–24

Cox RW. 2008. The point is not just to explain the world but to change it. In *The Oxford Handbook of International Relations*, ed. C Reus-Smit, D Snidal, pp. 84–93. Oxford, UK: Oxford Univ. Press

Dryzek JS. 2006. *Deliberative Global Politics: Discourse and Democracy in a Divided World.* Cambridge, UK: Polity

Dryzek JS, Downes D, Hunold C, Schlosberg D, Hernes H-K. 2003. *Green States and Social Movements: Environmentalism in the United States, United Kingdom, Germany, and Norway.* Oxford, UK: Oxford Univ. Press

Dryzek JS, Niemeyer S. 2008. Discursive representation. *Am. Polit. Sci. Rev.* 102:481–93

Falk R. 1998. Global civil society: Perspectives, initiatives, movements. *Oxf. Dev. Stud.* 26(1):99–110

Falk R, Strauss A. 2001. Toward global parliament. *For. Aff.* 80(1):212–20

Finnemore M, Sikkink K. 2001. Taking stock: The constructivist research program in international relations and comparative politics. *Annu. Rev. Polit. Sci.* 4:391–416

Gadafy S al-I. 2008. *The role of civil society in the democratisation of global governance institutions: From "soft power" to collective decision-making?* Unpub. PhD thesis, London School Econ. Polit. Sci.

Gallie WB. 1956. Essentially contested concepts. *Proc. Aristotelian Soc.* 56:121–46

Glasius M. 2009. What is global justice and who decides? Civil society and victim responses to the International Criminal Court. *Hum. Rights Q.* 31:496–520

Goodhart M. 2005. Civil society and the problem of global democracy. *Democratization* 12(1):1–21

Grant RW, Keohane RO. 2005. Accountability and the abuse of power in world politics. *Am. Polit. Sci. Rev.* 99:29–44

Heins V. 2004. Civil society's barbarisms. *Eur. J. Soc. Theory* 7:499–517

Heins V. 2005. Global civil society as politics of faith. In *Global Civil Society: Contested Futures*, ed. G Baker, D Chandler, pp. 186–201. London: Routledge

Held D. 1995. *Democracy and the Global Order: From the Nation-State to Cosmopolitan Governance.* Cambridge, UK: Polity

Huntington SP. 1996. *The Clash of Civilizations and the Remaking of World Order.* New York: Simon & Schuster

Jaeger H-M. 2007. "Global civil society" and the political depoliticization of global governance. *Int. Polit. Sociol.* 1:257–77

Jänicke M. 1996. Democracy as a condition for environmental policy success: The importance of non-institutional factors. In *Democracy and the Environment: Problems and Prospects*, ed. WM Lafferty, J Meadowcroft, pp. 71–85. Cheltenham, UK: Edward Elgar

Jordan L, van Tuijl P, eds. 2006. *NGO Accountability: Politics, Principles and Innovations.* London: Earthscan

Kaldor M. 2003. *Global Civil Society: An Answer to War.* Cambridge, UK: Polity

Kaldor M. 2007. *New and Old Wars: Organized Violence in a Global Era.* Cambridge, UK: Polity. 2nd ed.

Katz H. 2006. Gramsci, hegemony, and global civil society networks. *Voluntas* 17:333–48

Keane J. 2003. *Global Civil Society?* Cambridge, UK: Cambridge Univ. Press

Keane J. 2009. *The Life and Death of Democracy.* London: Simon & Schuster

Keck ME. 2003. Governance regimes and the politics of discursive representation. In *Transnational Activism in Asia*, ed. N Piper, A Uhlin, pp. 43–60. London: Routledge

Keck ME, Sikkink K. 1998. *Activists beyond Borders: Advocacy Networks in International Politics.* Ithaca, NY: Cornell Univ. Press

Khagram S, Riker JV, Sikkink K. 2002. *Restructuring World Politics: Transnational Social Movements, Networks and Norms.* Minneapolis: Univ. Minn. Press

Lipschutz R. 1992. Reconstructing world politics: The emergence of global civil society. *Millennium* 21(3):389–420

Lipschutz R. 2005. Global civil society and global governmentality: Resistance, reform, or resignation? In *Global Civil Society: Contested Futures*, ed. G Baker, D Chandler, pp. 171–85. London: Routledge

Lipschutz R, Mayer J. 1996. *Global Civil Society and Global Environmental Governance: The Politics of Nature from Place to Planet.* Albany: State Univ. New York Press

Mansbridge J. 2009. A "selection model" of political representation. *J. Polit. Phil.* 17(4):369–98

Montanero L. 2008. *The democratic legitimacy of "self-authorized" representatives.* Presented at Workshop on

Rethinking Representation: A North-South Dialogue, Bellagio, Italy, Sep. 30–Oct. 3

Munck R. 2006. *Globalization and Contestation: The New Great Counter-Movement.* London: Routledge

Newell P. 2000. *Climate for Change: Non-state Actors and the Global Politics of the Greenhouse.* Cambridge, UK: Cambridge Univ. Press

Omelicheva MY. 2009. Global civil society and democratization of world politics: A bona fide relationship or illusory liaison? *Int. Stud. Rev.* 11:109–32

Payne RA. 2001. Persuasion, frames and norm construction. *Eur. J. Int. Rel.* 7(1):37–61

Pettit P. 1997. *Republicanism: A Theory of Freedom and Government.* Oxford, UK: Oxford Univ. Press

Pettit P. 2006. Two-dimensional democracy and the international domain. *The Monist* 89(2):301–24

Pitkin HF. 1967. *The Concept of Representation.* Berkeley: Univ. Calif. Press

Price R. 1998. Reversing the gun sights: Transnational civil society targets land mines. *Int. Org.* 52(3):613–44

Reus-Smit C, Snidal D, eds. 2008. *The Oxford Handbook of International Relations.* Oxford, UK: Oxford Univ. Press

Rhodes RAW. 1997. *Understanding Governance: Policy Networks, Governance, Reflexivity, and Accountability.* Buckingham, UK: Open Univ. Press

Rosenau JN, Czempiel E-O. 1992. *Governance without Government: Order and Change in World Politics.* New York: Cambridge Univ. Press

Saward M. 2009. Authorisation and authenticity: Representation and the unelected. *J. Polit. Phil.* 17:1–22

Saward M. 2010. *The Representative Claim.* Oxford, UK: Oxford Univ. Press

Schlemmer-Schulte S. 2001. The impact of civil society on the World Bank, the International Monetary Fund, and the World Trade Organization: The case of the World Bank. *ILSA J. Int. Comp. Law* 7:399–428

Scholte JA. 2002. Civil society and democracy in global governance. *Glob. Governance* 8:281–304

Scholte JA. 2007. Civil society and the legitimation of global governance. *J. Civil Soc.* 3:305–26

Sending OJ, Neumannn IB. 2006. Governance to governmentality: Analyzing NGOs, states, and power. *Int. Stud. Q.* 50:651–72

Smith J. 1998. Global civil society? Transnational social movements and social capital. *Am. Behav. Sci.* 42(1):93–107

Smith J, Wiest D. 2005. The uneven geography of global civil society: National and global influences on transnational association. *Soc. Forces* 84(2):621–52

Stevenson H. 2011. *Representing "the peoples"? Post-neoliberal states in the international climate negotiations.* Work. Pap. 2011/1, Cent. Deliberative Democracy and Global Governance, Australian Natl. Univ.

Stiglitz J. 2002. *Globalization and Its Discontents.* New York: W.W. Norton

Taylor R. 2002. Interpreting global civil society. *Voluntas* 13(4):339–47

von Frantzius I. 2004. World Summit on Sustainable Development Johannesburg 2002: A critical assessment of the outcomes. *Environ. Polit.* 13:467–73

Wapner P. 2002. Introductory essay: Paradise lost? NGOs and global accountability. *Chicago J. Int. Law* 3(1):155–60

Weinstein MM, Charnovitz S. 2001. The greening of the WTO. *For. Aff.* 80(6):147–56

Willetts P. 2006. The Cardoso report on the UN and civil society: Functionalism, global corporatism, or global democracy? *Glob. Governance* 12:305–24

CREDITS